mar·ket·ing

Marketing is the activity, set of institutions, and processes for creating, *capturing*, communicating, delivering, and exchanging offerings that have value for customers, clients, partners, and society at large.

The definition of marketing, established by the American Marketing Association, October 2007. Word in italics was added by authors.

mhhe.com/grewal6e

Marketing

Sixth Edition

Dhruv Grewal, PhD
Babson College

Michael Levy, PhD
Babson College

MARKETING, SIXTH EDITION

Published by McGraw-Hill Education, 2 Penn Plaza, New York, NY 10121. Copyright © 2018 by McGraw-Hill Education. All rights reserved. Printed in the United States of America. Previous edition © 2016, 2014, 2012, 2010, and 2008. No part of this publication may be reproduced or distributed in any form or by any means, or stored in a database or retrieval system, without the prior written consent of McGraw-Hill Education, including, but not limited to, in any network or other electronic storage or transmission, or broadcast for distance learning.

Some ancillaries, including electronic and print components, may not be available to customers outside the United States.

This book is printed on acid-free paper.

1 2 3 4 5 6 7 8 9 LWI/LWI 21 20 19 18 17

ISBN 978-1-259-70907-4
MHID 1-259-70907-8

Chief Product Officer, SVP Products & Markets: *G. Scott Virkler*
Vice President, General Manager, Products & Markets: *Michael Ryan*
Vice President, Content Design & Delivery: *Betsy Whalen*
Managing Director: *Susan Gouijnstook*
Brand Manager: *Meredith Fossel*
Director, Product Development: *Meghan Campbell*
Lead Product Developer: *Kelly L. Delso*
Product Developer: *Lai T. Moy*
Director, Marketing: *Robin Lucas*
Marketing Manager: *Elizabeth Schonagen*
Market Development Manager: *Andrea Shieve*
Digital Product Analyst: *Kerry Shanahan*
Director, Content Design & Delivery: *Terri Schiesl*
Program Manager: *Mary Conzachi*
Content Project Managers: *Christine A. Vaughan; Danielle Clement*
Buyer: *Susan G. Culbertson*
Design: *Matt Diamond*
Content Licensing Specialists: *DeAnna Dausener; Ann Marie Jannette*
Cover Images: *Tomislav Forgo/Getty Images; Jack Anderson/Getty Images; habovka/Getty Images; Devan Muir/Getty Images*
Compositor: *Aptara®, Inc.*
Typeface: *10/12 STIX Mathjax Main*
Printer: *LSC Communications*
Section/chapter opener strawberry image: © *Himbeertoni/Getty Images RF*

All credits appearing on page or at the end of the book are considered to be an extension of the copyright page.

Library of Congress Cataloging-in-Publication Data

Names: Grewal, Dhruv, author. | Levy, Michael, 1950- author.
Title: Marketing / Dhruv Grewal, PhD, Babson College, Michael Levy, PhD,
    Babson College.
    Description: Sixth edition. | New York, NY : McGraw-Hill Education, [2018]
    Identifiers: LCCN 2016046062 | ISBN 9781259709074 (alk. paper) | ISBN
    1259709078 (alk. paper)
    Subjects: LCSH: Marketing.
    Classification: LCC HF5415 .G6753 2018 | DDC 658.8—dc23 LC record
    available at https://lccn.loc.gov/2016046062

The Internet addresses listed in the text were accurate at the time of publication. The inclusion of a website does not indicate an endorsement by the authors or McGraw-Hill Education, and McGraw-Hill Education does not guarantee the accuracy of the information presented at these sites.

mheducation.com/highered

To my family for their never-ending support; my wife Diana; and my children, Lauren and Alex.

—Dhruv Grewal

To Mark Levy, my best friend and brother.

—Michael Levy

Courtesy of Dhruv Grewal

Dhruv Grewal

Dhruv Grewal, PhD (Virginia Tech), is the Toyota Chair in Commerce and Electronic Business and a professor of marketing at Babson College. He is listed in The World's Most Influential Scientific Minds, Thompson Reuters 2014 (only eight from the marketing field and 95 from economics and business are listed). He was awarded the 2013 university-wide Distinguished Graduate Alumnus from his alma mater, Virginia Tech, the 2012 Lifetime Achievement Award in Pricing (AMA Retailing & Pricing SIG), the 2010 Lifetime Achievement Award in Retailing (AMA Retailing SIG), the 2010 AMS Cutco/Vector Distinguished Educator Award, the 2010 Lifetime Achievement Award in Retailing (AMA Retailing SIG), and in 2005 the Lifetime Achievement in Behavioral Pricing Award (Fordham University, November 2005). He is a Distinguished Fellow of the Academy of Marketing Science. He was ranked first in the marketing field in terms of publications in the top-six marketing journals during the 1991–1998 period and again for the 2000–2007 period. He ranked eighth in terms of publications in JM and JMR during the 2009–2013 period and ranked seventh in terms of publications in the *Journal of Public Policy & Marketing* for the period 1992–2001. He was also ranked first in terms of publications and third in citations for pricing research for the time period 1980–2010 in 20 marketing and business publications. He has served as VP, research and conferences, American Marketing Association Academic Council (1999–2001), and as VP, development for the Academy of Marketing Science (2000–2002). He was co-editor of *Journal of Retailing* from 2001 to 2007. He co-chaired the 1993 Academy of Marketing Science Conference, the 1998 Winter American Marketing Association Conference, the 2001 AMA doctoral consortium, the American Marketing Association 2006 Summer Educators Conference, the 2011 DMEF research summit, and the 2012 and 2015 AMA/ACRA Retailing Conference.

Professor Grewal has published over 140 articles in journals such as the *Journal of Retailing, Journal of Marketing, Journal of Consumer Research, Journal of Marketing Research, Journal of Consumer Psychology, Journal of Applier Psychology,* and *Journal of the Academy of Marketing Science,* as well as other journals. He currently serves on numerous editorial and advisory review boards, such as the *Journal of Retailing, Journal of Marketing* (area editor), *Journal of Marketing Research, Journal of Consumer Psychology, Journal of the Academy of Marketing Science* (area editor), *Academy of Marketing Science Review, Journal of Interactive Marketing, Journal of Business Research,* and *Journal of Public Policy & Marketing.* He has over 35,000 citations based on Google scholar.

He has won a number of awards for his teaching: 2005 Sherwin-Williams Distinguished Teaching Award, Society for Marketing Advances; 2003 American Marketing Association Award for Innovative Excellence in Marketing Education; 1999 Academy of Marketing Science Great Teachers in Marketing Award; Executive MBA Teaching Excellence Award (1998); School of Business Teaching Excellence Awards (1993, 1999); and Virginia Tech Certificate of Recognition for Outstanding Teaching (1989). He has won numerous awards for his research: 2016 *Journal of Marketing* Sheth Award; William R. Davidson *Journal of Retailing* Best Paper Awards 2010, 2012, and 2016; Luis W. Stern Awards 2011 and 2015 (AMA IO Sig); William R. Davidson *Journal of Retailing* Honorable Mention Awards 2010 and 2011; Babson College Faculty Scholarship Award (2010 and 2015); University of Miami School of Business Research Excellence Award for the years 1991, 1995, 1996, and 1998; Best Services Paper Award (AMA Services SIG 2002); Stanley C. Hollander Best Retailing Paper (AMS 2002 and 2008); and M. Wayne DeLozier Best Conference Paper (AMS 2002 and 2008). He also received Best Reviewer Awards (*Journal of Retailing* 2008, *Journal of Marketing* 2014), best area editor (*Journal of the Academy of Marketing Science* 2016), and a Distinguished Service Award (*Journal of Retailing* 2009).

Professor Grewal has taught executive seminars and courses and/or worked on research projects with numerous firms, such as Dell, ExxonMobil, IRI, Radio Shack, Telcordia, Khimetriks, Profit-Logic, McKinsey, Ericsson, Motorola, Nextel, FP&L, Lucent, Sabre, Goodyear Tire & Rubber Company, Sherwin-Williams and Asahi. He has delivered seminars in the United States, Europe, Latin America, and Asia. He has also served as an expert witness and worked as a consultant on numerous legal cases.

Courtesy of Michael Levy

Michael Levy

Michael Levy, PhD (Ohio State University), is the Charles Clarke Reynolds Professor of Marketing Emeritus at Babson College and CEO of RetailProf LLC. He received his PhD in business administration from The Ohio State University and his undergraduate and MS degrees in business administration from the University of Colorado at Boulder. He taught at Southern Methodist University before joining the faculty as professor and chair of the marketing department at the University of Miami.

Professor Levy received the inaugural ACRA Academic Lifetime Achievement Award presented at the 2015 AMA/ACRA (American Marketing Association/American Collegiate Retailing Association) Triennial Conference; was recognized for 25 years of dedicated service to the editorial review board of the *Journal of Retailing* in 2011. He won the McGraw-Hill Corporate Achievement Award for Grewal–Levy *Marketing 2e* with Connect in the category of excellence in content and analytics (2010); Revision of the Year for *Marketing 2e* (Grewal–Levy) from McGraw-Hill/Irwin (2010); the 2009 Lifetime Achievement Award, American Marketing Association, Retailing Special Interest Group (SIG); the Babson Faculty Scholarship Award (2009); and the Distinguished Service Award, *Journal of Retailing* (2009) (at winter AMA).

He was rated as one of the best researchers in marketing in a survey published in *Marketing Educator* (Summer 1997). He has developed a strong stream of research in retailing, business logistics, financial retailing strategy, pricing, and sales management. He has published over 50 articles in leading marketing and logistics journals, including the *Journal of Retailing, Journal of Marketing, Journal of the Academy of Marketing Science,* and *Journal of Marketing Research.* He has served on the editorial review boards of the *Journal of Retailing, Journal of the*

Academy of Marketing Science, International Journal of Physical Distribution and Materials Management, International Journal of Business Logistics, ECR Journal, European Business Review, and has been on the editorial advisory boards of *European Retail Research* and the *European Business Review.* He is co-author of *Retailing Management,* 9e (2014), the best-selling college-level retailing text in the world. Professor Levy was co-editor of the *Journal of Retailing* from 2001 to 2007. He co-chaired the 1993 Academy of Marketing Science conference and the 2006 summer AMA conference.

Professor Levy has worked in retailing and related disciplines throughout his professional life. Prior to his academic career, he worked for several retailers and a housewares distributor in Colorado. He has performed research projects with many retailers and retail technology firms, including Accenture, Federated Department Stores, Khimetrics (SAP), Mervyn's, Neiman Marcus, ProfitLogic (Oracle), Zale Corporation, and numerous law firms.

New to the Sixth Edition

Some exciting new additions to the Sixth Edition!

Chapter 1, "Overview of Marketing," starts with a discussion of one of the world's most successful chocolate brands, Godiva, which is in keeping with this edition's cover theme—how chocolate has gone from a commodity to a high-value branded product through marketing. The Superior Service, Adding Value, Social & Mobile Marketing, and Ethical & Societal Dilemma boxes now cover such new topics as in-flight WiFi, Whole Foods purpose-based marketing, the growth of mobile advertising, and free fruit offered by supermarkets to individuals shopping with children. A new section on marketing analytics is also accompanied in other chapters by new Marketing Analytics boxes. In this chapter the Marketing Analytics box discusses how Starbucks uses analytics to determine new store locations. Finally the chapter closes with a new case study on the global chocolate market, again in keeping with this edition's cover theme on how marketing has added value to the chocolate industry.

Chapter 2, "Developing Marketing Strategies and a Marketing Plan," opens with a discussion on PepsiCo, weaving in a comparison between PepsiCo and Coca-Cola throughout the chapter. We introduce a new Superior Service box highlighting Amazon's new home-service option, as well as a new Ethical & Social Dilemma box examining Volkswagen's Dieselgate scandal. The new Marketing Analytics box covers Google's predictive analytics. In addition, the chapter ends with a new case study on the coffee wars between Starbucks, Dunkin' Donuts, and McDonald's.

Chapter 3, "Social and Mobile Marketing," begins with a new opener on how Under Armour has successfully used social media in its marketing campaigns. The chapter also features a new section that details the wheel of social media engagement. The wheel of engagement highlights the information, connected, network, dynamic, and timeless effects of social media. The chapter also includes a new Adding Value box describing how Mercedes-Benz uses LinkedIn, an Ethical & Societal Dilemma box on how Disney appeals to moms, and two new Marketing Analytics boxes: one that covers eHarmony's analytics and the other on how Twitter and Billboard are teaming up to create real-time top music lists.

Chapter 4, "Conscious Marketing, Corporate Social Responsibility, and Ethics," is re-titled to reflect a new section on conscious marketing, which argues that firms have a sense of purpose that encompasses four key principles: (1) recognizing marketing's greater purpose, (2) considering stakeholders and their interdependence, (3) conscious leadership and its role in creating a corporate culture, and (4) understanding that decisions are ethically based. Chapter 4 also includes a new opener on the TOMS shoes company, a new Marketing Analytics box on how Kellogg's uses analytics to address GMO concerns, and a new Social & Mobile Marketing box on how cell phones are being used to help customers at the bottom of the pyramid.

Chapter 5, "Analyzing the Marketing Environment," starts with a discussion of Panera Bread's new clean menu. The chapter includes a new Superior Service box on CVS's mobile MinuteClinic app and a new Marketing Analytics box that highlights Netflix's predictive analytics. It also includes a new Adding Value box on Google's self-driving car.

Chapter 6, "Consumer Behavior," begins with a discussion of Nike's partnership with the Weather Channel and how it is using the Weather Channel app to advertise. A new Marketing Analytics box highlights how H&R Block uses analytics to create new tax services. A new Ethical & Societal Dilemma box discusses the allegations of unethical practices by pharmaceutical firms.

Chapter 7, "Business-to-Business Marketing," starts with an interesting application of a B2B market—how Amazon Business serves its partners. The chapter also includes two new boxes: Marketing Analytics on cloud computing and Adding Value on Xerox's fashion show to sell its latest printer. The chapter also includes a new case study on Staples' B2B business.

Chapter 8, "Global Marketing," examines how companies that either market the same products globally or have to change their products for the global market have different challenges from those that operate only in domestic markets. The new opener highlights the challenges faced by Netflix as it expands to the global economy. New examples include Chanel and how they are addressing the exchange rate in China, as well as Porsche's and Marks & Spencer's marketing fumbles when advertising to the Chinese market.

Chapter 9, "Segmentation, Targeting, and Positioning," opens with a discussion of how ABC Family's segmentation strategy has influenced its recent rebranding effort. A new Marketing Analytics box features Starbucks' wildly popular mobile app, and a new Superior Service box highlights how hotels leverage their proximity to universities. The chapter also includes a new case study on Mercedes-Benz's marketing strategy.

Chapter 10, "Marketing Research," begins with a discussion about how research has influenced the lingerie company Adore Me to use plus-sized models. A new Superior Service box explains how universities analyze usage data to identify when students use on-campus gyms to improve their college experience. Finally, the chapter concludes with a case study on how the YMCA is redefining itself.

Chapter 11, "Product, Branding, and Packaging Decisions" includes the following new boxes: Adding Value about the latest entry-level luxury cars, Marketing Analytics that discusses how Macy's uses analytics to determine its assortment, and Ethical & Societal Dilemma that highlights how Mars, Inc. is moving toward sugar labeling on its candy products. This chapter concludes with a new case study describing how Birkenstock has become a fashion brand.

Chapter 12, "Developing New Products," begins with a discussion of Xiaomi's affordable smartphones in Asia; a new Adding Value box explores how Disney licenses its movies and characters to toy companies; a new Ethical & Societal Dilemma box discusses concerns about the rise in the popularity of drones; a new Marketing Analytics box focuses on GM's use of big data to develop new cars and features; and a new Adding Value box features SkinnyPop snacks.

Chapter 13, "Services: The Intangible Product," opens with a new vignette about lululemon's new flagship store in New York City, which is designed to provide consumers with exceptional customer service. New boxes include Adding Value about Pepsi's new Kola House restaurant and Marketing Analytics about Kroger's use of analytics to determine how to reduce wait times during checkout. A new case study highlights the differences among Uber, Lyft, and traditional taxis.

Chapter 14, "Pricing Concepts for Establishing Value," describes pricing concepts using new examples from Coca-Cola in an Ethical & Societal Dilemma box, Amazon in a new Adding Value box, and airline ticket pricing in a Marketing Analytics box.

Chapter 15, "Strategic Pricing Methods," begins with a discussion of Disney's new surge pricing at its theme parks. Updated examples include two new Ethical & Societal Dilemma boxes: one about how Apple is conspiring with publishers to raise the price of e-books, and another about the gray market for luxury goods. Finally, the chapter ends with a new case study on the pizza industry, focusing specifically on Papa John's, Little Caesars, Domino's, Pizza Hut, and local pizzerias.

Chapter 16, "Supply Chain and Channel Management," opens with a vignette on IKEA's innovations in its supply chain. New boxes in this chapter include: Marketing Analytics on Amazon's anticipatory shipping, Ethical & Societal Dilemma on how consumer demands for organic products is affecting the supply chain, and Adding Value on e-tailing in the United States versus India.

Chapter 17, "Retailing and Omnichannel Marketing," begins with a discussion of a retail innovator–Amazon. It includes a new Superior Service box on how Burberry is seeking to access its customers directly, a new Marketing Analytics box discussing FreshDirect, a new Social & Mobile Marketing box detailing IKEA's online and in-store retailing strategies, and a new case study about how Macy's is taking initiatives to maintain its competitive advantage.

Chapter 18, "Integrated Marketing Communications," starts with Pepsi's emoji campaign to illustrate how integrated marketing communications is at the forefront of marketing. New boxes: Social & Mobile Marketing describing how Domino's uses Snapchat for a marketing campaign, Adding Value about Pepsi's endorsement on the television show *Empire*, Ethical & Societal Dilemma highlighting how companies take risks when developing their IMC programs, Adding Value on the partnership between the NBA and Kia, and Marketing Analytics describing how Puma uses Google's analytics. The chapter concludes with a new case study on Pepsi's Pepsi Max campaign.

Chapter 19, "Advertising, Public Relations, and Sales Promotions," starts with McDonald's "Our Food. Your Questions" campaign. There is a new Social & Mobile Marketing box on how mobile advertising is pushing out digital advertising, a new Adding Value box on the use of popular music in advertisements, and a new Marketing Analytics box on how CVS uses the data it collects from its loyalty program to target coupons to consumers.

Chapter 20, "Personal Selling and Sales Management," begins with a discussion of IBM's Watson. The chapter also includes a new Social & Mobile Marketing box highlighting how companies can use mobile CRM systems, and an Adding Value box on how selling Tupperware can empower women in Indonesia.

a letter from the authors

We are pleased to welcome you to the sixth edition of *Marketing*! Since the first edition, we have committed to emphasizing a basic, yet essential, theme: **Marketing adds value.** This theme comes through not only in our instructional features but also in our covers. With each edition's cover, we have featured a product that, because of marketing, has become more valuable in the eyes of consumers than it might have otherwise become. Last edition we featured coffee; in previous editions, we featured yogurt, water, and jeans. For this sixth edition, we feature chocolate. These are all familiar products that started out as commodities but became high-value branded products because of marketing.

How We Show That Marketing Adds Value

As with previous editions of *Marketing*, we continue to emphasize how marketing has evolved into its present-day, integral business function of creating value. We also focus on how firms maintain value and rely on value for establishing lasting relationships with their customers.

To keep students engaged with this theme, we offer the following features:

- **Adding Value**—illustrate how companies add value not only in providing products and services but also in making contributions to society.

- **Ethical & Societal Dilemmas**—emphasize the role of marketing in society.

- **Marketing Analytics**—feature companies that rely on sophisticated data analytics to define and refine their approaches to their customers and their markets.

- **Marketing Digitally**—illustrates how marketers successfully use digital media in their marketing campaigns and efforts.

- **Social & Mobile Marketing**—discuss how social media are used in marketing products.

- **Superior Service**—highlight the emerging role of the service industry.

How We Teach the Basics of Marketing

We understand that for students to appreciate discussions of how marketing adds value, they must first develop a basic understanding of key marketing principles and core concepts. In this effort, we believe students learn best when they see how a subject relates to them. Throughout this edition and all those prior, we provide numerous examples of how students engage in marketing activities every day of their lives—either as consumers or sellers of a product or service. In addition to providing the traditional study and reinforcement tools of most principles of marketing products, we also offer ways to help students think critically about and apply core concepts:

Chapter-Opening Vignettes focus on some of the marketplace challenges faced by such well-known companies as Under Amour, PepsiCo, TOMS, Netflix, Amazon, and others.

Marketing Applications encourage students to apply what they have learned to marketing scenarios that are relevant to their lives.

End-of-Chapter Cases help students develop analytical, critical-thinking, and technology skills.

Progress Checks throughout each chapter give students the opportunity to stop and consider whether their understanding of key concepts is progressing as it should.

Auto-graded Application Exercises in Connect (such as video cases, case analyses, and click-drags) challenge students to apply marketing concepts to real-life marketing scenarios, which fosters their critical-thinking skills in lecture and beyond.

Why We Believe in the Value of Marketing

Beyond teaching a principles of marketing course and developing a product to be taught, we also want to impress upon our students why marketing in and of itself is valuable. Marketing creates enduring and mutually valuable relationships between companies and their consumers. Marketing identifies what customers value at the local level in order to make it possible for firms to expand at the global level. Without marketing, it would be difficult for any of us to learn about new products and services. In fact, an understanding of marketing can help students find jobs after they finish school. If we can inspire this understanding of the value of marketing in our students, then we will have succeeded in demonstrating how *marketing adds value* . . . to their education, their careers, and to their lives.

Dhruv Grewal,
Babson College

Michael Levy,
Babson College

McGraw-Hill Connect®
Learn Without Limits

Connect is a teaching and learning platform that is proven to deliver better results for students and instructors.

Connect empowers students by continually adapting to deliver precisely what they need, when they need it, and how they need it, so your class time is more engaging and effective.

73% of instructors who use Connect require it; instructor satisfaction increases by 28% when Connect is required.

Connect's Impact on Retention Rates, Pass Rates, and Average Exam Scores

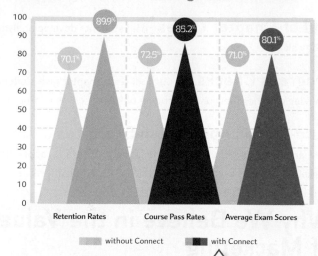

- 70.1% 89.9% Retention Rates
- 72.5% 85.2% Course Pass Rates
- 71.0% 80.1% Average Exam Scores

without Connect ▮ with Connect

Using Connect improves retention rates by 19.8%, passing rates by 12.7%, and exam scores by 9.1%.

Analytics

Connect Insight®

Connect Insight is Connect's new one-of-a-kind visual analytics dashboard—now available for both instructors and students—that provides at-a-glance information regarding student performance, which is immediately actionable. By presenting assignment, assessment, and topical performance results together with a time metric that is easily visible for aggregate or individual results, Connect Insight gives the user the ability to take a just-in-time approach to teaching and learning, which was never before available. Connect Insight presents data that empowers students and helps instructors improve class performance in a way that is efficient and effective.

Impact on Final Course Grade Distribution

	without Connect	with Connect
A	22.9%	31.0%
B	27.4%	34.3%
C	22.9%	18.7%
D	11.5%	6.1%
F	15.4%	9.9%

Students can view their results for any Connect course.

Mobile

Connect's new, intuitive mobile interface gives students and instructors flexible and convenient, anytime–anywhere access to all components of the Connect platform.

Adaptive

> More students earn **A's** and **B's** when they use McGraw-Hill Education **Adaptive** products.

SmartBook®

Proven to help students improve grades and study more efficiently, SmartBook contains the same content within the print book, but actively tailors that content to the needs of the individual. SmartBook's adaptive technology provides precise, personalized instruction on what the student should do next, guiding the student to master and remember key concepts, targeting gaps in knowledge and offering customized feedback, and driving the student toward comprehension and retention of the subject matter. Available on tablets, SmartBook puts learning at the student's fingertips—anywhere, anytime.

> Over **8 billion questions** have been answered, making McGraw-Hill Education products more intelligent, reliable, and precise.

Practice Marketing

Practice Marketing is a 3D, online, single- or multiplayer game that helps students apply the four Ps by taking on the role of Marketing Manager for a backpack company. By playing the game individually and/or in teams, students come to understand how their decisions and elements of the marketing mix affect one another. Practice Marketing is easy to use, fully mobile, and provides an interactive alternative to marketing plan projects. Log in to **mhpractice.com** with your Connect credentials to access a demo, or contact your local McGraw-Hill representative for more details.

www.mheducation.com

acknowledgments

We would like to acknowledge the considerable contributions of Elisabeth Nevins and Jenny Esdale for their help throughout the development of this edition of *Marketing*.

We wish to express our sincere appreciation to Leroy Robinson of the University of Houston–Clear Lake for his work on the instructor's manual and the PowerPoint slides; Melissa Martin of George Mason University for her contributions to the Connect instructor's manual, video guide, and Connect application exercises; and to Susan Simpfenderfer of ID8 for her contributions to the test bank. We are grateful to Kelly Luchtman at Lightfellow for her continuing hard work on video production. Our McGraw-Hill editorial and production staff also deserve recognition for their patient and professional support: executive brand manager, Meredith Fossel; marketing manager, Elizabeth Schonagen; senior product developer, Lai Moy; lead content project manager, Christine Vaughan; senior content project manager, Danielle Clement; senior designer, Matt Diamond; content licensing specialists, DeAnna Dausener and Ann Marie Jannette; and photo researchers, Danny Meldung and Julie De Adder.

Our colleagues in industry have been invaluable in providing us with case, video, advertising, and photo materials.

Over the years, we have had the opportunity to work with many talented and insightful colleagues. We have benefited from our research and discussions with them. Some of these colleagues are: Anne L. Roggeveen, Victoria Crittenden, Anjali Bal, Lauren S. Beitelspacher, Krista Hill, Rajendra Sisodia, Bala Iyer (Babson College); Ruth Bolton, Steve Brown, and Terry Bristol (Arizona State University); Ramon Avila (Ball State University); Joan Lindsey-Mullikin and Norm Borin (Cal Poly, San Luis Obispo); Ko de Ruyter (Cass Business School); Larry D. Compeau (Clarkson University); Don Lehmann and Keith L. Wilcox (Columbia); Praveen Kopalle, Scott Neslin, and Kusum Ailawadi (Dartmouth); Rajneesh Suri (Drexel); Rajesh Chandrashekaran (Fairleigh Dickinson University); Gopal Iyer and Tamara Mangleburg (Florida Atlantic University); Anthony Miyazaki and Walfried Lassar (Florida International University); Hooman Estelami (Fordham University); Ronnie Goodstein (Georgetown); V. Kumar (Georgia State University); Scott Motyka (KGI); K. Sivakumar (Lehigh University); Martin Wetzels and Dominik Mahr (Maastricht University); Yu Ma (McGill University); Maria Elena Vazquez Lira (Monterrey Tec); Douglas M. Lambert and Walter Zinn (Ohio State University); Wagner Kamakura (Rice); Thomas Rudolph (St. Gallen University); Jens Nordfält (Stockholm School of Economics); Zhen Zhu (Suffolk University); Venkatesh Shankar, Mark Houston, and Manjit Yadav (Texas A&M); Julie Baker and William Cron (Texas Christian University); Rodney C. Runyan (Texas State University); Kristy Reynolds (University of Alabama); Merrie Brucks and Ajith Kumar (University of Arizona); Dinesh Gauri (University of Arkansas); Nancy M. Puccinelli (University of Bath); Cheryl Nikata (University of Illinois, Chicago); David Hardesty (University of Kentucky); Arun Sharma, A. Parasuraman, R. Krishnan, Howard Marmorstein, Anuj Mehrotra, Claudia Townsend, and Michael Tsiros (University of Miami); Francisco Villarroel Ordenes (University of Massachusetts Amherst); A. C. Samli (University of North Florida); Monika Kukar Kinney and Kent Monroe (University of Richmond); Abhijit Guha (University of South Carolina); Valerie Folkes (University of Southern California); Stephanie Noble (University of Tennessee); Robert Peterson (University of Texas at Austin); Carolyn Costley (University of Waikato); Rob Palmatier (University of Washington); Abhijit Biswas and Sujay Dutta (Wayne State University); and M. Joseph Sirgy (Virginia Tech).

We would like to thank the following instructors for providing feedback to shape the fifth and sixth editions. A special thank you to:

Wendi L. Achey
Northampton Community College

Ebru Ulusoy Akgun
University of Maine

Audrey Ashton-Savage
Peter T. Paul College of Business and Economics, University of New Hampshire

Nisreen Bahnan
Salem State University

Linda Jane Coleman
Salem State University

Kevin Joseph Cumiskey
Eastern Kentucky University

Laura Dix
Ferris State University

Kim Donahue
Indiana University, Kelley School of Business Indianapolis

Jerome Gafford
University of North Alabama

James Gorman
Houson University of Alabama

Daniel E. Hallock
University of North Alabama

Dana L. E. Harrison
East Tennessee State University

Reba Heberlein
Madison Area Technical College

Tarique Hossain
California State Polytechnic University

Elizabeth Jane
Wilson Suffolk University

Mayuresh M. Kelkar
Salem State University

Todd Korol
Monroe Community College

Kathleen A. Krentler
San Diego State University

Jamie Lambert
Ohio University

Marilyn Lavin
University of Wisconsin-Whitewater

Patricia Marco
Madison College

Mary Christene Martin
Fort Hays State University

Carolyn A. Massiah
University of Central Florida

Maria McConnell
Lorain County Community College

Joyce L. Meyer
The University of Alabama

Susan Myrden
University of Maine

Steve Noll
Madison Area Technical College

Matthew O'Hern
University of Oregon

David Terry Paul
The Ohio State University

Frank Allen Philpot
George Mason University

Lori A. Radulovich
Baldwin Wallace University

Jean Marc Rejaud
Fashion Institute of Technology

Harper Andrew Roehm, Jr.
University of North Carolina–Greensboro

Donald Shemwell
East Tennessee State University

John Striebich
Monroe Community College

Robert Scott Taylor
Moberly Area Community College

Steven A. Taylor
Illinois State University

Deborah Utter
Boston University

For their contributions to previous editions of *Marketing,* we gratefully acknowledge:

Wendi Achey
Northampton Community College

Praveen Aggarwal
University of Minnesota, Duluth

Maria Aria
Camden County College

Dennis Arnett
Texas Tech University

Gerard Athaide
Loyola College of Maryland

Timothy W. Aurand
Northern Illinois University

Laurie Babin
University of Louisiana at Monroe

Ainsworth Bailey
University of Toledo

Aysen Bakir
Illinois State University

Joyce Banjac
Myers University

Harvey Bauman
Lees McRae College

Oleta Beard
University of Washington

Sandy Becker
Rutgers Business School

Hannah Bell-Lombardo
Bryant University

Ellen Benowitz
Mercer County Community College

Gary Benton
Western Kentucky University

Joseph Ben-Ur
University of Houston at Victoria

Patricia Bernson
County College of Morris

Harriette Bettis-Outland
University of West Florida

Parimal Bhagat
Indiana University of Pennsylvania

Amit Bhatnagar
University of Wisconsin, Milwaukee

Jan Bingen
Little Priest Tribal College

John Bishop
University of South Alabama–Mobile

Nancy Bloom
Nassau Community College

Claire Bolfing
James Madison University

Karen Bowman
University of California

Tom Boyd
California State University–Fullerton

Nancy Boykin
Tarleton State University

Cathy Brenan
Northland Community and Technical College

Martin Bressler
Houston Baptist University

Claudia Bridges
California State University

Glen H. Brodowsky
California State University, San Marcos

Greg Broekemier
University of Nebraska Kearney

Gary Brunswick
Northern Michigan University

Alan J. Bush
University of Memphis

John Buzza
Monmouth University

Linda Calderone
SUNY, Farmingdale

Nathaniel Calloway
University of Maryland, University College

Rae Caloura
Johnson & Wales University

Michaelle Cameron
St. Edwards University

Catherine Campbell
University of Maryland

Carlos Castillo
University of Minnesota, Duluth

Eve Caudill
Winona State University

Carmina Cavazos
University of Saint Thomas

Lindell Chew
Linn University of Missouri

Dorene Ciletti
Duquesne University

Melissa Clark
University of North Alabama

Terry Clark
Southern Illinois University–Carbondale

Joyce Claterbos
University of Kansas

Gloria Cockerell
Collin County College

Paul Cohen
Florida Atlantic University

Mark E. Collins
University of Tennessee

Clare Comm
University of Massachusetts, Lowell

Sherry Cook
Southwest Missouri State University

Stan Cort
Case Western Reserve University

Keith Cox
University of Houston

Ian Cross
Bentley College

Geoffrey Crosslin
Kalamazoo Valley Community College

Brent Cunningham
Jacksonville State University

Clayton L. Daughtrey
Metropolitan State College of Denver

Charlene Davis
Trinity University

Joseph DeFilippe
Suffolk County Community College

George Deitz
University of Memphis

Kathleen DeNisco
Erie Community College

Tilokie Depoo
Monroe College

Monique Doll
Macomb Community College

Kimberly Donahue
Indiana University–Purdue University at Indianapolis

Jim D'Orazio
Cleveland State University

Michael Dore
University of Oregon

James Downing
University of Illinois–Chicago

Michael Drafke
College of DuPage

Leon Dube
Texas A&M University

Colleen Dunn
Bucks County Community College

John Eaton
Arizona State University–Tempe

Kellie Emrich
Cuyahoga Community College

Nancy Evans
New River Community College

Keith Fabes
Berkeley College

Tina Facca
John Carroll University

Joyce Fairchild
Northern Virginia Community College

David J. Faulds
University of Louisville

Larry Feick
University of Pittsburgh

Karen Flaherty
Oklahoma State University–Stillwater

Leisa Flynn
Florida State University

William Foxx
Auburn University

Alan Friedenthal
Kingsborough Community College

Douglas Friedman
Penn State University

Stanley Garfunkel
Queensborough Community College

S. J. Garner
Eastern Kentucky University

David Gerth
Nashville State Community College

Peggy Gilbert
Missouri State University

Kelly Gillerlain
Tidewater Community College

George Goerner
Mohawk Valley Community College

Jana Goodrich
Penn State Behrend

Robin Grambling
University of Texas at El Paso

Kimberly D. Grantham
University of Georgia

James I. Gray
Florida Atlantic University

Kelly Gredone
Bucks County Community College

Tom Greene
Eastern Washington University

Michael Greenwood
Mount Wachusett Community College

Barbara Gross
California State University–Northridge

David Grossman
Florida Southern College

Hugh Guffey
Auburn University

Reetika Gupta
Lehigh University

John Hafer
University of Nebraska at Omaha

Allan Hall
Western Kentucky University

Joan Hall
Macomb Community College

Clark Hallpike
Elgin Community College

James E. Hansen
University of Akron

Don Hanson
Bryant University

Jeffrey Harper
Texas Tech University

Dorothy Harpool
Wichita State University

Lynn Harris
Shippensburg University

Linda Hefferin
Elgin Community College

Charlane Held
Onondaga Community College

Lewis Hershey
Fayetteville State University

Jonathan Hibbard
Boston University

Tom Hickman
Loyola University

Robbie Hillsman
University of Tennessee–Martin

Nathan Himelstein
Essex County College

Adrienne Hinds
Northern Virginia Community College at Annandale

John Hobbs
University of Oklahoma

Don Hoffer
Miami University

Craig Hollingshead
Texas A&M University, Kingsville

Donna Hope
Nassau Community College

Ronald Hoverstad
University of the Pacific

Kris Hovespian
Ashland University

James Hunt
University of North Carolina Wilmington

Shane Hunt
Arkansas State University

Julie Huntley
Oral Roberts University

Sean Jasso
University of California–Riverside

Carol Johanek
Washington University, St. Louis

Doug Johansen
University of North Florida

Candy Johnson
Holyoke Community College

Maria Johnson
*Macomb Commity College,
Clinton Township*

Keith Jones
North Carolina A&T University

Janice Karlen
CUNY–Laguardia Community College

Eric J. Karson
Villanova University

Rajiv Kashyap
William Paterson University

Josette Katz
Atlantic Cape Community College

Garland Keesling
Towson University

Imran Khan
University of South Alabama–Mobile

Todd Korol
Monroe Community College

Dennis Lee Kovach
Community College of Allegheny County

Dmitri Kuksov
Washington University–St Louis

Jeff Kulick
George Mason University

Michelle Kunz
Morehead State University

Ann T. Kuzma
Minnesota State University, Mankato

John Kuzma
Minnesota State University at Mankato

Sandie Lakin
Hesser College

Timothy Landry
University of Oklahoma

Don Larson
Ohio State University

Felicia Lassk
Northeastern University

J. Ford Laumer
Auburn University

Marilyn Lavin
University of Wisconsin, Whitewater

Kenneth Lawrence
New Jersey IT

Freddy Lee
California State University, Los Angeles

Rebecca Legleiter
Tulsa CC Southeast Campus

Hillary Leonard
University of Rhode Island

Natasha Lindsey
University of North Alabama

Guy Lochiatto
Massachusetts Bay Community College

Paul Londrigan
Mott Community College

Terry Lowe
Heartland Community College

Dolly Loyd
University of Southern Mississippi

Harold Lucius
Rowan University

Alicia Lupinacci
Tarrant Community College

Stanley Madden
Baylor University

Lynda Maddox
George Washington University

Moutusi Maity
University of Wisconsin, Whitewater

Cesar Maloles
California State University, East Bay

Karl Mann
Tennessee Tech University

Cathy Martin
University of Akron

Melissa Martin
George Mason University

Carolyn Massiah
University of Central Florida

Tamara Masters
Brigham Young University

Erika Matulich
University of Tampa

Bob Mayer
Mesa State College

Nancy McClure
University of Central Oklahoma

Maria McConnnell
Lorain County Community College

Dennis Menezes
University of Louisville, Louisville

Mohan Menon
University of South Alabama

Michelle Meyer
Joliet Junior College

Ivor Mitchell
University of Nevada Reno

Mark Mitchell
University of South Carolina

Steven Moff
Pennsylvania College of Technology

Rex Moody
University of Colorado

Rex Moody
Central Washington University at Ellensburg

Melissa Moore
Mississippi State University

Linda Morable
Richland College

Farrokh Moshiri
University of California–Riverside

Dorothy Mulcahy
Bridgewater State College

James Munch
Wright State University–Dayton

Brian Murray
Jefferson Community College

Suzanne Murray
Piedmont Technical College

James E. Murrow
Drury University

Noreen Nackenson
Nassau Community College

Sandra Blake Neis
*Borough of Manhattan Community
College*

John Newbold
Sam Houston State University

Keith Niedermeier
University of Pennsylvania

Martin Nunlee
Syracuse University

Hudson Nwakanma
Florida A & M University

Lois Olson
San Diego State University

Beng Ong
California State University, Fresno

Daniel Onyeagba
Argosy University, Atlanta

Karen Overton
Houston Community College

Deborah L. Owens
University of Akron

Esther Page-Wood
Western Michigan University

Richard Pascarelli
Adelphi University

Terry Paul
Ohio State University, Columbus

Michael Pearson
Loyola University

Jerry Peerbolte
University of Arkansas–Fort Smith

Glenn Perser
Houston Community College

Diane Persky
Yeshiva University

Susan Peters
California State Polytechnic University at Pomona

Renee Pfeifer-Luckett
University of Wisconsin at Whitewater

Frank Alan Philpot
George Mason University

Gary Pieske
Minnesota State Community and Technical College

Jeff Podoshen
Temple University

Carmen Powers
Monroe Community College

Mike Preis
University of Illinois–Champaign

Susan Price
California Polytechnic State University

Lori Radulovich
Baldwin-Wallace College

Bruce Ramsey
Franklin University

Rosemary Ramsey
Wright State University

Srikumar Rao
Long Island University

Kristen Regine
Johnston & Wales University

Joseph Reihing
Nassau Community College

William Rice
California State University–Fresno

Patricia Richards
Westchester Community College

Eric Rios
Eastern University

Ann Renee Root
Florida Atlantic University

Janet Robinson
Mount St. Mary's College

Tom Rossi
Broome Community College

Heidi Rottier
Bradley University

Juanita Roxas
California State Polytechnic University

Donald Roy
Middle Tennessee State University

Linda Salisbury
Boston College

Nick Sarantakes
Austin Community College

Shikhar Sarin
Boise State University

Carl Saxby
University of Southern Indiana

Diana Scales
Tennessee State University

Dwight Scherban
Central Connecticut State University

James Schindler
Columbia Southern University

Jeffrey Schmidt
University of Oklahoma–Norman

Laura Shallow
St. Xavier University

Dan Sherrell
University of Memphis

Philip Shum
William Paterson University

Lisa Simon
California Polytechnic State University, San Luis Obispo

Rob Simon
University of Nebraska–Lincoln

Erin Sims
Devry University at Pomona

Lauren Ruth Skinner
University of Alabama at Birmingham

Karen Smith
Columbia Southern University

Lois J. Smith
University of Wisconsin

Julie Z. Sneath
University of South Alabama

Brent Sorenson
University of Minnesota–Crookston

James Spiers
Arizona State University–Tempe

Geoffrey Stewart
University of Louisiana

John Striebich
Monroe Community College

Randy Stuart
Kennesaw State University

James Swanson
Kishwaukee College

James Swartz
California State Polytechnic University

Robert R. Tangsrud, Jr.
University of North Dakota

Steve Taylor
Illinois State University

Sue Taylor
Southwestern Illinois College

Sharon Thach
Tennessee State University

Mary Tharp
University of Texas at San Antonio

Frank Tobolski
Lake in the Hills

Louis A. Tucci
College of New Jersey

Sue Umashankar
University of Arizona

Deborah Utter
Boston University

Ven Venkatesan
University of Rhode Island at Kingston

Bronis Verhage
Georgia State University

Deirdre Verne
Westchester Community College

Steve Vitucci
Tarleton University Central Texas

Keith Wade
Webber International University

Suzanne Walchli
University of the Pacific

Wakiuru Wamwara-Mbugua
Wright State University–Dayton

Bryan Watkins
Dominican University, Priory Campus

Ron Weir
East Tennessee State University

Ludmilla Wells
Florida Gulf Coast University

Thomas Whipple
Cleveland State University

Tom Whitman
Mary Washington College

Kathleen Williamson
University of Houston–Clear Lake

Phillip Wilson
Midwestern State University

Doug Witt
Brigham Young University

Kim Wong
Albuquerque Tech Institute

Letty Workman
Utah Valley University

Courtney Worsham
University of South Carolina

Brent Wren
University of Alabama–Huntsville

Alex Wu
California State University– Long Beach

Joseph Yasaian
McIntosh College

Poh-Lin Yeoh
Bentley College

Paschalina Ziamou
Bernard M. Baruch College

We would like to thank all the professors who were instrumental in guiding our revision of
not only the text, but also Connect and other ancillary materials

Ivan Abel
St. John's University

Wendi Achey
Northampton Community College

Praveen Aggarwal
University of Minnesota, Duluth

Keanon Alderson
California Baptist University

Rosalyn Amaro
*Florida State College at
Jacksonville*

Maria Aria
Camden County College

Jill S. Attaway
Illinois State University

Michelle Barnhart
Oregon State University

Robert Belenger
Bristol Community College

Tom Bilyeu
Southwestern Illinois College

Mark Blake
York College of Pennsylvania

Maurice Bode
Delgado Community College

Brad Cox
Midlands Technical College

Jean M. Brown
University of Alabama in Huntsville

Gary Brunswick
Northern Michigan University

Desislava Budeva
Ramapo College of New Jersey

Melissa Burnett
Missouri State University

Susan Carder
Northern Arizona University

Ella Carter
Bowie State University

Debi Cartwright
Truman State University

Haozhe Chen
East Carolina University

Angeline Close
The University of Texas at Ausin

Kevin Coulson
Emporia State University

Brent Cunningham
Jacksonville State University

Datha Damron-Martinez
Truman State University

Beth Deinert
Southeast Community College

David DiRusso
Millersville University

Michael Dotson
Appalachian State University

Colleen Dunn
Bucks County Community College

Diane Edmondson
Middle Tennessee State University

Burcak Ertimur
Fairleigh Dickinson University

David J. Faulds
University of Louisville

Amy Feest
Tunxis Community College

Kathleen Ferris-Costa
Bridgewater State University

Troy A. Festervand
Middle Tennessee State University

Paul Fombelle
Northeastern University

John Fraedrich
Southern Illinois University–Carbondale

Theresa E. Frame
Horry Georgetown Technical College

Sheila Fry
Champlain College

Jerome Gafford
Univeristy of North Alabama

Tao (Tony) Gao
Northeastern University

Lance Gentry
Colorado State University–Pueblo

Nabarun Ghose
The University of Findlay

Connie Golden
Lakeland Community College

Lisa Goolsby
Southern Adventist University

Deborah M. Gray
Central Michigan University

Susan Greer
*Horry-Georgetown Technical
College*

Cynthia Grether
Delta College

Mike Griffith
Lone Star College–Kingwood

Barbara Gross
California State University, Northridge

Chiquan Guo
The University of Texas–Pan American

Jamey Halleck
Marshall University

Richard Hanna
Northeastern University

David Eric Hansen
Texas Southern University

Jeffrey Harper
Texas Tech University

Perry Hidalgo
Gwinnett Technical College

Diane Holtzman
*Richard Stockton College of
New Jersey*

Monica Hodis
St. John Fisher College

Donna Hope
Nassau Community College

Gorman Houston
University of Alabama

Erika Hovland
Temple University

Vince Howe
University of North Carolina, Wilmington

Miriam Huddleston
Harford Community College

James B. Hunt
University of North Carolina, Wilmington

Eva Hyatt
Appalachian State University

Roxanne Jackson
Vance-Granville Community College

Grace Jebakumari Johnson
University of Wisconsin–Milwaukee

Victoria Jones
University of North Carolina, Wilmington

Sungwoo Jung
Columbus State University

Vishal Kashyap
Xavier University

Mark Kay
Montclair State University

Sylvia Keyes
Bridgewater State University

Tina Kiesler
California State University, Northridge

Brian Kinard
University of North Carolina, Wilmington

John Kinnett
Columbus State University

Peter Knight
University of Wisconsin, Parkside

Michael W. Kroff
Montana State University

Ann T. Kuzma
Minnesota State University, Mankato

Theodore Labay
Bishop State Community College

Donald W. Larson
The Ohio State University

James R. Lashley
Bowie State University

E. Scott Lathrop
*Whitman School of Management,
Syracuse University*

Debra Laverie
Texas Tech University

Cary LeBlanc
Assumption College

David M. Lee
Sam Houston State University

Andrea Licari
St. John's University

Junsang Lim
Virginia State University

Bryan D. Little
Marshall University

Ruth Lumb
Minnesota State University, Moorhead

Guy Lochiatto
MassBay Community College

Anne Weidemanis Magi
University of South Florida

David Matthews
*SUNY Adirondack (Adirondack
Community College)*

Fredric Mayerson
Kingsborough Community College

Myke McMullen
Long Beach Community College

Rajiv Mehta
New Jersey Institute of Technology

Sanjay S. Mehta
Sam Houston State University

Jeffrey Meier
Fox Valley Technical College

Michael Mejza
*University of Nevada,
Las Vegas*

Robert Meyer
Parkland College

Elizabeth Miller
Boston College

Iris Mohr
St. John's University

Josefer Montes
Walla Walla University

Dorothy J. Mulcahy
Bridgewater State University

Jay Mulki
Northestern University–Boston

Benjamin Muller
Portland Community College

Gergana Nenkov
Boston College

John Newbold
Sam Houston State University

Hudson Nwakanma
Florida A&M University

Matt O'Hern
University of Oregon

Richard B. Osborn
York College of Pennsylvania

Rodney Oudan
Worcester State University

Lauren Paisley
Genesee Community College

Mahatapa Palit
*Borough of Manhattan Community
College*

Janet Parish
Texas A&M University

Raymond A. Parkins, Jr.
Florida State College at Jacksonville

Ed Petkus
Ramapo College of New Jersey

Julie M. Pharr
Tennessee Tech University

Rajani Ganesh Pillai
North Dakota State University

Sampath Ranganathan
University of Wisconsin–Green Bay

Mohammed Rawwas
University of Northern Iowa

Virginia Reilly
Ocean County College

John E. Robbins
Winthrop University

Ann R. Root
Florida Atlantic University

Robert Rouwenhorst
University of Iowa

Donald P. Roy
Middle Tennessee State University

Alberto Rubio-Sanchez
University of the Incarnate Word

Catherine Ruggieri
St. John's University, New York

Doreen Sams
Georgia College & State University

Robin Schallie
Fox Valley Technical College

Douglas Scott
State College of Florida

Christine Seel
Delaware Valley College

Daaim Shabazz
Florida A&M University

Abhay Shah
Colorado State University–Pueblo

Rick Shannon
Western Kentucky University

Kenneth Shaw
State University of New York, Oswego

Robert Simon
University of Nebraska–Lincoln

Peter D. Simonson
North Dakota State University

David Smith
Bemidji State University

Dennis Spector
Naugatuck Valley Community College

Vernon R. Stauble
San Bernardino Valley College

Susan Steiz
Norwalk Community College

Geoffrey Stewart
University of Louisiana

Karen L. Stewart
Richard Stockton College of New Jersey

Susan Stone
Shippensburg University of Pennsylvania

Ray Stroup, Jr.
University of Louisiana at Lafayette

James Swenson
Minnesota State University, Moorhead

Steven Taylor
Illinois State University

Ramendra Thakur
University of Louisiana–Lafayette

Norman Thiel
Walla Walla University

Dennis Tootelian
California State University, Sacramento

Philip Trocchia
University of South Florida, St. Petersburg

Sven Tuzovic
Pacific Lutheran University

Leo Vasquez
San Bernardino Valley College, San Bernardino

Franck Vigneron
California State University Northridge

Doug Wilson
*University of Oregon–Lundquist
College of Business*

Roger Wilson
Fairmont State University

Doug Witt
Brigham Young University

Mike Wittmann
The University of Southern Mississippi

Van R. Wood
Virginia Commonwealth University

Jefrey R. Woodall
York College of Pennsylvania

Kim Wong
Central New Mexico Community College

Ashley Wright
Spartanburg Community College

Elle Wu
Louisiana State University

Charles Wyckoff
Riverside Community College

Ge Xiao
Wilkes University

Jim Zemanek
East Carolina University

Lin Zhang
Truman State University

We express our thanks to all faculty who have contributed to the development of digital learning content:

Lauren Spinner Beitelspacher
Babson University

Barbara Black
University of Miami

Thomas Byrnes
North Carolina State University

Donna Haeger
Monroe Community College

Todd Korol
Monroe Community College

Melissa Martin
George Mason University

Leroy Robinson
University of Houston, Clear Lake

John Striebech
Monroe Community College

Lois Olson
San Diego State University

A special thank you to Steven A. Taylor of Illinois State University, Elizabeth Jane Wilson of Suffolk University, Kevin Bertotti of iTVk, and Becky and Patrick of We Write Good for their efforts in authoring and producing the iSee it! videos in Connect.

We'd also like to thank the team at Hurix—Sumesh Yoganath, Namrata Gunjal, and Ashwin Srivastav—for their contributions, as well as Sue Sullivan of Editors, Inc.

brief contents

table of contents

© Charley Gallay/Getty Images

© Craig Barritt/Getty Images

© VCG/Getty Images

4 CONSCIOUS MARKETING, CORPORATE SOCIAL RESPONSIBILITY, AND ETHICS   116

© jackie ellis/Alamy

© B. O'Kane/Alamy

© Zuma Press, Inc./Alamy

© dpa picture alliance/Alamy

8   GLOBAL MARKETING   234

© Pascal Sittler/REA/Redux

© ABC Family/Courtesy Everett Collection

© David Paul Morris/Getty Images

SECTION 4   VALUE CREATION   337

© Chris McLennan/Alamy

© Bloomberg/Getty Images

© Bloomberg/Getty Images

© McGraw-Hill Education

© Cui Hao/Getty Images

© Fox Network/Photofest

© Rick Diamond/WireImage/Getty Images

© Ben Hider/Getty Images

ASSESSING THE MARKETPLACE

Section One, Assessing the Marketplace, contains five chapters. Following an introduction to marketing in Chapter 1, Chapter 2 focuses on how a firm develops its marketing strategy and a marketing plan. A central theme of the chapter is how firms can effectively create, capture, deliver, and communicate value to their customers. Chapter 3 is devoted to understanding how one can develop social and mobile marketing strategies. Chapter 4 focuses attention on marketing ethics. An ethical decision framework is developed and presented, and the key ethical concepts are linked back to the marketing plan introduced in Chapter 2. Finally, Chapter 5, Analyzing the Marketing Environment, focuses on how marketers can systematically uncover and evaluate opportunities.

CHAPTER 1

OVERVIEW OF MARKETING

After reading this chapter, you should be able to:

LO1-1 Define the role of marketing in organizations.

LO1-2 Describe how marketers create value for a product or service.

LO1-3 Understand why marketing is important both within and outside the firm.

Nestled in their lovely and iconic little gold boxes, Godiva chocolates can spark the desires of nearly any chocolate lover, just by reminding them of the joy they are likely to experience from tasting the delicious, luxurious treats. It seems almost innate: think about Godiva, start to salivate in anticipation. But in fact, the appeal of Godiva chocolates, as well as every detail that we used to describe them in the first sentence of this opener, represents a nearly century-long marketing effort by a premium brand chocolatier that is determined to keep its customers happy and coming back for more.

When Pierre and Joseph Draps first started selling chocolate pralines in 1926, they insisted on the idea that "Chocolate is a dream."[1] Thus from the very start of the company, Godiva has aimed to create an image and an experience for consumers that is totally different from the humdrum of everyday existence. The chocolates themselves are made with very high-quality ingredients.[2] In addition, Godiva introduces specific innovations and recipes for special occasions—from the Signature Lait that was created specifically to be handed out to guests at the 1939 theatrical release of *Gone with the Wind* to the Egérie Noir, a raspberry ganache treat created in honor of the company's 90th anniversary.[3] Collections featuring examples of its various editions highlight Godiva's long-standing and storied history; people who buy them can feel connected to a sense of both luxury and nostalgia.

Its packaging, high-quality gold boxes, also evokes luxury.[4] Whether consumers buy a single piece of chocolate as a treat for themselves or a 140-piece Gold Ballotin collection as an impressive gift for someone else,[5] the package is fancy and pretty, suggesting that the company values their purchase, no matter how large or small.

If they buy the treats from a small Godiva chocolatier, they also receive personal service when the salesperson wraps up their individually chosen treats with a gold bow. If they visit the expansive Godiva counter in Macy's flagship New York store, they can sample a vast variety of options, from soft serve ice cream to just-dipped strawberries encased in milk or dark chocolate.[6] If instead consumers want something a little more accessible, Godiva makes sure that prepackaged offerings are available in grocery stores. These mass-produced desserts are not quite so personalized, but they also are relatively less expensive than the high-end option.

Thus Godiva tries to make sure it has an option for virtually anyone—a less expensive, mass-produced version for shoppers who need a break from their daily chores, but also more expensive, delicately made, individualized options for those who regard excellent chocolate as a necessary indulgence. And with its golden boxes and high-end image, Godiva also has long guaranteed Valentines and gift givers that their presents would be appreciated and enjoyed if they splurged on the "good" candy.[7]

Although Godiva embraces its heritage as a Belgian company,[8] it also has fans and consumers around the world. Accordingly, it makes sure that people living anywhere in the world can access not only its products but also the stories and experiences that go along with those products. For example, it uses social marketing tools to tell stories about the five classically trained chefs, each with a unique and varied background, who take charge of developing new recipes.[9]

Thus, by adopting the various marketing methods, tactics, and recommendations that we describe throughout this book, Godiva has survived and thrived for nearly a century, while making sure that it has a strong foundation to last for decades more.

LO1-1 Define the role of marketing in organizations.

WHAT IS MARKETING?

Unlike other subjects you may have studied, marketing already is very familiar to you. You start your day by agreeing to do the dishes if your roommate will make the coffee. Then you fill up your car with gas. You attend a class that you have chosen and paid for. After class, you pick up lunch and maybe a chocolate bar for dessert at the cafeteria, which you eat while reading a book on your iPad. Then you leave campus to have your hair cut and take in a movie. On your bus ride back to school, you pass the time by buying a few songs from Apple's iTunes. In each case, you have acted as the buyer and made a decision about whether you should part with your time and/or money to receive a particular product or service. If, after you return home, you decide to sell some clothes on eBay that you don't wear much anymore, you have become a seller. In each of these transactions, you were engaged in marketing.

The American Marketing Association (AMA) states that "**marketing** is the activity, set of institutions, and processes for creating, *capturing,* communicating, delivering, and exchanging offerings that have value for customers, clients, partners, and society at large."[10] What does this definition really mean? Good marketing is not a random activity; it requires thoughtful planning with an emphasis on the ethical implications of any of those decisions on society in general. Firms develop a **marketing plan** (Chapter 2) that specifies the marketing activities for a specific period of time. The marketing plan also is broken down into various components—how the product or service will be conceived or designed, how much it should cost, where and how it will be promoted, and how it will get to the consumer. In any exchange, the parties to the transaction should be satisfied. In our previous example, you should be satisfied or even delighted with the song you downloaded, and Apple should be satisfied with the amount of money it received from you. Thus, the core aspects of marketing are found in Exhibit 1.1. Let's see how these core aspects look in practice.

EXHIBIT 1.1 Core Aspects of Marketing

- Marketing helps create value.
- Marketing is about satisfying customer needs and wants.
- Marketing entails an exchange.
- Marketing requires product, price, place, and promotion decisions.
- Marketing can be performed by both individuals and organizations.
- Marketing affects various stakeholders.

Marketing

Some chocolate lovers prefer Hershey's over other brands because it is made in Hershey, Pennsylvania.

© Tim Shaffer/Reuters

Marketing Is about Satisfying Customer Needs and Wants

Understanding the marketplace, and especially consumer needs and wants, is fundamental to marketing success. In the broadest terms, the marketplace refers to the world of trade. More narrowly, however, the marketplace can be segmented or divided into groups of people who are pertinent to an organization for particular reasons. For example, the marketplace for soft drinks may include most people in the world, but as Godiva and Hershey's battle for chocolate lovers, they divide the population into a host of categories: luxury versus cost-conscious, service-oriented versus self-service, those who purchase chocolates for a quick energy-boosting snack versus those who purchase it as a reward for a hard day's work or as a gift for a friend or loved one, and those who prefer "Made in America" versus those who prefer the illusion that their chocolates are made in Belgium (even though Godiva has manufacturing facilities in the United States). If you manufacture chocolate, you want to know for which marketplace segments your product is most relevant, then make sure you build a marketing strategy that targets those groups.

Marketing Entails an Exchange

Marketing is about an **exchange**—the trade of things of value between the buyer and the seller so that each is better off as a result. As depicted in Exhibit 1.2, sellers provide

EXHIBIT 1.2   Exchange: The Underpinning of Seller–Buyer Relationships

Communications
and delivery

Goods/services
producers
(sellers)

Money and
information

Customers/
consumers (buyers)

If you can't wait for an Amazon delivery of Godiva chocolates, go to one of its mall store locations and buy them in person!

© Steve Vidler/Alamy

products or services, then communicate and facilitate the delivery of their offering to consumers. Buyers complete the exchange by giving money and information to the seller. Suppose you learn about a new Godiva chocolate from a friend's tweet, so you visit Godiva's website to check it out. From there you order a box from Amazon's website. Your billing information is already in the company's system, so you do not have to enter your credit card number or other information. Furthermore, Amazon creates a record of your purchase, which it uses, together with your other purchase trends, to create personalized recommendations of other luscious treats that you might like. Thus, Amazon uses the valuable information you provide to facilitate future exchanges and solidify its relationship with you. Nonetheless, not wanting to wait until tomorrow to receive your chocolates, you rush down to the Godiva store in the mall and buy some, consuming them all on your way home.

Marketing Requires Product, Price, Place, and Promotion Decisions

Marketing traditionally has been divided into a set of four interrelated decisions and consequent actions known as the **marketing mix**, or **four Ps**: product, price, place, and promotion (as defined in Exhibit 1.3).[11] The four Ps are the controllable set of decisions or activities that the firm uses to respond to the wants of its target markets. But what does each of these activities in the marketing mix entail?

Product: Creating Value The first of the four Ps is product. Although marketing is a multifaceted function, its fundamental

purpose is to create value by developing a variety of offerings, including goods, services, and ideas, to satisfy customer needs. Take, for example, chocolate. At one time,
people purchased simple chocolates and cocoa from a local
supplier and either ate it by itself or combined it with other
ingredients at home. Imagine the night that a bunch of kids
got together by a campfire and decided to make a sandwich
by melting chocolate and marshmallows and holding the
sweet, creamy, white and brown goop together with graham
crackers—the night s'mores were born. Today, Hershey's
and Mars make a range of chocolates and candies. Hershey's
Chocolate candies include Almond Joy, Cadbury, Reese's,
and more. Furthermore, Hershey's "sugar confectionery"
products range from Jolly Rancher to Twizzlers, its owns Ice
Breakers Bubble Yum Gum, a line of Hershey's chocolate
and Reese's peanut butter baking goods, and snacks such as
Mauna Loa mixed nuts.[12] Mars chocolate line of products
includes 3 Musketeers, Milky Way, Snickers, and M&M's.

*There is nothing like s'mores around a campfire to kindle one's
interest in chocolate.*

© Stephen Alvarez/National Geographic/Getty Images

However, Mars is not just in the chocolate business. It also owns Uncle Ben's; Wrigley
products that include Double Mint and 5 gum; Life Savers; Altoids; drinks such as Dove
hot chocolate; and even pet food, including Iams and Pedigree.[13] And these treats are
available both online and through a plethora of retail outlets from grocery to convenience
stores like 7-Eleven.

Goods are items that you can physically touch. A bag of Godiva chocolate, Nike
shoes, Pepsi-Cola, a Frappuccino, Kraft cheese, Tide, an iPad, and countless other products are examples of goods. As we describe at the start of this chapter, Godiva makes
chocolates—but it adds value to its products by using fresh and interesting ingredients of
the highest quality, packaging the chocolates in gold boxes, using personalized service in
its boutiques, and creating a nostalgic historical and quality image through its various
promotional outlets. Hershey's and Mars sell very good, affordable confections; Godiva
sells an experience.

Unlike goods, services are intangible customer benefits that are produced by people or
machines and cannot be separated from the producer. When people buy tickets—whether
for airline travel, a sporting event, or the theater—they are paying not for the physical ticket
stub but, of course, for the experience they gain, a lesson that JetBlue has taken to heart, as
we describe in Superior Service 1.1. For people who like to pick out their chocolates one at
a time, Godiva offers a full-service experience in their boutiques. Hotels, insurance agencies, and spas similarly provide services. Getting money from your bank, whether through
an ATM or from a teller, is another example of using a service. In this case, cash machines
usually add value to the banking experience because they are conveniently located, fast,
and easy to use.

Many offerings in the market combine goods and services.[14] When you go to an
optical center, you get your eyes examined (a service) and purchase new contact lenses

*Hershey's and Mars sell very
good but affordable confections.*

Left: © Dean Bertoncelj/Shutterstock RF;
right: © Kevin Wheal/Alamy

Superior Service 1.1

A Service for Fliers, a Moneymaker for JetBlue Airlines: WiFi-Enabled Shopping in the Air[i]

There is a new retail channel taking off—literally. The "onboard, online retail business" refers to the options that more and more airlines offer passengers to shop through their mobile devices while they fly toward their destination. The retail channel relies on technology that enables airlines to offer WiFi access to customers and cater to customers' evident desire to buy things while flying.

According to JetBlue, which began offering WiFi-enabled flights at no charge as a service to customers, the expectation was that people would check their social media or maybe get some work e-mails sent. Instead, it found that many passengers on flights were visiting shopping websites and picking up new items to be delivered to their homes. Evidently, those kitschy in-flight catalogs that had long been stuck in the seat pockets, with their silly gifts and travel kits, had strong market appeal. When consumers could go online, they wanted the same functions of the in-flight retail catalogs paired with the conveniences of ordering and paying online.

In response, various players in the market are seeking to attract sales by the captive audience of airline passengers. For example, in a partnership with Amazon, JetBlue pushes purchases of Amazon content, or else encourages customers to invest in purchasing a new Prime membership, which enables them to stream the content for free. According to a JetBlue spokesperson, a "surprising number" of customers take advantage of this offer, readily signing up to pay the annual fee in return for the chance to stream *House of Cards* on their flight to the real Washington, DC, for example.

Most carriers charge passengers for the right to access the WiFi, whereas JetBlue continues to offer it for free, in the belief that it can get more people to use the service that way. That means more people are looking at the product and service offers for sale, and that means that the resulting purchases are more likely to make up for the costs of the free service offer.

But there is something of a cost for consumers—namely, the prevalence and clutter of advertising that pops up every time they go online while onboard. For some, the annoyance of the advertising is enough to put them off the idea of shopping. Others, though, would even consider paying for the right to see that sort of marketing in the air.

JetBlue has enhanced its service experience by offering on-board WiFi.

© Blend Images/Alamy RF

When you attend a Bruno Mars concert, you are paying for a service.

© Rich Polk/Clear Channel/Getty Images

(a good). If you attend a Bruno Mars concert, you can be enthralled by the world-class performance. To remember the event, you might want to pick up a shirt or a souvenir from the concert. With these tangible goods, you can relive and remember the enjoyment of the experience over and over again.

Ideas include thoughts, opinions, and philosophies; intellectual concepts such as these also can be marketed. Groups promoting bicycle safety go to schools, give talks, and sponsor bike helmet poster contests for the members of their primary market—children. Then their secondary target market segment, parents and siblings, gets involved through their interactions with the young contest participants. The exchange of value occurs when the children listen to the sponsors' presentation and wear their helmets while bicycling, which means they have adopted, or become "purchasers," of the safety idea that the group marketed.

Marketing Analytics 1.1 | Location, Location, Analytics: Starbucks' Use of Data to Place New Stores[ii]

By now, nearly everyone on the planet recognizes the green mermaid logo that proudly sits atop every Starbucks sign, poster, and cup. The ubiquitous coffee giant maintains more than 22,000 locations in more than 66 countries. But its growth has not been without a few stumbles and bumps in the road. For example, in the last decade, hundreds of newly opened stores had to be closed because of their poor performance. In analyzing how the company got to that point, Patrick O'Hagan, Starbucks' manager of global market planning, explained that many of the stores never should have opened. However, the staff in charge of these location choices had been inundated with so much data, they were unable to use them to make profitable decisions. Thus, the Starbucks story reveals a great deal about the importance of data analytics.

Starbucks began using Esri's Geographic Information Systems (GIS) technology as far back as the 1990s. But it has perfected its applications of the GIS-provided predictive analytics only recently. Currently, it is using the information gleaned from the technology to plan 1,500 new locations. With the system's ArcGIS Online tool, Starbucks obtains a graphical summary of the GIS data in map form. These data include both location information and demographic details, which the software analyzes according to pertinent criteria. The applications allow Starbucks' staff to pinpoint ideal locations that are likely to attract substantial traffic and thus boost chainwide sales, such that "ArcGIS allows us to create replicable consumer applications that are exactly what they need." Because the GIS technology is accessible through desktops as well as mobile devices, location experts in the field also can combine the high-tech insights with their real-world observations.

Starbucks uses Geographic Information Systems (GIS) technology to pinpoint ideal locations and determine which kinds of stores to open in those locations.

© Bhandol/Alamy

Not only does the GIS technology help Starbucks determine the ideal locations for new stores, but it also can enable the company to decide which kinds of stores to open. For example, many of the 1,500 planned new stores will feature drive-through windows; others will be smaller stores, strategically placed to provide the greatest customer convenience. The new approach already has been proving effective, according to results that show that the most recently opened stores, particularly those in the Americas, consistently are producing great returns and exceeding hurdle rates.

Price: Capturing Value The second of the four Ps is price. Everything has a price, although it doesn't always have to be monetary. Price, therefore, is everything the buyer gives up—money, time, and/or energy—in exchange for the product.[15] Marketers must determine the price of a product carefully on the basis of the potential buyer's belief about its value. For example, JetBlue Airlines can take you from New York to Denver. The price you pay for that service depends on how far in advance you book the ticket, the time of year, and whether you want to fly coach or business class. If you value the convenience of buying your ticket at the last minute for a ski trip between Christmas and New Year's Day and you want to fly business class, you can expect to pay four or five times as much as you would for the cheapest available ticket. That is, you have traded off a lower price for convenience. For marketers, the key to determining prices is figuring out how much customers are willing to pay so that they are satisfied with the purchase and the seller achieves a reasonable profit.

Place: Delivering the Value Proposition The third P, place, represents all the activities necessary to get the product to the right customer when that customer wants it. As Marketing Analytics 1.1 describes, for Starbucks, that means expanding its storefronts constantly and proactively, so that it is easy for caffeine junkies to find their fix. Creative locations, such as kiosks at the baggage claim in airports or small booths in grocery stores, represent the chain's effort to improve its offering on this dimension of the marketing mix.

Place more commonly deals specifically with retailing and marketing channel management, also known as supply chain management. *Supply chain management* is the set of approaches and techniques that firms employ to efficiently and effectively integrate their suppliers, manufacturers, warehouses, stores, and other firms involved in the transaction (e.g., transportation companies) into a seamless value chain in which merchandise is produced and distributed in the right quantities, to the right locations, and at the right time, while minimizing systemwide costs and satisfying the service levels required by the customers. Many marketing students initially overlook the importance of marketing channel management because a lot of these activities are behind the scenes. But without a strong and efficient marketing channel system, merchandise isn't available when customers want it. Then customers are disappointed, and sales and profits suffer.

Promotion: Communicating the Value Proposition The fourth P is promotion. Even the best products and services will go unsold if marketers cannot communicate their value to customers. Promotion is communication by a marketer that informs, persuades, and reminds potential buyers about a product or service so as to influence their opinions and elicit a response. Promotion generally can enhance a product's or service's value. When the publisher of the well-known Babar books wanted to celebrate the 80th anniversary of the series, it initiated a $100,000 campaign. Working in collaboration with toy and bookstores, the campaign did not just suggest people buy the books and read about an elephant king. Instead, it embraced a sense of nostalgia and evoked a simpler time, in which grandparents might read pleasant stories to their grandchildren.[16]

Marketing Can Be Performed by Individuals and Organizations

Imagine how complicated the world would be if you had to buy everything you consumed directly from producers or manufacturers. You would have to go from farm to farm buying your food and then from manufacturer to manufacturer to purchase the table, plates, and utensils you needed to eat that food. Fortunately, marketing intermediaries such as retailers accumulate merchandise from producers in large amounts and then sell it to you in smaller amounts. The process by which businesses sell to consumers is known as **business-to-consumer (B2C) marketing**; the process of selling merchandise or services from one business to another is called **business-to-business (B2B) marketing**. When Keurig sells its machines and coffee to you on its website, it is a B2C sale, but when it sells similar items for office use, it is a B2B transaction. Through various Internet sites such as eBay and Etsy, consumers market their products and services to other consumers. This third category, in which consumers sell to other consumers, is **consumer-to-consumer (C2C) marketing**. These marketing transactions are illustrated in Exhibit 1.4.

When Keurig sells its machines and coffee to you on its website, it is a B2C sale, but when it sells similar items for office use, it is a B2B transaction.

Left: Source: Keurig Green Mountain, Inc.; right: © Sergi Alexander/Getty Images

EXHIBIT 1.4 Marketing Can Be Performed by Individuals and by Organizations

Individuals can also undertake activities to market themselves. When you apply for a job, for instance, the research you do about the firm, the résumé and cover letter you submit with your application, and the way you dress for the interview and conduct yourself during it are all forms of marketing activities. Accountants, lawyers, financial planners, physicians, and other professional service providers also constantly market their services one way or another.

Marketing Affects Various Stakeholders

Most people think of marketing as a way to facilitate the sale of products or services to customers or clients. But marketing can also affect several other stakeholders (e.g., supply chain partners, society at large). Partners in the supply chain include wholesalers, retailers, or other intermediaries such as transportation or warehousing companies. All of these entities are involved in marketing to one another. Manufacturers sell merchandise to retailers, but the retailers often have to convince manufacturers to sell to them. After many years of not being able to purchase products from Ralph Lauren because it sells below the manufacturers' suggested retail price (MSRP), TJX Companies, Inc., operators of Marshall's and TJMaxx, among others, is now Ralph Lauren's largest customer.[17]

Marketing also can aim to benefit an entire industry or society at large. The dairy industry targets its "Milk Life" and "Body by Milk" campaigns at different target segments, including parents, their children, and athletes. Through this campaign, the allied milk

The "Milk Life" and "Body by Milk" marketing campaigns create a high level of awareness for the milk industry.

Left: Courtesy of Lowe Campbell Ewald and MilkPEP; right: © Jonathan Ferrey/Getty Images producers have created high levels of awareness about the benefits of drinking milk, including the high levels of protein, potassium, and calcium it provides. The focus is largely on how drinking milk for breakfast fits in with a healthy lifestyle that helps people maintain their focus, weight, and muscle mass. Even the industry's charitable campaigns resonate with this notion: The Milk Drive, run in conjunction with Feeding America, seeks to ensure that local food banks are sufficiently stocked with this nutritious, frequently requested item. Such campaigns benefit the entire dairy industry and promote the health benefits of drinking milk to society at large.

Marketing Helps Create Value

Marketers and advertisers spend about $189 billion in the United States and $592 billion worldwide. Without such spending, and the marketing jobs associated with it, the global economy would plummet. If all ad spending on television and on streaming services like Hulu were to disappear, consumers would wind up paying around $1200 per year to access about a dozen channels each. Some currently available channels that appeal to relatively small, niche audiences likely would not be able to survive, though, so the options would shrink overall. Removing all marketing spending would also affect many websites. For example, Facebook is so widespread and popular, it likely could make up for any lost advertising revenues by charging users just about $12 per year, and most users likely would be willing to pay that rate. However, the charges would severely limit Facebook's spread into less developed nations, where $12 is more than many people earn in a fortnight. Other sites, such as Buzzfeed, would likely disappear altogether.[18]

But marketing didn't get to this current level of prominence among individuals, corporations, and society at large overnight.[19] To understand how marketing has evolved into its present-day, integral business function of creating value, let's look for a moment at some of the milestones in marketing's short history (see Exhibit 1.5).

Production-Oriented Era Around the turn of the 20th century, most firms were production oriented and believed that a good product would sell itself. Henry Ford, the founder of Ford Motor Company, once famously remarked, "Customers can have any color they want so long as it's black." Manufacturers were concerned with product innovation, not with satisfying the needs of individual consumers, and retail stores typically were considered places to hold the merchandise until a consumer wanted it.

Sales-Oriented Era Between 1920 and 1950, production and distribution techniques became more sophisticated; at the same time, the Great Depression and World War II

EXHIBIT 1.5   Marketing Evolution: Production, Sales, Marketing, and Value

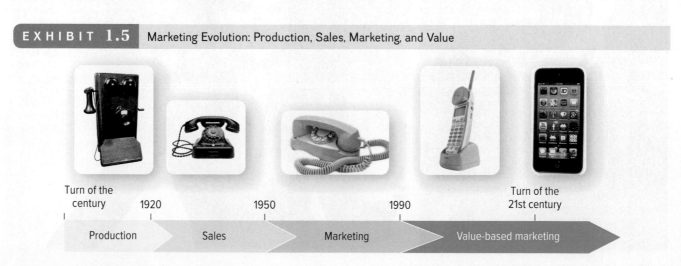

| Turn of the century | 1920 | 1950 | 1990 | Turn of the 21st century |

Production → Sales → Marketing → Value-based marketing →

Photos (left to right): © Ryan McVay/Getty Images RF; © CMCD/Getty Images RF; © Ted Dayton Photography/Beateworks/Corbis RF; © Ryan McVay/Getty Images RF; © McGraw-Hill Education/Mark Dierker, photographer

conditioned customers to consume less or manufacture items themselves, so they planted victory gardens instead of buying produce. As a result, manufacturers had the capacity to produce more than customers really wanted or were able to buy. Firms found an answer to their overproduction in becoming sales oriented: They depended on heavy doses of personal selling and advertising.

Market-Oriented Era After World War II, soldiers returned home, got new jobs, and started families. At the same time, manufacturers turned from focusing on the war effort toward making consumer products. Suburban communities, featuring cars in every garage, sprouted up around the country, and the new suburban fixture, the shopping center, began to replace cities' central business districts as the hub of retail activity and a place to just hang out. Some products, once in limited supply because of World War II, became plentiful. And the United States entered a buyers' market—the customer became king! When consumers again had choices, they were able to make purchasing decisions on the basis of factors such as quality, convenience, and price. Manufacturers and retailers thus began to focus on what consumers wanted and needed before they designed, made, or attempted to sell their products and services. It was during this period that firms discovered marketing.

Value-Based Marketing Era Most successful firms today are market oriented.[20] That means they generally have transcended a production or selling orientation and attempt to discover and satisfy their customers' needs and wants. Before the turn of the 21st century, better marketing firms recognized that there was more to good marketing than simply discovering and providing what consumers wanted and needed; to compete successfully, they would have to give their customers greater value than their competitors did. (The importance of value is appropriately incorporated into the AMA definition of marketing discussed earlier.)

Value reflects the relationship of benefits to costs, or what you *get* for what you *give*.[21] In a marketing context, customers seek a fair return in goods and/or services for their hard-earned money and scarce time. They want products or services that meet their specific needs or wants *and* that are offered at a price that they believe is a good value. A good value, however, doesn't necessarily mean the product or service is inexpensive. If it did, luxury goods manufacturers like Godiva would go out of business. There are customers willing to pay asking prices for all types of goods at all price levels because, to those individuals, what they get for what they give is a good value. This point is central to the marketing strategy adopted by Whole Foods, as Adding Value 1.1 explains.

A creative way to provide value to customers is to engage in value cocreation.[22] In this case, customers can act as collaborators to create the product or service. When clients work with their investment advisers, they cocreate their investment portfolios; when Nike allows customers to custom design their sneakers, they are cocreating.

In the next section, we explore the notion of value-based marketing further. Specifically, we look at various options for attracting customers by providing them with better value than the competition does. Then we discuss how firms compete on the basis of value. Finally, we examine how firms transform the value concept into their value-driven activities.

PROGRESS CHECK

1. What is the definition of marketing?
2. Marketing is about satisfying _____ and _____.
3. What are the four components of the marketing mix?
4. Who can perform marketing?
5. What are the various eras of marketing?

Adding Value 1.1   The Meaning of Best Value: Whole Foods' Purpose-Based Marketing [iii]

Some analysts looking at Whole Foods' dwindling sales numbers and decreased earnings would feel the solution to these issues is obvious: The grocery chain should lower its prices so that consumers consider it more valuable. Whole Foods rejects that notion though, arguing instead that value means far more than prices. And it has several ideas in mind to prove that it is right.

To start, it has introduced a new Responsibly Grown rating program, which identifies all fresh produce and flowers according to their environmental impact. The program is stringent in its demands. When vendors exert minor environmental impacts, they are rated good; those producers that go further by, for example, minimizing wasteful plastic usage or ensuring conservation areas for bees, earn a ranking of better. The producers identified as the best address a vast range of responsibility initiatives, from working conditions for farmers to conservation efforts to clean energy to renewable resources and so on. For example, one criterion asks farmers how many earthworms live in the soil on their farms.

e-oriented initiative follows Whole Foods' existing efforts such as its eco-scale applied to cleaning products and separate programs to determine the sustainability and responsibility associated with animal and fish products. Furthermore, by 2018, it plans to introduce labels that indicate whether any particular food item contains any genetically modified ingredients. This produce-oriented initiative follows Whole Foods' existing efforts such as its eco-scale applied to cleaning products and separate programs to determine the sustainability and responsibility associated with animal and fish products. Furthermore, by 2018, it plans to introduce labels that indicate whether any particular food item contains any genetically modified ingredients.

Whole Foods' Responsibly Grown rating program identifies all fresh produce and flowers according to their environmental impact.

© Justin Sullivan/Getty Images

In parallel with these new initiatives, Whole Foods has developed a revised advertising campaign, with a prominent tagline that reminds shoppers that "Values matter." The commercials emphasize that by shopping at Whole Foods, consumers can be confident that their food has been sourced responsibly and fairly. For example, any beef purchased in the stores has been raised by responsible ranchers who give the cows "room to roam."

By promoting the idea that "value is inseparable from values," Whole Foods seeks to remind shoppers of all that it provides, in exchange for a somewhat higher price point. In particular, it promises that they can make their food choices confidently, buoyed by a range of information that Whole Foods will make available to them at all times.

 LO1-2 Describe how marketers create value for a product or service.

Kroger collects massive amounts of data about how, when, why, where, and what people buy, and then analyzes those data to better serve its customers.

© Daniel Acker/Bloomberg/Getty Images

How Do Marketing Firms Become More Value Driven?

Firms become value driven by focusing on four activities. First, they share information about their customers and competitors across their own organization and with other firms that help them get the product or service to the marketplace, such as manufacturers and transportation companies. Second, they strive to balance their customers' benefits and costs. Third, they concentrate on building relationships with customers. Fourth, they take advantage of new technologies and connect with their customers using social and mobile media.

Marketing Analytics Modern marketers rely on sophisticated data analytics to define and refine their approaches to their customers and their markets. Companies such as Starbucks, CVS, Kroger, Netflix, and Amazon collect massive amounts of data about how, when, why, where, and what people buy, and then analyze those data to inform their choices.

Balancing Benefits with Costs Value-oriented marketers constantly measure the benefits that customers perceive against the cost of their offerings. They use available customer data to find opportunities to satisfy their customers' needs better, keep down costs, and develop long-term loyalties. For example, except in a few instances, Hershey's does not have fancy stores with highly paid salespeople to sell its chocolate, but its high-quality products are available in self-service stores wherever food items are sold.

Hershey's balances benefits with costs by placing its products in self-service stores.
© Lee Jae-Won/Reuters

Building Relationships with Customers During the past couple of decades, marketers have begun to develop a **relational orientation** as they have realized that they need to think about their customers in terms of relationships rather than transactions.[23] To build relationships, firms focus on the lifetime profitability of the relationship, not how much money is made during each transaction. Thus, Apple makes its innovations compatible with existing products to encourage consumers to maintain a long-term relationship with the company across all their electronic needs.

This relationship approach uses a process known as **customer relationship management (CRM)**, a business philosophy and set of strategies, programs, and systems that focus on identifying and building loyalty among the firm's most valued customers.[24] Firms that employ CRM systematically collect information about their customers' needs and then use that information to target their best customers with the products, services, and special promotions that appear most important to them.

Connecting with Customers Using Social and Mobile Media Marketers are steadily embracing new technologies such as social and mobile media to allow them to connect better with their customers and thereby serve their needs more effectively. Businesses take social and mobile media seriously and include these advanced tools in the development of their marketing strategies, though as Social and Mobile Marketing 1.1 explains, even these efforts might not be sufficient to keep up with consumers' rapidly changing demands. In turn, 97 percent of marketers assert that they use social media tools for their businesses.[25] That's largely because approximately 4.2 billion people link to some social media sites through their mobile devices.[26]

Apple makes its new products compatible with existing ones to maintain a long-term relationship with its customers.
© Spencer Platt/Getty Images

Social & Mobile Marketing 1.1   What Comes Around: Marketing Today[iv]

The signs of the growth of mobile advertising, at the expense of other digital forms such as desktops and laptops, have long been evident. But the speed with which this shift is occurring seemingly is taking many marketers by surprise, because it is virtually unprecedented. Consider some of the numbers: In 2009, mobile Internet ad spending was $1.3 billion, while in 2018 it is projected to be $125 billion. Within just a couple of years, mobile advertising will be a bigger market than digital advertising.

Both forms are similar, in the sense that they are clearly distinct from traditional marketing and seek to reach technologically savvy shoppers. But they require unique approaches and marketing plans, because a campaign that works well on a user's desktop computer might not function effectively on a tablet or smartphone. Furthermore, mobile marketing offers functionalities and advertising tactics that digital ads cannot provide. In addition, mobile advertising allows brands and marketers to send timely, location-based communications to consumers at the moment they enter a store or begin a search for a nearby restaurant on their phones.

Another trend occurring apace with this shift is the rise of ad-blocking technology. Apple now allows users to install software to block banner ads in digital channels. Although consumers indicate that they would like the ability to block advertising in mobile settings as well, marketing messages contained within apps continue to be prevalent. In this sense, advertisers might seek to expand and improve their mobile marketing so as to avoid the barriers that consumers can implement on their desktops. In the longer term, though, the shift to more mobile marketing likely implies the need for new forms of communication, including game-oriented, social content, and informational advertising that does not really look like advertising at all.

Yet even with this astounding penetration, only 20 percent of the world's population use Facebook—which means 80 percent still have not signed up.[27] The United States and United Kingdom may be approaching saturation, but there is still huge growth potential for social networks. Before users can sign up for Facebook, though, they need access to high-speed Internet. Other countries continue to experience higher Facebook growth rates as they gain greater Internet access and as Facebook becomes available in more languages (around 140 currently). The global average Internet penetration rate hovers below 50 percent, with massive populations in Africa and Asia still limited in their access.[28]

Beyond social media sites, online travel agencies such as Expedia, Travelocity, Orbitz, Priceline, and Kayak have become the first place that users go to book travel arrangements. In 2015, almost 150 million bookings, representing 57 percent of all travel bookings, were made on the Internet. Sixty-five percent of same-day booking were made from mobile devices.[29] Customers who book hotels using travel agencies become loyal to the agency that gives them the lowest prices rather than to any particular hotel brand. So hotels are using social media and mobile applications to lure customers back to their specific brands by engaging in conversations with them on Facebook and allowing fans of the page to book their hotel reservations through Facebook. Some hotel chains have mobile applications that allow customers to make changes to their reservations, shift check-in and check-out times, and add amenities or services to their stays. The hotels know a lot about their customers because they collect information about their previous visits, including the type of room they stayed in, their preferences (from pillows to drinks consumed from the minibar), and the type of room service they prefer.

Several restaurant chains are exploiting location-based social media applications such as HappyCow, Yelp, Foodspotting, Foursquare, OpenTable, and Seamless.[30] By using location-based apps on their mobile phones, customers can use, for

Marketers are increasingly connecting with their customers via mobile devices

© Tanya Constantine/Getty Images RF

Make travel arrangements on-line either through Facebook or your mobile app and check-in is a breeze.

© Erik Isakson/Getty Images RF

example, HappyCow to find nearby vegetarian restaurants or Yelp to find restaurants that are well rated by users. The result is that users are driving the way brands and stores are interacting with social media.

Buffalo Wild Wings suggests that its diners check in to its locations using their phones. The target customers for this chain are young and tech savvy, and with its in-house games and sports broadcasts, Buffalo Wild Wings is uniquely situated to encourage customers to connect and bring their friends along. It offers contests and encourages frequent visits to win. Customers can earn free chicken wings or soft drinks within their first three visits. Buffalo Wild Wings' Game Break allows customers to play fantasy-style and real-time games for prizes, whether they are in-store using a tablet or anywhere at all on their smartphones.[31]

Buffalo Wild Wings attracts young and tech-savvy customers to its restaurants by offering contests and games through mobile devices.

© dcwcreations/Shutterstock RF

PROGRESS CHECK

1. Does providing a good value mean selling at a low price?
2. How are marketers connecting with customers through social and mobile media?

WHY IS MARKETING IMPORTANT?

LO1-3 Understand why marketing is important both within and outside the firm.

Marketing once was only an afterthought to production. Early marketing philosophy went something like this: "We've made it; now how do we get rid of it?" However, marketing not only has shifted its focus dramatically but it also has evolved into a major business function

EXHIBIT 1.6   Importance of Marketing

Can be
entrepreneurial

Expands global
presence

Importance
of
marketing

Enriches society

Pervasive across
channel members

Top left: © Thinkstock/Jupiterimages RF; top right: © Jason Reed/Getty Images RF; middle right: © JG Photography/Alamy RF; bottom right: © McGraw-Hill Education/Andrew Resek, photographer; bottom left: © Purestock/SuperStock RF; middle left: © Blend Images/Ariel Skelley/Getty Images RF.

that crosses all areas of a firm or organization, as illustrated in Exhibit 1.6. Marketing advises production about how much of the company's product to make and then tells supply chain managers when to ship it. It creates long-lasting, mutually valuable relationships between the company and the firms from which it buys.[32] It identifies those elements that local customers value and makes it possible for the firm to expand globally. Marketing has had a significant impact on consumers as well. Without marketing, it would be difficult for any of us to learn about new products and services. Understanding marketing can even help you find a job after you finish school.

Marketing Expands Firms' Global Presence

A generation ago Coca-Cola was available in many nations, but Levi's and most other U.S. brands weren't. Blue jeans were primarily an American product—made in the United States for the U.S. market. But today most jeans, including those of Levi Strauss & Co., are made in places other than the United States and are available nearly everywhere. Thanks to MTV and other global entertainment venues, cheap foreign travel, and the Internet, you share many of your consumption behaviors with college students in countries all over the globe. The best fashions, music, and even food trends disseminate rapidly around the world. Take a look at your next shopping bag. Whatever it contains, you will find goods from many countries: produce from Mexico, jeans from Japan, electronics from Korea.

EXHIBIT 1.7 Supply Chain

Raw material → Manufacturer → Retailer → Consumer

Global manufacturers and retailers continue to make inroads into the U.S. market. The Dutch grocery store giant Ahold is among the top five grocery store chains in the United States, though you may never have heard of it because it operates under names such as Stop & Shop, Giant, and Peapod in the United States.[33] As marketing helps expand firms' global presence, it also enhances global career opportunities for marketing professionals.

Marketing Is Pervasive across Marketing Channel Members

Firms do not work in isolation. Manufacturers buy raw materials and components from suppliers, which they sell to wholesalers, retailers, or other businesses after they have turned the materials into products (see Exhibit 1.7). Every time materials or products are bought or sold, they are transported to different locations, which sometimes requires that they be stored in warehouses operated by yet other organizations. Such a group of firms that make and deliver a given set of goods and services is known as a supply chain or a marketing channel. All the various channel members (e.g., suppliers, manufacturers, wholesalers, and retailers) of the supply chain are firms that are likely to provide career opportunities to marketing professionals.

Effectively managing supply chain relationships often has a marked impact on a firm's ability to satisfy the consumer, which results in increased profitability for all parties. Consider the agreement between Amazon and the U.S. Postal Service (USPS) to expand their supply chain to provide Sunday delivery of Amazon orders. In a groundbreaking experiment, the USPS started delivering packages emblazoned with Amazon's smile logo to customers and businesses on Sundays, the first time it had assigned delivery drivers to work on that day. Neither of the USPS's main competitors, UPS and FedEx, offer Sunday delivery. For Amazon, the deal provides a stellar competitive benefit: Buyers can plan on receiving items they order every day of the week. The deal appears to be particularly appealing to Amazon's Prime customers, who pay an annual fee to guarantee two-day delivery. For a shopper browsing Amazon on Friday, it means receiving all purchases within those two days instead of having to discount Sunday and wait for Monday for the delivery.[34]

Marketing Enriches Society

Should marketing focus on factors other than financial profitability, like good corporate citizenry? Many of America's best-known corporations seem to think so—they have undertaken

You can now receive your Amazon orders on Sunday.
© John Gress/Corbis

Ethical & Societal Dilemma **1.1**   Free Fruit for Children: What Could Go Wrong?[v]

Childhood obesity is a serious and global problem. For parents, shopping with hungry kids who demand sugary snacks sometimes might seem like an equally vexing challenge. In an effort to help resolve both concerns, several grocery store chains are offering a new kind of appealing giveaway. Specifically, these grocers set up stands that display a range of fruits, with signs offering the produce for free to children under a certain age.

The idea is that a banana or apple at the start of the shopping trip can keep kids from getting hungry and cranky, thus making the shopping experience more pleasant for their parents. The fruit options are more healthful and less troublesome than other options, such as the free cookies or doughnuts that some in-store bakeries provide for young shoppers. Because the fruit is free, it also offers notable benefits over packaged chocolate bars, fruit snacks, or granola bars that parents might open up in the aisles even before they check out.

The fruit giveaway experiments have expanded globally, with chains in the United States, United Kingdom, and Australia all taking part. Although many responses have been positive, including parents' praise for stores that help them encourage healthful eating by their children, others question the tactic. The key complaint has been hygiene, in that there are few options for washing fruit like apples, peaches, and pears before children bite down. Still, the generally positive responses have led at least one chain to estimate that it will give away approximately 1 million pieces of fruit over the next year.

Should grocery stores offer free fruit to children?
© Hero Images Inc./Alamy RF

various marketing activities such as developing greener products, making healthier food options and safer products, and improving their supply chains to reduce their carbon footprint. At a more macro level, firms are making socially responsible activities an integral component of everything they do, as the grocers in Ethical and Societal Dilemma 1.1 exemplify.

Socially responsible firms recognize that including a strong social orientation in business is a sound strategy that is in both its own and its customers' best interest. It

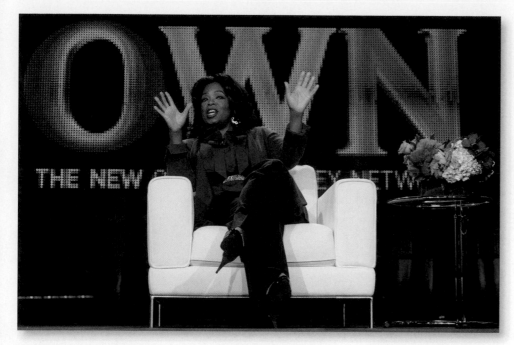

When you think of Oprah Winfrey, think big: Harpo Productions, Inc.; O, The Oprah Magazine; O at Home magazine; Harpo Films; the OWN television network; not to mention her philanthropic work with the Oprah Winfrey Foundation.
© Chris Pizzello/AP Photo

shows the consumer marketplace that the firm will be around for the long run and can be trusted with the marketplace's business. In a volatile market, investors view firms that operate with high levels of corporate responsibility and ethics as safe investments. Similarly, firms have come to realize that good corporate citizenship through socially responsible actions should be a priority because it will help their bottom line in the long run.[35]

Marketing Can Be Entrepreneurial

Whereas marketing plays a major role in the success of large corporations, it also is at the center of the successes of numerous new ventures initiated by **entrepreneurs**, or people who organize, operate, and assume the risk of a business venture.[36] Key to the success of many such entrepreneurs is that they launch ventures that aim to satisfy unfilled needs. Some examples of successful ventures (and their founders) that understood their customers and added value include: Ben & Jerry's (Ben Cohen and Jerry Greenfield); Birchbox (Hayley Barna and Katia Beauchamp); Amazon (Jeff Bezos); Netflix (Reed Hastings); and OWN (Oprah Winfrey).

An extraordinary entrepreneur and marketer, Oprah Winfrey was a self-made billionaire before she turned 50 years of age. Winfrey went from being the youngest person and first African American woman to anchor news at WTVF-TV in Nashville, Tennessee, to being only the third woman in history to head her own production studio. Under the Oprah banner are a variety of successful endeavors, including Harpo Films, Oprah's Book Club, Oprah.com, the Oxygen television network, and the Oprah Winfrey Network (OWN). In addition to producing two of the highest-rated talk shows ever on television, *The Oprah Winfrey Show* and *Dr. Phil*, Harpo Studios has produced films such as *Beloved* and *Tuesdays with Morrie*. Oprah's philanthropic contributions are vast and varied. Although the charity was dissolved in 2010 when Oprah's TV show ended, through the Oprah Winfrey Foundation and Oprah's Angel Network, people worldwide have raised more than $80 million for scholarships, schools, women's shelters, and youth centers.[37] Oprah's latest entrepreneurial venture includes a sizable ownership share in WeightWatchers, as we discuss in Chapter 5.

Great and distinguished entrepreneurs have visions of how certain combinations of products and services can satisfy unfilled needs.[38] They find and understand a marketing opportunity (i.e., the unfilled need), conduct a thorough examination of the marketplace, and develop and communicate the value of their products and services to potential consumers.

PROGRESS CHECK

1. List four functions that illustrate the importance of marketing.
2. A firm doing the right thing emphasizes the importance of marketing to _____.

Reviewing Learning Objectives

 LO1-1 Define the role of marketing in organizations.

Marketing is the activity, set of institutions, and processes for creating, capturing, communicating, delivering, and exchanging offerings that have value for customers, clients, partners, and society at large. Marketing strives to *create value* in many ways. If marketers are to succeed, their customers must believe that the firm's products and services are valuable; that is, they are worth more to the customers than they cost. Another important and closely related marketing role is to capture value of a product or service based on potential buyers' beliefs about its value. Marketers also enhance the value of products and services through various forms of *communication* such as advertising and personal selling. Through communications, marketers educate and inform customers about the benefits of their products and services and thereby increase their perceived value. Marketers facilitate the *delivery of value* by making sure the right products and services are available when, where, and in the quantities their customers want. Better marketers are not concerned about just one transaction with their customers; they recognize the value of loyal customers and strive to develop *long-term relationships* with them.

LO1-2 Describe how marketers create value for a product or service.

Value represents the relationship of benefits to costs. Firms can improve their value by increasing benefits, reducing costs, or both. The best firms integrate a value orientation into everything they do. If an activity doesn't increase benefits or reduce costs, it probably shouldn't occur. Firms become value driven by finding out as much as they can about their customers and those customers' needs and wants. They share this information with their partners up and down the marketing channel, so the entire chain collectively can focus on the customer. The key to true value-based marketing is the ability to design products and services that achieve precisely the right balance between benefits and costs. Value-based marketers aren't necessarily worried about how much money they will make on the next sale. Instead, they are concerned with developing a lasting relationship with their customers so those customers return again and again.

LO1-3 Understand why marketing is important both within and outside the firm.

Successful firms integrate marketing throughout their organizations so that marketing activities coordinate with other functional areas such as product design, production, logistics, and human resources, enabling them to get the right product to the right customers at the right time. Marketing helps facilitate the smooth flow of goods through the supply chain, all the way from raw materials to the consumer. From a personal perspective, the marketing function facilitates your buying process and can support your career goals. Marketing also can be important for society through its embrace of solid, ethical business practices. Firms "do the right thing" when they sponsor charitable events, seek to reduce environmental impacts, and avoid unethical practices; such efforts endear the firm to customers. Finally, marketing is a cornerstone of entrepreneurialism. Not only have many great companies been founded by outstanding marketers, but an entrepreneurial spirit pervades the marketing decisions of firms of all sizes.

Key Terms

- business-go-business (B2B) marketing, 10
- business-to-consumer (B2C) marketing, 10
- consumer-to-consumer (C2C) marketing, 10
- customer relationship management (CRM), 5

- entrepreneur, 21
- exchange, 5
- four Ps (see marketing mix), 6
- goods, 7
- ideas, 8
- marketing, 4
- marketing channel, 19

- marketing mix (four Ps), 6
- marketing plan, 4
- relational orientation, 15
- service, 7
- supply chain, 19
- value, 13
- value cocreation, 13

Marketing Digitally

1. Visit Godiva (www.godiva.com) and Hershey's (www.hersheys.com). What value do these chocolatiers provide customers? How is the value proposition different?

2. Go to Facebook.com and click on "About" at the bottom of the page and then click on the About tab. What is Facebook's mission? How could a marketer use Facebook, and what other social media tools could

they use? What are the drawbacks a marketer might face when using Facebook to communicate with their customers?

3. Visit Mondelēz International's website (www.mondelezinternational.com) and then click on the "Brand Family" link. In what major categories does Mondelēz have brands? Can you identify related categories in which the company should compete?

Marketing Applications

1. Do you know the difference between needs and wants? When companies that sell coffee develop their marketing strategy, do they concentrate on satisfying their customers' needs or wants? What about a utility company, such as the local power company? A humanitarian agency, such as Doctors without Borders?

2. People can apply marketing principles to finding a job. If the person looking for a job is the product, describe the other three Ps.

3. What is the difference between a good and a service? When you buy a music subscription on Pandora, are you buying a good or a service? Would your answer be different if you bought an MP3 album on Amazon?

4. One of your friends was recently watching TV and saw an advertisement that she liked. She said, "Wow, that was great marketing!" Was the ad, in fact, marketing?

5. Using the four Ps, discuss how the Apple iBeacon will create value for customers.

6. Columbia Sportswear sells a men's fleece vest for $36 and an Omni-Heat Jacket for $1,200. Is Columbia Sportswear providing the target markets for these products with a good value? Explain your answer.

7. Assume you have been hired into the marketing department of a major consumer products manufacturer such as Nike. You are having lunch with some new colleagues in other departments—finance, manufacturing, and logistics. They are arguing that the company could save millions of dollars if it just got rid of the marketing department. Develop an argument that would persuade them otherwise.

8. Why do marketers like Apple find it important to embrace societal needs and ethical business practices? Provide an example of a societal need or ethical business practice that Apple is addressing.

Quiz Yourself

1. Which of the following illustrates marketing's direct impact on consumers?

   a. Marketing advises production about how much product to manufacture.

   b. Marketing creates long-lasting relationships between the firm and its suppliers.

   c. Marketing helps firms expand globally.

   d. Marketing helps consumers learn about new products and services.

   e. Marketing advises logistics about when to ship products.

2. The _____ consists of the product, price, place, and promotion of an offering.

   a. marketing exchange

   b. marketing mix

   c. channel of distribution

   d. value proposition

   e. marketing plan

(Answers to these two questions can be found in the Quiz Yourself Answer Key section.)

Chapter Case Study   Mc Graw Hill Education **connect**

FROM BEANS TO PRALINES: THE GLOBAL CHOCOLATE MARKET

Three and a half million tons is a lot—more than most people can really understand. Perhaps a more comprehensible number is 11.5 pounds. But from a different perspective, that second number might be even more remarkable than the first one. The 3.5 million tons refer to how many cocoa beans—the raw material that represents the first step in the making of chocolate—are farmed, processed, shipped, and consumed worldwide every year. But that notable 11.5-pound figure indicates how much of the finished chocolate product, on average, a single consumer in the United States or Europe eats every year.[39]

That's a lot of chocolate, making for an expansive, massive market. The members of the market are diverse and varied, from the international farmers who produce the cocoa beans to the processing plants that transform the beans into edible treats to the well-known brands that design and produce the bars or candies to consumers who gobble up the finished product. Each transaction in the process involves some form of marketing, adding value along the way so that chocoholics never have to go without their favorite treat.

The earliest cocoa beans were grown in the Amazon basin, and farmers in Brazil and Ecuador still provide much of the world's supply. But the value and constantly increasing desire for chocolate products encouraged the expansion of the cocoa farming industry, spreading into Asia and West Africa.[40] The quality of the beans clearly affects the quality of the final product, leading many farmers and manufacturers to agree to follow Fair Trade or organic standards. For example, Fair Trade labels guarantee fair treatment of the farmers, most of whom work for minimal wages and live in underdeveloped nations. It also requires responsible farming practices. As a result of the benefits that these guarantees offer, farmers receive higher prices for their produce; currently, Fair Trade producers earn about $150 more per ton of beans than conventional growers would.[41] Organic farmers, who adopt the various national-level standards for organic farming (e.g., no pesticides), also earn more on the beans they sell—anywhere from $100 to $300 more per ton. The rationale behind both these initiatives is that consumers ultimately will pay more for Fair Trade and organic chocolate, though each of these forms

Chocolate consumers are demanding organic and fair traded products.

© Q-Images/Alamy

still account for tiny shares of the overall market. Still, estimates predict substantial growth in the organic chocolate market.[42]

However they choose to farm their beans, farmers then must sell their produce to processors. Those processors are located all over the world. The processors take the beans, add in sugar and dairy, and arrive at edible food products that they can sell under various brands. The number of these processors has grown remarkably in recent years in response to growing demand. In particular, less developed nations have sought to combine their farming with processing capabilities, such that factories have been popping up in various West African and Asian nations. As a result, in just five years, global processing capacity has grown by more than 400,000 metric tons.[43] Although the growth in the chocolate processing segment is a response to increased demand—sales of chocolate increased by 13 percent in the same five-year period—the capacity increases have been so massive that processing supply now outpaces demand. In turn, many processing plants, whether newly opened or decades old, are struggling to earn a profit.

All these shifts in supply mean that the prices that branded chocolate companies pay for their products are variable, and different companies have different needs. Whereas Godiva, as we explain in the opener to this chapter, demands the highest quality, other companies like Mars or Hershey's seek a level of quality that is sufficient but not overly expensive. These mass-market brands sell far more chocolate than their luxury competitors do; for example, in 2015, Mars' sales surpassed $18,400 million, and Nestlé brought in $11,041 million. These companies constantly compete for market share with their various brands, flavors, sizes, and product options. At the same time, luxury brands are engaging in their own competition,[44] such that Lindt has announced its goal to unseat Godiva as the top-selling premium chocolate brand.[45]

But that's not to suggest that mass-market brands compete with themselves or that premium brands do either. Almost regardless of their exact positioning and pricing, each chocolate brand seeks to be the one that appeals most to customers by finding just the right balance of quality, availability, and price.

As a result, customers face more choices than ever before when it comes to their chocolate fix. That's fortunate too, because even as health concerns and global obesity crises continue to be prominent news stories, people all over the world are eating more and more chocolate, possibly because chocolate, especially dark chocolate, is good for you.[46] For example, in Brazil—remember, one of the leading sources of cocoa beans—consumers used to eat about 10.5 ounces each year. Today, that amount has increased to 90 ounces on average.[47] In China, estimates suggest that international chocolate companies will sell $4.4 billion worth of candy by 2020.[48]

As this section reveals, everybody markets and everybody is subjected to the effects of marketing. Farmers try to market their beans as better by embracing Fair Trade or organic standards. Processors struggle to balance demand and supply and seek ways to earn enough profits to continue manufacturing. Chocolate brands aim to define their position in the market and appeal more to customers through the ways they combine the four Ps. And customers keep buying, faced with a wealth of choices, available only because marketing throughout the world makes sure they have access to just the kinds of treats they most desire.

Questions

1. Choose one of the supply chain members of the chocolate market described in this case study and detail how it adds value through its marketing efforts.

2. Describe the market for chocolates in the United States. In your discussion explain:

   - What type(s) of people do they sell to?
   - How do they appeal to those different groups of people?
   - How do those people typically procure the products?
   - Is there a difference between how and why different groups purchase chocolate?
   - Compare and contrast how those two "players" use the four Ps.

Endnotes

1. Tim Nudd, "At 90, Godiva Proudly Looks Back as It Charts a Path Forward," *AdWeek*, March 31, 2016.

2. Godiva, "Our Story," http://www.godiva.com/experience-godiva/ourStory.html.

3. Nudd, "At 90, Godiva Proudly Looks Back."

4. Robert Klara, "How a Naked Woman, a Horse, and a Family in Belgium Created Godiva Chocolate," *AdWeek*, February 10, 2015.

5. Godiva, "Collections," http://www.godiva.com/collections.

6. "Godiva Opens New Boutique at Macy's Herald Square," *PR Newswire*, November 2, 2015.

7. Klara, "How a Naked Woman, a Horse, and a Family in Belgium."

8. Godiva, "Our Belgian Heritage," http://www.godiva.com/our-story-our-belgian-heritage/OurStoryArticle2.html.

9. Godiva, "Meet our Chefs," http://www.godiva.com/experience-godiva/MeetOurChefs_RichArticle.html.

10. The American Marketing Association, http://www.marketing-power.com. We added the word in italics. Discussions of the latest revision of the AMA's marketing definition are wide-spread. See Gregory T. Gundlach and William L. Wilkie, "AMA's New Definition of Marketing: Perspective and Commentary on the 2007 Revision," *Journal of Public Policy & Marketing* 28, no. 2 (2008), pp. 259–64; see also the fall 2007 issue of the *Journal of Public Policy & Marketing* 26, no. 2, which contains eight different perspectives on the new definition.

11. The idea of the four Ps was conceptualized by E. Jerome McCarthy, *Basic Marketing: A Managerial Approach* (Homewood, IL: Richard D. Irwin, 1960).

12. https://www.thehersheycompany.com/brands/category.aspx#/Select.

13. http://www.mars.com/global/brands.aspx.

14. Wolfgang Ulaga and Werner Reinartz, "Hybrid Offerings: How Manufacturing Firms Combine Goods and Services Successfully," *Journal of Marketing* 75 (November 2011), pp. 5–23.

15. Anja Lambrecht and Catherine Tucker, "Paying with Money or Effort: Pricing When Customers Anticipate Hassle," *Journal of Marketing Research* 49 (February 2012), pp. 66–82.

16. Stuart Elliot, "A New Coronation for the King of Elephants," *The New York Times*, November 13, 2012.

17. Personal communication, Trang Connelly, TJX Companies, Inc., September 2013.

18. Simon Dumenco, "Ad Age Imagines a World Without Ads—And It's Not Cheap," *Advertising Age*, September 28, 2015.

19. Peter C. Verhoef et al., "A Cross-National Investigation into the Marketing Department's Influence within the Firm: Toward Initial Empirical Generalizations," *Journal of International Marketing* 19 (September 2011), pp. 59–86.

20. George S. Day, "Aligning the Organization with the Market," *Marketing Science Institute* 5, no. 3 (2005), pp. 3–20.

21. Kimmy Wa Chan, Chi Kin (Bennett) Yim, and Simon S. K. Lam, "Is Customer Participation in Value Creation a Double-Edged Sword? Evidence from Professional Financial Services across Cultures," *Journal of Marketing* 74, no. 3 (May 2010); Dhruv Grewal, Kent B. Monroe, and R. Krishnan, "The Effects of Price Comparison Advertising on Buyers' Perceptions of Acquisition Value and Transaction Value," *Journal of Marketing* 62 (April 1998), pp. 46–60.

22. Anne L. Roggeveen, Michael Tsiros, and Dhruv Grewal, "Understanding the Co-Creation Effect: When Does Collaborating with Customers Provide a Lift to Service Recovery?," *Journal of the Academy of Marketing Science* 40, no. 6 (2012), pp. 771–90; Sigurd Troye and Magne Supphellen, "Consumer Participation in Coproduction: 'I Made It Myself' Effects on Consumers' Sensory Perceptions and Evaluations of Outcome and Input Product," *Journal of Marketing* 76 (March 2012), pp. 33–46.

23. Anita Luo and V. Kumar, "Recovering Hidden Buyer-Seller Relationship States to Measure the Return on Marketing Investment in Business-to-Business Markets," *Journal of Marketing Research* 50, no. 1 (2013), pp. 143–60; V. Kumar and Denish Shah, "Can Marketing Lift Stock Prices?," *Sloan Management Review* 52, no. 4 (2011), pp. 24–26; V. Kumar et al., "Is Market Orientation a Source of Sustainable Competitive Advantage or Simply the Cost of Competing?," *Journal of Marketing* 75 (January 2011), pp. 16–30; Stephen A. Samaha, Robert W. Palmatier, and Rajiv P. Dant, "Poisoning Relationships: Perceived Unfairness in Channels of Distribution," *Journal of Marketing* 75 (May 2011), pp. 99–117.

24. Luo and Kumar, "Recovering Hidden Buyer-Seller Relationship States"; V. Kumar, Denish Shah, and Rajkumar Venkatesan, "Managing Retailer Profitability—One Customer at a Time!," *Journal of Retailing* 82, no. 4 (2006), pp. 277–94.

25. Harsh Ajmera, "Social Media Facts, Figures, and Statistics 2013," *Digital Insights*, http://blog.digitalinsights.in.

26. Kadie Regan, "10 Amazing Social Media Growth Stats from 2015," *Social Media Today*, August 10, 2015, http://www.socialmediatoday.com/social-networks/kadie-regan/2015-08-10/10-amazing-social-media-growth-stats-2015.

27. United States Census Bureau, "U.S. and World Population Clock," April 7, 2016, http://www.census.gov/popclock/; We Are Social. "Leading Social Networks Worldwide as of January 2016, Ranked by Number of Active Users (in Millions)," *Statista - The Statistics Portal*. January 2016, http://www.statista.com/statistics/272014/global-social-networks-ranked-by-number-of-users/.

28. "Internet Usage Statistics," *Internet World Stats*, November 30, 2015, http://www.internetworldstats.com/stats.htm.

29. "Internet Travel Hotel Booking Statistics," *Statistic Brain Research Institute*, March 3, 2015, http://www.statisticbrain.com/internet-travel-hotel-booking-statistics/.

30. Alex Heath, "8 Apps Every Food Lover Needs," June 29, 2015, http://www.businessinsider.com/the-best-food-apps-2015-6; http://www.foodspotting.com/about; http://www.happycow.net/.

31. http://www.bdubsgamebreak.com/Home/About.

32. Raji Srinivasan, Gary L. Lilien, and Shrihari Sridhar, "Should Firms Spend More on Research and Development and Advertising During Recessions?," *Journal of Marketing* 75 (May 2011), pp. 49–65.

33. http://www.ahold.com.

34. Ron Nixon, "Postal Service to Make Sunday Deliveries for Amazon," *The New York Times*, November 11, 2013.

35. Philip Kotler, "Reinventing Marketing to Manage the Environmental Imperative," *Journal of Marketing* 75 (July 2011), pp. 132–35; Katherine White, Rhiannon MacDonnell, and John H. Ellard, "Belief in a Just World: Consumer Intentions and Behaviors toward Ethical Products," *Journal of Marketing* 76 (January 2012), pp. 103–18.

36. http://dictionary.reference.com/search?q=Entrepreneurship.

37. http://www.oprah.com; https://web.archive.org/web/20110809132838/http://oprahsangelnetwork.org/how-to-help/thank-you-donors.

38. For a series of contributions about how entrepreneurs contribute to society, see the special section on social entrepreneurship in *Journal of Public Policy & Marketing*, 31 (Spring 2012).

39. Katy Barnado and Luke Graham, "Future of the Chocolate Industry Looks Sticky," *CNBC.com*, March 24, 2016, http://www.cnbc.com/2016/03/24/future-of-the-chocolate-industry-looks-sticky.html.

40. Cadbury, "Cocoa Growing Countries," https://www.cadbury.com.au/About-Chocolate/Cocoa-Growing-Countries.aspx.

41. International Cocoa Organization, "The Chocolate Industry," January 28, 2016, http://www.icco.org/about-cocoa/chocolate-industry.html.

42. Ibid.

43. Katherine Dunn, "Chocolate Processors Struggle with Factory Glut," *The Wall Street Journal*, March 24, 2016.

44. Nudd, "At 90, Godiva Proudly Looks Back."

45. Corinne Gretler, "Lindt Aims to Dethrone Godiva in High-End Chocolate Market," *Bloomberg.com*, March 8, 2016, http://www.bloomberg.com/news/articles/2016-03-08/lindt-profit-meets-analysts-estimates-on-russell-stover-revamp.

46. https://www.bulletproofexec.com/is-chocolate-good-for-you-health-benefits/; http://www.thedailybeast.com/articles/2012/03/28/11-reasons-chocolate-is-good-for-your-health.html.

47. "The BRIC Chocolate Market 2016," March 21, 2016, http://www.sbwire.com/press-releases/the-bric-chocolate-market-2016/release-674329.htm?utm_source=djournal&utm_medium=feed&utm_campaign=distribution.

48. Ibid.

i. Martha C. White, "Airlines Use Wireless Networks to Replace Seat-Back Catalogs," *The New York Times*, February 1, 2015.

ii. Barbara Thau, "How Big Data Helps Chains Like Starbucks Pick Store Locations—An (Unsung) Key to Retail Success," *Forbes*, April 24, 2014, http://www.forbes.com; Malcolm Wheatley, "Data-Driven Location Choices Drive Latest Starbucks Surge," *Data Informed*, January 10, 2013, http://data-informed.com/data-driven-location-choices-drive-latest-starbucks-surge/.

iii. Stephanie Strom, "Whole Foods to Rate Its Produce and Flowers for Environmental Impact," *The New York Times*, October 15, 2014; Stuart Elliot, "Whole Foods Asks Shoppers to Consider a Value Proposition," *The New York Times*, October 19, 2014, http://www.nytimes.com.

iv. Miriam Gottfried, "Publishers Face Moving Target in Mobile," *The Wall Street Journal*, July 7, 2015; eMarketer, September 2014.

v. Tom Ryan, "Does It Pay for Grocers to Give Free Fruit to Kids?," *Retail Wire*, February 4, 2016.

CHAPTER 2

DEVELOPING MARKETING STRATEGIES AND A MARKETING PLAN

LEARNING OBJECTIVES

After reading this chapter, you should be able to:

LO2-1 Define a marketing strategy.

LO2-2 Describe the elements of a marketing plan.

LO2-3 Analyze a marketing situation using SWOT analyses.

LO2-4 Describe how a firm chooses which consumer group(s) to pursue with its marketing efforts.

LO2-5 Outline the implementation of the marketing mix as a means to increase customer value.

LO2-6 Summarize portfolio analysis and its use to evaluate marketing performance.

LO2-7 Describe how firms grow their business.

We may be getting healthier. We might be ordering more salads, exercising a few more times a week, and drinking more water. But even as these healthy trends expand and persist, people still love their carbonated beverages—whether they call them sodas, pop, colas, or something else. Faced with these conflicting preferences and consumer demands, what's a cola company to do to appeal to buyers and make sure it provides them with what they want, where, how, and when they want it?

For PepsiCo, the latest strategy is to expand the market with high-end and special-edition product offerings. The company firmly believes that a premium space remains in the ongoing cola battle, created by consumers who want something a little distinctive and unique, rather than just the same mass-marketed brands. Accordingly, it has developed a range of smaller-batch, distinctive cola options, some of which it already has introduced, with others on their way.

For example, it recently released Caleb's Kola, which features African kola nuts, cane sugar, and unique spices, along with a slight citrus flavor. The drink is named after Caleb Bradham, the pharmacist who first started selling "Brad's Drink" in 1893 in his North Carolina drug store. That beverage, with a few tweaks, was renamed and released more widely as Pepsi just a few years later.

Bradham also may be the inspiration for Pepsi's next rollout. It has applied for a trademark for the name "1893 from the Makers of Pepsi Cola." The meaning of the trademark has not yet been confirmed by the company, but savvy observers recognize the year as the same one in which Bradham started selling Brad's Drink, which originally contained sugar, caramel, water, lemon, and nutmeg.

Although both Caleb's Kola and the 1893 line thus appear to hearken back to Pepsi's past, another recent launch of a premium option played on its hypothetical future. Noting the arrival of Marty McFly day (i.e., the future date set in the modified DeLorean time machine at the end of the first *Back to the Future* film), Pepsi introduced a very limited run of "Pepsi Perfect," which was the version of the beverage available in the anticipated future depicted in the second entry into the movie series. With a production run of only 6,500 bottles, Pepsi Perfect was tough to get, offering a clear distinction to those lucky few who snagged the collectible bottles (back) in time.

In contrast with the strategically limited release of Pepsi Perfect, both Caleb's Kola and 1893 appear designed to be broader in their distribution. In another, similar move, Pepsi announced that it would soon begin developing an additional line, called Stubborn Sodas. Thus, through its efforts to address declining consumption, Pepsi has devised a refreshed marketing strategy, one that involves diversifying and thereby appealing to those consumers who might dismiss conventional colas as too mainstream but love the notion of something special and nostalgic to drink.[1]

In this chapter, we start by discussing a *marketing strategy*, which outlines the specific actions a firm intends to implement to appeal to potential customers. Then we discuss how to do a *marketing plan*, which provides a blueprint for implementing the marketing strategy. The chapter concludes with a discussion of strategies firms use to grow.

Define a marketing strategy.

WHAT IS A MARKETING STRATEGY?

A **marketing strategy** identifies (1) a firm's target market(s), (2) a related marketing mix (its four Ps), and (3) the bases on which the firm plans to build a sustainable competitive advantage. A **sustainable competitive advantage** is an advantage over the competition that is not easily copied and can be maintained over a long period of time. A competitive advantage acts like a wall that the firm has built around its position in a market. This wall makes it hard for outside competitors to contact customers inside—otherwise known as the marketer's target market. Of course, if the marketer has built a wall around an attractive market, competitors will attempt to break down the wall. Over time, advantages will erode because of these competitive forces, but by building high, thick walls, marketers can sustain their advantage, minimize competitive pressure, and boost profits for a longer time. Thus, establishing a sustainable competitive advantage is key to long-term financial performance.

For Pepsi, this wall involves the bricks of a strong brand and a loyal customer base, which were built on the foundation of its strong innovative capabilities. Customers around the world know Pepsi and consider it a primary "go-to" brand if they want a refreshing drink. This positioning reflects Pepsi's careful targeting and marketing mix implementation. In terms of the four Ps (as we described them in Chapter 1), Pepsi already has achieved *product* excellence with its signature colas, Pepsi and Diet Pepsi. It also is constantly adding new products to its product line, as detailed in the opening vignette to this chapter. For example, it has launched Caleb's Kola already and appears poised to release its 1893 beverage soon.[2] Furthermore, the Pepsi brand is owned by a parent company, PepsiCo, that also owns many of the top snack brands; other cola lines; and additional beverage products such as Lays, Quaker, Mountain Dew, and Naked—among dozens of others.[3] To market its products, it relies on an extensive distribution network that *places* its familiar and appealing brands in stores in more than 200 countries.[4] Its pricing also is competitive and strategic. For example, customers can readily access a quick drink from a Pepsi soda fountain at a higher price by volume, or they can pay a little less per liter and buy larger, 2-liter bottles to store and consume at home. Central to its promotion efforts are Pepsi's celebrity endorsements. Pepsi partners with some of the world's biggest musicians, including Madonna, Beyonce, and Elton John,[5] and sponsors major sports events and leagues, such as the Super Bowl, as well as the NBA and WNBA, NHL, NFL, and MLB.[6]

There are four macro, or overarching, strategies that focus on aspects of the marketing mix to create and deliver value and to develop sustainable competitive advantages, as we depict in Exhibit 2.1:[7]

- **Customer excellence:** Focuses on retaining loyal customers and excellent customer service.

- **Operational excellence:** Achieved through efficient operations and excellent supply chain and human resource management.

- **Product excellence:** Having products with high perceived value and effective branding and positioning.

- **Locational excellence:** Having a good physical location and Internet presence.

Pepsico owns many brands including Gatorade, Lays, Quaker, Aunt Jemima, and Aquafina.

© Steven Senne/AP Photo

EXHIBIT 2.1 Macro Strategies for Developing Customer Value

Customer Excellence

Customer excellence is achieved when a firm develops value-based strategies for retaining loyal customers and provides outstanding customer service.

Retaining Loyal Customers Sometimes the methods a firm uses to maintain a sustainable competitive advantage help attract and maintain loyal customers. For instance, having a strong brand, unique merchandise, and superior customer service all help solidify a loyal customer base. In addition, having loyal customers is, in and of itself, an important method of sustaining an advantage over competitors.

Loyalty is more than simply preferring to purchase from one firm instead of another.[8] It means that customers are reluctant to patronize competitive firms. Loyal customers drink Pepsi even if Coca-Cola goes on sale. More and more firms realize the value of achieving customer excellence by focusing their strategy on retaining loyal customers. PepsiCo doesn't think in terms of selling a single case of Mountain Dew for $15; instead, it focuses on satisfying customers who buy various bottles or cans to keep in their homes all the time, including Mountain Dew for the kids, Diet Pepsi for the adults, and Pepsi for guests. It also considers whether those consumers might want some salty snacks to go with their beverages and how it can help them combine those desires through the purchase of multiple PepsiCo products. Even if we just consider cola purchases, it is reasonable to imagine that a household of cola consumers might buy 50 cases of carbonated beverages every year for something like 20 years. In this case, the consumer is not a $15 customer who bought a single case; by combining all purchases for the family over the years, we come to the determination that this household represents a $15,000 customer! Viewing customers with a lifetime value perspective rather than on a transaction-by-transaction basis is key to modern customer retention programs.[9] We will examine how the lifetime value of a customer is calculated in Chapter 10, Appendix 10A.

Another method of achieving customer loyalty creates an emotional attachment through loyalty programs. These loyalty programs, which constitute part of an overall customer relationship management (CRM) program, prevail in many industries, from airlines to hotels to movie theaters to retail stores. With such programs, firms can identify members through the loyalty card or membership information the consumer provides when he or she makes a purchase. Using that purchase information, analysts determine which types of merchandise certain groups of customers are buying and thereby tailor their offering to better meet the needs of their loyal customers. For instance, by analyzing their databases, banks develop profiles of customers who have defected in the past and use that information to identify customers who may defect in the future. Once it identifies these customers, the firm can implement special retention programs to keep them.

Providing Outstanding Customer Service Marketers also may build sustainable competitive advantage by offering excellent customer service,[10] though consistency in this area can prove difficult. Customer service is provided by employees, and, invariably, humans are less consistent than machines are. Firms that offer good customer service must instill its importance in their employees over a long period of time so that it becomes part of the organizational culture.

Disney offers excellent examples of both of these types of customer excellence. First, Disney's My Magic system enables visitors to swipe their Magic Band wristbands to make purchases, open their hotel room door, get dinner reservations, or check in for rides throughout the park and its grounds. The system also enables Disney to collect a remarkable amount of information about what each guest is doing at virtually every moment of his or her visit to its theme parks.[11]

Second, its customer service is virtually unparalleled. Visitors to Disney parks are greeted by "assertively friendly" staff who have been extensively trained to find ways to provide better service. The training includes information about how to recognize the signs that a visitor is lost, so the Disney employee

Disney's employees and cast members provide the highest level of customer service.

© Tao Images/agefotostock

Superior Service 2.1

Amazon Is about Products, Delivery, Prices, and Now Home Services[i]

Approximately 85 million customers buy items from Amazon that require some sort of installation or construction, from large screen televisions to children's bicycles. If a busy consumer shops on Amazon mainly because of the convenience it offers, is she or he likely to have the time and patience to install or assemble the product?

The gap implied by this question has led to the emergence of online home services markets at Amazon and other firms such as Google. Customers can now click a link to receive quotes for services from local professionals. The purchase of a big-screen television thus prompts a query about whether the buyer wants someone to hang it on the wall. If the customer expresses interest, the system provides a list of service providers as well as clear, detailed quotes for the price of the service.

Amazon hopes to extend its reach by convincing its customers to consider it for services as well as products. Accordingly, it already has a roster of providers offering about 700 types of services to customers, from the conventional to the obscure (just what does a "silk aerialist" do?). Just as it has with products, it will seek to offer the widest selection possible, ensure speedy delivery, and provide highly competitive prices.

For service providers, joining Amazon promises benefits as well as challenges. Local plumbers, lawn care services, and tile installers are likely to increase their business if they appear on these sites. However, they also face greater price competition, such that they likely need to underbid all their local competitors to earn the customer's business.

Although other review sites, such as Angie's List or Yelp, already offer a single source of a range of service provider options, sourcing these purchases from a well-known retailer offers some added benefits. In particular, people can sign up for a needed service during the very occasion during which they purchase the item; without pausing, they can buy a new stereo system and schedule its installation. In addition, Amazon offers the reassurance of its name and reputation. Consumers can feel safe, knowing that Amazon has registered the service providers on its site. Explaining how she overcame any reservations about buying an experiential service through Amazon, one first-time service buyer noted, "I thought, O.K., Amazon stands behind this." Because all services are guaranteed by Amazon, its smaller, service-specific competitors keep struggling, unable to compete with Amazon's reputation for meeting customers' needs and guaranteed ability to reduce buyers' purchase risks. As a result, Amazon appears poised to become a dominant provider of superior services.

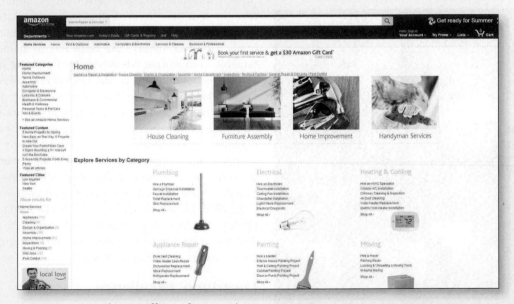

Amazon is extending its offering from products to services.

Source: Amazon

can offer help locating a destination. It also highlights the need to communicate frequently and collaboratively about every aspect of the park, so a custodian at one end of the Magic Kingdom likely knows what time a restaurant on the other side opens.[12] Although it may take considerable time and effort to build such a reputation for customer service, once a marketer has earned a good service reputation, it can sustain this advantage for a long time, because a competitor is hard pressed to develop a comparable reputation. Superior Service 2.1 describes Amazon's latest attempt to shore up and enhance its competitive barriers by introducing a home service marketplace that may help it achieve a lasting, powerful advantage.

Operational Excellence

Firms achieve **operational excellence**, the second way to achieve a sustainable competitive advantage, through their efficient operations, excellent supply chain management, and strong relationships with their suppliers.

All marketers strive for efficient operations to get their customers the merchandise they want, when they want it, in the required quantities, and at a delivered cost that is lower than that of their competitors. By so doing, they ensure good value to their customers, earn profitability for themselves, and satisfy their customers' needs.

Firms achieve efficiencies by developing sophisticated distribution and information systems as well as strong relationships with vendors. Like customer relationships, vendor relations must be developed over the long term and generally cannot be easily offset by a competitor.[13]

You are likely aware of, and perhaps have taken advantage of, Amazon's Prime shipping program that offers, for $99 a year, free two-day shipping on all orders. Perhaps you have paid for overnight delivery with Amazon, or if you live in one of the eleven cities in the United States that offer it, you may have paid for same-day shipping. With attractive shipping options like these, how are other online retailers able to compete? Operational excellence is required for Amazon to execute this program effectively. Not only does it need to have the technology to coordinate the personal buyers, but it needs to have an effective human resources hiring program that selects and trains employees capable of going the extra mile to please its customers.[14]

Product Excellence

Product excellence, the third way to achieve a sustainable competitive advantage, occurs by providing products with high perceived value and effective branding and positioning. Some firms have difficulty developing a competitive advantage through their merchandise and service offerings, especially if competitors can deliver similar products or services easily. However, others have been able to maintain their sustainable competitive advantage by investing in their brand itself; positioning their product or service using a clear, distinctive brand image; and constantly reinforcing that image through their merchandise, service, and promotion. For example, with its new product introductions, as described in the opening vignette to this chapter, Pepsi clearly is seeking to reinforce and emphasize its historical legacy and image as a provider of excellent, refreshing, distinctive beverages. *Bloomberg Businessweek*'s top global brands—such as Coca-Cola, IBM, Microsoft, Google, GE, McDonald's, Intel, Apple, Disney, and Samsung—are all leaders in their respective industries, at least in part because they have strong brands and a clear position in the marketplace.[15]

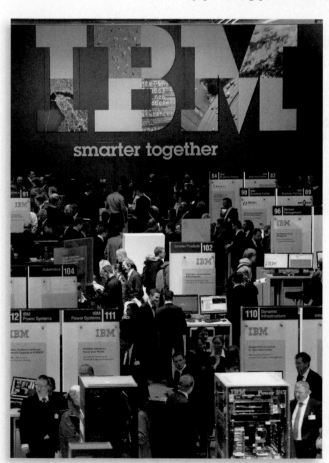

IBM is one of Bloomberg Businessweek's *top global brands.*

Locational Excellence

Locational excellence is particularly important for retailers and service providers. Many say, "The three most important things in retailing are location, location, location." For example, most people will not walk or drive very far when looking to buy a cup of coffee. A competitive advantage based on location is sustainable because it is not easily duplicated. Starbucks has developed a strong competitive advantage with its location selection. The high density of stores it has established in some markets makes it very difficult for a competitor to enter that market and find good locations. After all, if Starbucks has a store on the corner of a busy intersection, no other competitor can take that location and will instead have to settle for a less worthy spot.

Multiple Sources of Advantage

In most cases, a single strategy, such as low prices or excellent service, is not sufficient to build a sustainable competitive advantage. Firms require multiple approaches to build a "wall" around their position that stands as high as possible.

Southwest Airlines consistently has positioned itself as a carrier that provides good service at a good value—customers get to their destinations on time for a reasonable price without having to pay extra for checked luggage. At the same time, its customers know not to have extraordinary expectations, unlike those they might develop when they purchase a ticket from Singapore Airlines. They don't expect food service or seat assignments. But they do expect—and even more important, get—on-time flights that are reasonably priced. By developing its unique capabilities in several areas, Southwest has built a very high wall around its position as the premier value player in the airline industry, which has resulted in a huge cadre of loyal customers.

PROGRESS CHECK

1. What are the various components of a marketing strategy?
2. List the four macro strategies that can help a firm develop a sustainable competitive advantage.

THE MARKETING PLAN

 LO2-2 Describe the elements of a marketing plan.

Effective marketing doesn't just happen. Firms like Pepsi carefully plan their marketing strategies to react to changes in the environment, the competition, and their customers by creating a marketing plan. A **marketing plan** is a written document composed of an analysis of the current marketing situation, opportunities and threats for the firm, marketing objectives and strategy specified in terms of the four Ps, action programs, and projected or pro forma income (and other financial) statements.[16] The three major phases of the marketing plan are planning, implementation, and control.[17]

Although most people do not have a written plan that outlines what they are planning to accomplish in the next year, and how they expect to do it, firms do need such a document. It is important that everyone involved in implementing the plan knows what the overall objectives for the firm are and how they are going to be met. Other stakeholders, such as investors and potential investors, also want to know what the firm plans to do. A written marketing plan provides a reference point for evaluating whether or not the firm has met its objectives.

A marketing plan entails five steps, depicted in Exhibit 2.2. In Step 1 of the **planning phase**, marketing executives, in conjunction with other top managers, define the mission and/or vision of the business. For the second step, they evaluate the situation by assessing how various players, both in and outside the organization, affect the firm's potential for success. In the **implementation phase**, marketing managers identify and evaluate different opportunities by engaging in a process known as segmentation, targeting, and positioning (STP) (Step 3). They then are responsible for implementing the marketing mix using the four Ps (Step 4). Finally, the **control phase** entails evaluating the performance of the marketing strategy using marketing metrics and taking any necessary corrective actions (Step 5).

As indicated in Exhibit 2.2, it is not always necessary to go through the entire process for every evaluation (Step 5). For instance, a firm could evaluate its performance in Step 5, then go directly to Step 2 to conduct a situation audit without redefining its overall mission.

We first discuss each step involved in developing a marketing plan. Then we consider ways of analyzing a marketing situation, as well as identifying and evaluating marketing opportunities. We also examine some specific strategies marketers use to grow a business. Finally, we consider how the implementation of the marketing mix increases customer value.

EXHIBIT 2.2 The Marketing Plan

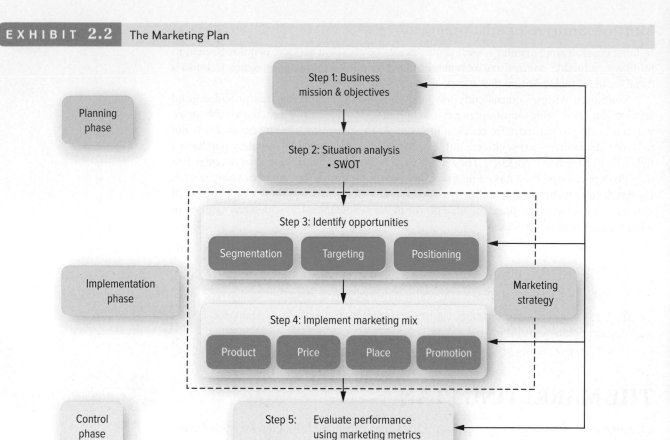

Planning phase

Step 1: Business mission & objectives

Step 2: Situation analysis
• SWOT

Step 3: Identify opportunities

Segmentation | Targeting | Positioning

Implementation phase

Marketing strategy

Step 4: Implement marketing mix

Product | Price | Place | Promotion

Control phase

Step 5: Evaluate performance using marketing metrics

Step 1: Define the Business Mission

The **mission statement**, a broad description of a firm's objectives and the scope of activities it plans to undertake,[18] attempts to answer two main questions: What type of business are we? What do we need to do to accomplish our goals and objectives? These fundamental business questions must be answered at the highest corporate levels before marketing executives can get involved. Most firms want to maximize stockholders' wealth by increasing the value of the firms' stock and paying dividends.[19] Let's look at the two very different mission statements of PepsiCo and Coca-Cola:

PepsiCo's Mission Statement emphasizes the global nature of its products, while Coke's evokes emotions like happiness.

Left: © Bloomberg/Getty Images; right: Image Courtesy of The Advertising Archives

- **PepsiCo's Mission Statement:** "To provide consumers around the world with delicious, affordable, convenient and complementary foods and beverages from wholesome breakfasts to healthy and fun daytime snacks and beverages to evening treats."[20]

- **Coke's Mission Statement:** "To refresh the world . . . To inspire moments of optimism and happiness . . . To create value and make a difference."[21]

For both of these firms, marketing is primarily responsible for enhancing the value of the company's offering for its customers and other constituents, whether in pursuit of a profit or not. Another key goal or objective often embedded in a mission statement relates to how the firm is building its sustainable competitive advantage.

However, owners of small, privately held firms frequently have other objectives, such as achieving a specific level of income and avoiding risks. Nonprofit organizations such as the "Pink Ribbon" campaign instead have nonmonetary objectives:

- **Pink Ribbon International's Mission Statement:**
"To create a global community to support breast cancer patients, survivors and their families all over the world . . . by facilitating forums and blogs where thoughts, experience and information can be shared."[22]

Step 2: Conduct a Situation Analysis

After developing its mission, a firm would perform a situation analysis using a SWOT analysis that assesses both the internal environment with regard to its **S**trengths and **W**eaknesses and the external environment in terms of its **O**pportunities and **T**hreats. In addition, it should assess the opportunities and uncertainties of the marketplace due to changes in **C**ultural, **D**emographic, **S**ocial, **T**echnological, **E**conomic, and **P**olitical forces (CDSTEP). These factors are discussed in more detail in Chapter 5. With this information, firms can anticipate and interpret change, so they can allocate appropriate resources.

Consider how PepsiCo might conduct a SWOT analysis, as outlined in Exhibit 2.3. We focus on PepsiCo here, but we also recognize that its marketing managers might find it helpful to perform parallel analyses for competitors, such as Coca-Cola.

A company's strengths (Exhibit 2.3, upper left) refer to the positive internal attributes of the firm. In this example, the strengths we might identify include PepsiCo's diversified product portfolio and celebrity endorsements. Pepsi has signed some of the world's most recognized musicians and athletes as spokespersons, from Beyoncé to Michael Jordan and David Beckham.[23] Building on this forte, it has launched its own Music Platform, Out of the Blue, that debuted during a recent Grammy Awards ceremony. The platform aims to connect fans with their favorite artists by giving away extravagant trips to major music festivals,

Pink Ribbon is a nonprofit organization that supports breast cancer patients, survivors, and their families.

© David Westing/Getty Images

 LO2-3   Analyze a marketing situation using SWOT analyses.

A PepsiCo strength is its portfolio of celebrity endorsers like Beyoncé (left) and David Beckham (right).

Left: © Wenn US/Alamy; right: © Clive Brunskill/Getty Images

EXHIBIT 2.3		Examples of Elements in a SWOT Analysis	
		Environment	**Evaluation**
		Positive	Negative
Pepsi	Internal	**Strengths** Brand product portfolio Strong celebrity endorsers Dedication to charitable and social projects	**Weakness** Relatively lower brand awareness Water source for bottled water
	External	**Opportunity** Emerging countries Health food segments Bottled water	**Threats** Water scarcity Changes to labeling regulations Increase competition
Coca-Cola	Internal	**Strengths** Very strong brand Strong global presence Excellent customer loyalty	**Weakness** Over-reliance on carbonated drinks Negative sugar-related publicity
	External	**Opportunity** Emerging countries	**Threats** Water scarcity Potential market saturation Changes to labeling regulations

SWOT analysis of Pepsi, Strategic Management Insight, February 15, 2013, http://www.strategicmanagementinsight.com/swot-analyses/pepsico-swot-analysis.html; SWOT analysis of Coca-Cola, Strategic Management Insight, February 15, 2013, http://www.strategicmanagementinsight.com/swot-analyses/coca-cola-swot-analysis.html.

concerts, and other fabulous experiences.[24] Another strength comes from its efforts to benefit society, such as the PepsiCo Foundation's Global Citizenship Initiatives, which encourage healthy lifestyles, clean water, and women's empowerment, among other positive goals.

Yet every firm has its weaknesses, and PepsiCo is no exception. Weaknesses (Exhibit 2.3, upper right) are negative attributes of the firm. Furthermore, PepsiCo has much lower global brand awareness and market share than does its main rival, Coca-Cola.[25] Also, PepsiCo's Aquafina water brand relies on a public water source. It has faced public criticism and negative press that jeopardizes its market position and has had to acknowledge that Aquafina is simply tap water in a bottle.[26]

One of PepsiCo's Global Citizenship Initiatives is its S.M.A.R.T program that identifies which Pepsi/Frito-Lay products are healthier. S.M.A.R.T. stands for five steps that encourage active living and better food choices: Start with a healthy breakfast, Move more, Add more fruits, vegetables and whole grains, Remember to hydrate, and try lower-calorie or lower-fat foods.

© Kayte Deioma/Zumapress/Newscomz

Adding Value 2.1   Small Coke Cans: Are Consumers Paying More for Less, or Are They Just Paying to Get What They Want?[ii]

When Coca-Cola checked its sales data recently, it found consistently over the past few quarters that sales of smaller containers, such as 7.5-ounce cans, were growing fast, while traditional packages kept suffering stagnant or even decreasing sales. The evidence has prompted the beverage company to revisit its approach, such that its goal is not just to sell Coke but rather to sell Cokes.

What's the difference? Consumer trends have led more people to request and purchase small containers of cola, so that they can limit their intake and achieve healthier lifestyles. In particular, parents wanted the smaller containers so that they could allow their children to have a treat without loading them up with more sugar and caffeine than would be good for the kids. Therefore, they sought to be able to buy a 12-pack of small cans or bottles rather than a 6-pack of the traditional 12-ounce packages. The volume of actual beverages being purchased might not change, or even might decline. But the number of packages being bought increases. As a result, approximately 14 percent of Coca-Cola's product mix now consists of the small servings—a move that also reflects the company's effort to live up to its pledge to reduce the number of calories people consume through carbonated beverages. As the president of Coca-Cola North America explained, "Having a 20 oz. bottle of Coca-Cola is pointless if half of it is never consumed."

In addition to revising its perspective on what customers actually want, Coke has reinvented its pricing approach. It enjoys a beneficial new price platform due to the switch. The cost to consumers for the small cans is approximately the same as that for the larger packages, meaning that shoppers pay approximately the same amount of money for substantially less product. But for the most part, shoppers appear willing to do so, because the smaller packaging meets their needs and represents a clear response to their requests. The 17 percent sales growth in the small size categories affirms this willingness.

Consumers are demanding smaller containers of Cola to limit their intake and achieve healthier lifestyles. So, Coke provides the smaller cans on the right.

© Matt Rourke/AP Photo

As a result of "more people, enjoying more Coke, more often, for a little more money," Coca-Cola also has increased its revenues, despite decreased volume sales. Customer research showed that consumers often equate finishing a drink with their sense of refreshment. Leaving customers wanting more, by giving them smaller containers, thereby helps encourage repurchase and consumption intentions while still making those consumers feel happier and more refreshed. The threat of cannibalization certainly remains pertinent, such that the sales growth in small packages might only come at the cost of lost sales of larger ones; yet the company appears confident that it is on the right path, ready to offer the "perfect pour" of carbonation.

Opportunities (Exhibit 2.3, lower left) pertain to positive aspects of the external environment. Among PepsiCo's opportunities is the rising demand for healthy food and drink options, as we indicated in the opening vignette. That is, the increasing interest for healthier options gives PepsiCo new opportunities to expand its product lines, introduce innovative new colas that appeal to people's preferences for premium options, and offer healthier options as well. For example, even with the public sourcing controversy, PepsiCo's bottled water brand Aquafina has seen significant growth.[27] Another notable opportunity for PepsiCo is the growth in global markets for snacks and beverages. In particular, it has invested strongly in Brazil, Russia, India, and China (i.e., the BRICs).[28] If these efforts are successful, PepsiCo can enjoy substantial growth while also reducing its nearly exclusive reliance on the U.S. market. There are multiple ways to take advantage of opportunities, though; Adding Value 2.1 describes how Coca-Cola is taking another approach to address the external environment and provide value to its customers.

Finally, threats (Exhibit 2.3, lower right) represent the negative aspects of the company's external environment. Water scarcity is a significant concern, because the production of cola demands substantial amounts of water.[29] In addition, increased attention to labeling and nutrition facts could threaten to undermine PepsiCo's appeal.[30] Finally, competition in the snack-food market continues to increase, not just among the existing members of the market but also by new entrants that are coming up with innovative, alternative snacks to appeal to consumers' specific preferences.[31] These are just some of the threats that PepsiCo is facing.

Step 3: Identify and Evaluate Opportunities Using STP (Segmentation, Targeting, and Positioning)

After completing the situation audit, the next step is to identify and evaluate opportunities for increasing sales and profits using segmentation, targeting, and positioning (STP). With STP, the firm first divides the marketplace into subgroups or segments, determines which of those segments it should pursue or target, and finally decides how it should position its products and services to best meet the needs of those chosen targets (more details on the STP process can be found in Chapter 9).

Segmentation   Many types of customers appear in any market, and most firms cannot satisfy everyone's needs. For instance, among Internet users some do research online, some shop, some look for entertainment, and many do all three. Each of these groups might be a market segment consisting of consumers who respond similarly to a firm's marketing efforts. The process of dividing the market into groups of customers with different needs, wants, or characteristics—who therefore might appreciate products or services geared especially for them—is called market segmentation.

Let's look at Hertz, the car rental company. The example in Exhibit 2.4 reveals some of the segments that Hertz targets. With the Adrenaline Collection, Hertz offers up the Chevrolet Camaro or Corvette, seeking to appeal to thrill seekers and gear heads on vacation. Its Prestige Collection features various Cadillac and Infiniti models, targeting business customers and families who prefer a luxurious ride. With its Green Collection of cars such as the Toyota Prius and Ford Fusion, and even some electric vehicle options in

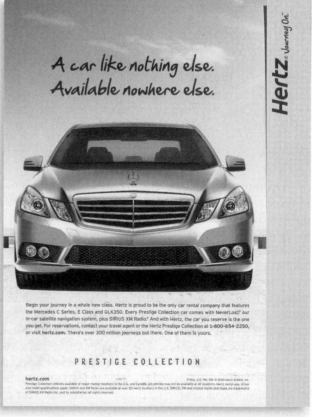

Hertz targets several markets. Its Adrenaline Collection appeals to single people and couples wanting to have fun, while its Prestige Collection appeals to its business customers and families who prefer a luxurious ride.

Source: The Hertz Corporation

EXHIBIT 2.4	Hertz Market Segmentation Illustration				
	Segment 1	Segment 2	Segment 3	Segment 4	Segment 5
Segments	Single thrill seekers and gear heads on vacation	Business customers and families who prefer a luxurious ride	Environmentally conscious customers	Families	Commercial customers
	Adrenaline Collection	Prestige Collection	Green Collection	SUV/Minivan/4x4	Commercial Van/Truck
Cars Offered	Corvette ZHZ	Infiniti QX56	Toyota Prius	Toyota Rav 4	
	Chevrolet Camaro	Cadillac Escalade	Ford Fusion	Ford Explorer	Ford Cargo Van

selected locations, Hertz appeals to environmentally conscious customers. It also offers commercial vans for service customers with its Commercial Van/Truck Collection.[32] Thus, Hertz uses a variety of demographics—gender, age, income, interests—to identify customers who might want the Prestige, Green, and Adrenaline Collections, but it also applies psychological or behavioral factors, such as a need to move possessions across town, to identify likely consumers of its commercial vans.

Targeting After a firm has identified the various market segments it might pursue, it evaluates each segment's attractiveness and decides which to pursue using a process known as **target marketing or targeting**. For example, Hertz realizes that its primary appeal for the SUV/Minivan/4x4 collection centers on young families, so the bulk of its marketing efforts for this business is directed toward that group.

Soft drink manufacturers also divide their massive markets into submarkets or segments. Coca-Cola, for instance, makes several different types of Coke, including regular, Coke II, and Cherry Coke. Among its diet colas, it targets Coke Zero to men and Diet Coke to women because men prefer not to be associated with diets. It also markets Sprite to those who don't like dark colas, Fruitopia and Minute Maid for more health-conscious consumers, and Dasani bottled water for purists.

Positioning Finally, when the firm decides which segments to pursue, it must determine how it wants to be positioned within those segments. **Market positioning** involves the process of defining the marketing mix variables so that target customers have a clear, distinctive, desirable understanding of what the product does or represents in comparison with competing products. Hertz positions itself as a quality car (and truck) rental company that is the first choice for each of its target segments. In its marketing communications it stresses that customers will get peace of mind when they rent from Hertz, the market leader in the car rental business, and be able to enjoy their journey (e.g., leisure consumers) and reduce travel time (e.g., business consumers).[33]

To segment the coffee-drinker market, Starbucks uses a variety of methods, including geography (e.g., college campuses versus shopping/business districts) and benefits (e.g., drinkers of caffeinated versus decaffeinated products). After determining which of those segments represent effective targets, Starbucks positions itself as a firm that develops a variety of products that match the wants and needs of the different market segments— espresso drinks, coffees, teas, bottled drinks, pastries, and cooler foods.

After identifying its target segments, a firm must evaluate each of its strategic opportunities. A method of examining which segments to pursue is described in the Growth Strategies section later in the chapter. Firms typically are most successful when they focus on opportunities that build on their strengths relative to those of their competition. In Step 4 of the marketing plan, the firm implements its marketing mix and allocates resources to different products and services.

Step 4: Implement Marketing Mix and Allocate Resources

When the firm has identified and evaluated different growth opportunities by performing an STP analysis, the real action begins. It has decided what to do, how to do it, and how

LO2-5 Outline the implementation of the marketing mix as a means to increase customer value.

Dyson creates value with its innovative products (top). It can therefore charge significantly more than the price charged for conventional fans (bottom).

Left: Source: Dyson, Inc.; right: © Stockbyte/PunchStock RF

many resources should be allocated to it. In the fourth step of the planning process, marketers implement the actual marketing mix—product, price, promotion, and place—for each product and service on the basis of what they believe their target markets will value. At the same time, marketers make important decisions about how they will allocate their scarce resources to their various products and services.

Product and Value Creation Products

These products include services and constitute the first of the four Ps. Because the key to the success of any marketing program is the creation of value, firms attempt to develop products and services that customers perceive as valuable enough to buy. Dyson fans and fan heaters draw in and redirect surrounding air without potentially dangerous or fast-spinning blades or visible heating elements. Although more expensive than conventional fans and space heaters, these sculpturally beautiful appliances are perceived by consumers to be a valuable alternative to products that haven't significantly changed since the early 1900s.

Price and Value Capture

Recall that the second element of the marketing mix is price. As part of the exchange process, a firm provides a product or a service, or some combination thereof, and in return, it gets money. Value-based marketing requires that firms charge a price that customers perceive as giving them a good value for the product they receive. Clearly, it is important for a firm to have a clear focus in terms of what products to sell, where to buy them, and what methods to use in selling them. But pricing is the only activity that actually brings in money and therefore influences revenues. If a price is set too high, it will not generate much volume. If a price is set too low, it may result in lower-than-optimal margins and profits. Therefore, price should be based on the value that the customer perceives. Dyson fans can retail for $150 or more; conventional fans retail for around $25. Customers can decide what they want from their fan and choose the one at the price they prefer.

Dyson invoked two of the 4Ps, price and place, by making a select number of fans available on Groupon at a heavily discounted price.

© digitallife/Alamy

Place and Value Delivery For the third P, place, the firm must be able, after it has created value through a product and/or service, to make the product or service readily accessible when and where the customer wants it. Dyson therefore features fans prominently on its website, but also makes sure to place them on Amazon and in Bed Bath and Beyond stores. In these locations, consumers previously found other Dyson products, and they likely would look for fans there too.

Promotion and Value Communication Integrated marketing communications (IMC) represents the fourth P, promotion. It encompasses a variety of communication disciplines—advertising, personal selling, sales promotion, public relations, direct marketing, and online marketing including social media—in combination to provide clarity, consistency, and maximum communicative impact.[34] Using the various disciplines of its IMC program, marketers communicate a *value proposition,* which is the unique value that a product or service provides to its customers and how it is better than and different from those of competitors.

To increase its exposure, Dyson not only offers promotions for its products on its website, but also on promotion websites such as coupon.com and Groupon. That is, it makes a select number of products available on several promotion channels at a discounted price to encourage people to try the innovations.

Step 5: Evaluate Performance Using Marketing Metrics

The final step in the planning process includes evaluating the results of the strategy and implementation program using marketing metrics. A metric is a measuring system that quantifies a trend, dynamic, or characteristic. Metrics are used to explain why things happened and also project the future. They make it possible to compare results across regions, strategic business units (SBUs), product lines, and time periods. The firm can determine why it achieved or did not achieve its performance goals with the help of these metrics. Understanding the causes of the performance, regardless of whether that performance exceeded, met, or fell below the firm's goals, enables firms to make appropriate adjustments. Procter & Gamble uses performance metrics to test its new geolocation method of reaching users of the popular social networking app Snapchat, as Social & Mobile Marketing 2.1 reveals.

Social & Mobile Marketing 2.1

Making Snapchat More Strategic: How CoverGirl Uses Geotargeting to Leverage the Marketing Potential of a Fun App[iii]

Companies know well that social media apps can be great for their marketing communications, enabling them to reach lots of customers in a fun and engaging way. But while some apps offer detailed data about how consumers behave, many others do not provide any such insights, because their primary goal is helping users have fun.

Take Snapchat for example. It allows visitors to overlay photo filters, but it has no capacity to calculate or show advertisers who is using its branded overlays or what consumers do after adopting such a filter. All it can tell them is how many people used the focal filter, which is not nearly enough information to be used to make any marketing decisions.

Recognizing that Snapchat lacked a user-friendly dashboard or summary statistics that might provide it with straightforward insights and marketing data, Procter & Gamble (P&G) decided that it needed to do the analytical work on its own. It devised an innovative marketing strategy: It would release *Star Wars*–themed lines of cosmetics under its CoverGirl brand, available only in Ulta retail stores. At the same time, it would allow Snapchat users to apply a related filter to their photos, all coinciding with the release of *Star Wars: The Force Awakens*. The social media move was likely to enhance brand awareness, by revealing to users that the *Star Wars*–linked products even existed. But P&G also wanted to increase sales. To measure these effects, it implemented a detailed, careful experiment.

First, it created geofilters that reflected the locations of the 868 Ulta stores in which the new eye and lip cosmetic product lines were available. If a consumer was located near one of these stores and also visited Snapchat to post a photo, she encountered the option to use a filter that featured logos for Ulta, CoverGirl, and *Star Wars*, as well as a frame that surrounded the picture with what looked like light saber rays. However, P&G did not make the filter available for every store that carried the makeup products. By strategically limiting the application of the campaign, it created what was essentially a control sample: stores whose consumers could not have seen the Snapchat-affiliated advertising campaign whose sales could be compared with those that had the campaign.

Second, it gathered data about how many Snapchat users saw a related ad on the social media site, how many times they swiped to look at the filter, and how many times they used that filter. Then it correlated these data with sales information available from Ulta stores that prompted the geolocated campaign and those that did not. By combining these data, P&G could obtain a pretty clear idea of how many of the sales stemmed from the Snapchat campaign because they took place in a focal store, versus how many sales would have occurred without the advertising, according to the sales data for similar but non-geolocation-linked stores.

Third, P&G compared the results of this social media campaign, timed to link with a major movie release, against a similar campaign that it conducted in 2013, in relation to the arrival of a new *Hunger Games* film in theaters. In that previous effort though, it relied on traditional television advertising and a brand-linked Tumblr blog instead of Snapchat. Although the company declined to release exact numbers, it determined that the new Snapchat strategy was more efficient, more effective, and less costly. Thus P&G might have invented the analytics that make it possible to calculate the returns on Snapchat campaigns, but the method holds great promise for any marketer willing to undertake similar efforts in social media channels.

Through the Snapchat platform, P&G's CoverGirl brand developed a Star Wars*–themed cosmetics line that is available only in Ulta stores. If a consumer was located near an Ulta store that had the cosmetics line, and also posted a photo on Snapchat, she could use a filter that featured logos for Ulta, CoverGirl, and* Star Wars, *as well as a frame that surrounded the picture with what looked like light saber rays.*

© Mim Friday/Alamy

Typically, managers begin by reviewing the implementation programs, and their analysis may indicate that the strategy (or even the mission statement) needs to be reconsidered. Problems can arise both when firms successfully implement poor strategies and when they poorly implement good strategies.

Who Is Accountable for Performance? At each level of an organization, the business unit and its manager should be held accountable only for the revenues, expenses, and

Ethical & Societal Dilemma 2.1   Volkswagen's "Dieselgate" Scandal[iv]

The automotive market really was rocked by scandal when the U.S. Environmental Protection Agency discovered that many of the cars that Volkswagen (VW) had sold in the United States contained faulty software, apparently installed purposefully. The purpose of the software was to detect the amount of emissions produced by the cars' diesel engines—information that is critical to regulators that enforce emissions standards, as well as to consumers who seek environmentally friendly transportation options. But when the cars underwent emissions tests, the software tweaked their performance, making it seem better than it was normally.

Instead, when driven under normal conditions, the diesel-engine cars were emitting approximately 40 times the legal limit imposed on nitrogen oxide pollutants. That is, the vehicles were polluting illegally, and then the integrated software was falsifying the data, so that no one could even identify the damage. But the evidence came to light, forcing VW to admit that approximately 11 million cars worldwide, sold over the course of nearly a decade, had been outfitted with the emissions-cheating software. The cars in question came with multiple brand names in the VW portfolio, including not just the VW brand but also Skoda, SEAT, and Audi. Soon thereafter, the company came under scrutiny again when it admitted to finding an irregularity in tests measuring carbon dioxide emissions that could affect an additional 800,000 vehicles, though subsequent investigations led VW to reduce that estimate to only 36,000 cars being affected.

In handling the situation, VW has provided examples of both what to do and what not to do. The company quickly instituted several internal changes, mainly designed to increase the amount of oversight and thereby prevent such unacceptable practices in the future. In implementing both structural and management changes, VW also replaced a number of key executives. Top executives also firmly asserted that the scandal was the result of poor choices by a relatively small group of middle managers, not indicative of a wider corporate ethical lapse.

Consumers protest Volkswagen's falsification of its cars' emissions.

© John MacDougall/Getty Images

The scandal has had powerful and drastic effects on the performance of the world's biggest car manufacturer. Sales in the United States dropped by nearly one-quarter, compared with same-month sales for the previous year, immediately following the scandalous announcement. The drop—resulting both from consumers' perception that the brand is not trustworthy and from the loss of sales that followed from the company pulling the affected engines off the market—is a particular concern for VW today, because the automotive industry as a whole is on track to post record sales. In addition, VW could owe an estimated $18.2 billion in fines related to the scandal, not to mention the further legal and reputational costs it is likely to accrue. Yet the company's chief executive remains remarkably confident, noting that "Although the current situation is serious, this company will not be broken by it." Only time will tell if he is right.

profits that they can control. Thus, expenses that affect several levels of the organization (such as the labor and capital expenses associated with operating a corporate headquarters) shouldn't be arbitrarily assigned to lower levels. In the case of a store, for example, it may be appropriate to evaluate performance objectives based on sales, sales associate productivity, and energy costs. If the corporate office lowers prices to get rid of merchandise and therefore profits suffer, then it's not fair to assess a store manager's performance based on the resulting decline in store profit.

Performance evaluations are used to pinpoint problem areas. Reasons performance may be above or below planned levels must be examined. If a manager's performance is below planned levels, was it because the sales force didn't do an adequate job, because the economy took a downward turn, because competition successfully implemented a new strategy, or because the managers involved in setting the objectives aren't very good at making estimates? The manager should be held accountable only in the case of the inadequate sales force job or setting inappropriate forecasts. When the fault is difficult to assign, the company faces a serious challenge, as Ethical & Societal Dilemma 2.1 explains in relation to Volkswagen's attempts to respond to the scandal surrounding falsified emissions data for diesel engines in its cars.

Promotional discounts are one way General Mills is trying to save the cereal industry.

© Joe Raedle/Getty Images

When it appears that actual performance is going to be below the plan because of circumstances beyond the manager's control, the firm can still take action to minimize the harm. Similar to the soft drink industry, the cereal industry has been beset by a number of setbacks due to trends in the wider consumer environment. People seek to cut carbohydrates out of their diets, but cereal is mostly carbs. Many consumers are recognizing their allergies to gluten, but many cereals include wheat as a main ingredient. In response, the largest cereal maker General Mills (GM) has called on its competitors to step up their marketing efforts to save the industry. Leading the way, it has increased its advertising budget and offers promotional discounts on some of its most popular cereal brands, including Cheerios.[35]

In remarkable cases such as this, marketing managers must ask themselves several relevant questions: How quickly were plans adjusted? How rapidly and appropriately were pricing and promotional policies modified? In short, did I react to salvage an adverse situation, or did my reactions worsen the situation?

Performance Objectives, Marketing Analytics, and Metrics Many factors contribute to a firm's overall performance, which makes it hard to find a single metric to evaluate performance.[36] One approach is to compare a firm's performance over time or to competing firms, using common financial metrics such as sales and profits. Another method of assessing performance is to view the firm's products or services as a portfolio. Depending on the firm's relative performance, the profits from some products or services are used to fuel growth for others.

With its extensive data, Google claims that it can use a combination of metrics to predict the performance of a major motion picture up to a month prior to the date it opens in theaters. Using search volume for the movie title in combination with several other metrics, such as the season and whether the movie is a sequel, Google promises a 94 percent accurate prediction of box office performance. Other proprietary metrics include the volume of clicks on search ads. If, for example, one movie prompted 20,000 more paid clicks than another film, it will bring in approximately $7.5 million more in revenues during its opening weekend. Beyond the implications for opening weekend, Google asserts that weekday searches in the weeks leading up to the release offer better predictors of continued revenues. That is, if a film fan searches for a movie title on a Tuesday, she or he is more likely to hold off on seeing the movie rather than rushing out during opening weekend.[37] Google's extensive analytics abilities support its competitive tactics in other markets too, as Marketing Analytics 2.1 describes.

Financial Performance Metrics Some commonly used metrics to assess performance include revenues, or sales, and profits. For instance, sales are a global measure of a firm's activity level. However, a manager could easily increase sales by lowering prices, but the profit realized on that merchandise (gross margin) would suffer as a result. An attempt to maximize one metric may therefore lower another. Thus, managers must understand how their actions affect multiple performance metrics. It's usually unwise to use only one metric, because it rarely tells the whole story.

In addition to assessing the absolute level of sales and profits, a firm may wish to measure the relative level of sales and profits. For example, a relative metric of sales or profits is its increase or decrease over the prior year. In addition, a firm may compare its growth in sales or profits relative to other benchmark companies (e.g., Coke may compare itself to Pepsi).

The metrics used to evaluate a firm vary depending on (1) the level of the organization at which the decision is made and (2) the resources the manager controls. For example, while the top executives of a firm have control over all of the firm's resources and resulting expenses, a regional sales manager has control over only the sales and expenses generated by his or her salespeople.

Let's look at Pepsi's sales revenue and profits (after taxes) and compare them with those of Coca-Cola (Exhibit 2.5).

Marketing Analytics 2.1 — The First Name in Predictive Analytics: Google[v]

In the world of analytics, Google has made a significant name for itself because, from the moment it was established, Google has put predictive analytics at the heart of the company. As the most widely used search engine, Google needs to be able to predict which websites and pages a person is seeking, based on just a few keywords. Google is so successful at this method that few users even bother going to the second page of the results list in a Google search. Google now offers Google Analytics for companies to help improve their online presence by providing insights into customers' web searching behavior. In addition, Google now uses its analytics for more than just its search engine. They were critical to the development of Android software, Apple's biggest competitor in the smartphone domain. Now with the help of its sophisticated analytics, Google is taking on Apple in another domain as well: cars.

In Google's 2015 Android boot camp, the company officially introduced its Android Auto dashboard interface, which will face off against Apple's CarPlay. Data analytics have played a big role in the development of these systems. Study after study has shown how dangerous it is to drive while using one's phone. Data even show that driving while using a smartphone is equitable to driving while under the influence of alcohol. These startling results have spurred top phone system manufacturers' interest in creating dashboard platforms. When Google debuted Android Auto, it was clear that extensive analytics went into the development of every feature.

For example, Google developed a driver distraction lab to learn what tasks people do frequently when driving. These data informed which functions would be included and how

Data analytics have played a big role in developing Google's Android Auto dashboard interface to help keep drivers safe while using electronic dashboard functions.

© Elijah Nouvelage/Reuters

they would work in the Android Auto system. According to Google's studies, no action should take longer than two seconds, so every function of Android Auto must be "glanceable." In addition, the interface does not include any "back" or "recent" buttons. Not only are social media apps blocked, but texting is accessible only through voice commands. With these improvements in the connection between phones and cars, data analytics are helping make the world both more convenient and safer.

EXHIBIT 2.5 Performance Metrics: Coke vs. Pepsi

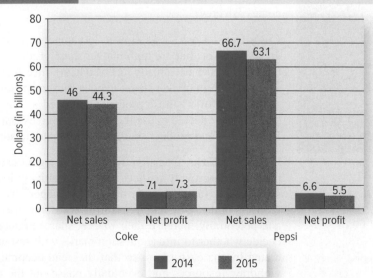

Dollars (in billions)

Coke:
- Net sales: 46 (2014), 44.3 (2015)
- Net profit: 7.1 (2014), 7.3 (2015)

Pepsi:
- Net sales: 66.7 (2014), 63.1 (2015)
- Net profit: 6.6 (2014), 5.5 (2015)

■ 2014 ■ 2015

LO2-6 Summarize portfolio analysis and its use to evaluate marketing performance.

Portfolio Analysis In portfolio analysis, management evaluates the firm's various products and businesses—its "portfolio"—and allocates resources according to which products are expected to be the most profitable for the firm in the future. Portfolio analysis is typically performed at the **strategic business unit (SBU)** or **product line** level of the firm, though managers also can use it to analyze brands or even individual items. An SBU is a division of the firm itself that can be managed and operated somewhat independently from other divisions and may have a different mission or objectives. For example, Goodyear is one of the largest tire firms in the world, selling its products on six continents and with sales of approximately $18 billion. Its four SBUs are organized by geography: North American; Europe, Middle East, African; Latin American; and Asia-Pacific.[38]

A product line, in contrast, is a group of products that consumers may use together or perceive as similar in some way. One line of product for Goodyear could be car, van, sport-utility vehicle (SUV), and light truck tires; another line could be high-performance tires or aviation tires.

One of the most popular portfolio analysis methods, developed by the Boston Consulting Group (BCG), requires that firms classify all their products or services into a two-by-two matrix, as depicted in Exhibit 2.6.[39]

The circles represent brands, and their sizes are in direct proportion to the brands' annual sales. The horizontal axis represents the relative market share. In general, **market share** is the percentage of a market accounted for by a specific entity,[40] and is used to establish the product's strength in a particular market. It is usually discussed in units, revenue, or sales. A special type of market share metric, **relative market share**, is used in this application because it provides managers with a product's relative strength compared with that of the largest firm in the industry.[41] The vertical axis is the **market growth rate**, or the annual rate of growth of the specific market in which the product competes. Market growth rate thus measures how attractive a particular market is. Each quadrant has been named on the basis of the amount of resources it generates for and requires from the firm.

Stars Stars (upper left quadrant) occur in high-growth markets and are high market share products. That is, stars often require a heavy resource investment in such things as promotions and new production facilities to fuel their rapid growth. As their market growth slows, stars will migrate from heavy users of resources to heavy generators of resources and become cash cows.

Cash Cows Cash cows (lower left quadrant) are in low-growth markets but are high market share products. Because these products have already received heavy investments to develop their high market share, they have excess resources that can be spun off to those products that need it. For example, the firm may decide to use the excess resources generated by Brand C to fund products in the question mark quadrant.

Question Marks Question marks (upper right quadrant) appear in high-growth markets but have relatively low market shares; thus, they are often the most managerially intensive products in that they require significant resources to maintain and potentially increase their market share. Managers must decide whether to infuse question marks with resources generated by the cash cows, so that they can become stars, or withdraw resources and eventually phase out the products.

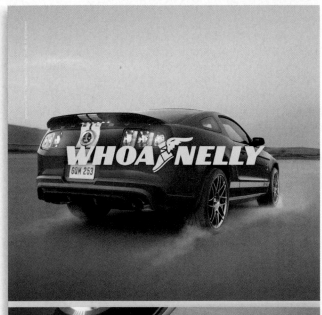

Goodyear, one of the largest tire firms in the world, organizes its strategic business units by geography. This ad for high-performance tires, one of Goodyear's many product lines, was designed for its North American SBU.

Source: 2008 The Goodyear Tire & Rubber Company. All rights reserved. Agency: McCann Erickson/New York, NY. Creative Director: Craig Markus; Art Director: Tim Dillingham; Copywriter: Mark Ronquillo; Photographer: © 2007 Graham Westmoreland/Friend and Johnson.

| EXHIBIT 2.6 | Boston Consulting Group Matrix |

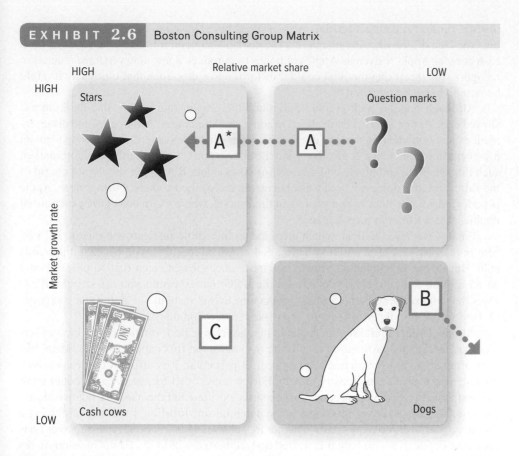

Brand A, for instance, is currently a question mark, but by infusing it with resources, the firm hopes to turn it into a star.

Dogs Dogs (lower right quadrant) are in low-growth markets and have relatively low market shares. Although they may generate enough resources to sustain themselves, dogs are not destined for "stardom" and should be phased out unless they are needed to complement or boost the sales of another product or for competitive purposes. In the case depicted in Exhibit 2.6, the company has decided to stop making Brand B.

Now let's look at Apple and some of its products.[42] The four that we will focus our attention on are: iPhone, iPod, iMac Desktop, and iPad.

Let's consider each of these products and place them into the BCG matrix based on the data. The iPhone has clearly been the star, with a steady growth rate of 35 percent each quarter.

The iPod tells a different story. With a staggering absolute market share consistently above 75 percent, its relative market share is 100 percent. More than 300 million iPods sold in a little over 10 years, so this product definitely has been important for Apple. Unfortunately,

In which Boston Consulting Group quadrant do these products fit?

© Stanca Sanda/Alamy

the MP3 market is contracting, and sales of iPods have slowed to their lowest level. Combine the lack of growth with a large relative market share and it is likely that the iPod is a cash cow for Apple.[43] Even as Apple continues to introduce a few new versions, it needs to recognize the threat that the iPod could transform into a dog, such that ultimately it might be wise to halt its production.[44]

Although popular with graphic designers, the growth rate of the Mac Desktop has slowed enough that it has even declined in some recent quarters. Although some disagreement exists about the exact rate of decline, it appears that sales have dropped by up to about 3 percent in recent years. It also has a small relative market share in the desktop market, such that the iMac tentatively could be classified as a dog. But Apple should not get rid of the iMac, because doing so would risk alienating its loyal customers. Furthermore, Apple is performing better than its competitors in this market, where PC makers have experienced double-digit declines in recent years.[45]

Finally, we have the iPad, which provided an incredible sales growth rate of 333 percent in the first year after its introduction. Sales peaked in 2014, with 67.99 million units sold. But its market share and growth rate have since slowed, such that Apple sold only 54.85 million units in 2015.[46] Where on the BCG matrix would you classify the iPad? Does the still excellent market for this product mean that it should be in the star category? Or is the erosion of its growth enough to make it a question mark?

Although quite useful for conceptualizing the relative performance of products or services and using this information to allocate resources, the BCG approach, and others like it, is often difficult to implement in practice. In particular, it is difficult to measure both relative market share and industry growth. Furthermore, other measures easily could serve as substitutes to represent a product's competitive position and the market's relative attractiveness. Another issue for marketers is the potential self-fulfilling prophecy of placing a product or service into a quadrant. Whether it is classified as a star or a question mark has profound implications on how it is treated and supported within the firm. Question marks require more marketing and production support.

Strategic Planning Is Not Sequential

The planning process in Exhibit 2.2 suggests that managers follow a set sequence when they make strategic decisions. Namely, after they've defined the business mission, they perform the situation analysis, identify strategic opportunities, evaluate alternatives, set objectives, allocate resources, develop the implementation plan, and, finally, evaluate their performance and make adjustments. But actual planning processes can move back and forth among these steps. For example, a situation analysis may uncover a logical alternative that perhaps was not included in the mission statement, which would mean that the mission statement would need to be revised. The development of the implementation plan also might reveal that insufficient resources have been allocated to a particular product for it to achieve its objective. In that case, the firm would need to either change the objective or increase the resources; alternatively, the marketer might consider not investing in the product at all.

Now that we have gone through the steps of the marketing plan, let's look at some growth strategies that have been responsible for making many marketing firms successful.

PROGRESS CHECK

1. What are the five steps in creating a marketing plan?
2. What tool helps a marketer conduct a situation analysis?
3. What is STP?
4. What do the four quadrants of the portfolio analysis represent?

GROWTH STRATEGIES

Firms consider pursuing various market segments as part of their overall growth strategies, which may include the four major strategies in Exhibit 2.7.[47] The rows distinguish those opportunities a firm possesses in its current markets from those it has in new markets, whereas the columns distinguish between the firm's current marketing offering and that of a new opportunity. Let's consider each of them in detail.

Market Penetration

A **market penetration strategy** employs the existing marketing mix and focuses the firm's efforts on existing customers. Such a growth strategy might be achieved by attracting new consumers to the firm's current target market or encouraging current customers to patronize the firm more often or buy more merchandise on each visit. A market penetration strategy generally requires greater marketing efforts, such as increased advertising and additional sales and promotions, or intensified distribution efforts in geographic areas in which the product or service already is sold.

To further penetrate its current customer base, the super-hero entertainment giant, Marvel, has expanded its movie offerings. In collaboration with several production companies, as well as talented directors and well-known star actors, Marvel has helped bring the X-Men, Spiderman, Superman, Iron Man, and other popular characters to the big screen, where they confront some relevant, modern-day topics such as discrimination, environmental destruction, and international wars—before ultimately kicking tail and saving the city. These films have grossed massive profits, ranging from $1.5 million to $4 million domestically.[48] Marvel has further increased its market penetration by expanding the distribution of its films. Today, Marvel movies can be seen in theaters, accessed on Xfinity, and viewed on DVDs available in discount stores, grocery stores, and a host of other stores, including book and comic stores.

Market Development

A **market development strategy** employs the existing marketing offering to reach new market segments, whether domestic or international. Marvel pursues such a market development strategy when it enhances the viewing of its movies in global markets. For example, the release of *The Avengers: Age of Ultron* proved to be one of the biggest movies of all time, grossing almost a half a billion dollars just in the domestic market. When we include the international appeal, the success of *The Avengers: Age of Ultron* is almost hard to comprehend: Its international box office sales were nearly $950 million, for a total box office of $1.4 billion.[49] These phenomenal results highlight the importance of expanding into new market segments.

Product Development

The third growth strategy option, a **product development strategy**, offers a new product or service to a firm's current target market. For example, Marvel has launched several

EXHIBIT 2.7 Markets/Products and Services Strategies

PRODUCTS AND SERVICES

	Current	New
Current	Market penetration	Product development
New	Market development	Diversification

MARKETS

LO2-7 Describe how firms grow their business.

Marvel pursues a market development strategy by releasing The Avengers: Age of Ultron *globally.*

© Marvel Studios/Photos 12/Alamy

Marvel has launched several series on Netflix including Daredevil.

© Netflix/Photofest

successful series on Netflix, including *Jessica Jones*, *Daredevil*, *Iron Fist*, and *Luke Cage*.[50] Unlike traditional network providers, Netflix (and its competitors, such as Hulu or Amazon) allows viewers to binge watch entire series in one sitting. Binge watching has become a phenomenally successful pastime for couch potatoes worldwide. Netflix has 69 million subscribers worldwide, including 43 million in the United States alone, making it an outstanding new service channel for Marvel character lovers. By developing series designed for this format, Marvel can connect with its customers in a new and important way.

Diversification

A diversification strategy, the last of the growth strategies from Exhibit 2.7, introduces a new product or service to a market segment that currently is not served. Diversification opportunities may be related or unrelated. In a related diversification opportunity, the current target market and/or marketing mix shares something in common with the new opportunity.[51] In other words, the firm might be able to purchase from existing vendors, use the same distribution and/or management information system, or advertise in the same newspapers to target markets that are similar to their current consumers. Marvel has pursued related diversification with its home décor, for example. Collectables and t-shirts have long been a staple of the comic market, but Marvel also has diversified its offerings, expanding to include lamp shades and throw pillows.[52]

In contrast, in an unrelated diversification, the new business lacks any common elements with the present business. Unrelated diversifications do not capitalize on either core strengths associated with markets or with products. Thus, they would be viewed as very risky. For instance, if Marvel ventured into the child day care service industry, it would be an unrelated diversification, because it is so different from its core business and therefore very risky.

PROGRESS CHECK

1. What are the four growth strategies?
2. What type of strategy is growing the business from existing customers?
3. Which strategy is the riskiest?

Reviewing Learning Objectives

 Define a marketing strategy.

A marketing strategy identifies (1) a firm's target markets(s), (2) a related marketing mix (four Ps), and (3) the bases on which the firm plans to build a sustainable competitive advantage. Firms use four macro strategies to build their sustainable competitive advantage: *Customer excellence* focuses on retaining loyal customers and excellent

customer service. *Operational excellence* is achieved through efficient operations and excellent supply chain and human resource management. *Product excellence* entails having products with high perceived value and effective branding and positioning. Finally, *locational excellence* entails having a good physical location and Internet presence.

Describe the elements of a marketing plan.

A marketing plan is composed of an analysis of the current marketing situation, its objectives, the strategy for the four Ps, and appropriate financial statements. A marketing plan represents the output of a three-phase process: planning, implementation, and control. The planning phase requires that managers define the firm's mission and vision and assess the firm's current situation. It helps answer the questions, "What business are we in now, and what do we intend to be in the future?" In the second phase, implementation, the firm specifies, in more operational terms, how it plans to implement its mission and vision. Specifically, to which customer groups does it wish to direct its marketing efforts, and how does it use its marketing mix to provide good value? Finally, in the control phase, the firm must evaluate its performance using appropriate metrics to determine what worked, what didn't, and how performance can be improved in the future.

LO2-3 Analyze a marketing situation using SWOT analyses.

SWOT stands for strengths, weaknesses, opportunities, and threats. A SWOT analysis occurs during the second step in the strategic planning process, the situation analysis. By analyzing what the firm is good at (its strengths), where it could improve (its weaknesses), where in the marketplace it might excel (its opportunities), and what is happening in the marketplace that could harm the firm (its threats), managers can assess their firm's situation accurately and plan its strategy accordingly.

LO2-4 Describe how a firm chooses which consumer group(s) to pursue with its marketing efforts.

Once a firm identifies different marketing opportunities, it must determine which are the best to pursue. To accomplish this task, marketers go through a segmentation, targeting, and positioning (STP) process. Firms segment various markets by dividing the total market into those groups of customers with different needs, wants, or characteristics who therefore might appreciate products or services geared especially toward them. After identifying the different segments, the firm goes after, or targets, certain groups on the basis of the firm's perceived ability to satisfy the needs of those groups better than competitors, and do so profitably. To complete the STP process, firms position their products or services according to the marketing mix variables so that target customers have a clear, distinctive, and desirable understanding of what the product or service does or represents relative to competing products or services.

LO2-5 Outline the implementation of the marketing mix as a means to increase customer value.

The marketing mix consists of the four Ps—product, price, promotion, and place—and each P contributes to customer value. To provide value, the firm must offer a mix of products and services at prices their target markets will view as indicating good value. Thus, firms make trade-offs between the first two Ps, product and price, to give customers the best value. The third P, promotion, informs customers and helps them form a positive image about the firm and its products and services. The last P, place, adds value by getting the appropriate products and services to customers when they want them and in the quantities they need.

 Summarize portfolio analysis and its use to evaluate marketing performance.

Portfolio analysis is a management tool used to evaluate the firm's various products and businesses—its "portfolio"—and allocate resources according to which products are expected to be the most profitable for the firm in the future. A popular portfolio analysis tool developed by the Boston Consulting Group classifies all products into four categories. The first, stars, are in high-growth markets and have high market shares. The second, cash cows, are in low-growth markets but have high market share. These products generate excess resources that can be spun off to products that need them. The third category, question marks, are in high-growth markets but have relatively low market shares. These products often utilize the excess resources generated by the cash cows. The final category, dogs, are in low-growth markets and have relatively low market shares. These products are often phased out.

LO2-7 Describe how firms grow their business.

Firms use four basic growth strategies: market penetration, market development, product development, and diversification. A market penetration strategy directs the firm's efforts toward existing customers and uses the present marketing mix. In other words, it attempts to get current customers to buy more. In a market development strategy, the firm uses its current marketing mix to appeal to new market segments, as might occur in international expansion. A product development growth strategy involves offering a new product or service to the firm's current target market. Finally, a diversification strategy takes place when a firm introduces a new product or service to a new customer segment. Sometimes a diversification strategy relates to the firm's current business, such as when a women's clothing manufacturer starts making and selling men's clothes, but a riskier strategy is when a firm diversifies into a completely unrelated business.

Key Terms

- control phase, 35
- customer excellence, 32
- diversification strategy, 52
- implementation phase, 35
- integrated marketing communications (IMC), 43
- locational excellence, 34
- market development strategy, 51
- market growth rate, 48
- market penetration strategy, 51
- market positioning, 41
- market segment, 40

- market segmentation, 40
- market share, 48
- marketing plan, 35
- marketing strategy, 30
- metric, 43
- mission statement, 36
- operational excellence, 34
- planning phase, 35
- product development strategy, 51
- product excellence, 34
- product line, 48
- related diversification, 52

- relative market share, 48
- segmentation, targeting, and positioning (STP), 40
- situation analysis, 37
- strategic business unit (SBU), 48
- sustainable competitive advantage, 30
- SWOT analysis, 37
- target marketing/targeting, 41
- unrelated diversification, 52

Marketing Digitally

1. The mission statement for The Estee Lauder Companies is "'Bringing the best to everyone we touch'. By 'The best', we mean the best products, the best people and the best ideas. These three pillars have been the hallmarks of our Company since it was founded by Mrs. Estee Lauder in 1946. They remain the foundation upon which we continue to build our success today." Harley-Davidson, Inc.'s mission statement is more straightforward: "We fulfill dreams through the experience of motorcycling, by providing to motorcyclists and to the general public an expanding line of motorcycles and branded products and services in selected market segments." (Both statements taken from: https://www.missionstatements.com/fortune_500_mission_statements.html) These different perspectives also reflect the quite different positioning adopted by each company. Visit the websites of each manufacturer and review the descriptions of the company, its mission, and its values. Do you believe these two disparate mission statements reflect what the firms do and how they are portrayed in the media? Justify your answer.

2. More and more firms seem to be entering the dating service industry. Visit http://www.eharmony.com and tour the website to find the types of activities and methods such companies use to help match compatible couples. Then visit http://www.match.com and do the same. What are the similarities and differences of these two online dating services? Pick one and perform a SWOT analysis for it.

3. Black and Decker (http://www.blackanddecker.com) and DeWalt (http://www.dewalt.com) are owned by the same parent company, and both sell similar products. Visit each of their websites and identify what markets each brand targets. Next, discuss how the two companies use the marketing mix differently to target these unique target markets.

Marketing Applications

1. How have PepsiCo and Coca-Cola created sustainable competitive advantages for themselves?

2. Perform a SWOT analysis for the company that makes your favorite shoes.

3. How does Coca-Cola segment its market? Describe the primary target markets for Coca-Cola. How does it position its various offerings so that it appeals to these different target markets?

4. How does Hertz add value for business customers through the implementation of the four Ps?

5. Dyson successfully sells its fans and heaters for $150 to $400, whereas most conventional fans sell for around $25. Explain what is the value it creates and how this affects the price it can charge.

6. Of the four growth strategies described in the chapter, which is the riskiest? Which is the easiest to implement? Why?

7. Choose three companies. You believe the first builds customer value through product excellence, the second through operational excellence, and the third through customer excellence. Justify your answer.

8. You are in the job market and have received offers from three very different firms. Develop a marketing plan to help market yourself to prospective employers.

Quiz Yourself

1. After a firm has conducted a SWOT analysis, it would typically progress to the next step of marketing planning, which is _____ and involves using STP (segmentation, targeting, and positioning).
   a. defining the mission
   b. conducting a situation analysis
   c. identifying and evaluating opportunities
   d. implementing the marketing mix
   e. evaluating performance

2. Which of the following is a marketing metric that might be used to evaluate the performance of a company's implementation of its marketing plan?
   a. Four Ps (price, product, promotion, place)
   b. SWOT analysis (strengths, weaknesses, threats, opportunities)
   c. STP (segmentation, targeting, positioning)
   d. GM (gross margin)
   e. SBU (strategic business unit)

(Answers to these two questions can be found in the Quiz Yourself Answer Key section.)

Chapter Case Study

THE COFFEE WARS

In the coffee and breakfast market, Starbucks vigorously competes with the likes of Dunkin' Donuts and, more recently, McDonald's. Independent coffeehouses and smaller regional chains, seen by many as more hip and less commercial, also continually nip at Starbucks' heels. However, the "coffee war" between Starbucks and Dunkin' Donuts is particularly fierce in the areas in which they compete head to head, even though each chain has its geographic strongholds—Dunkin' in the East and Starbucks in the West.[53] Part of the reason for this infamous battle might be the dominance of these two brands: Together, Starbucks and Dunkin' Donuts control well over half of the coffee market in the United States.[54] Moreover, Starbucks can claim some victories over Dunkin' Donuts, considering that its net revenues and stock prices have risen continuously since 2009.[55] By 2014, its global revenues had reached a record-setting $16.4 billion, and in 2015, its stock surged by more than 50 percent for the year.[56]

Starbucks' ubiquitous stores—from long-standing locations in U.S. cities and towns to international expansion into a vast range of new nations—are easy to locate and visit. A recent count showed that the chain maintains more than 22,000 stores, spanning 67 countries.[57] By making sure its stores, with their familiar siren logo, are easy to find, Starbucks guarantees that most people can readily find a place to get their coffee fix. For the vast majority of buyers, an addictive Salted Caramel Mocha, or just a great cup of black coffee, is convenient to find and very familiar.

There are plenty of jokes about how Starbucks manages to charge upwards of $5 for a jolt of caffeine, but a quick glance at its marketing methods and strategies helps explain why it can do so. The products it sells are appealing to customers and fulfill their needs: They taste good, are available readily and conveniently, and offer the benefit of helping them wake up to start their day (or stay awake for a long night of studying). Thus the exchange of money for coffee—or tea or juice or yogurt or a nice pastry—is a good value for consumers, despite the relatively high cost.

Starbucks also connects with fans through social marketing channels, including its popular My Starbucks Idea site. The site is an innovative approach to developing new products. Customers share ideas about everything "Starbucks," from store designs to new drink recipes. They can also join one of the many discussions in the customer forums. The site connects customers to its Twitter and Facebook sites too, and it also links users to its mobile apps. New capabilities available through the apps allow consumers to order their preferred beverage in advance and pay for their drinks or other products, then pop into the store to grab their purchases without ever having to wait in line.

When it comes to Starbucks' competition with Dunkin' Donuts, history shows that the two early morning giants actually had coexisted nicely for many years: Dunkin' Donuts made the donuts, and Starbucks brewed the coffee. Starting in 2000 though, Dunkin' Donuts slowly started encroaching on the upscale coffee market with the Dunkaccino. It also joined the "espresso revolution" in 2003, before formally declaring in 2006 its explicit intent to enter a head-to-head competition with Starbucks.[58]

Along with expanding its menu to feature specialty espresso drinks, Dunkin' Donuts launched a smartphone app that competes directly with Starbucks' widely popular version. In particular, the new Dunkin' Donuts app aims to extend the battle to the mobile field. It offers not just mobile ordering but also mobile delivery services, called Door-Dash. The delivery service began in Dallas, Texas; plans are in place to expand it to other major U.S. cities.[59]

Although Dunkin' Donuts still trails Starbucks as a global company—with only 3,100 stores in 30 countries[60]—it uses this relatively small size and regional feel strategically, leveraging these attributes to adjust flexibly and integrate itself with local communities. Accordingly, it has ranked tops in the market for customer loyalty since 2007.[61] This focus on loyalty also resonates with the company's chosen sponsorship efforts. It lends its support to professional sports teams with strong local and national followings, including all the major league Boston-area teams (Red Sox, Patriots, Celtics, and Bruins), the Dallas Cowboys, New York's Yankees and Mets, and the Tampa Bay Rays. Expanding on the strategy, both abroad and to less famous leagues, Dunkin' Donuts partners with the Liverpool football club and the National Women's Hockey League.

Through these partnerships with sports teams, Dunkin' Donuts encourages consumers to interact more closely with it. For example, New England customers receive inducements to become DD Perks members and use its mobile app. With its "Pats Win, You Win" promotion, DD Perks members who pay through the app receive a free cup of coffee each time the New England Patriots win a game. The popular, vastly successful promotion has continued for several seasons, during which the Patriots continue winning lots of games, thus bringing lots of excited fans into Dunkin' Donuts stores.[62]

The competition between these two brands is well established and likely to continue, especially as Dunkin' Donuts continues to move away from being exclusively a donut shop and toward becoming a more coffee-centered business. As big new competitors such as McDonald's and Taco Bell enter the breakfast, coffee, and espresso markets, both Starbucks and Dunkin' Donuts are likely to continue coming up with new ways to maintain their existing customer base, then expand it in the United States and abroad.

Questions

1. Perform a SWOT analysis for Starbucks and Dunkin' Donuts. Based on your analysis, in which company would you invest? Justify your answer.

2. Which growth strategies have been pursued by Starbucks and Dunkin' Donuts in the past? Which strategies do you believe will be most successful for the two firms in the future? Why?

3. Which marketing metrics would be most helpful for an executive in charge of developing new products for a coffee chain?

Endnotes

1. E. J. Schultz, "Pepsi Plans New '1893' Soda," *Advertising Age*, November 4, 2015; Laura Northrup, "The Sale Event for Pepsi Perfect Was Deeply Flawed," *Consumerist.com*, October 25, 2015.

2. E. J. Schultz, "Pepsi Plans New '1893' Soda," *Advertising Age*, November 4, 2015; PepsiCo, "Who We Are," http://www.pepsico.com/Company.

3. PepsiCo, "The PepsiCo Advantage," https://www.pepsico.com/docs/album/Investor/barclays_bts_presentation.pdf?sfvrsn=0.

4. PepsiCo, "Who We Are," http://www.pepsico.com/Company.

5. Robert Klara, "Why Celebrities Want to Be in PepsiCo's Ads," *Advertising Age*, June 8, 2015.

6. Beth Kowitt, "PepsiCo Nabs NBA Sponsorship Rights from Coca-Cola," *Fortune*, April 13, 2015.

7. Michael Treacy and Fred Wiersema, *The Disciplines of Market Leaders* (Reading, MA: Addison-Wesley, 1995). Treacy and Wiersema suggest the first three strategies. We suggest the fourth—locational excellence.

8. V. Kumar et al., "Establishing Profitable Customer Loyalty for Multinational Companies in the Emerging Economies: A Conceptual Framework," *Journal of International Marketing* 21 (March 2013), pp. 57–80; Yuping Liu-Thompkins and Leona Tam, "Not All Repeat Customers Are the Same: Designing Effective Cross-Selling Promotion on the Basis of Attitudinal Loyalty and Habit," *Journal of Marketing* 77 (September 2013), pp. 21–36.

9. Melea Press and Eric J. Arnould, "How Does Organizational Identification Form? A Consumer Behavior Perspective," *Journal of Consumer Research* 38 (December 2011), pp. 650–66.

10. Valarie A. Zeithaml, Mary Jo Bitner, and Dwayne D. Gremler, *Services Marketing: Integrating Customer Focus across the Firm*, 5th ed. (Burr Ridge, IL: McGraw-Irwin, 2009).

11. Brooks Barnes, "At Disney Parks, a Bracelet Meant to Build Loyalty (and Sales)," *The New York Times*, January 7, 2013.

12. Carmine Gallo, "Customer Service the Disney Way," *Forbes*, April 14, 2011.

13. Diane M. Martin and John W. Schouten, "Consumption-Driven Market Emergence," *Journal of Consumer Research* 40 (February 2014), pp. 855–70. Also see articles in special issue edited by John T. Mentzer and Greg Gundlach, "Exploring the Relationship between Marketing and Supply Chain Management: Introduction to the Special Issue," *Journal of the Academy of Marketing Science* 38, no. 1 (2010), pp. 1–4.

14. Hilary Stout, "In War for Same-Day Delivery, Racing Madly to Go Last Mile," *The New York Times*, November 23, 2013, http://www.nytimes.com.

15. http://www.interbrand.com.

16. "Marketing Plan," *American Marketing Association Dictionary*, http://www.marketingpower.com.

17. Donald Lehman and Russell Winer, *Analysis for Marketing Planning*, 7th ed. (Burr Ridge, IL: McGraw-Hill/Irwin, 2008).

18. Nancy J. Sirianni et al., "Branded Service Encounters: Strategically Aligning Employee Behavior with the Brand Positioning," *Journal of Marketing* 77 (November 2013), pp. 108–23; Andrew Campbell, "Mission Statements," *Long Range Planning* 30 (1997), pp. 931–33.

19. Gene R. Laczniak and Patrick E. Murphy, "Stakeholder Theory and Marketing: Moving from a Firm-Centric to a Societal Perspective," *Journal of Public Policy & Marketing* 31 (Fall 2012), pp. 284–92; Alfred Rappaport, *Creating Shareholder Value: The New Standard for Business Performance* (New York: Wiley, 1988).

20. PepsiCo, "Our Mission & Values," http://www.pepsico.com/Purpose/Our-Mission-and-Values.

21. Coca-Cola, "Mission, Vision & Values," http://www.coca-colacompany.com/our-company/mission-vision-values/.

22. Pink Ribbon International, http://www.pinkribbon.org.

23. Robert Klara, "Why Celebrities Want to Be in PepsiCo's Ads: A 'Symbiotic Relationship' with Stars Like Beckham, Beyoncé and Jordan," *Ad Week*, June 8, 2015, http://www.adweek.com/news/advertising-branding/why-celebrities-want-be-pepsicos-ads-165217.

24. "Pepsi Launches New Music Platform "Out of the Blue" To Debut During the 57th Annual Grammy Awards," *PR Newswire*, Feb. 4, 2015, http://www.prnewswire.com/news-releases/pepsi-launches-new-music-platform-out-of-the-blue-to-debut-during-the-57th-annual-grammy-awards-300031079.html.

25. StreetAuthority, "Coke vs. Pepsi: By the Numbers," *Nasdaq*, March 24, 2014, http://www.nasdaq.com/article/coke-vs-pepsi-by-the-numbers-cm337909.

26. RT, "PepsiCo Admits Public Source Origins of Its Aquafina Bottled Water," https://www.rt.com/usa/319980-aquafina-tap-water-origins/.

27. Trefis Team, "Non-Carbonated Beverages Spearhead Growth for PepsiCo's North America Business," *Forbes*, Dec. 10, 2015, http://www.forbes.com/sites/greatspeculations/2015/12/10/non-carbonated-beverages-spearhead-growth-for-pepsicos-north-america-business/.

28. http://www.pepsico.com/Company/Global-Divisions.

29. Brian Dumaine, "The Water Conservation Challenge of Coke vs. Pepsi," *Fortune*, Aug. 20, 2015, http://fortune.com/2015/08/20/coca-cola-vs-pepsi/.

30. Ilan Brat and Mike Esterl, "FDA Proposes Placing Sugar Guide on Food Labels," *The Wall Street Journal*, July 24, 2015, http://www.wsj.com/articles/fda-proposes-listing-added-sugar-on-food-labels-1437774370.

31. Stephanie Strom, "Small Food Brands, Big Successes," *The New York Times*, Aug. 24, 2015, http://www.nytimes.com/2015/08/26/dining/start-up-food-business-changing-appetites.html?_r=0.

32. https://www.hertz.com/rentacar/productsandservices/productsandservicesRegions.do.

33. https://images.hertz.com/pdfs/VMVWeb.pdf; http://www.adweek.com/aw/content_display/creative/new-campaigns/e3i21cea1586dd4edf5d50f9a17e7f18bf3.

34. Terence A. Shimp, *Advertising Promotion and Other Aspects of Integrated Marketing Communication,* 8th ed. (Mason, OH: South-Western, 2008); T. Duncan and C. Caywood, "The Concept, Process, and Evolution of Integrated Marketing Communication," in *Integrated Communication: Synergy of Persuasive Voices,* ed. E. Thorson and J. Moore (Mahwah, NJ: Erlbaum, 1996); see also various issues of the *Journal of Integrated Marketing Communications,* http://jimc.medill.northwestern.edu.

35. Nathalie Tadena, "Cheerios Is King of Commercial Spending Among Cereal Brands," *The Wall Street Journal*, July 17, 2014, http://blogs.wsj.com/cmo/2014/07/17/cheerios-is-king-of-commercial-spending-among-cereal-brands/.

36. Ofer Mintz and Imran S. Currim, "What Drives Managerial Use of Marketing and Financial Metrics and Does Metric Use Affect Performance of Marketing-Mix Activities?," *Journal of Marketing* 77 (March 2013), pp. 17–40.

37. Kirsten Acuna, "Google Says It Can Predict Which Films Will Be Huge Box Office Hits," *Business Insider,* June 6, 2013.

38. Goodyear, Annual Report 2014.

39. This discussion is adapted from Roger A. Kerin, Steven W. Hartley, and William Rudelius, *Marketing,* 10th ed. (Burr Ridge, IL: McGraw-Hill/Irwin, 2011).

40. P. Farris et al., *Marketing Metrics: 50+ Metrics Every Executive Should Master* (Upper Saddle River, NJ: Pearson, 2006), p. 17.

41. Relative market share = Brand's market share ÷ Largest competitor's market share. If, for instance, there are only two products in a market, A and B, and product B has 90 percent market share, then A's relative market share is 10 ÷ 90 = 11.1 percent. If, on the other hand, B only has 50 percent market share, then A's relative market share is 10 ÷ 50 = 20 percent. P. Farris et al., *Marketing Metrics: 50+ Metrics Every Executive Should Master* (Upper Saddle River, NJ: Pearson, 2006), p. 19.

42. Apple Inc., "Form 10-K 2011 Annual Report," October 30, 2013.

43. Sherilynn Macale, "Apple Has Sold 300M iPods, Currently Holds 78% of the Music Player Market," *The Next Web*, October 4, 2011, http://thenextweb.com; Chris Smith, "iPad Tablet Market Share Down to 57 Per-cent," *Techradar.com*, February 16, 2012, http://www.techradar.com; Ken Yeung, "Apple Sold 4.6M Macs and 3.49M iPods in Q4 FY2013," *The Next Web*, October 28, 2013, http://thenextweb.com.

44. "iPhone, iPad and iPod Sales from 1st Quarter 2006 to 4th Quarter 2015 (in Million Units)," *Statista*, December 4, 2015, http://www.statista.com/statistics/253725/iphone-ipad-and-ipod-sales-comparison/

45. Katie Collins, "Apple Mac Sales Down, but the Broader PC Market is Even Worse," *CNET*, October 9, 2015, http://www.cnet.com/news/apple-mac-sales-reportedly-hit-two-year-low/.

46. Chuck Jones, "Morgan Stanley Survey Shows Strong Demand for Apple's iPhone and Expects Growth in 2016," *Forbes*, September 6, 2015, http://www.forbes.com/sites/chuckjones/2015/09/06/morgan-stanley-survey-shows-strong-demand-for-apples-iphone-and-expects-growth-in-2016/

47. Roger Kerin, Vijay Mahajan, and P. Rajan Varadarajan, *Contemporary Perspectives on Strategic Market Planning* (Boston: Allyn & Bacon, 1991), Chapter 6; Susan Mudambi, "A Topology of Strategic Choice in Marketing," *International Journal of Market & Distribution Management* (1994), pp. 22–25.

48. Devin Leonard, "Calling All Superheroes," *Fortune*, May 23, 2007; Box Office Mojo, "X-Men (2000)," http://www.boxofficemojo.com/movies/?id=xmen.htm

49. The Numbers, "The Avengers: Age of Ultron (2015)," http://www.the-numbers.com/movie/Avengers-Age-of-Ultron-The#tab=summary

50. Patrick Cavanaugh, "Netflix Orders a Second Season of 'Marvel's Daredevil'," *Marvel.com*, April 21, 2015; Todd Spangler, "Netflix, Marvel Pick 'Luke Cage' Showrunner, Cheo Hodari Coker," *Variety*, March 31, 2015.

51. A. A. Thompson et al., *Crafting and Executing Strategy,* 18th ed. (New York: McGraw-Hill/Irwin, 2012).

52. Marvel, "Home Décor," http://shop.marvel.com/home-decor/

53. Alvin Chang and Matt Carroll, "Split Country: Dunkin' vs. Starbucks," *Boston Globe*/Boston.com (n.d.).

54. Christine Champagne and Teressa Iezzi, "Dunkin' Donuts and Starbucks: A Tale of Two Coffee Marketing Giants," *Fast Company Co Create*, August 21, 2014, http://www.fastcocreate.com/3034572/coffee-week/dunkin-donuts-and-starbucks-a-tale-of-two-coffee-marketing-giants.

55. Starbucks, "Fiscal Year 2015 Annual Report," http://investor.starbucks.com

56. Justin Bariso, "The Strategy that Led Starbucks's Stock Price to Jump 50 Percent?" *Inc.,* December 7, 2015,

http://www.inc.com/justin-bariso/what-you-can-learn-from-star-bucks-continued-success.html.

57. Starbucks, "Starbucks Company Profile," https://news.starbucks.com/uploads/documents/AboutUs-Company_Profile-Q32015-8.6.2015.pdf.

58. Champagne and Iezzi, "Dunkin' Donuts and Starbucks."

59. "Dunkin' Donuts Tests On-The-Go Ordering and Delivery Service in Select Markets," Dunkin' Donuts Newsroom, November 18, 2015, http://news.dunkindonuts.com/news/dunkin-donuts-tests-on-the-go-ordering-and-delivery-service-in-select-markets-3105177.

60. "Global Presence," https://www.dunkindonuts.com/dunkindonuts/en/company/global.html.

61. "Dunkin' Donuts," Dunkin' Brands, http://dunkinbrands.com/about/donuts.

62. Frank O'Laughlin, "Dunkin' Donuts to Give Away Free Coffee When Patriots Win," *Woburn Patch*, September 8, 2015, http://patch.com/massachusetts/woburn/dunkin-donuts-give-away-free-coffee-when-patriots-win-0.

i. Hilary Stout, "Amazon, Google, and More Are Drawn to Home Services Market," *The New York Times*, April 12, 2015; Laura Lorenzetti, "Amazon's Handyman Service Is Expanding to 15 Cities," *Fortune*, July 22, 2015; Harriet Taylor, "Amazon, Google Move into On-Demand Home Services," *CNBC*, October 1, 2015.

ii. Seb Joseph, "Coca-Cola Has an Internal Strategy Called 'Marketing in Smaller Sizes' to Make People Buy Its Soda More Often for More Money," *Business Insider*, November 18, 2015; Rachel Arthur, "Coca-Cola Sees Big Success with Small Pack Sizes, Celebrating a 'Tremendous Amount of Positive Growth'," BeverageDaily.com, July 23, 2015; Brooke Metz, "Less Is More: For Coca-Cola, Small Packs Mean Big Business," July 22, 2015, http://www.coca-colacompany.com/stories/less-is-more-for-coca-cola-small-packs-mean-big-business/; Associated Press, "Coke, Pepsi, Pledge to Shrink Can and Bottle Sizes to Cut Calories," *CBC News,* September 23, 2014, http://www.cbc.ca/news/health/coke-pepsi-pledge-to-shrink-can-and-bottle-sizes-to-cut-calories-1.2775467

iii. Tim Peterson, "How P&G Is Tying Snapchat Ads to In-Store Sales," *Advertising Age*, November 18, 2015.

iv. William Boston, Hendrink Varnhot, and Sarah Sloat, "Volkswagen Blames 'Chain of Mistakes' for Emissions Scandal," *The Wall Street Journal*, December 10, 2015; Russell Hotten, "Volkswagen: The Scandal Explained," *BBC News*, December 10, 2015; Alex Davis, "Volkswagen's US Sales Plummet 25 Percent as Dieselgate Rolls On," *Wired*, December 1, 2015; Stephen Edelstein, "Used VW Prices Fall More, with No End to Diesel Scandal in Sight," *Green Car Reports*, December 9, 2015, http://www.greencarreports.com/news/1101315_used-vw-prices-fall-more-with-no-end-to-diesel-scandal-in-sight.

v. Aaron M. Kessler and B.X. Chen, "Google and Apple Fight for the Car Dashboard," *The New York Times*, February 22, 2015, http://www.nytimes.com; Tim Stevens, "2014's Battle for Dashboard Supremacy: Apple's CarPlay vs. Google's OAA vs. MirrorLink," *CNET*, March 4, 2014, http://www.cnet.com/news/2014s-battle-for-dashboard-supremacy-apples-carplay-vs-googles-oaa-vs-mirrorlink/.

APPENDIX 2A

WRITING A MARKETING PLAN

Have a plan. Follow the plan, and you'll be surprised how successful you can be. Most people don't have a plan. That's why it's easy to beat most folks.

—Paul "Bear" Bryant, football coach, University of Alabama

WHY WRITE A MARKETING PLAN?[1]

As a student, you likely plan out much in your life—where to meet for dinner, how much time to spend studying for exams, which courses to take next semester, how to get home for winter break, and so on. Plans enable us to figure out where we want to go and how we might get there.

For a firm, the goal is not much different. Any company that wants to succeed (which means any firm whatsoever) needs to plan for a variety of contingencies, and marketing represents one of the most significant. A marketing plan—which we defined in Chapter 2 as a written document composed of an analysis of the current marketing situation, opportunities and threats for the firm,

marketing objectives and strategy specified in terms of the four Ps, action programs, and projected or pro forma income (and other financial) statements—enables marketing personnel and the firm as a whole to understand their own actions, the market in which they operate, their future direction, and the means to obtain support for new initiatives.[2]

Because these elements—internal activities, external environments, goals, and forms of support—differ for every firm, the marketing plan is different for each firm as well. However, several guidelines apply to marketing plans in general; this appendix summarizes those points and offers an annotated example.

MARKETING PLAN VERSUS BUSINESS PLAN

Of course, firms consider more than marketing when they make plans and therefore commonly develop business plans as well. Yet as this book highlights, marketing constitutes such an important element of business that business plans and marketing plans coincide in many ways.[3] Marketing plans as well as business plans generally encompass:

1. Executive summary.
2. Company overview.
3. Objectives or goals, usually according to strategic plan and focus.
4. Situation analysis.
5. Customer segmentation, target marketing, and positioning analysis.
6. Marketing strategy.
7. Financial projections.
8. Implementation plan.
9. Evaluation and control metrics.
10. Appendix

A business plan also includes details about R&D and operations, and both may feature details about other key topics, depending on the focus of the company and the plan.

STRUCTURE OF A MARKETING PLAN

This section briefly describes each of the elements of a marketing plan.[4]

Executive Summary

The executive summary essentially tells the reader why he or she is reading this marketing plan—what changes require consideration, what new products need discussion, and so forth—and suggests possible actions to take in response to the information the plan contains.

Company Overview

The company overview provides a brief description of the company, including perhaps its mission statement, background, and competitive advantages.

Objectives/Goals

The objectives/goals section offers more specifics about why readers are reading the marketing plan. What does the company want to achieve, both overall and with this particular marketing plan?

Situation Analysis

Recall from the chapter text that a situation analysis generally relies on SWOT considerations; the situation section, then, describes the strengths, weaknesses, opportunities, and threats facing the company.

STP Analysis

The analysis proceeds by assessing the market in which the company functions, the products it currently offers or plans to offer in the future, and the characteristics of current or potential customers.

Marketing Strategy

The marketing strategy may be very specific, especially if the plan pertains to, for example, a stable product in a familiar market, or it may be somewhat open to varied possibilities, such as when the firm plans to enter a new market with an innovative product.

Financial Projections

On the basis of the knowledge already obtained, the marketing plan should provide possible developments and returns on the marketing investments outlined in the marketing strategy.

Implementation Plan

The implementation plans includes the timing of promotional activities, when monitoring will take place, and how expansions likely will proceed.

Evaluation and Control Metrics

The firm must have a means of assessing the marketing plan's recommendations; the marketing plan therefore must indicate the methods for undertaking this assessment, whether quantitatively or qualitatively.

Appendix

The final section(s) offers additional information that might be of benefit, such as a list of key personnel; data limitations that may influence the findings; and suggestions of the plan, relevant legislation, and so forth.

INFORMATION SOURCES[5]

When writing a marketing plan, you likely can turn to a variety of your firm's in-house information sources, including annual reports, previous marketing plans, published mission statements, and so on. In addition, various sources offer suggestions and examples that may provide you with direction and ideas. A reference librarian can help you find many of these sources, which likely are available through your university's library system.

- Knowthis.com—"a knowledge source for marketing," http://www.knowthis.com/ tutorials/principles-of-marketing/how-to-write-a-marketing-plan/21.htm.
- Encyclopedia of American Industries—introduces industry structure; arranged by SIC and NAICS codes.
- Standard & Poor's NetAdvantage—surveys of more than 50 industries, with financial data about companies in each industry.
- Investext Plus—brokerage house reports.
- IBISWorld—market research on thousands of industries; classified by NAICS code.
- Statistical Abstract of the United States—a vast variety of statistics on a wealth of topics.
- U.S. Bureau of the Census—detailed statistical data gathered every 10 years on all aspects of the U.S. population.
- County Business Patterns: U.S. Bureau of the Census—payroll and employee numbers for most NAICS codes.
- Consumer Expenditure Study: U.S. Bureau of Labor Statistics—income and expenditures by household, classified by various demographics.
- LifeStyle Market Analyst—lifestyle information about geographic areas, lifestyle interest groups, and age and income groups.

- Mediamark Reporter—information about demographics, lifestyles, product and brand usage, and advertising media preferences.

- Scarborough Arbitron—local market consumer information for various media in 75 local markets for consumer retail shopping behavior, product consumption, media usage, lifestyle behavior, and demographics.

- Simmons Study of Media and Markets—products and consumer characteristics; various media audiences and their characteristics.

- Sourcebook America—demographic data, including population, spending potential index, income, race, and *Tapestry* data, presented by state, county, DMA, and zip code, as well as business data by county and zip code.

- Rand McNally Commercial Atlas and Marketing Guide—maps and tables showing demographic, industrial, transportation, railroad, airline, and hospital data.

- "Survey of Buying Power," Sales and Marketing Management—current state, county, city, and town estimates of population by age, retail sales by store group, effective buying income, and buying power index.

- Annual & 10-K reports from *Thomson One Banker, Edgar,* and *LexisNexis*—business descriptions, product listings, distribution channels, possible impact of regulations and lawsuits, and discussions of strategic issues.

- MarketResearch.com Academic—market research reports on a variety of consumer products.

- Mintel Reports Database—market research reports focusing on consumer products, lifestyles, retailing, and international travel industry.

LINGUISTIC AND VISUAL SUGGESTIONS

Again, recall that all marketing plans differ because all firms differ. However, just as rules exist that dictate what makes for good writing, some rules or guidelines apply to all well-written marketing plans.

- Maintain a professional attitude in the writing and presentation.

- Keep descriptions and summaries concise. Get to the point.

- Use standard English in a professional tone.

- Proofread the entire plan multiple times to catch grammatical, spelling, or other such errors that could dampen the professionalism of the writing.

- Adopt a businesslike tone; avoid flowery or jargon-filled writing.

- Employ active voice rather than passive voice, and present tense rather than past tense whenever possible (e.g., "We plan to achieve 30 percent growth in two years" rather than "The plan was that 30 percent growth would be achieved by the firm within two years").

- Be positive.

- Avoid meaningless adjectives (e.g., "Our goal is tremendous growth").

- Be specific; use quantitative information whenever possible.

- Insert graphics to convey important concepts succinctly, including photos, graphs, illustrations, and charts.

- Avoid using so many visual elements that they clutter the plan.

- Lay out the plan clearly and logically.

- Organize sections logically, using multiple levels of headings, distinguished clearly by font differences (e.g., bold for first-level heads, italics for second-level heads).

- Consider the use of bullet points or numbered lists to emphasize important points.

- Exploit modern technology (e.g., graphics software, page layout software, laser printers) to ensure the plan looks professional.

- Adopt an appropriate font to make the text easy to read and visually appealing—avoid using anything smaller than 10-point font at a minimum.

- Avoid unusual or decorative fonts; stick with a common serif type to make the text easy to read.

- Consider binding the report with an attractive cover and clear title page.

- Generally, aim for a plan that consists of 15–30 pages.

Endnotes

1. This appendix was written by Tom Chevalier, Britt Hackmann, and Elisabeth Nevins Caswell, in conjunction with the textbook authors (Dhruv Grewal and Michael Levy) as the basis of class discussion, rather than to illustrate either effective or ineffective marketing practice.

2. http://www.knowthis.com (accessed May 16, 2008); see also "Marketing Plan Online," http://www.quickmba.com (accessed May 16, 2008); "Marketing Plan," http://www.businessplans.org (accessed May 18, 2008).

3. Roger Kerin, Steven Hartley, and William Rudelius, *Marketing* (New York: McGraw-Hill/Irwin, 2008), p. 53.

4. Roger A. Kerin, Steven W. Hartley, and William Rudelius, *Marketing* 12e, Burr Ridge, Il.: McGraw-Hill Education, 2015; http://www.knowthis.com (accessed May 16, 2008).

5. This listing of sources largely comes from the Babson College Library Guide, http://www3.babson.edu, May 12, 2008 (accessed May 15, 2008). Special thanks to Nancy Dlott.

6. This marketing plan presents an abbreviated version of the actual plan for PeopleAhead. Some information has been changed to maintain confidentiality.

7. Publishers' and Advertising Directors' Conference, September 21, 2005.

8. Mintel International Group, "Online Recruitment–US," January 1, 2005, http://www.marketresearch.com (accessed September 1, 2005).

9. Corzen Inc., May 1, 2004, http://www.wantedtech.com (accessed May 17, 2004).

10. Mintel International Group, "Online Recruitment–US."

PEOPLEAHEAD MARKETING PLAN ILLUSTRATION[6]

PeopleAhead Marketing Plan: Condensed

1. Executive Summary

PeopleAhead focuses on career advancement done right. Instead of making the job search a one-time event, PeopleAhead provides a platform for people to find, advance, and develop their careers by sharing career goals, discussing professional development plans, and socializing with other professionals.

PeopleAhead culminates the career advancement experience with its proprietary TrueMatch® technology, which identifies synergies between the companies hiring talent (employers) and PeopleAhead members (job candidates) who wish to be hired. By anonymously presenting only prequalified career opportunities to members, who confirm their interest and recommend others, PeopleAhead transforms the ineffective online hiring process into a highly efficient career-matching system. PeopleAhead was founded by Carlos Larracilla and Tom Chevalier to improve people's lives by helping them achieve their career aspirations. The vision for PeopleAhead was conceived of in January 2006, with a notion that personality alignment is critical to matching the right people with the right career opportunities. Since then, the idea has grown and morphed into a company that matches the right person with the right career opportunity by aligning personality, competencies, experience, and interests.

Tom and Carlos combine human resources, system development, and sales experience to deliver a groundbreaking, TrueMatch®-branded talent matching network that makes it easier for people to achieve their career aspirations and improves the way companies identify individuals who will be able to contribute to their long-term success. The organizational chart of PeopleAhead is available in Appendix A.

Side annotations:

Instead of using separate "Executive Summary" and "Company Overview" sections, this marketing plan begins with a general overview that includes both aspects and answers the key questions: "What type of business are we?" and "What do we need to do to accomplish our objectives?" (see Chapter 2).

As this plan does, a marketing plan should start with a positive, upbeat assessment of what the company does and what it hopes to continue doing.

Note the personalization of the company founders, which may help readers feel connected to the company.

2. Strategic Objectives

2.1. Mission

PeopleAhead's mission is to help individuals with career advancement and improve the human capital in companies. The site will act as a networking platform for professionals and career matching as opposed to job and resume-posting searches.

2.2. Goals:

- Use brand-matching technology: TrueMatch®
- Build critical mass of users.
- Drive traffic to the Web site through marketing blitzes.
- Utilize word-of-mouth advertising from satisfied users.

2.3. Business Summary

- **Business customers:** This group provides PeopleAhead's revenues. Customers purchase contact information about the Top Ten PROfiles gleaned from the individual member base that have been sorted and ranked by the TrueMatch® technology. PeopleAhead will focus on small and medium businesses (see Market Segmentation section), because these entities are underserved by large competitors in the online recruitment market, and because research shows that this demographic has a less efficient recruitment process that would benefit most readily from PeopleAhead's services. Within this segment, customers include HR managers who are responsible for the sourcing of candidates, functional area managers who require new talent for their team, and executives whose business objectives rely on human capital and efficiency of operations.
- **Individual members:** This group does not pay for services but is the main source of data points for PeopleAhead's TrueMatch® system. PeopleAhead will focus on building a base of individual members who range from recent graduates to individuals with 5–7 years of continuous employment. Ideal members are those who are currently employed or will be graduating within nine months and are "poised" to make a career change. These individuals can utilize the services to the fullest extent and are valuable candidates for business customers.

2.4. Competitive Advantage

- **TrueMatch® offers a branded technology,** marketed to both business customers and individual candidates for its "black box" value proposition, which establishes PeopleAhead as the category leader for recruitment-matching software. This technology provides a point of differentiation from competitors, which may have technically similar matching software but constantly need to reinforce their marketing messages with explanations of their value proposition.
- **For individual candidates,** PeopleAhead will be the favored career advancement platform online, where individuals enthusiastically create a history and have connections (invited friends, coworkers, and mentors) in place that will make PeopleAhead a staple among their favorite Web sites. PeopleAhead delivers TrueMatch® career opportunities, professional development plans that let people establish a professional record, and valuable career advancement tools, including automatic position feedback, "recommend-a-friend," and team-based career networking.
- **For business customers,** PeopleAhead makes online sourcing and qualification of candidates quick and efficient by prequalifying potential candidates, seeking recommendations for hard-to-find individuals, and delivering only the Top 10 most highly qualified candidates who have

The paragraph provides a general outline of the firm's objectives; the bulleted list offers more specific goals, and the subsequent sections go into more detail about the various factors that may influence these objectives.

By referring to another section, the plan makes clear where it is heading and enables readers to cross-reference the information.

The plan acknowledges both a general, potential target market and the ideal targets.

As Chapter 2 suggests, the plan notes PeopleAhead's sustainable competitive advantage as part of its overall mission statement.

preconfirmed interest in the available position. PeopleAhead will be the most effective candidate-company matching platform available in the market, delivering prequalified, preconfirmed candidates.

3. Situation Analysis—Online Recruitment

Online recruitment is the system whereby companies use the Web to locate and qualify prospective candidates for available positions. The methods employed by online recruitment service providers to serve this market range from resume aggregation to assessment test application to linking strategies. However, the common underlying objective is to locate candidates who would not be found by traditional recruitment methods and use computing power to qualify candidates quickly and with more accuracy than would be possible manually.

3.1. Industry Analysis

Large online recruitment Web sites make this a tedious process by requiring companies to search through many resumes manually to find the right candidate. Other sites solicit recommendations for positions. However, resumes are often "enhanced," such that almost all candidates appear qualified, and information found in the resume or provided through a recommendation is simply not sufficient to make an educated hiring decision. Companies need more information and intelligent tools that make this screening process more accurate.

3.1.1. Market Size:

The market size for both member segments in 2005 was as follows:

Individual members segments

7.4 M   1.3 M

24.4 M

3.7 M

134.5 M

- ■ Senior college students
- □ Other college students
- ■ Graduate program students
- □ Current employees
- ■ Unemployed

In discussing both the external market and the internal advantages of PeopleAhead, the plan carefully distinguishes between individual job candidates and businesses, thus differentiating the focus and objectives according to this segmentation.

Figures provide a visually attractive break in the text and summarize a lot of information in an easy-to-read format.

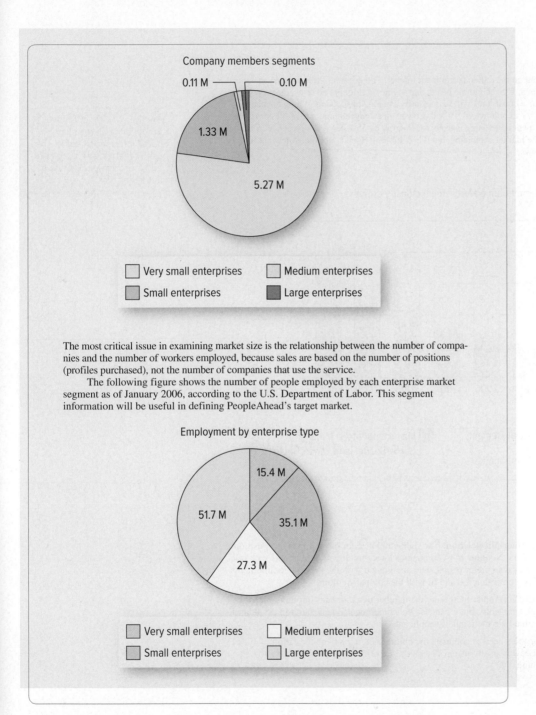

Company members segments

0.11 M — ⌐ 0.10 M

1.33 M

5.27 M

- ☐ Very small enterprises
- ☐ Small enterprises
- ☐ Medium enterprises
- ☐ Large enterprises

The most critical issue in examining market size is the relationship between the number of companies and the number of workers employed, because sales are based on the number of positions (profiles purchased), not the number of companies that use the service.

The following figure shows the number of people employed by each enterprise market segment as of January 2006, according to the U.S. Department of Labor. This segment information will be useful in defining PeopleAhead's target market.

Employment by enterprise type

15.4 M

51.7 M

35.1 M

27.3 M

- ☐ Very small enterprises
- ☐ Small enterprises
- ☐ Medium enterprises
- ☐ Large enterprises

3.1.2. Market Growth

PeopleAhead will operate in the online recruitment market. The growth of this industry is subject to two primary constraints: U.S. economic health and online recruitment advertisement adoption rates. Understanding these constraints will help identify PeopleAhead's opportunity. General indicators suggest the U.S. economy (GDP) will grow at an average annual rate of 4% for the next decade.[7] Online recruitment advertising is expected to grow by 35% per year to reach $7.6 billion by 2010.[8] Not only is the market expanding, but it is exhibiting rapid adoption by new entities, as the following graph shows.[9]

> Another visually attractive graph summarizes complicated information easily. The use of high-quality color can add a professional feel to a marketing plan.

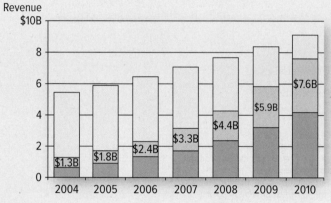

Recruitment advertisement industry growth

Legend:
- ☐ Total recruitment advertisement
- ☐ Total online recruitment market
- ▨ Main competitors: Monster, CareerBuilder, and Yahoo/HotJobs

3.1.3. Market Needs

- **The right person for the right position:** The right employee for one company or position is not the same for all others. Not only must companies locate intelligent individuals with relevant experience, but they also prefer people who are aligned with the position requirements in terms of personality, competencies, and fit with the company culture.

- **Prescreening qualification tools:** Increasing the number of candidates through online recruitment can be advantageous, but it can also be a hindrance. When sourcing candidates, recruiters need tools that help them qualify applicants.

- **Time savings:** Companies need to complete the online sourcing and qualification of candidates quickly. Leaving positions unfilled can cause critical performance gaps to emerge within the company.

3.1.4. Market Trends

The methods by which online recruitment service providers deliver candidates has been undergoing a migration from resume aggregation and search services like Monster and CareerBuilder to new Web 2.0 methodologies that include passive recruitment, "meta tagging," and social networking.

The underlying objective of these Web 2.0 services is to allow individuals to remain on a few, trusted Web sites while enabling companies to access those individuals for financial purposes. In parallel, the focus is moving from aggregation of unique visitors toward engaging existing users more intensively. Internet users are growing familiar with sites that encourage socializing, collaborating, and distributing private information online to help improve network benefits and need to be engaged to maintain contact.

3.2. SWOT Analysis

	Positive	Negative
Internal	**STRENGTHS** • Industry best practices: The networking model used by PeopleAhead draws on the industry accepted best practices contact protocols drawn from multiple industries, including online feedback, recruitment, and social networking and offline professional networking. True-Match® software aligns business objectives with appropriate candidates. • Team expertise: The combined talents of the founders include human resources, system development, sales, and marketing. • Web development expertise: PeopleAhead has partnered with an award-winning European software development provider. This company provides quality usually reserved for high-budget projects, at terms that are favorable for a start-up company.	**WEAKNESSES** • Absence of industry "influentials": As a start-up, PeopleAhead does not currently have resources to attract influential industry managers. • Inability to guarantee critical mass: As is true of many Internet companies, the business must solve the "chicken and egg" puzzle to build critical mass. • Verifying efficiency of matching capabilities: In theory, the system has an absolute guarantee of effectivity; computations make decisions rather than humans. However, the matching capabilities must be verified as accurate to gain widespread acceptance. • Broad target market: Because PeopleAhead is targeting a wide range of businesses, the product being developed has not been "customized" ideally for each segment.
External	**OPPORTUNITIES** • Service gap: Recruiters are not pleased with current online recruitment vendors. • Industry gap: Job turnover is every 3.5 years per person. • Demand for productive candidates. • Online recruitment advertising: Growing by 35% per year, to reach $7.6 billion by 2010.[10]	**THREATS** • Convergence: Existing competitors may form strategic alliances and establish powerful positions before PeopleAhead can establish itself. • Inability to protect model: Very little intellectual property created by Web sites is protected by law. Although PeopleAhead will pursue aggressive

(continued)

Before engaging in a firm-specific SWOT analysis (see Chapter 2), this marketing plan assesses the external market environment further and thus establishes a basis for the subsequent SWOT analysis.

Using a table and bullet points, the plan summarizes a lot of information succinctly and clearly.

Note that the analysis uses outside sources to support its claims.

External   **OPPORTUNITIES**
- Fragmented business models: Online recruitment is fragmented by recruitment methodology: active (people who need jobs), passive (people who are not looking but would move if enticed), poised (people unsatisfied with jobs they have), and network (finding people of interest based on who or what they know).

THREATS

IP protection strategies, the model could be copied or mimicked by competitors.
- Inadequate differentiation: Inability to explain our differentiation would relegate PeopleAhead to (unfair) comparisons with competitors. Without differentiation, PeopleAhead will not be able to create scale through network effects.

3.3. Competition

Most online recruitment Web sites compete in the active recruitment market, including Monster, CareerBuilder, and Yahoo/HotJobs. The pervasive segment includes job seekers who actively look for jobs, post their resumes, and search for jobs on company Web sites. Most active recruiters offer free services to users and charge companies on a fee basis. Companies can post jobs and search for candidate resumes in the database (average fee for local searches is $500 and nationwide is $1,000). In this first-generation online recruitment business model, competitors face the challenge to make the process more user-friendly and reduce the effort required to make these sites deliver results.

- **Monster:** Monster.com is the sixteenth most visited Web site in the United States, with more than 43 million professionals in its viewer base. Monster earns revenue from job postings, access to its resume database, and advertisements on Web sites of partner companies.
- **Careerbuilder:** Careerbuilder.com has experienced 75% growth for the past five years. This job post/resume search company uses its media ownership to attract passive candidates from partner Web sites. It achieves growth through affiliate partnerships that host job searches on affiliated Web pages, such as Google, MSN, AOL, *USA Today,* Earthlink, BellSouth, and CNN. Job posting is the primary activity, sold together with or separately from resume searches.
- **Passive recruitment:** The second generation of online recruitment locates candidates who are not necessarily looking for jobs but who could be convinced to move to a new position if the right opportunity was presented. The most recognized competitors in this category include Jobster, LinkedIn, and H3 (Appendix B).

3.4. Company Analysis

PeopleAhead's mission is simple: improve people's lives through career advancement. PeopleAhead recognizes that career advancement means many things to many people and provides a fresh perspective on career networking that is flexible yet powerful:

- **Users are not alone:** Finding a job is not easy. Why search solo? PeopleAhead unites groups of friends, coworkers, and mentors to create natural, team-based career discovery.
- **Job posting is not natural:** People spend countless hours searching job listings and posting resumes, only to be overlooked because their writing style or resume format does not match an overburdened recruiter's preference. Good people, not resumes, make great companies. PeopleAhead's TrueMatch technology matches the right people with the right position. No posting, no applying—just good, quality matches.

If PeopleAhead chooses to adopt a competitor-based pricing strategy (see Chapter 13), detailed information about how other recruitment firms work will be mandatory.

Information about competitors' revenues, customers, growth, and so forth often is available publicly through a variety of sources.

For information that may not belong in the main text, an appendix offers an effective means to provide detail without distracting readers.

This section offers the "product" component of the market/product/customer analysis. Because PeopleAhead's product is mostly a service (see Chapter 12), it focuses on some intangible features of its offering.

- **Professionals being professionals:** There is a place online for social networking, pet networking, and music networking. So why is there no outlet for career networking online—the activity that consumes the majority of our professional lives? PeopleAhead is a place where professionals share their experiences, achievements, and objectives with other professionals that care and can be found by employers who value their professionalism.

3.5. Customer Analysis

PeopleAhead's R&D efforts show that the impetus to improve recruitment effectivity is pervasive and that unmet needs revolve around a few core issues: the ability to find qualified talent, establishing a fit between the candidate and the company culture, verifying the candidate's career progression, and working quickly and cost effectively. The following customer characteristics represent ideal attributes that align with PeopleAhead's service offering. This information might be used in conjunction with the Marketing Strategy.

3.5.1. Business Customer

- **Industry:** Because companies that value human capital are more likely to take a chance on a start-up that promotes professional development, the broadly defined professional services industry, including insurance, banking, and consulting, is the primary focus.
- **Functional area:** PeopleAhead's system identifies "people" people, so positions that require human interaction are more aligned with system capabilities than those with stringent skill requirements, sets such as programming or accounting.
- **Size:** Large businesses (>1000 employees) have high volume requirements and demand vendors with proven track records; small businesses (<25 employees) hire fewer people and may not justify acquisition costs. PeopleAhead aligns best with medium-sized customers.
- **Hiring need:** PeopleAhead serves two types of searches very well: those with too many applicants and those with too few applicants. By drawing applicants that most systems overlook and delivering only the most qualified applicants, the system assures the right candidate is identified quickly.

3.5.2. Individual Member

- **Background:** People who value professional development and are familiar with computer networking technologies; most are likely college educated, motivated by career success, and aware of their professional competencies/deficiencies.
- **Situation:** Members should have a professional development plan to share with others who can help them achieve their objectives—likely people who are inquisitive about their professional future and not content with their current situation. The common industry terminology for this group of people is "poised candidates."
- **Outlook:** Proactive people who research, plan, self-educate, and talk about their career. Probably the clearest example of proactivity is a student who devotes time, effort, and financial resources toward career advancement.

The last—and some would say most important—piece of the analysis puzzle: customers.

Although the introduction to this appendix and the plan's organization suggest that analyses of competitors, products, and customers are separate, as this plan shows, a firm usually cannot address one without considering the other. Here, in the "customer" section, the plan notes what its competitors fail to do and therefore why it offers a more valuable service.

Understanding a target customer is not just about numbers. PeopleAhead tries to consider what customers think and feel when searching for jobs too.

4. Marketing Strategy

4.1. Market Segmentation

4.1.1. Business Customers

- **Small enterprises.** Businesses with 10–99 employees. Companies with fewer than 10 employees are categorized as "Very Small Enterprises" and will not be a primary target market.
- **Medium enterprises.** Businesses with 100–1,000 employees.

4.1.2. Individual Members

- **Senior college students.** Students in the process of searching for a first career.
- **Graduate program students.** Mid-career candidates searching for new career opportunities, such as internships, part-time during enrollment, or full-time after graduation.
- **Current employees.** Persons who are currently employed but are poised to locate better career opportunities.
- **Unemployed.** Persons searching for jobs not included in previous segments.

4.2. Target Market

PeopleAhead plans to focus resources on small to medium enterprises (SMEs) in the New England metro market, including Boston, Providence, Hartford, Stamford, Norwalk, Worcester, and Springfield. Online recruitment companies compete for national recruitment spending, but most job seekers are locally based, so market penetration is possible by covering a single geographical location. By maintaining this focus, PeopleAhead will be better equipped to build a critical mass of users that represent the job-seeking population and thus improve both users' and customers' experience, customer service, and the use of financial resources.

4.3. User Positioning

To the proactive professional, PeopleAhead is career advancement done right—providing a platform to discover, plan, and advance careers by uniting friends, coworkers, and mentors with companies searching for the right talent.

5. Marketing Mix

5.1. Products/Services Offered

The first planned offering is **group profiling;** users self-associate with groups to share development plans. Access to groupings is permission based and similar to social networking. Members will be able to share professional experiences with people they know. Group profiling may prompt "voyeur" networking, such that members join to view the profiles of the people they know.

PeopleAhead will then open **group profiling to business customers,** who will be granted access to groups of members to target people they want to hire.

The next added feature will be **user feedback** on professional development plans. PeopleAhead will track data from successful member profile matches to provide feedback for members who have not been matched successfully.

The plan continues with the same segmentation throughout. Here the plan discusses targeting and what makes each segment attractive.

By already identifying key markets in the previous section, the plan provides a foundation for a more specific targeting statement in this section.

The final step in the STP process: Positioning for the segmented, targeted market.

PeopleAhead's mission

Given its own section in this plan, a discussion of the marketing mix constitutes a key element of the strategic planning process (see Chapter 2).

According to well-known marketing concepts, the marketing mix consists of the four Ps: product (service here), price, place (distribution here), and promotion.

The product (service) offering must establish the value for consumers: Why should they expend effort or resources to obtain the offering?

5.2. Price

In addition to a basic pricing schedule, PeopleAhead will offer bulk pricing and contract pricing to business customers to satisfy unique customer needs. The pricing model is expected to remain constant, but customer feedback will be analyzed to ensure alignment with their requirements.

Continuing the new customer acquisition plan, PeopleAhead will encourage new trials by offering promotional pricing to new customers.

5.3. Distribution

- **PeopleAhead Challenge:** The PeopleAhead Challenge will act as a primary user acquisition strategy. Selection will be focused on successful target segments demanded by customers.

- **Direct sales:** Direct customer contact is the preferred method of communication during the first six months. Telesales is the anticipated eventual sales model, due to reduced costs and quicker customer sales cycle, but it limits intimacy between the customer and PeopleAhead. During the initial stages, intimacy and excellent customer service are more highly desired than reduced cost, and direct sales achieves that objective.

- **Industry events:** Attendance at HR industry and recruitment events will supplement direct sales efforts.

- **Challenge groups:** Word-of-mouth distribution by PeopleAhead members.

5.4. Promotion

- **Public profiling:** When the product is ready, with proper precautions for protecting competitive advantages, PeopleAhead can increase its Web presence. Strategies include contributing articles to recruitment publishers, writing op/ed pieces, public profiling of the founders on Web sites like LinkedIn, Ziggs, and zoominfo, and blogging.

- **Blogger community testimonials:** Influential users of blogs will be invited to try the system and be granted "exclusive" access to the inner workings of the site. A subsequent linking blitz will put opinion pieces in front of recruiters, job seekers, and the investment community.

- **Strategic alliances:** PeopleAhead offers a product that complements the services offered by many large organizations. Partner opportunities exist with

  a. Universities, colleges, academic institutions

  b. Professional associations, clubs, industry affiliation groups

  c. Online associations, groups, blogs

  d. Professional services firms, outplacement firms, and executive search firms

Strategic alliances serve multiple purposes: They can help PeopleAhead increase public exposure, increase the user base, expand product offerings, and increase revenue opportunities. These benefits will be considered and partnerships proposed prior to the official launch. For strategic purposes, PeopleAhead prefers to focus on product development in the near term (3 months) and then reassess potential alliances after system efficacy has been proven.

> Making the product (service) available where and when consumers want it may seem somewhat easier for PeopleAhead because of the vast development of the Internet; however, the firm still needs to consider how it can ensure people know where and how to access its offering.

> The plan offers a specific time frame, which recognizes the potential need to make changes in the future, as the market dictates.

delivers:

》Target marketing for hard-to-fill positions

》Qualified & pre-confirmed candidates

》Intelligent candidate ranking tools

》Results

6. Financials

Start-up costs consist primarily of Web site design and development, legal representation (business formation, contract negotiation, and intellectual property protection), and general overhead. PeopleAhead projects start-up expenditures of $70,000 during inception, of which $30,000 has been funded by the founding team.

    After the Web site launches, the cost structure will consist of sales agent salaries, general and administrative operating costs, and marketing. In the first year, marketing expenses are projected to be $6,250 per month. Monthly overhead likely will reach $24,750 and remain constant.

    A.   **Projected Income Statement**

Pro Forma Income Statement

	Year 1	Year 2	Year 3	Year 4	Year 5
Sales	**$56,453**	**$2,683,665**	**$8,170,655**	**$16,312,843**	**$30,921,013**
Gross Margin	$54,194	$2,316,318	$7,383,829	$14,780,329	$28,244,172
Gross Margin %	96.00%	86.31%	90.37%	90.61%	91.34%
Net Profit	**($156,906)**	**$717,403**	**$3,356,768**	**$7,035,155**	**$14,180,041**

The marketing plan needs to identify not only costs but also potential revenues to cover those costs.

Certain assumptions or marketing research form the basis for its estimation of start-up costs.

This section contains a lot of numbers in a small space; the graphs and tables help depict those numbers clearly and visually.

Revenue and net income projections

7. Implementation Plan

The launch of PeopleAhead will use a phased approach, beginning with building brand awareness. Brand awareness should be developed through the founders' visible presence at professional events, online searches, membership in professional associations, networking, and strategic alliances. This visibility will help gain investment capital.

7.1. Objective—Growth

- During the first six months of commercial availability, the primary objective is to expand both the user and customer base to maintain a 100:1 user to customer ratio.

  - **Business customers:** Sign 24 regular customers and 72 occasional customers. Execute 117 position matches.

  - **Individual members:** Convert 10,000 people to PeopleAhead members.

7.2. Marketing Objectives—Growth

- **PeopleAhead Challenge:** Pursue groups that were effective during beta trial and represent a cohesive set of profiles. Expand and refine the Challenge to reflect lessons learned.

- **Increase member networking activity:** Increase user numbers through networking initiated by existing members. Improve user experience to promote networking.

- **Increase profile completeness:** Increase user engagement with platform.

- **Generate traffic.**

- **Public relations campaign (PR):** Increase awareness of PeopleAhead brand through concentrated PR efforts directed at the target market of customers and users.

> This plan divides the objectives into three categories: overall objective, marketing, and financial. Although this is a marketing plan, it must also include other aspects that influence marketing, such as financial status.

7.3. Financial Objectives

- **Efficient marketing expenditures:** 9,000 target users (10,000 year-end total − 1,000 during beta) × $5.00 target acquisition cost = $45,000 budget.
- **Revenue:** $482.50 per position × 117 positions = $56,452.50 revenue.

> By offering quantitative, direct goals, PeopleAhead ensures that it can measure its progress toward those goals.

7.4. Key Success Factors:

- **Economical marketing to relevant constituents:** PeopleAhead needs to establish communication (distribution) channels that pinpoint relevant constituents in a manner consistent with mission values. Limited by resources, chosen channels must aggregate many relevant eyes with free, minimal, or deferred costs involved.

- **Crafting of brand identity:** The contrast between PeopleAhead and competitors lies not only in product differentiation but also in the company's mission statement and delivery. One-time job search is available from thousands of online recruitment sources. Social networking has been covered from diverse angles, attracting many different audiences. The challenge is to associate www.PeopleAhead.com and TrueMatch technology with "career advancement done right." The goal is to become the only company that a person thinks of for long-term career discovery, advancement, and development.

- **Efficient value delivery:** The base of customers (both individual and business) needs to receive the proposed value in a timely manner, with consideration given to quality versus quantity of results, alignment with existing objectives, and overall experience with the PeopleAhead brand.

- **Critical mass of business customers and individual users:** The matching process requires that both customers and users exist in the system from the outset of commercialization. This need brings to the forefront the "chicken and egg" scenario; establishing either customers or users requires the other constituent to exist already. The exact number that constitutes "critical mass" ranges from 100 users per position to 10 users per position, depending on compatibility between each constituency.

- **System effectivity:** The ability of PeopleAhead's TrueMatch software to provide relevant candidate recommendations is critical. The effectiveness of the software depends on the algorithms that match users with positions and the networking protocol that initiates recommendations between users and the people they know. Proposing an inappropriate match could jeopardize the credibility of the system.

- **Intellectual property (IP) strategy:** PeopleAhead is engaged in two primary segments of online enterprise: online recruitment and social networking. Existing competitors have made many efforts to protect their methodologies through U.S. patents. However, precedent has not been established for the legal assertions made by these companies. As a result, PeopleAhead will assume an offensive IP strategy, consisting of diligent IP infringement review, patent application where appropriate, and aggressive trade secret protection of best practices.

- **Financial support:** The founders' investment is sufficient to form the business core and take delivery of PeopleAhead's Web site and software. Financial support will be required to fund operations, execute the IP strategy, and secure customers and users to meet financial targets. Without funding, PeopleAhead will not be able to proceed beyond the product development stage.

- **Sales process:** PeopleAhead's business model requires the acquisition of both business customers who have available positions and users who will be matched with those positions. These two constituents may be reached through different sales processes without overlap.

8. Evaluation & Control

PeopleAhead will evaluate user profiles to identify sets of profiles that are valuable to new business customers, which will aid in the selection of subsequent target market customers.

8.1. Business Customers

> The evaluation section retains the segmentation scheme established previously between business customers and individual members.

Face-to-face meetings, phone conversations, and e-mail survey contacts with people from a range of industries, company sizes, and functional areas provide a means to (1) build relationships with prospective customers, (2) understand customer needs, and (3) ensure alignment between PeopleAhead's product and customers' recruitment preferences. A summary of the key findings is listed here:

- **Employee fit:** Will the applicant fit our corporate culture? Will the applicant fit with the team we're considering? Will the applicants' competencies fit with the position requirements?

- **Pay for performance:** Objections to recruitment services focus not on price (though it is a consideration) but rather on lack of performance.

- **Unqualified applicants:** Many people who want a job apply, whether they are qualified or not. Recruiters then must scan resumes and weed out unqualified applicants instead of getting to know the qualified applicants.

- **Hard costs vs. soft costs:** Most companies track the recruitment costs of hiring providers, but few measure the time costs of hiring, opportunity costs of hiring the wrong employee, or productivity costs of leaving a position unfilled. Recruitment performance must be easy to measure. Value selling is difficult in the human resources departments.

- **Valuable recommendations:** Most recruiters use online recruitment as a necessary but ineffective means of candidate sourcing, secondary to recommendations. Recommendations include the recommender's judgment of the candidate's fit with the available position.

8.2. Individual Members

Periodic surveys of various prospective users of online recruitment services indicate (1) current services, (2) methods that work well, and (3) biggest problems with online recruitment providers. The following is a qualitative summary of the key findings:

- **Willingness to try:** Careers are important to people; they are averse to spending time uploading resume information to online recruitment Web sites only because of the lack of perceived value. They will spend time when the career opportunities are perceived as valuable.

- **Frustration:** Job seekers are frustrated with available online recruitment providers. Networking is the favored method for career advancement.

- **Lack of differentiation:** Regardless of the qualifications a job seeker possesses, it is difficult to make them evident in a traditional resume.

- **Motivation shift over time:** Early professionals are motivated by financial rewards. Mid-career professionals recommend people because it helps the people they know. Late-career professionals hope to improve their own job search opportunities.

Appendix A. Organizational Chart of PeopleAhead

Appendix B. Competition: Passive Recruiters

> Additional useful information that might clutter the plan should appear in an appendix, but is not included in this illustration.

CHAPTER 3

SOCIAL AND MOBILE MARKETING

LEARNING OBJECTIVES

After reading this chapter, you should be able to:

LO3-1 Describe the 4E framework of social media marketing.

LO3-2 Understand the drivers of social media engagement.

LO3-3 Understand the types of social media.

LO3-4 Understand various motivations for using mobile applications and how they are priced.

LO3-5 Recognize and understand the three components of a social media strategy.

Social media have revolutionized how companies communicate with, listen to, and learn from customers. The influence is far-reaching, whether firms are selling online or in stores, providing services or products, or dealing primarily with consumers or business customers. Modern listening and analysis tools allow firms to identify salient, pertinent trends and customer input through social media.

For example, Under Armour's carefully designed social media plan enables it to connect effectively with customers, control buzz, and respond to trends as they arise. Largely through its stellar social media use, applied in combination and parallel to various other marketing tactics, Under Armour has overtaken adidas and moved in to second place in the sportswear market.[1]

Some elements of Under Armour's basic marketing strategy, such as leveraging the popularity and authenticity of famous athletic spokespersons, also constitute key aspects of its social media strategy.[2] Under Armour might

have half a million Twitter followers,[3] but the athletes it sponsors have far more; Stephan Curry, pictured above for example, has 3.4 million followers.[4] As part of the NBA phenom's partnership with Under Armour, in his Twitter profile and cover pictures, Curry sports Under Armour gear. In parallel, Under Armour's Twitter cover picture has featured Curry prominently.[5]

Curry's profile also includes Under Armour's current slogan, #IWILL.[6] The brand constantly seeks to develop and spread encouraging and inspiring taglines, including "I Will," in its marketing communication.[7] Its Facebook page contains little explicit advertising; instead, the brand posts inspirational quotes, videos, and graphics in an attempt to engage customers with its products and brand.[8] In contrast, Nike, the top brand in the market, uses its Facebook page primarily to promote its latest products.[9] On YouTube, Under Armour offers easy access to some of its most famous commercials, including the "I will what I want" and "Rule Yourself" campaigns. The channel also includes a series of interviews with top athletes. Such inspirational approaches in turn inform the multiple, specific social media accounts that Under Armour develops for various target markets. For example, different Twitter accounts highlight Under Armour's links to basketball, baseball, football, and running.

Inspiring storylines and exciting brand images are clearly important, but success on social media also demands the ability to respond actively and promptly to customers' comments. In this sense, Under Armour again achieves notable advantages, because it takes this aspect seriously. A designated Twitter handle @AskTeamUA connects customers directly with customer service representatives.[10] Customers expect responses from brands on Twitter, especially if they tweet a complaint.[11] Therefore, Under Armour's ability to respond to both negative and positive feedback, often within an hour, is fundamental to the success of its social media presence.

When consumers search for Under Armour on popular search engines, they usually see a page of company-sponsored results. The brand has done the preliminary work, through search engine optimization and brand building, to control most of the brand-related content people see online. Even if an uncontrolled story pops up (e.g., when Nike spokesperson LeBron James mockingly asked "Who's that?" in response to a reporter's question about Under Armour), the brand's own communications dominate the first page of results.[12] No company can prevent negative comments completely, but Under Armour has managed to ensure that most of them are hidden under a wave of positive, company-approved messages. Thus the @AskTeamUA service is available, but browsers must look a bit harder to find the criticisms.

LO3-1 Describe the 4E framework of social media marketing.

THE 4E FRAMEWORK FOR SOCIAL MEDIA

As we will see throughout the book and as we saw in the chapter opener, social media are becoming integral components of any integrated marketing communications strategy. The term social media refers to the online and mobile technologies that distribute content to facilitate interpersonal interactions. These media use various firms that offer services or tools to help consumers and firms build connections. Through these connections, marketers and customers share information of all forms—from their thoughts about products or images to uploaded pictures, music, and videos.

The changes and advances in social, mobile, and online technologies have created a perfect storm, forcing firms to change how they communicate with their customers. Traditional ways to market their products using brick-and-mortar stores, traditional mass media (e.g., print, television, radio), and other sales promotional vehicles (e.g., mail, telemarketing) are no longer sufficient for many firms. The presence of social, mobile, and online marketing is steadily expanding relative to these more traditional forms of integrated marketing communications (IMC).

The changing role of traditional media, sales promotions, and retail, coupled with the new social, mobile, and online media, has led to a different way of thinking about the objectives of marketing communications: the 4E framework (see Exhibit 3.1):

- **E**xcite customers with relevant offers.
- **E**ducate them about the offering.

EXHIBIT 3.1 The 4E Framework for Social Media

- Help them **e**xperience products, whether directly or indirectly.
- Give them an opportunity to **e**ngage with their social network.

Social and Mobile Marketing 3.1 recounts how Jimmy Fallon got viewers more excited and engaged with his late-night talk show by leveraging the power of social media.

Excite the Customer

Marketers use many kinds of social media–related offers to excite customers, including mobile applications ("apps") and games to get the customers excited about an idea, product, brand, or company. Firms actively use social networks such as Facebook, Pinterest, and Google+ to communicate deals that are likely to excite consumers, such as when the Minnesota Timberwolves encouraged Facebook fans to post a great shot of a dunk onto their Pinterest page for a chance to win tickets to a game.[13]

To excite customers, an offer must be relevant to its targeted customer. Relevancy can be achieved by providing personalized offers, which are determined through insights and information obtained from customer relationship management and/or loyalty programs. To obtain these insights and information, the firm might use online analytic tools such as Google Analytics.

The Minnesota Timberwolves excited Facebook fans by offering a chance to win tickets by posting pictures of a dunk to its Pinterest page.

© Genevieve Ross/AP Photo

Social & Mobile Marketing 3.1   Late-Night Laughs to Order[i]

Social media appear to have brought us full circle. In the early days of television, nearly all the advertisements were live. Then taping became the main method. But as recent technologies have made it easy for viewers to speed past or completely skip the advertising messages, some marketers are revisiting the idea of live advertising. This isn't the same old notion though. By recombining an idea from broadcast media with new functionalities enabled by social media, marketers seek to ensure that viewers are not only interested in the new content but even might determine it.

A Lexus-sponsored program, "It's Your Move After Dark," ran on *Late Night with Jimmy Fallon* over the course of four weeks. During the first commercial break on each Thursday's show, a Lexus advertisement prominently displayed a hashtag. By linking to it, viewers could submit their ideas for commercials. Then in a later advertising break during the same show, an improvisational comedy troupe acted out the chosen ideas. The acting troupes—Fun Young Guys, Magnet Theater Touring Company, MB's Dream, and Stone Cold Fox—were all from New York and well known for their comedy. In actuality, their performances took place under the Brooklyn Bridge, adding to the vibrancy and reality of the setting.

To appeal to the widest audience of Fallon fans possible, separate advertisements were chosen and enacted for the East and West Coast broadcasts. The submissions came through a wide variety of media channels, including Facebook, Twitter, and Tumblr. Such ready access, real-time interactivity, and potential influence—together with the promise of funny, totally new advertising content and perhaps even a live, on-air goof—promised that Fallon's youthful, edgy audience wanted to tune in to the commercials as much as they did to the show.

The advertisements are not the only way Fallon has relied on social media to connect with his audience of course. He has nearly 10 million Twitter followers, and on a regular basis he challenges them to post the funniest, silliest, or craziest responses to topics he provides, such as "#howigotfired," "#whydonttheymakethat," and "#awkwardate." The best contributions are highlighted on Fallon's Twitter feed but also might make it onto the network broadcast when he reads out his favorite bits. That is, the consumers of his content also provide some of that content.

On the flip side, content from the traditional television channel constantly makes it onto social media sites. Excerpts from Fallon's shows are some of the most popular YouTube

In an innovative campaign, Jimmy Fallon viewers could submit ideas for Lexus commercials via Twitter and see an improvised version later in the night on the show.

© Theo Wargo/Getty Images

videos, including a skit in which President Barack Obama "slow jams" the news, a sing-along with Carly Rae Jepson and the Roots of "Call Me Maybe" using found materials as instruments, and of course, any skits featuring his pal Justin Timberlake.

Fallon has continued these antics and tactics on the *The Tonight Show*. As long as he keeps his viewers excited and willing to contribute and engage with him, his social media dominance appears likely to persist, regardless of what time he appears on people's televisions.

In some cases location-based software and applications help bring the offer to the customers when they are in the process of making a purchase decision. For instance, Staples may provide a loyal customer a relevant coupon, based on previous purchases through his or her mobile phone, while the customer is in the store—a very relevant and hopefully exciting experience.

Educate the Customer

An imperative of well-designed social media marketing offers is that they have a clear call to action to draw customers through their computers, tablets, and mobile devices into online websites or traditional retail stores. When potential customers arrive at the websites or stores, the marketer has a golden opportunity to educate them about its value proposition and communicate the offered benefits. Some of this information may be new, but in some cases, education is all about reminding people about what they already know. Therefore, by engaging in appropriate education, marketers are expanding the overlap of the benefits that they provide with the benefits that customers require. In this sense, the second E of the 4E framework constitutes a method to develop a sustainable competitive advantage. Several social media tools are critical in helping marketers educate their potential customers, such as blogs and blogging tools (e.g., WordPress, Twitter), HubSpot (all-in-one marketing software), YouTube, and Google+, as well as some lesser known options such as Roost or Schedulicity. Adding Value 3.1 highlights how HubSpot can be used to educate customers better.

Experience the Product or Service

Although most of the top videos on YouTube are funny, silly, or otherwise entertaining, the site's most useful contributions may be the vivid information it provides about a firm's goods and services—how they work, how to use them, and where they can be obtained. YouTube and similar sites can come relatively close to simulating real, rather than virtual, experiences. Such benefits are very common for products that have long been sold online—so much so that we might forget that it used to be difficult to assess these products before buying them. But today, consumers can download a chapter of a new book to their tablet before buying it. They can try out a software option for a month before buying it. They often view tutorials on everything from how to purchase caviar to cowboy boots. Being able to experience a product or service before buying it has expanded the market significantly.

Staples excites its customers by giving them instant rewards through their mobile phone while they are in the store.

Courtesy of Staples, Inc.

Adding Value 3.1   Educating Customers Using HubSpot[ii]

HubSpot is driven by its motto: "Solve for the customer." This attitude has provided a foundation for the company's enormous success as it has become the largest provider of inbound marketing software and support. Consider one example of how it helps companies educate their own consumers.

Hy-Line Cruises is a ferry company with vessels for travel to and from Cape Cod and regional islands, deep-sea fishing trips, and sightseeing. Although it had a strong Internet presence through its website and on Facebook and Twitter, it didn't know if its efforts were leading to increased sales. Using HubSpot's SEO (search engine optimization) and blogging tools, Hy-Line began to match its blogging content to the keywords and phrases its potential customers were using. Not only did the new blogging content contain information about ferry services, but it also made recommendations about where to eat and what to do once on the Cape and islands. It also developed a free downloadable Insider's Guide for each destination, and it kept track of and—through e-mail—thanked each potential customer. Compared with the previous year, before it started using HubSpot's services, Hy-Line quickly generated 5 times more cruise offers to Nantucket and 17 times more Fall Daytrip Specials to Martha's Vineyard.

HubSpot thus has grown to more than 15,000 business customers, spanning more than 90 countries. The constant

Hy-Line Cruises uses HubSpot to enhance its social media presence.

© Oleg Albinsky/Getty Images RF

growth it has enjoyed since its founding encompasses both the number of customers and revenues, which grew by approximately two-thirds in a recent one-year span. Its prospects for continued success also appear excellent, as its stock keeps soaring and its business customers keep looking for help reaching their own target markets.

Sephora maintains its own You-Tube channel with dedicated videos that encourage customers to experience specific product lines, such as the "Kat Von D playlist."

© Steve Jennings/Getty Images

For other offerings, such as services, social media again offer experience-based information that was not previously available unless consumers bought and tried the product or service. Sephora has perfected the art of customer service in-store, online, and in social media. Customers know they can find beauty advice and makeovers in Sephora stores. But they can also visit Sephora.com for information. The advice section contains nearly 1 million conversations among Sephora customers, and to facilitate these conversational experiences, Sephora suggests a featured topic each week, asking contributors to indicate their favorite eyebrow products, for example. The how-to section contains video tutorials by customers who offer testimonials about their experiences, as well as from beauty professionals who describe how viewers can achieve similar experiences with their hair, nail, makeup, and skincare beauty tools.[14] For customers seeking an experience in other settings, Sephora also maintains its own YouTube channel featuring not only all the tutorial videos but also dedicated videos that encourage them to experience specific product lines, such as the "Kat Von D playlist."[15]

Engage the Customer

In a sense, the first three Es set the stage for the last one: engaging the customer. With engagement comes action, the potential for a relationship, and possibly even loyalty and commitment. Through social media tools such as blogging and microblogging, customers actively engage with firms and their own social networks. Such engagement can be negative or positive. Positively engaged consumers tend to be more profitable consumers, purchasing 20 to 40 percent more than less engaged customers do.[16]

But negative engagement has the potential to be even more damaging than positive engagement is beneficial. American Apparel has come under fire on several occasions for its social media posts. In the aftermath of Hurricane Sandy, in 2012, it sent out an e-mail blast to customers on the East Coast, promising 20 percent off all online purchases, "in case you're bored during the storm." The company again faced backlash when it posted what it thought to be an artistic image of a firework on Tumblr for the Fourth of July—but the image turned out to be of the tragic explosion of the Challenger space shuttle.[17] Many companies also seek to leverage the viral appeal of hashtag campaigns, sometimes without thinking through the potential consequences. When McDonald's launched a Twitter campaign to highlight its supply chain, using the hashtag #McDstories, the vagueness of the hashtag allowed consumers to move the conversation in a very different direction, sharing horror stories about their negative experiences eating at the fast food chain.[18]

Furthermore, social media engagement is moving past talking with companies, as the Wheel of Social Media Engagement in the next section reveals. After years of watching users express their deep desire to purchase the products highlighted on their sites, the social media powerhouses Pinterest and Instagram are adopting new initiatives to facilitate purchase transactions. Specifically, they both plan to install "buy buttons" that will enable users to click on a featured post or picture to initiate a sales process. On Instagram, the button is similar in function to the Facebook buy button. Advertisers on the site can include buy buttons in their ads, and when users click, the button links them to an external website where they can complete their purchase. The process is a little different on Pinterest. The presence of "buyable" pins signals to users that they may click on the link to receive detailed information about available colors, sizes, and other information. If they choose to purchase, the order goes directly to the merchant without ever taking the user off the Pinterest site. In a recent survey, 93 percent of Pinterest users—or pinners—noted that they would like to use the site to make their purchases. However, these links are unpaid thus far, so Pinterest will not earn any revenues on the transaction. Both Instagram and Facebook instead can leverage advertising dollars to support their buying capabilities.[19]

Buy it
Buy it in just a few taps, right on Pinterest

Pay with Apple Pay™ or credit card

To engage its customers, Pinterest uses "buyable" pins, which signal users that they may click on the link to receive detailed information about products.

Source: Pinterest

PROGRESS CHECK

1. What are the 4Es?
2. What social media elements work best for each of the 4Es?

LO3-2 Understand the drivers of social media engagement.

THE WHEEL OF SOCIAL MEDIA ENGAGEMENT[20]

Marketers recognize the importance of engaging customers; social media engagement offers a profitable way to engage customers by taking their current behavior into account while also setting the stage for future behavior. Firms work hard to engage customers, and social media provide them with unique abilities to target and participate in dynamic conversations with individual customers, leading to excellent returns on their investments in social media efforts. The growth of social media and their effects in turn stems from several related factors.

A unifying framework, the Wheel of Social Media Engagement, comprises these fundamental drivers of social media engagement as five related effects, as Exhibit 3.2 shows. In the Wheel of Social Media Engagement, we propose that the hub is a repository of past and current social media engagements, and the circles around the wheel are the five effects that drive social media, as detailed next.

The Information Effect

The information effect is the outcome of social media in which relevant information is spread by firms or individuals to other members of its social network. Information–whether because it is funny, cute, instructive, surprising, or interesting—is the key to turning the wheel. But the relevance of the information, and therefore its impact, depends on its context and the receiver. Marketers work hard to provide information that is somehow contextually relevant, such as interjecting a humorous advertisement into a social network of users who like to joke around and share funny pictures.

As we think further about the information effect and the incredible magnitude of information being conveyed through reviews, Facebook posts, tweets, and so on, it raises the

---

EXHIBIT 3.2   The Wheel of Social Media Engagement

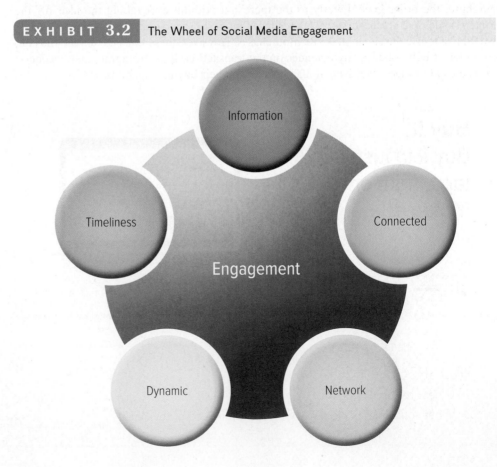

question: What can and should marketers do with all of it? The amount of information available can be overwhelming, even for the best marketers. Even when they know a lot about potential customers, marketers continue to find it challenging to create appeals that consumers embrace and to leverage the information they obtain from consumers in ways that encourage shoppers to purchase from them.

For example, BMW gained in-depth information about visitors to a popular Chinese social media site. Using those data, which included income and prior purchase behaviors, it determined which visitors were likely to be luxury car buyers and targeted advertising at them. That sounds great, except that other visitors, who were not targeted, protested vehemently. By not showing them luxury car ads, they asserted, the car brand and the social media site combined to make them feel like "losers."[21]

BMW gains information about visitors to a Chinese social media site to target advertising to them.
Source: BMW Group China

The Connected Effect

The **connected effect** is an outcome of social media that satisfies humans' innate need to connect with other people. This connection in social media is bidirectional: People learn what their friends are interested in, but they also broadcast their own interests and opinions to those friends. Humans seek connections to other people, and social media have provided them with a new, easy, and engaging way to do so. In particular,

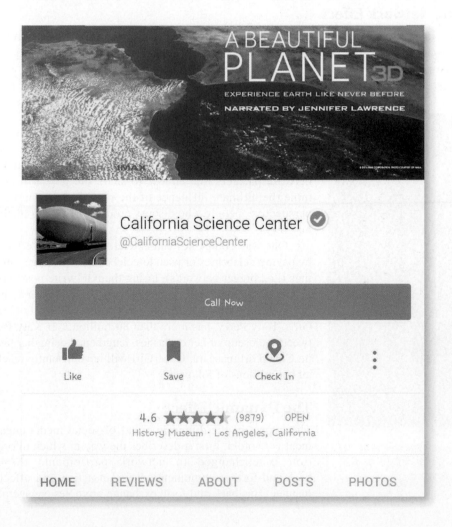

People connect through social media by "liking" or "checking in" on Facebook.
© Tashauna Johnson Photography/ Photoedit

people can connect by sharing different types of information, whether their location, the food they have consumed, exercises they have completed, or a news article that they find interesting. And they achieve this connection by checking in, posting a picture to Instagram, uploading a video to YouTube, or sharing a link to an article they have liked on Facebook.

The need to connect with others has been a powerful evolutionary force throughout human history, driving communities as well as civilizations, including our modern technology civilization. Today, humans are less physically connected, because they shop online and have products delivered instead of interacting with the local shopkeeper, and they telecommute instead of working in an office with colleagues. But social media empower them to connect in novel ways. Some connections involve existing friends and colleagues; others refer to acquaintances who might not have been connected in an offline world or with firms, brands, or news outlets that were not available before social media created the link.

This increased connection allows consumers to seek social approval for themselves and provide social approval to others. For example, consumers click to express their liking of various posts by members of their social networks. However, the increased forms of connections created by this effect also might threaten to annoy users who start looking at their smartphones every time they ding. Markets for filters could emerge to help consumers categorize posts and updates in ways that reflect their own preferences. Furthermore, whereas different platforms currently serve distinct purposes (e.g., Facebook for personal and LinkedIn for business), these social media outlets might seek to grow by encouraging users to visit their platform exclusively, then sort the various purposes from that point.

The Network Effect

The connected effect enhances human interaction on a one-to-one basis. But the network effect enables the impact of the interaction to expand exponentially. The **network effect** is the outcome of social media engagement in which every time a firm or person posts information, it is transferred to the poster's vast connections across social media, causing the information to spread instantaneously. That is, when a person or company posts something on social media, other people or firms in their network might repost it, as when one "shares" on Facebook. The credibility and influence of the original poster and the network partners that choose to share the post will determine the ultimate influence of the post. From a marketing perspective, people who discuss products are more likely to buy them.[22]

One way companies can extend their network effects is by paying celebrities or pseudo-celebrities with large followings (i.e., bigger networks), hiring them to write posts about or upload pictures with their products. CoverGirl may have fewer than 2,000 Twitter followers,[23] but one of its Cover-Girls, Katy Perry, has more than 80 million.[24] If Katy Perry tweets a closeup of her eyelashes, lengthened using her favorite CoverGirl mascara, CoverGirl will have instantly reached all her millions of followers.

If Katy Perry tweets a closeup of her eyelashes, lengthened using her favorite CoverGirl mascara, CoverGirl will have instantly reached all her millions of followers.
© Photoshot

The Dynamic Effect

The impact of the **dynamic effect** of social media engagement is twofold. First it describes the way in which information is exchanged to network participants through back-and-forth communications in an active and effective manner. This back-and-forth exchange promotes engagement, which makes consumers more likely to buy. The dynamic nature of social media is a very efficient way to get information or to resolve disputes, and can provide the firm with insights into how to best provide a product or service in the future. Customers can communicate their level of satisfaction with an issue and suggest further actions to be taken. For instance, at the Sol Wave House hotel on the beautiful island of Majorca, Spain, a Twitter concierge stays in constant contact with its guests. If a guest has a problem or a question, the answer is just a hashtag away.[25]

Second, the dynamic effect expands the impact of the network effect by examining how people flow in and out of networked communities as their interests change.[26] Consider a social network community that is concerned with everything chocolate. As it evolves and matures, its members develop varied interests—some want to know where to buy the best chocolates, while others are concerned about its health benefits. New people join the community, while others leave; and people's interests change, causing them to seek out new and different information. Since the community is dynamic, chocolate social media sites can specialize to meet the needs of its varied constituents. From a marketing perspective, this dynamic effect is very powerful. Marketers can provide very specific information, which should be well received by the interested parties.

Need information from the concierge on best place to dine? At the Sol Wave House it's only a tweet away.

© Ignacio Izquierdo/Rex Features/AP Photo

The Timeliness Effect

The **timeliness effect** of social media engagement is concerned with the firm being able to engage with the customer at the right place and time—that is, 24/7 from any location. To be effective, firms must, in fact, respond quickly, or the timeliness effect benefit diminishes. Responding in a timely manner can positively impact customers' buying intentions: 24 percent of Twitter users who fail to get a quick response say they would not buy as much from the company in the future, and 35 percent of them who receive fast responses note that they would buy more.[27] Further, 70 percent of Twitter users expect a response from companies—53 percent of them within an hour! Among customers who tweet a complaint, the number who expect responses within an hour jumps to 72 percent. Responding quickly

Coca-Cola engages customers in a timely manner by offering moviegoers a free Coke at the moment they walk through a movie theater.

© SeongJoon Cho/Bloomberg/ Getty Images

can pay off far better than a slow response in that nearly 50 percent of consumers recommend brands that respond quickly.[28]

Many customers enjoy the timely interactions with firms when they engage with them at the point of purchase. To reach customers at the right time, Coca-Cola relies on beacon technology—that is, technology that allows companies to detect where customers (who have enabled the feature) are at each moment, through their smartphones.[29] In 2015, Coca-Cola's pilot campaign offered moviegoers a free Coke at the moment they walked through the movie house if they had already downloaded the appropriate app from the brand.[30]

As the Wheel of Social Media Engagement shows, intimate connections can arise between a firm and customers. Firms increasingly are not only investing time and money in creating engagement, but also in capturing engagement data. Social media posts contain rich information that a well-equipped company can mine to understand its customers better. As a consequence, firms are striving to make profitable customers even more profitable through increased engagement. The power of the Internet, mobility, computing, and analytics that harness the power of social connections all have led to a leapfrog advance in the potential to create meaningful engagement with customers. According to the Wheel of Social Media Engagement, understanding how to engage effectively with consumers thus is important for marketing managers.

PROGRESS CHECK

1. What are the five drivers of social media engagement described in the Wheel of Social Media Engagement?

LO3-3 Understand the types of social media.

CATEGORIES OF SOCIAL MEDIA

Consider your own Facebook site. Are all your real-life friends your online friends too? Do you actually know all the friends registered on your online site? In all likelihood, you host online friends you've never met, and your circle of virtual friends may be larger than the number of people you see regularly or talk to personally. Accordingly, the audience for marketers could be bigger on social media sites than through other, more traditional forms of media. Such a huge potential audience has gotten the attention of marketers.

Marketers rely on the three types of social media: social networking sites, media-sharing sites, and thought-sharing sites (or blogs) (see Exhibit 3.3) to achieve three objectives. First, members promote themselves to gain more friends. Second, the sites promote to get more members. Third, outside companies promote their products and services to appeal to the potential consumers who are active on the sites.

EXHIBIT 3.3 Types of Social Media

Social Network Sites

Social network sites are an excellent way for marketers to create *excitement,* the first of the 4Es. People can interact with friends (e.g., Facebook) or business acquaintances (e.g., LinkedIn). Although the amount of time people spend on such sites varies, research indicates they are widely used—between one and four hours every day.[31]

Facebook On this well-known social network platform, more than 1.5 billion monthly active users give companies a forum for interacting with their fans.[32] Thus Facebook not only ensures individual users a way to

Forever 21 excites its customers on Facebook.
© Weng lei/Imaginechina/AP Photo

connect with others, but it also gives marketers the ability to target their audience carefully. Companies have access to the same features that regular users do, including a "wall" where they can post company updates, photos, and videos or participate in a discussion board. Only the fans of its page generally have access to such information, so the company can specifically target its fans.

Successful companies on Facebook attempt to excite their customers regularly. On the fan page for the discount clothing retailer Forever 21, for example,[33] when a fan clicks to indicate that he or she "likes" a certain post, the message gets relayed to a news feed. Then every friend of that user sees what he or she likes, creating an exciting and huge multiplier effect.

Display advertising with "Facebook ads" instead targets specific groups of people according to their profile information, browsing histories, and other preferences. If online users reveal an interest in ski equipment or Burton snowboards, marketers can target both groups. Facebook offers a variation on more traditional forms of promotion, with the promise of more accurate targeting and segmentation.

LinkedIn A professional instead of casual or friendship-based site, LinkedIn allows users to share their professional lives. With approximately 400 million users, it is a place where users can post their résumés, network with other professionals, and search for jobs.[34] Users post to question-and-answer forums, job search, and post personal intellectual property such as presentations they have given.

The professional networking benefits of LinkedIn are particularly valuable for small-business owners.

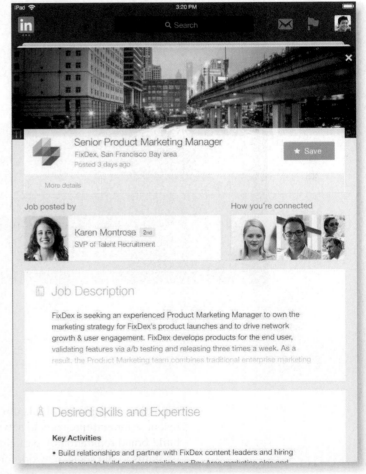

LinkedIn is an excellent place to begin your search for a marketing job.
Source: LinkedIn

Adding Value 3.2   Mercedes-Benz Is LinkedIn[iii]

With all of the social networking sites available now, it can be difficult for marketers to decide which one to use to connect with its target demographic. Facebook undoubtedly has the most users of all social networking sites, so it might seem like the smartest choice when launching a social media campaign. However, if looking to target a specific audience, the number of users on Facebook might in and of itself be a reason not to turn to the social networking giant as a platform for a marketing campaign.

For example, when the luxury auto brand Mercedes-Benz needed to target affluent potential customers with the launch of its new E- and C-class models, it turned to LinkedIn. Although LinkedIn has a smaller network, its users spend more online—more than 2.5 times as much as an average U.S. consumer—which likely signals their relative affluence.

Mercedes's LinkedIn ad campaign used sponsored updates and display ads with product videos. With the sponsored updates, Mercedes could reach more customers and gain real-time insights, according to sophisticated analytics, to improve its future content. Furthermore, the company was able to target professionals and senior executives and drive them to the company's website.

The high level of engagement that customers exhibited with this campaign in turn inspired Mercedes to employ LinkedIn's platform for a giveaway contest, in which the top prize was a new C-class car. The "Driven to Perform" contest was unique; users nominated others in their LinkedIn network, based on their professional achievements and how they embodied the sophistication of the Mercedes brand. In this sense, it represented a perfect fit with LinkedIn, which already provides a function that enables users to recommend or praise colleagues for their professional skills. The contest thus did not require LinkedIn users to change their behaviors; it simply leveraged those behaviors to target the ideal customers for Mercedes-Benz.

To inspire a high level of involvement, Mercedes employed LinkedIn's platform to give away a new C-class car.

© Harold Cunningham/Getty Images

More than 12 million of LinkedIn's users are small-business owners, making it an excellent resource for entrepreneurs to network with like-minded firms, identify the best vendors, or build brand reputation by participating in LinkedIn's professional association groups. But its status as the social network for professionals also makes it attractive to marketers seeking to access such consumers, as Adding Value 3.2 explains.

Google+ With Google+, the company that essentially defined search engines sought to compete in the social media realm. Although it has attracted hundreds of millions of users, most analysts suggest it is not an effective competitor thus far. Even when users register, they do not engage closely with the site; Google+ accounted for a small percent of all social media shares.[35]

Yet it would be risky to ignore Google+ completely. It offers several functions that other social networking sites do not. For example, its "Communities" feature lets people interested in similar topics form their own groups. Unlike Facebook, Google+'s Communities allow brands to join as members—for example, a paddle brand or seller of suntan lotion could easily interact with the members of a group devoted to paddleboarding. Moreover, with Google+'s unique "Hangouts" feature, brands can host discussions or focus groups and also post live product demonstrations.[36]

Media-Sharing Sites

The World Wide Web has the ability to connect people more easily and in more ways than have ever been possible before. Media-sharing sites explicitly rely on this capability to enable users to share content they have generated, from videos on YouTube to pictures on Flickr and so on. In terms of the 4E framework, companies use such sites to highlight how consumers can *experience* their goods or services as well as encourage consumers to *engage* with the firm, its other social media outlets, and other consumers.

YouTube On this video-sharing social media platform with more than 1 billion unique monthly visitors, companies gain a chance to express themselves in different ways than they have in the past. Because YouTube is owned by Google, its videos show up prominently in Google searches, making it an appealing vehicle for retailers.[37] The site's demographics indicate visitors are affluent, of the age range most appealing to retailers, and racially reflective of the wider U.S. population.[38]

Companies can broadcast from their own channels—that is, a YouTube site that contains content relevant only to the company's own products.[39] For example, Home Shopping Network (HSN) offers consumers an interesting vehicle to utilize the 4E framework. As competition in this field has increased, HSN has added to its communication arsenal an integrated social media component that includes Facebook, Instagram, Twitter, and Pinterest. But perhaps the most powerful tool it has added is its dedicated YouTube channel. Products promoted on HSN are available on YouTube almost immediately after they appear on television. Then HSN marketers can use the information gathered from YouTube to target its direct mail campaigns. For example, it could send jewelry promotions to households that viewed the YouTube video clip for a necklace. Consumer responses get monitored 24/7 and measured against hourly sales goals. Thus there's never a dull moment.

Products promoted on Home Shopping Network (HSN) are available on its dedicated YouTube channel almost immediately after they appear on television.

Courtesy of HSN, Inc.

Innocent uses Flickr to post photos for its Big Knit charity promotion.

© John Boud/Alamy

Instagram With Instagram, people who have downloaded the app (more than 400 million and counting) can take a photo of themselves or their surroundings.[40] Then they can upload the photo to various social networking sites, including Twitter, Tumblr, or Facebook.

The name of this app evokes the founders' idea of its use: a sort of modern-day, immediate telegram.[41] It has attracted the attention of some of the most famous names in media sharing, including Kim Kardashian, Adele, and The Rock—which has increased its popularity even more. When Dr. Dre launched his Beats brand, the Beats by Dre Instagram page was instrumental in building brand awareness, attracting approximately 2.5 million followers.[42] The brand posts pictures and videos of celebrities using the products, as well as information about current events.[43] When Eminem released his album SHADYXV, he teamed up with Beats by Dre to promote it with a video in which the rapper told the back story to his hit single "Lose Yourself." The video, which was released on the Beats Instagram page, garnered massive publicity for both parties.[44]

Flickr and Other Photo Sites Whereas YouTube allows users to share videos, Imgur, Flickr, Photobucket, Picasa, and TwitPic allow them to share photos.[45] They tend to be less popular as marketing tools, yet some innovative companies have found ways to engage with customers, such as by hosting picture-posting competitions or using photos to communicate core tenets and values.[46]

The U.K. brand Innocent, known for selling pure, 100 percent fruit smoothies, uses Flickr to communicate its quirky brand image. Its photo-posting competitions, such as the Funny Shaped Fruit Competition (http://www.flickr.com/groups/funnyshapedfruit/), provide significant entertainment value. But it also uses Flickr for more serious purposes, such as to post photos related to its Big Knit charity promotion.

Thought-Sharing Sites

Thought-sharing sites consist of different types of blogs: corporate, professional, personal, and micro. In terms of the 4E framework, blogs are particularly effective at *educating* and *engaging* users, and in many cases enhance their *experience* with the products and services being discussed.

Blogs Originally confined to a journal or diary in a person's room, the blog (from "weblog") on the Internet has allowed us to make our thoughts open to the world through thought-sharing websites. For corporations, the comment section allows marketing managers to create a two-way dialogue directly with the end users. Blogs provide firms the opportunity to *educate* their customers about their offers and offerings by explaining their offerings, and to *engage* them by responding to their communications, both positive and negative. The reach that marketers have to their customer from blogs can be categorized by the level of control they offer.

Corporate blogs, which are created by the companies themselves, have the highest level of control because, to a large degree, they can control the content posted on them. Of course, blogs also allow customers to respond to posts, so the content can never be completely controlled, but marketing managers have a good opportunity to pepper their blogs with the messages they wish their customers to see. The best corporate blogs illustrate the importance of engaging customers around the core brand tenets without being overly concerned with a hard sell.

As a trendy provider of clothing, accessories, and home décor, Anthropologie uses its blog to educate customers on the latest trends. Rather than sticking just to fashion in its online content though, some of Anthropologie's most successful blog posts have been for do-it-yourself recipes for signature cocktails. The posts are successful because they keep with the unique and eclectic feel of the brand overall, without being too obvious in their marketing or sales-related intentions.[47]

Lana Del Ray's Tumblr page might seem like a personal blog, as we define later in this section, but it actually represents a corporate blog, because its goal is primarily to help launch the musician's latest releases. Although some of the images are seemingly

Lana Del Ray's Tumblr page seems like a personal blog but is actually a corporate blog because it helps launch the musician's latest releases.
Source: Tumblr

personal photographs, the page highlights images that will get fans excited about and engaged with the products that Del Ray sells. She controls the content, and she can respond to the thousands of comments her posts spark. For example, to promote the single "West Coast," Del Ray created excitement by taking a few screen captures from the yet-to-be-released video and providing them exclusively to fans, on a platform already popular with these consumers.[48]

From a marketing perspective, **professional blogs** are those written by people who review and give recommendations on products and services. Marketers often offer free products or provide modest remuneration to top-rated professional bloggers in the hopes of getting a good product review. Marketers have less control over professional bloggers than they do their own corporate blogs. But consumers seem to trust professional bloggers' reviews much more than corporate blogs and other more traditional media, like advertising.

Such trust may be fleeting, however, as more consumers realize that professional bloggers are often compensated for positive reviews. That is, by using social media influencers such as bloggers, marketers can achieve significant rewards. But such tactics require some ethical considerations, especially as companies come under fire for paying professional bloggers to use and review products without disclosing the monetary benefits they have provided to them. Ethical & Societal Dilemma 3.1 explains how Disney has sought to address these concerns in relation to its Social Media Moms.

Finally, **personal blogs** are written by people who receive no products or remuneration for their efforts. Thus, of the three types of blogs, marketers have the lowest level of control over this type. However, personal blogs are useful for monitoring what is going on in the marketplace and for responding to customer complaints or compliments.

Microblogs As the name implies, a **microblog** differs from a traditional blog in size—a microblog uses short sentences, short videos, or individual images. The most popular microblogging site, Twitter, provides another option for companies to *educate* their customers by providing corporate and product information, and to *engage* them by providing a platform for two-way communications.

To drive awareness about serious problems in the developing world, the nonprofit organization Water is Life launched a "Hashtag Killer" campaign. It created a YouTube video in which people in Haiti, still struggling to obtain basic housing and security needs in the aftermath of a devastating earthquake, read tweets that had been tagged as

Ethical & Societal Dilemma 3.1   The Most Powerful and Appealing Target Market Might Be . . . Your Mom?[iv]

There are a lot of moms out there. And in a breathtakingly clever way, Disney has figured out a way to leverage the interest that many of those moms express in Mickey Mouse—and all that goes with him—to expand its market, increase its sales, enhance its name recognition, and increase its online and social media presence.

The Disney Social Media Moms is a group of approximately 1,300 parents who receive perks (but not pay) from the entertainment conglomerate. In turn, the company encourages (but does not require) them to blog, post, and comment about all things Disney. Popular topics include reviews of cruises, tips for moving easily through the theme parks, and Pinterest boards with ideas for themed birthday parties.

The criteria for being chosen as a Disney Social Media Mom are not made public, and competition to be picked is fierce. According to some analyses of the existing group and its members, the preferred moms are very active on social media and do not limit their online conversations to topics surrounding Disney. Rather, these bloggers, authors, and Internet personalities write about parenting, of course, as well as cooking, crafting, and travel. They also attract substantial followings;

an average among recently invited Social Media Moms was 27,000 followers on Twitter.

As a Social Media Mom, a consumer might receive an invitation to a special event at Disney World, featuring motivational sessions, updates on new Disney plans, and talks by Disney film producers. They also get substantial discounts in the parks and other retail settings and passes that allow them to skip many of the lines for rides and other attractions. However, even after receiving an invitation, attendees still must pay entrance fees to get into the park and cover all travel expenses for themselves and any family members who join them.

Still, the 200 or so moms who attended a recent event shared overwhelmingly positive assessments of their experience, including 88 blog posts, nearly 5,000 pictures uploaded to Instagram, and 28,500 tweets on Twitter. Marketing like this, by regular consumers who share their own experiences and thus strongly influence purchases by their peers, is unmatchable by traditional marketing efforts. But is it ethical to offer special treatment to people who claim simply to be reporting on their experiences?

"#firstworldproblems." In one, a child sitting on a mound of dirt reads, "I hate when my leather seats aren't heated." Many Haitians engaged with the campaign, offering consolation with tweets such as, "I'm sorry your leather seats weren't heated . . . I hope your day gets better!" In turn, the campaign invoked the engagement of citizens of wealthier nations, leading to its remarkable success, such that people donated enough to ensure more than 1 million days of clean water for people in less developed locations.[49]

Water is Life's "Hashtag Killer" campaign posted videos on YouTube of Haitians reading and responding to tweets to excite individuals to donate to their cause.

Courtesy of WATERisLIFE

GOING MOBILE AND SOCIAL

LO3-4 Understand various motivations for using mobile applications and how they are priced.

Of the more than 184 million people who have smartphones in the United States,[50] approximately 60 percent of them make purchases on these devices.[51] About 180 billion apps were downloaded globally in 2015.[52] In the United States alone, almost $10 billion of mobile downloads and in-app revenues were accrued in 2015, even though nearly 93 percent of apps downloaded are free.[53] Mobile app downloads are expected to grow to 286 billion annually by 2017.[54] Thus, mobile marketing is significant and growing.

As Exhibit 3.4 illustrates, there are seven primary needs that apps meet: the need to find "me time," socialize, shop, accomplish, prepare, discover, and self-express.

- The most popular need is all about entertainment and relaxation—that is, *"me time."* People spend nearly half their time on their smartphones seeking fun, whether by playing *Candy Crush Saga* or watching *American Horror Story* through their Netflix app.

- Because apps enable people to stay connected with friends both near and far, specialized entrants are growing to meet people's need to *socialize.* For example, in China, the social networking app Weixin (pronounced way-SHEEN) allows users to send videos, photos, messages, web links, status updates, and news; it has been released as WeChat

With more than 500 million downloads, Candy Crush Saga *clearly fulfills for many people an important need for unproductive "me time."*

© Gabriel Bouys/AFP/Getty Images

EXHIBIT 3.4 Seven Primary Motivations for Mobile App Usage

Source: "Vision Statement: How People Really Use Mobile," *Harvard Business Review,* January/February 2013, http://www.hbr.org.

Growing faster than Twitter and Facebook, Weixin has 300 million users, mainly in China, and allows people to send videos, photos, messages, web links, status updates, and news to friends.

© Keepin sh/Imaginechina/AP Photo

in the United States. Weixin has had a faster adoption rate than either Facebook or Twitter have, with more than 300 million users in only three years.[55]

- Shoppers want to *shop* anytime they choose. In a process called showrooming, a customer visits a store to touch, feel, and even discuss a product's features with a sales associate, and then instantly compares the prices online to see whether a better deal is available. Using the showrooming Amazon app, if the Amazon price is better, the customer can buy the product online with a single click.

- On the flip side of the need for fun, the need to *accomplish* means that people seek to manage their finances, improve their health, or become more productive through apps.[56] MyFitnessPal allows users to track their daily exercise, calories, and weight loss, and its social component enables people to post their successes. This app also can interact with Fitbit, Jawbone UP, and iHealth Wireless Scales.

- Calendars, flight trackers, and trip planning apps help consumers meet their need to *prepare*.[57] For example, Business Calendar helps people plan their days with an interactive app that integrates multiple calendars (e.g., Google Calendar, Outlook Calendar) and allows users to link an event to people in their contacts list and put a daily agenda widget on their smartphone home screen.

- When people seek information, due to their need to *discover*, they now turn to weather and news apps. Flipboard produces a full-screen magazine, aggregating multiple news and entertainment sources to provide top stories, entertainment, local news, and business news. Its social component also allows readers to send selected stories to friends.

- Finally, people have diverse interests and tastes and thus a need for apps that allow them to *express themselves*. Tapatalk aggregates tens of thousands of interest groups into a single app, making it easy to connect aficionados of just about any interest or hobby.

As you can see from this discussion, apps can meet several needs at once. Sharing an interesting story with friends via Flipboard can meet the needs of discovery and socialization. Consider the person who purchases Chinese food via GrubHub's app on her ride home; she's not only shopping, but she's also avoiding making dinner to get some extra me time. With this information in mind, apps (and advertising within those apps) can be designed and targeted in ways that better apply the 4Es.

Not only does Flipboard aggregate all of the news important to you in one place, its unique format also gives the app the look and feel of a printed magazine.

© Alliance Images/Alamy

App Pricing Models

A key decision for firms producing apps is what to charge for them. There are four basic ways of generating revenue from apps—ad-supported apps, freemium apps, paid apps, and paid apps with in-app purchases.

Ad-supported apps are free to download, but appear as ads on the screen. They generate revenues while users interact with the app. Although there are many of these types of apps, the majority of app revenue is generated from the remaining three pricing models, discussed next.

Freemium apps are apps that are free to download but include in-app purchases that enables the user to enhance an app or game. In *Candy Crush Saga*, you get five lives to play in the game. When you lose a life, it takes 30 minutes in real-life time to get that life back. This is where in-app purchases come in. For just $0.99, you can get all five lives back immediately so you can keep playing.[58] *Candy Crush Saga* is estimated to earn the developer between $623,000 and $850,000 *a day* in revenue from in-app purchases.[59]

EXHIBIT 3.5   Apple App Store Revenue by App Category Pricing Models

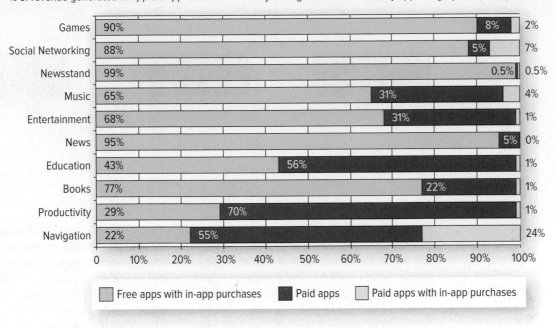

% of revenue generated in Apple's App Store from January through November 2013, by app category and pricing model

	Free apps with in-app purchases	Paid apps	Paid apps with in-app purchases
Games	90%	8%	2%
Social Networking	88%	5%	7%
Newsstand	99%	0.5%	0.5%
Music	65%	31%	4%
Entertainment	68%	31%	1%
News	95%	5%	0%
Education	43%	56%	1%
Books	77%	22%	1%
Productivity	29%	70%	1%
Navigation	22%	55%	24%

Source: Adapted from Christel Schoger, "2013 Year in Review," *Distimo Report,* December 2013, http://www.distimo.com.

Paid apps charge the customer an upfront price to download the app ($0.99 is the most common), but offer full functionality once downloaded. Similar to the freemium model, **paid apps with in-app purchases** require the consumer to pay initially to download the app and then offer the ability to buy additional functionality.

Which is the best pricing model? Time will tell, but it appears that freemium apps may be the winner. As Exhibit 3.5 shows, free apps with in-app purchases make up the vast majority of revenue from Apple's App Store in 8 of 10 app categories. According to Distimo, a research firm specializing in the mobile app market, 71 percent of apps in Apple's App Store implement a freemium pricing model, and 92 percent of revenues from Apple's App Store and 98 percent from Google's Play App Store come from freemium pricing.[60]

PROGRESS CHECK

1. What are the seven types of customer motivations for using mobile apps?
2. What are the four options for pricing mobile apps?
3. What are some of the most popular types of mobile applications?

HOW DO FIRMS ENGAGE THEIR CUSTOMERS USING SOCIAL MEDIA?

LO3-5   Recognize and understand the three components of a social media strategy.

Now that we have an understanding of the various social and mobile media that are at the firm's disposal, it is important to determine how firms should go about engaging customers through social and mobile media. The three-stage process found in Exhibit 3.6 involves *listening* to what customers have to say, *analyzing* the information available through various touch points, and implementing (or *doing*) social media tactics to excite customers.

EXHIBIT 3.6   Social Media Engagement Process

Listen

From a market research point of view, companies can learn a lot about their customers by listening to (and monitoring) what they say on their social networks, blogs, review sites, and so on. Customers appear willing to provide their opinions on just about anything that involves their interests and purchases—both their own and their friends'. Writing blogs and providing opinions via polls about such diverse topics as BOTOX treatments, ASICS running shoes, or a particular play of an NFL team during the playoffs all constitute new ways that customers communicate with one another—and with marketers who are paying attention.

Using a technique known as **sentiment analysis**, marketers can analyze the content found on sites like Facebook, Twitter, and online blogs and reviews to assess the favorableness or unfavorableness of the sentiments. Sentiment analysis allows marketers to analyze data from these sources to collect consumer comments about companies and their products. The data are then analyzed to distill customer attitudes and preferences, including reactions to specific products and campaigns. Scouring millions of sites with sentiment

The NFL blog is one way fans communicate with each other during and after games.
Courtesy of NFL Properties, LLC

analysis techniques provides new insights into what consumers really think. Companies plugged into this real-time information and these insights can become more nimble, allowing for numerous quick changes such as a product rollout, a new advertising campaign, or reactions to customer complaints.

Several companies specialize in monitoring social media.[61] For example, Salesforce .com offers sentiment analysis and then helps its clients such as GE, Kodak, Microsoft, and PepsiCo engage with their customers.[62] Using sentiment analysis techniques, it processes a constant stream of online consumer opinion from blogs, Facebook, and other networking sites, including 90 million Twitter tweets a day. The Salesforce.com tools for managing consumer sentiment data allow companies to identify opinion trends that might warrant an online corporate response.

Analyze

Fortunately, the companies that help facilitate listening also provide analytic tools to assess what customers are saying about the firm and its competitors. There are three main categories of analysis used for understanding data collected from social media.[63]

First, it is important to determine the amount of traffic using their sites, visiting their blogs, or tweeting about them. Measures used for this purpose include **hits** (i.e., total requests for a page), visits to a particular site or page, unique visitors to the site, and **page views** (i.e., the number of times any page gets viewed by any visitor).

Second, while knowing how many people are using a firm's social media is important, it is even more critical to learn who those visitors are, what they are doing, and what engages and excites them. For example, eHarmony works hard to understand what its clients want, both in a service provider and in a mate, as Marketing Analytics 3.1 details. To analyze these factors, social media marketers use metrics such as the **bounce rate**, which refers to the percentage of times a visitor leaves the site almost immediately, such as after viewing only one page. Analyzing which pages are the most frequent entry and exit locations provides direction on how to make a website more effective. In addition, following visitors' **click paths** shows how users proceed through the information—not unlike how grocery stores try to track the way shoppers move through their aisles. A firm can use this information to provide users with an easier navigation experience through the site so they can more quickly find what they are looking for. The data analysis can also reveal **conversion rates**, a measure that indicates what percentage of visitors or potential customers act as the marketer hopes, whether by clicking, buying, or donating. Click paths and conversion rates can also reveal what users might have wanted but did not find at the site.

Marketing Analytics 3.1

Finding a Perfect Match: How eHarmony Leverages Users' Data to Identify Dates—and Their Consumption Patterns[v]

Some of the same information that enables eHarmony, the online dating service, to connect romantic partners is exactly the same sort of detail that enables eHarmony, the marketer, to communicate most effectively with its clients and prospective customers. The company is upfront in revealing that it collects a lot of data about users—that collection is one of its selling points. By gathering so much insightful information about users, it can better match them with their perfect mates. As a result, it possesses massive amounts of information—approximately 125 terabytes of data, according to one estimate.

To leverage those data for its own benefit, eHarmony switched from an external data analysis service and brought the process in house. Its sophisticated data analytics enable the firm's seven-person team to determine which communications media sparked responses from which users and when. Whereas previously it struggled to grasp when and why people became loyal customers depending on the channel they used to access its services, today the team gains real-time alerts about whether this person used a smartphone to access its app, or if that person relied on a tablet to visit its website. It carefully calculates the return on its investment in each media buy, according to the lifetime value of each customer, classified according to the route this customer used to access the service, as well as where and when she or he did so.

By enhancing the efficiency of its efforts, eHarmony was able to cut its marketing budget by approximately $5 million. Furthermore, clients' requests for additional information have dropped by around 75 percent, because eHarmony now knows in advance what sorts of details they want and provides it to them predictively.

These data also inform the personalized service the company provides. For example, eHarmony has learned that users who click onto the website through a display ad are more flexible in terms of their requirements in a potential mate. In contrast, users who purchase the service after seeing a televised advertisement are much more particular and specific with regard to the range of ages they will consider in a partner. For users who rely on the eHarmony app, the company offers a shorter questionnaire but a wider range of potential

eHarmony uses its clients' data for matchmaking and more precise target marketing.

© iPhone/Alamy

dates, because these users tend to be younger and more open-minded when it comes to dating.

Its confidence in its data analytics capabilities is pushing eHarmony's future moves as well. In addition to adding a Spanish-language service, it plans to grow internationally. With a commitment to add one new country each quarter for the next several years, eHarmony is also learning all sorts of new things about its clients. Did you know, for example, that people outside the United States are more willing to date a smoker than are members of the U.S. dating population? eHarmony does.

Third, some companies want to analyze data that come from other sites, such as measuring where people have come from to get to the company's site. Did they search through Google or Amazon? Did they receive a referral from a friend? Which keywords did they use to find the firm? Firms can use **keyword analysis** to determine what keywords people use to search on the Internet for their products and services. With this information, they can refine their websites by choosing keywords to use on their site that their customers use. Then they can assess the return on investment (ROI) made by improving the site. This would be done by calculating the incremental profit increase divided by the investment on the site improvement. For social media, it is more challenging to determine ROI than for more traditional marketing applications because the revenue

EXHIBIT 3.7	Analytics	
Type of Analytic	**How It's Used**	**Competitors Offering Similar Analytics**
Content	Understand what's popular and what's not on a firm's website, including page load times and site navigation.	Adobe SiteCatalyst, Clickstream, Coremetrics, IBM SurfAid, Mtracking, VisiStat
Social	Track effectiveness of social media programs, including information on social media–referred conversion rates and engagement metrics.	Facebook Insights, Twitter Web Analytics, Webtrends, HootSuite, TweetDeck
Mobile	Track website access from mobile devices, track which ads direct people to a firm's app, and understand what mobile platform performs best.	AppClix, Bango, Flurry, Localytics, Medialets, Webtrends
Conversion	Measure sales, downloads, video plays, or other actions important to a firm.	ClickTale, KeyMetric, Latitude
Advertising	Track the effectiveness of social, mobile, and search and display ads and divide ad effectiveness by device, platform, or type.	ad:tech, MediaMelon, MediaCloud, Metronome, Snoobi, Adomic

Source: http://www.google.com/analytics/features/index.html.

generated by social media is often not directly related to the expenditure. So, instead of traditional ROI measures, firms often examine questions like: Does having more Twitter followers correlate with having higher sales? Do the company's Facebook fans buy more than nonfans do?[64]

These analyses require well-trained marketing managers, marketing analytic software, and perhaps some help with consulting specialists (e.g., IBM, SAS, PricewaterhouseCoopers). But almost everyone seems to be turning to Google Analytics these days because it offers a sophisticated, in-depth form of analysis, all for free. Not only does Google Analytics track the elements included in Exhibit 3.7, but it also is highly customizable.[65]

Do

Even the greatest analysis has little use if firms fail to implement what they have learned from analyzing their social and mobile media activity. That is, social media may be all about relationships, but ultimately, firms need to use their connections to increase their business.[66] They might launch a new Facebook campaign, actively blog, or provide mobile offers.

YouTube still earns more daily video views than Facebook does, and being second is not a position that Facebook enjoys. Accordingly, it has launched a new program entitled Anthology to facilitate the production of marketing videos for advertisers by well-known content providers such as College Humor, Vice, Funny or Die, Vox Media, The Onion, Tastemade, and Oh My Disney. The resulting videos must be made available through Facebook. However, in addition to running the communications on Facebook, the advertiser also can run them on its own websites, insert them into traditional channels (e.g., television), or pay the content provider to run the videos on its site. Such links can benefit advertisers, which obtain high-quality marketing communications designed specifically for a social media platform. They also help content providers find new clients and outlets for their creativity. But for Facebook, the benefits might be even more critical: By requiring that the videos run through its platform, it nearly inevitably increases the number of daily views it can attract from consumers.[67]

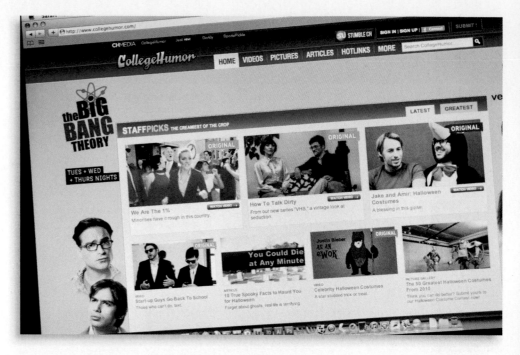

To illustrate how firms might go about undertaking such campaigns, consider the steps involved in developing and implementing a Facebook marketing campaign (Exhibit 3.8).[68] These steps are not unlike the steps used in any integrated marketing communications (IMC) program. (See Chapter 17 for more details.) Assume a marketer was developing a Facebook marketing campaign for a new product that his or her firm has designed.

1. **Identify strategy and goals.** The firm has to determine exactly what it hopes to promote and achieve through its campaign. Does it want to increase awareness of the product? Is it hoping more potential customers might visit and "like" its Facebook page? Is its focus mainly on increasing sales of the product? Depending on what the company aims to achieve, it might focus on developing a Facebook page, creating a Facebook app, or hosting a Facebook event.

2. **Identify target audience.** The next step is to determine whom the firm is targeting. As Exhibit 3.9 shows, Facebook enables the firm to perform targeting that is based on location, language, education, gender, profession, age, relationship status, likes/dislikes, and friends or connections. The marketer's aim is to find an audience big

EXHIBIT 3.8   How to Do a Social Media Marketing Campaign

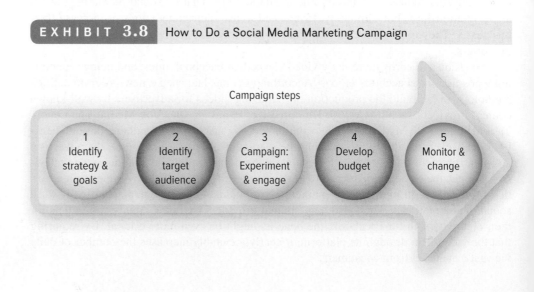

Campaign steps

1 Identify strategy & goals

2 Identify target audience

3 Campaign: Experiment & engage

4 Develop budget

5 Monitor & change

EXHIBIT 3.9   Example Facebook Targeting Choices

2. Targeting

Location

Country: (?)   [New York]
- ○ Everywhere
- ○ By State/Province (?)
- ● By City (?)

Demographics

Age: (?)   [24 ↕] – [35 ↕]

Demographics

Age: (?)   [24 ↕] – [35 ↕]
☐ Require exact age match

Sex: (?)   ● All   ○ Men   ○

Interests

Precise interests: (?)   [Cooking]

Switch to Broad Category Targeting (?)

Estimated Reach (?)

266,920 people
- ▪ who live in the United States
- ▪ who live within 50 miles of New York, NY
- ▪ between the ages of 24 and 35 inclusive
- ▪ who are in the category Cooking

Source: From http://www.facebook.com/business/ads/.

enough that they reach all those who might adopt their product, but not so big that they end up trying to appeal to someone way outside their target audience.

3. **Develop the campaign: Experiment and engage.** Now that the firm knows who it is targeting, the next step is to develop the communications, including the copy and images. Here again, the process is not very different from any other IMC campaign. There should be a call to action that is clear and compelling. Strong, eye-catching images and designs are important. And the campaign must appeal to the right customers. However, an aspect that is more critical with social media than with other forms of IMC is that the images and messages need to be updated almost constantly. Because people expect changing content online, it would be inappropriate to run the same campaign for several months, as the firm might if it was advertising on television, for example.

4. **Develop the budget.** Budgeting is key. Facebook allows advertisers to set a daily budget: Once their costs (usually per click) reach a certain level, the ad disappears for the rest of the day. Of course, this option can be risky if the firm is getting great feedback, and all of a sudden, a compelling ad disappears. Therefore, similar to the campaign content, budgets demand nearly constant review. For example, if a competitor lowers its price significantly, it might be necessary to follow suit to avoid being excluded from customers' consideration sets.

5. **Monitor and change.** The final step is to review the success of the campaign and make changes as necessary. Facebook's Ad Manager offers various metrics and reports, such as number of clicks on ads, audience demographics, and ad performance for specific time periods. As Marketing Analytics 3.2 details, Billboard is turning to Twitter to improve and expand its ability to help brands (i.e., musicians) monitor their performance in real time.

Marketing Analytics 3.2

Measuring the Coolest Tunes: A Billboard Chart for the Popularity of Music-Related Tweets[vi]

Reaching the top of the Billboard charts is the ultimate goal for any kid with a tune in his head or a song just dying to be played on her guitar. For years, these ranking charts have relied on traditional metrics: number of plays on radio stations and album sales. Clearly, in the modern music market, such measurements are out of date and unlikely to provide insightful assessments of which songs are truly generating the most interest among the coolest fans.

After several false starts, Billboard and Twitter have collaborated to come up with what they believe will be the best solution. Billboard will rank mentions and shares of music communicated through Twitter. The social media site is rich with discussions of music. According to informal estimates, music is the most discussed topic, and 7 of the top 10 accounts are held by musicians.

The charts will break new ground in several ways. In particular, they will reflect real-time trends. That is, bands can track at virtually every moment how many mentions their latest singles are getting. Billboard already integrates information from YouTube, but this advance helps solidify its position as a list maker for modern music listeners too, not just those who rely on the radio. Because they are based on users' own tweets, the charts level the playing field, at least

somewhat, for newer and unconventional artists. If a trend-setting consumer gets lots of his or her followers to start talking about an exciting new band, that band is not limited to the rules that a music publisher or label establishes for them.

To access these charts, interested readers—fans, music professionals, and artists alike—can visit Billboard.com directly. Of course, they can also reach them through Billboard's own Twitter feed.

The first real-time chart to launch was the Billboard Trending 140, which ranked the songs moving at the fastest speed, in terms of how many times they have been mentioned on Twitter in the previous hour. The Trending 140 chart also can be filtered to show the rankings of songs over the previous 24 hours. Then the list specifies a ranking of budding artists, defined by Billboard as artists with fewer than 100,000 followers on Twitter who have not been featured previously on Billboard's Hot 100 or 200 lists.

With this approach, Twitter has staked out its official claim: It "wants music business decisions to be based on Twitter data."

Billboard's music popularity rankings are based on the number of mentions and shares of music communicated through Twitter.

Source: Billboard

Reviewing Learning Objectives

LO3-1 **Describe the 4E framework of social media marketing.**

The 4E framework recognizes that marketers must **e**xcite customers with relevant offers; **e**ducate them about the offering; help them **e**xperience products, whether directly or indirectly; and give them an opportunity to **e**ngage.

LO3-2 **Understand the drivers of social media engagement.**

The Wheel of Social Media Engagement highlights five factors that focus on the uniqueness of social media in driving engagement. The five spokes of the wheel are: the information effect, connected effect, the network effect, the dynamic effect, and the timeliness effect.

LO3-3 **Understand the types of social media.**

Users of social media employ them to promote themselves or their products and services. They do so through three main categories: social networking sites (e.g., Facebook, LinkedIn), media-sharing sites (e.g., YouTube), and thought-sharing sites (e.g., blogs, Twitter).

LO3-4 **Understand various motivations for using mobile applications and how they are priced.**

As mobile users increase in number and diversity, the applications developed to appeal to them are spreading as well. Although there are well over a million apps, they meet seven basic customer motivations: for "me time" and to socialize, shop, accomplish, prepare, discover, and self-express. By meeting a multiple of these motivations, companies can attract large numbers of customers. When choosing how to charge for apps, firms have four options: ad-supported, freemium, paid apps, and paid apps with in-app purchases.

LO3-5 **Recognize and use the three components of a social media strategy.**

Firms engage with customers through social and mobile media using a three-step process. First, they listen to the customer using techniques like sentiment analysis. Second, they analyze the data collected in the first step using metrics like the bounce rate, click paths, and conversion rates. Finally, they use this information to develop tactics to engage their customers in a way very similar to the process described in Chapter 18.

Key Terms

- ad-supported apps, 100
- blog, 96
- bounce rate, 103
- click path, 103
- conversion rate, 103
- connected effect, 89
- corporate blog, 96
- dynamic effect, 90

- freemium apps, 100
- hit, 103
- in-app purchases, 100
- information effect, 88
- keyword analysis, 104
- microblog, 97
- network effect, 90
- page view, 103

- paid apps, 101
- paid apps with in-app purchases, 101
- personal blog, 97
- professional blog, 97
- sentiment analysis, 102
- showrooming, 100
- social media, 82
- timeliness effect, 91

Marketing Digitally

1. Go to http://www.facebook.com/business and learn about how to build pages, ads, and sponsored stories and how to take advantage of mobile applications. What are some of the steps that Facebook suggests a person consider when using ads for marketing?

2. Go to Hubspot.com and check out its top case studies. How do these case studies provide insights into how listening and analytics can help firms improve their social media marketing?

3. Learn about Coca-Cola's "#shareacoke" social media campaign on YouTube (https://www.youtube.com/watch?v=5l0cCyElfgg). Which of the 4E components does this campaign leverage?

4. A student who graduates with a marketing degree likely has a good foundation for jobs that utilize social media. Go to Monster.com and search for jobs in your area, using the keyword "social media." Would you be interested in pursuing one or more of these positions? Why or why not?

Marketing Applications

1. Evaluate Under Armour's social media strategy using the 4E framework.

2. Using the components of the 4E framework, outline how an entrepreneur marketing low-sugar candy might apply it to their marketing mix efforts.

3. Suppose an herbal tea company introduced a new product called Mint-Enhanced Tea—a mint and lemon herbal tea. How should it go about creating excitement using various social and mobile media tools?

4. If you were marketing a new running shoe, what sort of mobile applications might enhance your marketing efforts?

5. Assume you work for a large consumer packaged-goods firm that has discovered that its latest line of snack foods is moving very slowly off store shelves. Recommend a strategy for listening to what consumers are saying on blogs, review sites, and the firm's website. Describe how your strategy might provide insights into consumers' sentiments about the new product line.

6. As an intern for Starbucks, you have been asked to develop a social media campaign for a new latte. The objective of the campaign is to increase awareness and trial of this new line. Use the listen-analyze-do framework to outline a new campaign.

7. You were just hired by a company that wants to produce apps that help people become healthier by exercising, eating well, and reducing stress. On which customer motivations would you recommend the company focus? Describe the app you would design, the customer motivations it meets, and why your app is the right design for your potential customers.

8. The company loves the idea for the app you suggested in the previous question, but is concerned about how it will make money on the app. Suggest a pricing model for the app and discuss why this model will maximize profits.

Quiz Yourself

1. Through its Facebook page, a major restaurant chain is offering its customers a Groupon coupon for 50 percent off the purchase of a meal. In doing so, the restaurant is focusing on which aspect of the 4E framework?
   a. Educating
   b. Enlightening
   c. Experiencing
   d. Employing
   e. Exciting

2. To get customers excited about a social media–related offer, the offer must be:
   a. innovative and substantial.
   b. timely and aimed at a broad-based audience.
   c. relevant and aimed at a target audience.
   d. isolated and trendy.
   e. general and unique.

(Answers to these two questions can be found in the Quiz Yourself Answer Key section.)

Chapter Case Study

IMAGES, SALES, BRANDS: HOW RED BULL USES VARIOUS SOCIAL MEDIA TECHNIQUES TO ACHIEVE ALL ITS OBJECTIVES

It isn't as if the social media strategy adopted by Red Bull—the energy drink that "gives you wings"—is a trade secret. Granted, the private company has a policy that discourages employees from giving interviews. But its overall strategy is clear from its actions and their outcomes. The success it has accrued from this strategy therefore isn't a matter of doing things differently from anyone else. It's a function of doing them better.

To begin, Red Bull distinguishes its goals for leveraging social media contacts. Is it hoping for more brand exposure, or is it pursuing sales increases? Depending on its focus, it adopts distinct, appealing methods that are specific and unique to each social media platform. Then it implements these tactics consistently and comprehensively, to increase the chances that they will be widely shared and recognized.

Social Media for Name Recognition

When Felix Baumgartner (purposefully) fell to Earth from 127,852 feet up, he broke all sorts of records. His jump was from the highest height ever achieved by a human. During the 4-minute, 20-second freefall, he also reached greater speeds—up to Mach 1.25, faster than the speed of sound—than anyone else ever has. The event was a breakthrough on various levels. Baumgartner's pressure suit was the first version to be able to protect the human body in space but still enable maneuverability. To address the threat of ebullism (i.e., when liquid in the body evaporates due to high altitudes, causing a person's blood to literally boil), Baumgartner and his team derived new medical techniques with widespread applications. His parachute also adopted a new "reefed" design to reduce drifting, with clear implications for airdrops of materials and supplies.[69]

In reporting on all these remarkable feats, Baumgartner's name was mentioned frequently—though not as frequently as the project that sponsored his jump and all the technology that went into supporting it: the Red Bull Stratos project. Every official mention of the event included the full name, such that Red Bull Stratos often appeared as a single term. It was not just the Stratos project. It was the Red Bull Stratos project.

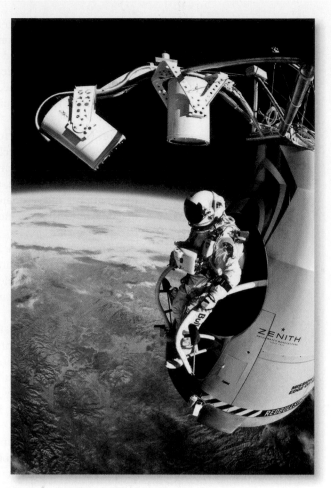

Sponsored by Red Bull, Felix Baumgartner's jump reached speeds of Mach 1.25.

© Jay Nemeth/Zumapress/Newscom

And what a project it was, leading to the creation of not just scientific advances but also a remarkable video. That video, taken from the camera mounted on Baumgartner's helmet, features vast, picturesque views of Earth and the sense of plummeting. Red Bull immediately made it available for people to check out at their leisure. But the real targets—the people whom Red Bull hoped would be most engaged by the video and the stunt in general—were extreme sports fanatics. These folks willingly put their bodies at risk on a regular basis to perform some cool stunt to cause their friends to marvel. For them, there may be no better stunt than having some guy fall from space.[70] In full awareness of this appeal, Red Bull made sure that the video was prominent on its YouTube channel. On the day of the jump itself, approximately 8 million viewers streamed the video live and in real time. Also on that day, the number of subscribers to Red Bull's YouTube channel increased by a remarkable 87,801.[71]

On Twitter, recognizing that 140 characters was not nearly enough to communicate the awesomeness of the stunt, it simply used hashtags and links to connect followers to the video, whether through YouTube or on a Red Bull site. Although Red Bull's main Twitter feed did not exhibit any notable differences, the dedicated Red Bull Stratos Twitter feed prompted more than 20,000 mentions in tweets by others on that day.

The Red Bull Stratos Facebook page featured several photos during and after the jump. Just one shot of a landed Baumgartner, still in his space suit and on his knees beside his reefed parachute, prompted more than 20,000 comments, more than 50,000 shares, and nearly half a million likes.[72]

Thus the example of the Red Bull Stratos project and its attendant coverage through social media suggests several things Red Bull did well. It knew its audience and its own goals and it understood how different channels could help it attain those goals. To ensure that it appealed to the target audience, it engaged them in an exciting, never-before-tried, daredevil experience. Moreover, it shared the scientific lessons learned through the project, to give those who wanted it an education.

But it also spent a lot of money to get Baumgartner to space and back down again. And that meant that it needed to translate some of the brand awareness it developed into sales. Luckily for Red Bull, its social media strategy also has room for that effort.

Social Media for Performance

Red Bull does not just send athletes to space. It also sponsors them on the pitch, in the form of the New York Red Bull MLS team, which plays in Red Bull Arena in Harrison, New Jersey. In one recent game, the team's star forward Thierry Henry scored yet another goal. Afterward, he leaned, with his right arm up against the goal post and left hand on his hip. The pose, caught on camera, almost immediately became a Twitter meme as amateur photo editors placed him against a variety of backgrounds.[73]

The team was quick to move on this social media coup. It rapidly posted the photo to its website and encouraged fans to vote for it as their favorite shot of the season. Immediately above and below the encouragement to engage with the brand also appeared links that would allow fans to purchase tickets for a full season, half season, or individual games.[74]

Beyond these consumer-related uses of social and mobile media, Red Bull's international sales efforts depend on "SoLoMo" (referring to social, location, and mobile) software. Users who download the Red Bull app receive alerts on their smartphones about in-store promotions as soon as they arrive at the retail site. If they also attend Red Bull events, such as a flugtag or BMX race, selected patrons might even receive a special invitation to come backstage to meet some of the stars of the show.

Each of Red Bull's mobile sales representatives is equipped with her or his own tablet computer loaded with mobile software. Thus on visits to retail sites and vendors, the salespeople can provide the latest inventory information. They also present detailed analytics to show vendors how best to position their coolers of Red Bull products and how to line up the cans in the display case to encourage sales.[75]

Combining the Uses of Social Media

When you are as good at engaging and exciting people through social media as Red Bull is, the next step might be to make social media your main focus. Although the privately held company has not publicized any such plans, commentators suggest that it appears poised to transform itself into a media company that just happens to sell energy drinks.[76] The extent and amount of content it creates, featuring extreme sports and even sports it has created (ever hear of ice racing?), is similar in quality to sports videos produced by well-known networks. If Red Bull can convince networks to purchase its coverage of Shaun White on the half-pipe, it enters a new market. If Shaun White happens to be wearing a hat with the Red Bull logo, well then that's just an added bonus.

Such predictions actually resonate quite well with what Red Bull already does in social media. For example, though it maintains a plethora of Facebook pages and Twitter accounts for various events and locations, virtually none of them ever feature pictures of its drink product. Instead, they offer exciting in-sport shots or humorous images. Fans can—and do—comment, but Red Bull rarely responds. That may be because its primary goal is to establish an edgy, exciting image as a lifestyle brand, which it feels confident will translate into product sales.[77]

Questions

1. What social and mobile media tools is Red Bull using?

2. Evaluate Red Bull's social media marketing strategy using the 4E framework.

3. How should Red Bull assess the effectiveness of these campaigns? Describe how it should respond to insights gained by this assessment.

Endnotes

1. Sarah Germano, "Under Armour Overtakes Adidas in U.S. Sportswear Market," *The Wall Street Journal*, January 8, 2015.

2. Ibid.

3. https://twitter.com/UnderArmour.

4. https://twitter.com/StephenCurry30.

5. https://twitter.com/UnderArmour.

6. Ibid.

7. Yuyu Chen, "How Does Under Armour Differentiate Itself from Nike Via Digital Marketing?" *ClickZ*, October 30, 2015, https://www.clickz.com/clickz/news/2432655/how-does-under-armour-differentiate-itself-from-nike-via-digital-marketing.

8. https://www.facebook.com/Underarmour/; Artemiss Berry, "How Under Armour and Warby Parker Win with Social Media," *National Retail Federation*, February 29, 2015, https://nrf.com/news/how-under-armour-and-warby-parker-win-social-media.

9. Chen, "How Does Under Armour Differentiate Itself."

10. https://twitter.com/AskTeamUA/with_replies.

11. Pamela Vaughan, "72% of People Who Complain on Twitter Expect a Response Within an Hour," *HubSpot*, July 23, 2014, http://blog.hubspot.com/marketing/twitter-response-time-data.

12. https://www.google.com/#q=under+armour.

13. We Are Social, and IAB Singapore, "Leading Social Networks Worldwide as of March 2015, Ranked by Number of Active Users (in Millions)," *Statista*, Accessed 19 March 2015, http://www.statista.com/statistics/272014/global-social-networks-ranked-by-number-of-users/.

14. www.sephora.com.

15. www.youtube.com/user/sephora.

16. Chris Barry et al., "Putting Social Media to Work," 2011, Bain & Co., http://www.bain.com/Images/BAIN_BRIEF_Putting_social_media_to_work.pdf.

17. Meg Wagner, "Corporate Social Media Fails of 2014: Big Brands Make Big Mistakes," *New York Daily News*, December 20, 2014, http://www.nydailynews.com/.

18. Seth Fendley, "7 Hilarious Twitter Brand Hashtag Fails," *HubSpot*, March 12, 2015, http://blog.hubspot.com/marketing/hilarious-twitter-brand-hashtag-fails.

19. Matthew Stern, "Social Sites Move to Boost Retail Sales," *Retail Wire*, June 5, 2015, http://www.retailwire.com/discussion/18327/social-sites-move-to-boost-retail-sales.

20. This section draws heavily from Anne L. Roggeveen and Dhruv Grewal, "Engaging Customers: The Wheel of Social Media Engagement," *Journal of Consumer Marketing*, forthcoming.

21. Peter Schrank, "A Brand New Game: As People Spend More Time on Social Media, Advertisers Are Following Them," *The Economist*, August 29, 2015.

22. See reviews: Dhruv Grewal, Yakov Bart, Martin Spann, and Peter Pal Zubcsek (2016), "Mobile Advertising: A Framework and Research Agenda," *Journal of Interactive Marketing*, 34 (May), 3–14; Aguirre, Elizabeth M., Dhruv Grewal, Anne L. Roggeveen and Martin Wetzels (2016), "Personalizing Online, Social, and Mobile Communications: Opportunities and Challenges," *Journal of Consumer Marketing*, 33(2), 98–110.

23. https://twitter.com/covergirl.

24. http://twittercounter.com/pages/100?version=1&utm_expid=102679131-65.MDYnsQdXQwO2AlKoJXVpSQ.1&utm_referrer=http%3A%2F%2Fwww.google.com%2Furl%3Fsa%3Dt%26rct%3Dj%26q%3D%26esrc%3Ds%26source%3Dweb%26cd%3D3%26ved%3D0ahUKEwiv9Pr4ipbKAhUKbj4KHUnPCkkQFggoMAI%26ur.

25. Stephanie Rosenbloom, "A Hotel Room with 140 Characters," *The New York Times*, October 3, 2013.

26. "Social Media and Dynamic Social Communities," SAM (Socializing Around Media). http://samproject.net/social-media-and-dynamic-social-communities/.

27. Vaughan, "72% of People Who Complain."

28. Ibid.

29. H.O. Maycotte, "Beacon Technology: The Where, What, Who, How and Why," *Forbes*, September 1, 2015, http://www.forbes.com/sites/homaycotte/2015/09/01/beacon-technology-the-what-who-how-why-and-where/.

30. Seb Joseph, "Coca-Cola Has Taken a Step Closer to Using Beacons to Turn Location-Based Marketing on its Head," *The Drum*, August 13, 2015, http://www.thedrum.com/news/2015/08/13/coca-cola-has-taken-step-closer-using-beacons-turn-location-based-marketing-its-head.

31. Shea Bennett, "28% of Time Spent Online Is Social Networking," *Ad Week*, January 27, 2015, http://www.adweek.com/socialtimes/time-spent-online/613474.

32. We Are Social, and IAB Singapore, "Leading Social Networks Worldwide as of March 2015, Ranked by Number of Active Users (in Millions)," *Statista—The Statistics Portal*, http://www.statista.com/statistics/272014/global-social-networks-ranked-by-number-of-users/ (accessed March 19, 2015).

33. Forever 21 Facebook Fan Page, http://www.facebook.com/#!/Forever21?rcf=ts.

34. Mike Gingerich, "4 Ways to Boost Your Facebook Engagement with Promotions," *Social Media Examiner*, January 8, 2013, http://www.socialmediaexaminer.com/boost-your-facebook-engagement-with-promotions/.

35. Experian, "Most Popular Social Media Websites in the United States in December 2014, Based on Share of Visits," *Statista—The Statistics Portal*, http://www.statista.com/statistics/265773/market-share-of-the-most-popular-social-media-websites-in-the-us/ (accessed March 19, 2015).

36. Dorie Clark, "Why You Should Be on Google Plus (Even Though No One Else Is)," *Forbes*, January 14, 2013.

37. Ross Blum, "Where Have All the Customers Gone?," p. 8.

38. "In The Know," YouTube, Fall 2009, http://www.gstatic.com/youtube/engagement/platform/autoplay/advertise/downloads/YouTube_InTheKnow.pdf.

39. "Brand Channels," YouTube, http://www.gstatic.com/youtube/engagement/platform/autoplay/advertise/downloads/YouTube_BrandChannels.pdf.

40. Instagram. "Number of Monthly Active Instagram Users from January 2013 to September 2015 (in Millions)." Statista, January 7, 2016. http://www.statista.com/statistics/253577/number-of-monthly-active-instagram-users/.

41. Somini Sengupta, Nicole Perlroth, and Jenna Wortham, "Behind Instagram's Success, Networking the Old Way," *The New York Times*, April 13, 2012, http://www.nytimes.com/2012/04/14/

technology/instagram-founders-were-helped-by-bay-area-connections.html?pagewanted=all&_r=2&.

42. Instagram, "beatsbydre," https://www.instagram.com/beatsbydre/.

43. Heike Young, "The 30 Most Genius Content Marketing Examples of 2014 (So Far)," *Salesforce Marketing Cloud*, August 6, 2014, http://www.exacttarget.com/blog/the-30-most-genius-content-marketing-examples-of-2014-so-far/.

44. Shirley Ju, "Instagram Flexin': Eminem Readies Story Behind 'Lose Yourself' for Beats by Dre," *HipHopDX*, November 15, 2014, http://hiphopdx.com/editorials/id.2647/title.instagram-flexin-eminem-readies-story-behind-lose-yourself-for-beats-by-dre.

45. "Top 15 Most Popular Photo Sharing Sites | January 2016," http://www.ebizmba.com/articles/photo-sharing-sites.

46. "Brands on Flickr," *Supercollider*, July 12, 2008, http://geoffnorthcott.com/blog/2008/07/brands-on-flickr/.

47. Young, "The 30 Most Genius."

48. Ibid.

49. Digital Training Academy, "Social Media Marketing: How #FirstWorldProblems Was Hijacked by WATERisLIFE," *Digital marketing industry case study library*, http://www.digitaltrainingacademy.com/casestudies/2015/03/social_media_marketing_how_firstworldproblems_was_hijacked_by_waterislife.php.

50. David H Deans, "184 Million People in America Own a Smartphone," *Social Media Today*, March 15, 2015, http://www.socialmediatoday.com/technology-data/2015-03-15/184-million-people-america-own-smartphone.

51. Bill Siwicki, "On Smartphones, More Older Folks Make Purchases Than Youngsters," *Internet Retailer*, April 17, 2014, https://www.internetretailer.com/2014/04/17/smartphones-more-older-folks-make-purchases-youngsters.

52. http://www.statista.com/statistics/266488/forecast-of-mobile-app-downloads/.

53. http://www.statista.com/statistics/241587/number-of-free-mobile-app-downloads-worldwide/.

54. http://www.statista.com/statistics/266488/forecast-of-mobile-app-downloads/.

55. David Barboza, "A Popular Chinese Social Networking App Blazes Its Own Path," *The New York Times*, January 20, 2014.

56. "Vision Statement: How People Really Use Mobile." *Harvard Business Review*, January-February 2013, https://hbr.org/2013/01/how-people-really-use-mobile/ar/1.

57. Ibid.

58. Ashley Feinberg, "I Just Spent $236 on Candy Crush, Help," *Gizmodo*, August 7, 2013, http://www.gizmodo.com.

59. Stuart Dredge, "Candy Crush Saga: '70% of People on the Last Level Haven't Paid Anything,'" *The Guardian*, September 10, 2013, http://www.theguardian.com; "Candy Crush Saga Most Popular Game App on the Planet," *Metro*, January 30, 2014, http://www.metro.co.uk.

60. Josh Wolonick, "Here's How Big the In-App Purchases Market Is for Apple and Google," *Minyanville*, January 16, 2014, http://www.minyanville.com.

61. Katie Van Domelin, "Social Media Monitoring Tools—How to Pick the Right One," July 7, 2010, http://www.convinceandconvert.com/social-media-monitoring/social-media-monitoring-tools-how-to-pick-the-right-one/.

62. "New Salesforce.com Features Help to Scale 'Social' across the Enterprise," Salesforce.com website, November 12, 2011, http://www.Salesforce.com.com.

63. Laura S. Quinn and Kyle Andrei, "A Few Good Web Analytics Tools," *TechSoup* May 19, 2011, http://www.techsoup.org.

64. Christina Warren, "How to Measure Social Media ROI," *Mashable* October 27, 2009, http://mashable.com/2009/10/27/social-media-roi/.

65. "iNoobs: What Is Google Analytics?," http://inspiredm.com; http://www.google.com/analytics/features/index.html; http://www.advanced-web-metrics.com; Kevin Ryan, "What Can the Average Marketer Learn from Google Creative Lab?," *Advertising Age*, April 19, 2013.

66. Amy Porterfield, "3 Steps to an Effective Social Media Strategy," *Social Media Examiner*, March 1, 2012, http://www.socialmediaexaminer.com.

67. Tim Peterson, "Facebook Opens Branded Video Program on YouTube's Anniversary," *Advertising Age*, April 23, 2015, http://www.adage.com.

68. Andy Shaw, "How to Create a Facebook Ad Campaign," *Social Media Tips*, September 23, 2011, http://exploringsocialmedia.com/how-to-create-a-facebook-ad-campaign/.

69. Red Bull Stratos, "Scientific Data Review," http://www.redbullstratos.com.

70. Rick Mulready, "The Secret to Red Bull's Media Success Is There Is No Secret," November 6, 2013, http://rickmulready.com.

71. SocialBakers, "Red Bull Stratos on Social Media,"http://www.socialbakers.com.

72. Ibid.

73. Jack Bell, "Red Bulls' Henry Strikes a Pose, and Starts a Trend," *The New York Times*, September 21, 2013.

74. http://www.newyorkredbulls.com/.

75. Clint Boulton, "Red Bull Eyes 'SoLoMo' Software to Grow Business," *The Wall Street Journal*, April 30, 2012.

76. *Wall Street Journal Live*, "Lunch Break: Interview with John Jurgensen," December 20, 2013, http://online.wsj.com.

77. David Moth, "How Red Bull Uses Facebook, Twitter, Pinterest, and Google+," *eConsultancy.com*, February 21, 2013, http://econsultancy.com.

i. Stuart Elliot, "Live Commercials Coming to 'Late Night,'" *The New York Times*, September 18, 2013; Jeanine Poggi, "Lexus to Air Live Ads, Fueled by Social Suggestions, during NBC's 'Late Night,'" *Advertising Age*, September 18, 2013; Chris Perry, "How Social Media Propelled Fallon's Tonight Show Takeover," *Forbes*, April 6, 2013; YouTube, "Late Night with Jimmy Fallon," http://www.youtube.com/user/latenight.

ii. http://www.hubspot.com/customers/hy-line-cruises; "Inbound in Number," *HubSpot*, http://www.hubspot.com/internet-marketing-company; *Hubspot* Inc. 2014 Annual Report. http://s2.q4cdn.com/235752014/files/doc_financials/2015/HubSpot-2014-AR_v001_b3808p.pdf; "HubSpot Inc." *Google Finance*. December 14, 2015, www.google.com/finance.

iii. LinkedIn Marketing Solution, "Mercedes-Benz USA Gets More Mileage from Shareable Content with Sponsored Updates from LinkedIn," https://business.linkedin.com/content/dam/business/marketing-solutions/global/en_US/site/pdf/cs/LinkedIn-MercedesBenz%20SU-CaseStudy-130919.pdfl; Andrew Adam Newman, "Mercedes Looks for Up-and-Comers on LinkedIn," *The New York Times*, July 14, 2014, http://www.nytimes.com/2014/07/18/business/media/mercedes-looks-for-up-and-comers-on-linkedin.html; We Are Social, "Leading Social Networks Worldwide as of November 2015, Ranked by Number of Active Users (in Millions)," *Statista—The Statistics Portal*, December 14, 2015, http://www.statista.com/statistics/272014/global-social-networks-ranked-by-number-of-users/.

iv. Lisa Richwine, "Disney's Powerful Marketing Force: Social
Media Moms," *Reuters*, June 15, 2015; Ernan Roman, "How
Disney Influences Small Customer Segments for Major Impact,"
The Huffington Post, August 18, 2015, http://www.huffington-
post.com/; Nadia Cameron, "How to Engage in Influencer
Marketing: The Controversy and the Opportunity," *CMO*,
June 19, 2015, http://www.cmo.com.au/article/577875/
how-engage-influencer-marketing-controversy-opportunity/.

v. Kate Kaye, "eHarmony's Love for Data Goes Beyond Dating: It's
Good for Marketing Too," *Advertising Age*, February 18, 2015,

http://adage.com; Samuel Greengard, "eHarmony Enhances Its
Relationship with Big Data," *Baseline*, February 2, 2015, http://
www.baseline.com; "IBM Big Data & Analytics Helps eHarmony
Identify More Compatible Matches in Real Time," *IBM Big
Data & Analytics Hub*, September 8, 2014, http://www.
ibmbigdatahub.com.

vi. Ben Sisario, "Tweets About Music to Get a Billboard Chart," *The
New York Times*, March 27, 2014, https://www.nytimes.com;
http://www.billboard.com/billboard-twitter-chart-faq.

CHAPTER 4

CONSCIOUS MARKETING, CORPORATE SOCIAL RESPONSIBILITY, AND ETHICS

LEARNING OBJECTIVES

After reading this chapter, you should be able to:

LO4-1 Define conscious marketing.

LO4-2 Describe what constitutes marketing's greater purpose.

LO4-3 Differentiate between conscious marketing and corporate social responsibility.

LO4-4 Describe the ways in which conscious marketing helps various stakeholders.

LO4-5 Explain how conscious leadership can produce a conscious culture in the firm.

LO4-6 Describe how ethics constitute an integral part of a firm's conscious marketing strategy.

LO4-7 Identify the four steps in ethical decision making.

Blake Mycoskie doesn't just want his customers to buy his shoes; he wants to turn customers into benefactors. In this innovative, conscious approach to marketing, his company, TOMS Shoes, does more than engage in charitable acts. The charitable acts *are* the company. There is no separating TOMS from the social responsibility it embraces.

Mycoskie started out manufacturing a revised version of a traditional Argentinean shoe called *alpargatas* and selling them to consumers outside their generally impoverished source nation. The combination of the comfortable shoes and the extreme poverty he observed led to a simple code: "With every pair you purchase, TOMS will give a pair to a child in need. One for One." Thus, consumers who buy TOMS Shoes do so because they know that with their purchase, they help donate shoes to people in need. Their choices reflect their desire to make their money count for something and to embrace a higher purpose.[1]

As the company has grown, it also has added lines of vegan and recycled shoes. It expanded into sunglasses, where its One for One philosophy dictates that for every pair sold, TOMS provides eye care, such as medicines, glasses, or surgery, to someone else in the world at risk of losing his or her sight. TOMS has also included coffee, bags, and backpacks among its offerings.[2] When a customer makes a purchase from the TOMS line of coffee, a week's worth of safe water goes to someone in need.[3] For each bag purchased, TOMS helps provide the materials and training that health care providers require to help mothers give birth safely.[4] Backpack purchases help prevent bullying, because TOMS provides teachers, school counselors, and other school staff with bullying prevention and intervention training in return for the purchases.[5]

More recently, TOMS launched its Animal Initiative, in support of National Geographic's nonprofit Big Cat Collection. The nonprofit works to conserve big cat populations, including lions, mainly through poaching prevention efforts. The Animal Initiative is unique among all of the TOMS initiatives in that the lines dedicated to support this effort span a variety of products, including shoes, sunglasses, and backpacks, all with animal-inspired designs.[6]

Despite the expanding range of products associated with TOMS, its offerings still remain somewhat focused. Thus, when it comes to procuring other products—those that TOMS doesn't sell—finding a socially responsible seller that actively engages in tactics to benefit people and communities is still challenging for individual shoppers. To extend his vision more broadly, Mycoskie determined that he would bring together sellers and vendors whose work benefited communities onto one online platform. Then shoppers could visit a single site, where they knew that each item they purchased had social as well as consumption benefits.

On the TOMS Marketplace website, visitors can search by product line (e.g., apparel, tech, accessories), by their preferred cause (e.g., education, job creation, water), by global region, or by brand. The approximately 200 different products benefit diverse causes: Buying a backpack from Stone + Cloth funds education initiatives in East Africa; the purchase of handmade wooden headphones from LSTN means that LSTN will help restore the hearing of a person with hearing impairment.

Although the TOMS model remains dedicated to a buy one, give one approach, the Marketplace does not require the same commitment from all its 30 or so sellers. Instead, Mycoskie reviews each provider to ensure it has an appropriate culture that features "a mission of improving people's lives baked into its business model." Furthermore, TOMS purchases all the products on the site. In that sense, it functions like a wholesaler that not only procures supplies but also takes responsibility for storing, warehousing, shipping, and other logistics.[7]

Detractors argue that TOMS actually may do some harm, in that its provisions might reduce demand for locally produced products. But TOMS already has restored 275,000 people's eyesight and provided 67,000 weeks of clean water.[8] It also has given away 35 million pairs of shoes, so consumers have bought at least that many—at an average price of $55 per pair. Clearly, the value that consumers find in these cloth shoes goes well beyond the simple linen and canvas parts that go into making them.

Which is the more important corporate objective: making a profit or protecting customers, employees, and the broader needs of society and the environment?[9] This question underlies a primary dilemma that marketers have long faced. At one point, they might have argued that profit was the primary goal of any firm. But over time, firms—and society as a whole—came to agree that corporations have social responsibilities to a range of stakeholders that they must meet.

Doing so can be harder than it sounds, especially because the goals of different shareholder groups often can be at odds. For example, employees in the coal industry want to keep their jobs; consumers want cheap energy; society wants clean, sustainable energy; and shareholders who own stock in a coal company want to earn profits. But those goals often come in conflict, because coal will never be a clean or sustainable energy, so to satisfy society, shareholders by definition would lose their source of income. Accordingly, some industries and companies resist the idea that they need to acknowledge the impact of their actions on others. However, in the long term, if customers believe they can no longer trust a company or that the company is not acting responsibly, they will no longer support that company by purchasing its products or services or investing in its stock.

Ultimately then, modern firms and their marketing efforts must address these notions. For corporate leaders, their firm's ability to balance the needs of various stakeholders—while building and maintaining consumer trust by conducting ethical, transparent, clear transactions that have a positive impact on society and the environment—must be of paramount importance. It is the role of the firm's leadership to weigh the trade-offs among stakeholders and establish a culture that encourages the company to function in a responsible, ethical way.[10] Throughout history, regardless of the objectives they embrace, companies and marketers have needed to be ethical in their actions if they hope to survive.

As these corporate social responsibilities have grown, and ideas about how they should be implemented have expanded, the progression in thinking has moved to encompass the relatively more recent concept of conscious marketing. This chapter details these developments over time, in an effort to describe and explain what conscious marketing means and how it depends on ethics and corporate social responsibility. We start by defining conscious marketing and its four main components (a higher purpose, stakeholders, conscious leadership, and a conscious culture). In particular, we explain why behaving consciously is so important to successful marketing. We then examine how a firm can balance the sometimes disparate needs of various stakeholders to create an offering that sustains the company financially in the long term while also benefiting society and the environment (i.e., the triple bottom line). Then we turn our attention to the leaders who establish a conscious marketing culture in the firm. Coming full circle, we describe how conscious marketing can be integrated into a firm's marketing strategy and marketing plan (from Chapter 2). Finally, we consider ethics as a crucial component of conscious marketing. To help you make ethical marketing decisions, we also provide a framework for ethical decision making. In Appendix 4A, we present some scenarios that highlight typical ethical challenges marketing managers often must face.

CONSCIOUS MARKETING

 Define conscious marketing.

Conscious marketing entails a sense of purpose for the firm that is higher than simply making a profit by selling products and services. It encompasses four overriding principles:[11]

1. **Recognition of marketing's greater purpose.** When the marketing function recognizes that the purpose of business should be more than just making profits—whether the purpose is providing shoes for residents of poor nations, as TOMS does, or ensuring employment opportunities for local communities, or making strides toward greener production—the actions it undertakes change in focus. The resulting engagement improves inputs as well as outcomes of marketing actions.

2. **Consideration of stakeholders and their interdependence.** Conscious marketers consider how their actions will affect the expansive range of potential stakeholders, which are the broad set of people who might be affected by a firm's actions, including not just corporate shareholders and customers but also past, current, and prospective employees and their families; supply chain partners; government agencies; the physical environment; and members of the communities in which the firm operates (defined either locally or on a global scale). Marketers increasingly acknowledge that to serve as many stakeholders as possible and avoid inflicting severe damage on any others, they must give up their exclusive focus on maximizing profits.[12] Rather, they engage in conscious marketing, such that they attend to the broad implications of their actions. By considering these impacts as a foundation for any marketing decisions, conscious marketers achieve the most benefits for the largest numbers of stakeholders while also ensuring that they avoid causing significant harm to any group. For example, when Walmart issued new standards for farms that supply

it with livestock products, the effects were felt by the supply chain partners who might need to adjust their practices, competitors that might need to adopt similar protections, consumers who can take more assurance that the animals raised for their food will not have been fed antibiotics, and animal welfare groups that call the new standards "a step in the right direction."[13]

3. **The presence of conscious leadership, creating a corporate culture.** A conscious marketing approach implies that the firm's leaders are dedicated to the proposition of being conscious at all levels of the business, throughout its entire culture. For example, Elon Musk, the visionary head of a range of innovative companies (e.g., Tesla, SpaceX, Solar City, Hyperloop), explains, "I like to be involved in things that change the world."[14] Therefore, regardless of whether his firm is selling electric vehicles, investigating realistic options for building renewable public transportation systems, or seeking to colonize space, the vision remains the same: to change the world for the better. The resulting conscious culture remains dedicated to the notion that the choices the firm makes reflect its conscious consideration of stakeholders, in line with its higher purpose and in accordance with the leader's ideals. As a result, every member of the firm embodies the ideas of conscious marketing, and every stakeholder affected by that marketing can recognize the higher principles involved.

When Walmart issued new standards for livestock products that were raised on food without antibiotics or artificial growth hormones, it considered multiple stakeholder groups including the ranchers that supply the food, its customers, and animal welfare groups.

© Don Ryan/AP Photo

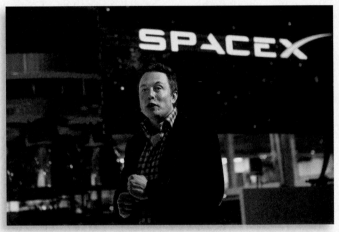

Elon Musk, the head of SpaceX, wants to be involved in things that change the world.

© Patrick T. Fallon/Bloomberg/Getty Images

4. **The understanding that decisions are ethically based.** Conscious marketers must make decisions that are based on sound marketing ethics. **Business ethics** is concerned with distinguishing between right and wrong actions and decisions that arise in a business setting, according to broad and well-established moral and ethical principles that might arise in a business setting, and any special duties or obligations that apply to persons engaged in commerce. **Marketing ethics**, in contrast, examines ethical situations that are specific to the domain of marketing, including societal, global, or individual consumer issues. They can involve societal issues such as the sale of products or services that may damage the environment, global issues such as the use of child labor (see Chapter 8), or individual consumer issues such as misrepresenting a product in advertising or marketing dangerous products.

MARKETING'S GREATER PURPOSE: CORPORATE SOCIAL RESPONSIBILITY AS AN ELEMENT OF CONSCIOUS MARKETING

LO4-2 Describe what constitutes marketing's greater purpose.

As we noted previously, the notion of conscious marketing has evolved over time. At one point, a popular view held that the only responsibility of a business was to its shareholders, so its only purpose was to make a profit.[15] In many parts of the world, that view has been supplanted with the idea that companies must consider their responsibilities to a wider range of stakeholders who make up society. Although there are many and varied definitions of corporate social responsibility (CSR),[16] firms generally acknowledge that, in addition to economic and legal duties, they have responsibilities to society. These responsibilities are not mandated by any law or regulation but instead are associated with the demands, expectations, requirements, and desires of various stakeholders. For example, one definition describes CSR as context-specific actions and policies, taking stakeholders' expectations into account, to achieve what is referred to as the triple bottom line: economic, social, and environmental performance.[17]

Today, virtually all large and well-known companies engage in some form of CSR. The available initiatives are vast in their spread, from establishing charitable foundations to supporting and associating with existing nonprofit groups to supporting the rights of minority groups to adopting responsible marketing, sales, and production practices. Exhibit 4.1 provides several illustrations of the CSR programs undertaken by major firms.

Although CSR is an important element of conscious marketing, it is not the same thing. Becoming a conscious marketing organization is a complex effort, and for some firms, it may prove virtually impossible to achieve. When marketers work in controversial or polluting industries such as tobacco or fossil fuels, their central activities largely bar them from becoming conscious marketers. However, they might engage in CSR in an effort to mitigate the damage that their products cause, such as when cigarette companies sponsor public information campaigns or oil companies plant trees to balance out their

EXHIBIT 4.1	Sampling of Major Companies' CSR Programs
Company	**Illustration of CSR Program**
Amazon.com	Developed nonprofit Simple Pay Donation system to help nonprofits raise money easily
BMW	Light Up Hope and BMW Children's Safety programs
Coca-Cola	Spent $102 million through The Coca-Cola Campaign focusing on water stewardship, healthy and active lifestyles, community recycling, and education
FedEx	Transported more than 67 planes' worth of aid to disaster victims
General Electric	Ecomagination campaign, GE Volunteers Foundation
Google	Google.org funds for pro-profit entrepreneurship in Africa, Google China Social Innovation Cup for College Students
McDonald's	99 percent of fish come from MSC-fisheries, transitioning to sustainable food and packaging sources, Ronald McDonald House charities
Proctor & Gamble	Live, Learn, and Thrive improves the lives of children worldwide
Southwest Airlines	Employees donate volunteer hours to Ronald McDonald Houses throughout the U.S.
Starbucks	Develops ecologically friendly growing practices, LEED certified stores

Source: Adapted from http://money.cnn.com/magazines/fortune/most-admired/.

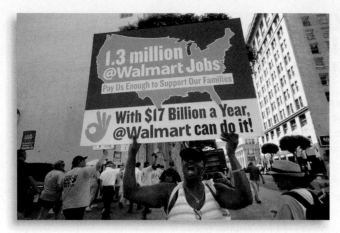

Walmart employees protest low wages.
© Jae C. Hong/AP Photo

carbon footprint.[18] In addition, these companies might undertake efforts in other sectors, such as donating time in local communities or guaranteeing fair wages, because they recognize the importance of such socially responsible efforts.

Walmart offers an interesting example in this discussion. The retail giant has been widely criticized as the worst-paying company in the United States.[19] Yet it also engages in extensive CSR programs across the triple bottom line. It has committed to reducing its carbon footprint (environmental performance), donates more than $1 billion in cash and in-kind items to charitable causes per year (social performance), and still earns strong profits (economic performance).[20]

Thus, though conscious marketing and CSR have some clear connections, they also differ in critical ways, as Exhibit 4.2 summarizes.

 LO4-3 Differentiate between conscious marketing and corporate social responsibility.

EXHIBIT 4.2 How Conscious Marketing Differs from CSR[21]

Corporate Social Responsibility	Conscious Marketing
Independent of corporate purpose or culture	Incorporates higher purpose and a caring culture
Reflects a mechanistic view of business	Takes a holistic, ecosystem view of business as a complex adaptive system
Often grafted on to traditional business model, usually as a separate department or part of PR	Social responsibility is at the core of the business through the higher purpose and viewing the community and the environment as stakeholders
Sees limited overlap between the business and society, and between business and the planet	Recognizes that business is a subset of society, and that society is a subset of the planet

PROGRESS CHECK

1. What are the criteria for being a conscious marketer?
2. Is Walmart a conscious marketer or is it a practitioner of CSR?

 LO4-4 Describe the ways in which conscious marketing helps various stakeholders.

THE STAKEHOLDERS OF CONSCIOUS MARKETING

Among the key differences between conscious marketing and CSR, we can highlight the unique view on shareholders that is absolutely critical to conscious marketing. That is, when companies embrace conscious marketing, they appeal not only to their shareholders but also to all of their key stakeholders (Exhibit 4.3), including their own employees, consumers, the marketplace, and society at large. The choices they make with regard to what they produce and how, and then how they seek to sell those offerings, take a broad range of elements into consideration.

A prominent example appears in the supply chain for processed foods (e.g., cereals, salad dressings). For decades, most of these foods have contained ingredients made from

EXHIBIT 4.3 Key CSR Stakeholders

- Employees
- Their families

- Current customers
- Potential customers

Employees

Customers

Marketplace

Society

- Partners
- Competitors

- Community
- Environment

plants whose DNA has been manipulated in a laboratory. For example, to help them weather frosts better and produce a greater yield of crops, tomatoes might be spliced with salmon genes. Such genetically modified organisms, or GMOs, appear in many of the foods that U.S. consumers eat daily. The U.S. Food and Drug Administration does not require GMO food product labeling,[22] so legally, food manufacturers do not have to identify which of their products contain GMOs. Many consumers express a preference to know this information; they also have concerns about the potential negative health effects of GMOs. No available scientific evidence confirms these threats. Genetic modifications also increase crop yields for farmers and lower production costs. Avoiding a GMO label might help companies sell more of their products. Thus far, many food manufacturers seem to be fighting GMO labeling, as Marketing Analytics 4.1 describes. However, in 2014 General Mills decided to make some of its products, such as Cheerios, completely free of GMOs, and Whole Foods has committed to issuing labels, by 2018, on all GMO-containing foods it sells.[23]

In this example, the stakeholders have contrasting preferences and demands, and they are diverse—they include farmers, consumers, manufacturing companies, shareholders, retailers, and the environment. Let's consider five stakeholder categories in more depth to understand the meaning and effects of conscious marketing in the modern marketing arena, as well as how conscious marketing ultimately can benefit firms that undertake it.

Employees

Perhaps the most basic responsibility of a firm is to employees: to ensure a safe working environment free of threats to their physical safety, health, or well-being. In some cases, this basic level of safety seems insufficient to ensure responsibility to workers. For example, more firms today realize that happy employee families make happy and productive employees, so they are offering new benefits and options, such as on-site daycare[24] or flextime arrangements. When REI thought more consciously about its practices, it determined that living up to its higher purpose—that

Whole Foods has committed to issuing labels, by 2018, on all GMO-containing foods it sells.

© Ralph Barrera/MCT/Newscom.

Marketing Analytics **4.1**   How Kellogg's Uses Analytics to Address GMO Concerns[i]

Analytics are a valuable tool for helping manufacturers understand the relationship their customers have with their brands. For example, Kellogg's recently suffered its first sales and profit decreases in decades. The unprecedented drop in these key metrics prompted the company to decide to revamp its brand, cleanly and clearly. But what exactly did it need to change? Using advanced analytics, Kellogg's realized that one of its brands was getting creamed on social media: Reports showed that Kashi, which Kellogg's has promoted as an all-natural option, contained genetically modified organisms (GMOs). Consumers were furious, and they made their opinions clear on various social media.

In response, Kellogg's undertook a complete overhaul in an attempt to redefine its brands' core purpose. It consolidated its 42 separate company websites into a single umbrella site. And it made social media a focal point in its brand overhaul. To manage this social media reinvention, Kellogg's hired a computer whiz to serve as its director of digital and social-media strategy. The strategy first went into effect in the United Kingdom. To encourage trial of its Krave cereal, it released the hashtag "#KravetheSmiler," then awarded prizes to customers who used the hashtag. Throughout the campaign, Kellogg's constantly gathered data, including daily summaries of tweets that featured the hashtag, the daily top tweeters, how many tweets per hour they received, and so forth.

The well-planned campaign worked: Kellogg's received more than 35,000 tweets about Krave cereal. Using specially designed algorithms, Kellogg's could quickly and effectively comb through all the data and award prizes fairly and effectively.

Kellogg's used social media to introduce and gather data about its new Krave cereal.

© studiomode/Alamy

Although the campaign improved customer relations, the more important result might have been the way it provided Kellogg's with new insights and data. With this information, Kellogg's is likely to be able to replicate this success in other social media campaigns. For example, it could identify the products in which consumers would be willing to allow GMOs and those in which they absolutely would reject GMOs. Analytics also might show Kellogg's how to seed communication campaigns to give consumers accurate information about GMOs' actual threats and benefits. Thus far, though, its implementation of careful data-based strategies has boosted the return on investment for Kellogg's brands—in some cases, up to six times more than previous methods ever achieved.

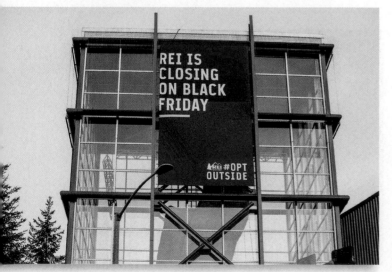

REI closes on Black Friday, the day after Thanksgiving, so its employees can enjoy time outdoors with their families.

© Suzi Pratt/Getty Images

is, helping people enjoy outdoor adventures—meant closing its stores on Thanksgiving and the day after, popularly known as Black Friday. Although closing meant that REI lost some sales, the conscious culture in the firm emphasized that employees should be enjoying time outdoors with their families too.[25]

Customers

Especially as changes in the marketing environment emerge, firms must consider the effects on their current customers as well as future customers they have targeted. Conscious marketing programs must take such shifts and trends into account and react to them quickly. Some trends receiving substantial attention in modern times include respecting and protecting privacy in an electronic world and ensuring the healthiness of products, especially those aimed at children. When conscious marketing takes on such pertinent issues, it often increases consumer awareness of the firm, which can lead to better brand equity and sales in the long run. The Walt Disney

Company appears to be a strong proponent: In one year, Disney gave more than $370 million to charity, and its employees donated 667,013 hours of their time through Disney's VoluntEAR program. Reflecting its higher purpose of ensuring the happiness and enjoyment of children, Disney has partnered with Give Kids the World, and its employees have renovated 88 vacation villas that the charitable organization offers to the families of children with life-threatening illnesses, so that they can take life-affirming vacations.[26]

Marketplace

When one firm in the industry leads the way toward conscious marketing, its partners and competitors often have no choice but to follow—or run the risk of not doing business or being left behind. To address issues such as global warming, water scarcity, and energy, GE uses a program it calls ecomagination. Reflecting the company's higher purpose, ecomagination encompasses a business strategy composed of four commitments: to double investments in clean research and development (R&D), increase revenues from ecomagination products, reduce greenhouse gas emissions, and inform the public about these issues.[27] The initiative for the program came from conscious leaders who recognized that the energy field had great potential to exert long-lasting effects on the world. When confronted with such initiatives, other energy companies are forced to

Walt Disney's VoluntEAR program is one of the best CSR programs in the world.

© Deshakalyan Chowdhury/Stringer/Getty Images

GE is the industry leader in CSR with its ecomagination program.

Source: General Electric Company

Adding Value **4.1**   Walmart Wants to Be the Corporate "Good Guy"[ii]

Walmart is known for its low prices and for driving its vendors nearly to tears to get them. Now it is pressuring its vendors to supply it with environmentally friendly merchandise with labels to prove it. In the future, merchandise sold at Walmart will have the environmental equivalent of nutrition labels, providing information on the product's carbon footprint, the amount of water and air pollution used to produce it, and other environmental issues. To measure how a vendor's products are doing, it has developed a sustainability index that simultaneously takes several issues into consideration. In particular, Walmart required its top 200 factories to cut their energy usage by 20 percent by 2012. Walmart achieved this amazing goal, reducing energy consumption by 2.168 billion kilowatt-hours, or the equivalent amount of energy that would be needed to power 1.46 million homes for a whole year.

It also has committed to buying more of the products it sells in its U.S. stores from U.S. suppliers, in an effort to address high unemployment rates. More directly, it has promised to hire up to 100,000 U.S. veterans, which will help address the job challenges many soldiers face upon leaving the military.

Nor has Walmart limited its efforts to the United States. It has sought to increase food safety in China, where the relatively underdeveloped infrastructure can create the danger of contamination of fresh and packaged food products. Walmart created a fleet of customized vans outfitted with the latest tools for conducting food safety inspections. The vans, staffed by trained specialists, deliver the "China Mobile Labs" to 33 stores throughout Guangzhou, Dongguan, and Shenzhen and ensure the safety and quality of the products they sell.

To reduce the use of plastic bags and thereby mitigate harm to the environment, Walmart has initiated several campaigns. In particular, plastic bag usage has dropped significantly throughout Asia—by 40 percent in Japan, 86 percent in China, and 90 percent in India.

Walmart has not always been touted as a good corporate citizen, though. In the 1990s, workers at some factories producing clothing for Walmart alleged that they had been

Why is Walmart attempting to position itself as the retail industry's sustainability leader?

Source: Walmart Corporation/Flickr/CC BY 2.0

subjected to inhumane conditions. More recently, two governmental organizations accused Walmart of buying from 15 factories that engage in abuse and labor violations, including child labor, 19-hour shifts, and below-subsistence wages. It and other companies have also been accused of dumping hazardous waste in Oklahoma City.

So why is Walmart attempting to position itself as the retail industry's sustainability leader? The initiatives and related publicity position Walmart as a good corporate citizen and thereby enhance its image. But the retail giant expects its moves to be good for business as well. Its customers, especially younger consumers, are increasingly concerned about how the products they use affect the environment and the people who produce them. Furthermore, Walmart believes that many of these initiatives can help streamline its supply chain processes and therefore provide additional financial benefits to its suppliers and customers.

make a decision: continue as they have been doing or adopt more responsible practices themselves. In either case, the initiating firm enjoys an advantage by gaining a reputation for being on the cutting edge of CSR efforts.

Society

Firms expend considerable time and energy engaging in activities aimed at improving the overall community and the physical environment, which suggests their increasing recognition of the importance of a broad range of varied stakeholders. According to a McKinsey & Co. survey, 95 percent of CEOs believe that society expects companies to take on public responsibilities.[28] Broader society, a key stakeholder, demands that companies act responsibly, and companies cannot ignore this. A firm that fails to act responsibly causes damage to all the preceding stakeholders as well as to itself. For example, reports that the artificial sweeteners in diet sodas might have ill effects, such as long-term weight gain and possible links to developing cancer, have led customers to alter their buying habits. Specifically, sales of diet soda have dropped 6.8 percent in a year, more than three times the decline in regular soda sales. Even though organizations such as the American Diabetic Association and the U.S. Food and Drug Administration have affirmed that diet sodas are safe, the broader shift in societal opinions demands that beverage companies seek new options. In particular, many companies are researching the potential use of stevia, a plant with naturally sweet properties, to replace the artificial versions.[29]

Environment

A special category that combines considerations of all these stakeholders is sustainability. According to the U.S. Environmental Protection Agency, "Sustainability is based on a simple principle: Everything that we need for our survival and well-being depends, either directly or indirectly, on our natural environment." Therefore, sustainable actions, including sustainable marketing, allow "humans and nature [to] exist in productive harmony, that permit fulfilling the social, economic and other requirements of present and future generations."[30] When marketing is truly sustainable, it can benefit all stakeholders: employees, customers, the marketplace, and society, as Adding Value 4.1 details in relation to Walmart's sustainability efforts. We discuss sustainable, or "green," marketing further in Chapter 5.

PROGRESS CHECK

1. What is the difference between conscious marketing and corporate social responsibility?
2. Provide a specific example of a conscious marketing firm that considers the needs of each of its stakeholders.

INTEGRATING CONSCIOUS MARKETING THROUGHOUT THE FIRM: LEADERSHIP AND CULTURE

 Explain how conscious leadership can produce a conscious culture in the firm.

For new firms founded on conscious marketing principles, their leaders, who are also their founders, establish the standard from the very start. But even if an existing firm seeks to move toward a conscious approach to marketing, it can adopt decision rules (as we discuss in the next section) and norms that encourage consciousness throughout its entire corporate culture. For example, to ensure that conscious marketing is infused into all levels of the firm, it can be integrated into each stage of the marketing plan (introduced in Chapter 2), as we detail here. In their constant pursuit of conscious marketing, firms can address relevant questions at each stage of the strategic marketing planning process. For instance, in the planning stage, the firm will decide what level of commitment to its ethical policies and standards it is willing to declare publicly and how the firm plans to balance the needs of its various stakeholders. In the implementation stage, the tone of the questions switches from "can we?" serve the market with the firm's products or services in a conscious marketing manner to "should we?" be engaging in particular marketing practices. The key task in the control phase is to ensure that all potential conscious marketing issues raised during the planning process have been addressed and that all employees of the firm have acted ethically.

Planning Phase

With strong leadership, marketers can introduce conscious marketing at the beginning of the planning process by including statements in the firm's mission or vision statements (recall our discussion of various mission statements in Chapter 2). For instance,

Since 1982, Newman's Own has given more than $400 million to charities like Newman's Hole in the Wall Gang camps for children with life-threatening diseases.

(left): © Food Collection/Alamy;
(right): © Lamperti Francois-Xavier/
Abaca/Newscom

Was it unethical for Grey Poupon to allow only those customers whom it considered to have Facebook posting history that was in good taste to "like" its Facebook page?

Source: Grey Poupon

the mission statement for natural skin care company Burt's Bees is to "create natural, Earth-friendly personal care products formulated to help you maximize your well-being and that of the world around you,"[31] which reflects not only what is good for its customers but for society in general.

For General Electric, the complexity of its organization and the wealth of ethical issues it faces necessitated an entire booklet, "The Spirit and the Letter." This booklet presents not only a statement of integrity from the CEO and a code of conduct, but also details policies for dealing with everything from international competition laws to security and crisis management to insider trading. In addition, GE publishes an annual citizenship report to determine the scope of its impacts, "produced for the benefit of all stakeholders, including GE employees—the people whose actions define GE every day."[32]

Newman's Own mission takes a fairly straightforward perspective: Its simple but powerful purpose was to sell salad dressing (initially; it expanded later to many other product lines) and use the proceeds to benefit charities. This simple idea began with the leadership of Paul Newman, the late actor who whipped up a batch of salad dressing to give as holiday gifts one year. When he and a friend decided to check with a local grocer to see if it would be interested in the product, they found they could sell 10,000 bottles in two weeks. Thus Newman's Own Foundation, the nonprofit organization, grew quickly; today, dozens of products with the Newman's Own and Newman's Own Organic brands are sold in countries around the world, from coffee to popcorn to dog food. Profits from Newman's Own—over $430 million since 1982—have been donated to thousands of charities, especially Newman's Hole in the Wall Gang camps for children with life-threatening diseases.[33] The unique mission of the company and the entrepreneurial flair of the founders, along with their conscious leadership, made this nonprofit a smashing, ongoing success. Employees of Newman's Own have the great satisfaction of giving back to society, various charities benefit from the donations, and customers enjoy good food with a clear conscience.

Implementation Phase

In the implementation phase of the marketing strategy, when firms are identifying potential markets and ways to deliver the four Ps to them, firms must consider several pertinent issues. Sometimes a firm's choice of target market and how it pursues it can lead to charges of unethical behavior. For instance, to "like" Grey Poupon's Facebook page, consumers had to apply through their Facebook app. This app then examined the customers' post history and decided whether each person had "good taste." If they had good taste, they could like the page; if not, they were not allowed to be part of, as Grey Poupon put it, "the most discerning page on Facebook." Although it may sound fun, several privacy issues challenged the ethics of the campaign and created threats to certain stakeholders, because users had to allow Grey Poupon to post on their timelines, and Grey Poupon gained open access to their post histories.[34]

Social & Mobile Marketing 4.1

How Mobile Phones and Payments Have Created a Viable New Market at the Bottom of the Pyramid[iii]

We might imagine that the greatest spread of mobile technology is among middle-class and wealthy consumers who demand the most advanced phones with innumerable gadgets and added features. But in truth, the biggest jumps might be coming from the opposite side of the economic divide—namely, from some of the poorest consumers in the world.

For people living in extreme poverty, basic, functional phones offer a vast opportunity for consumption. In sub-Saharan Africa for example, consumers rely on text messages to communicate with distant contacts, because texts are less expensive than phone calls.

More notably, mobile payment services allow these consumers to load as little as a dollar on their phones, which they can then use to pay for services that improve their quality of life. One woman described her ability to pay less than 50 cents daily to receive electricity from a solar panel provider. In the past, taking such small daily payments would have been too much work and too inefficient for the service provider. By linking to a mobile payment system, neither the consumer nor the supplier needs to engage in additional effort. And if the consumer isn't able to load enough onto her phone on one day, she can go without electricity until she can reload her mobile account with funds, without risk of harming her credit or losing access to her account. As one Kenyan investment firm, which helps poor consumers gain access to micro-insurance and savings plans, explains, "If you're taking a dollar off a million people, that's a reasonable revenue stream, but it wasn't possible to do that without the mobile phone."

Among these consumers, bank accounts are unusual, so the mobile payment systems allow them to load funds with the assistance of agents that work in local gas stations and stores. Once the funds are loaded, they can pay for groceries at the point of sale by tapping their phones, or they can send funds electronically. This latter functionality is critical, because for many Africans, making a trip to pay a bill might mean an entire day of lost labor due to travel times.

In sub-Saharan Africa, consumers rely on text messages to communicate with distant contacts, because texts are less expensive than phone calls.

© Jake Lyell/Alamy

These benefits have turned Africa into the source of some astounding innovations, especially for microbusiness concepts. Sub-Saharan Africa accounts for about 70 percent of the world's poor population, but nearly 65 percent of these households have access to at least one mobile phone. In addition, Africa is the fastest growing mobile market in the world.

Mobile payments are being introduced in other impoverished areas as well. India has a large impoverished population. Out of the 1.2 billion people living in the country, 600 million people do not have access to basic necessities such as drinking water and toilets. However, there are 1 billion cell phone subscribers in the country, making the number of people with access to a cell phone significantly higher than the number of those with bank accounts. To push for financial inclusion of the impoverished population, a network is being put in place to allow for digital payments possible across the country.

In other situations, an implementation can have unforeseen benefits. A conscious marketer might predict some of those benefits, but as Social and Mobile Marketing 4.1 explains, sometimes positive situations that arise for an entire population can lead to more conscious practices by firms.

Once the strategy is implemented, controls must be in place to be certain that the firm has actually done what it has set out to do. These activities take place in the next phase of the strategic marketing planning process: the control phase.

Control Phase

During the control phase of the strategic marketing planning process, managers must be evaluated on their actions from a conscious marketing perspective. Systems must be in place to check whether each conscious marketing issue raised in the planning process was actually successfully addressed. Systems used in the control phase must also react to change. The emergence of new technologies and new markets ensures that new potentially troubling issues continually arise. In particular, people expect to be able to move normally in public spaces without their location being recorded for subsequent use. Yet marketers regularly collect data on people's location through purchase transactions and posts on social and mobile sites such as Facebook, Twitter, and Flickr. Additionally, several retailers' credit card systems have been violated, resulting in the theft of consumer data of millions of people, the most egregious of which were the estimated 110 million at Target and 1.1 million at Neiman Marcus at the end of 2013.[35] Although most experts blamed the thefts on U.S.-based credit card companies' reticence to adopt a more secure type of credit card that is used in Europe and elsewhere, the retailers and their customers suffer the consequences.

Many firms have emergency response plans in place just in case they ever encounter a crisis that would negatively impact its conscious marketing philosophy. Conscious marketers adopt such contingency plans from the start, reflecting their conscious leadership and conscious culture. In this sense, conscious marketing remains an ongoing crucial component of the strategic marketing planning process and should be incorporated into all the firm's decision making down the road.

PROGRESS CHECK

1. What ethical questions should a marketing manager consider at each stage of the marketing plan?

LO4-6 Describe how ethics constitute an integral part of a firm's conscious marketing strategy.

MARKETING ETHICS AS A CONSCIOUS MARKETING PRINCIPLE

Decision making according to conscious marketing might sound easy, but as this chapter has shown, it is often difficult to balance the needs and preferences of various stakeholders. A key component for making any conscious marketing decision can be very personal in that individuals must decide whether their actions are right or wrong based on their moral principles. In other words, are they making ethically correct decisions? As noted earlier in this chapter, like CSR, marketing ethics is an integral component of a conscious marketing initiative. To begin our discussion, we examine the nature of ethical and unethical marketing decisions and the difference between marketing ethics and CSR.

The Nature of Ethical and Unethical Marketing Decisions

People are expected to know what is and is not ethical behavior based on their ability to distinguish right from wrong in a particular culture. Consider product recalls of toys, for example. How can certain manufacturers engage in such egregious behavior as using lead paint on toys or including magnets that can be swallowed in toys marketed toward young children? What makes people take actions that create so much harm? Are all the individuals who contributed to that behavior just plain unethical?

There are no ready answers to such philosophical questions. But when asked in a survey whether they had seen any unethical behavior among their colleagues, chief marketing officers responded that they had observed employees participating in high-pressure, misleading, or deceptive sales tactics (45 percent); misrepresenting company earnings, sales, and/or revenues (35 percent); withholding or destroying information that could hurt company sales or image (32 percent); and conducting false or misleading advertising (31 percent).[36] Did all the marketers in these situations view their actions as unethical? Probably not. There may have been extenuating circumstances. In marketing, managers often face the choice of doing what is beneficial for them and possibly the firm in the short run and taking a conscious marketing perspective by doing what is right and beneficial for the firm and society in the long run.

For instance, a manager might feel confident that earnings will increase in the next few months and therefore believe it benefits himself, his branch, his employees, and his shareholders to exaggerate current earnings just a little. Another manager might feel considerable pressure to increase sales in a retail store, so she brings in some new merchandise, marks it at an artificially high price, and then immediately puts it on sale, deceiving consumers into thinking they are getting a good deal because they view the initial price as the real price. These decisions may have been justifiable at the time and to some stakeholders, but they have serious long-term consequences for the company and are therefore not in concert with a conscious marketing approach.

What is the "real" price? Did the manager bring the T-shirts in at an artificially high level and then immediately mark them down?

© Dennis MacDonald/PhotoEdit

To avoid such potentially unethical behaviors, conscious marketing seeks to align the short-term goals of each employee with the long-term, overriding goals of the firm. To align personal and corporate goals, firms need to have a strong ethical climate exemplified by the actions of corporate leaders and filtered through an ethically based corporate culture. There should be explicit rules for governing transactions; these rules should include a code of ethics and a system for rewarding and punishing inappropriate behavior. The American Marketing Association (AMA) provides a detailed, multipronged "Statement of Ethics" that can serve as a foundation for marketers, emphasizing that "As marketers . . . we not only serve our organizations but also act as stewards of society in creating, facilitating and executing the transactions that are part of the greater economy."[37]

Ethics and Corporate Social Responsibility

Although both fall under the conscious marketing umbrella, it is important to distinguish between ethical marketing practices and corporate social responsibility programs. When a firm embraces conscious marketing, it implements programs that are socially responsible, and its employees act in an ethically responsible manner. (See Exhibit 4.4, upper left quadrant.) None of the other quadrants in Exhibit 4.4 embodies conscious marketing principles.

A firm's employees may conduct their activities in an ethically acceptable manner, but it may not be considered socially responsible, because its activities have little or no impact

EXHIBIT 4.4   Ethics versus Social Responsibility

on anyone other than its closest stakeholders: its customers, employees, and stockholders. It does not engage in programs that better society or the environment as a whole (Exhibit 4.4, upper right quadrant).

Employees at firms that are perceived as socially responsible can nevertheless take actions that are viewed as unethical (Exhibit 4.4, lower left quadrant). For instance, a firm might be considered socially responsible because it makes generous donations to charities, but if it is simultaneously involved in questionable sales practices it cannot be seen as ethical. The worst situation, of course, is when firms behave both unethically and in a socially unacceptable manner (Exhibit 4.4, lower right quadrant).

Customers may be willing to pay more if they can be assured the companies truly are ethical.[38] According to a poll conducted by *Time* magazine, even in economically constrained settings, 38 percent of U.S. consumers actively tried to purchase from companies they considered responsible. The magazine cites the rise of the "ethical consumer" and the evolution of the social contract "between many Americans and businesses about what goes into making the products we buy."[39]

Embracing conscious marketing is one way to enforce this social contract. However, even in the most conscious of firms, individual members may face challenges in their efforts to act ethically. Therefore, a framework for ethical decision making can help move people to work toward common ethical goals.

LO4-7 Identify the four steps in ethical decision making.

A Framework for Ethical Decision Making

Exhibit 4.5 outlines a simple framework for ethical decision making. Let's consider each of the steps.

Step 1: Identify Issues   The first step is to identify the issue. Imagine the use (or misuse) of data collected from consumers by a marketing research firm. One of the issues that might arise is the way the data are collected. For instance, are the respondents told about the real purpose of the study? Another issue might be whether the results will be used in a way that might mislead or even harm the public, such as selling the information to a firm to use in soliciting the respondents.

Step 2: Gather Information and Identify Stakeholders   In this step, the firm focuses on gathering facts that are important to the ethical issue, including all relevant legal information. To get a complete picture, the firm must identify all the individuals and groups that have a stake in how the issue is resolved.

As we detailed previously, stakeholders typically include the firm's employees, suppliers, the government, customer groups, stockholders, and members of the community in which the firm operates. Beyond these, many firms now also analyze the needs of the industry and the global community, as well as one-off stakeholders such as future generations and the natural environment. In describing its sustainability and transparency efforts, for example, the electronics firm Philips notes that it tries to communicate with and consider "anyone with an interest in Philips."[40]

Step 3: Brainstorm Alternatives   After the marketing firm has identified the stakeholders and their issues and gathered the available data, all parties relevant to the

EXHIBIT 4.5   Ethical Decision-Making Framework

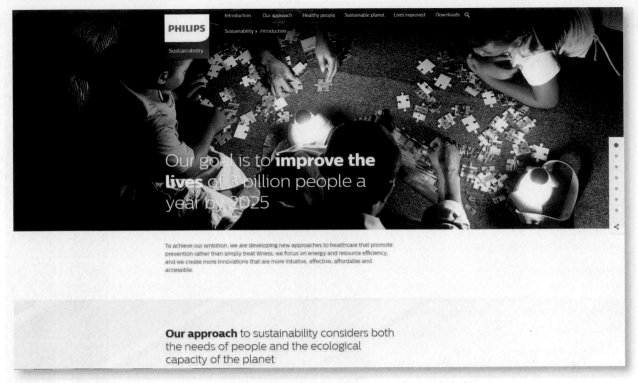

With its sustainability and transparency efforts, Philips takes a global view of its stakeholders.
Source: Philips

decision should come together to brainstorm any alternative courses of action. In our example, these might include halting the market research project, making responses anonymous, instituting training on the AMA Code of Ethics for all researchers, and so forth. The company leaders and managers then can review and refine these alternatives, leading to the final step.

Step 4: Choose a Course of Action
The objective of this last step is to weigh the various alternatives and choose a course of action that generates the best solution for the stakeholders, using ethical practices based on a conscious marketing approach. Management—ideally, conscious leaders—rank the alternatives in order of preference, clearly establishing the advantages and disadvantages of each. It is also crucial to investigate any potential legal issues associated with each alternative. Of course, any illegal activity should be rejected immediately.

To choose the appropriate course of action, marketing managers will evaluate each alternative by using a process something like the sample ethical decision-making metric in Exhibit 4.6. The conscious marketer's task here is to ensure that he or she has applied all relevant decision-making criteria and to assess his or her level of confidence that the decision being made meets those stated criteria. If the marketer isn't confident about the decision, he or she should reexamine the other alternatives. Using Exhibit 4.6, you can gauge your own ethical response. If your scores tend to be in the "Yes" area (columns 1 and 2), then the situation is not ethically troubling for you. If, in contrast, your scores tend to be in the "No" area (columns 6 and 7), it is ethically troubling, and you know it. If your scores are scattered or are in the "Maybe" area (columns 3, 4, and 5), you need to step back and reflect on how you wish to proceed. In using such an ethical metric or framework, decision makers must consider the relevant ethical issues, evaluate the alternatives, and then choose a course of action that will help them avoid serious ethical lapses.

Next, let's illustrate how the ethical decision-making metric in Exhibit 4.6 can be used to make ethical business decisions.

EXHIBIT 4.6 Ethical Decision-Making Metric

Test	Decision						
	Yes		Maybe			No	
	1	2	3	4	5	6	7
The Publicity Test Would I want to see this action that I'm about to take described on the front page of the local paper or in a national magazine?							
The Moral Mentor Test Would the person I admire the most engage in this activity?							
The Admired Observer Test Would I want the person I admire most to see me doing this?							
The Transparency Test Could I give a clear explanation for the action I'm contemplating, including an honest and transparent account of all my motives, that would satisfy a fair and dispassionate moral judge?							
The Person in the Mirror Test Will I be able to look at myself in the mirror and respect the person I see there?							
The Golden Rule Test Would I like to be on the receiving end of this action and all its potential consequences?							

Source: Adapted from The Art of Achievement: Mastering the 7 Cs of Business and Life. © *2002 by Tom Morris, published by Andrews McMeel Publishing LLC, an Andrews McMeel Universal company, Kansas City, Missouri.*

Myra Jansen, the head cook at Lincoln High School in Anytown, USA, has had enough. Reports showing that children rarely eat enough vegetables have combined with studies that indicate school kids have a limited amount of time to eat their lunches. The combination has led to increasing obesity rates and troublesome reports about the long-term effects. Myra has therefore decided that the Tater Tots and hot dogs are out. Vegetables and healthy proteins are in.

If schools want children to eat more healthy foods, should they switch to healthier options without telling them, or tell them even though the children might reject the changes?

© Citizen of the Planet/Alamy

The problem, of course, is getting the kids to eat raw vegetables, plant proteins, and lean meat. For many teenagers, recommending that they eat healthy food at lunch is akin to calling detention a play date. But Myra has a plan: She's going to reformulate various menu items using different ingredients and just never tell the students. Thus the regular hot dogs will be replaced with turkey or soy dogs. The Tater Tots will contain the more nutrient-dense sweet potatoes instead of the vitamin-deficient regular spuds they used to be made out of. She is convinced she can make such switches for most of the menu items, and none of the children need to know.

Most of the kitchen staff members are on board with the idea and even have suggested other possible menu switches that would benefit the students by ensuring that they receive a well-balanced meal at school. School board members, when apprised of the idea, got very excited and praised Myra for her innovative thinking. But the community liaison for the school, Salim Jones, whose job it is to communicate with parents and other members of the community, is not so sure. Salim is nervous about how students will react when they learn that they have been deceived. He also has two small children of his own, one of whom has a severe wheat allergy. Thus the Joneses are extremely cautious about eating out, always asking for a detailed, specific list of ingredients for anything they order.

Using his training in ethical decision making, Salim sits down to evaluate his alternatives, beginning with identifying possible options available to the school district as well as the various stakeholders who might be affected by the decision. He comes up with the following list:

1. Switch out the food without telling students.

2. Leave menus as they are.

3. Switch out the food ingredients but also tell students exactly what is in each item in the cafeteria.

To make a clear recommendation to the board about what would be the best ethical choice, Salim decides to evaluate each alternative using a series of questions similar to those in Exhibit 4.6.

Question 1: Would I want to see this action described on the front page of the local paper? The school board's reaction caused Salim to think that the larger community would appreciate the effort to improve students' health. Thus, option 1 appears best for these stakeholders, and possibly for society, which may reduce the prevalence of obesity among these students. However, he shudders to think about how angry students might be if they learned they had been tricked. They also likely are accustomed to their menu as it is, and therefore, they would prefer option 2.

Question 2: Would the person I admire most engage in this activity, and would I want him or her to see me engage in this activity? For most of his life, Salim has held up Mahatma Gandhi as his ideal for how to act in the world. For Gandhi, truth was an absolute concept, not something that could be changed depending on the situation. Therefore, Salim believes Gandhi would strongly disapprove of option 1. However, Gandhi also worried about the ethics of eating and avoided food choices that had negative effects on society, so he might reject option 2 as well.

Question 3: Can I give a clear explanation for my action, including an honest account of my motives? In thinking about his children, Salim realizes that he is prioritizing their needs more than he is the needs of other children, such as those who struggle with weight issues. That is, he worries that his daughter might unknowingly be exposed to wheat in a school cafeteria, so he prefers option 3.

Question 4: Will I be able to look at myself in the mirror and respect what I see? By bringing up the ethics of this decision, even when it seems as if everyone else has agreed with it, Salim feels confident that he has taken the right first step. The option chosen is still important, but it is a group decision, and Salim thinks he is doing his part.

Question 5: Would I want to be on the receiving end of this action and its conse-quences? Salim struggles most with this question. He remembers the kind of junk foods he chose when he was in college and the 20 pounds he put on as a result. He wishes now that his parents had given him rules to follow about what to eat at school. But he also remembers how rebellious he was and knows that he probably would not have followed those rules. And at the same time, he hates the idea that someone could give him food to eat with falsified ingredients.

On the basis of this exercise, Salim decides that he wants to recommend option 3 to the school board. When he does so, Myra Jansen protests loudly: "This is ridiculous! I know better what kids should be eating, and I know too that some community liaison has no idea what they are willing to eat. You've got to trick them to get them to eat right." Another school board member agrees, noting, "They're just kids. They don't necessarily have the same rights as adults, so we are allowed to decide what's best for them. And hiding the healthy ingredients to get the kids to eat healthy foods is what's best."

So what does the school board decide?

PROGRESS CHECK

1. Identify the steps in the ethical decision-making framework

Reviewing Learning Objectives

 Define conscious marketing

Conscious marketing involves a sense of purpose for the firm that is more than simply making a profit by selling products and services. It consists of four main principles: a greater purpose, consideration of stake-holders, conscious leadership and culture, and ethics.

 Describe what constitutes marketing's greater purpose.

Marketers must recognize that the purpose of busi-ness is more than making profits. The actual pur-pose might vary, such as providing necessary products, ensuring employment opportunities, or achieving greener production methods, but in all of these cases, the engagement improves the inputs as well as the outcomes of marketing actions.

 Differentiate between conscious marketing and corporate social responsibility.

Although CSR is an important element of conscious marketing, they are different from one another. CSR implies a focus on the triple bottom-line of good performance according to economic, environmental, and social criteria. Thus good CSR can support and

help promote conscious marketing. But conscious marketing goes beyond just CSR to refer to the over-all meaning and purpose of the company and its marketing.

 Describe the ways in which conscious marketing helps various stakeholders.

To describe the ways, we first have to identify the various stakeholders of a company—namely, cus-tomers, employees, the marketplace, society, and the environment:

- *Customers:* When companies exhibit con-scious marketing principles, customers know that they can trust the firms to provide healthy, ethically acceptable products and services. Many customers also feel better about buying from a company that engages in responsible practices, which provides them with the addi-tional value of feeling good about buying from that company.

- *Employees:* A firm committed to conscious marketing treats its employees with decency and respect. For many employees, working for an irresponsible firm would be antithetical to their own morals and values.

- *Marketplace:* An industry improves its practices and avoids scandals when it ensures that the participating firms act responsibly and appropriately in all areas.
- *Society:* This stakeholder is local, national, or global communities who benefit when conscious marketers give thought to how their practices might influence values or connections, such as providing aid to underprivileged communities.
- *Environmental Sustainability.* The benefits of conscious marketing might include cleaner air and water as well as healthier product options.

LO4-5 Explain how conscious leadership can produce a conscious culture in the firm.

Conscious marketing should be integrated into the very foundation of the firm by its leaders, such as in the firm's mission statement. Then top management must follow through and commit to supporting CSR, a strong ethical climate in the organization, and conscious marketing principles. When considering their strategy, conscious marketing firms ask not only "can we implement a certain policy?" but also "should we do it?" If any action is not ethical or socially responsible, the conscious firm will make changes to its marketing strategy.

LO4-6 Describe how ethics constitute an integral part of a firm's conscious marketing strategy.

Being a part of an ethically responsible firm should be important to every employee, but it is particularly important to marketers because they interact most directly with customers and suppliers and make decisions about how their products impact society and the environment. Thus marketing issues present a multitude of ethical questions and opportunities to handle.

LO4-7 Identify the four steps in ethical decision making.

First, firms can include ethics and social responsibility in their corporate mission. Second, they should institute policies and procedures to ensure that everyone working for the firm is acting in an ethically responsible manner. Third, firms can model their ethical policies after a well-established code of ethics like the one provided by the American Marketing Association. Fourth, when making ethically sensitive decisions, firms can utilize a metric such as the ethical decision-making metric in Exhibit 4.6.

Key Terms

- business ethics, 120
- conscious marketing, 119
- corporate social responsibility (CSR), 121
- marketing ethics, 120
- stakeholders, 119
- triple bottom line, 121

Marketing Digitally

1. Perhaps no subdiscipline of marketing receives more scrutiny regarding ethical compliance than does direct marketing, a form of nonstore retailing in which customers are exposed to and purchase merchandise or services through an impersonal medium such as telephone, mail, or the Internet.[41] Ethical issues in direct marketing cover a broad spectrum because this means of selling is conducted through all forms of communication. The Direct Marketing Association (DMA) takes ethics very seriously and has numerous programs to ensure that its member organizations comply with its Code of Ethics. Go to the website for the DMA (http://www.the-dma.org/).

   Click on "Advocacy." List the different ways that the DMA is involved in assisting consumers and the industry to create a more ethical marketplace.

2. An increasing number of firms are stating their strong commitment to corporate social responsibility initiatives. The Corporate Social Responsibility Newswire Service keeps track of these various initiatives and posts stories on its website about what various corporations are doing. Go to http://www.csrwire.com/ and choose one story. Write a description of the corporation and the initiative.

Marketing Applications

1. Distinguish among conscious marketing, CSR, and marketing ethics.

2. Develop an argument for why a cosmetics manufacturer should build and maintain an ethical climate.

3. A clothing company gives generously to charities and sponsors donation drives to help lower-income teen girls get reasonably priced prom dresses. It also locates its manufacturing plants in countries with few labor laws, such that it does not know whether children are working in its factories, and works to prevent union activity among its employees in the United States. Evaluate this company from an ethical and social responsibility perspective.

4. Based on the evaluation you developed for Question 3, provide responses to the ethical decision-making metric from Exhibit 4.6. Provide a rationale for your score for each question.

5. A company that makes vitamin-infused drinks and other "healthy" snacks has the following mission statement: "Our goal is to profitably sell good-tasting, healthy products and to better society." Although its products are organic, they also are relatively high in sugar and calories. The company gives a small portion of its profits to the United Way. Evaluate its mission statement in terms of the four principles of conscious marketing.

6. Choose a company that you believe is particularly adept at conscious marketing that is not discussed in this chapter. How do you justify your choice? What counterarguments might someone make to suggest that your chosen company is not responsible? Consider all key stakeholders in developing both sides of the argument.

Quiz Yourself

1. As noted in your text, which of the following ranks as the top unethical behavior by employees as reported by chief marketing officers?
   a. Misrepresenting company earnings.
   b. Withholding information that could hurt the company's image.
   c. Participating in misleading or deceptive sales tactics.
   d. Conducting false or misleading advertising.
   e. Misrepresenting company sales figures.

2. A firm makes generous donations to charities, but its employees are always being scrutinized for engaging in questionable sales practices. This firm would be considered:
   a. Ethical but socially irresponsible.
   b. Ethical and socially responsible.
   c. Unethical but socially responsible.
   d. Unethical and socially irresponsible.
   e. Neither ethical nor socially responsible.

(Answers to these two questions can be found in the Quiz Yourself Answer Key section.)

Chapter Case Study

IS THERE AN APP FOR GOOD PARENTING?

If you've gone to a mall or family restaurant recently, it's likely that you have seen children playing games or watching videos on tablets. Whereas it used to be difficult to get children to behave in stores or at restaurants, parents are finding that a tablet or smartphone can be an effective babysitter. Manufacturers have picked up on this trend and offer several tablets designed specifically for kids: Samsung has the Galaxy Tab 3 Kids Edition, LeapFrog sells the LeapPad3 PowerLearning Tablet, nabi provides the nabi 2, and Amazon has the Fire Kids Edition, to name just a few.

Producing and selling technology for kids has proven to be a profitable business. But when is it too much technology? Both the American Academy of Pediatrics and the Mayo Clinic urge parents to not allow children younger than two years of age to interact with any device with a screen (television, computer, tablet), out of concern that it will have negative effects on children's brain development, including possible language delays and damage to their social, emotional, and cognitive skills.[42] Furthermore, research has shown that increased "screen time" (defined as the number of hours children spend interacting with any device with an electronic screen) leads to increased risks of obesity, irregular sleep, behavioral problems, and impaired academic performance.

Despite such warnings, companies continue to produce technology products geared toward younger and younger children.[43] One of the latest is Fisher-Price's Newborn-to-Toddler Apptivity Seat[44]—essentially a small chair for newborns, with a bar that hangs an iPad a few inches from the child's face. As might be expected, the introduction prompted a massive outcry from child advocacy groups such as the Campaign for a Commercial-Free Childhood (CCFC), which filed complaints with the Federal Trade Commission about claims Fisher-Price has posted on its website asserting that the chair, in concert with a tablet, actually helps babies' brain development.

Fisher-Price's response? It has added a "note to customers" on the product's web page. After suggesting that parents limit their children's screen time, it goes on to state, "we realize this type of technology in infant products isn't for everyone. That's why our Apptivity Seat is just one of more than a dozen baby seats we make, giving parents lots of choices with the options they prefer for their family's lifestyle."[45]

The company is not alone in its efforts. With the 2-in-1 iPotty, CTA Digital suggests that parents affix their tablet to their children's potty-training seats. Then the children can play with an app or watch a video while learning how to use the potty—often a challenging task for parents as well as children. Since its introduction, the potty seat has been extremely popular, becoming one of the company's top-selling products.[46]

The offerings also do not stop at products. Mattel (the parent company of Fisher-Price) has developed a suite of iPad Apptivity apps, available for free to parents who buy the seat. The early development content shows high-contrast patterns, so babies' young eyes can follow them, and features soothing sounds of nature. For slightly older children, the app advances to introduce numbers and letters. Each visual presentation times out after 10 to 12 minutes.

On an even more advanced level, Netflix has expanded its line of self-produced content, beyond fan favorites such as *Arrested Development* or *Orange Is the New Black,* to include series for children.[47] By appealing to young consumers, Netflix hopes to increase the loyalty of the entire household, reasoning that parents are unlikely to cancel their subscription if Netflix is the only place kids can get the latest episodes of some of their favorite shows.

For parents, innovative products for children can be a lifesaver: They keep kids entertained, help with potty training, and offer a convenient distraction. Moreover, many parents today already rely heavily on tablets and other screens for their own purposes, making it difficult for them to avoid screen time for their children. In this sense, companies are merely providing the products and services that parents, and their children, want.

Although parents may want devices that keep their children entertained, screen time at such a young age may be harmful to children's cognitive development.

© Minneapolis Star Tribune/Zumapress/ Newscom

Questions

1. Who benefits from products designed to give children and babies more screen time? Who is harmed?

2. Who has a greater ethical responsibility in relation to children and screen time: companies or parents? Present arguments for both sides.

Endnotes

1. TOMS, "Our Movement," http://www.toms.com/our-movement; Andrew Adam Newman, "'Buy One, Give One' Spirit Imbues an Online Store," *Los Angeles Times,* November 4, 2013.

2. TOMS, "Home Page," http://www.toms.com/?cid=mozilla_suggested&utm_medium=suggested&utm_source=mozilla&utm_campaign=retail_apparel1.

3. TOMS, "What We Give: The Gift of Water," http://www.toms.com/what-we-give-water.

4. TOMS, "What We Give: Safe Births," http://www.toms.com/what-we-give-safe-births.

5. TOMS, "What We Give: Preventing Bullying," http://www.toms.com/what-we-give-preventing-bullying.

6. TOMS, "The TOMS Animal Initiative," http://www.toms.com/the-toms-animal-initiative.

7. George Anderson, "Toms Offers a Different Way to Shop," *Retail Wire,* November 6, 2013.

8. TOMS, "Corporate Responsibility," http://www.toms.com/corporate-responsibility.

9. Theodore Levitt, *Marketing Imagination* (Detroit, MI: Free Press, 1983).

10. See John Mackey and Raj Sisodia, *Conscious Capitalism: Liberating the Heroic Spirit of Business* (Boston, MA: Harvard Business Review Press, 2014).

11. The first three principles draw on Raj Sisodia, "Conscious Capitalism: A Better Way to Win," *California Management Review* 53 (Spring 2011), pp. 98–108.

12. Gene R. Laczniak and Patrick E. Murphy, "Stakeholder Theory and Marketing: Moving from a Firm-Centric to a Societal Perspective," *Journal of Public Policy & Marketing* 31 (Fall 2012), pp. 284–92.

13. Stephanie Strom, "Walmart Pushes for Improved Animal Welfare," *The New York Times,* May 22, 2015.

14. Andrew Khouri and Samantha Masunaga, "Tesla's Elon Musk and His Big Ideas: A Brief History," *Los Angeles Times,* May 1, 2015.

15. The most famous proponent of this view was Milton Friedman. See, for example, *Capitalism and Freedom* (Chicago: University of Chicago Press, 2002); or *Free to Choose: A Personal Statement* (Orlando, FL: Harcourt, 1990).

16. For a broad discussion of the range of CSR definitions, see "Communicating Corporate Social Responsibility," University Catholique de Louvain, https://www.edx.org/course/communicating-corporate-social-louvainx-louv12x.

17. H. Aguinis, "Organizational Responsibility: Doing Good and Doing Well," in *APA Handbook of Industrial and Organizational Psychology,* Vol. 3, S. Zedeck, ed. (Washington, DC: American Psychological Association, 2011), pp. 855–79.

18. For a collection of articles discussing such challenges, see the "Special Issue on Corporate Social Responsibility in Controversial Industry Sectors," *Journal of Business Ethics* 110, no. 4 (November 2012).

19. Thomas C. Frohlich, Michael B. Sauter, and Sam Stebbins, "Companies Paying Americans the Least," 247WallSt.com, September 3, 2015.

20. Thomas C. Frohlich, Michael B. Sauter, and Sam Stebbins, "Companies Paying Americans the Least," 247WallSt.com, September 3, 2015.

21. This table was adapted from John Mackey and Rajendra Sisodia, (2013), *Conscious Capitalism: Liberating the Heroic Spirit of Business* (Boston MA: Harvard Business Review Press).

22. U.S. Food and Drug Administration, "Guidance for Industry: Voluntary Labeling Indicating Whether Foods Have or Have Not Been Derived from Genetically Engineered Plants," November 2015, http://www.fda.gov/food/guidanceregulation/guidancedocumentsregulatoryinformation/ucm059098.htm.

23. Laura Parker, "The GMO Labeling Battle Is Heating Up—Here's Why," *National Geographic,* January 11, 2014; Stefanie Strom, "Major Grocer to Label Foods with Gene-Modified Content," *The New York Times,* March 8, 2013; Amy Harmon and Andrew Pollack, "Battle Brewing over Labeling of Genetically Modified Food," *The New York Times,* May 24, 2012.

24. Rana Florida, "The Case for On-Site Day Care," *Fast Company,* October 1, 2014.

25. Aaron Katersky and Susannah Kim, "Slew of Retailers Say No to Black Friday," *ABC News,* October 27, 2015.

26. https://thewaltdisneycompany.com/blog/infographic-disneys-charitable-giving-reaches-370-million-2013; http://disneyparks.disney.go.com/blog/galleries/2014/01/disney-cast-members-create-an-extreme-village-makeover-for-give-kids-the-world/#photo-5.

27. http://www.ge.com/news/our_viewpoints/energy_and_climate.html; "GE Launches New Ecomagination Healthcare Products, Opens Renewable Energy HQ," *GreenBiz,* February 2, 2010, http://www.greenbiz.com.

28. D.B. Bielak, S. Bonini, and J.M. Oppenheim, "CEOs on Strategy and Social Issues," *McKinsey Quarterly,* 2007, http://www.mckinseyquarterly.com.

29. United Press International, "Diet Soda Sales: Flat Would Be Better," December 9, 2013, http://www.upi.com.

30. U.S. Environmental Protection Agency, "What Is Sustainability?," http://www.epa.gov/sustainability/basicinfo.htm.

31. http://www.burtsbees.com.

32. See for example General Electric, "2014 Performance," http://www.gecitizenship.com; General Electric, "The Spirit and the Letter," http://integrity.ge.com.

33. http://newmansownfoundation.org.

34. Ross Wilson, "The Best and Worst of Facebook 2012," *Ignite Social Media,* December 13, 2012, http://www.ignitesocialmedia.com.

35. Elizabeth A. Harris, Nicole Perlroth, and Nathaniel Popper, "Neiman Marcus Data Breach Worse Than First Said," *The New York Times,* January 23, 2014.

36. http://www.cmomagazine.com. This survey was conducted in 2006; more recent reports suggest that 41 percent of respondents to a 2013 survey reported having seen ethical misconduct overall, and 26 percent of these general employees considered the misconduct to represent a repeated pattern of behavior. See Ethics Resource Center, "2013 National Business Ethics Survey," http://www.ethics.org.

37. American Marketing Association, "Statement of Ethics," April 8, 2014, https://archive.ama.org/archive/AboutAMA/Pages/Statement%20of%20Ethics.aspx.

38. Nielsen, "Global Customers Are Willing to Put Their Money Where Their Heart Is When It Comes to Goods and Services Committed to Social Responsibility," June 17, 2014, http://www.nielsen.com/us/en/press-room/2014/global-consumers-are-willing-to-put-their-money-where-their-heart-is.html; Michael

Connor, "Survey: U.S. Consumers Willing to Pay for Corporate Responsibility," *Business Ethics,* March 29, 2010, http://business-ethics.com.

39. Richard Stengel, "Doing Well by Doing Good," *Time,* September 10, 2009, http://www.time.com. More recent surveys affirm this consumer preference too. See for example, "2015 Cone Communications/Ebiquity Global CSR Survey," http://www.conecomm.com/2015-global-csr-study.

40. "2011 World's Most Ethical Companies," *Ethisphere,* http://ethisphere.com/2011-worlds-most-ethical-companies.

41. http://www.marketingpower.com/_layouts/Dictionary.aspx.

42. See http://www.mayoclinic.org/children-and-tv/art-20047952.

43. Cecilia Kang, "Infant iPad Seats Raise Concerns about Screen Time for Babies," *The Washington Post,* December 10, 2013.

44. http://www.fisher-price.com/img/product_shots/X7045-newborn-to-toddler-apptivity-seat-d-2.jpg.

45. http://www.fisher-price.com/en_US/brands/babygear/products/78030.

46. Kang, "Infant iPad Seats Raise Concerns about Screen Time for Babies."

47. "Dreamworks Animation to Create Netflix's First Original Kids' Show," *Advertising Age,* February 12, 2013.

i. Hannah Tregear, "Case Study/Kellogg's: Kellogg's Boosts Social Media Campaign ROI," *Brandwatch,* November 23, 2013, http://www.brandwatch.com/wp-content/uploads/2013/11/Brandwatch_CS_Kelloggs.pdf; Jennifer Rooney, "Kellogg's Completes Major Brand Overhaul," *Forbes,* May 10, 2012, http://www.forbes.com/; E.J. Schultz, "Media Maven Bob Arnold Leads Kellogg Into Digital-Buying Frontier," *Advertising Age,* September 23, 2013, http://adage.com/; Larisa Bedgood, "5 Compelling Reasons to Ramp Up Your Digital Marketing Strategy," *SmartData Collective,* March 18, 2015, http://smartdatacollective.com/lbedgood/305186/5-compelling-reasons-ramp-your-digital-marketing-strategy.

ii. "Walmart Energy Efficiency Program Achieves Energy Savings of 20% across 210 Supplier Factories in China," *PR Newswire,* April 22, 2013; Jessica Wohl, "Walmart Announces $50 Billion Buy American Campaign," *The Huffington Post,* January 15, 2013; "Walmart Launches Major Initiative to Make Food Healthier and Healthier Food More Affordable," http://walmartstores.com.

iii. Heidi Vogt, "Making Change: Mobile Pay in Africa," *The Wall Street Journal,* January 2, 2015; Leslie Shaffer, "Consumer Companies Struggle to Tap Aspirational Middle-Class India," *CNBC,* November 25, 2015, http://www.cnbc.com/2015/11/25/consumer-companies-struggle-to-tap-aspirational-middle-class-india.html; "How Digital Revolution Can Push Financial Inclusion," *CNBC,* December 7, 2015, http://www.moneycontrol.com/news/economy/how-digital-revolution-can-push-financial-inclusion_4472241.html.

APPENDIX 4A

UNDERSTANDING ETHICS USING SCENARIOS

I n this appendix, we present nine ethical scenarios designed to assist you in developing your skills at identifying ethical issues. There is no one right answer to the dilemmas below, just as there will be no correct answers to many of the ethical situations you will face throughout your career. Instead, these scenarios can help you develop your ethical reasoning skills as well as your sensitivity toward ethical issues. As mentioned throughout the chapter, Exhibit 4.4 provides an ethical decision-making metric to assist you in evaluating the following and all such ethical dilemmas you may face.

Scenario 1: R.J. Reynolds: Promotions to the Youth Market

Tobacco giant R.J. Reynolds sent a set of coasters featuring its cigarette brands and recipes for mixed drinks with high alcohol content to young adults, via direct mail, on their 21st birthdays (the legal age for alcohol consumption). The alcohol brands in the recipes included Jack Daniels, Southern Comfort, and Finlandia Vodka. The reverse side of the coaster read, "Go 'til Daybreak, and Make Sure You're Sittin'." The campaign, called "Drinks on Us," clearly promoted abusive and excessive drinking. This campaign was eventually stopped because the cigarette company did not have permission to use the alcohol brands.

The Federal Drug Administration (FDA) has been given the authority to regulate tobacco, including banning certain products, limiting nicotine, and blocking labels such as "low tar" and "light" that could wrongly imply certain products are less harmful.[1] The law doesn't let the FDA ban nicotine or tobacco entirely. A committee has been formed to study several issues, including dissolvable tobacco products, product changes, and standards, and report back to the FDA. Of particular interest is the increase in the share of smokers using menthol cigarettes from 31 percent to almost 34 percent in four years, with more pronounced increases among young smokers. It also showed that among black smokers, 82.6 percent used menthol cigarettes, compared with 32.3 percent for Hispanic smokers and 23.8 percent for white smokers.[2] A ban on cigarettes with flavors such as clove, chocolate, or fruit took effect in 2009 because they are believed to appeal to youth.

After graduation, you have an offer to work in either marketing or sales at R.J. Reynolds, the tobacco company that sells many popular brands of cigarettes. The pay and benefits are very competitive. The job market is tight, and if you don't get a job right away, you will have to live with your parents. Should you take the job?

Scenario 2: Car Manufacturer Gives Bribes for Contracts

A car and truck manufacturer just found out that two of its overseas business units have been engaging in bribery over a 10-year period of time. The company paid $56 million in bribes to more than 20 countries to gain government contracts for their vehicles.[3] The company is now paying millions in criminal and civil charges because of its violation of the Foreign Corrupt Practices Act (FCPA), and it admits to earning more than $50 million in profits based on its corrupt transactions. The car company recorded the bribe payments as commissions, special discounts, or necessary payments. Should the manufacturer discontinue its operations with the countries that were unlawfully bribed to buy its cars? Are financial fines sufficient to repair the problem? How can companies be sure the commissions they earn are true commissions and not a bribe?

Scenario 3: Retailers Lack Ethical Guidelines

Renata has been working at Peavy's Bridal for nearly a year now. Her sales figures have never been competitive with those of her coworkers, and the sales manager has called her in for several meetings to discuss her inability to close the sale. Things look desperate; in the last meeting, the sales manager told her that if she did not meet her quota next month, the company would likely have to fire her.

In considering how she might improve her methods and sales, Renata turned to Marilyn, the salesperson in the store who had the most experience. Marilyn has been with Peavy's for nearly 30 years, and she virtually always gets the sale. But how?

"Let me tell you something sweetie," Marilyn tells her. "Every bride-to-be wants one thing: to look beautiful on her wedding day so that everyone gasps when they first see her. And hey, the husband is going to think she looks great. But let's be honest here—not everyone is all that beautiful. So you have to convince them that they look great in one, and only one, dress. And that dress had better be the most expensive one they try, or they won't believe you anyway! And then you have to show them how much better they look with a veil. And some shoes. And a tiara . . . you get the picture! I mean, they need all that stuff anyway, so why shouldn't we make them feel good while they're here and let them buy from us?"

Should she follow Marilyn's advice and save her job?

Scenario 4: Giving Credit Where Credit Isn't Due

A catalog retailer that carries home and children's items, such as children's furniture, clothing, and toys, was seeking a way to reach a new audience and stop the declining sales and revenue trends it was suffering. A market research firm hired by the cataloger identified a new but potentially risky market: lower-income single parents. The new market seemed attractive because of the large number of single parents, but most of these homes were severely constrained in terms of their monetary resources.

The research firm proposed that the cataloger offer a generous credit policy that would allow consumers to purchase up to $500 worth of merchandise on credit without a credit check, provided they signed up for direct payment of their credit account from a checking account. Because these were high-risk consumers, the credit accounts would carry extremely high interest rates. The research firm believed that even with losses, enough accounts would be paid off to make the venture extremely profitable for the catalog retailer.

Should the cataloger pursue this new strategy?

Scenario 5: The Jeweler's Tarnished Image

Sparkle Gem Jewelers, a family-owned and -operated costume jewelry manufacturing business, traditionally sold its products only to wholesalers. Recently however, Sparkle Gem was approached by the charismatic Barb Stephens, who convinced the owners to begin selling through a network of distributors she had organized. The distributors recruited individuals to host jewelry parties in their homes. Sparkle Gem's owners, the Billing family, have been thrilled with the revenue generated by these home parties and started making plans for the expansion of the distributor network.

However, Mrs. Billing just received a letter from a jewelry party customer, who expressed sympathy for Mrs. Billing's loss. Confused, Mrs. Billing contacted the letter writer, who told her that Barb Stephens had come to the jewelry party at her church and told the story of Sparkle Gem. According to Stephens's story, Mrs. Billing was a young widow struggling to keep her business together after her husband had died on a missionary trip. The writer had purchased $200 worth of jewelry at the party and told Mrs. Billing that she hoped it helped. Mrs. Billing was stunned. She and her very-much-alive husband had just celebrated their 50th wedding anniversary.

What should Mrs. Billing do now?

Scenario 6: No Wonder It's So Good

Enjoy Cola is a new product produced by ABC Beverage and marketed with the slogan "Relax with Enjoy." Unlike other colas on the market, Enjoy does not contain caffeine and therefore is positioned as the perfect beverage to end the day or for a slow-paced weekend and as a means to help consumers relax and unwind. The market response has been tremendous, and sales of Enjoy have been growing rapidly, especially among women.

ABC Beverage decided not to list on the ingredients label that Enjoy contains a small amount of alcohol, because it is not required to do so by the government unless the alcohol content is more than 1 percent.

Mia Rodriguez, the marketing director for Enjoy, only recently learned that Enjoy contains small amounts of alcohol and is troubled about ABC's failure to disclose this information on the ingredients list. She worries about the impact of this omission on consumers who have alcohol sensitivities or those who shouldn't be consuming alcohol, such as pregnant women and recovering alcoholics.

What should Rodriguez do? What would you do in her position?

Scenario 7: Bright Baby's Bright Idea

Bartok Manufacturing produces a line of infant toys under the Bright Baby brand label. The Consumer Product Safety Commission (CPSC) recently issued a recall order for the Bright Baby car seat gym, a very popular product. According to the CPSC, the gym contains small parts that present a choking hazard. The CEO of Bartok Manufacturing, Bill Bartok, called an executive meeting to determine the firm's strategy in response to the recall.

Mike Henderson, Bartok's CFO, stated that the recall could cost as much as $1 million in lost revenue from the Bright Baby line. Noting that there had been no deaths or injuries from the product, just the potential for injury, Henderson proposed that the remaining inventory of car seat gyms be sold in regions where there are no rules such as the CPSC's. Sue Tyler, the marketing director for Bartok, recommended that the product be repackaged and sold under a different brand name so that the Bright Baby name would not be associated with the product. Bartok, though a bit leery of the plan, agreed to go along with it to avoid the monetary losses.

What would you have recommended to the CEO?

Scenario 8: Money from Mailing Lists[4]

Sports Nostalgia Emporium sells autographed sports memorabilia online. Recently, the director of marketing, John Mangold, started using a mailing list he had purchased from Marketing Metrix, a marketing research firm that sells consumer information. Mangold relies on such purchased mailing lists to grow the company and sends printed catalogs to thousands of people each month. The mailing lists he gets from Marketing Metrix are much more effective than other mailing lists and generate almost twice as much revenue.

In a recent conversation with a sales representative from Marketing Metrix, Mangold discovered the reason its lists were so effective: Marketing Metrix tracks the online behavior of consumers and uses that information to create targeted lists. The mailing lists that Mangold has been using consist of consumers who visited the websites of Sports Nostalgia Emporium's competitors. Based on what he can discern, Mangold believes that these consumers are not aware that someone is collecting information about their online behavior, along with their names and addresses, and selling it to other firms.

Should Mangold continue to use the Marketing Metrix mailing list? If so, should he tell his new customers how he got their names and addresses? Do consumers need to give consent before firms can collect information about their behavior?

Scenario 9: The Blogging CEO[5]

David Burdick is the CEO of ACME Bubblegum, a successful public company. As one of the cofounders of the company, Burdick has enjoyed speaking and writing about the success of ACME Bubblegum for several years. Typically, he speaks at conferences or directly to the press, but recently he has been blogging about his firm anonymously. Specifically, he defended a recent advertising campaign that was unpopular among consumers and pointedly attacked one of ACME Bubblegum's competitors. Burdick deeply enjoys his anonymous blogging and believes that none of his readers actually know that he works for ACME Bubblegum.

Should Burdick be allowed to praise his company's performance anonymously online? Should he be allowed to attack his competitors without disclosing his relationship with the company? How would you feel if the CEO of a company at which you shopped was secretly writing criticisms of his or her competition? How would you feel if you knew a writer for your favorite blog was actually closely involved in a company that the blog community discussed?

Endnotes

1. Michael Felberbaum, "Panel to Examine Menthol Cigarettes' Impact," *Associated Press*, March 29, 2010.

2. Ibid., based on a study by the Substance Abuse and Mental Health Services Administration in November, 2009.

3. Department of Justice, Office of Public Affairs, "Daimler AG and Three Subsidiaries Resolve Foreign Corrupt Practices Act Investigation and Agree to Pay $93.6 Million in Criminal Penalties," press release, April 1, 2010; Michael Connor, "Daimler Agrees to Pay $185 Million to Settle Bribery Charges," *Business Ethics*, March 26, 2010, http://businessethics.com.

4. Emily Steel, "How Marketers Hone Their Aim Online," *The Wall Street Journal*, June 19, 2007, p. B6.

5. "Mr. Mackey's Offense," *The Wall Street Journal*, July 16, 2007, p. A12.

CHAPTER 5

ANALYZING THE MARKETING ENVIRONMENT

After reading this chapter, you should be able to:

LO5-1 Outline how customers, the company, competitors, and corporate partners affect marketing strategy.

LO5-2 Explain why marketers must consider their macroenvironment when they make decisions.

LO5-3 Describe the differences among the various generational cohorts.

LO5-4 Identify various social trends that impact marketing.

There is no denying that healthy eating is a growing trend. Consumers seek out foods that contain less sugar and fat, demand fresh produce and meats, and express concerns about genetically modified organisms. Noting consumers' efforts to avoid processed foods as well, Panera has introduced a new "clean menu," using marketing communications that focus mainly on what the food items do *not* feature rather than what they do.

In particular, Panera has developed a "No No List" of ingredients that may not appear anywhere in its clean menu. Some of the food culprits are familiar, such as too much sugar or too many calories. But the list also reflects consumers' growing awareness of and education about the potential negative effects of complex preservatives and artificial colorings or flavors. Eliminating all these ingredients has required an intricate, in-depth, and lengthy development process.

For its broccoli cheddar soup for example, Panera had to take great care: It is one of its top selling menu items, so the taste, consistency, and appearance could not change. But to make its way onto the clean menu, the soup also had to exclude all sodium phosphate, a very common preservative. Finding cheese that did not contain any of this preservative was a significant challenge for the company. Furthermore, it excluded bleached wheat flour, which of course altered the color of the soup. Because of these detailed analyses and complicated requirements to achieve "clean" status, the

redevelopment of the soup underwent more than 60 different iterations. And that was before Panera realized it also needed to revise the Dijon mustard it included as an ingredient in the soup, because that condiment also contained preservatives.

The effort may prove worthwhile though. Panera sells approximately 200 million servings of soup each year, and it might be able to charge more for clean versions of those soups. According to some polls, 88 percent of consumers indicated they would happily pay more for healthier food options. Although these polls tend to refer to products on supermarket shelves, they reflect broader trends in the market. Furthermore, this expressed willingness to pay more spans virtually all age ranges, from Generation 7 to Baby Boomers.

In addition to excluding artificial preservatives, sweeteners, and flavors, Panera is expanding its notion of healthy menus to include more plant-based, and fewer animal-based, protein sources on its menu board. The company has announced new animal welfare standards for its suppliers as well. Such moves reflect consumer demands for foods that are healthy not just for them but also for society and the environment in general. That is, vegetarian options tend to be better for consumers and the environment, and ethically sourced meat provides health as well as societal benefits.

In these adjustments, Panera is responding to various trends in its consumer markets, especially the growing focus on clean eating and healthy alternatives to traditional fast food menus. Although it is not the only company to move toward healthier options, it claims to be the first to publish a comprehensive list of the ingredients that its menu items will no longer include. In this sense, marketing today can be just as much about what products don't contain as it is about the specific features and ingredients they do offer.[1]

 LO5-1 Outline how customers, the company, competitors, and corporate partners affect marketing strategy.

A MARKETING ENVIRONMENT ANALYSIS FRAMEWORK

As the opening vignette illustrates, marketers continue to find changes in what their customers demand or expect and adapt their product and service offerings accordingly. By paying close attention to customer needs and continuously monitoring the business environment in which the company operates, a good marketer can identify potential opportunities.

Exhibit 5.1 illustrates factors that affect the marketing environment. The centerpiece, as always, is consumers. Consumers may be influenced directly by the immediate actions of the focal company, the company's competitors, or corporate partners that work with the firm to make and supply products and services to consumers. The firm, and therefore consumers indirectly, is influenced by the macroenvironment, which includes various impacts of culture; demographics; and social, technological, economic, and political/legal factors. We discuss each of these components in detail in this chapter and suggest how they might interrelate.

Because the consumer is the center of all marketing efforts, value-based marketing aims to provide greater value to consumers than competitors offer. Therefore, the marketing firm must consider the entire business process, all from a consumer's point of view.[2]

EXHIBIT 5.1 Understanding the Marketing Environment

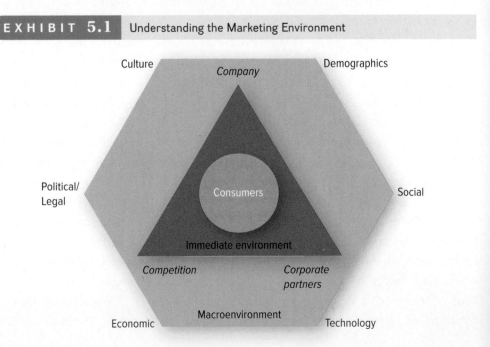

150

Consumers' needs and wants, as well as their ability to purchase, depend on a host of factors that change and evolve over time. Firms use various tools to keep track of competitors' activities and consumer trends, and they rely on various methods to communicate with their corporate partners. Furthermore, they monitor their macroenvironment to determine how such factors influence consumers and how they should respond to them. Sometimes, a firm can even anticipate trends.

THE IMMEDIATE ENVIRONMENT

Exhibit 5.2 illustrates the factors that affect consumers' immediate environment: the company's capabilities, competitors, and corporate partners.

Company Capabilities

In the immediate environment, the first factor that affects the consumer is the firm itself. Successful marketing firms focus on satisfying customer needs that match their core competencies. The primary strength of Corning is its ability to manufacture glass. The company initially made its name by producing the glass enclosure to encase Thomas Edison's lightbulb. But by successfully leveraging its core competency in glass manufacturing while also recognizing marketplace trends toward mobile devices, Corning shifted its focus. As a result, Corning is one of the leading producers of durable, scratch-resistant glass on the faces of smartphones and tablets. More than 1 billion mobile devices feature its Gorilla Glass.[3] Marketers can use analyses of their external environment, like the SWOT analysis described in Chapter 2, to categorize any opportunity as attractive or unattractive. If it appears attractive, they also need to assess it in terms of their existing competencies.

Competitors

Competition also significantly affects consumers in the immediate environment. It is therefore critical that marketers understand their firm's competitors, including their strengths, weaknesses, and likely reactions to the marketing activities that their own firm undertakes.

For example, in one of the most competitive markets, the weight loss industry, the current ruling competitors are Jenny Craig and Weight Watchers. As both companies work to gain market share in this competitive industry, they tend to avoid direct confrontations. Thus when asked about Weight Watchers, the Jenny Craig CEO Monty Sharma has chosen not to comment, other than to explain that the differences in their programs make any such

EXHIBIT 5.2   Understanding the Immediate Environment

Weight Watchers' partnership with Oprah Winfrey is expected to help rejuvenate the weight-loss company.

© Michael Nagle/Bloomberg/Getty Images

Jenny Craig's spokesperson, Kirstie Alley, has been credited with expanding its membership rolls.

© Charles Sykes/Invision for Curves Jenny Craig/AP Photo

comparison unfair.[4] In particular, whereas Jenny Craig focuses on delivered meals and personal consultants, Weight Watchers is famous for its point system. Yet Weight Watchers' recent partnership with Oprah Winfrey has prompted more comparisons. That is, Jenny Craig has long relied on Kristie Alley as a spokesperson, a marketing strategy that has been credited with helping the company expand its membership rolls by 25 percent.[5] This success of a well-know spokesperson for one diet company likely was instrumental in Weight Watchers' decision to team up with Winfrey. Although Weight Watchers experienced revenue and profit declines in recent years, following the announcement of its partnership with Winfrey, the price of the company's stock more than tripled.[6] These efforts represent the companies' recognition of what their closest competitor is doing. But at the same time, each company touts its benefits over its competitors because the ultimate goal, of course, is to appeal to consumers.

Corporate Partners

Few firms operate in isolation. For example, automobile manufacturers collaborate with suppliers of sheet metal, tire manufacturers, component part makers, unions, transport companies, and dealerships to produce and market their automobiles successfully. Parties that work with the focal firm are its corporate partners.

Consider an example that demonstrates the role these partners play and how they work with the firm to create a single, efficient manufacturing system. Unlike most outdoor clothing manufacturers that use synthetic, nonrenewable materials, Nau makes modern urban+outdoor apparel from renewable sources such as sustainably harvested eucalyptus and recycled plastic bottles. It was founded by a team of entrepreneurs who left companies such as Nike and Patagonia. To develop rugged and beautiful clothing from sustainable materials, these founders turned to manufacturing partners around the world to develop new fabrics that are performance-driven and technical. One example of an innovative fabric used in Nau's jackets is a blend of recycled polyester and organic

Nau works with its corporate partners to develop socially responsible outdoor (left) and urban (right) apparel.

Courtesy of Nau International, Inc. Photography by Matthew D'Annunzio.

cotton that is coated and bonded to recycled polyester knit. The result is a water-resistant, breathable technical soft shell material that is ideal for outdoor activities. To complement the new fabrics, the company uses only organic cotton and wool from "happy sheep," provided by partners in the ranching industry that embrace animal-friendly practices. Not only does Nau represent the cutting edge of sustainability and green business, it also clearly demonstrates how "going green" can prompt companies to work more closely with their partners to innovate.[7]

PROGRESS CHECK

1. What are the components of the immediate environment?

MACROENVIRONMENTAL FACTORS

 LO5-2 Explain why marketers must consider their macroenvironment when they make decisions.

In addition to understanding their customers, the company itself, their competition, and their corporate partners, marketers must understand the macroenvironmental factors that operate in the external environment. These factors are **c**ulture, **d**emographics, **s**ocial trends, **t**echnological advances, **e**conomic situation, and **p**olitical/regulatory environment, or CDSTEP, as shown in Exhibit 5.3.

Culture

We broadly define culture as the shared meanings, beliefs, morals, values, and customs of a group of people.[8] Transmitted by words, literature, and institutions, culture is passed down from generation to generation and learned over time. You participate in many cultures: Your family has a cultural heritage, so perhaps your mealtime traditions include eating rugelach, a traditional Jewish pastry, or sharing corned beef and cabbage to celebrate your Irish ancestry on St. Patrick's Day. In addition, your school or workplace shares its own common culture. In a broader sense, you also participate in the cultural aspects of the town and country in which you live. The challenge for marketers is to have products or services identifiable by and relevant to a particular group of people. Our various cultures

EXHIBIT 5.3   The Macroenvironment

Some firms, like Disney, bridge the cultural gap by using the same advertising in different countries. Only the language is different, as illustrated by these two ads for The Avengers. *The left photo is for the Russian market; the right photo is for the Portuguese market.*

(Both): © Walt Disney Studios Motion Pictures/Courtesy Everett Collection

influence what, why, how, where, and when we buy. Two dimensions of culture that marketers must take into account as they develop their marketing strategies are the culture of the country and that of a region within a country.

Country Culture The visible nuances of a country's culture, such as artifacts, behavior, dress, symbols, physical settings, ceremonies, language differences, colors, tastes, and food preferences, are easy to spot. But the subtler aspects of **country culture** generally are trickier to identify and navigate. Sometimes the best answer is to establish a universal appeal within the specific identities of country culture. Disney and other global firms have successfully bridged the cultural gap by producing advertising that appeals to the same target market across countries. The pictures and copy are the same. The only thing that changes is the language.

Regional Culture The region in which people live in a particular country has its own **regional culture** that affects many aspects of people's lives, including their dietary tastes and preferences. For national and global restaurant chains, it is particularly important to cater to these preferences. But implementing completely different menus for each region would create significant strains on supply chains. To resolve this dilemma, McDonald's keeps the staple elements of its menu consistent throughout the United States, but it offers slightly different variations to appeal to specific regions.[9] In the south and southwestern regions of the United States, McDonald's offers a Hot 'n Spicy variant of the McChicken sandwich that is not available other areas.[10] Such variation is relatively easy for McDonald's to offer, because the only real difference between the Hot 'n Spicy McChicken and the regular McChicken is

To accommodate regional cultures, McDonald's offers regional specialties such as Spam for breakfast in Hawaii (left) and lobster rolls in Maine (right).

(left): © Phil Mislinski/Getty Images; (right): © Felix Choo/Alamy

the spicy breading on the chicken patty. Furthermore, McDonald's has pledged to continue personalizing offerings according to regional tastes,[11] even expanding menus in select areas with completely new items. For example, in Maine, McDonald's menu includes a lobster roll; in parts of Delaware, Virginia, and Maryland, it features a seasonal crab cake sandwich; and in Hawaii—which arguably gets the most regional U.S. customization—McDonald's offers noodle soup and vegetable pie. The chain can sustain these vastly different menu items by turning to local sources for the ingredients in the relevant regions.[12]

Demographics

Demographics indicate the characteristics of human populations and segments, especially those used to identify consumer markets. Typical demographics such as age (which includes generational cohorts), gender, race, and income are readily available from market research firms such as IRI. Many firms undertake their own market research as well. For example, with its Clubcard loyalty program, U.K.-based grocery chain Tesco collects massive amounts of data about shoppers who visit its stores. It uses this information to target offers. For Tesco's 16 million cardholders, 9 million different versions of its newsletter

Tesco uses the demographic information it collects from its 16 million cardholders to create 9 million different versions of its newsletter that offers customized discounts.

© NetPhotos/Alamy

Social & Mobile Marketing 5.1   Understanding Connections, Both with and by Young Consumers[i]

For marketing executives, choices about where and how much to spend to appeal to consumers should depend mainly on a careful analysis of where those consumers are exposed to marketing messages. But when a generation gap appears between marketing executives and consumers, advertising choices may reflect marketers' preferences more than consumers'.

A clear manifestation comes from advertising for beauty products. Previous generations of consumers often relied on insights and advice from big, glossy fashion magazines. Lush, expensive, two-page spreads, with glamorous shots of beauty products in use seemed effective and appropriate. But Millennials (Gen Y) who still read such magazines likely access them online and skip quickly over such long and intrusive ads, with little appreciation for the quality of the shot. Furthermore, recent research shows that such high-quality visual tactics used in print advertisements do not translate particularly well to online product sites. On retail websites, the pretty pictures are largely ineffective because shoppers seek concrete information about their purchase decisions.

According to Forrester Research, 91 percent of Millennials are active Internet users. To reach the web, 59 percent of them use smartphones, 35 percent rely on tablets, and 70 percent employ their laptops. Across these various uses,

this younger generation of consumers spends an average of 25 hours online every week.

Their electronic media usage is not the only impressive number describing these consumers: The Millennial market encompasses approximately 105 million consumers, with annual buying power of about $200 billion. Yet even when they recognize and appreciate the size and opportunity that these consumers represent, many marketers—especially those who have reached executive positions after long careers—continue to devote the bulk of their media spending to channels that Millennials simply don't use that much anymore, such as magazines and television.

The main reason for this error might be a somewhat clichéd image of Baby Boomers, confused and overwhelmed by the new options created through technological advances. Faced with a wealth of choices, such as small independent blogs, content-generating sites, and aggregators, these marketing executives retreat to familiar ground. If they aren't sure what each type of site does, they can't determine which is the best option.

Even marketers who embrace technology channels for advertising exhibit a tendency to prefer well-established, widely known spaces such as Facebook or Google. For young consumers who seek exciting, interactive media content, such options have little chances of success.

---

offer customized discounts for, say, cosmetics to young female shoppers.[13] It also uses these data to cut food waste, such that by analyzing location and customer data, Tesco can create a sales forecast and stocks stores appropriately.[14] Not all firms are quite as effective in their efforts though, as Social and Mobile Marketing 5.1 describes.

Demographics thus provide an easily understood snapshot of the typical consumer in a specific target market, as the next few sections detail.

LO5-3
Describe the differences among the various generational cohorts.

Generational Cohorts   Consumers in a *generational cohort*—a group of people of the same generation—have similar purchase behaviors because they have shared experiences and are in the same stage of life. Applying age as a basis to identify consumers is quite useful to marketers, as long as it is used in conjunction with other consumer characteristics. For example, most media are characterized by the consumers who use them.[15] Age groups can identify appropriate media in which firms should advertise, as discussed in Social and Mobile Marketing 5.1. Although there are many ways to cut the generational pie, we describe four major groups, as listed in Exhibit 5.4.

Members of **Generation Z (Gen Z)** are also known as **Digital Natives** because people in this group were born into a world that already was full of electronic gadgets and digital technologies such as the Internet and social networks.[16] These technologies are being developed and adopted at an unprecedented rate. Whereas

EXHIBIT 5.4   Generational Cohorts

Generational cohort	Gen Z	Gen Y	Gen X	Baby Boomers
Range of birth years	2001–2014	1977–2000	1965–1976	1946–1964
Age in 2017	0–15	16–39	40–51	52–70

it took 38 years for the radio to be adopted by 50 million people and 13 years for television, it only took 2 years for the same number of consumers to sign up for Facebook.

Members of Generation Y (Gen Y), also called Millennials, include the more than 60 million people born in the United States between 1977 and 2000. As the children of the Baby Boomers, this group is the biggest cohort since the original postwar World War II boom. It also varies the most in age, ranging from teenagers to adults who have their own families.[17]

The next group, Generation X (Gen X), includes people born between 1965 and 1976 and represents some 41 million Americans. Vastly unlike their Baby Boomer parents, Xers are the first generation of latchkey children (those who grew up in homes in which both parents worked), and 50 percent of them have divorced parents.

After World War II, the birthrate in the United States rose sharply, resulting in a group known as the Baby Boomers, the 78 million Americans born between 1946 and 1964. Now that the oldest Boomers are collecting Social Security, it is clear that this cohort will be the largest population of 50-plus consumers the United States has ever seen.

Digital natives are always connected.
© Alberto Pomares/E+/Getty Images RF

Income Income distribution in the United States has grown more polarized—the highest-income groups are growing, whereas many middle- and lower-income groups' real purchasing power keeps declining. Although the trend of wealthy households outpacing both poor and middle classes is worldwide, it is particularly prominent in the United States. For 2014, the average weekly income of the richest 5 percent of the population was more than $3970, the average (median) weekly income for the United States as a whole was $1031, and the poorest 10 percent of the population earned less than $412 per week.[18] Furthermore, the number of people who earn less than the poverty line ($24,230 for a family of four in 2014) continues to grow.[19] The wealthiest 1 percent control 34.6 percent of Americans' total net worth; in comparison, the bottom 90 percent control only 26.9 percent.[20] The increase in wealthy families may be due to the maturing of the general population, the increase in dual-income households, and the higher overall level of education. It also may prompt some ethical concerns about the distribution of wealth. However, the broad range in incomes creates marketing opportunities at both the high and low ends of the market.

Although some marketers choose to target only affluent population segments, others have had great success delivering value to middle- and low-income earners. Consider, for example, SC Johnson, the parent company of many familiar household brands such as Glade, Ziploc, Windex, and Raid. SC Johnson has long been working at the bottom of the income pyramid; in the 1960s it began establishing locations in impoverished countries. Its most successful project has been in Ghana, where SC Johnson uses a direct-sales model and coaches to sell and teach customers about the benefits of pest control products and how to use them. Furthermore, SC Johnson sells these products in refillable containers and bundles them with air fresheners, in an effort to boost sales.[21]

SC Johnson targets the bottom of the income pyramid by selling pest control products in Ghana.
© Danita Delimont/Alamy

Education Studies show that higher levels of education lead to better jobs and higher incomes.[22] According to the U.S. Bureau of Labor Statistics, employment that requires a college or secondary degree accounts for nearly half of all projected job growth in the near future. Moreover, average annual earnings are higher for those with degrees than for those without. Young adults who did not graduate from high school have an average annual salary of about $23,900, high school grads earn $30,000, and those with bachelor's degrees earn around $48,500.[23]

Best Buy has redesigned its stores to appeal to its female shoppers by making its appliance sections look more like kitchens than like industrial shipyards.

© Bruce Bisping/MCT/Newscom

For some products, marketers can combine education level with other data such as occupation and income and obtain pretty accurate predictions of purchase behavior. For instance, a full-time college student with a part-time job may have relatively little personal income but will spend his or her disposable dollars differently than would a high school graduate who works in a factory and earns a similar income. Marketers need to be cognizant of the interaction among education, income, and occupation.

Gender Years ago gender roles appeared clear, but those male and female roles have been blurred. In particular, women today outperform men scholastically, earn higher grades on average, and graduate from both high school and college at greater rates. Perhaps unsurprisingly, recent studies also show that approximately 15 percent of married women in Western economies earn more than their husbands do in the workplace.[24] These shifts in status, attitudes, and behaviors affect the way many firms need to design and promote their products and services. More firms are careful about gender neutrality in positioning their products and attempt to transcend gender boundaries, especially through increased interactions with their customers. On the basis of its research with men, for example, the children's stroller company Bugaboo International designed a high-tech, black-and-chrome contraption with dirt bike tires.

Best Buy has recognized that women are a massive market for electronics, smartphones, and mobile devices. But its stores tended to attract very few female shoppers. Therefore, its recent store design revisions aim to appeal to women with household appliance sections that look more like kitchens than like industrial shipyards, and they place hand sanitizer dispensers next to the videogame test consoles.[25]

Ethnicity Because of immigration and increasing birthrates among various ethnic and racial groups, the United States continues to grow more diverse. Approximately 80 percent of all population growth in the next 20 years is expected to come from African American, Hispanic, and Asian communities. Minorities now represent approximately one-quarter of the population; by 2050 they will represent about 50 percent, and nearly 30 percent of the population will be Hispanic.[26] The United Nations also estimates that approximately 1 million people per year will emigrate from less developed nations to the United States over the next 40 years.[27] Many foreign-born Americans and recent immigrants tend to concentrate in a handful of metropolitan areas, such as New York, Los Angeles, San Francisco, and Chicago.

Among the different groups, Hispanic buying power was projected to reach $1.3 trillion in 2015, a cumulative increase of around 25 percent compared with 2010.[28] The 50 million Hispanic consumers in the United States have increasing influences on mainstream U.S. culture.

LO5-4 Identify various social trends that impact marketing.

The Hispanic market is so large in some areas of the United States that some firms, like McDonald's, develop entire marketing programs just to meet their needs.

© Ethel Wolvovitz/The Image Works

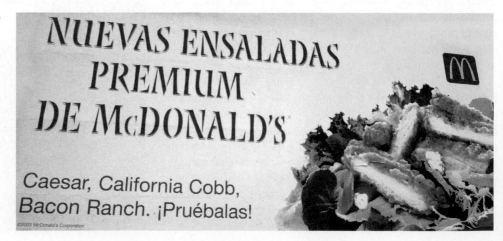

Many families have been in the United States for multiple generations, and the consumer behavior of these highly acculturated Hispanics differs little from that of other groups of Americans. For example, they use credit cards, are minimally influenced by advertising and product placements, exhibit greater sensitivity to in-store promotions, and are likely to shop online and from catalogs.

The census of 2010 counts 42 million African American U.S. households, who are more affluent and suburban than previous studies have suggested. They also tend to be younger, such that 47 percent are between the ages of 18 and 49 years (a key age demographic for many marketers). The number of black households earning more than $75,000 has increased by 47 percent since 2005, and it is expected that a majority of black Americans now live in the suburbs.[29] For example, in the Atlanta metropolitan area the city lost 8 percent of its African American households, while the surrounding suburbs gained a remarkable 40 percent.[30] For this demographic segment, especially as it moves increasingly to the suburbs, Home Depot has developed particular appeals featuring national figures such as Tom Joyner and Steve Harvey.

Asian Americans make up only about 5.6 percent of the U.S. population, but they also represent the fastest-growing minority population, tend to earn more, have more schooling, and are more likely to be professionally employed or own a business.

The United States is like a salad bowl, a mix made up of people from every corner of the world.

© Andrea Laurita/Getty Images RF

Social Trends

Various social trends appear to be shaping consumer values in the United States and around the world, including a greater emphasis on health and wellness concerns, greener consumers, and privacy concerns.

Health and Wellness Concerns

As the opening vignette for this chapter indicated, health concerns, especially those pertaining to children, are prevalent, critical, and widespread. In the past 20 years, child obesity has doubled and teenage obesity tripled in the United States, leading to skyrocketing rates of high blood pressure, high cholesterol, early signs of heart disease, and type 2 diabetes among children. The U.S. Centers for Disease Control and Prevention (CDC) also estimates that approximately one-third of U.S. adults are obese, and the incidence of diabetes has reached 8.3 percent—with much higher rates for people still undiagnosed or classified as having prediabetes.[31] It is also increasing at alarming rates in other countries and among consumers who adopt more Western diets.

New advertising guidelines therefore require marketers to produce food in reasonably proportioned sizes. Advertised food items must provide basic nutrients, have less than 30 percent of their total calories from fat, and include no added sweeteners. The advertising also cannot be aired during children's programming, and companies cannot link unhealthy foods with cartoon and celebrity figures. For example, the SUBWAY FRESH FIT FOR KIDS™ offerings meet the American Heart Association's criteria for a heart-healthy meal, since it includes lean protein, fruits, vegetables, grains, and milk, all for less than 500 calories.[32] It has even partnered with Disney in a *Star Wars*-related TV ad promoting healthy children's meals.[33]

This Subway ad speaks directly to the issue of childhood obesity and responds to the new advertising guidelines adopted by marketers. The SUBWAY FRESH FIT FOR KIDS™ meal, which meets the American Heart Association's criteria for a heart-healthy meal, provides a nutritional choice for customers wanting a quick service food alternative for their children.

Source: Subway Franchise Advertising Fund Trust

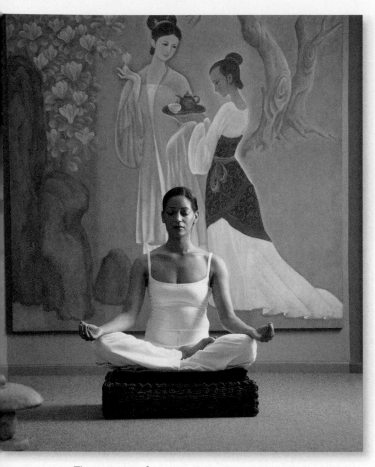

The practice of yoga is growing as more consumers embrace healthy lifestyles.

© Plush Studios/Blend Images LLC RF

Accordingly, consumers' interest in improving their health has opened up several new markets and niches focused on healthy living. For example, consumer spending on yoga classes, mats, and clothing has increased consistently in recent years.[34] Yoga studios actually combine multiple modern trends: As the economy sours, people face increasing stress, which they hope to reduce through yoga. In addition, yoga studios are relatively inexpensive to open and operate, so entrepreneurs and consumers appreciate the value for the money they offer. And of course, Americans remain consistently on the lookout for exercise mechanisms that can help them shed pounds and match media images of athletic prowess and beautiful bodies. Thus competition is growing in this industry, and some studios have begun to combine their basic yoga classes with additional offers to attract clients such as food services, acupuncture, or massages.[35]

Health and wellness concerns have also spurred a number of mobile apps, many of which help customers get or stay in shape by tracking exercise, calorie intake, and sleep cycles. Superior Service 5.1 describes how CVS's MinuteClinic apps helps its patients stay well.

Greener Consumers   **Green marketing** involves a strategic effort by firms to supply customers with environmentally friendly, sustainable merchandise and services.[36] As we noted in Chapter 4, sustainability is a critical ethical consideration for marketers. Many consumers, concerned about everything from the purity of air and water to the safety of beef and salmon, believe that each person can make a difference in the environment. For example, nearly half of U.S. adults now recycle their soda bottles and newspapers, and European consumers are even more green. Germans are required by law to recycle bottles, and the European Union does not allow beef raised on artificial growth hormones to be imported.

Demand for green-oriented products has been a boon to the firms that supply them. Marketers encourage consumers to replace older versions of washing machines and dishwashers with water- and energy-saving models and to invest in phosphate-free laundry powder and mercury-free and rechargeable batteries. New markets emerge for recycled building products, packaging, paper goods, and even sweaters and sneakers as well as for more efficient appliances, lighting, and heating and cooling systems in homes and offices. Jumping on the green bandwagon, Frito-Lay's SunChips line of snack foods uses solar power at one of its eight production facilities to harness the sun's energy to produce its products.[37] Ethical and Societal Dilemma 5.1 examines some of the challenges companies face in making green products.

These green products and initiatives suggest a complicated business model. Are they good for business? Some green options are more expensive than traditional products and initiatives. Are consumers interested in or willing to pay the higher prices for green products? Are firms really interested in improving the environment? Or are they disingenuously marketing products or services as environmentally friendly, with the goal of gaining public approval and sales rather than actually improving the environment? This type of exploitation is common enough that it even has produced the term **greenwashing**. Consumers need to question whether a firm is spending significantly more money and time advertising being green and operating with consideration for the environment than actually spending these resources on environmentally sound practices.

Privacy Concerns   More and more consumers worldwide sense a loss of privacy. At the same time that the Internet has created an explosion of accessibility to consumer information, improvements in computer storage facilities and the manipulation of information have

Superior Service 5.1 | The MinuteClinic Mobile App: The Latest Service Expansion by CVS[ii]

There are some apps that are really exciting and "sexy," promising vast leaps in technological innovation, achieving new capabilities mainly to prove that it can be done. And then there are apps that seem a lot less exciting but enable users to get far more done. In modern marketing environments, companies seek a balance between these types of innovations for their apps, as is demonstrated readily by CVS Health and the range of apps it continues to introduce in connection with its onsite MinuteClinics.

On the exciting and thrilling side, CVS Health is experimenting with an app that would enable consumers to attach specialty lenses and scopes to their smartphones. Then when confronted with another earache or a sore throat, they could snap a picture of the affected area. The app would provide this visual information to a health care provider on duty at a local MinuteClinic, who could make an initial diagnosis and recommendations for treatment. This prototype conceivably could change the way people receive health care (and virtually eliminate late-night trips to emergency rooms), but its implementation remains uncertain, so CVS Health has not rolled it out quite yet.

Instead, it already has established a means for consumers to receive a text message when their prescriptions are ready. By adding their mobile device number into the system, they get timely alerts, so they know when to swing by the store for their medications. The adoption of this app has been so extensive—more than 3 million people used the service within a few months of its introduction—that CVS determined other service-oriented apps were a good place to expand its offerings.

The latest entry gives consumers a means to check the schedules at MinuteClinics near their homes or offices: They can gauge wait times if they need to stop in immediately or else make an appointment if they have a little flexibility. The app also sends them a reminder message 30 minutes in advance of their appointment, prompting the patients to make their way over to their local CVS. The app thus helps the company leverage its MinuteClinics in additional ways by improving the service that consumers receive from this health care option. In particular, it enables CVS Health to balance the demand for its clinic services more effectively with its supply of those services. For example, data gathered from usage of the app could help the company redefine the hours of operation for its MinuteClinics or adjust the staffing levels to reflect heavy and light demand times.

As the president of the MinuteClinic division of CVS has noted in describing these new service-oriented apps, "I know this isn't as sexy as a new service clinically, but these transactional things are making a big difference in healthcare,

CVS Health offers a range of apps in connection with its onsite MinuteClinics.

Source: MinuteClinic

because mostly what people want to know is 'Are you going to be able to see them promptly? What's the service experience like?' Especially in relatively commoditized ambulatory care activities, that service is important."

Along similar lines, CVS plans to extend the functions of its app even further in the near future. Users soon will be able to scan their insurance cards or driver's licenses, such that the app will help them make sure their insurance and contact information is up to date in the pharmacy's system. Another promising service function would help patients link with health care providers in video conferences, such that a worried parent might ask a nurse to take a look at a child's rash to help determine if a visit to the doctor is necessary.

Yet another new app spans the gap between radical and more functional innovations: Nicknamed "Ellen," after a company executive's mother, this new function gives users the option to share their prescription and health information with friends or family. Then, if they fail to pick up or refill their prescriptions in a timely manner, it sends a report to those friends and family, giving them all the information they need to nag the patient to take better care of him- or herself.

led to more and better security and credit check services. In recent years there have been a number of hacking scandals, perhaps most notably the 2013 Target breach that put millions of customers' credit and personal information at risk. Although companies continuously develop new ways to keep customer information safe, some observers suggest hackers are just getting more effective. For example in early 2016 it was revealed that some online

Ethical & Societal Dilemma 5.1   Green Cereal?[iii]

At times it may seem that massive conglomerates are slow to change, but some companies are clearly learning some lessons when it comes to responsible sourcing. Just a few years ago, Nestlé suffered terrible consumer backlash when it agreed to purchase a small amount of palm oil (used in its chocolate candies) from a company that cleared rain forests to access the palms.

Wary of such reactions, General Mills (GM) quickly promised that all the palm oil used in any of its products and packaging would come from responsible, sustainable sources by 2015. Recent estimates suggest that such moves are achieving some success. The rate of Amazonian deforestation in 2012 was lower than at any other point since the Brazilian government started tracking this statistic in 1988. But neither GM nor any of its competitors in the consumer packaged-goods industry have reached the goal of complete sustainability quite yet.

Determined not to limit itself to palm oil, GM also committed to improving the trade conditions for vanilla farmers who supply the raw material for the traditional favorite flavor of its Häagen-Dazs ice cream. With a two-year investment of $125 million in Madagascar, GM plans to train small vanilla farmers in sustainable methods that also increase crop quality, such as yield improvements and curing techniques. Ideally, these tactics also will enhance the earnings of local farmers and their communities.

Next, GM helped found—in collaboration with the U.S. Department of Agriculture (USDA) and Environmental Protection Agency (EPA)—the U.S. Food Waste Challenge. This initiative seeks not only to reduce the environmental impacts of waste collected in landfills but also to address spreading food insecurity concerns. By reducing the waste and loss of food products, the collaborators hope to feed more people or at least use the edible remainders for productive uses such as animal feed.

The demand for palm oil can often lead to rain forests such as this one being clear cut.

© Warwick Lister-Kaye/Getty Images RF

These examples reflect GM's overall sustainability mission and efforts. It has released Global Responsibility Reports annually for more than 40 years. It also touts its efforts widely through its blog, press releases, and other communications. GM does run the risk that skeptical consumers will come to believe it publicizes its good works to cover up bad behavior. But as the CEO of General Mills has readily acknowledged, "We're finding opportunities to collaborate with business, government and non-governmental organizations on important systemic solutions. While we're proud of our progress, we also know there is still much more to be done. We are committed to continued progress in these areas. Our business requires it and future generations depend on it."

Fitbit accounts were hacked. The hackers attempted to use the accounts to make fraudulent claims on the customer's warranty for new devices. However, they also gained access to the customers' GPS histories, including typical running routes and sleep history.[38]

Every time a consumer surfs the web and clicks on a site, online marketers can place "cookies" on that user's computer, showing them where the user starts, proceeds, and ends the online encounter—as well as what the user buys and doesn't buy. For many consumers, such close access to their behaviors is an unacceptable invasion of privacy.

Realizing consumers are upset about this issue, the marketing industry as a whole has sought to find solutions and self-regulations that would calm customers, satisfy cautious regulators, and still enable marketing firms to gain access to invaluable information about consumer behaviors. Those attempts appear to have stalled. The online marketing industry simply has not been able to agree about how to police itself. It looks like it may be up to Congress to address this growing issue.[39]

Technological Advances

Technological advances have accelerated during the past decade, improving the value of products as well as services. Consumers have constant access to the Internet everywhere through services such as wifi, mobile hotspots, 4G, and LTE. Smartphones using the iOS and Android systems allow for greater computing, data storage, and communication. Tablet

Marketing Analytics 5.1 | When the Best Is Good Enough: Netflix's Stellar Predictive Analytics[iv]

Netflix's data analytics are groundbreaking. In academic circles, its influence has been called a "scientific renaissance" because of the techniques the streaming service has pioneered in its efforts to handle the massive amounts of data it deals in and process payments from across the globe. The power and precision of Netflix's predictive analytics have become such common knowledge that even Netflix pokes fun at itself. In one April Fool's joke, it revised its recommended television and movie categories to include classifications such as "TV Shows Where Defiantly Crossed Arms Mean Business!" Netflix gathers data about every aspect of the viewing process, including not just the basics, such as customer ratings, searches, time of day and week, and location, but also customer behaviors that take place during the movie, such as rewinds, fast-forwards, pauses, and how long they let the credits roll. Going even a step further, Netflix analyzes every hue of color contained in the cover art of the options that it offers and can create a profile of the average color of titles viewed by each customer.

Netflix clearly relies on such customer data to create its hallmark personalized suggestions. But in 2010, Netflix chose not to enhance its ability to personalize any further. In 2009, a team of mathematicians created a new algorithm that would have improved Netflix's personalization by 10 percent, in response to a company-sponsored contest. But Netflix never implemented the improved algorithm. Why? There simply wasn't enough value to be gained from it. Various studies show that, even for the most personal choices, including their love lives, people often forgo what they know already for the thrill of what's new. Thus, Netflix decided that it could deliver more value to its customers by offering something new rather than a personalized version of what they wanted yesterday. Accordingly, it has changed its strategy and its uses of predictive analytics to focus more on creating original content.

Netflix challenges traditional approaches to content development by using data to help make new shows as well as production decisions. This approach has almost guaranteed the success of the shows, as evidenced by the release of the third season of the award-winning series *House of Cards*. Before this release, the show experienced an unprecedented increase in fans on Facebook and Twitter, approximately double the increase that occurred prior to the start of the second season. This jump was especially notable, because a show's social growth usually slows after its first or second season. Even though the third season initially brought some mixed reviews, many viewers already had finished watching the entire season just a week or so after its release.

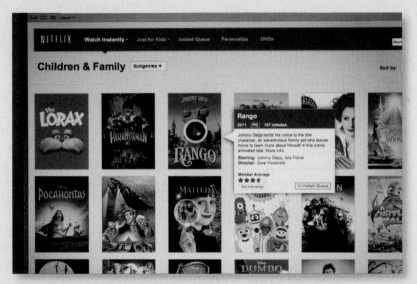

Netflix relies on its advanced technological capabilities not just to suggest which movies we should watch but also to develop new content that it is confident we will like.

© Victor J. Blue/Bloomberg/Getty Images

computers, starting with the iPad, have extended mobile computing even further by offering a larger mobile interface in environments that traditionally have limited access.

These examples of advanced technology make consumers increasingly dependent on the help they receive from the providers of the technology. As Marketing Analytics 5.1 details, Netflix relies on its advanced technological capabilities not just to suggest which movies we should watch but also to develop new content that it is confident we will like.

Adding Value 5.1   Are We There Yet? Google's Moves to Get Us Closer to Driverless Cars[v]

Self-driving cars were the central focus at the 2016 Consumer Electronics Show (CES). Google's self-driving cars have been the most widely talked-about product, in part because its driverless car program, which began in 2009, is the oldest. Its self-driving cars currently being tested include modified Lexus SUVs as well as Google-designed prototype vehicles. Google's self-driving cars have logged a significant amount of mileage, with an average of 30,000–40,000 miles driven each month (the average American drives about 13,500 miles a year). Currently Google is in talks with Ford to produce the self-driving cars—Google gets Ford's manufacturing expertise; Ford gets the self-driving technology. Although Ford already has a fleet of self-driving cars, it has announced plans to triple its production by the end of 2016.

Although Google has the most advanced driverless car program, the latest report shows that there is still plenty of work to be done before the cars are completely driverless. From September to November 2014, Google reported 341 self-driving disengagements, where the driver had to take over control of the car. More than 270 of these disengagements were reportedly due to lapses in the technology; only 69 were due to the test drivers opting to take control. On average there was one disengagement experienced every 1,244 miles. However, these numbers are significantly better than with other self-driving cars. For example Bosch's model had one disengagement every 41 miles, Nissan experienced a disengagement every 14 miles, Mercedes-Benz disengaged every 1 to 2 miles, and Volkswagen disengaged once every 57 miles. A Tesla was involved in a fatal accident when the car was in self-driving mode.

Automakers such as Toyota are collaborating with companies such as Apple and Google to create a self-driving car.

© Karen Bleier/AFP/Getty Images

The Google car might not be ready yet, but it seems to be leading the pack and improving rapidly. The 2015 reports of self-driving disengagement show a considerable drop from the 2014 reports, down to just one human intervention every 5,318 miles. Furthermore, Google recognizes these disengagements as an important aspect of its testing. Driver interventions give Google critical data and insight into the strengths and weaknesses of its software, allowing the company to make improvements. Google is undoubtedly one of the best companies at using data, and as seen by the rapid decline in driver intervention, its self-driving cars may soon be ready for the general public.

Near-field communication technology takes payments, coupons, and loyalty card data from customers as they walk by the scanner. The next broad wave of mobile applications is likely to expand the use of wireless payments through applications such as Apple Pay, Google Wallet, Master Card's Easy Pay, and Softcard Mobile Wallet, all of which enable customers' phones to serve as m-wallets.

From the firm's perspective, the technology called radio frequency identification device (RFID) enables the firm to track an item from the moment it was manufactured, through the distribution system, to the retail store, and into the hands of the final consumer. Because they are able to determine exactly how much of each product is at a given point in the supply chain, retailers can also communicate with their suppliers and collaboratively plan to meet their inventory needs.

Mobile devices enhance the customer's experience by making it easier to interact with the manufacturer or retailer or other customers, and they add a new channel of access, which makes customers more loyal and more likely to spend more with a particular retailer. Walgreens' applications and Web Pickup service allow customers to order prescriptions or review their prescription history, check the in-store inventories, and print photos. As Adding Value 5.1 summarizes, ever more new and exciting technologies seem poised to enter the consumer market.

Economic Situation

Marketers monitor the general economic situation, both in their home country and abroad, because it affects the way consumers buy merchandise and spend money. Some major factors that influence the state of an economy include the rate of inflation, foreign currency exchange rates, and interest rates.

Inflation refers to the persistent increase in the prices of goods and services. Increasing prices cause the purchasing power of the dollar to decline; in other words, the dollar buys less than it used to.

In a similar fashion, foreign currency fluctuations can influence consumer spending. For instance, in the summer of 2002 the euro was valued at slightly less than US$1. By 2008, it had risen to an all-time high of $1.60, but in early 2016, the euro and the dollar were nearly equivalent.[40] When the euro is more expensive than the dollar, merchandise made in Europe is more costly for Americans, but European shoppers enjoy bargains on U.S. products. When the dollar is worth more than the euro, American-made products become more costly for European consumers, but U.S. buyers can get great deals in Europe.

U.S. tourists are flocking to other countries such as the UK to shop because the value of the dollar is high compared to other currencies like the pound sterling.

© Samir Hussein/Getty Images Entertainment/Getty Images

Interest rates represent the cost of borrowing money. When customers borrow money from a bank, they agree to pay back the loan, plus the interest that accrues. The interest, in effect, is the cost to the customers or the fee the bank charges those customers for borrowing the money. Likewise, if a customer opens a savings account at a bank, he or she will earn interest on the amount saved, which means the interest becomes the fee the consumer gets for loaning the money to the bank. If the interest rate goes up, consumers have an incentive to save more because they earn more for loaning the bank their money; when interest rates go down, however, consumers generally borrow more.

How do these three important economic factors—inflation, foreign currency fluctuations, and interest rates—affect firms' ability to market goods and services? Shifts in the three economic factors make marketing easier for some and harder for others. For instance, when inflation increases, consumers probably don't buy less food, but they may shift their expenditures from expensive steaks to less expensive hamburgers. Grocery stores and inexpensive restaurants win, but expensive restaurants lose. Consumers also buy less discretionary merchandise, though off-price and discount retailers often gain ground at the expense of their full-price competitors. Similarly, the sales of expensive jewelry, fancy cars, and extravagant vacations decrease, but the sale of low-cost luxuries, such as personal care products and home entertainment, tends to increase.

Political/Regulatory Environment

The political/regulatory environment comprises political parties, government organizations, and legislation and laws. Organizations must fully understand and comply with any legislation regarding fair competition, consumer protection, or industry-specific regulation. Since the turn of the 20th century, the government has enacted laws that promote both fair trade and competition by prohibiting the formation of monopolies or alliances that would damage a competitive marketplace, which fosters fair pricing practices for all suppliers and consumers.

The government enacts laws focused on ensuring that companies compete fairly with one another. Although enacted in the early part of the 20th century, these laws remain the backbone of U.S. legislation protecting competition in commerce: The 1890 Sherman Antitrust Act prohibits monopolies and other activities that would restrain trade or competition and makes fair trade within a free market a national goal; the 1914 Clayton Act supports the Sherman Act by prohibiting the combination of two or more competing corporations through pooling ownership of stock and restricting pricing policies such as price discrimination, exclusive dealing, and tying clauses to different buyers; and the 1936 Robinson-Patman Act specifically outlaws price discrimination toward wholesalers, retailers, or other producers and requires sellers to make ancillary services or allowances available to all

EXHIBIT 5.5   Consumer Protection Legislation

Year	Law	Description
1906	Federal Food and Drug Act	Created the Food and Drug Administration (FDA); prohibited the manufacture or sale of adulterated or fraudulently labeled food and drug products.
1914	Federal Trade Commission Act	Established the Federal Trade Commission (FTC) to regulate unfair competitive practices and practices that deceive or are unfair to consumers.
1966	Fair Packaging and Labeling Act	Regulates packaging and labeling of consumer goods; requires manufacturers to state the contents of the package, who made it, and the amounts contained within.
1966	Child Protection Act	Prohibits the sale of harmful toys and components to children; sets the standard for child-resistant packaging.
1967	Federal Cigarette Labeling and Advertising Act	Requires cigarette packages to display this warning: "Warning: The Surgeon General Has Determined That Cigarette Smoking Is Dangerous to Your Health."
1972	Consumer Product Safety Act	Created the Consumer Product Safety Commission (CPSC), which has the authority to regulate safety standards for consumer products.
1990	Children's Television Act	Limits the number of commercials shown during children's programming.
1990	Nutrition Labeling and Education Act	Requires food manufacturers to display nutritional contents on product labels.
1995	Telemarketing Sales Rule	Regulates fraudulent activities conducted over the telephone. Violators are subject to fines and actions enforced by the FTC.
2003	Controlling the Assault of Non-Solicited Pornography and Marketing Act of 2003 (CAN-SPAM Act)	Prohibits misleading commercial e-mail, particularly misleading "subject" and "from" lines.
2003	Amendment to the Telemarketing Sales Rule	Establishes a National Do Not Call Registry, requiring telemarketers to abstain from calling consumers who opt to be placed on the list.
2003	Do Not Spam Law	Laws created to reduce spam or unwarranted e-mails.
2010	Financial Reform Law	Created the Consumer Financial Protection Bureau whose aim is to enforce appropriate consumer-oriented regulations on a number of financial firms such as banks, mortgage businesses, and payday and student lenders. It also set up the Financial Services Oversight Council to act as an early warning system.

buyers on proportionately equal terms. These laws have been used specifically to increase competition. For example, the telephone and energy industries were deregulated, which resulted in massive conglomerates such as Ma Bell (the nickname for AT&T) being broken into smaller, competing companies.

Legislation has also been enacted to protect consumers in a variety of ways. First, regulations require marketers to abstain from false or misleading advertising practices that might mislead consumers, such as claims that a medication can cure a disease when in fact it causes other health risks. Second, manufacturers are required to refrain from using any harmful or hazardous materials (e.g., lead in toys) that might place consumers at risk. Third, organizations must adhere to fair and reasonable business practices when they communicate with consumers. For example, they must employ reasonable debt-collection methods and disclose any finance charges, and they are limited with regard to their telemarketing and e-mail solicitation activities. A summary of the most significant legislation affecting marketing interests appears in Exhibit 5.5.

Responding to the Environment

As the examples throughout this chapter show, many companies engage in tactics and marketing strategies that attempt to respond to multiple political, regulatory, economic, technical, and social developments and trends in the wider environment. For example, in 2011, responding to several of these trends—pressures from the FCC, the economic status of some consumers, increasing capabilities for accessing faster broadband capabilities, and calls for greater social responsibility—14 cable companies agreed to provide low-cost Internet access to impoverished families.[41] Although the program was due to expire in 2014, Comcast chose to continue to run the program indefinitely, spurring other cable companies to do the same.[42] This remarkable agreement allows the cable companies to promote their social responsibility. But it also ensures that families whose children are eligible for free lunch programs can gain access to the services, opportunities, and options available only online. In a constantly changing marketing environment, the marketers that succeed are the ones that respond quickly, accurately, and sensitively to their consumers.

PROGRESS CHECK

1. What are the six key macroenvironmental factors?
2. Differentiate between country culture and regional culture.
3. What are some important social trends shaping consumer values and shopping behavior?

Reviewing Learning Objectives

LO5-1 Outline how customers, the company, competitors, and corporate partners affect marketing strategy.

Everything a firm does should revolve around the customer; without the customer, nothing gets sold. Firms must discover their customers' wants and needs and then be able to provide a valuable product or service that will satisfy those wants or needs. If there were only one firm and many customers, a marketer's life would be a piece of cake. But because this situation rarely occurs, firms must monitor their competitors to discover how they might be appealing to their customers. If a firm does not monitor its competitors, the firm's customers might soon belong to its competitors. Though life certainly would be easier without competitors, it would be difficult, if not impossible, without corporate partners. Good marketing firms or departments work closely with suppliers, marketing research firms, consultants, and transportation firms to coordinate the extensive process of discovering what customers want and finally getting it to them when and where they want it. Each of these activities—discovering customer needs, studying competitors' actions, and working with corporate partners—helps add value to firms' products and services.

LO5-2 Explain why marketers must consider their macroenvironment when they make decisions.

What are the chances that a fast-food hamburger restaurant would be successful in a predominantly Hindu neighborhood? Not good. Marketers must be

sensitive to such cultural issues to be successful, and they must also consider customer demographics—age, income, market size, education, gender, and ethnicity—to identify specific customer target groups. In any society, major social trends influence the way people live. In no other time in history has technology moved so rapidly and had such a pervasive influence on the way we live. Not only do marketers help identify and develop technologies for practical, everyday uses, but technological advances help marketers provide consumers with more products and services more quickly and efficiently. The general state of the economy influences how people spend their discretionary income. When the economy is healthy, marketing success comes relatively easily. But when the economy gets bumpy, only well-honed marketing skills can yield long-term successes. Naturally, all firms must abide by the law, and many legal issues affect marketing directly. These laws pertain to competitive practices and protecting consumers from unfair or dangerous products.

LO5-3 Describe the differences among the various generational cohorts.

Generational cohorts are groups of consumers of the same generation. They are likely to have similar purchase and consumption behaviors due to their shared experiences and stages of life. The four main types include Gen Z (born 2001–2016), Gen Y (born 1977–2000), Gen X (1965–1976), and Baby Boomers (1946–1964). Each of these segments exhibits different consumption patterns, attitudes toward the world, and preferences with regard to marketing efforts.

LO5-4 **Identify various social trends that impact marketing.**

Social trends have a tremendous impact on what consumers purchase and consume. Understanding these trends—health and wellness, green marketing, and privacy issues—can help marketers serve their customers better.

Key Terms

- Baby Boomers, 157
- country culture, 154
- culture, 153
- demographics, 155
- Digital Native, 156
- economic situation, 164
- foreign currency fluctuations, 165

- Generation X (Gen X), 157
- Generation Y (Gen Y), 157
- Generation Z (Gen Z), 156
- generational cohort, 156
- green marketing, 160
- greenwashing, 160
- inflation, 165

- interest rates, 165
- macroenvironmental factors, 153
- Millennials, 157
- political/regulatory environment, 165
- regional culture, 154
- technological advances, 162

Marketing Digitally

1. Seventh Generation is the leading brand of nontoxic, environmentally safe household products in the United States. Visit its website (http://www.seventhgeneration.com) and review the philosophy behind the business. Next, review the site to identify the products the company offers. Briefly summarize some of the consumer trends you think are reflected. Describe the ways in which Seventh Generation's products address the wants and needs of its customers.

2. Visit The Cool Hunter (http://www.thecoolhunter.net) and identify examples that would provide marketers insights regarding social trends.

3. Visit and explore the website of your favorite breakfast cereal. Identify the demographics of its target customer. Evaluate the effectiveness of its marketing strategy.

Marketing Applications

1. Assume you are going to open a new store selling fitness products. Describe it. Who are your competitors? What would you do to monitor your competitors' actions? Who are your customers? What are you going to do to appeal to them? What are your social responsibilities, and how will you meet them?

2. How would your approach to buying a computer differ from your parents' approach? What about buying an outfit to wear to a party? How can firms use their knowledge of different age or generational cohorts to market their products and services better?

3. How can firms use customer demographics like income, market size, education, and ethnicity to market to their customers better?

4. Identify some of the ethnicity changes in the United States. Describe how they might affect the marketing practices of (a) a radio station in Texas, (b) food retailers in cities, and (c) a home furnishing store in New York City.

5. Identify some recent technological innovations in the marketplace and describe how they have affected consumers' everyday activities.

6. Why should a T-shirt shop in the United States care about the value of the Hong Kong dollar?

7. Several social trends were discussed in the chapter. For each of these trends, choose a retailer or service provider that you believe has seized the moment by grasping the importance of the trend and successfully marketing to its customers as a result.

8. Identify a company that you believe does a particularly good job of marketing to different cultural groups. Justify your answer.

9. Examine the consumer protection legislation in Exhibit 5.5. Which law do you believe has had the biggest impact on society in general? Which has had the largest impact on you personally? Justify your answer.

Quiz Yourself

1. ABC Company knew that its customers were interested in environmentally friendly business practices, so it began marking all of its products as environmentally friendly because they were made with all-natural ingredients, even though ABC's plant was one of the worst polluters in town. The new term for this practice is

   a. deceptive advertising.

   b. greenwashing.

   c. environmental exploitation.

   d. virtual greening.

   e. enviromarketing.

2. One of the goals of value-based marketing is

   a. to provide the greatest value for the least profit.

   b. to sell products for the highest possible price.

   c. to offer greater value than competitors offer.

   d. to determine the value of the brand.

   e. to sell to all consumers, regardless of their needs.

(Answers to these two questions can be found in the Quiz Yourself Answer Key section.)

Chapter Case Study

A NEXT-GENERATION CLEANSER[43]

Taking an Iroquois directive—"In our every deliberation, we must consider the impact of our decisions on the next seven generations"—the consumer product company Seventh Generation has applied a distinctly modern sensibility to derive a long-term approach to the marketing environment. Although its mission statement might be focused on future generations, its efforts to appeal to current consumers are always responsive to their immediate demands.

From its start in Vermont in 1988, Seventh Generation has grown to become a national brand with more than $200 million in revenues.[44] Its growth has been sparked largely by consumer desires to buy more sustainable, environmentally safe green products. Approximately 71 percent of consumers in a recent survey indicated that they thought it was important to buy green offerings (up from 66 percent in 2008), and consumer demand for products in a wide range of categories continues to grow.[45]

But even as more categories appear to offer promising green opportunities for marketers, the primary purchase area continues to be groceries and household products—exactly the space that Seventh Generation dominates. As it has gained brand recognition and trust, it also has proactively altered its market. That is, Seventh Generation does not simply wait for customers to request options. It creates entirely new categories.

With a new line of detergents, Seventh Generation began promoting the idea that perhaps chemical brighteners—common to virtually all commercially available detergents, even those that avoid dyes or fragrances—are not necessary. The company took care not to suggest these chemicals were dangerous. It just says they're unnecessary, and for consumers interested in environmental concerns, that may be enough.

Previously, household magazines such as *Good Housekeeping* or *Real Simple* might have ranked the best detergent, the best dishwashing soap, and the best surface cleaner. But

Seventh Generation dominates the environmentally friendly cleaning products market in the United States.

© HO Marketwire/Newscom

the entry of companies such as Seventh Generation has created new categories: best green detergent, best green dishwashing soap, and best green cleaner. Seventh Generation products consistently emerge victorious in these new category contests.[46]

In addition, to maintain its brand recognition, it uses extensive multimedia marketing initiatives. In print ads, it highlights the environmentally friendly contents of its laundry detergent. It provides free samples to active bloggers, along with blacklights so these consumers can test their own clothes to see the residues left by other detergents. Dozens have posted the results of their own in-home experiments.[47]

Yet its products also cost more, which offers a significant challenge in the very price-competitive cleaning products market. Even as many consumer product companies increasingly tout their down-market brands, Seventh Generation introduced a 4× concentrated laundry detergent that costs significantly more. The new derivation avoids all volatile organic compounds and relies on enzymes to get clothes clean.[48]

In 2013, Seventh Generation spent a significant sum to acquire bobble, a company that produces reusable, self-filtering water bottles. Because many consumers worry about using environmentally unfriendly plastic water bottles, but also are not willing to trust unfiltered tap water, the new product provides an effective solution. With this move, Seventh Generation also appears poised to "extend our influence and spread our practices more broadly by acquiring innovative brands in the sustainability space," in the words of the company CEO.[49]

Questions

1.   What consumer trends does Seventh Generation respond to most effectively?
2.   Which consumer trends might it be missing?

Endnotes

1.   Beth Kowitt, "Panera Really Wants You to Know What's Not in Its Soups," *Fortune*, January 5, 2016; "Panera Changing Soup to 'Clean' Recipe," *Fox2Now.com* (St. Louis), January 7, 2016; Nancy Gagliardi, "Consumers Want Healthy Foods—And Will Pay More for Them," *Forbes.com*, February 18, 2015.

2.   Peter F. Drucker, *The Essential Drucker* (New York: HarperCollins, 2001).

3.   "Corning Announces Third-Quarter Results," *Corning News Release*, October 24, 2012, http://www.corning.com.

4.   Mallory Schlossberg, "One of the Oldest Diet Companies in America is Thriving Without Organic Food or Going Carb-Free," *Business Insider*, January 10, 2016, http://www.businessinsider.com/jenny-craig-ceo-interview-2016-1.

5.   Jessica Wohl, "Oprah vs. Kirstie: Let the Celebrity 'Wellness' Battle Begin," *AdvertisingAge*, December 30, 2015, adage.com/article/cmo-strategy/oprah-vs-kirstie-celebrity-wellness-battle/301961/.

6.   Ibid.

7.   http://www.nau.com; Chris Dannen, "Wanted: The Light, Recycled Trench," *Fast Company*, November 19, 2010, http://www.fastcompany.com; Polly Labarre, "Leap of Faith," *Fast Company*, June 2007.

8.   Del I. Hawkins and David L. Mothersbaugh, *Consumer Behavior: Building Marketing Strategy*, 11th ed. (Burr Ridge, IL: McGraw-Hill/Irwin, 2009); Philip Cateora and John Graham, *International Marketing*, 16th ed. (Burr Ridge, IL: McGraw-Hill/Irwin, 2012).

9.   Katie Little, "Hot McDonald's Items You (Probably) Can't Order," *CNBC*, July 30, 2015, http://www.cnbc.com/2015/04/16/hot-mcdonalds-items-you-probably-cant-order.html.

10.   "Fast Food Review: Hot 'n Spicy McChicken from McDonald's," *GrubGrade*, March 7, 2011, http://www.grubgrade.com/reviews/fast-food-review-hot-n-spicy-mcchicken-from-mcdonalds/.

11.   Katie Little, "Hot McDonald's Items You (Probably) Can't Order," *CNBC*, July 30, 2015, http://www.cnbc.com/2015/04/16/hot-mcdonalds-items-you-probably-cant-order.html.

12.   "Fast Food Reference: McDonald's U.S. Regional/Seasonal Menu Items," *Brand Eating*, August 2, 2011, http://www.brandeating.com/2011/08/fast-food-reference-mcdonalds-us.html#2DvdA6r3JuFR6squ.99.

13.   "The Top Customer Loyalty Programs and Why they Work," *Consumer Strategist*, March 3, 2015, http://www.consumer-strategist.com/top-customer-loyalty-programs/.

14.   Mark van Rijmenam, "Tesco and Big Data Analytics, a Recipe for Success?" *DataFloq*, December 22, 2014, https://datafloq.com/read/tesco-big-data-analytics-recipe-success/665.

15.   Geoffrey E. Meredith, Charles D. Schewe, and Janice Karlovich, *Defining Markets, Defining Moments: America's 7 Generational Cohorts, Their Shared Experiences, and Why Businesses Should Care* (New York: Wiley, 2002).

16.   "Consumers of Tomorrow: Insights and Observations about Generation Z," *Grail Research*, June 2010.

17.   Suzy Menkes, "Marketing to the Millennials," *The New York Times*, March 2, 2010; Pamela Paul, "Getting Inside Gen Y," *American Demographics* 23, no. 9; Sharon Jayson, "A Detailed Look at the Millennials," *USA Today*, February 23, 2010.

18.   Carmen DeNavas-Walt and Bernadette D. Proctor, "Income and Poverty in the United States: 2014," September 2015, https://www.census.gov/content/dam/Census/library/publications/2015/demo/p60-252.pdf.

19.   Ibid.

20.   Dave Gilson and Carolyn Perot, "It's the Inequality, Stupid," *Mother Jones* (March/April 2011), http://motherjones.com;

Organisation for Economic Co-operation and Development, "Growing Unequal? Income Distribution and Poverty in OECD Countries," 2008, http://www.oecd.org.

21. Erik Simanis and Duncan Duke, "Profits at the Bottom of the Pyramid," *Harvard Business Review*, October 2014, https://hbr.org/2014/10/profits-at-the-bottom-of-the-pyramid.

22. http://www.census.gov; http://www.infoplease.com.

23. "Income of Young Adults," *National Center for Education Statistics* (n.d.), https://nces.ed.gov/fastfacts/display.asp?id=77.

24. Richard Thaler, "Breadwinning Wives and Nervous Husbands," *The New York Times*, June 1, 2013, http://www.nytimes.com.

25. Miguel Bustillo and Mary Ellen Lloyd, "Best Buy Tests New Appeals to Women," *The Wall Street Journal*, June 16, 2010.

26. Jeffrey S. Passel and D'Vera Cohn, "U.S. Population Projections: 2005–2050," Pew Research Center, http://pewhispanic.org.

27. Joel Kotkin, "The Changing Demographics of America," *Smithsonian Magazine* (August 2010), http://www.smithsonianmag.com.

28. Julie Jargon, "Pizza Chain Seeks Slice of Bicultural Pie," *The Wall Street Journal*, December 30, 2010, http://online.wsj.com.

29. Todd Wasserman, "Report: Shifting African American Population," *Adweek*, January 12, 2010, http://www.adweek.com; U.S. Bureau of the Census, "Annual Social and Economic Supplement to the Current Population Survey," http://www.census.gov.

30. Nielsen, "The State of the African-American Consumer," September 2011, p. 5.

31. Centers for Disease Control and Prevention, "National Diabetes Fact Sheet, 2011," http://www.cdc.gov.

32. http://www.subway.com/subwayroot/about_us/Social_Responsibility/NutritionalLeadership.aspx.

33. Dan Galbraith, "Subway Partners with Disney on *Star Wars*–Themed Fresh Fit for Kids Meal Promotion," *The Packer*, December 21, 2015.

34. Yoga Buzz, "Yoga Biz Thrives Despite Economy," October 24, 2011, http://blogs.yogajournal.com.

35. Catherine Clifford, "Yoga: The Booming Business of Zen," *CNNMoney*, October 18, 2011, http://money.cnn.com.

36. This definition of green marketing draws on work by Jacquelyn A. Ottman, *Green Marketing: Opportunity for Innovation* (Chicago: NTC Publishing, 1997).

37. "SunChips Marketing Campaign Brings Light to Its Solar Energy Efforts," PR Newswire, April 3, 2008, http://www.prnewswire.com/news-releases/sunchips-marketing-campaign-brings-light-to-its-solar-energy-efforts-57042102.html.

38. Dan Mangan, "There's a Hack for That: Fitbit User Accounts Attacked," *CNBC*, January 8, 2016, http://www.cnbc.com/2016/01/08/theres-a-hack-for-that-fitbit-user-accounts-attacked.html.

39. John Bussey, "Taming the Spies of Web Advertising," *The Wall Street Journal*, August 8, 2013.

40. http://www.irs.gov/.

41. Brendan Greeley, "Providing Internet Access to the Poor," *Bloomberg Businessweek*, November 17, 2011, http://www.businessweek.com.

42. Brian Fung, "It Shouldn't Take a Merger for Low-Income Americans to Get Cheap Broadband," *The Washington Post*, March 5, 2014, https://www.washingtonpost.com/news/the-switch/wp/2014/03/05/it-shouldnt-take-a-merger-for-low-income-americans-to-get-cheap-broadband/.

43. http://www.seventhgeneration.com.

44. Serena Ng, "Seventh Generation Picks Up Bobble Brand," *The Wall Street Journal*, May 30, 2013, http://online.wsj.com.

45. "71% of Consumers Think Green When Purchasing," *Environmental Leader*, April 3, 2013; "Seventh Gen, Whole Foods Top Green Brands Ranking," *Environmental Leader*, June 10, 2011, http://www.environmentalleader.com.

46. "The Best Cleaning Products," *Real Simple*, http://www.realsimple.com.

47. Andrew Adam Newman, "Seventh Generation Highlights Its Chemical-Free Detergent," *The New York Times*, December 29, 2010, http://www.nytimes.com/2010/12/30/business/media/30adco.html; "Seventh Generation Promotes Eco-Friendly Detergents through Multichannel Marketing Initiative," December 30, 2010, http://www.ricg.com.

48. Dan D'Ambrosio, "Seventh Generation Looks to Buck Trend in Concentrated Laundry Detergent Market," *Burlington Free Press*, October 13, 2011.

49. "Seventh Generation Acquires bobble for Undisclosed Sum," press release, May 31, 2013, http://seventhgeneration.mwnews-room.com/press-releases/seventh-generation-acquires-bobble-for-undisclosed-1022443.

i. Bonnie Fuller, "Baby-Boomer Marketers Are Misreading Millennials' Media Behavior," *Advertising Age*, May 13, 2013; Chingching Chang, "Dual System Model Comparisons of Print Advertisements and e-Store Product Pages: The Influence of Dominant Pictures on Decision Making," working paper (under review at *Journal of Advertising*).

ii. Michael Fitzgerald, "Not Just a Pharmacy: CVS Unveils Its Digital Innovation Lab," *Fast Company*, June 19, 2015; Jonah Comstock, "CVS MinuteClinic App to Get New Wait Times, Remote Scheduling Features," *Mobile Health News*, December 10, 2015.

iii. Emily Steel, "Nestlé Takes a Beating on Social-Media Sites," *The Wall Street Journal*, March 29, 2010, http://online.wsj.com; Jerry Lynch, "Achieving a Sustainable Palm Oil Commitment," *Taste of General Mills*, December 7, 2012, http://www.blog.generalmills.com; "Haagen-Dazs and General Mills to Help Smallholder Vanilla Farmers Increase Yields and Improve Sustainability Practices in Madagascar," *MarketWatch*, press release, February 20, 2013; "General Mills Joins U.S. Food Waste Challenge as Founding Partner," *The Wall Street Journal*, June 4, 2013, http://online.wsj.com; "General Mills Reports Progress on Global Responsibility Efforts," *The New York Times*, April 30, 2013, http://markets.on.nytimes.com.

iv. Scott M. Fulton III, "Netflix Has an Exchange So Complex That It Has Triggered a Scientific Renaissance," *The New Stack*, February 24, 2015, http://thenewstack.io/netflix-exchange-complex-triggered-scientific-renaissance/; Ben Kunz, "Why Netflix Walked Away from Personalization," *ThoughtGadgets*, January 4, 2014, http://www.thoughtgadgets.com/why-netflix-walked-away-from-personalization/; Amol Sharma, "Amazon Mines Its Data Trove to Bet on TV's Next Hit," *The Wall Street Journal*, November 1, 2013, http://www.wsj.com/; Derrick Harris, "Netflix Analyzes a Lot of Data about Your Viewing Habits," *Gigaom*, June 14, 2012, https://gigaom.com/2012/06/14/netflix-analyzes-a-lot-of-data-about-your-viewing-habits/; Phil Simon, "Big Data Lessons from Netflix," *Wired*, March 11, 2014, http://www.wired.com/; Marianne Zumberge, "'House of Cards' Sees Unusual Social-Media Spike Ahead of Season 3," *Boston Herald*, February 27, 2015, http://www.bostonherald.com/.

v. John Greenough, "Self-Driving Cars Took Center Stage at CES," *Business Insider*, Jan. 14, 2015, http://www.businessinsider.com/self-driving-cars-ces-2016-01; https://www.google.com/selfdrivingcar/where/; Alyssa Newcomb, "Google Self-Driving Cars: What We Learned from Latest Report," *ABC News*, Jan. 14, 2015, http://abcnews.go.com/Technology/google-driving-cars-learned-latest-report/story?id=36285705; U.S. Department of Transportation Federal Highway Administration, "Average Annual Miles per Driver by Age Group," https://www.fhwa.dot.gov/ohim/onh00/bar8.htm; Samantha Masunaga, "Self-Driving Cars Aren't Ready Yet: Here's How Often Human Drivers Need to Grab the Wheel," *Los Angeles Times*, January 14, 2016, http://www.latimes.com/business/autos/la-fi-hy-self-driving-cars-20160113-story.html; Bill Vlasic and Neal E. Boudette, "Self-Driving Tesla Was Involved in Fatal Crash, U.S. Says," *The New York Times*, June 30, 2016.

UNDERSTANDING THE MARKETPLACE

The three chapters in Section Two, Understanding the Marketplace, focus on three levels of marketing: to individual consumers; from business to business; and on the global playing field. Chapter 6, Consumer Behavior, discusses why individual consumers purchase products and services. The consumer decision process is highlighted. Chapter 7, Business-to-Business Marketing, explores the whys and hows of business-to-business buying. Finally, Chapter 8, Global Marketing, focuses on global markets. Thus, the three chapters in Section Two move from creating value for the individual consumer, to creating value for the firm or business, to creating value on the global level.

CHAPTER 6

CONSUMER BEHAVIOR

You get up in the morning, gearing up in your mind for a good run to start your day. But what do you put on: shorts or sweats? Do you need a sweatshirt, or would your technical top be a better option? And what about rain gear? To answer these questions, you need information about the weather, and because you're a modern consumer, you likely pick up your phone to check your favorite weather prediction app. Like a lot of people, maybe you click on the Weather Channel's app to find the temperature, rain chances, or humidity.

And that's exactly why Nike has begun posting advertisements in the Weather Channel's app and developing a

Source: Nike

simultaneous weather-oriented campaign for various advertising channels. Nike recognizes that consumers frequently face a key decision at the point at which they check the weather on their phones or mobile devices. This decision often revolves around what they should wear, and Nike wants to make sure that its brand is prominent and evident, prompting people to lean toward Nike's undershirts or gym shorts as they select their apparel.

Furthermore, the app is specific to the weather conditions the consumer sees. If an early morning jogger checks the weather and finds that it is cold and dark out, the embedded link to Nike's site will take him or her directly to the page featuring a cold weather vest with reflective stripes, for example.

Around the same time it started inserting its advertising on the Weather Channel app, Nike also released a new advertising campaign, "Snow Day," in which dozens of star athletes from various sports awaken to snowy conditions but head out, equipped in Nike gear, to enjoy a quick pick-up game. The idea is to remind consumers that even in terrible weather, exercising can be fun and safe, especially if they are wearing the cold weather gear that Nike sells.

The parallel campaigns reflect several insights Nike has gained. First, virtually everybody complains, thinks, and talks about the weather, so it can reach a broad audience by cooperating with the Weather Channel. Second, Nike recognizes the potential limitations imposed by new ad-blocking software for apps. By integrating its marketing communications within the app, it can sidestep those blockades and ensure that consumers see its advertising. Third, recent evidence indicates that people using apps engage more with the brands appearing within them than do consumers in most other channels. According to some reports, U.S. consumers spend approximately 60 percent of their time online interacting with mobile apps. Therefore, to drive its broader e-commerce strategy, Nike is looking to interact with potential users in the channels that they use the most.[1]

We are all consumers, and we take this status for granted. But we are also complex and irrational creatures who cannot always explain our own choices and actions. This inability makes the vitally important job of marketing managers even more difficult, in that they must be able to explain consumers' behavior to give marketers as clear an understanding of their customers as possible.

To understand consumer behavior, we must ask *why* people buy goods or services. Using principles and theories from sociology and psychology, marketers have been able to decipher many consumer choices and develop basic strategies for dealing with consumer behavior. Generally, people buy one product or service instead of another because they perceive it to be the better value for them; that is, the ratio of benefits to costs is higher for a particular product or service than for any other.

However, benefits can be subtle and less than rationally assessed, as we shall see. Consider Katie Smith, who is thinking of buying a new outfit for a job interview. She requires something fashionable but professional looking and doesn't want to spend a lot of money. In making the decision about where she should buy the outfit, Katie asks herself:

- Which alternative gives me the best overall value—the most appropriate yet fashionable outfit at the lowest price?

- Which alternative is the best investment—the outfit that I can get the most use of?

Because Katie might have several reasons to choose a particular store or outfit, it is critical for companies such as Banana Republic or Macy's to key in on the specific benefits that are most important to her. Other factors that might influence Katie go beyond her conscious awareness, which means that the retailers need to be even more well versed in her decision process than she is.[2] Only then can they create a marketing mix that will satisfy Katie.

In this chapter, we explore the process that consumers go through when they buy products and services. Then we discuss the psychological, social, and situational factors that influence this consumer decision process. Throughout the chapter, we emphasize what firms can do to influence consumers to purchase their products and services.

EXHIBIT 6.1   The Consumer Decision Process

Need recognition

↓

Information search

↓

Alternative evaluation

↓

Purchase and consumption

↓

Post-purchase

THE CONSUMER DECISION PROCESS

The consumer decision process model represents the steps that consumers go through before, during, and after making purchases.[3] Because marketers often find it difficult to determine how consumers make their purchasing decisions, it is useful for us to break down the process into a series of steps and examine each individually, as in Exhibit 6.1.

Need Recognition

The consumer decision process begins when consumers recognize they have an unsatisfied need and they would like to go from their actual, needy state to a different, desired state. The greater the discrepancy between these two states, the greater the need recognition will be. For example, your stomach tells you that you are hungry, and you would rather not have that particular feeling. If you are only a little hungry, you may pass it off and decide to eat later. But if your stomach is growling and you cannot concentrate, the *need*—the difference between your actual (hungry) state and your desired (not hungry) state—is greater and you'll want to eat immediately to get to your desired state. Furthermore, your hunger conceivably could be satisfied by a nice, healthy salad, but what you really want is a bowl of ice cream. *Wants* are goods or services that are not necessarily needed but are desired.[4] Regardless of the level of your hunger, your desire for ice cream will never be satisfied by any type of salad. Consumer needs like these can be classified as functional, psychological, or both.[5]

Functional Needs Functional needs pertain to the performance of a product or service. For years, BMW has made functionally superior motorcycles. BMW's K1600 model has an inline six-cylinder motor, something previously available only in BMW automobiles, combined with a stiff aluminum frame. Thus it offers remarkable power on a lightweight bike, enabling it to outperform the best luxury touring bikes in terms of comfort as well as serious sporty motorcycles in terms of speed. Of course, not everyone in need of a transportation function needs the power and speed of a BMW. A bicycle, a motor scooter, or a car can perform this function as well. It just depends on the specific needs of the purchaser.

As Marketing Analytics 6.1 notes, virtually everyone must pay taxes, and H&R Block seeks to convince taxpayers to let it help them meet this highly functional need.

What needs does a BMW K1600 satisfy?
© Zuma Press, Inc./Alamy

LO6-1 Articulate the steps in the consumer buying process.

LO6-2 Describe the difference between functional and psychological needs.

Do Lana Marks bags, like this one carried by Bingbing Li, satisfy psychological or functional needs?

© Ethan Miller/Getty Images

Psychological Needs Psychological needs pertain to the personal gratification consumers associate with a product and/or service.[6] Purses, for instance, provide a functional need—to transport wallets and other personal items and keep them organized and safe. So why would anyone pay more than $5,000 for a purse that does not perform these tasks any better than a $100 purse? Because they seek to satisfy psychological needs. Each year, Lana Marks produces a single Cleopatra clutch purse valued at $250,000. The purse is extravagantly embellished; one version featured more than 1,500 black and white diamonds, 18-carat gold, and alligator skin. The company permits one star each year to bring its purse to the Oscars; recent winners of this informal contest were Charlize Theron and Helen Mirren.[7] Even though these bags are not known for being particularly practical, strong demand for Lana Marks bags persists among women who love exciting (and expensive) purses.

These examples highlight that most goods and services seek to satisfy functional as well as psychological needs, albeit to different degrees. Whereas the functional characteristics of a BMW K1600 are its main selling point, it also maintains a fashionable appeal for bikers and comes in several colors to match buyers' aesthetic preferences. Lana Marks purses satisfy psychological needs that overshadow the functional needs, though they still ultimately serve the function of carrying personal items.

Successful marketing requires determining the correct balance of functional and psychological needs that best appeal to the firm's target markets.

Marketing Analytics 6.1   Tax Time Tactics by H&R Block[i]

Taxes may be among the few certainties in life, but they usually are not considered one of the more fun features. But in an attempt to make the inevitable a little less painful, H&R Block is seeking to make "tax season" a time that regular consumers actually can enjoy, if they do it right. The basis for the claim stems mostly from the company's in-depth analysis of its customer data. An elite analytics team, The Tax Institute at H&R Block, learned by poring over reams of data that approximately half of the consumers who do their own taxes make mistakes in their returns. Then the team of tax attorneys and CPAs went deeper into the data and determined that about half of those mistaken returns led to people receiving smaller refunds than they actually deserved. In turn, it developed an advertising campaign that promises to "get your billions back" for taxpayers who rely on its professional services.

But H&R Block also acknowledges that more than one-third of U.S. taxpayers continue to do their taxes themselves, so it offers online assistance too. With H&R Block's software, taxpayers can complete and submit their federal and state income tax returns for less than $10, while still receiving some limited online help from the tax professionals. Although it has been offering the online service for more than 15 years, its more recent analysis of customer data showed that a $9.99 price would be likely to drive interest while also reinforcing the enjoyable idea of saving money. Moreover, confusion among taxpayers about new laws and regulations (especially those related to the Affordable Care Act) created another opening for H&R Block to attract potential customers, promising that it can help them understand their tax liabilities and responsibilities, whether they come in to brick-and-mortar

H&R Block uses analytics to make tax preparation more enjoyable, at a price that its customers deem reasonable.
© Paul Sakuma/AP Photo

storefronts with all their receipts or aim to complete their paperwork at home.

These moves reflect the tax service's recent adoption of an advanced data analytics platform called Domo, which combines various sources and types of information into a single, straightforward format. According to H&R Block's manager of analytics and operations, "With Domo, we already have alignment on what we are measuring, so we no longer spend time each week discussing the data itself. Instead, we can ask better questions about the business and make decisions based on the information we have."

Search for Information

The second step, after a consumer recognizes a need, is to search for information about the various options that exist to satisfy that need. The length and intensity of the search are based on the degree of perceived risk associated with purchasing the product or service. If the way your hair is cut is important to your appearance and self-image, you may engage in an involved search for the right salon and stylist. Alternatively, an athlete looking for a short buzz cut might go to the closest, most convenient, and cheapest barber shop. Regardless of the required search level, there are two key types of information search: internal and external.

Internal Search for Information In an internal search for information, the buyer examines his or her own memory and knowledge about the product or service gathered through past experiences. For example, every time Katie wants to eat salad for lunch, she and her friends go to Sweet Tomatoes, but if she's craving dessert, she heads straight to The Cheesecake Factory. In making these choices, she relies on her memory of past experiences when she has eaten at these restaurant chains.

External Search for Information In an external search for information, the buyer seeks information outside his or her personal knowledge base to help make the buying decision. Consumers might fill in their personal knowledge gaps by talking with friends, family, or a salesperson. They can also scour commercial media for unsponsored and (it is hoped) unbiased information, such as that available through *Consumer Reports,* or peruse sponsored media such as magazines, television, or radio. Perhaps the most common sources of external information these days are online search engines, such as Google and Bing.

The Internet provides information in various ways.[8] For example, while watching an episode of Fox's *Scream Queens,* Katie saw one of the Chanels wearing a fantastic outfit that included a flare dress and pearl choker. She pulled her laptop over, went to WornOnTv.net, and found the focal episode, which in turn told her where to purchase the items she loved. The choker was designed by Baroni and available for $119, and the dress cost $48.[9] But Katie is also a savvy shopper, so when she searched for "Baroni pearl choker" on Bing, she found that she could get it at a lower price from another retailer. Satisfied with that purchase, she began flipping through a magazine and saw Reese Witherspoon wearing a pair of adorable jeans. This time she navigated directly to TrueFit.com, which featured those very jeans, designed by 7 For All Mankind, on its home page.[10] Katie entered her measurements and style preferences, and the website returned recommendations of jeans that would be a good fit for her.

All these examples are external searches for information. Katie used the television show's dedicated site to find a style she liked; she referred to a magazine for additional style tips; and, using the web, she found jeans that would be a perfect fit for her. All these events took place without Katie ever leaving her home to go to the store or try on dozens of pairs of pants.

Factors Affecting Consumers' Search Processes It is important for marketers to understand the many factors that affect consumers' search processes. Among them are the following three factors: perceived benefits versus perceived costs of search, the locus of control, and the actual or perceived risk.

Katie liked the picture of Reese Witherspoon in jeans that she found in a magazine so much that she navigated to TrueFit.com and purchased them.

© JB Lacroix/WireImage/Getty Images

 LO6-3 Describe factors that affect information search.

The Perceived Benefits versus Perceived Costs of Search Is it worth the time and effort to search for information about a product or service? For instance, most families spend a lot of time researching the housing market in their preferred area before they make a purchase, because homes are a very expensive and important purchase with significant safety and enjoyment implications. They likely spend much less time researching which inexpensive dollhouse to buy for the youngest member of the family.[11]

The Locus of Control People who have an internal locus of control believe they have some control over the outcomes of their actions, in which case they generally engage in more search activities. With an external locus of control, consumers believe that fate or other external factors control all outcomes. In that case, they believe it doesn't matter how much information they gather; if they make a wise decision, it isn't to their credit, and if they make a poor one, it isn't their fault. People who do a lot of research before purchasing individual stocks have an internal locus of control; those who purchase mutual funds are more likely to believe that they can't predict the market and probably have an external locus of control. These beliefs have widespread effects. For example, when people believe that they can choose their own consumption goals (internal locus of control), they work

Social & Mobile Marketing 6.1   The Future of Health Is Mobile[ii]

A host of new applications and mobile links make it easier than ever for consumers to maintain their own health and well-being with just a few clicks. Whether the condition is chronic or new, these health-related offerings seek to make it easier for health care consumers to understand their options, consider solutions, and recognize when to seek immediate medical care. They also facilitate providers' efforts to stay up to date with the latest treatments and advances. Consider a few examples:

- The award-winning app mySugr turns the tedious task of glucose monitoring into a game for diabetics. They earn points for each data entry they make that helps them tame a monster named Diabetes. The app enables users to record their food consumption and take snapshots of what they have eaten, provides immediate data analyses, produces a summary report that users can send to their doctors, and maintains the data in a central location.

- Doctor Mole allows people to take a selfie (i.e., self-portrait) of any suspicious skin growth. Using augmented reality technology, the app applies the well-established criteria for assessing the risk associated with each mole (i.e., asymmetry, borders, color, diameter). Users can determine whether they have a potentially cancerous malignancy or just a new freckle.

- With BurnMed, users draw on a displayed image of a body to indicate the extent of the burn suffered, whether by themselves, a friend, or a patient. This app seeks to target laypeople as well as medical practitioners. In a lay setting, users can determine the seriousness of a burn they might have suffered at home. In a medical practice, emergency staff can quickly determine the appropriate treatment when faced with a crisis such as a tanker explosion that burns hundreds of victims.

- The vCath training tool is expressly for medical students who need to learn to insert neurosurgical catheters. In patients this step is critical and risky because students have little opportunity for practicing their technique. The

app enables them to do so virtually, as many times as they wish, before facing actual patients.

Along with these dedicated apps, various hospitals and doctors are experimenting with software that reminds patients to take their medicine or when their next appointments are. By encouraging positive behaviors, these technology advances should lead to greater consumer health and happiness as well as benefits for society as a whole.

Smartphone apps empower consumers to take control of their health in exciting new ways.

Source: mySugr/GmbH. -K. Rose

harder to achieve them than if those goals feel imposed upon them (external locus of control).[12] Social and Mobile Marketing 6.1 discusses how consumers are gaining a greater internal locus of control over their health by using smartphone apps.

Actual or Perceived Risk Five types of risk associated with purchase decisions can delay or discourage a purchase: performance, financial, social, physiological, and psychological. The higher the risk, the more likely the consumer is to engage in an extended search.

Performance risk involves the perceived danger inherent in a poorly performing product or service. An example of performance risk is the possibility that Katie Smith's new interview outfit is prone to shrinking when dry cleaned.

Financial risk is risk associated with a monetary outlay and includes the initial cost of the purchase as well as the costs of using the item or service.[13] Katie is concerned not only that her new outfit will provide her with the professional appearance she is seeking but also that the cost of dry cleaning will not be exorbitant. Retailers recognize that buying professional apparel can be a financial burden and therefore offer guarantees that the products they sell will perform as expected. Their suppliers are also well aware that dry cleaning is expensive and can limit the life of the garment, so many offer easy-to-care-for washable fabrics.

Social risk involves the fears that consumers suffer when they worry others might not regard their purchases positively. When buying a fashionable outfit, consumers like Katie consider what their friends would like. Alternatively, because this job interview is so important, Katie might make a conscious effort to assert a distinctive identity or make a statement by buying a unique, more stylish, and possibly more expensive outfit than her friends would typically buy. She also hopes to impress her prospective boss rather than her pals with her choice.

Physiological risk could also be called safety risk. Whereas performance risk involves what might happen if a product does not perform as expected, physiological (or safety) risk refers to the fear of an actual harm should the product not perform properly. Although physiological risk is typically not an issue with apparel, it can be an important issue when buying other products, such as a car. External agencies and government bodies publish safety ratings for cars to help assuage this risk. Consumers compare the safety records of their various choices because they recognize the real danger to their well-being if the automobile they purchase fails to perform a basic task, such as stopping when the driver steps on the brakes or protecting the passengers in the cabin even if the car flips.

Finally, psychological risks are those risks associated with the way people will feel if the product or service does not convey the right image. Katie Smith, thinking of her outfit purchase, read several fashion magazines and sought her friends' opinions because she wanted people to think she looked great in the outfit—and she wanted to get the job!

Recent research suggests that psychological risks might help explain why consumers often think that "bigger is better." In particular, this research helps explain why some enjoy buying large-sized menu items at restaurants. Especially when consumers feel powerless or more vulnerable, they equate larger sizes—whether in televisions, houses, or menu items—with improved status.[14]

Evaluation of Alternatives

Once a consumer has recognized a problem and explored the possible options, he or she must sift through the choices available and evaluate the alternatives. Alternative evaluation often occurs while the consumer is engaged in the process of information search. For example, Katie Smith would rule out various stores because she knows they won't carry the style she needs for the job interview. Once in the right kind of store, she would try on lots of outfits and eliminate those that do not fit, do not look good on her, or are not appropriate attire for the occasion. Consumers forgo alternative evaluations altogether when buying habitual (convenience) products; you'll rarely catch a loyal Pepsi drinker buying Coca-Cola.

Attribute Sets Research has shown that a consumer's mind organizes and categorizes alternatives to aid his or her decision process. Universal sets include all possible choices for a product category, but because it would be unwieldy for a person to recall all possible alternatives for every purchase decision, marketers tend to focus on only a subset of choices. One important subset is retrieval sets, which are those brands or stores that can be readily brought forth from memory. Another is a consumer's evoked set, which comprises the alternative brands or stores that the consumer states he or she would consider when making a purchase decision. If a firm can get its brand or store into a consumer's evoked set, it has increased the likelihood of purchase and therefore reduced search time because the consumer will think specifically of that brand when considering choices.

Katie Smith knows that there are a lot of apparel stores (universal set). However, only some have the style that she is looking for, such as Macy's, The Gap, and Banana Republic

Macy's is part of the retrieval set of stores available to women for business apparel, but Banana Republic is in the evoked set for young women looking for business apparel.

Left: © McGraw-Hill Education/Mark Dierker, photographer; right: © Sang Tan/AP Photo

(retrieval set). She recalls that Macy's is where her mother shops and The Gap is a favorite of her younger sister. But she is sure that Banana Republic and Macy's carry business attire she would like, so only those stores are in her evoked set.

When consumers begin to evaluate different alternatives, they often base their evaluations on a set of important attributes or evaluative criteria. **Evaluative criteria** consist of salient, or important, attributes about a particular product. For example, when Katie is looking for her outfit, she might consider things like the selling price, fit, materials and construction quality, reputation of the brand, and the service support that the retailer offers. At times, however, it becomes difficult to evaluate different brands or stores because there are so many choices,[15] especially when those choices involve aspects of the garment that are difficult to evaluate, such as materials and construction quality.

Consumers use several shortcuts to simplify the potentially complicated decision process: determinant attributes and consumer decision rules. **Determinant attributes** are product or service features that are important to the buyer and on which competing brands or stores are perceived to differ.[16] Because many important and desirable criteria are equal among the various choices, consumers look for something special—a determinant attribute—to differentiate one brand or store from another. Determinant attributes may appear perfectly rational, such as health and nutrition claims offered by certain foods and beverages, or they may be more subtle and psychologically based, such as the stitching on the rear pockets of those 7 For All Mankind jeans that Reese Witherspoon was wearing. Ethical and Societal Dilemma 6.1 highlights the use of determinant attributes describing food and beverages marketed as natural when in fact they are not.

Consumer Decision Rules **Consumer decision rules** are the set of criteria that consumers use consciously or subconsciously to quickly and efficiently select from among several alternatives. These rules are typically either compensatory or noncompensatory.

Compensatory A **compensatory decision rule** assumes that the consumer, when evaluating alternatives, trades off one characteristic against another, such that good characteristics compensate for bad characteristics.[17] For instance, Hanna Jackson is looking to buy breakfast cereal and is considering several factors such as taste, calories, price, and natural/organic claims. But even if the cereal is priced a little higher than Hanna was planning to spend, a superb overall rating offsets, or compensates for, the higher price.

Ethical & Societal Dilemma 6.1

Wearing the "Healthy" Label: Natural and Organic Foods[iii]

With competition for shelf space always at a premium, today's supermarket aisles are more crowded than ever. Much of the new competition comes from natural and organic foods, which comprised about 10 and 5 percent, respectively, of the more than $700 billion U.S. food industry in 2013.

For a consumer facing a dizzying array of choices, these natural foods offer a unique appeal: They promise to improve personal and planetary health. Organic and natural food companies claim that their foods are safer and more nutritious because they are produced with only natural ingredients.

Consumers generally believe that these claims mean the food contains no artificial or highly processed ingredients. Yet Snapple's "natural" bottled iced tea contains high-fructose corn syrup, a highly processed and controversial form of sugar. In California, most organic strawberry farmers use seeds and plants from nurseries that are not organic, including growers producing fruit for Driscoll Strawberry Associates, the largest berry distributor in the world. The farmers argue that once their plants bear fruit, they halt their use of chemical pesticides and herbicides, so the berries themselves

How healthful is Snapple?

© Bloomberg/Getty Images

are still organic. These companies thus might be contradicting consumer expectations, but they are not actually violating federal requirements.

The U.S. Department of Agriculture (USDA) regulates the production of organic foods. Products bearing the USDA Organic label must be grown using organic, not conventional, farming methods. That regulation means using natural fertilizers such as manure or compost, beneficial insects or birds rather than chemical herbicides to control insects, and crop rotation or other manual methods rather than chemical herbicides to control weeds. Animals raised for meat production must be given organic feed and access to the outdoors rather than antibiotics, growth hormones, and other medications.

Yet the USDA's National Organic Program (NOP) regulations do not explicitly govern the production of seeds and planting stock. Advocates who want to see sustainable production methods used throughout the food-growing process have called on the USDA to outlaw the use of chemical fumigants, including methyl bromide, a widely used pesticide and soil sterilizer known to deplete the ozone layer. Furthermore, NOP regulations allow conventional agricultural stock to be used whenever organically grown seeds and plants are not commercially available.

Nor does the USDA regulate the production of foods labeled "natural," except for meats and poultry, which must be minimally processed and free of artificial colors, flavors, sweeteners, preservatives, and ingredients. No such specifics govern other foods that choose to carry the natural label rather than an organic claim.

For the consumer, the organic and natural food experience is also about perception. Some shoppers may believe these foods deliver healthful benefits, but studies also reveal that simply identifying a grocery item as a healthy food option may affect their eating experience. Specifically, people may perceive that health-oriented foods do not taste good or satisfy their need to curb their appetites. Students given snacks labeled "health bars" reported feeling hungry afterward and craving foods they enjoyed more. In another study, respondents widely perceived "that 'healthy' isn't going to meet enjoyment goals," which likely reflects consumers' assumption that healthy foods won't taste good.

Although Hanna probably would not go through the formal process of making the purchasing decision based on the **multi-attribute model** described in Exhibit 6.2, this exhibit illustrates how a compensatory model would work.[18] Hanna assigns weights to the importance of each factor. These weights must add up to 1.0. So, for instance, for Hannah, taste is the most important, with a weight of 0.4, and calories are least important, with a weight of 0.1. She assigns weights to how well each of the cereals might perform, with 1 being very poor and 10 being very good. Hanna thinks Cheerios has the best taste, so she assigns it a 10. Then she multiplies each performance rating by its importance rating to get an overall score for each cereal. The rating for Cheerios in this example is the highest of the

EXHIBIT 6.2	Compensatory Purchasing Multi-Attribute Model for Buying Cereal				
	Taste	Calories	Natural/Organic Claims	Price	Overall Score
Importance Weight	0.4	0.1	0.3	0.2	
Cheerios © Michael J. Hruby	10	8	6	8	8.2
Post © Michael J. Hruby	8	9	8	3	7.1
Kashi © Michael J. Hruby	6	8	10	5	7.2

three cereals $[(0.4 \times 10) + (0.1 \times 8) + (0.3 \times 6) + (0.2 \times 8) = 8.2)]$. This multi-attribute model allows the trade-off between the various factors to be incorporated explicitly into a consumer's purchase decision.

Noncompensatory Sometimes, however, consumers use a **noncompensatory decision rule** in which they choose a product or service on the basis of one characteristic or one sub-set of a characteristic, regardless of the values of its other attributes.[19] So although Cheerios received the highest overall score of 8.2, Hanna might still pick Kashi because she is particularly sensitive to claims of natural or organic contents, and this brand earned the highest score on this attribute (i.e., a 10). Once a consumer has considered the possible alternatives and evaluated the pros and cons of each, he or she can move toward a purchase decision.

Purchase and Consumption

After evaluating the alternatives, customers are ready to buy. However, they don't always patronize the store or purchase the brand or item on which they had originally decided. It may not be available at the retail store, for example. Retailers therefore turn to the **conversion rate** to measure how well they have converted purchase intentions into purchases. One method of measuring the conversion rate is the number of real or virtual abandoned carts in the retailer's store or website.

When it realized that approximately two-thirds of decisions about home improvements are made by women, Home Depot embarked on a strategy to increase its conversion rate by appealing more to women. It has implemented in-store renovations to ensure that female consumers not only visit its stores but also make their purchases there rather than from its main rival, Lowe's. In particular, whereas Home Depot once purposefully embraced a sort of construction site feel, with wheeled pallets and jumbled displays of nuts and bolts, the renovated stores feature better lighting and cleaner product displays. In addition, greeters at

When Home Depot realized that the majority of home improvement decisions are made by women, it implemented changes from its traditional construction site feel (left) to include cleaner product displays (right).

Left: © Capture +/Alamy; right: © Paul Bersebach/Zumapress/Newscom

the entrance help people find what they need. In addition to the greeters, Home Depot is enhancing customer service by mounting devices throughout stores to enable shoppers to check prices or find particular items, and it is providing more training to employees, encouraging them to provide more effective assistance to shoppers who might be less familiar with hardware and home improvement projects.

To make sure that shoppers can find everything they want and therefore don't have the desire to shop elsewhere, Home Depot is expanding its product lines to feature familiar names such as Martha Stewart and include more décor and convenience items for the household. The idea is that a trip to Home Depot can be a family event, because it carries items for parents of either gender, as well as small projects for kids. If these family members want to install their new purchases on their own, Home Depot offers do-it-yourself workshops in stores as well as video tutorials online. If they want to have the product installed by professionals, Home Depot provides a list of qualified, rated subcontractors available for the work. Thus the retailer seeks to become the sole source for all its customers' home improvement needs, from the smallest project to the largest remodeling.[20]

EXHIBIT 6.3 Components of Postpurchase Outcomes

Customer satisfaction

Postpurchase cognitive dissonance

Customer loyalty

Postpurchase

The final step of the consumer decision process is postpurchase behavior. Marketers are particularly interested in postpurchase behavior because it entails actual rather than potential customers. Satisfied customers, whom marketers hope to create, become loyal, purchase again, and spread positive word of mouth, so they are quite important. There are three possible postpurchase outcomes, as illustrated in Exhibit 6.3: customer satisfaction, postpurchase cognitive dissonance, and customer loyalty (or disloyalty).

 Discuss postpurchase outcomes.

Customer Satisfaction Setting unrealistically high consumer expectations of the product through advertising, personal selling, or other types of promotion may lead to higher initial sales, but it eventually will result in dissatisfaction if the product fails to achieve high performance expectations. (For a related discussion about communication gaps, see Chapter 13.) This failure can lead to dissatisfied customers and the potential for negative word of mouth.[21] Setting customer expectations too low is an equally dangerous strategy. Many retailers fail to put their best foot forward. For instance, no matter how good the merchandise and service may be, if a store is not clean and appealing from the entrance, customers are not likely to enter.

Marketers can take several steps to ensure postpurchase satisfaction:

- Build realistic expectations, not too high and not too low.

- Demonstrate correct product use—improper usage can cause dissatisfaction.

- Stand behind the product or service by providing money-back guarantees and warranties.

- Encourage customer feedback, which cuts down on negative word of mouth and helps marketers adjust their offerings.

- Periodically make contact with customers and thank them for their support. This contact reminds customers that the marketer cares about their business and wants them to be satisfied. It also provides an opportunity to correct any problems. Customers appreciate human contact, though it is more expensive for marketers than are e-mail or postal mail contacts.

Postpurchase Cognitive Dissonance Postpurchase cognitive dissonance is an internal conflict that arises from an inconsistency between two beliefs or between beliefs and behavior. For example, you might have buyer's remorse after purchasing an expensive television because you question whether this high-priced version offers appreciably better quality than does a set of similar size but at a lower price—or whether you need a television at all, considering your ability to stream content through your computer. Postpurchase cognitive dissonance generally occurs when a consumer questions the appropriateness of a purchase after his or her decision has been made.

Postpurchase cognitive dissonance is especially likely for products that are expensive, are infrequently purchased, do not work as intended, or are associated with high levels of risk. Marketers direct efforts at consumers after the purchase is made to address this issue.[22] General Electric sends a letter to purchasers of its appliances, mentioning the high quality that went into the product's design and production, thus positively reinforcing the message that the customer made a wise decision. Some clothing manufacturers include a tag on their garments to offer the reassurance that because of their special manufacturing process, perhaps designed to provide a soft, vintage appearance, there may be variations in color that have no effect on the quality of the item. After a pang of dissonance, satisfaction may then set in.

Let's check back in with our friend Katie to recognize these effects. After Katie purchased her interview outfit at Macy's, she tried it on for some of her friends. Her boyfriend said he loved it, but several of her girlfriends seemed less impressed. Katie thought it made her look more mature. Because of these mixed signals, some dissonance resulted and manifested itself as an uncomfortable, unsettled feeling. To reduce the dissonance, Katie could:

- Take back the outfit.

- Pay attention to positive information, such as looking up ads and articles about this particular designer.

- Seek more positive feedback from friends.

- Seek negative information about outfits made by designers not selected.

Customer Loyalty In the postpurchase stage of the decision-making process, marketers attempt to solidify loyal relationships with their customers. They want customers to be satisfied with their purchases and buy from the same company again. Loyal customers will buy only certain brands and shop at certain

Stores collect customer information for their CRM programs from their loyalty cards.

© Mark Lennihan/AP Photo

stores, and they include no other firms in their evoked set. As we explained in Chapter 2, such customers are therefore very valuable to firms, and marketers have designed detailed analytics software and customer relationship management (CRM) programs specifically to acquire and retain them.

Undesirable Consumer Behavior Although firms want satisfied, loyal customers, sometimes they fail to attain them. Passive consumers are those who don't repeat purchase or recommend the product to others. More serious and potentially damaging, however, is negative consumer behavior such as negative word of mouth and rumors.

Negative word of mouth oc-

curs when consumers spread negative information about a product, service, or store to others. When customers' expectations are met or even exceeded, they often don't tell anyone about it. But when consumers believe that they have been treated unfairly in some way, they usually want to complain, often to many people. The Internet and social media have provided an effective method of spreading negative word of mouth to millions of people instantaneously through personal blogs, Twitter, and corporate websites. In turn, some firms rely on listening software offered by companies like Salesforce.com (as we discussed in Chapter 3), then respond to negative word of mouth through customer service representatives— whether online, on the phone, or in stores—who have the authority to handle complaints. Many companies also allow customers to post comments and complaints to proprietary social media sites.

For example, Whirlpool set up Facebook pages for its appliance brands Maytag, KitchenAid, and Whirlpool. Customers may share their thoughts on these sites without fear that their negative feedback will be deleted from the site. Whirlpool believes that it should keep the bad comments to open up discussions and emphasize the proactive measures the company is taking to remedy service or product failures.[23] If a customer believes that positive action will be taken as a result of the complaint, he or she is less likely to complain to family and friends or through the Internet. (A detailed example of word of mouth appears in Chapter 13.)

Whirlpool posts good as well as bad comments on Twitter. It believes that posting negative comments opens up discussions and emphasizes the proactive measures the company is taking to remedy service or product failures.

Source: Whirlpool

PROGRESS CHECK

1. Name the five stages in the consumer decision process.
2. What is the difference between a need and a want?
3. Distinguish between functional and psychological needs.
4. What are the various types of perceived risk?
5. What are the differences between compensatory and noncompensatory decision rules?
6. How do firms enhance postpurchase satisfaction and reduce cognitive dissonance?

FACTORS INFLUENCING THE CONSUMER DECISION PROCESS

The consumer decision process can be influenced by several factors, as illustrated in Exhibit 6.4. First are psychological factors, which are influences internal to the customer, such as motives, attitudes, perception, learning, and lifestyle. Second are situational factors, such as the specific purchase situation, a particular shopping situation, or temporal state (the time of day), that affect the decision process. Third are social factors, such as family, reference groups, and culture, that also influence the decision process. And fourth are the elements of the marketing mix, which we discuss throughout this book.

Every decision people make as consumers will take them through some form of the consumer decision process. But, like life itself, this process does not exist in a vacuum.

EXHIBIT 6.4   Factors Affecting the Consumer Decision Process

Psychological Factors

Although marketers can influence purchase decisions, a host of psychological factors affect the way people receive marketers' messages. Among them are motives, attitudes, perception, learning, and lifestyle. In this section, we examine how such psychological factors can influence the consumer decision process.[24]

Motives In Chapter 1 we argued that marketing is all about satisfying customer needs and wants. When a need, such as thirst, or a want, such as for a Diet Pepsi, is not satisfied, it motivates us, or drives us, to get satisfaction. So, a *motive* is a need or want that is strong enough to cause the person to seek satisfaction.

People have several types of motives. One of the best-known paradigms for explaining these motive types, developed by Abraham Maslow over 70 years ago, is called **Maslow's hierarchy of needs**.[25] Maslow categorized five groups of needs: physiological (e.g., food, water, shelter), safety (e.g., secure employment, health), love (e.g., friendship, family), esteem (e.g., confidence, respect), and self-actualization (people engage in personal growth activities and attempt to meet their intellectual, aesthetic, creative, and other such needs).

The pyramid in Exhibit 6.5 illustrates the theoretical progression of those needs.

Physiological needs deal with the basic biological necessities of life—food, drink, rest, and shelter. Although for most people in developed countries these basic needs are generally met, there are those in developed as well as less developed countries who are less fortunate. However, everyone remains concerned with meeting these basic needs.[26] Marketers seize every opportunity to convert these needs into wants by reminding us to eat at Taco Bell, drink milk, sleep on a Beautyrest mattress, and stay at a Marriott.

Safety needs pertain to protection and physical well-being. The marketplace is full of products and services that are designed to make you safer, such as airbags in cars and burglar alarms in homes, or healthier, such as vitamins and organic meats and vegetables.

Love needs relate to our interactions with others. Haircuts and makeup make you look more attractive, deodorants prevent odor, and greeting cards help you express your feelings toward others.

Esteem needs allow people to satisfy their inner desires. Yoga, meditation, health clubs, and many books appeal to people's desires to grow or maintain a happy, satisfied outlook on life.

Finally, **self-actualization** occurs when you feel completely satisfied with your life and how you live. You don't care what others think. You drive a Ford Fusion because it suits the person you are, not because some celebrity endorses it or because you want others to think better of you.

EXHIBIT 6.5 Maslow's Hierarchy of Needs

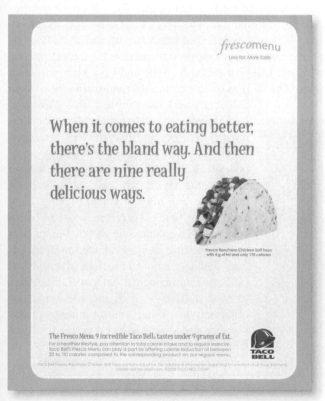

In this ad, Taco Bell satisfies the physiological need of food while letting the consumer know that healthy eating can also be delicious.

Source: Taco Bell

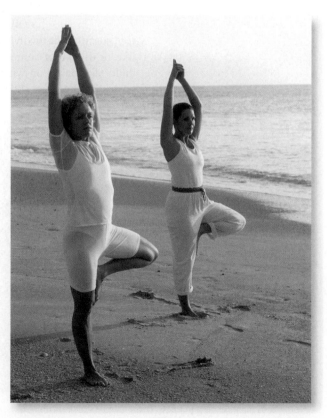

Yoga satisfies esteem needs by helping people satisfy their inner desires.

© Purestock/SuperStock RF

Which category of Maslow's hierarchy of needs are satisfied by a visit to Starbucks?

© Bandphoto/UPPA/Photoshot

Which of these needs apply when a consumer makes a purchase from Starbucks? On the surface, Starbucks satisfies physiological needs by providing food and drink. But Starbucks also satisfies safety needs, such as those related to healthier living, by publishing the calorie, fat, and sugar contents of all of its products and offering healthy alternatives, such as a spinach, feta, and egg white breakfast wrap.[27] Furthermore, Starbucks satisfies love needs through its powerful focus on creating relationships with customers: Baristas call each customer by his or her name, and the store environment encourages customers to sit a while, talk, and work together while enjoying their beverages. For many customers, Starbucks' in-store environment even encourages them to better themselves. The music at low volume as well as warm beverages create an ideal setting in which to read a book or work on a project, such that it helps people satisfy their esteem needs. Good marketers add value to their products or services by nudging people up the needs hierarchy and offering information on as many of the pyramid of needs as they can.

Attitude We have attitudes about almost everything. For instance, we like this class, but we don't like the instructor. We like where we live, but we don't like the weather. An **attitude** is a person's enduring evaluation of his or her feelings about and behavioral tendencies toward an object or idea. Attitudes are learned and long lasting, and they might develop over a long period of time, though they can also abruptly change. You might like your instructor for much of the semester—until she returns your first exam. The one thing attitudes have in common for everyone is their ability to influence our decisions and actions.

An attitude consists of three components. The **cognitive component** reflects our belief system, or what we believe to be true; the **affective component** involves emotions,[28] or what we feel about the issue at hand, including our like or dislike of something; and the **behavioral component** pertains to the actions we undertake based on what we know and feel. For example, Matt and Lisa Martinez see a poster for the latest *Avengers* movie. The ad lists quotes from different movie critics who call it a great and exciting film. Matt and Lisa therefore come to believe that the critics must be correct and that the new *Avengers* movie will be a good movie (cognitive component). Later they catch an interview with Robert Downey Jr., who talks about making the movie and his enjoyment playing Tony Stark (Iron Man). Therefore, Matt and Lisa start to believe the movie will be fun and engaging because they appreciate action adventures and have enjoyed previous Marvel films (affective component). After weighing their various options—which include numerous other movies, other entertainment options such as attending a concert instead, or just staying home—Matt and Lisa decide to go see the movie (behavioral component).

Ideally, agreement exists among these three components. But when there is incongruence among the three—if Matt and Lisa read positive reviews and like action films but do not find Robert Downey Jr. an appealing actor—cognitive dissonance might occur.

Based on positive reviews (cognitive component) and positive feelings (affective component), many movie watchers will go see the latest Avengers *movie (behavioral component) and come away with a positive attitude.*

© Collection Christophel/Alamy

Ethical & Societal Dilemma **6.2**   Can Marketing Be Life Threatening? Allegations of Unethical Practices by Pharmaceutical Firms[iv]

In separate lawsuits brought in Illinois and California, local authorities have charged that five large pharmaceutical firms behaved illegally in promoting painkilling drugs to consumers and health care providers. Specifically, the suits assert that through "aggressive marketing" tactics, the pharmaceutical companies pushed doctors to prescribe powerful opioid drugs to patients whose ailments did not meet the extreme conditions for which these drugs initially were developed. The result, according to the attorneys bringing the suits, has been a vast increase in addiction rates and incalculable damage to society.

Opioid painkillers originally emerged as solutions for patients suffering from extreme, acute pain that could not be relieved by other drugs. These patients were severely disabled by their pain or suffered from serious conditions such as cancer. The prescriptions were intended to be limited because of the substantial risk of addiction that the painkilling drugs created.

According to the recent lawsuits, though, the pharmaceutical companies put their desire for increased profits ahead of their responsibility to help doctors prescribe their products appropriately. They allege that pharmaceutical sales representatives encouraged doctors to prescribe the drugs for less severe pain and injuries to create a broader market of end users for their products. In addition, the lawsuits argue that some of the companies tried to downplay the risk of addiction in their general marketing communications.

These misleading claims in turn have led to significantly negative implications for society, according to the lawsuits. No one questions the fact that rates of opioid addiction have increased rapidly in recent years. What is at question is why. According to the city of Chicago and two California counties, these increased rates can be attributed directly to the misleading, irresponsible, and unethical marketing practices of the drug companies. As a result, because taxpayers must pay the millions of dollars in health care costs associated with dealing with drug addiction, even people who are not directly affected by the epidemic suffer. For example, Chicago has asserted that more than 1,000 emergency room visits in one year stemmed from opioid abuse or overdoses. According to one of the district attorneys bringing suit in California, the goal of these legal efforts is not to limit the company's ability to sell but rather to "require these companies to change their conduct and to tell people—to tell the doctors, to tell the patients—tell them that these drugs are dangerous. Tell them they are addictive, and you could overdose on them, and you could die."

Matt and Lisa might decide their reviews and their liking of action films will outweigh their dislike of Robert Downey Jr. and go see the movie. If they then find the movie unenjoyable because he is a primary star, they may feel foolish for having wasted their money.

Such dissonance is a terrible feeling that people try to avoid, often by convincing themselves that the decision was a good one in some way.[29] In this example, Matt and Lisa might focus on the special effects and the romantic elements of the movie while mentally glossing over the parts that featured the actor they did not enjoy. In this way, they can convince themselves that the parts they liked were good enough to counterbalance the part they didn't like, and thus they make their moviegoing experience a positive event overall.

Although attitudes are pervasive and usually slow to change, the important fact from a marketer's point of view is that they can be influenced and perhaps changed through persuasive communications and personal experience. Marketing communication—through salespeople, advertisements, free samples, or other such methods—can attempt to change what people believe to be true about a product or service (cognitive) or how they feel toward it (affective). Because of these effects, marketers have an ethical responsibility to communicate truthfully, as Ethical and Societal Dilemma 6.2 reflects. If the marketing communication is successful, the cognitive and affective components work in concert to affect behavior. Continuing with our example, suppose that prior to viewing the movie ad, Matt and Lisa thought they wanted to see *Fast and Furious,* but when they heard such good things about *Avengers,* they decided to see it instead. The ad positively influenced the cognitive component of their attitude toward *Avengers,* making it consistent with their affective component.

Perception Another psychological factor, perception, is the process by which we select, organize, and interpret information to form a meaningful picture of the world. Perception in marketing influences our acquisition and consumption of goods and services through our tendency to assign meaning to such things as color, symbols, taste, and packaging. Culture, tradition, and our overall upbringing determine our perception of the world. For instance, Lisa Martinez has always wanted an apartment in the Back Bay neighborhood of

Boston because her favorite aunt had one, and they had a great time visiting for Thanksgiving one year. However, from his past experiences Matt has a different perception. Matt thinks Back Bay apartments are small, expensive, and impractical for a couple thinking about having children—though they would be convenient for single people who work in downtown Boston. In recent years, however, the city of Boston, working with developers to create larger, modern, and more affordable apartments and using promotion to reposition the perception of apartments in the Back Bay for young couples, has labored to overcome the long-standing negative perceptual bias that Matt and many others hold.[30]

Learning Learning refers to a change in a person's thought process or behavior that arises from experience and takes place throughout the consumer decision process. After Katie Smith recognized that she needed an outfit for her job interview, she started looking for ads and searching for reviews and articles on the Internet. She learned from each new piece of information, so her thoughts about the look she wanted in an outfit were different from those before she had read anything. She liked what she learned about the clothing line from Macy's. She learned from her search, and it became part of her memory to be used in the future, possibly so she could recommend the store to her friends.

Learning affects attitudes as well as perceptions. Throughout the buying process, Katie's attitudes shifted. The cognitive component came into play for her when she learned Macy's had one of the most extensive collections of career apparel. Once she was in the store and tried on some outfits, she realized how much she liked the way she looked and felt in them, which involved the affective component. Then she made her purchase, which involved the behavioral component. Each time she was exposed to information about the store or the outfits, she learned something different that affected her perception. Before she tried them on, Katie hadn't realized how easy it would be to find exactly what she was looking for; thus, her perception of Macy's selection of career clothing changed through learning.

Lifestyle Lifestyle refers to the way consumers spend their time and money to live. For many consumers, the question of whether the product or service fits with their actual lifestyle (which may be fairly sedentary) or their perceived lifestyle (which might be outdoorsy) is an important one. Some of the many consumers sporting North Face jackets certainly need the high-tech, cold weather gear because they are planning their next hike up Mount Rainier and want to be sure they have sufficient protection against the elements. Others, however, simply like the image that the jacket conveys—the image that they might be leaving for their own mountain-climbing expedition any day now—even if the closest they have come has been shoveling their driveway.

A person's perceptions and ability to learn are affected by his or her social experiences, which we discuss next.

Social Factors

The consumer decision process is influenced from within by psychological factors but also by the external social environment, which consists of the customer's family, reference groups, and culture.[31] (Recall Exhibit 6.4.)

Family Many purchase decisions are made about products or services that the entire family will consume or use. Thus, firms must consider how families make purchase decisions and understand how various family members might influence these decisions.

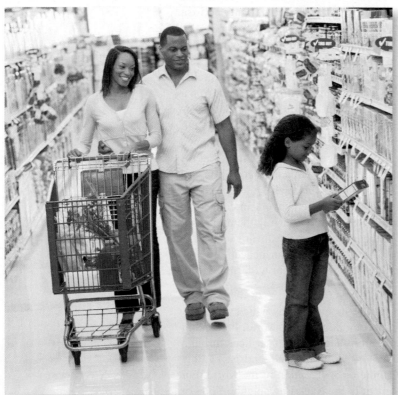

Gen Xers tend to shop at Target, Kmart, and Walmart.

© Stockbroker/Purestock/SuperStock RF

When families make purchase decisions, they often consider the needs of all the family members. In choosing a restaurant, for example, all the family members may participate in the decision making. In other situations, however, different members of the family may take on the purchasing role. For instance, the husband and teenage child may look through car magazines and *Consumer Reports* to search for information about a new car. But once they arrive at the dealership, the husband and wife, not the child, decide which model and color to buy, and the wife negotiates the final deal.[32]

Influencing a group that holds this much spending power is vitally important. Traditional food retailers are already caught in a squeeze between Walmart, which lures low-end customers, and specialty retailers like Whole Foods, which targets the high end. Knowing how children influence food-buying decisions is a strategic opportunity for traditional supermarkets and their suppliers to exploit. Currently, the age cohorts referred to as Gen Xers and Millennials (remember from Chapter 5 that these groups were born anywhere between 1965 and 2000) tend to shop at Target, Kmart, and Walmart and spend more at those stores than do other generational groups.[33] Getting these groups to prefer one store, chain, or product over another can make a difference in the bottom line as well as in the chances for survival in a difficult marketplace.

Reference Groups A reference group is one or more persons whom an individual uses as a basis for comparison regarding beliefs, feelings, and behaviors. A consumer might have various reference groups, including family, friends, coworkers, or famous people the consumer would like to emulate. These reference groups affect buying decisions by (1) offering information and (2) enhancing a consumer's self-image.[34]

Reference groups provide information to consumers directly through conversation, either face-to-face or electronically, or indirectly through observation. For example, Katie received valuable information from a friend about where she should shop for her interview outfit. On another occasion, she heard a favorite cousin who is a fashionista praising the virtues of shopping at Macy's, which solidified her decision to go there.

With the increasing popularity of blogs, more and more people also get recommendations for products from their favorite bloggers. When you follow a blog about kittens, you might notice that the author posts a scathing review of a particular cat tree or strongly recommends a product that encourages kittens to use their litter boxes. Because this blogger offers insights you appreciate, you go out to buy the litter box product but avoid adding that cat tree to your shopping cart. In realizing the vast influence of this reference group, companies today offer prominent bloggers free products and sometimes even pay them to write positive reviews.[35]

Bloggers can influence their readers to buy or not buy certain products or services.

© geekygirlreviewsblog.com

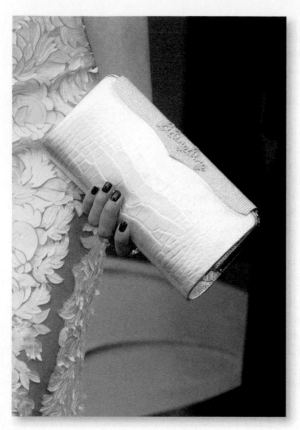

If you aspire to a high fashion image, carry a Lana Marks bag.
© Michael Buckner/Getty Images

Consumers can identify and affiliate with reference groups to create, enhance, or maintain their self-image. Customers who want to be seen as earthy might buy Birkenstock sandals, whereas those wanting to be seen as high fashion might buy Lana Marks bags.

Reference groups are a powerful force, especially among young consumers. For example, the primary way teenagers have expressed their personalities has long been through their fashion choices, which has made them an appealing market for retailers such as Abercrombie and Fitch and American Eagle. The teen market is also using social media, smartphones, and various apps to communicate and express their self image. As a consequence teens seek out places that offer free Wi-Fi, such as fast food restaurants, coffee shops, and casual eateries.[36]

Culture We defined culture in Chapter 5 as the shared meanings, beliefs, morals, values, and customs of a group of people. As the basis of the social factors that affect your buying decisions, the culture or cultures in which you participate are not markedly different from your reference groups. That is, your cultural group might be as small as your reference group at school or as large as the country in which you live or the religion to which you belong. Like reference groups, cultures influence consumer behavior. For instance, the culture at Katie's college is rather fashion conscious. This influences, to some extent, the way she spends, how she dresses, and where she shops.

Situational Factors

Psychological and social factors typically influence the consumer decision process the same way each time. For example, your motivation to quench your thirst usually drives you to drink a Coke or a Pepsi, and your reference group at the workplace coerces you to wear appropriate attire. But sometimes situational factors, or factors specific to the situation, override or at least influence psychological and social issues. These situational factors are related to the purchase and shopping situation as well as to temporal states.[37]

Purchase Situation Customers may be predisposed to purchase certain products or services because of some underlying psychological trait or social factor, but these factors may change in certain purchase situations. For instance, Samantha Crumb considers herself a

Situational factors may influence your purchase decisions. If you are buying jewelry for yourself, you might browse the clearance counter at Macy's (left). But if you are buying a gift for your best friend's birthday, you may go to Tiffany & Co (right).
Left: © RosalreneBetancourt 4/Alamy; right: © Victor J. Blue/Bloomberg/Getty Images

Adding Value **6.1**   Doing Everything Right—H-E-B Supermarkets^v

When it comes to consumer behavior, the research is clear: If they want to succeed, companies selling to consumers need to attract consumers' attention, affection, and commitment; put them in a great mood, perhaps by offering them something for nothing; and help people make their decisions easily and in a way that causes them to feel smart and informed. It may be clear, but few companies are applying these lessons as effectively as a regional grocery store chain in Texas, H-E-B.

First, H-E-B gets its regional customers excited and entranced by playing on their shared identity of being from Texas. This option might be less effective in other regions with a weaker sense of identity, but in Texas, the idea that H-E-B is just like its consumers garners it substantial attention and affection. Then once it has people in its stores, it gets them to engage and commit to actually buying by adding tear-off coupons to its displays. Rather than just seeing a sale sign, customers must undertake the action of tearing off a coupon. This action is not particularly strenuous of course, but the simple move increases the chances that shoppers will follow through on their already committed effort by completing the purchase.

Second, H-E-B sets up an appealing and enjoyable atmosphere that seeks to put shoppers in a better mood. In particular, a plethora of coupons give buyers an additional item for free after they purchase. People simply love things for free, so the constant reminder of how much they can get, seemingly at no cost, enhances their moods. As if that were not enough, H-E-B also gives away lots of free samples. In addition to food samples, to keep shoppers' blood sugar levels up it specializes in wine samples. Because alcohol releases dopamine in people's brains, just a small sip of a nice Zinfandel can leave shoppers in a better mood.

Third, the entire operation seeks to make it easier for consumers to buy the products they want and feel pleased with

Fabio Viviani, TopChef's fan favorite, cooks up Italian meatballs at H-E-B.
© Rachel Denny Clow/AP Photo

their purchases. H-E-B has avoided loyalty cards and instead simply offers all consumers in the store the same deals on the same items. Thus, shoppers do not need to remember to bring their store coupons or stick their loyalty cards in their wallets before they leave for their grocery run. The fresh food displays also offer obvious highlights of their freshness: a constant smell of rotisserie chicken near the deli display, a guacamole prepping station featuring chefs carving out the avocados right in front of shoppers, and sushi chefs working in the center of the store.

As a result, even though H-E-B remains a regional chain with limited name recognition outside Texas, its ranking on a recent "consumer delight index" placed it on par with such well-known customer favorites as Trader Joe's and Whole Foods.

thrifty, cautious shopper—someone who likes to get a good deal. But her best friend is having a birthday, and she wants to get her some jewelry. If she were shopping for herself, she might seek out the clearance merchandise at Macy's. But because it is for her best friend, she went to Tiffany & Co. Why? She wanted to purchase something fitting for the special occasion of having a birthday.

Shopping Situation Consumers might be ready to purchase a product or service but be completely derailed once they arrive in the store. Marketers use several techniques to influence consumers at this choice stage of the decision process, as Adding Value 6.1 describes using one example.[38]

Store Atmosphere Some retailers and service providers have developed unique images that are based at least in part on their internal environment, also known as their atmospherics.[39] Research has shown that, if used in concert with other aspects of a retailer's strategy, music, scent, lighting, and even color can positively influence the decision process.[40] Restaurants such as Outback Steakhouse and The Cheesecake Factory have developed internal environments that are not only pleasant but also consistent with their food and service. Some Wegmans and Whole Foods stores have built bars and restaurants inside their stores, where customers can stop and relax, have a glass of wine or a bite to eat, but still get their shopping done for the week.[41]

Salespeople Well-trained sales personnel can influence the sale at the point of purchase by educating consumers about product attributes, pointing out the advantages of one item over another, and encouraging multiple purchases. Each Apple store features a simple layout that enables shoppers to play with the latest gadgets, though the real key to success is the salespeople. Apple keeps its product lines relatively minimal so salespeople can become familiar with every product in the store. For more technical questions, Apple Geniuses are available and consultations can be scheduled.[42] The company takes nothing for granted when training its employees, such that it uses role-playing scenarios, lists banned words, and specifies exactly how to communicate with agitated customers. Although technical expertise is a must, Apple also looks for salespeople with "magnetic personalities" and trains them in a five-point selling technique: **a**pproach customers warmly, **p**robe politely to assess their needs, **p**resent solutions the customer can do today, **l**isten and resolve worries the customer may still have, **e**nd by giving the customer a warm goodbye and invite them back.[43] What's that spell?

Crowding Customers can feel crowded because there are too many people, too much merchandise, or lines that are too long. If there are too many people in a store, some people become distracted and may even leave.[44] Others have difficulty purchasing if the merchandise is packed too closely together. This issue is a particular problem for shoppers with disabilities.

In-Store Demonstrations The taste and smell of new food items may attract people to try something they normally wouldn't. Similarly, some fashion retailers offer trunk shows, during which their vendors show their whole line of merchandise on a certain day. During these well-advertised events, customers are often enticed to purchase that day because they get special assistance from the salespeople and can order merchandise that the retailer otherwise does not carry.

In-store demonstrations, such as this one in an Albertson's grocery store, attract consumers to try and buy.

Source: Albertson's, Inc.

Promotions Retailers employ various promotional vehicles to influence customers once they have arrived in the store. An unadvertised price promotion can alter a person's preconceived buying plan. Multi-item discounts, such as "buy one, get one free" sales, are popular means to get people to buy

Social & Mobile Marketing 6.2 Ensuring Mobile Dominance through In-Store Promotion[vi]

Some consumers rely on websites to reach their favorite retailers. Others like to head to the stores themselves to check out the options. Still others want a mobile app that enables them to shop quickly and on the go. And increasingly, today's customers demand that retailers offer them all of these options, consistently and constantly, so that they can pick and choose the channel they want to use at any specific time.

This demand is the impetus for the latest developments in the marketing strategy of Sephora, the specialized beauty product retailer. Although it has long maintained a good reputation for its interactive website, the company remains in constant pursuit of a strategy that enables it to reach all its customers through the most channels and as frequently as possible. It integrates these efforts with its constantly evolving loyalty program, in an effort to become nearly irresistible to beauty product consumers.

Sephora engages its customers in the store with its mobile app, Sephora to Go.

© Victor J. Blue/Bloomberg/Getty Images

Users of the most recent version of its mobile app, Sephora to Go, can engage in any activities they would pursue in stores. The close alignment across these channels provides a seamless experience. In addition, the app encourages customers to sign up for the loyalty program and create a Beauty Insider account. Once they have done so, they gain a mobile version of their loyalty card. They can check their loyalty points at any time and redeem them however they wish. Downloadable bar codes also are available, which can be scanned in stores.

Simultaneously, Sephora's in-store signage encourages shoppers to sign up for the loyalty program and create a Beauty Insider account. That is, both channels issue similar calls to action. Moreover, the in-store signs encourage brick-and-mortar shoppers to take advantage of the benefits they can gain from interacting with the retailer, either online or through mobile apps.

---

more than they normally would.[45] Because many people regard clipping coupons from the newspaper as too much trouble, some stores make coupons available in the store, on the Internet, or on their cell phones. Another form of promotion is offering a free gift with the purchase of a good or service. This type of promotion is particularly popular with cosmetics, and Sephora has worked hard to integrate various elements of its shopping situation to encourage purchase, as Social and Mobile Marketing 6.2 shows.

Packaging It is difficult to make a product stand out in the crowd when it competes for shelf space with several other brands.[46] Customers spend just a few seconds standing in front of products as they decide whether to buy them.[47] This problem is particularly difficult for consumer packaged goods such as groceries and health and beauty products. Marketers therefore spend millions of dollars designing and updating their packages to be more appealing and eye catching. This is why Pringles keeps packaging its chips in tubes that differ greatly from the formless bags farther down the aisle. But not all product packaging can, or should, remain the same, the way Pringles has. Doublemint Gum undertook its first packaging redesign nearly a century after its 1914 product launch. The move was designed to help the chewing gum appeal to a younger audience, even while it maintained its loyal base of older consumers. Another aging brand, Kraft's Macaroni & Cheese, similarly redesigned its packaging, which it launched originally in 1937.[48]

Temporal State Our state of mind at any particular time can alter our preconceived notions of what we are going to purchase. For instance, some people are morning people, whereas others function better at night. Therefore, a purchase situation may have different appeal levels

Doublemint Gum changed its packaging after 100 years to appeal to a younger audience, while still being attractive to its older customers.

© Mahathir Mohd Yasin/Shutterstock RF

depending on the time of day and the type of person the consumer is. Mood swings can alter consumer behavior.[49] Suppose Samantha received a parking ticket just prior to shopping at Tiffany & Co. It is likely that she would be less receptive to the salesperson's influence than if she came into the store in a good mood. Her bad mood might even cause her to have a less positive postpurchase feeling about the store. Because retailers cannot affect what happens outside the store very much, they should do everything possible to make sure their customers have a positive shopping experience once they are in the store.

The factors that affect the consumer decision process—the marketing mix, psychological factors, social factors, and situational factors—are all affected by the level of consumer involvement, the subject of the next section.

PROGRESS CHECK

1. What are some examples of specific needs suggested by Maslow's hierarchy of needs?

2. Which social factors likely have the most influence on (a) the purchase of a new outfit for a job interview and (b) the choice of a college to attend?

3. List some of the tactics stores can use to influence consumers' decision processes.

 LO6-6 Describe how involvement influences the consumer decision process.

INVOLVEMENT AND CONSUMER BUYING DECISIONS

Consumers make two types of buying decisions, depending on their level of involvement: extended problem solving or limited problem solving (which includes impulse purchases and habitual decision making). **Involvement** is the consumer's degree of interest in the product or service.[50] Consumers may have different levels of involvement for the same type of product. One consumer behavior theory, the elaboration likelihood model illustrated in Exhibit 6.6, proposes that high- and low-involvement consumers process different aspects of a message or advertisement.

If both types of consumers viewed ads for career clothing, the high-involvement consumer (e.g., Katie, who is researching buying an outfit for a job interview) will scrutinize

EXHIBIT 6.6 Elaboration Likelihood Model

all the information provided (price, fabric quality, construction) and process the key elements of the message more deeply. As an involved consumer, Katie likely ends up judging the ad as truthful and forming a favorable impression of the product, or else she regards the message as superficial and develops negative product impressions (i.e., her research suggests the product is not as good as it is being portrayed).

In contrast, a low-involvement consumer will likely process the same advertisement in a less thorough manner. Such a consumer might pay less attention to the key elements of the message (price, fabric quality, construction) and focus on elements such as brand name (Macy's I·N·C) or the presence of a celebrity endorser. The impressions of the low-involvement consumer are likely to be more superficial.

Extended Problem Solving

The buying process begins when consumers recognize that they have an unsatisfied need. Katie Smith recognized her need to buy a new outfit for a job interview. She sought information by asking for advice from her friends, reading fashion magazines, and conducting research online. She visited several stores to determine which had the best options for her. Finally, after considerable time and effort analyzing her alternatives, Katie purchased an outfit at Macy's. This process is an example of extended problem solving, which is common when the customer perceives that the purchase decision entails a lot of risk. The potential risks associated with Katie's decision to buy the outfit include financial (did I pay too much?) and social (will my potential employer and friends think I look professional?) risks. To reduce her perceived risk, Katie spent a lot of effort searching for information before she actually made her purchase.

Limited Problem Solving

Limited problem solving occurs during a purchase decision that calls for, at most, a moderate amount of effort and time. Customers engage in this type of buying process when they have had some prior experience with the product or service and the perceived risk is moderate. Limited problem solving usually relies on past experience more than on external information. For many people, an apparel purchase, even an outfit for a job interview, could require limited effort.

A common type of limited problem solving is impulse buying, a buying decision made by customers on the spot when they see the merchandise.[51] When Katie went to the

Typically, fashion apparel purchases (left) require extended problem solving, whereas grocery shopping normally requires limited problem solving (right).

grocery store to do her weekly shopping, she saw a display case of popcorn and Dr Pepper near the checkout counter. Knowing that some of her friends were coming over to watch a movie, she stocked up. The popcorn and soda were an impulse purchase. Katie didn't go through the entire decision process; instead, she recognized her need and jumped directly to purchase without spending any time searching for additional information or evaluating alternatives. The grocery store facilitated this impulse purchase by providing easily accessible cues (i.e., by offering the popcorn and soda in a prominent display, at a great location in the store, and at a reasonable price).

Some purchases require even less thought. **Habitual decision making** describes a purchase decision process in which consumers engage in little conscious effort. On her way home from the grocery store, for example, Katie drove past an In-N-Out Burger and swung into the drive-through for a cheeseburger and Diet Coke. She did not ponder the potential benefits of going to Wendy's instead for lunch. Rather, she simply reacted to the cue provided by the sign and engaged in habitual decision making. Marketers strive to attract and maintain habitual purchasers by creating strong brands and store loyalty (see Chapters 11 and 12) because these customers don't even consider alternative brands or stores.

Picking up a hamburger at a drive-through fast-food restaurant like In-N-Out Burger requires little thought. It is a habitual decision.

© K. Rousonelos

PROGRESS CHECK

1. How do low- versus high-involvement consumers process the information in an advertisement?
2. What is the difference between extended versus limited problem solving?

Reviewing Learning Objectives

  LO6-1 **Articulate the steps in the consumer buying process.**

The consumer buying process consists of five main steps: First, during need recognition, consumers simply realize they have an unsatisfied need or want that they hope to address. Second, they begin to search for information to determine how to satisfy that need. Third, during the alternative evaluation stage, they assess the various options available to them to determine which is the best for their purposes. Fourth, the purchase stage involves obtaining and using the product. Finally, consumers enter the postpurchase stage, during which they determine whether they are satisfied or dissatisfied with their choice.

LO6-2 **Describe the difference between functional and psychological needs.**

Functional needs pertain to the performance of a product or service. Psychological needs pertain to the personal gratification consumers associate with a product and/or service.

LO6-3 **Describe factors that affect information search.**

The information search that people undertake varies depending on both external and internal factors. Among the former, the type of product or service dictates whether people can make an easy, quick decision or instead must undertake significant research to find the best purchase option. A person's perceptions of the benefits versus the costs of the search also determine how much effort they undertake. These perceptions often relate closely to their perception of the risk involved in their purchase. Finally, people's locus of control, whether external or internal, strongly influences their information search actions.

LO6-4 **Discuss postpurchase outcomes.**

Marketers hope that after their purchase, consumers are satisfied and pleased with their purchase, which can lead to customer loyalty, a positive postpurchase outcome. However, consumers also may suffer postpurchase dissonance, or buyer's remorse.

LO6-5 **List the factors that affect the consumer decision process.**

The elements of the marketing mix (product, place, promotion, and price) have significant effects, of course. In addition, social factors, such as family and culture, influence not only what a consumer buys but also how a consumer goes about making a purchase decision. The psychological factors that influence purchase decisions include motives, attitudes, perceptions, learning, and lifestyle. Finally, the specific factors that mark the purchase situation, like the store setting or even the time of day, can alter people's decision process.

LO6-6 **Describe how involvement influences the consumer decision process.**

More involved consumers, who are more interested or invested in the product or service they are considering, tend to engage in extended problem solving. They gather lots of information, scrutinize it carefully, and then make their decisions with caution, to minimize any risk they may confront. In contrast, less involved consumers often engage in limited problem solving, undertake impulse purchases, or rely on habit to make their purchase decisions.

Key Terms

- affective component, 190
- attitude, 190
- behavioral component, 190
- cognitive component, 190
- compensatory decision rule, 182
- consumer decision rules, 182
- conversion rate, 184
- culture, 194
- determinant attributes, 182
- esteem needs, 189
- evaluative criteria, 182
- evoked set, 181
- extended problem solving, 199
- external locus of control, 179
- external search for information, 178
- financial risk, 180
- functional needs, 177
- habitual decision making, 200
- impulse buying, 199
- internal locus of control, 179
- internal search for information, 178
- involvement, 198
- learning, 192
- lifestyle, 192
- limited problem solving, 199
- love needs, 189
- Maslow's hierarchy of needs, 188
- motive, 188
- multi-attribute model, 183
- need recognition, 176
- negative word of mouth, 187
- noncompensatory decision rule, 184
- perception, 191
- performance risk, 180
- physiological needs, 189
- physiological risk, 181
- postpurchase cognitive dissonance, 186
- psychological needs, 177
- psychological risk, 181
- reference group, 193
- retrieval sets, 181
- safety needs, 189
- safety risk, 181
- self-actualization, 189
- situational factors, 194
- social risk, 181
- universal sets, 181

Marketing Digitally

1. Visit the Shopkick site (http://www.shopkick.com) and describe the benefits it offers consumers. How are these offers likely to influence consumers' behavior? Click on the Download tab. What kinds of need appeals does this company make to encourage shoppers to join?

2. Customers use a variety of methods to provide feedback to companies about their experiences. Planetfeedback.com was developed as one such venue. Visit its website (http://www.planetfeedback.com) and identify the types of feedback that customers can provide. Look over the feedback for Verizon by typing "Verizon" in the company search space. Summarize some of the most recent comments. What is the ratio of positive to negative comments about Verizon during the last year or so? Describe the effects these comments might have on customer perceptions of Verizon.

3. Different companies emphasize different aspects of attitude in making decisions. Explore the Microsoft (http://www.microsoftstore.com) and Apple (store.apple.com) stores online. Discuss the primary attitude components they are targeting and how the two stores differ.

4. Companies often emphasize either the functional or psychological needs their products fulfill. Go to *Car and Driver*'s website (http://www.caranddriver.com) and identify a luxury car company that emphasizes functional needs and one that emphasizes psychological needs.

Marketing Applications

1. Does buying Kashi cereal satisfy a consumer's functional or psychological needs? How might this information help a Kashi brand manager better promote the product?

2. When consumers buy a new notebook computer, what sort of information search (internal versus external) would they conduct? If you were a marketing manager for Sony, how would you use this information?

3. Explain the factors that affect the amount of time and effort a consumer might take when choosing an oral surgeon to get his or her wisdom teeth removed. How would your answer change if the consumer were looking for a dentist to get a cleaning? How should the office manager for a dental practice use this information?

4. When evaluating different alternatives for a Saturday night outing at a fine restaurant, explain the difference between the universal set, the retrieval set, and the evoked set. From which set of alternatives will the consumer most likely choose the restaurant?

5. What can retailers do to make sure they have satisfied customers after the sale is complete?

6. Tazo makes a blend of exotic green teas, spearmint, and rare herbs into a tea called Zen. Using Maslow's hierarchy of needs, explain which need(s) is (are) being fulfilled by this tea.

7. You recently were invited to a formal event at the home of the president of your university. You decide such an event warrants a completely new outfit. Describe three social factors that might influence your purchase decision.

8. Trek has designed a new off-road bicycle designed to stand up to the rugged conditions of trail riding. Develop a theme for an advertising strategy that covers all three components of attitude.

9. What can a marketer do to positively influence a situation in which a consumer is ready to buy but has not yet done so?

10. You were recently hired by a multichannel retailer that promotes itself as an American firm selling only American-made goods. The products featured in advertising and in catalogs tell stories of the firms that produced the goods in the United States. The sales response to the firm's Made in the USA position has been incredible because it resonates with its customers' values. As a result, growth has been impressive. One day while speaking to a vendor, you find out a shipment of merchandise will be delayed because the product is coming from overseas and is late. A few days later you hear a similar story. As it turns out, the firm just barely earns the Made in the USA label. Though technically the products meet a standard to be classified as American made, you worry that the firm is not being truthful to its customers. You decide to write a letter to the VP of marketing detailing your concerns. What would you put in the letter?

Quiz Yourself

1. The salient or important attributes about a particular product that consumers use to make product evaluations are called:

   a. attribute set.

   b. affective components.

   c. evaluative criteria.

   d. psychological decision rules.

   e. situational factors.

2. Because not all purchase intentions result in an actual purchase, marketers calculate the _____ to measure how effectively a decision to purchase a specific product results in a completed purchase.

   a. performance risk

   b. compensatory decision rate

   c. noncompensatory decision rate

   d. decision heuristic

   e. conversion rate

(Answers to these two questions are provided in the Quiz Yourself Answer Key section.)

Chapter Case Study

THE DIET BATTLE—WEIGHT WATCHERS, JENNY CRAIG, AND SLIM-FAST[52]

Want to lose weight? For about half of the U.S. population, the answer is yes,[53] and for weight-loss companies, that's the right answer. The weight-loss industry, worth over $60 billion,[54] is growing steadily because lifestyles and food choices keep working against people's desire to lose weight. Many Americans spend their days sitting in front of a computer and their evenings sitting in front of a television. Restaurant meals, prepared foods, and high-fat, high-sugar snacks have replaced home-cooked meals, whole grains, and fresh produce. Exercise is limited to clicking a mouse or turning an ignition key. These habits are fattening (both literally and figuratively) the profits for the weight-loss industry, as well as expanding belt sizes. By the time we factor in diet pills, specially packaged weight-loss meals and snacks, diet programs, and the whole range of products and services promising bathing-suit bodies, we've got a highly lucrative market.

Three recognized diet aid behemoths, Weight Watchers, Jenny Craig, and Slim-Fast, share a substantial piece of the pie. These companies stress their flexibility and ability to accommodate a wide range of lifestyles. They also showcase success stories.[55] But they approach dieting differently in their quest for new members.

The Big Three The current market leader, Weight Watchers International, now boasts groups in more than 30 countries worldwide. The program teaches portion control and the basics of good nutrition, allowing members to select their own foods. A point system, based on nutritional value, encourages members to select healthy foods, exercise appropriately, and control portions.[56] Dieters record meals and snacks in a paper journal or on their mobile app. Although members can follow the Weight Watchers regimen without support, the company notes that the most successful members are those who weigh in at weekly group sessions and attend meetings. Weight Watchers members can prepare their own food, dine out, or purchase Weight Watchers-prepared or -endorsed dinners, snacks, and desserts at most grocery stores. To further support dieters in making healthy food choices, Weight Watchers increased the number of points for fat content and reduced them for fiber.

Weight Watchers has recently teamed up with Oprah Winfrey, causing the company's stock price to triple almost instantly.[57] The company had been struggling to stand out, especially among younger audiences that found the appeal of wearable health-tracking devices like the Fitbit highly compelling.[58] Winfrey's first commercial for the company was

If you want to lose weight, which company would you prefer, Weight Watchers (left) or Slim Fast (right)?

Left: © Michael Nagle/Bloomberg/Getty Images; right: © Perry Correll/Shutterstock RF

met with an outpouring of excitement and support on Twitter.[59] Thus, the partnership seems likely to be a success for Weight Watchers, though what continues to set it apart remains its core offering of meetings, personal coaching, and branded food.[60]

Jenny Craig instead promises a unique and comprehensive plan for food, body, and mind.[61] Members eat meals and snacks prepared and packaged by Jenny Craig, supplemented by fresh fruits and vegetables. Jenny Craig's offerings provide portion control and accommodate busy schedules by reducing meal prep time. Members meet weekly on a one-on-one basis with a personal counselor and are encouraged to develop an exercise program. Like Weight Watchers, Jenny Craig offers customized programs for men and teenagers and for those who prefer to lose weight on their own rather than travel to a center. In its efforts to retake the market leadership position from Weight Watchers, Jenny Craig is promoting itself as the "don't-do-it-yourself" weight loss option. It also has reenlisted Kristie Alley as a spokesperson.[62]

Slim-Fast offers dieters a combination of three small and healthy snacks, two meal-replacement shakes, and one 500-calorie meal daily.[63] By eating six small meals daily, dieters maintain steady glucose levels, and the plan ensures adequate intakes of carbohydrates, protein, and fiber.[64]

Other diet programs abound, but even when people lose weight on these regimens, the losses tend to be temporary because the diets are based on unsustainable eating patterns, such as eliminating major food groups (e.g., no carbohydrates). Two of the big diet companies also offer social reinforcement and flexibility, which appears to help people remain committed to their weight-loss programs.

Defining the Difference Perhaps the most significant difference among Jenny Craig, Slim-Fast, and Weight Watchers is the amount of effort required. Jenny Craig dieters don't have to think about what they eat; everything is prepared for them. Dieters on the Weight Watchers plan must learn how to make the right choices from among the foods that surround them in their daily lives. Slim-Fast combines both ease and education, but it provides fewer choices for controlled meals than Jenny Craig does. Each program competes heavily for members, particularly in the early months of the year, when Americans return to the scales after indulging for the holidays.

The diet giants are locked in another battle as well, this one targeted at men. Although a completely different program isn't necessary—both genders need to cut calories and increase exercise to lose weight—marketing specifically to men has the power to bring in new members.

While the Weight Watchers programs are identical for men and women, the men's website is tailored to their interests and concerns, focusing more on working out and less on the eating plan. The men's site also mentions the link between obesity and erectile dysfunction, implying that a man's sex life might improve if he loses weight.[65]

Jenny Craig's men's program also is very similar to its women's program, but tweaked to accommodate differences in food cravings and issues with portion control. Men on this program, Jenny Craig promises, can still have a beer and fries once in a while.[66]

The Slim-Fast program tends to appeal to men because they like to lose weight on their own rather than participating in group meetings.[67] The company has used male celebrities, including a former New York mayor, to sell its products.

Technology Support for Dieters Dieters have a variety of electronic devices to help track food consumption and exercise. Using any Internet-ready device, Weight Watchers members can check point values for foods, including meals at popular restaurants, and add snacks or meals to their daily journal. Similar services and applications for fitness training are available via mobile apps. Using a camera-equipped cell phone, for example, dieters can photograph a meal and send the picture to a registered dietitian, who replies with recommendations for modifying portions or food choices. Theoretically this approach is more honest than keeping a food diary, because dieters may be tempted not to record full amounts. These services require additional fees though.

Questions

1. Trace how you might go through the steps in the consumer decision process if you were thinking of going on a diet and using any of these diet programs.

2. How have Weight Watchers, Slim-Fast, and Jenny Craig created value?

3. Identify the determinant attributes that set the Weight Watchers, Slim-Fast, and Jenny Craig programs apart. Use those attributes to develop a compensatory purchasing model similar to the one in Exhibit 6.2.

4. How can Weight Watchers, Slim-Fast, and Jenny Craig increase the probability of customer satisfaction?

5. Which factors examined in this chapter might have the most impact on consumers' propensity to go on a diet and choose one of these diet programs?

Endnotes

1. Sydney Ember, "Nike Embraces Weather App in Campaign to Sell Gear Suited to Local Conditions," *The New York Times*, October 29, 2015.

2. For example, when trying on a dress, Katie might be influenced by the way that same dress looks on a salesperson in the store. See Darren W. Dahl, Jennifer J. Argo, and Andrea C. Morales, "Social Information in the Retail Environment: The Importance of Consumption Alignment, Referent Identity, and Self-Esteem,"*Journal of Consumer Research* 38, no. 5 (February 2012), pp. 860–71.

3. For a detailed discussion of customer behavior, see Michael R. Solomon, *Consumer Behavior: Buying, Having, and Being,* 11th ed. (Upper Saddle River, NJ: Pearson Prentice Hall, 2014).

4. Martin R. Lautman and Koen Pauwels, "Metrics That Matter: Identifying the Importance of Consumer Wants and Needs,"*Journal of Advertising Research* 49, no. 3 (2009), 339–59.

5. Liz C. Wang et al., "Can a Retail Web Site Be Social?" *Journal of Marketing* 71, no. 3 (2007), pp. 143–57; Barry Babin, William Darden, and Mitch Griffin, "Work and/or Fun: Measuring Hedonic and Utilitarian Shopping Value," *Journal of Consumer Research* 20 (March 1994), pp. 644–56.

6. Jing Xu and Norbert Schwarz, "Do We Really Need a Reason to Indulge?" *Journal of Marketing Research* 46, no. 1 (February 2009), pp. 25–36.

7. "Lana Marks Cleopatra Bag," *Lord Glamour*, February 8, 2014, http://www.lordglamour.com/; Lopa Mohanty, "10 Most Expensive Handbag Brands in the World," *Fashion Lady*, May 31, 2013, http://www.fashionlady.in/; "Celebrities," *Lana Marks*, http://www.lanamarks.com/.

8. Peng Huang, Nicholas H. Lurie, and Sabyasachi Mitra, "Searching for Experience on the Web: An Empirical Examination of Consumer Behavior for Search and Experience Goods," *Journal of Marketing* 73, no. 2 (March 2009), pp. 55–69.

9. http://www.nordstrom.com; http://www.baronidesigns.com.

10. http://www.truefit.com.

11. Lan Luo, Brian T. Ratchford, and Botao Yang, "Why We Do What We Do: A Model of Activity Consumption," *Journal of Marketing Research* 50 (February 2013), pp. 24–43.

12. Ying Zhang et al., "Been There, Done That: The Impact of Effort Investment on Goal Value and Consumer Motivation," *Journal of Consumer Research* 38, no. 1 (June 2011), pp. 78–93.

13. Debabrata Talukdar, "Cost of Being Poor: Retail Price and Consumer Price Search Differences across Inner-City and Suburban Neighborhoods," *Journal of Consumer Research* 35, no. 3 (October 2008), pp. 457–71.

14. David Dubois, Derek D. Rucker, and Adam D. Galinsky, "Super Size Me: Product Size as a Signal of Status," *Journal of Consumer Research* 38, no. 6 (April 2012), pp. 1047–62.

15. Benjamin Scheibehenne, Rainer Greifeneder, and Peter M. Todd, "Can There Ever Be Too Many Options? A Meta-Analytic Review of Choice Overload," *Journal of Consumer Research* 37, no. 3 (October 2010), pp. 409–45.

16. The term *determinance* was first coined by James Myers and Mark Alpert nearly three decades ago; http://www.sawtooth-software.com.

17. http://www.sawtoothsoftware.com.

18. Julie R. Irwin and Rebecca Walker Naylor, "Ethical Decisions and Response Mode Compatibility: Weighting of Ethical Attributes in Consideration Sets Formed by Excluding versus Including Product Alternatives," *Journal of Marketing Research* 46, no. 2 (April 2009), pp. 234–46; Richard Lutz, "Changing Brand Attitudes through Modification of Cognitive Structure," *Journal of Consumer Research* 1, no. 1 (1975), pp. 125–36.

19. Caroline Goukens, Siegfried Dewitte, and Luk Warlop, "Me, Myself, and My Choices: The Influence of Private Self-Awareness on Choice," *Journal of Marketing Research* 46, no. 5 (October 2009), pp. 682–92.

20. James M. Kerr, "How Appealing to Women Has Helped The Home Depot," ManagementIssues.com, October 3, 2014.

21. "Beware of Dissatisfied Consumers: They Like to Blab," *Knowledge@Wharton*, March, 8, 2006, based on the "Retail Customer Dissatisfaction Study 2006" conducted by the Jay H. Baker Retailing Initiative at Wharton and The Verde Group.

22. Goutam Challagalla, R. Venkatesh, and Ajay K. Kohli, "Proactive Postsales Service: When and Why Does It Pay Off?" *Journal of Marketing* 73, no. 2 (March 2009), pp. 70–87.

23. Randall Stross, "Consumer Complaints Made Easy. Maybe Too Easy," *The New York Times*, May 28, 2011, http://www.nytimes.com.

24. For a more extensive discussion on these factors, see Banwari Mittal, *Consumer Behavior* (Cincinnati, OH: Open Mentis, 2008); J. Paul Peter and Jerry C. Olson, *Consumer Behavior and Marketing Strategy*, 9th ed. (Burr Ridge, IL: McGraw-Hill Education, 2010.

25. A. H. Maslow, *Motivation and Personality* (New York: Harper & Row, 1970).

26. Kelly D. Martin and Ronald Paul Hill, "Life Satisfaction, Self-Determination, and Consumption Adequacy at the Bottom of the Pyramid," *Journal of Consumer Research* 38, no. 6 (April 2012), pp. 1155–68; Hazel Rose Markus and Barry Schwartz, "Does Choice Mean Freedom and Well-Being?" *Journal of Consumer Research* 37, no. 2 (August 2010), pp. 344–55.

27. http://www.starbucks.com/menu/nutrition/35-under-350.

28. For recent research on the link between emotions and consumer behavior, see the "Emotions and Consumer Behavior" special issue of *Journal of Consumer Research* 40 (February 2014).

29. Leonard Lee, On Amir, and Dan Ariely, "In Search of Homo Economicus: Cognitive Noise and the Role of Emotion in Preference Consistency," *Journal of Consumer Research* 36, no. 2 (2009), pp. 173–87; Anish Nagpal and Parthasarathy Krishnamurthy, "Attribute Conflict in Consumer Decision Making: The Role of Task Compatibility," *Journal of Consumer Research* 34, no. 5 (February 2008), pp. 696–705.

30. http://www.bostonbackbay.com/.

31. For more discussion on these factors, see Mittal, *Consumer Behavior;* Peter and Olson, *Consumer Behavior and Marketing Strategy;* Michael Levy, Barton A. Weitz, and Dhruv Grewal, *Retailing Management*, 9th ed. (Burr Ridge, IL: Irwin/McGraw-Hill, 2013), Chapter 4; and the "Social Influence and Consumer Behavior" special issue of *Journal of Consumer Research* 40 (August 2013).

32. Juliano Laran, "Goal Management in Sequential Choices: Consumer Choices for Others Are More Indulgent than Personal Choices," *Journal of Consumer Research* 37, no. 2 (August 2010), pp. 304–14.

33. Todd Hale, "Mining the U.S. Generation Gaps," *Nielsen Wire*, March 4, 2010, http://blog.nielsen.com.

34. Gokcen Coskuner-Balli and Craig J. Thompson, "The Status Costs of Subordinate Cultural Capital: At-Home Fathers' Collective Pursuit of Cultural Legitimacy through Capitalizing Consumption Practices," *Journal of Consumer Research* 40 (June 2013), pp. 19–41.

35. Carol Bryant, "The Truth about Paid Product Reviews and Disclosure," *Blog Paws,* September 5, 2013, http://www.blog-paws.com; see sites that recruit bloggers to do paid reviews: http://www.sponsoredreviews.com, http://www.payperpost.com, http://www.reviewme.com.

36. Elizabeth A. Harris and Rachel Abrams, "Plugged-In Over Preppy: Teenagers Favor Tech Over Clothes," *The New York Times*, August 27, 2014, http://www.nytimes.com.

37. For an expanded discussion on these factors, see Peter and Olson, *Consumer Behavior and Marketing Strategy.* For some interesting experiments involving consumers' physical positioning and its effects on behavior, see Jeffrey S. Larson and Darron M. Billeter, "Consumer Behavior in 'Equilibrium': How Experiencing Physical Balance Increases Compromise Choice," *Journal of Marketing Research* 50 (August 2013), pp. 535–47.

38. Tracey S. Dagger and Peter J. Danaher, "Comparing the Effect of Store Remodeling on New and Existing Customers," *Journal of Marketing* (forthcoming). doi: http://dx.doi.org/10.1509/jm.13.0272.

39. The concept of atmospherics was introduced by Philip Kotler, "Atmosphere as a Marketing Tool," *Journal of Retailing* 49 (Winter 1973), pp. 48–64.

40. Sylvie Morin, Laurette Dubé, and Jean-Charles Chebat, "The Role of Pleasant Music in Servicescapes: A Test of the Dual Model of Environmental Perception," *Journal of Retailing 83*, no. 1 (2007), pp. 115–30.

41. http://www.wegmans.com; http://wholefoodsmarket.com/stores/cooking-classes/; Tracy Turner, "New Hangout Supermarket," *Columbus Dispatch*, March 20, 2011.

42. Tim Bajarin, "6 Reasons Apple Is So Successful," *Time*, May 7, 2012, http://techland.time.com.

43. Carmine Gallo, "Apple's Secret Employee Training Manual Reinvents Customer Service in Seven Ways," *Forbes*, August 30, 2012.

44. Ahreum Maeng, Robin J. Tanner, and Dilip Soman, "Conservative When Crowded: Social Crowding and Consumer Choice," *Journal of Marketing Research* 50 (December 2013), pp. 739–52; Alexander Chernev and Ryan Hamilton, "Assortment Size and Option Attractiveness in Consumer Choice among Retailers," *Journal of Marketing Research* 46, no. 3 (June 2009), pp. 410–20; Marc-Andre Kamel, Nick Greenspan, and Rudolf Pritzl, "Standardization Is Efficient but Localization Helps Shops to Stand Out," *The Wall Street Journal*, January 21, 2009.

45. Jeffrey Trachtenberg, "Publishers Bundle E-Books to Boost Sales, Promote Authors," *The Wall Street Journal*, February 11, 2011.

46. Pierre Chandon et al., "Does In-Store Marketing Work? Effects of the Number and Position of Shelf Facings on Brand Attention and Evaluation at the Point of Purchase," *Journal of Marketing* 73, no. 6 (November 2009), pp. 1–17.

47. Kirk Henderson and Kusum Ailawadi, "Shopper Marketing: Six Lessons for Retail from Six Years of Mobile Eye Tracking Research," *Review of Marketing Research* 12 (2014).

48. Christine Birkner, "Thinking Outside of the Box," *Marketing News*, March 30, 2011.

49. Dan King and Chris Janiszewski, "Affect-Gating," *Journal of Consumer Research* 38, no. 4 (December 2011), pp. 697–711.

50. Mittal, *Consumer Behavior*; Peter and Olson, *Consumer Behavior and Marketing Strategy*.

51. Yuping Liu-Thompkins and Leona Tam, "Not All Repeat Customers Are the Same: Designing Effective Cross-Selling Promotion on the Basis of Attitudinal Loyalty and Habit," *Journal of Marketing* 77 (September 2013), pp. 21–36; Karen M. Stilley, J. Jeffrey Inman, and Kirk L. Wakefield, "Planning to Make Unplanned Purchases? The Role of In-Store Slack in Budget Deviation," *Journal of Consumer Research* 37, no. 2 (2010), pp. 264–78; doi: 10.1086/651567.

52. This case was written by Kate Woodworth in conjunction with Dhruv Grewal and Michael Levy as the basis of class discussion rather than to illustrate either effective or ineffective marketing practices.

53. Justin McCarthy, "Fewer Americans Say They Want to Lose Weight," *Gallop*, November 27, 2015, http://www.gallup.com/poll/186920/fewer-americans-say-lose-weight.aspx?g_source=WEIGHT&g_medium=topic&g_campaign=tiles.

54. John Kell, "Lean Times for the Diet Industry," *Fortune*, May 22, 2015, http://fortune.com/2015/05/22/lean-times-for-the-diet-industry/.

55. PR Newswire, "Jenny Craig Showcases Real Member Success Stories in 2016 & Announces New Foods, Plus Introduces a New Retail Starter Kit," January 5, 2016, http://www.multivu.com/players/English/7727051-jenny-craig-campaign-kirstie-alley-cheers/.

56. https://www.weightwatchers.com/us/our-approach.

57. Tara Lachapelle, "Weight Watchers Gets Pounded," *Bloomberg*, January 21, 2016, http://www.bloomberg.com/gadfly/articles/2016-01-21/weight-watchers-turnaround-trouble-reveals-its-flaws.

58. John Kell, "Lean Times for the Diet Industry," *Fortune*, May 22, 2015, http://fortune.com/2015/05/22/lean-times-for-the-diet-industry/.

59. Megan McCluskey, "Oprah's New Weight Watchers Commercial Is Sending the Internet on an Emotional Roller Coaster," *Time*, December 29, 2015, http://time.com/4163543/oprah-weight-watchers-commercial-making-internet-emotional/.

60. Tara Lachapelle, "Weight Watchers Gets Pounded," *Bloomberg*, January 21, 2016, http://www.bloomberg.com/gadfly/articles/2016-01-21/weight-watchers-turnaround-trouble-reveals-its-flaws.

61. http://www.jennycraig.com/site/corporate/company-profile.

62. Tara Lachapelle, "Weight Watchers Gets Pounded," *Bloomberg*, January 21, 2016, http://www.bloomberg.com/gadfly/articles/2016-01-21/weight-watchers-turnaround-trouble-reveals-its-flaws; Jade Scipioni, "Kirstie Alley on Jenny Craig, Oprah, & 'Cheers' Reunion," *Fox Business*, January 14, 2016, http://www.foxbusiness.com/features/2016/01/14/kirstie-alley-on-jenny-craig-oprah-cheers-reunion.html.

63. http://www.slim-fast.com/plan/.

64. "Slim-Fast Diet," *US News Wellness*, http://health.usnews.com/best-diet/slim-fast-diet?utm_source=huffingtonpost.com&utm_medium=referral&utm_campaign=pubexchange_article.

65. http://weightwatchers.com/men/.

66. http://www.jennycraig.com/site/learn/article/a-healthy-diet-for-men.

67. Chris Sherwood, "Does Slim-Fast Work for Men?" *Live Strong*, November 12, 2015, http://www.livestrong.com/article/284239-does-slim-fast-work-for-men/.

i. Kathy Collins, "Here's How to Use Analytics to Tell a Brand Story," *Forbes*, April 4, 2014, http://www.forbes.com/sites/onmarketing/2014/04/07/heres-how-to-use-analytics-to-tell-a-brand-story/; Ashley Rodriguez, "H&R Block Ushers in 'Refund Season' with Slew of New Ads," *Advertising Age*, January 9, 2015, http://adage.com; "H&R Block Turns to Domo to Make Data Avalanche Less Taxing," June 25, 2013, http://www.domo.com/news/press/hr-block-turns-to-domo-to-make-data-avalanche-less-taxing.

ii. Bianca Banova, "The Future of Mobile Technology in Medicine: Innovative Medical Apps," *MedCity News*, April 24, 2013, http://medcitynews.com; William Cook, "Is That Little Mole a Big Problem?" *Daily Mail*, October 3, 2012, http://www.dailymail.co.uk; "mySugr App, Award-Winning iPhone App That Gamifies Blood Sugar Monitoring for People with Diabetes, Launches in US," *The Wall Street Journal*, June 6, 2013, press release, http://online.wsj.com; Mike H, "'Diabetes Monster' App Actually Motivates!" *Diabetes Mine*, June 19, 2013, http://www.diabetesmine.com.

iii. Ronnie Cummins, "ORCA to Attack 'Natural' Products Labeling Fraud," *Organic Consumers Association*, March 7, 2013, http://www.organicconsumers.org; Ashby Jones, "Is Your Dinner 'All Natural'?" *The Wall Street Journal*, September 20, 2011; "Diet and Nutrition Report," *Consumer Reports*, February 2009, http://www.consumerreports.org; Rachel Gross, "Farmers Seek to Raise Standards for Berries," *The New York Times*, September 23, 2011, http://www.nytimes.com; Mayo Clinic Staff, "Organic Foods: Are They Safer? More Nutritious?" http://www.mayoclinic.com; Natural and Organic Foods Backgrounder, Food Marketing Institute, http://www.fmi.org; Stacey R. Finkelstein and Ayelet Fishbach, "When Healthy Food Makes You Hungry," *Journal of Consumer Research* 37, no. 3 (October 2010), pp. 357–67.

iv. John Schwartz, "Chicago and 2 California Counties Sue Over Marketing of Painkillers," *The New York Times*, August 24, 2014, http://www.nytimes.com.

v. Roger Dooley, "The Smartest Supermarket You Never Heard Of," *Forbes*, January 28, 2014, http://www.forbes.com.

vi. Lauren Johnson, "Sephora Magnifies Mobile Ambitions via In-Store Signage, Updated App," *Mobile Commerce Daily*, August 23, 2013.

CHAPTER 7

BUSINESS-TO-BUSINESS MARKETING

After reading this chapter, you should be able to:

LO7-1 Describe the ways in which business-to-business (B2B) firms segment their markets.

LO7-2 List the steps in the B2B buying process.

LO7-3 Identify the roles within the buying center.

LO7-4 Describe the different types of organizational cultures.

LO7-5 Detail different buying situations.

f you haven't shopped at Amazon recently, you know someone who has. Amazon.com is the largest Internet retailer in the United States; it even is the ninth largest retailer of any type, earning $49.3 million in annual U.S. sales (accounting for a little more than half of its total annual sales of $83.3 million).[1] When most of us think of Amazon, we think about what we, as consumers, can buy there—currently, just about anything. But

© dpa picture alliance/Alamy

Amazon is much more than just a company that supplies consumers with books, household products, clothing, and so forth. Its business-to-business (B2B) transactions are significant and permeate multiple areas.

When you purchase a book on Amazon, you generally have two choices: Buy it directly from Amazon, or purchase it through Amazon but from a third-party vendor. If you go the direct route, Amazon has already purchased the book from a publisher and is holding it in an Amazon fulfillment center[2]—a B2B transaction. If you take the third-party route, Amazon acts as an agent for the supplier and takes a commission of about 10 percent of the value of the merchandise for the right to sell it on Amazon's platform—another B2B transaction.

The symbiotic relationships that Amazon has with its third-party providers are significant and likely to continue expanding in the future. Similar to other online marketplaces such as eBay, Amazon derives significant revenues by using third-party providers. These entities expand its marketplace presence by providing its customers a larger assortment of merchandise. Although Amazon makes less money by selling a book through a third party than if it sold that book itself, it does not have to incur the expenses of storing merchandise, fulfilling orders, or transporting it to the customer. The third-party providers benefit from their exposure on Amazon's website. If, in the future, Internet sales are taxed by state governments, Amazon is poised to help its smaller and often less sophisticated third-party providers collect the taxes, a service for which it will derive significant additional revenues.

Amazon Business is strictly a B2B operation. Competing with the likes of Staples (see this chapter's case study), Amazon Business sells millions of products necessary to run a business, from janitorial supplies to tools to soft drinks.[3] Similar to its business-to-consumer cousin Amazon Prime, Amazon Business offers free two-day shipping on orders over $49 and extra discounts for buying large quantities. Any B2B customers can compare prices from multiple sellers just like on Amazon.com. In addition, customers can chat with product experts, a feature that often is very necessary when purchasing technical products.

Amazon also has close B2B relationships with traditional delivery services, even though it has been expanding its own delivery capabilities. It continues to rely heavily on the U.S. Postal Service. Because of this close connection, the Postal Service even altered operating procedures that it had maintained for centuries and agreed to deliver Amazon packages on Sundays.[4] It also keeps up its links with other delivery companies such as UPS, recognizing that it might need them in the future. Finally, it is investing in its own delivery trucks, another B2B transaction.[5]

But as an alternative to these traditional B2B delivery companies, Amazon is experimenting with an alternative delivery mechanism called Prime Air, which promises to offer same-day delivery with the help of Amazon drones.[6] The development of drones has been managed internally under a cloak of secrecy. It has required close B2B relationships and commitments by partners not to disclose any information, so that Amazon could gather raw materials and parts and engage in necessary technical consulting.[7]

Another piece of Amazon's B2B puzzle is its robot army. Okay, it might not be an army, but over the course of a decade, it has purchased and put into service more than 30,000 Kiva warehouse robots to automate its fulfillment centers. The Kiva robots perform relatively complex but still standard tasks, such as moving merchandise throughout the distribution centers. But they also are equipped with language perception, object recognition, and software that enable them to gain a basic semantic understanding of voice commands.[8] At one point, Amazon cultivated B2B relationships with other companies by selling them robots so that they could automate their own supply chains. More recently though, having recognized that the Kivas are part of its own sustainable competitive advantage, it has renamed them simply Amazon robots, stopped supplying them to other firms, and are using all of Kiva's production internally. In this way, rather than expand its B2B sales, Amazon has attempted to limit the sale of robots (and patented its technology) so that it can maintain its dominance in other categories.[9]

Even though virtually everyone has heard of Amazon, most consumers have no idea of its true reach. With these varied and extensive B2B operations, Amazon stretches even further than you knew. It's the best B2B company that you never heard of, but knew all along.

Business-to-business (B2B) marketing refers to the process of buying and selling goods or services to be used in the production of other goods and services for consumption by the buying organization and/or resale by wholesalers and retailers. Therefore, a typical B2B marketing transaction involves manufacturers (e.g., GE, Levi's, Siemens, IBM, Ford) selling to wholesalers that, in turn, sell products to retailers. B2B transactions can also involve service firms (e.g., UPS, Oracle, Accenture) that market their services to other businesses but not to the ultimate consumer (e.g., you). The distinction between a B2B and a business-to-consumer (B2C) transaction is not the product or service itself; rather, it is the ultimate user of that product or service. Another key distinction is that B2B transactions tend to be more complex and involve multiple members of both the buying organization (e.g., buyers, marketing team, product developers) and the selling organization (e.g., sellers, R&D support team), whereas B2C often entails a simple transaction between the retailer and the individual consumer.

The demand for B2B sales is often derived from B2C sales in the same supply chain. More specifically, **derived demand** reflects the link between consumers' demand for a company's output and the company's purchase of necessary inputs to manufacture or assemble that particular output. For example, if more customers want to purchase staplers

Apple (left) and Google (right) both offer smartphone connectivity for specific car manufacturers.
Left: © Fabrice Coffrini/AFP/Getty Images; right: © Kyodo/AP Photo

(a B2C transaction), a company that produces them must purchase more metal from its supplier to make additional staplers (a B2B transaction).

Similar to organizations that sell directly to final consumers in B2C transactions, B2B firms focus on serving specific types of customer markets by creating value for those customers. Recognizing the growing demand for ever-increasing smartphone connectivity in cars, both Apple (with its CarPlay) and Google (with its Android-based Open Automotive Alliance) are making deals to integrate their operating systems into cars. Ferrari, Audi, Mercedes-Benz, and Volvo all offer CarPlay in select models, and it can also be added as an aftermarket system; Google has deals with Lexus, Honda, Hyundai, and General Motors.[10]

Also like B2C firms, many B2B companies find it productive to focus their efforts on key industries or market segments. Although the average large corporation has over 175 social media accounts, small-business owners often struggle to maintain a single social media account on each of the major networks.[11] Enter the B2B firm Constant Contact.[12] This firm provides a centralized dashboard for small businesses to manage their social media accounts as well as templates for posts and help on creating social media campaigns. Constant Contact could target businesses of any size, but it has become one of the leaders in small-business social media management by narrowing its efforts on this key market segment.[13]

In this chapter, we look at the different types of B2B markets and examine the B2B buying process, with an eye toward how it differs from the B2C buying process we discussed in Chapter 6. Several factors influence the B2B buying process, and we discuss these as well.

B2B MARKETS

LO7-1 Describe the ways in which business-to-business (B2B) firms segment their markets.

The most visible types of B2B transactions are those in which manufacturers and service providers sell to other businesses. However, resellers, institutions, and governments also may be involved in B2B transactions. Therefore, in the next sections we describe each of these B2B organizations (see Exhibit 7.1).

Manufacturers and Service Providers

Manufacturers buy raw materials, components, and parts that allow them to make and market their own goods and ancillary services. For example, the German-based Volkswagen Group, the largest auto manufacturer in Europe, owns and distributes the Audi, Bentley, Bugatti, Lamborghini, Seat, Skoda, Scania, VW, and VW Commercial Vehicles brands.[14] Whereas purchasing agents formerly spent 70 percent of their time

EXHIBIT 7.1   B2B Markets

German-based Volkswagen Group, the largest auto manufacturer in Europe, owns and distributes numerous brands.

© Oliver Hardt/AFP/Getty Images/ Newscom

searching for, analyzing, validating, and forwarding information about parts and components, today they can use VWSupplyGroup.com to communicate with suppliers for all transactions, from procurement to logistics. The VW Group system is used by 45,600 suppliers.[15] Purchasing agents receive product descriptions directly from suppliers online, which means search processes that used to take two hours now require about nine minutes. Users of the system receive alerts of potential parts shortages before they occur and thus can focus on efficiencies instead of redundant paperwork.

IBM provided the consulting services necessary to design the Volkswagen Group's system. IBM, which was once a major manufacturer of computers and related products, now generates 90 percent of its profits from its software, consulting, and financing businesses—all of which are considered services. Like Volkswagen Group, it requires a host of B2B products and services to support these businesses. For instance, the airlines that IBM consultants and service providers rely on to shuttle them around the globe also use a mix of products such as airplanes and fuel as well as consulting, legal, and other services. As Marketing Analytics 7.1 describes, IBM is constantly working to ensure that it can provide the features, data, and capabilities its business customers need.

Marketing Analytics 7.1 | Clouding over Computing Power [i]

As their computing power and security demands escalate, few businesses want to maintain their own hardware and servers anymore. Instead, they look to the cloud, where they seek to purchase more computing power, provided at a faster speed, with lower costs.

In response, traditional mainframe providers such as IBM are moving to expand their presence in the cloud. In particular, IBM has devoted billions of dollars to enhancing its cloud capabilities. First, it purchased a cloud company called SoftLayer for $2 billion to add that firm's 13 cloud computing centers to IBM's own 12 data centers. Second, it is allocating an additional $1.2 billion to expand its cloud computing centers worldwide.

The services provided by these cloud centers will include not just power and data storage but also access to some of IBM's proprietary software and related products. Perhaps most famously, for some of the best IBM clients it will offer access to Watson, IBM's famous *Jeopardy*-winning computer.

The Singaporean bank DBS Group Holdings plans to use Watson to provide up-to-date insights and lessons to its financial planners, who in turn will share that information with high-net-worth clients. With Watson analyzing the massive amounts of financial data available in nearly real time, DBS hopes to improve the customized advising services it provides to wealthy clients, who then may agree to do more of their investing with the bank. To gain this access, DBS will pay around $12 million over three years. It also agreed to share its own data, contributing and updating Watson's knowledge stores constantly.

Because Watson is only as good as the data that feeds it, IBM also has followed an acquisitive path, purchasing and obtaining rights to ever-increasing amounts of data. One of its recent acquisitions, the digital assets of The Weather Company, includes approximately four gigabytes of data every second from approximately 40 million smartphones, nearly 150,000 weather stations, and 50,000 daily airline flights. The Weather Company currently collects all these data to offer up-to-the-minute weather information to consumers who subscribe to its services. In return, those consumers actually provide much of the data through their linked smartphones. These weather-related offerings certainly remain valuable, but IBM plans to take the big data even further by combining them

Watson, IBM's super computer, is being used by some of its best customers including the Singaporean bank DBS Group Holdings and Under Armour.

© Andrew Spear/The Washington Post/Getty Images

with other reams of information. For example, IBM already has partnerships in place that allow it to receive data from diverse firms such as Johnson & Johnson, Apple, and Twitter.

Under Armour has announced it will be relying on Watson to expand its analytics capabilities too. In this new collaboration, Under Armour will introduce a personal fitness app that enables users to measure their activity and receive real-time instruction from coaches. They also can enter their information into the system and agree to participate in app-based competitions with other people of the same age or from the same city. Beyond activity levels, the app allows users to track and compare their sleep habits, meals, and nutrition levels.

With its massive data, one of the primary goals for IBM—and Watson—is better targeted, more informative, and more helpful advertising. In one example suggested by the Weather Company CEO, by combining health information, sentiment analysis from Twitter, weather data, and details of a user's buying habits, Watson could identify and recommend preventative practices or medications to help a consumer avoid catching the flu or limit seasonal allergies.

Resellers

Resellers are marketing intermediaries that resell manufactured products without significantly altering their form. For instance, **wholesalers** and **distributors** buy Xerox products and sell them to retailers (B2B transaction), then retailers resell those Xerox products to the ultimate consumer (B2C transaction). Alternatively, these retailers may buy directly from Xerox. Thus, wholesalers, distributors, and retailers are all resellers. Retailers represent resellers and engage in B2B transactions when they buy fixtures, capital investments, leasing locations, financing operations, and merchandise for their stores. To appeal to resellers and keep them interested in what it has to offer, Xerox works hard to ensure that its innovative products appeal to them and their customers. Adding Value 7.1 explains how it is promoting its HD printer technology to enhance its value, its commercial customers' value, and in the end, the consumers' value.

Adding Value 7.1   The "Alfonso Versant" Fashion Show: Creating Excitement for a New Xerox Printer[ii]

Xerox enjoys a strong reputation as a steady provider of equipment to business customers—but steady also can mean boring. Drumming up excitement for new products in its core market, document management, isn't exactly easy. Therefore, when a New Zealand branch of Xerox launched its new HD printer, the Versant 2100, it decided to get creative and host a fashion show, designed and produced fully through the use of the new printer.

Noting that the name Versant had a high fashion ring to it, the Xerox team decided to make up a designer, Alfonso Versant. It sent out glossy lookbooks of the designer's fashions, all printed on the Versant 2100. The direct mail campaign also included invitations to a fashion show, sent to business customers that might consider purchasing the products. These customers all were in the business of printing high-quality materials themselves, so the key was to demonstrate the remarkable and added-value capabilities of the Versant 2100. In support of this effort, Xerox solicited designs for a fashion show from fashion school students, who had to produce everything they designed by using only materials that came out of the Versant 2100. Highlighting the varieties of paper the printer could use, the students integrated not just traditional paper but also tissue paper and card stock in their designs.

Thus the direct mail campaign with the lookbook of designs clearly highlighted what the Versant 2100 could do, appealing to business customers who wanted to be able to promise their own customers that they could undertake complex print jobs easily and professionally. The lookbook included some traditional information about the printer too, but the main focus was on the creative and fun products that the project would

Xerox created excitement for its HD printer, the Versant 2100, by hosting a fashion show for the fictitious designer, Alfonso Versant.

Courtesy of MarketingSherpa and Fuji Xerox

produce. By the time the fashion show rolled around, Xerox was able to showcase 14 dresses and demonstrate how its new printer could offer value to its customers—while also achieving the added social benefit of collaborating with students to give them some real-world experience.

Overall, the event was a huge success for Xerox. Three months after the event, the New Zealand branch had surpassed its sales targets by a remarkable 240 percent; it alone accounted for 34 percent of total sales in the Asia-Pacific region, even though New Zealand makes up less than 1 percent of the region in area.

The U.S. Department of Defense spends over $500 billion a year on everything from nuts and bolts to this F-14 Tomcat jetfighter.

© Stocktrek Images/Getty Images RF

Institutions

Institutions such as hospitals, educational organizations, and religious organizations also purchase all kinds of goods and services. A public school system might have a $40 million annual budget for textbooks alone, which gives it significant buying power and enables it to take advantage of bulk discounts. However, if each school makes its own purchasing decisions, the system as a whole cannot leverage its combined buying power. Public institutions also engage in B2B relationships to fulfill their needs for capital construction, equipment, supplies, food, and janitorial services.

Government

In most countries, the central government is one of the largest purchasers of goods and services. For example, the U.S. federal government spends nearly $4 trillion annually on procuring goods and services. If you add in what state and local governments spend, these numbers

Social & Mobile Marketing 7.1 iPads Go to Work[iii]

Since their introduction, iPads have rocketed into widespread use for gaming, online access, music, videos, and e-mail. Tech-savvy business executives and educators also have noted some advantages of these devices that could make them useful at work as well as at play. Tablet computers weigh less and cost less than laptop computers. Uploaded e-books can be more up to date and are less expensive than physical textbooks. And in both the classroom and the workplace, the use of iPads extends the enthusiastic adoption of technology that is already occurring naturally in social contexts.

These devices, educators have learned, go beyond delivery of course materials: They save additional funds for schools and increase the value for students. Students can watch videos or tutorials, take notes, or use interactive programs that demonstrate particular skills. They can scroll effortlessly through documents or between texts to reach a section relevant to the current class discussion. Part-time and distance students can communicate more readily with their classmates, potentially enhancing collaboration and team-based learning. Visual learners, children with autism spectrum disorders or learning disabilities, and students who have grown up using electronic devices in various facets of their lives all can benefit from the interactive nature of iPads. And all students benefit from developing comfort with technology, a vital skill set in tomorrow's workforce.

The iPad is finding fans in the workplace as well. Executives, staff members, and clients at companies as diverse as Wells Fargo Bank, the business management software developer SAP, and Daimler's Mercedes-Benz have adopted the device. Airplane pilots have begun replacing paper binders full of flight manuals, navigation charts, and other materials with iPads. Siemens Energy has equipped some of its wind turbine service technicians with iPads so that they have convenient access to manuals, checklists, and cameras, even from atop a 300-foot tower. iPad's manufacturer, Apple, claims that

Eighty percent of Fortune *100 companies are either using the iPad or have launched pilot projects to try it.*
© Ariel Skelley/Getty Images RF

80 percent of *Fortune* 100 companies are either using the device or have launched pilot projects to try it.

Whether in the classroom or in the workplace, iPads are not without their disadvantages. Schools may save money in textbook costs but will need funding for repairs and wireless infrastructure. Tablets may enhance learning, but they cannot replace teachers or peer-to-peer interactions. Academic and business users find that the virtual keyboard is challenging for composing longer text, sharing applications is burdensome, and multitasking is impossible. Some companies are put off by iPad security breaches; others reject Apple's traditional focus on the consumer market, which is often at the expense of business sales. Despite these challenges, the iPad has gained a strong foothold in both the classroom and the workplace.

reach staggering proportions. For example, the Department of Defense was slated to receive $561 billion in fiscal year 2016, and $14 billion of that amount was to be dedicated to working with cybersecurity firms that can provide services to help the U.S. government protect against cyberterrorism attacks.[16] Thus the government, and the Department of Defense in particular, represents a spending force to be reckoned with.

Across these various B2B markets, purchasing methods might vary with the range of options being pursued. As Social and Mobile Marketing 7.1 highlights, iPads are playing increasing roles in educational institutions and businesses, which suggests that institutions need to start making thoughtful purchasing decisions about them too.

PROGRESS CHECK

1. What are the various B2B markets?

LO7-2 List the steps in the B2B buying process.

THE BUSINESS-TO-BUSINESS BUYING PROCESS

As noted in the previous section, the B2B buying process is unique (Exhibit 7.2): It both parallels the B2C process and differs in several ways. Both start with need recognition, but the information search and alternative evaluation steps are more formal and structured in the B2B process. Typically, B2B buyers specify their needs in writing and ask potential suppliers to submit formal proposals, whereas B2C buying decisions are usually made by individuals or families and do not need formal proposals. Thus, for an individual to buy a tablet computer, all that is required is a trip to the store or a few minutes online and perhaps some preliminary research about iPads versus competitors.

For a school to buy thousands of tablet computers, however, it must complete requisition forms, accept bids from manufacturers, and obtain approval for the expenditure. The final decision rests with a committee, as is the case for most B2B buying decisions, which often demand a great deal of consideration. Finally, in B2C buying situations, customers evaluate their purchase decision and sometimes experience postpurchase cognitive dissonance. But formal performance evaluations of the vendor and the products sold generally do not occur in the B2C setting, as they do in the B2B setting. Let's examine all six stages in the context of a university buying tablets for its incoming first-year students to use as resources.

Stage 1: Need Recognition

In the first stage of the B2B buying process, the buying organization recognizes, through either internal or external sources, that it has an unfilled need. Hypothetical University wants to ensure that its students are well educated and able to participate in a technologically connected workforce. It also seeks to grant them affordable access to required educational resources, from textbooks to library access to administrative tasks. The administration of the university also has reviewed research suggesting that portable devices, including tablet computers, can enhance students' in-class learning because they can directly and constantly interact with the materials and take notes in conjunction with the lecture and text, rather than only hearing information or seeing it on a whiteboard. The tablets also support innovative learning methodologies, such as the uses of interactive clickers in lecture-based courses. Using this information, the university has determined it will issue a tablet to each of the 1,200 students entering as its next freshman class.

Stage 2: Product Specification

After recognizing the need and considering alternative solutions, including laptop computers, the university wrote a list of potential specifications that vendors might use to develop their proposals. The school's specifications include screen size, battery life, processor speed, how the device connects to the Internet, and delivery date. In addition, the board of directors of the university has requested that a bundle of educational apps be preloaded on the tablets, that all other apps be removed, and that each tablet come equipped with a

The first step in the B2B decision process is to recognize that the university needs to purchase 1,200 tablets.

© McGraw-Hill Education/Mark Dierker, photographer

EXHIBIT 7.2 Business-to-Business Buying Process

Need recognition → Product specification → RFP process → Proposal analysis and supplier selection → Order specification → Vendor performance assessment using metrics

screen protector, power cord, cover, stand, keyboard, and headphones. The school hopes to obtain a four-year service contract that includes replacement within 24 hours for any tablets that are returned to the vendor for servicing.

Stage 3: RFP Process

The **request for proposals (RFP)** is a common process through which organizations invite alternative vendors or suppliers to bid on supplying their required components or specifications. The purchasing company may simply post its RFP needs on its website or work through various B2B web portals or inform their preferred vendors directly. Because the university does not have a preferred vendor for tablets yet, it issues an RFP and invites various tablet suppliers, technology companies, and other interested parties to bid on the contract.

Smaller companies may lack the ability to attract broad attention to their requests, so they might turn to a **web portal**, an Internet site whose purpose is to be a major starting point for users when they connect to the web. Although there are general portals such as Yahoo! or MSN, B2B partners connect to specialized or niche portals to participate in on-line information exchanges and transactions. These exchanges help streamline procurement or distribution processes. Portals can provide tremendous cost savings because they eliminate periodic negotiations and routine paperwork, and they offer the means to form a supply chain that can respond quickly to the buyer's needs.

Small- to medium-sized companies looking for skilled service workers also can use portals such as Guru.com, started to help freelance professionals connect with companies that need their services, whether those services entail graphic design and cartooning or finance and accounting advice. Currently, more than 1.5 million professionals list their offerings on this service-oriented professional exchange, and more than 30,000 companies regularly visit the site to post work orders. Guru.com thus provides value to both companies and freelancers by offering not only a site for finding each other but also dispute resolution, escrow for payments, and a means to rate freelancer quality.[17]

Stage 4: Proposal Analysis, Vendor Negotiation, and Selection

The buying organization, in conjunction with its critical decision makers, evaluates all the proposals it receives in response to its RFP. Hypothetical University reviews all proposals it receives, together with the board of directors, representatives from the teachers' union, and members of the student government. Many firms narrow the process to a few suppliers, often those with which they have existing relationships, and discuss key terms of the sale, such as price, quality, delivery, and financing. The university likely considers the bid by the company that installed computers in its library, assuming that provider performed well. Some firms have a policy that requires them to negotiate with several suppliers, particularly if the product or service represents a critical component or aspect of the business. This policy keeps suppliers on their toes; they know that the buying firm can always shift a greater portion of its business to an alternative supplier if it offers better terms.

The university evaluates proposals on the basis of the amount of experience the vendor has with tablet computers and similar technology products because it wants to make sure that its investment is reliable in the short term and flexible enough to accommodate new apps or updates. In addition, the school wants to be sure the technology will remain relevant in the longer term and not become obsolete. The vendor's ability to meet its specifications also is important because if the processor is too slow, students are unlikely to make use of the devices. The vendor's financial position provides an important indication of whether the vendor will be able to stay in business.

Stage 5: Order Specification

In the fifth stage of the B2B buying process, the firm places its order with its preferred supplier (or suppliers). The order includes a detailed description of the goods, prices, delivery dates, and, in some cases, penalties for noncompliance. The supplier then sends an acknowledgment that it has received the order and fills it by the specified date. In the case

EXHIBIT 7.3   Evaluating a Vendor's Performance

(1) Key Issues	(2) Importance Score	(3) Vendor's Performance	(4) Importance × Performance (2) × (3)
Customer service	0.40	5	2.0
Issue resolution	0.20	4	0.8
Delivery	0.10	5	0.5
Quality	0.30	3	0.9
Total	1.0		4.2

of the school's tablets, the terms are clearly laid out regarding when and how the vendor is expected to perform any preventive maintenance, who the contact person is for any problems with delivery or the tablets themselves, and under what circumstances the vendor will be expected to provide a replacement for a malfunctioning tablet. Issues such as maintenance and replacement are important, because the university does not plan to keep any inventory of extra tablets on hand.

Stage 6: Vendor Performance Assessment Using Metrics

Just as in the consumer buying process, firms analyze their vendors' performance so they can make decisions about their future purchases. The difference is that in a B2B setting, this analysis is typically more formal and objective. Let's consider how Hypothetical University might evaluate the tablet vendor's performance, as in Exhibit 7.3, using the following metrics: delivery (based on promised delivery date), quality, customer service, and issue resolution.

1. The buying team develops a list of issues that it believes are important to consider in the vendor evaluation.

2. To determine the importance of each issue (column 1), the buying team assigns an importance score to each (column 2). The more important the issue, the higher its score, but the importance scores must add up to 1. In this case, the buying team believes that customer service and quality are most important, whereas the issue resolution and delivery are comparatively less important.

3. In the third column, the buying team assigns numbers that reflect its judgments about how well the vendor performs. Using a 5-point scale, where 1 equals poor performance and 5 equals excellent performance, the university decides that the tablet vendor performs quite well on all issues except product quality.

4. To calculate an overall performance score in the fourth column, the team combines the importance of each issue and the vendor's performance scores by multiplying them. Because the tablet vendor performed well on the most important issues, when we add the importance/performance scores in column 4, we find that the overall evaluation is pretty good—4.2 on a 5-point scale.

PROGRESS CHECK

1. Identify the stages in the B2B buying process.
2. How do you perform a vendor analysis?

THE BUYING CENTER

LO7-3 Identify the roles within the buying center.

In most large organizations, several people are responsible for buying decisions. These **buying center** participants can range from employees who have a formal role in purchasing decisions (i.e., the purchasing or procurement department) to members of the design team who will specify the equipment or raw materials needed for employees who will be using a new machine that is on order. All these employees are likely to play different roles in the buying process, which vendors must understand and adapt to in their marketing and sales efforts.

We can categorize six buying roles within a typical buying center (see Exhibit 7.4). One or more people may take on a certain role, or one person may take on more than one of the following roles: (1) **initiator**, the person who first suggests buying the particular product or service; (2) **influencer**, the person whose views influence other members of the buying center in making the final decision; (3) **decider**, the person who ultimately determines any part of or the entire buying decision—whether to buy, what to buy, how to buy, or where to buy; (4) **buyer**, the person who handles the paperwork of the actual purchase; (5) **user**, the person who consumes or uses the product or service; and (6) **gatekeeper**, the person who controls information or access, or both, to decision makers and influencers.[18]

To illustrate how a buying center operates, consider purchases made by a hospital. Where do hospitals obtain their X-ray machines, syringes, and bedpans? Why are some medical procedures covered in whole or in part by insurance, whereas others are not? Why might your doctor recommend one type of allergy medication instead of another?

The Initiator—Your Doctor When you seek treatment from your physician, he or she initiates the buying process by determining the products and services that will best address and treat your illness or injury. For example, say you fell backward off your snowboard

EXHIBIT 7.4 Buying Center Roles

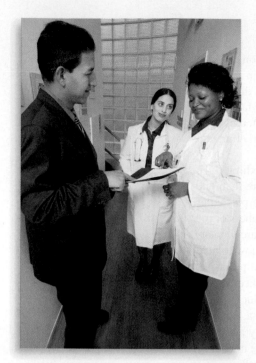

In the buying center, the medical device supplier is the influencer, whereas the doctor is the initiator.

© Custom Medical Stock Photo RF

and, in trying to catch yourself, you shattered your elbow. You require surgery to mend the affected area, which includes the insertion of several screws to hold the bones in place. Your doctor promptly notifies the hospital to schedule a time for the procedure and specifies the brand of screws she wants on hand for your surgery.

The Influencer—The Medical Device Supplier, the Pharmacy For years your doctor has been using ElbowMed screws, a slightly higher-priced screw. Her first introduction to ElbowMed screws came from the company's sales representative, who visited her office to demonstrate how ElbowMed screws were far superior to those of its competition. Your doctor recognized ElbowMed as a good value. Armed with empirical data and case studies, ElbowMed's sales rep effectively influenced your doctor's decision to use that screw.

The Decider—The Hospital Even though your doctor requested ElbowMed screws, the hospital ultimately is responsible for deciding whether to buy ElbowMed screws. The hospital supplies the operating room, instrumentation, and surgical supplies, and, therefore, the hospital administrators must weigh a variety of factors to determine whether the ElbowMed screw is not only best for the patients but also involves a cost that is reimbursable by various insurance providers.

The Buyer The actual buyer of the screw will likely be the hospital's materials manager, who is charged with buying and maintaining inventory for the hospital in the most cost-effective manner. Whereas ElbowMed screws are specific to your type of procedure, other items, such as gauze and sutures, may be purchased through a group purchasing organization (GPO), which obtains better prices through volume buying.

The User—The Patient Ultimately, the buying process for this procedure will be greatly affected by the user, namely you, and your broken elbow. If you are uncomfortable with the procedure or have read about alternative procedures that you prefer, you may decide that ElbowMed screws are not the best treatment.

The Gatekeeper—The Insurance Company Your insurer may believe that ElbowMed screws are too expensive and that other screws deliver equally effective results and therefore refuse to reimburse the hospital in full or in part for the use of the screws.

In the end, the final purchase decision must take into consideration every buying center participant. Ethical and Societal Dilemma 7.1 examines the unethical, illegal, but also international practice of influencing the influencers through expensive gifts and payments.

LO7-4 Describe the different types of organizational cultures.

Organizational Culture

A firm's **organizational culture** reflects the set of values, traditions, and customs that guide its employees' behavior. The firm's culture often comprises a set of unspoken guidelines that employees share with one another through various work situations. For example, Walmart buyers are not allowed to accept even the smallest gift from a vendor, not even a cup of coffee. This rule highlights its overall corporate culture: It is a low-cost operator whose buyers must base their decisions only on the products' and vendors' merits.

At GE, the culture aims to ensure that members and partners regard B2B as a source of innovation, not a "boring-to-boring" proposition. Rather than lament the relatively less glamorous process of B2B, GE has "decided we are geeky and we are proud of it."[19] Therefore, rather than turning to some of the more conventional uses of Instagram, General Electric (GE) relies on the social media site to communicate with "its people," those followers it affectionately refers to as #AVgeeks. What GE offers to its business customers is mainly advanced technology and scientifically based products and services. But those sorts of offerings are exactly what get geeks excited, so it offers content that they can share with other geeks, as well as with their own customers. In addition to uploading quotes from

Ethical & Societal Dilemma **7.1**   Is It Business or Bribery?[iv]

In some parts of the world, accepting money, offering expensive gifts, or distributing payments to government and business officials to influence business decisions is considered an acceptable business practice. In other nations, these practices are unethical and illegal. As the world moves to a more global economy, pressure is mounting to level the playing field by eliminating bribery. Yet companies that have traditionally relied on business bribery argue that criminalizing this activity will negatively affect their ability to compete. How do executives doing business on an international scale respond when a behavior that could earn them a lucrative contract in one country could earn them jail time in another?

Whenever businesses cooperate with one another or companies intersect with governments, the opportunity exists for bribery. An extravagant gift or economic incentive may mean one contractor lands a lucrative contract. A private exchange of money between an executive and a public official may result in the official driving a new car while the executive's company bypasses a restriction that could hinder its growth. These types of interactions occur behind closed doors and between two people, yet they can have significant repercussions, including unsafe infrastructure, bridges, and buildings, if they

Although in some parts of the world bribes are part of doing business, in the United States they are unethical and illegal.

© James Lauritz/Photodisc/Getty Images RF

occur in the context of large business transactions. Increasingly, players in the world's economies thus are pushing for an end to foreign bribery.

Perceived corruption levels by country and companies' propensity to bribe

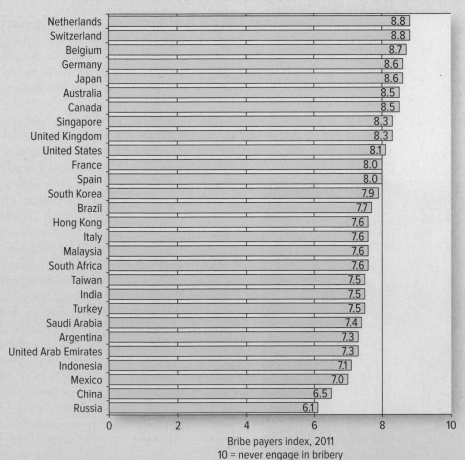

Country	Bribe payers index, 2011
Netherlands	8.8
Switzerland	8.8
Belgium	8.7
Germany	8.6
Japan	8.6
Australia	8.5
Canada	8.5
Singapore	8.3
United Kingdom	8.3
United States	8.1
France	8.0
Spain	8.0
South Korea	7.9
Brazil	7.7
Hong Kong	7.6
Italy	7.6
Malaysia	7.6
South Africa	7.6
Taiwan	7.5
India	7.5
Turkey	7.5
Saudi Arabia	7.4
Argentina	7.3
United Arab Emirates	7.3
Indonesia	7.1
Mexico	7.0
China	6.5
Russia	6.1

Bribe payers index, 2011
10 = never engage in bribery

Source: Bribes Payers Index Report 2011. Transparency International. http://www.transparency.org/bpi2011/results.

(continued)

One tactic they are using is a public report called the Bribe Payers Index, published by Transparency International, that compares corruption rates of countries and industries. This investigation reveals unexpected trends, such as evidence that bribes passing from one business to another are almost as common as bribes slipped to public officials. By highlighting those business sectors or countries perceived as the worst offenders, the Bribe Payers Index also aims to bring about change, whether through embarrassment or economic repercussions that result when companies refuse to do business in corrupt economies. Finally, this report highlights suggestions for reducing corruption and incentives for improvement.

As summarized in the graph opposite, the Transparency International Bribe Payers Index reveals that all the world's 28 largest economies engage in bribery; China and Russia emerged as those most likely to be using money and gifts to influence decisions. Both countries have recently begun enforcing legal repercussions for companies and individuals that engage in international business bribery. For example,

when reports surfaced that representatives of GlaxoSmith-Kline (GSK) had bribed doctors, medical practices, and hospitals to prescribe only GSK drugs, China's news media and central government reacted with anger. Calling the drug company a "criminal godfather," Chinese authorities encouraged consumers to boycott its products. A **boycott** occurs when a group refuses to deal commercially with an organization to protest against its policies. As a result, GSK's business revenues fell by two-thirds in China.

The Transparency International report also highlights positive results of reduced corruption: A business survey conducted in Europe found that two-thirds of respondents believe that a company with a reputation for ethical behavior enjoys a commercial advantage. Findings such as these, along with improved transparency added to business practices, international anticorruption standards, monitoring and enforcement of anticorruption business policies and laws, and empowerment of whistle-blowers, may also help reduce international bribery rates.

Marie Curie on International Women's Day for example,[20] the @generalelectric Instagram page highlights pictures taken on its production floor and research labs. It encourages customers to submit depictions of how they use GE products in their own locations, from a monorail in Sydney to oil rigs in Singapore.[21] Employees upload their own shots, giving business customers an insider's view of what is going on with GE and how the products they purchase get made.[22]

Organizational culture also can have a profound influence on purchasing decisions. Corporate buying center cultures can be divided into four general types: autocratic, democratic, consultative, and consensus (as illustrated in Exhibit 7.5). Knowing which buying center culture is prevalent in a given organization helps the seller decide how to approach that particular client, how and to whom to deliver pertinent information, and to whom to make sales presentations.

In an **autocratic buying center**, even though there may be multiple participants, one person makes the decision alone, whereas the majority rules in a **democratic buying center**. **Consultative buying centers** use one person to make a decision but solicit input from others before doing so. Finally, in a **consensus buying center**, all members of the team must reach a collective agreement that they can support a particular purchase.

Cultures act like living, breathing entities that change and grow, just as organizations do. Even within some companies, culture may vary by geography, by division, or by functional department. Whether you are a member of the buying center or a supplier trying to sell to it, it is extremely important to understand the buying center's culture and the roles of the key players in the buying process. Not knowing the

GE communicates with its B2B customers via Instagram by providing interesting pictures that geeks love, like its Guinness World Record holder combined-cycle, the most efficient in the world.

Source: General Electric Company/Instagram

EXHIBIT 7.5 Organizational Buying Culture

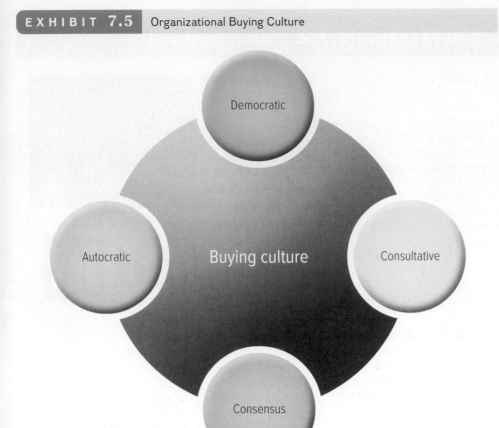

roles of the key players could waste a lot of time and even alienate the real decision maker.

Building B2B Relationships

In B2B contexts there are a multitude of ways to enhance relationships, and these methods seem to be advancing and evolving by the minute. For example, blogs and social media can build awareness, provide search engine results, educate potential and existing clients about products or services, and warm up a seemingly cold corporate culture. Fiberlink offers document and mobile enterprise management services. To make its offerings and content more engaging, it launched a series of fun webinars and video campaigns filled with pop culture references. One webinar, "Game of Phones," used comparisons from the popular HBO series *Game of Thrones* to highlight the different mobile operating systems and detail how Fiberlink's platform could enable business customers to leverage their content on all of them. Thus Apple, as the current market leader, was presented as the House Lannister; Android was the House Targaryen because the factors that kept it on the sidelines also have helped it gain power; and Windows was House Stark because it is "full of battle scars." The engaging campaign allowed the company to generate 20 percent more new leads than previous campaigns had achieved.[23]

An expert who offers advice and knowledge about products increases brand awareness, and a blog is a great medium for this information. Web analytics, such

To make its offerings more engaging, Fiberlink launched a series of fun webinars and video campaigns, like this one that "plays" with the popular HBO series Game of Thrones.

Source: androidcentral.com

Social & Mobile Marketing 7.2   Making the Most of LinkedIn[v]

Business-to-business (B2B) marketing may seem relatively impersonal, but even in formalized, standardized buying situations, personal relationships count. Social media, with a bit of a tweak, play a key role in this setting, just as they do in consumer contexts. Perhaps the best example is LinkedIn, the social media site for business professionals. Launched in 2003, the site attracts approximately two new members every single second. It has more than 400 million members worldwide, about 10 percent of whom are college students or recent graduates. The site is available in more than 19 languages and more than 200 countries, which means that it can help B2B interactions overcome geographic boundaries.

In particular, LinkedIn can boast that executives from all the *Fortune* 500 companies have memberships on its site. Accordingly, its promise for networking, whether individually or for the company, is virtually unsurpassed. Such networking entails several key groups:

LinkedIn is perhaps the best social media site for networking with business professionals.

© Paul Sakuma/AP Photo

- *Customers and prospective customers.* LinkedIn allows a firm or its representatives to introduce themselves to possible buyers, using a credible and easily accessible format. The Q&A option on LinkedIn pages also allows customers to ask questions and suppliers to demonstrate their expertise.

- *Investors.* The LinkedIn page offers tangible evidence of the firm's existence and its promise, which is critical information for outsiders who might be willing to invest in its development.

- *Suppliers.* By starting their own group on LinkedIn, B2B buyers might better identify which suppliers in the market are best matched with their needs and most interested in providing the resources they need.

- *Employees and prospective employees.* LinkedIn is a great source for finding employees who are diligent,

professional, interested, and qualified. Furthermore, if a firm retains its links to former employees, it can gain a good source of referrals—assuming those employees left on good terms.

- *Analysts.* The job of an analyst is to find detailed information about a company and then recommend it, or not, to the market. LinkedIn gives firms a means to provide that information in a credible but still firm-controlled context.

The site also provides sophisticated analytics for keeping track of all these networking opportunities. Users can see who visits their pages, which descriptions they view, and even compare their LinkedIn performance against competitors' pages.

---

as traffic on the website and the number of comments, can offer tangible evaluations, but a better measure is how often the blog gets mentioned elsewhere, the media attention it receives, and the interaction, involvement, intimacy, and influence that it promotes.

The LinkedIn.com social network is mainly used for professional networking in the B2B marketplace (see Social and Mobile Marketing 7.2). Twitter, the microblogging site, is also valuable for B2B marketers because they can communicate with other businesses as often as they want. Companies such as HootSuite make it easier for companies using Twitter to manage their followers, update their posts, track analytics, and even schedule tweets, just as they would to manage a traditional marketing campaign.[24]

When executives confront an unfulfilled business need, they normally turn to **white papers** prepared by potential B2B marketers.[25] White papers are a promotional technique used by B2B sellers to provide information about a product or service in an educational context, thereby not appearing like a promotion or propaganda. The goal of white papers is to provide valuable information that a potential B2B buyer can easily understand and that will help the company address its problems with new solutions. For instance, say a B2B seller has a technologically advanced solution for an inventory problem. Since the executives of the potential B2B buying firm are not technologically oriented, the B2B seller creates a white paper to explain the solution in nontechnological terms so that the buying firm's executives can understand and appreciate the solution before they consider a purchase.

PROGRESS CHECK

1. What are the six buying roles?
2. What are the types of cultures that exist in buying centers?

THE BUYING SITUATION

LO7-5 Detail different buying situations.

The type of buying situation also affects the B2B decision process. Most B2B buying situations can be categorized into three types: new buys, modified rebuys, and straight rebuys (see Exhibit 7.6). To illustrate the nuances among these three buying situations, consider how colleges and universities develop relationships with some of their suppliers. Most universities negotiate with sports apparel manufacturers, such as Nike, Reebok, and New Balance, to establish purchasing agreements for their sports teams. Those with successful sports teams have been very successful in managing these relationships, to the benefit of both the team and the company.[26] Large universities that win national championships, such as the University of Alabama or University of Southern California (USC), can solicit sponsorships in exchange for free athletic equipment, whereas less popular teams or smaller schools typically must accept an upfront sponsorship and then agree to buy from that vendor for a specified period of time. In exchange for this sponsorship, the vendors gain the right to sell apparel with the university logo and require the school's team to purchase only their equipment. Many apparel companies make a significant portion of their revenue through sponsorship deals that grant them the right to sell apparel with popular university logos.

EXHIBIT 7.6   Buying Situations

In a **new buy** situation, a customer purchases a good or service for the first time,[27] which means the buying decision is likely to be quite involved because the buyer or the buying organization does not have any experience with the item. In the B2B context, the buying center is likely to proceed through all six steps in the buying process and involve many people in the buying decision. Typical new buys might range from capital equipment to components that the firm previously made itself but now has decided to purchase instead. For example, a small college might need to decide which apparel company to approach for a sponsorship. For smaller colleges, finding a company that will sponsor multiple sports teams—such as women's soccer as well as men's basketball—is a priority, though it also must balance other considerations such as the length of the contract. Some vendors offer perks to attract new buyers; New Balance offers teams that sign up for long-term contracts custom fittings for their players' shoes. Each season, a sales team from New Balance visits the school and custom fits each player to achieve the best fit possible.

With another sort of example, Adding Value 7.2 highlights how HubSpot helps buyers become more informed about products before engaging in the B2B buying process.

Another example of a new buy occurs in the fashion industry, where runway shows offer wholesale buyers an opportunity to inspect new lines of clothing and place orders. Designer sales often occur during private meetings with buyers, both before and after runway shows. Buyers meet with the designers, discuss the line, and observe a model wearing the clothing. The buyer's challenge, then: determine which items will sell best in the retail stores he or she represents while trying to imagine what the item will look like in regular, as opposed to model, sizes. Buyers must also negotiate purchases for orders that may not be delivered for as long as six months. Buyers can suggest modifications to make the clothing more or less expensive or more comfortable for their customers. Buyers and designers recognize the significant value of this relationship, which occasionally prompts buyers to purchase a few items from a designer even if those items do not exactly fit the store's core customers' tastes. Doing so ensures that the buyer will have access to the designer's collection for the next season.[28]

In a **modified rebuy**, the buyer has purchased a similar product in the past but has decided to change some specifications such as the desired price, quality level, customer service level, options, and so forth. Current vendors are likely to have an advantage in acquiring the sale in a modified rebuy situation as long as the reason for the modification is not dissatisfaction with the vendor or its products. The Ohio State University's sports department might ask adidas to modify the specifications for its basketball shoes after noticing some improvements made to the adidas shoes used by the University of Michigan.

Adding Value 7.2   Getting Out the Message with Inbound Marketing[vi]

Search engines, company web pages, social media sites, and the blogosphere have transformed the way businesses learn about and shop for products and services. Unlike in the not-so-distant past, when a prospective customer had little knowledge of a vendor's products at first contact, today's customers have searched the Internet using relevant keywords and reviewed company websites by the time they speak with a vendor. As a result, they are well informed and seriously interested in a purchase, adding new efficiency to B2B transactions. But this development works only if companies have the marketing savvy to use today's technology to their advantage.

Two entrepreneurs noticed that small companies and start-ups without the skills to use these tools effectively get lost in the noise, even if prospective customers are searching for vendors in their niche. Furthermore, companies that enlist marketing firms are disadvantaged if those firms rely solely on traditional best practices such as print advertising, telemarketing, and trade shows. To help these businesses, the two entrepreneurs launched a software marketing program, HubSpot, designed to help companies transform their marketing approach. The idea was to abandon intrusive outbound marketing, which people are increasingly able to screen out, and replace it with inbound marketing. Inbound marketing, defined as any marketing tactic that relies on earning customer interest rather than buying it, is built on the understanding that Facebook, Twitter, online user reviews, smartphones, blogs, and websites are the true force behind the way consumers in today's marketplace actually learn and shop.

HubSpot's software contains easy-to-use tools that help companies get noticed, convert website visitors to customers, and analyze the effectiveness of marketing efforts across channels. Among the tools in the first category, for example, is a keyword grader that helps companies create content and a list of relevant keywords to improve search engine odds and ranking. Using the lead conversion tools, marketers without technical skills can create landing pages with customizable lead capture forms, auto-response e-mails, and thank-you pages. These tools can also be used to send customized e-mails to new leads on a self-selected schedule. The marketing analytics tools allow HubSpot's customers to track competitors, evaluate the impact of a blog, and compare the effectiveness of all marketing channels to provide important insight into the behaviors of customers and the value of each channel to the bottom line.

HubSpot's approach has been successful for both the founders and their customers. The company, launched in June 2006, currently has over 13,000 customers.

One customer, the nonprofit National Institute for Fitness and Sport (NIFS), wanted to increase its visibility with corporate and retirement fitness centers. After experiencing difficulty driving traffic to the company website—and after an expensive marketing company campaign proved ineffective—NIFS turned to HubSpot. The results were increases in traffic and leads by more than 200 percent and an increase in social media traffic of 16 percent. According to NIFS's director of media, the fitness company "picked up a number of requests for proposals from businesses that never would have paid attention to us initially because we were able to raise where we sit in the search engines."

Companies such as HubSpot are taking advantage of changes that have already occurred in the marketplace to reduce costs and improve the effectiveness of marketing. As technology evolves and more business and individual shoppers use online information to make their purchasing decisions, businesses will have to adapt their marketing strategies to encompass new technologies and new shopping behaviors.

HubSpot helps its customers get noticed on the Internet.

© Hubspot

Straight rebuys occur when the buyer or buying organization simply buys additional units of products that had previously been purchased. Many B2B purchases are likely to fall in the straight rebuy category. For example, sports teams need to repurchase a tremendous amount of equipment that is not covered by apparel sponsorships, such as tape for athletes' ankles or weights for the weight room. The purchase of bottled water also typically involves a straight rebuy from an existing supplier.

These varied types of buying situations call for very different marketing and selling strategies. The most complex and difficult is the new buy because it requires the buying organization to make changes in its current practices and purchases. As a result, several members of the buying center will likely become involved, and the level of their involvement will be more intense than in the case of modified and straight rebuys. In new buying situations, buying center members also typically spend more time at each stage of the B2B buying process, similar to the extended decision-making process that consumers use in the B2C process. In comparison, in modified rebuys the buyers spend less time at each stage of the B2B buying process, similar to limited decision making in the B2C process (see Chapter 6).

In straight rebuys, however, the buyer is often the only member of the buying center involved in the process. Like a consumer's habitual purchase, straight rebuys often enable the buyer to recognize the firm's need and go directly to the fifth step in the B2B buying process, skipping the product specification, RFP process, proposal analysis, and supplier selection steps.

Over the course of a B2B relationship, the type of buying process also can change. The buying process for restaurants appears poised to undergo a significant transformation because of the potential mergers between food distributors in the United States. Restaurants that once considered their purchases of hamburger meat a straight rebuy might find that they need to reconsider the process. Because the merger would create a single, dominant food supplier, the new company will gain much more power over pricing. In turn, restaurants might need to enter into a modified rebuy (e.g., purchase lower-quality hamburger to cut costs).

Thus, in various ways B2B marketing both differs from and mirrors the consumer behavior (B2C) process we detailed in Chapter 6. The differences in the six stages of the buying process make sense in view of the many unique factors that come into play. The constitution of the buying center (initiator, influencer, decider, buyer, user, and gatekeeper), the culture of the purchasing firm (autocratic, democratic, consultative, or consensus), and the context of the buying situation (new buy, modified rebuy, straight rebuy) all influence the B2B buying process in various ways, which means that sellers must be constantly aware of these factors if they want to be successful in their sales attempts.

PROGRESS CHECK

1. How do new buy, straight rebuy, and modified rebuy differ?

Reviewing Learning Objectives

 Describe the ways in which business-to-business (B2B) firms segment their markets.

All firms want to divide the market into groups of customers with different needs, wants, or characteristics who therefore might appreciate products or services geared especially toward them. On a broad level, B2B firms divide the market into four types:

manufacturers or service providers, resellers, institutions, and government. Manufacturers and service providers purchase materials to make their products and components and offer expertise to help run their businesses, such as computer and telephone systems. Resellers are primarily wholesalers, distributors, or retailers that sell the unchanged products. Institutions include nonprofit organizations such as hospitals, schools, or churches. Finally, governments purchase all types of goods and services; in the United States, defense is among the largest expenditures.

 List the steps in the B2B buying process.

Similar to the B2C buying process, the B2B process consists of several stages: need recognition; product specification; the RFP process; proposal analysis, vendor negotiation, and selection; order specification; and vendor performance assessment using metrics. The B2B process tends to be more formalized and structured than the customer buying process.

 Identify the roles within the buying center.

The initiator first suggests the purchase. The influencer affects important people's perceptions and final decisions. The decider ultimately determines at least some of the buying decision—whether, what, how, or where to buy. The buyer handles the details of the actual purchase. The user consumes or employs the product or service. The gatekeeper controls information and access to decision makers and influencers. In B2B situations, it is likely that several people, organized into a buying center, will be involved in making the purchase decision. The vendor must understand the relationships among the

participants of the buying center to be effective. A firm's organizational culture can also influence the decision process. For instance, if a firm is trying to sell to a young, high-tech computer component manufacturer, it might be well advised to send salespeople who are fluent in technology-speak and can easily relate to the customer.

 Describe the different types of organizational cultures.

Firm culture consists of unspoken guidelines that employees share through various work situations. They generally can be classified as autocratic, in which one person makes most decisions; democratic, where the majority rules; consultative, in which one person makes decisions based on the input of others; or consensus, which requires all members of the team to reach collective agreement.

 Detail different buying situations.

The buying process depends to a great extent on the situation. If a firm is purchasing a product or service for the first time (i.e., new buy), the process is much more involved than if it is engaging in a straight rebuy of the same item again. A modified rebuy falls somewhere in the middle, such that the buyer wants essentially the same thing but with slightly different terms or features.

Key Terms

- autocratic buying center, 222
- boycott, 222
- business-to-business (B2B) marketing, 210
- buyer, 219
- buying center, 219
- consensus buying center, 222
- consultative buying center, 222
- decider, 219

- democratic buying center, 222
- derived demand, 210
- distributor, 213
- gatekeeper, 219
- inbound marketing, 227
- influencer, 219
- initiator, 219
- modified rebuy, 226
- new buy, 226

- organizational culture, 220
- request for proposals (RFP), 217
- reseller, 213
- straight rebuy, 228
- user, 219
- web portal, 217
- white papers, 224
- wholesaler, 213

Net Savvy

1. Ballymaloe Country Relish is an Irish delicacy sold in fine food stores throughout Ireland. For consumers outside Ireland, it also lists various sellers in different countries. Visit ballymaloecountryrelish.ie and click on "Stocklist" to find the most convenient source for you personally. Why does Ballymaloe offer such information and direct links to other retailers? What benefits does doing so provide the relish maker, the retailer, and customers?

2. Siemens worked with the custom motorcycle manufacturer Orange County Chopper to build the Smart Chopper—the first electric motorcycle. Visit http://www.usa .siemens.com/smartchopper/ to learn about the specifications and details of this new form of chopper. How is Siemens using this innovation to improve its relationships with its business customers? What other outcomes might this services provider expect from its efforts?

Marketing Applications

1. Provide an example of each of the four types of B2B organizations.

2. What are the major differences between the consumer buying process discussed in Chapter 6 and the B2B buying process discussed in this chapter? Use buying iPads for personal use versus buying more than 100 iPads for a firm to illustrate the key points.

3. Assume you have written this textbook and are going to attempt to sell it to your school. Identify the six members of the buying center. What role would each play in the decision process? Rank them in terms of how much influence they would have on the decision, with 1 being most influential and 6 being least influential. Will this ranking be different in other situations?

4. Now provide an example of the three types of buying situations that the bookstore at your school might face when buying textbooks.

5. Finally, discuss for which types of products the bookstore would do a straight rebuy and for which it would pursue a modified rebuy.

6. Mazda is trying to assess the performance of two manufacturers that could supply music systems for its vehicles. Using the information in the accompanying table, determine which manufacturer Mazda should use.

Performance Evaluation of Brands			
Issues	Importance Weights	Manufacturer A's Performance	Manufacturer B's Performance
Sound	0.4	5	3
Cost	0.3	2	4
Delivery time	0.1	2	2
Brand cachet	0.2	5	1
Total	1		

7. Describe the organizational culture at your school or job. How would knowledge of this particular organization's culture help a B2B salesperson sell products or services to the organization?

8. You have just started to work in the purchasing office of a major pharmaceutical firm. The purchasing manager has asked you to assist in writing an RFP for a major purchase. The manager gives you a sheet detailing the specifications for the RFP. While reading the specifications, you realize that they have been written to be extremely favorable to one bidder. How should you handle this situation?

Quiz Yourself

1. Which of the following statements regarding the B2B buying process is true?
   a. The B2B buying process is identical to the B2C buying process.
   b. The B2B buying process is less complex than the B2C buying process.
   c. In the B2B buying process, decisions are made quickly and without much consideration.
   d. In the B2B buying process, formal performance evaluations of the vendor generally do not occur.
   e. In the B2B buying process, the search for information and evaluation of alternatives is more formal and structured.

2. In a _____ situation, the buying center is likely to proceed through all six steps in the buying process and involve many people in the buying decision.
   a. straight rebuy
   b. standard rebuy
   c. modified rebuy
   d. new buy
   e. capital buy

(Answers to these two questions can be found in the Quiz Yourself Answer Key section.)

Chapter Case Study

STAPLES: THE BIG BOX RETAILER THAT'S REALLY A B2B POWERHOUSE

Probably every reader of this book has visited a Staples store or its website at least once, needing to stock up on back-to-school supplies, grab a roll of packing tape, or take a look at the newest printers available in the market. Clearly, selling to individual consumers is important to Staples. But some of its greatest growth, and some of its most important marketing efforts, relate to its Staples Advantage division, which provides business customers with services and support.

This support may be most valuable for small businesses, which often lack the resources to manage all their various functions on their own. Most straightforwardly, Staples Advantage provides companies with the behind-the-scenes supplies that are necessary to keep the doors open: coffee machines, sugar, and creamer to stock employee break rooms; janitorial supplies and floor mats that keep the place looking clean; paper towels and soap dispensers in restrooms; and office equipment to ensure that workers can keep their files organized and their workspaces productive. To facilitate these offerings, Staples has begun equipping all its B2B sales associates in the field with iPads that are loaded with a virtual assistant. Thus, rather than relying on their recall or a bulky product catalog, they can depend on the virtual tool to determine which type of furniture polish will save their business clients the most money while still enabling them to keep all their surfaces free of dirt.[29]

To appeal even more to these small-business owners and provide them with not just office supplies but also ideas on how to run their offices, Staples has introduced the Quick Wins app. The app tracks the small businesses' performances on a range of measures, including social media engagement, website traffic, and financial metrics, all in one place. In this case, the innovative offering is a clear response to customer demand. Through its research, Staples determined that approximately 41 percent of its small-business customers expressed their need for help with these measures of performance, but they also did not know which metrics were most important or how to measure them accurately. Worried about their ability to keep up with the information, respondents to Staples' surveys also noted that they would prefer for all the information to be available in one easy-to-read dashboard. In helping business customers track key data regularly, Staples promises to develop customized, specific suggestions for how the business customers can expand their firms and increase business. Furthermore, through the Quick Wins app, users can interact with other small-business owners, seeking answers and support from their peers.[30]

Once they determine their performance, small-business owners likely identify sources of improvement. Pursuing such improvements often requires new investments, especially monetary ones—a resource that small-business owners usually lack. Therefore, Staples' latest service introduction is Lendio, an online financing arm that facilitates loans for these customers. Accessing the loan forms through Staples' main website, business customers can provide the necessary information.[31] Lendio then forwards the information to a relevant lender and maintains the financing agreement. In just a few months, Lendio had facilitated close to $1.5 million in loans to small firms, such as Bubba Nubb's Lunch Wagon, which used the loan to equip its food truck, or Hitt Medical Writing, which spent the money to hire new employees and expand its capacity to provide content to medical publications.[32]

By spreading and expanding its B2B offerings, Staples effectively protects against upheaval in any one market. Sales that it categorizes as B2B account for approximately one-third of its $23 billion in annual revenue. The revenues earned through Lendio for example are still just a tiny percentage of those totals, but by adding this service, Staples achieves two critical goals. First, it establishes itself as a source for such services, so the contributions to its bottom line might grow over time. Second, it makes sure that it is available for every need that a business customer might imagine. By doing so, it becomes a true partner that businesses turn to so that they can serve their own customers.

Questions

1. Imagine a small business that has long bought its office supplies from Staples. It reads about Lendio and considers whether to solicit a loan. What kind of buying situation has this small business entered?

2. What attributes should this small business use to evaluate Staples as vendor? What about Lendio? Using those attributes for Staples and Lendio, perform two separate vendor analyses.

Endnotes

1. David Schultz, "Top 100 Retailers 2015," *Stores Magazine*, July 1, 2015; National Retail Foundation, "Top 100 Retailers Chart 2015," https://nrf.com/2015/top100-table.

2. Pierre Mitchell, "Amazon Takes Stage with Oracle, Enters B2B Market—So What?" *Spend Matters*, February 3, 2015.

3. Clare O'Connor, "Amazon Launches Amazon Business Marketplace, Will Close AmazonSupply," *Forbes*, April 28, 2015.

4. Ron Nixon, "Postal Service to Make Sunday Deliveries for Amazon," *The New York Times*, November 11, 2013.

5. Marshall Hargrave, "Amazon.com, Inc. (AMZN): Sights Set On The Shipping Industry," *ETF Daily News*, January 7, 2016, http://etfdailynews.com/2016/01/07/amazon-com-inc-amzn-sights-set-on-the-shipping-industry/.

6. "Amazon Unveils Futuristic Plan: Delivery by Drone," *CBS News*, December 1, 2013, http://www.cbsnews.com/news/amazon-unveils-futuristic-plan-delivery-by-drone/.

7. "Amazon Prime Air," http://www.amazon.com/b?node=8037720011.

8. "Our Vision," https://www.amazonrobotics.com/#/vision.

9. Steve Banker, "Robots In the Warehouse: It's Not Just Amazon," *Forbes*, January 11, 2016, http://www.forbes.com/sites/stevebanker/2016/01/11/robots-in-the-warehouse-its-not-just-amazon/3/#51e85eff4550.

10. Samuel Gibs, "Battle for the Car: Will Google, Apple, or Microsoft Dominate?" *The Guardian*, March 6, 2014, http://www.theguardian.com.

11. Corey Eridon, "The Average Large Company Has 178 Social Media Accounts," *Hub Spot*, January 10, 2012, http://blog.hubspot.com.

12. http://www.constantcontact.com.

13. Ibid.

14. http://www.volkswagenag.com.

15. http://www.volkswagenag.com/content/vwcorp/content/en/brands_and_products.html.

16. "The President's Budget for Fiscal Year 2016," Office of Management and Budget, February 2, 2015, https://www.whitehouse.gov/sites/default/files/omb/budget/fy2016/assets/budget.pdf.

17. http://www.guru.com.

18. These definitions are provided by http://www.marketingpower.com (the American Marketing Association's website). We have bolded the key terms.

19. E. J. Schultz, "GE Tells the Secret of Making Geeky Cool," *Advertising Age*, October 5, 2013, http://adage.com.

20. Meghan Keaney Anderson, "10 Exceptional B2B Content Marketing Examples," *HubSpot*, June 9, 2015, http://blog.hubspot.com/blog/tabid/6307/bid/33505/10-B2B-Companies-That-Create-Exceptional-Content.aspx.

21. https://www.pinterest.com/generalelectric/geinspiredme/.

22. http://blog.business.instagram.com/post/30960118045/ge-instagrapher-contest-a-look-inside-general.

23. Erin Hogg, "Case Study–B2B Content Marketing: Video Campaign Leveraging Pop Culture Lifts New Leads Generated 20%," *Marketing Sherpa*, February 4, 2015, http://www.marketingsherpa.com/article/case-study/video-campaign-leverages-pop-culture.

24. http://www.hootsuite.com.

25. Tracey Peden, "The Use of White Papers in Today's B2B Market," *Marketing Resources Blog*, May 28, 2013, http://blog.ubmcanon.com/bid/285080/.

26. Michael Krause, "How Does Oregon Football Keep Winning? Is It the Uniforms?," *Grantland*, August 30, 2011, http://www.grantland.com.

27. Fabiana Ferreira et al., "The Transition from Products to Solutions: External Business Model Fit and Dynamics," *Industrial Marketing Management* 42, no. 7 (2013), pp. 1093–1101; Mark W. Johnston and Greg W. Marshall, *Contemporary Selling: Building Relationships, Creating Value* (New York: Routledge, 2013); Barton A. Weitz, Stephen B. Castleberry, and John F. Tanner, *Selling Building Partnerships*, 6th ed. (Burr Ridge, IL: McGraw-Hill /Irwin, 2005), p. 93.e

28. Leslie Kaufman, "Stone Washed Blue Jeans (Minus the Wash)," *The New York Times*, November 1, 2011, http://www.nytimes.com.

29. Robert Hackett, "Staples, Never Stationary," *Forbes*, March 9, 2015.

30. Mike Troy, "Staples' New Digital Tool to Help Small Biz," *Retailing Today*, January 4, 2016.

31. See http://www.staples.com/sbd/cre/business-loans/.

32. Paul Demery, "Staples Connects Growing Businesses with Its Online Financing Service," *Internet Retailer*, May 28, 2015, https://www.internetretailer.com/2015/05/28/staples-connects-growing-businesses-its-online-financing-se.

i. Quentin Harvey, "IBM Plans Big Spending for the Cloud," *The New York Times*, January 17, 2014, http://www.nytimes.com; Alex Barinka, "IBM's Watson to Help Rich DBS Clients with 'Jeopardy' Smarts," *Bloomberg Technology*, January 8, 2014, http://www.bloomberg.com/; Robert McMillan, "IBM Buys Weather Company's Digital Assets, Expanding Move into Data

Crunching," *The Wall Street Journal*, October 28, 2015; Dan Berthiaume, "Under Armour Seeks Deep Understanding of Customer Fitness," *Retailing Today*, January 8, 2016; Lauren Goode, "IBM's Watson Will Tell You When to Sleep, Exercise, and Eat," *The Verge*, January 7, 2016, http://www.theverge.com/2016/1/7/10726592/ibm-under-armour-watson-ua-record-app-ces-2016.

ii. Kayla Cobb, "Case Study–Event Marketing: Fuji Xerox Achieves 240% of Sales Target Via a Fashion Show," *Marketing Sherpa*, September 16, 2015, http://www.marketingsherpa.com/article/case-study/b2b-achieves-target-with-fashion-show#; Courtney Eckerle, "Fuji Xerox Launches New B2B Product with a Fashion Show," *Marketing Sherpa Blog*, December 29, 2015, http://sherpablog.marketingsherpa.com/marketing/fuji-xerox-fashion-show/; http://www.xerox.com/about-xerox/75th-anniversary/enus.html.

iii. Stephanie Reitz, "Many US Schools Adding iPads, Trimming Textbooks," *Yahoo Finance*, September 3, 2011, http://finance.yahoo.com; "Do iPads in Schools Change Behavior?," February 22, 2011, http://www.ipadinschools.com; Nick Wingfield, "Once Wary, Apple Warms Up to Business Market," *The New York Times*, November 15, 2011, http://www.nytimes.com; Rachel King, "Apple Woos Businesses Despite Security Worries," *Bloomberg Businessweek*, July 7, 2010, http://www.msnbc.msn.com; Dawn Kawamoto, "iPad 2 Launch Adds Muscle to Apple's Invasion of Corporate America," *Daily Finance*, March 10, 2011, http://www.dailyfinance.com; Leander Kahney, "iPad May Replace Computers and Textbooks in Schools, Experts Predict," *Cult of Mac*, http://www.cultofmac.com.

iv. Sean Silverthorne, "Business Ethics: Pay the Bribe?," *CBS Money Watch*, http://www.cbsnews.com; Stephen H. Unger, "Ethical Aspects of Bribing People in Other Countries," http://www1.cs.columbia.edu; Transparency International, "Bribe Payers Index 2011," http://bpi.transparency.org/; "International Back Scratching," *The Economist*, November 2, 2011, http://www.economist.com; Julia Kollewe, "GlaxoSmithKline's Boss's 2013 Bonus Doubled, Despite Scandal in China,"*The Guardian*, February 27, 2014, http://www.theguardian.com; Ernst and Young, "European Fraud Survey 2011: Recovery, Regulation and Integrity," http://www.ey.com.

v. LinkedIn Press Center, "About Us," http://press.linkedin.com; Heidi Cohen, "5 LinkedIn Business Goals," March 25, 2011, http://heidicohen.com; Maria Tabaka, "How to Launch a Linked-In Company Page," *Inc.*, April 17, 2011, http://www.inc.com.

vi. http://www.hubspot.com; http://www.hubspot.com/customer-case-studies/; "Should Your Startup Be Hubspotting?" *Tech Cocktail*, May 6, 2013, http://www.tech.co; "2013 State of Inbound Marketing," *HubSpot*, May 2013, http://www.stateofinboundmarketing.com, http://www.hubspot.com/2014-year-in-review.

CHAPTER 8

GLOBAL MARKETING

LEARNING OBJECTIVES

After reading this chapter, you should be able to:

LO8-1 Describe the components of a country market assessment.

LO8-2 Understand the marketing opportunities in BRIC countries.

LO8-3 Identify the various market entry strategies.

LO8-4 Highlight the similarities and differences between a domestic marketing strategy and a global marketing strategy.

In its home country, Netflix has approximately 34 million U.S. subscribers. That's a lot of streaming viewers, but it isn't nearly enough to ensure the company's long-term survival. Accordingly, Netflix has initiated a staged approach to going global, entering one or two international markets at a time, in an attempt to ensure that its positioning and offers align with each market's demands and regulations.

In 2012, Netflix started with six international markets: Norway, Finland, Sweden, Denmark, the United Kingdom, and Ireland. In 2013, Netflix limited its expansion to just one nation, the Netherlands. Now it is heading farther across the Continent, with introductions in Germany and France, which rank fourth and sixth worldwide, respectively, in the sizes of their broadband markets. The promise is seemingly too great for Netflix to ignore: millions of European households that, because of their existing access to broadband services in Europe, already represent a strong potential market.

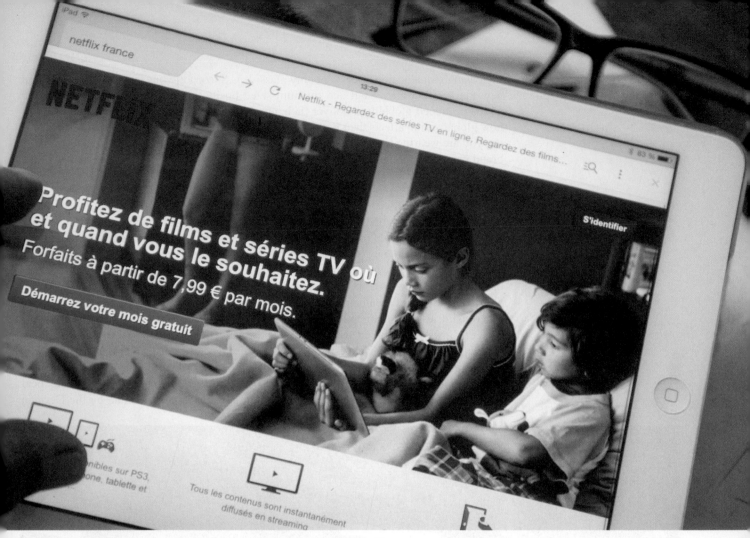

Yet as its staggered approach reflects, entering the European Union is not a simple matter of one offer for everyone. Instead, each nation has its own rules and regulations regarding streaming content, as well as its own existing competitive market. In France for example, Netflix cannot legally stream any movie until at least three years after the movie's theatrical release. Furthermore, Netflix already sold the rights to some of its most popular original programming, such as *House of Cards,* to the French pay-television provider Canal Plus, so it cannot air those episodes either. In Germany, the challenge is less legal and more competitive. Previously established services, including the Amazon-owned Lovefilm, a streaming service called Watchever, and the satellite television service Sky Deutschland, already own much of the potential market.

More broadly, with each new entry, Netflix must commit to substantial local investments. Beyond buying the

rights to traditional Hollywood blockbusters and independent films, it needs to purchase access to local televised content and national movies to appeal to each country's viewers. Moreover, it has to gain name recognition through national-level marketing. Due to such investments, its international streaming unit already has been operating at an annual loss of several hundred million dollars.

Yet Netflix exhibits great confidence that it will be able to meet these national-level challenges and emerge victorious. In particular, it notes that the European Union has committed to net neutrality, which is a distinct benefit for the streaming service. Thus, it plans to expand its European presence to Belgium, Austria, Luxembourg, and Switzerland within the next year or so. Furthermore, Netflix CEO Reed Hastings predicts that the company soon will earn 80 percent of its revenue from international units—a massive leap compared with the 27 percent achieved recently.[1]

Increasing globalization affects not only massive U.S. corporations that actively search out new markets but also small and medium-sized businesses that increasingly depend on goods produced globally to deliver their products and services. Few people think about how globalization affects their daily lives, but take a minute to read the labels on the clothing you are wearing right now. Chances are that most of the items, even if they carry U.S. brand names, were manufactured in another part of the world.

In the United States, the market has evolved from a system of regional marketplaces to national markets to geographically regional markets (e.g., Canada and the United States together) to international markets and finally to global markets. Globalization refers to the processes by which goods, services, capital, people, information, and ideas flow across national borders. Global markets are the result of several fundamental changes such as reductions or eliminations of trade barriers by country governments, the decreasing concerns of distance and time with regard to moving products and ideas across countries, the standardization of laws across borders, and globally integrated production processes.[2]

Each of these fundamental changes has paved the way for marketing to flourish in other countries. The elimination of trade barriers and other governmental actions, for instance, allows goods and ideas to move quickly and efficiently around the world, which in turn facilitates the quick delivery of goods to better meet the needs of global consumers.

As a consequence, consumers have easy access to global products and services. When we walk into a toy store, we expect to find LEGO brand toys from Denmark. In the local sporting goods store we anticipate finding running shoes made in China by the German

These 25-foot-tall replicas of the New York skyline are made completely out of Legos and have been on display at the Times Square Toys"R" Us in New York City. How do Legos get from their manufacturer in Denmark to toy stores in the United States?

© Dennis Van Tine/Newscom

firm adidas. In the grocery store, we demand out-of-season produce such as blueberries from Chile in January. Or consider how a $12 digital camera for your keychain, made in Taiwan, could be produced, transported halfway around the world, and sold for so little money at your local Target. These are the questions we will be examining in this chapter.

We begin by looking at how firms assess the potential of a given market, with particular attention to the BRIC countries (Brazil, Russia, India, and China). Next we examine how firms make decisions to go global and choose how and what they will sell globally. Then we explore how to build the marketing mix for global products.

ASSESSING GLOBAL MARKETS

LO8-1 Describe the components of a country market assessment.

Because of globalization, marketers are presented with a variety of opportunities, which means that firms must assess the viability of various potential market entries. As illustrated in Exhibit 8.1, we examine four sets of criteria necessary to assess a country's market: economic analysis, infrastructure and technological analysis, government actions or inactions, and sociocultural analysis. Information about these four areas offers marketers a more complete picture of a country's potential as a market for products and services.

Economic Analysis Using Metrics

The greater the wealth of people in a country, generally, the better the opportunity a firm will have in that particular country. A firm conducting an economic analysis of a country market must look at three major economic factors using well-established metrics: the general economic environment, the market size and population growth rate, and real income.

EXHIBIT 8.1 Components of a Country Market Assessment

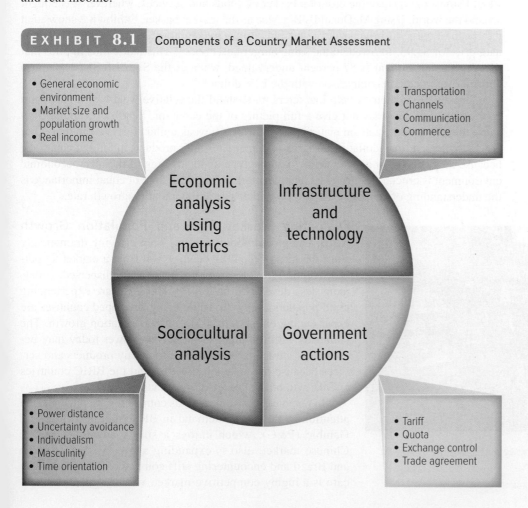

- General economic environment
- Market size and population growth
- Real income

- Transportation
- Channels
- Communication
- Commerce

Economic analysis using metrics

Infrastructure and technology

Sociocultural analysis

Government actions

- Power distance
- Uncertainty avoidance
- Individualism
- Masculinity
- Time orientation

- Tariff
- Quota
- Exchange control
- Trade agreement

Evaluating the General Economic Environment In general, healthy economies provide better opportunities for global marketing expansions, and there are several ways a firm can use metrics to measure the relative health of a particular country's economy. Each way offers a slightly different view, and some may be more useful for some products and services than for others.

To determine the market potential for its particular product or service, a firm should use as many metrics as it can obtain. One metric is the relative level of imports and exports. The United States, for example, suffers a **trade deficit**, which means that the country imports more goods than it exports.[3] For U.S. marketers this deficit can signal the potential for greater competition at home from foreign producers. Firms would prefer to manufacture in a country that has a **trade surplus**, or a higher level of exports than imports, because it signals a greater opportunity to export products to more markets.

The most common way to gauge the size and market potential of an economy, and therefore the potential the country has for global marketing, is to use standardized metrics of output. **Gross domestic product (GDP)**, the most widely used of these metrics, is defined as the market value of the goods and services produced by a country in a year. **Gross national income (GNI)** consists of GDP plus the net income earned from investments abroad (minus any payments made to nonresidents who contribute to the domestic economy).[4] In other words, U.S. firms that invest or maintain operations abroad count their income from those operations in the GNI but not the GDP.

Another frequently used metric of an overall economy is the **purchasing power parity (PPP)**, a theory that states that if the exchange rates of two countries are in equilibrium, a product purchased in one will cost the same in the other, if expressed in the same currency.[5] A novel metric that employs PPP to assess the relative economic buying power among nations is *The Economist*'s Big Mac Index, which suggests that exchange rates should adjust to equalize the cost of a basket of goods and services, wherever it is bought around the world. Using McDonald's Big Mac as the market basket, Exhibit 8.2 shows that the cheapest burger is in Venezuela, where it costs $0.66, compared with an average American price of $4.93. In Sweden, the same burger costs $5.23. This index thus implies that the Venezuelan Bolivar is 87 percent undervalued, whereas the Swedish SKr is about 6 percent overvalued, in comparison with the U.S. dollar.[6]

These various metrics help marketers understand the relative wealth of a particular country, though they may not give a full picture of the economic health of a country because they are based solely on material output. Nor is a weak dollar always a bad thing. For U.S. exporters, a weak dollar means greater demand for their products in foreign countries, because they can sell at a lower price.[7] Although an understanding of the macroeconomic environment is crucial for managers facing a market entry decision, of equal importance is the understanding of economic metrics of market size and population growth rate.

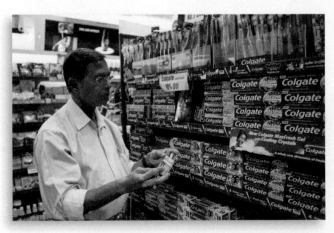

Procter & Gamble is expanding aggressively into India and encountering stiff competition.

Evaluating Market Size and Population Growth Rate The global population has been growing dramatically since the turn of the 20th century. But from a marketing perspective, this growth has never been equally dispersed. Today, many less developed nations by and large are experiencing rapid population growth, while many developed countries are experiencing either zero or negative population growth. The countries with the highest purchasing power today may become less attractive in the future for many products and services because of stagnated growth. And the BRIC countries are likely to be the source of most market growth.

In response, consumer goods companies are paying close attention to the strong demand in BRIC nations. Procter & Gamble (P&G), which enjoys a strong advantage in the Chinese market, also is expanding aggressively into India and Brazil and encountering stiff competition. In Brazil oral care is a highly competitive market, with Colgate and P&G

EXHIBIT 8.2   Big Mac Index

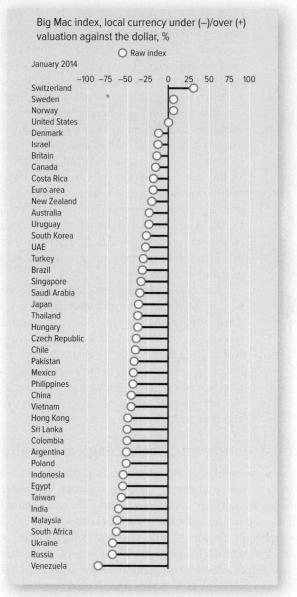

Big Mac index, local currency under (–)/over (+)
valuation against the dollar, %

○ Raw index

January 2014

| | –100 –75 –50 –25 0 25 50 75 100 |

Switzerland
Sweden
Norway
United States
Denmark
Israel
Britain
Canada
Costa Rica
Euro area
New Zealand
Australia
Uruguay
South Korea
UAE
Turkey
Brazil
Singapore
Saudi Arabia
Japan
Thailand
Hungary
Czech Republic
Chile
Pakistan
Mexico
Philippines
China
Vietnam
Hong Kong
Sri Lanka
Colombia
Argentina
Poland
Indonesia
Egypt
Taiwan
India
Malaysia
South Africa
Ukraine
Russia
Venezuela

Source: © The Economist Newspaper Limited, London (Jan 2014).

competing. In India, big-name Western firms are competing for market share of laundry products.[8]

   Another aspect related to market size and population growth pertains to the distribution of the population within a particular region: Is the population located primarily in rural or urban areas? This distinction determines where and how products and services can be delivered. Long supply chains, in which goods pass through many hands, are often necessary to reach rural populations in less developed countries and therefore add to the products' cost. India's 1.2 billion people live overwhelmingly in rural areas, although the population is moving toward urban areas to meet the demands of the growing industrial and service centers located in major cities such as Bangalore and New Delhi. This population shift, perhaps not surprisingly, is accompanied by rapid growth in the middle class. Furthermore, relatively careful banking policies and minimal dependence on exports have helped protect India from the global financial crisis. The business impacts of these combined trends of increasing urbanization, a growing middle class, a degree of protectionism

For the Chinese market, Haier sells washing machines that can wash both clothes and vegetables.

Courtesy of Haier America

by the central government, and a youthful populace make India an absolutely enormous market for consumer goods.

Evaluating Real Income Firms can make adjustments to an existing product or change the price to meet the unique needs of a particular country market. Such shifts are particularly common for low-priced consumer goods. In settings in which consumers earn very low wages, the market is known as the bottom of the pyramid. That is, there is a large, impoverished population that still wants and needs consumer goods but cannot pay the prices that the fewer, wealthier consumers in developed nations can. Thus P&G developed a single-use shampoo packet for consumers who cannot afford an entire bottle at one time. To increase consumption of Coca-Cola in rural India, the company lowered its price to the equivalent of about 10 cents per bottle; Cadbury International introduced Dairy Milk Shots for the equivalent of about 4 cents.[9] Textbook publishers sell paperback versions of U.S. books for a fraction of their U.S. price to countries where students would not otherwise be able to afford a textbook.

But pricing adjustments aren't only for inexpensive products. Fashion and jewelry manufacturers also make downward adjustments to their prices in countries where the incomes of their target markets cannot support higher prices. Nor is price the only factor that companies adjust to appeal to lower income markets. Haier sells washing machines that also have the capacity to wash vegetables to Chinese consumers who confront limited access to resources such as water and electricity.[10]

Analyzing Infrastructure and Technological Capabilities

The next component of any market assessment is an infrastructure and technological analysis. Infrastructure is defined as the basic facilities, services, and installations needed for a community or society to function, such as transportation and communications systems, water and power lines, and public institutions such as schools, post offices, and prisons.

Marketers are especially concerned with four key elements of a country's infrastructure: transportation, distribution channels, communications, and commerce. First, there must be a system to transport goods throughout the various markets and to consumers in geographically dispersed marketplaces—trains, roads, refrigeration. Second, distribution channels must exist to deliver products in a timely manner and at a reasonable cost. Third, the communications system, particularly media access, must be sufficiently developed to allow consumers to find information about the products and services available in the marketplace. Fourth, the commercial infrastructure, which consists of the legal, banking, and regulatory systems, allows markets to function. In the next section, we focus on how issues pertaining to the political and legal structures of a country can affect the risk that marketers face in operating in a given country.

Analyzing Governmental Actions

Governmental actions, as well as the actions of nongovernmental political groups, can significantly influence firms' ability to sell goods and services because they often result in laws or other regulations that either promote the growth of the global market or close off the country and inhibit growth. Some of the effects are difficult to predict in advance, as Ethical and Societal Dilemma 8.1 describes.

Tariffs A tariff, also called a duty, is a tax levied on a good imported into a country. In most cases, tariffs are intended to make imported goods more expensive and thus less

Ethical & Societal Dilemma 8.1   How Chinese Regulations Change Car-Buying Practices[i]

As the Scottish poet Robert Burns wrote, "The best laid schemes of mice and men/Go often awry." That is, we might have the best intentions to produce beneficial outcomes, but sometimes those plans have a way of leading to the opposite effect. It's a truth that consumer behavior researchers and marketers know only too well.

Consider, for example, the case of China and its latest attempt to limit automobile-induced air pollution. The expansion of China's middle class has created a vast new population of consumers who can now afford cars. The nation's roads, especially in urban centers such as Shanghai, Guangzhou, Guiyang, and Beijing, have become clogged with vehicles. Pollution levels also have reached critical proportions. And China has moved into the top spot in terms of consumer car purchases, with some estimates suggesting that Chinese consumers will buy 30 million vehicles annually by 2020.

In response to these concerns, Chinese government officials have begun testing a licensing regulation that requires people to enter a lottery for a limited number of car registration tags. Without the license plate, drivers would face severe penalties. Thus, officials hoped to halt the growth in this sector and thereby limit pollution and congestion on the roads. Instead, consumers have taken the threat that the regulations would spread as a great reason to buy a new car immediately. If they might not be able to next year, they had better snag a car right now! In cities in which the regulations are already in place, the lucky license lottery winners also are buying bigger (i.e., more polluting), more expensive vehicles. As one consumer noted, "Would you want to put a 100,000 yuan plate on a 50,000 yuan car?" Because these consumers already are spending more than they might have planned, just to have the chance to enter the lottery for a license, they feel more justified spending more on the car itself. Average prices paid per car thus have leapt up approximately 88 percent in just two years.

These trends are great news for foreign luxury carmakers like Audi and Mercedes-Benz, whose sales in China have jumped. It is not so great for Chinese carmakers, which have long provided the lower-end, functional vehicles that China's population previously demanded. It also might not be great news for the environment, which was not at all what authorities planned when they implemented these regulations. The best-laid schemes, indeed.

In an attempt to limit air pollution by reducing the number of vehicles on the road, the Chinese government has imposed a lottery for car buyers. The license lottery winners are buying bigger, more expensive vehicles like Audi and Mercedes-Benz.

© Chen Jianli Xinhua News Agency/Newscom

competitive with domestic products, which in turn protects domestic industries from foreign competition. In other cases, tariffs might be imposed to penalize another country for trade practices that the home country views as unfair. For example, when the U.S. government determined the prices of solar panels imported from China were artificially low due to illegal subsidies, it imposed a tariff to help domestic firms compete.[11]

Quotas A quota designates a minimum or maximum quantity of a product that may be brought into a country during a specified time period. The United States, for instance, has committed to allowing at least 1.23 million tons of sugar to be imported (the quota) without a tariff because the country generally consumes more than it produces.[12] It then monitors consumption closely to protect domestic sugar farmers. If demand exceeds supply, it increases the quota, but the level depends on annual consumption and production rates.[13]

Tariffs and quotas can have fundamental and potentially devastating impacts on a firm's ability to sell products in another country. Tariffs artificially raise prices and therefore lower demand, and quotas reduce the availability of imported merchandise. Conversely, tariffs and quotas benefit domestically made products because they reduce foreign competition.

Exchange Control Exchange control refers to the regulation of a country's currency exchange rate, the measure of how much one currency is worth in relation to another.[14] A designated agency in each country, often the central bank, sets the rules for currency exchange. In the United States, the Federal Reserve sets the currency exchange rates. In recent years the value of the U.S. dollar has changed significantly compared with other important world currencies. When the dollar falls, it has a twofold effect on U.S. firms' ability to conduct global business. For firms that depend on imports of finished products, raw materials that they fabricate into other products, or services from other countries, the cost of doing business goes up dramatically. At the same time, buyers in other countries find the costs of U.S. goods and services to be much lower than they were before.

Prices are nearly always lower in the country of origin, because there are no customs or import duties to pay, and international transportation expenses are less than domestic ones. For many products, the price difference might not be significant. But for luxury items that cost thousands of euros (or tens of thousands of Chinese yuan), buying overseas thus has long been a habit for consumers. As the euro dropped, international shopping excursions have become especially appealing for consumers from China, where the yuan remains strong. As a result, for Chinese shoppers seeking Italian designer clothing or French handbags, it literally is worth the cost of flying to Milan and Paris and buying the items there rather than shopping in Shanghai. But that's not what the luxury fashion houses want, so they are revising their pricing schemes. Chanel announced it would raise its retail prices in Europe but cut them in China, in an attempt to level the playing field, so that the same

In the past, Chinese customers seeking luxury goods, such as Chanel, would fly to Europe to shop because the prices were lower there. But Chanel is raising its retail prices in Europe while cutting them in China to encourage its Chinese customers to buy at home, like at this Chanel store in Shanghai.

© Aly Song/Reuters

EXHIBIT 8.3	Trade Agreements
Name	**Countries**
European Union	There are 28 member countries of the EU: Austria, Belgium, Bulgaria, Croatia, Cyprus, Czech Republic, Denmark, Estonia, Finland, France, Germany, Greece, Hungary, Ireland, Italy, Latvia, Lithuania, Luxembourg, Malta, Netherlands, Poland, Portugal, Romania, Slovakia, Slovenia, Spain, Sweden, and the United Kingdom. There are five official candidate countries to join the EU: Macedonia, Serbia, Turkey, Iceland, Montenegro, and Albania. Bosnia and Herzegovina and Kosovo are also potential candidates.
NAFTA	United States, Canada, and Mexico.
CAFTA	United States, Costa Rica, the Dominican Republic, El Salvador, Guatemala, Honduras, and Nicaragua.
Mercosur	Full members: Argentina, Brazil, Paraguay, Uruguay, and Venezuela.
ASEAN	Brunei Darussalam, Cambodia, Indonesia, Laos, Malaysia, Myanmar, Philippines, Singapore, Thailand, and Vietnam.

Source: Information about EU members is from http://europa.eu/about-eu/countries/./index_en.htm.

handbag would cost approximately the same amount wherever people buy it.[15] As economies and currencies continue their constant rising and falling relative to one another, marketers must keep revising their pricing strategies to reflect the current international conditions.

Trade Agreements Marketers must consider the trade agreements to which a particular country is a signatory or the trading bloc to which it belongs. A trade agreement is an intergovernmental agreement designed to manage and promote trade activities for a specific region, and a trading bloc consists of those countries that have signed the particular trade agreement.[16] Together, the following major trade agreements cover two-thirds of the world's international trade: the European Union (EU), the North American Free Trade Agreement (NAFTA), Central America Free Trade Agreement (CAFTA), Mercosur, and the Association of Southeast Asian Nations (ASEAN).[17] These trade agreements are summarized in Exhibit 8.3. The EU represents the highest level of integration across individual nations; the other agreements vary in their integration levels.

Currency fluctuations enhance or impede tourists.

© J. Hardy/PhotoAlto RF

Entering the Chinese market can be difficult. This Porsche ad left more Chinese consumers confused than intrigued because the Great Wall of China has little in common with Porsche.

Source: Porsche AG

Analyzing Sociocultural Factors

Understanding another country's culture is crucial to the success of any global marketing initiative. Culture, or the shared meanings, beliefs, morals, values, and customs of a group of people, exists on two levels: visible artifacts (e.g., behavior, dress, symbols, physical settings, ceremonies) and underlying values (thought processes, beliefs, and assumptions).[18] Visible artifacts are easy to recognize, but businesses often find it more difficult to understand the underlying values of a culture and appropriately adapt their marketing strategies to them.[19]

For example, though the opening of China's market to foreign brands has been a boon, it also represents a very risky proposition for firms that forget to take their international expansion seriously enough. For example, when Porsche filmed an advertisement in which its vehicles ran over the Great Wall of China, Chinese consumers were left more confused than intrigued. The ancient site had little in common with Porsche's own storied history. It also had little to do with Uncle Ben's Rice or FedEx, but that did not stop those brands from featuring the Great Wall in their advertising either. By the same token, hiring Western spokespeople who are unfamiliar to Chinese audiences to introduce a brand offers few benefits. Marks & Spencer paid substantial sums to hire Oscar-winner Emma Thompson to appear in Chinese advertisements, but because few Chinese consumers knew who she was, those investments were likely wasted.[20]

To address or avoid such issues, one important cultural classification scheme that firms can use is Geert Hofstede's cultural dimensions concept, which sheds more light on these underlying values. Hofstede initially proposed that cultures differed on four dimensions, but he has added two more dimensions in recent years.[21] Despite some arguments for using other models,[22] Hofstede's cultural dimensions offer a foundation for most research into culture:

1. **Power distance:** willingness to accept social inequality as natural.

2. **Uncertainty avoidance:** the extent to which the society relies on orderliness, consistency, structure, and formalized procedures to address situations that arise in daily life.

3. **Individualism:** perceived obligation to and dependence on groups.

4. **Masculinity:** the extent to which dominant values are male oriented. A lower masculinity ranking indicates that men and women are treated equally in all aspects of society; a higher masculinity ranking suggests that men dominate in positions of power.

5. **Time orientation:** short- versus long-term orientation. A country that tends to have a long-term orientation values long-term commitments and is willing to accept a longer time horizon for, say, the success of a new product introduction.

6. **Indulgence:** the extent to which society allows for the gratification of fun and enjoyment needs or else suppresses and regulates such pursuits.[23]

To illustrate two of the six dimensions, consider the data and graph in Exhibit 8.4. Power distance is on the vertical axis and individualism is on the horizontal axis. Several Latin American countries, including Brazil, cluster high on power distance but low on individualism; the United States, Australia, Canada, and the United Kingdom, in contrast, cluster high on individualism but low on power distance. Using this information, firms should expect that if they design a marketing campaign that stresses equality and individualism, it will be well accepted in English-speaking countries, all other factors being equal, but not be as well received in Latin American countries.

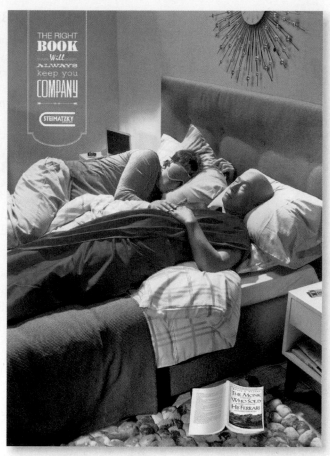

Ads from Steimatzky, the oldest and largest bookstore chain in Israel, illustrate marketing along one of Hofstede's cultural dimensions: one is highly feminine (left) and the other masculine (right).

Source: Agency: ACW Grey Tel-Aviv, Israel; Production Company: We Do Production; Photographer: Shai Yehezkelli.

Another means of classifying cultures distinguishes them according to the importance of verbal communication.[24] In the United States and most European countries, business relationships are governed by what is said and written down, often through formal contracts. In countries such as China and South Korea, however, most relationships rely on nonverbal cues, so that the situation or context means much more than mere words. For instance, business relationships in China often are formalized by just a handshake, and trust and honor are often more important than legal arrangements.

Overall, culture affects every aspect of consumer behavior: why people buy; who is in charge of buying decisions; and how, when, and where people shop. After marketing managers have completed the four parts of the market assessment, they are better able to make informed decisions about whether a particular country possesses the necessary characteristics to be considered a potential market for the firm's products and services. In the next section, we assess the market potential in the BRIC countries.

EXHIBIT 8.4   Country Clusters

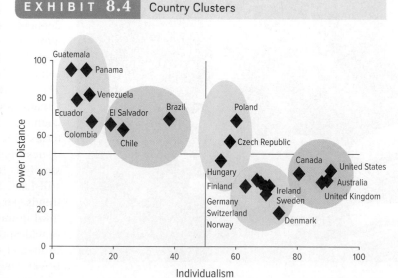

Source: Geert Hofstede, Geert Jan Hofstede, and Michael Minkov, Cultures and Organizations, Software of the Mind, *Third Revised Edition, McGraw-Hill 2010, ISBN: 0-07-166418-1.* © Geert Hofstede B.V. quoted with permission.

Understand the
marketing opportunities
in BRIC countries.

The Appeal of the BRIC Countries

Changes in technology, especially communications, have been a driving force for growth in global markets for decades. The telegraph, radio, television, computers, and the Internet have increasingly connected distant parts of the world. Today, communication is instantaneous. Sounds and images from across the globe are delivered to televisions, radios, and computers in real time, which enables receivers in all parts of the world to observe how others live, work, and play.

Perhaps the greatest change facing the global community in recent years has been the growth and expansion of four countries that together have come to be known as the BRIC countries: Brazil, Russia, India, and China. Some commentators suggest adding South Africa, to make BRICS, because of that nation's remarkable transformation into a functioning democracy.[25] The inspiring changes to South Africa suggest its increasing promise as a market, but its relatively smaller size leads us to focus on the four BRIC nations, which seem to have the greatest potential for growth. Let's examine each in turn.

Brazil[26] Long a regional powerhouse, Brazil's ability to weather, and even thrive, during economic storms has transformed it into a global contender. Currently, Brazil is the world's seventh largest economy,[27] but high inflation and political crises have prompted Brazil to project some significant economic declines in the near future.[28] Still, Brazil's impressive economic growth in the 21st century largely can be attributed to the expansion of its literate population and the impositions of social programs that have allowed more than half of the 201 million Brazilians to enter the middle class.[29] Even as the nation struggles with a recession, it continues to experiment with innovative financial approaches in an effort to ensure that the Brazilian economy rebounds.[30] This large South American democracy also welcomes foreign investors.

Russia[31] The relations between the United States and Russia are a little more complicated than for Brazil. Since the fall of the former Soviet Union, Russia has undergone multiple upturns and downturns in its economy. However, its overall growth prospects appear promising, especially as a consumer market. Long denied access to consumer goods, the well-educated population of 143 million exhibits strong demand for U.S. products and brands. In particular, the number of Russian Internet users, presently at 83 million,[32] is growing at a rate of approximately 10 percent annually,[33] and is already Europe's largest Internet market.[34] The country also is negotiating to enter the World Trade Organization (WTO) to improve trade relations with other countries. In 2015 it ranked as one of the top countries in terms of retail growth; even though economic and political issues challenge its retail growth prospects, the market simply is too big for most firms to disregard.[35] Yet Russia still faces an aging population and low birthrates. If these trends persist, Russia's population could decline by one-third in the next half century. At the same time, corruption is widespread, creating ethical dilemmas for firms trying to market their goods and services. Furthermore, international sanctions on Russia, in response to its occupation of Ukraine and its involvement in the Middle East, and fluctuations in oil prices threaten the country with a financial crisis.[36]

Like other countries in which McDonald's thrives, Brazil has a strong and growing middle class.

© Bloomberg/Getty Images

In which of the BRIC countries does each of these classic structures reside?

(Top left): © McGraw-Hill Education/Barry Barker, photographer; (top right): © McGraw-Hill Education/Barry Barker, photographer; (bottom left): © Travelif/iStock Exclusive/ Getty Images; (bottom right): © Martin Child/Getty Images RF

India[37] With more than 1.2 billion people, or approximately 15 percent of the world's population, together with expanding middle and upper classes, India is one of the world's fastest-growing markets. India also has one of the youngest populations in the world, with a median age of 26.7 years. Its young inhabitants increasingly are adopting global attitudes while living in growing urban centers and shopping at large malls. The well-educated, modern generation is largely fluent in English, and the highly skilled work-force holds great attraction for firms that hope to expand using local talent, especially in technical fields.

India's retail environment is still dominated by millions of small stores and lacks modern supply chain management facilities and systems.[38] Recent changes by the Indian government, however, have the potential to significantly modernize the retail landscape. For example, foreign retailers that carry multiple brands, like Walmart, are now allowed to own up to 51 percent of joint ventures in India, and retailers that carry only their own

Relaxed Indian governmental restrictions now allow foreign retailers that carry their own brand, like Levi's, to own 100 percent of their Indian businesses.

© Aijaz Rahi/AP Photo

brand, like adidas and Reebok, can now own 100 percent of their Indian businesses.[39] India is also projected to become the fastest growing e-commerce market in the world, with e-commerce sales forecasted to reach $55 billion by 2018.[40]

China[41] For most of the 20th century, China experienced foreign occupation, civil unrest, major famine, and a strict one-party Communist regime. However, since 1978, China's leadership, while maintaining communist political ideals, has embraced market-oriented economic development, which has led to startlingly rapid gains. For many Chinese, recent developments have dramatically improved their living standards and their levels of personal freedom. Increasing liberalization in the economy has prompted a large improvement in China's Global Retail Development Index (GRDI); it enjoyed the greatest retail growth in 2014. Even as growth in its gross domestic product has slowed, China maintains a thriving retail market, likely to reach the $8 trillion mark soon and surpass the United States as the world's largest.[42]

Yet the country continues to suffer from drastically unequal economic distribution, which has led to a significant migrant workforce that subsists on part-time, low-paying jobs. These workers were hit hard by the global financial crisis, which reduced demand for Chinese exports for the first time in years. Furthermore, actual growth of the 1.3 billion-strong Chinese population slowed as a result of government population controls that limit each family to one child. Although China's median age is slightly younger than that of the United States currently, at 36.3 years, its population has been aging as a result of its one-child policy, and will likely continue to do so for many years, even though the government has recently rescinded the policy and will now allow two children per couple.[43]

Even as vast numbers of U.S. companies actively target BRIC countries or explore options for entering them, as Social and Mobile Marketing 8.1 highlights, some challenges remain. In the next section, we detail the market entry decision process, beginning with a discussion of the various ways firms might enter a new global market.

China's population has been aging as a result of its one-child policy, and will likely continue to do so for many years, even though the government has recently rescinded the policy and will now allow two children per couple.

© Images by Tang Ming Tung/Getty Images RF

Social & Mobile Marketing 8.1

The Growth of Social Networking— Brazil's Free Market versus China's Restrictions[ii]

By Facebook CEO Mark Zuckerberg's own admission, Facebook grew exponentially for years without a strategic plan for international growth. As the company has matured, however, Facebook has refocused its attention on global markets. Two countries offer a short course on how that attention must shift with the specific global target.

In Brazil, Facebook already has 65 million members, making the South American nation its second-largest market, behind the United States. It also ranks among the top markets for YouTube, Google, and Twitter. Part of the explanation for this great growth is Brazil's status as one of the most rapidly developing economies in the world. As people gain economic security, they have more resources to spend on social networking gadgets, as well as more leisure time to play with them.

But it also has to do with the culture. Brazil is known for the open, friendly attitudes of its people. For these "hypersocial" consumers, new ways to connect with friends and loved ones represent an important form of need fulfillment. International companies can enter freely, function according to a relatively well-established legal structure, and enjoy a pretty strong infrastructure as well.

In contrast, when companies confront the inherent openness of social networking with China's strict censorship rules, significant challenges arise. Successful entry by social and mobile marketers into China requires a particular blend of timing, skill, cultural understanding, and political savvy. These factors may not be quite in alignment for Facebook. The timing may be wrong because China's autocratic leaders have enforced greater controls on social networking and blogging recently. Nor do Facebook executives appear to have a full grasp of the political and cultural nuances of business in China, despite a good track record of respecting local cultural values, such as when it agreed to block content about Nazism in Germany or drawings of Muhammad in Pakistan. And even if Facebook were to navigate these challenges safely, China has

a strong, enduring preference for companies owned and run by its own people.

Censorship issues are highly complex. For instance, how would Facebook respond to retaliation against users who criticize the government? For Google, whose mission statement simply advises "Don't Be Evil," such questions became all too pertinent when hackers in China gained access to the e-mail accounts of prominent human rights activists. When Western companies have cooperated with the Chinese government, some operations have led to the imprisonment of online activists.

In Brazil, the question is how many users the company can encourage to enjoy all the fun of Facebook. In China, a post on Facebook can lead to jail time. Thus, it becomes a question of basic human rights.

CEO Mark Zuckerberg (center) claims that Facebook will employ diplomacy in China, but censorship issues are highly complex.
© Lao Chen/ChinaFotoPress/Zumapress/Newscom

PROGRESS CHECK

1. What metrics can help analyze the economic environment of a country?
2. What types of governmental actions should we be concerned about as we evaluate a country?
3. What are some important cultural dimensions?
4. Why are each of the BRIC countries viewed as potential candidates for global expansion?

LO8-3 Identify the various market entry strategies.

CHOOSING A GLOBAL ENTRY STRATEGY

When a firm has concluded its assessment analysis of the most viable markets for its products and services, it must then conduct an internal assessment of its capabilities. As we discussed in Chapter 2, this analysis includes an assessment of the firm's access to capital, the current markets it serves, its manufacturing capacity, its proprietary assets, and the commitment of its management to the proposed strategy. These factors ultimately contribute to the success or failure of a market expansion strategy, whether at home or in a foreign market. After these internal market assessments, it is time for the firm to choose its entry strategy.

A firm can choose from many approaches when it decides to enter a new market, which vary according to the level of risk the firm is willing to take. Many firms actually follow a progression in which they begin with less risky strategies to enter their first foreign markets and move to increasingly risky strategies as they gain confidence in their abilities and more control over their operations, as illustrated in Exhibit 8.5. We examine these different approaches that marketers take when entering global markets, beginning with the least risky.

Exporting

Exporting means producing goods in one country and selling them in another. This entry strategy requires the least financial risk but also allows for only a limited return to the exporting firm. Global expansion often begins when a firm receives an order for its product or service from another country, in which case it faces little risk because it has no investment in people, capital equipment, buildings, or infrastructure.[44] By the same token, it is difficult to achieve economies of scale when everything has to be shipped internationally. The Swiss watchmaker Rolex sells relatively small numbers of expensive watches all over the world. Because its transportation costs are relatively small compared with the cost of the watches, the best way for it to service any market is to export from Switzerland.

Rolex exports its watches to countries all over the world from its factory in Switzerland.
Source: Rolex USA

KFC and Pizza Hut are successful global franchisors.

(Left): © Yang zheng/AP Photo; (right): © Zhou junxiang/AP Photo

Franchising

Franchising is a contractual agreement between a firm, the franchisor, and another firm or individual, the franchisee. A franchising contract allows the franchisee to operate a business—a retail product or service firm or a B2B provider—using the name and business format developed and supported by the franchisor. Many of the best-known retailers in the United States are also successful global franchisors, including McDonald's, Pizza Hut, Starbucks, Domino's Pizza, KFC, and Holiday Inn, all of which have found that global franchising entails lower risks and requires less investment than does opening units owned wholly by the firm. However, when it engages in franchising, the firm has limited control over the market operations in the foreign country, its potential profit is reduced because it must be split with the franchisee, and, once the franchise is established, there is always the threat that the franchisee will break away and operate as a competitor under a different name.

Strategic Alliance

Strategic alliances refer to collaborative relationships between independent firms, though the partnering firms do not create an equity partnership; that is, they do not invest in one another. Therefore, when Cisco Systems Inc. of San Jose, California, and Tata Consultancy Services of Mumbai, India, entered into their strategic alliance, they both continued to develop market-ready infrastructure and network solutions for customers, but they relied on each other to provide the training and skills that one or the other might have lacked. At the same time, Cisco maintains alliances with various other companies, including Microsoft, Nokia, IBM, and Accenture.

Joint Venture

A joint venture is formed when a firm entering a market pools its resources with those of a local firm. As a consequence, ownership, control, and profits are shared. In addition to sharing financial burdens, a local partner offers the foreign entrant greater understanding of the market and access to resources such as vendors and real estate.

Some countries require joint ownership of firms entering their domestic markets, as is the case with the new regulations affecting multi-line retailers entering India, though many of these restrictions have loosened as a result of WTO negotiations and ever-increasing

Adding Value 8.1   Tata Starbucks and the Indian Coffee Culture[iii]

Starbucks traditionally has relied on a franchising model to expand internationally. But when it came to India, the coffee chain took another approach. It allied with Tata Group, another huge international name, to create the Tata Starbucks Limited joint venture. The two conglomerates are equal partners in the venture—which celebrated its first anniversary not with champagne but by releasing a new coffee blend: India Estates, made from only Indian-sourced coffee.

Since its initial launch with one store in October 2012, the joint venture has grown exponentially. Its store count reached 25 within a year, with stores in Delhi, Pune, and Mumbai. It also promises frequent new openings, including greater spread throughout the nation and localized offerings. For example, when the first store opened in Bangalore, in southern India, it offered more food options containing specific local flavors.

But it remains an international joint venture, and some marketing appeals span virtually every culture. Thus in autumn, Salted Caramel Mochas rolled out in India, just as they have done throughout the world for the past several years.

Starbucks has a joint venture with Tata Group to open stores in India.

© Sajjad Hussain/AFP/Getty Images

globalization pressures. Problems with this entry approach can arise when the partners disagree or if the government places restrictions on the firm's ability to move its profits out of the foreign country and back to its home country.

Yet joint ventures also can provide highly promising insights and benefits for all the partners, as Adding Value 8.1 suggests.

Direct Investment

Direct investment requires a firm to maintain 100 percent ownership of its plants, operation facilities, and offices in a foreign country, often through the formation of wholly owned subsidiaries. This entry strategy requires the highest level of investment and exposes the firm to significant risks, including the loss of its operating and/or initial investments. A dramatic economic downturn caused by a natural disaster, war, political instability, or changes in the country's laws can increase a foreign entrant's risk considerably. Many firms believe that in certain markets, these potential risks are outweighed by the high potential returns. With this strategy, none of the potential profits must be shared with other firms. In addition to the high potential returns, direct investment offers the firm complete control over its operations in the foreign country.

Although we often tend to think of direct investment flowing from more to less developed economies, the dynamic international market means that sometimes it goes the other way. The computer maker Lenovo started in China but has since expanded its operations. In addition to purchasing IBM's PC division and Motorola's handset business unit, it established parallel headquarters in both Beijing and North Carolina. When it entered Brazil it quickly established separate manufacturing plants to keep its costs low.[45]

As we noted, each of these entry strategies entails different levels of risk and rewards for the foreign entrant. But even after a firm has determined how much risk it is willing to take, and therefore how it will enter a new global market, it still must establish its marketing strategy, as we discuss in the next section.

PROGRESS CHECK

1. Which entry strategy has the least risk and why?
2. Which entry strategy has the most risk and why?

CHOOSING A GLOBAL MARKETING STRATEGY

LO8-4 Highlight the similarities and differences between a domestic marketing strategy and a global marketing strategy.

Just like any other marketing strategy, a global marketing strategy includes two components: determining the target markets to pursue and developing a marketing mix that will sustain a competitive advantage over time. In this section, we examine marketing strategy as it relates specifically to global markets.

Target Market: Segmentation, Targeting, and Positioning

Global segmentation, targeting, and positioning (STP) are more complicated than domestic STP for several reasons. First, firms considering a global expansion have much more difficulty understanding the cultural nuances of other countries. Second, subcultures within each country also must be considered. Third, consumers often view products and their role as consumers differently in different countries.[46] A product, service, or even a retailer often must be positioned differently in different markets.

Even when an STP strategy appears successful, companies must continually monitor economic and social trends to protect their position within the market and adjust products and marketing strategies to meet the changing needs of global markets. In this sense, global marketing is no different from local or national marketing.

When any firm identifies its positioning within the market, it then must decide how to implement its marketing strategies using the marketing mix. Just as firms adjust their products and services to meet the needs of national target markets, they must alter their marketing mix to serve the needs of global markets.

Adding Value 8.2   Ponying Up the Latest Ford Mustang[iv]

When the 2015 model of the classic American muscle car hit the streets, it wasn't only on Route 66. Instead, Ford's latest iteration of its iconic car was introduced simultaneously in six global cities spanning four continents. The worldwide move aims to both acknowledge the car's 50-year history and expand its appeal to a broader market in the future.

In keeping with its tradition, the redesign retains most of the visual features that consumers have come to associate with the Mustang: blunt-nosed and stylish, with a substantial grille and a profile low to the ground. Despite some buzz that Ford would completely redesign the look (and apparently there was some debate about doing so inside the company), ultimately it chose to keep things visually similar.

In contrast, another recent version of a storied muscle car, the Chevy Camaro, broke with its historical look to adopt a more angular profile. This change seems popular. In the head-to-head-to-head competition among the Mustang, the Camaro, and the Dodge Charger, the Camaro seems to be pulling out ahead. Not only is the Camaro tops in sales among pony cars, but it also attracts a greater percentage of female drivers and a younger demographic than either of the other two options.

Ford's response was to introduce the newest Mustang as a global car, not just an American one. Along with its simultaneous grand release events in far-flung places such as Shanghai, Barcelona, and Sydney, Ford undertook a social media blitz, mostly targeting Mustang fan clubs and car groups worldwide. Even if it predicts that international sales will be responsible for only about 10 percent of revenues, Ford hopes the Mustang will serve as a sort of "ambassador," opening parking spaces and garages to other Ford models.

Chevrolet redesigned its classic Camaro (a 1969 version is pictured on the left) to have a more angular profile (right), making it popular with female and younger car buyers.

(Left): © Ken Babione/Getty Images RF; (right): © Imaginechina/AP Photo

Global Product or Service Strategies There are three potential global product strategies: (1) sell the same product or service in both the home-country market and the host country, referred to as **glocalization**; (2) sell a product or service similar to that sold in the home country but include minor adaptations; and (3) sell totally new products or services. The strategy a firm chooses depends on the needs of the target market. Ford Motor Co., for example, envisions a world car that will sell everywhere, as we discuss in Adding Value 8.2. The level of economic development, as well as differences in product and technical standards, helps determine the need for and level of product adaptation. Cultural differences such as food preferences, language, and religion also play a role in product strategy planning.

Same Product or Service The most typical method of introducing a product outside the home country is to sell the same product or service in other countries. However, in **reverse innovation**, companies initially develop products for niche or underdeveloped markets and then expand them into their original or home markets. For example, General Electric realized that adapting medical diagnostic equipment that had been developed in the United States to sell it in India was ineffective. Few Indian medical providers had sufficient resources to pay $20,000 for the massive machinery. Therefore, GE undertook innovation specific to the Indian market to develop a battery-operated, portable EKG (electrocardiogram) machine for $500. Then it realized that the small, affordable machines would appeal as well to U.S. emergency medical personnel in the field and therefore globalized its offer.[47]

Similar Product or Service with Minor Adaptations

Campbell Soup discovered that even though Russia and China are two of the largest markets for soup in the world, cooks in those countries have unique demands. Chinese consumers drink 320 billion bowls of soup each year, and Russian buyers consume 32 billion servings, compared with only 14 billion bowls of soup served in the United States. However, Chinese cooks generally refuse to resort to canned soup; the average Chinese consumer eats soup five times each week, but he or she also takes great pride in preparing it personally with fresh ingredients. In contrast, Russian consumers, though they demand very high quality in their soups, had grown tired of spending hours preparing their homemade broths. To identify

Campbell's research found that Russians eat a lot of soup, and they want time-saving preparation help. So it developed broths to enable cooks to prepare soups with their own flair.

Source: Campbell Soup Company

opportunities in these markets, Campbell sent teams of social anthropologists to study how Chinese and Russian cooks prepare and consume soup. When it faced further hurdles, it entered into a joint venture with the Swire soup company in China. But its efforts in Russia never panned out, forcing Campbell to withdraw after around four years. That is, even with extensive, devoted efforts by an industry giant, global marketing remains a challenge.[48]

Referred to as glocalization, some firms also standardize their products globally but use different promotional campaigns to sell them. The original Pringles potato chip product remains the same globally, as do the images and themes of the promotional campaign, with limited language adaptations for the local markets, although English is used whenever possible. However, the company does change Pringles' flavors in different countries, including paprika-flavored chips sold in Italy and Germany.[49]

Totally New Product or Service The level of economic development and cultural tastes also affects global product strategy because it relates directly to consumer behavior. For example, although you are likely to know Heinz for its tomato ketchup, as you traveled the globe you would find they sell many unique products in different countries. If you taste the ketchup in the Philippines, you'll be surprised to find it's made with bananas instead of tomatoes (and sold under Heinz's Jufran label). In many East Asian countries, Heinz competes by selling soy sauce. The size of the package varies by country as well. Whereas in the United States big bottles of condiments are sold, in poorer countries, such as Indonesia, condiments such as soy sauce are sold in single-serve packets for a few pennies.[50]

Global Pricing Strategies

Determining the selling price in the global marketplace is an extremely difficult task.[51] Many countries still have rules governing the competitive marketplace, including those that affect pricing. For example, in parts of Europe, including Belgium, Italy, Spain, Greece, and France, sales are allowed only twice a year, in January and June or July. In most European countries retailers can't sell below cost, and in others they can't advertise reduced prices in advance of sales or discount items until they have been on the shelves for more than a month. For firms such as Walmart and other discounters, these restrictions threaten their core competitive positioning as the lowest-cost provider in the market. Other issues, such as tariffs, quotas, antidumping laws, and currency exchange policies, can also affect pricing decisions.[52]

Competitive factors influence global pricing in the same way they do home country pricing, but because a firm's products or services may not have the same positioning in the global marketplace as they do in their home country, market prices must be adjusted to reflect the local pricing structure. Spain's fashion retailer Zara, for instance, is relatively

Pringles sometimes changes flavors to reflect local tastes and demand, for example, these paprika-flavored chips are sold in Italy and Germany.

© Whitebox Media/Mediablitzimages/ Alamy

Zara is relatively inexpensive in its home country, Spain, but is more expensive in North America because of transportation expenses and currency fluctuations.

Source: Inditex

inexpensive in the EU but is priced about 40 percent higher in the United States, putting it right in the middle of its moderately priced competition.[53] Zara is dedicated to keeping production in Spain, but it also must get its fashions to the United States quickly, so it incurs additional transportation expenses, which it passes on to its North American customers. Finally, as we discussed previously in this chapter, currency fluctuations affect global pricing strategies.

Global Distribution Strategies

Global distribution networks form complex value chains that involve middlemen, exporters, importers, and different transportation systems. These additional middlemen typically add cost and ultimately increase the final selling price of a product. As a result of these cost factors, constant pressure exists to simplify distribution channels wherever possible.

The number of firms with which the seller needs to deal to get its merchandise to the consumer determines the complexity of a channel. In most developing countries, manufacturers must go through many types of distribution channels to get their products to end users, who often lack adequate transportation to shop at central shopping areas or large malls. Therefore, consumers shop near their homes at small, family-owned retail outlets. To reach these small retail outlets, most of which are located far from major rail stations or roads, marketers

Tupperware provides an acceptable way for women in Indonesia to make money, because the traditional culture discourages women's participation in the workforce.

© Lam Yik Fei/The New York Times/Redux Pictures

have devised a variety of creative solutions. For example, Tupperware parties offer an acceptable way for women in Indonesia—where the traditional culture discourages women's participation in the workforce—to sell and distribute the plastic food storage containers, benefiting both the firm and these entrepreneurs.[54]

Global Communication Strategies The major challenge in developing a global communication strategy is identifying the elements that need to be adapted to be effective in the global marketplace. For instance, literacy levels vary dramatically across the globe. Consider again the BRIC nations: In India, approximately 71 percent of the adult population is literate, compared with 86 percent in Brazil, over 90 percent in China, and over 99 percent in Russia.[55] Media availability also varies widely; some countries offer only state-controlled media.

Differences in language, customs, and culture also complicate marketers' ability to communicate with customers in various countries. Language can be particularly vexing for advertisers. For example, in the United Kingdom a thong is only a sandal, whereas in the United States it can also be an undergarment. To avoid the potential embarrassment that language confusion can cause, firms spend millions of dollars to develop brand names that have no preexisting meaning in any known language, such as Accenture (a management consulting firm) or Avaya (a subsidiary of Lucent Technologies, formerly Bell Labs).

Within many countries there are multiple variants on a language or more than one language. For example, China has three main languages; the written forms produce meaning through the characters used but the spoken forms depend on tone and pronunciation. Some firms choose names that sound similar to their English-language names, such as Nike, whose Chinese brand name is pronounced *nai-ke*. Others focus on the meanings of the characters, such that Citibank is known as *hui-qi-yinhang,* which means "star-spangled banner bank." Still other firms, such as Mercedes-Benz, have adapted their names for each language: *peng-zee* in Cantonese for Hong Kong, *peng-chi* in Mandarin for Taiwan, and *ben-chi* in Mandarin for mainland China. Naming is a constant challenge in China, especially to avoid the threat that a brand name evokes unwanted connotations, such as when Microsoft realized that the sound of its search engine name, Bing, meant "virus" in China—not the best image for an online company![56]

Even with all these differences, many products and services serve the same needs and wants globally with little or no adaptation in their form or message. Firms with global appeal can run global advertising campaigns and simply translate the wording in the advertisements and product labeling.

Nike's Chinese brand name is pronounced "nai ke," which is very similar to the English pronunciation, and means "Enduring and Persevering."
© Shiho Fukada/Redux Pictures

Other products require a more localized approach because of cultural and religious differences. In a classic advertisement for Longines watches, a woman's bare arm and hand appear, with a watch on her wrist. The advertisement was considered too risqué for Muslim countries, where women's bare arms are never displayed in public, but the company simply changed the advertisement to show a gloved arm and hand wearing the same watch.

Even among English speakers, there can be significant differences in the effectiveness of advertising campaigns. Take the popular "What Happens in Vegas Stays in Vegas" advertising campaign, which has been very successful and spawned numerous copycat slogans in the United States. Essentially, the U.S. mass market thought the provocative campaign pushed the envelope, but just far enough to be entertaining. However, when the Las Vegas tourism group extended its advertising to the United Kingdom, it found that the ad campaign was not nearly as effective. After conducting focus groups, the group found that British consumers did not find the advertisements edgy enough for their more irreverent British tastes. In response, the advertising agency began studying British slang and phrases to find ways to make the campaign even sexier and more provocative.[57]

PROGRESS CHECK

1. What are the components of a global marketing strategy?
2. What are the three global product strategies?

Reviewing Learning Objectives

 Describe the components of a country market assessment.

First, firms must assess the general economic environment. For instance, countries with a trade surplus, strong domestic and national products, growing populations, and income growth generally are relatively more favorable prospects. Second, firms should assess a country's infrastructure. To be successful in a particular country, the firm must have access to adequate transportation, distribution channels, and communications. Third, firms must determine whether the proposed country has a political and legal environment that favors business. Fourth, firms should be cognizant of the cultural and sociological differences between their home and host countries and adapt to those differences to ensure successful business relationships.

 Understand the marketing opportunities in BRIC countries.

Technology, particularly in the communication field, has facilitated the growth of global markets. Firms can communicate with their suppliers and customers instantaneously, easily take advantage of production efficiencies in other countries, and bring together parts and finished goods from all over the globe. Four countries that provide tremendous

marketing opportunities are the BRIC nations—Brazil, Russia, India, and China. These countries have large populations that are increasingly interested in the latest goods and services.

 Identify the various market entry strategies.

Firms have several options for entering a new country, each with a different level of risk and involvement. Direct investment is the riskiest but potentially the most lucrative. Firms that engage in a joint venture with other firms already operating in the host country share the risk and obtain knowledge about the market and how to do business there. A strategic alliance is similar to a joint venture, but the relationship is not as formal. A less risky method of entering a new market is franchising, in which, as in domestic franchise agreements, the franchisor allows the franchisee to operate a business using its name and strategy in return for a fee. The least risky method of entering another country is simply exporting.

 Highlight the similarities and differences between a domestic marketing strategy and a global marketing strategy.

The essence of a global marketing strategy is no different from that of a domestic strategy. The firm starts by identifying its target markets, chooses specific markets to pursue, and crafts a strategy to meet the needs of those markets. However, additional issues make global expansion more problematic. For instance, should the product or service be altered to fit the new market better? Does the firm

need to change the way it prices its products in different countries? What is the best way to get the product or service to the new customers? How should the firm publicize its product or service offering in various countries?

Key Terms

■■LEARNSMART

- bottom of the pyramid, 240
- direct investment, 252
- duty, 240
- exchange control, 242
- exchange rate, 242
- exporting, 250
- franchisee, 251
- franchising, 251

- franchisor, 251
- globalization, 236
- glocalization, 254
- gross domestic product (GDP), 238
- gross national income (GNI), 238
- infrastructure, 240
- joint venture, 251
- purchasing power parity (PPP), 238

- quota, 242
- reverse innovation, 254
- strategic alliance, 251
- tariff, 240
- trade agreements, 243
- trade deficit, 238
- trade surplus, 238
- trading bloc, 243

Net Savvy

1. For many small businesses, the idea of entering a foreign market is intimidating. The U.S. government and most state governments now offer assistance designed specifically for small-business owners. Visit the website of the Massachusetts Export Center at http://www.mass.gov/export/ and examine the types of services it provides. Click on the Export Statistics link. To what five countries did Massachusetts export the most? Are you surprised?

2. Nike is a global brand, yet it alters its promotions to meet local tastes. Go to http://store.nike.com/gb/en_gb/ and explore the UK site. Now go to the U.S. site. How are these websites different?

Marketing Applications

1. What is globalization? Why is it important for marketers to understand what globalization entails?

2. Moots is a high-end bicycle manufacturer located in Steamboat Springs, Colorado. Assume the company is considering entering the Brazilian, Chinese, and Indian markets. When conducting its market assessment, what economic factors should Moots consider to make its decision? Which market do you expect will be more lucrative for Moots? Why?

3. Now consider the political, economic, and legal systems of China, India, and Brazil. Explain why you think one country might be more hospitable to Moots than the others.

4. Colgate sells its products in many countries throughout the world. How would you expect its marketing strategy to differ in various countries, compared with that in the United States? Consider various areas across the globe in formulating your answer.

5. How does Coca-Cola market its products differently in the BRIC countries? In formulating your answer, go to: http://www.cocacola.com.br/; https://www.coca-cola.ru/; http://www.coca-cola.in/en/home/; and http://www.icoke.cn/. What are the benefits of being able to offer a globally standardized product? What types of products easily lend themselves to global standardization?

6. What are some examples of companies that use a glocalization strategy?

7. Choose a firm that currently manufactures and sells its products or services only in the United States. Choose and defend a global entry strategy for the firm.

Quiz Yourself

1. The shift of population from rural to urban areas in countries such as India helps global marketers by:
    a. Decreasing pollution.
    b. Simplifying the supply chain needed to make goods and services available.
    c. Increasing the human development index.
    d. Decreasing competition for intellectual capital.
    e. Increasing nonmaterial GDP output.

2. Why should marketers be aware of the BRIC countries?
    a. They are a microcosm of the rest of the world.
    b. They represent almost half the world's population.

    c. They are likely to be the source of most market growth.
    d. They have had the most dramatic changes in culture and consumer buying patterns.
    e. They have stable population growth, which makes them easier to study.

(Answers to these two questions can be found in the Quiz Yourself Answers section.)

Chapter Case Study

THE GLOBALIZATION OF THE MOST UBIQUITOUS OF AMERICAN CUISINES—THE HAMBURGER

McDonald's France has its own version of the "I'm lovin' it" slogan.
© Bill Ryall/William Ryall RF

From the Maharaja Mac in India to the Prosperity Burger prepared especially for Chinese New Year celebrations, McDonald's has built a global fast-food empire under its golden arches. Only 31 percent of McDonald's revenue now comes from sales in the United States, and most of its international growth has come from the surging economies of Brazil, Russia, China, and India.[58] A pioneer in overseas franchising, McDonald's has spared no effort in its attempts to penetrate foreign markets. In China, it opened one new outlet a day to meet its goal of 2,000 stores.[59] In Brazil, it created Latin America's first environmentally certified fast-food restaurant. A vast market defined by stark cultural differences, India has required a more modest approach that would allow McDonald's to develop its real estate and supply infrastructure, train its local workforce and management at its famed Hamburger University, and adjust the menu for vegetarian customers.[60] The McAloo Tikki Burger has been a great success, and the company has started opening more McCafe storefronts.[61]

But McDonald's growth strategy relies on more than just added locations. In crowded cities, with real estate prices too high to build drive-through restaurants, the company has hired droves of motorbike drivers to bring Big Macs to customers. This nimble delivery approach is now a mainstay in cities from Beijing to Kuwait City. Online ordering will be next, though the challenge will be to reduce the cost of call centers to support this new distribution model.[62] In addition, McDonald's keeps looking for new mobile innovations, such as mobile ordering or payment options, to keep up with consumer demand.[63]

Fast-food restaurants enjoy some segment-specific benefits as they pursue such international expansion. Unlike retail brands, such as Walmart or Carrefour, restaurants pose less perceived competitive threats. Local eateries can exist side-by-side with a McDonald's in a way that a mom-and-pop grocer cannot survive if an international hypermarket moves in next door.[64]

But even considering the massive growth in rapidly transitioning economies, Europe still generates the bulk of foreign sales for McDonald's. In France, for example, "MacDo" restaurants attract crowds that line up outside for a bite of lunch. But lunch might mean something a little different in this case: French McDonald's offer menus that feature Camembert cheese on the burgers, Heineken, a McBaguette, and macaroons for dessert.[65] Once, the secret to McDonald's success was "lockstep" consistency—the fact that a meal in Memphis tasted the same as it did in Moscow or Madrid. But the novelty of the American hamburger stand has worn off in the new millennium, and with it McDonald's ability to export American culture as its staple commodity. A cheeseburger, fries, and Coke don't register

McDonald's is successful in Israel because of its kosher offerings.

© David Silverman/Getty Images

the same level of excitement when the café next door and the bistro down the block are also serving burgers. More and more, the key to McDonald's future appears to be found in the DNA of the places it inhabits, like the sweet potato soft serve now available in Hong Kong.[66] And with it, suddenly the fast-food giant that to many represents the globalization of taste suddenly finds itself in a very unlikely position: as a defender of local cuisine.[67]

The kosher burger has been a hit in Israel, and Indian consumers seem to appreciate the opening of McDonald's first vegetarian restaurant. However, most new growth comes from Russia, where the company has 245 locations and controls 70 percent of the booming fast-food business. Even as fast-food competitors face potential market saturation in the United States, Russian demand for quick burgers appears to be insatiable.[68] Driving this Russian appetite has been the growth of a newly affluent middle class with money to spend to dine out. Infrastructure development in Russia also has been a boon as cities open malls with food courts, highways are constructed with drive-through locations, and specialty suppliers of frozen food and packaging have appeared.

In the early years of Russian expansion, few private businesses existed to supply all the ingredients McDonald's needed to produce Big Macs and fries. The company solved the problem by building an enormous food processing plant outside Moscow. But it also worked to cultivate relationships with local Russian vendors and contractors to which it eventually could outsource its supply chain. Today, a grower who began selling cucumbers to McDonald's in 1990 has become the Pickle King of Russia, dominating the processed foods market.[69]

Even when faced with some politically sensitive challenges—such as suspicious inspections by Russian agencies that alleged code violations in several McDonald's stores, seemingly in response to the strained relations between the Russian and U.S. governments[70]—McDonald's has continued with its plans to expand in the country. Most recently, it signed an agreement to open 20 new restaurant locations in remote Siberian regions.[71] International enrollment in Hamburger University thus shows no signs of slowing.

Questions

1. Which sociocultural factors have informed McDonald's global expansion?

2. Describe some of the global distribution strategies that McDonald's uses or might consider using to spread throughout the world.

3. Explain McDonald's global marketing strategy. Compare McDonald's strategy in the United States (http://www.mcdonalds.com/us/en/home.html) to McDonald's strategy in India (http://www.mcdonaldsindia.com/).

Endnotes

1. Mark Scott, "Netflix Faces Hurdles, Country by Country, in Bid to Expand in Europe," *The New York Times*, May 21, 2014, http://www.nytimes.com; Amol Sharma, "Netflix to Expand to France, Germany Later This Year," *The Wall Street Journal*, May 21, 2014, http://online.wsj.com.

2. Pierre-Richard Agenor, *Does Globalization Hurt the Poor?* (Washington, DC: World Bank, 2002); "Globalization: Threat or Opportunity," International Monetary Fund, http://www.imf.org.

3. http://www.census.gov.

4. https://stats.oecd.org/glossary/detail.asp?ID=1176

5. http://siteresources.worldbank.org/DATASTATISTICS/Resources/GNIPC.pdf; Arthur O'Sullivan, Steven Sheffrin, and Steve Perez, *Macroeconomics: Principles and Tools*, 8th ed. (Upper Saddle River, NJ: Prentice Hall, 2013).

6. *The Economist*, "The Big Mac Index," January 7, 2016, http://www.economist.com/content/big-mac-index.

7. Justin Dove, "Taking Advantage of Dollar Weakness," *Investor U*, July 28, 2011, http://www.investmentu.com.

8. Jack Neff, "Emerging-Market Growth War Pits Global Brand Giants against Scrappy Local Rivals," *Advertising Age*, June 13, 2011, http://adage.com.

9. "Coca-Cola Tackles Rural Indian Market" (video), *The Wall Street Journal*, May 3, 2010.

10. Melissa Ip, "Bottom of the Pyramid—a Decade of Observations," *Social Enterprise Buzz*, January 21, 2013, http://www.socialenterprisebuzz.com.

11. Wayne Ma, "China Levies 6.5% Tariff on U.S. Solar-Panel Materials," *The Wall Street Journal*, September 18, 2013, http://www.online.wsj.com.

12. Leslie Josephs, "U.S. Increases Sugar Quota for Second Time," *The Wall Street Journal*, June 23, 2011, http://online.wsj.com.

13. Leslie Josephs, "U.S. Unlikely to Raise Sugar-Import Quota," *The Wall Street Journal*, February 19, 2013, http://online.wsj.com.

14. "Exchange Rate," http://en.wikipedia.org/wiki/Exchange_rate.

15. Jason Chow and Nadya Masidlover, "Chanel Acts on Prices as Euro Worsens Gray Market," *The Wall Street Journal*, March 17, 2015.

16. https://ustr.gov/trade-agreements: provides information on US trade agreements.

17. http://www.unescap.org.

18. Johny Johansson, *Global Marketing*, 5th ed. (New York: McGraw-Hill/Irwin, 2008).

19. Philip R. Cateora, Mary C. Gilly, and John L. Graham, *International Marketing*, 17th ed. (New York: McGraw-Hill, 2015); Danielle Medina Walker and Thomas Walker, *Doing Business Internationally: The Guide to Cross-Cultural Success*, 2nd ed. (Princeton, NJ: Trade Management Corporation, 2003).

20. Angela Doland, "Six Cringeworthy Blunders Brands Make in China," *Advertising Age*, July 8, 2014, http://adage.com.

21. For a website dedicated to Hofstede's research, see http://www.geert-hofstede.com/.

22. Rosalie L. Tung and Alain Verbeke, eds., "Beyond Hofstede and GLOBE: Improving the Quality of Cross-Cultural Research," *Journal of International Business Studies* 41 (Special Issue, 2010).

23. Note that the time orientation and indulgence dimensions are relatively more recent additions to the categorization. See Geert Hofstede, "Dimensions of National Cultures," http://www.geerthofstede.eu/dimensions-of-national-cultures.

24. James W. Carey, *Communication as Culture*, rev. ed. (New York: Routledge, 2009).

25. *The Economist*, "Why Is South Africa Included in the BRICS?" March 29, 2013, http://www.economist.com/blogs/economist-explains/.

26. "Brazil," U.S. Department of State, http://www.state.gov; CIA, *The CIA World Factbook*, https://www.cia.gov/library/publications/the-world-factbook/.

27. Prableen Bajpai, "The World's Top 10 Economies," *Investopedia*, January 22, 2016, http://www.investopedia.com/articles/investing/022415/worlds-top-10-economies.asp.

28. "Brazil Economic Outlook," *FocusEconomics*, January 19, 2016, http://www.focus-economics.com/countries/brazil; "Brazil Economic Growth," *FocusEconomics*, January 19, 2016.

29. Asher Levine, "Brazil's 'New Middle Class' Struggles as Economy Plunges," *Reuters*, October 12, 2015, http://www.reuters.com/article/us-brazil-economy-fears-idUSKCN0S61QF20151012.

30. "Brazil Economic Outlook," *FocusEconomics*, January 19, 2016, http://www.focus-economics.com/countries/brazil; "Brazil Economic Growth," *FocusEconomics*, January 19, 2016.

31. "Russia," U.S. Department of State, http://www.state.gov; CIA, *The CIA World Factbook*, https://www.cia.gov.

32. eMarketer, "Number of Internet Users in Russia from 2013 to 2019 (in Millions)," *Statista*, February 4, 2016, http://www.statista.com/statistics/251818/number-of-internet-users-in-russia/.

33. "Russia," Internet Live Stats, http://www.internetlivestats.com/internet-users/russia/.

34. "Internet in Europe Stats," *Internet World Stats*, January 8, 2016, http://www.internetworldstats.com/stats4.htm#europe.

35. Marianne Wilson, "China Is Top Emerging Retail Market," *The New York Times*, June 1, 2015.

36. Paul Gregory, "A Russian Crisis with No End In Sight, Thanks to Low Oil Prices and Sanctions," *Forbes*, May 14, 2015, http://www.forbes.com/sites/paulroderickgregory/2015/05/14/a-russian-crisis-with-no-end-in-sight-thanks-to-low-oil-prices-and-sanctions/3/#5502e1f66d5e.

37. "India," U.S. Department of State, http://www.state.gov; CIA, *The CIA World Factbook*, https://www.cia.gov.

38. Megha Bahree, "India Unlocks Door for Global Retailers," *The Wall Street Journal*, November 25, 2011.

39. "Retail Industry in India" *India Brand Equity Foundation*, January 2016, http://www.ibef.org/industry/retail-india.aspx.

40. Ibid.

41. "China," U.S. Department of State, http://www.state.gov; CIA, *The CIA World Factbook* https://www.cia.gov.

42. Marianne Wilson, "China Is Top Emerging Retail Market," *The New York Times*, June 1, 2015.

43. Laurie Burkitt, "Tapping China's 'Silver Hair' Industry," *The Wall Street Journal*, January 19, 2015, http://www.wsj.com; Laurie Burkitt, "China's Aging Future," *The Wall Street Journal*, January 19, 2015, http://www.wsj.com/video, Steven Jiang and Susannah Cullinane, "China's One-child Policy to End," *CNN*, October 30, 2015.

44. Lance Eliot Brouthers et al., "Key Factors for Successful Export Performance for Small Firms," *Journal of International Marketing* 17, no. 3 (2009), pp. 21–38; "Selling Overseas," November 12, 2009, http://www.entrepreneur.com.

45. Juro Osawa and Lorraine Luk, "How Lenovo Built a Tech Giant," *The Wall Street Journal*, January 30, 2014, http://online.wsj.com; Juro Osawa and Yun-Hee Kim, "PC Firm Lenovo Hunts for Brazil Acquisitions," *The Wall Street Journal*, May 28, 2012, http://online.wsj.com.

46. Philip R. Cateora, Mary C. Gilly, and John L. Graham, *International Marketing*, 14th ed. (New York: McGraw-Hill, 2009).

47. Natalie Zmuda, "P&G, Levi's, GE Innovate by Thinking in Reverse," *Advertising Age*, June 13, 2011, http://adage.com.

48. Julie Jargon, "Can M'm, M'm Good Translate?" *The Wall Street Journal*, July 9, 2007, p. A16; Brad Dorfman and Martinne Geller, "Campbell Soup in Joint Venture to Expand in China," *Reuters*, January 12, 2011, http://www.reuters.com; Julie Jargon, "Campbell Soup to Exit Russia," *The Wall Street Journal*, June 29, 2011, http://online.wsj.com.

49. http://www.pringles.it/.

50. Bill Johnson, "The CEO of Heinz on Powering Growth in Emerging Markets," *Harvard Business Review*, October 2011.

51. Silvia Fabiana et al., eds., *Pricing Decisions in the Euro Era: How Firms Set Prices and Why* (Oxford: Oxford University Press, 2007); Cateora et al., *International Marketing*.

52. Ibid.; Amanda J. Broderick, Gordon E. Greenley, and Rene Dentiste Mueller, "The Behavioural Homogeneity Evaluation Framework: Multi-Level Evaluations of Consumer Involvement in International Segmentation," *Journal of International Business Studies* 38 (2007), pp. 746–63; Terry Clark, Masaaki Kotabe, and Dan Rajaratnam, "Exchange Rate Pass-Through and International Pricing Strategy: A Conceptual Framework and Research Propositions," *Journal of International Business Studies* 30, no. 2 (1999), pp. 249–68.

53. Sarah Morris, "How Zara Clothes Turned Galacia into a Retail Hotspot," *Reuters*, October 31, 2011, http://www.reuters.com.

54. Joe Cochrane, "Tupperware's Sweet Spot Shifts to Indonesia," *The New York Times*, February 28, 2015, http://www.nytimes.com.

55. CIA, *The CIA World Factbook*, https://www.cia.gov/library/publications/the-world-factbook/fields/2103.html.

56. Michael Wines, "Picking Brand Names in Asia Is a Business Itself," *Advertising Age*, November 11, 2011, http://www.nytimes.com; Brand Channel, http://www.brandchannel.com.

57. Joan Voight, "How to Customize Your U.S. Branding Effort to Work around the World," *Adweek*, September 3, 2008.

58. *Statista*, "Revenue of McDonald's Corporation Worldwide from 2008 to 2014, by Geographic Region (in Billion U.S. Dollars)," http://www.statista.com/statistics/219453/revenue-of-the-mcdonalds-corporation-by-geographic-region/.

59. "McDonald's China Plans to Open a New Store Every Day in Four Years," *The Huffington Post*, September 28, 2011, http://www.huffingtonpost.com.

60. "McDonald's Best Practices," http://bestpractices.mcdonalds.com; Annie Gasparro, "Yum Splits India into Separate Division, Names New International CEO," *The Wall Street Journal*, November 23, 2011.

61. Neha Thirani Bagri, "A Growing Taste for U.S. Fast Food in India," *The New York Times*, January 8, 2014, http://india.blogs.nytimes.com/.

62. Julie Jargon, "For Food Delivery, China Calls McDonald's," *The Wall Street Journal*, December 12, 2011, http://online.wsj.com.

63. Nat Rudarakanchana, "McDonald's (MCD) Going Mobile, Expanding in China and Three Other Takeaways from Last Scheduled Consumer Presentation of Uninspiring 2013," *International Business Times*, September 11, 2013, http://www.ibtimes.com.

64. Neha Thirani Bagri, "A Growing Taste for U.S. Fast Food in India," *The New York Times*, January 8, 2014, http://india.blogs.nytimes.com/.

65. Hannah Fleishman, "13 Businesses With Brilliant Global Marketing Strategies," *HubSpot*, July 29, 2015, http://blog.hubspot.com/blog/tabid/6307/bid/33857/10-Businesses-We-Admire-for-Brilliant-Global-Marketing.aspx.

66. Charles Passy, "How Fast Food Chains Cook Up New Menu Items," *The Wall Street Journal*, August 24, 2015; McDonald's, "What a Twist! McDonald's Hong Kong Launches Sweet Potato Sensation Ice Cream," January 22, 2016, http://news.mcdonalds.com/Corporate/Feature-Stories-Articles/2016/What-a-twist-McDonald-s-Hong-Kong-Launches.

67. Matt Goulding, "Why the French Secretly Love the Golden Arches," *Slate*, August 2013, http://www.slate.com.

68. "McDonald's Sees Strong Revenue on Global Demand," Associated Press, December 8, 2011, http://www.msnbc.msn.com; Ravi Krishnani, "McDonald's in Russia: Defeated Communism with a 'Happy' Meal," *Business Today*, http://www.businesstoday-eg.com; McDonald's Europe Virtual Press Office, press brief, http://www.mcdpressoffice.eu.

69. Andrew E. Kramer, "Russia's Evolution, Seen through Golden Arches," *The New York Times*, February 2, 2010, http://www.nytimes.com.

70. "For First Time Ever, McDonald's Closes a Restaurant in Russia," The Moscow Times, April 14, 2015, http://www.themoscowtimes.com/business/article/for-first-time-ever-mcdonalds-closes-a-restaurant-in-russia/519066.html.

71. Olga Razumovskaya, "McDonald's Extends Reach in Russia," *The Wall Street Journal*, August 21, 2015, http://www.wsj.com/articles/mcdonalds-extends-reach-in-russia-1440174904.

i. Rose Yu and Colum Murphy, "In China, Air Pollution Rules Spur Big Car Purchases," *The Wall Street Journal*, August 7, 2013, http://online.wsj.com.

ii. Jason Kincaid, "Mark Zuckerberg on Facebook's Strategy for China (and His Wardrobe)," *Tech Crunch*, October 16, 2010, http://techcrunch.com; Loretta Chao, "Brazil: The Social Media Capital of the Universe," *The Wall Street Journal*, February 4, 2013, http://online.wsj.com; Normandy Madden, "What Will Facebook Find if It Ventures into China?" *Advertising Age Global*, June 13, 2011, http://adage.com; Chloe Albanesius, "Human Rights Group Slams Facebook over China Strategy," *PCMag.com*, June 3, 2011, http://www.pcmag.com.

iii. Anil Urs and K. Giriprakash, "Tata Starbucks CEO: Our Business in India Continues to Exceed Expectations," *Hindu Business Line*, November 27, 2013, http://www.thehindubusinessline.com; Starbucks, "Starbucks Celebrates Its First Year in India with Launch of India Estates Blend," October 21, 2013, http://news.starbucks.com.

iv. Mike Ramsay, "Ford to Take Mustang Sports Car Global," *The New York Times*, December 4, 2013; "With 2015 Mustang, Ford Puts American Icon on Global Path," *Advertising Age*, December 5, 2013.

TARGETING THE MARKETPLACE

CHAPTER 9
Segmentation, Targeting, and Positioning

CHAPTER 10
Marketing Research

Section Three, Targeting the Marketplace, contains two chapters. Chapter 9 focuses on segmentation, targeting, and positioning. In this chapter, we examine how firms segment the marketplace, then pick a target market, and finally position their goods/services in line with their customers' needs and wants. Chapter 10, on marketing research, identifies the various tools, techniques, and metrics that marketers use to uncover customers' needs and wants and to ensure that they create goods and services that provide value to their target markets.

CHAPTER 9

SEGMENTATION, TARGETING, AND POSITIONING

After reading this chapter, you should be able to:

LO9-1 Outline the different methods of segmenting a market.

LO9-2 Describe how firms determine whether a segment is attractive and therefore worth pursuing.

LO9-3 Articulate the differences among targeting strategies: undifferentiated, differentiated, concentrated, or micromarketing.

LO9-4 Determine the value proposition.

LO9-5 Define positioning and describe how firms do it.

The president of the ABC Family television network summed up a recent epiphany about the Millennial generation, that popular target of vast marketing efforts, with a clear and funny comment: "We looked up from our research," he explained, "and said, 'Oh golly, they're turning 40.'" That is, the Millennials keep getting older, which means that another generational cohort must be coming up behind

To appeal to aging Millennials, ABC Family has rebranded itself with a new name, Freeform, but will continue to feature successful shows like Pretty Little Liars, *starring (from left to right) Shay Mitchell, Keegan Allen, Ashley Benson, Lucy Hale, Ian Harding, and Troian Bellisario.*

them ready to check out the shows, and the accompanying advertising, on channels that their parents let them watch.

ABC Family is one of those channels, available in approximately 94 million households. But its name signals its appeal to parents, and that's never a recipe for appealing successfully to kids. Therefore, the network is undergoing a rebranding effort, in which it will become a network called Freeform. The new network will still air many of the shows that have supported the success of ABC Family, such as *Pretty Little Liars, The Fosters,* and *Switched at Birth.* The network also plans to persist in successful marketing tactics like its *25 Days of Christmas* programming. However, the name and renewed vision for Freeform will reflect the more "fluid" approach that young viewers bring to their television watching habits. In particular, studies suggest that young viewers, usually defined as those born since 1995, are unlikely to accept vast cable packages filled with lots of channels they do not find interesting. Instead, they seek "skinny" packages that contain only those offerings they actually want. They also are exposed to content in various forms, screens, and channels that allow them to select from entertainment options that reflect their fluid preferences.

In researching who these consumers are and what they want, ABC Family executives also derived a view of the cohort that highlighted the developments they would undergo. Rather than strictly defining the target market by their age, Freeform hopes to define it according to the experiences they will be undergoing now and in the future. With that view, it adopted the term *becomers* to refer to them—that is, young people who are undertaking experiences and making choices that will enable them to become who they want to be. They are, as one executive noted, "somewhere between their first kiss and their first kid."

The new name of the network reflects this particular target market by acknowledging both their freely forming identities and their freedom with various forms of information. Freeform also seeks to evoke a spontaneous mood that is in line with the wide-open possibilities for its target audience, who are still figuring out who they want to be and how to develop that identity.

Although much of the programming will remain acceptable to families, the family-oriented targeting will be less explicit and obvious. The rebranding is not a response to falling sales or customer churn. Instead, it represents Freeform's recognition that as its audience shifts, it needs to do the same. In so doing, it hopes to maintain its ability to attract young viewers: Millennials when they were younger, becomers today, and the next generational cohort when the time comes. Whoever those young viewers are, they are the same ones that advertisers will pay the network to be able to reach.[1]

We learned in Chapter 1 that marketing is about satisfying consumers' wants and needs. Chapter 2 noted how companies analyze their markets to determine the different kinds of products and services people want. But it is not sufficient just to produce such an offering. Firms must also position their offerings in the minds of customers in their target market in such a way that these consumers understand why the thing the company is providing meets their needs better than other competitive offerings do.

This process requires a marketing plan, as we discussed in Chapter 2. You should recall that the third step of this plan is to identify and evaluate opportunities by performing an STP (segmentation, targeting, and positioning) analysis. This chapter focuses on that very analysis.

 LO9-1 Outline the different methods of segmenting a market.

THE SEGMENTATION, TARGETING, AND POSITIONING PROCESS

In this chapter, we discuss how a firm conducts a market segmentation or STP analysis (see Exhibit 9.1). We first outline a firm's overall strategy and objectives, methods of segmenting the market, and which segments are worth pursuing. Then we discuss how to choose a target market or markets by evaluating each segment's attractiveness and, on the basis of this evaluation, choose which segment or segments to pursue. Finally, we describe how a firm develops its positioning strategy.

Although the STP process in Exhibit 9.1 implies that the decision making is linear, this need not be the case. For instance, a firm could start with a strategy but then modify it as it gathers more information about various segments' attractiveness.

Step 1: Establish the Overall Strategy or Objectives

The first step in the segmentation process is to articulate the vision or objectives of the company's marketing strategy clearly. The segmentation strategy must be consistent with and derived from the firm's mission and objectives as well as its current situation—its strengths, weaknesses, opportunities, and threats (SWOT). Botticelli's objective, for instance, is to increase sales in a mature industry. The company, which sells olive oil, pasta, pasta sauces, and roasted red peppers,[2] knows its strengths are its reputation for using quality ingredients.[3] However, a weakness is that it may not currently have a product line that appeals to those who like Italian food but not the traditional options that are high in carbohydrates and heavy sauces. Identifying this potentially large and profitable market segment, and doing so before many of its mainstream competitors do, offers a great

EXHIBIT 9.1   The Segmentation, Targeting, and Positioning (STP) Process

Step 1: Establish strategy or objectives

Step 2: Use segmentation methods

Segmentation

Step 3: Evaluate segment attractiveness

Step 4: Select target market

Targeting

Step 5: Identify and develop positioning strategy

Positioning

opportunity. However, following through on that opportunity could lead to a significant threat: competitive retaliation. Botticelli's recent choice to pursue health-conscious and vegan customers with a vegan-friendly Bolognese sauce made with soy is consistent with its overall strategy and objectives.[4]

To thwart the competition and pursue the health-conscious market, Botticelli has introduced a vegan-friendly Bolognese sauce made with soy.

Courtesy of Borticelli

Now let's take a look at methods for segmenting a market.

Step 2: Use Segmentation Methods

The second step in the segmentation process is to use a particular method or combination of methods to segment the market. This step also develops descriptions of the different segments, which helps firms better understand the customer profiles in each segment. With this information, firms can distinguish customer similarities within a segment and dissimilarities across segments. Marketers use geographic, demographic, psychographic, benefits, and behavioral segmentation methods, as Exhibit 9.2 details.

Food marketers, for instance, divide the traditional pasta sauce landscape into with or without meat, original or light/heart healthy, and marinara versus something else (e.g., Alfredo, pesto). This segmentation method is based on the benefits that consumers derive from the products.

Geographic Segmentation Geographic segmentation organizes customers into groups on the basis of where they live. Thus, a market could be grouped by country, region (northeast, southeast), or areas within a region (state, city, neighborhoods, zip codes). Not surprisingly, geographic segmentation is most useful for companies whose products satisfy needs that vary by region.

Firms can provide the same basic goods or services to all segments even if they market globally or nationally, but better marketers make adjustments to meet the needs of smaller geographic groups.[5] A national grocery store chain such as Safeway or Kroger runs similar stores with similar assortments in various locations across the United States. But within those similar stores, a significant percentage of the assortment of goods will vary by region, city, or even neighborhood, depending on the different needs of the customers who surround each location.

Demographic Segmentation Demographic segmentation groups consumers according to easily measured, objective characteristics such as age, gender, income, and education. These variables represent the most common means to define segments because they are easy to identify, and demographically segmented markets are easy to reach. Kellogg's uses age segmentation for its breakfast cereals: Cocoa Krispies and Froot Loops are for kids; Special K and All-Bran are for adults. It also tends to adopt a gender-based segmentation; for example, marketing communications about Special K appeal almost exclusively to women.

Gender plays a very important role in how most firms market products and services.[6] For instance, TV viewing habits vary significantly between men and women. Men tend to channel surf—switching quickly from channel to channel—and watch prime-time shows

EXHIBIT 9.2 Methods for Describing Market Segments

Segmentation Method	Sample Segments
Geographic	Continent: North America, Asia, Europe, Africa Within the United States: Pacific, mountain, central, south, mid-Atlantic, northeast
Demographic	Age, gender, income, education
Psychographic	Lifestyle, self-concept, self-values
Benefits	Convenience, economy, prestige
Behavioral	Occasion, loyalty

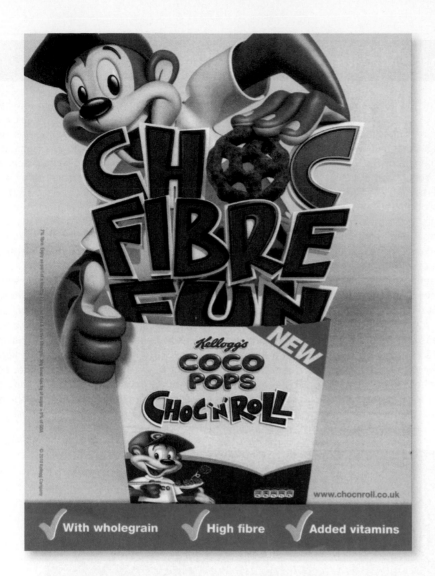

that are action oriented and feature physically attractive cast members. Women, in contrast, tend to view shows to which they can personally relate through the situational plot or characters and those recommended by friends. Print media are similar: A company such as Proactiv, which seeks to appeal to men as well as women who are worried about the condition of their skin, therefore carefully considers the gender-based appeal of different magazines when it purchases advertising space.

However, demographics may not be useful for defining the target segments for other companies. They are poor predictors of the users of activewear such as jogging suits and athletic shoes. At one time, firms such as Nike assumed that activewear would be purchased exclusively by young, active people, but the health and fitness trend has led people of all ages to buy such merchandise. Even relatively inactive consumers of all ages, incomes, and education find activewear to be more comfortable than traditional street clothes.

Rethinking some stereotypical ideas about who is buying thus has become a relatively common trend among firms that once thought their target market was well defined. As Social and Mobile Marketing 9.1 shows, even some of the most well-known companies in the world must continually reconsider the true identity of their prime targets.

Psychographic Segmentation Of the various methods for segmenting, or breaking down, the market, **psychographic segmentation** is the one that delves into how consumers actually describe themselves. Usually marketers determine (through demographics, buying patterns, or usage) into which segment an individual consumer falls.

Social & Mobile Marketing 9.1   Is Facebook Over?[i]

According to a recent study funded by the European Union, the terms that UK teens (16–18 years of age) use to describe Facebook include *embarrassing, old,* and *dead and buried.* These are not exactly the sorts of images that a company that revolutionized social media prefers to embrace. So what has led Facebook, once the social media home base of teens, to become the last place they want to be seen?

Most analyses suggest the main problem was its growing popularity—and more specifically, its growing popularity among their parents' generation. As mom, dads, aunts, uncles, and even grandparents joined the network, teens quickly became less willing to share quite so much. Humor sites collect various awkward moments when a teenager rails against an unfair parent on Facebook, only to have that parent respond with deeply embarrassing accounts of the teen's behavior or the imposition of a new punishment.

Beyond these direct contacts, teens tend to assume that anything their parents like cannot also be cool for them. If their grandmother posts pictures of her vacation to Facebook, seemingly by definition the site cannot be cool anymore.

As challenging as these trends are for Facebook, it could always rebrand itself as the social media location for middle-aged users who want to share their thoughts about their children or grandchildren. The larger question is where teens will go next to get their social media fix. The growing popularity of Snapchat implies that teens might begin preferring temporary, ephemeral sharing, possibly in reaction to the lessons learned when Facebook posts remain accessible to employers and school administrators. They also appreciate sites that allow in-the-moment connectivity, such as Periscope and its ability to live-stream exciting events as they happen. Moreover, teens seemingly use various sites for different purposes: Twitter for wide broadcasts, Instagram for visual sharing, WhatsApp for more personal interactions.

Of course, many of these sites have been or are poised to be acquired by the social media giants. Twitter bought Periscope, and Facebook continues to seek ways to expand its functions, both through internal innovation and acquisitions of other popular social media apps. The big names in social media are not ready to give up their valuable target market of teenaged users just yet. Finally, the variety of sites that continue to emerge suggests a gap in the market, waiting for some innovative entrepreneur to devise the next big thing, a site that teens consider cool and compelling—until their parents find it and ruin it too, of course.

Have you used WhatsApp to do real-time messaging?

Source: WhatsApp

Psychographics studies how people self-select, as it were, based on the characteristics of how they choose to occupy their time (behavior) and what underlying psychological reasons determine those choices.[7] For example, a person might have a strong need for inclusion or belonging, which motivates him or her to seek out activities that involve others, which in turn influences the products he or she buys to fit in with the group. Determining psychographics involves knowing and understanding three components: self-values, self-concept, and lifestyles.

Self-values are goals for life, not just the goals one wants to accomplish in a day. They are the overriding desires that drive how a person lives his or her life. Examples might be the need for self-respect, self-fulfillment, or a specific sense of belonging. This motivation causes people to develop self-images of how they want to be and then images of a way of life that will help them arrive at these ultimate goals. From a marketing point of view, self-values help determine the benefits the target market may be looking for from a product. The underlying, fundamental, personal need that pushes a person to seek out certain products or brands stems from his or her desire to fulfill a self-value.

People's self-image, or **self-concept**, is the image people ideally have of themselves.[8] A person who has a goal to belong may see, or want to see, himself as a fun-loving, gregarious type whom people wish to be around. Marketers often make use of this particular self-concept through communications that show their products being used by groups of laughing people who are having a good time. The connection emerges between the group fun and the product being shown and connotes a lifestyle that many consumers seek.

Such tactics need to balance the ideal with the realistic. Advertisements for women's skincare products tend to feature salacious shots of extraordinarily beautiful women. As we know, however, few women reach this ideal, and many of those who do actually think they don't. After some preliminary research in 2000, Unilever's Dove soap brand initiated its Campaign for Real Beauty campaign. It first placed billboards in the United States, Canada, and the United Kingdom featuring photos of "real" rather than "aspirational" women and two tick-box options such as "flawed?" or "flawless?"; 1.5 million observers texted their vote, and the vote tally appeared on the billboard. Based on this initial campaign, Dove recognized that it hit a raw nerve with many women. The campaign has been expanded to television and online videos, and is still one of the most talked about success stories in modern marketing.[9]

Lifestyles, the third component of people's psychographic makeup, are the ways we live.[10] If values provide an end goal, and self-concept is the way one sees oneself in the context of that goal, lifestyles are how we live our lives to achieve goals.

One of the most storied lifestyles in American legend is the Harley way of life: the open road, wind in your hair, rebelling against conventions. But the notions of freedom,

Dove's Campaign for Real Beauty features photos of "real" rather than "aspirationally" beautiful women.

Source: Dove/Unilever

Using lifestyle segmentation, Harley-Davidson has four main target markets: On the left is its core segment consisting of men older than 35 years. On the right are women older than 35 years.

(Left): © Bloomberg/Getty Images; (right): © Jeffrey Phelps/AP Photo

rebellion, and standing out from a crowd vastly appeal to all sorts of people. In response, Harley-Davidson has shifted its STP methods to define four main target markets: core (men older than 35 years), young adults (both genders, 18–34 years), women (older than 35 years), and diverse (men and women, African American and Hispanic, older than 35 years).[11]

For women, for example, it encourages lifestyle events such as Garage Parties, women's-only social gatherings hosted in the evenings at dealerships to teach women the basics of motorcycling. The company publication *We Ride* focuses solely on female Hogs, and the HD-1 Customization website offers a separate process for women to build their cycles to match their build, power preferences, and color desires.[12]

The most widely used tool to support such psychographic segmentation efforts is owned and operated by Strategic Business Insights (SBI).[13] Called **VALS**™, it examines the intersection of psychology, demographics, and lifestyles. Consumers can be classified into the eight segments shown in Exhibit 9.3 based on their answers to the questionnaire (http://www.strategicbusinessinsights.com/vals/presurvey.shtml). The vertical dimension of the VALS framework indicates level of resources, including income, education, health, energy level, and degree of innovativeness. The upper segments have more resources and are more innovative than are those on the bottom.

The horizontal dimension shows the segments' primary psychological motivation for buying. Consumers buy products and services because of their primary motivations—that is, how they see themselves in the world and how that self-image governs their activities. The three primary motivations of U.S. consumers are ideals, achievement, and self-expression. People who are primarily motivated by ideals are guided by knowledge and principles.

EXHIBIT 9.3 VALS Framework

US VALS™ Framework

High Resources

Innovators

Ideals   Achievement   Self-Expression

Thinkers   Achievers   Experiencers

Believers   Strivers   Makers

Survivors   Low Resources

The VALS survey places individuals into one of the eight groups. The VALS framework is the visualization of the consumer groups. Consumers with abundant resources—psychological, emotional, and material means and capabilities—are near the top of the framework and those with minimal resources are at the bottom. Consumer groups within a motivation can be targeted together. For instance, a marketer may target Thinkers and Believers together. Do you want to know your VALS type? If you do, respond to the questions at http://www.strategicbusinessinsights.com/vals/presurvey.shtml. Simply click on "Take the survey." You will receive your primary and secondary types in real time. In order to receive an accurate VALS type, your first language must be American English. If you are not a resident of the United States or Canada, residency should be for enough time to know the culture and its idioms.

Those who are motivated by achievement look for products and services that demonstrate success to their peers. Consumers who are primarily motivated by self-expression desire social or physical activity, variety, and risk.

VALS enables firms to identify target segments and their underlying motivations. It shows correlations between psychology and lifestyle choices. For instance, a European luxury automobile manufacturer used VALS to identify online, mobile applications that would appeal to affluent, early-adopter consumers within the next five years.[14] The VALS analysis enabled the company to prioritize the most promising applications to develop. In another case, VALS was used to help a medical center identify customers most interested and able to afford cosmetic surgery. Based on the underlying motivations of its target customers, the center and its ad agency developed an ad campaign so successful that it had to be pulled early to avoid overbooking at the surgical center.

Firms are finding that psychographic segmentation schemes like VALS are often more useful for predicting consumer behavior than are demographics. This is because people who share demographics often have very different psychological traits. Take, for example, Jack and John, both 30-year-old, married college graduates. Demographically they are the same, but Jack is risk-averse and John is a risk taker. Jack is socially conscious and John is

It is just as easy to identify Thinkers (left) as it is Makers (right). A person is given the VALS questionnaire, and the VALS program at SBI runs the answers through the computer for scoring to determine the VALS type.

(Left): © Sam Edwards/Getty Images RF; (right): © Huntstock/Getty Images RF

focused on himself. Lumping Jack and John together as a target does not make sense, because the ways they think and act are totally different.

There are limitations to using psychographic segmentation, however. Psychographics is more expensive as a means to identify potential customers. With demographics, a firm like Nike can easily identify its customers as, say, men or women and then direct its marketing strategies to each group differently. The problem is that not all men are alike, as we saw with Jack and John. Women are not all alike either! To identify VALS Thinkers or Makers, companies use the VALS questionnaire in surveys or focus groups. Then VALS provides robust segment descriptions, linkages with consumer product and media–use data, and communication tools to create consistent messages that build brand awareness and customer loyalty.[15]

Benefit Segmentation   Benefit segmentation groups consumers on the basis of the benefits they derive from products or services. Because marketing is all about satisfying consumers' needs and wants, dividing the market into segments whose needs and wants are best satisfied by the product benefits can be a very powerful tool.[16] It is effective and relatively easy to portray a product's or service's benefits in the firm's communication strategies.

Hollywood in particular is a constant and effective practitioner of benefit segmentation. Although all movies may seem to provide the same service—entertainment for a couple of hours—film producers know that people visit the theater or rent films to obtain a vast variety of benefits, and market them accordingly. Need a laugh? Try the latest comedy from Adam Sandler or Melissa McCarthy. Want to cry and then feel warm and fuzzy? Go see *Joy* starring Jennifer Lawrence, Bradley Cooper, and Robert De Niro, for by the time you leave the theater, you are likely to feel quite happy: The lead characters will have faced obstacles, overcome them, and ultimately found success.

The movie industry pursues a benefit segmentation strategy. Want to cry and then feel warm and fuzzy? Go see Joy *starring Jennifer Lawrence, Bradley Cooper, and Robert De Niro.*

© Twentieth Century Fox Film Corporation/Photofest

Behavioral Segmentation

Behavioral Segmentation Behavioral segmentation divides customers into groups on the basis of how they use the product or service. Some common behavioral measures include occasion and loyalty.

Occasion Behavioral segmentation based on when a product or service is purchased or consumed is called occasion segmentation. Men's Wearhouse uses this type of segmentation to develop its merchandise selection and its promotions. Sometimes men need a suit for their everyday work, but other suits are expressly for special occasions such as a prom or a wedding. Snack food companies such as Frito-Lay also make and promote snacks for various occasions—individual servings of potato chips for a snack on the run but 16-ounce bags for parties.

Restaurants offer loyalty programs because it is less expensive to retain customers than to attract new ones.
© Eric Audras/Onoky/SuperStock RF

Loyalty Firms have long known that it pays to retain loyal customers. Loyal customers are those who feel so strongly that the firm can meet their relevant needs best that any competitors are virtually excluded from their consideration; that is, these customers buy almost exclusively from the firm. These loyal customers are the most profitable in the long term.[17] In light of the high cost of finding new customers and the profitability of loyal customers, today's companies are using loyalty segmentation and investing in retention and loyalty initiatives to retain their most profitable customers. From simple, "buy 10 sandwiches, get the 11th free" punchcards offered by local restaurants to the elaborate travel-linked programs run by hotel and airline affiliates, such loyalty segmentation approaches are ubiquitous. Starbucks is using its loyalty programs and mobile apps to enhance value for its customers, as highlighted in Marketing Analytics 9.1.

Using Multiple Segmentation Methods

Using Multiple Segmentation Methods Although all segmentation methods are useful, each has its unique advantages and disadvantages. For example, segmenting by demographics and geography is easy, because information about who the customers are and where they are located is readily available; however, these characteristics don't help marketers determine their customers' needs. Knowing what benefits customers are seeking or how the product or service fits a particular lifestyle is important for designing an overall marketing strategy, but such segmentation schemes present a problem for marketers attempting to identify specifically which customers are seeking these benefits. Thus, firms often employ a combination of segmentation methods, using demographics and geography to identify and target marketing communications to their customers, then using benefits or lifestyles to design the product or service and the substance of the marketing message.

One very popular mixture of segmentation schemes is geodemographic segmentation. Based on the adage "birds of a feather flock together," geodemographic segmentation uses a combination of geographic, demographic, and lifestyle characteristics to classify consumers. Consumers in the same neighborhoods tend to buy the same types of cars, appliances, and apparel and shop at the same types of retailers.

One widely used tool for geodemographic market segmentation is the Tapestry™ Segmentation system developed and marketed by ESRI.[18] Tapestry Segmentation classifies all U.S. residential neighborhoods into 65 distinctive segments based on detailed demographic data and lifestyles of people who live in each U.S. block tract (zip code +4).[19] Each block group then can be analyzed and sorted by many characteristics, including income, home value, occupation, education, household type, age, and several key lifestyle characteristics. The information in Exhibit 9.4 describes three Tapestry segments.

Geodemographic segmentation can be particularly useful for retailers, because customers typically patronize stores close to their neighborhoods. Thus, retailers can use geodemographic segmentation to tailor each store's assortment to the preferences of the local community. If a toy store discovers that one of its stores is surrounded by Inner City

Marketing Analytics 9.1

A Complete Ecosystem for Coffee Drinkers: The Starbucks Mobile Plan[ii]

When it comes to mobile marketing, few brands are more successful than Starbucks. Reportedly, Starbucks customers make payments using a mobile device 7 million times per week, accounting for 20 percent of all transactions. These staggering numbers far exceed any of Starbucks' competitors, indicating that it has overcome one of the biggest hurdles in mobile marketing—namely, getting customers to engage frequently with it on their mobile devices. One observer attributes this level of success to Starbucks' creation of "a digital ecosystem that entwines the payment platform with their rewards program."

The loyalty program, My Starbucks Rewards, allows members to pay via their mobile device and earn points toward discounts and free offers. The integration of My Starbucks Rewards with the mobile app has been crucial to the app's success, because the moment customers use their mobile payment operation, Starbucks can gather the purchase behavior data, appropriately segment that customer, and offer customers deals immediately. Previously it would have taken at least a week for the company to even receive the purchase information. In the past year, Starbucks also introduced another way for customers to engage with the loyalty program: When they buy packages of Starbucks coffee in grocery stores, they can earn rewards points toward drinks and snacks in Starbucks stores. This feature has helped increase the My Starbucks Rewards program membership to over 9 million people.

To integrate the mobile app even more closely with the in-store experience, Starbucks also introduced a mobile ordering feature that allows customers to place their orders in advance. Their personalized drink then will be ready when they arrive at the store, eliminating the need to wait in line. This behavior represents yet another piece of information that Starbucks gains about its customers: Who are the ones in the biggest hurry, unwilling to stand in line for a few minutes to place their order and wait for it to be

Starbucks is using its loyalty programs and mobile apps to enhance value for its customers.

© Kevin Schafer/Moment Mobile ED/Getty Images

brewed up? With all these data collected about its My Starbucks Rewards customers, Starbucks can shape its marketing tactics, promotions, and store locations in optimal ways.

Tenants (Exhibit 9-4), it might adjust its offering to include less expensive toys. Stores surrounded by Top Rung (Exhibit 9-4) would warrant a more expensive stock selection.

This kind of segmentation is also useful for finding new locations; retailers identify their best locations and determine what types of people live in the area surrounding those stores, according to the geodemographic clusters. They can then find other potential locations where similar segments reside.

However, such treasure troves of data introduce a host of ethical concerns, as highlighted in Ethical and Societal Dilemma 9.1.

PROGRESS CHECK

1. What are the various segmentation methods?

EXHIBIT 9.4 Examples of Tapestry

	Segment 01 - *Top Rung*	Segment 18 - *Cozy and Comfortable*	Segment 52 - *Inner City Tenants*
LifeMode Summary Group	L1 *High Society*	L2 *Upscale Avenues*	L8 *Global Roots*
Urbanization Summary Group	U3 *Metro Cities I*	U8 *Suburban Periphery II*	U4 *Metro Cities II*
Household Type	Married-Couple Families	Married-Couple Families	Mixed
Median Age	44.6	41.7	28.8
Income	High	Upper Middle	Lower Middle
Employment	Prof/Mgmt	Prof/Mgmt	Srvc/Prof/Mgmt/Skilled
Education	Bach/Grad Degree	Some College	No HS Diploma; HS; Some Coll
Residential	Single Family	Single Family	Multiunit Rentals
Race/Ethnicity	White	White	White; Black; Hispanic
Activity	Participate in public/civic activities	Dine out often at family restaurants	Play football, basketball
Financial	Own stock worth $75,000+	Have personal line of credit	Have personal education loan
Activity	Vacation overseas	Shop at Kohl's	Go dancing
Media	Listen to classical, all-news radio	Listen to sporting events on radio	Read music, baby, fashion magazines
Vehicle	Own/Lease luxury car	Own/Lease minivan	Own/Lease Honda

Source: Esri, "Tapestry Segmentation: The Fabric of America's Neighborhoods."

Step 3: Evaluate Segment Attractiveness

The third step in the segmentation process involves evaluating the attractiveness of the various segments. To undertake this evaluation, marketers first must determine whether the segment is worth pursuing, using several descriptive criteria: Is the segment identifiable, substantial, reachable, responsive, and profitable (see Exhibit 9.5)?

Identifiable Firms must be able to identify who is within their market to be able to design products or services to meet their needs. It is equally important to ensure that the segments are distinct from one another, because too much overlap between segments means that distinct marketing strategies aren't necessary to meet segment members' needs. As Superior Service 9.1 details, an effective marketing strategy to distinct segments might even offer similar options but with different mascots and colors, if those identifiable segments are connected with particular universities.

Substantial Once the firm has identified its potential target markets, it needs to measure their sizes. If a market is too small or its buying power insignificant, it won't generate sufficient profits or be able to support the marketing mix activities. As China's economy started growing, there were not enough middle-class car buyers to push foreign automakers to design an entry-level vehicle. It was only after that number grew substatially that it became worthwhile for them to market to these identified consumers.

 LO9-2 Describe how firms determine whether a segment is attractive and therefore worth pursuing.

Ethical & Societal Dilemma 9.1   Congressional Hearings and the Ethical Considerations for Modern Loyalty Programs[iii]

Loyalty programs are so widespread, spanning so many industries, that they may seem unquestionable. But recent hearings held by the U.S. Congress Commerce Committee created some challenging questions, especially for the data warehouses that help companies target their ideal markets.

Part of the impetus for this questioning is the increased insights that marketers gain about their customers using technologically advanced data-gathering methods. Especially when consumers opt in to a loyalty program, they grant data brokers access to vast amounts of information about them. These brokers, including Experian, Acxiom, and Epsilon, earn their revenues by gathering and warehousing these massive amounts of consumer data and then selling selected slices to companies that want to target a particular audience.

The chair of the hearings, Democratic senator John Rockefeller of West Virginia, voiced concerns that the practices of the data brokers were shrouded in secrecy, such that there was insufficient oversight of how they collected and used information about consumers. But his challenges also extended to some central tactics embraced by marketers.

By segmenting populations by gender, race, ethnicity, and income, Rockefeller asserted, data gatherers were inherently discriminatory. Predatory lenders who identify a population of lower-income, less educated consumers might target them unfairly, such as by promising loans but only at very high interest rates. A list of people suffering from a genetic disease might attract the attention of unethical peddlers of "miracle cures." Because so much personal data are now available online, oversight of the uses of the data becomes even more difficult.

Rockefeller also objected to the defining feature of loyalty programs—namely, the provision of benefits to customers that the provider deems "better." Using the example of airlines, the hearing noted that in the aftermath of a flight cancellation, airlines often give priority to their best customers to help them find another route to their destination. Such practices in turn make the industry more frustrating and less serviceable for occasional or infrequent fliers. Overall, then, the harms to the broader society might outweigh the benefits to the individual or the firm.

Or perhaps the problem is merely unethical implementation, and the segmentation and targeting that Rockefeller decries is merely part of doing business.

EXHIBIT 9.5   Evaluation of Segment Attractiveness

Superior Service 9.1 — Symbiosis in Your Stay: How Hotels Leverage Their Proximity to Universities[iv]

Orientation. Move-in day. Parents' day. Moving-out day. Commencement. Reunion. Over the spans of time that students and their families interact with their colleges or universities, there are innumerable situations in which someone needs an extra room. Whether parents are dropping their first-year students off for their first taste of campus life, picking up their new graduates, or even returning as alumni, they represent a steady, predictable stream of potential revenue for the hotels located close to campus. These clearly identifiable parents and families are vast in number and tend to be highly responsive to offers that highlight their favorite university.

Recognizing the vast opportunity associated with this captive market, hotels are getting better at presenting themselves as virtual extensions of the school. From keeping sports memorabilia in the front lobby to decorating with school colors, these hotels seek to make devoted fans, students, and parents feel connected. One hotel near Boston University has established a dedicated room, the Terrier Suite, to honor the school's mascot. On its walls hang historical photographs of the school, and the minibar has glassware etched with the university emblem. The Nashville Marriot promotes its symbiosis with Vanderbilt University by decorating the lobby with one wall of equations, balanced by another wall of Vandy football helmets.

Beyond décor, hotels also are finding ways to pitch offers to parents that are valuable enough to encourage them to keep coming back for all four (or five or six) years that their students are enrolled in the school. A hotel located next to Bucknell University hands out cards, preprinted with the dates of key events for the upcoming year, such as homecoming or graduation, so that parents can book their next trips well in advance. The Revere Hotel Boston Common is in close proximity to several schools, such as Suffolk University, Tufts University, and Emerson College. For each guest, it determines his or her school loyalty, then hands out welcome packages stuffed with school merchandise, museum passes, and access to other local area attractions. It even solicited help designing staff members' uniforms from the design students attending the nearly Massachusetts College of Art and Design.

These moves appear popular among independent hotel operators as well as national chains. They reflect an increasing focus in the hotel industry to address the customer experience, in an effort to enhance customer loyalty and thereby buffer themselves from the dynamic demand they usually face. The targeted group of consumers also is strongly appealing. These parents already might be spending thousands to help pay for their children's educations, suggesting their strong promise for profit for the hotels as well. And ultimately, who can resist a hotel room festooned with balloons and streamers in their school colors?

To target visitors to Boston University, one hotel features the Terrier Suite, to honor the school's mascot. In addition to terrier décor, on its walls hang historical photographs of the school, and the minibar has glassware etched with the university emblem.

Courtesy of the Hotel Commonwealth

Reachable The best product or service cannot have any impact, no matter how identifiable or substantial the target market is, if that market cannot be reached (or accessed) through persuasive communications and product distribution. The consumer must know that the product or service exists, understand what it can do for him or her, and recognize how to buy it. If Victoria's Secret fails to tell women that it is offering some less luxurious, more affordable options, shoppers will just walk right past the store and buy basic bras from the Macy's store in the same mall.

Responsive For a segmentation strategy to be successful, the customers in the segment must react similarly and positively to the firm's offering. If, through the firm's distinctive competencies, it cannot provide products or services to that segment, it should not target it. For instance, the Cadillac division of General Motors (GM) has introduced a line of cars to the large and very lucrative luxury car segment. People in this market typically purchase Porsches, BMWs, Audis, and Lexuses. In contrast, GM has been somewhat successful competing for the middle-priced family-oriented car and light truck segments. Thus, even though the luxury car segment meets all the other criteria for a successful segment, GM took a big risk in attempting to pursue this market.

Profitable Marketers must also focus their assessments on the potential profitability of each segment, both current and future. Some key factors to keep in mind in this analysis include market growth (current size and expected growth rate), market competitiveness (number of competitors, entry barriers, product substitutes), and market access (ease of developing or accessing distribution channels and brand familiarity). Some straightforward calculations can help illustrate the profitability of a segment:

$$\text{Segment profitability} = (\text{Segment size} \times \text{Segment adoption percentage} \times \text{Purchase behavior} \times \text{Profit margin percentage}) - \text{Fixed costs}$$

where

Segment size = Number of people in the segment

Segment adoption percentage = Percentage of customers in the segment who are likely to adopt the product/service

Purchase behavior = Purchase price × number of times the customer would buy the product/service in a year

EXHIBIT 9.6 Profitability of Two Market Segments for Camillo's Lawn Service

	Homeowners	Businesses
Segment size	75,000	1,000
Segment adoption percentage	1%	20%
Purchase behavior Purchase price Frequency of purchase	$100 12 times	$500 20 times
Profit margin percentage	60%	80%
Fixed costs	$400,000	$1,000,000
Segment profit	$140,000	$600,000

Profit margin percentage = (Selling price − variable costs) ÷ selling price

Fixed costs = Advertising expenditure, rent, utilities, insurance, and administrative salaries for managers

To illustrate how a business might determine a segment's profitability, consider Camillo's start-up lawn service. He is trying to determine whether to target homeowners or businesses in a small midwestern town. Exhibit 9.6 estimates the profitability of the two segments. The homeowner segment is much larger than the business segment is, but several lawn services with established customers already exist. There is much less competition in the business segment. So, the segment adoption rate for the homeowner segment is only 1 percent, compared with 20 percent for the business segment. Camillo can charge a much higher price to businesses, and they use lawn services more frequently. The profit margin for the business segment is higher as well, because Camillo can use large equipment to cut the grass and therefore save on variable labor costs. However, the fixed costs for purchasing and maintaining the large equipment are much higher for the business segment. Furthermore, he would need to spend more money obtaining and maintaining the business customers, whereas he would use less expensive door-to-door flyers to reach household customers. On the basis of these informed predictions, Camillo decides the business segment is more profitable for his lawn service.

This analysis provides an estimate of the profitability of two segments at one point in time. It is also useful to evaluate the profitability of a segment over the lifetime of one of its typical customers. To address such issues, marketers consider factors such as how long the customer will remain loyal to the firm, the defection rate (percentage of customers who switch on a yearly basis), the costs of replacing lost customers (advertising, promotion), whether customers will buy more or more expensive merchandise in the future, and other such factors.

Now that we've evaluated each segment's attractiveness (Step 3), we can select the target markets to pursue (Step 4).

Step 4: Select a Target Market

LO9-3 Articulate the differences among targeting strategies: undifferentiated, differentiated, concentrated, or micromarketing.

The fourth step in the STP process is to select a target market. The key factor likely to affect this decision is the marketer's ability to pursue such an opportunity or target segment. Thus, as we mentioned in Chapter 2, a firm very carefully assesses both the attractiveness of the target market (opportunities and threats based on the SWOT analysis and the profitability of the segment) and its own competencies (strengths and weaknesses based on the SWOT analysis).

Determining how to select target markets is not always straightforward, as we discuss in more detail next and illustrate in Exhibit 9.7 with several targeting strategies.

Undifferentiated Targeting Strategy, or Mass Marketing When everyone might be considered a potential user of its product, a firm uses an **undifferentiated targeting**

EXHIBIT 9.7   Targeting Strategies

Condé Nast has more than 20 niche magazines focused on different aspects of life.

© Alberto Coto/Getty Images RF

strategy (mass marketing). (See Exhibit 9.7.) Clearly, such a targeting strategy focuses on the similarities in needs of the customers as opposed to the differences. If the product or service is perceived to provide similar benefits to most consumers, there simply is little need to develop separate strategies for different groups.

Although not a common strategy in today's complex marketplace, an undifferentiated strategy is used for many basic commodities such as salt or sugar. However, even those firms that offer salt and sugar now are trying to differentiate their products. Similarly, everyone with a car needs gasoline. Yet gasoline companies have vigorously moved from an undifferentiated strategy to a differentiated one by targeting their offerings to low-, medium-, and high-octane gasoline users.

Differentiated Targeting Strategy Firms using a **differentiated targeting strategy** target several market segments with a different offering for each (again see Exhibit 9.7). Condé Nast has more than 20 niche magazines focused on different aspects of life—from *Vogue* for fashionistas to *Bon Appetit* for foodies to *GQ* for fashion-conscious men to *The New Yorker* for literature lovers to *Golf Digest* for those who walk the links.

Firms embrace differentiated targeting because it helps them obtain a bigger share of the market and increase the market for their products overall. Readers of *Golf Digest* probably are unlike readers of *Architectural Digest* in their interests, as well as in such demographics as gender, age, and income. Providing products or services that appeal to multiple segments helps diversify the business and therefore lowers the company's (in this case, Condé Nast's) overall risk. Even if one magazine suffers a circulation decline, the impact on the firm's profitability can be offset by revenue from another publication that continues to do well. But a differentiated strategy is likely to be more costly for the firm.

Concentrated Targeting Strategy When an organization selects a single, primary target market and focuses all its energies on providing a product to fit that market's needs, it is using a concentrated targeting strategy. Entrepreneurial start-up ventures often benefit from using a concentrated strategy, which allows them to employ their limited resources more efficiently. Newton Running, for instance, has concentrated its targeting strategy to runners—but not all runners. It focuses only on those who prefer to land on their forefeet while running, a style that has been suggested as more natural, efficient, and less injury-prone than the style encouraged by more traditional running shoes with their heel-first construction and substantial cushioning. In comparison, though it also is known for its running shoes, Nike uses a differentiated targeting strategy. It makes shoes for segments that include basketball and football players and skateboarders; it also makes shoes for fashion-conscious white-collar workers with its subsidiary brand Cole Haan.

Micromarketing[20] Take a look at your collection of belts. Have you ever had one made to match your exact specifications? (If you're interested, try http://www.leathergoodsconnection.com.) When a firm tailors a product or service to suit an individual customer's wants or needs, it is undertaking an extreme form of segmentation called micromarketing or one-to-one marketing.

CVS uses micromarketing to each customer by analyzing what they are buying and the profitability of each item purchased from its loyalty card data.[21] If a customer shops relatively infrequently, for example, once a month for her prescriptions, it may provide incentives that expire in a week. Alternatively, if another customer buys frequently, but with a relatively low market basket value of less than $20 per visit, it provides incentives to increase each visit's purchases to, say, $25. It may provide incentives to get customers who are purchasing only national brands to purchase more private label merchandise.

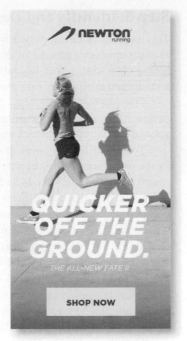

Which segment is Newton targeting?
© Newton Running

CVS uses micromarketing to each customer by analyzing what they are buying and the profitability of each item purchased from its loyalty card data.

© Sonda Dawes/The Image Works

LO9-4   Determine the value proposition.

Step 5: Identify and Develop Positioning Strategy

The last step in developing a market segmentation strategy is positioning. **Market positioning** involves a process of defining the marketing mix variables so that target customers have a clear, distinctive, desirable understanding of what the product does or represents in comparison with competing products.

The positioning strategy can help communicate the firm's or the product's **value proposition**, which communicates the customer benefits to be received from a product or service and thereby provides reasons for wanting to purchase it.

To visualize the value proposition, examine the Circles for a Successful Value Proposition framework in part A of Exhibit 9.8.[22] The bottom left circle in part A represents the customer needs and wants, the bottom right circle represents the company's offerings (i.e., its capabilities), and the top circle represents the benefits offered by competitors. The best situation is if a company's product or service offering overlaps with customer needs and wants but suffers no overlap with competitors' offerings (Exhibit 9.8). The shaded portion reflects the value proposition, or the intersection of what the customer needs and wants with what the company can offer. Unfortunately, even if the situation depicted in part A of Exhibit 9.8 existed, and the product or service is currently successful, that success would not be sustainable because competitors would attempt to copy the important product or service attributes and therefore begin to encroach on the firm's value proposition. Maintaining a unique value proposition can be sustained in the long term only in monopoly situations or possibly monopolistic competition situations.

In part B of Exhibit 9.8, the intersection of customer needs, the benefits provided by our focal firm, and the benefits provided by a competing firm reveal seven specific spaces where a product or service might be located. Let's look at each one in turn, using the offerings of the airline industry as hypothetical examples to understand each space.

EXHIBIT 9.8   Circles for a Successful Value Proposition

A. No overlap with competition

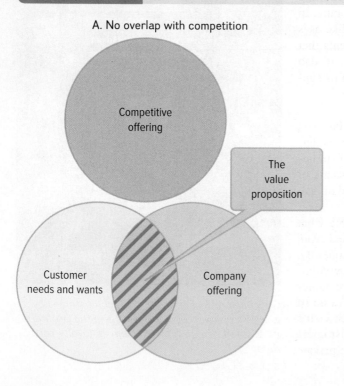

B. Determining the value proposition

#1: Firm's value proposition.
#2: Customer's unmet needs (marketing opportunity).
#3: Firm's benefits that are not required—educate customer or redesign product.
#4: Key benefits that both the firm and competitor provide that customers require—carefully monitor performance relative to competitor on these benefits.
#5: Competitor's value proposition—monitor and imitate if needed.
#6: Benefits both firms provide that customers do not appear to need.
#7: Competitor benefits that are not required.

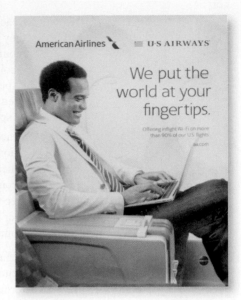

A firm's value proposition is represented by the benefits that a firm provides but that its competitors do not. Airline customers who are looking for a good value and will therefore tolerate a cattle-call approach to seating, which allows them to choose their own seats on the plane as long as they get an early check-in, turn to Southwest for their flights (left). Alternatively, customers who are looking for lots of world-wide flight options will turn to American Airlines/US Airways (right).

(Left): © Buskirk Services, Inc./PhotoEdit; (right): © Ashok Saxena/Alamy

Space 1. Representing the firm's value proposition, this space reveals which customer needs are effectively met by the benefits that the firm provides but not by the benefits provided by competitors. That is, there is no overlap between competitors. When airline customers prefer a cattle-call approach to seating, which allows them to choose their own seats on the plane as long as they get an early check-in, they turn to Southwest, and Southwest alone, for their flights.

Space 2. These customer needs are unmet. It represents an important marketing opportunity in that the firm could create new products or services or augment existing ones to better satisfy these needs. A direct route between two cities that currently are not connected by any airline represents a prime example of such a space.

Space 3. Customers express little need or desire for these company benefits. The firm thus has several options. It might educate customers about the importance and benefits that it provides with this space, to encourage customers to develop a sense of their need. Alternatively, it could reengineer its approach to stop providing these unwanted benefits, which likely would enable it to save money. For example, when airlines realized that passengers cared little about the appearance of a piece of lettuce underneath the in-flight sandwiches they were served, they saved millions of dollars they had previously spent on unwanted produce.

Space 4. These needs are being met by the benefits of the firm as well as by competitors. Many customers make frequent trips between major cities, like New York and Washington, DC, and many airlines offer multiple direct flights each day between these hubs. Each firm therefore works to compete effectively, such as by offering convenient flight times or striving to increase its on-time rates to make it easier for customers to compare firms on these specific features.

Space 5. This space constitutes the competitor's value proposition: the needs of customers that are met by benefits a competitor provides but not by the benefits provided by our focal firm. For example, only a few airlines host separate lounges for their best customers; a lower-cost airline cannot compete in this space. However, if more and more customers start to make demands for these benefits, the focal firm needs to monitor developments carefully and match some benefits if possible.

Space 6. Although both the focal firm and its competitors provide these benefits, they somehow are not meeting customer needs. The stringent security screening requirements aim to increase passenger safety, but they also represent a significant inconvenience that many fliers associate with airlines rather than federal regulators. Expending significant efforts to educate customers by the focal firm about these needs would also benefit competitors, so they likely are lower in the priority list of spending.

Space 7. Finally, some competitor benefits are either undesired or unnecessary among customers. Similar to Space 3, the competitor could invest money to educate customers about the importance of these benefits and highlight their needs through advertising and promotional campaigns. If so, the focal firm should recognize that this need is moving to Space 5. Alternatively, the competitor could reengineer its products to eliminate these benefits, in which case it requires no response from the focal firm.

Regardless of their existing space, firms must constantly and closely monitor their competitors' offerings. If competitors offer features that the firm does not, it is important to determine their importance to customers. Important attributes should be considered for inclusion in the firm's offering—or else they will provide a unique value proposition for competitors.

In Exhibit 9.9, we highlight the elements of developing and communicating a firm's value proposition. The main value proposition components are:

1. Target market
2. Offering name or brand
3. Product/service category or concept
4. Unique point of difference/benefits

Let's focus on a couple of well-known products, Gatorade and 7-Up, and their potential value propositions (brackets are added to separate the value proposition components):

- **Gatorade:**[23] To [athletes around the world] [Gatorade] is the [sports drink] [representing the heart, hustle, and soul of athleticism and gives the fuel for working muscles, fluid for hydration, and electrolytes to help replace what is lost in sweat before, during, and after activity to get the most out of your body].

- **7UP:**[24] To [non-cola consumers] [7-Up] is a [non-caffeinated soft drink] that is [light, refreshing, lemon-lime flavored, and has a crisp, bubbly, and clean taste].

EXHIBIT 9.9   Value Proposition Statement Key Elements

	Gatorade	7-Up
Target market	Athletes around the world	Non-cola consumers
Offering name or brand	Gatorade	7-Up
Product/service category or concept	Sports drink	Non-caffeinated soft drink
Unique point of difference/ benefits	Representing the heart, hustle, and soul of athleticism and gives the fuel for working muscles, fluid for hydration, and electrolytes to help replace what is lost in sweat before, during, and after activity to get the most out of your body.	Light, refreshing, lemon-lime flavored, and has a crisp, bubbly, and clean taste.

Positioning Methods

Firms position products and services based on different methods such as the value proposition, salient attributes, symbols, and competition.

Value Proposition Value is a popular positioning method because the relationship of price to quality is among the most important considerations for consumers when they make a purchase decision. But value is in the eyes of the beholder. Some chocolate lovers buy only Hershey's. It has a made-in-the-U.S.A. heritage. It offers a wide assortment—something for everyone. It is perceived to be of good quality and have great taste. And, importantly, it is relatively inexpensive. Other chocoholics wouldn't think of buying such a low-priced treat, but instead portion their disposable calorie intake to only higher-priced brands such as Godiva. Godiva has stores in high-end malls, offers some handmade items such as fresh berries dipped in chocolate, and has a loyalty

 LO9-5 Define positioning, and describe how firms do it.

Hershey's and Godiva both offer their respective target markets a good value. Hershey's (left) is a lower-priced option with a made-in-the-U.S.A. heritage, as depicted by this chocolate Statue of Liberty in the Hershey's Chocolate World store in the New York-New York hotel in Las Vegas. Godiva (right) offers handmade items, such as the strawberry dipped in chocolate on the book's cover, and beautiful traditional stores like this one in Brussels, Belgium.

program. Each market, the Hershey's and the Godiva lovers, would argue that their brand is the best value, and to them, it is. Recall from our discussion in Chapter 1, value does not necessarily mean low priced. But both of these chocolatiers position their products based on value.

Salient Attributes Another common positioning strategy focuses on the product attributes that are most important to the target market. With its all-wheel drive Quattro, Audi has positioned itself on performance and handling. Targeting a different market, Subaru positions its all-wheel drive slightly differently, instead focusing on safety and handling.

How does Saddleback Leather position itself?

© Saddleback Leather Company

Symbols A well-known symbol can also be used as a positioning tool. What comes to mind when you think of Colonel Sanders, the Jolly Green Giant, the Gerber Baby, or Tony the Tiger? Or consider the Texaco star, the Nike swoosh, or the Ralph Lauren polo player. These symbols are so strong and well known that they create a position for the brand that distinguishes it from its competition. Many such symbols are registered trademarks that are legally protected by the companies that developed them.

Competition Firms can choose to position their products or services against a specific competitor or an entire product/service classification. For instance, although most luggage companies focus on building lightweight and functional designs, Saddleback Leather focuses on rugged durability and a classic look. Offering a 100-year guarantee on its products, the owner Dave positions his bags as something "they'll fight over when you're dead."[25] This craftsmanship comes at a cost—its suitcases sell for more than $1,000.

Marketers must be careful, however, that they don't position their product too closely to their competition. If, for instance, their package or logo looks too much like a competitor's, they might be opening themselves up to a trademark infringement lawsuit. Many private-label and store brands have been challenged for using packaging that appears confusingly similar to that of the national brand leaders in a category. Similarly, McDonald's sues anyone who uses the *Mc* prefix, including McSleep Inns and McDental Services, even though in the latter case there was little possibility that consumers would believe the fast-food restaurant company would branch out into dental services.

Positioning Using Perceptual Mapping

Now that we have identified the various methods by which firms position their products and services, we discuss the actual steps they go through to establish that position. When developing a positioning strategy, firms go through six important steps. But before you read about these steps, examine Exhibits 9.10A through 9.10D, a hypothetical perceptual map of the soft drink industry. A **perceptual map** displays, in two or more dimensions, the position of products or brands in the consumer's mind. We have chosen two dimensions for illustrative purposes: sweet versus light taste (vertical) and less natural versus healthy (horizontal). Also, though this industry is quite complex, we have simplified the diagram to include only a few players in the market. The position of each brand is denoted by a small circle, except for the focal brand, Gatorade, which is denoted by a star. The numbered circles denote consumers' **ideal points**—where a particular market segment's ideal product would lie on the map. The larger the numbered circle, the larger the market size.

To derive a perceptual map such as shown in Exhibits 9.10A through 9.10D, marketers follow six steps.

Gatorade and Powerade are positioned similarly and compete with each other for customers who seek healthy sweet drinks.

© Rachel Epstein/PhotoEdit

1. **Determine consumers' perceptions and evaluations of the product or service in relation to competitors' product or service.** Marketers determine their brand's position by asking a series of questions about their firm's and the competitors' products. For instance, they might ask how the consumer uses the existing product or services, what items the consumer regards as alternative sources to satisfy his or her needs, what the person likes or dislikes about the brand in relation to competitors, and what might make that person choose one brand over another. Exhibit 9.10A depicts the five products using two dimensions (light taste–sweet taste; and less natural–healthy).

EXHIBIT 9.10A   Perceptual Map, Chart A

EXHIBIT 9.10B Perceptual Map, Chart B

◯ Target market size indicated by size of oval

2. **Identify the market's ideal points and size.** On a perceptual map, marketers can represent the size of current and potential markets. For example, Exhibit 9.10B uses differently sized ovals that correspond to the market size. Ideal point 1 represents the largest market, so if the firm does not already have a product positioned close to this point, it should consider an introduction. Point 3 is the smallest market, so there are relatively few customers who want a healthy, light-tasting drink. This is not to suggest that this market should be ignored; however, the company might want to consider a niche market rather than mass market strategy for this group of consumers.

3. **Identify competitors' positions.** When the firm understands how its customers view its brand relative to competitors', it must study how those same competitors position themselves. For instance, Powerade positions itself closely to Gatorade, which means they appear next to each other on the perceptual map and appeal to target market 2 (see Exhibit 9.10C). They are also often found next to each other on store shelves, are similarly priced, and are viewed by customers as sports drinks. Gatorade also knows that its sports drink is perceived to be more like Powerade than like its own Propel Fitness Water (located near target market 3) or Coke (target market 1).

EXHIBIT 9.10C Perceptual Map. Chart C

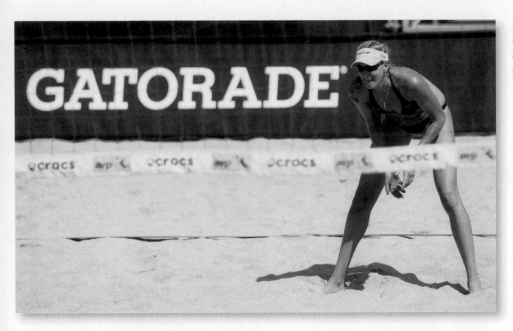

Gatorade uses athletes to compete for target markets in Exhibit 9.10.

© Jed Jacobsohn/Getty Images

4. **Determine consumer preferences.** The firm knows what the consumer thinks of the products or services in the marketplace and their positions relative to one another. Now it must find out what the consumer really wants—that is, determine the ideal product or service that appeals to each market. For example, a huge market exists for traditional Gatorade, and that market is shared by Powerade. Gatorade also recognizes a market, depicted as the ideal product for segment 4 on the perceptual map, of consumers who would prefer a less sweet, less calorie-laden drink that offers the same rejuvenating properties as Gatorade. Currently, no product is adequately serving market 4.

5. **Select the position.** Continuing with the Gatorade example, the company has some choices to appeal to the "less sweet sports drink" target market 4. It could develop a new product to meet the needs of market 4 (see Exhibit 9.10D, option 1). Alternatively, it could adjust or reposition its marketing approach—its product and promotion—to sell original Gatorade to market 4 (option 2). Finally, it could ignore what target market 4 really wants and hope that consumers will be attracted to the original Gatorade because it is closer to their ideal product than anything else on the market.

EXHIBIT 9.10D   Perceptual Map, Chart D

Chart D

Sweet taste

○ Coke
  ○ Pepsi   ○ Powerade

①

#1: Gatorade introduces new product   ② ┼ Gatorade

                                          #2: Gatorade repositions itself

Less natural   Gatorade

                                                      Healthy

                                          ④

                              ○ Propel Fitness
                          ③   Water
                              ○ Bottled water

Light taste

6. **Monitor the positioning strategy.** Markets are not stagnant. Consumers' tastes shift, and competitors react to those shifts. Attempting to maintain the same position year after year can spell disaster for any company. Thus, firms must always view the first three steps of the positioning process as ongoing, with adjustments made in step four as necessary.

Despite the apparent simplicity of this presentation, marketers should recognize that changing their firm's positioning is never an easy task.

PROGRESS CHECK

1. What is a perceptual map?
2. Identify the six positioning steps.

Reviewing Learning Objectives

 Outline the different methods of segmenting a market.

There is really no one "best" method to segment a market. Firms choose from various methods on the basis of the type of product/service they offer and their goals for the segmentation strategy. For instance, if the firm wants to identify its customers easily, demographic or geographic segmentation likely will work best. But if it is trying to dig deeper into why customers might buy its offering, then psychographic, geodemographic, benefits, or behavioral segmentation (occasion and loyalty) work best. Typically, a combination of several segmentation methods is most effective.

 Describe how firms determine whether a segment is attractive and therefore worth pursuing.

Marketers use several criteria to assess a segment's attractiveness. First, the customer should be identifiable—companies must know what types of people are in the market so they can direct their efforts appropriately. Second, the market must be substantial enough to be worth pursuing. If relatively few people appear in a segment, it is probably not cost effective to direct special marketing mix efforts toward them. Third, the market must be reachable—the firm must be able to reach the segment through effective communications and distribution. Fourth, the firm must be responsive to the needs of customers in a segment. It must be able to deliver a product or service that the segment will embrace. Finally, the segment must be profitable, both in the near term and over the lifetime of the customer.

 Articulate the differences among targeting strategies: undifferentiated, differentiated, concentrated, or micromarketing.

Firms use a targeting strategy after they have identified its segments. An undifferentiated strategy uses no targeting at all and works only for products or services that most consumers consider to be commodities. The difference between a differentiated and a concentrated strategy is that the differentiated approach targets multiple segments, whereas the concentrated targets only one. Larger firms with multiple product/service offerings generally use a differentiated strategy; smaller firms or those with a limited product/service offering often use a concentrated strategy. Firms that employ a micromarketing, or one-to-one, marketing strategy tailor their product/service offering to each customer—that is, it is custom-made. In the past, micromarketing was reserved primarily for artisans, tailors, or other craftspeople who would make items exactly as the customer wanted. Recently, however, larger manufacturers and retailers have begun experimenting with custom-made merchandise as well. Service providers, in contrast, are largely accustomed to customizing their offering.

 Determine the value proposition.

A firm's value proposition communicates the customer benefits to be received from a product or service and thereby provides reasons for the customer to want to purchase it. It consists of the attributes of a product or service that are desired by the target market but not available from competitors. Firms could attempt to offer attributes that are important to its customers, whether or not they are offered by competitors. For attributes that are not important to its customers, it should either educate its customers about the importance of those attributes, deemphasize them, or not offer those product or service attributes.

LO9-5 **Define positioning, and describe how firms do it.**

Positioning is the *P* in the STP (segmentation, targeting, and positioning) process. It refers to how customers think about a product, service, or brand in the market relative to competitors' offerings. Firms position their products and services according to several criteria. Some focus on their offering's value—customers get a lot for what the product or service costs. Others determine the most important attributes for customers and position their offering on the basis of those attributes. Symbols can also be used for positioning, though few products or services are associated with symbols that are compelling enough to drive people to buy. Finally, one of the most common positioning methods relies on the favorable comparison of the firm's offering with the products or services marketed by competitors. When developing a positioning strategy and a perceptual map, firms go through six steps. First, they determine consumers' perceptions and evaluations of the product or service in relation to competitors. Second, they identify the market's ideal points and market sizes for those products or services. Third, they identify competitors' positions. Fourth, they determine consumer preferences. Fifth, they select the position. Finally, they monitor the positioning strategy.

Key Terms

LEARNSMART

- behavioral segmentation, 277
- benefit segmentation, 276
- concentrated targeting strategy, 284
- demographic segmentation, 270
- differentiated targeting strategy, 284
- geodemographic segmentation, 277
- geographic segmentation, 270

- ideal point, 291
- lifestyle, 273
- loyalty segmentation, 277
- market positioning, 286
- micromarketing, 285
- occasion segmentation, 277
- one-to-one marketing, 285
- perceptual map, 291
- psychographics, 273

- psychographic segmentation, 271
- self-concept, 273
- self-values, 273
- undifferentiated targeting strategy (mass marketing), 283
- value, 289
- Value and Lifestyle Survey (VALS), 274
- value proposition, 286

Marketing Digitally

1. Go to http://www.esri.com/library/fliers/pdfs/tapestry_segmentation.pdf, and identify five segments that you would expect to find in your zip code. Then go to http://www.esri.com/data/tapestry/zip-lookup, and type in your zip code. Compare the segments that are found in your zip code with your initial prediction. Are they similar or different? Discuss the extent to which you believe these are accurate descriptions of the main segments of people who reside in your zip code.

2. Go to the VALS website (http://www.strategicbusinesssinsights.com/vals/presurvey.shtml), and click on the link to complete the VALS survey. After you submit your responses, a screen will display your primary and secondary VALS types. Click on the colored names of each segment to get additional information about them, and print out your results. Assess the extent to which these results reflect your lifestyle, and identify which characteristics accurately reflect your interests and activities and which do not.

Marketing Applications

1. What segmentation methods would you suggest for a small entrepreneur starting her own business selling gourmet chocolates? Justify why you would recommend those methods.

2. You have been asked to identify various segments in the market and then a potential targeting strategy. Describe the segments for a pet supply store, and then justify the best targeting strategy to use.

3. What types of products would you use demographic segmentation for? How about psychographic segmentation? Explain how these products differ.

4. You have been asked to evaluate the attractiveness of a group of identified potential market segments. What criteria will you use to evaluate those segments? Why are these appropriate criteria?

5. A small-business owner is trying to evaluate the profitability of different segments. What are the key factors you would recommend she consider? Over what period of time would you recommend she evaluate?

6. Think about the various soft drinks that you know (e.g., Coca-Cola, Pepsi, 7-Up, Gatorade, Powerade). How do those various brands position themselves in the market?

7. Put yourself in the position of an entrepreneur who is developing a new product to introduce into the market. Briefly describe the product. Then, develop the segmentation, targeting, and positioning strategy for marketing the new product. Be sure to discuss (a) the overall strategy, (b) characteristics of the target market, (c) why that target market is attractive, and (d) the positioning strategy. Provide justifications for your decisions.

8. Think of a specific company or organization that uses various types of promotional material to market its offerings. The web, magazine ads, newspaper ads, catalogs, newspaper inserts, direct-mail pieces, and flyers might all be sources for a variety of promotional materials. Locate two or three promotional pieces for the company and use them as a basis to analyze the segments being targeted. Describe the methods used for segmenting the market reflected in these materials, and describe characteristics of the target market according to the materials. Be sure to include a copy of all the materials used in the analysis.

9. You have been hired recently by a large bank in its credit card marketing division. The bank has relationships with a large number of colleges and prints a wide variety of credit cards featuring college logos, images, and the like. You have been asked to oversee the implementation of a new program targeting first-year college students at the schools with which the bank has a relationship. The bank has already purchased the names and home addresses of the incoming class. You have been told that no credit checks will be required for these cards as long as the student is over 18 years of age. The bank plans a first-day-of-school marketing blitz that includes free hats, T-shirts, and book promotions, as well as free pizza, if the students simply fill out an application. Do you think it is a good idea to target this program to these new students?

Quiz Yourself

1. For the _____ criteria to be met when evaluating segment attractiveness, the consumer must know the product or service exists, understand what it can do for him or her, and recognize how to buy it.
   a. substantial
   b. identifiable
   c. reachable
   d. responsive
   e. profitable

2. Which step in the STP process develops descriptions of the different segments, which in turn helps firms better understand the customer profiles in each segment?
   a. Establish overall strategy or objectives.
   b. Select segmentation method.
   c. Develop positioning strategy.
   d. Evaluate segment attractiveness.
   e. Select target market.

(Answers to these two questions can be found in the Quiz Yourself Answer Key section.)

Chapter Case Study

MERCEDES-BENZ

From Janis Joplin to Jay-Z, The Eagles to Outcast, Kanye West to Mariah Carey, generations of singers and songwriters have been inspired to mention Mercedes-Benz in their lyrics. Whether the brand offers a dreamed-of aspiration that they hope to access some day, or a signal of their wealth and power, Mercedes appeals to the musicians as well as their audiences. When lyricists beg for a Mercedes, or brag about how many sit in their garages, listeners around the world know exactly what they mean.

Mercedes-Benz has launched a multichannel campaign targeted specifically at women that includes the "She's Mercedes" website.

Source: Mercedes

The diversity of musicians and musical styles represented in the overall list of songs about Mercedes reflects just how effective the car brand has been at establishing a strong image as a luxury vehicle. But simultaneously, Mercedes-Benz also has developed a specific and strategic segmentation, targeting, and positioning approach that allows it to access unique and diverse markets of consumers and potential buyers. With its various models and strategic marketing plan, Mercedes considers ways to segment customers by gender, location, age, and economic strata, among other factors. Then it determines appropriate methods to appeal to each of those segments with dedicated communications, designs, and car models. Let's consider some examples of its STP efforts.

Gender[26]

As a function of its "Best Customer Experience" initiative, Mercedes-Benz has launched a multichannel campaign targeted specifically at women. The brand owners expressed their desire to make sure that all customers receive precisely the car buying and owning experience they want. In an attempt to ensure such access and experiences for women, the "She's Mercedes" campaign features a dedicated website, a print magazine, and sponsored events. The events are mostly networking opportunities, and the magazine prominently features successful women (who also own Mercedes, of course) and their efforts to balance work, family, and other commitments. In addition to similar sorts of stories, the website hosts a platform for consumers to share their ideas and impressions.

But the website also features a clever tool designed to target women buyers and position Mercedes as a brand that is friendly to female consumers. Specifically, it gives women the option to use a dedicated configurator—that is, a tool that many car companies provide to help customers build the exact car they want, using virtual tools. On the conventional Mercedes tool, a similar tool allows potential buyers to select their model, color, wheels, audio package, transmission, and so on. On the She's Mercedes site, the configurator instead focuses more on lifestyle questions rather than soliciting preferred drive train sizes. For example, a potential buyer can list her favorite music, hobbies, and travel plans. An algorithm then proposes several models of Mercedes cars that are likely to fit her preferences. She can add options to those models, or else accept the prespecified car that the company has targeted especially for her—or at least segments of consumers like her.

Location[27] Mercedes already is nearly everywhere. But it also develops distinct targeting and positioning strategies in the various locations in which it appears. Thus for example, it notes upward trends in its worldwide sales, but it also acknowledges that sales grew by 14 percent in the United States, 3 percent in Canada, 27 percent in South Korea, 4 percent in Japan, and so on. It also pays particular attention to the BRIC nations (Brazil, Russia, India, and China; see Chapter 8). In all these countries, it has enjoyed strong, double-digit sales growth. Furthermore, Mercedes specifies that in these markets, the luxury car market itself is growing much faster than in other traditional markets. For example, while the U.S. market for luxury automobiles might be growing at a respectable 6 percent annually, India shows promise of increasing by a remarkable 24 percent.

Noting the importance of the Indian luxury car market in particular, Mercedes has developed unique and specific methods to appeal to these consumers. For example, it pursued local production options to avoid the high import taxes and keep the cars affordable. Acknowledging the high "chauffeur share," such that many Indians have drivers to maneuver their cars about, Mercedes made sure to devote attention to the backseats of the high-end sedans it sells there. Similarly, to broaden its appeal in China, where the growing market demands a wider variety of options, Mercedes introduced 15 models in a single year, while also expanding its sales network in that country with 50 new dealerships.[28]

Age[29] When research showed Mercedes that its average customer in the United States was 52 years of age, the company also adopted a more explicit age-based segmentation approach that would help it appeal to younger buyers. Somewhat ironically, its investigation of buyers in their 30s showed that they actually had strongly nostalgic leanings. They liked the idea of Mercedes as a heritage brand. Accordingly, to position the brand as nostalgic, advertising targeting these buyers features glamour shots of the Mercedes legacy, as manifested in row upon row of beautifully designed cars, from the past to the present.

In addition, Mercedes has vastly expanded its product lines to introduce some sportier models and provide a clear contrast to the "boring" sedans that young consumers might associate with the brand. For example, its A-class is smaller but still powerful, available in hatchback versions, and totally equipped with the latest in smart technology. Noting younger consumers' interest in environmental sustainability, Mercedes also has improved the emissions rate for most of its models and touts its energy-saving innovations.

Economic Strata[30] For luxury carmakers, the lowest end models in their product lines often represent only a small portion of their sales. Yet these models are critically important when it comes to attracting new customers and, potentially, establishing their lifelong loyalty to the brand. Accordingly, Mercedes has developed some comparatively less option-laden options to lure first-time and unconventional buyers to their dealerships. It introduced its CLA model at a base price of less than $40,000. When consumers realized that they could purchase or lease a Mercedes-Benz for approximately the same monthly price that they would spend for a high-end Toyota or Honda, many of them switched happily.

For the most part, the target market for such models includes young professionals. These consumers earn a steady income that enables them to take on a car payment—but they cannot pay for a new car outright, and the monthly payments must fit their budgets. Mercedes accordingly has enjoyed sales increases due to the introductions of the lower-end models. Furthermore, these purchases are not repeat buys: Approximately 75 percent of CLA purchasers are new to the brand. Such statistics suggest an expanded market for the brands. As these buyers age, advance in their careers, and consider more expensive car purchases, they should be more likely to continue visiting the dealerships that provided them with their very first luxury automobile.

Questions

1. What are the main ways Mercedes-Benz segments its customers? Are there any other methods in this chapter that it might use?

2. How can Mercedes-Benz position itself effectively to appeal to consumers who are (a) men, (b) younger than 30, (c) from China, or (d) very wealthy?

Endnotes

1. Brooks Barnes, "Disney's Family Channel Aims Younger Than Millennials with New Name," *The New York Times*, October 6, 2015; Dave Walker, "ABC Family to Freeform: Six Things to Know About the New Name of the 'Pretty Little Liars' Network," *Forbes*, January 11, 2016; Eric Deggans, "ABC Family Channel to Change Its Name to Freeform," *NPR*, January 12, 2016.

2. http://www.botticelli-foods.com/index.html.

3. Isaac Thompson, "Botticelli Foods Olive Oil: Sourced from Italy or Tunisia? Pricing Differences?" World Trade Daily, July 25, 2012, http://worldtradedaily.com/2012/07/25/botticelli-foods-olive-oil-sourced-from-italy-or-tunisia-pricing-differences/.

4. http://www.botticelli-foods.com/pastasauces.html.

5. James Agarwal, Naresh K. Malhotra, and Ruth N. Bolton, "A Cross-National and Cross-Cultural Approach to Global Market Segmentation: An Application Using Consumers' Perceived Service Quality," *Journal of International Marketing* 18, no. 3 (September 2010), pp. 18–40.

6. Bill Carter, "ABC Viewers Tilt Female for a Network Light on Sports," *The New York Times*, December 17, 2013, http://www.nytimes.com; Alex Sood, "The Lost Boys Found: Marketing to Men through Games," *Fast Company*, March 10, 2011, http://www.fastcompany.com; Jeanine Poggi, "Men's Shopping Shrines," *Forbes*, September 30, 2008, http://www.forbes.com.

7. Michael R. Solomon, *Consumer Behavior*, 10th ed. (Upper Saddle River, NJ: Prentice Hall, 2012).

8. Rosellina Ferraro, Amna Kirmani, and Ted Matherly, "Look at Me! Look at Me! Conspicuous Brand Usage, Self-Brand Connection, and Dilution," *Journal of Marketing Research* 50, no. 4 (2013), pp. 477–88; Keith Wilcox and Andrew T. Stephen, "Are Close Friends the Enemy? Online Social Networks, Self-Esteem, and Self-Control," *Journal of Consumer Research* 40, no. 1 (2013), pp. 90–103.

9. Eric Wilson, "Less Ab, More Flab," *The New York Times*, May 22, 2013.

10. Michael R. Solomon, *Consumer Behavior: Buying, Having, and Being*, 10th ed. (Upper Saddle River, NJ: Prentice Hall, 2012).

11. James M. Hagerty, "Harley, with Macho Intact, Tries to Court More Women," *The Wall Street Journal*, October 31, 2011, http://online.wsj.com; Harley-Davidson, "Global Customer Focus," http://investor.harley-davidson.com.

12. Harley-Davidson, "Women Riders," http://www.harley-davidson.com.

13. http://www.strategicbusinessinsights.com/vals/store/USconsumers/intro.shtml.

14. http://www.strategicbusinessinsights.com/vals/applications/apps-pos.shtml.

15. "Segmentation and Targeting," http://www.kellogg.northwestern.edu; Carson J. Sandy, Samuel D. Gosling, and John Durant, "Predicting Consumer Behavior and Media Preferences: The Comparative Validity of Personality Traits and Demographic Variables," *Psychology & Marketing* 30, no. 11 (2013), pp. 937–49.

16. For an interesting take on this issue, see Joseph Jaffe, *Flip the Funnel* (Hoboken, NJ: Wiley, 2010).

17. V. Kumar, Ilaria Dalla Pozza, and Jaishankar Ganesh, "Revisiting the Satisfaction–Loyalty Relationship: Empirical Generalizations and Directions for Future Research," *Journal of Retailing* 89,

no. 3 (2013), pp. 246–62; Irit Nitzan and Barak Libai, "Social Effects on Customer Retention," *Journal of Marketing* 75, no. 6 (November 2011), pp. 24–38.

18. ESRI, "Tapestry Segmentation Reference Guide" and "Tapestry Segmentation: The Fabric of America's Neighborhood," www.esri.com.

19. ESRI, "Lifestyles-Esri Tapestry Segmentation," http://www.esri.com/data/esri_data/tapestry.

20. Thorsten Blecker, *Mass Customization: Challenges and Solutions* (New York: Springer, 2006).

21. Personal Communication, Robert Price, CVS Caremark's SVP of Marketing and Advertising, 2010.

22. This circular depiction of the value proposition is based on work by John Bers (Vanderbilt University) and adaptation and development of circles of success by Ronald Goodstein (Georgetown University).

23. http://www.gatorade.com/frequently_asked_questions/default.aspx.

24. http://www.drpeppersnapplegroup.com/brands/7up/.

25. http://www.saddlebackleather.com/.

26. Mercedes, "About She's Mercedes," September 15, 2015, https://www.mercedes-benz.com/en/mercedes-me/inspiration/she/about-shes-mercedes/; "Mercedes Wants to Be the Car for Women," *AutoBlog*, September 16, 2015, http://www.autoblog.com/2015/09/16/mercedes-luxury-car-for-women/.

27. Joachim Schmidt, "Mercedes-Benz Cars: Sales and Marketing Strategy," March 29, 2012, https://www.daimler.com/dokumente/investoren/kapitalmarkttage/daimler-ir-mercedesbenzcarsdivisiondayhungaryschmidt-20120329.pdf.

28. Daimler Chrysler, "Annual Report 2015: Mercedes-Benz Cars," http://ar2015.daimler.com/divisions/mercedes-benz-cars.

29. Vanessa Fuhrmans, "German Auto Makers to Shake Up Luxury Market," *The Wall Street Journal*, January 14, 2013.

30. Mark Clothier, "The Downside of Low-End Luxury Cars," *Bloomberg Businessweek*, July 17, 2014, http://www.businessweek.com.

i. Chris Matyszczyk, "For Teens, Facebook Is 'Dead and Buried,'" *CNET*, December 27, 2013, http://news.cnet.com; Jayson DeMers, "The Top 7 Social Media Marketing Trends that Will Dominate 2016," *Forbes*, September 28, 2015.

ii. Sarah Halzack, "Starbucks Has Managed to Get You Addicted to Its Coffee—And Its App," *Washington Post*, January 23, 2015, http://www.washingtonpost.com; Kate Kaye, "At Starbucks, Data Pours In. But What to Do With It?" *Advertising Age*, March 22, 2013, http://adage.com; WBAL NewsRadio 1090, "Why Consumers Are Addicted To Starbucks App," *WBAL News*, February 19, 2015, http://www.wbal.com/article/113508/21/why-consumers-are-addicted-to-starbucks-app; Sarah Perez, "Starbucks' Mobile Order & Pay Now Live Nationwide, Delivery Service in Testing by Year-End," *TechCrunch.com*, September 25, 2015.

iii. Kate Kaye, "Rockefeller to Marketing Data Giants: You're on Notice," *Advertising Age*, December 18, 2013; Kate Kaye, "7 Reasons This Senior Senator Hates Your Loyalty Program," *Advertising Age*, December 20, 2013.

iv. Julie Weed, "Hotels Embrace the Campus Nearby," *The New York Times*, May 19, 2014, http://www.nytimes.com.

MARKETING RESEARCH

After reading this chapter, you should be able to:

LO10-1 Identify the five steps in the marketing research process.

LO10-2 Describe the various secondary data sources.

LO10-3 Describe the various primary data collection techniques.

LO10-4 Summarize the differences between secondary data and primary data.

LO10-5 Examine the circumstances in which collecting information on consumers is ethical.

Although marketing researchers draw conclusions from their data, those conclusions tend to change over time as customer preferences and trends are constantly changing. For years, researchers and marketers agreed that featuring very thin, very attractive models in underwear advertising was the best route to selling more. Indeed, research had indicated that even though the images of highly attractive, glamorized models made people feel worse about themselves and their bodies, those advertisements also prompted consumers to buy more bras, panties, underwear, and shapewear than advertising that featured more realistically proportioned or unretouched models. No wonder the women in the photo look angry and anxious.[1]

AdoreMe.com

However, the marketplace is changing with the rise of selfies, societal efforts to counteract the negative effects of damaging body images, and expanding definitions of gender and gender roles. As a consequence, instead of preferring to buy underwear because of of ads featuring beautiful and stylized models, consumers increasingly prefer to buy their undergarments from companies that feature models whose body types are somewhat more realistic and whose beauty appears more achievable.

The evidence of this shift is perhaps clearest in market research performed by Adore Me, a start-up firm that sells subscriptions to customers, who then receive monthly packages of women's lingerie. Before it initiated its first national advertising campaign, Adore Me undertook experimental research in which it ran multiple versions of a similar advertisement that varies on specific elements, then watched its website to determine immediate reactions. For this campaign, Adore Me ran three advertisements for lingerie: one with highly attractive, very thin, blond models; another with a group of brunette models without any retouching efforts applied; and a third with a plus-size brunette model.[2] The results of their experiment demonstrated that the advertisement with the thin blond models led to the lowest response. The advertisement with the plus-size brunette model provoked more than four times as many sales as did the "traditional" advertisement, and the unretouched, multiple-model advertisement did even better than that.

Adore Me also conducts research to determine which voiceover leads people to purchase. That is, the research it conducts is not limited to just visual images but also accounts for customers' preferences for certain voices and types of information provided. Furthermore, based on the data it collects regularly from its online customers, it determined that they would like to interact with the products in person. So Adore Me decided to experiment with a pop-up store—a retail space located in a temporary location. The insights gained from the experimental shop in turn led the retailer to open its first physical location in New York City.[3]

Underwear advertising is undergoing some radical changes at other firms as well. As we noted in Chapter 9, in their underwear commercials, companies like 2(x)ist and Mack Weldon feature handsome but slightly flabby men.[4] In a recent edition, even that bastion of gorgeous but unrealistic images of beauty, the *Sports Illustrated* swimsuit edition, features three different cover models,

Marketing research is a prerequisite of successful decision making. It consists of a set of techniques and principles for systematically collecting, recording, analyzing, and interpreting data that can aid decision makers who are involved in marketing goods, services, or ideas. When marketing managers attempt to develop their strategies, marketing research can provide valuable information that will help them make segmentation, positioning, product, place, price, and promotion decisions.

Firms invest billions of dollars in marketing research every year. The largest U.S.-based marketing research firm, the Nielsen Company, earns annual worldwide revenues of over $6 billion.[7] Why do marketers find this research valuable? First, it helps reduce some of the uncertainty under which they currently operate. Successful managers know when research might help their decision making and then take appropriate steps to acquire the information they need. Second, marketing research provides a crucial link between firms and their environments, which enables them to be customer oriented because they build their strategies by using customer input and continual feedback. Third, by constantly monitoring their competitors, firms can anticipate and respond quickly to competitive moves.

If you think market research is applicable only to corporate ventures though, think again. Nonprofit organizations and governments also use research to serve their constituencies better. The political sector has been slicing and dicing the voting public for decades to determine relevant messages for different demographics. Politicians desperately want to understand who makes up the voting public to determine how to reach them. But they do not want to know only your political views—they also want to understand your media habits, such as what magazines you subscribe to, so they can target you more effectively.

To do so, they rely on the five-step marketing research process we outline in this chapter. We also discuss some of the ethical implications of using the information that these databases can collect.

THE MARKETING RESEARCH PROCESS

Managers consider several factors before embarking on a marketing research project. First, will the research be useful; will it provide insights beyond what the managers already know and reduce uncertainty associated with the project? Second, is top management committed to the project and willing to abide by the results of the research? Related to both of these questions is the value of the research. Marketing research can be very expensive, and if the results won't be useful or management does not abide by the findings, it represents a waste of money. Third, should the marketing research project be small or large? A project might involve a simple analysis of data that the firm already has, or it could be an in-depth assessment that costs hundreds of thousands of dollars and takes months to complete.

The marketing research process itself consists of five steps (see Exhibit 10.1). Although we present the stages of the marketing research process in a step-by-step progression, of course research does not always, or even usually, happen that way. Researchers go back and forth from one step to another as the need arises. For example, marketers may establish a specific research objective, which they follow with data collection and preliminary analysis. If they uncover new information during the collection step or if the findings of the analysis spotlight new research needs, they might redefine their objectives and begin again from a new starting point. Another important requirement before embarking on a research project is to plan the entire project in advance. By planning the entire research process prior to starting the project, researchers can avoid unnecessary alterations to the research plan as they move through the process.

Marketing Research Process Step 1: Defining the Objectives and Research Needs

Because research is both expensive and time-consuming, it is important to establish in advance exactly what problem needs to be solved. For example, Adding Value 10.1 details how, McDonald's conducted careful research in its effort to address a critical consumer concern: breakfast service that used to end before noon. In general, marketers must clearly define the objectives of their marketing research project.

Consider a scenario: McDonald's is the global leader in the fast-food market, with more than 36,000 stores in more than 100 countries, earning close to $30 billion in annual revenues.[8] But it wants a better understanding of its customers' experience. It also needs to understand how customers view the experience at Wendy's, a main competitor, operating in 30 countries and earning approximately $2 billion in annual revenues, even after Wendy's discontinued its breakfast menu.[9] Finally, McDonald's hopes to gain some insight into how it should set a price for and market its latest combo meal of a hamburger, fries, and drink. Any one of these questions could initiate a research project. The complexity of the project that the company eventually undertakes depends on how much time and resources it has available, as well as the amount of in-depth knowledge it needs.

Researchers assess the value of a project through a careful comparison of the benefits of answering some of their questions and the costs associated with conducting the research. When researchers have determined what information they need in order to address a particular problem or issue, the next step is to design a research project to meet those objectives.

Marketing Research Process Step 2: Designing the Research

The second step in the marketing research project involves design. In this step, researchers identify the type of data needed and determine the research necessary to collect them. Recall that the objectives of the project drive the type of data needed, as outlined in Step 1.

Let's look at how this second step works, using the McDonald's customer experience. McDonald's needs to ask its customers about their McDonald's experience. However, because people don't always tell the whole truth in surveys, the company also may want to observe customers to see how they actually enter the stores, interact

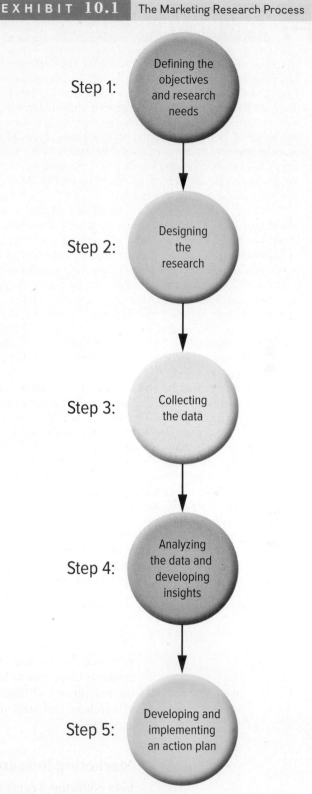

EXHIBIT 10.1 The Marketing Research Process

Step 1: Defining the objectives and research needs

Step 2: Designing the research

Step 3: Collecting the data

Step 4: Analyzing the data and developing insights

Step 5: Developing and implementing an action plan

LO10-1 Identify the five steps in the marketing research process.

Adding Value 10.1 A Key Motivation for Waking Teens Early on Weekends Disappears: Breakfast All Day at McDonald's[i]

Once upon a time, McDonald's did not offer any breakfast: no pancakes, no links, no nothing. Then in 1973 it introduced the Egg McMuffin, and today it generates almost a quarter of its revenues from its breakfast offerings. But since that introduction, one persistent problem had plagued night owls and morning laggards: Breakfast stopped at 10:30 a.m. sharp. After years of listening to complaints—and especially in the social media age, where consumers could communicate their desire for all-day breakfast directly to the company—McDonald's decided to make the dream a reality.

Following several years of research into what changes would be required, including test runs in limited markets, a "Breakfast After Midnight" initiative, and continued solicitations of feedback from customers, McDonald's announced that its entire breakfast menu would be available all day in all of its locations. Following the announcement, and before the change even was instituted, research into consumer perceptions of fast-food outlets showed that McDonald's score has increased. Simply hearing that McDonald's was going to go to a full-day breakfast enabled the chain to improve its perceptions among consumers, surpassing competitors such as Burger King and Taco Bell.

By the time it had finished collecting all these data, McDonald's believed it had powerful evidence to support its latest menu expansion. Despite the strong research-based evidence though, some franchisees still complained that the move imposed significant burdens on them. Store operators worried that McDonald's had paid so much attention to its customer research that it forgot to research how stores would be able to increase their capacity to prep and sell hotcakes alongside burgers throughout the entire day. In response, the corporate offices can point to research that shows the increasing presence of breakfast items as a percentage of total sales. That is, by selling breakfast foods, the local restaurants are likely to increase their overall sales. Thus the menu expansion has

After years of research, McDonald's now offers breakfast all day.

© Vivien Killilea/Getty Images

been valuable and beneficial pretty much across the board: for hungry consumers, franchisees that can sell more meals, and the national chain that listened to what its customers were asking for—and as a result is enjoying an improved image.

The challenge is capacity. According to one franchise owner, because McDonald's continues to ask employees to use toasters and griddles to prepare its fast-food offerings—rather than faster options such as microwaves—selling breakfast and dinner items simultaneously would strain the preparation capabilities of stores. Furthermore, McDonald's has already expanded its menu into other categories, such as wraps and salads. Perhaps adding another entire category of items would overly tax the busy employees.

with employees, and consume the product. The project's design might begin with available data, such as information that shows that people with children often come into the restaurants at lunchtime and order Happy Meals. Then McDonald's marketing researchers can start to ask customers specific questions about their McDonald's experience.

Marketing Research Process Step 3: Collecting the Data

Data collection begins only after the research design process. Based on the design of the project, data can be collected from secondary or primary data sources. **Secondary data** are pieces of information that have been collected prior to the start of the focal research project. Secondary data include external as well as internal data sources. **Primary data**, in contrast, are those data collected to address specific research needs. Some common primary data collection methods include focus groups, in-depth interviews, and surveys.

If McDonald's were to do research to better understand its customers' experience, it would study both the McDonald's experience (left) and that of its major competitors, like Wendy's (right).

(Left): © David Paul Morris/Getty Images; (right): © Jay Laprete/Bloomberg/Getty Images

For our hypothetical fast-food scenario, McDonald's may decide to get relevant secondary data from external providers such as National Purchase Diary Panel and Nielsen. The data might include the prices paid for menu items, sales figures, sales growth or decline in the category, and advertising and promotional spending. McDonald's is likely to gather pertinent data about sales from its franchisees. However, it also wants competitor data, overall food consumption data, and other information about the quick-service restaurant category, which it likely obtains from appropriate syndicated data providers. Based on the data, it might decide to follow up with some primary data using a survey.

No company can ask every customer his or her opinion or observe every customer, so researchers must choose a group of customers who represent the customers of interest, or a **sample**, and then generalize their opinions to describe all customers with the same characteristics. They may choose the sample participants at random to represent the entire customer market. Or they may choose to select the sample on the basis of some characteristic, such as their age, so they can research how Millennials experience buying Value Meals.

Marketing researchers use various methods of asking ques-
tions to measure the issues they are tackling. In our hypothetical McDonald's scenario, assume the research team has developed a questionnaire (see Exhibit 10.2), using a few different types of questions. Section A measures the customer's experience in McDonald's, Section B measures the customer's experience in Wendy's, Section C measures the customer's habits at McDonald's, and Section D measures customer demographics.[10]

Marketing Research Process Step 4: Analyzing the Data and Developing Insights

The next step in the marketing research process—analyzing and interpreting the data—should be both thorough and methodical. To generate meaningful information, researchers analyze and make use of the collected data. Superior Service 10.1 details how universities leverage

*McDonald's assesses its customers' market experience by examin-
ing available data and then asks customers about their experience with products such as Value Meals.*

© Michael J. Hruby

EXHIBIT 10.2	A Hypothetical Fast-Food Survey

Please Evaluate Your Experience at McDonald's

A. McDonald's	Strongly Disagree 1	Disagree 2	Neither Agree nor Disagree 3	Agree 4	Strongly Agree 5
McDonald's food tastes good	☐	☐	☐	☐	☐
McDonald's is clean	☐	☐	☐	☐	☐
McDonald's has low prices	☐	☐	☐	☐	☐

B. Wendy's	Strongly Disagree 1	Disagree 2	Neither Agree nor Disagree 3	Agree 4	Strongly Agree 5
Wendy's food tastes good	☐	☐	☐	☐	☐
Wendy's is clean	☐	☐	☐	☐	☐
Wendy's has low prices	☐	☐	☐	☐	☐

C. McDonald's

	Never	1–2 times	3–4 times	More than 5 times
In the last month, how many times have you been to McDonald's?	☐	☐	☐	☐
In the last month, how often did you order breakfast items at McDonald's?	☐	☐	☐	☐
If McDonald's offered breakfast items all the time, how often would you order them outside of normal breakfast times in a typical month?	☐	☐	☐	☐

On average, how much do you spend each visit at McDonald's? $_____

What is your favorite item at McDonald's?   _____

D. Please tell us about yourself

	Under 16	17–24	25–35	36+
What is your age?	☐	☐	☐	☐

	Male	Female		
What is your gender?	☐	☐		

the data they gain from students' uses of on-campus gyms and facilities to discover new insights into both what students want and how the schools can help them succeed. In this context, **data** can be defined as raw numbers or other factual information that, on their own, have limited value to marketers. However, when the data are interpreted, they become **information**, which results from organizing, analyzing, and interpreting data and putting them into a form that is useful to marketing decision makers. For example, a checkout scanner in the grocery store collects sales data about individual consumer purchases. Not until those data are categorized and examined do they provide

Superior Service 10.1

Did You Hit the Weights or Swim a Lap Today? Your University Wants to Know—For a Good Reason[ii]

When universities and colleges announce the opening of a new sports facility or recreational center, students might feel reassured that their "student activity fees" have gone to good use. But to prove it, the schools are stepping up their efforts to learn exactly how and when students use these services, which enables them to offer the elements that students demand as well as justify their capital expenditures.

By tracking student usage, the schools gather a wealth of valuable data that inform their next steps. For example, students at the University of Florida had begun complaining that their activity fee was too high. When the school reviewed the data showing who was using its health facilities, it realized that graduate students came around 7:00 a.m., when the gym opened, but undergraduates did not. When it moved the opening an hour earlier to 6:00 a.m., undergraduates flooded the facility, because they still had enough time to get in a workout, shower, and make their early morning classes. In addition, complaints about the fees dropped off, because the students believed they were getting their money's worth.

For North Carolina State University in Raleigh, the usage data showed that far more students were taking fitness classes than were joining intramural sports teams. Thus, the rec center cut back the resources it allocated to intramurals and tripled the number of fitness classes, making sure that it offered what its students wanted, when and where they wanted it.

The GymFlow app available through the University of California Los Angeles shows school administrators how many people are using each section of its gym at different times. In addition, it tabulates exactly how many students and employees—43,734—visited the center in a year. With this information, UCLA was able to show critics that its expenditures were worthwhile. For students, the same app reveals when their favorite piece of equipment is being used by lots of others, as well as when the quiet times are at the facility.

Purdue went a step beyond tracking usage to link exercise with scholastic performance. When it built a $98 million facility, not everyone thought it was a good idea. But the university was able to demonstrate that students who swiped their ID cards to access the gym also earned higher grade point averages than did students who never came to work out. In a parallel study, a professor investigated the attitudes of participants in one of the gym's kickboxing classes and found that regular participants indicated substantially lower stress levels.

It might seem strange that a school would keep track of when its students are running around the track. But in truth, the information it gathers is valuable for justifying its resource allocations as well as determining future investments in services for students.

Research at North Carolina State University showed that more students were taking fitness classes than were joining intramural sports teams, so the university tripled the number of fitness classes offered.

© Phovoir/Shutterstock RF

EXHIBIT 10.3   Survey Results for McDonald's and Wendy's

■ Wendy's
■ McDonald's

(bar chart with y-axis from 1 to 5; categories: Cleanliness, Taste, Low price)

information about which products and services were purchased together or how an in-store promotional activity translated into sales.

For the McDonald's example, we can summarize the results of the survey (from Exhibit 10.2) in Exhibit 10.3. Both McDonald's and Wendy's scored the same on the cleanliness of their restaurants, but McDonald's had lower prices, whereas Wendy's food tasted better. McDonald's may want to improve the taste of its food, without raising prices too much, to compete more effectively with Wendy's.

Marketing Research Process Step 5: Developing and Implementing an Action Plan

In the final phase in the marketing research process, the analyst prepares the results and presents them to the appropriate decision makers, who undertake appropriate marketing strategies. A typical marketing research presentation includes an executive summary, the body of the report (which discusses the research objectives, methodology used, and detailed findings), the conclusions, the limitations, and appropriate supplemental tables, figures, and appendixes.

In the McDonald's hypothetical scenario, according to the research findings, the company is doing fine in terms of cleanliness (comparable to its competitors) and is perceived to have lower prices, but the taste of its food could be improved. It also found that of those customers who purchased breakfast items relatively frequently (at least three times per month), 35 percent would go for breakfast outside the normal breakfast times frequently. Also, of those who never ordered breakfast items, 25 percent would order breakfast items outside the normal breakfast times occasionally (at least once a month). Using this analysis and the related insights gained, McDonald's might consider hiring some gourmet chefs as consultants to improve the menu and offerings.[11] It then could highlight its efforts to improve the taste of the food and add desired offerings (e.g., breakfast items) through marketing communications and promotions. McDonald's also should consider undertaking additional pricing research to determine whether its lower prices enhance sales and profits or whether it could increase its prices and still compete effectively with Wendy's.

McDonald's marketing research will show how to better compete against Wendy's.

© Michael Neelon/Alamy

Now let's take a closer look at sources of secondary and primary data.

PROGRESS CHECK

1. What are the steps in the marketing research process?
2. What is the difference between data and information?

SECONDARY DATA

 LO10-2 Describe the various secondary data sources.

A marketing research project often begins with a review of the relevant secondary data. Secondary data might come from free or very inexpensive external sources such as census data, information from trade associations, and reports published in magazines. Although readily accessible, these inexpensive sources may not be specific or timely enough to solve the marketer's research needs and objectives. Firms also can purchase more specific or applicable secondary data from specialized research firms. Finally, secondary sources can be accessed through internal sources, including the company's sales invoices, customer lists, and other reports generated by the company itself.

In political settings, such secondary data can be critical for candidates running for office. Both major political parties thus have developed proprietary databases that contain vast information about voters, broken down by demographic and geographic information. Before a local politician, canvasser, or poll taker even knocks on doors in a neighborhood, he or she likely knows which houses are inhabited by retirees, who has a subscription to *The Wall Street Journal* or *The New York Times,* for whom the residents said they voted in the last election, or whether they served in the military. All these traits can give hints about the voters' likely concerns, which a good politician can address immediately upon knocking on the door. Such research also can dictate tactics for designing broader campaign materials or to zero in on very specific issues. Social media campaigns are a growing mechanism used to interact with potential voters in a more timely manner than is possible with more traditional methods. Monitoring tweets after a major address by a candidate, for instance, would provide instant feedback and direction for future communications.

Inexpensive External Secondary Data

Some sources of external secondary data can be quickly accessed at a relatively low cost. The U.S. Bureau of the Census (http://www.census.gov), for example, provides data about businesses by county and zip code. If you wanted to open a new location for a business you are already operating, such data might help you determine the size of your potential market.

Often, however, inexpensive data sources are not adequate to meet researchers' needs. Because the data initially were acquired for some purpose other than the research question at hand, they may not be completely relevant or timely. The U.S. Census is a great source of demographic data about a particular market area, and it can be easily accessed at a low cost. However, the data are collected only at the beginning of every decade, so they quickly become outdated. If an entrepreneur wanted to open a retail flooring store in 2017, for example, the data would already be seven years old, and the housing market likely would be stronger than it was in 2010. Researchers must also pay careful attention to how other sources of inexpensive secondary data were collected. Despite the great deal of data available on the Internet, easy access does not ensure that the data are trustworthy.

Syndicated External Secondary Data

Although the secondary data described previously are either free or inexpensively obtained, marketers can purchase external secondary data called **syndicated data**, which are available for a fee from commercial research firms such as IRI, the National Purchase Diary Panel, and

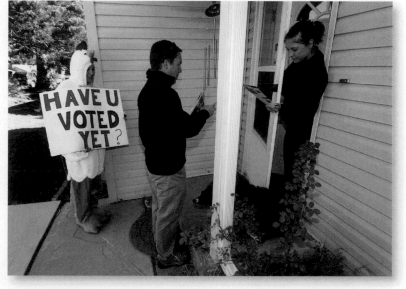

Secondary data are useful to politicians so they know who they are talking to before they knock on any doors.
© Cathleen Allison/AP Photo

EXHIBIT 10.4	Syndicated Data Providers and Some of Their Services
Name	**Services Provided**
Nielsen (http://www.nielsen.com)	With its *Market Measurement Services*, the company tracks the sales of consumer packaged goods, gathered at the point of sale in retail stores of all types and sizes.
IRI (http://www.iriworldwide.com)	*InfoScan* store tracking provides detailed information about sales, share, distribution, pricing, and promotion across a wide variety of retail channels and accounts.
J.D. Power and Associates (http://www.jdpower.com)	Widely known for its automotive ratings, it produces quality and customer satisfaction research for a variety of industries.
Mediamark Research Inc. (http://www.mediamark.com)	Supplies multimedia audience research pertaining to media and marketing planning for advertised brands.
National Purchase Diary Panel (http://www.npd.com)	Based on detailed records consumers keep about their purchases (i.e., a diary), it provides information about product movement and consumer behavior in a variety of industries.
NOP World (http://www.nopworld.com)	The *mKids US* research study tracks mobile telephone ownership and usage, brand affinities, and entertainment habits of American youth between 12 and 19 years of age.
Research and Markets (http://www.researchandmarkets.com)	Promotes itself as a one-stop shop for market research and data from most leading publishers, consultants, and analysts.
Roper Center for Public Opinion Research (http://www.ropercenter.uconn.edu)	The *General Social Survey* is one of the nation's longest running surveys of social, cultural, and political indicators.
Simmons Market Research Bureau (http://www.smrb.com)	Reports on the products American consumers buy, the brands they prefer, and their lifestyles, attitudes, and media preferences.
Yankelovich (http://thefuturescompany.com/products/us-yankelovich-monitor/)	The *MONITOR* tracks consumer attitudes, values, and lifestyles shaping the American marketplace.

Nielsen. Exhibit 10.4 contains information about various firms that provide syndicated data.

Consumer packaged-goods firms that sell to wholesalers often lack the means to gather pertinent data directly from the retailers that sell their products to consumers, which makes syndicated data a valuable resource for them. Some syndicated data providers also offer information about shifting brand preferences and product usage in households, which they gather from scanner data, consumer panels—and several other cutting-edge methods, as detailed in Social and Mobile Marketing 10.1.

Scanner data are used in quantitative research obtained from scanner readings of Universal Product Code (UPC) labels at checkout counters. Whenever you go into your local grocery store, your purchases are rung up using scanner systems. The data from these purchases are likely to be acquired by leading marketing research firms such as IRI or Nielsen, which use this information to help leading consumer packaged-goods firms (e.g., Kellogg's, Pepsi, Kraft) assess what is happening in the marketplace. For example, a firm can use scanner data to determine what would happen to its sales if it reduced the price of its least popular product by 10 percent in a given month. In the test market in which it lowers the price, do sales increase, decrease, or stay the same?

Social & Mobile Marketing 10.1

Nielsen Seeks to Track Viewership, Regardless of the Media People Use to Watch[iii]

As television viewers have changed their practices—such that more and more people catch the latest shows on their tablets or smartphones rather than home-based television screens—marketing researchers have unfortunately failed to keep up. For example, Nielsen, the most famous provider of ratings that reflect people's viewing patterns, maintained two separate measures: one for regular television and one for online viewing. It had no metric for views through other forms of streaming media.

That gap may be about to disappear, though. In the immediate future, Nielsen plans to introduce a Twitter-based measure that will assess the number of tweets about a show as a measure of popularity. Its initial metric suggests that every tweet represents about 50 people watching the show, regardless of where or how. The new system is similar to the collaboration that we described in Chapter 3 between Billboard and Twitter, which charts tweets about music and musicians in an effort to provide new research insights into trends and listeners' preferences.

Nielsen also plans to introduce a mobile-linked measurement system. With this proprietary method, Nielsen will enable the networks to issue their content through mobile applications that contain a preexisting link back to Nielsen's data collection methods. When a viewer downloads the app with the content, Nielsen knows it and can add that viewership to the show's and its network's ratings.

Such measures are critical for content providers, because ratings determine advertising sales and rates. A show or network with higher ratings attracts more potential advertisers and can charge more. In recent months, when the traditional ratings formats showed that viewership was declining, advertisers grew concerned. At the same time, the networks protested loudly that the ratings were undercutting the extent of their true market by ignoring the people watching on their tablets.

Nielsen's moves seek to address those complaints, but they also have sparked some new concerns. In particular, insufficient evidence exists to confirm whether Twitter numbers are really a good representation of viewership. Without strong support for the link between tweets and the actual popularity of a show, the new measure might be meaningless. In addition, some observers suggest that it could be blocked by security features in Apple operating systems that prevent metering software from running simultaneously with other programs.

Thus marketing researchers face a problem without a ready solution. They know that consumers are moving away from their televisions, but they have no perfect way to measure what they do after those viewers move.

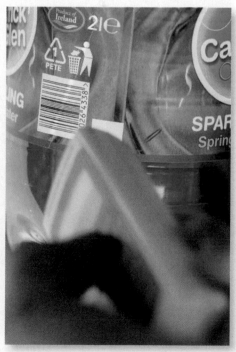

Syndicated external secondary data are acquired from scanner data obtained from scanner readings of UPC codes at checkout counters (left) and from panel data collected from consumers that electronically record their purchases (right).

Panel data are information collected from a group of consumers, organized into panels, over time. Data collected from panelists often include their records of what they have purchased (i.e., secondary data) as well as their responses to survey questions that the client gives to the panel firm to ask the panelists (i.e., primary data). Secondary panel data thus might show that when Diet Pepsi is offered at a deep discount, 80 percent of usual Diet Coke consumers switch to Diet Pepsi. Primary panel data could give insights into what they think of each option. We discuss further how marketing researchers use scanner and panel data to answer specific research questions in the primary data section.

Overall, both panel and scanner data, as well as their more advanced methods gathered through social media and online usage patterns, provide firms with a comprehensive picture of what consumers are buying or not buying. The key difference between scanner research and panel research is how the data are aggregated. Scanner research typically focuses on weekly consumption of a particular product at a given unit of analysis (e.g., individual store, chain, region); panel research focuses on the total weekly consumption by a particular person or household.

Internal Secondary Data

Internally, companies also generate a tremendous amount of secondary data from their day-to-day operations. One of the most valuable resources such firms have at their disposal is their rich cache of customer information and purchase history. However, it can be difficult to make sense of the millions and even billions of pieces of individual data, which are stored in large computer files called **data warehouses**. For this reason, firms find it necessary to use data mining techniques to extract valuable information from their databases.

Data mining uses a variety of statistical analysis tools to uncover previously unknown patterns in the data or relationships among variables. Some retailers try to customize their product and service offerings to match the needs of their customers. For instance, the U.K. grocer Tesco uses its loyalty card to collect massive amounts of information about its individual customers. Every time a loyalty card member buys something, the card is scanned and the store captures key purchase data specific to that member. But these specific data are basically useless until Tesco mines and analyzes them to identify, for instance, three income groups: upscale, middle income, and less affluent. With this mined information, Tesco has been able to create appealing private-label product offerings for each group, according to their preferences, and has begun targeting promotions to each customer according to his or her income classification.

Data mining can also enable a home improvement retailer such as Lowe's to learn that 25 percent of the time its customers buy a garden hose, they also purchase a sprinkler. With such information, the retailer may decide to put the garden hoses next to the sprinklers in the store. Outside the retail realm, an investment firm might use statistical techniques to group clients according to their income, age, type of securities purchased, and prior investment experience. This categorization identifies different segments to which the firm can offer valuable packages that meet their specific needs. The firm also can tailor separate marketing programs to each of these segments.

By analyzing the enormous amount of information that they possess about customers, companies have developed

Marketers use data mining techniques to determine what items people buy at the same time so they can be promoted and displayed together.

© B2M Productions/Photographer's Choice/Getty Images RF

statistical models that help identify when a customer is dissatisfied with his or her service. Once the company identifies an unhappy customer, it can follow up and proactively address that customer's issues. By mining customer data and information, the company also reduces its churn levels. Churn is the number of participants who discontinue use of a service, divided by the average number of total participants. With this knowledge, the company can focus on what it does best and improve potential problem areas. Overall, firms hope to use data mining to generate customer-based analytics that they can apply to their strategic decision making and thereby make good customers better and better customers their best.

Big Data The field of marketing research has seen enormous changes in the last few years because of (1) the increase in the amounts of data to which retailers, service providers, and manufacturers have access; (2) their ability to collect these data from transactions, customer relationship management (CRM) systems, websites, and social media platforms that firms increasingly use to engage with their customers;[12] (3) the ease of collecting and storing these data; (4) the computing ability readily available to manipulate data in real time; and (5) access to in-house or available software to convert the data into valuable decision-making insights using analytic dashboards.

To specify this explosion of data, which firms have access to but cannot handle using conventional data management and data mining software, the term big data has arisen in the popular media. Leading firms such as Amazon, Netflix, Google, Nordstrom, Kroger, Tesco, Macy's, American Express, and Walmart already are converting their big data into customer insights—and the list of firms keeps growing.[13]

Amazon may be the poster child for big data. Any Amazon shopper is familiar with its recommendation engine, which notes what the consumer is purchasing, analyzes purchase patterns by similar customers, suggests other items the customer might enjoy, and indicates what other people who bought the focal item also added to their shopping carts.[14] With more than 200 million active customers and billions of pieces of shopping data,[15] Amazon certainly qualifies as a big data user; its item-to-item collaborative filtering helps it determine which relevant products to suggest, generating almost one-third of its sales.[16]

The U.K. grocery retailer Tesco processes its data at a rate of approximately 100 customer baskets per second, to cover its 6 million daily transactions.[17] Furthermore, each purchased product can feature up to 45 data attributes: Is it Tesco's own brand, an ethnic recipe, exotic (e.g., star fruit) or basic (e.g., apple), and so on? On the basis of the attributes of the items customers purchase, Tesco filters them to define who they are, who else lives in their household, and what hobbies they have, then provides specific incentives that match these characteristics.[18]

To enable these efforts, firms such as SAP, Splunk, and GoodData offer a host of software solutions to help firms better integrate their data, visualize them, and then move from data to real-time insights.[19] The suite of options previously were available only to the largest firms, but falling costs mean they are now more accessible to smaller firms.

The big data explosion also stems from the growth of online and social media. In response, Google, Facebook, and Twitter all provide analytic dashboards designed to help their customers understand their own web traffic. In particular, Google has developed tremendous marketing analytical capabilities that it makes available to partner firms. Google helps firms attract customer traffic to their sites through the use of more relevant keywords, the purchase of Google AdWords, and better conversion methods.[20] Using Google Analytics, Puma has gained insights into which online content and products most engaged its web visitors, while also defining where these visitors lived. With these visitor behavioral data in hand, Puma has revised its website to be more dynamic (http://www.Puma.com) and has created unique identifiers for its various product categories (e.g., PUMA Golf), targeting them in accordance with the home region of the visitor.[21]

As Marketing Analytics 10.1 explains, sometimes the "internal" data can be gathered by a partner firm too, providing deeper insights than an individual firm can derive.

Marketing Analytics 10.1   Google Analytics Promises Movie Studios the Ability to Predict Performance Weeks Prior to Opening[iv]

A lot of movie watchers searching for the trailer for a film in the month before the movie opens means a bigger opening weekend. Such a claim might seem somewhat self-evident, but Google has announced that it has the means to quantify this effect and thereby help movie studios predict their profits up to a month prior to the opening day.

More precisely, Google asserts that search volume for the movie title (combined with a few other metrics, such as the season and whether the movie is a franchise) offers a 94 percent accurate prediction of box office performance.

Other proprietary information that Google can use to predict success is the volume of clicks on search ads. If, for example, one movie prompted 20,000 more paid clicks than another film did, it will bring in approximately $7.5 million more in revenues during its opening weekend. Furthermore, the search effects are not limited to Google; YouTube searches reveal similar predictive information. From its analysis, Google recommends that studios need to go beyond just a one-week window, because studying the search and click trends for a month increases the accuracy and power of its predictions significantly.

Moving beyond the implications for opening weekend, Google asserts that weekday searches in the weeks leading up to the release offer better predictors of continued revenues. That is, if a film fan searches for a movie title on a Tuesday, she or he is more likely to hold off on seeing the movie rather than rushing out during opening weekend. On a related note, Google says that nearly half of all moviegoers choose the film they will see that night on the same day. Thus, studios need to maintain a marketing presence far past opening day, to be sure to catch the laggard customers' attention.

But unless the movie is a big name, an anticipated release, or a franchise, most people have no idea of what is coming to their local cineplex. Instead, during weeks without a major movie release, Google notes that consumers undertake more generic searches to gather information about what new movies might be available. On average, these film buffs consider 13 sources of information before they select a specific film to watch.

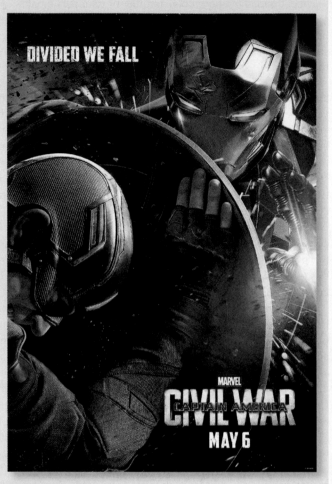

Google analytics are increasingly used to predict the success of movies.

© Marvel Entertainment Pictures/Zuma Press, Inc./Alamy

PROGRESS CHECK

1. What is the difference between internal and external secondary research?

LO10-3 Describe the various primary data collection techniques.

PRIMARY DATA COLLECTION TECHNIQUES

In many cases, the information researchers need is available only through primary data or data collected to address specific research needs. Depending on the nature of the research problem, the primary data collection method can employ a *qualitative* or a *quantitative* research method.

EXHIBIT 10.5   Qualitative versus Quantitative Data Collection

Qualitative research   Quantitative research

Observation   In-depth interviews   Data collection research   Experiments   Survey

Focus groups   Social media   Scanner   Panel

As its name implies, **qualitative research** uses broad, open-ended questions to understand the phenomenon of interest. It provides initial information that helps the researcher more clearly formulate the research objectives. Qualitative research is more informal than quantitative research methods and includes observation, following social media sites, in-depth interviews, and focus groups (see Exhibit 10.5, left side).

Once the firm has gained insights from doing qualitative research, it is likely to engage in **quantitative research**, which are structured responses that can be statistically tested. Quantitative research provides information needed to confirm insights and hypotheses generated via qualitative research or secondary data. It also helps managers pursue appropriate courses of action. Formal studies such as specific experiments, surveys, scanner and panel data, or some combination of these are quantitative in nature (see Exhibit 10.5, right side). We now examine each of these primary data collection techniques in order.

Observation

Observation entails examining purchase and consumption behaviors through personal or video camera scrutiny, or by tracking customers' movements electronically as they move through a store. For example, researchers might observe customers while they shop or when they go about their daily lives, during which processes they use a variety of products. Observation can last for a very brief period of time (e.g., two hours watching teenagers shop for clothing in the mall), or it may take days or weeks (e.g., researchers live with families to observe their use of products). When consumers are unable to articulate their experiences, observation research becomes particularly useful; how else could researchers determine which educational toys babies choose to play with or confirm details of the buying process that consumers might not be able to recall accurately?

Although traditionally firms might videotape customers' movements, Microsoft's Kinect sensors are providing a less intrusive option. Discretely embedded in aisles of retail stores, the sensors provide three-dimensional spatial recognition. Thus retailers and their

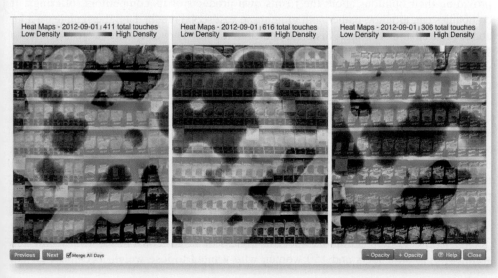

Using Microsoft Kinect sensors, firms like Shopperception create heatmaps of shopper interactions with the products (touches, pickups, and returns). The red represents the hot zones where shoppers touch the most, yellow less, and blue not at all.

Source: Shopperception

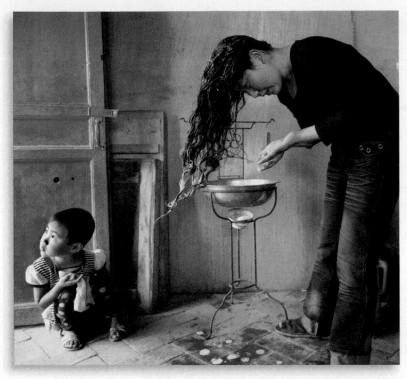

By watching women in rural China wash their hair, Procter & Gamble learned that even their poorest customers wanted beautiful hair, but it has to be packaged affordably.

© Benjamin Lowy/Getty Images

suppliers can unobtrusively track the amount of time people spend in front of a shelf, which products they touch or pick up, the products they return to shelves, and finally what they add to their carts and purchase.[22] The data gathered can be used to improve store layouts because they can identify causes of slow-selling merchandise, such as poor shelf placement. By studying customers' movements, marketers can also learn where customers pause or move quickly or where there is congestion. This information can help them decide if the layout and merchandise placement is operating as expected, such as whether new or promoted merchandise is getting the attention it deserves.

Observation may be the best—and sometimes the only—method to determine how customers might use a product; therefore it is useful for designing and marketing products. By watching women wash their hair in a rural town in China, Procter & Gamble recognized the fallacy of its assumption that the poorest consumers were interested only in functionality of a product—how to get hair clean. One woman struggled to find ways to wash her long hair effectively, even in the face of severe water shortages, rather than cut off what she considered the source of her beauty. Based on its research, P&G has added value by selling Rejoice shampoo inexpensively ($1.50) to a market that was using alternative options such as laundry detergent. Other observations pushed P&G to develop a more skin-sensitive laundry detergent after noting how many people in developing markets wash their clothes by hand.[23] These insights might be helpful, both for the company that gathers them and for consumers who ultimately benefit from better products.

Social Media

Social media sites are a booming source of data for marketers. Marketers have realized that social media can provide valuable information that could aid their marketing research and strategy endeavors. In particular, contributors to social media sites rarely are shy about providing their opinions about the firm's own products or its competitors' offerings. If companies can monitor, gather, and mine these vast social media data, they can learn a lot about their customers' likes, dislikes, and preferences. They then might cross-reference such social media commentary with consumers' past purchases to derive a better sense of what they want. Customers also appear keen to submit their opinions about their friends' purchases, interests, polls, and blogs.

Blogs in particular represent valuable sources of marketing research insights. Marketers are paying attention to online reviews about everything from restaurants to running shoes to recycling. *The Truth About Cars* blog is known for its unflinchingly objective reviews of various makes and models as well as discussions about the industry as a whole, marketing tactics, and global competition, among other topics.[24] Analyzing the content of this and similar blogs provides an excellent source of ideas and information for auto industry executives. Another creative use of social media for market research involves building online communities for companies. When it considered the launch of its South Beach product line, Kraft hired Communispace to create a **virtual community** (an online network of people who communicate about specific topics) of target consumers: 150 health and wellness opinion leaders and 150 women who wanted to lose weight became a virtual community. The participants openly shared their frustrations and difficulties managing their weight because the community environment prompted them to sense that everyone else on the site struggled with similar issues and concerns. By monitoring the community, Kraft learned that it would need to educate consumers about the South Beach Diet and offer products that could address cravings throughout the day, not just at mealtimes. Six months after the line's introduction, Kraft had earned profits of $100 million.[25]

When Kraft considered the launch of its South Beach product line, it created a virtual community of health and wellness opinion leaders and women who wanted to lose weight.

© Michael J. Hruby

Noting these various opportunities and marketing research sources online, many companies—including Ford Motor Co., PepsiCo, Coca-Cola, and Southwest Airlines—have added heads of social media to their management teams. These managers take responsibility for scanning the web for blogs, postings, tweets, or Facebook posts in which customers mention their experience with a brand. By staying abreast of this continuous stream of information, companies can gather the most up-to-date news about their company, products, and services as well as their competitors. These social media searches allow companies to learn about customers' perceptions and resolve customer complaints they may never have heard about through other channels.

The data gathered through the searches also undergo careful analyses: Are customer sentiments generally positive, negative, or neutral? What sort of intensity or interest levels do they imply? How many customers are talking about the firm's products, and how many focus instead on competitors'? This data analysis is understandably challenging, considering the amount of data available online. However, monitoring consumer sentiments has grown easier with the development of social media monitoring platforms.

Using a technique known as sentiment mining, firms collect consumer comments about companies and their products on social media sites such as Facebook, Twitter, and online blogs. The data are then analyzed to distill customer attitudes toward and preferences for products and advertising campaigns. Scouring millions of sites by combining automated online search tools with text analysis techniques, sentiment mining yields qualitative data that provide new insight into what consumers really think. Companies plugged into this real-time information can become more nimble, allowing for quick changes in a product rollout or a new advertising campaign.[26]

In-Depth Interviews

Although relatively expensive, in-depth interviews can reveal information that would be difficult to obtain with other methods.

© Jeff Greenberg/agefotostock

In an in-depth interview, trained researchers ask questions and listen to and record the answers and then pose additional questions to clarify or expand on a particular issue. For

instance, in addition to simply watching teenagers shop for apparel, interviewers might stop them one at a time in the mall to ask them a few questions, such as: "We noticed that you went into and came out of Abercrombie & Fitch very quickly without buying anything. Why was that?" If the subject responds that no one had bothered to wait on her, the interviewer might ask a follow-up question like, "Oh? Has that happened to you before?" or "Do you expect more sales assistance there?"

In-depth interviews provide insights that help managers better understand the nature of their industry as well as important trends and consumer preferences, which can be invaluable for developing marketing strategies. Specifically, they can establish a historical context for the phenomenon of interest, particularly when they include industry experts or experienced consumers. They also can communicate how people really feel about a product or service at the individual level. Finally, marketers can use the results of in-depth interviews to develop surveys.

In-depth interviews are, however, relatively expensive and time-consuming. The interview cost depends on the length of the interaction and the characteristics of the people included in the sample. If the sample must feature medical doctors, for example, the costs of getting sufficient interviews will be much higher than the costs associated with intercepting teenagers in a mall.

Focus Group Interviews

In **focus group interviews**, a small group of people (usually 8 to 12) come together for an intensive discussion about a particular topic. Using an unstructured method of inquiry, a trained moderator guides the conversation according to a predetermined, general outline of topics of interest. Researchers usually record the interactions by videotape or audiotape so they can carefully comb through the interviews later to catch any patterns of verbal or nonverbal responses. In particular, focus groups gather qualitative data about initial reactions to a new or existing product or service, opinions about different competitive offerings, or reactions to marketing stimuli, such as a new ad campaign or point-of-purchase display materials.[27]

To obtain new information to help it continue its innovative success derived from its introduction of low-sodium choices, Campbell Soup conducted extensive focus groups with female shoppers who indicated they would buy ready-to-eat soups. The groups clearly revealed the women's top priorities: a nutritious soup that contained the ingredients they would use if they made soup. They wanted, for example, white meat chicken, fresh vegetables, and sea salt. In addition, focus group participants were equally clear about what they did *not* want, like high fructose corn syrup, MSG, and other ingredients whose names they could not even pronounce.[28]

The growth of online technology, as well as computer and video capabilities, have provided tremendous benefits for focus group research, which now often takes place online. Online focus group firms offer a secure site as a platform for companies to listen in on focus groups and even interact with consumers, without anyone having to travel. The client company not only saves costs but also gains access to a broader range of potential customers who live in various neighborhoods, states, or even countries.

PROGRESS CHECK

1. What are the types of qualitative research?

Survey Research

Arguably the most popular type of quantitative primary collection method is a **survey**—a systematic means of collecting information from people using a questionnaire. A **questionnaire** is a document that features a set of questions designed to gather information from respondents and thereby accomplish the researchers' objectives. Individual questions on a questionnaire can be either unstructured or structured. **Unstructured questions** are open ended and allow respondents to answer in their own words. An unstructured question like "What are the most important characteristics for choosing a brand of shampoo?" yields an unstructured response. However, the same question could be posed to respondents in a structured format by providing a fixed set of response categories, such as price, fragrance, ability to clean, or dandruff control, and then asking respondents to rate the importance of each. **Structured questions** are closed-ended questions for which

EXHIBIT 10.6 Structured versus Unstructured Response

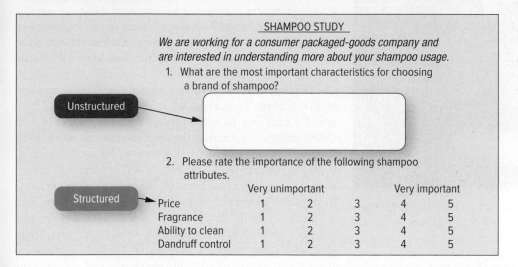

a discrete set of response alternatives, or specific answers, is provided for respondents to evaluate (see Exhibit 10.6).

Developing a questionnaire is part art and part science. The questions must be carefully designed to address the specific set of research questions. Moreover, for a questionnaire to produce meaningful results, its questions cannot be misleading in any fashion (e.g., open to multiple interpretations), and they must address only one issue at a time. They also must be worded in vocabulary that will be familiar and comfortable to those being surveyed. The questions should be sequenced appropriately: general questions first, more specific questions next, and demographic questions at the end. Finally, the layout and appearance of the questionnaire must be professional and easy to follow, with appropriate instructions in suitable places. For some tips on what to avoid when designing a questionnaire, see Exhibit 10.7.[29]

EXHIBIT 10.7 What to Avoid When Designing a Questionnaire

Issue	Good Question	Bad Question
Avoid questions the respondent cannot easily or accurately answer.	When was the last time you went to the grocery store?	How much money did you spend on groceries last month?
Avoid sensitive questions unless they are absolutely necessary.	Do you take vitamins?	Do you dye your gray hair?
Avoid double-barreled questions, which refer to more than one issue with only one set of responses.	1. Do you like to shop for clothing? 2. Do you like to shop for food?	Do you like to shop for clothing and food?
Avoid leading questions, which steer respondents to a particular response, irrespective of their true beliefs.	Please rate how safe you believe a BMW is on a scale of 1 to 10, with 1 being not safe and 10 being very safe.	BMW is the safest car on the road, right?
Avoid one-sided questions that present only one side of the issue.	To what extent do you believe fast food contributes to adult obesity using a five-point scale? 1: Does not contribute 5: Main cause	Fast food is responsible for adult obesity: Agree/Disagree

Survey research uses questionnaires to collect primary data. Questions can be either unstructured or structured.

© Kayte Deioma/PhotoEdit

Similar to focus groups, marketing surveys can be conducted either online or offline, but online marketing surveys offer researchers the chance to develop a database quickly with many responses. Web surveys have steadily grown as a percentage of all quantitative surveys. Online surveys have a lot to offer marketers with tight deadlines and small budgets.[30]

In particular, the response rates for online surveys are relatively high. Typical response rates run from 1 to 2 percent for mail and 10 to 15 percent for phone surveys. For online surveys, in contrast, the response rate can reach 30 to 35 percent or even higher in business-to-business research. It also is inexpensive. Costs likely will continue to fall as users become more familiar with the online survey process. Results are processed and received quickly. Reports and summaries can be developed in real time and delivered directly to managers in simple, easy-to-digest reports, complete with color, graphics, and charts. Traditional phone or mail surveys require laborious data collection, tabulation, summary, and distribution before anyone can grasp their results.

Diverse online survey software, such as Qualtrics, SurveyMonkey, and Zoomerang, make it very easy to draft an online survey using questions from existing survey libraries. A survey link can be sent easily in an e-mail to potential respondents or panelists as well as posted on specific sites that are likely to attract the target audience or people who are willing to perform online work (e.g., Amazon's Mechanical Turk Site).

Panel- and Scanner-Based Research

As noted previously, panel and scanner research can be either secondary or primary. An example of the use of a panel to collect primary data would be Walmart's subsidiary Asda, which uses an 18,000-customer panel, called "Pulse of the Nation," to help determine which products to carry. Asda sends e-mails to each participant with product images and descriptions of potential new products. The customers' responses indicate whether they think each product should be carried in stores. As an incentive to participate, Asda enters respondents automatically in a drawing for free prizes.[31]

Walmart's U.K. subsidiary Asda uses an 18,000-customer panel, which it calls "Pulse of the Nation," to help determine which products to carry.

© David Levenson/Alamy

Experimental Research

Experimental research (an **experiment**) is a type of quantitative research that systematically manipulates one or more variables to determine which variables have a causal effect on other variables. For example, in our earlier scenario, one thing the hypothetical McDonald's research team was trying to determine was the most profitable price for a new menu combo item (hamburger, fries, and drink). Assume that the fixed cost of developing the item is $300,000 and the variable cost, which is primarily composed of the cost of the food itself, is $2. McDonald's puts the item on the menu at four prices in four markets. (See Exhibit 10.8.) In general, the more expensive the item, the less it will sell. But by running this experiment, the restaurant chain determines that the most profitable price is the second least expensive ($5). These findings suggest some people may have believed that the most expensive item ($7) was too expensive, so they refused to buy it. The least expensive item ($4) sold fairly well, but McDonald's did not make as much money on each item sold. In this experiment, the changes in price likely caused the

EXHIBIT 10.8 Hypothetical Pricing Experiment for McDonald's

Market	1 Unit Price	2 Market Demand at Price (in Units)	3 Total Revenue (Col. 1 × Col. 2)	4 Total Cost of Units Sold ($300,000 Fixed Cost + $2.00 Variable Cost)	5 Total Profits (Col. 3 − Col. 4)
1	$4	200,000	$800,000	$700,000	$100,000
2	5	150,000	750,000	600,000	150,000
3	6	100,000	600,000	500,000	100,000
4	7	50,000	350,000	400,000	(50,000)

changes in quantities sold and therefore affected the restaurant's profitability.

Firms are also actively using experimental techniques on Facebook. Once a firm has created its Facebook page, it can devise advertisements and rely on Facebook's targeting options to deliver those ads to the most appropriate customer segments. To make sure the communication is just right, companies can experiment with alternative versions and identify which advertisement is most effective, just as Adore Me has done, as we described in the chapter opener. State Bicycle Co., a manufacturer in Arizona, similarly needed to determine what other interests its customers had and who its main competitors were. Therefore, it tested a range of ads targeting customers who searched for different bands (e.g., did more Arcade Fire or Passion Pit fans click their link?) and other bicycle manufacturers. With this information, it devised new contests and offerings on its own homepage to attract more of the visitors who were likely to buy.[32] Facebook tries to help its corporate clients enhance their own customers' engagement and influence through a variety of options: check-ins, asking for customer comments,

Using an experiment, McDonald's would test the price of new menu items to determine which is the most profitable.
© Mary Altaffer/AP Photos

EXHIBIT 10.9 Advantages and Disadvantages of Secondary and Primary Data

Type	Examples	Advantages	Disadvantages
Secondary research	☐ Census data ☐ Sales invoices ☐ Internet information ☐ Books ☐ Journal articles ☐ Syndicated data	☐ Saves time in collecting data because they are readily available ☐ Free or inexpensive (except for syndicated data)	☐ May not be precisely relevant to information needs ☐ Information may not be timely ☐ Sources may not be original, and therefore usefulness is an issue ☐ Methodologies for collecting data may not be appropriate ☐ Data sources may be biased
Primary research	☐ Observed consumer behavior ☐ Focus group interviews ☐ Surveys ☐ Experiments	☐ Specific to the immediate data needs and topic at hand ☐ Offers behavioral insights generally not available from secondary research	☐ Costly ☐ Time-consuming ☐ Requires more sophisticated training and experience to design study and collect data

Facebook analytics help firms increase customer engagement.

Courtesy of True Digital Communications, www.truedigitalcom.com

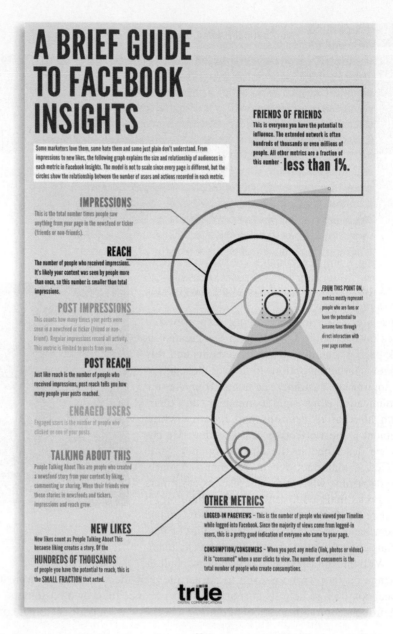

sharing information with friends, and so on.[33] It measures all these forms of data, contributing even further to the information businesses have about their page visitors.

Advantages and Disadvantages of Primary and Secondary Research

Now that we have discussed the various secondary and primary data collection methods, think back over our discussion and ask yourself what seem to be the best applications of each and when you would want to go to secondary sources or use primary collection methods. We can see that both primary data and secondary data have certain inherent and distinct advantages and disadvantages. For a summary of the advantages and disadvantages of each type of research, see Exhibit 10.9.

 LO10-4 Summarize the differences between secondary data and primary data.

PROGRESS CHECK

1. What are the types of quantitative research?
2. What are the advantages and disadvantages of primary and secondary research?

THE ETHICS OF USING CUSTOMER INFORMATION

LO10-5 Examine the circumstances in which collecting information on consumers is ethical.

As we noted in Chapter 4, upholding strong business ethics requires more than a token nod to ethics in the mission statement. A strong ethical orientation must be an integral part of a firm's marketing strategy and decision making. It is particularly important for marketers to adhere to ethical practices when conducting marketing research. The American Marketing Association provides three guidelines for conducting marketing research: (1) It prohibits selling or fund-raising under the guise of conducting research, (2) it supports maintaining research integrity by avoiding misrepresentation or the omission of pertinent research data, and (3) it encourages the fair treatment of clients and suppliers.[34] Numerous codes of conduct written by various marketing research societies all reinforce the duty of researchers to respect the rights of the subjects in the course of their research. The bottom line: Marketing research should be used only to produce unbiased, factual information.

As technology continues to advance, the potential threats to consumers' personal information grow in number and intensity. Ethical and Societal Dilemma 10.1 discusses an interesting example of how retailers are using mannequins with hidden cameras to monitor shoppers. Marketing researchers must be vigilant to avoid abusing their access to these data. From charitable giving to medical records to Internet tracking, consumers are more anxious than ever about preserving their fundamental right to privacy. They also demand increasing control over the information that has been collected about them.

Many firms voluntarily notify their customers that any information provided to them will be kept confidential and not given or sold to any other firm. As more firms adopt advanced marketing research technology, such as facial recognition software, they also are working to ensure they receive permission from consumers. Facial recognition software is used to detect individuals from a video frame or digital images.[35] For example, Coca-Cola's experiments using facial recognition software record participants' faces as they watch advertisements or prototypes, then assess how their eyes moved, when they smiled or frowned, and so on—but only after those participants have agreed to be recorded.[36]

In contrast, consumers have little control over facial recognition software that allows companies to detect demographic information based on their appearances. For example, digital billboards embedded with such software can identify passersby and then display ads targeted to them based on their age, gender, and attention level.[37] The resulting communication is precisely targeted, which should make the advertisement more interesting to the

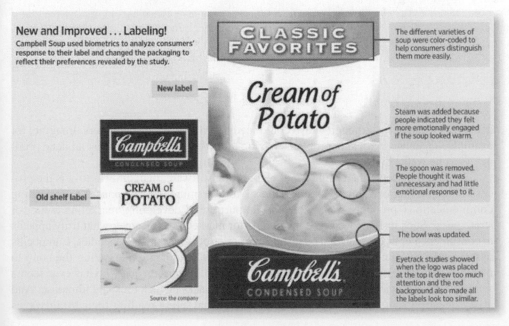

New and Improved . . . Labeling!
Campbell Soup used biometrics to analyze consumers' response to their label and changed the packaging to reflect their preferences revealed by the study.

CLASSIC FAVORITES

Cream of Potato

New label

Campbell's
CONDENSED SOUP
CREAM of POTATO

Old shelf label

Campbell's
CONDENSED SOUP

Source: the company

The different varieties of soup were color-coded to help consumers distinguish them more easily.

Steam was added because people indicated they felt more emotionally engaged if the soup looked warm.

The spoon was removed. People thought it was unnecessary and had little emotional response to it.

The bowl was updated.

Eyetrack studies showed when the logo was placed at the top it drew too much attention and the red background also made all the labels look too similar.

Campbell's redesigned its cans based on information it obtained through neuromarketing studies.
Source: Campbell Soup Company.

Ethical & Societal Dilemma 10.1   Oh, Say, Can You See? The Implications of Mannequins That Capture Shoppers' Demographic Data[v]

The basic elements of a new data-gathering tool for retailers are not in any real contention. By spending about $5,000 to purchase an EyeSee mannequin from a provider called Almax, retailers gain not only a place to display clothing but also a discreet recording tool that indicates the genders, ages, and ethnicities of the customers who walk by the display.

Rather more controversial are the implications of this innovation. On one side, consumer privacy advocates complain that the mannequins obtain information about shoppers without their permission. Because the mannequins do not look any different from regular mannequins, shoppers have no way of knowing whether someone (or something) is watching them as they walk through the store. Furthermore, consumers have no control over what retailers do with the aggregated data.

On the other side, retailers note that because the mannequins do not record specifics to identify any given individual, their use is no different from that of a closed-circuit system. Furthermore, some commentators argue that consumers should have no expectation of privacy in public spaces. Certainly, a staffer could similarly mark down people's ages, races, and genders as they walk through the shop doors. The electronic form simply does this work better and more accurately.

In implementing the new technology, one retailer recognized the predominance of Asian shoppers after about 4:00 p.m., so it hired more Chinese-speaking staffers to put on the floor to assist them. Another retailer realized that a lot of children were walking through its stores, so it added an entirely new children's clothing line to its offerings. Buoyed by its early successes, Almax also plans to add a function that would capture shoppers' conversations as they pass by the mannequins.

Current legislation allows retailers to maintain cameras and record customers for security purposes as long as they post warnings that customers might be recorded. However, the use of the mannequins is clearly for marketing purposes, not security. And most retailers seem to prefer to keep their usage of the new technology under wraps. Almax has not officially released the names of any of its clients—perhaps somewhat ironically, citing their need for privacy.

EyeSee mannequins do not record or store any images, so the privacy of the customer is protected.

Courtesy of Almax S.p.A.

From your perspective as a consumer, do you believe that mannequins that record your movements, image, and possibly conversations in a store invade your privacy? If so, would you avoid stores that use this technology?

consumer walking by—though it also could lead to embarrassing encounters. Imagine, for example, a teenager with skin problems having a billboard loudly broadcast an acne product ad as he walks by!

Going even deeper than using facial recognition software, **neuromarketing** is the process of examining consumers' brain patterns to determine their responses to marketing communications, products, or services for the purpose of developing marketing tactics or strategies.[38] Such insights would be invaluable for marketers to discover what truly appeals to consumers. For example, based on results of a series of neuromarketing studies, Campbell's has recently changed its soup labels by shrinking the logo and emphasizing the soup to increase customers' emotional responses to the cans.[39] But as anyone who has ever seen a science fiction movie can imagine, the potential for abuses of such tools are immense. And a key question remains: Do any consumers want marketers reading their brain waves

Findings from neuromarketing studies by NeuroFocus.

and marketing goods and services to them in a manner that bypasses their conscious thoughts? One firm, NeuroFocus, used neuromarketing techniques with several global firms to garner customer information that would be difficult, if not impossible, to obtain using more traditional research methods.

Several organizations, including the Center for Democracy & Technology (CDT) and the Electronic Privacy Information Center (EPIC), have emerged as watchdogs over data mining of consumer information. In addition, national and state governments in the United States play a part in protecting privacy. Companies are legally required to disclose their privacy practices to customers on an annual basis.[40] As the U.S. federal government has failed to enact comprehensive privacy laws for the Internet, several states are starting to consider legislation. While this may be good for the consumer, companies will have to deal with adherence to a complex patchwork of different privacy regulations across the country, making business on the Internet harder to conduct.[41]

PROGRESS CHECK

1. Under what circumstances is it ethical to use consumer information in marketing research?
2. What challenges do technological advances pose for the ethics of marketing research?

Reviewing Learning Objectives

 Identify the five steps in the marketing research process.

The first step is to define objectives and research needs, which sounds so simple that managers often gloss over it. But this step is crucial to the success of any research project because, quite basically, the research must answer those questions that are important for making decisions. In the second step, designing the research project, researchers identify the type of data that are needed, whether primary or secondary, on the basis of the objectives of the project from Step 1, and then determine the type of research that enables them to collect those data. The third step involves deciding on the data collection process and then collecting the data. The process usually starts with qualitative research methods such as observation, in-depth interviews, or focus groups. The information gleaned from the qualitative research is then used in quantitative research, which may include a survey, an experiment, or the use of scanner and panel data. The fourth step is to analyze and interpret the data and develop insights. The fifth and final step is to develop and implement an action plan. Although these steps appear to progress linearly, researchers often work backward and forward throughout the process as they learn at each step.

Describe the various secondary data sources.

External secondary data comprise information that has been collected from outside sources, such as the U.S. census, the Internet, books, articles, trade associations, or syndicated data services. Internal secondary data can also be derived from internal company records such as sales, customer lists, and other company reports and are analyzed using data mining and big data software.

Describe the various primary data collection techniques.

Primary data are collected to address specific research needs. Techniques used for primary qualitative research include observation, social media, in-depth interviews, and focus groups. Techniques used for primary quantitative research include surveys (both offline and online), scanner, panel, and experiments.

Summarize the differences between secondary data and primary data.

Compared with primary research, secondary research is quicker, easier, and generally less expensive. However, if you are using secondary data using big data, then the investment in programs supporting secondary data can be expensive. However, because secondary research is collected for reasons other than those pertaining to the specific problem at hand, the information may be dated, biased, or simply not specific enough to answer the research questions. Primary research, in contrast, can be designed to answer very specific questions, but it also tends to be more expensive and time-consuming.

Examine the circumstances in which collecting information on consumers is ethical.

Marketing researchers should gain permission to collect information on consumers, and it should be for the sole purpose of conducting marketing research endeavors. Information should not be collected under the guise of marketing research when the intent is to sell products or to fund-raise. In addition, marketers must take responsibility for protecting any information they collect.

Key Terms   ■LEARNSMAR┐

- big data, 313
- churn, 313
- customer lifetime value (CLV), 332
- data, 306
- data mining, 312
- data warehouses, 312
- experiment, 320
- experimental research, 320
- facial recognition software, 323

- focus group interview, 318
- in-depth interview, 317
- information, 306
- marketing research, 302
- neuromarketing, 324
- observation, 315
- panel data, 313
- primary data, 304
- qualitative research, 315
- quantitative research, 315

- questionnaire, 318
- sample, 305
- scanner data, 310
- secondary data, 304
- sentiment mining, 317
- structured questions, 318
- survey, 318
- syndicated data, 309
- unstructured questions, 318
- virtual community, 316

Marketing Digitally

1. Go to the website for the marketing research company Kantar (http://www.kantar.com). Click on "Company News," and then click on one of the recent press releases. What types of research does Kantar conduct, and what types of insights does it develop for its clients?

2. The epinions.com website (http://www.epinions.com) is a clearinghouse for consumer reviews about different products and services. Think of a particular business with which you are familiar, and then review the ratings and comments for that business on the epinions website. Discuss the extent to which this site might be useful to a marketer for that company who needs to gather market research about the company and its competitors. Identify the type of research this process involves—secondary or primary.

Marketing Applications

1. A large hardware store collects data about what its customers buy and stores these data in a data warehouse. If you were the store's buyer for lawn equipment, what would you want to know from the data warehouse that would help you be a more successful buyer?

2. Identify a nonprofit organization that might use marketing research, and describe one example of a meaningful research project that it might conduct. Discuss the steps it should undertake in this project.

3. Marketing researchers do not always go through the steps in the marketing research process in sequential order. Provide an example of a research project that might not follow this sequence.

4. A sunglasses retailer is trying to determine if there is a significant market for its merchandise in a specific mall location where it is considering opening a store. It has an active Facebook page where customers routinely visit to get coupons and comment on the latest sunglasses offered. How can this retailer use Facebook and Facebook Insights to decide if it should open the new store?

5. A consumer packaged-goods company (e.g., Pepsi) has just developed a new beverage. The company needs to estimate the demand for such a new product. What sources of syndicated data could it explore?

6. A bank manager notices that by the time customers get to the teller, they seem irritated and impatient. She wants to investigate the problem further, so she hires you to design a research project to figure out what is bothering the customers. The bank wants three studies: (a) several focus groups of their customers, (b) observation using a hidden camera, and (c) an online survey of 500 customers. Which studies are qualitative, and which are quantitative?

7. Best Buy has an extensive loyalty program, Best Buy Reward Zone, that allows it to track its customers' purchasing habits over time. How can Best Buy use such big data to improve sales?

8. Suppose your university wants to modify its course scheduling procedures to better serve students. What are some secondary sources of information that might be used to conduct research into this topic? Describe how these sources might be used. Describe a method you could use to gather primary research data about the topic. Would you recommend a specific order in obtaining each of these types of data? Explain your answer.

9. Manuel is planning to launch a new gourmet taco truck and is trying to decide where he should park his truck and what features and prices would entice consumers. He sends a request for proposal to four marketing research vendors, and three respond, as described in the table below. Which vendor should Manuel use? Explain your rationale for picking this vendor over the others.

Vendor A	Vendor B	Vendor C
The vendor that Manuel has used in the past estimates it can get the job done for $200,000 and in two months. The vendor plans to do a telephone-based survey analysis and use secondary data from the U.S. Census.	Manuel's key competitor has used this vendor, which claims that it can get the job done for $150,000 and in one month. This vendor plans to do a telephone-based survey analysis and use secondary data. During a discussion pertaining to its price and time estimates, the vendor indicates it will draw on insights it has learned from a recent report prepared for one of Manuel's competitors.	This well-known vendor has recently started to focus on the restaurant industry. It quotes a price of $180,000 and a time of one month. The vendor plans to conduct a web-based survey analysis and use secondary data.

Quiz Yourself

1. Which of the following is not a disadvantage of using secondary research data?
   a. The information may not be timely.
   b. The process is costly and time-consuming.
   c. The data sources may be biased.
   d. The methodologies for collecting the data may not be appropriate.
   e. The sources may not be original, and therefore usefulness is an issue.

2. The key difference between scanner and panel research is that scanner research typically focuses on a particular _____, while panel research typically focuses on a particular _____.
    a. product; person or household
    b. product; service

c. person; household
d. person; product
e. service; product

(Answers to these two questions can be found in the Quiz Yourself Answer Key section.)

Chapter Case Study

McGraw Hill Education **connect**

SWIM, LIFT, PLAY—BUT ALSO DONATE: USING MARKET RESEARCH TO REDEFINE THE YMCA

Over the years, the YMCA has come to mean different things to different people. Depending on the meanings that people embrace, the charitable organization sometimes struggles to achieve its mission and goals. Accordingly, a key element of its efforts, at both national and local levels, is to conduct ongoing and persistent research into what people perceive when they think of the Y.

Founded in the mid-nineteenth century in response to the new challenges of an industrial society, the YMCA sought to give young men coming to the city for work a place where they could stay safely and for a reasonable rate. In the United States, local YMCAs quickly became known as sources of assistance for new immigrants; though segregated, they also provided meeting places for African Americans and eventually emerged as important rallying sites for the civil rights movement. Once barriers to race and gender fell, the Y embraced its role as a place that every member of the family could find the resources, self-fulfillment, and support that they needed.[42]

Many of those resources historically and still today have focused on exercise and health. Different employees of YMCA facilities have contributed to exercise culture:

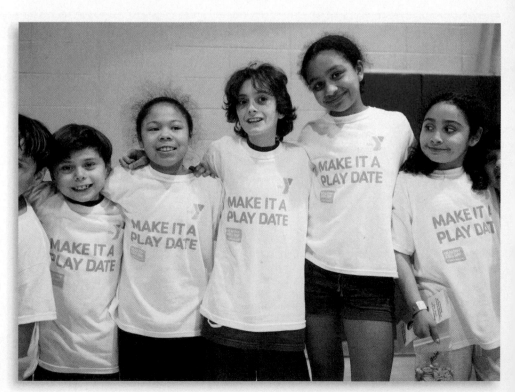

Based on market research, the YMCA has been rebranded to the Y, and local branches are encouraged to focus on its core values: caring, honesty, respect, and responsibility.

© Kevin Wolf/AP Photo

one originated the term "body building"; others invented games that we now know as volleyball, racquetball, and basketball in Y gymnasiums; and its initiative to help everyone learn to swim led to the vast expansion of public pools and swim classes throughout the nation.

This focus on exercise and health remains a primary element of the reputation of the Y in most Americans' minds. Approximately 13 million adults and 9 million children in the United States turn to their local Y to lift weights, shoot hoops, swim laps, or jog around a track.[43] But the national organization also began to suspect that those purposes were all that members, and other stakeholders, were seeing. As the president of the national organization explained, even as membership numbers were climbing, other data related to charitable donations suggested some concerns. That is, people were perceiving the Y "as a gym and swim place. We're also a charity, and that is the missing ingredient. We want people to realize that we're deserving of their charitable donations."[44]

To make that case, the Y (which rebranded in 2010 to take the single-letter moniker, though it also still relies on the longer YMCA acronym to maintain links to its historical functions) relies substantially on research. The goal is to show, with data, facts, figures, and graphics, how programs run by the Y and sponsored by charitable donations actually change lives and improve communities.

For example, a vast survey of consumers across the nation showed that 98 percent of people knew of the YMCA, and 92 percent of them had favorable impressions of it. But only 50 percent indicated that they understood why the Y offered the programs that it did.[45] The national organization considered its mission—to give families resources that they needed to build self-esteem and self-confidence, and thus build communities—evident, but the market research showed that these notions were not widespread among people who might use or contribute to their local organizations. In response, it encouraged the local branches (each of which is run autonomously) to emphasize four core values: caring, honesty, respect, and responsibility. It also recommended that local branches consider conducting their own research projects, to ensure they were providing the types of resources their local members wanted and needed most.[46]

In other, more targeted, market research projects, the national and local arms of the Y also have sought to determine which price points will attract the most members. For example, the Boston branch cited extensive market research that showed that if it cut membership fees by 11 percent, it could attract 10,000 new members. The research got it a little bit wrong though: After it reduced the fees, the membership rolls swelled by more than 20,000 users.[47]

Research also has informed which initiatives the Y has made its primary focus for the near future. First, noting extensive academic literature that shows that impoverished students retain less of the education they have received during the summer months, the Y is expanding a summer camp program in an effort to reduce the well-documented "achievement gap" between children from poor and wealthy families.[48] To support this initiative, the Y also instituted its first national advertising campaign, in which one televised advertisement highlights the various after-school, summer, and meal programs available for children. It also ends with a clear call for contributions to support such programs.[49]

Second, the Y cites national statistics about the number of people with diabetes or pre-diabetes, as well as scientific evidence that shows that losing even 5 percent of their body weight can help at-risk people avoid becoming diabetic. Accordingly, its second main initiative is to expand its diabetes prevention programs, in collaboration with national health care organizations such as the Centers for Disease Control and the Let's Move campaign.

Some evidence suggests its efforts are paying off. Visits to the Y's website increased in just the two months after it launched the national advertising campaigns.[50] In addition, the new communications are attracting attention to the Y in various outlets and sources, including a prominent role in a documentary about a swim team for people with autism.[51]

So the Y means a lot of things to a lot of people. The national organization continues to find out what people think of when they think of the Y. In addition, it seeks to learn how it can convince them to think about the Y and its valuable programs as a destination for their charitable donations.

Questions

1. What kinds of market research has the Y conducted?

2. Which questions has the Y sought to answer with each different type of market research it has conducted?

3. Who are the main stakeholders that the Y is attempting to reach with the information it has gained through its market research?

4. Are there other types of market research that the Y could conduct in the future to answer other important questions? Give some examples of both the questions it still faces and the research methods it could use to answer them.

Endnotes

1. Elizabeth Olson, "A Lingerie Brand that Offers Real Women as (Role) Models," *The New York Times,* February 21, 2016.

2. Sara Ashley O'Brien, "Plus-Size Models Sell More Bras," *CNN Money,* May 5, 2015.

3. Teresa Novellino, "Adore Me Pop-Up Is No Tease: Lingerie Brand Plans N.Y.C. Store," *New York Business Journal,* February 4, 2016.

4. Eric Wilson, "Less Ab, More Flab," *The New York Times,* May 22, 2013.

5. "Ashley Graham, Hailey Clauson, & Rhonda Rousey Land Sports Illustrated Covers," *Harper's Bazaar,* February 14, 2016.

6. Sara Ashley O'Brien, "Plus-Size Models Sell More Bras," *CNN Money,* May 5, 2015.

7. Nielsen Holding plc, "2015 10-K Annual Report," The Nielsen Company, February 19, 2016.

8. McDonald's Corporation, "Our Company," http://www.aboutmcdonalds.com/mcd/our_company.html; McDonald's Corporation, "2014 Annual Report," February 24, 2015.

9. The Wendy's Company, "Corporate Profile," https://www.wendys.com/en-us/about-wendys/the-wendys-company; The Wendy's Company, "2014 Annual Report," February 26, 2015.

10. Detailed illustrations of scales are provided in two books: Gordon C. Bruner, *Marketing Scales Handbook: A Compilation of Multi-Item Measures,* vol. 7 (Carbondale, IL: GCBII Productions, Fort Worth, TX: 2013); William O. Bearden, Richard G. Netemeyer, and Kelly L. Haws, *Handbook of Marketing Scales: Multi-Item Measures for Marketing and Consumer Behavior Research* (Thousand Oaks, CA: Sage, 2011).

11. John Cloud, "McDonald's Chef: The Most Influential Cook in America?" *Time,* February 22, 2010, http://www.time.com.

12. Jeff Kelly, "Big Data: Hadoop, Business, Analytics, and Beyond," *Wikibon,* February 5, 2014, http://wikibon.org.

13. Rachel Wolfson, "Retailers Using Big Data: The Secret Behind Amazon and Nordstrom's Success," *Big Data News,* December 11, 2014, http://www.bigdatanews.com.

14. "How Amazon Is Leveraging Big Data," *BigData Startups,* http://www.bigdata-startups.com/BigData-startup/amazon-leveraging-big-data/.

15. Amazon, http://www.amazon.com.

16. Rachel Wolfson, "Retailers Using Big Data: The Secret Behind Amazon and Nordstrom's Success," *Big Data News,* December 11, 2014,http://www.bigdatanews.com.

17. "Tesco Doubles Customer Rewards in Further Boost to Clubcard," press release, August 14, 2009.

18. Jenny Davey, "Every Little Bit of Data Helps Tesco Rule Retail," *TimesOnline.com,* October 4, 2009.

19. Quentin Hardy, "Big Data Picks Up the Pace," *The New York Times,* March 5, 2014, http://bits.blogs.nytimes.com.

20. Google, "Analytic Guide," http://www.google.com.

21. Google, "Puma Kicks Up Order Rate 7% with Insights from Google Analytics and Viget," case study, 2013.

22. "In Retail Stores, Research Tool Uses Kinect to Track Shoppers' Behavior," *Retail,* December 29, 2011, http://www.springwise.com.

23. Jennifer Reingold, "Can P&G Make Money in a Place Where People Earn $2 Per Day?" *CNN Money,* January 6, 2011, http://features.blogs.fortune.cnn.com.

24. http://www.thetruthaboutcars.com/.

25. "Client Story: Kraft," http://www.communispace.com.

26. Rachael King, "Sentiment Analysis Gives Companies Insight into Consumer Opinion," *Bloomberg Businessweek,* March 1, 2011, http://www.businessweek.com.

27. Richard A. Krueger and Mary Anne Casey, *Focus Groups: A Practical Guide for Applied Research* (Thousand Oaks, CA: Sage, 2009).

28. http://www.campbellsoup.com.

29. Adapted from A. Parasuraman, Dhruv Grewal, and R. Krishnan, *Marketing Research,* 2nd ed. (Boston: Houghton Mifflin, 2007), Ch. 10.

30. Floyd J. Fowler, *Survey Research Methods* (Thousand Oaks, CA: Sage, 2009); Don A. Dillman et al., "Response Rate and *Measurement Differences* in Mixed-Mode Surveys Using Mail, Telephone, Interactive Voice Response (IVR), and the Internet," *Social Science Research* 38 (March 2009), pp. 1–18.

31. https://pulse.asda.com; "Asda Wins Vision Critical's European Insight Community Award," press release, *Research,* September 30, 2013, http://www.research-live.com/news/.

32. Facebook, "State Bicycle Co.: Building a Strong Customer Base," case study, https://www.facebook.com/advertising/success-stories/state-bicycle.

33. Facebook, https://www.facebook.com/business/a/online-sales.

34. http://www.marketingpower.com/AboutAMA/Pages/Statement%20of%20Ethics.aspx; http://www.helleniccomserve.com.

35. https://www.techopedia.com/definition/26948/facial-recognition-software.

36. Roger Dooley, "Neuromarketing: For Coke, It's the Real Thing," *Forbes,* March 7, 2013, http://www.forbes.com.

37. Natasha Singer, "Face Recognition Makes the Leap from Sci-Fi," *The New York Times,* November 12, 2011.

38. http://dictionary.reference.com/browse/neuromarketing.

39. Ilan Brat, "The Emotional Quotient of Soup Shopping," *The Wall Street Journal,* February 17, 2010, http://online.wsj.com.

40. Cecilia Kang, "Library of Congress Plan for Twitter: A Big, Permanent Retweet," *The Washington Post,* April 16, 2010; http://www.cdt.org; Mark Penn, "Did Google Violate Privacy Laws?" http://www.politicallyillustrated.com, April 2, 2010; Lona M. Farr, "Whose Files Are They Anyway? Privacy Issues for the Fundraising Profession," *International Journal of Nonprofit and Voluntary Sector Marketing* 7, no. 4 (November 2002), p. 361.

41. Somini Sengupta, "No U.S. Action, So States Move on Privacy Law," *The New York Times,* October 30, 2013, http://www.nytimes.com.

42. YMCA, "History," http://www.ymca.net/history.

43. YMCA, "Organizational Profile," http://www.ymca.net/organizational-profile.

44. Alina Tugent, "The Y Embarks on Its First National Advertising Campaign," *The New York Times,* January 23, 2016.

45. Aaron K. Olson and B. Keith Simerson, *Leading with Strategic Thinking: Four Ways Effective Leaders Gain Insight, Drive Change, and Get Results* (New York: John Wiley & Sons, 2015).

46. FourSquare, "What Is a FourSquare Market Research Study?" http://foursquareresearch.com/FourSquare%20Market%20Study%20for%20YMCAs.pdf.

47. Melissa Harris, "Kevin Washington Sets Agenda for YMCA's National Organization," *Chicago Tribune,* November 21, 2014.

48. Ibid.

49. Alina Tugent, "The Y Embarks on Its First National Advertising Campaign," *The New York Times,* January 23, 2016.

50. Adrianne Pasquarelli, "Move Over Clinton and Trump: YMCA Backs a Toddler's Run in New Spot," *Advertising Age,* February 25, 2016.

51. Shanna Belott, "The Best Place for Community Is the One You Grew Up In," *Huffington Post,* February 18, 2016.

i. Martha White, "There's Scientific Proof the All-Day McMuffin Is a Brilliant Idea," *Time,* April 7, 2015; Trefis Team, "Is McDonald's All Day Breakfast Strategy Working?" *Forbes,* December 16, 2015; Hayely Peterson, "McDonald's Franchisees Say All-Day Breakfast Is a Nightmare," *Business Insider,* August 16, 2015; Ashley Lutz, "McDonald's Comes Even Closer to Offering a 24-Hour Breakfast," *Business Insider,* June 6, 2013; Robert Lara, "The True Steamy Story of the Egg McMuffin Hockey Puck Breakfast Turns 40," Adweek.com, August 9, 2013.

ii. Colleges Are Tracking When Students Work Out at Rec Centers," *The Wall Street Journal,* October 28, 2014, http://wsjonline.com.

iii. Amol Sharma and Suzanne Vranica, "Nielsen to Add Data for Mobile TV Viewing," *The Wall Street Journal,* September 19, 2013; Ben Sisario, "Tweets About Music to Get a Billboard Chart," *The New York Times,* March 27, 2014.

iv. Kirsten Acuna, "Google Says It Can Predict Which Films Will Be Huge Box Office Hits," *Business Insider,* June 6, 2013.

v. Andrew Roberts, "In Some Stores, the Mannequins Are Watching You," *Bloomberg Businessweek,* December 6, 2012, http://www.businessweek.com; Amar Toor, "EyeSee Mannequin Silently Collects Customer Data for Overzealous Retailers," *The Verge,* November 20, 2012, http://www.theverge.com; Joanna Stern, "Department Store Mannequins Are Watching You. No, Really," *ABC News,* November 26, 2012, http://abcnews.go.com.

APPENDIX 10A

USING SECONDARY DATA TO ASSESS CUSTOMER LIFETIME VALUE (CLV)

This appendix examines how secondary data from customer transactions can help determine the value of a customer over time. Specifically, **customer lifetime value (CLV)** refers to the expected financial contribution from a particular customer to the firm's profits over the course of their entire relationship.[52]

To estimate CLV, firms use past behaviors to forecast future purchases, the gross margin from these purchases, and the costs associated with servicing the customers. Some costs associated with maintaining customer relationships include communicating with customers through advertising, personal selling, or other promotional vehicles to acquire their business initially and then retain them over time.

Measures of customer lifetime value typically apply to a group or segment of customers and use available secondary data. A basic formula for CLV, with the assumption that revenues and profits arrive at the start of the year, is as follows:[53]

$$CLV = \frac{\sum_{t=1}^{T} [\text{profit at t} \times \text{retention rate}^{t-1}]}{(1+i)^{t-1}} - \begin{array}{c}\text{acquisition} \\ \text{costs}\end{array}$$

To implement this CLV formula, we must answer the following questions:

1. How many years (t) can we expect to do business with a customer? The total number of years is denoted by T.

2. What can we expect the annual profits to be from an individual customer or an average

customer? These profits are based on sales minus the costs of merchandise and the costs of serving and retaining the customer.

3. What is the retention rate—that is, the average percentage of customers who continue to purchase from the firm from one time period to another? A 90 percent retention rate means that if we have 100 customers in the first year, we will have 90 at the beginning of the second year.

4. What is the discount rate (i)? The discount rate is based on the idea that a dollar is worth less in the future than it is today, so the company can use it to adjust future profits and determine a customer's value today for the customer's purchases in the future. For example, if the discount rate is 10 percent, $100 in profits at the beginning of year 2 are worth only $90.91 (100/(1 + .1)) at the beginning of year 1.

Consider Gregory Missoni, a fairly new client of Very Clean Cleaners who switched from his other dry cleaner because Very Clean sent him $100 worth of coupons in a direct mailing.

Greg just picked up his $200 shirt from Very Clean and found that the dry cleaner had broken a brown button and replaced it with a white button. When he complained, the clerk acted as if it were no big deal. Greg explained to the clerk that it was a very expensive shirt that deserved more careful handling, then asked to speak with the manager. At this point, how important is it for the manager to make sure Greg is satisfied, so that he will continue to bring his dry cleaning to Very Clean Cleaners? To answer this question, the manager uses the following information:

Very Clean Cleaners should consider a customer's lifetime value to determine its service levels.

© Don Mason/Corbis

- It cost Very Clean $100 to acquire Greg as a customer. Thus, the acquisition cost is $100.

- Very Clean expects Greg to remain a client for 5 years (time horizon T = 5 years).

- Very Clean expects to make a $1,000 profit each year from Greg's dry cleaning.

- On average, 10 percent of customers defect to another cleaner each year. Therefore, the expected retention rate is 90 percent.

- The discount rate is 10 percent per year (i in this illustration). For simplicity, Very Clean assumes all profits are accrued at the beginning of the year.

Applying the formula, such that CLV equals the profits from years 1–5, less the acquisition costs, we obtain:

$$CLV = \frac{\$1{,}000 \times (.90)^0}{(1 + .1)^0} + \frac{\$1{,}000 \times (.90)^1}{(1 + .1)^1} + \frac{\$1{,}000 \times (.90)^2}{(1 + .1)^2}$$
$$\underset{\textbf{Year 1}}{} \qquad \underset{\textbf{Year 2}}{} \qquad \underset{\textbf{Year 3}}{}$$

$$\frac{\$1{,}000 \times (.90)^3}{(1 + .1)^3} + \frac{\$1{,}000 \times (.90)^4}{(1 + .1)^4} - \$100$$
$$\underset{\textbf{Year 4}}{} \qquad \underset{\textbf{Year 5}}{}$$

Or

$$CLV = \$1,000 + \$818.2 + \$669.4 + \$547.7 + \$448.1 - \$100 = \$3,383.40$$

Let's see how the formula works. The expected profit from Greg is $1,000 per year. Very Clean assumes profits accrue at the beginning of the year, so the profits for the first year equal $1,000; they are not affected by the retention rate or the discount rate.

However, the retention and discount rates have effects on the profits for the subsequent time periods. In the second year, the retention rate, which Very Clean determined was 90 percent (i.e., 90 percent of customers continue to do business with it) modifies profits, such that expected profits in the second year equal $1,000 × 90% = $900. Moreover, the discount rate is applied such that the profits received in the second year are worth less than if they had been received in the first year. Therefore, the $900 received at the beginning of the second year must be divided by 1.1, which is equivalent to $818.20.

Using similar calculations for the third year, the expected profits adjusted for retention are $1,000 × .9 × .9 = $810. The discount rate then reduces the profit to $810 ÷ $1.1^2 = $669.40 in today's dollars. (Note that the discount rate is squared because it refers to two years in the future.) After calculating the adjusted and discounted profits for the fourth and fifth years in similar fashion, we realize the sum of estimated discounted profits for five years is $3,483.40. However, we still must subtract the $100 spent to acquire Greg, which provides a CLV of $3,383.40.

According to this analysis, it would be a good idea for the manager to take a long-term perspective when evaluating how to respond to Greg's complaint about his button. Greg cannot be viewed as a $2.50 customer, as he would be if Very Clean determined his value based on the cost of laundering his shirt, nor should he be viewed as a $200 customer, based on the cost of the shirt. He actually is worth a lot more than that.

For illustrative purposes, we have simplified the CLV calculations in this example. We assumed that the average profits remain constant at $1,000. But firms usually expect profits to grow over time or else grow, level off, and then perhaps decline. Retention costs, such as special promotions used to keep Greg coming back, also do not appear in our illustration, though such additional costs would reduce annual profits and CLV. Finally, we assume a five-year time horizon; the CLV obviously would differ for longer or shorter periods. For an infinite time horizon, with first period payments upfront, the formula becomes fairly simple:[54]

$$CLV = profits \times \left[1 + \frac{retention\ rate}{(\$1 + discount\ rate - retention\ rate)}\right]$$

$$- \ acquisition\ costs$$

$$= \$1,000 \times \left[1 + \frac{.9}{(1 + .1 - .9)}\right] - \$100$$

$$= \$1,000 \times (1 + 4.5) - \$100$$

$$= \$5,500 - \$100 = \$5,400$$

This illustration thus explains how firms can use secondary data to calculate CLV; it further demonstrates the importance of knowing a customer's lifetime value when executing marketing tactics and strategies.

Endnotes

52. V. Kumar, A. Petersen and R. P. Leone, "How Valuable Is Word of Mouth?" *Harvard Business Review*, October 2007, pp. 139–46; V. Kumar and M. George, "Measuring and Maximizing Customer Equity: A Critical Analysis," *Journal of the Academy of Marketing Science* 35, no. 2 (June 2007), pp. 157–71; V. Kumar, D. Shah, and R. Venkatesan, "Managing Retailer Profitability: One Customer at a Time!" *Journal of Retailing* 82, no. 4 (October 2006), pp. 277–94; V. Kumar, "Profitable Relationships," *Marketing Research: A Magazine of Management and Applications* 18, no. 3 (Fall 2006), pp. 41–46;

V. Kumar, "Customer Lifetime Value: A Databased Approach," *Journal of Relationship Marketing* 5, no. 2/3 (2006), pp. 7–35; S. Gupta, D. Hanssens, B. Hardie, W. Kahn, V. Kumar, N. Lin, N. Ravishanker, and S. Sriram, "Modeling Customer Lifetime Value," *Journal of Service Research* 9 (November 2006), pp. 139–55; V. Kumar, R. Venkatesan, and W. Reinartz, "Knowing What to Sell, When and to Whom," *Harvard Business Review,* March, 2006, pp. 131–37; W. Reinartz, J. Thomas, and V. Kumar, "Balancing Acquisition and Retention Resources to Maximize Profitability," *Journal of Marketing* 69 (January 2005), pp. 63–79; R. Venkatesan and V. Kumar, "A Customer Lifetime Value Framework for Customer Selection and Resource Allocation Strategy," *Journal of Marketing* 68 (October 2004), pp. 106–25; V. Kumar and J. A. Petersen, "Maximizing ROI or Profitability: Is One Better Than the Other," *Marketing Research: A Magazine of Management and Applications* 16, no. 3 (Fall 2004), pp. 28–34; V. Kumar, G. Ramani, and T. Bohling, "Customer Lifetime Value Approaches and Best Practice Applications," *Journal of Interactive Marketing* 18, no. 3 (Summer 2004), pp. 60–72; J. Thomas, Werner Reinartz, and V. Kumar, "Getting the Most Out of All Your Customers," *Harvard Business Review* (July–August 2004), pp. 116–23; Werner Reinartz and V. Kumar, "The Impact of Customer Relationship Characteristics on Profitable Lifetime Duration," *Journal of Marketing* 67 (January 2003), pp. 77–99; W. Reinartz and V. Kumar, "The Mismanagement of Customer Loyalty," *Harvard Business Review* (July 2002), pp. 86–97; W. Reinartz and V. Kumar, "On the Profitability of Long Lifetime Customers: An Empirical Investigation and Implications for Marketing," *Journal of Marketing* 64 (October 2000), pp. 17–32.

53. We have made some minor adjustments to the formula suggested by Gupta et al., "Modeling Customer Lifetime Value."

54. S. Gupta and D. R. Lehmann, *Managing Customers as Investments* (Philadelphia, PA: Wharton School Publishing, 2005); Gupta et al., "Modeling Customer Lifetime Value."

VALUE CREATION

Section Four devotes three chapters to how marketing contributes to value creation. Chapters 11 and 12 explore strategies and tactics in the development and management of successful products and their brands. Although many of the concepts involved in developing and managing services are similar to those of physical brands, Chapter 13 addresses the unique challenges of the marketing of services.

CHAPTER 11

PRODUCT, BRANDING, AND PACKAGING DECISIONS

© Chris McLennan/Alamy

To convey its brand of unconscious cool and radical adventure, Red Bull embraces daredevil stunts but also seeks to avoid making it look as if it is trying too hard to promote itself in so doing. Thus its branding operations walk a delicate line: Make a name for the brand but without appearing to do so.

Consider the Red Bull Stratos project. Over a period of approximately five years, Red Bull bankrolled the experimental development of a flight suit that would enable daredevil and skydiver Felix Baumgartner to free fall from 24 miles up, break the sound barrier, and still survive his jump from space.[1]

A camera mounted on his helmet recorded the entire experience, including the early moments, when he spun out of control in the thin stratosphere, until nearly five minutes later, when he landed. Approximately 8 million people watched the jump live.[2]

The company has continually sought to reinforce its image as a cutting-edge, danger-seeking, boundary-pushing entity. The data gathered through the Stratos project were made available to pilots and astronauts who might need to bail out of a disabled aircraft. The newly designed space suit also revealed that it could protect the human body against the extreme conditions in the stratosphere.[3]

Pushing the envelope is just what Red Bull wants its brand to be known for doing. Red Bull has found new ways to emphasize this image by diving into new areas. Although Red Bull continues to sponsor extreme sporting and events and stunts, it also has its own record label, which produces artists who make high-energy music.[4] Red Bull has been able to pair its music label with their many events and even create playlists for skydiving and X-fighters on their Red Bull Records YouTube channel, which integrates music from their artists and other popular musicians.[5]

By sponsoring events such as the space jump, its annual Flugtag competition, and music festivals, Red Bull brands itself as fun, a little crazy, and ready for anything. But by letting the events speak largely for themselves rather than promoting its participation in a traditional sense, it also maintains an image of slightly detached cool. It hopes that consumers who would like to think of themselves the same way will find this branding deeply compelling.

As a key element of a firm's marketing mix (the four Ps), product strategies are central to the creation of value for the consumer. A **product** is anything that is of value to a consumer and can be offered through a voluntary marketing exchange. In addition to goods, such as soft drinks, or services, such as a stay in a hotel, products might be places (e.g., Six Flags theme parks), ideas (e.g., stop smoking), organizations (e.g., MADD), people (e.g., Oprah Winfrey), or communities (e.g., Facebook) that create value for consumers in their respective competitive marketing arenas.

This chapter begins with a discussion of the complexity and types of products. We then examine how firms adjust their product lines to meet and respond to changing market conditions. Then we turn our attention to branding—why are brands valuable to the firm, and what are the different branding strategies firms use? We also never want to underestimate the value of a product's package and label. These elements should send a strong message from the shelf: Buy me! The final section of this chapter examines packaging and labeling issues.

 Describe the components of a product.

COMPLEXITY AND TYPES OF PRODUCTS

Complexity of Products

There is more to a product than its physical characteristics or its basic service function. Marketers involved with the development, design, and sale of products think of physical characteristics and service functions in an interrelated fashion, as depicted in Exhibit 11.1. At the center is the **core customer value**, which defines the basic problem-solving benefits that consumers are seeking. When Mars manufactures M&M's, Snickers, and other confectionary products, or when Trek designs bicycles, each company's core question is: What are customers looking for? With Mars, is it a sweet, great tasting snack, or is it an energy boost? With Trek, is the bike being used for basic green transportation (a cruiser), or is it for speed and excitement (a road, hybrid, or mountain bike)?

Marketers convert core customer value into an **actual product**. Attributes such as the brand name, features/design, quality level, and packaging are important, but the level of their importance varies, depending on the product. The Trek Madone 7 Series, for instance, is positioned as "see how fastest feels."[6] It features a carbon frame that is light, stiff, and comfortable; an advanced shifting system; and other high-tech features. Not only is it beautiful to look at, but customers can choose from three fits—pro, performance, and touring.

EXHIBIT 11.1 Product complexity

Actual product

Brand name   Packaging
Quality level   Features/Design

Core
customer
value

Associated services

Financing
Product warranty
Product support

Photos: Left: © Photodisc/Getty Images RF; Right: © Michael Blann/Getty Images RF

The **associated services** in Exhibit 11.1, also referred to as the **augmented product**, include the nonphysical aspects of the product, such as product warranties, financing, product support, and after-sale service. The amount of associated services also varies with the product. The associated services for a package of M&M's may include only a customer complaint line, which means they are relatively less important than the associated services for a Trek bicycle. The frame of the Madone 7 Series bicycle is guaranteed for the lifetime of the original owner. Trek sells its bikes only in shops that have the expertise to service them properly. Every possible consumer question is answered on Trek's comprehensive website. Trek even has a financing program that allows customers to purchase new bikes on credit.

When developing or changing a product, marketers start with the core customer value to determine what their potential customers are seeking. Then they make the actual physical product and add associated services to round out the offering.

Types of Products

  Identify the types of consumer products.

Marketers consider the types of products they are designing and selling because these types affect how they will promote, price, and distribute their products. There are two primary categories of products and services that reflect who buys them: consumers or businesses. Chapter 7 discussed products for businesses. Here we discuss consumer products.

Consumer products are products and services used by people for their personal use. Marketers further classify consumer products by the way they are used and how they are purchased.

Specialty Products/Services **Specialty products/services** are those for which customers express such a strong preference that they will expend considerable effort to search for the best suppliers. Road bike enthusiasts, like those interested in the Trek Madone 7 Series, devote lots of time and effort to selecting just the right one. Other examples might include luxury cars, legal or medical professionals, or designer apparel.

Shopping Products/Services **Shopping products/services** are products or services for which consumers will spend a fair amount of time comparing alternatives, such as furniture, apparel, fragrances, appliances, and travel. When people need new sneakers, for instance, they often go from store to store shopping—trying on shoes, comparing alternatives, and chatting with salespeople.

A medical professional is a specialty service. Soda is a convenience product. Insurance is an unsought service. Apparel is a shopping product.

Top left: © Comstock Images/SuperStock RF; Top right: © McGraw-Hill Education/Jill Braaten, photographer; Bottom left: © numbeos/E-plus/Getty Images RF; Bottom right: © Big Cheese Photo/SuperStock RF

Convenience Products/Services **Convenience products/services** are those products or services for which the consumer is not willing to expend any effort to evaluate prior to purchase. They are frequently purchased commodity items, usually bought with very little thought, such as common beverages, bread, or soap.

Unsought Products/Services **Unsought products/services** are products or services that consumers either do not normally think of buying or do not know about. Because of their very nature, these products/services require lots of marketing effort and various forms of promotion. When new-to-the-world products are first introduced, they are unsought products. Do you have cold hands and don't know what to do about it? You must not have heard yet of HeatMax HotHands Hand Warmers, air-activated packets that provide warmth for up to 10 hours. Do you have an internship in a less developed country and your regular insurance cannot give you the coverage you may need in case of an emergency? You now can turn to a Medex insurance policy.

PROGRESS CHECK

1. Explain the three components of a product.
2. What are the four types of consumer products?

PRODUCT MIX AND PRODUCT LINE DECISIONS

 LO11-3 Explain the difference between a product mix's breadth and a product line's depth.

The complete set of all products and services offered by a firm is called its **product mix**. An abbreviated version of the product mix for Daimler AG, the company that owns Mercedes-Benz, appears in Exhibit 11.2. The product mix typically consists of various **product lines**, which are groups of associated items that consumers tend to use together or think of as part of a group of similar products or services. Daimler's product lines (brands) for consumers include, for example, Mercedes-Benz cars, Mercedes-AMG cars, smart cars, and Mercedes-Benz vans and camper vans.

The product mix reflects the breadth and depth of the company's product lines. A firm's product mix **breadth** represents a count of the number of product lines offered by the firm; the four columns in Exhibit 11.2 depict just four of the lines offered by Daimler AG. Product line **depth**, in contrast, equals the number of products within a product line. Daimler AG clearly maintains the most products under its Mercedes-Benz line of cars, and it adds more as needed to appeal to various consumers, as Adding Value 11.1 explains.

However, adding unlimited numbers of new products can have adverse consequences. Too much breadth in the product mix becomes costly to maintain, and too many brands may weaken the firm's reputation.[7] If the products are too similar, sales of one brand may **cannibalize**, or take away sales from the other brand, with no net sales, profit, or market share increase. As described in Adding Value 11.1, the Audi A3 may cannibalize sales from the A4, which is a more expensive model, but looks remarkably like the A3. With more products and product lines, the firm must keep track of trends and developments in various industries, which might tax its resources. Marketing Analytics 11.1 describes how Macy's uses advanced methods to fine-tune its product lines.

So why do firms change their product mix's breadth or depth?[8]

Increase Depth Firms might add items to address changing consumer preferences or to preempt competitors while boosting sales (see the addition of product A4 in Exhibit 11.3). For Philadelphia brand cream cheese, adding a new jalapeno-flavored cream cheese enables it to appeal better to hot-and-spicy-loving consumers. The product is still essentially the same (cream cheese), but the availability of 35 different flavors significantly increases the product line's depth.[9]

Kraft has increased the depth of its Philadelphia brand cream cheese by introducing a new jalapeño flavor.

© Danny Meldung/Photo Affairs, Inc.

EXHIBIT 11.2	Abbreviated List of Daimler AG Product Mix		
Product Lines			
Mercedes-Benz Cars	Mercedes-AMG cars	Smart Cars	Mercedes-Benz Vans
A-Class	C 63	Smart ForTwo	Sprinter Worker
B-Class	CLS 63	Smart ForTwo Cabrio	Sprinter Cargo Van
C-Class	GLE 450	Smart ForFour	Sprinter Crew Van
CLA	SL Convertible	Smart ForTwo Electric Drive	Sprinter Passenger Van
CLS	GT		Metro Passenger Van
G-Class			Metro Cargo Van
E-Class			Marco Polo Camper Van
GLA			
R-Class			
S-Class			
V-Class			

Adding Value 11.1   An Entryway to Luxury: The Latest Entry-Level Models from High-End Car Brands[i]

For luxury carmakers, the lowest-end models in their product lines often represent only a small portion of their sales. Yet these models are critically important when it comes to attracting new customers and, potentially, establishing their lifelong loyalty to the brand. Accordingly, more high-end, traditionally expensive brands have developed comparatively less option-laden alternatives to lure first-time and nontraditional buyers to their dealerships.

The most prominent automobile brand to adopt this strategy was Mercedes-Benz, which introduced its CLA model at a base price of less than $40,000. When consumers realized that they could purchase or lease a Mercedes-Benz for approximately the same monthly price that they would spend for a high-end Toyota or Honda, many of them switched happily. For the most part, the target market for such models includes young professionals. These are consumers who earn a steady income that enables them to take on a car payment but not pay for a new car outright, and their monthly payments must fit their budgets.

Noting the success Mercedes was enjoying, Audi added the A3, for a base price of less than $30,000. With a stated goal of appealing to young, cool, urban drivers, Audi promised that they could "upgrade" from their non-luxury brands, though the differences between the A3 and high-end versions of comparable Hondas or Toyotas have little to do with actual upgrades to the cars—that is, both likely provide leather interiors and sunroofs. Rather, the key difference is the image benefits that driving a luxury brand offer to consumers.

The lack of distinction in the amenities offered by the luxury brands might constitute a risk too. One test driver, after cruising around in a Mercedes CLA, deemed it similar to the experience of driving a Honda. Such attitudes could readily overturn the distinctive and long-standing advantages that luxury brands have enjoyed. If enough people come to perceive that driving a luxury car is no different from driving a midrange car, those image-based benefits from luxury branding would disappear.

For Mercedes and Audi though, the risks appear subordinate to the potential and realized benefits. Both brands have enjoyed sales increases due to the introductions of these low-end models. Furthermore, these purchases are not repeat buys: Approximately 60 percent of new A3 drivers and 75 percent of CLA purchasers are new to the brands. Such statistics suggest an expanded market for the brands. As these buyers age, advance in their careers, and consider more expensive car purchases, they should be more likely to continue visiting the dealerships that provided them with their very first luxury automobile.

Do the risks outweigh the rewards of Mercedes-Benz and Audi to introduce lower-priced models like the CLA (left) and the A3 (right) to lure first-time buyers?

Left: © Wing Lun Leung/Alamy; Right: © Jonathan Thurlow/Alamy

Decrease Depth From time to time, it is also necessary to delete products within a product line to realign the firm's resources (see the deletion of products B5 and B6 in Exhibit 11.3). The decision is never taken lightly. Generally, substantial investments have been made to develop and manufacture the products. Yet firms often must prune their product lines to eliminate unprofitable or low-margin items and refocus their marketing efforts on their more profitable items. When Procter & Gamble (P&G) announced that it would be merging, eliminating, or selling many of its brands and only keeping the top performing 70–80 brand names, it may have seemed at first that the historically underperforming Duracell brand would be cut. However, recent merchandising efforts, such as signing an exclusive distribution agreement with Sam's Club, pushed Duracell's annual sales up to $2.3 billion, guaranteeing its continuation as a P&G brand. This quick shift

Marketing Analytics 11.1

How Macy's Defines Its Assortment through Analytics[ii]

In the current marketing landscape, it is critical that retailers have a well-developed understanding of their customers. Macy's uses **predictive analytics** to gain more insight into its customers and improve the buying experience across all channels. Predictive analytics is the use of statistics on data to determine patterns and predict future outcomes and trends. For years, Macy's has been collecting data to create a customer-centric in-store experience. Specifically, Macy's uses predictive analytics to create its assortment. The retailer collects data on details such as out-of-stock rates, price promotions, and sell-through rates, then combines those data with stock-keeping unit (SKU) information from each location to segment customers and create personalized store assortments.

As sales continue to shift to digital platforms, Macy's also uses predictive analytics to create an engaging online experience through Macys.com. The company analyzes visit frequency, style preferences, and shopping motivations in its website data, then seeks to apply the insights to ensure that every customer has an enjoyable, effortless shopping experience. Macys.com does more than just use predictive analytics to create personalized purchase suggestions, though. It calculates the likelihood that each customer will spend a specific amount in a particular product category, then uses that information to present the customer with personalized offers on the checkout page. Furthermore, analytics enable Macy's to send registered users of Macys.com even more personalized e-mail offers. For example, it can send up to 500,000 unique versions of the same mailing.

Macy's already has enjoyed significant success as a result of its implementation of advanced predictive analytics. It has continued to experience increases in store sales and online sales, at least partially due to its targeted e-mails. Looking to the future, Macy's plans to improve its online and mobile shopping experiences even further while enhancing the integration of these various shopping platforms to create a seamless experience with just the right product mix.

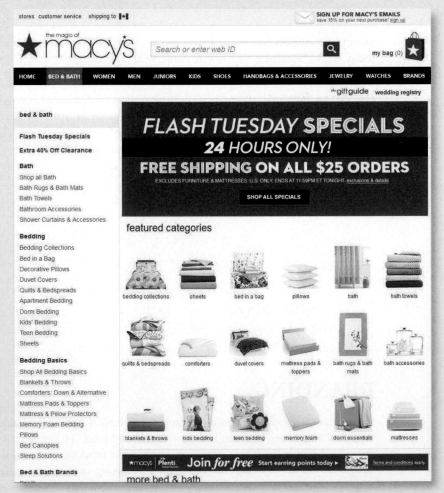

Macys.com analyzes visit frequency, style preferences, and shopping motivations in its website data to develop promotions like the one pictured here.

Source: Macy's

EXHIBIT 11.3   Changes to a Product Mix

Added depth:
New product (A4)

Decreased depth:
Dropped B5 & B6

Decreased breadth:
Dropped product
line C (C1 & C2)

Added breadth:
New line (D1, D2,
D3, & D4)

exemplifies the challenges of brand and product line choices: An underperforming brand today might become a superior revenue generator a year later.[10] Thus, marketers need to think very carefully as they decrease the depth of a given product line.

Decrease Breadth   Sometimes it is necessary to delete entire product lines to address changing market conditions or meet internal strategic priorities (e.g., deleting product line C in Exhibit 11.3). Thus, the firm drops its line of protein bars and focuses its attention on its energy drinks and vitamin water (product lines A and B).

Increase Breadth   Firms often add new product lines to capture new or evolving markets and increase sales (e.g., product line D in Exhibit 11.3). The firm adds a whole new line of yogurt.

PROGRESS CHECK

1.   What is the difference between product mix breadth and product line depth?
2.   Why change product mix breadth?
3.   Why change product line depth?

BRANDING

A company lives or dies based on brand awareness. Consumers cannot buy products that they don't know exist. Even if the overall brand name is familiar, it won't help sales of individual products unless consumers know what products are available under that name. Sports fans have long been familiar with the rallying cry for Under Armour and its line of athletic gear: "Protect this house." But when the company chose to refresh its tagline, it undertook a massive ad campaign to introduce its new slogan, "I will." In addition to extensive online and outdoor advertising, Under Armour has intensified its branding efforts by signing Washington Nationals baseball star Bryce Harper to the biggest endorsement deal for an MLB player.[11]

Branding also provides a way for a firm to differentiate its product offerings from those of its competitors. Both Snapple and Tropicana make and sell fruit drinks, yet consumers may choose one over the other because of the associations the brands invoke. As we discuss in more detail subsequently, brand names, logos, symbols, characters, slogans, jingles, and even distinctive packages constitute the various brand elements firms use,[12] which they usually choose to be easy for consumers to recognize and remember. Most consumers know the Nike swoosh and would recognize it even if the word *Nike* did not appear on the product or in an advertisement. Exhibit 11.4 summarizes some of these brand elements.

 LO11-4 Identify the advantages that brands provide firms and consumers.

Value of Branding for the Customer

Brands add value to merchandise and services, for consumers as well as sellers, beyond physical and functional characteristics or the pure act of performing the service.[13] Let's examine some ways in which brands add value for customers as well as the firm.

Brands Facilitate Purchases Brands are often easily recognized by consumers and, because brands signify a certain quality level and contain familiar attributes, they help consumers make quick decisions, especially about their purchases.[14] The cola market is a particularly strong example of this benefit. Some people think cola is cola, such that one brand is not too different from another. But branding has made it easy for Pepsi drinkers to find the familiar logo on the store shelf and make it more likely that they simply buy one of Pepsi's other products, should they decide to switch to a diet soda or a flavored version. From promotions, past purchases, or information from friends and family, they recognize the offering before they even read any text on the label, and they likely possess a perception of the brand's level of quality, how it tastes, whether it is a good value, and, most important, whether they like it and want to buy it. Brands enable customers to differentiate one firm or product from another. Without branding, how could we easily tell the difference between Coca-Cola and Pepsi before tasting them?

Brands Establish Loyalty Over time and with continued use, consumers learn to trust certain brands. They know, for example, that they wouldn't consider switching brands and, in some cases, feel a strong affinity to certain brands.

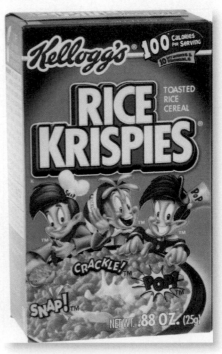

Characters like Rice Krispies' Snap, Crackle, and Pop help build a brand.

EXHIBIT 11.4   What Makes a Brand?

Brand Element	Description
Brand name	The spoken component of branding, it can describe the product or service characteristics and/or be composed of words invented or derived from colloquial or contemporary language. Examples include Comfort Inn (suggests product characteristics), Apple (no association with the product), or Zillow.com (invented term).
URLs (uniform resource locators) or domain names	Locations of pages on the Internet, which often substitute for the firm's name, such as Toyota (http://www.toyota.com).
Logos and symbols	Visual branding elements that stand for corporate names or trademarks. Symbols are logos without words. Examples include the McDonald's arches.
Characters	Brand symbols that could be human, animal, or animated. Examples include the Energizer Bunny and Rice Krispies' Snap, Crackle, and Pop.
Slogans	Short phrases used to describe the brand or persuade consumers about some characteristics of the brand. Examples include State Farm's "Like A Good Neighbor" and Dunkin' Donuts' "America Runs On Dunkin'."
Jingles/Sounds	Audio messages about the brand that are composed of words or distinctive music. An example is Intel's four-note sound signature that accompanies the Intel Inside slogan.

LO11-5 Explain the various components of brand equity.

Source: Adapted from Kevin Lane Keller, *Strategic Brand Management*, 4th ed. (Upper Saddle River, NJ: Prentice Hall, 2012).

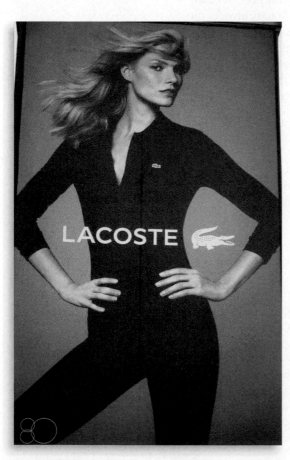

Lacoste has a superior-quality image that helps protect it from competition and enables it to command relatively high prices.

© Bryn Colton/Bloomberg/Getty Images

Amazon.com has a loyal following because its reputation for service prompts customers to turn to it first.

Brands Protect from Competition and Price Competition

Strong brands are somewhat protected from competition from other firms and price competition. Because such brands are more established in the market and have a more loyal customer base, neither competitive pressures on price nor retail-level competition is as threatening to the firm. Lacoste is widely known for its cotton knit shirts. Although many similar brands are available and some retailers offer their own brands, Lacoste is perceived to be of superior quality, garners a certain status among its users, and therefore can command a premium price.

Brands Are Assets

For firms, brands are also assets that can be legally protected through trademarks and copyrights and thus constitute a unique form of ownership. Firms sometimes have to fight to ensure their brand names are not being used, directly or indirectly, by others. McDonald's, for instance, has a long history of fighting trademark infringements. It recently won a trademark case with a Singapore-based restaurant chain that wanted to use the term "MACCOFFEE."[15]

Brands Affect Market Value

Having well-known brands can have a direct impact on the company's bottom line. The value of a company is its overall monetary worth, comprising a vast number of assets. When the brand loses value, it also threatens other assets. RadioShack was once the first destination for consumers seeking a Walkman or boom box; however, the loss of brand value as it has struggled to maintain relevance as a provider of modern, cutting-edge technology has ultimately led to its demise in bankruptcy.

The value of a brand can be defined as the earning potential of that brand over the next 12 months.[16] The world's 10 most valuable brands for 2015 appear in Exhibit 11.5.

EXHIBIT 11.5	The World's 10 Most Valuable Brands				
2015 Rank	2013 Rank	Brand	Country	Sector	Brand Value (in $ Billions)
1	1	Apple	United States	Technology	$170.3
2	2	Google	United States	Technology	$120.3
3	3	Coca-Cola	United States	Beverages	$ 78.4
4	5	Microsoft	United States	Technology	$ 67.7
5	4	IBM	United States	Business Services	$ 65.1
6	10	Toyota	Japan	Automotive	$ 49.0
7	8	Samsung	South Korea	Technology	$ 45.3
8	6	GE	United States	Diversified	$ 42.3
9	7	McDonald's	United States	Restaurants	$ 39.8
10	n.a.	Amazon	United States	Retail	$ 37.9

Source: From Interbrand.com, http://interbrand.com/best-brands/best-global-brands/2015/ranking/#?listFormat=ls.

Brand Equity for the Owner

The value of a brand translates into **brand equity**, or the set of assets and liabilities linked to a brand that add to or subtract from the value provided by the product or service.[17] Like the physical possessions of a firm, brands are assets a firm can build, manage, and harness over time to increase its revenue, profitability, and overall value. For example, firms spend millions of dollars on promotion, advertising, and other marketing efforts throughout a brand's life cycle. Marketing expenditures allocated carefully can result in greater brand recognition, awareness, perceived value, and consumer loyalty for the brand, which all enhance the brand's overall equity. Such benefits can be particularly strong if the brand markets itself ethically, as Ethical and Societal Dilemma 11.1 notes.

How do we know how good a brand is or how much equity it has? Experts look at four aspects of a brand to determine its equity: brand awareness, perceived value, brand associations, and brand loyalty.

Brand Awareness **Brand awareness** measures how many consumers in a market are familiar with the brand and what it stands for and have an opinion about it. The more aware of or familiar with it they are, the easier their decision-making process is, which improves the chances of purchase. Familiarity matters most for products that are bought without much thought, such as soap or chewing gum, but brand awareness is also critical for infrequently

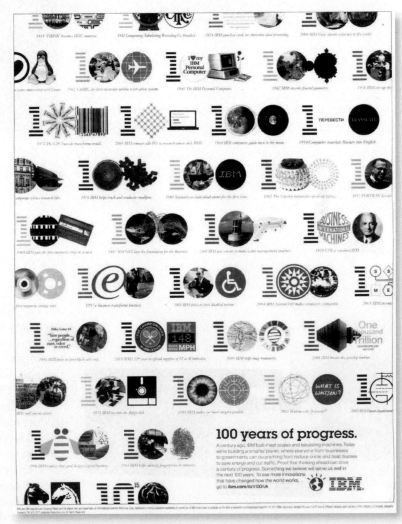

IBM is one of the world's most valuable brands.

Image Courtesy of The Advertising Archives

Ethical & Societal Dilemma 11.1   (Not) Marketing Sugary Drinks to Kids[iii]

Obesity rates are often highest in the nations and regions that drink the most soda. The sugary, high-calorie versions of popular carbonated beverage brands in turn have been widely blamed for the growing rates of obesity, especially among children. Those complaints also are growing as brands expand outside the United States and potentially threaten the long-term health of kids across the globe.

Even as it strongly maintains that sodas are not the main culprit in rising obesity rates, Coca-Cola has acknowledged its own limited responsibility and therefore vowed not to advertise in settings in which children make up more than 35 percent of the anticipated audience (previously, it set this standard at 50 percent). Thus Coke ads have disappeared from cartoon networks and youth-oriented shows, children's magazines, and so forth.

In addition to its commitment not to advertise directly to children younger than 12 years of age, Coke has invested in initiatives to promote more physical activity and to encourage consumers to consider lower calorie alternatives, whether Diet Coke or Minute Maid juices (which Coca-Cola also owns). Beyond advertising, Coke's new product development efforts are largely focused on identifying and integrating natural low-calorie sweeteners. In some countries, its packaging also will feature more prominent information about calorie contents.

Yet critics point out that even as Coke promises to stop targeting children, it has confirmed that it has no plans to stop relying on its popular polar bear advertisements during the holiday season, nor will it eliminate images of children enjoying Coke in its ads. Thus while Coca-Cola might be working to reduce the amount of marketing children might see during their favorite programs, it certainly does not plan to stop appealing to young consumers altogether.

Should Coca-Cola and other consumer packaged-goods companies be allowed to advertise to children?

© GL Archive/Alamy

These brands are so strong that they have become synonymous with the product itself.

© McGraw-Hill Education

purchased items or those the consumer has never purchased before. If the consumer recognizes the brand, it probably has attributes that make it valuable.[18] For those who have never purchased a Toyota, the simple awareness that it exists can help facilitate a purchase. Marketers create brand awareness through repeated exposures of the various brand elements (brand name, logo, symbol, character, packaging, or slogan) in the firm's communications to consumers through advertising, publicity, or other methods (see Chapters 17, 18, and 19).

Certain brands gain such predominance in a particular product market over time that they become synonymous with the product itself; that is, the brand name starts being used as the generic product category. Examples include Kleenex tissues, Clorox bleach, Band-Aid adhesive bandages, and the Google search engine. Companies must be vigilant in protecting their brand names because if they are used so generically, over time the brand itself can lose its trademark status. For competitors, this trend similarly is destructive: If everyone with an upset stomach asks for Pepto-Bismol and never considers any alternatives, brands such as Activia suffer smaller chances of making it into customers' shopping baskets. To counteract such concerns, Activia uses well-known celebrities such as Columbian singer Shakira,[19] retired boxer Laila Ali, singer and actress Reba McEntire, and TV host Dr. Travis Stork in its advertisements to make sure it is recognizable and prominent.[20]

Perceived Value The **perceived value** of a brand is the relationship between a product's or service's benefits and its cost. Customers usually determine the offering's value in relation to the value of its close competitors. If they believe a less expensive brand is about the same quality as a premium brand, the perceived value of that cheaper choice is high. Merchandise sold by Target and Kohl's is not always perceived to be the highest quality, nor is the apparel the most fashion-forward. But not every customer needs to show up at school looking like they came from a fashion show runway. At the same time, these retailers hire high-fashion designers to create reasonably priced lines to feature in their stores—as Target did with Adam Lippes and his "all about plaid" collection to create well-designed pieces at Target-level prices.[21]

Brand Associations **Brand associations** reflect the mental and emotional links that consumers make between a brand and its key product attributes, such as a logo and its color, slogan, or famous personality. These brand associations often result from a firm's advertising and promotional efforts. Toyota's hybrid car, the Prius, is known for being economical, a good value, stylish, and good for the environment. But firms also attempt to create specific associations with positive consumer emotions such as fun, friendship, good feelings, family gatherings, and parties. Jingles can establish particularly strong associations, especially when they are catchy and get stuck in consumers' heads. State Farm Insurance continues to rely on the jingle that Barry Manilow wrote for it in the 1970s: In modern advertisements, young customers in trouble sing the phrase "like a good neighbor, State Farm is there," and an agent magically appears on scene.[22]

Because of his vast viral popularity, Grumpy Cat (real name: Tardar Sauce) has been approached by several brands that seek to be associated with him so they can benefit from his entertaining, satirical, and hip image. The feline's naturally unhappy looking mouth now appears across Friskies' product line. Mashable featured Grumpy Cat in its tent at South by Southwest, and a bidding process led to the *Grumpy Cat's Worst Christmas Ever* movie in 2014.

Brand Loyalty **Brand loyalty** occurs when a consumer buys the same brand's product or service repeatedly over time rather than buying from multiple suppliers within the same category.[23] Therefore, brand-loyal customers are an important source of value for firms. First, firms such as airlines, hotels, long-distance telephone providers, credit card companies, and retailers reward loyal consumers with loyalty or customer relationship management (CRM) programs, such as points customers can redeem for extra discounts or free services, advance

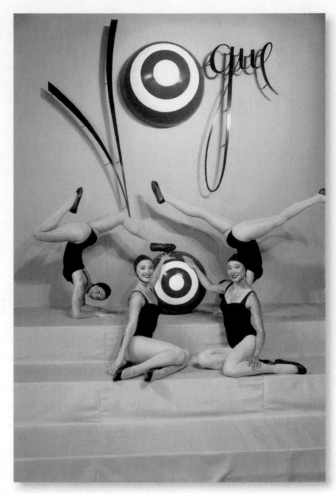

Target is advertising in Vogue *magazine in a clear attempt to enhance the perceived value of its products by featuring them in a magazine that normally features higher-priced, very fashionable products.*
© Neilson Barnard/Getty Images

Friskies cat food is associated with its famous "spokesperson," Grumpy Cat.
© Robin Marchant/Getty Images

notice of sale items, and invitations to special events sponsored by the company. Second, the marketing costs of reaching loyal consumers are much lower because the firm does not have to spend money on advertising and promotion campaigns to attract these customers. Loyal consumers simply do not need persuasion or an extra push to buy the firm's brands. Third, loyal customers tend to praise the virtues of their favorite products, retailers, or services to others. This positive word of mouth reaches potential customers and reinforces the perceived value of current customers, all at no cost to the firm. Fourth, a high level of brand loyalty insulates the firm from competition because, as we noted in Chapter 2, brand-loyal customers do not switch to competitors' brands, even when provided with a variety of incentives.

PROGRESS CHECK

1. How do brands create value for the customer and the firm?
2. What are the components of brand equity?

LO11-6 Determine the various types of branding strategies used by firms.

BRANDING STRATEGIES

Firms institute a variety of brand-related strategies to create and manage key brand assets. The decisions surrounding these strategies are: whether to use manufacturer brands or retailer/store brands, how to name brands and product lines, whether or not to extend the brand name to other products and markets, should the brand name be used with another firm or licensed to another firm, and whether or not the brand be repositioned.

Brand Ownership

Brands can be owned by any firm in the supply chain, whether manufacturers, wholesalers, or retailers. There are two basic brand ownership strategies: manufacturer brands and retailer/store brands, as Exhibit 11.6 shows. Additionally, the brands can be marketed using a common/family name or as individual brands.

EXHIBIT 11.6 Who Owns the Brand?

Who Owns the Brand?		Manufacturer/National Brand	Retailer/Store Brand
Common Name or Not?	Family Brands	Kraft's family line	Kroger's line
	Individual Brands	Kraft's individual brand	Kroger's individual brand

Top left: © Steve Cukrov/Shutterstock RF; Top right: © McGraw-Hill Education; Bottom left: © Ian Dagnall/Alamy; Bottom right: © Food Collection/Alamy

Manufacturer Brands Manufacturer brands, also known as national brands, are owned and managed by the manufacturer. Some famous manufacturer brands are Kraft, Nike, Coca-Cola, KitchenAid, and Sony. With these brands, the manufacturer develops the merchandise, produces it to ensure consistent quality, and invests in a marketing program to establish an appealing brand image. The majority of the brands marketed in the United States are manufacturer brands, and manufacturing firms spend millions of dollars each year to promote their brands. By owning their brands, manufacturers retain more control over their marketing strategy, are able to choose the appropriate market segments and positioning for the brand, and can build the brand and thereby create their own brand equity.

Retailer/Store Brands Retailer/store brands, also called private-label brands, are products developed by retailers. In some cases, retailers manufacture their own products; in other cases they develop the design and specifications for their retailer/store brands and then contract with manufacturers to produce those products. Some national brand manufacturers work with retailers to develop a special version of their standard merchandise offering to be sold exclusively by the retailer.

In the past, sales of store brands were limited. But in recent years, as the size of retail firms has increased through growth and consolidation, more retailers have the scale economies to develop private-label merchandise and use this merchandise to establish a distinctive identity. In addition, manufacturers are more willing to accommodate the needs of retailers and develop co-brands for them.[24] At Kroger, 35 percent of sales in in its nearly 2,500 stores come from store brand options.[25] Both Costco and Trader Joe's have based their brand identities around their store brands.

Naming Brands and Product Lines

Although there is no simple way to decide how to name a brand or a product line, the more the products vary in their usage or performance, the more likely it is that the firm should use individual brands. For example, General Motors uses several individual brands (Cadillac, Chevrolet, Buick, and GMC), each catering to very different target markets and meeting different needs. Hyundai, on the other hand, uses only one brand, because the usage and level of performance are relatively homogeneous across all its cars.

Family Brands A firm can use its own corporate name to brand all its product lines and products; for example, Kraft incorporates the company name into the brand name of its various salad dressings (refer to Exhibit 11.6). When all products are sold under one family brand, the individual brands benefit from the overall brand awareness associated with the family name. Kraft Foods also uses its family brand name prominently on its

Kraft uses a family branding strategy in which several product lines are sold under one name.

© Michael Neelon(misc)/Alamy

cheese, pasta, and condiment brands (e.g., Kraft Macaroni & Cheese, Kraft Singles, Kraft Mayo).

Individual Brands A firm can use **individual brand** names for each of its products. For example, Kraft makes good use of the family branding strategy, but it also allows other products, such as Philadelphia cream cheese, Cracker Barrel restaurants, A.1. steak sauce, and Planters nuts (Exhibit 11.6), to keep their individual identities, which are not readily regarded as falling under the Kraft umbrella.[26]

Distinguish between brand extension and line extension.

Brand and Line Extensions[27]

A **brand extension** refers to the use of the same brand name in a different product line. It is an increase in the product mix's breadth.[28] The dental hygiene market, for instance, is full of brand extensions; Colgate and Crest sell toothpaste, toothbrushes, and other dental hygiene products, even though their original product line was just toothpaste. A **line extension** is the use of the same brand name within the same product line and represents an increase in a product line's depth.

There are several advantages to using the same brand name for new products. First, because the brand name is already well established, the firm can spend less in developing consumer brand awareness and brand associations for the new product.[29] Kellogg's has branched out from the cereal company it once was. Its strategy of branding the corporate name into the product name has allowed it to introduce new products quicker and more easily. Kellogg's Eggo Syrup was a natural extension to its product line of breakfast foods.

Second, if either the original brand or the brand extension has strong consumer acceptance, that perception will carry over to the other product. Ferrari is well known as a brand of luxury sports cars; accordingly, it has leveraged its brand name to introduce clothing offerings emblazoned with its horse logo, which allows enthusiasts to show their devotion to the brand through their apparel. The high cost of luxury cars makes them out of reach for most customers, but clothing-related line extensions give aspirational buyers a pathway to connect with the brand while also helping provide "brand awareness, brand enhancement and, sometimes, brand reinvigoration."[30]

Third, when brand extensions are used for complementary products, a synergy exists between the two products that can increase overall sales. For example, Frito-Lay markets both chips and dips under its Frito-Lay and Tostitos brand names. When people buy the chips, they tend to buy the dips as well.

Not all brand extensions are successful, however. Some can dilute brand equity.[31] **Brand dilution** occurs when the brand extension adversely affects consumer perceptions about the attributes the core brand is believed to hold.[32] Ferrari might be at risk of this effect, because it has gone far past clothing to offer brand licenses for sunglasses, perfume and cologne, skis, hotel suites, guitars, phones, LEGOs, leather bags, watches, jewelry boxes, and dice—among other things. It has licensed its logo to 68 different products, prompting Ferrari's chief executive to admit that cars are "almost incidental" to the brand.[33] Here are some examples of unsuccessful brand extensions:[34]

Using a brand extension strategy, Frito-Lay markets chips as well as dips under its Frito-Lay and Tostitos brand names.
© Michael J. Hruby

- Lifesavers Soda did well in prelaunch taste tests but didn't in subsequent sales.
- Harley Davidson's cake decorating kit tried to appeal to the brand's unparalleled consumer loyalty, but it was considered too tame by their consumer base.
- The Virgin Group has successfully entered many markets, from mobile phones with Virgin Mobile to travel with Virgin cruises, but its entry into the wedding-dress market with Virgin Brides is just one of the firm's failures.
- Zippo believed that its iconic lighter design would be an appealing design for a woman's perfume. Although the perfume didn't smell like lighter fluid, it turns out lighters aren't something that many women want to associate with perfume.
- Dr Pepper's barbeque marinades hoped to utilize the brand's "one of a kind" image, but it never took off with consumers.

To prevent the potentially negative consequences of brand extensions, firms should consider the following:

- Marketers should evaluate the fit between the product class of the core brand and that of the extension.[35] If the fit between the product categories is high, consumers will consider the extension credible, and the brand association will be stronger for the extension. Thus, when Starbucks introduced its line of instant coffee, VIA, it made sense to its customers.

Life Savers unsuccessfully attempted a brand extension strategy with its line of soda.
© GfK Custom Research

- Firms should evaluate consumer perceptions of the attributes of the core brand and seek out similar attributes for the extension, because brand-specific associations are very important for extensions.[36] For example, if HP printers were associated with reliability, performance, and value, consumers would expect the same brand-specific attributes in other products that carried the HP brand name.

- To avoid diluting the brand and damaging brand equity, firms should refrain from extending the brand name to too many products and product categories. At its founding, the Kate Spade brand offered aspirational luxury, selling nearly luxury handbags for $2,000 instead of $20,000. Kate Spade sought to expand its reach, opening a range of Kate Spade Saturday stores as well as Jack Spade shops for men to offer lower-priced versions of its designs. Within two years though, the company has decided to close all these stand-alone storefronts and integrate any remaining inventory into its traditional, central line stores.[37]

- Firms should consider whether the brand extension will be distanced from the core brand, especially if the firm wants to use some but not all of the existing brand associations. Marriott has budget, midtier, and luxury hotels. Its luxury hotels, including the Ritz-Carlton, Edition, and Renaissance, do not use the name Marriott at all.[38]

Co-Branding

Co-branding is the practice of marketing two or more brands together on the same package, promotion, or store. Co-branding can enhance consumers' perceptions of product quality by signaling unobservable product quality through links between the firm's brand and a well-known quality brand. For example, Yum! Brands frequently combines two or more of its restaurant chains, including A&W, KFC, Long John Silver's, Pizza Hut, and Taco Bell, into one store space. This co-branding strategy is designed to appeal to diverse market segments and extend the hours during which each restaurant attracts customers. Yet co-branding also creates risks, especially when the customers of each of the brands turn out to be vastly different. For example, the Burger King and Häagen-Dazs co-branding strategy failed because the customer profiles for each brand were too different.[39] Co-branding may also fail when there are disputes or conflicts of interest between the co-brands.

Brand Licensing

Brand licensing is a contractual arrangement between firms whereby one firm allows another to use its brand name, logo, symbols, and/or characters in exchange for a negotiated fee.[40] Brand licensing is common for toys, apparel, accessories, and entertainment products such as video games. The firm that provides the right to use its brand (licensor) obtains revenues through royalty payments from the firm that has obtained the right to use the brand (licensee). These royalty payments may take the form of upfront, lump-sum licensing fees or be based on the dollar value of sales of the licensed merchandise.

The NBA's New Orleans Pelicans (licensor) provides the right to use its brand to apparel manufacturers (licensee) in return for royalty payments.
© Stacy Revere/Getty Images

One very popular form of licensing is the use of characters created in books and other media. Such entertainment licensing has generated tremendous revenues for movie studios. Disney, for instance, flooded retail stores with products based on its *Frozen* movie.[41] *Star Wars* memorabilia has been continually successful since the first film was released in the 1970s, and the most recent film releases have led to a massive increase in sales. A long-standing staple of licensing has been major league sports teams that play in the MLB, NBA, NFL, or NHL as well as various collegiate sports teams.

Licensing is an effective form of attracting visibility for the brand and thereby building brand equity while also generating additional revenue. There are, however, some risks associated with it. For the licensor, the major risk is the dilution of its brand equity through overexposure of the brand, especially if the brand name and characters are used inappropriately.[42]

Brand Repositioning

Brand repositioning, or **rebranding**, refers to a strategy in which marketers change a brand's focus to target new markets or realign the brand's core emphasis with changing market preferences.[43] The cereal-flavored milk Cow Wow seeks to evoke the liquid left

Cow Wow repositioned its product from appealing to children (left) to appealing to adult Millennials (right).
Source: Cow Wow Cereal Milk

Manufacturers of high fructose corn syrup attempted to reposition their product as high fructose corn sugar using the tagline "Your body can't tell the difference," but it didn't work. Instead, it sparked a series of legal suits between the corn and sugar industries and failed to convince consumers.

© Big Ryan/Getty Images RF

over after a breakfast eater finishes all the grains but still has some milk in the bowl. It originally was targeted for children between 5 and 12 years of age, but the company struggled to reach the parents of this target market. After an unexpected endorsement by late-night talk show host Jimmy Kimmel, who described enjoying the flashback to his childhood, Millennials suddenly started seeking out Cow Wow, ready to purchase a fun treat that reminded them of slurping milk from their cereal bowls after they finished their Froot Loops as kids. Thus Cow Wow decided to reposition and transform the product, using regular 1 percent milk and repackaging it in a larger carton with a screw top, to sell to adult Millennial consumers instead of to children.[44]

Although repositioning can improve the brand's fit with its target segment or boost the vitality of old brands, it is not without costs and risks. Firms often need to spend tremendous amounts of money to make tangible changes to the product and packages as well as intangible changes to the brand's image through various forms of promotion, as Adding Value 11.2 details. These costs may not be recovered if the repositioned brand and messages are not credible to consumers or if the firm has mistaken a fad for a long-term market trend. An example of a recent rebranding effort that provoked consumers' disdain was the attempted repositioning of high fructose corn syrup as "corn sugar."

High fructose corn syrup first became popular when customers began reducing their sugar intake. However, in recent years, concerns surrounding the consumption of high fructose corn syrup have changed customers' preferences, and they began embracing traditional cane sugar as a more natural option. In response to this shift, the corn industry initiated an advertising campaign that featured healthy-looking people strolling through corn fields and asserting that human bodies process sugars produced by cane and sugars produced by corn in exactly the same way. Along with the tagline, "Your body can't tell the difference," the advertising campaign attempted to rebrand high fructose corn syrup as "corn sugar." Not only did the campaign spark a series of legal suits between the corn and sugar industries, but it also failed to convince consumers. Consumption of high fructose corn syrup has decreased from 6.7 billion metric tons to 5.2 billion. This shift, together with consumers' continued demands, has prompted many food manufacturers to cut corn syrup out of their products and accordingly advertise them as "natural." For example, Heinz promises that its ketchup avoids high fructose corn syrup, and both Coca-Cola and Pepsi have introduced line extensions based on the promise of being made with "real sugar."[45]

PROGRESS CHECK

1. What are the differences between manufacturer and private-label brands?
2. What is co-branding?
3. What is the difference between brand extension and line extension?
4. What is brand repositioning?

Adding Value 11.2   The Global Appeal and Rebranding Efforts of American Airlines[iv]

For more than 40 years, American Airlines had used the same logo: a pair of capital *A*s, one red and one blue, surrounding the silhouette of a diving eagle. When the airline purchased 550 new planes, made from a new composite material, it had to change the look of the finish, so it decided to change its look altogether, including a new logo, new designs for the plane interiors, a new website, and new kiosk interfaces in terminals.

The most visible element thus far is the new logo, which removes the double *A* and offers a more abstract version of an eagle. The abstract image is oriented more horizontally, rather than vertically downward. On the new planes, this eagle logo will appear near the front, as if pointing in the direction of the flight. Furthermore, the tails of each airplane will feature another abstract image, evocative of the U.S. flag with blue and red stripes (but no stars).

The abstraction of the images reflects American Airlines' goals for the rebranding—namely, to emphasize the "American spirit" without evoking negative images of the United States in global markets. Futurebrand, the agency that American

Airlines hired to assist it with its efforts, polled consumers around the world to identify positive traits they associated with the United States. The effort sought to determine not just how people view American products and services but also how they view America in a global age.

The results highlighted images of progress, technology, and entertainment, but they also cautioned against any implication of attack or aggression. Therefore the downward-diving eagle needed to go because it could be interpreted as attacking. A direct representation of the U.S. flag might have been perceived as jingoistic, whereas the abstracted version simply provides a more neutral identifying hint.

In eliminating a widely familiar logo along with its well-known letter typeface, American Airlines clearly is taking a risk that it will lose brand recognition among customers who unconsciously seek the same look they have always seen at the airport. But in a global economy, a company with an American identity, in all senses of the term, needs to take care to emphasize the positives while avoiding more controversial elements.

American Airlines' new logo is an abstract version of an eagle. The tail of each plane features an abstraction of the U.S. flag.
© Kevin Clark/Alamy RF

PACKAGING

LO11-8 Indicate the advantages of a product's packaging and labeling strategy.

Packaging is an important brand element that has more tangible or physical benefits than other brand elements have. Packages come in different types and offer a variety of benefits to consumers, manufacturers, and retailers. The **primary package** is the one the consumer uses, such as the toothpaste tube. From the primary package, consumers typically seek convenience in terms of storage, use, and consumption.

The **secondary package** is the wrapper or exterior carton that contains the primary package and provides the UPC label used by retail scanners. Consumers can use the secondary package to find additional product information that may not be available on the primary package. Like primary packages, secondary packages add consumer value by facilitating the convenience of carrying, using, and storing the product.

Whether primary or secondary, packaging plays several key roles: It attracts the consumers' attention. It enables products to stand out from their competitors. It offers a promotional tool (e.g., "NEW" and "IMPROVED" promises on labels). Finally, it

Kraft's Philadelphia cream cheese changed its packaging from round to oval to ensure front-facing displays that can't spin and fits more into the same shelf space.

© Edible images/Alamy

Morton Salt changed its packaging to celebrate its 100th anniversary.

© Mike Mozart/Flickr/CC BY 2.0

allows for the same product to appeal to different markets with different sizes, such that convenience stores stock little packages that travelers can buy at the last minute, whereas Costco sells extra-large versions of products.

Firms occasionally change or update their packaging as a subtle way of repositioning the product. A change can be used to attract a new target market and/or appear more up to date to its current market. For instance, to help consumers find their preferred taste among the vast variety of flavor options it now sells (as we discussed previously in this chapter), Philadelphia cream cheese has undertaken another change—namely, to the packaging of its products. Rather than round tubs—which can easily get spun around on store shelves, such that consumers have trouble seeing exactly which variety is in front of them—the brand is introducing an oval tub, to ensure front-facing displays. In addition to preventing spin, the oval shape means that more products can fit into the same shelf space.[46]

Changes also can make consumers feel like they are receiving something tangible in return for paying higher prices, even when the product itself remains untouched. Whether true or not, consumers see new packaging and tend to think that the "new" product may be worth trying. In honor of its 100th birthday, Morton has redesigned the packaging of over 100 individual items to give a clean, modern feel.[47]

Some packaging changes are designed to make the product more recognizable, such as L'eggs pantyhose iconic egg-shaped container and Daisy Brand's redesign of its

Daisy Brand simplified its cottage cheese containers and added colored lids to make them more recognizable.

© Daisy Brand

L'eggs pantyhose packaging makes the product more recognizable with its iconic egg shape.

© McGraw-Hill Education

cottage cheese containers. Known for using no more than four ingredients in any of its cottage cheese products, Daisy Brand redesigned its containers to present a simple, Spartan look and paired it with blue lids. The shade of the blue lid varies by the fat content of the cottage cheese. Combining a simple container and varying colored lids, Daisy Brand expects its new containers will grab consumers' attention in the dairy case and increase sales.[48]

An interesting recent development in packaging is a move to "sustainable packaging." Sustainable packaging is product packaging that has less of a negative impact on the environment. Leaders in this area of innovation include Coca-Cola, Microsoft, Waste Management, Aveda, and Zappos. These firms host a sustainable packaging conference that brings together more than 250 firms to discuss new methods to produce environmentally responsible packaging that is also cost effective. Ideas from this conference include returnable packaging, use of 3D printing, and flexible packaging. They have also set up a website with information on future conferences and information for the industry at http://www .sustainability-in-packaging.com.[49]

Packaging can also be used in a far subtler way—namely, to help suppliers save costs. When the costs of producing a product rise significantly, manufacturers are faced with either raising prices—something customers don't usually like—or reducing the amount of product sold in a package. Chobani reduced the size of its Greek yogurt containers by 12 percent. When customers noticed the decrease, they took to Twitter and Facebook to complain about the change.[50]

Product Labeling

Labels on products and packages provide information the consumer needs for his or her purchase decision and consumption of the product. Because they identify the product and brand, labels are also an important element of branding and can be used for promotion. The information required on them must comply with general and industry-specific laws and regulations, including the constituents or ingredients contained in the product, where the product was made, directions for use, and/or safety precautions.

Many labeling requirements stem from various laws, including the Federal Trade Commission Act of 1914, the Fair Packaging and Labeling Act of 1967, and the Nutrition Labeling Act of 1990. Several federal agencies, industry groups, and consumer watchdogs carefully monitor product labels. The Food and Drug Administration is the primary federal agency that reviews food and package labels and ensures that the claims made by the manufacturer are true.

A product label is much more than just a sticker on the package; it is a communication tool. Many of the elements on the label are required by laws and regulations (i.e., ingredients, fat content, sodium content, serving size, calories), but other elements remain within the control of the manufacturer. Ethical and Societal Dilemma 11.2 describes how some food companies are responding proactively to the potential of new regulations. In addition, the way manufacturers use labels to communicate the benefits of their products to consumers varies with the product. Many products highlight specific ingredients, vitamin content or nutrient content (e.g., iron), and country of origin. This focus signals to consumers that the product offers these benefits. The importance of the label as a communication tool should not be underestimated.

PROGRESS CHECK

1. Why do firms change packaging?
2. What objectives do product labels fulfill?

Ethical & Societal Dilemma 11.2

Mars Inc., an Unlikely but Powerful Proponent of Sugar Labeling on Packages[v]

When U.S. regulators recently proposed changes to the nutrition labels on food, a key element was adding a new line to the familiar table that would quantify how much sugar had been added to the product. Although the U.S. Food and Drug Administration does not have a set amount that it recommends, the U.S. Dietary Guidelines Advisory Committee calls for consumers to obtain no more than 10 percent of their daily calories from sugars. Observers predicted quick responses from food producers, especially those that add substantial sugar to their products.

They might not have predicted exactly the response that Mars, Inc., offered though. The maker of M&M's, Snickers, and other candies rapidly came out in favor of the recommendations, in contrast with most of its big food peers. Asserting that even a candymaker knows that people should not consume too much sugar, a senior executive at Mars noted that more transparency about food ingredients was always a good thing for consumers, and therefore something that the company would support.

The regulations would pertain only to added sugars, though human bodies process all sugars the same way, whether they derive naturally from the ingredients or are added during the production process. Some other well-known companies have yet to announce their reactions to the regulations, but their actions suggest they are aware of the trend to find ways to reduce sugar intake. For example, Nestlé says it will aim to remove all artificial coloring and flavors, and Mondelez plans to introduce more 200-calorie serving sizes for its popular Oreo and Cadbury product lines.

These moves all refer to products that consumers expect will contain sugar—that is, few people are likely to be surprised that M&M's candies exceed the 10 percent limit, with 30 grams of sugar in a serving that contains 240 calories. But if the nutrition guidelines come to pass, the requirements also would apply to products whose sugar content might seem less obvious. For example, manufacturers often add sugar to products such as yogurts, pasta sauces, crackers, and breads. If the added sugar content were evident on the labels, consumers might be unpleasantly surprised to realize how much had been added to products that they likely assume are relatively healthy.

But another perspective suggests that it won't matter much. The past history of nutrition guidelines suggests that consumers rarely pay much attention to the information provided on labels. In that case, requiring packaged food companies to change their labels might be an expensive demand that feels like the right thing to do but actually has little benefit for society or consumer health.

When U.S. regulators proposed quantifying the amount of sugar that is added to a product by printing it on nutrition labels, Mars, Inc., makers of M&M's and other candies, supported the initiative, noting that transparency about food ingredients is always a good thing for consumers.

© Roman Samokhin/123RF.com

Reviewing Learning Objectives

LO11-1 **Describe the components of a product.**

The product itself is important, but so are its associated services, such as support or financing. Other elements combine to produce the core customer value of a product: the brand name, quality level, packaging, and additional features.

LO11-2 **Identify the types of consumer products.**

Consumer products tend to be classified into four groups: specialty, shopping, convenience, and unsought products. Each classification involves a different purchase situation and consumer goal.

LO11-3 **Explain the difference between a product mix's breadth and a product line's depth.**

Breadth, or variety, entails the number of product lines that a company offers. Depth involves the number of categories within one specific product line.

LO11-4 **Identify the advantages that brands provide firms and consumers.**

Brands play important roles in enabling people to make purchase decisions more easily and encouraging customer loyalty. For firms specifically, they also constitute valuable assets and improve a company's bottom line and help protect against competition.

LO11-5 **Explain the various components of brand equity.**

Brand equity summarizes the value that a brand adds or subtracts from the offering's value. It comprises brand awareness, or how many consumers in the market are familiar with the brand; brand associations, which are the links consumers make between the brand and its image; and brand loyalty, which occurs when a consumer will only buy that brand's offer. Brand equity also encompasses the concept of perceived value, which is a subjective measure that consumers develop to assess the costs of obtaining the brand.

LO11-6 **Determine the various types of branding strategies used by firms.**

Firms use a variety of strategies to manage their brands. First, they decide whether to offer manufacturer and/or private-label brands. Second, they have a choice of using an overall family brand or a collection of product line or individual brands. Third, to reach new markets or extend their current market, they can extend their current brands to new products. Fourth, firms can co-brand with another brand to create sales and profit synergies for both. Fifth, firms with strong brands have the opportunity to license their brands to other firms. Finally, as the marketplace changes, it is often necessary to reposition a brand.

LO11-7 **Distinguish between brand extension and line extension.**

Whereas a brand extension uses the same brand name for a new product that gets introduced into new or the same markets, a line extension is simply an increase of an existing product line by the brand.

LO11-8 **Indicate the advantages of a product's packaging and labeling strategy.**

Similar to brands, packaging and labels help sell the product and facilitate its use. The primary package holds the product, and its label provides product information. The secondary package provides additional consumer information on its label and facilitates transportation and storage for retailers as well as their customers. Labels have become increasingly important to consumers because they supply important safety, nutritional, and product usage information.

Key Terms

LEARNSMART

Marketing Digitally

1. Visit Mac Cosmetic's website (http://www.maccosmetics.com). Identify and briefly describe the depth and the breadth of its product lines.

2. Go to BMW's website (http://www.bmwusa.com) and identify a few recently introduced brand extensions to the marketplace. Discuss whether you believe the brand extension examples you provided will benefit or harm the firm.

Marketing Applications

1. L.L.Bean has a 100% satisfaction guaranteed policy on all of its products. What features of a pair of pants from L.L.Bean would be part of the actual product and which would be part of the associated services?

2. Classify each of the following products into either convenience, shopping, specialty, or unsought goods: toothpaste, life insurance, Sharp TV, Eggo waffles, lettuce, Coach handbag, adidas soccer cleats, furniture.

3. Study the following two product mixes. For Product Mix 1: A, B, C and D are the lines; and for Product Mix 2: X, Y and Z are the lines.

A	B	C	D
a1	b1	c1	d1
a2	b2	c2	d2
a3	b3	c3	

Product Mix 1

X	Y	Z
x1	y1	z1
x2	y2	z2
x3	y3	z3
x4	y4	

Product Mix 2

Which mix has more *breadth* and why? Which mix is *deeper* and why?

4. Suppose you are the coffee buyer for Kroger's. There is a strong corporate initiative to increase store-label merchandise. Discuss the advantages and disadvantages of offering private-label coffee.

5. Identify a specific brand that has developed a high level of brand equity. What specific aspects of that brand establish its brand equity?

6. Are you loyal to any brands? If so, pick one and explain why you believe you are loyal, beyond that you simply like the brand. If not, pick a brand that you like and explain how you would feel and act differently toward the brand if you were loyal to it.

7. Sears owns several store brands, including DieHard, Kenmore, and Craftsman. Each brand features many models that may appeal to various customer groups. Wouldn't it be easier to just identify them all as Sears? Justify your answer.

8. Do you think all edible items sold in a grocery store should have an ingredient and nutrition label? Consider the perspectives of consumers, the manufacturer, and the store.

9. You are the brand manager for a firm that makes herbs, spices, and other food additives. You have had complaints from some of your retail outlets that they are finding empty bottles of pure vanilla extract stashed around the store. Apparently, due to the high (35 percent) alcohol content of pure vanilla extract, people are grabbing the cute little bottles, having a drink, and getting rid of the evidence. Anecdotal evidence from store employees indicates that the majority of the imbibers are teenagers. The cost of placing a tamperproof cap on the extract is a relatively insignificant percentage of the purchase price but will make it more difficult to open, particularly for older customers. Also, there has been a significant rise in sales to retailers as a result of the vanilla "addicts." What should you do?

Quiz Yourself

1. As the size of retail firms has increased through growth and consolidation, more retailers have developed ____ merchandise, which they use to establish a distinctive identity.
   a. generic
   b. copycat
   c. private-label
   d. manufacturer
   e. co-branded

2. Brand equity is determined by four aspects of a brand. Which of the following is not one of the four aspects?

   a. Brand awareness
   b. Perceived value
   c. Brand associations
   d. Brand quality
   e. Brand loyalty

(Answers to these questions can be found in the Quiz Yourself Answer Key section.)

Chapter Case Study

FROM THE COUNTERCULTURE TO THE RUNWAY: HOW DID BIRKENSTOCKS BECOME FASHIONABLE?

Hippies wear them. Rebels, dropouts from conventional consumerism, flower children—all images traditionally associated with Birkenstocks, the clunky, cork-soled sandals that have been issuing forth from German factories for 240 years. Although the company has introduced a few variations, such as a clog or rubberized straps, the look of a Birkenstock is immediately recognizable and little changed from its humble beginnings.[51]

All these features suggest it is a poor candidate as a fashion product. Rather than changing every season, the footwear has stayed largely the same. Rather than focusing on the appearance of the offering, the product design stems solely from considerations of comfort and orthopedic safety. Furthermore, they continue to be made in relatively expensive German factories rather than having production shipped overseas to lower the costs.

Considering these factors, it seems strange that *Vogue* has called Birks "sexy" and *Glamour* named it the shoe of the summer recently. Explanations for this newfound popularity with fashion's elite are varied and unproven. One fashion blogger explained that after years of wearing only uncomfortable, tight, high-heeled shoes, slipping on a pair of Birkenstocks was a life-changing experiment in comfort, so she could not imagine going back. Other fashion leaders, including Manolo Blahnik—known for his sky-high heels and creative shoe designs—has offered his endorsement, asserting that as long as the wearers have nice toes and a good pedicure, the sandals can look nice.

The approval from these fashion leaders has led more and more famous people to name-drop the brand. In popular magazines that feature interviews with trendy celebrities like Keke Palmer and Lorraine Pascale, the Birkenstock name pops up as the shoe of preference on set.[52]

The shift certainly did not result from a conscious effort by Birkenstock though. Rather, it caught the company somewhat by surprise, because it had been doing business the same way it had for more than two centuries. It has a virtually nonexistent marketing budget, does not advertise widely, and did not pursue the endorsements it has received from fashion trendsetters. Its CEO asserts that the popularity is a reaffirmation of a basic, and seemingly outdated, marketing lesson: Build a great product, and people will seek it out on their own.

Still, the company is not immune to the appeal of being known as fashionable. Accordingly, it is happy to tout its mentions in popular media on the Birkenstock website. It also has developed a nice collection of Instagram shots that emphasize its diverse assortment options. Along with fashion shots of models wearing its silver sandals with high-fashion dresses, it also features hikers in remote locations, sporting its comfortable-looking, well-worn footwear.

The combination of great product and strong branding has been highly effective. Birkenstock's sales have grown by anywhere from 40 percent to 50 percent over the past year in different regions of the world, and it estimates that it will sell 20 million pairs annually by 2020. That's a lot of toes to show.[53]

Birkenstock has gone high fashion. Pictured here is British-American actress Lily Collins sporting the 240-year-old brand on her feet.
© OPC/ZOJ/WENN/Newscom

Questions

1. Visit the company website (https://www.birkenstockusa.com/) and identify and describe the different product lines that it markets.

2. Describe its product line breadth.

3. Review the different product categories in each of the company's product lines. Which has the greatest depth? Which has the least?

4. How has the company positioned its brand? How does it go about communicating its position?

Endnotes

1. John Tierney, "24 Miles, 4 Minutes, and 834 M.P.H., All in One Jump," *The New York Times*, October 14, 2012, http://www.nytimes.com.

2. Catharine Smith, "Red Bull Stratos YouTube Live Stream Attracts Record Number Of Viewers (UPDATE)," *Huffington Post*, October 15, 2012, http://www.huffingtonpost.com/2012/10/14/red-bull-stratos-youtube_n_1965375.html.

3. John Tierney, "24 Miles, 4 Minutes, and 834 M.P.H., All in One Jump," *The New York Times*, October 14, 2012, http://www.nytimes.com.

4. http://redbullrecords.com/.

5. https://www.youtube.com/channel/UC7qn3NBI3XV7d8I3cvZeABw.

6. http://www.trekbikes.com.

7. Sharon Ng, "Cultural Orientation and Brand Dilution: Impact of Motivation Level and Extension Typicality," *Journal of Marketing Research* 47, no. 1 (February 2010), pp. 186–98.

8. Michael A. Wiles, Neil A. Morgan, and Lopo L. Rego, "The Effect of Brand Acquisition and Disposal on Stock Returns," *Journal of Marketing* 76, no. 1 (2012), pp. 38–58.

9. E.J. Schultz, "Spread Some Bacon on that Bagel: Kraft's New Philly Flavor," *Advertising Age*, October 8, 2014, http://adage.com.

10. Jack Neff, "As P&G Looks to Cut More Than Half Its Brands, Which Should Go?" *Advertising Age*, August 4, 2014, http://adage.com.

11. Darren Rovell, "Source: Bryce Harper Signs Biggest Endorsement Deal for MLB Player," *ESPN*, May 4, 2016.

12. Kevin Lane Keller, *Strategic Brand Management: Building, Measuring, and Managing Brand Equity*, 4th ed. (Upper Saddle River, NJ: Prentice Hall, 2012); David A. Aaker, *Building Strong Brands* (New York: Simon & Schuster, 2012).

13. This discussion of the advantages of strong brands is adapted from Kevin Lane Keller, *Strategic Brand Management: Building, Measuring, and Managing Brand Equity*, 4th ed. (Upper Saddle River, NJ: Prentice Hall, 2012)

14. Kevin Lane Keller and Donald R. Lehmann, "Assessing Long-Term Brand Potential," *Journal of Brand Management* 17 (2009), pp. 6–17.

15. "McDonald's Just Won a Big Trademark Turf Fight," Reuters, July 5, 2016.

16. http://www.interbrand.com. The net present value of the earnings over the next 12 months is used to calculate the value.

17. David Aaker, *Brand Portfolio Strategy: Creating Relevance, Differentiation, Energy, Leverage, and Clarity* (New York: Free Press, 2004); David A. Aaker, *Managing Brand Equity* (New York: Free Press, 1991).

18. Rong Huang and Emine Sarigöllü, "How Brand Awareness Relates to Market Outcome, Brand Equity, and the Marketing Mix," *Journal of Business Research* 65, no. 1 (2012), pp. 92–99; Lopo L. Rego, Matthew T. Billett, and Neil A. Morgan, "Consumer-Based Brand Equity and Firm Risk," *Harvard Business Review* 73, no. 6 (November 2009), pp. 47–60; Natalie Mizik and Robert Jacobson, "Valuing Branded Businesses," *Harvard Business Review* 73, no. 6 (November 2009), pp. 137–53.

19. David Kiefaber, "Activia Shows That Inside Shakira's Famous Stomach Are . . . More Shakiras!," *Adweek*, March 18, 2014, http://www.adweek.com.

20. Stuart Elliott, "New Campaign Markets Activia to Wider Audience," *The New York Times*, January 5, 2014.

21. Stephanie Eckart, "Target's Fall Collaboration Is Full of Plaid," *nymag.com*, August 13, 2015.

22. Tim Nudd, "Zoinks! State Farm Saves Scooby-Doo and the Gang in Groovy Animated Spot," *Adweek*, October 29, 2013, http://www.adweek.com.

23. http://www.marketingpower.com/_layouts/Dictionary.aspx?dLetter=B.

24. Lien Lamey et al., "How Business Cycles Contribute to Private-Label Success: Evidence from the United States and Europe," *Journal of Marketing* 71 (January 2007), pp. 1–15; PLMA (2009), http://www.plmainternational.com.

25. "Kroger Cranks Up Store-Brand Manufacturing, *NBCNews.com*, October 7, 2009.

26. http://www.kraftfoodsgroup.com/brands/index.aspx.

27. The distinction between brand and line extensions is clarified in Barry Silverstein, "Brand Extensions: Risks and Rewards," *Brandchannel.com*, January 5, 2009.

28. See Alokparna Basu Monga and Deborah Roedder John, "What Makes Brands Elastic? The Influence of Brand Concept and Styles of Thinking on Brand Extension Evaluation," *Journal of Marketing* 74, no. 3 (May 2010), pp. 80–92; Thorsen Hennig-Thurau, Mark B. Houson, and Torsten Heitjans, "Conceptualizing and Measuring the Monetary Value of Brand Extensions: The Case of Motion Pictures," *Journal of Marketing* 73, no. 6 (November 2009), pp. 167–83; Rajeev Batra, Peter Lenk, and Michel Wedel, "Brand Extension Strategy Planning: Empirical Estimation of Brand–Category Personality Fit and Atypicality," *Journal of Marketing Research* 47, no. 2 (April 2010), pp. 335–47.

29. David Aaker, *Aaker on Branding: 20 Principles That Drive Success* (Morgan James, 2014); David A. Aaker, *Building Strong Brands* (New York: Simon & Schuster, 2012).

30. Rebecca R. Ruiz, "Luxury Cars Imprint Their Brands on Goods from Cologne to Clothing," *The New York Times*, February 20, 2015, http://www.nytimes.com.

31. Rosellina Ferraro, Amna Kirmani, and Ted Matherly, "Look at Me! Look at Me! Conspicuous Brand Usage, Self-Brand Connection, and Dilution," *Journal of Marketing Research* 50, no. 4 (August 2013), pp. 477–88; Sanjay Sood and Kevin Lane Keller, "The Effects of Brand Name Structure on Brand Extension Evaluations and Parent Brand Dilution," *Journal of Marketing Research* 49, no. 3 (June 2012), pp. 373–82.

32. Rosellina Ferraro, Amna Kirmani, and Ted Matherly, "Look at Me! Look at Me! Conspicuous Brand Usage, Self-Brand Connection, and Dilution," *Journal of Marketing Research* 50, no. 4 (August 2013), pp. 477–88; Sharon Ng, "Cultural Orientation and Brand Dilution: Impact of Motivation Level and Extension Typicality," *Journal of Marketing Research* 47, no. 1 (February 2010), pp. 186–98.

33. Rebecca R. Ruiz, "Luxury Cars Imprint Their Brands on Goods from Cologne to Clothing," *The New York Times*, February 20, 2015, http://www.nytimes.com.

34. Shané Schutte, "6 Worst Brand Extensions from Famous Companies," *Real Business*, June 16, 2014, http://realbusiness.co.uk/article/26961-6-worst-brand-extensions-from-famous-companies; Emily Marchak, "The Pros and Cons of Sub-Branding and Brand Extension," *Brogan & Partners*, October 13, 2015, http://brogan.com/blog/pros-and-cons-sub-branding-and-brand-extension.

35. Susan Spiggle, Hang T. Nguyen, and Mary Caravella. "More Than Fit: Brand Extension Authenticity," *Journal of Marketing Research* 49, no. 6 (2012), pp. 967–83; Franziska Völckner et al., "The Role of Parent Brand Quality for Service Brand Extension Success," *Journal of Service Research* 13, no. 4 (2010), pp. 379–96.

36. Guoqun Fu, Jiali Ding, and Riliang Qu, "Ownership Effects in Consumers' Brand Extension Evaluations," *Journal of Brand Management* 16 (2009), pp. 221–33; Christoph Burmann, Sabrina Zeplin, and Nicola Riley, "Key Determinants of Internal Brand Management Success: An Exploratory Empirical Analysis," *Journal of Brand Management* 16 (2009), pp. 264–84.

37. Kim Bhasin, "For Kate Spade, a Move Downmarket Goes Bust," *Bloomberg Businessweek*, February 5, 2015.

38. http://www.marriott.com/corporateinfo/glance.mi.

39. David A. Aaker, *Building Strong Brands* (New York: Simon & Schuster, 2012).

40. Kevin Lane Keller, *Strategic Brand Management: Building, Measuring, and Managing Brand Equity*, 4th ed. (Upper Saddle River, NJ: Prentice Hall, 2012)

41. Rachel Abrams and Gregory Schmidt, "Superhero Movies Create Opportunity for Toymakers," *The New York Times*, February 13, 2015, http://www.nytimes.com.

42. Ibid.

43. Mukesh Kumar Mishra and Dibyendu Choudhury, "The Effect of Repositioning on Brand Personality: An Empirical Study on BlackBerry Mobile Phones," *IUP Journal of Brand Management* 10, no. 2 (2013); Pascale G. Quester and Nathalie Fleck, "Club

Med: Coping with Corporate Brand Evolution," *Journal of Product & Brand Management* 19, no. 2 (2010), pp. 94–102.

44. John Grossman, "A Sweet Breakfast Memory that Connects with the Wrong Market," *The New York Times*, November 12, 2014; John Grossman, "Should Cow Wow Sell to Little Children or Big Children," *The New York Times*, November 12, 2014; John Grossman, "Cow Wow Picks a Target Audience for its Flavored Milk," *The New York Times*, November 19, 2014, http://www.nytimes.com.

45. E.J. Schultz, "Corn and Sugar Industries Battle in Court over Ad Claims," *Advertising Age*, November 3, 2015.

46. Schultz, "Spread Some Bacon on that Bagel: Kraft's New Philly Flavor."

47. "Morton Salt Girl Birthday Brings Brand Refresh," *Packaging World*, March 12, 2014, http://www.packworld.com.

48. "Daisy Updates Cottage Cheese Pack," *Packaging World*, March 13, 2014, http://www.packworld.com.

49. "Microsoft, Waste Management, The Coca-Cola Company and More at Sustainability in Packaging 2014," *Sustainability in Packaging*, January 6, 2014.

50. Kate Little, "Chobani Yogurt Is Latest Victim in Shrinking Grocery Case," CNBC, January 4, 2014, http://www.cnbc.com.

51. Rebecca Mead, "Sole Cycle," *The New Yorker*, March 23, 2015.

52. Birkenstock USA, "Press," https://www.birkenstockusa.com/press.

53. Ellen Emmerentze Jervell, "Birkenstock Doesn't Care If Fashionistas Stop Wearing Its Sandals," *The Wall Street Journal*, May 11, 2015.

i. Mark Clothier, "The Downside of Low-End Luxury Cars," *Bloomberg Businessweek*, July 17, 2014, http://www.businessweek.com.

ii. Mark van Rijmenam, "Macy's Is Changing the Shopping Experience with Big Data Analytics," *DataFloq*, March 14, 2014, https://datafloq.com/read/macys-changing-shopping-experience-big-data-analyt/286; Nicole Marie Melton, "Macy's Boosts Web Sales, Email Marketing with Predictive Analytics," *FierceRetailT*, May 14, 2014, http://www.fierceretail.com/retailit/story/macys-boosts-web-sales-email-marketing-predictive-analytics/2014-05-14; Joe Keenan, "Customer Retention: Macy's Uses Predictive Analytics to Grow Customer Spend," *Retail Online Integration*, August 2014, http://www.retailonlineintegration.com/article/macys-uses-predictive-analytics-grow-customer-spend/1.

iii. Tiffany Hsu, "Coca-Cola Anti-Obesity Promises Include No Advertising to Kids," *Los Angeles Times*, May 8, 2013, http://articles.latimes.com; Mike Esterl and Paul Ziobro, "Coke to Limit Ads to Kids, Push Diet Drinks," *The Wall Street Journal*, http://online.wsj.com.

iv. Mark Wilson, "American Airlines Rebrands Itself, and America Along with It," *Fast Company*, January 22, 2012.

v. Annie Gasparro, "M&M Maker Wants Labels for Added Sugar," *The Wall Street Journal*, May 8, 2015.

CHAPTER 12

DEVELOPING NEW PRODUCTS

LEARNING OBJECTIVES

After reading this chapter, you should be able to:

LO12-1 Identify the reasons firms create new products.

LO12-2 Describe the different groups of adopters articulated by the diffusion of innovation theory.

LO12-3 Describe the various stages involved in developing a new product or service.

LO12-4 Explain the product life cycle.

You may not have heard of Xiaomi yet, but that is likely to change soon. The company appeared on the scene only in 2014, and within a few years was already the fifth-largest smartphone maker in the world.[1] Most of its products still sell in its home market of China, but it has expanded to 58 countries,[2] with expectations to move into the United States, Eastern Europe, and Latin America.[3] Though the start-up firm has adopted a unique path to growth that its founder has insisted is the key to its future success, even as critics suggest it will need to become far more conventional if it is to get substantially larger. The strategy began with its product: offer smartphones comparable to those produced by rivals such as Apple and Samsung, but at approximately half the price. With this introduction, Xiaomi emerged as the most valuable start-up in the world, with an initial valuation of $46 billion.

But part of the strength of the brand was that its new product offerings have been especially popular among "regular" consumers and young purchasers, many of whom simply cannot afford the high prices demanded for more traditional smartphone brands. These consumers appreciate various aspects of the newly introduced Mi phones: their equivalent functionality, their lower price, and their added benefits in the form of value-added social events and services provided to customers of the new company. For example, Xiaomi hosts parties every few weeks in different locations across China, inviting hundreds of customers to each. These customers are not necessarily those with the most expensive plans; one guest arrived at a party at a high-end nightclub still in his work clothes, noting that he had worked 29 out of the previous 30 days.[4]

In addition to providing social events to go along with their products, senior executives at Xiaomi answer customers' online questions personally and commit a certain amount of time each week to meet with visitors. When users provide assistance to the company, such as

answering additional questions in fan forums, Xiaomi shows its appreciation by sending them gifts and honoring them with VIP titles. In return, these dedicated fans spread the word about the company far and wide, which has meant that Xiaomi seemingly did not need to spend much on advertising to get its products to spread.

But then an interesting thing happened: Faced with remarkable growth and dedicated to the proposition that it had to make its customers feel embraced and valued, Xiaomi struggled to maintain its innovation pace.[5] Furthermore, with its focus on keeping prices low, Xiaomi did not aggressively patent its new products. Therefore, as it sought to expand beyond China, it struggled to avoid potential lawsuits or copycats in other nations. For example, it initiated forays into the Philippines and Malaysia but has yet to earn any more than about 5 percent market share in each of these markets.[6] Growth in India has been somewhat stronger, where fans have enjoyed and appreciated the product offerings.

In response, Xiaomi notes that a key effort is "to understand the fans and to make friends with them, instead of talking as a brand."[7] The founder and CEO Lei Jun even has asserted that his goal is less to build market share and more to introduce "thrilling" new products and make sure that Xiaomi earns the continued support of its loyal fans.[8] For about a year, Xiaomi had not introduced any new offerings, so when it announced its Mi5 phone in early 2016, consumers got pretty excited. The latest version features a better camera, a fingerprint sensor, a cool look, and updated processing capabilities. Although many of these options already are available in Apple and Samsung products, the Mi5 is innovative in that it still brings these offerings to customers at approximately half the price of the other brands' options.

In addition, Xiaomi has filed for approximately 3,600 patents recently, mostly in China but also in several international markets. It is determined that it can bring "the good life" to consumers across the developing world by offering them not just smartphones but also technologically advanced light bulbs and television sets at reasonable prices.[9] Lei also has made a point of encouraging Xiaomi researchers to renew their focus on "cool stuff," from virtual reality to robotics to potentially developing a new and proprietary processing chip.[10]

Few three-letter words are more exciting than *new*. It brings forth an image of freshness, adventure, and excitement. Yet *new* also is a complex term when it comes to market offerings because it might mean adding something new to an existing product, introducing a flavor never offered before, or relying on different packaging that provides added value. But the most exhilarating type of new product is something never seen before. Thousands of patent applications pursue this elusive prize: a successful and truly innovative new product.

To think about how once-new products have changed the world, imagine living 200 years ago: You cook meals on a stove fueled by coal or wood; you write out homework by hand (if you are lucky enough to attend school) and by candlelight. To get to school, you hike along unpaved roads to reach a small, cold, basic classroom with just a few classmates who listen to a lecture from a teacher writing on a blackboard.

Today, you finish your homework on a laptop computer with word processing software that appears to have a mind of its own and can correct your spelling automatically. Your climate-controlled room has ample electric light. While you work on your laptop, you also talk with a friend using the hands-free headset of your wireless phone. As you drive to school in your car, you pick up fast food from a convenient drive-through window while browsing and listening to your personal selection of songs playing through your car speakers, connected wirelessly to your iPhone. Your friend calls to discuss a slight change to the homework, so you pull over to grab your iPhone, make the necessary change to your assignment, and e-mail it from your smartphone to your professor. When you arrive at school, you sit in a 200-person classroom, where you can plug in your laptop, take notes on your iPad, or digitally record the lecture. The professor adds notes on the day's PowerPoint presentations using her tablet computer. You have already downloaded the PowerPoint presentations and add similar notes through your own laptop. After class, to complete your planning for a last-minute party, you send out a Facebook invitation to your friends and ask for responses to get a head count. You then text your roommate, telling her to get food and drinks for the right number of people, which she orders through an online grocer that will deliver later in the day.

Our lives are defined by the many new products and services developed through scientific and technological advances and by the added features included in products that we have always used. In this second chapter dealing with the first P in the marketing mix (product), we continue our discussion from the preceding chapter and explore how companies add value to product and service offerings through innovation. We also look at how firms develop new products and services on their own. We conclude the chapter with an examination of how new products and services get adopted by the market and how firms can change their marketing mix as the product or service moves through its life cycle.

WHY DO FIRMS CREATE NEW PRODUCTS?

LO12-1 Identify the reasons firms create new products.

New market offerings provide value to firms as well as to customers. But the degree to which they do so depends on how new they really are. When we say a "new product/ service," we don't necessarily mean that the market offer has never existed before. Completely new-to-the-market products represent fewer than 10 percent of all new product introductions each year. It is more useful to think of the degree of newness or innovativeness on a continuum from truly new-to-the-world—as Fitbits are—to slightly repositioned, such as when Kraft's Capri Sun brand of ready-to-drink beverages were repackaged in a bigger pouch to appeal to teens.

Regardless of where on the continuum a new product lies, firms have to innovate. **Innovation** refers to the process by which ideas are transformed into new offerings, including products, services, processes, and branding concepts that will help firms grow. Without innovation and its resulting new products and services, firms would have only two choices: continue to market current products to current customers or take the same product to another market with similar customers.

Fitbits are new-to-the-world. How in the world did we ever get by without them?
© Cultura RM/Alamy

Although innovation strategies may not always work in the short run—some estimates indicate that only about 3 percent of new products actually succeed—various overriding and long-term reasons compel firms to continue introducing new products and services, as the following sections describe.

The iPhone is an easily accessible, affordable, easy-to-use tool that has changed the phone, camera, communication, and technology markets forever.

© Rawpixel.com/Shutterstock RF

Changing Customer Needs

When they add products, services, and processes to their offerings, firms can create and deliver value more effectively by satisfying the changing needs of their current and new customers or by keeping customers from getting bored with the current product or service offering. Sometimes companies can identify problems and develop products or services that customers never knew they needed. When Apple first introduced its handheld smartphone with advanced camera capabilities, virtually no market research provided any hint that consumers wanted one. But with the fervent belief that people would enjoy the convenience of snapping and reviewing a photo or getting online at any particular moment, the company's founder and visionary leader, Steve Jobs, insisted on developing the iPhone as an easily accessible, affordable, easy-to-use tool that consumers could enjoy[11]—and thus changed the phone, camera, communication, and technology markets forever.

In other cases, customers enter new stages in their lives that intensify their demand for such innovations. For example, as life expectancy increases due to technology and health care advances, the senior population is increasing at unprecedented rates. The World Health Organization says that 2 billion people will be older than 60 years of age by 2050, and yet most inventors are ignoring this growing market segment. The 91-year-old inventor Barbara Beskind therefore has taken it upon herself to improve one of the most common items used by the elderly: the cane. Traditional canes require the user to lean on them, promoting poor posture. Beskind's walking sticks instead have rockers on the bottom that users can push off against, and they are made from modified ski poles. In turn, they promote a proper posture and a more natural walking gait.[12]

On the other end of the age spectrum, the market for product and services targeting parents of infants, seems relatively stable, in the sense that most products have been around for years. But Huggies recognized that parents of toddlers often struggled to get their wriggly babies to stay still for diaper changes, so it introduced Little Movers Slip-Ons, to help make the change a fun game rather than a frustrating struggle. The per-diaper price is about 16 cents more than a regular diaper, but Huggies knows that if it can appeal to the relatively loyal parent segment (approximately 55 percent of whom nearly always buy their preferred brand), its innovation can help it maintain market share.[13]

How can a walking stick be improved? Barbara Beskind, a 91-year-old inventor, did it by developing walking sticks that have rockers on the bottom that users can push against for better posture and a more natual gait.

© IDEO

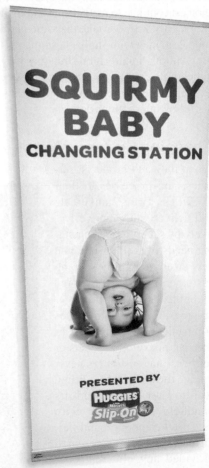

Huggies Little Movers Slip-On diapers are designed to make life easier for parents.

© Jemal Countess/Getty Images

Market Saturation

The longer a product exists in the marketplace, the more likely it is that the market will become saturated. Without new products or services, the value of the firm will ultimately decline.[14] Imagine, for example, if car companies simply assumed and expected that people would keep their cars until they stopped running. If that were the case, there would be no need to come up with new and innovative models; companies could just stick with the models that sell well. But few consumers actually keep the same car until it stops running. Even those who want to stay with the same make and model often want something new, just to add some variety to their lives. Therefore, car companies revamp their models every year, whether with new features like advanced GPS or a more powerful engine or by redesigning the entire look of the vehicle. The firms sustain their growth by getting consumers excited about the new looks and new features, prompting many car buyers to exchange their old vehicle years before its functional life is over.

General Mills provides a number of gluten-free options at www.chex.com/recipes/gluten-free.

© Bruce Bisping/Zuma Press/Newscom

Saturated markets can also offer opportunities for a company that is willing to adopt a new process or mentality. At one point in time, mass marketers would not even consider entering a market that they believed would not earn at least $50 million. But General Mills is looking to niche markets for its future growth. Whereas only 1 percent of the U.S. population suffers from celiac disease—a condition in which ingested gluten damages the digestive system—a much higher percentage of U.S. consumers say they want to reduce or eliminate gluten, a wheat protein, from their diet. As awareness increases, those percentages are growing, such that the U.S. market for gluten-free products could be broadly worth up to $10 billion.[15] General Mills has created more than 600 gluten-free products, including variations on its regular offerings, like Chex cereals and Nestle Gluten Free Cornflakes, as well as Larabars and Betty Crocker pancake mixes.

Managing Risk through Diversity

Through innovation, firms often create a broader portfolio of products, which help them diversify their risk and enhance firm value better than a single product can.[16] If some products in a portfolio perform poorly, others may do well. Firms with multiple products can better withstand external shocks like changes in consumer preferences or intensive competitive activity. For this reason, firms such as Keebler offer many variations of its basic product, cookies, including Animals, Chips Deluxe, E.L. Fudge, Gripz, Sandies, Vanilla Wafers, and Vienna Fingers. This diversification enables Keebler to enjoy more consistent performance than it would with just one kind of cookie.

The Keebler line's risk is lessened by offering many variations of its basic product, cookies.

© Michael J. Hruby

Adding Value 12.1 — No Fairy Godmother Needed: How Disney Is Leveraging Its Inventory of Animated Films to Develop New Live-Action Products[i]

While its partner company Pixar continues to break new ground in animated movies, Walt Disney Pictures is taking a different path. Rather than keep making the sort of well-known, traditional animations that essentially created the movie studio, it is reformulating those tales as live-action films.

One of the first examples was *Cinderella*, whose live-action version hewed closely to Disney's 1950 animated version, from the coach that turns into a pumpkin to the sky blue color of Cinderella's dress at the ball. The goal in making the new version with actors instead of animation was to pay tribute to and resonate with the nostalgic original while still offering something new. That is, the studio's new product strategy is strongly premised in the safe familiarity of well-known and beloved characters.

The company has embraced this potentially risky strategy wholeheartedly, with many other titles in development or having been recently introduced with similar cartoon-to-live action transformations, including *The Jungle Book*, *Beauty and the Beast*, *Dumbo*, and *Pete's Dragon*. It has already introduced a sequel to *Alice in Wonderland* with its *Alice Through the Looking Glass* film.

The source material in many of these cases is both a benefit and a threat to Disney. Because it made fairy tale films in the early days of movies, it has a strong reputation in this market.

When people think *Sleeping Beauty*, they are often imagining the Disney version. Thus, by releasing *Maleficent*, Disney could count on people's knowledge of its previous movie while expanding its reach to more adult audiences.

However, since fairy tales are in the public domain, anyone can make a movie based on the story. Thus Universal Pictures has a new version of *The Little Mermaid* in development, and the movie it ultimately releases does not have to follow the Disney version of the story in any way. This risk may explain Disney's choice to remake some other childhood favorites, such as *Mary Poppins*, for which it owns actual copyrights.

To maximize the profitability of the new films, Disney also leverages its existing access to its target demographic. Store displays of popular *Frozen* toys featured new *Cinderella* paraphernalia immediately adjacent. Before the movie opened, Disney theme parks played up Cinderella's re-emergence. And the trailers preceding Disney movies in theaters for months before its release encouraged viewers to consider the new live-action fairy tale for their future entertainment needs.

The goal is to keep audiences—especially young children who love fairy tales—engaged with Disney films, products, and theme park attractions. In this light, one Disney executive explains, "We view the fairy tale space as our arena."

Disney creates new products out of old ones by recycling earlier movies like Alice in Wonderland *into new ones like* Alice Through the Looking Glass.

© Walt Disney Studios Motion Pictures/Photofest

Fashion Cycles

In industries that rely on fashion trends and experience short product life cycles—including apparel, arts, books, and software markets—most sales come from new products. For example, a motion picture generates most of its theater, DVD, and cable TV revenues within a year of its release. If the same selection of books were always for sale, with no new titles, there would be no reason to buy more. But as Adding Value 12.1 explains, new versions of familiar titles also can be a powerful means to prompt consumers to purchase: Having loved the cartoon version of *Cinderella* as small children, teens and adults might find a new product prompted by a new live-action movie of substantial interest. Consumers of computer software and video games demand new offers because once they have beaten the game, they want to be challenged by another game or experience the most recent version, as the remarkable sales of successive versions of the Call of Duty game exemplify.[17] In the case of apparel, fashion designers produce entirely new product selections a few times per year.

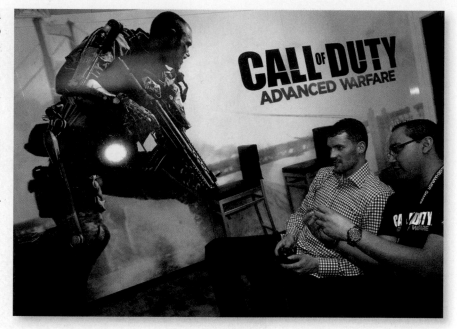

Improving Business Relationships

New products do not always target end consumers; sometimes they function to improve relationships with suppliers. For example, Kraft, the maker of Capri Sun, found that its lemonade flavor was selling poorly. Through a little market research, it realized that the reason was the placement of the packages in pallets. Because it was placed at the bottom of the stack in pallets, lemonade was the last flavor retailers would sell. By changing and innovating its pallet, Kraft offered chimney stacks for each flavor, enabling the retail stockers to reach whichever flavor they needed easily. Sales of Capri Sun's lemonade improved by 162 percent.[18]

Even if they succeed in innovating and creating new products, new-to-the-world products are not adopted by everyone at the same time. Rather, they diffuse or spread through a population in a process known as *diffusion of innovation*, which will be discussed next.

Video games like Call of Duty Advanced Warfare are "fashionable" because consumers demand new versions. Once they "beat" the game, they want to be challenged with a new experience.

© Imeh Akpanudosen/Getty Images

PROGRESS CHECK

1. What are the reasons firms innovate?

DIFFUSION OF INNOVATION

LO12-2 Describe the different groups of adopters articulated by the diffusion of innovation theory.

The process by which the use of an innovation—whether a product, a service, or a process—spreads throughout a market group, over time and across various categories of adopters, is referred to as **diffusion of innovation**.[19] The theory surrounding diffusion of innovation helps marketers understand the rate at which consumers are likely to adopt a new product or service. It also gives them a means to identify potential markets for their new products or services and predict their potential sales, even before they introduce the innovations.[20]

Truly new product introductions—that is, new-to-the-world products that create new markets—can add tremendous value to firms. These new products, also called **pioneers** or **breakthroughs**, establish completely new markets or radically change the rules of competition

Clairol's Touch of Yogurt
Shampoo failed because
consumers didn't like the
idea of washing their
hair with yogurt.

as well as consumer preferences in a market.[21] The Apple iPod is a pioneer product. Not only did it change the way people listen to music but it also created an entirely new industry devoted to accessories such as cases, ear buds, docking stations, and speakers. Although Apple offers many of these accessories itself, other companies have jumped on the bandwagon, ensuring that you can strap your iPod to your arm while on the move or insert it into the base of a desk lamp equipped with speakers to get music and light from your desk. And don't forget: The iPod also launched perhaps the most notable other recent pioneer, the iPhone, along with the innovative iTunes service, the iPod Touch, and the iPad.[22]

Pioneers have the advantage of being **first movers**; as the first to create the market or product category, they become readily recognizable to consumers and thus establish a commanding and early market share lead. Studies also have found that market pioneers can command a greater market share over a longer time period than later entrants can.[23]

Yet not all pioneers succeed. In many cases, imitators capitalize on the weaknesses of pioneers and subsequently gain advantage in the market. Because pioneering products and brands face the uphill task of establishing the market alone, they pave the way for followers, who can spend less marketing effort creating demand for the product line and focus directly on creating demand for their specific brand. Also, because the pioneer is the first product in the market, it often has a less sophisticated design and may be priced relatively higher, leaving room for better and lower-priced competitive products.

An important question to ask is, Why is the failure rate for new products so high? One of the main reasons is the failure to assess the market properly by neglecting to do appropriate product testing, targeting the wrong segment, and/or poor positioning.[24] Firms may also overextend their abilities or competencies by venturing into products or services that are inconsistent with their brand image and/or value proposition. We discuss some infamous product failures in Exhibit 12.1.

As the diffusion of innovation curve in Exhibit 12.2 shows, the number of users of an innovative product or service spreads through the population over a period of time and generally follows a bell-shaped curve. A few people buy the product or service at first, then more buy, and finally fewer people buy as the degree of the diffusion slows. These purchasers can be divided into five groups according to how soon they buy the product after it has been introduced: innovators, early adopters, early majority, late majority, and laggards.

EXHIBIT 12.1 Illustrative Product Failures

Product	Concept	Why It Failed
New Coke	In response to growing market pressure, Coca-Cola launched a reformulated version of its classic cola in 1985.	Coke underestimated the consumers' affinity to the original formulation and their unwillingness to change. It was pulled from shelves three months after its introduction.
Sony Betamax	In 1975, Sony bet big on the Betamax, one of the first ever mass-produced home video recording systems.	Unfortunately, the next year, JVC launched the VHS player, ensuring a format war similar to the Blu-ray and HD-DVD format wars of 2006.
Harley-Davidson Perfume	After being successful with lighters and T-shirts bearing the Harley logo, Harley-Davidson branched out into its own line of perfumes associated with the motorcycle lifestyle.	Although lighters and T-shirts may resonate with the Harley image, customers were not as attracted to smelling like a motorcycle.
Bic Underwear	Bic is well known for its disposable products: pens, lighters, and razors. Capitalizing on its ability to cross product categories, Bic began producing underwear.	The concept of buying underwear from a company well known for disposable pens was confusing and off-putting to consumers.
Bottled Water for Pets	Trying to capitalize on the pet pampering craze, makers of *Thirsty Cat!* and *Thirsty Dog!* launched a line of bottled water for cats and dogs. No longer did owners need to give their pet tap water; instead they could give them a daily pet drink in flavors such as Crispy Beef, Tangy Fish, and Grilled Chicken.	Although people do indeed desire to pamper their pets, the idea of purchasing bottled water for them never caught on. The associations generated by their flavors, such as tangy fish-tasting water, probably did not help either.
Frito-Lay Lemonade	To Frito-Lay, lemonade seemed like a reasonable-enough brand extension. After all, the high salt content of corn chips often leads consumers to search out something to quench their thirst.	Associating a salty snack with a supposed thirst quencher did not go over well.
Kellogg's Breakfast Mates	Capitalizing on the convenience market, Kellogg's Breakfast Mates launched a line of cereal products in 1998 that came with cereal, spoon, and milk.	Sometimes a good idea is poorly executed. The milk was usually warm because it did not require refrigeration and the product was not child-friendly, making its appeal very limited.
Apple Newton	Launched in 1993 with a price tag of more than $700, the Apple Newton was one of the first PDAs, which then led the way for the Palm Pilot, BlackBerry, and iPad.	The Newton concept was ahead of its time. Unfortunately, due to its bulky size and ridicule by comedians, the Newton lasted only until 1998.
Colgate Kitchen Entrees	Colgate launched a line of frozen dinners. Apparently the idea was that consumers would enjoy eating a Colgate meal and then using Colgate on their toothbrush afterward.	The association of toothpaste with a chicken stir-fry was something customers did not find appetizing.
Clairol's Touch of Yogurt Shampoo	Clairol marketed a shampoo with a touch of yogurt to improve hair quality.	Consumers were not enticed with the idea of washing their hair with yogurt, something Clairol should have known after its Look of Buttermilk failed in test markets a few years earlier.

Source: DailyFinance.com, "Top 25 Biggest Product Flops of All Time," http://www.dailyfinance.com/photos/top-25-biggest-product-flops-of-all-time/3662621.

Innovators

Innovators are those buyers who want to be the first on the block to have the new product or service. These buyers enjoy taking risks and are regarded as highly knowledgeable. You probably know someone who is an innovator—or perhaps you are one for a particular product or service category. For example, the person who stood in line overnight to be sure to get a ticket for the very first showing of the latest superhero movie is an innovator in that context. Those consumers who already fly drones off their back porches are likely innovators too, a development covered in Ethical and Societal Dilemma 12.1. Firms that invest in the latest technology, either to use in their products or services or to make the firm more efficient, also are considered innovators. Typically, innovators keep themselves very well informed about the product category by subscribing to trade and specialty magazines, talking to other experts, visiting product-specific blogs and forums that describe the coolest new products,[25] and attending product-related forums, seminars, and special events. Yet innovators represent only about 2.5 percent of the total market for any new product or service.

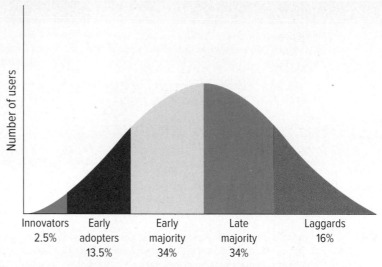

EXHIBIT 12.2 Diffusion of Innovation Curve

Number of users

| Innovators 2.5% | Early adopters 13.5% | Early majority 34% | Late majority 34% | Laggards 16% |

Time of adoption of the innovation

Source: Adapted from Everett M. Rodgers, *Diffusion of Innovation* (New York: Free Press, 1983).

These innovators are crucial to the success of any new product or service, though, because they help the product gain market acceptance. Through talking about and spreading positive word of mouth about the new product, they prove instrumental in bringing in the next adopter category, known as early adopters.[26]

Early Adopters

The second subgroup that begins to use a product or service innovation is **early adopters**. They generally don't like to take as much risk as innovators do but instead wait and purchase the product after careful review. Thus, this market waits for the first reviews of the latest movie before purchasing a ticket, though they likely still go a week or two after it

Early adopters for Samsung 65 Curve televisions typically wait for reviews before they purchase.

Ethical & Societal Dilemma 12.1 Drones in the Sky, Questions on the Ground[ii]

Among the newest and hottest products on the market, personal drones are selling out worldwide, with sales numbers hitting more than 4 million in 2015—a 167 percent surge compared with the year before. The global spread is remarkable too: Its biggest market is the United States, which accounts for 35 percent of the market, followed by Europe with 30 percent of the market, and China with 15 percent. Furthermore, drones were listed as one of the best holiday gifts for 2015 by both *The Wall Street Journal* and the popular gadget retailer *Brookstone*.

The uses of the brand-new consumer product have revolutionized many areas, from photography and videography to Amazon's proposed plan to use drones for package delivery. However, their uses also have created some new privacy concerns. Although drones have enabled people to take beautiful images of natural events such as whale migrations and glacier collapses with unprecedented ease, people cannot always be trusted to limit their image captures to nature and art. Unfortunately, drones also enable unethical users to capture unsolicited and unwarranted images of others, intruding on the privacy and threatening the safety of some of their subjects.

From stories of people spying on their neighbors to the drone that landed on the White House lawn in 2015, serious concerns surrounding the use of private drones continue, without a clear resolution. The company that made the drone involved in the White House event responded by remotely installing software on all its drones that prohibits them from flying within a 15.5-mile radius of downtown Washington, DC. Yet this move was voluntary by the company; no governmental policies have been passed that regulate their usage. The current lack of legislation has implications for matters of personal privacy and security, but it also could be a factor when it comes to the use of drones by major companies. For now, for example, Amazon's Prime Air drone delivery system remains stalled, primarily due to a lack of regulatory support and questions about airspace and privacy rights.

Drones are among the hottest new products on the market, particularly at gadget retailer Brookstone.

© Kimihiro Hoshino/AFP/Getty Images

opens. They do not stand in line to grab the first Samsung 65 Curve televisions; only after reading the innovators' complaints and praises do they decide whether the new technology is worth the cost. But most of them go ahead and purchase because early adopters tend to enjoy novelty and often are regarded as the opinion leaders for particular product categories.

This group, which represents about 13.5 percent of all buyers in the market, spreads the word. As a result, early adopters are crucial for bringing the other three buyer categories to the market. If the early adopter group is relatively small, the number of people who ultimately adopt the innovation likely will also be small.

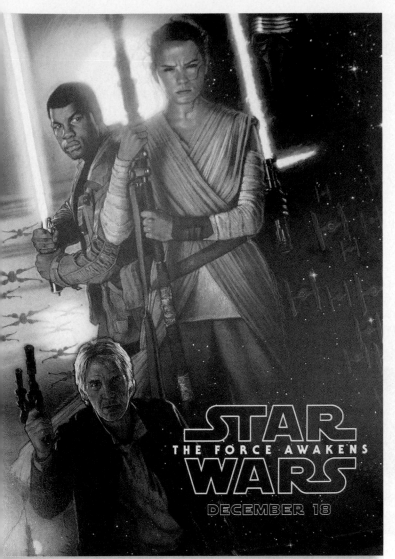

The early majority group would probably wait to rent the latest
Star Wars movie during the first week it comes out on video.

© Walt Disney Studios Motion Pictures/Photofest

Consumers who are fixated on cleaning will spend substantial
amounts for the most technologically advanced machines, like this
Dyson Ball Vacuum.

© Hugh Threlfall/Alamy

Early Majority

The early majority, which represents approximately 34 percent of the population, is crucial because few new products and services can be profitable until this large group buys them. If the group never becomes large enough, the product or service typically fails.

The early majority group differs in many ways from buyers in the first two stages. Its members don't like to take as much risk and therefore tend to wait until the bugs are worked out of a particular product or service. This group probably rents the latest *Star Wars* movie during the first week it comes out on video. Thus, early majority members experience little risk because all the reviews are in, and their costs are lower because they're renting the movie instead of going to the theater. When early majority customers enter the market, the number of competitors in the marketplace usually also has reached its peak, so these buyers have many price and quality choices.

Late Majority

At 34 percent of the market, the late majority is the next group of buyers to enter a new product market. When they do, the product has achieved its full market potential. Perhaps these movie watchers wait until the newest movie is available on Netflix. By the time the late majority enters the market, sales tend to level off or may be in decline.

Laggards

Laggards make up roughly 16 percent of the market. These consumers like to avoid change and rely on traditional products until the products are no longer available. In some cases, laggards may never adopt a certain product or service. When the sequel to *Star Wars: The Force Awakens* eventually shows up on their regular television networks, they might watch it.

Using the Diffusion of Innovation Theory

Using the diffusion of innovation theory, firms can predict which types of customers will buy their new product or service immediately after its introduction as well as later as the product is more and more accepted by the market. With this knowledge, the firm can develop effective promotion, pricing, and other marketing strategies to push acceptance among each customer group. Let's consider an example of some everyday products that nearly all of us use at some point.

Although they are not as flashy as the latest iPhone, cleaning supplies are used by everyone. Often the innovators who adopt new cleaning products are the ones who are the most fanatical about cleaning. Firms conduct in-depth research into how people clean their homes to identify such segments. This research

Products like the Swiffer have a relative advantage over the competition because they make cleaning faster, easier, and more efficient, especially for seniors and other consumers with mobility issues.

Source: Swiffer

finds that some people are so obsessive about cleaning that they spend nearly 20 hours every week doing it, while others are so reluctant that they avoid cleaning as much as they can; their average weekly cleaning time is about 2.5 hours.[27] Their options with regard to the products to purchase to assist them in their cleaning tasks are vast, from scrubbers to sprays to vacuums to dusters. Thus, in the vacuum cleaner market, manufacturers recognize that the segment of consumers who will spend substantial amounts for the most technologically advanced, powerful, easy-to-maneuver machines, such as the latest Dyson model, are likely to be the segment of consumers that is most fixated on cleaning.[28] But another segment just wants some basic suction to get the grit out of their rugs.

Relative Advantage If a product or service is perceived to be better than substitutes, then the diffusion will be relatively quick. As advertising for Swiffer products emphasizes, its mops and dusters promise to make cleaning faster, easier, and more efficient. In featuring real families, it seeks to highlight the relative advantage for all types of cleaners. Older people who might once have gotten on their hands and knees to scrub the floor can now rely on the design of the cleaning pads on the end of the mop to get the job done. Their children, who have never been very good at cleaning, can swipe a few surfaces and get the house looking clean before their parents visit. And a man who has lost an arm to cancer can still help his family keep the house clean, because the duster does not require him to use a spray or climb a ladder to dust the ceiling fan.[29]

Compatibility A diffusion process may be faster or slower, depending on various consumer features, including international cultural differences. Electrolux's latest bagless vacuums offer a key innovation and solve the age-old problem of how to empty the chamber without having a cloud of particles fly out: compact the dirt into a "pellet." To make the product more compatible with the needs of people in different cultures, it is made in various sizes. The U.S. version offers a carpet nozzle with a motor, to deal with the dirt accumulated in Americans' larger, often carpeted homes. Because in many Asian "megacities" consumers live in tiny apartments, Electrolux has introduced a smaller version that is also very quiet.[30]

Observability When products are easily observed, their benefits or uses are easily communicated to others, which enhances the diffusion process. To demonstrate to consumers why they should spend $400 on a blender, Blendtec launched an extensive YouTube campaign titled "Will It Blend?" to demonstrate the effectiveness of the blender. In each video, a spokesperson in a white lab coat blends a different product in the Blendtec—from iPads to golf balls to Justin Bieber's autobiography—and gives visible proof to consumers of the quality of the product. The humor and innovativeness of this product demonstration has

caused these videos to go viral, with over 230 million views and 700,000 subscribers.[31] Yet
some cleaning products face a serious challenge in making their innovations widely ob-
servable, because few consumers spend a lot of time talking about the products that are of
a more personal nature, such as what they use to clean their toilets. Even a great product
might diffuse more slowly if people feel uncomfortable talking about what they perceive to
be involved in their personal care.

Complexity and Trialability Products that are relatively less complex are also relatively
easy to try. These products will generally diffuse more quickly and lead to greater and
faster adoption than will those that are not so easy to try. In the cleaning products range, it
is far easier to pick up a new spray cleaner at the grocery store to try at home than it is to
assess and test a new vacuum. In response, manufacturers seek ways to help people conduct trials. For example, Dyson's displays in national retailers such as Bed, Bath, & Beyond
often include floor space that allows shoppers to run the machine to see how well the roller
ball works and watch it pick up dirt.

   Knowledge of how a product or service will diffuse is useful for developing marketing
strategies. But even before a new product or service is introduced, firms must actually develop those new offerings. In the next section, we detail the process by which most firms
develop new products and services and how they introduce them into the market.

PROGRESS CHECK

1. What are the five groups on the diffusion of innovation curve?
2. What factors enhance the diffusion of a good or service?

Describe the various
stages involved in
developing a new
product or service.

HOW FIRMS DEVELOP NEW PRODUCTS

The new product development process begins with the generation of new product ideas and
culminates in the launch of a new product and the evaluation of its success. The stages of
the new product development process, along with the important objectives of each stage,
are summarized in Exhibit 12.3.

EXHIBIT 12.3 The Product Development Process

Idea generation	Concept testing	Product development	Market testing	Product launch	Evaluation of results
Development of viable new product ideas.	*Testing the new product idea among a set of potential customers.*	*Development of prototypes and/or the product.*	*Testing the actual products in a few test markets.*	*Full-scale commercialization of the product.*	*Analysis of the performance of the new product and making appropriate modifications.*

Idea Generation

To generate ideas for new products, a firm can use its own internal research and development (R&D) efforts, collaborate with other firms and institutions (R&D consortia), license technology, brainstorm, outsource, research competitors' products and services, and/or conduct consumer research; see Exhibit 12.4. In many cases these practices for identifying new product ideas cascade into other aspects of the product development process. Firms that want to be pioneers rely more extensively on R&D efforts, whereas those that tend to adopt a follower strategy are more likely to scan the market for ideas. Let's look at each of these idea sources.

Internal Research and Development Many firms have their own R&D departments in which scientists and engineers work to solve complex problems and develop new ideas. Historically, firms such as Black and Decker in the consumer goods industry, 3M in the industrial goods industry, and Merck and Pfizer in the pharmaceuticals industry have relied on R&D development efforts for their new products. In the fast-food industry, many chains run vast test kitchens that experiment with various flavors, concepts, and food groups to create potential new offerings. Furthermore, the industry uses its common franchise models to support new product development. For example, Arby's hosts an annual contest for

EXHIBIT 12.4 Sources of New Product Ideas

To identify new product ideas, many firms use their own internal R&D, like this test kitchen at CKE, the parent company of Hardee's.

© Tom Gannam/AP Photo

the best menu idea introduced by one of its franchise locations. And in perhaps the most famous example, the Egg McMuffin was created by a franchisee in the early 1970s.[32] In other industries, such as software, music, and motion pictures, product development efforts also tend to come from internal ideas and R&D financial investments. According to Marketing Analytics 12.1, General Motors is leveraging the data it gathers from customers as a sort of internal research source to support its designs.

The product development costs for these firms are quite high, but the resulting new product or service are expected to have a good chance of being a technological or market breakthrough. Firms expect such products to generate enough revenue and profits to make the costs of R&D worthwhile. R&D investments generally are considered continuous investments, so firms may lose money on a few new products. In the long run, though, these firms are betting that a few extremely successful new products, often known as blockbusters, can generate enough revenues and profits to cover the losses from other introductions that might not fare so well.

Some global firms also are taking an approach called reverse innovation, as we discussed in Chapter 8. They turn to subsidiaries in less developed markets for new product ideas. From its Shanghai research center, Coca-Cola developed Minute Maid Pulpy, a juice drink that the corporation has moved into 19 countries and is now worth more than $1 billion. Levi's Denizen brand got its start in India and China, where the company worked on ideas for producing more affordable jeans. In the U.S. market, Denizen jeans sell for about half the cost of a pair of regular Levi's and are available exclusively at Target.[33]

R&D Consortia To develop new product ideas, more and more firms have been joining an **R&D consortia**, or groups of other firms and institutions, possibly including government and educational institutions, to explore new ideas or obtain solutions for developing new products. Here, the R&D investments come from the group as a whole, and the participating firms and institutions share the results.

In many cases, the consortia involve pharmaceutical or high-tech members, whose research costs can run into the millions—too much for a single company to bear. The National Institutes of Health (NIH) sponsors medical foundations to conduct research to treat rare diseases. The research is then disseminated to the medical community, thus encouraging the development of drugs and therapies more quickly and at a lower cost than would be possible if the research were privately funded.

Licensing In the search for new products, firms buy the rights to use a technology or ideas from other firms through a **licensing** agreement. This approach saves the high costs of in-house R&D, but it means that the firm is banking on a solution that already exists but has not been marketed.

Brainstorming Firms often engage in **brainstorming** sessions during which a group works together to generate ideas. One of the key characteristics of a brainstorming session is that no idea can be immediately accepted or rejected. The moderator of the session may channel participants' attention to specific product features and attributes, performance expectations, or packaging. Only at the end of the session do the members vote on the best ideas or combinations of ideas. Those ideas that receive the most votes are carried forward to the next stage of the product development process.

Outsourcing When companies have trouble moving through these steps alone, they turn to **outsourcing**, a practice in which they hire an outside firm to help generate ideas and develop new products and services. IDEO, a design firm, does not sell ready-made product ideas but rather a service that helps clients generate new product and service ideas in industries such as health care, toys, and computers. IDEO employs anthropologists, graphic

Marketing Analytics 12.1 | Data That Help the Brand and the Customer: GM's Big Data Use[iii]

With its famous brands, such as Chevrolet and Cadillac, General Motors (GM) is a staple in the U.S. car industry. It also was one of the companies hit the hardest by the 2008 recession, following which it filed for bankruptcy and received a government bailout. In 2012, GM announced a new business strategy, a major component of which was more efficient and effective uses of big data. The importance of analytics again came to center stage in 2013, when the company faced legal allegations regarding the recall of the Chevy Cobalt. After the crisis, GM stressed the importance of big data even more and promised that analytics would be at the heart of all its future product development.

In particular, data analytics at GM support the development of new cars. Through GM's newly centralized data warehouse, it can analyze trends in both production and customer behavior. Furthermore, GM manufacturer data can be segmented at the individual vehicle identification number (VIN) level and then analyzed to improve quality and safety. For example, manufacturer data analytics helped GM develop tools that reduce the complexity associated with the mechanics of vehicle design. General Motors also is collecting data about its sales and dealerships and uses these data to create detailed customer profiles. The level of customer insight that these profiles provide enables GM to develop new products that then grant customers sufficient value. For example, GM's applied market information influenced its development of high-efficiency products that help reduce pollution.

All of this is just the start. New "connected cars" are generating even more data for the car industry, and the analyses of these data will likely define the cars found on the roads of the future. Connected cars communicate with the manufacturers directly through 4G or LTE. Currently, there are 9 million of

General Motors uses its OnStar system for remote communication with customers and diagnoses of problems. It analyzes the data it collects from its OnStar database to support the development of new cars.

© Bloomberg/Getty Images

these cars on the road, with 35 million projected by 2020. With its subscription-based, in-car security system, OnStar, GM has an advantage in this effort: It already uses OnStar for remote communication and diagnoses of problems. Thus it gains real-time information, which GM can use to improve its future car designs, even as the predictive diagnosis and preventive maintenance offer customers value by saving them money or preventing them from being stranded by a car that won't start.

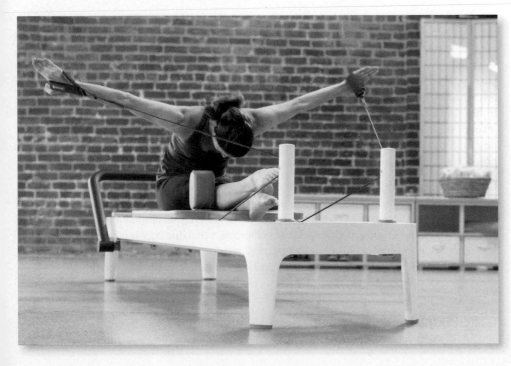

Balance Body partnered with IDEO to develop a less-intimidating, more-user-friendly reformer to be used with Pilates.

Courtesy of Balanced Body, Inc.

Social & Mobile Marketing 12.1   When Microsoft Plays Catch-Up[iv]

Microsoft is one of the most innovative companies of all time. After revolutionizing the home computer industry, it set out to be a leader in the information-technology and home-entertainment fields. It seems like not a year goes by without something new from the brain of Bill Gates.

But one area in which Microsoft has been behind the curve is the search-engine market. Google, with its nearly 70 percent market share and massive name recognition, does not appear to be in any real danger from competitors, including Microsoft's Bing.com. But Bing already has outpaced Yahoo.com for the remainder of the market, and as its market share keeps growing, it is beginning to encroach on Google's dominance. Perhaps most important, it is distinguishing itself by providing more frequent updates and feature additions than the other search engines do. Consumers benefit overall because Bing is forcing competitors to improve their offering to keep pace with Microsoft or prevent it from stealing market share from them.

Its efforts have paid off somewhat: Bing now attracts an approximately 21 percent market share among U.S. users, whereas Yahoo! accounts for only about 10 percent. Google maintains a remarkably high share, though that level has decreased in recent years. Despite these seeming successes, the costs of its copycat efforts have meant that the division responsible for Bing lost $2.56 billion in one recent fiscal year.

To differentiate itself better, Bing is being promoted as a decision engine rather than a search engine. It integrates Foursquare, a location-based phone application, into Bing Maps results. Users can focus on a particular area, such as South Boston, which means Bing can act like an integrative

Microsoft's Bing competes with Google in the search-engine market.

© M4OS Photos/Alamy

day planner and list the best things to do in that area. It is working on developing a desktop application, and Bing links seamlessly with Facebook to show users which search outcome their friends like best. Despite Microsoft's problems developing search engines, Bing suggests it intends to stay aggressive in this market. Other new products by Microsoft, such as Windows 10 and the Surface line of tablets, also bode well for the search engine, because these products come pre-equipped with Bing as their default search engine.

designers, engineers, and psychologists whose special skills help foster creativity and innovation. As exercise is becoming more and more popular, companies are looking for ways to capitalize on the beginner's market. Balanced Body is a company that makes and sells reformers, devices that help develop good alignment, core strength, and flexibility for Pilates participants. When Balanced Body did research and found that people starting Pilates found the reformers currently on the market to be too intimidating, it partnered with IDEO to develop a reformer that allowed for better user experience while maintaining the high level of functionality its products engender.[34] In an eight-week period, IDEO created a redesigned model with fewer wheels while improving functionality and adjustability of the product and reducing the cost of the machine.

Competitors' Products A new product entry by a competitor may trigger a market opportunity for a firm, which can use reverse engineering to understand the competitor's product and then bring an improved version to market. **Reverse engineering** involves taking apart a product, analyzing it, and creating an improved product that does not infringe on the competitor's patents, if any exist. This copycat approach to new product development is widespread and practiced by even the most research-intensive firms. Copycat consumer goods show up in apparel, grocery, and drugstore products as well as in technologically more complex products such as automobiles and computers, as Social and Mobile Marketing 12.1 notes.

Customer Input Listening to the customer in both B2B and B2C markets is essential for successful idea generation and throughout the product development process.[35] Because customers for B2B products are relatively few, firms can follow their use of products closely and solicit suggestions and ideas to improve those products either by using a formal approach, such as focus groups, interviews, or surveys, or through more informal discussions. The firm's design and development team then works on these suggestions, sometimes in consultation with the customer. This joint effort between the selling firm and the customer significantly increases the probability that the customer eventually will buy the new product.

Customer input in B2C markets comes from a variety of sources, though increasingly through social media. By monitoring online feedback, whether requested by the firm or provided voluntarily in customer reviews, companies can get better ideas about new products or necessary changes to existing ones. The recent introduction of Green Giant snack chips provides a good example of using inputs from various types of partners. General Mills (which owns the Green Giant brand) heard a pitch for a new vegetable-based snack chip from its supplier, Shearer's Chips. The chip manufacturer developed 10 options for its business customer, General Mills. Then General Mills solicited input from its end consumers to find out which flavors they might like best. Online reviews suggested the need for a much zestier version of the roasted vegetable tortilla chips, which ultimately appeared on store shelves.[36]

In some cases, consumers may not expressly demand a new product even though their behavior demonstrates their desire for it. For example, when market researchers observed the popularity of pretzel rolls, the corporate headquarters of several restaurant chains introduced new buns and mandated that all their locations carry them. Noting the increasing numbers of vegetarian and vegan eaters, a few chains also have expanded their non-meat offerings.[37]

Another particularly successful customer input approach is to analyze **lead users**, those innovative product users who modify existing products according to their own ideas

Customers are an important source of new product ideas. General Mills solicited input from consumers to find out which flavors they like best, and Green Giant Toasted Veggie Tortilla Chips was one of the winners.

Source: Green Giant

Innovative customers called lead users are especially influential in the fashion industry because designers frequently change their designs based on trends they see on the street.

© *Big Cheese Photo/Superstock RF*

to suit their specific needs.[38] If lead users customize a firm's products, other customers might wish to do so as well. Thus, studying lead users helps the firm understand general market trends that might be just on the horizon. Manufacturers and retailers of fashion products often spot new trends by noticing how innovative trendsetters have altered their clothing and shoes. Designers of high-fashion jeans distress their products in different ways depending on signals they pick up on the street. One season jeans appear with whiskers, the next season they have holes, the next, paint spots.

At the end of the idea-generation stage, the firm should have several ideas that it can take forward to the next stage: concept testing.

Concept Testing

An idea with potential is developed further into a concept, which in this context refers to a brief written description of the product; its technology, working principles, and forms; and what customer needs it would satisfy.[39] A concept might also include visual images of what the product would look like.

Concept testing refers to the process in which a concept statement is presented to potential buyers or users to obtain their reactions. These reactions enable the developer to estimate the sales value of the product or service concept, possibly make changes to enhance its sales value, and determine whether the idea is worth further development.[40] If the concept fails to meet customers' expectations, it is doubtful it would succeed if it were to be produced and marketed. Because concept testing occurs very early in the new product introduction process, even before a real product has been made, it helps the firm avoid the costs of unnecessary product development.

The concept for an electric scooter might be written as follows:

> The product is a lightweight electric scooter that can be easily folded and taken with you inside a building or on public transportation. The scooter weighs 25 pounds. It travels at speeds of up to 15 miles per hour and can go about 12 miles on a single charge. The scooter can be recharged in about two hours from a standard electric outlet. The scooter is easy to ride and has simple controls—just an accelerator button and a brake. It sells for $299.[41]

Concept testing progresses along the research techniques described in Chapter 10. The firm likely starts with qualitative research such as in-depth interviews or focus groups to test the concept, after which it can undertake quantitative research through Internet or mall-intercept surveys. Video clips on the Internet might show a virtual prototype and the way it works so that potential customers can evaluate the product or service. In a mall-intercept survey, an interviewer would provide a description of the concept to the respondent and then ask several questions to obtain his or her feedback.

The most important question pertains to the respondent's purchase intentions if the product or service were made available. Marketers also should ask whether the product would satisfy a need that other products currently are not meeting. Depending on the type of product or service, researchers might also ask about the expected frequency of purchase, how much customers would buy, whether they would buy it for themselves or as a gift, when they would buy, and whether the price information (if provided) indicates a good value. In addition, marketers usually collect some information about the customers so they can analyze which consumer segments are likely to be most interested in the product.

Some concepts never make it past the concept testing stage, particularly if respondents seem uninterested. Those that do receive high evaluations from potential consumers, however, move on to the next step, product development.

Product Development

Product development or product design entails a process of balancing various engineering, manufacturing, marketing, and economic considerations to develop a product's form and features or a service's features. An engineering team develops a product prototype that is based on research findings from the previous concept testing step as well as their own knowledge about materials and technology. A prototype is the first physical form or service description of a new product, still in rough or tentative form, which has the same properties as a new product but is produced through different manufacturing processes—sometimes even crafted individually.[42]

Product prototypes are usually tested through alpha and beta testing. In alpha testing, the firm attempts to determine whether the product will perform according to its design and whether it satisfies the need for which it was intended.[43] Rather than use potential consumers, alpha tests occur in the firm's R&D department. For instance, Ben & Jerry's Ice Cream alpha tests all its proposed new flavors on its own (lucky) employees at its corporate headquarters in Vermont.

In contrast, beta testing uses potential consumers who examine the product prototype in a real-use setting to determine its functionality, performance, potential problems, and other issues specific to its use. The firm might develop several

Is Ben & Jerry's Ice Cream doing alpha or beta testing?
© Nick Wass/AP Photo

prototype products that it gives to users, then survey those users to determine whether the product worked as intended and identify any issues that need resolution.

The advent of the Internet has made recruiting beta testers easier than ever. Through sites such as OnlineBeta (http://www.onlinebeta.com), everyday people can sign up to become beta testers for products from companies such as Dell, Kodak, and TomTom. To further automate the beta testing process, YouEye is developing eye tracking technology that works with an individual's webcam. Instead of needing to spend thousands of dollars on eye tracking equipment and having customers come into labs, firms will be able to utilize everyday webcams to track not only what a person attends to on a computer screen but also his or her emotional reactions to these products.[44]

Market Testing

The firm has developed its new product or service and tested the prototypes. Now it must test the market for the new product with a trial batch of products. These tests can take two forms: premarket testing and test marketing.

Premarket Tests

Firms conduct premarket tests before they actually bring a product or service to market to determine how many customers will try and then continue to use the product or service according to a small group of potential consumers. One popular proprietary premarket test version is called Nielsen BASES. During the test, potential customers are exposed to the marketing mix variables, such as advertising, then surveyed and given a sample of the product to try.[45] After some period of time, during which the potential customers try the product, they are surveyed about whether they would buy or use the product again. This second survey provides an estimation of the probability of a consumer's repeat purchase. From these data, the firm generates a sales estimate for the new product that enables it to decide whether to introduce the product, abandon it, redesign it before introduction, or revise the marketing plan. An early evaluation of this sort—that is, before the product is introduced to the whole market—saves marketers the costs of a nationwide launch if the product fails.

Sometimes firms simulate a product or service introduction, in which case potential customers view the advertising of various currently available products or services along with advertising for the new product or service. They receive money to buy the product or service from a simulated environment, such as a mock web page or store, and respond to a survey after they make their purchases. This test can determine the effectiveness of a firm's advertising as well as the expected trial rates for the new product.

Test Marketing

A method of determining the success potential of a new product, test marketing introduces the offering to a limited geographical area (usually a few cities) prior to a national launch. Test marketing is a strong predictor of product success, because the firm can study actual purchase behavior, which is more reliable than a simulated test. A test marketing effort uses all the elements of the marketing mix: It includes promotions such as advertising and coupons, just as if the product were being introduced nationally, and the product appears in targeted retail outlets with appropriate pricing. On the basis of the results of the test marketing, the firm can estimate demand for the entire market. Test marketing is widely used by fast food chains. Many restaurants roll out new ideas first in Orlando, Florida, a location that attracts a vast range of diverse tourists and thus might offer insights into what various consumers will like.[46]

Test marketing costs more and takes longer than premarket tests do, which may provide an advantage to competitors that could get a similar or better product to market first without test marketing. For this reason, some firms might launch new products without extensive consumer testing and rely instead on intuition, instincts, and guts.[47]

Product Launch

If the market testing returns with positive results, the firm is ready to introduce the product to the entire market. This most critical step in the new product introduction requires tremendous financial resources and extensive coordination of all aspects of the marketing mix. For any firm, if the new product launch is a failure, it may be difficult for the product—and perhaps the firm—to recover. For example, though the number of 3D movie theaters continues to grow, ticket sales for these offerings first leveled off and now have started to decline. The introduction of the new technology was popular enough that sellers invested heavily in building more than 15,000 3D screens, and Hollywood promised a wider range of 3D film options. But if—as appears to be the case—moviegoers have decided that the realistic, three-dimensional images are not worth the higher ticket price, such investments might be painful for both movie studios and movie theaters.[48]

So what does a product launch involve? First, on the basis of the research it has gathered on consumer perceptions, the tests it has conducted, and competitive considerations, the firm confirms its target market (or markets) and decides how the product will be positioned. Then the firm finalizes the remaining marketing mix variables for the new product, including the marketing budget for the first year.[49]

The timing of the launch may also be important, depending on the product.[50] Hollywood studios typically release movies targeted toward general audiences (G- or PG-rated movies) during the summer when children are out of school. New automobile models traditionally are released for sale during September, and fashion products are launched just before the season of the year for which they are intended.

Is the 3D experience worth the price?

© Jasper White CM/Image Source RF

Some products never make it out of the introduction stage, like Kwispelbier, an alcohol-free beer for dogs from The Netherlands.

© Michel Porro/Getty Images

Evaluation of Results

After the product has been launched, marketers must undertake a critical postlaunch review to determine whether the product and its launch were a success or failure and what additional resources or changes to the marketing mix are needed, if any. Many firms use panel data to improve the probability of success during the test marketing phase of a new product introduction. The consumer panel data are collected by panelists scanning in their receipts using a home scanning device. This information is used to measure individual household first-time trials and repeat purchases. Through such data, market demand can be estimated, so the firm can figure out how best to adjust its marketing mix. Some products never make it out of the introduction stage, especially those that seem almost laughable in retrospect. Alcohol-free beer for pets? Harley-Davidson perfume?[51]

For those products that do move on, firms can measure the success of a new product by three interrelated factors: (1) its satisfaction of technical requirements, such as performance; (2) customer acceptance; and (3) its satisfaction of the firm's financial requirements, such as sales and profits.[52] If the product is not performing sufficiently well, poor customer acceptance will result, which in turn leads to poor financial performance.

The new product development process, when followed rationally and sequentially, helps avoid failures. The product life cycle, discussed in the next section, helps marketers manage their products' marketing mix during and after introduction.

PROGRESS CHECK

1.   What are the steps in the new product development process?
2.   Identify different sources of new product ideas.

THE PRODUCT LIFE CYCLE

 LO12-4   Explain the product life cycle.

The **product life cycle** defines the stages that products move through as they enter, get established in, and ultimately leave the marketplace. It thereby offers marketers a starting point for their strategy planning. The stages of the life cycle often reflect marketplace trends, such as the healthy lifestyle trend that today places organic and green product

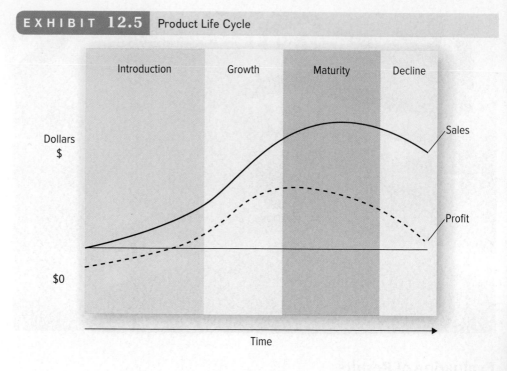

EXHIBIT 12.5 Product Life Cycle

categories in their growth stages. Exhibit 12.5 illustrates a typical product life cycle, including the industry sales and profits over time. In their life cycles, products pass through four stages: introduction, growth, maturity, and decline. When the product category first launches and innovators start buying the product, the **introduction stage** begins. In the **growth stage**, the product gains acceptance, demand and sales increase, and more competitors emerge in the product category. In the **maturity stage**, industry sales reach their peak, so firms try to rejuvenate their products by adding new features or repositioning them. If these efforts succeed, the product achieves new life.[53] If not, it goes into the **decline stage** and eventually exits the market.

Not every product follows the same life cycle curve. Many products, such as home appliances, stay in the maturity stage for a very long time. Manufacturers may add features to dishwashers and washing machines, but the mature product category remains essentially the same and seems unlikely to enter the decline stage unless some innovative, superior solution comes along to replace them.

The product life cycle offers a useful tool for managers to analyze the types of strategies that may be required over the life of their products. Even the strategic emphasis of a firm and its marketing mix (the four Ps) strategies can be adapted from insights about the characteristics of each stage of the cycle, as we summarize in Exhibit 12.6.

Let's look at each of these stages in depth.

EXHIBIT 12.6   Characteristics of Different Stages of the Product Life Cycle

	Introduction	Growth	Maturity	Decline
Sales	Low	Rising	Peak	Declining
Profits	Negative or low	Rapidly rising	Peak to declining	Declining
Typical consumers	Innovators	Early adopters and early majority	Late majority	Laggards
Competitors (number of firms and products)	One or few	Few but increasing	High number of competitors and competitive products	Low number of competitors and products

Introduction Stage

The introduction stage for a new, innovative product or service usually starts with a single firm, and innovators are the ones to try the new offering. Some new-to-the-world products and services that defined their own product category and industry are the telephone (invented by Alexander Graham Bell in 1876), the transistor semiconductor (Bell Laboratories in 1947), the Walkman portable cassette player (Sony in 1979), the Internet browser (Netscape in 1994), the personal digital assistant (Palm in 1996), iTunes (Apple in 2001), Facebook (2004), Blu-ray (Sony in 2006), iPad (Apple in 2010), and smartwatches (Pebble in 2013). Sensing the viability and commercialization possibilities of some market-creating new product, other firms soon enter the market with similar or improved products at lower prices. The same pattern holds for less innovative products such as apparel, music, and even a new soft drink flavor. The introduction stage is characterized by initial losses to the firm due to its high start-up costs and low levels of sales revenue as the product begins to take off. If the product is successful, firms may start seeing profits toward the end of this stage.

Growth Stage

The growth stage of the product life cycle is marked by a growing number of product adopters, rapid growth in industry sales, and increases in both the number of competitors and the number of available product versions.[54] The market becomes more segmented and consumer preferences more varied, which increases the potential for new markets or new uses of the product or service.[55] Adding Value 12.2 outlines how a couple of entrepreneurs had to take a trial-and-error approach before they ultimately found the segment of the popcorn market that would allow their SkinnyPop brand to grow massively and quickly.

Also during the growth stage, firms attempt to reach new consumers by studying their preferences and producing different product variations—varied colors, styles, or features—which enable them to segment the market more precisely. The goal of this segmentation is to ride the rising sales trend and firmly establish the firm's brand so as not to be outdone by competitors. For example, many food manufacturers are working hard to become the first brand that consumers think of when they consider organic products. Del Monte was the first of the major canned vegetable sellers to go organic. The cans feature bold "organic" banners across the front and promise that no pesticides were used to produce the food items. Even though Del Monte products have been around for over 100 years, in this growth category the company is a newer entrant in the organic market, so it must work to establish its distinctive appeal.[56]

As firms ride the crest of increasing industry sales, profits in the growth stage also rise because of the economies of scale associated with manufacturing and marketing costs, especially in promotion and advertising. At the same time, firms that have not yet established a stronghold in the market, even in narrow segments, may decide to exit, in what is referred to as an industry shakeout.

Recognizing that shampoo is a mature product category, Alterna and other manufacturers have introduced antiaging hair products.

© Alterna Haircare

Maturity Stage

The maturity stage of the product life cycle is characterized by the adoption of the product by the late majority and intense competition for market share among firms. Marketing costs (e.g., promotion, distribution) increase as these firms vigorously defend their market share against competitors. They also face intense competition on price as the average price of the product falls substantially compared with the shifts during

Adding Value 12.2   Skinny on Ingredients, Thick on Promise: The Growth of SkinnyPop Snacks[v]

Anyone who has ever wandered Chicago's streets—or flown through its Midway Airport for that matter—likely has at least a vague sense memory of the delicious scent of fresh popcorn, spreading out from the doors of the shops run by the local favorite, Garrett's Popcorn. A tin of Garrett's is a salty, buttery, guilt-inducing pleasure that can be hard to resist in the moment but isn't likely to be a daily snack that health-conscious consumers would stock in their pantries.

Still, when Andrew Friedman and Pam Netzky started up their Wells Street Popcorn brand, their initial goal was to launch a product that could compete with Garrett's. To differentiate themselves, they planned to offer even higher-quality ingredients and promote a sort of luxury version of the local snack. Unlike Garrett's neon-orange cheese corn, for example, Well Street would offer a version that was milder and less stain-likely. Wells Street products achieved mediocre performance; the founders were able to convince a few high-end, local grocers to stock the products. But the expensive ingredients meant that Wells Street was selling small bags of caramel corn for about $10 each, limiting its expansion opportunities. There just wasn't that big of a market for gourmet popcorn at a high price point, and when another company with a similar product entered the New York market and failed dismally, Netzky and Friedman realized they needed another option.

That option presented itself in the form of customer requests for healthier snacks. Customers liked the flavors of the fancy popcorn, but they hated the artificial ingredients, high levels of saturated fats, and massive amounts of sodium contained in each serving. To come up with an entry into the emerging, "better-for-you" snack market, the founders experimented for months, adjusting the precise recipes and ingredients until they achieved an offering that mimicked the taste of gourmet and movie theater popcorn but did so with "skinny" ingredients. Recognizing that this new product was vastly distinct from, and needed to be marketed separately from, the Wells Street line, Friedman and Netzky launched a new brand, SkinnyPop.

Despite the name, the products are not necessarily lower in calories. Rather, the "skinny" part of the name refers to what goes into the snacks—or perhaps more accurately, what doesn't go into them. Manufactured in a dedicated facility (to avoid any contamination with excluded ingredients), SkinnyPop popcorn contains no gluten, cholesterol, dairy, genetically modified organisms, trans fat, peanuts, or preservatives.

Even once they had the right recipe though, getting SkinnyPop onto grocers' shelves was a struggle. According to Friedman, retailers simply didn't know what to do with the product. Was it a health food? A snack? A natural product? On a visit to one local store, Friedman took advantage of a store manager's vacation, noting that while the manager was gone, "I moved stuff around, put them on the shelves and ran out of the store. Within a couple of days, they were calling to reorder." If you can excuse the pun, the success of the brand

Although it took a lot of trial and error in product development, marketing, and distribution, SkinnyPop is now firmly in the growth phase of the product life cycle.

© Keith Homan/Alamy RF

just popped from there. Within a year, SkinnyPop had sold $55.7 million in snacks, and then experienced explosive growth of 137.6 percent to earn $132.4 million in sales just a year after that.

The level of growth was so massive and quick that Friedman and Netzky sold their brand to a national company in 2014. And still the brand and its products continue to grow: Currently found in nearly 50,000 retail stores in North America, with plans to double that number before also moving into international markets, SkinnyPop seemingly has no cause to stop.

the previous two stages of the life cycle. Lower prices and increased marketing costs begin to erode the profit margins for many firms. In the later phases of the maturity stage, the market has become quite saturated, and practically all potential customers for the product have already adopted the product. Such saturated markets are prevalent in developed countries.

In the United States, most consumer packaged goods found in grocery and discount stores are already in the maturity stage. For example, in the well-established hair care products market, consumer goods companies constantly search for innovations to set themselves apart and extend the time in which they maintain their position in the maturity stage. Observing the popularity of new skin care products, hair care manufacturers have integrated similar product benefits to their products. These companies have introduced antiaging shampoos and conditioners, prewash hair masks, serums, and multiple-step solutions that go beyond the old mantra of lather, rinse, and repeat.[57]

Firms pursue various strategies during this stage to increase their customer base and/or defend their market share. Other tactics include entry into new markets and market segments and developing new products. (Refer to Growth Strategies in Chapter 2.)

Entry into New Markets or Market Segments

Because a market is saturated, firms may attempt to enter new geographical markets, including international markets (as we discussed in Chapter 8), that may be less saturated. For example, pharmaceutical companies are realizing that they need to turn to BRIC countries for continued growth in the coming years. While the U.S. and European markets are fairly saturated, the BRIC countries are expected to go from representing 5 percent of the total pharmaceutical market in 2005 to 30 percent in 2016.[58]

However, even in mature markets, firms may be able to find new market segments. Apple is well known for releasing new versions of its iPhone and iPad yearly, and development cycles are getting even shorter. Although people still get excited over these new products, they are also beginning to suffer from "device exhaustion," in which they are becoming progressively less likely to continue to upgrade their phones and tablets. As a result, the smartphone and tablet markets appear nearly or completely mature.[59] Although the market may be mature, for many people these new versions are prohibitively expensive, even when signing a two-year contract. To expand to these lower-income market segments, Apple doesn't get rid of its older devices when a new one comes along. Instead, it reduces the price on the older versions that are cheaper to produce. As a result, it is able to reach customers that would never be able to afford the latest iPhone model.

Development of New Products

Despite market saturation, firms continually introduce new products with improved features or find new uses for existing products because they need constant innovation and product proliferation to defend market share from intense

To reach new market segments, Apple reduces the price of older versions of its products when new ones are released.

© McGraw-Hill Education/Mark Dierker, photographer

Hallmark's "Life Is a Special Occasion" campaign moves beyond the idea that cards are only for holidays or birthdays. It encourages consumers to connect with loved ones all the time.

Source: Hallmark Cards, Inc.

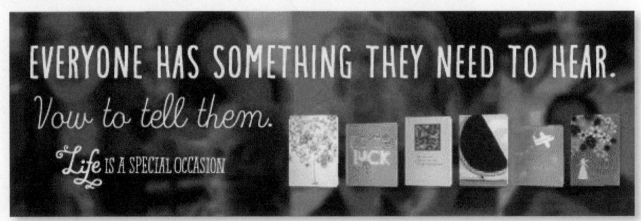

competition. Firms continually introduce new products to ensure that they are able to retain or grow their respective market shares. Hallmark, which has been the hallmark name for greeting cards for a long time, is trying a variety of innovations. They include customizable greeting cards, plates, and interactive storybooks that can be personalized for various recipients, as well as greeting applications that are available for both iPod and iPad users.[60]

Decline Stage

Firms with products in the decline stage either position themselves for a niche segment of diehard consumers or those with special needs or they completely exit the market. The few laggards who have not yet tried the product or service enter the market at this stage. Take vinyl long-playing records (LPs), for example. In an age of Internet-downloaded music files, it may seem surprising that vinyl records are still made and sold. Sales of vinyl LPs had long been declining, but they have enjoyed a resurgence in just the past few years as diehard music lovers demand the unique sound of a vinyl record rather than the digital sound of CDs and music files. Still, the 5.5 million LPs sold in the United States per year pales in comparison with the 1.26 billion digital downloads.[61] The grooves in vinyl records create sound waves that are similar to those of a live performance, however, which means they provide a more authentic sound, which in turn means nightclub DJs, discerning music listeners, and collectors will always prefer them.[62]

Aiding this continued demand is the fact that there are simply too many albums of music from the predigital era that are available only on vinyl. It may take many years, maybe even decades, for all the music from earlier generations to be digitized. Until that time, turntable equipment manufacturers, small record-pressing companies such as Music Connection in Manhattan, and new and emerging record companies such as Premier Crue Music continue to have a market that demands their LPs.[63]

The Shape of the Product Life Cycle Curve

In theory, the product life cycle curve is bell shaped with regard to sales and profits. In reality, however, each product or service category has its own individual shape; some move more rapidly through their product life cycles than others, depending on how different the category is from offerings currently in the market and how valuable it is to the consumer. New products and services that consumers accept very quickly have higher consumer adoption rates very early in their product life cycles and move faster across the various stages.

Although most would argue that LPs are in the declining stage of the product life cycle, there has been a resurgence in sales in recent years.
© Keystone/Getty Images

For example, Blu-ray players and Blu-rays moved much faster than DVDs across the life cycle curve and have already reached the maturity stage, likely because consumers who already owned DVDs were accustomed to playing prerecorded movies and TV shows. It also was easy to switch DVD customers to Blu-ray technology because DVDs played on Blu-ray players, and Blu-rays had better video and audio quality than DVDs had. With the advent of 4K televisions that offer resolutions four times higher than current 1080p HD TVs, it is likely we may see another fast adoption of a new video format, such as 4K Blu-ray.

Strategies Based on Product Life Cycle: Some Caveats

Although the product life cycle concept provides a starting point for managers to think about the strategy they want to implement during each stage of the life cycle of a product, this tool must be used with care. The most challenging part of applying the product life cycle concept is that managers do not know exactly what shape each product's life cycle will take, so there is no way to know precisely what stage a product is in. If, for example, a product experiences several seasons of declining sales, a manager may determine that it has moved from the growth stage to decline and so decides to stop promoting the product. As a result, of course, sales decline further. The manager then believes he or she made the right decision because the product continues to follow a predetermined life cycle. But what if the original sales decline was due to a poor strategy or increased competition—issues that could have been addressed with positive marketing support? In this case, the product life cycle decision became a self-fulfilling prophecy, and a growth product was doomed to an unnecessary decline.[64] Fortunately, new research, based on the history of dozens of consumer products, suggests that the product life cycle concept is indeed a valid idea, and new analytical tools now provide rules for detecting the key turning points in the cycle.[65]

DVD customers quickly switched to Blu-rays because of the enhanced picture and sound quality.

© Leon Neal/Alamy

PROGRESS CHECK

1. What are the key marketing characteristics of products or services at each stage of the product life cycle?

2. Why might placement decisions for products or services into stages of the product life cycle become a self-fulfilling prophecy?

Reviewing Learning Objectives

LO12-1 **Identify the reasons firms create new products.**

Firms need to innovate to respond to changing customer needs, prevent declines in sales from market saturation, diversify their risk, and respond to short product life cycles, especially in industries such as fashion apparel, arts, books, and software markets, where most sales come from new products. Finally, innovations can help firms improve their business relationships with suppliers.

LO12-2 **Describe the different groups of adopters articulated by the diffusion of innovation theory.**

The diffusion of innovation theory can help firms predict which types of customers will buy their products or services immediately upon introduction, as well as later as they gain more acceptance in the market. Innovators are those buyers who want to be the first to have the new product or service. Early adopters do not take as much risk as innovators do but instead wait and purchase the product after careful review. The members of the early majority don't like to take risks and therefore tend to wait until the bugs have been worked out of a particular product or service. The late majority are buyers who purchase the product after it has achieved its full market potential. Finally, laggards like to avoid change and rely on traditional products until those products are no longer available. Laggards may never adopt certain products or services.

LO12-3 **Describe the various stages involved in developing a new product or service.**

When firms develop new products, they go through several steps. First, they generate ideas for the product or service using several alternative techniques, such as internal research and development, R&D consortia, licensing, brainstorming, tracking competitors' products or services, or working with customers. Second, firms test their concepts by either describing the idea of the new product or service to potential customers or showing them images of what the product would look like. Third, the design process entails determining

what the product or service will actually include and provide. Fourth, firms test-market their designs. Fifth, if everything goes well in the test market, the product is launched. Sixth, firms must evaluate the new product or service to determine its success.

LO12-4 **Explain the product life cycle.**

The product life cycle helps firms make marketing mix decisions on the basis of the product's stage in its life cycle. In the introduction stage, companies attempt to gain a strong foothold in the market quickly by appealing to innovators. During the growth stage, the objective is to establish the brand firmly. When the product reaches the maturity stage, firms compete intensely for market share, and many potential customers already own the product or use the service. Eventually, most products enter the decline phase, during which firms withdraw marketing support and eventually phase out the product. Knowing where a product or service is in its life cycle helps managers determine its specific strategy at any given point in time.

Key Terms   ■SMARTBOOK

- alpha testing, 389
- beta testing, 389
- brainstorming, 384
- concept, 388
- concept testing, 388
- decline stage, 392
- diffusion of innovation, 375
- early adopters, 378
- early majority, 380
- first movers, 376

- growth stage, 392
- innovation, 371
- innovators, 377
- introduction stage, 392
- laggards, 380
- late majority, 380
- lead users, 387
- licensing, 384
- maturity stage, 392
- outsourcing, 384

- pioneers (breakthroughs), 375
- premarket test, 389
- product design, 388
- product development, 388
- product life cycle, 391
- prototype, 389
- R&D consortia, 384
- reverse engineering, 386
- test marketing, 389

Marketing Digitally

1. Go to http://www.quirky.com and read about how Quirky develops new products. How is this different from traditional new-product development?

2. The automotive industry is constantly adding new and different products and technologies to their cars—above as well as under the hood. Conduct an Internet or library database search and discuss two innovative new automotive technologies that are changing the industry.

Marketing Applications

1. Some people think that a product should be considered "new" only if it is completely new to the market and has never existed before. Describe or give examples of other types of new products.

2. Android Wear is a new category of wearable computing devices that link to Android smartphones. How quickly do you think this product will diffuse among the U.S. population? Describe the types of people that

you expect will be in each of the diffusion of innovation stages.

3. What are the advantages and disadvantages for companies that are the first to introduce products that create new markets?

4. Identify and describe the ways that companies generate new product ideas. Which of these ways involve the customer? How can firms assess the value of the ideas that customers generate?

5. Describe an example of a new product or service that is targeted at the college-student market. Using the concept-testing discussion in the chapter, describe how you would conduct a concept test for this product or service.

6. Using the same product or service you used in question 5, use the diffusion of innovation theory to assess how quickly it will diffuse based on its relative advantage, compatibility, observability, complexity, and trialability.

7. How does the Internet help companies gain customer input on their existing and new products?

8. Nature's Path is about to introduce a type of granola and is in the market-testing phase of the new product-development process. Describe two ways that Nature's Path might conduct initial market testing prior to launching this new product.

9. In what stage of the product life cycle is the PlayStation 4 video game console? Is Sony's marketing strategy— its four Ps—consistent with the product's stage in its life cycle? Explain.

10. You have recently been hired by a cosmetics company in the product-development group. The firm's brand is a top-selling, high-end line of cosmetics. The head of the development team has just presented research that shows that "tween" girls, aged 11 to 15, are very interested in cosmetics and have the money to spend. The decision is made to create a line of tween cosmetics based on the existing adult line. As the product moves through development you begin to notice that the team seems to lean toward a very edgy and sexual theme for the line, including naming the various lines "envy," "desire," "prowess," and "fatal attraction." You begin to wonder, is this concept too much for girls in the targeted age group?

Quiz Yourself

1. In the United States, most consumer packaged goods found in grocery and discount stores are already in the _____ stage, which is characterized by the adoption of the product by the late majority and intense competition for market share among firms.
   a. introduction
   b. growth
   c. maturity
   d. first
   e. decline

2. Although they enjoy novelty and are considered to be opinion leaders, _____ are not the first to purchase new product innovations.
   a. laggards
   b. innovators
   c. early adopters
   d. the late majority
   e. the early majority

(Answers to these two questions can be found in the Quiz Yourself Answer Key section.)

Chapter Case Study

Mc Graw Hill Education **connect**

IS THE GLASS HALF FULL? THE LAUNCH, DEATH STRUGGLES, AND POTENTIAL REEMERGENCE OF GOOGLE GLASS

From its very start, Google has embraced the idea of innovation actively. The founders began their company with the (at the time) totally innovative concept of an online search engine. Then they instituted the "20 percent" rule, according to which all employees had to spend at least one workday per week on creative, off-the-wall project ideas. With such a foundation, Google's record of innovation is naturally impressive, from Google Maps to Street View to driverless cars, from the Android operating system to Chromebooks. And then came Google Glass.

Even before the wearable technology was introduced in any form, it seemed as if everyone knew what it was—and had an opinion about its efficacy, appeal, and look. The wearable product would allow users to surf the Internet and gather information simply by looking up and to the right. They could swipe their finger over a sensor behind their ears to pull up a Google map and navigate, take pictures, or initiate the embedded Bluetooth technology to make a call.[66]

The initial rollout of Google Glass was limited, purposefully, by a couple of factors. First, Google set the price very high, at around $1,500. That meant that only the most dedicated tech geeks, and those with plenty of disposable income, would be the ones first sporting the headband-like devices. Second, Google required people to register for the chance to receive a set.[67] Even if thousands wanted to spend the money, Google allowed only a select few to receive them at any one time.

This slow, measured rollout was designed to provide several benefits for Google. Because it sought to minimize the supply available, Google created a perception that Glass was extremely popular and stirred up excitement in potential customers. The press buzz and word of mouth spread remarkably far and quickly. Furthermore, it identified a ready-made segment of beta testers. By making sure that those who used the early versions of Google Glass were really interested in it, Google knew that the feedback they provided was more likely to be insightful and related to the underlying technology. Thus it did not have to filter out, initially, complaints about it being too hard to use from people without much technological savvy or other reviews that seemed less important to the developers.

But the results were not exactly as Google planned. Google assumed most comments would be about technology improvements. Instead, much of the information it gleaned involved the look of the device and the alternative uses it could support. For example, though there was never any danger that Google Glass would become a high-fashion option, people sought to make them at least a little more attractive. The solution was an easy one: offer Google Glass in several colors, so that fashionable folks could coordinate with their phones, purses, or favorite hues.

In terms of the functions for which people actually use Google Glass, the innovator's predictions again were inaccurate. Google anticipated that Glass would resonate most with busy business professionals who found the act of taking their smartphones out of their pockets too inefficient. But it learned quickly that even these professional segments used Glass in far more casual manners. In one example, a pet lover explained that it was far easier to take funny cat videos when both hands were free to tempt the feline with a toy.[68]

Along with this feedback, Google noted some surprise at the diversity of people interested in Glass. As Leila Takayama, a researcher with Google, explained, "We were expecting the people to be extremely tech savvy—to kind of look like us Googlers. But what we actually saw were people who were much more diverse. They were people who were just sort of curious."[69] Although diversity of users seemingly should have been a benefit, instead it meant that Google Glass was not satisfying any market segment's needs precisely. Casual users found it ugly and awkward; high-tech early adopters complained about its short battery life and expressed their disgust with the "terrible product" online, noting that it was plagued by defects, bugs, and poor performance.

Google Glass is one of the latest of many significant Google innovations.

© *Michal Krakowiak/Getty Images RF*

In the wake of this negative press, Google pulled Glass nearly completely from the world. Not only did it stop producing new versions of the product, but it also removed dedicated social media pages on Facebook and Twitter, as if to pretend the launch had never happened. In so doing, it prompted many observers to proclaim the death of Google Glass.[70]

But not so fast. Post-mortem accounts suggest that the tremendous buzz and highly touted launch of the product—those marketing techniques that seemingly promised its success—actually were exactly what Google Glass engineers had hoped to avoid.[71] The research and development team knew that the initial product had lots of bugs; they never intended it to be released for widespread use. Instead, they called for a slow, quiet rollout, in which selected users would beta test the prototypes and provide specific feedback and information that would enable Google to create a more functional product for the wider market. Somewhere along the line though, the quiet rollout transformed into a media blitz, and the expectations for Google Glass rose well above any potential benefits that it was even designed to offer at that point in its life cycle.

Today, Google has basically no official comment to offer about the future of Google Glass. But a dedicated team still exists at Google,[72] overseen by two managers: a former jewelry designer and a former Apple product developer. These hires suggest that Google might be focusing more on the design appeal of potential new versions.

Moreover, the continued growth of wearable technology—from the Apple Watch to the Fitbit to Samsung's Gear—reinforce the appeal of the underlying concept: Modern users love their personal technology, and they want a viable, effective means to use their personal devices in hands-free, convenient ways. Google thus might emerge as an early entrant and innovator in this market. It also seemingly has broken open the path for other technology firms that look at its example and find inspiration for entering product markets on their own. For example, recent reports suggest that Snapchat has been hiring hardware experts and engineers with vast experience working on other wearable technology projects.[73] Does that mean Snap Glass might be the next new thing on the market?

Questions

1. What kind of testing did Google perform for Google Glass? What other methods might it have used?

2. At what stage of its product life cycle is Google Glass today?

3. What can later entrants into the wearable technology market learn from Google's new product introduction?

Endnotes

1. Eva Dou, "Xiaomi: The Secret to the World's Most Successful Startup," *The Wall Street Journal*, April 6, 2015, http://wsj.com.

2. Roberto A. Ferdman, "Who knew That Chinese Mobile Company Xiaomi Has Users in 58 Countries," QZ.com, January 4, 2014.

3. David Gilbert, "Xiaomi Misses Sales Target, Sells 70 Million Smartphones in 2015," IB Times, January 15, 2016.

4. Dou, "Xiaomi: The Secret to the World's Most Successful Startup."

5. Jonathan Cheng, "Xiaomi Launches New Flagship Smartphone at Mobile World Congress," *The Wall Street Journal*, February 24, 2016.

6. Dou, "Xiaomi: The Secret to the World's Most Successful Startup."

7. Ibid.

8. Bloomberg News, "Xiaomi Unveils Mi5 Phone to Spearhead Sales Drive Beyond China," *Bloomberg Business*, February 24, 2016, http://www.bloomberg.com/news/articles/2016-02-24/xiaomi-unveils-mi5-phone-to-spearhead-sales-drive-beyond-china.

9. Dou, "Xiaomi: The Secret to the World's Most Successful Startup."

10. Bloomberg News, "Xiaomi Unveils Mi5 Phone to Spearhead Sales Drive Beyond China."

11. Michael Beschloss, "The Polaroid Swinger: Changing the Market in an Instant," *The New York Times*, July 2, 2015.

12. Timothy Hay, "Technology Innovations That Could Help the Elderly," *The Wall Street Journal*, June 29, 2015.

13. Andrew Adam Newman, "Making the Diaper Change Easier for the Changer," *The New York Times*, July 28, 2011, http://www. nytimes.com; "The Huggies Brand Encourages Parents to Showcase Their Active Babies," *The New York Times*, January 19, 2012, http://markets.on.nytimes.com.

14. Koen Pauwels, et al., "New Products, Sales Promotions, and Firm Value: The Case of the Automobile Industry," *Journal of Marketing* 68, no. 4 (2008), p. 142.

15. Elaine Watson, "What's the Size of the US Gluten-Free Prize? $490m, $5bn, or $10bn?" *Food Navigator USA*, February 17, 2014, http://www.foodnavigator-usa.com.

16. Kalpesh Kaushik Desai and Kevin Lane Keller, "The Effects of Ingredient Branding Strategies on Host Brand Extendibility," *Journal of Marketing* 66, no. 1 (2002), pp. 73–93.

17. Erik Kain, " 'Madden NFL 25' Sales Down over Last Year, First Week Still Tops 1M Units," *Forbes*, September 5, 2013, http://www.forbes.com.

18. http://www.ideo.com/work/featured/kraft.

19. http://www.marketingpower.com/_layouts/Dictionary. aspx?dLetter=D.

20. Michael J. Barone and Robert D. Jewell, "The Innovator's License: A Latitude to Deviate from Category Norms," *Journal of Marketing* 77 (January 2013), pp. 120–34; Barak Libai, Eitan Muller, and Renana Peres, "The Diffusion of Services," *Journal of Marketing Research* 46 (April 2009), pp. 163–75; Yvonne van Everdingen, Dennis Fok, and Stefan Stemersch, "Modeling Global Spillover of New Product Takeoff," *Journal of Marketing Research* 46 (October 2009), pp. 637–52.

21. Stanley F. Slater, Jakki J. Mohr, and Sanjit Sengupta, "Radical Product Innovation Capability: Literature Review, Synthesis, and Illustrative Research Propositions," *Journal of Product Innovation Management* 31, no. 3 (May 2014), pp. 552–66;

Rosabeth Moss Kanter, *SuperCorp: How Vanguard Companies Create Innovation, Profits, Growth, and Social Good* (New York: Crown Business, 2009); Rajesh K. Chandy, Jaideep C. Prabhu, and Kersi D. Antia, "What Will the Future Bring? Dominance, Technology Expectations, and Radical Innovation," *Journal of Marketing* 67, no. 3 (2003), pp. 1–18; Harald J. van Heerde, Carl F. Mela, and Puneet Manchanda, "The Dynamic Effect of Innovation on Market Structure," *Journal of Marketing Research* 41, no. 2 (2004), pp. 166–83.

22. http://www.apple.com; Clayton M. Christensen and Michael E. Raynor, *The Innovator's Solution* (Boston: Harvard Business School Press, 2003).

23. Rajan Varadarajan, Manjit S. Yadav, and Venkatesh Shankar, "First-Mover Advantage in the Internet-Enabled Market Environment," in *Handbook of Strategic e-Business Management* (Heidelberg: Springer, 2014), pp. 157–85; James L. Oakley et al., "Order of Entry and the Moderating Role of Comparison Brands in Brand Extension Evaluation," *Journal of Consumer Research* 34, no. 5 (2008), pp. 706–12; Fernando F. Suarez and Gianvito Lanzolla, "Considerations for a Stronger First Mover Advantage Theory," *Academy of Management Review* 33, no. 1 (2008), pp. 269–70; Ralitza Nikolaeva, "The Dynamic Nature of Survival Determinants in E-commerce," *Journal of the Academy of Marketing Science* 35, no. 4 (2007), pp. 560–71.

24. "Top 10 Reasons for New Product Failure," *The Marketing Fray*, January 7, 2010, http://www.marketingfray.com.

25. http://smashinghub.com/10-coolest-upcoming-gadgets-of-2011.htm.

26. Barak Libai, Eitan Muller, and Renana Peres, "Decomposing the Value of Word-of-Mouth Seeding Programs: Acceleration versus Expansion," *Journal of Marketing Research* 50, no. 2 (2013), pp. 161–76; Jacob Goldenberg, et al., "The Role of Hubs in the Adoption Process," *Journal of Marketing* 73 (March 2009), pp. 1–13.

27. Ellen Byron, "The Cleanest House of All," *The Wall Street Journal*, March 20, 2013, http://online.wsj.com.

28. Carol Matlack, "Electrolux's Holy Trinity for Hit Products," *Bloomberg Businessweek*, October 31, 2013, http://www.businessweek.com.

29. Gabriel Beltrone, "Most Inclusive Ad Ever? Swiffer Spot Stars Interracial Family, and Dad's an Amputee," *Adweek*, January 21, 2014, http://www.adweek.com.

30. Carol Matlack, "Electrolux's Holy Trinity for Hit Products," *Bloomberg Businessweek*, October 31, 2013, http://www.businessweek.com.

31. https://www.youtube.com/user/Blendtec.

32. Charles Passy, "How Fast Food Chains Cook Up New Menu Items," *The Wall Street Journal*, August 24, 2015.

33. Natalie Zmuda, "P&G, Levi's, GE Innovate by Thinking in Reverse," *Advertising Age*, June 13, 2011, http://adage.com; "Minute Maid Pulpy Joins Growing List of Billion Dollar Brands for the Coca-Cola Company," press release, February 1, 2011, http://www.thecoca-colacompany.com.

34. "Pilates Allegra 2 Reformer for Balanced Body," IDEO Case Study, 2011.

35. Dominik Mahr, Annouk Lievens, and Vera Blazevic, "The Value of Customer Cocreated Knowledge during the Innovation Process," *Journal of Product Innovation Management* (2013); Pilar Carbonell, Ana I. Rodríguez-Escudero, and Devashish Pujari, "Customer Involvement in New Service Development: An Examination of Antecedents and Outcomes," *Journal of Product Innovation Management* 26 (September 2009), pp. 536–50; Glen L. Urban and John R. Hauser, " 'Listening In' to Find and Explore New Combinations of Customer Needs," *Journal of Marketing* 68, no. 2 (2004), p. 72.

36. Jeff Bellairs, "Innovation and Collaboration Swiftly Launch Green Giant Snack Chips," *Taste of General Mills*, June 19, 2013, http://www.blog.generalmills.com.

37. Passy, "How Fast Food Chains Cook Up New Menu Items."

38. Michael Nir, *Agile Project Management* (New York: CreateSpace, 2013); Jim Highsmith, *Agile Product Management: Creating Innovative Products* (Boston, Addison-Wesley, 2009); http://www.betterproductdesign.net; Eric von Hippel, *The Sources of Innovation* (New York: Oxford University Press, 1988); Eric von Hippel, "Successful Industrial Products from Consumers' Ideas," *Journal of Marketing* 42, no. 1 (1978), pp. 39–49.

39. Karl T. Ulrich and Steven D. Eppinger, *Product Design and Development*, 5th ed. (Boston: Irwin/McGraw-Hill, 2011).

40. http://www.marketingpower.com.

41. Ulrich and Eppinger, *Product Design and Development*.

42. Min Zhao, Steven Hoeffler, and Darren W. Dahl, "The Role of Imagination-Focused Visualization on New Product Evaluation," *Journal of Marketing Research* 46 (February 2009), pp. 46–55; http://www.marketingpower.com.

43. Ulrich and Eppinger, *Product Design and Development*.

44. Frederic Lardinois, "YouEye Raises $3M for Its Webcam-Based Usability Testing Service with Emotion Recognition," *Tech Crunch*, May 7, 2013, http://www.techcrunch.com.

45. http://en-us.nielsen.com/tab/product_families/nielsen_bases.

46. Passy, "How Fast Food Chains Cook Up New Menu Items."

47. Gernot H. Gessinger, *Materials and Innovative Product Development: From Concept to Market* (Oxford: Elsevier, 2009).

48. Michael Cieply, "New Challenge for Filmmakers: Adding Dimension to 3-D Movies," *The New York Times*, August 11, 2013, http://www.nytimes.com.

49. Product Development Management Association, *The PDMA Handbook of New Product Development*, 3rd ed., Kenneth K. Kahn, ed. (New York: Wiley, 2012).

50. Jan Hendrik Fisch and Jan-Michael Ross, "Timing Product Replacements under Uncertainty—the Importance of Material–Price Fluctuations for the Success of Products That Are Based on New Materials," *Journal of Product Innovation Management* (2014); Yuhong Wu, Sridhar Balasubramanian, and Vijay Mahajan, "When Is a Preannounced New Product Likely to Be Delayed?" *Journal of Marketing* 68, no. 2 (2004), p. 101.

51. http://www.walletpop.com/specials/top-25-biggest-product-flops-of-all-time.

52. http://www.pdma.org/.

53. Theodore Levitt, *Marketing Imagination* (New York: Free Press, 1986).

54. Donald R. Lehmann and Russell S. Winer, *Analysis for Marketing Planning*, 7th ed. (Burr Ridge IL: McGraw-Hill/Irwin, 2008).

55. Lehmann and Winer, *Analysis for Marketing Planning*; Glen L. Urban and John R. Hauser, *Design and Marketing of New Products*, 2nd ed. (Upper Saddle River, NJ: Prentice Hall, 1993), pp. 120–21.

56. http://www.organicearthday.org/DelMonteFoods.htm; http://www.delmonte.com/Products/.

57. Euromonitor International, "A Revival in Hair Care Innovation," August 12, 2013, http://blog.euromonitor.com.

58. "Winning in Emerging Markets to Drive Growth in the Life Sciences Industry," *Accenture*, 2013, http://www.accenture.com; Eric D. Beinhocker, Diana Farrell, and Adil S. Zainulbhai, "Tracking the Growth of India's Middle Class," *McKinsey Quarterly* (August 2007).

59. Wallace Witkowski, "iPhones and Other Portables Suffering from 'Device Exhaustion,' Analyst Says," *The Wall Street Journal*, August 20, 2013, http://blogs.marketwatch.com; Jon Gold, "Is the Smartphone Market Saturated?" *Network World*, July 30, 2015, http://www.networkworld.com/article/2954568/smartphones/is-the-smartphone-market-saturated.html.

60. Natalie Zmuda and Jennifer Rooney, "Hallmark Breaks Out of Special Occasion Mold," *Advertising Age*, July 6, 2011, http://adage.com.

61. Alan Kozzin, "Weaned on CDs, They're Reaching for Vinyl," *The New York Times*, June 9, 2013, http://www.nytimes.com; Ed Christman, "Digital Music Sales Decrease for First Time in 2013," *BillboardBiz*, January 3, 2014, http://www.billboard.com.

62. Yvonne Zipp, "As Vinyl Records Get Back in the Groove, Kalamazoo Record Stores See Sales Climb," *MLive*, January 15, 2012, http://www.mlive.com.

63. Steven Levenstein, "Sony's New USB Turntable Sparks Vinyl Revival," March 14, 2008, http://www.inventospot.com; http://www.electronichouse.com; Roy Bragg, "LP Vinyl Records Are Making a Comeback in Audiophile Circles," *Knight Ridder Tribune Business News*, January 3, 2004 (ProQuest Document ID: 521358371); Susan Adams, "You, the Record Mogul," *Forbes*, October 27, 2003, p. 256ff.

64. Goutam Challagalla, R. Venkatesh, and Ajay Kohli, "Proactive Postsales Service: When and Why Does It Pay Off?," *Journal of Marketing* 73 (March 2009), pp. 70–87; Kevin J. Clancy and Peter C. Krieg, "Product Life Cycle: A Dangerous Idea," *Brandweek*, March 1, 2004, p. 26; Nariman K. Dhalla and Sonia Yuseph, "Forget the Product Life-Cycle Concept," *Harvard Business Review* (January/February 1976), p. 102ff.

65. Jan R. Landwehr, Daniel Wentzel, and Andreas Herrmann, "Product Design for the Long Run: Consumer Responses to Typical and Atypical Designs at Different Stages of Exposure," *Journal of Marketing* 77, no. 5 (2013), pp. 92–107; Peter Golder and Gerard Tellis, "Cascades, Diffusion, and Turning Points in the Product Life Cycle," MSI Report No. 03-120, 2003.

66. David Pogue, "Google Glass and the Future of Technology," *The New York Times*, September 12, 2012, http://pogue.blogs.nytimes.com.

67. http://www.google.com/glass/start/how-to-get-one/.

68. David Zax, "Google Glass's Unexpected Lessons in Product Launching," *Fast Company*, February 3, 2014, http://www.fastcompany.com.

69. Ibid.

70. Lance Ulanoff, "Google Glass Disappears from Twitter and Facebook," *Mashable*, January 26, 2016, http://mashable.com/2016/01/26/google-glass-social-accounts/#q6OQsKlrlsqW.

71. Nick Bilton, "Why Google Glass Broke," *The New York Times*, February 5, 2015, http://www.nytimes.com/2015/02/05/style/why-google-glass-broke.html?_r=0.

72. Eric Johnson, "Google Glass Isn't Dead—But It's All About the Enterprise for Now," *Re/Code*, July 30, 2015, http://recode.net/2015/07/30/google-glass-isnt-dead-but-its-all-about-the-enterprise-for-now/.

73. Sean Hollister, "SnapGlass? HoloChat? Snapchat Is Secretly Hiring Wearable Technology Experts," *cnet*, March 11, 2016, http://www.cnet.com/news/snapchat-glasses-vergence-snap-labs-hints-wearable/.

i. Ben Fritz, "With 'Cinderella,' Disney Recycles Fairy Tales, Minus the Cartoons," *The Wall Street Journal*, March 10, 2015, https://www.wsj.com; Alan French, "Plenty on the Line for Disney's 2016 Live-Action Releases," *Inside the Magic*, February 23, 2016, http://www.insidethemagic.net/2016/02/plenty-on-the-line-for-disneys-2016-live-action-releases/; Drew Mackie, "Here Is a Complete List of All the Disney Classics Being Remade (So Far)," *People*, September 23, 2015, http://www.people.com/article/all-disney-classics-live-action-remake;

ii. Ryan Mac, "Bow to Your Billionaire Drone Overlord: Frank Wang's Quest to Put DJI Robots into the Sky," *Forbes*, May 6, 2015; Paul Bedard, "Drone Sales Surge 167% to 4.3 Million, U.S. Leads but China Catching Up," *Washington Examiner*, May 29, 2015; Geoffrey Fowler and Joanna Stern, "Best Tech Gifts of 2015: Our Favorite Gadgets," *The Wall Street Journal*, November 24, 2015; Brookstone, http://www.brookstone.com/best-seller-gifts?srule=highest-rating&sz=24&start=0; Amazon, http://www.amazon.com/b?node=8037720011.

iii. Chris Murphy, "GM's Data Strategy Pushed to Center Stage," *Information Week*, March 27, 2014, http://www.information-week.com/; Mark van Rijmenam, "Three Use Cases of How General Motors Applies Big Data to Become Profitable Again," *DataFloq*, August 25, 2014, https://datafloq.com/; Jonathan H. Owen, David J. VanderVeen, and Lerinda L. Frost, "General Motors: Using O.R. to Meet Auto Industry Challenges and Provide Value to Customers and the Company," *Informs Online*, December 2013, http://www.orms-today.org/.

iv. Jack Adams, "US Search Engine Market Share Figures Steady in February," *Clickthrough*, March 21, 2014, http://www.click-through-marketing.com; Steve Lohr, "Can Microsoft Make You 'Bing'?" *The New York Times*, July 30, 2011, http://www.nytimes.com; Renay San Miguel, "Bing's New Bells and Whistles Could Leave Searchers' Heads Ringing," *TechNewsWorld*, March 29, 2010; Jared Newman, "How Microsoft Plans to Beat Google with Bing," *PCWorld*, August 1, 2011, http://www.pcworld.com; Vamien McKalin, "Bing Slowly Eating Away at Google Search with New Market Share Gain," *TWCN Tech News*, January 2, 2016, http://news.thewindowsclub.com/bing-slowly-eating-away-google-search-new-market-share-gain-81397/.

v. Melissa Harris, "Business Is Popping for Healthier Snack," *Chicago Tribune*, February 8, 2012, http://articles.chicagotribune.com/2012-02-08/business/ct-biz-0209-confidential-skinnypop-20120204_1_grocery-stores-garrett-popcorn-bags; Ellen Rogan, "SkinnyPop's Success: Lessons I Learned," May 21, 2014, http://www.ellenrogin.com/skinny-pops-success-lessons-i-learned/; Tomi Kilgore, "5 Things to Know About SkinnyPop-Maker Amplify Ahead of Its IPO," *Market Watch*, August 4, 2015, http://www.marketwatch.com/story/5-things-to-know-about-skinnypop-maker-amplify-ahead-of-its-ipo-2015-08-03; Peter Frost, "SkinnyPop's Parent Company Goes Public, with a 10-Figure Valuation," *Crain's Chicago Business*, August 5, 2015, http://www.chicagobusiness.com/article/20150805/NEWS07/150809926/skinnypops-parent-company-goes-public-with-a-10-figure-valuation.

CHAPTER 13

SERVICES: THE INTANGIBLE PRODUCT

LEARNING OBJECTIVES

After reading this chapter, you should be able to:

LO13-1 Describe how the marketing of services differs from the marketing of products.

LO13-2 Discuss the four gaps in the Service Gaps Model.

LO13-3 Examine the five service quality dimensions.

LO13-4 Explain the zone of tolerance.

LO13-5 Identify three service recovery strategies.

Lululemon's newly opened flagship store in Manhattan does more than sell exercise clothing and yoga equipment, which make up only about two thirds of their business. Part of the facility is taken up with concierge services, available to recommend a nearby gym or help shoppers book class time. On another floor, the Hub Seventeen space is used for yoga classes, demonstrations, concerts, and other community-building events.

Lululemon believes that it can increase the sense of community surrounding its stores in various areas, especially with its concierge service. Concierges on staff suggest places in any local area where shoppers could take a jog or find a healthy meal. In invoking this sense of community, lululemon hopes to become a new "third place" for its consumers and fans after their home and work, such that they might feel comfortable stopping by to have a cup of tea and relax in the store, even if they are not going to make a purchase.

Although the Hub Seventeen space may not expand to all stores, it does point to the company's service-oriented efforts to make its stores more than just retail outlets. In particular, with the offer of yoga classes, lululemon gives its customers what they clearly want, namely, a space to practice the type of exercise for which they already have purchased the gear.

In addition to responding to customer demand for dedicated services, such efforts might reflect the company's attempt to overcome some bad press that it has suffered recently, including the fallout that resulted from thoughtless comments by a former executive who implied that overweight people were not the company's target market. Lululemon also invoked serious customer complaints when it raised the price of a popular pant style, as well as when consumers discovered a production error that resulted in multiple batches of its yoga pants being embarrassingly transparent.[1] With product and service failures like these, lululemon has recognized that it has some work to do if it hopes to keep customers centered, aligned, and happy.

Whereas a **service** is any intangible offering that involves a deed, performance, or effort that cannot be physically possessed,[2] **customer service** specifically refers to human or mechanical activities firms undertake to help satisfy their customers' needs and wants. By providing good customer service, firms add value to their products. Although Amazon may have built its reputation on being able to provide a vast range of products, it also has developed capabilities that allow customers to click a link to receive quotes for services, such as electronic installation, home repairs, yard work, or dog walking, from local professionals. Google already provides a service, in the form of its famous search engine, but it also is experimenting with ways to compete in other service spaces. For example, it recently invested heavily in Thumbtack, a platform that allows customers to post their service needs and job offers, then receive bids for those jobs from service providers that have registered with the site.[3]

Exhibit 13.1 illustrates the continuum from a pure service to a pure good. Most offerings lie somewhere in the middle and include some service and some good (i.e., a hybrid of the two). Even those firms that are engaged primarily in selling a good, such as an apparel store, typically view service as a method to maintain a sustainable competitive advantage. Although lululemon is working extraordinarily hard to provide community-oriented services, any clothing retailer needs to provide basic customer service to help shoppers find the items they want and complete their transaction. Therefore, this chapter takes an inclusive view of services as anything from pure service businesses, such as Twitter, to a business that uses service as a differentiating tool to help it sell physical goods.

Economies of developed countries such as of the United States have become increasingly dependent on services. Services account for nearly 80 percent of the U.S. gross domestic product (GDP), a much higher percentage than was true 50, 20, or even 10 years ago.[4] In turn, the current list of *Fortune* 500 companies contains more service companies and fewer manufacturers than it did in previous decades.[5] This dependence and the growth of service-oriented economies in developed countries have emerged for several reasons.

First, it is generally less expensive for firms to manufacture their products in less developed countries. Even if the goods are finished in the United States, some of their components likely were produced elsewhere. In turn, the proportion of service production to goods production in the United States and other similar economies has steadily increased over time.

Second, people place a high value on convenience and leisure. For instance, household maintenance activities, which many people performed themselves in the past, have become more popular and quite specialized. Food preparation, lawn

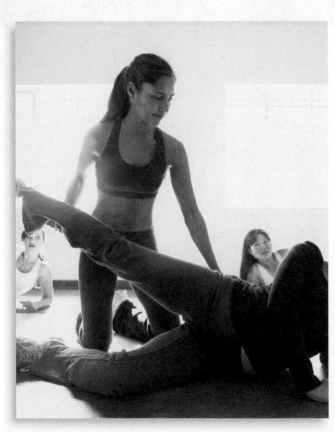

Specialized services like personal training are thriving.
© John Lund/Drew Kelly/Blend Images RF

EXHIBIT 13.1 The Service–Product Continuum

Doctor   Hotel   Dry cleaners   Restaurant   Apparel specialty store   Grocery store

Service dominant   Product dominant

(Doctor): © Dynamic Graphics/JupiterImages RF; (Hotel): © Jose Fuste Raga/Getty Images; (Dry cleaners): © McGraw-Hill Education/Andrew Resek, photographer; (Restaurant): © John A. Rizzo/Getty Images RF; (Apparel): © Charles Bowman/Alamy RF; (Grocery store): © Photodisc/Getty Images RF

maintenance, house cleaning, pet grooming, laundry and dry cleaning, hair care, and automobile maintenance are all often performed by specialists.

Third, as the world has become more complicated, people are demanding more specialized services—everything from plumbers to personal trainers, from massage therapists to tax preparation specialists, from lawyers to travel and leisure specialists, and even to health care providers. The aging population in particular has increased the need for health care specialists, including doctors, nurses, and caregivers in assisted living facilities and nursing homes, and many of those consumers want their specialists to provide personalized, dedicated services.

SERVICES MARKETING DIFFERS FROM PRODUCT MARKETING

 LO 13-1 Describe how the marketing of services differs from the marketing of products.

The marketing of services differs from product marketing because of the four fundamental differences involved in services: Services are intangible, inseparable, heterogeneous, and perishable.[6] (See Exhibit 13.2.) This section examines these differences and discusses how they affect marketing strategies.

Intangible

As the title of this chapter implies, the most fundamental difference between a product and a service is that services are intangible—they cannot be touched, tasted, or seen like a pure product can. When you get a physical examination, you see and hear the doctor, but the service itself is intangible. This intangibility can prove highly challenging to marketers, especially if they are more accustomed to selling products, as in the example in Adding Value 13.1. For instance, it makes it difficult to convey the benefits of services—try describing whether the experience of visiting your dentist was good or bad and why. Service providers (e.g., physicians, dentists) therefore offer cues to help their customers experience and perceive their service more positively, such as a waiting room stocked with television sets, beverages, and comfortable chairs to create an atmosphere that appeals to the target market.

A service that cannot be shown directly to potential customers also is difficult to promote. Marketers must creatively employ symbols and images to promote and sell services, as Six Flags does in using its advertising to evoke images of happy families and friends enjoying a roller coaster ride. Professional medical services provide appropriate images of personnel doing their jobs in white coats surrounded by high-tech equipment.

Some services have found excellent ways to make their offerings more tangible to their customers. For example, Carbonite provides simple, affordable, unlimited online backup for individual home computer users as well as small businesses, for which it keeps its services, prices, and customer support well within reach. The basic yearly rate for a home

EXHIBIT 13.2   Core Differences between Services and Goods

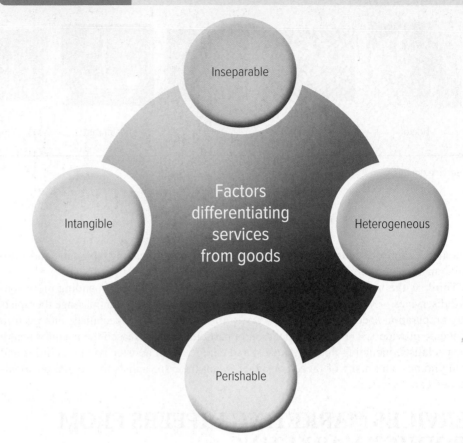

Inseparable

Intangible

Factors differentiating services from goods

Heterogeneous

Perishable

customer is $59 per computer; a business pays $269 a year to cover all company computers. Its software runs invisibly on both Macs and PCs, performing backups automatically. For portable digital access, the company offers free mobile applications for BlackBerry, iPad, iPhone, and Android devices. In addition, it has expanded its capabilities as it has grown, such that it now helps clients in medical professions ensure the security of patients'

Because it is difficult to show a service, Six Flags evokes images in its advertising of happy families and friends enjoying a ride at one of its amusement parks.

© Ken James/Bloomberg/Getty Images

Adding Value 13.1 | Kola House Restaurant: Ensuring a Service Experience That Includes Pepsi[i]

The terms and names that marketers use to describe their offerings are often critically important. Consumers might refer to carbonated beverages as colas, sodas, or pop, but in a new experimental expansion, PepsiCo. is emphasizing the term "kola" in an effort to highlight the kola nut that is the source of the flavor and body of traditional cola drinks. It isn't emphasizing the Pepsi name or any of the valuable brands that the company owns. And perhaps most remarkably, it isn't selling a product, in the traditional sense of the word.

Instead, at Kola House, a restaurant, bar, and event space in New York's trendy Chelsea neighborhood, Pepsi runs a traditional restaurant in conjunction with a product testing ground. The food and beverage menus revolve around the kola nut and related ingredients. This single space is the only Kola House planned so far, though Pepsi notes that if it achieves success here, it would consider expanding the idea to other cities.

Pepsi hired a head "alchemist"—a position that most people would likely call the head bartender. It also has plans for "modular" Kola Houses (a design that most people would call a pop-up) to appear at major sporting events like the Super Bowl, as well as at Lollapalooza and similar music festivals. Furthermore, the entire enterprise is being run by Pepsi's marketing department, not by a product division or specialized restaurant arm.

With this explicit marketing orientation, Pepsi is not only taking care with the words it uses but also taking a unique perspective on the entire restaurant experience. The physical space is largely designed to be so compelling and interesting that it drives consumers to report about it through social media. The very essence of the planning thus was not what products the restaurant will serve but rather what service experience it can create to excite and thrill consumers. The design firm that helped Pepsi create the space is owned by Lenny Kravitz, and it includes subtle hints of the ownership without emblazoning the Pepsi logo everywhere.

The initiative is thus both innovative and risky. As this article asserts, "Essentially, Pepsi is trying to market its product without marketing its product."

---

information. As for security, Carbonite's system is comparable to the safeguards used by major banks, credit card companies, and online retailers. All files are encrypted with two layers of technology, stored on enterprise-grade servers to protect against mechanical disk failure, and kept in state-of-the-art data centers guarded 24 hours a day, 365 days a year. Personnel must pass through biometric scans and electronic pin coding to enter. Carbonite thus has firmly established its market position by delivering a reliable, secure, easy-to-use service, combined with reasonable pricing and easily accessible technical support.[7]

Inseparable Production and Consumption

Unlike chocolates that may have been made halfway around the world six months prior to their purchase, services are produced and consumed at the same time; that is, service and consumption are *inseparable*. When getting a haircut, the customer is not only present but also may participate in the service process. Furthermore, the interaction with the service provider may have an important impact on the customer's perception of the service outcome. If the hairstylist appears to be having fun while cutting hair, it may affect the experience positively.

Because the service is inseparable from its consumption, customers rarely have the opportunity to try the service before they purchase it. And after the service has been performed, it can't be returned. Imagine telling your hairstylist that you want to have the hair around your ears trimmed as a test before he or she does your entire head. Because the purchase risk in these scenarios can be relatively high, service firms

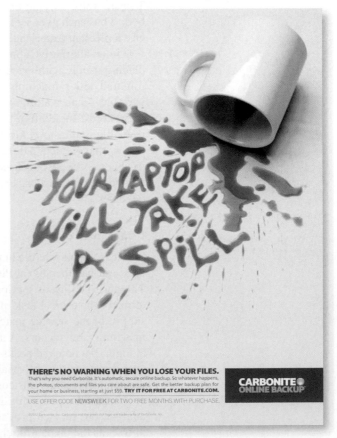

Carbonite backs up computer data on remote servers.

Source: Carbonite, Inc.

sometimes provide extended warranties and 100 percent satisfaction guarantees. The Choice Hotels chain, for instance, states: "When you choose to stay at a Comfort Inn, Comfort Suites, Quality, Clarion, or Sleep Inn hotel, we are committed to making you feel understood, welcome, and important."[8]

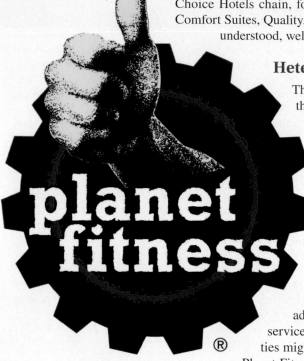

Planet Fitness' service offerings are customized to their customers' needs.
© Hand-out/Planet Fitness/Newscom

Heterogeneous

The more humans are needed to provide a service, the more likely there is to be **heterogeneity** or variability in the service's quality. A hairstylist may give bad haircuts in the morning because he or she went out the night before. Yet that stylist still may offer a better service than the undertrained stylist working in the next station over. A restaurant, which offers a mixture of services and products, generally can control its food quality but not the variability in food preparation or delivery. If a consumer has a problem with a product, it can be replaced, redone, destroyed, or, if it is already in the supply chain, recalled. In many cases, the problem can even be fixed before the product gets into consumers' hands. An inferior service can't be recalled; by the time the firm recognizes a problem, the damage has been done.

Marketers also can use the variable nature of services to their advantage. A micromarketing segmentation strategy can customize a service to meet customers' needs exactly (see Chapter 9). Exercise facilities might generally provide the same weights, machines, and mats, but at Planet Fitness, customers know that the gym explicitly seeks to offer a laid-back, less intense setting. Planet Fitness actively avoids targeting hardcore gym rats with its service offering. Instead, local storefronts offer pizza nights and bowls of free Tootsie Rolls, varying the details to match the needs and preferences of their local members. Thus each gym seeks to live up to the chain's overall promise to make going to exercise a pleasant experience rather than an intimidation festival.[9]

In an alternative approach, some service providers tackle the variability issue by replacing people with machines. For simple transactions such as getting cash, using an automated teller machine (ATM) is usually quicker and more convenient—and less variable—than waiting in line for a bank teller. Many retailers have installed kiosks in their stores: In addition to offering customers the opportunity to order merchandise not available in the store, kiosks can provide routine customer service, freeing employees to deal with more demanding customer requests and problems and reducing service variability. Kiosks can also be used to automate existing store services such as gift registry management, rain checks, credit applications, and preordering service for bakeries and delicatessens.

Perishable

Services are **perishable** in that they cannot be stored for use in the future. You can't stockpile your membership at Planet Fitness like you could a six-pack of V8 juice, for instance. The perishability of services provides both challenges and opportunities to marketers in terms of the critical task of matching demand and supply. As long as the demand for and supply of the service match closely, there is no problem, but unfortunately this perfect matching rarely occurs. A ski area, for instance, can be open as long as there is snow, even at night, but demand peaks on weekends and holidays, so ski areas often offer less expensive tickets during off-peak periods to stimulate demand. Airlines, cruise ships, movie theaters, and restaurants confront similar challenges and attack them in similar ways.

Certainly, providing great service is not easy, and it requires a diligent effort to analyze the service process piece by piece. In the next section, we examine what is known as the Gaps Model, which is designed to highlight those areas where customers believe they are getting less or poorer service than they should (the gaps) and how these gaps can be closed.

Because services are perishable, service providers like ski areas offer less expensive tickets at night to stimulate demand.

© Buddy Mays/Corbis

PROGRESS CHECK

1. What are the four marketing elements that distinguish services from products?
2. Why can't we separate firms into just service or just product sellers?

PROVIDING GREAT SERVICE: THE GAPS MODEL

LO13-2 Discuss the four gaps in the Service Gaps Model.

Customers have certain expectations about how a service should be delivered. When the delivery of that service fails to meet those expectations, a **service gap** results. The **Service Gaps Model** (Exhibit 13.3) is designed to encourage the systematic examination of all aspects of the service delivery process and prescribes the steps needed to develop an optimal service strategy.[10]

As Exhibit 13.3 shows, there are four service gaps:

1. The **knowledge gap** reflects the difference between customers' expectations and the firm's perception of those customer expectations. Firms can close this gap by determining what customers really want by doing research using marketing metrics such as service quality and the zone of tolerance (discussed later).

2. The **standards gap** pertains to the difference between the firm's perceptions of customers' expectations and the service standards it sets. By setting appropriate service standards, training employees to meet and exceed those standards, and measuring service performance, firms can attempt to close this gap.

3. The **delivery gap** is the difference between the firm's service standards and the actual service it provides to customers. This gap can be closed by getting employees to meet or exceed service standards when the service is being delivered by empowering service providers, providing support and incentives, and using technology where appropriate.[11]

4. The **communication gap** refers to the difference between the actual service provided to customers and the service that the firm's promotion program promises. If firms are more realistic about the services they can provide and at the same time manage customer expectations effectively, they generally can close this gap.

EXHIBIT 13.3   Service Gaps Model for Improving Retail Service Quality

Sources: Adapted from Valarie Zeithaml, A. Parasuraman, and Leonard Berry, *Delivering Quality Customer Service* (New York: The Free Press, 1990); and Valarie Zeithaml, Leonard Berry, and A. Parasuraman, "Communication and Control Processes in the Delivery of Service Quality," *Journal of Marketing* 52, no. 2 (April 1988), pp. 35–48.

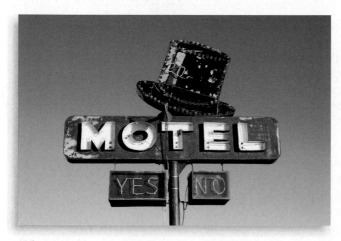

What service gaps did Marcia experience while on vacation at the motel in Maine?

© Sascha Burkard/Getty Images RF

As we discuss the four gaps subsequently, we will apply them to the experience that Marcia Kessler had with a motel in Maine. She saw an ad for a package weekend that quoted a very reasonable daily rate and listed the free amenities available at Green Valley Motel: free babysitting services, a piano bar with a nightly singer, a free continental breakfast, a heated swimming pool, and newly decorated rooms. When she booked the room, Marcia discovered that the price advertised was not available during the weekend, and a three-day minimum stay was required. Because of the nice amenities, however, she went ahead. After checking in with a very unpleasant person at the front desk, Marcia and her husband found that their room appeared circa-1950 and had not been cleaned, so they had to wait for several hours before they could use their room.. When she complained, all she got was attitude from the assistant manager. Resigned to the fact that they were slated to spend the weekend, she decided to go for a swim. Unfortunately, the water was heated by Booth Bay and stood at around 50 degrees. No one was using the babysitting services because there were few young children at the resort. It turns out the piano bar singer was the second cousin of the owner, and he couldn't carry a tune, let alone play the piano very well. The continental breakfast must have come all the way from the Continent, because everything was stale and tasteless. Marcia couldn't wait to get home.

The Knowledge Gap: Understanding Customer Expectations

An important early step in providing good service is knowing what the customer wants. It doesn't pay to invest in services that don't improve customer satisfaction. To reduce the knowledge gap, firms must understand customers' expectations. To understand those expectations, firms undertake customer research and increase the interaction and communication between managers and employees.

Customers' expectations are based on their knowledge and experiences.[12] Marcia's expectations were that her room at the motel in Maine would be ready when she got there, the swimming pool would be heated, the singer would be able to sing, and the breakfast would be fresh. Not a lot to expect, but in this extreme example, the Green Valley Motel was suffering a severe knowledge gap, perhaps based on its assumption that being on the ocean in Maine was enough. If the resort never understood her expectations, it is unlikely it would ever be able to meet them.

Expectations vary according to the type of service. Marcia's expectations might have been higher, for instance, if she were staying at a Ritz-Carlton rather than the Green Valley Motel. At the Ritz, she might have expected employees to know her by name, be aware of her dietary preferences, and to have placed fresh fruit of her choice and fresh-cut flowers in her room before she arrived. At the Green Valley Motel, she expected easy check-in/checkout, easy access to a major highway, a clean room with a comfortable bed, and a TV, at a bare minimum.

People's expectations also vary depending on the situation. If she had been traveling on business, the Green Valley Motel might have been fine (had the room at least been clean and modern), but if she were celebrating her 10th wedding anniversary, she probably would prefer the Ritz. Thus, the service provider needs to know and understand the expectations of the customers in its target market.

Evaluating Service Quality Using Well-Established Marketing Metrics

To meet or exceed customers' expectations, marketers must determine what those expectations are. Yet because of their intangibility, the service quality, or customers' perceptions of how well a service meets or exceeds their expectations, is often difficult for customers to evaluate.[13] Customers generally use five distinct service dimensions to determine overall service quality: reliability, responsiveness, assurance, empathy, and tangibles (see Exhibit 13.4). The Broadmoor Hotel in Colorado Springs, Colorado, maintains its five-star rating by focusing on these five service characteristics. In operation for more than a century, the Broadmoor is one of the world's premier resorts.[14] It has received more than 50 consecutive

LO13-3 Examine the five service quality dimensions.

EXHIBIT 13.4 Building Blocks of Service Quality

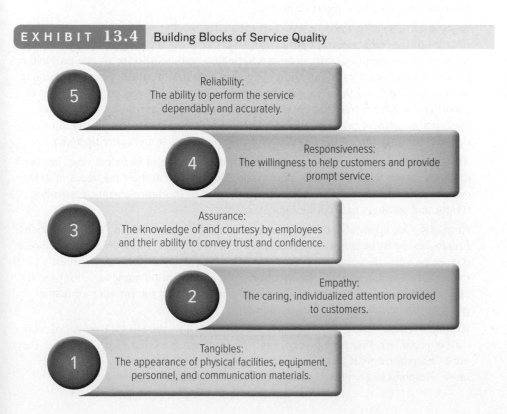

5 Reliability:
The ability to perform the service dependably and accurately.

4 Responsiveness:
The willingness to help customers and provide prompt service.

3 Assurance:
The knowledge of and courtesy by employees and their ability to convey trust and confidence.

2 Empathy:
The caring, individualized attention provided to customers.

1 Tangibles:
The appearance of physical facilities, equipment, personnel, and communication materials.

The Broadmoor in Colorado Springs, Colorado, is known for exceptional service quality.

Courtesy of The Broadmoor

years of five-star ratings from the Forbes Travel Guide—a record unmatched by any other hotel.[15] The aspects of its stellar service quality include:

- **Reliability** Every new Broadmoor employee, before ever encountering a customer, attends a two-and-a-half-day orientation session and receives an employee handbook. Making and keeping promises to customers is a central part of this orientation. Employees are trained always to give an estimated time for service, whether it be room service, laundry service, or simply how long it will take to be seated at one of the resort's restaurants. When an employee makes a promise, he or she keeps that promise. If they don't know the answer to a question, employees are trained to never guess. When an employee is unable to answer a question accurately, he or she immediately contacts someone who can.

- **Assurance** The Broadmoor conveys trust by empowering its employees. An example of an employee empowerment policy is the service recovery program. If a guest problem arises, employees are given discretionary resources to rectify the problem or present the customer with something special to help mollify them. For example, if a meal is delivered and there's a mistake in the order or how it was prepared, a server can offer the guest a free item such as a dessert or, if the service was well below expectations, simply take care of the bill. Managers then review each situation to understand the nature of the problem and help prevent it from occurring again.

- **Tangibles** One of the greatest challenges for the Broadmoor in recent years has been updating rooms built in the early part of the 20th century to meet the needs of 21st-century visitors. To accomplish this, it spent millions in improvements, renovating rooms, and adding a new outdoor pool complex.

- **Empathy** One approach used to demonstrate empathy is personalizing communications. Employees are instructed to always address a guest by name, if possible. To accomplish this, employees are trained to listen and observe carefully to determine a guest's name. Subtle sources for this information include convention name tags, luggage ID tags, credit cards, or checks. In addition, all phones within the Broadmoor display a guest's room number and name on a screen.

- **Responsiveness** Every employee is instructed to follow the HEART model of taking care of problems. First, employees must "Hear what a guest has to say." Second, they must "Empathize with them" and then "Apologize for the situation." Fourth, they must "Respond to the guest's needs" by "Taking action and following up."

Marketing Analytics 13.1 Using Analytics to Reduce Wait Time at Kroger[ii]

Shopping for groceries is rarely considered a pleasant task. But what makes the experience so odious? As Kroger found out when it asked customers, the answer is often the long checkout lines. To help alleviate the problem, it began analyzing customer data to find an answer to a simple question: What would happen if it could open up a lane exactly when needed? The answer was that it could significantly improve customer satisfaction. So Kroger developed QueVision.

QueVision combines infrared sensors over store doors and cash registers, predictive analytics, and real-time data feeds from point-of-sale systems to calculate how many registers are needed and what the actual wait times are, all in real time. Wait times appear on a screen at the front of the store. The overall goal of the combined system is to ensure there is never more than one person ahead of any shopper in the checkout line.

This technology has been so successful that it has cut the average wait time for customers from more than 4 minutes to less than 30 seconds. QueVision also has had some unexpected positive consequences, in the form of happier employees. Friendly associates are really important for defining customer-oriented metrics. Although the math might not have predicted it, the cashier friendliness metric, as measured by customer surveys, has improved throughout the company by approximately 24 percent. Shorter lines make customers happy, and when employees encounter happy customers,

Grocery shoppers really hate long checkout lines, so Kroger developed a system to calculate how many registers are needed and what the actual wait times are, all in real time.
© Zuma Press, Inc/Alamy

they're happier too. Kroger also uses its QueVision data in more detailed simulations. It has correlated enough data to keep people moving in the front of stores, including checkout lines, even in stores with unusual layouts. QueVision data also have helped Kroger evaluate new shopping systems, such as self-checkout.

Marketing research (see Chapter 10) provides a means to better understand consumers' service expectations and their perceptions of service quality. In Marketing Analytics 13.1, we describe how Kroger uses data to learn about customers' expectations. This research can be extensive and expensive, or it can be integrated into a firm's everyday interactions with customers. Today, most service firms have developed voice-of-customer programs and employ ongoing marketing research to assess how well they are meeting their customers' expectations. A systematic **voice-of-customer (VOC) program** collects customer inputs and integrates them into managerial decisions.

An important marketing metric to evaluate how well firms perform on the five service quality dimensions (again see Exhibit 13.4) is the **zone of tolerance**, which refers to the area between customers' expectations regarding their desired service and the minimum level of acceptable service—that is, the difference between what the customer really wants and what he or she will accept before going elsewhere. To define the zone of tolerance, firms ask a series of questions about each service quality dimension that relate to

LO13-4 Explain the zone of tolerance.

- The desired and expected level of service for each dimension, from low to high.

- Customers' perceptions of how well the focal service performs and how well a competitive service performs, from low to high.

- The importance of each service quality dimension.

Exhibit 13.5 illustrates the results of such an analysis for Lou's Local Diner, a family-owned restaurant. The rankings on the left are based on a nine-point scale, on which 1 is low and 9 is high. The length of each box illustrates the zone of tolerance for each service quality dimension. For instance, according to the short length of the reliability box, customers expect a fairly high level of reliability (top of the box) and will accept only a fairly

EXHIBIT 13.5   Customers' Evaluation of Service Quality

Note: The scale ranges from a 9 indicating very high service quality on a given
service quality dimension, to a 1 indicating very low service quality.

high level of reliability (bottom of the box). On the other end of the scale, customers expect
a high level of assurance (top of the box) but will also accept a fairly low level (bottom of
the box). This difference is to be expected because the customers also were asked to assign
an importance score to the five service quality dimensions so that the total equals 100 percent (see bottom of Exhibit 13.5). Looking at the average importance score, we conclude
that reliability is relatively important to these customers but assurance is not. So customers
have a fairly narrow zone of tolerance for service dimensions that are fairly important to
them and a wider range of tolerance for those service dimensions that are less important.
Also note that Lou's Local Diner always rates higher than its primary competitor, Well-
Known National Chain, on each dimension.

Further note that Well-Known National Chain scores below the zone of tolerance
on the tangibles dimension, meaning that customers are not willing to accept the way
the restaurant looks and smells. Lou's Local Diner, in contrast, performs above the zone
of tolerance on the responsiveness dimension—maybe even too well. Lou's may wish to
conduct further research to verify which responsiveness aspects it is performing so
well, and then consider toning those aspects down. For example, being responsive to
customers' desires to have a diner that serves breakfast 24 hours a day can be expensive
and may not add any further value to Lou's Diner, because customers would accept
more limited times.

*Lou's Local Diner always rates
higher than its primary competitor, Well-Known National
Chain, on each service quality
dimension.*

© *McGraw-Hill Education/Gideon Kindall,
photographer*

A very straightforward and inexpensive method of collecting consumers' perceptions of service quality is to gather them at the time of the sale. Service providers can ask customers how they liked the service—though customers often are reticent to provide negative feedback directly to the person who provided the service—or distribute a simple questionnaire. Regardless of how information is collected, companies must take care not to lose it, which can happen if there is no effective mechanism for filtering it up to the key decision makers. Furthermore, in some cases, customers cannot effectively evaluate the service until several days or weeks later. Automobile dealers, for instance, often call their customers a week after they perform a service such as an oil change to assess their service quality.

Another excellent method for assessing customers' expectations is making effective use of customer complaint behavior. Even if complaints are handled effectively to solve customers' problems, the essence of the complaint is too often lost on managers. For instance, an airline established a policy that customer service reps could not discuss any issues involving fees to travel agents with customers. So when a customer calls to complain about these fees, the representative just changes the subject, and management therefore never finds out about the complaint.[16]

Even firms with the best formal research mechanisms in place must put managers on the frontlines occasionally to interact directly with the customers. The late Sam Walton, founder of Walmart, participated in and advocated this strategy, which is known as "management by walking around."[17] Unless the managers who make the service quality decisions know what their service providers are facing on a day-to-day basis, and unless they can talk directly to the customers with whom those service providers interact, any customer service program they create will not be as good as it could be.

The Standards Gap: Setting Service Standards

Getting back to the Green Valley Motel in Maine for a moment, suppose because of a number of complaints or because business was falling off, it set out to determine customers' service expectations and gained a pretty good idea of them. The next step would be to set its service standards accordingly and develop systems to meet the customers' service expectations. How, for instance, can it make sure that every room is cleaned and ready by an optimum time of day in the eyes of the customers, or that the breakfast is checked for freshness and quality every day? To consistently deliver service that meets customers' expectations, firms must set specific, measurable goals. For instance, for the Green Valley Motel, the most efficient process might have been to start cleaning rooms at 8:00 a.m. and finish by 5:00 p.m. But many guests want to sleep late, and new arrivals want to get into their room as soon as they arrive, often before 5:00 p.m. So a customer-oriented standard would mandate that the rooms get cleaned between 10:00 a.m. and 2:00 p.m.

Service providers generally want to do a good job as long as they know what is expected of them. Motel employees should be shown, for instance, exactly how managers expect them to clean a room and what specific tasks they are responsible for performing. In general, more employees will buy into a quality-oriented process if they are involved in setting the goals. For instance, suppose an important employee of the motel objects to disposable plastic cups and suggests that actual drinking glasses in the rooms would be classier as well as more ecological. There might be a cost–benefit trade-off to consider here, but if management listens to her and makes the

Service providers, like this room service delivery person at a hotel, generally want to do a good job, but they need to be trained to know what exactly a good job entails.

© Chris Ryan/OJO Images/Getty Images RF

change in this case, it should likely make the employee all the more committed to other tasks involved in cleaning and preparing rooms.

The employees must be thoroughly trained not only to complete their specific tasks but also how to treat guests, and the manager needs to set an example of high service standards, which will permeate throughout the organization. The kind of attitude Marcia got, for instance, when she registered a complaint with the assistant manager at the Green Valley is not a recipe for generating repeat customers and should not be tolerated. For frontline service employees under stress, however, pleasant interactions with customers do not always come naturally. Although people can be taught specific tasks related to their jobs, this is not easily extended to interpersonal relations. But it is simply not enough to tell employees to be nice or do what customers want. A quality goal should be specific, such as: Greet every customer/guest you encounter with "Good morning/afternoon/evening, Sir or Ma'am." Try to greet customers by name.

The Delivery Gap: Delivering Service Quality

The delivery gap is where the rubber meets the road, where the customer directly interacts with the service provider. Even if there are adequate standards in place, the employees are well trained, and management is committed to meeting or exceeding customers' service expectations, there can still be delivery gaps. It could very well have been that Marcia experienced several delivery gaps at the Green Valley Motel. It could have been that the unclean room, the assistant manager's attitude, the unheated swimming pool, the poor piano bar singer, or the stale food resulted from unforeseen or unusual circumstances. Although some of these issues such as an unclean room or the attitude Marcia encountered should have been avoided, it is possible that the motel had a power outage resulting in the unheated swimming pool, the regular piano bar singer was ill, and the breakfast was stale because of a missed delivery. The maid could not vacuum the room because of the lack of power, and the assistant manager felt assaulted on all sides by these problems. But the result was a lost customer. Even if there are no other gaps, a delivery gap always results in a service failure.

Delivery gaps can be reduced when employees are empowered to spontaneously act in the customers' and the firm's best interests when problems or crises are experienced. Such empowerment might have saved the day for Marcia and the Green Valley Motel. Empowerment means employees are supported in their efforts to do their jobs effectively.[18]

Empowering Service Providers   In the service context, empowerment means allowing employees to make decisions about how service is provided to customers. When frontline employees are authorized to make decisions to help their customers, service quality generally improves. Empowerment becomes more important when the service is more individualized. Nordstrom provides an overall objective—satisfy customer needs—and then encourages employees to do whatever is necessary to achieve the objective. For example, a Nordstrom shoe sales associate decided to break up two pairs of shoes, one a size 10 and the other a size 10½, to sell a hard-to-fit customer. Although the other two shoes were unsalable and therefore it made for an unprofitable sale, the customer purchased five other pairs that day and became a loyal Nordstrom customer as a result. Empowering service providers with only a rule like "Use your best judgment" (as Nordstrom does) might cause chaos. At Nordstrom, department managers avoid abuses by coaching and training salespeople to understand what "Use your best judgment" specifically means.

Support and Incentives for Employees   To ensure that service is delivered properly, management needs to support the service providers in several ways and give them incentives. This is basic. A service provider's job can often be difficult, especially when customers are unpleasant or less than reasonable. But the service provider cannot be rude or offensive just because the customer is. The old cliché "Service with a smile" remains the best approach, but for this to work, employees must feel supported.

First, managers and coworkers should provide emotional support to service providers by demonstrating a concern for their well-being and standing behind their decisions. Because it can be very disconcerting when, for instance, a server is abused by a customer who believes her food was improperly prepared, restaurant managers must be supportive and help the employee get through his or her emotional reaction to the berating experienced.[19] Such support can extend to empowering the server to rectify the situation by giving the customer new food and a free dessert, in which case the manager must understand the server's decision, not punish him for giving away too much.

Second, service providers require instrumental support—the systems and equipment to deliver the service properly. Many retailers provide state-of-the-art instrumental support for their service providers. In-store kiosks help sales associates provide more detailed and complete product information and enable them to make sales of merchandise that is either not carried in the store or is temporarily out of stock.

Third, the support that managers provide must be consistent and coherent throughout the organization. Patients expect physicians to provide great patient care using state-of-the-art procedures and medications, but because they are tied to managed-care systems (health maintenance organizations [HMOs]), many doctors must squeeze more people into their office hours and prescribe less optimal, less expensive courses of treatment. These conflicting goals can be very frustrating to patients.

Finally, a key part of any customer service program is providing rewards to employees for their excellent service. Numerous firms have developed a service reputation by ensuring that their employees are themselves recognized for recognizing the value the firm places on customer service. Travelocity, for example, features employees who champion the customer service experience in a weekly e-mail. Believing that engaged employees are the key to customer satisfaction, it works to create an atmosphere that reinforces the commitment to customers by encouraging employees to nominate colleagues who exemplify this commitment. Through constant feedback about who is serving the customer best, as well as smaller events such as monthly lunches with the CEO for selected employees, Travelocity creates a business environment that recognizes and rewards customer service.[20] The results for Travelocity have been a wealth of awards, such as a top ranking on the Customer Online Respect Survey and a designation as the World's Leading Travel Internet Site for several consecutive years.[21]

Use of Technology

Technology can be employed to reduce delivery gaps, and has become an increasingly important facilitator of the delivery of services. Using technology to facilitate service delivery can provide many benefits, such as access to a wider variety of services, a greater degree of control by the customer over the services, and the ability to obtain information. The use of technology also improves the service provider's efficiency and reduces servicing costs; in some cases, it can lead to a competitive advantage over less service-oriented competitors.[22]

Technological advances that help close the delivery gap are expanding. Macy's has installed Look Book displays, which act like an interactive digital catalogue in the store. These displays enable customers to find fashionable ideas, ways to extend their existing wardrobes, and images from forward-thinking fashion icons. Touching the screen allows them to check the availability of various colors and sizes, as well as receive more detailed information about items that are of interest. Macy's has paired these larger displays with smaller point-of-purchase kiosks, which focus more on functionality than fashion. These smaller kiosks indicate which colors and styles are available, as well as identifying which items have prompted the most Facebook likes or customer favorite rankings.[23]

Panera Bread has developed a program that allows customers to order from their website in advance and have their take-out meal ready when they arrive. For those who prefer to dine in, this technology will make it possible to order using an in-store kiosk or a dedicated mobile app. Regardless of how they order, people can track the progress of their orders on in-store screens. All these elements also allow people to pay readily and ensure that their orders are prepared correctly.

Technological advances can also help with the delivery gap by improving supply chain efficiency. For example, grocery store chain Cisco is developing a shelf sensor that allows the retailer to determine the moment at which the supply of milk is getting low. Obviously, that information prompts the grocer to restock. In addition though, when the milk is moving

Which bank has better customer service: the one with self-checkout (left), or the bank offering a face-to-face interaction with the customer? It depends on whom you ask.

Left: © Picturenet/Blend Images/Getty Images RF; Right: © Keith Brofsky/Photodisc/Getty Images RF

quickly, it tells the store to open more checkout counters, because most customers grab this perishable necessity just before they leave the store.[24]

The technological delivery of services can cause problems though. Some customers either do not embrace the idea of replacing a human with a machine for business interactions or have problems using the technology, such as supermarket self-checkout devices that are too challenging for some customers. In other cases, the technology may not perform adequately, such as ATMs that run out of money or are out of order.

The Communications Gap: Communicating the Service Promise

Poor communication between marketers and their customers can result in a mismatch between an ad campaign's or a salesperson's promises and the service the firm can actually offer. Although firms have difficulty controlling service quality because it can vary from day to day and provider to provider, they have nearly constant control over how they communicate their service package to their customers. This control involves a significant responsibility, as Ethical and Societal Dilemma 13.1 notes.

If a firm promises more than it can deliver, customers' expectations won't be met. An advertisement may lure a customer into a service situation once, but if the service doesn't deliver on the promise, the customer will never return. Dissatisfied customers also are likely to tell others about the underperforming service using word of mouth or,

Panera Bread has developed a program that allows customers to order from their website in advance and have their take-out meal ready when they arrive.

Source: Panera.com

Ethical & Societal Dilemma 13.1   Fake Reviews[iii]

Yelp, TripAdvisor, and Amazon have all made user ratings and reviews a familiar—and even essential—part of the online toolbox for shoppers and other consumers. From the consumer's perspective, what better preparation could there be for a major purchase than to see what other, objective customers have to say about the product or service under consideration?

For retailers and service professionals, online reviews offer a huge benefit too. For some companies, especially small service providers that cannot afford much marketing, online reviews function as a low-cost form of advertising. A business seeking to meet or exceed customer expectations receives valuable, candid feedback from customers, which it can use to measure how well it is meeting customer expectations. Some firms even use this feedback in their formal marketing research process to improve company operations.

From this straightforward perspective, honest reviews are the most valuable resource that exists in review sites. But such straightforwardness is not enough for companies that provide poor service and attract reviews befitting their abilities. Rather than improving their service, many of these companies engage in the unethical practice of writing fake reviews themselves, hiring dedicated companies to flood sites with positive fake reviews, or bribing customers to pad their comments with positive assertions. Considering this unethical practice just another example—though in a modern form—of false advertising, state and federal regulators are taking action to ensure that such deceptive advertising does not pay. Moreover, as customers get wise to these moves, companies that fake their reviews often get caught.

VIP Deals, an online retailer that sells leather cases for digital tablets on Amazon, invited its customers to post reviews—and promised that if those reviews were positive, the customer would receive a complete refund. Within weeks, nearly all of the company's 355 online reviews gave the VIP Deals leather case four or five stars. But Amazon guidelines prohibit compensation for customer reviews, and the VIP Deals page soon disappeared.

A leather case for your iPad is one thing. Accurate, truthful information takes on paramount importance for a service like

Online reviews like this one from Yelp benefit consumers, retailers, and service providers as long as the reviews are written by unbiased customers.

© Yelp.com

plastic surgery. But Lifestyle Lift seemed to disregard customers' expectations that they could receive truthful information. When unhappy customers started posting too many negative comments on its website, the company launched a coverup rather than investigating the complaints to help its physicians and staff address the problems. On bogus websites, fictitious posters gave high praise to the company while also asserting that previously posted complaints had been phony. The state of New York soon filed suit and prompted a $300,000 settlement from Lifestyle Lift. New York's attorney general also has announced that his office will be pursuing such false advertisers more actively in the future, doling out stringent penalties as it finds them.

Online opinions of consumers have become a major source of information about products and services. When that information is authentic, it serves consumers and companies both. But when companies manipulate online reviews, it seems as if all of society is harmed. What—if anything—should be done about it?

increasingly, social media, which has become an important channel for dissatisfied customers to vent their frustrations.

The communications gap can be reduced by managing customer expectations and by promising only what you can deliver, or possibly even a little less. Suppose you need an operation, and the surgeon explains, "You'll be out of the hospital in five days and back to your normal routine in a month." You have the surgery and feel well enough to leave the hospital three days later. Two weeks after that, you're playing tennis again. Clearly, you will tend to think your surgeon is a genius. However, regardless of the operation's success, if you had to stay in the hospital for 10 days and it took you two months to recover, you would undoubtedly be upset.

A relatively easy way to manage customer expectations is to coordinate how the expectation is created and the way the service is provided. Expectations typically are created through promotions, advertising, or personal selling. Delivery is another function altogether. If a salesperson promises a client that an order can be delivered in one day, and that delivery actually takes a week, the client will be disappointed. However, if the salesperson coordinates the order with those responsible for the service delivery, the client's expectations likely will be met.

Customer expectations can be managed when the service is delivered. Recorded messages tell customers who have phoned a company with a query how many minutes they will have to wait before the next operator is available. Sellers automatically inform online customers of any items that are out of stock. Whether online or in a store, retailers can warn their customers to shop early during a sale because supplies of the sale item are limited. People are generally reasonable when they are warned that some aspect of the service may be below their expectations. They just don't like surprises!

Service Quality and Customer Satisfaction and Loyalty

Good service quality leads to satisfied and loyal customers. As we discussed in Chapter 6, customers inevitably wind up their purchase decision process by undertaking a postpurchase evaluation. This evaluation after the purchase may produce three outcomes: satisfaction, dissonance, and loyalty (see again Exhibit 6.3 in Chapter 6). Dissonance may just be a passing emotion that is overcome; we will discuss recovery from an actual service failure in the next section. Satisfaction, on the other hand, often leads to loyalty.

Assuming that none of the service gaps that we have discussed occur, or at least are not too wide, customers should be more or less satisfied. Surveys of customers that ask them to identify the retailer that provides the best customer service thus often show some consistency. A service provider that does a good job one year is likely to keep customers satisfied the next year too. Some of the best service providers year after year include Amazon, Zappos, L.L.Bean, and Nordstrom.

If a firm not only minimizes but also eliminates any service gaps, customers are likely to exhibit significant loyalty to it. Customers want to continue receiving such superior service and have no desire to go elsewhere for the offerings it provides them.

PROGRESS CHECK

1. Explain the four service gaps identified by the Service Gaps Model.
2. List at least two ways to overcome each of the four service gaps.

SERVICE RECOVERY

Despite a firm's best efforts, sometimes service providers fail to meet customer expectations. When this happens, the best course of action is to attempt to make amends with the customer and learn from the experience. Of course, it is best to avoid a service failure altogether, but when a failure does occur, the firm has a unique opportunity to demonstrate its customer commitment. Effective service recovery efforts can significantly increase customer satisfaction, purchase intentions, and positive word of mouth, though customers' postrecovery satisfaction levels usually fall lower than their satisfaction level prior to the service failure.

Remember the Green Valley Motel in Maine? It could have made amends with Marcia Kessler after its service failures if it had taken some relatively simple, immediate steps: The assistant manager could have apologized for his bad behavior and quickly upgraded her to a suite and/or given her a free night's lodging for a future stay. The motel could also have given her a free lunch or dinner to make up for the bad breakfast. Alternatively, the assistant manager could have asked Marcia how he could resolve the situation and worked with her to come up with an equitable solution. None of these actions would have cost the motel much money.

Had it used the customer lifetime value approach we described in Chapter 10, the motel would have realized that by not taking action, it lost Marcia as a customer forever. Over the next few years, she could have been responsible for several thousand dollars in sales. Instead, Marcia is now likely to spread negative word of mouth about the motel to her friends, family, and through online review sites, such as Yelp.com, because of its failure to recover. Effective service recovery thus demands (1) listening to the customers and involving them in the service recovery, (2) providing a fair solution, and (3) resolving the problem quickly.[25]

Listening to the Customers and Involving Them in the Service Recovery

Firms often don't find out about service failures until a customer complains. Whether the firm has a formal complaint department or the complaint is offered directly to the service provider, the customer must have the opportunity to air the complaint completely, and the firm must listen carefully to what he or she is saying.

Customers can become very emotional about a service failure, whether the failure is serious (a botched surgical operation) or minor (the wrong change at a restaurant). In many cases, the customer may just want to be heard, and the service provider should give the customer all the time he or she needs to get it out. The very process of describing a perceived wrong to a sympathetic listener or on social media is therapeutic in and of itself. Service providers therefore should welcome the opportunity to be that sympathetic ear, listen carefully, and appear (and actually be) eager to rectify the situation to ensure it doesn't happen again.[26]

When the company and the customer work together, the outcome is often better than either could achieve on their own. This cocreation logic applies especially well to service recovery. A service failure is a negative experience, but when customers participate in its resolution, it results in a more positive outcome than simply listening to their complaint and providing a preapproved set of potential solutions that may satisfy them.

Suppose, for instance, that when you arrived at the airport in San Francisco, your flight had been overbooked and you were bumped. Of course, good customer service required the ticket agent to listen to your frustration and help provide a fair solution. But the most obvious potential solution from the airline's perspective might not have been the best solution for you. It might have been inclined to put you on the next available flight, which would be a red-eye that left at midnight and got you to New York at 6:30 a.m. But if you don't sleep well on planes and you have an important business meeting the next afternoon, the best solution from your perspective would be to have the airline put you up in an airport hotel so you can get a good night's sleep and then put you on an early morning flight that would get you to New York in time for your meeting, well-rested and ready to go. Thus, by working closely with you to understand your needs, the ticket agent would be able to cocreate a great solution to the service failure.

Finding a Fair Solution

Most people realize that mistakes happen. But when they happen, customers want to be treated fairly, whether that means *distributive* or *procedural* fairness.[27] Their perception of what "fair" means is based on their previous experience with other firms, how they have seen other customers treated, material they have read, and stories recounted by their friends.

Distributive Fairness Distributive fairness pertains to a customer's perception of the benefits he or she received compared with the costs (inconvenience or loss). Customers want to be compensated a fair amount for a perceived loss that resulted from a service failure. If, for instance, a person arrives at the airport gate and finds her flight is overbooked, she may believe that taking the next flight that day and receiving a travel voucher is adequate compensation for the inconvenience. But if no flights are available until the next day, the traveler may require additional compensation, such as overnight accommodations, meals, and a round-trip ticket to be used at a later date.[28]

The key to distributive fairness, of course, is listening carefully to the customer. One customer, traveling on vacation, may be satisfied with a travel voucher, whereas another may need to get to the destination on time because of a business appointment. Regardless of how the problem is solved, customers typically want tangible restitution—in this case, to get to their destination—not just an apology. If providing tangible restitution isn't possible, the next best thing is to assure the customer that steps are being taken to prevent the failure from recurring.

Procedural Fairness With regard to complaints, procedural fairness refers to the perceived fairness of the process used to resolve them. Customers want efficient complaint procedures over whose outcomes they have some influence. Customers tend to believe they have been treated fairly if the service providers follow specific company guidelines. Nevertheless, rigid adherence to rules can have deleterious effects. Have you ever returned an item to a store, even a very inexpensive item, and been told that the return needed a manager's approval? The process likely took several minutes and irritated everyone in the checkout line. Furthermore, most managers' cursory inspection of the item or the situation would not catch a fraudulent return. In a case like this, the procedure the company uses to handle a return probably overshadows any potential positive outcomes. Therefore, as we noted previously, service providers should be empowered with some procedural flexibility to solve customer complaints.

A no-questions-asked return policy has been offered as a customer service by many retailers such as L.L.Bean. But because of its high cost as a result of customers abusing the policy, many retailers such as L.L.Bean's competitor REI have modified their return policies.[29] Some large retailers now limit their returns to 90 days, considered a reasonable amount of time for customers to return an item. Others will grant only a store credit based on the lowest selling price for the item if the customer doesn't have a receipt. In addition, for some consumer electronics products that have been opened, customers must pay a 15 percent restocking fee.

Resolving Problems Quickly

The longer it takes to resolve a service failure, the more irritated the customer will become and the more people he or she is likely to tell about the problem. To resolve service failures quickly, firms need clear policies, adequate training for their employees, and empowered employees. Health insurance companies, for instance, have made a concerted effort in recent years to avoid service failures that occur because customers' insurance claims have not been handled quickly or to the customers' satisfaction.

PROGRESS CHECK

1. Why is service recovery so important to companies?
2. What can companies do to recover from a service failure?

Reviewing Learning Objectives

 Describe how the marketing of services differs from the marketing of products.

Unlike products, services are intangible, inseparable, variable, and perishable. They cannot be seen or touched, which makes it difficult to describe their benefits or promote them. Service providers therefore enhance service delivery with tangible attributes, like a nice atmosphere or price benefits. Services get produced and consumed at the same time, so marketers must work quickly, and they are more variable than products, though service providers attempt to reduce this variability as much as possible. Finally, because consumers cannot stockpile perishable services, marketers often provide incentives to stagger demand.

LO13-2 Discuss the four gaps in the Service Gaps Model.

The knowledge gap reflects the difference between customers' expectations and the firm's perception of those customer expectations. Firms need to match customer expectations with actual service through research. The standards gap is the difference between the firm's perceptions of customers' expectations and the service standards it sets. Appropriate service standards and measurements of service performance help close this gap. The delivery gap is the difference between the firm's service standards and the actual service it provides to customers. Closing this gap requires adequate training and empowerment of employees. The communication gap refers to the difference between the actual service provided to customers and the service that the firm's promotion program promises. Firms close the communications gap by managing customer expectations and promising only what they can deliver.

LO13-3 Examine the five service quality dimensions.

First, reliability refers to whether the provider consistently provides an expected level of service. Second, responsiveness means that the provider notes consumers' desires and requests and then addresses them. Third, assurance reflects the service provider's own confidence in its abilities. Fourth, empathy entails the provider's recognition and understanding of consumer needs. Finally, tangibles are the elements that go along with the service, such as the magazines in a doctor's waiting room.

LO13-4 Explain the zone of tolerance.

The area between customers' desired service and the minimum level of service they will accept is the zone of tolerance. It is the difference between what the customer really wants and what he or she will accept before going elsewhere. Firms can assess their customers' zone of tolerance by determining the desired and expected level of service for each service dimension, their perceptions of how well the focal service performs and how well a competitive service performs, and the importance of each service quality dimension.

LO13-5 Identify three service recovery strategies.

In a best-case scenario, the service never fails. But some failures are inevitable and require the firm to make amends to the customer by (1) listening carefully and involving the customer in the service recovery; (2) finding a fair solution to the problem that compensates the customer for the failure and follows procedures the customer believes are fair; and (3) resolving the problem quickly.

Key Terms

 LEARNSMART

- communication gap, 411
- customer service, 406
- delivery gap, 411
- distributive fairness, 424
- emotional support, 418
- empowerment, 418
- heterogeneity, 410

- inseparable, 409
- instrumental support, 419
- intangible, 407
- knowledge gap, 411
- perishable, 410
- procedural fairness, 424
- service, 406

- service gap, 411
- Service Gaps Model, 411
- service quality, 413
- standards gap, 411
- voice-of-customer (VOC) program, 415
- zone of tolerance, 415

Marketing Digitally

1. What services does Zipcar (www.zipcar.com) offer? Go to Zipcar's website and click on "for everybody." Evaluate how quick it is to reserve a car in a major city or at a university that has a dedicated Zipcar car pickup/dropoff location.

2. Go to Zappos' website, http://www.zappos.com, and examine its customer service offerings. Next, go to Reseller Ratings, http://www.resellerratings.com, and look up Zappos. Based on these reviews, does Zappos have a service gap? If so, how can the company close it?

Marketing Applications

1. Those companies from which you purchase products and services are not pure sellers of services, nor are they pure sellers of products. What services does Home Depot provide? What goods does a health club provide?

2. You have been sitting in the waiting room of your mechanic's shop for more than an hour. With the knowledge that products are different from services, develop a list of the things the shop manager could do to improve the overall service delivery. Consider how the shop might overcome problems associated with the tangibility, separability, heterogeneity, and perishability of services.

3. You have conducted a zone of tolerance analysis for your local pizza restaurant. You find that the lengths of the reliability and responsiveness boxes are much greater than those of the other three service quality dimensions. You also find that the restaurant is positioned above the zone box on reliability but below the box on responsiveness. What should you tell the manager to do?

4. Assume you were hired by the local grocery store to help assess their service quality. How would you go about undertaking this project?

5. What should a restaurant server do who is faced with an irate customer who has received undercooked food after a long wait? How can he or she avoid a service failure by being empowered? What should the server do?

6. What types of support and incentives could your university provide advisers to help make them more attentive to students' needs?

7. What mobile apps do you use that help facilitate your transactions with a specific retailer or service provider? Would you rather use the apps or engage in a face-to-face relationship with a person? How, if at all, would your parents' answer to these two questions differ?

8. A local health club is running a promotional campaign that promises you can lose an inch a month off your waist if you join the club and follow its program. How might this claim cause a communications gap? What should the club do to avoid a service failure?

9. Suppose the health club didn't listen to your advice and ran the promotional campaign as is. A new member has come in to complain that not only did he not lose inches off his waist, he actually gained weight. How should the health club manager proceed?

10. You are hired by a career consulting firm that promises to market new graduates to high-paying employers. The firm provides potential clients with an impressive list of employers. It charges the clients a fee, and then a separate finder's fee if the client gets a position. The firm aggressively markets its services and has a large client base. You learn that the firm simply takes submitted résumés and posts them to a variety of online job search engines. The firm never actually contacts any firms on its clients' behalf. The CEO, himself a recent college grad, tells you that the firm never promises to actually contact potential employers, only that it has access to employers and will distribute clients' résumés. What do you think of the career consulting firm's practices?

Quiz Yourself

1. Which of the following represents the most fundamental difference between a product and a service?
   a. heterogeneity
   b. tangibility
   c. perishability
   d. serviceability
   e. inseparability

2. The Gaps Model is designed as a diagnostic tool to highlight specific areas where
   a. marketers deliver better quality service compared to the physical goods they sell.
   b. manufacturers are cutting costs on product quality.
   c. marketers are falling short in their service delivery.
   d. marketers can take advantage of unsuspecting customers.
   e. there is a gap in product quality compared to service quality.

(Answers to these two questions can be found in the Quiz Yourself Answer Key section.)

Chapter Case Study

TRANSPORTATION NETWORK SERVICES: UBER VS. LYFT VS. TAXIS

America might be a car culture, but there are plenty of times that people simply don't want to drive themselves. Whether they live in an urban environment that makes driving and parking difficult, want to avoid the costs of insurance and maintenance associated with owning a car, or just need rides in particular situations like after a night out on the town, people have long required the services of drivers. But whereas in the past their options were largely limited to taxi services, today the transportation industry is in the midst of a radical transformation, due largely to the impacts of Uber and Lyft.

The idea for Uber began with the frustration of a couple of tech-industry friends who could not get a cab on a snowy night in Paris. They developed an app for a car-sharing service and began introducing the option in major cities around the world. Within a year of establishing its New York City operations with three cars, Uber had raised tens of millions of dollars in financing, and it was rapidly expanding into many cities.[30]

With a presence in approximately 400 cities worldwide, Uber touts its benefits for riders, drivers, and communities. In particular, it highlights its ability to offer affordable, flexible rides to people at exactly the moment and place they need them. For drivers, Uber is an employment alternative that enables them to work exactly when and as much as they want, for a reasonable compensation. In addition, Uber asserts that its services make cities safer and expand transportation options.[31]

Lyft followed Uber into the market, but its expansion is not quite as extensive. Available in approximately 200 cities, Lyft seeks to differentiate itself from its bigger rival mainly in the friendly image it evokes.[32] Drivers adorn their cars with fuzzy pink moustaches, and riders are encouraged to sit up front and chat during the trip.[33]

In general though, the services are remarkably similar. Both transportation network companies (the formal name established for these services by the state of California, which was the first to start regulating the offerings) rely on app-based demand channels to link riders with drivers. Both of them allow drivers to work as much or as little as they want. In addition, both companies currently rely on surge pricing to balance out their supply and demand—although Uber has plans to phase out this practice because consumers dislike it so much.[34] With surge pricing, the companies charge higher rates during busy periods. Doing so can discourage some riders, who might be willing to wait a little while to get a lower rate. It also encourages more drivers to provide additional supply, because they can earn what is in essence time and a half for driving during rush hour or on Saturday nights.

In their efforts to gain share in each market in which they compete head to head, Uber and Lyft rely on various marketing tactics. They have cut prices in highly competitive markets, and they continue to work to recruit new drivers to reduce riders' wait times.[35]

Despite some attempts to regulate these services, the rules and norms remain somewhat uncertain. To address the concerns that such lack of regulation might induce, Uber offers a unique rating system, in which drivers have a means to rate riders, just as riders can rate drivers. When a driver's rating falls below a certain level, Uber contacts that driver to help ensure a satisfactory level of service. But when a rider earns a low rating, he or she may just find that no drivers respond to requests for a pick up, leaving the passenger stranded.

Who will win the transportation service war: Uber, Lyft, or taxis?

© Justin Sullivan/Getty Images

However, the rating system also might have some unintended consequences.[36] First, because there are few rules for how to establish review of customers, drivers and renters can issue negative reviews for virtually any reason. One Uber driver noted that he gave bad reviews to riders who entered the vehicle with "negative energy," for example. Nor are there any protections in place to avoid negative reviews based on race, gender, or physical disability. Thus consumers might be unfairly discriminated against in the reviews, creating a powerful ethical and legal concern. Second, the two-sided review system might lead to rating inflation. That is, riders want to earn positive reviews from the providers so that they can continue using the service in the future. To encourage such positive reviews, they might provide positive ratings of the providers, to avoid any negative retaliation, or feel compelled to leave larger tips. Third, customers do not have any control over, or in some cases knowledge of, how their reviews get used.

Across the board though, transportation network services continue to expand and grow in terms of both their reach in existing locales and their expansion into new markets. The need to grow has led to poaching efforts, such that Uber sends out "ambassadors" to try to lure Lyft drivers away to work for Uber. In addition, both companies try to empower drivers by granting them access to updated technology for their phones, to ensure they can find their riders. They also have started some collaborations with car dealers, to give their drivers good deals on new car purchases.[37]

Questions

1. How can Uber and Lyft apply the Service Gaps Model to identify potential service failures? Using the building blocks of service quality, how can Uber and Lyft ensure high service quality?

2. If Uber or Lyft fails to pick up a customer in a timely fashion, what should they do to rectify the service failure?

Endnotes

1. Adrianne Pasquarelli, "Lululemon Tries New Store Concept in Efforts to Woo Shoppers," *Advertising Age,* November 17, 2015; Mallory Scholossberg, "Lululemon Has Unveiled Its New Store of the Future," *Business Insider,* November 18, 2015; Nicole Santos, "Grand Opening for lululemon Draws Crowds to Fig Garden," *Fresno Bee,* July 3, 2015.

2. Valarie A. Zeithaml, Mary Jo Bitner, and Dwayne D. Gremler, *Services Marketing: Integrating Customer Focus across the Firm,* 6th ed. (Burr Ridge, IL: McGraw-Hill/Irwin, 2012).

3. Hilary Stout, "Amazon, Google, and More Are Drawn to Home Services Market," *The New York Times,* April 12, 2015.

4. The World Bank, "Services, etc., Value Added (% of GDP)," http://data.worldbank.org/indicator/NV.SRV.TETC.ZS.

5. *Fortune*, "*Fortune* 500: 2015," https://www.aei.org/publication/fortune-500-firms-in-1955-vs-2015-only-12-remain-thanks-to-the-creative-destruction-that-fuels-economic-growth/; Bureau of Economic Analysis, news release, January 27, 2012, http://www.bea.gov; "Fortune 500," *CNNMoney*, May 23, 2011, http://money.cnn.com.

6. Zeithaml et al., *Services Marketing: Integrating Customer Focus across the Firm.*

7. Ramon Ray, "Carbonite Offers Data Peace of Mind: A Solid Solution for Small Biz," *Business Insider*, January 24, 2012, http://www.businessinsider.com; "Carbonite Gains from HIPAA Regulations," *Zacks*, March 24, 2014, http://www.zacks.com; "Pricing," http://www.carbonite.com.

8. Choice Hotels, "Special Guest Policies," http://www.choicehotels.com.

9. Andrew Adam Newman, "A Gym for People Who Don't Like Gyms," *The New York Times*, January 2, 2013, http://www.nytimes.com.

10. The discussion of the Gaps Model and its implications draws heavily from Michael Levy, Barton A. Weitz, and Dhruv Grewal, *Retailing Management*, 9th ed. (Burr Ridge, IL: Irwin/McGraw-Hill, 2013); it is also based on the classic work of Zeithaml, Parasuraman, and Berry, *Delivering Quality Service*; Valarie Zeithaml, Leonard Berry, and A. Parasuraman, "Communication and Control Processes in the Delivery of Service Quality," *Journal of Marketing* 52, no. 2 (April 1988), pp. 35–48.

11. Zhen Zhu et al., "Fix It or Leave It? Customer Recovery from Self-Service Technology Failures," *Journal of Retailing* 89, no. 1 (2013), pp. 15–29.

12. Velitchka D. Kaltcheva, Robert D. Winsor, and A. Parasuraman, "Do Customer Relationships Mitigate or Amplify Failure Responses?" *Journal of Business Research* 66, no. 4 (2013), pp. 525–32; Ruth N. Bolton, et al., "Small Details That Make Big Differences: A Radical Approach to Consumption Experience as a Firm's Differentiating Strategy," *Journal of Service Management* 25, no. 2 (2014), pp. 253–74; Lance A. Bettencourt, Stephen W. Brown, and Nancy J. Sirianni, "The Secret to True Service Innovation," *Business Horizons* 56, no. 1 (2013), pp. 13–22.

13. Zeithaml et al., *Services Marketing: Integrating Customer Focus across the Firm.*

14. The Broadmoor Hotel, https://www.broadmoor.com.

15. Rich Laden, "Forbes Travel Guide Gives the Broadmoor Its 55th Consecutive Five-Star Rating" *[Colorado Springs] Gazette*, February 2, 2015, http://gazette.com/forbes-travel-guide-gives-the-broadmoor-its-55th-consecutive-five-star-rating/article/1546162.

16. Janelle Barlow, "A Complaint Is a Gift Corner," http://www.tmius.com.

17. Michael Bergdahl, *The Retail Revolution: How Wal-Mart Created a Brave New World of Business* (New York: Metropolitan Books, 2009); Michael Bergdahl, *The 10 Rules of Sam Walton: Success Secrets for Remarkable Results* (Hoboken, NJ: Wiley, 2006).

18. Steven W. Rayburn, "Improving Service Employee Work Affect: The Transformative Potential of Work Design," *Journal of Services Marketing* 28, no. 1 (2014), pp. 71–81; Zhen Zhu, et al., "Fix It or Leave It? Customer Recovery from Self-Service Technology Failures," *Journal of Retailing* 89, no. 1 (2013), pp. 15–29; Ying Hong, et al., "Missing Link in the Service Profit Chain: A Meta-Analytic Review of the Antecedents, Consequences, and Moderators of Service Climate," *Journal of Applied Psychology* 98, no. 2 (2013), p. 237.

19. Jason Colquitt, Jeffery LePine, and Michael Wesson, *Organizational Behavior: Improving Performance and Commitment in the Workplace*, 3rd ed. (Burr Ridge, IL: McGraw-Hill, 2012); Felicitas M. Morhart, Walter Herzog, and Torsten Tomczak, "Brand-Specific Leadership: Turning Employees into Brand Champions," *Journal of Marketing* 73 (September 2009), pp. 122–42.

20. Daisy Wademan Dowling, "The Best Advice I Ever Got: Michelle Peluso, President and Chief Executive Officer, Travelocity," The Harvard Business Review, October 2008, https://hbr.org

21. "Travelocity," http://www.sabre-holdings.com/ourBrands/travelocity.html; "Awards," http://svc.travelocity.com.

22. Suzanne C. Makarem, Susan M. Mudambi, and Jeffrey S. Podoshen, "Satisfaction in Technology-Enabled Service Encounters," *Journal of Services Marketing* 23, no. 1 (2009).

23. Alexander Coolidge, "Hate Checkout Lines? Macy's Can Help," *Cincinnati Inquirer*, October 3, 2014.

24. M.V. Greene, "Drawing a Line on Checkout," *Stores*, August 11, 2015.

25. Zhen Zhu et al., "Fix It or Leave It? Customer Recovery from Self-Service Technology Failures"; María Leticia Santos-Vijande et al., "An Integrated Service Recovery System (ISRS): Influence on Knowledge-Intensive Business Services Performance," *European Journal of Marketing* 47, no. 5/6 (2013), pp. 934–63.

26. Christian Grönroos and Päivi Voima, "Critical Service Logic: Making Sense of Value Creation and Co-creation," *Journal of the Academy of Marketing Science* 41, no. 2 (2013), pp. 133–50; Anne L.. Roggeveen, Michael Tsiros, and Dhruv Grewal, "Understanding the Co-Creation Effect: When Does Collaborating with Customers Provide a Lift to Service Recovery?" *Journal of the Academy of Marketing Science* 40, no. 6 (2012), pp. 771–90.

27. Kaltcheva et al., "Do Customer Relationships Migrate or Amplify Failure Responses?"; Yany Grégoire, Thomas M. Tripp, and Renaud Legoux, "When Customer Love Turns into Lasting Hate: The Effects of Relationship Strength and Time on Customer Revenge and Avoidance," *Journal of Marketing* 73 (November 2009), pp. 18–32.

28. Roggeveen et al., "Understanding the Co-Creation Effect: When Does Collaborating with Customers Provide a Lift to Service Recovery?"

29. Amy Martinez, "REI Now Limiting Returns to One Year," *Seattle Times*, June 3, 2013.

30. Julian Chokkattu and Jordan Crook, "A Brief History of Uber," *TechCrunch*, August 14, 2014, http://techcrunch.com/gallery/a-brief-history-of-uber/slide/33/.

31. Uber, "Our Trip History," https://www.uber.com/our-story/.

32. "Lyft," https://en.wikipedia.org/wiki/Lyft.

33. "Lyft Vs. Uber: Comparison Guide," *RideShare*, February 2, 2016, http://rideshare.services/lyft-vs-uber-comparison/.

34. Aarti Shahani, "Uber Plans to Kill Surge Pricing, Though Drivers Say It Makes Job Worth It," *NPR Morning Edition*, May 3, 2016.

35. Jen Wieczner, "Lyft Is Growing at a Crazy Pace in New York and San Francisco," *Fortune*, March 8, 2016, http://fortune.com/2016/03/08/lyft-vs-uber-new-york/.

36. David Streitfeld, "Ratings Now Cut Both Ways, So Don't Sass Your Uber Driver," *The New York Times*, January 30, 2015.

37. Aarti Shahani, "In the Battle Between Lyft and Uber, The Focus Is on Drivers," *All Things Considered*, January 18, 2016, http://www.npr.org/sections/alltechconsidered/2016/01/18/463473462/is-uber-good-to-drivers-it-s-relative.

i. Sydney Ember, "Pepsi Turns Restaurateur, to Serve Up Some Buzz," *The New York Times*, January 28, 2016

ii. "About Kroger," http://www.thekrogerco.com/about-kroger; Laurianne McLaughlin, "Kroger Solves Top Customer Issue: Long Lines," *InformationWeek*, April 2, 2014, http://www.information-week.com/strategic-cio/executive-insights-and-innovation/kroger-solves-top-customer-issue-long-lines/d/d-id/1141541?page_number=1.

iii. David Streitfeld, "For $2 a Star, an Online Retailer Gets 5-Star Product Reviews," *The New York Times*, January 26, 2012, http://www.nytimes.com; David Streitfeld, "Faking It to Make It: A Beautiful Try," *The New York Times*, January 27, 2012, http://bits.blogs.nytimes.com; David Streitfeld, "Give Yourself 5 Stars? Online, It Might Cost You," *The New York Times*, September 22, 2013, http://www.nytimes.com.

VALUE CAPTURE

Section Five contains two chapters on pricing dedicated to value capture. Chapter 14 examines the importance of setting the right price, the relationship between price and quantity sold, break-even analysis, the impact of price wars, and how the Internet has changed the way people shop. Chapter 15 looks specifically at how to set prices.

PRICING CONCEPTS FOR ESTABLISHING VALUE

After reading this chapter, you should be able to:

LO14-1 List the four pricing orientations.

LO14-2 Explain the relationship between price and quantity sold.

LO14-3 Explain price elasticity.

LO14-4 Describe how to calculate a product's break-even point.

LO14-5 Indicate the four types of price competitive levels.

P ricing is a key part of the value proposition for any purchase. After all, among the other definitions we have used in this book, value reflects the relationship between benefits and costs. When the economy sours and consumer income drops, no sticker prices can escape sharp scrutiny, especially in the supermarket. For example, shoppers on tight budgets still need to buy cleaning supplies, but when they do so, they tend to be much more sensitive to the prices for the various detergents their households need.

In such price-sensitive and highly competitive markets, companies must be creative in finding ways to balance profits and consumers. Procter & Gamble (P&G) had long floated high above its competitors in the sea of laundry detergents, with its Tide brand enjoying a 38 percent share of the laundry soap market in North America.[1] However, a wave of lower-priced competitors crashed into P&G when consumers began looking more actively for better deals. Thrifty shoppers began turning from their trusty Tide brand to cheaper alternatives, such as Arm & Hammer detergent, made by Church & Dwight, Co.

Not a company to rest on its laurels, P&G pursued several strategic responses to the challenge. For consumers interested in convenience, it introduced, developed, and expanded on the concept of laundry detergent pods—single-use packs that eliminate the mess and the need for measuring associated with liquids or powders. Tide's latest Pods, which add in Febreze, even won product of the year in the newly created "Laundry Pacs" category.[2] Although this option has expanded the breadth of Tide's product lines and established an approximately $1 billion market for P&G, the pods create higher per-wash costs for consumers.[3]

Therefore, for consumers determined to use cheaper detergents, it also has developed and introduced Tide Simply Clean & Fresh, a liquid detergent that retails for about 35 percent less than the $12 price of a 100-ounce bottle of regular Tide.[4] In an effort to reduce the risk of sales cannibalization of its premium higher-priced products, P&G makes sure that Simply Clean never appears for sale alongside other Tide brands, nor does it sport the easily recognizable orange Tide-branded container. In stores, Simply Clean is placed alongside its competitor brand on store shelves, despite its higher price point. The primary target markets are consumers from hard-working households, many of whom work in tough, odor-generating jobs and environments. With this approach, P&G can ensure that it never turns its back on its flagship brand.

Although P&G's product portfolio is broad, including various detergent brands such as Gain, Era, and Ace, it has chosen to focus where consumers are most invested, namely, in its Tide products. In trying to ensure Tide's market share advantage, P&G has shown its willingness to adjust its regular pricing strategies, develop new products with varying profit margins, and reduce bottle sizes while maintaining the same retail price. In essence, Procter & Gamble is keeping an eye on the way the tides are turning in the laundry detergent market.

Although knowing how consumers arrive at their perceptions of value is critical to developing successful pricing strategies, sellers also must consider other factors—which is why developing a good pricing strategy is such a formidable challenge to all firms. Do it right, and the rewards to the firm will be substantial. Do it wrong, and failure will be swift and severe. But even if a pricing strategy is implemented well, consumers, economic conditions, markets, competitors, government regulations, and even a firm's own products change constantly—and that means that a good pricing strategy today may not remain an effective pricing strategy tomorrow.

So much rides on marketers setting the right price that we take two chapters to explain the role of price in the marketing mix. In this chapter we explain what "price" is as a marketing concept, why it is important, how marketers set pricing objectives, and how various factors influence price setting. In the next chapter, we extend this foundation by focusing on specific pricing strategies that capitalize on capturing value.

Imagine that a consumer realizes that to save money on a particular item, she will have to drive an additional 20 miles. She may determine that her time and travel costs are not worth the savings, so even though the price tag is higher at the nearby store, she judges the overall cost of buying the product close by to be lower. To include aspects of price such as this, we may define **price** as the overall sacrifice a consumer is willing to make to acquire a specific product or service. This sacrifice necessarily includes the money that must be paid to the seller to acquire the item, but it also may involve other sacrifices, whether non-monetary, like the value of the time necessary to acquire the product or service, or monetary, like travel costs, taxes, shipping costs, and so forth, all of which the buyer must give up to take possession of the product.[5] It's useful to think of overall price in this way to see how the narrower sense of purchase price fits in.

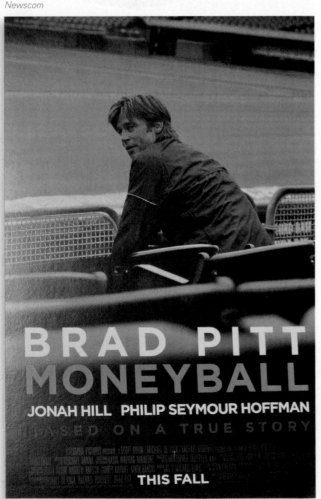

Demonstrating that price is often used to judge quality, in the movie Moneyball, Jonah Hill explains to Brad Pitt's character that baseball teams often overpay for young, untested talent or big-name players because they don't know how else to gauge an appropriate salary.

© Gregorio Binuya/Everett Collection/Newscom

Because price is the only element of the marketing mix that does not generate costs but instead generates revenue, it is important in its own right. Every other element in the marketing mix may be perfect, but with the wrong price, sales and thus revenue will not accrue. Consumers generally believe that price is one of the most important factors in their purchase decisions.

Knowing that price is so critical to success, why don't managers put greater emphasis on it as a strategic decision variable? Price is the most challenging of the four Ps to manage, partly because it is often the least understood. Historically, managers have treated price as an afterthought to their marketing strategy, setting prices according to what competitors were charging or, worse yet, adding up their costs and tacking on a desired profit to set the sales price. Prices rarely changed except in response to radical shifts in market conditions. Even today, pricing decisions are often relegated to standard rules of thumb that fail to reflect our current understanding of the role of price in the marketing mix.

Price is a particularly powerful indicator of quality when consumers are less knowledgeable about the product category—a lesson brought home by the movie (based on the book of the same name) *Moneyball*. As the character played by Jonah Hill argues convincingly to Brad Pitt's character, baseball teams often overpay for young, untested talent or big-name players because they don't know how else to set an accurate price.[6]

In summary, marketers should view pricing decisions as a strategic opportunity to create value rather than as an afterthought to the rest of the marketing mix. Let us now turn to the five basic components of pricing strategies.

EXHIBIT 14.1 The Five Cs of Pricing

Competition

Costs

Company objectives

Value

Customers

Channel members

THE FIVE Cs OF PRICING

Successful pricing strategies are built around the five critical components (the five Cs) of pricing, found in Exhibit 14.1. We examine these components in some detail because each makes a significant contribution to formulating good pricing policies.[7] To start, the first step is to develop the company's pricing objectives.

Company Objectives

By now, you know that different firms embrace very different goals. These goals should spill down to the pricing strategy, such that the pricing of a company's products and services should support and allow the firm to reach its overall goals. For example, a firm with a primary goal of very high sales growth will likely have a different pricing strategy than will a firm with the goal of being a quality leader.

Each firm then embraces objectives that seem to fit with where management thinks the firm needs to go to be successful, in whatever way it defines success. These specific objectives usually reflect how the firm intends to grow. Do managers want it to grow by increasing profits, increasing sales, decreasing competition, or building customer satisfaction?

Company objectives are not as simple as they might first appear. They often can be expressed in slightly different forms that mean very different things. Exhibit 14.2 introduces some common company objectives and corresponding examples of their implications for pricing strategies. These objectives are not always mutually exclusive, because a firm may embrace two or more noncompeting objectives.

Profit Orientation Even though all company methods and objectives may ultimately be oriented toward making a profit, firms implement a **profit orientation**

LO14-1 List the four pricing orientations.

EXHIBIT 14.2 Company Objectives and Pricing Strategy Implications

Company Objective	Examples of Pricing Strategy Implications
Profit-oriented	Institute a companywide policy that all products must provide for at least an 18 percent profit margin to reach a particular profit goal for the firm.
Sales-oriented	Set prices very low to generate new sales and take sales away from competitors, even if profits suffer.
Competitor-oriented	To discourage more competitors from entering the market, set prices very low.
Customer-oriented	Target a market segment of consumers who highly value a particular product benefit and set prices relatively high (referred to as premium pricing).

specifically by focusing on target profit pricing, maximizing profits, or target return pricing.

- Firms usually implement **target profit pricing** when they have a particular profit goal as their overriding concern. To meet this targeted profit objective, firms use price to stimulate a certain level of sales at a certain profit per unit.

- The **maximizing profits** strategy relies primarily on economic theory. If a firm can accurately specify a mathematical model that captures all the factors required to explain and predict sales and profits, it should be able to identify the price at which its profits are maximized. Of course, the problem with this approach is that actually gathering the data on all these relevant factors and somehow coming up with an accurate mathematical model is an extremely difficult undertaking.

- Other firms are less concerned with the absolute level of profits and more interested in the rate at which their profits are generated relative to their investments. These firms typically turn to **target return pricing** and employ pricing strategies designed to produce a specific return on their investment, usually expressed as a percentage of sales.

Sales Orientation Firms using a **sales orientation** to set prices believe that increasing sales will help the firm more than will increasing profits. Tide laundry detergent might adopt such an orientation selectively when it introduces new products that it wants to establish in the market. A new health club might focus on unit sales, dollar sales, or market share and therefore be willing to set a lower membership fee and accept less profit at first to focus on and generate more unit sales. In contrast, a high-end jewelry store might focus on dollar sales and maintain higher prices. The jewelry store relies on its prestige image, as well as the image of its suppliers, to provoke sales. Even though it sells fewer units, it can still generate high dollar sales levels.

Some firms may be more concerned about their overall market share than about dollar sales per se (though these often go hand in hand) because they believe that market share better reflects their success relative to the market conditions than do sales alone. A firm may set low prices to discourage new firms from entering the market, encourage current firms to leave the market, and/or take market share away from competitors—all to gain overall market share. For example, as low-cost, no-frills airlines like Frontier and Spirit have changed travelers' perspectives on what prices are reasonable and necessary to pay, the major airlines such as United, American, and Delta have had to work hard to keep increasing their market share. Delta now offers a Basic Economy fare on most routes that the discount airlines also fly. In exchange for the lower price, passengers lose the right to make changes to their itinerary, and they cannot obtain seat assignments in advance. Both American and United have indicated that they are developing similar economy fares to widen the range of prices that their consumers can access. In addition to lowering the prices they charge consumers, the major carriers are seeking to increase the number of seats in each plane, thus increasing their revenue per flight.[8]

Yet adopting a market share objective does not always imply setting low prices. Rarely is the lowest-price offering the dominant brand in a given market. Heinz ketchup, Philadelphia cream cheese, Crest toothpaste, and Nike athletic shoes have all dominated their markets, yet all are premium-priced brands. On the services side, IBM claims market dominance in human resource outsourcing, but again, it is certainly not the lowest-price competitor.[9] **Premium pricing** means the firm deliberately prices a product above the prices set for competing products so as to capture those customers who always shop for the best or for whom price does not matter. Thus, companies can gain market share by offering a high-quality product at a price that is perceived to be fair by its target market as long as they use effective

P&G increases sales by introducing new Tide products.

© Rob Kim/Getty Images

communication and distribution methods to generate high-value perceptions among consumers. Although the concept of value is not overtly expressed in sales-oriented strategies, it is at least implicit because, for sales to increase, consumers must see greater value.

Competitor Orientation When firms take a competitor orientation, they strategize according to the premise that they should measure themselves primarily against their competition. Some firms focus on competitive parity, which means they set prices that are similar to those of their major competitors. Another competitor-oriented strategy, status quo pricing, changes prices only to meet those of the competition. For example, when Delta increases its average fares, American Airlines and United often follow with similar increases; if Delta rescinds that increase, its competitors tend to drop their fares too.[10] Value is only implicitly considered in competitor-oriented strategies, but in the sense that competitors may be using value as part of their pricing strategies, copying their strategy might provide value.

Customer Orientation A firm uses customer orientation when it sets its pricing strategy based on how it can add value to its products or services. When CarMax promises a "no-haggle" pricing structure, it exhibits a customer orientation because it provides additional value to potential used car buyers by making the process simple and easy.[11]

Firms may offer very high-priced, state-of-the-art products or services in full anticipation of limited sales. These offerings are designed to enhance the company's reputation and image and thereby increase the company's value in the minds of consumers. Paradigm, a

Philadelphia brand cream cheese dominates its market and is a premium-priced brand.

© Michael J. Hruby

Canadian speaker manufacturer, produces what many audiophiles consider to be a high-value product, yet offers speakers priced as low as $320 per pair. However, Paradigm also offers a very high-end speaker for $8,500 per pair. Although few people will spend $8,500 on a pair of speakers, this "statement" speaker communicates what the company is capable of and can increase the image of the firm and the rest of its products—even that $320 pair of speakers. Setting prices with a close eye to how consumers develop their perceptions of value can often be the most effective pricing strategy, especially if it is supported by consistent advertising and distribution strategies.

After a company has a good grasp on its overall objectives, it must implement pricing strategies that enable it to achieve those objectives. As the second step in this process, the firm should look toward consumer demand to lay the foundation for its pricing strategy.

> **PROGRESS CHECK**
> 1. What are the five Cs of pricing?
> 2. Identify the four types of company objectives.

Can you tell the difference between the $8,500 and the $320 speakers?

Source: Paradigm Electronics, Inc.

 LO14-2 Explain the relationship between price and quantity sold.

Customers

When firms have developed their company objectives, they turn to understanding consumers' reactions to different prices. The second C of the five Cs of pricing focuses on the customers. Customers want value, and as you likely recall, price is half of the value equation.

To determine how firms account for consumers' preferences when they develop pricing strategies, we must first lay a foundation of traditional economic theory that helps explain how prices are related to demand (consumers' desire for products) and how managers can incorporate this knowledge into their pricing strategies. But first read through Adding Value 14.1, which considers how Amazon leverages its renowned algorithms to develop a sophisticated value-based pricing strategy.[12]

Demand Curves and Pricing   A **demand curve** shows how many units of a product or service consumers will demand during a specific period of time at different prices. Although we call them "curves," demand curves can be either straight or curved, as Exhibit 14.3

EXHIBIT 14.3 | Demand Curve for Teeth-Whitening Kits

Adding Value 14.1 Changing Once, Changing Twice, Changing 3 Million Times: How Amazon Prices to Win[i]

On a recent Black Friday (i.e., the day after Thanksgiving, when many retailers make enough profit for the year to exceed their costs, known as getting in the black), Amazon actively changed the prices of one-third of the products in its seemingly endless supply. Try to imagine what that means. Amazon, the marketplace for virtually everything, engaged in literally millions of price changes, on what would already be probably its busiest shopping day. Why?

Here's the thing: It isn't all that unusual for Amazon. Every single day, it changes the prices of 15 to 18 percent of its products. With its famous algorithms and remarkable data warehouses, Amazon evidently believes it has better insights into what consumers will pay at any particular moment for a vast range of products.

Some product categories come in for more changes than others. Some are subject to change every day, others undergo price alterations every third day, another set shifts once a week, and still others experience changes only once or twice a month. Perhaps unsurprisingly, considering its investment in the Kindle, the most frequently changed product category is tablets, for which Amazon changes the prices of 15 percent of its stock every one to two days.

But the really remarkable transitions are the ones that take place around the holidays. Reports from holiday trends indicate that Amazon literally changed more than 3 million prices each and every day in November—of course, with the previously mentioned jump in activity on the day after Thanksgiving. Pleased with how well these changes have worked, Amazon promises to continue making them, and perhaps even ramp up its efforts.

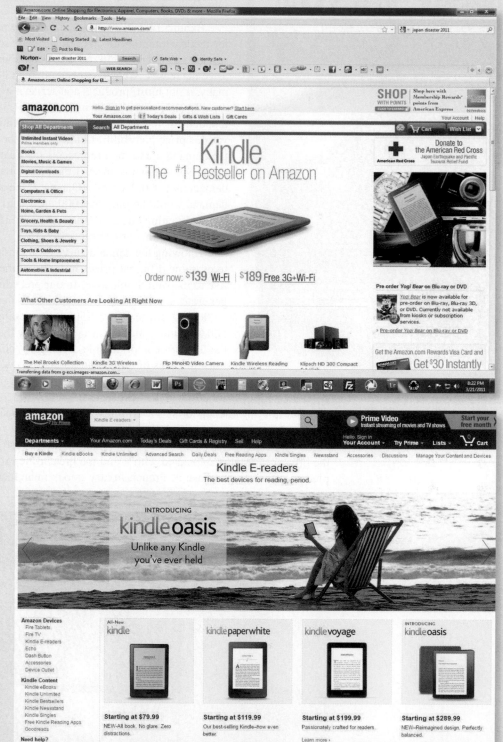

Amazon changes prices of 15 percent of its stock of Kindle tablets every one to two days. Note, the Kindle Oasis ranges from $139 and $189 (top) to $289.99 (bottom).

Top: © indiaforte/Alamy; Bottom: Source: Amazon

Based on Exhibit 14.3, what is the best price for WhiteLight?

© Miami Herald/McClatchy-Tribune/ Getty Images

shows. Of course, any demand curve relating demand to price assumes that everything else remains unchanged. For the sake of expediency, marketers creating a demand curve assume that the firm will not increase its expenditures on advertising and that the economy will not change in any significant way.

Exhibit 14.3 illustrates a classic downward-sloping demand curve for teeth-whitening kits. As price increases, demand for a product or service will decrease. In the case here, consumers will buy more as the price decreases. We can expect a demand curve similar to this one for many, if not most, products and services.

The horizontal axis in Exhibit 14.3 measures the quantity demanded for the teeth-whitening kits in units and plots it against the various price possibilities indicated on the vertical axis. Each point on the demand curve then represents the quantity demanded at a specific price. So, in this instance, if the price of a kit is \$10 per unit (P_1), the demand is 1,000,000 units (Q_1), but if the price were set at \$15 (P_2), the demand would be only 500,000 units (Q_2). The firm will sell far more teeth-whitening kits at \$10 each than at \$15 each. Why? Because of the greater value this price point offers.

Knowing the demand curve for a product or service enables a firm to examine different prices in terms of the resulting demand and relative to its overall objective. In our preceding example, the retailer will generate a total of \$10,000,000 in sales at the \$10 price (\$10 × 1,000,000 units) and \$7,500,000 in sales at the \$15 price (\$15 × 500,000 units). In this case, given only the two choices of \$10 or \$15, the \$10 price is preferable as long as the firm wants to maximize its sales in terms of dollars and units. But what about a firm that is more interested in profit? To calculate profit, it must consider its costs, which we cover in the next section.

But not all products or services follow the downward-sloping demand curve for all levels of price depicted in Exhibit 14.3. Consider **prestige products or services**, which consumers purchase for their status rather than for their functionality. The higher the price, the greater the status associated with it and the greater the exclusivity, because fewer people can afford to purchase it. French luxury goods manufacturer and retailer Hermès is

Hermès uses prestige pricing for its handbags, like this one that sold for more than \$300,000 at auction, which is more than \$20,000 above the standard retail price.

© Lam Yik Fei/The New York Times/Redux

known for making expensive leather goods. But paying $300,168 for a handbag at auction, which is over the standard retail price of $280,000, is extraordinary, and not for the casual shopper. Of course, the matte Himalayan crocodile handbag was finished using white-gold hardware set with 245 F-color diamonds.[13]

With prestige products or services, a higher price may lead to a greater quantity sold, but only up to a certain point. The price demonstrates just how rare, exclusive, and prestigious the product is. When customers value the increase in prestige more than the price differential between the prestige product and other products, the prestige product attains the greater value overall.

However, prestige products can also run into pricing difficulties. The Fender Telecaster and Stratocaster guitars are absolute necessities for any self-respecting guitar hero, but for hobbyists or students just learning to play, the price of owning a Fender "axe" was simply too much. In response, Fender introduced a separate, budget-priced line of similar guitars under a different brand name, so as not to dilute the prestige of the Fender name. The Squier line, made in Japan with automated manufacturing and less expensive parts, offers a look similar to the famous Fender guitars and performance just a notch below the originals. Today, an American-made Vintage Hot Rod '57 Fender Stratocaster lists for $1,700, more than 14 times as much as a Squier Bullet Strat model, which retails for around $120.[14]

Jimi Hendrix used a left-handed Fender guitar.

© David Redfern/Getty Images

Exhibit 14.4 illustrates a demand curve for a hypothetical prestige service, a Club Med vacation. As the graph indicates, when the price increases from $1,000 (P$_1$) to $5,000 (P$_2$), the quantity demanded actually increases from 200,000 (Q$_1$) to 500,000 (Q$_2$) units. However, when the price increases to $8,000 (P$_3$), the demand then decreases to 300,000 (Q$_3$) units.

Although the firm likely will earn more profit selling 300,000 vacation packages at $8,000 each than 500,000 vacation packages at $5,000 each, we do not know for sure until we bring costs into the picture. However, we do know that more consumers are willing to book the vacation as the price increases initially from $1,000 to $5,000 and that more consumers will choose an alternative vacation as the price increases further from $5,000 to $8,000.

EXHIBIT **14.4** Demand Curve for a Club Med Vacation

LO14-3   Explain price elasticity.

We must consider this notion of consumers' sensitivity to price changes in greater depth.

Price Elasticity of Demand

Although we now know something about how consumers react to different price levels, we still need to determine how consumers respond to actual changes in price. These responses vary depending on the product or service. For example, consumers are generally less sensitive to price increases for necessary items, such as milk, because they have to purchase the items even if the price climbs. When the price of milk goes up, demand does not fall significantly, because people still need to buy milk. However, if the price of T-bone steaks rises beyond a certain point, people will buy fewer of them because they can turn to the many substitutes for this cut of meat. Marketers need to know how consumers will respond to a price increase or decrease for a specific product or brand so they can determine whether it makes sense for them to raise or lower prices.

Price elasticity of demand measures how changes in a price affect the quantity of the product demanded. Specifically, it is the ratio of the percentage change in quantity demanded to the percentage change in price. We can calculate it with the following formula:

$$\text{Price elasticity of demand} = \frac{\%\ \text{Change in quantity demanded}}{\%\ \text{Changes in price}}$$

The demand curve provides the information we need to calculate the price elasticity of demand. For instance, what is the price elasticity of demand if we increase the price of our teeth-whitening kit from Exhibit 14.3 from $10 to $15?

$$\%\ \text{Change in quantity demanded} = \frac{(500,000 - 1,000,000)}{1,000,000} = -50\%, \text{ and}$$

$$\%\ \text{Change in price} = \frac{(\$15 - \$10)}{10} = 50\%, \text{ so}$$

$$\text{Price elasticity of demand} = \frac{-50\%}{50\%} = -1.$$

Thus, the price elasticity of demand for our teeth-whitening kit is −1.

In general, the market for a product or service is price sensitive, or **elastic**, when the price elasticity is less than −1. Thus, an elasticity of −5 would indicate that a 1 percent decrease in price produces a 5 percent increase in the quantity sold. In an elastic scenario, relatively small changes in price will generate fairly large changes in the quantity demanded, so if a firm is trying to increase its sales, it can do so by lowering prices. However, raising prices can be problematic in this context because doing so will lower sales. To refer back to our grocery examples, a retailer would significantly decrease its sales of T-bone steaks by raising its price by a relatively small amount, because T-bones are elastic.

The market for a product is generally viewed as price insensitive, or **inelastic**, when its price elasticity is greater than −1. For example, an elasticity of −.50 indicates that a 1 percent increase in price results in one-half a percent decrease in quantity sold. Generally, if a firm must raise prices, it is helpful to do so with inelastic products or services, because in such a market, fewer customers will stop buying or will reduce their purchases. However, if the products are inelastic, lowering prices will not appreciably increase demand; customers just don't notice or care about the lower price.

Consumers are generally more sensitive to price increases than to price decreases.[15] That is, it is easier to lose current customers with a price increase than it is to gain new customers with a price decrease. Also, the price elasticity of demand usually changes at different points in the demand curve unless the curve is actually a straight line, as in Exhibit 14.3. For instance, a prestige product or service, like our Caribbean cruise example in Exhibit 14.4, enjoys a highly inelastic demand curve up to a certain point, so price increases do not affect sales significantly. But when the price reaches that certain point, consumers start turning to other alternatives, because the value of the cruise has finally been reduced by the extremely high price.

Ideally, firms could maximize their profits if they charged each customer as much as the customer was willing to pay. The travel industry and airlines realize this benefit particularly well, as Marketing Analytics 14.1 explains. For instance, if a wealthy, price-insensitive customer wants to buy a

Consumers are less sensitive to the price of milk than they are to that of steak. When the price of milk goes up, demand does not fall significantly, because people still need to buy milk. However, if the price of steak rises beyond a certain point, people will buy less because they can turn to many substitutes for steak.

Left: © McGraw-Hill Education/Bob Coyle, photographer; Right: © FoodCollection/StockFood RF

new car, a Ford dealer might like to price a particular car at $40,000, but then price the same car at $35,000 to a more price-sensitive customer. Such a practice is legal when retailers sell to consumers such as in an eBay auction, but it is permitted only under certain circumstances in B2B settings.[16]

Although charging different prices to different customers is legal and widely used in some retail sectors, such as automobile and antique dealers, it has not been very practical in most retail stores until recently. Retailers have increased their use of dynamic pricing techniques due to the information that is available from point-of-sale data collected on the Internet purchases and in stores (as we discussed in Adding Value 14.1). **Dynamic pricing**, also known as **individualized pricing**, refers to the process of charging different prices for goods or services based on the type of customer; time of the day, week, or even season; and level of demand.

Factors Influencing Price Elasticity of Demand

We have illustrated how price elasticity of demand varies across different products and at different points along a demand curve, as well as how it can change over time. What causes these differences in the price elasticity of demand? We discuss a few of the more important factors next.

Income Effect The **income effect** refers to the change in the quantity of a product demanded by consumers due to changes in their incomes. Generally, as people's incomes increase, their spending behavior changes: They tend to shift their demand from lower-priced products to higher-priced alternatives. That is, consumers buy hamburger when they're stretching their money but steak when they're flush. Similarly, they may increase the

Marketing Analytics **14.1**   Airlines Use Price Elasticities to Price Tickets[ii]

The airline industry has been using analytics to influence pricing for decades. Early implementers of data-based pricing strategies, such as American Airlines, enjoyed a significant advantage over their competitors who maintained a single, flat rate for all tickets. By predicting demand for each particular flight, American Airlines could price different tickets at different rates and ensure that it sold as many tickets as possible. For example, when its analytics system identified which tickets might not sell, American Airlines began offering those seats at a significant discount, but it increased the rates for seats that were very likely to be purchased.

American Airlines' pricing strategy grew so effective that every other airline faced an obvious choice: Adopt it or go out of business. Some of the popularity of data-based pricing is the result of a key feature that it provides: It allows customers the freedom to determine the price they will pay. Travelers well know that they will find vast discrepancies in flight prices, depending on when they travel (spring break or the off-season?), when they book (Tuesday nights or Saturday mornings?), and where they want to sit (pay a lot extra for first class, a little extra for the exit row, or just the base fare for a middle seat?). Customers can weigh the value of the convenience of these various factors for themselves and then select the flight that best fits their own individual needs.

Despite the great deals offered and the resultant benefits for firms as well as customers, the use of strategic pricing analytics can require time-consuming hunts for the best deal. To combat the hassle of searching for airline deals, many service providers have introduced travel booking sites. Some are specific to a particular airline; others compile pricing information about various flights between two locations to make the price comparison evident and convenient for the customer. Kayak.com has taken it a step further and begun implementing predictive pricing analytics of its own in the form of its price forecast feature. Kayak takes information from the billions of requests for travel information that it processes each day and then predicts whether the price for a given destination on a particular date is likely to go up or down over the next seven days. It computes the accuracy of its predictions daily in an effort to perfect its use of these analytics.

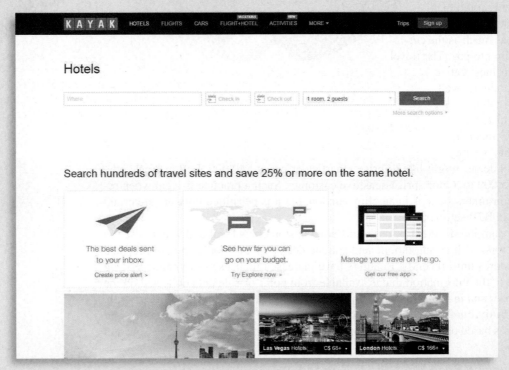

Kayak.com predicts when travel prices will change based on the information it processes each day.

Source: kayak.com

quantity they purchase and splurge on a five-star hotel during their six-day Las Vegas trip rather than three-star lodging over a weekend visit. Conversely, when incomes drop, consumers turn to less expensive alternatives or purchase less.

Substitution Effect The substitution effect refers to consumers' ability to substitute other products for the focal brand. The greater the availability of substitute products, the higher the price elasticity of demand for any given product will be. For example, there are many close substitutes in the laundry detergent category, as we discussed in the chapter opener. If Tide raises its prices, many consumers will turn to competing brands (e.g., Arm & Hammer Detergent), because they are more sensitive to price increases when they can easily find lower-priced substitutes. Extremely brand-loyal consumers, however, are willing to pay a higher price, up to a point, because in their minds, Tide still offers a better value than the competing brands do, and they believe the other brands are not adequate substitutes.

Keep in mind that marketing plays a critical role in making consumers brand loyal. And because of this brand loyalty and the lack of what consumers judge to be adequate substitutes, the price elasticity of demand for some brands is very low. For example, Polo/Ralph Lauren sells millions of its classic polo shirts at $85, while shirts of equal quality but without the polo-player logo sell for much less. Getting consumers to believe that a particular brand is unique, different, or extraordinary in some way makes other brands seem less substitutable, which in turn increases brand loyalty and decreases the price elasticity of demand.

ILacostena fights the price substitution effect by being one of the most recognized Mexican brands and a leading producer of canned products.

© Photodisc/Getty Images RF

Cross-Price Elasticity Cross-price elasticity is the percentage change in the quantity of Product A demanded compared with the percentage change in price in Product B. If Product A's price increases, Product B's price could either increase or decrease, depending on the situation and whether the products are complementary or substitutes. We refer to products like Blu-ray discs and Blu-ray players as complementary products, which are products whose demands are positively related, such that they rise or fall together. In other words, a percentage increase in the quantity demanded for Product A results in a percentage increase in the quantity demanded for Product B.[17] However, when the price for Blu-ray players dropped, the demand for DVD players went down, so DVD players and Blu-ray players are substitute products because changes in their demand are negatively related. That is, a percentage increase in the quantity demanded for Product A results in a percentage decrease in the quantity demanded for Product B.[18] In addition, on the Internet, shopping bots like TheFind.com and Bizrate.com have made it much easier for people to shop for substitutable products like consumer electronics, which likely has affected the price elasticity of demand for such products.[19]

The way a product or service is marketed to customers can have a profound effect on its price elasticity. Superior Service 14.1 describes how good marketing by Universal Theme Parks in the form of greater customer convenience can make customers less sensitive to price.

Prior to this point, we have focused on how changes in prices affect how much customers buy. Clearly, knowing how prices affect sales is important, but it cannot give us the whole picture. To know how profitable a pricing strategy will be, we must also consider the third C, costs.

Superior Service 14.1

The Increasing Costs of Play: New Offers and Pricing by Disney and Universal Theme Parks[iii]

As we discuss in the opening vignette for the next chapter, the price to get into Disneyland, in Anaheim, California, or Disney World, in Orlando, Florida, keeps increasing. At Universal Studios Hollywood, a one-day pass is $80. But instead of just raising its prices to match Disney, Universal has introduced a new pricing plan that offers greater access to those willing to pay more—quite a lot more.

The VIP service at Universal allows park visitors to bypass every line in the park—after having their car parked by a valet. They get free breakfast and lunch in a luxury lounge that features such offerings as scallops and short ribs. Then they can access the backlots while toting their free gift bags that contain mints, hand sanitizer, and a poncho to wear on water rides—all this at a cost of $299 per ticket. For those who don't worry about their breath or eating fancy meals, a $149 option offers just line-jumping privileges.

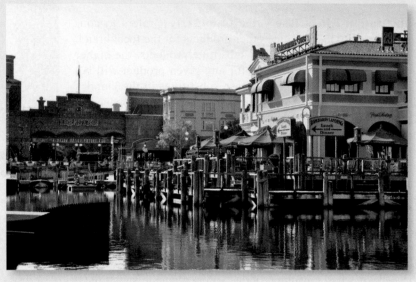

Universal Theme Parks offer premium service options at a premium price.
© Melanie Eldred Photography/Alamy

Even as it introduced this new service, Universal noted that it had no plans to expand its primary offering. That is, it did not plan to open any new rides or attractions this year. Its parks pulled in approximately 20 million people in 2012, which represented a nearly 20 percent increase over the year before. And according to some of these visitors, they simply would not attend without a VIP option, because they hate dealing with the crowds.

Such benefits raise some questions about the economic stratification Universal is promoting, such that only the wealthy get to enjoy all the perks. For Disney, concerns about damage to its "magical" image have halted it from classifying different price points for tickets based on different levels of access. Yet as a recent controversy—in which wealthy families hired people with disabilities to join their trips so that they could skip lines—showed, demand for such special treatment exists.

Even though theme parks are enjoying record attendance and revenue levels, they keep looking for ways to increase their appeal. New rides and attractions are expensive and in many cases can seem out of date pretty quickly. In this case, the magic may be in the pricing.

PROGRESS CHECK

1. What is the difference between elastic demand and inelastic demand?
2. What are the factors influencing price elasticity?

Costs

To make effective pricing decisions, firms must understand their cost structures so they can determine the degree to which their products or services will be profitable at different prices. In general, prices should *not* be based on costs, because consumers make purchase decisions based on their perceived value; they care little about the firm's costs to produce and sell a product or deliver a service. Although companies incur many different types of costs as a natural part of doing business, there are two primary cost categories: variable and fixed.

Variable Costs Variable costs are those costs, primarily labor and materials, that vary with production volume. As a firm produces more or less of a good or service, the total variable costs increase or decrease at the same time. Because each unit of the product produced incurs the same cost, marketers generally express variable costs on a per-unit basis. Consider a bakery like Entenmann's: The majority of the variable costs are the cost of the ingredients, primarily flour. Each time Entenmann's makes a loaf of bread, it incurs the cost of the ingredients.

In the service industry, variable costs are far more complex. A hotel, for instance, incurs certain variable costs each time it rents a room, including the costs associated with the labor and supplies necessary to clean and restock the room. Note that the hotel does not incur these costs if the room is not booked. Suppose that a particular hotel calculates its total variable costs to be $10 per room; each time it rents a room, it incurs another $10 in variable costs. If the hotel rents out 100 rooms on a given night, the total variable cost is $1,000 ($10 per room × 100 rooms).

In either case, however, variable costs tend to change depending on the quantity produced. If Entenmann's makes 100,000 loaves of bread in a month, it would have to pay a higher price for ingredients on a per pound basis than if it were producing a million loaves, because the more ingredients it purchases, the less expensive those ingredients become. Similarly, a very large hotel will be able to get a lower per unit price on most, if not all, the supplies it needs to service the room because it purchases such a large volume. However, as the hotel company continues to grow, it may be forced to add more benefits for its employees or increase wages to attract and keep long-term employees. Such changes will increase its overall variable labor costs and affect the total variable cost of cleaning a room. Thus, though not always the case, variable costs per unit may go up or down (for all units) with significant changes in volume.

Fixed Costs Fixed costs are those costs that remain essentially at the same level, regardless of any changes in the volume of production. Typically, these costs include items such as rent, utilities, insurance, administrative salaries (for executives and higher-level managers), and the depreciation of the physical plant and equipment. Across reasonable fluctuations in production volume, these costs remain stable; whether Entenmann's makes 100,000 loaves or a million, the rent it pays for the bakery remains unchanged.

Total Cost Finally, the total cost is simply the sum of the variable and fixed costs. For example, in one year, our hypothetical hotel incurred $100,000 in fixed costs. We also know that because the hotel booked 10,000 room nights, its total variable cost is $100,000 (10,000 room nights × $10 per room). Thus, its total cost is $200,000.

Next, we illustrate how to use these costs in simple analyses that can inform managerial decision making about setting prices.

Break-Even Analysis and Decision Making

LO14-4 Describe how to calculate a product's break-even point.

A useful technique that enables managers to examine the relationships among cost, price, revenue, and profit over different levels of production and sales is called break-even analysis. Central to this analysis is the determination of the break-even point, or the point at which the number of units sold generates just enough revenue to equal the total costs. At this point, profits are zero. Although profit, which represents the difference between the total cost and the total revenue (Total revenue or sales = Selling price of each unit sold × Number of units sold), can indicate how much money the firm is making or losing at a single period of time, it cannot tell managers how many units a firm must produce and sell before it stops losing money and at least breaks even, which is what the break-even point does.

How do we determine the break-even point? Exhibit 14.5 presents in graphic format the various cost and revenue information we have discussed. The graph contains three curves (recall that even though they are straight, we still call them curves): fixed costs, total costs, and total revenue. The vertical axis measures the revenue and costs in dollars, and the horizontal axis measures the quantity of units sold. The fixed cost curve will always

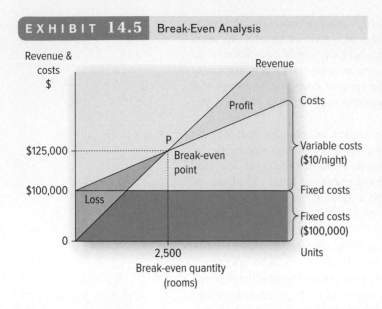

appear as a horizontal line straight across the graph, because fixed costs do not change over different levels of volume.

The total cost curve starts where the fixed cost curve intersects the vertical axis at $100,000. When volume is equal to zero (no units are produced or sold), the fixed costs of operating the business remain and cannot be avoided. Thus, the lowest point the total costs can ever reach is equal to the total fixed costs. Beyond that point, the total cost curve increases by the amount of variable costs for each additional unit, which we calculate by multiplying the variable cost per unit by the number of units, or quantity.

Finally, the total revenue curve increases by the price of each additional unit sold. To calculate it, we multiply the price per unit by the number of units sold. The formulas for these calculations are as follows:

$$\text{Total variable costs} = \text{Variable cost per unit} \times \text{Quantity}$$

$$\text{Total costs} = \text{Fixed costs} + \text{Total variable costs}$$

$$\text{Total revenue} = \text{Price} \times \text{Quantity}$$

We again use the hotel example to illustrate these relationships. Recall that the fixed costs are $100,000 and the variable costs are $10 per room rented. If the rooms rent for $50 per night, how many rooms must the hotel rent over the course of a year to break even? If we study the graph carefully, we find the break-even point at 2,500, which means that the hotel must rent 2,500 rooms before its revenues equal its costs. If it rents fewer rooms, it loses money (the pink area); if it rents more, it makes a profit (the gold area). To determine the break-even point in units mathematically, we must introduce one more variable, the **contribution per unit**, which is the price less the variable cost per unit.

In this case,

$$\text{Contribution per unit} = \$50 - \$10 = \$40$$

Therefore, the break-even point becomes

$$\text{Break-even point (units)} = \frac{\text{Fixed costs}}{\text{Contributions per unit}}$$

That is,

$$\text{Break-even point (units)} = \frac{\$100,000}{\$40} = 2,500 \text{ room nights}$$

When the hotel has crossed the break-even point of 2,500 rooms, it will start earning profit at the same rate of the contribution per unit. So if the hotel rents 4,000 rooms—that is, 1,500 rooms more than the break-even point—its profit will be $60,000 (1,500 rooms × $40 contribution per unit).

$$\text{Profit} = (\text{Contribution per unit} \times \text{Quantity}) - \text{Fixed costs}$$

$$\text{Profit} = (\$40 \times 4,000) - \$100,000 = \$60,000$$

Or an alternative formula would be:

$$\text{Profit} = (\text{Price} \times \text{Quantity}) - (\text{Fixed costs} + (\text{Variable costs} \times \text{Quantity}))$$

$$\text{Profit} = (\$50 \times 4,000) - (\$100,000 + (\$10 \times 4,000))$$

$$\text{Profit} = \$200,000 - (\$100,000 + \$40,000) = \$60,000$$

In a hotel, the cost of the physical structure, including the lobby, is fixed—it is incurred even if no rooms are rented. The costs of washing the towels and sheets are variable—the more rooms that are rented, the more the costs.

Left: © Erik Isakson/Blend Images/Getty Images RF; Right: © Eric Audras/Onoky/SuperStock RF

Let's extend this simple break-even analysis to show how many units a firm must produce and sell to achieve a target profit. Say the hotel wanted to make $200,000 in profit each year. How many rooms would it have to rent at the current price? In this instance, we need only add the targeted profit to the fixed costs to determine that number:

$$\text{Break-even point (units)} = \frac{\text{(Fixed costs + Target profit)}}{\text{Contributions per unit}}$$

or

$$7,500 \text{ rooms} = \frac{(\$100,000 + \$200,000)}{\$40}$$

Although a break-even analysis cannot actually help managers set prices, it does help them assess their pricing strategies because it clarifies the conditions in which different prices may make a product or service profitable. It becomes an even more powerful tool when performed on a range of possible prices for comparative purposes. For example, the hotel management could analyze various prices, not just $50, to determine how many hotel rooms it would have to rent at what price to make a $200,000 profit.

Naturally, however, there are limitations to a break-even analysis. First, it is unlikely that a hotel has one specific price that it charges for each and every room, so the price it would use in its break-even analysis probably represents an "average" price that attempts to account for these variances. Second, prices often get reduced as quantity increases, because the costs decrease, so firms must perform several break-even analyses at different quantities. Third, a break-even analysis cannot indicate for sure how many rooms will be rented or, in the case of products, how many units will sell at a given price. It only tells the firm what its costs, revenues, and profitability will be, given a set price and an assumed quantity. To determine how many units the firm actually will sell, it must bring in the demand estimates we discussed previously.

Markup and Target Return Pricing

In many situations, the manufacturer may want to achieve a standard markup—let's say 10 percent of cost. In our example of the teeth-whitening kit, let's assume:

Variable costs per unit:	$8.00
Fixed costs:	$1,000,000.00
Expected sales:	1,000,000 units

The teeth-whitening kit manufacturer would like to calculate the price at which it would make a 10 percent markup.

The formula for calculating a target return price based on a markup on cost is:

Target return price = (Variable costs + (Fixed costs ÷ Expected Unit sales))
× (1 × Target return % [expressed as a decimal])

In this example, this would result in the firm charging $9.90.

Target return price = ($8.00 + ($1,000,000.00 ÷ 1,000,000.00)) × (1 + 0.10)
Target return price = $9.00 × 1.1 = $9.90

PROGRESS CHECK

1. What is the difference between fixed costs and variable costs?
2. How does one calculate the break-even point in units?

LO14-5 Indicate the four types of price competitive levels.

Competition

Because the fourth C, competition, has a profound impact on pricing strategies, we use this section to focus on its effect, as well as on how competitors react to certain pricing strategies. There are four levels of competition—monopoly, oligopolistic competition, monopolistic competition, and pure competition—and each has its own set of pricing challenges and opportunities (see Exhibit 14.6).

EXHIBIT 14.6   Four Levels of Competition: Can you match each photo to its respective type of competition?

Less price competition   More price competition

| Monopoly
One firm controls
the market | Oligopoly
A handful of firms
control the market | Fewer firms |
| Monopolistic competition
Many firms selling
differentiated products
at different prices | Pure competition
Many firms selling
commodities for the
same prices | Many firms |

Photos (top to bottom): © Steve Cole/Getty Images RF; © Corbis RF; © Ingram Publishing/SuperStock RF; © Brand X Pictures/PunchStock RF

In a **monopoly**, one firm provides the product or service in a particular industry, which results in less price competition. For example, there is often only one provider of cable television services in each region of the country: Time Warner is in New York, Comcast is in most of New England, and so forth. When Comcast recently proposed a plan to buy Time Warner, the purchase ultimately could not be completed, mostly due to concerns that it would have caused Comcast to become an overly large monopolist with too much power. That is, with the merger, Comcast would have become the primary cable company for more than half of the country. Comcast frequently has been challenged for allegedly seeking to achieve a monopoly that restricts competition by controlling the industry. Were these allegations to be proven conclusively, it legally could be broken apart by the government.[20]

When a market is characterized by **oligopolistic competition**, only a few firms dominate. Firms typically change their prices in reaction to competition to avoid upsetting an otherwise stable competitive environment. Examples of oligopolistic markets include the soft drink market and commercial airline travel. Sometimes reactions to prices in oligopolistic markets can result in a **price war**, which occurs when two or more firms compete primarily by lowering their prices. Firm A lowers its prices; Firm B responds by meeting or beating Firm A's new price. Firm A then responds with another new price, and so on. In some cases though, these tactics result in **predatory pricing**, which occurs when a firm sets a very low price for one or more of its products with the intent of driving its competition out of business. Predatory pricing is illegal in the United States under both the Sherman Antitrust Act and the Federal Trade Commission Act.

Monopolistic competition occurs when there are many firms competing for customers in a given market but their products are differentiated. When so many firms compete, product differentiation rather than strict price competition tends to appeal to consumers. This is the most common form of competition. Hundreds of firms make sunglasses, thus the market is highly differentiated. Ray-Ban offers its iconic, thick-rimmed, black Wayfarer-style sunglasses. Oakley sells sunglasses that are sporty, with varied lens colors that promise to protect wearers' eyes better when they are engaging in outdoor activities. For consumers looking for more style, fashion designers such as Prada and Gucci have their own sunglasses. Depending on the features, style, and quality, companies compete for very different market segments. By differentiating their products using various attributes, prices, and brands, they create unique value propositions in the minds of their customers.

With **pure competition**, a large number of sellers offer standardized products or commodities that consumers perceive as substitutable, such as grains, gold, meat, spices, or minerals. In such markets, price usually is set according to the laws of supply and demand. For example, wheat is wheat, so it does not matter to a commercial bakery whose wheat it buys. However, the secret to pricing success in a pure competition market is not necessarily to offer the lowest price, because doing so might create a price war and erode profits. Instead, some firms have brilliantly decommoditized their products. For example, most people feel that all salt purchased in a grocery is the same. But companies like Morton have branded their salt to move into a monopolistically competitive market.

The sunglasses market is characterized by monopolistic competition with hundreds of firms with differentiated products. Ray-Ban's Wayfarer sunglasses (left) are classic, Oakley's sunglasses (middle) are sporty, and Gucci's sunglasses (right) are very, very fashionable.

When a commodity can be differentiated somehow, even if simply by a sticker or logo, there is an opportunity for consumers to identify it as distinct from the rest, and in this case, firms can at least partially extricate their product from a pure competitive market.

PROGRESS CHECK

1. What are the four different types of competitive environments?

Channel Members

How does DeWalt determine the suggested retail price so that all channel members make their required profit?

© S K D/Alamy

Channel members—manufacturers, wholesalers, and retailers—have different perspectives when it comes to pricing strategies. Consider a manufacturer that is focused on increasing the image and reputation of its brand but working with a retailer that is primarily concerned with increasing its sales. The manufacturer may desire to keep prices higher to convey a better image, whereas the retailer wants lower prices and will accept lower profits to move the product, regardless of consumers' impressions of the brand. Unless channel members carefully communicate their pricing goals and select channel partners that agree with them, conflict will surely arise.

Developing a price that allows all channel members to earn their requisite profits requires careful planning. Imagine that the electric tool manufacturer DeWalt is reconsidering the price of its 1/2-inch, 18-volt, Heavy Duty Cordless Drill that it sells through Ace Hardware stores. Using several pricing experiments (as described in Chapter 10), it determines that the profit maximizing retail price is $100 (see Exhibit 14.7). Ace Hardware is a **retailers' cooperative**, such that it helps its members achieve economies of scale by buying as a group. In a sense, a retailers' cooperative thus is similar to a wholesaler,

EXHIBIT 14.7   Pricing through the Channels

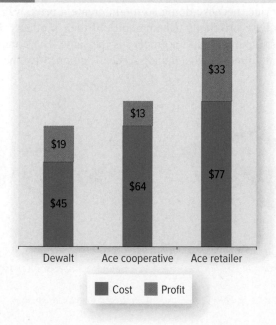

except that in this case, the retailers have some control over, and sometimes ownership in, the operation of the cooperative. For Ace Hardware to sell the DeWalt drill to consumers for $100, each retail store must purchase it for $77 at most, to be sure it can earn a 30 percent profit margin ($77 cost to retailer + [30 percent profit × $77 = $23 profit] = $100). The Ace Hardware cooperative in turn requires a 20 percent profit margin on its cost, so it must purchase the drill from DeWalt for $64 ($64 cost to Ace + [20 percent profit × $64 = $13 profit] = $77). The drill costs DeWalt $45 to produce, leaving DeWalt a profit of $19 ($64 − $45), or 42 percent (19/45), which is slightly above its benchmark profit of 40 percent. As this relatively simple example reveals, determining prices throughout the marketing channel that will enable all channel members to make a reasonable profit requires thought, cooperation, and strong negotiating skills by everyone involved.

Reviewing Learning Objectives

LO14-1 List the four pricing orientations.

A profit-oriented pricing strategy focuses on maximizing, or at least reaching, a target profit for the company. A sales orientation instead sets prices with the goal of increasing sales levels. With a competitor-oriented pricing strategy, a firm sets its prices according to what its competitors do. Finally, a customer-oriented strategy determines consumers' perceptions of value and prices accordingly.

LO14-2 Explain the relationship between price and quantity sold.

Generally, when prices go up, quantity sold goes down. Sometimes, however—particularly with prestige products and services—demand actually increases with price.

LO14-3 Explain price elasticity.

Changes in price generally affect demand; price elasticity measures the extent of this effect. It is based on the percentage change in quantity divided by the percentage change in price. Depending on the resulting value, a market offering can be identified as elastic, such that the market is very price sensitive, or inelastic, in which case the market cares little about the price.

LO14-4 Describe how to calculate a product's break-even point.

Because the break-even point occurs when the units sold generate just enough profit to cover the total costs of producing those units, it requires knowledge of the fixed cost, total cost, and total revenue curves. When these curves intersect, the marketer has found the break-even point.

LO14-5 Indicate the four types of price competitive levels.

In a monopoly setting, one firm controls the market and sets the price. In an oligopolistic competitive market, a few firms dominate and tend to set prices according to a competitor-oriented strategy. Monopolistic competition occurs when there are many firms competing for customers in a given market but their products are differentiated. Finally, pure competition means that consumers likely regard the products offered by different companies as basic substitutes, so the firms must work hard to achieve the lowest price point, limited by the laws of supply and demand.

Key Terms

LEARNSMART

- break-even analysis, 447
- break-even point, 447
- competitive parity, 437
- competitor orientation, 437
- complementary products, 445
- contribution per unit, 448
- cross-price elasticity, 445
- customer orientation, 437
- demand curve, 438
- dynamic pricing, 443
- elastic, 442
- fixed costs, 447

- income effect, 443
- individualized pricing, 443
- inelastic, 442
- maximizing profits, 436
- monopoly, 451
- monopolistic competition, 451
- oligopolistic competition, 451
- predatory pricing, 451
- premium pricing, 436
- prestige products or services, 440
- price, 434
- price elasticity of demand, 442

- price war, 451
- profit orientation, 435
- pure competition, 451
- retailers' cooperative, 452
- sales orientation, 436
- status quo pricing, 437
- substitute products, 445
- substitution effect, 445
- target profit pricing, 436
- target return pricing, 436
- total cost, 447
- variable costs, 447

Marketing Digitally

1. Several different pricing models can be found on the Internet. Each model appeals to different customer groups. Go to www.eBay.com and try to buy this book. What pricing options and prices are available? Do you believe that everyone will choose the least expensive option? Why or why not? Now go to www.Amazon.com. Is there more than one price available for this book? If so, what are those prices? Are different versions available? If you had to buy another copy of this book, where would you buy it and why would you buy it there?

2. Prices can vary, depending on the market being served and the novelty of the products. Shapeways allows anyone to upload a design and get it 3D printed. The best designs then are available to other customers to have printed in a variety of materials. Go to https://www.youtube.com/v/qJuTM0Y7U1k and learn more about Shapeways. Then go to its website, www.shapeways.com, and search for "Inception" and click on the design by the user roessnakhan. Note the difference in prices of the item to be printed in plastic versus metal. Now go to Amazon (www.Amazon.com) and search for "Inception Totem" and note the prices for a similar metal totem. How does the price of the item vary between Shapeways and Amazon? What would account for these differences in price? Why would a consumer purchase the product from Shapeways instead of Amazon? How is Shapeways communicating value?

Marketing Applications

1. You and your two roommates are starting a pet grooming service to help put yourselves through college. There are two other well-established pet services in your area. Should you set your price higher or lower than that of the competition? Justify your answer.

2. One roommate believes the most important objective in setting prices for your new pet grooming business is to generate a large profit while keeping an eye on your competitors' prices; the other roommate believes it is important to maximize sales and set prices according to what your customers expect to pay. Who is right and why?

3. Assume you have decided to buy an advertisement in the local newspaper to publicize your new pet grooming service. The cost of the ad is $1,000. You have decided to charge $40 for a dog grooming, and your variable costs are $20 for each dog. How many dogs do you have to groom to break even on the cost of the ad? What is your break-even point if you charge $60 per dog?

4. The local newspaper ad for your pet grooming business isn't helping much, so you decide to post your services on an auction site, where customers can bid for your services. What should the starting price of the auction be?

5. Is there a difference between a $5,900 Loro Piana vicuña sweater and a $150 cashmere sweater from L.L.Bean? Have you ever purchased a higher-priced product or service because you thought the quality was better than that of a similar, lower-priced product or service? What was the product or service? Do you believe you made a rational choice?

6. A soft drink manufacturer opened a new manufacturing plant in the Midwest. The total fixed costs are $100 million. It plans to sell the drinks to retailers for $6.00 for a package of 10 12-ounce cans. Its variable costs for the ingredients are $4.00 per package. Calculate the break-even volume. What would happen to the break-even point if the fixed costs decreased to $50 million, or the variable costs decreased to $3.00 due to declines in commodity costs. What would the break-even volume be if the firm wanted to make $20 million?

7. On your weekly grocery shopping trip, you notice that the price of spaghetti has gone up 50 cents a pound. How will this price increase affect the demand for spaghetti sauce, rice, and Parmesan cheese? Explain your answer in terms of the price elasticity of demand.

8. How do pricing strategies vary across markets that are characterized by monopolistic, oligopolistic, monopolistic competition, and pure competition?

9. Suppose you are in the market for a new Sharp LCD television. You see one advertised at a locally owned store for $300 less than it costs at hhgregg. The salesperson at the local store tells you that the television came from another retailer in the next state that had too many units of that model. Explain who benefits and who is harmed from such a gray market transaction: you, Sharp, hhgregg, the local store?

10. Has the Internet helped lower the price of some types of merchandise? Justify your answer.

11. Imagine that a pharmaceutical company has just developed a cure to a major fatal disease. Because the firm is the only one even close to a cure for this disease, price is inelastic, meaning it could virtually charge any price and people would pay. Discuss the ethical implications of choosing a price.

Quiz Yourself

1. A _____ orientation explicitly invokes the concept of value such as when a firm uses a "no-haggle" pricing structure to make the purchase process simpler and easier.
   a. profit
   b. sales
   c. competitor
   d. customer
   e. market

2. The most common form of competition is _____, where many firms compete for customers in a given market but with differentiated products.
   a. oligopolistic competition
   b. market saturation
   c. pure competition
   d. competitive parity
   e. monopolistic competition

(Answers to these two questions can be found in the Quiz Yourself Answer Key section.)

Chapter Case Study

PLANET FITNESS: PRICING FOR SUCCESS[21]

How does going completely against the grain of a typical fitness club strategy lead to success? That's the question that Planet Fitness appears uniquely positioned to answer. Most health clubs provide members with vast and seemingly valuable extra amenities such as child care, juice bars and protein supplements, on-staff professional trainers, and a broad range of fitness classes.[22] But many customers find the prices too high because they see little value in some of these amenities. Further reducing the value of traditional gym memberships, many consumers regard the social aspects unpleasant and offputting—whether that means observing others with nearly perfect bodies posturing in the mirror or listening to grunting exercisers huff with every lift.

While its competitors target upscale fitness buffs working on their six-pack abs, Planet Fitness successfully pursues an entirely different market: those who do not really enjoy going to the gym but know they need to do so to stay healthy. These exercisers are unlikely to hit the gym five or six times a week, making conventional gym memberships, which demand yearly contracts and fees of $49 to $95 per month, appear more expensive on a per-visit basis. Planet Fitness's formula is different: At $10 a month, the membership offers good value even if customers get to the club only a couple of times each week.[23]

In combination with its low price point, Planet Fitness promises a clean, friendly, laid-back workout environment featuring brand-name cardiovascular and strength equipment. Although it does not have the high-end amenities its competitors promise (e.g., pools, juice bars), the clubs maintain the key elements its members want: brand-name equipment, unlimited fitness training, flat-screen televisions, and large locker rooms. Its customers know from its advertising that they can expect a nonintimidating workout environment, or, as Planet Fitness promises, "No gymtimidation. No lunks. Just $10 a month."[24] With its foundation in the idea that simple is better,[25] Planet Fitness has become the fastest-growing full-sized fitness club in the United States. Exhibit 14.8 compares the prices of several major gyms.

For those who want a little more, Planet Fitness also offers a premium PF BlackCard membership for $19.99 a month, which promises access to nearly all the clubs in the Planet Fitness chain, unlimited guest privileges, use of tanning and massage chairs, and half-priced drinks.[26]

In addition to these in-club benefits, Planet Fitness's growth has been reinforced by its effective location strategy and marketing efforts that focus on attracting new customers. The low-cost monthly membership makes it easy to draw new members. Because most members come in only a couple of times each week, Planet Fitness also enjoys operating

EXHIBIT 14.8	Membership Costs of Planet Fitness and Competition in New York City	
Gym	Monthly Cost	Up-Front Cost
24 Hour Fitness	$44.99	$99.77
Bally Total Fitness	$29.99	$88.98
LA Fitness	$12.95/wk	$25.90
Planet Fitness	$10.00	$29.00
Snap Fitness	$39.99	$ 0.00

efficiencies and economies of scale, achieved by welcoming a high volume of members on any one day.[27]

Planet Fitness treats customers like real people. What kind of fitness club offers members pizza on the first Monday of every month, bagels on the first Tuesday, and Tootsie Rolls on a regular basis?[28] The kind of gym that plans to expand to 1,000 locations, with an eventual goal of more than 2,000, and that attracts more than 5 million members and systemwide sales approaching $700 million.[29]

Questions

1. What benefits do customers receive in return for the sacrifice they make when buying a membership at Planet Fitness?

2. How does this benefit–sacrifice ratio give Planet Fitness a competitive advantage in its industry?

3. Given its price strategy, why is it essential for Planet Fitness to continually attract new members? Do its high-end pricing competitors face the same need? Why or why not?

Endnotes

1. Serena Ng, "At P&G, New Tide Comes In, Old Price Goes Up," *The Wall Street Journal,* February 10, 2014, http://wsj.online.com.

2. http://productoftheyearusa.com/winners-2016/.

3. Dale Buss, "P&G Looks to Wring More Value out of Tide Brand with Lower-Priced Detergent," *BrandChannel,* September 4, 2013, http://www.brandchannel.com.

4. Ng, "At P&G, New Tide Comes In, Old Price Goes Up."

5. R. Suri and M. V. Thakor, "'Made in Country' versus 'Made in County': Effects of Local Manufacturing Origins on Price Perceptions," *Psychology & Marketing* 30, no. 2 (2013), pp. 121–32; R. Suri, K. B. Monroe, and U. Koc, "Math Anxiety and Its Effects on Consumers' Preference for Price Promotion Formats," *Journal of the Academy of Marketing Science* 41, no. 3 (2013), pp. 271–82; Kent B. Monroe, *Pricing: Making Profitable Decisions,* 3rd ed. (New York: McGraw-Hill, 2003); Dhruv Grewal, Kent B. Monroe, and R. Krishnan, "The Effects of Price Comparison Advertising on Buyers' Perceptions of Acquisition Value and Transaction Value," *Journal of Marketing* 62 (April 1998), pp. 46–60.

6. *Moneyball,* directed by Bennett Miller (2011; Sony Pictures). See also Michael Lewis, *Moneyball* (New York: Norton, 2004).

7. Dhruv Grewal et al., "Evolving Pricing Practices: The Role of New Business Models," *Journal of Product & Brand Management* 20, no. 7 (2011), pp. 510–13; Bang-Ning Hwang et al., "An Effective Pricing Framework in a Competitive Industry: Management Processes and Implementation Guidelines," *Journal of Revenue and Pricing Management* (November 2009).

8. Susan Carey, "Airlines Challenge Low-Cost Foes on Fares," *The Wall Street Journal,* December 29, 2015.

9. "IBM Market Share Leader in Human Resources (HR) Business Transformation Outsourcing, Enterprise Sector," press release. www.ibm.com.

10. Carey, "Airlines Challenge Low-Cost Foes on Fares."

11. https://www.carmax.com/car-buying-process

12. Jenn Markey, "Three Things You Need to Know About Amazon's Price Strategy," *Retail Customer Experience,* April 21, 2014, http://www.retailcustomerexperience.com.

13. Desiree Au, "Who Would Pay $300,000 for a Handbag?," *The New York Times,* June 3, 2016, http://www.nytimes.com/2016/06/05/fashion/hermes-birkin-most-expensive-bag-ever-sold.html

14. Fender Electric Guitars, http://www.fender.com.

15. Kent B. Monroe, *Pricing: Making Profitable Decisions*, 3rd ed. (New York: McGraw-Hill, 2003)

16. This type of B2B price discrimination is illegal under the Robinson-Patman Act of 1936. B2B sellers are allowed to charge different prices for merchandise of the same "grade and quality" if (1) the price difference is justified by different costs in manufacture, sale, or delivery (e.g., volume discounts); or (2) the price concession was given in good faith to meet a competitor's price. See http://www.ftc.gov/tips-advice/competition-guidance/guide-antitrust-laws/price-discrimination-robinson-patman.

17. http://www.marketingpower.com/_layouts/Dictionary.aspx?dLetter=C.

18. http://www.marketingpower.com/_layouts/Dictionary.aspx?dLetter=S.

19. Joan Lindsey-Mullikin and Dhruv Grewal, "Market Price Variation: The Availability of Internet Market Information," *Journal of the Academy of Marketing Science* 34, no. 2 (2006), pp. 236–43.

20. Drew Guarini, "This Is the United States of Comcast, Depressing Map Shows," *The Huffington Post*, March 5, 2014, http://www.huffingtonpost.com/2014/03/04/cable-company-map_n_4892435.html; Richard Greenfield, "How the Cable Industry Became a Monopoly," *Fortune*, May 19, 2015, http://fortune.com/2015/05/19/cable-industry-becomes-a-monopoly/.

21. This case was written by Jeanne L. Munger (University of Southern Maine) in conjunction with the textbook authors Dhruv Grewal and Michael Levy, as a basis for class discussion rather than to illustrate effective or ineffective marketing practices.

22. "Planet Fitness Continues Successful Growth with Puerto Rico Expansion," press release, http://www.marketwatch.com/story/.

23. http://www.planetfitness.com/.

24. Andrew Adam Newman, "A Gym for People Who Don't Like Gyms," *The New York Times*, January 3, 2013, http://www.nytimes.com.

25. Judith Ohikuare, "The Secret of Planet Fitness's Success," *Inc.*, February 2013, http://www.inc.com/magazine/.

26. "Planet Fitness Continues Successful Growth with Puerto Rico Expansion," press release, http://www.marketwatch.com/story/.

27. Beth Kowitt, "The Southwest Airlines of the Gym Business," *Fortune*, November 21, 2013, http://features.blogs.fortune.cnn.com/.

28. Andrew Adam Newman, "A Gym for People Who Don't Like Gyms," *The New York Times*, January 3, 2013, http://www.nytimes.com.

29. Kowitt, "The Southwest Airlines of the Gym Business."

i. Jenn Markey, "Three Things You Need to Know About Amazon's Price Strategy," *Retail Customer Experience*, April 21, 2014, http://www.retailcustomerexperience.com.

ii. "A Look Back: How Predictive Analytics Transformed the Airline Industry," Cusotra, https://www.custora.com/university/for-marketers/predictive-analytics/basic/predictive-analytics-and-the-airline-industry; "Price Trends & Tips Explanation," Kayak, 2015, http://www.kayak.com.

iii. Brooks Barnes, "At Theme Parks, a V.I.P. Ticket to Ride," *The New York Times*, June 9, 2013; "Ticket to Disneyland: Now $92," *The Wall Street Journal*, June 3, 2013; https://www.universalorlando.com/Theme-Park-Tickets/Vip-Experience.aspx.

CHAPTER 15

STRATEGIC PRICING METHODS AND TACTICS

LEARNING OBJECTIVES

After reading this chapter, you should be able to:

LO15-1 Identify three methods that firms use to set their prices.

LO15-2 Describe the difference between an everyday low pricing (EDLP) strategy and a high/low strategy.

LO15-3 Explain the difference between a price skimming and a market penetration pricing strategy.

LO15-4 Identify tactics used to reduce prices to consumers.

LO15-5 Identify tactics used to reduce prices to businesses.

LO15-6 List the pricing practices that are illegal or unethical.

Some companies choose to raise prices to earn more profits. Others do so in response to increased prices on their raw materials or components. But for Walt Disney, its latest price increase might not have really been the company's choice. The theme parks are bursting at the seams with visitors, and in an attempt to ensure that all these vacationers find the "Happiest Place on Earth" when they visit, Disney is implementing a demand-based pricing model to try to even out its supply.

The new model creates three main tiers for admission prices to the parks. The "value" tier refers to visits on regular work days (Monday–Thursday) during the traditional school year. "Regular" prices instead apply on weekends and most of the summer. And then there are the "peak" tickets, charged to visitors who want to visit on traditional spring break weeks, over Christmas, or during weekends in July.

The price tiers are about $10 apart, and the exact prices are little different for Disney World (in Orlando, Fla.) and Disneyland (in Anaheim, Calif.). For example, the peak price is $124 in Orlando but $119 in Anaheim. The Disney World value price of $105 is the same as the regular price at Disneyland. These variations in location reflect the slightly different popularity of the two parks, as well as their offerings. For example, the Florida location features four unique parks (Magic Kingdom, Epcot, Animal Kingdom, and Hollywood Studio), such that visitors have more choices.

But have no doubt: All the parks are popular. Attendance rates keep rising; Disney World welcomed approximately 20 million visitors last year. As the numbers climb, the parks struggle to keep the experience enjoyable, especially during the peak times. When so many people visit on the same day, there is little that Disney can do to keep the wait times reasonable and the lines moving.

Therefore, its primary goal with the demand-based pricing tiers is to encourage price-conscious travelers and those with more flexible schedules to plan their trips during regular work weeks. If Disney can convince even some of them to move their visits, it can better accommodate travelers across all the periods and likely earn better customer satisfaction.

Furthermore, Disney believes it has plenty of room to raise its prices. Admission prices traditionally have increased every year, and though of course some fans complain, prices have never jumped enough to cause demand to drop—as evidenced by the continued popularity of these destinations.[1]

Coming up with the "right" price is never easy, as this opening example shows. How can a firm determine what consumers are willing to pay and how much firms can charge? To answer such questions, we examine various pricing strategies and tactics in this chapter. We focus on specific considerations for setting pricing strategies, then discuss several specific pricing strategies. We also examine the implications of various pricing tactics—for consumers as well as businesses—and discuss some of the more important legal and ethical issues associated with pricing.

 LO15-1 Identify three methods that firms use to set their prices.

CONSIDERATIONS FOR SETTING PRICE STRATEGIES

Firms embrace different objectives, face different market conditions, and operate in different manners. Thus, they employ unique pricing strategies that seem best for the particular set of circumstances in which they find themselves. Even a single firm needs different strategies across its products and services and over time as market conditions change. The choice of a pricing strategy thus is specific to the product/service and target market. Although firms tend to rely on similar strategies when they can, each product or service requires its own specific strategy, because no two are ever exactly the same in terms of the marketing mix. Three different methods that can help develop pricing strategies—cost based, competition based, and value based—are discussed in this section (see Exhibit 15.1).

Cost-Based Methods

As their name implies, **cost-based pricing methods** determine the final price to charge by starting with the cost. Relevant costs (e.g., fixed, variable, overhead) and a profit are added. Then this total amount is divided by the total demand to arrive at a cost-plus price. For example, assume the fixed costs to produce an item are $200,000, the variable costs add up to $100,000, and the estimated number of units to be produced is 30,000. Then,

$$(100{,}000 + 200{,}000) \div 30{,}000 = \$10$$

which is the total allocated cost per unit when 30,000 units are produced. If the desired markup is 20 percent, we multiply $10 by 1.20 (i.e., by $100 + 20 = 120$ percent) to attain the cost-plus price for this item: $12. This sales price represents a cost-plus-percentage markup.

Cost-based methods do not recognize the role that consumers' or competitors' prices play in the marketplace, though. Although they are relatively simple, compared with other methods used to set prices, cost-based pricing requires that all costs be identified and

EXHIBIT 15.1 Pricing Strategies

calculated on a per-unit basis. Moreover, the process assumes that these costs will not vary much for different levels of production. If they do, the price might need to be raised or lowered according to the production level. Thus, with cost-based pricing, prices are usually set on the basis of estimates of average costs.

Competition-Based Methods

Recall from Chapter 14 that some firms set prices according to their competitors' prices. But even if they do not have a strict competitor orientation, most firms still know that consumers compare the prices of their products with the different product/price combinations that competitors offer. Thus, using a competition-based pricing method, they may set their prices to reflect the way they want consumers to interpret their own prices relative to competitors' offerings. For example, setting a price very close to a competitor's price signals to consumers that the product is similar, whereas setting the price much higher signals greater features, better quality, or some other valued benefit.

Value-Based Methods

Value-based pricing methods are approaches to setting prices that focus on the overall value of the product offering as perceived by the consumer. Consumers determine value by comparing the benefits they expect the product to deliver with the sacrifice they will need to make to acquire the product. Of course, different consumers perceive value differently. So how does a manager use value-based pricing methods? We consider two key approaches here: the improvement value and the cost of ownership methods. The experimental approach in which different prices are introduced into the marketplace to determine which is the most profitable based on consumer demand was discussed in Chapter 10.

Improvement Value Method With the first method, the manager must estimate the improvement value of a new product or service. This improvement value represents an estimate of how much more (or less) consumers are willing to pay for a product relative to other comparable products. For example, suppose a major telecommunications company has developed a new cell phone. Using any of a host of research methods—such as consumer surveys—the manager could get customers to assess the new product relative to an existing product and provide an estimate of how much better it is; that is, its improvement value.

Exhibit 15.2 illustrates how to calculate the improvement value. Consumers evaluate how much better (or worse) the new cell phone is than an existing product on five dimensions: clarity, range, security, battery life, and ease of use. According to the respondents to the survey, the new cell phone has 20 percent more clarity than the comparison phone has. These consumers also weight the importance of the five attributes by allocating 100 points among them to indicate their relative importance; for the clarity dimension, this weighting is 0.40. When the manager multiplies the improvement weight by the relative importance percentage,

EXHIBIT 15.2 Improvement Value

Incremental Benefits	Improved Value	Benefit Weight	Weighted Factor
Clarity	20%	0.40	8%
Range	40%	0.20	8%
Security	10%	0.10	1%
Battery life	5%	0.20	1%
Ease of use	30%	0.10	3%
Overall		1.00	21%

clarity (20 × 0.40) emerges with a weighted factor of 8 percent. The marketer repeats the process for each benefit and sums the weighted factors to arrive at an approximation of the improvement value of the new product from customers' points of view. In this illustration, the improvement value is equal to 21 percent, so if the other cell phone costs $100, the firm should be able to charge customers a value-based price as high as $121 ($100 × 1.21).

Cost of Ownership Method   Another value-based method for setting prices determines the total cost of owning the product over its useful life. Using the **cost-of-ownership method**, consumers may be willing to pay more for a particular product because, over its entire lifetime, it will eventually cost less to own than will a cheaper alternative.[2]

Consider, for example, that an energy-efficient LED lightbulb costs $3 and is expected to last 6,000 hours. Alternatively, a conventional lightbulb costs $1 but its average life is only 1,500 hours. The LED bulb is expected to last four times longer than a conventional bulb, but it costs three times as much. Using the cost of ownership method, and considering the cost per hour, the LED bulb manufacturer could charge $4 for each bulb if it wanted to be equivalent to the cost of the conventional bulb. But research also has indicated that many consumers are reluctant to spend $4 for a bulb when they have been used to getting them for $1, so the manufacturer chose to charge only $3.

Implementing Value-Based Pricing Methods   Although value-based pricing methods can be quite effective, they also necessitate a great deal of consumer research to be implemented successfully. Sellers must know how consumers in different market segments will attach value to the benefits delivered by their products, as Adding Value 15.1 describes. They also must account for changes in consumer attitudes, because the way customers perceive value today may not be the way they perceive it tomorrow.

PROGRESS CHECK

1. What are the three different considerations for setting prices?
2. How can you use value-based methods for setting prices?

Adding Value 15.1 — Value at a Premium Price: Moving Consumers Away from a View of Cheap as Valuable[i]

Value, as we know, is the relationship of benefits to costs, or what consumers get for what they give. But in consumer situations, value pricing and value options often imply the cheapest offerings. A value menu seems to mean really low prices rather than referring to the benefits that the menu items provide to consumers. But this common misunderstanding may be changing.

As the slow economic recovery continues to plod along, marketers cannot simply keep their fingers crossed and hope that eventually buyers will be willing to pay more for their products. Instead, as Procter & Gamble has profitably learned with its Tide Pods, as discussed in the opener in Chapter 14, they need to offer more value, which will prompt consumers to pay more because they are getting more. The added convenience of the single-use pods, together with the detergent's effective cleaning technology and the brand's high-quality image, have convinced household laundry buyers to pay more per wash—and be happy about their choice.

To provide more value options to its customers, Wendy's has expanded its pricing options. If fast-food patrons want a smaller item on a particular visit, they can purchase from the 99¢ menu. But if they are much hungrier or in the mood for a fresher option, they can jump up to a $1.99 menu item. Each option provides value, but the value is perceived differently by different people and in different situations. In a sense, these moves mimic the trends in dollar stores, which quickly realized that limiting themselves to only $1 options also limited the depth of their offerings and made them less appealing to consumers who sought a great deal, not just a way to get rid of all their single dollar bills.

Ford has enjoyed higher revenues from adding its Sync hands-free communication technology. Approximately 50 percent of Ford buyers cite the technology as a primary reason for their purchase choice. The associated price increase for this feature is reportedly around $4,000—not cheap, but apparently perceived to be a good value by many. Marketers can charge more and increase profits by providing more benefits when they are perceived to add value to consumers in some meaningful way. For modern marketers, this lesson may seem basic, but it is also one that they need to be reminded of regularly.

Adding value doesn't necessarily mean a low price. Ford added value with its Sync hands-free communication technology. It is not cheap, but it is perceived to be a good value by its customers.

© Chris O'Meara/AP Photo

PRICING STRATEGIES

A **pricing strategy** is a long-term approach to setting prices broadly in an integrative effort (across all the firm's products) based on the five Cs (company objectives, costs, customers, competition, and channel members) of pricing discussed in Chapter 14. In this section, we discuss a number of commonly used price strategies: everyday low pricing, high/low pricing, and new product strategies.[3]

LO15-2 Describe the difference between an everyday low pricing (EDLP) strategy and a high/low strategy.

Everyday Low Pricing (EDLP)

With an **everyday low pricing (EDLP)** strategy, companies stress the continuity of their retail prices at a level somewhere between the regular, nonsale price and the deep-discount sale prices their competitors may offer.[4] By reducing consumers' search costs, EDLP adds value; consumers can spend less of their valuable time comparing prices, including sale prices, at different stores. With its EDLP strategy, Walmart communicates to consumers that, for any given group of often-purchased items, its prices will tend to be lower than those of any other company in that market. This claim does not necessarily mean that every item that consumers may purchase will be priced lower at Walmart than anywhere else—in fact, some competitive retailers will offer lower prices on some items. However, for an average purchase, Walmart's prices tend to be lower overall. Adding Value 15.2 describes Walmart's foray into organic produce using its EDLP strategy.

A high/low pricing strategy relies on the promotion of sales, during which prices are temporarily reduced to encourage purchases.

© Jeff Greenberg/PhotoEdit

LO15-3 Explain the difference between a price skimming and a market penetration pricing strategy.

High/Low Pricing

An alternative to EDLP is a **high/low pricing** strategy, which relies on the promotion of sales, during which prices are temporarily reduced to encourage purchases. A high/low strategy is appealing because it attracts two distinct market segments: those who are not price sensitive and are willing to pay the "high" price and more price-sensitive customers who wait for the "low" sale price. High/low sellers can also create excitement and attract customers through the "get them while they last" atmosphere that occurs during a sale.

Sellers using a high/low pricing strategy often communicate their strategy through the creative use of a **reference price**, which is the price against which buyers compare the actual selling price of the product and that facilitates their evaluation process. The seller labels the reference price as the "regular price" or an "original price." When consumers view the "sale price" and compare it with the provided reference price, their perceptions of the value of the deal increase.[5]

In the advertisement on this page, Kohl's has provided a reference price, in smaller print and labeled "Reg.," to indicate that $355 is the regular price of a diamond ring. In addition, the advertisement highlights the current "sale" price of $69.99. Thus, the reference price suggests to consumers that they are getting a good deal and will save money. Thus, it is crucial that retailers and manufacturers provide genuine advertised reference prices in their ads and signage.

New Product Pricing Strategies

Developing pricing strategies for new products is one of the most challenging tasks a manager can undertake. When the new product is similar to what already appears on the market, this job is somewhat easier, because the product's approximate value has already been established and the value-based methods described earlier in this chapter can be employed. But when the new product is truly innovative, or what we call "new to the world," determining consumers' perceptions of its value and pricing it accordingly become far more difficult.

Adding Value 15.2   Walmart Offers Low-Priced Organic Foods[ii]

One word can strike fear into the heart of any small retailer: Walmart! Because it enjoys massive economies of scale, Walmart's entry into a market can cause tremors for even other large retailers, because somehow it always manages to underprice everyone else with the everyday low pricing (EDLP) strategy for which it has become famous. Long a consumer-goods giant, the Arkansas-based behemoth also has turned its massively successful EDLP practices to the grocery industry, where it quickly became the country's largest grocer as well.

Not satisfied with being just the largest grocer, Walmart aims to gain a substantial share of the lucrative organic food market. In true Walmart fashion, it intends to do so using its well-known, EDLP strategies. Organic products typically feature premium prices, but at Walmart, "there will be no premium for the customer to purchase organic products," according to the executive vice president of grocery at Walmart U.S. "They will be able to purchase organic at non-organic prices." In-house research indicated that consumers would overwhelmingly purchase organic products if they cost less, so Walmart responded.

But how can Walmart be the only retailer to offer organic products at nonorganic prices? It will deliver organic items through an atypical "bigger is better" mentality. That is, organic foods typically come from small farms, which send their products out to be processed at facilities that simultaneously process conventional foods. The switches from organic to conventional processing and back again require a great deal of labor, which increases costs and thus prices. Because of their economies of scale, Walmart can work with larger farms and processing

At Walmart you can buy organic produce without the typical premium organic food prices.

© Robert Hughes/Zuma Press/Newscom

plants that cater only to organic food production, saving time, labor, and money—by a margin of as much as 20 to 30 percent.

As is also its habit, Walmart is thinking long term and locking its suppliers into agreements that will enable it to meet the enormous requirements associated with its lofty organic goals.

Now you can visit your local Walmart to grab not just a DVD, diapers, and oil for your car, but also the ingredients for a gourmet organic meal. That's one-stop shopping at its finest.

The reference price for the diamond ring (left) is $355, and the reference prices for the toys are from $39.99 to $59.99. They provide potential customers with an idea of the "regular price" before it was put on sale.

Source: Kohl's

Two distinct new product pricing strategies are discussed next: penetration pricing and price skimming.

Penetration Pricing Firms using a **penetration pricing strategy** set the initial price low for the introduction of the new product or service. Their objective is to build sales, market share, and profits quickly and deter competition from entering the market. The low penetration price is an incentive to purchase the product immediately. Firms using a penetration pricing strategy expect the unit cost to drop significantly as the accumulated volume sold increases, an effect known as the **experience curve effect**. With this effect, as sales continue to grow, the costs continue to drop.

In addition to offering the potential to build sales, market share, and profits, penetration pricing discourages competitors from entering the market because the profit margin is relatively low. Furthermore, if the costs to produce the product drop because of the accumulated volume, competitors who enter the market later will face higher unit costs, at least until their volume catches up with the early entrant.

A penetration strategy has its drawbacks. First, the firm must have the capacity to satisfy a rapid rise in demand—or at least be able to add that capacity quickly. Second, low price does not signal high quality. Of course, a price below their expectations decreases the risk for consumers to purchase the product and test its quality for themselves. Third, firms should avoid a penetration pricing strategy if some segments of the market are willing to pay more for the product; otherwise, the firm is just "leaving money on the table."

Price Skimming In many markets, and particularly for new and innovative products or services, innovators and early adopters (see Chapter 12) are willing to pay a higher price to obtain the new product or service. This strategy, known as **price skimming**, appeals to these segments of consumers who are willing to pay the premium price to have the innovation first. This tactic is particularly common in technology markets, where sellers know that customers of the hottest and coolest products will wait in line for hours, desperate to be the first to own the newest version. These innovators are willing to pay the very highest prices to obtain brand-new examples of technology advances and exciting product enhancements. However, after this high-price market segment becomes saturated and sales begin to slow down, companies generally lower the price to capture (or skim) the next most price-sensitive market segment, which is willing to pay a somewhat lower price. For most companies, the price-dropping process can continue until the demand for the product has been satisfied, even at the lowest price points.

Price skimming is often used for high-demand video games like Call of Duty Black Ops III *because fans will pay a higher price to be one of the first to own the newest version.*
© Chesnot/Getty Images

The spread of new media for movies illustrates a price-skimming strategy. As with VCRs in the 1970s and DVD players in the 1990s, consumers were slow to embrace the new, more expensive Blu-ray discs. But enough early adopters purchased the Blu-ray discs that manufacturers continued to refine Blu-ray players to penetrate wider target markets. Consumers are buying the devices at a faster pace than they did the earlier movie-playing devices. One obvious reason for this sales growth is that prices for high-quality Blu-ray players have dropped below $80,[6] down sharply from the $300-plus that retailers charged for debut models.[7]

For price skimming to work though, the product or service must be perceived as breaking new ground in some way, offering consumers new benefits currently unavailable in alternative products. When they believe it will work, firms use skimming strategies for a variety of reasons. Some may start by pricing relatively high to signal high quality to the market. Others may decide to price high at first to limit demand, which gives them time to build their production capacities. Similarly, some firms employ a skimming strategy to try to quickly earn back some of the high research and development investments they made for the new product. Finally, firms employ skimming strategies to test consumers' price sensitivity. A firm that prices too high can always lower the price, but if the price is initially set too low, it is almost impossible to raise it without significant consumer resistance.

Furthermore, for a skimming pricing strategy to be successful, competitors cannot be able to enter the market easily; otherwise, price competition will likely force lower prices and undermine the whole strategy. Competitors might be prevented from entering the market through patent protections, their inability to copy the innovation (because it is complex to manufacture, its raw materials are hard to get, or the product relies on proprietary technology), or the high costs of entry.

Skimming strategies also face a significant potential drawback in the relatively high unit costs associated with producing small volumes of products. Therefore, firms must consider the trade-off between earning a higher price and suffering higher production costs. Finally, firms using a skimming strategy for new products must face the consequences of ultimately having to lower the price as demand wanes. Margins suffer, and customers who purchased the product or service at the higher initial price may become irritated when the price falls.

PROGRESS CHECK

1. Explain the difference between EDLP and high/low pricing.
2. What pricing strategies should be considered when introducing a new product?

PRICING TACTICS

LO15-4 Identify tactics used to reduce prices to consumers.

It is important to distinguish clearly between pricing strategies and pricing tactics. A pricing strategy, as we have discussed, is a long-term approach to setting prices broadly in an integrative effort (across all the firm's products) based on the five Cs (company objectives, costs, customers, competition, and channel members) of pricing discussed in Chapter 14. **Pricing tactics**, in contrast, offer short-term methods to focus on select components of the five Cs. Generally, a pricing tactic represents either a short-term response to a competitive threat (e.g., lowering price temporarily to meet a competitor's price reduction) or a broadly accepted method of calculating a final price for the customer that is short term in nature. We separate our discussion of pricing tactics into those directed at end consumers and those aimed at intermediaries in a business-to-business (B2B) setting.

Pricing Tactics Aimed at Consumers

When firms sell their products and services directly to consumers rather than to other businesses, the pricing tactics they use naturally differ. Some of the tactics aimed directly at consumers—such as markdowns, quantity discounts, seasonal discounts, coupons, rebates, leasing, price bundling, leader pricing, and price lining—continue to be important factors.

Markdowns Markdowns are the reductions retailers take on the initial selling price of the product or service. An integral component of the high/low pricing strategy we described previously, markdowns enable retailers to get rid of slow-moving or obsolete merchandise, sell seasonal items after the appropriate season, and match competitors' prices on specific merchandise. Retailers must get rid of merchandise that isn't selling, because holding on to such items hurts the retailer's image and ties up money in inventory that could be used more productively elsewhere. Retailers also use markdowns to promote merchandise and increase sales. Particularly when used in conjunction with promotions, markdowns can increase traffic into the store or onto their websites, which many retailers view as half the battle. Once customers are in the store or on their websites, retailers always hope they will purchase other products at regular prices.

Customers get a size discount for buying larger sizes. With Cheerios, the larger the box, the less it costs per ounce.

© Michael J. Hruby

Quantity Discounts for Consumers The most common implementation of a quantity discount at the consumer level is the size discount. Take, for example, three sizes of General Mills' popular cereal Cheerios: 10-, 14-, and 18-ounce boxes are priced at approximately $2.99, $3.99, and $4.49, respectively. The larger the quantity, the less the cost per ounce, which means the manufacturer is providing a quantity discount. The goal of this tactic is to encourage consumers to purchase larger quantities each time they buy. In turn, these consumers are less likely to switch brands and often tend to consume more of the product, depending on the product usage characteristics. Typically, buying a larger package of toilet tissue does not mean consumers will use it faster, but buying a larger box of cereal may encourage them to eat more of it or eat it more often.[8]

Seasonal Discounts Seasonal discounts that are offered to consumers are price reductions offered on products and services to stimulate demand during off-peak seasons. You can find hotel rooms, ski lift tickets, snowmobiles, lawn mowers, barbeque grills, vacation packages, flights to certain destinations, and Christmas cards at discounts during their "off" seasons. Some consumers even plan their buying around these discounts, determined to spend the day after Christmas stocking up on discounted wrapping paper and bows for the following year.

Coupons Coupons offer a discount on the price of specific items when they're purchased. Coupons are issued by manufacturers and retailers in newspapers, on products, on the shelf, at the cash register, over the Internet, and through the mail.[9] Retailers use coupons because they can induce customers to try products for the first time, convert those first-time users to regular users, encourage large purchases, increase usage, and protect market share against competition. However, the impact of coupons on profitability is questionable. Coupon promotions, like all temporary promotions, may be stealing sales from a future period without any net increase in sales. Coupons also may annoy, alienate, and confuse consumers and therefore do little to increase store loyalty. Customers see an ad for a supermarket with a headline reading "Double Coupons" but don't realize there might be conditions, such as a minimum purchase required, or that it may apply only to certain manufacturers.

Recognizing these problems, some retailers have reduced coupon usage and cut the number of days in which customers can redeem coupons. Other retailers, like CVS, are making coupons more attractive to loyal customers by customizing their content to be in line with their unique needs. For instance, if a customer typically spends a small amount during each shopping trip, the customer will receive coupons that encourage larger purchases, such as "buy one, get one free." Unique coupons will also encourage customers to try new brands within categories that they normally purchase, or products that complement their usual purchases, such as shampoo to customers who purchase hair color.[10]

Internet sites provide customers with instant coupons. For instance, a customer might go to a Walmart and find the latest Lego video game for $29.99. A scan of the bar code on his cell phone to ShopSavvy.com might find the same item at a Target a mile away for $19.99. Another scan to MyCoupons.com provides a coupon for $10.00, thus saving the customer $20.00 in a matter of minutes.

Coupons offer a discount on the price of specific items when they're purchased.
© Michael J. Hruby

Rebates Rebates provide another form of discounts for consumers off the final selling price. In this case, however, the manufacturer, instead of the retailer, issues the refund as a portion of the purchase price returned to the buyer in the form of cash. A rebate promises savings, usually mailed to the consumer at some later date, only if the consumer carefully follows the rules. The "hassle factor" for rebates thus is higher than for coupons. The consumer must first buy the item during a specified time period, then mail in the required documentation—which usually includes the original sales receipt—and finally wait four to six weeks (or more!) for a check to arrive.

Manufacturers generally like rebates because as much as 90 percent of consumers never bother to redeem them. Manufacturers also embrace this form of price reduction because it lets them offer price cuts to consumers directly. With a traditional wholesale price cut from its vendors, retailers can keep the price on the shelf the same and pocket the difference. Rebates can also be rolled out and shut off quickly. That allows manufacturers to fine-tune inventories or respond quickly to competitors without actually cutting prices. Finally, because buyers are required to fill out forms with names, addresses, and other data, rebates become a great way for vendors to build a customer data warehouse. From the retailer's perspective, rebates are more advantageous than coupons since they increase demand in the same way coupons may, but the retailer has no handling costs.

Leasing For some products, discounts, coupons, and rebates may not be sufficient to bring the price to within consumers' reach. With a lease, consumers pay a fee to purchase the right to use a product for a specific amount of time. They never own the product, they are just renting it. Leasing products opens up new, less price-sensitive target markets. Some consumers also like leases because they get tired of the product before its useful life is over, and they don't have to worry about selling it, trading it, or throwing it away. Car companies have used leasing options for years to appeal to consumers who plan to keep their cars for only a few years and will want to trade in for a new model sooner rather than later. Other industries are recognizing that what works for Toyotas and Chevy trucks also works for gowns, handbags, art, and luxury cars.

Price Bundling When you signed up for your high-speed Internet connection, did you also get cable TV and telephone? If so, you probably pay less than if you were to get the three services separately. This practice of selling more than one product for a single, lower price is called price bundling.[11] Firms bundle products or services together to encourage customers to stock up so they won't purchase competing brands, to encourage trial of a new product, or to provide an incentive to purchase a less desirable product or service to obtain a more desirable one in the same bundle.

Leader Pricing Leader pricing is a tactic that attempts to build store traffic by aggressively pricing and advertising a regularly purchased item, often priced at or just above the store's cost. Leader pricing fuels happy hours at restaurants and bars all over the country.

Maison Premiere in Brooklyn, New York, uses leader pricing on its oysters to build traffic, but makes a profit on other items customers order.

© Toss Heisler/The New York Times/Redux

At Maison Premiere in Brooklyn New York, customers down a selection of 15 different kinds of oysters, most priced at $1 per oyster, with $15 glasses of wine.[12] The rationale behind this tactic argues that, to get the great deal on oysters, the consumer will order other items that sell at a higher margin. The higher margins and profits on these other items then will more than cover the lower markup on the oysters. Leader pricing can be illegal under some circumstances though, as discussed subsequently in this chapter.

Price Lining When marketers establish a price floor and a price ceiling for an entire line of similar products and then set a few other price points in between to represent distinct differences in quality, the practice is called price lining. Imagine that you need a new dress shirt because you have an important job interview. You go to brooksbrothers.com and find similar-looking shirts for $92 (non-iron), $185 (Egyptian cotton), and $278 (luxury). Which are you going to buy? Are you going to risk the success of the interview by purchasing the least expensive shirt? Probably not. Will the interviewee be able to tell the difference between the $135 classic cotton and the $295 Sea Island cotton shirt? Probably not. You will probably purchase the middle-quality shirt because you don't want to look cheap, but you really can't afford the highest-priced shirt.[13]

Business Pricing Tactics and Discounts

Identify tactics used to reduce prices to businesses.

The pricing tactics employed in B2B settings differ significantly from those used in consumer markets. Among the most prominent are seasonal and cash discounts, allowances, quantity discounts, and uniform delivered versus zone pricing. (See Exhibit 15.3.)

Seasonal Discounts Unlike seasonal discounts offered to consumers, a seasonal discount to a business is an additional reduction offered as an incentive to retailers to order merchandise in advance of the normal buying season. For instance, Lennox may offer its air conditioner dealers an additional seasonal discount if they place their orders and receive delivery before April 1, prior to the warm months when air conditioner sales are highest. If it can ship earlier in the season, Lennox can plan its production schedules more easily and

EXHIBIT 15.3	Business-to-Business Pricing Tactics
Tactic	**Description**
Seasonal discounts	An additional reduction offered as an incentive to retailers to order merchandise in advance of the normal buying season.
Cash discounts	An additional reduction that reduces the invoice cost if the buyer pays the invoice prior to the end of the discount period.
Allowances	Advertising or slotting allowances (additional price reductions) offered in return for specific behaviors. Advertising allowances are offered to retailers if they agree to feature the manufacturer's product in their advertising and promotional efforts. Slotting allowances are offered to get new products into stores or to gain more or better shelf space.
Quantity discounts	Providing a reduced price according to the amount purchased.
Uniform delivered versus zone pricing	Uniform delivered price: shipper charges one rate, no matter where the buyer is located. Zone price: different prices depending on the geographical delivery area.

lessen its finished goods inventory. Its dealers, however, must weigh the benefits of a larger profit because of the discount versus the extra cost of carrying the inventory for a longer period of time.

Cash Discounts A **cash discount** reduces the invoice cost if the buyer pays the invoice prior to the end of the discount period. Typically, it is expressed in the form of a percentage, such as "3/10, n/30," or "3%, 10 days, net 30," which means the buyer can take a 3 percent discount on the total amount of the invoice if the bill is paid within 10 days of the invoice date; otherwise the full, or net, amount is due within 30 days. Why do B2B sellers offer cash discounts to customers? By encouraging early payment, they benefit from the time value of money. Getting money earlier rather than later enables the firm to either invest the money to earn a return on it or avoid borrowing money and paying interest on it. In both instances, the firm is better off financially.

Allowances Another pricing tactic that lowers the final cost to channel members is allowances, such as advertising or slotting allowances, offered in return for specific behaviors. An **advertising allowance** offers a price reduction to channel members if they agree to feature the manufacturer's product in their advertising and promotional efforts. Advertising allowances are legal as long they are available to all customers and not structured in such a way that they consistently and obviously favor one or a few buyers over others. **Slotting allowances** are fees paid to retailers simply to get new products into stores or to gain more or better shelf space for their products. Some argue that slotting allowances are unethical because they put small manufacturers that cannot readily afford allowances at a competitive disadvantage. Demanding large slotting allowances could be considered a form of bribery—"paying off" the retailer to get preferential treatment.

Quantity Discounts A **quantity discount** provides a reduced price according to the amount purchased. The more the buyer purchases, the higher the discount and, of course, the greater the value.

A **cumulative quantity discount** uses the amount purchased over a specified time period and usually involves several transactions. This type of discount particularly encourages resellers to maintain their current supplier because the cost to switch must include the loss of the discount. Recall that we noted that automobile dealers must buy the products they hope to sell to consumers from the manufacturer. They often attempt to meet a quota or a sales goal for a specific time period, such as a quarter or a year, because if they meet those quotas, they earn discounts on all the cars they purchased from the manufacturer, in the form of a cumulative quantity discount. For this very reason, you will often find good deals on cars at the end of a quarter or fiscal year. If the dealership can just sell a few more cars to meet its quota, the cumulative quantity discount earned can be substantial, so taking a few hundred dollars less on those last few cars is well worth the opportunity to receive a check worth many times the amount of the losses.

A **noncumulative quantity discount**, though still a quantity discount, is based only on the amount purchased in a single order. It therefore provides the buyer with an incentive to purchase more merchandise immediately. Such larger, less frequent orders can save manufacturers order processing, sales, and transportation expenses. For example, a retail store might get a 40 percent discount off the manufacturer's suggested retail price for placing a $500 order, a 50 percent discount for an order of $501 to $4,999, and a 60 percent discount for an order of greater than $5,000.

Uniform Delivered versus Zone Pricing These pricing tactics are specific to shipping, which represents a major cost for many manufacturers. With a **uniform delivered pricing** tactic, the shipper charges one rate, no matter where the buyer is located, which makes things very simple for both the seller and the buyer. **Zone pricing**, however, sets different prices depending on a geographical division of the delivery areas. For example, a manufacturer based in New York City might divide the United States into seven different zones and use different shipping rates for each zone to reflect the average shipping cost for customers located therein. This way, each customer in a zone is charged the same cost for shipping. Zone pricing can be advantageous to the shipper because it reflects the actual shipping charges more closely than uniform delivered pricing can.

PROGRESS CHECK

1. What are some consumer-oriented pricing tactics?
2. What are some B2B-oriented pricing tactics?

LO15-6 List the pricing practices that are illegal or unethical.

LEGAL AND ETHICAL ASPECTS OF PRICING

With so many different pricing strategies and tactics, it is no wonder that unscrupulous firms find ample opportunity to engage in pricing practices that can hurt consumers. We now take a look at some of the legal and ethical implications of pricing.

U.K.-based Tesco wasn't allowed to make the claim that it is "Britain's Biggest Discounter" because it was considered to be misleading. Such a claim probably would be considered puffery in the United States, and therefore would be allowed.
© Alex Segre/Alamy

Prices tend to fluctuate naturally and respond to varying market conditions. Thus, though we rarely see firms attempting to control the market in terms of product quality or advertising, they often engage in pricing practices that can unfairly reduce competition or harm consumers directly through fraud and deception. A host of laws and regulations at both the federal and state levels attempt to prevent unfair pricing practices, but some are poorly enforced, and others are difficult to prove.

Deceptive or Illegal Price Advertising

Although it is always illegal and unethical to lie in advertising, a certain amount of "puffery" is typically allowed (see Chapter 19).[14] But price advertisements should never deceive consumers to the point of causing harm. For example, a local car dealer's advertising that it had the "best deals in town" would likely be considered puffery. In contrast, advertising "the lowest prices, guaranteed" makes a very specific claim and, if not true, can be considered deceptive.

Deceptive Reference Prices Previously, we introduced reference prices, which create reference points for the buyer against which to compare the selling price. If the reference price is bona fide, the advertisement is informative. If the reference price has been inflated or is just plain fictitious, however, the advertisement is deceptive and may cause harm to consumers. But it is not easy to determine whether a reference price is bona fide. What standard should be used? If an advertisement specifies a "regular price," just what qualifies as regular? How many units must the store sell at this price for it to be a bona fide regular price—half the stock? A few? Just one? Finally, what if the store offers the item at the regular price but customers do not buy any? Can it still be considered a regular price? In general, if a seller is going to label a price as a regular price, the Better Business Bureau suggests that at least 50 percent of the sales have occurred at that price.[15]

Is this a legitimate sale, or is the retailer using deceptive reference prices?
© Jeff Greenberg/PhotoEdit

Loss-Leader Pricing As we discussed previously, leader pricing is a legitimate attempt to build store traffic by pricing a regularly purchased item aggressively but still above the store's cost. **Loss-leader pricing** takes this tactic one step further by lowering the price *below* the store's cost. No doubt you have seen "buy one, get one free" offers at grocery and discount stores. Unless the markup for the item is 100 percent of the cost, these sales obviously do not generate enough revenue from the sale of one unit to cover the store's cost for both units, which means it has essentially priced the total for both items below cost, unless the manufacturer is absorbing the cost of the promotion to generate volume. In some states, this form of pricing is illegal.

Bait and Switch Another form of deceptive price advertising occurs when sellers advertise items for a very low price without the intent to really sell any. This **bait-and-switch** tactic is a deceptive practice because the store lures customers in with a very low price on an item (the bait), only to aggressively pressure these customers into purchasing a higher-priced model (the switch) by disparaging the low-priced item, comparing it unfavorably with the higher-priced model, or professing an inadequate supply of the lower-priced item. Again, the laws against bait-and-switch practices are difficult to enforce because salespeople, simply as a function of their jobs, are always trying to get customers to trade up to a higher-priced model without necessarily deliberately baiting them. The key to proving deception centers on the intent of the seller, which is also difficult to prove.

Predatory Pricing

When a firm sets a very low price for one or more of its products with the intent to drive its competition out of business, it is using **predatory pricing**. Predatory pricing is illegal under both the Sherman Antitrust Act and the Federal Trade Commission Act because it constrains free trade and represents a form of unfair competition. It also tends to promote a concentrated market with a few dominant firms (an oligopoly).

But again, predation is difficult to prove. First, one must demonstrate intent; that is, that the firm intended to drive out its competition or prevent competitors from entering the market. Second, the complainant must prove that the firm charged prices lower than its average cost, an equally difficult task.

The issue of predatory pricing has arisen anew because of Google's dominance in the search engine market. Advertisers on Google bid on specific keywords; if they win the auction, their product appears first in the paid results section on the search engine. However, Google also includes a "quality handicap" and charges poor-quality advertisers more. It claims this tactic ensures that users are more likely to find high-quality results from their searches. The algorithm it uses to define quality is confidential, but some experts allege that Google has manipulated the paid search results in such a way that it undermines competitors' offerings while promoting its own. It appears these claims may be true; in 2012 the Federal Trade Commission (FTC) found enough evidence for search results manipulation that it recommended the government sue Google, and in 2013 a European Commission came to similar conclusions.[16] Despite significant documented evidence against Google, the FTC decided to close the case in 2015.[17] The unresolved question is: Because of Google's dominance in the search engine market, with its resulting ability to control prices, would its practice of charging more for its "quality handicap" be predatory?

Price Discrimination

There are many forms of price discrimination, but only some of them are considered illegal under the Clayton Act and the Robinson-Patman Act. When firms sell the same product to different resellers (wholesalers, distributors, or retailers) at different prices, it can be considered **price discrimination**; usually, larger firms receive lower prices.

Is this price discrimination illegal?
© Tom Prettyman/PhotoEdit

We have already discussed the use of quantity discounts, which is a legitimate method of charging different prices to different customers on the basis of the quantity they purchase. The legality of this tactic stems from the assumption that it costs less to sell and service 1,000 units to one customer than 100 units to 10 customers. But quantity discounts must be available to all customers and not be structured in such a way that they consistently and obviously favor one or a few buyers over others.

The Robinson-Patman Act does not apply to sales to end consumers, at which point many forms of price discrimination occur. For example, students and seniors often receive discounts on food and movie tickets, which is perfectly acceptable under federal law. Those engaged in online auctions like eBay are also practicing a legal form of price discrimination, because sellers are selling the same item to different buyers at various prices.

Price Fixing

Price fixing is the practice of colluding with other firms to control prices. Price fixing might be either horizontal or vertical. Whereas horizontal price fixing is clearly illegal under the Sherman Antitrust Act, vertical price fixing falls into a gray area.[18]

Horizontal price fixing occurs when competitors who produce and sell competing products or services collude, or work together, to control prices, effectively taking price out of the decision process for consumers. This practice clearly reduces competition and is illegal. Six South African airlines were accused of colluding to hike the price of fares for flights within the country during the World Cup.[19] The major tobacco companies also have been accused of colluding to fix the prices of cigarettes worldwide.[20] As a general rule of thumb, competing firms should refrain from discussing prices or terms and conditions of sale with competitors. If firms want to know competitors' prices, they can look at a competitor's advertisements, its websites, or its stores.

Vertical price fixing occurs when parties at different levels of the same marketing channel (e.g., manufacturers and retailers) agree to control the prices passed on to consumers. Manufacturers often encourage retailers to sell their merchandise at a specific price, known as the **manufacturer's suggested retail price (MSRP)**. Manufacturers set MSRP prices to reduce retail price competition among retailers, stimulate retailers to provide complementary services, and support the manufacturer's merchandise. Manufacturers enforce MSRPs by withholding benefits such as cooperative advertising or even refusing to deliver merchandise to noncomplying retailers. The Supreme Court has ruled that the ability of a manufacturer to require retailers to sell merchandise at MSRP should be decided on a case-by-case basis, depending on the individual circumstances.[21]

According to the U.S. Department of Justice, Apple and several publishing agencies have engaged in vertical price fixing, as outlined in Ethical and Societal Dilemma 15.1.

As these legal issues clearly demonstrate, pricing decisions involve many ethical considerations. In determining their pricing strategies and their pricing tactics, marketers must always balance their goal of inducing customers, through price, to find value and the need to deal honestly and fairly with those same customers. Whether another business or an individual consumer, buyers can be influenced by a variety of pricing methods. It is up to marketers to determine which of these methods works best for the seller, the buyer, and the community.

Gray Market Pricing Channels can be very difficult to manage, and distribution outside normal channels does occur. A **gray market** employs irregular but not necessarily illegal methods; generally, it legally circumvents authorized channels of distribution to sell goods at prices lower than those intended by the manufacturer.[22] Many manufacturers of consumer electronics therefore require retailers to sign an agreement that demands certain activities (and prohibits others) before the retailers may become authorized dealers. But if a retailer has too many high-definition televisions in stock, it may sell them at just above its

Ethical & Societal Dilemma 15.1

The Verdict: Apple Conspired to Raise Prices on eBooks[iii]

In a long-running court case, Amazon, Apple, a group of book publishers, and customers fought a tough battle over the price of reading.

Compared with Amazon, Apple was a late entrant to the ebook market. Amazon, with its Kindle devices and well-known reputation as a bookseller (which was how the online giant started), dominated the market of books sold to be read on Kindles as well as on other devices, including Apple's phones and tablets. Amazon also offered great prices, with many popular titles priced at under $10. Faced with this tremendous dominance, Apple believed it needed to find a way to compete. It worked with five major book publishers to decide on a minimum price below which they would not sell. With the agreement, publishers like Simon & Schuster, Penguin, and Macmillan began insisting on higher prices for their titles, and Apple took a percentage of each sale. This pricing method also meant that Amazon had to raise the prices it charged consumers, because it was paying more for the rights to the electronic content.

Amazon immediately brought the situation to the attention of the U.S. Department of Justice, alleging that the agreement represented price fixing and illegal conspiracy. Apple defended its actions vigorously; by entering a market that had been essentially a monopoly, with Amazon as the only seller, Apple asserted that it was increasing competition, not harming it. It also alleged that the effect on the price was not the issue. Whether its entry led to higher or lower prices, the key point—according to Apple's argument—was that, previously, consumers had only one source for ebooks, and now they had two, and that was an improvement.

Various levels of the U.S. court system have disagreed with Apple's assertions though, and recently the U.S. Supreme Court refused to hear an appeal. Thus the most recent decision by the lower appellate court stands. That decision establishes that the agreement among Apple and the five big publishers represented collusion. Previously the publishers had been forced by Amazon to sell at low prices. The deal with Apple benefited them by allowing them to charge what they wanted. It also benefited Apple, which received a percentage of each sale. But the Court's interest is mostly in the effects on consumers, and for those stake-

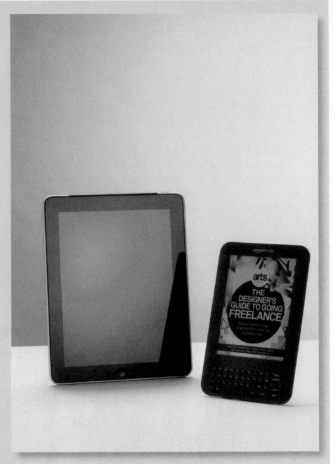

Who will ultimately win the Apple/Amazon pricing war? Currently, the court's decision is that the agreement among Apple and the five big publishers represents collusion.
© Joby Sessions/Computer Arts Magazine/Getty Images

holders, the conspiracy had negative effects in the form of higher prices.

As a result, Apple is liable to pay a $450 million settlement to ebook consumers. The publishers already had settled with the government.

own cost to an unauthorized discount dealer. This move places the merchandise in the market at prices far below what authorized dealers can charge and in the long term may tarnish the image of the manufacturer if the discount dealer fails to provide sufficient return policies, support, service, and so forth.

To discourage this type of gray market distribution, many manufacturers have resorted to large disclaimers on their websites, packaging, and other communications to warn consumers that the manufacturer's product warranty becomes null and void unless the item has been purchased from an authorized dealer. Another method is to equalize worldwide prices so the gray market advantage evaporates, as we describe in Ethical and Societal Dilemma 15.2.

Ethical & Societal Dilemma 15.2   Impeding the Gray Market for Luxury Goods[iv]

The euro is lower than it has been in over a decade. As a result, for Asian shoppers seeking Italian designer clothing or French handbags, it is literally worth the cost of flying to Milan and Paris to buy the items there rather than shopping in Shanghai. Prices are nearly always lower in the country of origin, because there are no customs or import duties to pay, and transportation is relatively inexpensive. Currently, prices for Chanel items in China are approximately 63 percent higher than prices for comparable items sold in Paris. When the item is a €4,000 handbag, this difference is great enough that a shopper from Beijing could buy a ticket to Paris, fly over, purchase the bag, and fly home—and still save money compared with buying the item in the local store.

An alternative to a shopping trip to Europe is to buy at home in the gray market. Because of the vast gap between their European and Asian prices, gray market players can readily buy up goods at the lower European cost, increase the price slightly—still remaining below the Asian retail level—and

earn massive profits by selling it in China on the gray market. China's well-known Taobao shopping site is a ready source for such gray market goods.

Although this gray market does move a lot of merchandise, it is not in the best interest of the European luxury goods manufacturers. Their reputation is diminished by having merchandise sold at lower prices through nontraditional channels. Service is nonexistent in such markets, and warranties are null and void. If the gray market thrives, their traditional channels suffer as customers are drawn to the cheaper prices. Ultimately, customers might no longer find value in traditional stores.

In response to these market developments, Chanel has announced it will be raising its retail prices in Europe but cutting them in China. In so doing, it seeks to level the playing field so that the same handbag costs approximately the same amount wherever people buy it. In the end, who benefits from the gray market?

In an attempt to equalize prices across global markets, Chanel is raising its retail prices in Europe but cutting them in China.

© David Hogsholt/Reportage/Getty Images

PROGRESS CHECK

1. What common pricing practices are considered to be illegal or unethical?

Reviewing Learning Objectives

LO15-1 Identify three methods that firms use to set their prices.

The various methods of setting prices have their advantages and disadvantages. The three primary methods are cost based, competition based, and value based. The cost-based techniques are quick and easy but fail to reflect the competitive environment or consumer demand. Although it is always advisable to be aware of what competitors are doing, using competition-based pricing should not occur in isolation without dealing with cost considerations and consumer reactions. Taking a value-based approach to pricing, whether the improvement value, the total cost of ownership approach, or the experimental approach described in Chapter 10 in conjunction with these other methods provides a nicely balanced method of setting prices.

LO15-2 Describe the difference between an everyday low pricing (EDLP) strategy and a high/low strategy.

An everyday low pricing strategy is maintained when a product's price stays relatively constant at a level that is slightly lower than the regular price from competitors using a high/low strategy, and is less frequently discounted. Customers enjoy an everyday low pricing strategy because they know that the price will always be the about the same and will be and a better price than the competition's. High/low pricing strategy starts out with a product at one (higher) price, and then discounts the product. This strategy first attracts a less price-sensitive customer who pays the regular price, and then a very price-sensitive customer who pays the low price.

LO15-3 Explain the difference between a price skimming and a market penetration pricing strategy.

When firms use a price skimming strategy, the product or service must be perceived as breaking new ground, or customers will not pay more than what they pay for other products. Firms use price skimming to signal high quality, limit demand, recoup their investment quickly, and/or test people's price sensitivity. Moreover, it is easier to price high initially and then lower the price than vice versa. Market penetration, in contrast, helps firms build sales and market share quickly, which may discourage other firms from entering the market. Building demand quickly also typically results in lowered costs as the firm gains experience making the product or delivering the service.

LO15-4 Identify tactics used to reduce prices to consumers.

Marketers use a variety of tactics to provide lower prices to consumers. The tactics include markdowns, quantity discounts, seasonal discounts, coupons, rebates, leasing, price bundling, leader pricing, and price lining. For example, leader pricing involves retailers pricing certain products or services at very low prices, with the hope that these same customers will also buy other, more profitable items.

LO15-5 Identify tactics used to reduce prices to businesses.

Seasonal discounts give retailers an incentive to buy prior to the normal selling season, cash discounts prompt them to pay their invoices early, and allowances attempt to get retailers to advertise the manufacturer's product or stock a new product. In addition, quantity discounts can cause retailers to purchase a larger quantity over a specific period of time or with a particular order. Finally, zone pricing bases the cost of shipping the merchandise on the distance between the retailer and the manufacturer—the farther away, the more it costs.

LO15-6 List the pricing practices that are illegal or unethical.

There are almost as many ways to get into trouble by setting or changing a price as there are pricing strategies and tactics. Some common legal issues pertain to advertising deceptive prices. Specifically, if a firm compares a reduced price with a "regular" or reference price, it must actually have sold that product or service at the regular price. Bait and switch is another form of deceptive price advertising, where sellers advertise items for a very low price without the intent to really sell any at that price. Collusion among firms to fix prices is always illegal.

Key Terms

LEARNSMART

- advertising allowance, 471
- bait and switch, 473
- cash discount, 471
- competition-based pricing method, 461
- cost-based pricing method, 460
- cost of ownership method, 462
- coupon, 468
- cumulative quantity discount, 471
- everyday low pricing (EDLP), 464
- experience curve effect, 466
- gray market, 474
- high/low pricing, 465
- horizontal price fixing, 474
- improvement value, 461

Marketing Digitally

1. Go to www.coupons.com. In which product categories does this website offer coupons? Choose a product from each category.
   - How effective are coupons for selling these types of products? Why?
   - Do any sellers offer rebates through this website? Why or why not?
   - What are the benefits to the seller of using Coupons.com instead of offering coupons in a newspaper?
   - How do you think Coupons.com makes money? For example, consider what companies are advertising on the site. Do the same companies who advertise on their site offer coupons?

2. Visit the website for Bag, Borrow, or Steal (www.bagborroworsteal.com) and select handbags. Click on the "Handbags," then choose "Gucci," in the Designer category on the left column, and then "Sort by" Price. What is the difference between Gucci's highest and lowest priced bags? Notice that if a product says "Waitlist," it has already been borrowed, but if it says "Borrow," then it is available for you to borrow. Are the bags that are waitlisted the highest priced or the lowest priced? How would you determine the price it charges to rent a bag?

Marketing Applications

1. Suppose you have been hired as the pricing manager for a drugstore chain that typically adds a fixed percentage onto the cost of each product to arrive at the retail price. Evaluate this technique. What would you do differently?

2. Some high-fashion retailers, notably H&M and Zara, sell what some call "disposable fashion"—apparel priced so reasonably low that it can be disposed of after just a few wearings. Here is your dilemma: You have an important job interview and need a new suit. You can buy the suit at one of these stores for $129 or at Brooks Brothers for $500. Of course, the Brooks Brothers suit is of higher quality and will therefore last longer. How would you use the two value-based approaches described in this chapter to determine which suit to buy?

3. A phone manufacturer is determining a price for its product, using a cost-based pricing strategy. The fixed costs are $100,000, and the variable costs are $50,000. If 1,000 units are produced and the company wants to have a 30 percent markup, what is the price of the phone?

4. Identify two stores at which you shop, one of which uses everyday low pricing and another that uses a high/low pricing strategy. Do you believe that each store's chosen strategy is appropriate for the type of merchandise it sells and the market of customers to whom it is appealing? Justify your answer.

5. As the product manager for Whirlpool's line of washing machines, you are in charge of pricing new products. Your product team has developed a revolutionary new washing machine that relies on radically new technology and requires very little water to get clothes clean. This technology will likely be difficult for your competition to copy. Should you adopt a skimming or a penetration pricing strategy? Justify your answer.

6. What is the difference between a cumulative and a noncumulative quantity discount?

7. If you worked for a manufacturing firm located in Oregon and shipped merchandise all over the United States, which would be more advantageous, a zone or a uniform delivered pricing policy? Why? What if your firm were located in Kansas—would it make a difference?

8. Coupons and rebates benefit different distribution channel members. Which would you prefer if you were a manufacturer, a retailer, and a consumer? Why?

9. Suppose the president of your university got together with the presidents of all the universities in your athletic conference for lunch. They discussed what each university was going to charge for tuition the following year. Are they in violation of federal laws? Explain your answer.

10. Imagine that you are the newly hired brand manager for a restaurant that is about to open. Both the local newspaper and a gourmet food magazine recently ran articles about your new head chef, calling her one of the best young chefs in the country. In response to these positive reviews, the company wants to position its brand as a premium, gourmet restaurant. Your boss asks what price you should charge for the chef's signature filet mignon dish. Other restaurants in the area charge around $40 for their own filet offerings. What steps might you undertake to determine what the new price should be?

11. You have been hired by a regional supermarket chain as the candy and snack buyer. Your shelves are dominated by national firms such as Wrigley's and Nabisco. The chain imposes a substantial slotting fee to allow new items to be added to their stock selection. Management reasons that it costs a lot to add and delete items, and besides, these slotting fees are a good source of revenue. A small, minority-operated, local firm produces several potentially interesting snack crackers and a line of gummy candy, all with natural ingredients, added vitamins, reduced sugar, and a competitive price—and they also happen to taste great. You'd love to give the firm a chance, but its managers claim the slotting fee is too high. Should your firm charge slotting fees? Are slotting fees fair to the relevant shareholders—customers, stockholders, vendors?

Quiz Yourself

1. A(n) _____ strategy is attractive because it attracts two distinct market segments: customers who are not price-sensitive customers and customers who are price sensitive.
   a. cost-based pricing
   b. high/low pricing
   c. predatory pricing
   d. EDLP
   e. competitor-based pricing

2. When using a market penetration strategy, as sales continue to grow, the costs continue to drop, allowing even further reductions in the price. This is due to
   a. markdowns.
   b. price lining.
   c. seasonal discounts.
   d. improvement value.
   e. experience curve effects.

(Answers to these two questions can be found in the Quiz Yourself Answer Key section.)

Chapter Case Study

PIZZA PLAYERS, PIZZA PRICES

For most of us, "pizza wars" suggest the fight over which toppings to put on a shared pie. But in truth, the pizza industry is in the midst of a battle, for which the weapons of choice are mainly pricing tactics. In addition to the small, local pizzerias that appear in nearly every town, there are four major chains that pursue pizza-loving consumers in the United States (see Exhibit 15.4), a massive market in which approximately 1 in 8 people eat pizza on any particular day.[23] Running the gamut from a low-price promise to a higher price and higher quality appeal, these four chains all seek to price their offerings in ways that promise to increase their sales and market share.

How exactly are they doing so? Let's consider their pricing tactics in turn, moving in order from the smallest of the big four (in terms of market share) to the biggest.

Papa John's With its well-known spokespeople, from Peyton Manning and J.J. Watt to the founder himself, "Papa" John Schnatter, Papa John's is a familiar name to many advertising viewers, even though it accounts for only about 6 percent of the national market. Along with these recognizable faces, Papa John's has established a motto and tagline that most consumers can repeat from memory: "Better Ingredients, Better Pizza." In accordance with this focus on quality, Papa John's rarely tries to offer the lowest price in

EXHIBIT 15.4 Top Pizza Chains by Market Share

Source: Andrew Alvarez, "BISWorld Industry Report OD4320 Pizza Restaurants in the US," IBISWorld, November 2015.

a market. Constantly lowering prices means, according to Schnatter, that "you are either serving ingredients that are not high quality or you're putting less on."[24] Arguing that it is not willing to make such quality-related sacrifices, Papa John's says that it will never seek to reach the $5 pizza threshold that many of its national competitors offer.

But to gain ground, it cannot just ignore the price interests of its consumers. In response, Papa John's promises that if consumers order one large pizza at the regular price, they can get a second for just $.50.[25] The combined deal still remains above that $5 threshold, but it brings the overall cost to consumers more in line with competitors' prices. Furthermore, Papa John's has introduced a quality guarantee: Any consumer dissatisfied with the quality of the pie he or she receives may call the store within a half-hour to complain. That complaint automatically gives them the option of getting another delivery immediately or having their account credited, such that they may receive another pie for free in the future.

Finally, Papa John's seeks to introduce various innovations to get people calling for an order. For example, during a recent one-month promotional run, it offered the Brookie—a combination chocolate chip cookie and brownie—for $6 with the order of any pizza.[26]

Little Caesars Little Caesars also has a well-known tagline ("Pizza! Pizza!"), but its offer is premised almost completely on convenience. With a different business model than any of the other big players in the market, the restaurant chain promises that its food is "hot and ready," thus eliminating the need to place an order. At the moment a consumer walks in to a store, the pizza will be ready for her or him to take, for just about $5. For a little more, they can upgrade their pie, such as selecting the cheese-stuffed crust or bacon-wrapped deep-dish versions.

In parallel with this relatively simple sales model, Little Caesars embraces a sort of absurdist image. Its advertising often features unrealistic or fantastic sequences, such as when two disembodied heads floated above a pie in a campaign to introduce the new cheese-stuffed crust.[27] To promote the notion that avoiding ordering is more convenient—even though it requires consumers to go out and pick up their food, rather than having it delivered to them at home—another advertising campaign shows a couple desperately trying to remember the password for an online ordering site, typing in name after name of the hundreds of cats who appear to be living in the house with them.

It also likes to play with its "underdog," overlooked status, despite its prominence.[28] In one promotion, it promised an even lower price—free—if any team that was seeded sixteenth in the men's college basketball tournament won in the first round, which would mean that it would have unseated the top ranked team in its division.[29] The risk was relatively low, considering that no team has ever done so. Still, it put the idea in people's minds and offered the chance of a free Hot-N-Ready lunch if the upset occurred. (It didn't.)

Domino's While Papa John's focuses on quality and Little Caesars goes for convenience, Domino's is relying on its delivery reputation and its head start in terms of mobile commerce capabilities to compete more effectively for orders. In the past, Domino's was known for its promise to deliver pizzas in 30 minutes or less, though it ultimately removed the guarantee for safety reasons. Still, it built its reach throughout the market by promising to make it easy for people at home to get their pizza fix. That reputation continues to inform its approach to growth today.

By "utilizing mobile better than their competitors,"[30] Domino's restaurants make it easy for tech-savvy consumers to gain access to the offerings. For example, its well-developed Pizza Tracker app, which is available on all the major mobile platforms, gives users one-touch ordering functions. Then the app keeps consumers appraised of the progress of their pie, constantly updating the expected delivery times. It also has begun experimenting with other mobile channels, such as Snapchat, seeking to find ways to connect with consumers in unexpected, entertaining, and more appealing channels and manners.[31]

In the course of developing these mobile capabilities, Domino's pricing strategy has not changed substantively. As one spokesperson noted, in response to new promotions by Pizza Hut, Domino's does not "play the price or product-of-the-month gimmick game others seem to. The limited-time-only tactic is something we left behind years ago."[32] Instead, since about 2010, Domino's has continued to offer the same baseline: medium cheese pizzas for around $5.99 each. Increasing the size or adding more toppings increases the price, but the pricing is clearly transparent and mostly consistent over time and geographic locations.

Pizza Hut And finally we come to the biggest player, the world's largest pizza chain. Pizza Hut started the most recent pizza war by creating a new pricing and promotion initiative. As long as consumers bought at least one other item (e.g., breadsticks, wings, another pizza), they could get a medium, one-topping pizza for just $5.[33] The promotion is part of the launch of a wider, $5 "flavor menu" that includes multiple options. Similar to single-price menus in other fast food settings, this approach allows consumers to decide which items they prefer to purchase for their set budget. One consumer might want the variety of wings and pizza, another might need a couple of pizzas to feed multiple people, and yet another could want both a meal and a dessert.

With its more than 15,000 stores, Pizza Hut enjoys vast reach, excellent brand awareness, and a market-leading position. It also asserts that it has been "serving the same great-tasting pizza, at a great value" for its entire history.[34] Yet for several quarters, the performance of the chain had not met the expectations of either its investors or its corporate brand owner, Yum Brands. To address these concerns, Pizza Hut not only introduced its new price promotion but also adopted a "focused emphasis on making it easier to get a better pizza."[35]

The Rest of the Market Of course, local pizzerias also remain in play. Unlike many local retailers, restaurants offer greatly differentiated options. For consumers who want a basic meal, the large chains offer consistency at a reasonable price, but for those who want something unique and different on their plates, the local pizzeria generally has represented a more appealing option. Patxi's is a chain operating 17 restaurants in California, Colorado, and Washington that is small enough that it can still be considered "local." Unlike its national competitors vying for the five dollars per pie market, Patxi's is a full-service sit-down restaurant that serves gourmet Chicago-style deep dish and New York style pizzas made from fresh, natural ingredients with no preservatives. There is no rushing these pizzas, which can take up to 40 minutes to serve. Pizzas can run up to $28. An order of Brussels sprouts is $14, and salads can run up to $15—a far cry from the basic $5 offering of the national chains.[36]

Besides their relatively low prices, the national chains have also increased the convenience of ordering by using online and mobile systems, which is cutting into the local pizzeria's market. These ordering systems are quick and easy. Consumers do not need to worry about having all their topping preferences ready to shout out quickly, to a harried and possibly rude order taker. Nor do they need to be concerned that someone will mishear their desire for "pepperocini" and load up their pizza with "pepperoni" instead. Once they plug in their credit card information, those data get stored, so ordering the next time around is even more convenient and quick. Faced with such efficient systems, many of the small restaurants simply cannot compete on price or fast service.[37]

Patxi's is a small pizzeria chain operating in California, Colorado, and Washington. It is a full-service sit-down restaurant serving gourmet pizzas made from fresh, natural ingredients with no preservatives. Its prices are commensurate with its quality.

Courtesy of Patxi

Most local pizzerias can't afford to establish their own online ordering systems, which would require significant investments in software, technology, and new staff. As an alternative, some restaurants turn to intermediaries like GrubHub or Seamless, which link hungry customers with various food purveyors on a single platform. Such platforms enable online ordering, but they also charge the restaurants a percentage of their sales.

The number of small pizza stores in operation has decreased by nearly 7 percent in recent years. Their best bet to compete with the national chains is to differentiate themselves with great and unusual offerings coupled with an interesting dining experience.

The Results In recent quarters, Papa John's announced a 5 percent growth rate.[38] Little Caesars' sales increased from $2.9 million to $3.4 million over a two-year period.[39] Domino's enjoyed 13 percent revenue growth. Pizza Hut reported flat sales.[40] Will the outcome of the pizza battle change these trends?

Questions

1. Which pricing tactics does each company utilize? Evaluate the effectiveness of each one of these tactics for the particular pizza chain.

2. How might the current price wars change the pricing tactics used by the major pizza chains?

Endnotes

1. Brooks Barnes, "Disney Introduces Demand-Based Pricing at Theme Parks," *The New York Times*, February 27, 2016.

2. Thomas T. Nagle, John E. Hogan, and Joseph Zale, *The Strategy and Tactics of Pricing: A Guide to Growing More Profitability*, 5th ed. (Upper Saddle River, NJ: Pearson, 2010).

3. R. Hamilton and A. Chernev, "Low Prices Are Just the Beginning: Price Image in Retail Management," *Journal of Marketing* 77, no. 6 (2013), pp. 1–20; Dinesh K. Gauri, Minakshi Trivedi, and Dhruv Grewal, "Understanding the Determinants of Retail Strategy: An Empirical Analysis," *Journal of Retailing* 84, no. 3 (2008), pp. 256–67.

4. Michael Levy, Barton A. Weitz, and Dhruv Grewal, *Retailing Management,* 9th ed. (Burr Ridge, IL: Irwin/McGraw-Hill, 2014).

5. Abhijit Biswas et al., "Consumer Evaluations of Sale Prices: Role of the Subtraction Principle," *Journal of Marketing* 77, no. 4 (2013), pp. 49–66.

6. http://www.amazon.com.

7. Eric A. Staub, "As Prices Fall, Blu-Ray Players Are Invited Home," *The New York Times,* December 13, 2009.

8. Nailya Ordabayeva and Pierre Chandon, "Predicting and Managing Consumers' Package Size Impressions," *Journal of Marketing* 77, no. 5 (2013), pp. 123–37; Xiaoyan Deng and Raji Srinivasan, "When Do Transparent Packages Increase (or Decrease) Food Consumption?" *Journal of Marketing* 77, no. 4 (2013), pp. 104–17; Sha Yang and Priya Raghubir, "Can Bottles Speak Volumes? The Effect of Package Shape on How Much to Buy," *Journal of Retailing* 81, no. 4 (2005), pp. 269–81.

9. This section is adapted from Michael Levy, Barton A. Weitz, and Dhruv Grewal, *Retailing Management,* 9th ed. (Burr Ridge, IL: Irwin/McGraw-Hill, 2014).

10. Personal communication with Rob Price, VP of Retail Marketing, CVS, June 16, 2009.

11. Marco Bertini and Luc Wathieu, "Research Note: Attention Arousal through Price Partitioning," *Marketing Science* 27, no. 2 (2008), pp. 236–46; Rebecca W. Hamilton and Joydeep Srivastava, "When 2+2 Is Not the Same as 1+3: Variations in Price Sensitivity across Components of Partitioned Prices," *Journal of Marketing Research* 45, no. 4 (2008), pp. 450–61.

12. Karen Stabiner, "Loss Leaders on the Half Shell, *The New York Times,* February 22, 2014.

13. http://www.brooksbrothers.com.

14. Alison Jing Xu and Robert S. Wyer Jr., "Puffery in Advertisements: The Effects of Media Context, Communication Norms and Consumer Knowledge," *Journal of Consumer Research,* August 2010.

15. J. Lindsey-Mullikin and R. D. Petty, "Marketing Tactics Discouraging Price Search: Deception and Competition," *Journal of Business Research* 64, no. 1 (2011), pp. 67–73. doi: 10.1016/j.jbusres.2009.10.003.

16. Steve Lohr, "Drafting Antitrust Case, F.T.C. Raises Pressure on Google," *The New York Times,* October 12, 2012, http://www.nytimes.com; Claire Cain Miller, "Europeans Reach Deal with Google on Searches," *The New York Times,* April 14, 2013, http://www.nytimes.com.

17. Brody Mullins, Rolfe Winkler, and Brent Kendall, "Inside the U.S. Antitrust Probe of Google," *The Wall Street Journal,* March 19, 2915.

18. Daniel M. Garrett, Michelle Burtis, and Vandy Howell, "Economics of Antitrust: An Economic Analysis of Resale Price Maintenance," http://www.GlobalCompetitionReview.com, 2008; Stephen Labaton, "Century-Old Ban Lifted on Minimum Retail Pricing," *The New York Times,* June 29, 2007.

19. "South African Airlines to Be Investigated for Alleged World Cup Price-Fixing, Report DialAFlight," *Business Wire,* February 1, 2010.

20. Tom Bawden, "Bloody Nose for OFT in Row over Tobacco Price-Fixing," *The Independent* (London), December 13, 2011, http://www.independent.co.uk; "The Marlboro Cartel," http://tobacco.cleartheair.org.hk/wp-content/uploads/2012/01/Smokingate2.pdf.

21. Daniel M. Garrett, Michelle Burtis, and Vandy Howell, "Economics of Antitrust: An Economic Analysis of Resale Price Maintenance," http://www.GlobalCompetitionReview.com, 2008; Stephen Labaton, "Century-Old Ban Lifted on Minimum Retail Pricing," *The New York Times,* June 29, 2007.

22. *Merriam-Webster's Dictionary of Law,* 1996.

23. Hollis Johnson, "We Taste-Tested Pizzas from Papa John's, Pizza Hut, and Domino's—Here's Who Does It Best," *Business Insider,* November 13, 2015.

24. Aamer Madhani, "Papa John's Tries New Tack to Challenge Pizza Hut, Domino's for Pizza Supremacy," *USA Today,* January 30, 2016.

25. Fast Food, "2016 Pizza Wars: Who Will Win," February 12, 2016, http://www.fastfoodmenuprices.com/2016-pizza-war-who-will-win/.

26. Fast Food, "Papa John's Rings 2016 with the Launching of its New Dessert," February 12, 2016, http://www.fastfoodmenuprices.com/2016-pizza-war-who-will-win/.

27. Erik Oster, "Barton F. Graf Hypes Little Caesars Stuffed Crust Deep! Deep! Dish with 'Faces'," *Ad Week,* March 25, 2016, http://www.adweek.com/agencyspy/barton-f-graf-hypes-little-caesars-stuffed-crust-deep-deep-dish-with-faces/105328.

28. Jonathan Maze, "The Most Underappreciated Growth Restaurant in the Country," *Nation's Restaurant News,* July 22, 2015, http://nrn.com/blog/most-underappreciated-growth-restaurant-country.

29. Brian Manzullo, "Little Caesars Will Give You Free Lunch if No. 16 Seed Scores an Upset," *Detroit Free Press,* March 16, 2016.

30. Rebecca Borison, "Domino's Earns Customer Loyalty with Mobile at the Forefront," *Mobile Commerce Daily,* October 21, 2013, http://www.mobilecommercedaily.com/domino's-leads-the-mobile-way-for-pizza-chains.

31. Seb Joseph, "Domino's Says Its Snapchat Test Led to a 'Surprising' Surge in Pizza Orders," *Business Insider,* February 18, 2016.

32. Chris Isidore, "Pizza War! Pizza Hut and Papa John's Slash Prices," *CNN Money,* January 4, 2016.

33. Ibid.

34. Madhani, "Papa John's Tries New Tack to Challenge Pizza Hut, Domino's for Pizza Supremacy."

35. Monica Watrous, "Pizza Hut's Performance Warms Up," *Food Business News,* February 5, 2016, http://www.foodbusinessnews.net/articles/news_home/Financial-Performance/2016/02/Pizza_Huts_performance_warms_u.aspx?ID=%7B406380A3-B93E-4EAA-A162-97E225B69B2E%7D&cck=1.

36. Patxispizza.com.

37. Julie Jargon, "Big Chains Use Web Ordering to Slice Out Bigger Market Share," *The Wall Street Journal,* February 6, 2014, http://online.wsj.com.

38. Isidore, "Pizza War! Pizza Hut and Papa John's Slash Prices."

39. Jonathan Maze, "The Most Underappreciated Growth Restaurant in the Country," *Nation's Restaurant News,* July 22, 2015, http://nrn.com/blog/most-underappreciated-growth-restaurant-country.

40. Isidore, "Pizza War! Pizza Hut and Papa John's Slash Prices."

i. Maureen Morrison and Matthew Creamer, "How P&G, Ford, and Wendy's Are Redefining Value," *Advertising Age,* April 22, 2013.

ii. Elizabeth A. Harris and Stephanie Strom, "Walmart to Sell Organic Food, Undercutting Big Brands," *The New York Times,* April 10, 2014, http://www.nytimes.com; Dan Charles, "Can Wal-Mart Really Make Organic Food Cheap for Everyone?" *NPR,* April 19, 2014, http://www.wbur.org/npr/; Steven Overly, "Wal-Mart Plans to Bring Its Compete-on-Price Approach to Organic Food: Here's How," *The Washington Post,* April 10, 2014, http://www.washingtonpost.com.

iii. Adam Liptak and Vindu Goel, "Supreme Court Declines to Hear Apple's Appeal in E-Book Pricing Case," *The New York Times,* March 7, 2016; Reuters, "Supreme Court Rejects Apple e-Books Price-Fixing Appeal," *The New York Times,* March 8, 2016.

iv. Jason Chow and Nadya Masidlover, "Chanel Acts on Prices as Euro Worsens Gray Market," *The Wall Street Journal,* March 17, 2015.

VALUE DELIVERY: DESIGNING THE CHANNEL AND SUPPLY CHAIN

CHAPTER 16
Supply Chain and Channel Management

CHAPTER 17
Retailing and Omnichannel Marketing

Section Six deals with the value delivery system. It is critical that merchandise is delivered in time to stores to meet customer demand. To achieve this, retailers have initiated many innovative programs with their vendors and have developed sophisticated transportation and warehousing systems. We devote two chapters to value delivery. Chapter 16 takes a look at marketing channels and how to manage the supply chain, while Chapter 17 concentrates on retailing and omnichannel marketing.

CHAPTER 16

SUPPLY CHAIN AND CHANNEL MANAGEMENT

LEARNING OBJECTIVES

After reading this chapter, you should be able to:

LO16-1 Understand the importance of marketing channels and supply chain management.

LO16-2 Understand the difference between direct and indirect marketing channels.

LO16-3 Describe how marketing channels are managed.

LO16-4 Describe the flow of information and merchandise in the marketing channel.

In its efforts to provide "affordable solutions for better living," the Swedish furniture retailer IKEA has radically changed the way many people furnish and decorate their homes. As the chain grew and spread, from its single-operation origins in Sweden to a global presence of more than 350 stores in nearly 50 countries,[1] it has prompted millions of customers to regard furniture as something they can put together on their own rather than as items they should purchase preassembled. In addition to this innovative approach to selling furniture, which moves responsibility for the assembly process further down the supply chain, to the customer, IKEA also embodies a modern approach to sustainability. Thus when devising shipping policies, it pursues both the lowest costs and the least negative impact on the environment.[2]

As a result of its innovative approaches, relatively inexpensive products, and appealing assortment of merchandise, IKEA is quite successful.[3] It is also determined to meet ambitious growth goals of $56.2 billion by 2020, which would require nearly 10 percent growth every year until then, compared to an average of around 5 percent in recent years.

How does an already large company literally double its growth rate? It starts by looking at the things it can control, including its supply chain practices. When the CEO of IKEA asserts, "We hate air," what he means is that the company wants to eliminate any dead spaces anywhere in its packaging and shipping containers.[4] Thus for example, it has redesigned a popular sofa to be sold in pieces instead of as a single unit. In so doing, it could fit all the pieces into a much smaller box, without any dead air in the box. The smaller boxes, in turn, allow the company to fit more units onto trucks, reducing the number of

trips required to restock stores—a significant reduction in transportation costs.

Size is not the only issue though; weight also increases transportation costs. Therefore, IKEA engineers have replaced solid table legs with hollow ones, reducing both the weight of the tables it was shipping and the amount of raw materials required to make them. In turn, it passed the cost savings on to customers, encouraging more people to purchase the lighter-weight but otherwise similar products.

The concern, according to several commentators, is that if IKEA pursues only the most efficient packing design, its famous reputation for requiring shoppers to spend all night putting their furniture together will eventually alienate customers. There is only so much frustration customers will accept in building their inexpensive furniture before they agree to pay a little more to receive an already completed bed or bookshelf. Accordingly, to help reduce this frustration, IKEA introduced the Regissör series, in which the products require very simple assembly, such as screwing legs into a table.[5]

Efficiency is not the only route to growth that IKEA is pursuing. It also plans to expand into new regions, such as India, and increase online sales and click-and-collect options that allow people to order online and pick up items in the stores. Furthermore, it strongly believes that its supply chain efficiency efforts ultimately lead to better products at better prices. Thus it hopes to put the right products in the right place with the lowest cost and the least damage to the environment. That's a nearly irresistible recipe for growth.

Accordingly, in this chapter, we discuss the third P in the marketing mix, *place*, which includes all activities required to get the right product to the right customer when that customer wants it.[6] As we noted in Chapter 1, **marketing channel management**, which also has been called **supply chain management**, refers to a set of approaches and techniques firms employ to efficiently and effectively integrate their suppliers, manufacturers, warehouses, stores, and transportation intermediaries into a seamless operation in which merchandise is produced and distributed in the right quantities, to the right locations, and at the right time, as well as to minimize systemwide costs while satisfying the service levels their customers require.[7] Students of marketing often overlook or underestimate the importance of place in the marketing mix simply because it happens behind the scenes. Yet marketing channel management adds value because it gets products to customers efficiently, quickly, and at low cost.

LO16-1 Understand the importance of marketing channels and supply chain management.

THE IMPORTANCE OF MARKETING CHANNEL/SUPPLY CHAIN MANAGEMENT

So far in this book we have reviewed the methods companies use to conduct in-depth market research, gain insights into consumer and business behaviors, segment markets, select the best target markets, develop new products and services, and set prices that provide good value. But even if firms execute these activities flawlessly, unless they can secure the placement of products in appropriate outlets in sufficient quantities exactly when customers want them, they are likely to fail. Adding Value 16.1 examines how Goya Foods recognized it needed to do a better job at getting products into stores to satisfy customers' demands and what it did about it.

Convincing wholesalers and retailers to carry new products can be more difficult than you might think. **Wholesalers** are firms that buy products from manufacturers and resell them to retailers; retailers sell products directly to consumers. Consider some familiar examples: Walmart is a massive retailer, and many of its products come from massive partners such as Procter & Gamble (P&G). In this relationship, Walmart certainly needs P&G to supply it with toothpaste, diapers, paper towels, and other consumer goods marketed under P&G's various brand names. But P&G also desperately needs Walmart to agree to stock its products, because the retailer represents its largest purchaser, accounting for about $12 billion in annual sales.[8] When P&G introduces a totally new product, such as teeth-whitening strips, it has to convince Walmart to create space in its stores for the innovation without giving up too much space for its other products.[9]

When P&G introduces a totally new product, such as teeth-whitening strips, it has to convince Walmart to create space in its stores for the innovation without giving up too much space for its other products.

© Tom Uhlman/AP Photo

Adding Value 16.1 The Beans May Be Slow Cooked, but the Delivery Is Quick[i]

As Goya Foods celebrated its 75th year in business, its top managers were dealing with some very serious growing pains. Selling a wide variety of Hispanic and Latin foods, the company had achieved a dominant market share, was the largest Hispanic-owned company in the United States, and had annual sales of around $1 billion. In specific local and regional markets, demand for its products was substantial—a great success that also came with a notable challenge.

That is, many of the markets that loved Goya products had slightly different preferences, reflecting the diversity of Hispanic consumers in the United States. People of Cuban heritage wanted items made somewhat differently than consumers whose families originated in Mexico, and so on. Thus, the number of unique inventory items or stock keeping units (SKUs) that Goya provided reached over 1,600. The supply chain network grew more complex. And in all the confusion, service levels, as measured by its in-stock availability, dropped. Quite simply, with all the complexity, buyers were spending too much time manually calculating and determining shipments and inventory levels, leaving them insufficient time or energy to think strategically. Making decisions without sophisticated analytics was not something that Goya could sustain anymore.

For Goya, the solution was to automate the transportation and inventory planning processes, using software that enabled it to keep track of demand, order fulfillment, and replenishment with minimal effort. By automating its ordering processes, Goya's buyers could work smarter. For example,

To satisfy its diverse market of Hispanic consumers, Goya expanded the number of unique inventory items it carried to 1,600. To keep service levels high, Goya implemented an automated transportation and inventory planning system.

© Goya Foods Inc

making sure delivery trucks were more efficiently used resulted in millions of dollars in transportation savings. The new system also improved its in-stock availability to 98 percent, which resulted in a proportional increase in sales.

For other wholesalers and manufacturers, the effort to convince Walmart to stock their products might be even more challenging, because they lack the leverage and power of P&G. For example, PenAgain, a small California-based manufacturer of ergonomic pens and other writing instruments, wanted to put its offerings in Walmart stores, but first it had to get Walmart to buy what it was selling.[10] After a tough selling session, Walmart agreed to give PenAgain a one-month trial in 500 stores, but only if it lowered its costs. Walmart also provided no marketing support, and PenAgain was too small to afford traditional print or television advertising, so it developed a viral marketing program and produced displays to use in the stores. A **viral marketing program** is one that encourages people to pass along a marketing message to other potential consumers. To keep track of sales, it relied on Walmart's Internet-based Retail Link system, though it also hired a firm that sends representatives into stores to check out display placement and customer traffic. Finally, PenAgain agreed to adhere to strict packaging, labeling, and shipping requirements. And remember, for all this effort, its entry in stores was only a test, and a very expensive gamble! But if it could succeed in Walmart stores, PenAgain would be well on its way to prosperity.

In the simplified supply chain in Exhibit 16.1, manufacturers make products and sell them to retailers or wholesalers. The exhibit would be much more complicated if we had included the suppliers of materials to manufacturers; all the various manufacturers, wholesalers, and stores in a typical marketing channel; and digital channels through which customers order products and receive them directly with the assistance of delivery providers such as UPS, FedEx, or the U.S. Postal Service.

EXHIBIT 16.1 Simplified Supply Chain

Exhibit 16.1 represents a typical flow of manufactured goods: Manufacturers ship to a wholesaler or to a retailer's distribution center (e.g., Manufacturer one and Manufacturer three) or directly to stores (Manufacturer two). In addition, many variations on this supply chain exist. Some retail chains, such as Home Depot or Costco, function as both retailers and wholesalers. They act as retailers when they sell to consumers directly and as wholesalers when they sell to other businesses such as building contractors or restaurant owners. When manufacturers such as Avon sell directly to consumers, they perform production as well as retailing activities. When Lenovo sells computers to a university or business, it engages in a business-to-business (B2B) transaction, but when it sells to students or employees individually, it is a B2C (business-to-consumer) operation.

Marketing Channels Add Value

Why do manufacturers use wholesalers or retailers? Don't these added channel members just cut into their profits? Wouldn't it be cheaper for consumers to buy directly from manufacturers? In a simple agrarian economy, the best supply chain likely does follow a direct route from manufacturer to consumer: The consumer goes to the farm and buys food directly from the farmer. Modern eat-local environmental campaigns suggest just such a process. But before the consumer can eat a fresh steak procured from a local farm, she needs to cook it. Assuming the consumer doesn't know how to make a stove and lacks the materials to do so, she must rely on a stove maker. The stove maker, which has the necessary knowledge, must buy raw materials and components from various suppliers, make the stove, and then make it available to the consumer. If the stove maker isn't located near the consumer, the stove must be transported to where the consumer has access to it. To make matters even more complicated, the consumer may want to view a choice of stoves, hear about all their features, and have the stove delivered and installed.

How many companies are involved in making and getting a stove to your kitchen?

Each participant in the channel adds value.[11] The components manufacturer helps the stove manufacturer by supplying parts and materials. The stove maker turns the components into the stove. The transportation company gets the stove to the retailer. The retailer stores the stove until the customer wants it, educates the customer about product features, and delivers and installs the stove. At each step, the stove becomes more costly but also more valuable to the consumer.

Marketing Channel Management Affects Other Aspects of Marketing

Every marketing decision is affected by and has an effect on marketing channels. When products are designed and manufactured, how and when the critical components reach the factory must be coordinated with production. The sales department must coordinate its delivery promises with the factory or distribution or fulfillment centers. A **distribution center**, a facility for the receipt, storage, and redistribution of goods to company stores, may be operated by retailers, manufacturers, or distribution specialists.[12] Similar to a distribution center, instead of shipping to stores, **fulfillment centers** are used to ship directly to customers. Furthermore, advertising and promotion must be coordinated with those departments that control inventory and transportation. There is no faster way to lose credibility with customers than to promise deliveries or run a promotion and then not have the merchandise when the customer expects it.

DESIGNING MARKETING CHANNELS

 LO16-2 Understand the difference between direct and indirect marketing channels.

When a firm is just starting out or entering a new market, it doesn't typically have the option of designing the best marketing channel structure—that is, choosing from whom it buys or to whom it sells. A new sporting goods retailer may not have the option of carrying all the manufacturer lines it wants, because other competing retailers in its market area might carry the same products. On the other side, a small specialty sporting goods apparel manufacturer may not be able to place its products in major stores like Sports Authority because its line is unproven, and the products might duplicate lines that the retailer already carries. Chapter 17 discusses in more depth how manufacturers choose their retailer partners.

Although there are thus various constraints on marketing channel partners with regard to the design of the best channel structure, all marketing channels take the form of a direct channel, an indirect channel, or some combination thereof.

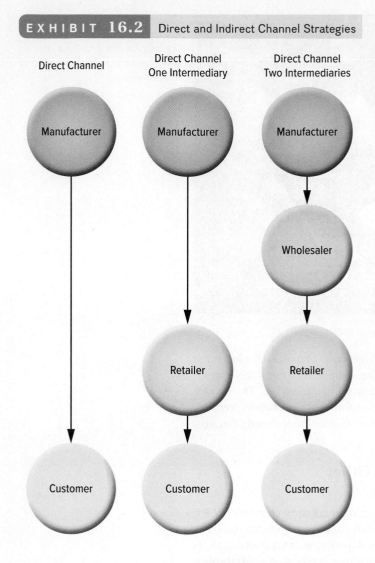

EXHIBIT 16.2 Direct and Indirect Channel Strategies

Direct Marketing Channel

As shown on the left side of Exhibit 16.2, there are no intermediaries between the buyer and seller in a **direct marketing channel**. Typically, the seller is a manufacturer, such as when a carpentry business sells bookcases through its own store and online to individual consumers. The seller also can be an individual, such as when a knitter sells blankets and scarves at craft fairs, on Etsy, and through eBay. (Recall our discussion of consumer-to-consumer [C2C] transactions in Chapter 1.) When the buyer is another business, such as when Boeing sells planes to JetBlue, the marketing channel still is direct, but in this case, the transaction is a business-to-business one (see Chapter 7).

Noting that people increasingly use online channels to purchase the consumer goods that it manufactures (e.g., diapers, detergent, paper towels), P&G seeks to enhance its direct-to-consumer online sales. Rather than adding shampoo to a repeat purchase list on Amazon or Walmart.com, P&G hopes consumers might buy it directly from it, the manufacturer. In so doing, it might increase its own margins, because it would not need to share the revenue with the retailer. In addition, it likely could undercut any retailer on price, because it would not need to maintain retail stores. Considering the long-standing, close relationship between P&G and Walmart though, such moves might make for some awkward strategy meetings between the two companies in the near future. It also requires P&G to build some new infrastructure, including an $89 million distribution center, that it needs to staff and operate so that it can be sure to get the products into customers' homes as quickly as Amazon or Walmart.com promises to do.[13]

Indirect Marketing Channel

In **indirect marketing channels**, one or more intermediaries work with manufacturers to provide goods and services to customers. In some cases, only one intermediary might be involved. Automobile manufacturers such as Ford and General Motors often use indirect distribution, such that dealers act as retailers, as shown in the middle of Exhibit 16.2. The right side of Exhibit 16.2 reveals how wholesalers are more common when the company does not buy in sufficient quantities to make it cost effective for the manufacturer to deal directly with them—independent book sellers, wine merchants, or independent drug stores, for example. Wholesalers are also prevalent in less developed economies, in which large retailers are rare.

LO16-3 Describe how marketing channels are managed.

MANAGING THE MARKETING CHANNEL AND SUPPLY CHAIN

Marketing channels and supply chains comprise various buying entities such as retailers and wholesalers, sellers such as manufacturers or wholesalers, and facilitators of the exchange such as transportation companies. Similar to interpersonal interactions, their relationships can range from close working partnerships to one-time arrangements. Marketing Analytics 16.1 details how Amazon is attempting to combine all these roles by leveraging its access to massive amounts of customer data. In most cases though, interactions occur

Marketing Analytics 16.1 | Analytics in Support of Anticipatory Shipping by Amazon[ii]

Already well established as an efficient shipper of orders, Amazon continues to seek to do even better. Currently, Amazon receives an order, labels and packages it, loads it onto a delivery truck (run by UPS or the U.S. Postal Service, depending on the day and delivery details), and waits for confirmation that this third-party logistics provider has delivered the product directly to the customer's door. In this traditional process, the online retail giant seeks to improve by adding more warehouses that can provide more customers with overnight or same-day delivery.

But recently, a striking innovation instead aims to reinvent the supply chain completely, to benefit customers as well as itself. That is, Amazon recently applied for and received a patent for its "anticipatory shipping" system, which starts readying packages for delivery before the customer even adds the item to his or her virtual cart. With anticipatory shipping, Amazon boxes and ships out products that it expects customers will want, according to their previous purchases, in the

belief that they are likely to order them soon. To determine what to ship, Amazon uses information from customers' previous orders, product searches, shopping cart contents, and previous returns.

This innovation promises to be particularly beneficial for popular books, movies, and games, which people clearly have announced their desire to have in hand the very day they are released. If Amazon can get it to their homes on that same day, it might discourage customers from visiting physical retail locations, because their wait times would be even shorter than brick-and-mortar stores can offer. In this sense, Amazon is using big data to predict demand and thus edge out its rivals. However, critics caution that when Amazon's algorithms are incorrect, the necessary returns could grow rapidly to become quite costly. In response, Amazon has suggested that it might simply convert any unwanted deliveries into gifts, thus building goodwill among customers who receive a desirable new order for no cost.

With Amazon's "anticipatory shipping" system, packages are shipped before the customer even adds the item to his or her virtual cart.

© Geoffrey Robinson/Alamy

across the supply chain because the parties want something from each other: Home Depot wants hammers from Stanley Tool Company; Stanley wants an opportunity to sell its tools to the general public; both companies want UPS to deliver the merchandise.

Each member of the marketing channel also performs a specialized role. If one member believes that another has failed to do its job correctly or efficiently, it can replace that member. So, if Stanley isn't getting good service from UPS, it can switch to FedEx. If Home Depot believes its customers do not perceive Stanley tools as a good value, it may

The Home Depot and Stanley Tool Company have a mutually beneficial partnership. Home Depot buys tools from Stanley because its customers find value in Stanley products. Stanley sells tools to Home Depot because Home Depot has established an excellent market for its products.

Source: The Stanley Works

buy from another tool company. Home Depot even could decide to make its own tools or use its own trucks to pick up tools from Stanley. However, any time a marketing channel member is replaced, the function it has performed remains, so someone needs to complete it.[14] As noted in the opening vignette, if IKEA does not build the bookcase or table, it means the consumer has more work to do.

If a marketing channel is to run efficiently, the participating members must cooperate. Often, however, supply chain members have conflicting goals, and this may result in channel conflict (Exhibit 16.3). For instance, Stanley wants Home Depot to carry all its tools but not the tools of its competitors so that Stanley can maximize its sales. But Home Depot carries a mix of tool brands so it can maximize the sales in its tool category. When supply chain members that buy and sell to one another are not in agreement about their goals, roles, or rewards, **vertical channel conflict** or discord results.

Horizontal channel conflict can also occur when there is disagreement or discord among members at the same level in a marketing channel, such as two competing retailers or two competing manufacturers. Another recent innovation by Amazon, the Vendor Flex program, seeks to lower overall transportation costs but also creates new forms of channel conflict with competitors.[15] As a partner in the Vendor Flex program, P&G agreed to allow Amazon to build fulfillment centers within P&G's own warehouses. The new system thus helped eliminate some of the costs of transporting P&G's products to Amazon's fulfillment centers. But companies such as Target and Walmart, which have enjoyed long-term relationships with P&G, found the move frustrating. Believing that the program was giving its competitor Amazon an unfair advantage, Target reacted vigorously, moving all P&G products from prominent end-cap positions in its stores to less prestigious and less visible

EXHIBIT 16.3   Vertical versus Horizontal Channel Conflict locations. Target also stopped using P&G as its primary source of advice for planning merchandising strategies within each category.[16]

Avoiding vertical channel conflicts demands open, honest communication. Buyers and vendors all must understand what drives the other party's business, their roles in the relationship, each firm's strategies, and any problems that might arise over the course of the relationship. Amazon and P&G recognize that it is in their common interest to remain profitable business partners. Amazon's customers demand and expect to find P&G products on its website; P&G needs the sales generated through Amazon. Amazon cannot demand prices so low that P&G cannot make money, and P&G must be flexible enough to accommodate the needs of this important customer. With a common goal, both firms have the incentive to cooperate because they know that by doing so, each will boost its sales.[17]

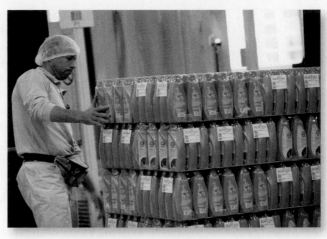

Amazon and Procter & Gamble recognize that it is in their common interest to remain profitable business partners.

© Daniel Mihailescu/AFP/Getty Images

Common goals also help sustain the relationship when expected benefits fail to arise. If one P&G shipment fails to reach the Amazon section of one of its fulfilment centers due to an uncontrollable event such as a demand forecasting miscalculation, Amazon does not suddenly call off the whole arrangement. Instead, it recognizes the incident as a simple, isolated mistake and maintains the good working relationship, because Amazon knows that both it and P&G are committed to the same goals in the long run.

In this sense, their partnership exhibits both of the nonmutually exclusive ways that exist to manage a marketing channel or supply chain: Coordinate the channel using a vertical marketing system and develop strong relationships with marketing channel partners—topics we now examine.

Managing the Marketing Channel and Supply Chain through Vertical Marketing Systems

Although conflict is likely in any marketing channel, it is generally more pronounced when the channel members are independent entities. Marketing channels that are more closely aligned, whether by contract or ownership, share common goals and therefore are less prone to conflict.

In an **independent (conventional) marketing channel**, several independent members—a manufacturer, a wholesaler, and a retailer—attempt to satisfy their own objectives and maximize their profits, often at the expense of the other members, as we portray in Exhibit 16.4 (left). None

EXHIBIT 16.4 Independent versus Vertical Marketing Channels

Independent marketing channel

Manufacturer

Wholesaler

Retailer

Consumer

Vertical marketing channel

Manufacturer

Wholesaler

Retailer

Consumer

of the participants have any control over the others. Before any sort of relationship develops, or in one-time interactions, both parties likely try to extract as much profit from the deal as possible. After the deal is consummated, neither party feels any responsibility to the other.

Over time though, many parties develop relationships marked by routinized, automatic transactions, such as those that take place between Walmart and P&G. Walmart's customers thus come to expect to find P&G products in stores, and P&G depends on Walmart to purchase a good portion of its output to sell to its own customers. This scenario represents the first phase of a vertical marketing system, a marketing channel in which the members act as a unified system, as in Exhibit 16.4 (right). Three types of vertical marketing systems— administered, contractual, and corporate—reflect increasing phases of formalization and control. The more formal the vertical marketing system, the less likely conflict is to ensue.

Administered Vertical Marketing System Walmart's various marketing channel relationships offer examples of different forms of an administered vertical marketing system: There is no common ownership or contractual relationships, but the dominant channel member controls or holds the balance of power. Because of its size and relative power, Walmart can easily impose controls on small manufacturers, such as PenAgain, but with large, powerful suppliers such as P&G, the control is more balanced between parties. Power in a marketing channel exists when one firm has the means or ability to dictate the actions of another member at a different level of distribution (Exhibit 16.5). A retailer like Walmart exercises its power over suppliers in several ways.

- With its reward power, Walmart offers rewards, often a monetary incentive, if the wholesalers or manufacturers do what Walmart wants them to do. For example, it might promise to purchase larger quantities if a manufacturer will lower its wholesale price.

- Coercive power arises when Walmart threatens to punish or punishes the other channel member for not undertaking certain tasks, such as if it were to delay payment for a late delivery.

- Walmart may also have referent power if a supplier desperately wants to be associated with Walmart, because being known as an important Walmart supplier enables that supplier to attract other retailers' business. In this sense, P&G might be playing its retailer partners against one another to enhance its own performance.

- If Walmart exerts expertise power, it relies on its vast experience and knowledge to decide how to market a particular supplier's products, without giving the supplier much of a say.

- Because Walmart has vast information about the consumer goods market, it might exert information power over P&G by providing or withholding important market information. At the same time, P&G might have its own information power that it could exert over Walmart, depending on which company has the most or most updated data.

- Legitimate power is based on getting a channel member to behave in a certain way because of a contractual agreement between the two firms. As Walmart deals with its suppliers, it likely exerts multiple types of power to influence their behaviors. If either party dislikes the way the relationship is going, though, it can simply walk away.

EXHIBIT 16.5 Bases of Power

Contractual Vertical Marketing System Over time, members of the supply chain often formalize their relationship by entering into contracts that dictate various terms,[18] such as how much Walmart will buy from P&G each month and at what price, as well as the penalties for late deliveries. In contractual vertical marketing systems like this, independent firms at different levels of the marketing channel join through contracts to obtain economies of scale and coordination and to reduce conflict.[19]

Franchising is the most common type of contractual vertical marketing system. Franchising is a contractual agreement between a franchisor and a franchisee that allows the franchisee to operate a retail outlet using a name and format developed and supported by the franchisor. Exhibit 16.6 lists the United States' top franchise opportunities. These rankings, determined by *Entrepreneur* magazine, are created using a number of objective measures such as financial strength, stability, growth rate, and size of the franchise system.[20]

In a franchise contract, the franchisee pays a lump sum plus a royalty on all sales in return for the right to operate a business in a specific location. The franchisee also agrees to operate the outlet in accordance with the procedures prescribed by the franchisor. The franchisor typically provides assistance in locating and building the business, developing the products or services sold, management training, and advertising. To maintain the franchisee's reputation, the franchisor also makes sure that all outlets provide the same quality of services and products.

A franchise system combines the entrepreneurial advantages of owning a business with the efficiencies of vertical marketing systems that function under single ownership (i.e., a corporate system, as we discuss next). Franchisees are motivated to make their stores successful because they receive the profits after they pay the royalty to the franchisor. The franchisor is motivated to develop new products, services, and systems and to promote the franchise because it receives royalties on all sales. Advertising, product

EXHIBIT 16.6	Top 10 Franchises for 2014		
Rank	Franchise Name	Number of U.S. Outlets	Start-Up Costs
1	Jimmy John's Gourmet Sandwiches Sandwiches	2,238	$326K–555K
2	Hampton Hotels Mid-price hotels	1,939	$3.8M–14.1M
3	Supercuts Hair salon	1,474	$144K–294K
4	Servpro Insurance/disaster restoration and cleaning	1,683	$156K–210K
5	Subway Subs, salads	26,972	$117K–263K
6	McDonald's Burgers, chicken, salads, beverages	12,899	$989K–2.2M
7	7-Eleven Convenience stores	8,109	$38K–1.1M
8	Dunkin' Donuts Coffee shop	8,308	$217K–1.6M
9	Denny's Inc. Family restaurant	1,428	$1.2M–2.1M
10	Anytime Fitness Fitness centers	2,139	$63K–418K

Source: Entrepreneur's 2016 Franchise 500, https://www.entrepreneur.com/franchise500.

development, and system development are all done efficiently by the franchisor, with costs shared by all franchisees.

Corporate Vertical Marketing System

In a **corporate vertical marketing system**, the parent company has complete control and can dictate the priorities and objectives of the marketing channel because it owns multiple segments of the channel, such as manufacturing plants, warehouse facilities, and retail outlets. By virtue of its ownership and resulting control, potential conflict among segments of the channel is lessened.

Tesla Motors, manufacturer of luxury electric automobiles, represents a corporate vertical marketing system because it manufactures its own cars in Fremont, California, and it operates its own retail stores in high foot-traffic locations like malls and shopping streets.[21] The Tesla Product Specialists that work in these stores are trained to answer questions, not sell cars per se. They could not even sell a car on the spot if they wanted to, because there is no inventory on hand. They would, of course, be happy to take an order though. Tesla also owns and operates its own service centers. With this corporate ownership structure, it is able to maintain control of every aspect of Tesla ownership, thus ensuring satisfied and loyal customers.

Managing Marketing Channels and Supply Chains through Strategic Relationships

There is more to managing marketing channels and supply chains than simply exercising power over other members in an administered system or establishing a contractual or corporate vertical marketing system. There is also a human side.

In a conventional marketing channel, relationships between members reflect their arguments over the split of the profit pie: If one party gets ahead, the other party falls behind. Sometimes this type of transaction is acceptable if the parties have no interest in a long-term relationship. But as Ethical and Societal Dilemma 16.1 highlights, such attitudes can limit the success of the supply chain as a whole.

Therefore, firms frequently seek a strategic relationship, also called a partnering relationship, in which the marketing channel members are committed to maintaining the relationship over the long term and investing in opportunities that are mutually beneficial. In a conventional or administered marketing channel, there are significant incentives to establish a strategic relationship, even without contracts or ownership relationships. Both parties benefit because the size of the profit pie has increased, so both the buyer and the seller increase their sales and profits. These strategic relationships are created explicitly to uncover and exploit joint opportunities, so members depend on and trust each other heavily; share goals and agree on how to accomplish those goals; and are willing to take risks, share confidential information, and make significant investments for the sake of the relationship. Successful strategic relationships require mutual trust, open communication, common goals, interdependence, and credible commitments.

Mutual Trust
Mutual trust holds a strategic relationship together. Trust is the belief that a partner is honest (i.e., reliable, stands by its word, sincere, fulfills obligations) and benevolent (i.e., concerned about the other party's welfare). When vendors and buyers trust each other, they are more willing to share relevant ideas, clarify goals and problems, and communicate efficiently. Information shared between the parties, such as inventory positions in stores, thus becomes increasingly comprehensive, accurate, and timely.

With trust, there's also less need for the supply chain members to constantly monitor and check up on each other's actions, because each believes the other won't take advantage, even if given the opportunity. Although it is important in all relationships, monitoring supply chain members becomes particularly pertinent when suppliers are located in less developed countries, where issues such as the use of child labor, poor working conditions, and below-subsistence wages have become a shared responsibility.

Open Communication
To share information, develop sales forecasts together, and coordinate deliveries, Walmart and its suppliers maintain open and honest communication. This maintenance may sound easy in principle, but some businesses don't tend to share information with their business partners. But open, honest communication is a key to developing successful relationships because supply chain members need to understand what is driving each other's business, their roles in the relationship, each firm's strategies, and any problems that arise over the course of the relationship.

Common Goals
Supply chain members must have common goals for a successful relationship to develop. Shared goals give both members of the relationship an incentive to pool their strengths and abilities and exploit potential opportunities together. Such commonality also offers an assurance that the other partner won't do anything to hinder the achievement of those goals within the relationship.

Ethical & Societal Dilemma 16.1   Shrinking the Supply Chain to Supply Organic Demand[iii]

The consumer market for organic products—fruit, vegetables, eggs, animal products, broth, and so forth—continues to expand at an amazing rate. Between 2000 and 2013, consumption of organic products tripled in the United States. Consumers, worried about their health and food quality, actively seek more supply chains that are willing to guarantee that the food they eat does not contain adulterants such as synthetic hormones, genetically modified organisms, or pesticides. But these supply chains are struggling to meet this demand, even as it continues to grow.

That creates a problem for organic brands: If they cannot source enough organic raw materials to make their products, they cannot get their products to consumers. For example, the Garden of Eatin' brand underwent nearly constant stockouts on store shelves when it could not procure enough organic blue corn to make its popular tortilla chips. To find organic sources, some companies look to farms overseas. But such purchases increase costs and logistics concerns and do not align with the company's fresh images.

In response to this challenge, manufacturers are reimagining their supply chains in several ways. The most dramatic response is by manufacturers that literally "buy the farm." Nature's Path recently purchased 2,800 acres of farmland in Montana, for $2 million, so that it could control the cultivation of organic wheat and oats for its cereal products. It also plans to dedicate an additional $2 million each year to the purchase of cropland so that it can ensure the continued supply of organic resources to its supply chain.

Similarly, Pacific Foods decided to build its own henhouses to be able to source organic chicken to make into broth. Its organic chicken broth accounts for about half of the manufacturer's sales. However, its own production was insufficient, so Pacific Foods also offered incentives to local chicken farmers who agreed to adopt organic practices. Specifically, Pacific Foods pays for the feed and supplies, and then it guarantees that it will cover any losses if the production fails.

For Chipotle, buying a lot of farmland seemed too far beyond its core competencies, so it instead has entered into beneficial agreements with farmers who agree to transform their conventional farms into organic ones. For example, for a black-bean farmer who was undergoing the transition to organic methods, Chipotle paid a 10 percent premium for the beans

To encourage egg farmers to sell organic eggs, Pete and Gerry's promises to provide them with blueprints and guarantees for bank loans.
© Gary Cameron/Reuters

even though it could not market those beans as fully organic. Instead, its goal was to encourage this farm to continue its organic efforts, which should ensure a more stable supply in the future. In a similar trend, egg farmers can charge more for their organic eggs, and the brand Pete and Gerry's promises to provide them with blueprints and guarantees for bank loans if they agree to build organic-friendly chicken coops.

Such forms of assistance appear especially necessary for the organic food supply chain, because, unlike conventional agriculture, the crops and products are not traded on futures markets. In addition, bank loans continue to be more difficult for organic farmers to obtain, because of their substantially higher production costs, compared with conventional farmers. But if demand continues to grow as it has—and it shows few signs of stopping—these financial players might find that they have some catching up to do. If organic brands can control their entire supply chains, why would they need outsiders?

Walmart and P&G recognize that it is in their common interest to be strategic partners. Walmart needs P&G to satisfy its customers, and P&G recognizes that if it can keep Walmart happy, it will have more than enough business for years to come. With common goals, both firms have an incentive to cooperate, because they know that by doing so, both can boost sales. If Walmart needs a special production run of detergent to meet demand following a natural disaster for example, P&G will work to meet the challenge. If P&G is determined to introduce radically new products, it is in Walmart's best interest to help it, because they are committed to the same goals in the long run.

Interdependence When supply chain members view their goals and ultimate success as intricately linked, they develop deeper long-term relationships. Interdependence between supply chain members that is based on mutual benefits is key to developing and sustaining the relationship.[22] Walmart's suppliers recognize that without Walmart, their sales would be significantly less. Although it is the more powerful member of most of its supply chains, Walmart also recognizes that it can depend on these suppliers to be a dependable source of supply, thus enabling it to have a very efficient marketing channel.

Credible Commitments Successful relationships develop because both parties make credible commitments to, or tangible investments in, the relationship. These commitments go beyond just making the hollow statement, "I want to be your partner"; they involve spending money to improve the products or services provided to the customer and on information technology to improve supply chain efficiency.[23] As we described previously, Amazon and P&G have worked closely to set up their Vendor Flex program, enabling Amazon to operate fulfillment centers within P&G's own warehouses and thereby lower transportation expenses.

Similar to many other elements of marketing, managing the marketing channel can seem like an easy task at first glance: Put the right merchandise in the right place at the right time. But the various elements and actors involved in a marketing channel create its unique and compelling complexities and require firms to work carefully to ensure they are achieving the most efficient and effective chain possible.

We now turn our attention to how information and merchandise flow through marketing channels.

PROGRESS CHECK

1. What is the difference between an indirect and a direct marketing channel?

2. What are the differences among the three types of vertical marketing systems?

3. How do firms develop strong strategic partnerships with their marketing channel partners?

MAKING INFORMATION FLOW THROUGH MARKETING CHANNELS

 Describe the flow of information and merchandise in the marketing channel.

Information flows from the customer to stores, to and from distribution centers, possibly to and from wholesalers, to and from product manufacturers, and then on to the producers of any components and the suppliers of raw materials. To simplify our discussion—and because information flows are similar in other marketing channel links, such as through the Internet and catalogs, as well as in B2B channels—we shorten the supply chain in this section to exclude wholesalers as well as the link from suppliers to manufacturers. Exhibit 16.7 illustrates the flow of information that starts when a customer buys a Sony HDTV at Best Buy. The flow follows these steps:

Flow 1 (Customer to Store): The sales associate at Best Buy scans the Universal Product Code (UPC) tag on the HDTV packaging, and the customer receives a receipt. The UPC tag is the black-and-white bar code found on most merchandise. It contains a 13-digit code that indicates the manufacturer of the item, a description of the item, information about special packaging, and special promotions.[24] In the future, RFID tags, discussed later in this chapter, may replace UPC tags.

EXHIBIT 16.7 Information Flows

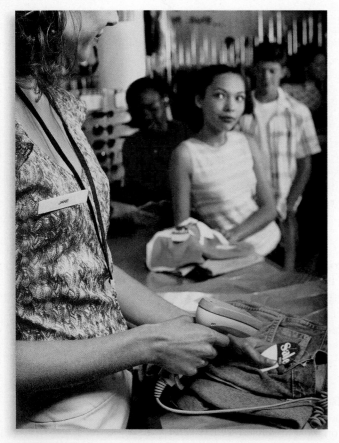

The flow of information starts when the UPC tag is scanned at the point of purchase.

Flow 2 (Store to Buyer): The point-of-sale (POS) terminal records the purchase information and electronically sends it to the buyer at Best Buy's corporate office. The sales information is incorporated into an inventory management system and used to monitor and analyze sales and decide to reorder more HDTVs, change a price, or plan a promotion. Buyers also send information to stores about overall sales for the chain, ways to display the merchandise, upcoming promotions, and so on.

Flow 3 (Buyer to Manufacturer): The purchase information from each Best Buy store is typically aggregated by the retailer as a whole, which creates an order for new merchandise and sends it to Sony. The buyer at Best Buy may also communicate directly with Sony to get information and negotiate prices, shipping dates, promotional events, or other merchandise-related issues.

Flow 4 (Store to Manufacturer): In some situations, the sales transaction data are sent directly from the store to the manufacturer, and the manufacturer decides when to ship more merchandise to the distribution centers and the stores. In other situations, especially when merchandise is reordered frequently, the ordering process is done automatically, bypassing the buyers. By working together, the retailer and manufacturer can better satisfy customer needs.

Flow 5 (Store to Distribution Center): Stores also communicate with the Best Buy distribution center to coordinate deliveries and check inventory status. When the store inventory drops to a specified level, more HDTVs are shipped to the store, and the shipment information is sent to the Best Buy computer system.

Flow 6 (Manufacturer to Distribution Center and Buyer): When the manufacturer ships the HDTVs to the Best Buy distribution center, it sends an advanced shipping notice to the distribution centers. An **advanced shipping notice (ASN)** is an electronic document that the supplier sends the retailer in advance of a shipment to tell the retailer exactly what to expect in the shipment. The center then makes appointments for trucks to make the delivery at a specific time, date, and loading dock. When the shipment is received at the distribution center, the buyer is notified and authorizes payment to the vendor.

Data Warehouse

Purchase data collected at the point of sale (information flow 2 in Exhibit 16.7) goes into a huge database known as a data warehouse, similar to those described in Chapter 10. Using the data warehouse, the CEO not only can learn how the corporation is generally doing but also can look at the data aggregated by quarter for a merchandise division, a region of the country, or the total corporation. A buyer may be more interested in a particular manufacturer in a certain store on a particular day. Analysts from various levels of the retail operation extract information from the data warehouse to make a plethora of marketing decisions about developing and replenishing merchandise assortments.

In some cases, manufacturers also have access to this data warehouse. They communicate with retailers by using electronic data interchange (EDI) and supply chain systems known as vendor-managed inventory.

In information flows 3, 4, and 6 in Exhibit 16.7, the retailer and manufacturer exchange business documents through EDI. **Electronic data interchange (EDI)** is the computer-to-computer exchange of business documents from a retailer to a vendor and back. In addition to sales data, purchase orders, invoices, and data about returned merchandise can be transmitted back and forth. With EDI, vendors can transmit information about on-hand inventory status, vendor promotions, and cost changes to the retailer, as well as information about purchase order changes, order status, retail prices, and transportation routings. Thus EDI enables channel members to communicate more quickly and with fewer errors than in the past, ensuring that merchandise moves from vendors to retailers more quickly.

Vendor-managed inventory (VMI) is an approach for improving marketing channel efficiency in which the manufacturer is responsible for maintaining the retailer's inventory levels in each of its stores.[25] By sharing the data in the retailer's data warehouse and communicating that information via EDI, the manufacturer automatically sends merchandise to the retailer's store or distribution or fulfillment center when the inventory at the store reaches a prespecified level.[26]

In ideal conditions, the manufacturer replenishes inventories in quantities that meet the retailer's immediate demand, which reduces stockouts with minimal inventory. In addition to providing a better match between retail demand and supply, VMI can reduce the vendor's and the retailer's costs. Manufacturer salespeople no longer need to spend time generating orders on items that are already in the stores, and their role shifts to selling new items and maintaining relationships. Retail buyers and planners no longer need to monitor inventory levels and place orders.

PROGRESS CHECK

1. What are the marketing channel links associated with each information flow?
2. How do marketing channel members use data warehouses to make decisions?
3. What is EDI and how is it used?
4. Why do some marketing channels use VMI and others do not?

MAKING MERCHANDISE FLOW THROUGH MARKETING CHANNELS

Exhibit 16.8 illustrates the merchandise flow steps for a large retailer, such as Best Buy, that relies largely on its physical store operations. The flow of merchandise and pertinent decision variables in an Internet channel are similar, except that orders arrive from customers one at a time and go out in relatively small quantities, so the facility used to store and process these orders—that is, the fulfillment center—works a little differently. In general though, the merchandise flow steps are:

1. Sony to Best Buy's distribution centers, or
2. Sony directly to stores.
3. If the merchandise goes through distribution centers, it is then shipped to stores,
4. and then to the customer.

Making merchandise flow involves first deciding whether the merchandise will go from the manufacturer to a retailer's distribution center or directly on to stores. Once in a distribution center, multiple activities take place before it is shipped on to a store. Adding Value 16.2 describes how merchandise flows in India are inherently more complicated than they are in the United States.

Distribution Centers versus Direct Store Delivery

As indicated in Exhibit 16.8, manufacturers can ship merchandise directly to a retailer's stores—direct store delivery (flow 2)—or to their distribution centers (flow 1). Although manufacturers and retailers may collaborate, the ultimate decision is usually up to the retailer and depends on the characteristics of the merchandise and the nature of demand. To determine which distribution system—distribution centers or direct store delivery—is better, retailers consider the total cost associated with each alternative and the customer service criterion of having the right merchandise at the store when the customer wants to buy it.

There are several advantages to using a distribution center:

- More accurate sales forecasts are possible when retailers combine forecasts for many stores serviced by one distribution center rather than doing a forecast for each store. Consider a set of 50 Target stores, serviced by a single distribution center that each carries Dualit toasters. Each store normally stocks 5 units, for a total of 250 units in

EXHIBIT 16.8 Merchandise Flows

Distribution centers

Store

Customer

Manufacturing

Adding Value 16.2   E-Tailing in the United States versus India[iv]

In the expanding e-commerce universe, India appears poised to be the next China—that is, a developing economy with millions of consumers seeking access to varied products to purchase. But India is not China, and neither nation is following the path cut by U.S. e-commerce retailers, so the next steps remain uncertain, both literally and figuratively.

The literal next steps are getting purchases packed and shipped from retailers to customers. Such steps are particularly difficult in India. The nation's infrastructure is notably underdeveloped, featuring poor roads, outdated trucking fleets, insufficient air transport capacity, and insufficient legal protections for shippers. The threat of every monsoon season also means that logistics providers have trouble keeping delivery promises, especially if the buyer expects rapid delivery. As a result, many e-commerce companies spend the equivalent of a whopping 30 percent of their sales on logistics, approximately three times as much as Amazon does in the United States.

Figuratively, e-commerce in India also is uncertain because of the structure adopted by the existing start-ups. Most

of them still rely heavily on venture capital; virtually none of them are profitable on their own. Although nationwide e-tailers such as Flipkart and Snapdeal assert that they plan to be profitable within two to three years, they have not released their plans for doing so. But as these competitors seek to become the first site that shoppers visit, they are offering great deals and discounts, along with free shipping to buyers across the country. In many cases, they thus take a loss on each sale, especially if a buyer purchases a single, inexpensive item.

The consumer base also remains something of a question mark. Web penetration is still comparatively slight in India. Whereas China's e-commerce market has exploded in the past decade, growing in value from $7 million to $458 million, India's e-commerce is worth only about $4 million today. Part of this difference stems from the individual level. The average Indian consumer's online order is worth the equivalent of about $20. In the United States, each order instead averages around $100.

E-commerce is difficult in India due to poor roads, outdated trucking fleets, insufficient air transport capacity, and insufficient legal protections for shippers.

© Hemis/Alamy

the system. By carrying the item at each store, the retailer must develop individual forecasts, each with the possibility of errors that could result in either too much or too little merchandise. Alternatively, by delivering most of the inventory to a distribution center and feeding the stores merchandise as they need it, the effects of forecast errors for the individual stores are minimized, and less backup inventory is needed to prevent stockouts.

- Distribution centers enable the retailer to carry less merchandise in the individual stores, which results in lower inventory investments systemwide. If the stores get frequent deliveries from the distribution center, they need to carry relatively less extra merchandise as backup stock.

    - It is easier to avoid running out of stock or having too much stock in any particular store because merchandise is ordered from the distribution center as needed.

    - Retail store space is typically much more expensive than is space at a distribution center, and distribution centers are better equipped than stores to prepare merchandise for sale. As a result, many retailers find it cost effective to store merchandise and get it ready for sale at a distribution center rather than in individual stores.

Should Target stock Dualit toasters in distribution centers or keep all its backup stock in stores?

© Lee Hacker/Alamy

But distribution centers aren't appropriate for all retailers. If a retailer has only a few outlets, the expense of a distribution center is probably unwarranted. Also, if many outlets are concentrated in metropolitan areas, merchandise can be consolidated and delivered by the vendor directly to all the stores in one area economically. Direct store delivery gets merchandise to the stores faster and thus is used for perishable goods (meat and produce), items that help create the retailer's image of being the first to sell the latest product (e.g., video games), or fads. Superior Service 16.1 explores how the two retail giants Amazon and Walmart are vying to win the same-day grocery delivery battle. Finally, some manufacturers provide direct store delivery for retailers to ensure that their products are on the store's shelves, properly displayed, and fresh. For example, employees delivering Frito-Lay snacks directly to supermarkets replace products that have been on the shelf too long and are stale, replenish products that have been sold, and arrange products so they are neatly displayed.

The Distribution (or Fulfillment) Center

The distribution center performs the following activities: managing inbound transportation; receiving and checking; storing and cross-docking; getting merchandise floor-ready; ticketing and marking; preparing to ship merchandise to stores; and shipping merchandise to stores. Fulfillment centers perform the same functions, but because they deliver directly to customers rather than to stores, they do not have to get merchandise floor ready. To illustrate these activities being undertaken in a distribution center, we'll continue our example of Sony HDTVs being shipped to a Best Buy distribution center.

Walmart speeds merchandise from its distribution centers to stores.

Source: Wal-Mart Stores, Inc.

Managing Inbound Transportation Traditionally, when working with vendors, buyers focused their efforts on developing merchandise assortments, negotiating prices, and arranging joint promotions. Now, buyers and planners are much more involved in coordinating the physical flow of merchandise to stores. **Planners** are employees responsible for the financial planning and analysis of merchandise and its allocation to stores. The TV buyer has arranged for a truckload of HDTVs to be delivered to its Houston, Texas, distribution center on Monday between 1:00 and 3:00 p.m. The buyer also specifies how the merchandise should be placed on pallets for easy unloading.

The truck must arrive within the specified time because the distribution center has all of its 100 receiving docks allocated throughout the day, and much of the merchandise on this particular truck is going to be shipped to stores that evening. Unfortunately, the truck was delayed in a snowstorm. The **dispatcher**—the person who coordinates deliveries to the distribution center—reassigns the truck delivering the HDTVs to a Wednesday morning delivery slot and charges the firm several hundred

Superior Service 16.1 | Who Will Win the Same-Day Grocery Delivery War?[v]

Amazon has more than 89 fulfillment centers, with more to come. The complex machinery and supply chain mechanisms allow Amazon to ship out products in less than 2.5 hours from the time a customer clicks "Place Your Order." Yet, fulfillment center teams are always working to develop innovative ways to cut the time down even further. In addition to warehouse speed, these centers excel in proximity. Amazon has spent billions building centers closer and closer to customers.

Now Amazon is expanding its grocery delivery business, AmazonFresh. Previously available only in Seattle, Amazon sees AmazonFresh as the future of shopping. Customers

AmazonFresh is expanding its grocery delivery business to several U.S. cities.
© Silicon Valley Stock/Alamy

can get whatever they want, whenever they want, wherever they want, and as fast as they demand it. During a recent launch in Los Angeles, customers enjoyed free trials of PrimeFresh, the upgraded version of Amazon Prime, including free shipping of products and free delivery of groceries for orders over $35. In both Los Angeles and Seattle, Amazon maintains a fleet of Fresh trucks that deliver everything from full-course meals to chocolate from local merchants. As Amazon evolves into a same-day delivery service, its fleet could become yet another competitive advantage.

Yet AmazonFresh remains a challenge, mainly because of the differences associated with grocery products: It cannot ship milk the same way it ships diapers. Despite the tremendous logistical and economic hurdles to creating a same-day delivery service, Amazon hopes to expand its grocery customers and turn monthly customers to weekly or even twice-weekly buyers.

In Mexico, Walmart has achieved the goal of same-day grocery delivery, where Superama, its high-end grocery chain, delivers groceries in as little as three hours. When Superama first began home delivery in 1993, managers would take orders by telephone or fax. As volume increased, it created a web page and then a mobile application that today accounts for approximately 20 percent of Superama's online orders.

Much of this delivery success in Mexico is a result of the nation's densely populated urban areas. Demand is highest in Mexico City, which also accounts for much of Mexico's wealth.

Due to traffic congestion and more dual-income families, demand for grocery deliveries is high; most of the deliveries are made by freelance drivers who get $1.50 per delivery, using their own transportation rather than relying on a fleet of Walmart-owned trucks.

Walmart is betting big on the Mexican market as a "detonator for growth" and seeks to triple the number of stores offering grocery delivery in Mexico within a year. Superama's target market is households with incomes of $3,000 a month, or 35 percent of the nation's population. As one of Walmart's largest foreign markets, Mexico contributes $27 billion (or 6 percent) to the retailer's annual sales. Superama also has helped Walmart dominate the market (92 percent share) for online grocery shopping in Mexico.

Thus two retail giants have staked their claims, relying on their distinct capabilities. Other competitors in selected regional markets include eBay Now (offering one-hour delivery by couriers for about $5 per delivery), Peapod and FreshDirect (dedicated grocery delivery services), and Google Shopping Express (offering Bay Area deliveries from Staples, Walgreens, Target, Whole Foods, and American Eagle). But considering the delivery cost advantages in Mexico and Amazon's head start in the United States, can Walmart or any of these other competitors catch up with their Internet-only rival in the U.S. same-day grocery delivery market? And just as important, how much do they need to do so?

dollars for missing its delivery time. Although many manufacturers pay transportation expenses, some retailers negotiate with their vendors to absorb this expense. These retailers believe they can lower their net merchandise cost and better control merchandise flow if they negotiate directly with trucking companies and consolidate shipments from many vendors.

Receiving and Checking Using UPC or RFID

Receiving is the process of recording the receipt of merchandise as it arrives at a distribution center. Checking is the process of going through the goods upon receipt to make sure they arrived undamaged and that the merchandise ordered was the merchandise received.

In the past, checking merchandise was a very labor-intensive and time-consuming process. Today, however, many distribution systems using EDI are designed to minimize, if not eliminate, these processes. The advance shipping notice (ASN) tells the distribution center what should be in each carton. A UPC label or radio frequency identification (RFID) tag on the shipping carton that identifies the carton's contents is scanned and automatically counted as it is being received and checked. Radio frequency identification (RFID) tags are tiny computer chips that automatically transmit to a special scanner all the information about a container's contents or individual products. Approximately as large as a pinhead, these RFID tags consist of an antenna and a chip that contains an electronic product code that stores far more information about a product than bar (UPC) codes can. The tags also act as passive tracking devices, signaling their presence over a radio frequency when they pass within a few yards of a special scanner. The tags have long been used in high-cost applications such as automated highway toll systems and security identification badges. As the cost of the tags and implementation technology has decreased, their uses have become more prevalent in retail supply chain applications.

Storing and Cross-Docking

After the merchandise is received and checked, it is either stored or cross-docked. When merchandise is stored, the cartons are transported by a conveyor system and forklift trucks to racks that go from the distribution center's floor to its ceiling. Then, when the merchandise is needed in the stores, a forklift driver or a robot goes to the rack, picks up the carton, and places it on a conveyor system that routes the carton to the loading dock of a truck going to the store.

Using a cross-docking distribution center, merchandise cartons are prepackaged by the vendor for a specific store. The UPC or RFID labels on the carton indicate the store to which it is to be sent. The vendor also may affix price tags to each item in the carton. Because the merchandise is ready for sale, it is placed on a conveyor system that routes it from the unloading dock at which it was received to the loading dock for the truck going to the specific store—hence the name *cross-docked*. The cartons are routed on the conveyor system automatically by sensors that read the UPC or RFID label on the cartons. Cross-docked merchandise is in the distribution center only for a few hours before it is shipped to the stores.

Merchandise sales rate and degree of perishability or fashionability typically determine whether cartons are cross-docked or stored. For instance, because Sony's HDTVs sell so quickly, it is in Best Buy's interest not to store them in a distribution center. Similarly, cross-docking is preferable for fashion apparel or perishable meat or produce.

Getting Merchandise Floor-Ready

For some merchandise, additional tasks are undertaken in the distribution center to make the merchandise floor-ready. Floor-ready merchandise is merchandise that is ready to be placed on the selling floor. Getting merchandise floor-ready entails ticketing, marking, and, in the case of some apparel, placing garments on hangers (or maybe attaching RFID chips). For the UK-based grocery chain Tesco, it is essential that products ship in ready-to-sell units so that there is little manipulation or sorting to do at the distribution center or in the stores. To move the store-ready merchandise it receives from suppliers quickly into the store, Tesco demands that products sit on roll cages rather than pallets. Then, store employees can easily wheel them onto the retail floor. The stores' backrooms only have two or three days' worth of backup inventory, and it is important to keep inventory levels low and receive lots of small, accurate deliveries from its suppliers—which also helps cut costs.[27]

Ticketing and Marking Ticketing and marking refers to affixing price and identification labels to the merchandise. It is more efficient for a retailer to perform these activities at a distribution center than in its stores. In a distribution center, an area can be set aside and a process implemented to efficiently add labels and put apparel on hangers. Conversely, getting merchandise floor-ready in stores can block aisles and divert sales people's attention from their customers. An even better approach from the retailer's perspective is to get vendors to ship floor-ready merchandise, thus totally eliminating the expensive, time-consuming ticketing and marking process.

Preparing to Ship Merchandise to a Store At the beginning of the day, the computer system in the distribution center generates a list of items to be shipped to each store on that day. For each item, a pick ticket and shipping label is generated. The pick ticket is a document or display on a screen in a forklift truck indicating how much of each item to get from specific storage areas. The forklift driver goes to the storage area, picks up the number of cartons indicated on the pick ticket, places UPC shipping labels on the cartons that indicate the stores to which the items are to be shipped, and puts the cartons on the conveyor system, where they are automatically routed to the loading dock for the truck going to the stores. In some distribution and fulfillment centers, these functions are performed by robots.

Robots are often used to help prepare merchandise to be shipped to stores.
© Quiet Logistics

Shipping Merchandise to Stores Shipping merchandise to stores from a distribution center has become increasingly complex. Most distribution centers run 50 to 100 outbound truck routes in one day. To handle this complex transportation problem, the centers use sophisticated routing and scheduling computer systems that consider the locations of the stores, road conditions, and transportation operating constraints to develop the most efficient routes possible. As a result, stores are provided with an accurate estimated time of arrival, and vehicle usage is maximized.

Customer Store Pickup

Technology advances have changed consumers' expectations of their shopping experience. They want the option of making the purchase online and then picking up in store. Retailers that can offer this option drive additional sales, as customers who come into the store to pick up online orders are more likely to make additional purchases while in store. For retailers to be successful with the buy-online-and-pick-up-in-store option, they need to invest in technology that enables order allocation systems to locate every item in stock so as to fulfill the order in a timely manner.

Consumers have been spoiled by technology that allows them to shop for anything, anywhere, anytime, and they want it delivered now. Multichannel retailers that offer the buy-online-and-pick-up-in-store option will be appealing to these spoiled customers. For this option to be successful, retailers need to ensure that the products that show up as being available online will actually be available in stock and ready for pick up. This requires a high level of accuracy inherent in the retailer's inventory management system.

The notification of sales to stores quickly and accurately is crucial for retailers to differentiate themselves. Retailers need to equip themselves with mobile task management technology to deliver outstanding customer experience. Mobile task management technology is a wireless network and a mobile device that receives demand notification and enables a speedy response. This solution allows the associate closest to the ordered item to physically pull it and verify its availability.

Walmart offers customer store pickup.

© Danny Johnston/AP Photo

For the buy-online-and-pick-up-in-store option to be successful, the retailer must be able to move the product along its supply chain smoothly, effectively, and efficiently with the intention of delivering a single order to an individual customer. That is what enables the retailer to deliver an outstanding in-store pick-up experience, and in return, brings the customer back to the store in the future.[28]

Inventory Management through Just-in-Time Inventory Systems

Marketing channel management offers the 21st century's answer to a host of distribution problems faced by firms. As recently as the early 1990s, even the most innovative firms needed 15 to 30 days—or even more—to fulfill an order from the warehouse to the customer. The typical order-to-delivery process had several steps: order creation, usually using a telephone, fax, or mail; order processing, using a manual system for credit authorization and assignment to a warehouse; and physical delivery. Things could, and often did, go wrong. Ordered goods were not available. Orders were lost or misplaced. Shipments were misdirected. These mistakes lengthened the time it took to get merchandise to customers and potentially made the entire process more expensive.

Faced with such predicaments, firms began stockpiling inventory at each level of the supply chain (retailers, wholesalers, and manufacturers), but keeping inventory where it is not needed becomes a huge and wasteful expense. If a manufacturer has a huge stock of items stuck in a warehouse, it not only is not earning profits by selling those items but also must pay to maintain and guard that warehouse.

Therefore many firms, such as H&M, Zara, Mango, and Forever 21, have adopted a practice developed by Toyota in the 1950s. **Just-in-time (JIT) inventory systems**, also known as **quick response (QR) inventory systems** in retailing, are inventory management systems that deliver less merchandise on a more frequent basis than in traditional inventory systems. The firm gets the merchandise just in time for it to be used in the manufacture of another product or for sale when the customer wants it. The benefits of a JIT system include reduced **lead time** (the amount of time between the recognition that an order needs to be placed and the arrival of the needed merchandise at the seller's store, available for sale), increased product availability, and lower inventory investment.[29]

Firms such as H&M have adopted a just-in-time (JIT) or quick response inventory system.

© Victor J. Blue/Bloomberg/Getty Images

Reduced Lead Time By eliminating the need for paper transactions, the EDI in the JIT systems reduces lead time. Even better, the shorter lead times further reduce the need for inventory, because the shorter the lead time, the easier it is for the retailer to forecast its demand.

Increased Product Availability and Lower Inventory Investment In general, as a firm's ability to satisfy customer demand by having stock on hand increases, so does its inventory investment; that is, it needs to keep more backup inventory in stock. But with JIT, the ability to satisfy demand can actually increase while inventory decreases. Because a firm like H&M can make purchase commitments or produce merchandise closer to the time of sale, its own inventory investment is reduced. H&M needs less inventory because it's getting less merchandise in each order but receiving those shipments more often. Because firms using JIT order merchandise to cover shorter-term demand, their inventory is reduced even further.

The ability to satisfy customer demand by keeping merchandise in stock also increases in JIT systems as a result of the more frequent shipments. For instance, if an H&M store runs low on a medium-sized red T-shirt, its JIT system ensures a shorter lead time than for those of more traditional retailers. As a result, it is less likely that the H&M store will be out of stock for its customers before the next T-shirt shipment arrives.

Costs of a JIT System Although firms achieve great benefits from a JIT system, it is not without its costs. The distribution function becomes much more complicated with more frequent deliveries. With greater order frequency also come smaller orders, which are more expensive to transport and more difficult to coordinate. Therefore, JIT systems require a strong commitment by the firm and its vendors to cooperate, share data, and develop systems.

PROGRESS CHECK

1. How does merchandise flow through a typical marketing channel?
2. Why have just-in-time inventory systems become so popular?

Reviewing Learning Objectives

 Understand the importance of marketing channels and supply chain management.

Marketing channels allow companies to get their products in the appropriate outlets in sufficient quantities to meet consumer demand. To anticipate this demand, advertising and promotions must be coordinated with the departments that control inventory and transportation. Otherwise, customers would come in seeking a promotion and not find the product.

Without the members in a marketing channel, consumers would be forced to find raw materials, manufacture products, and somehow get them to where they could be used all on their own. Thus, each marketing channel member adds value to the product by performing one or more of these functions. Marketing channel management also creates value for each firm in the chain and helps bind together many company functions, including manufacturing, inventory management, transportation, advertising, and marketing.

 Understand the difference between direct and indirect marketing channels.

There are ways by which businesses get their goods to consumers. Using a direct marketing channel, a customer can purchase goods from the manufacturer without needing to go through a retailer or intermediary, generally online (e.g., Ascend speakers) or at company stores (e.g., Apple). More commonly, manufacturers choose to offer their goods to consumers through an intermediary, such as a retailer (e.g., Walmart), implementing an indirect marketing channel strategy.

 Describe how marketing channels are managed.

The more closely aligned the marketing channel members are with each other, the less likely there will be significant conflict. An administered marketing channel occurs when a dominant and powerful marketing channel member has control over the other members. In a contractual marketing channel (e.g., franchising), coordination and control are dictated by contractual relationships between members. Corporate marketing channels can operate relatively smoothly because one firm owns the various levels of the chains. Marketing channels also can be effectively managed through strong relationships developed with marketing channel partners. To create such relationships, the partners must trust each other, communicate openly, have compatible goals, realize there is benefit in being interdependent, and be willing to invest in each other's success.

 Describe the flow of information and merchandise in the marketing channel.

Information flow involves: flow 1 (customer to store), flow 2 (store to buyer), flow 3 (buyer to manufacturer), flow 4 (store to manufacturer), flow 5 (store to distribution center), and flow 6 (manufacturer to distribution center and buyer). Merchandise flow involves flow 1 (manufacturer to retailer distribution centers), flow 2 (manufacturer directly to stores), flow 3 (distribution centers to stores, when shipped first to distribution centers), and flow 4 (retailer to customer).

Key Terms

■SMARTBOOK

- administered vertical marketing system, 496
- advanced shipping notice (ASN), 503
- checking, 508
- coercive power, 496
- contractual vertical marketing system, 497
- corporate vertical marketing system, 498
- cross-docking distribution center, 508
- direct marketing channel, 492
- dispatcher, 506
- distribution center, 491

- electronic data interchange (EDI), 503
- expertise power, 496
- floor-ready merchandise, 508
- franchising, 497
- fulfillment center, 491
- horizontal channel conflict, 494
- independent or conventional marketing channel, 495
- indirect marketing channel, 492
- information power, 496
- just-in-time (JIT) inventory system, 510
- lead time, 510
- legitimate power, 496

- marketing channel management, 488
- mobile task management, 509
- pick ticket, 509
- planner, 506
- power, 496
- quick response (QR) inventory system, 510
- radio frequency identification (RFID) tag, 508
- receiving, 508
- referent power, 496
- reward power, 496
- strategic or partnering relationship, 499
- supply chain management, 488

Marketing Digitally

1. Zappos.com, an online shoe seller, has received praise for its stellar supply chain management. Go to http://about.zappos.com/zappos-story/fulfillment-facility, read the "In the Beginning," "Looking Ahead," and "Customer Testimonial" sections, and see how a shoe ultimately reaches the customer. How does its fulfillment center enable Zappos to adhere to its marketing communications message and provide excellent customer service?

2. The case study for this chapter examines how Zara International, a division of Inditex, successfully manages its supply chain. Visit Inditex's website (http://www.inditex.com) and go to "Sustainability," then review the company's commitment to sustainable management, particularly the section that pertains to its suppliers and the code of conduct for its suppliers. Considering the discussion in this chapter about strategic relationships, how does Inditex address the factors necessary for mutually beneficial partnerships, according to its code of conduct?

Marketing Applications

1. Describe marketing channel management by identifying the major activities that it involves. Identify several ways that marketing channel management adds value to a company's offerings, with regard to consumers as well as business partners.

2. In what ways can the flow of information be managed in the supply chain? How can the ready flow of information increase a firm's operating efficiencies?

3. Describe how B2B transactions might employ EDI to process purchase information. Considering the information discussed in Chapter 7 about B2B buying situations, determine which buying situation (new task, modified rebuy, or straight rebuy) would most likely align with the use of EDI technology. Justify your answer.

4. What are the differences between the use of a traditional distribution center and one that relies on cross-docking? Discuss the extent to which one is more efficient than the other, being sure to detail your reasoning.

5. Discuss the advantages to a retailer like Macy's of expending the time and effort to get merchandise floor-ready at either the point of manufacture or in the distribution center rather than having retail store staff members do it in the stores. Provide the logic behind your answer.

6. A just-in-time (JIT) inventory system appears to be an important success factor for retailers like H&M and Forever 21. Choose a local retailer and examine the advantages and disadvantages of its use of a JIT system. Do you believe it should use JIT? Why?

7. Give an example of a retailer that participates in an independent (conventional) supply chain and one involved in a vertical marketing system. Discuss the advantages and disadvantages of each.

8. For each of the following consumer products, identify the type of vertical marketing system used, and justify your answer: (a) Bertolli pasta sold through grocery stores, (b) Krispy Kreme donuts sold through franchises, and (c) www.polo.com by Ralph Lauren.

9. Why might a big company like Lenovo want to develop strategic partnerships with locally owned computer stores? Describe what Lenovo would have to do to maintain such relationships.

10. You are hired as an assistant brand manager for a popular consumer product. One day in an emergency meeting, the brand manager informs the group that there is a problem with one of the suppliers and that he has decided to send you over to the manufacturing facilities to investigate the problem. When you arrive at the plant, you learn that a key supplier has become increasingly unreliable in terms of quality and delivery. You ask the plant manager why the plant doesn't switch suppliers, because it is becoming a major problem for your brand. He informs you that the troubled supplier is his cousin, whose wife has been very ill, and he just can't switch right now. What course of action should you take?

Quiz Yourself

1. All of the following are examples of the value provided by a supply chain in the production of kitchen stoves except

   a. the transportation company gets the stove to the retailer.

   b. the retailer educates the customer about product features, and delivers and installs the stove.

   c. the product design team develops initial drawings for a new product offering.

   d. the stove maker turns the components into the stove.

   e. the components manufacturer helps the stove manufacturer by supplying parts and materials.

2. When supply chain members that buy and sell to one another are not in agreement about their goals, _____ channel conflict can occur.

   a. vertical

   b. independent

   c. competitive

   d. horizontal

   e. administered

(Answers to these two questions can be found in the Quiz Yourself Answer Key section.)

Chapter Case Study

ZARA DELIVERS FAST FASHION[30]

In the fast fashion retail business strategy, supply chain management processes serve to introduce fashionable merchandise rapidly so that stores can respond immediately to customer demand for merchandise. This was pioneered by Zara, a global specialty apparel chain located in La Coruna, Spain, but it also has been adopted by other retailers, including H&M (headquartered in Sweden), TopShop (UK), and Forever 21 (United States).

The approach is particularly effective for specialty apparel retailers that target fashion-conscious consumers who simply must have the latest looks—but they want to do so on a very limited budget. These shoppers load up on new fast fashions every few weeks instead of purchasing a few higher-priced basics every few months.

To fit with such short cycles and meet customers' demands, the fast fashion process starts with the receipt of timely information from store managers. At Zara, store managers always have their reporting devices literally in hand. These handheld devices, which are linked directly to the company's corporate office in Spain, enable daily reports on what customers are buying (or not) and what they are asking for but not finding.

For example, customers might want a purple version of a pink shirt that they see on the shop floor. Managers immediately pass the information on to the designers in Spain. Those designers then communicate electronically with the factory that produces fabric for shirts. This factory starts up its automated equipment, which is run by assemblers who live in close proximity to the factory. (The undyed fabric comes from Asia, where Zara finds inexpensive sources, and then bulk fabric ships to Spain and Portugal to be manufactured into apparel.) The robots in the company's 23 highly automated factories start cutting out shirts and mixing purple dye. For final construction, a network of 300 or so small assemblers, located near the factories in Galicia, Spain, and northern Portugal, takes responsibility for making the final product. Finally, to ensure timely delivery, the shirts get shipped by truck to stores in Europe and by air express to stores in the rest of the world.

The Benefits of Fast Fashion for Zara Zara's main advantage over its competitors, such as The Gap, Abercrombie & Fitch, and American Eagle Outfitters, has resulted from its highly responsive and tightly organized supply chain. Unlike these competitors, Zara selects factory locations that are in close geographic proximity to the company's headquarters in Spain. Although this approach increases labor costs, compared with outsourced production in lower-cost countries in Asia, it also improves communication, reduces shipping costs and time, and reduces the time before new fashions appear in stores. It also gives

Zara's competitive advantage in specialty apparel retailing is based on its efficient supply chain that delivers fashionable merchandise to its stores frequently.

© Denis Doyle/AP Photo

Zara the flexibility to modify its operations in one supply chain function to expedite processes in another, such as pricing or tagging. It might hang merchandise on racks in the warehouse so that store employees can move apparel directly from delivery to the sales floor. And it can do all this because it maintains complete control over the entire process.

Furthermore, instead of shipping new products a few times a season, as many of its competitors do, Zara makes deliveries to every one of its stores every few days. The purple shirts would be in stores in two weeks—compared with the several months it would take for most department stores and other specialty apparel stores to accomplish the same feat. Because its fast fashion system also ensures shorter lead times, it's less likely that any Zara store will be out of stock before the next sweater shipment arrives. Limiting the stock in stores even can create a sense of scarcity among its customers. If they don't buy now, the item might not be available next time they visit the store. By producing and shipping in these small quantities, Zara can quickly recover from its (rare) fashion faux pas.

Finally, the efficiency of its supply chain means Zara rarely has to discount merchandise that is not selling. At Zara, the number of items that end up marked down is about half the industry average. Even with these results, Zara still manages to introduce around 10,000 new designs and 40,000 new SKUs each year.

Moving Too Fast? The Negative Effects of Fast Fashion Despite some strong signals of success—including annual growth rates of approximately 20 percent in terms of sales and number of stores—Zara started to outgrow its own strategy. By their very nature, fashion trends change rapidly and constantly, and so must the merchandise on Zara's shop floors. Faced with disappointed customers, some sales managers ordered extra quantities of hot items so as to avoid stockouts. Even with this attempt to circumvent the replenishment system, some stores still suffered from stockouts, because they received fewer units than they had ordered when overall demand exceeded inventory levels. For some items, Zara even confronted perhaps the most frustrating scenario in a supply chain: Inventory sat unused, eating up storage costs at one location even as another store desperately pleaded for the same inventory to meet its customers' demand.

As noted among the benefits, the company launches as many as 10,000 new styles annually, with a range of colors and sizes, resulting in hundreds of thousands of SKUs in the system. If we add in replenishment orders, which are received twice weekly, Zara's average shipping total reached nearly 2.5 million items per week, all coming from the company's distribution center. Its legendary supply chain efficiency thus was in danger of a clogged artery.

In response, Zara has adopted some new mathematical processes that turn human experience and mountains of data into actionable information. These models factor in store managers' unique requests for merchandise replenishments, together with historical trends in the sales of the same item. Merchandise display practices have been altered, such as removing all sizes of a garment from the sales floor if a popular size is not available. This practice helps reduce customer frustration, in that they never see an item that might not be available in their size. It also diminishes shipping; if the medium size is unavailable, the small and large sizes do not get shipped either. Instead, these remaining sizes head toward the stores that still have all sizes in stock so they can be available to customers there.

Furthermore, Zara is making more effective uses of RFID technology. Because Zara manufacturers its own clothing, it can insert RFID tags into the security tags that already appear on each piece of clothing. Thus the very act of inserting the tags becomes viable as a parallel step to the attachment of the security tags. In contrast, retailers that previously tried to insert RFID tags struggled to find efficient methods and had trouble deciding exactly when in the supply chain they should be inserted. Walmart, for example, demanded that suppliers add them, but suppliers balked at the added expense associated with the additional step.[31]

In addition, by including the RFID elements within the security tags, Zara has found a way to reuse the still relatively expensive RFID technology. In previous experiments, the tags left the store with customers who purchased the related item. At Zara, employees remove the security tag as they check out customers, so the RFID chips also stay in the store, available for reuse.

These methods give Zara a distinct advantage. The task of taking inventory has become so much faster and easier—rather than actively scanning each item's barcode, inventory takers simply walk through the store with an RFID device that passively gathers information from each rack—that Zara can perform it every six weeks instead of twice a year, as is common in the industry. In turn, its inventory tracking is drastically more accurate, and it knows exactly what styles and items are selling best (or worst).

Growth, costs, market demand, and technology advances all can push retail executives to rethink their business processes. But truly savvy managers search for ways to optimize operations, even when business is running smoothly. As Zara learned, current approaches will not necessarily work tomorrow. As the founder of Zara's corporate owner, Inditex, told the company's first deputy chair and CEO, "Once a month, come here thinking that we are near bankruptcy. You will find a lot of things to change."[32]

Questions

1. How does an individual firm like Zara manage a supply chain? How does it get new products from design to store so quickly?

2. What are some of the ways that Zara's supply chain management system has helped create value for its customers? Provide specific examples.

3. What challenges did Zara's focus on supply chain efficiency create? Are all such systems destined to suffer such growing pains?

Endnotes

1. "IKEA," https://en.wikipedia.org/wiki/IKEA.

2. IKEA, "Flat Packs, Stacks and How We Ship Them," http://www.ikea.com/ms/en_US/the_ikea_story/working_at_ikea/work_areas_logistics.html.

3. Matt McCue, "Ikea: For Delighting Customers at Each and Every Turn," *Fast Company*, February 9, 2015, http://www.fastcompany.com/3039598/most-innovative-companies-2015/ikea.

4. Saabira Chaudhuri, "IKEA's Favorite Design Idea: Shrink the Box," *The Wall Street Journal*, June 18, 2015.

5. McCue, "Ikea: For Delighting Customers at Each and Every Turn."

6. This chapter draws from Michael Levy, Barton A. Weitz, and Dhruv Grewal, *Retailing Management*, 9th ed. (Burr Ridge, IL: McGraw-Hill/Irwin, 2012).

7. This chapter draws from Levy et al., *Retailing Management*, 9th ed. See also the special issue, "Past, Present, and Future of Marketing Channels," *Journal of Retailing* 91 (December 2015), for insightful summaries of research into related topics.

8. Alexander Coolidge, "Walmart's Strategy May Squeeze P&G, Other Suppliers," *Cincinnati Enquirer*, April 13, 2015, http://www.cincinnati.com/story/money/2015/04/11/walmarts-back-basics-strategy-may-squeeze-pg-suppliers/25632645/.

9. Procter & Gamble, "Recent Innovations," http://us.pg.com/who_we_are/our_approach/our_approach_innovation/recent_innovations.

10. Based on Barton A. Weitz, "PenAgain Sells to Walmart," in Michael Levy and Barton A. Weitz, *Retailing Management*, 8th ed. (Burr Ridge, IL: McGraw-Hill/Irwin, 2012), pp. 564–65; http://www.Penagain.com; Gwendolyn Bounds, "The Long Road to Walmart," *The Wall Street Journal*, September 19, 2005, p. R1; Gwendolyn Bounds, "One Mount to Make It," *The Wall Street Journal*, May 30, 2006, p. B1.

11. Terry L. Esper et al., "Demand and Supply Integration: A Conceptual Framework of Value Creation through Knowledge Management," *Journal of the Academy of Marketing Science* 38, no. 1 (2010), pp. 5–18.

12. http://www.marketingpower.com/_layouts/Dictionary.aspx.

13. Andrew Elliot, "Does P&G Need Retailers Anymore?" *Retail Wire*, November 3, 2014.

14. George E. Stigler, "The Division of Labor Is Limited by the Extent of the Market," *Journal of Political Economy* 59, no. 3 (1951), pp. 185–93.

15. Dan Berthiaume, "Three Reasons Amazon Is Everyone's Competitor" *Chain Store Age*, November 9, 2015.

16. Greg Besinger, "Amazon Wants to Ship Your Package Before You Buy It," *The Wall Street Journal*, January 17, 2014, http://wsjonline.com.

17. Angus Loten and Adam Janofsky, "Sellers Need Amazon, But at What Cost?" *The Wall Street Journal*, January 15, 2015.

18. Tereza Dean, David A. Griffith, and Roger J. Calantone, "New Product Creativity: Understanding Contract Specificity in New Product Introductions," *Journal of Marketing* 80 (March 2016), pp. 39–58.

19. http://www.marketingpower.com/live/mg-dictionary.

20. "2016 Top Franchises from Entrepreneur's Franchise 500 List," https://www.entrepreneur.com/franchise500.

21. https://www.teslamotors.com/blog/tesla-approach-distributing-and-servicing-cars.

22. Lisa Scheer, Fred Miao, and Jason Garrett, "The Effects of Supplier Capabilities on Industrial Customers' Loyalty: The Role of Dependence," *Journal of the Academy of Marketing Science* 38, no. 1 (2010), pp. 90–104; Robert W. Palmatier, Rajiv Dant, and Dhruv Grewal, "A Longitudinal Analysis of Theoretical Perspectives of Interorganizational Relationship Performance," *Journal of Marketing* 71 (October 2007), pp. 172–94; Robert W. Palmatier et al., "A Meta-Analysis on the Antecedents and Consequences of Relationship Marketing Mediators: Insight into Key Moderators," *Journal of Marketing* 70 (October 2006), pp. 136–53.

23. Donna Davis and Susan Golicic, "Gaining Comparative Advantage in Supply Chain Relationships: The Mediating Role of Market-Oriented IT Competence," *Journal of the Academy of Marketing Science* 38, no. 1 (2010), pp. 56–70; Beth Davis-Sramek, Richard Germain, and Karthik Iyer, "Supply Chain Technology: The Role of Environment in Predicting Performance," *Journal of the Academy of Marketing Science* 38, no. 1 (2010), pp. 42–55; Erin Anderson and Barton Weitz, "The Use of Pledges to Build and Sustain Commitment in Distribution Channels," *Journal of Marketing Research* 29 (February 1992), pp. 18–34.

24. http://www.marketingpower.com/_layouts/Dictionary.aspx.

25. http://www.vendormanagedinventory.com.

26. G. P. Kiesmüller and R. A. C. M. Broekmeulen, "The Benefit of VMI Strategies in a Stochastic Multi-Product Serial Two Echelon System," *Computers and Operations Research* 37, no. 2 (2010), pp. 406–16; Dong-Ping Song and John Dinwoodie, "Quantifying the Effectiveness of VMI and Integrated Inventory Management in a Supply Chain with Uncertain Lead-Times and Uncertain Demands," *Production Planning & Control* 19, no. 6 (2008), pp. 590–600.

27. J. Lindsey-Mullikin and R. D. Petty, "Marketing Tactics Discouraging Price Search: Deception and Competition," *Journal of Business Research* 64, no. 1 (2011), pp. 67–73. doi: 10.1016/j.jbusres.2009.10.003.

28. Jen Mosscrop, "The Fulfillment Option That Brings Customers Back in Store," *Chain Store Age*, March 25, 2014.

29. Steve Lohr, "Drafting Antitrust Case, F.T.C. Raises Pressure on Google," *The New York Times*, October 12, 2012, http://www.nytimes.com; Claire Cain Miller, "Europeans Reach Deal with Google on Searches," *The New York Times*, April 14, 2013, http://www.nytimes.com.

30. Ben Latham, "How Retailers Can Learn from Fast Fashion to Beat the Weather," *Retail Week*, April 20, 2016; Vertica Bhardwaj and Ann Fairhurst, "Fast Fashion: Response to Changes in the Fashion Industry," *International Review of Retail, Distribution and Consumer Research* 20 (February 2010), pp. 165–73; Felipe Caro et al., "Zara Uses Operations Research to Reengineer Its Global Distribution Process," *Interfaces* 40 (2010), pp. 71–84; Carmen Lopez and Ying Fan, "Case Study: Internationalisation of the Spanish Fashion Brand Zara," *Journal of Fashion Marketing and Management* 13, no. 2 (2009), pp. 279–96.

31. Christopher Bjork, "Zara Builds Its Business Around RFID," *The Wall Street Journal*, September 17, 2014.

32. Zeynep Ton, Elena Corsi, and Vincent Dessain, "Zara: Managing Stores for Fast Fashion," Harvard Business School Case, March 2011.

i. SCDigest, "Supply Chain News: Goya Foods Shows Path to Success for Mid-Market Companies from New Supply Chain Planning Tools," July 13, 2011, http://www.scdigest.com.

ii. Taylor Soper, "Amazon's Dominance of Online Shopping Starts with Product Searches, Study Shows," *Geek Wire*, October 6, 2015; Greg Besinger, "Amazon Wants to Ship Your Package Before You Buy It," *The Wall Street Journal*, January 17, 2014, http://wsjonline.com.

iii. Ilan Brat, "Hunger for Organic Foods Stretches the Supply Chain," *The Wall Street Journal*, April 3, 2015.

iv. Sean McLain and Newley Purnell, "Indian Startups View to Win E-Commerce Battle," *The Wall Street Journal*, October 23, 2015.

v. Todd Sherman, "Which Same-Day Service Will Deliver the Goods for Retailers?" *RetailWire*, January 28, 2014; J.J. McCorvey, "AmazonFresh is Jeff Bezos' Last Mile Quest for Total Retail Domination," *Fast Company*, August 5, 2013; Amy Guthrie and Shely Banjo, "Mexico Delivers for Walmart," *The Wall Street Journal*, February 15, 2014; James B. Stewart, "Walmart Plays Catch Up with Amazon," *The New York Times*, October 22, 2015.

CHAPTER 17

RETAILING AND OMNICHANNEL MARKETING

After reading this chapter, you should be able to:

LO17-1 Discuss the four factors manufacturers should consider as they develop their strategies for working with retailers.

LO17-2 Outline the considerations associated with choosing retail partners.

LO17-3 List the three levels of distribution intensity.

LO17-4 Describe the various types of retailers.

LO17-5 Describe the components of a retail strategy.

LO17-6 Identify the benefits and challenges of omnichannel retailing.

When it comes to competition among retailers, pretty much everyone competes with Amazon. From small sellers of personalized gifts to service retailers to massive consumer goods providers, the retail market must recognize that Amazon is a dominant actor, specialized in getting the products that customers want to them quickly, efficiently, and exactly when and where they want those items. In particular, Amazon offers three key benefits to retail customers.

First, Amazon is incredibly convenient, available to meet shoppers' every product need, at any time. Second, it is increasing its remarkable availability even further, such as with its expansion into services and its introduction of new tools and channels to help customers interact with it more often. Third, just in case people want to interact personally, Amazon is gaining steam as a brick-and-mortar retailer as well.

Let's consider these benefits in turn. Not only is Amazon's inventory unsurpassed, but it makes ordering easy with checkout tools such as one-click and automatically repeated purchases on frequently bought items. Then it gets the ordered products to customers quickly and conveniently. For a fee, many customers even can get the products on the same day. But with its expanding roster of fulfillment centers, Amazon ensures that even its free, standard shipping service is pretty fast.

So why does it need physical stores? It recognizes that some customers like to shop in an actual environment rather than a virtual one. Accordingly, Amazon plans to apply its remarkable facility with integrating and leveraging customer data to make recommendations to its brick-and-mortar stores. In so doing, it appears poised to make a successful transition from a mainly online presence to a truly omnichannel source.

It also is making its presence felt in other ways, especially in customers' homes. With its Echo service, Amazon customers who pay for Prime Now service can place orders by calling out their grocery list to an artificial intelligence device installed in their homes. With records of prior purchases, Echo can also suggest alternative options and apply previously set shipping preferences. The

Dash device is another means for retail consumers to reorder various items with literally a push of a button.

And in terms of services, Amazon already functions as some users' primary search engine. Among 2000 respondents, 44 percent indicated that when they begin a product search, they start on Amazon rather than on traditional search engines such as Google or on specific retailers' own websites. If a shopper starts the purchase process with a search on Amazon, he or she is highly likely to remain with Amazon through the final steps of the process—namely, making the purchase and even reviewing it thereafter. Furthermore, when asked why they chose Amazon, most of these respondents noted that the retailer offered great personalization. When they enter a search term, Amazon knows how to suggest related and pertinent products that help them make good purchase decisions.[1]

As consumers invite Amazon in and solicit further services from it, the effect the retail giant has on the market appears destined to increase. For retailers seeking to compete with it—and by definition, that means pretty much every retailer in the world—paying attention to what Amazon is doing now is a necessary task. That is, because Amazon competes with literally every retailer, every retailer needs to understand what makes Amazon work so well if they are going to remain competitive and hold on to at least some of their market share.[2]

Retailing sits at the end of the supply chain, where marketing meets the consumer.[3] But there is far more to retailing than just manufacturing a product and making it available to customers. It is primarily the retailer's responsibility to make sure that customers' expectations are fulfilled.

Retailing is defined as the set of business activities that add value to products and services sold to consumers for their personal or family use. Our definition includes products bought at stores, through catalogs, and over the Internet, as well as services such as fast-food restaurants, airlines, and hotels. Some retailers claim they sell at wholesale prices, but if they sell to customers for their personal use, they are still retailers, regardless of their prices. Wholesalers (see Chapter 16) buy products from manufacturers and resell them to retailers or industrial or business users.

LO17-1 Discuss the four factors manufacturers should consider as they develop their strategies for working with retailers.

Retailing today is changing, both in the United States and around the world. Manufacturers no longer rule many supply chains as they once did. Retailers such as Walmart (U.S. superstore), Costco (U.S. warehouse club), Kroger (U.S. grocery chain), Schwarz (German conglomerate), Tesco (U.K.-based food retailer), Carrefour (French hypermarket), Aldi Enkauf (German discount food retailer), Metro (German retail conglomerate), Home Depot (U.S. home improvement), Walgreens (U.S. drugstore), Target (U.S. discount retailer), and Amazon (U.S. e-tailer)[4]—the largest retailers in the world—dictate to their suppliers what should be made, how it should be configured, when it should be delivered, and, to some extent, what it should cost. These retailers are clearly in the driver's seat.

This chapter extends Chapter 16's discussion of supply chain management by examining why and how manufacturers use retailers. The manufacturer's strategy depends on its overall market power and how consistent a new product or product line is with current offerings. Consider the following scenarios:

M-A-C will use different criteria than will either Coach for Men or Eva's green cosmetics for placing products in retail stores.

© Linda Matlow/Alamy

- Scenario 1: Cosmetics conglomerate Estée Lauder's subsidiary brand M-A-C is introducing a new line of mascara.

- Scenario 2: Coach, well known for its women's handbags, has introduced a line of men's leather goods, apparel, gifts, shoes, and other accessories—products not previously in its assortment.

EXHIBIT 17.1 Factors for Establishing a Relationship with Retailers

1. Choosing retailing partners → 2. Identifying types of retailers → 3. Developing a retail strategy → 4. Managing an omnichannel strategy

- Scenario 3: Eva, a young entrepreneur, is launching a new line of environmentally friendly (green) cosmetics.

Each of these scenarios is different and requires the manufacturer to consider alternatives for reaching its target markets through retailers.

Exhibit 17.1 illustrates four factors manufacturers consider to establish their strategies for working with retailers. In choosing retail partners, the first factor, manufacturers assess how likely it is for certain retailers to carry their products. Manufacturers also consider where their target customers expect to find the products, because those are exactly the stores in which they want to place their products. The overall size and level of sophistication of the manufacturer will determine how many of the marketing channel functions it performs and how many it will hand off to other channel members. Another aspect in choosing retail partners: The type and availability of the product and the image the manufacturer wishes to portray will determine how many retailers within a geographic region will carry the products.

For the second factor, manufacturers identify the types of retailers that would be appropriate to carry their products. Although the choice is often obvious—such as a supermarket for fresh produce—manufacturers may have a choice of retailer types for some products.

As we discussed in Chapter 16, a hallmark of a strong marketing channel is one in which manufacturers and retailers coordinate their efforts. In the third factor, manufacturers and retailers therefore develop their strategy by implementing the four Ps.

Many retailers and some manufacturers use an **omnichannel or multichannel strategy**, which involves selling in more than one channel (e.g., store, catalog, and Internet). The fourth factor therefore consists of examining the circumstances in which sellers may prefer to adopt a particular strategy.

Although these factors for establishing a relationship with retailers are listed consecutively, manufacturers may consider them all simultaneously or in a different order.

LO17-2 Outline the considerations associated with choosing retail partners.

CHOOSING RETAILING PARTNERS

Imagine, as a consumer, trying to buy a new leather jacket without being able to visit a retailer or buy online. You would have to figure out exactly what size, color, and style of jacket you wanted. Then you would need to contact various manufacturers, whether in person, by phone, or over the Internet, and order the jacket. If the jacket fit you reasonably well but not perfectly, you still might need to take it to a tailor to have the sleeves shortened. You wouldn't find this approach to shopping very convenient. However, as Superior Service 17.1 explains, consumers are asking for other benefits from fashion brands that represent challenges to traditional retail channel structures.

Most manufacturers like Coach use retailers such as Macy's to undertake partnerships that create value by pulling together all the actions necessary for the greatest possible customer convenience and satisfaction. The store offers a broad selection of purses, leather jackets, scarves, and other accessories that its buyers have carefully chosen in advance. Customers

Coach partners with retailers to help conveniently deliver its products to satisfied customers.
© MaximImages/Alamy

Superior Service 17.1   Removing the Retailer, Burberry Seeks to Access Consumers Directly[i]

The catwalks at the big fashion shows have long been exciting, experiential events. Celebrities and fashion mavens stake out seats in the front rows, and critics and fashion photographers weigh in on the looks that are destined to catch on, as well as the radically creative designs that are unlikely to ever be re-created in the real world.

But the modern state of the world means that nearly anyone can join in on these sorts of experiences, at least virtually and at some level, by live streaming the events or following social media updates by attendees, posted in real time. As a result, the fashion houses are confronting a new and vexing problem: They can no longer "talk to a customer and say, 'We're really excited, we're going to stimulate you and inspire you, but you can't touch it or feel it for another six months.'" That is, the excitement created by fashion shows is now so widespread and encompassing that consumers are demanding immediate access to the looks that appear on the models striding down the runway.

In response, Burberry is giving it to them. In a radical departure from its traditional mode of operation—in which it would feature the season's looks at a fashion show, receive orders from retailers, produce the goods, and then make them available to consumers about six months after the show—the fashion house has promised a "wear-now" option. Shoppers can see an outfit or piece in the fashion show, order it immediately, and have it in hand within a few weeks. For the privilege of doing so, wear-now customers will pay full price. Burberry hopes that this option will help mitigate the trend in which customers have gotten so accustomed to end-of-season sales that they simply wait to buy products until they are available at a discounted price.

The move implies major changes for other members of the fashion world too. For example, fashion magazines have long been the arbiters of what is or is not great fashion. But if consumers can order the pieces on their own, will those magazines continue to play their powerful role? If consumers can make their own choices from the runway, will they even need to keep buying the magazines?

The other key player is the retailers that traditionally stock fashion brands. Although Burberry largely sells through its

Burberry's customers can now order fashion show items and have them within a few weeks.
© Catwalking/Getty Images

own stores, if other fashion brands adopt a similar direct runway-to-consumer approach, retailers might struggle to find customers who are willing to wait for the longer production process required before they can gain access to the latest fashions in stores.

can see, touch, feel, and try on any item while in the store. They can buy one scarf or leather jacket at a time or buy an outfit that works together. Finally, the store provides a salesperson to help customers coordinate their outfits and a tailor to make the whole thing fit perfectly.

When choosing retail partners, manufacturers look at the basic channel structure, where their target customers expect to find the products, channel member characteristics, and distribution intensity.

Channel Structure

The level of difficulty a manufacturer experiences in getting retailers to purchase its products is determined by the degree to which the channel is vertically integrated, as described in Chapter 16; the degree to which the manufacturer has a strong brand or is otherwise desirable in the market; and the relative power of the manufacturer and retailer.

Scenario 1 represents a corporate vertical marketing system. Because M-A-C is made by Estée Lauder and operates its own stores, when the new mascara line is introduced, the stores receive the new line automatically with no decision on the part of the retailer. In contrast, Revlon would have a much more difficult time getting CVS to buy a new mascara line, because these supply chain partners are not vertically integrated.

When an established firm such as Coach enters a new market with men's leather goods, apparel, gifts, shoes, and other accessories, as is the case in Scenario 2, it must determine where its customers would expect to find these products and then use its established relationships with women's handbag buyers, the power of its brand, and its overall reputation to leverage its position in this new product area.

Eva (Scenario 3) would have an even more difficult time convincing a retailer to buy and sell her green cosmetics line because she lacks power in the marketplace—she is small, and her brand is unknown. She would have trouble getting buyers to see her, let alone consider her line. She might face relatively high slotting allowances just to get space on retailers' shelves. But like Coach in Scenario 2, Eva should consider where the end customer expects to find her products, as well as some important retailer characteristics.

Customer Expectations

Retailers should also know customer preferences regarding manufacturers. Manufacturers, in contrast, need to know where their target market customers expect to find their products and those of their competitors. As we see in the hypothetical example in Exhibit 17.2, Coach currently sells handbags at stores such as Dillard's, Neiman Marcus, and Marshalls as well as in its own stores (red arrows). Its competitor Cole Haan sells at Dillard's and Neiman Marcus (teal arrows). A survey of male Coach customers shows that they would expect to find its products at Saks Fifth Avenue, Dillard's, Neiman Marcus, and its own Coach stores (all of the stores in the light blue box). On the basis of this information, Coach decides to try selling at Saks Fifth Avenue but to stop selling at Marshalls to better meet customers' expectations.

Customers generally expect to find certain products at some stores but not at others. For example, Estée Lauder would not choose to sell to CVS or Dollar General because its customers would not expect to shop at those stores for high-end cosmetics such as Estée Lauder's. Less expensive cosmetic brands such as Revlon and Maybelline, on the other hand are sold at CVS and probably even appear as bargain closeouts at Dollar General. But male Coach customers definitely expect to find the brand's clothing offerings at major department stores and at Coach stores.

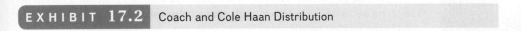

EXHIBIT 17.2   Coach and Cole Haan Distribution

Customer expectations of where they would find the product

Saks Fifth Avenue

Coach

Dillard's

Neiman Marcus

Cole Haan

Coach stores

Marshalls

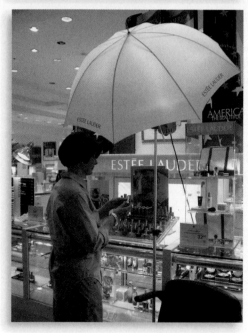

Most consumer packaged-goods companies, such as Pepsi (top), strive for intensive distribution—they want to be everywhere. But cosmetics firms such as Estée Lauder (bottom) use an exclusive distribution strategy by limiting their distribution to a few select higher-end retailers in each region.

(Top): © Kristoffer Tripplaar/Alamy; (Bottom): © Susan Van Etten/PhotoEdit

LO17-3 List the three levels of distribution intensity.

Channel Member Characteristics

Several factors pertaining to the channel members themselves help determine the channel structure. Generally, the larger and more sophisticated the channel member, the less likely that it will use supply chain intermediaries. Eva will probably use a group of independent salespeople to help sell her line of green cosmetics, whereas a large manufacturer such as Estée Lauder will use its own sales force that already has existing relationships in the industry. In the same way, an independent grocery store might buy merchandise from a wholesaler, but Walmart, the world's largest grocer, only buys directly from the manufacturer. Larger firms often find that by performing the channel functions themselves, they can gain more control, be more efficient, and save money.

Distribution Intensity

When setting up distribution for the first time, as is the case with Eva's green cosmetics (Scenario 3), or introducing a new product line, as is the case with Coach for men (Scenario 2), firms decide the appropriate level of **distribution intensity**—the number of channel members to use at each level of the marketing channel. Distribution intensity commonly is divided into three levels: intensive, exclusive, and selective.

Intensive Distribution
An **intensive distribution** strategy is designed to place products in as many outlets as possible. Most consumer packaged-goods companies, such as Pepsi, Procter & Gamble, Kraft, and other nationally branded products found in grocery and discount stores, strive for and often achieve intensive distribution. Pepsi wants its product available everywhere—grocery stores, convenience stores, restaurants, and vending machines. The more exposure the products get, the more they sell.

Exclusive Distribution
Manufacturers also might use an **exclusive distribution** policy by granting exclusive geographic territories to one or very few retail customers so that no other retailers in the territory can sell a particular brand. Exclusive distribution can benefit manufacturers by assuring them that the most appropriate retailers represent their products. Luxury goods firms such as Coach limit distribution to a few select, higher-end retailers in each region. The company believes that selling its products to full-line discount stores or off-price retailers would weaken its image.

When supply is limited or a firm is just starting out, providing an exclusive territory to one retailer or retail chain helps ensure enough inventory to provide the buying public an adequate selection. By granting exclusive territories, Eva guarantees her retailers will have an adequate supply of her green cosmetics. This guarantee gives these retailers a strong incentive to market her products. The retailers that Eva uses know there will be no competing retailers to cut prices, so their profit margins are protected. This knowledge gives them an incentive to carry more inventory and use extra advertising, personal selling, and sales promotions.

Selective Distribution
Between the intensive and exclusive distribution strategies lies **selective distribution**, which relies on a few selected retail customers in a territory to sell products. Like exclusive distribution, selective distribution helps a seller maintain a particular image and control the flow of merchandise into an area. These advantages make this approach attractive to many shopping goods manufacturers. Recall that shopping goods are those products for which consumers are willing to spend time comparing alternatives, such as most apparel items, home items like branded pots and pans or sheets and towels, branded hardware and tools, and consumer electronics. Retailers still have a strong incentive to sell the products, but not to the same extent as if they had an exclusive territory.

As we noted in Chapter 16, like any large, complicated system, a marketing channel is difficult to manage. Whether the balance of power rests with large retailers such as Walmart or with large manufacturers such as Procter & Gamble, channel members benefit by working together to develop and implement their channel strategy. In the next section, we explore the different types of retailers with an eye toward which would be most appropriate for each of our scenarios: M-A-C Cosmetics, Coach's products for men, and Eva's new line of environmentally friendly cosmetics.

PROGRESS CHECK

1. What issues should manufacturers consider when choosing retail partners?
2. What are the differences among intensive, exclusive, and selective levels of distribution intensity?

IDENTIFY TYPES OF RETAILERS

 LO17-4 Describe the various types of retailers.

At first glance, identifying the types of retailers that Coach and Eva may wish to pursue when attempting to place their new lines seems straightforward. But the choice is not always easy. Manufacturers need to understand the general characteristics of different types of retailers to determine the best channels for their product. The characteristics of a retailer that are important to a food manufacturer may be quite different from those considered valuable by a cosmetics manufacturer. In the next few sections, we examine the various types of retailers, identify some major players, and discuss some of the issues facing each type (Exhibit 17.3).

Food Retailers

The food retailing landscape is changing dramatically. Twenty years ago, consumers purchased food primarily at conventional supermarkets. Now conventional supermarkets account for only slightly more than 60 percent of food sales (not including restaurants).[5] Not only do full-line discount stores like Walmart and Target offer a full assortment of grocery items in their superstores, but traditional supermarkets also are carrying more nonfood items. Many supermarkets offer pharmacies, health care clinics, banks, and cafés.

The world's largest food retailer, Walmart, attains more than $485 billion in sales of supermarket-type merchandise.[6] On this measure, it is followed by Costco (United States),

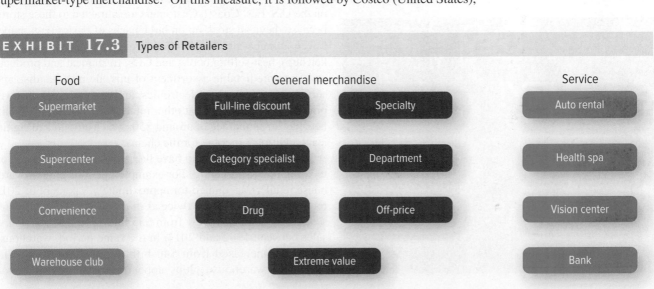

EXHIBIT 17.3 Types of Retailers

Food	General merchandise		Service
Supermarket	Full-line discount	Specialty	Auto rental
Supercenter	Category specialist	Department	Health spa
Convenience	Drug	Off-price	Vision center
Warehouse club		Extreme value	Bank

Carrefour (France), Kroger (United States), Tesco (United Kingdom), Seven & I (Japan), and Schwartz Group (Germany).[7] In North America specifically, the largest supermarket chains in order are Walmart, Kroger, Costco, Loblaw, Safeway, Publix, Ahold US, C&S Wholesale Grocers, Albertsons, and H-E-B.[8]

Supermarkets

A **conventional supermarket** is a large, self-service retail food store offering groceries, meat, and produce, as well as some nonfood items such as health and beauty aids and general merchandise.[9] Perishables including meat, produce, baked goods, and dairy products account for almost 54 percent of supermarket sales and typically have higher margins than packaged goods do.[10]

Whereas conventional supermarkets carry about 30,000 SKUs, **limited-assortment supermarkets**, or **extreme-value food retailers**, stock only about 1,500 SKUs.[11] The two largest limited-assortment supermarket chains in the United States are Save-A-Lot and ALDI. Rather than carrying 20 brands of laundry detergent, limited-assortment supermarkets offer one or two brands and sizes, one of which is a store brand. By trimming costs, limited-assortment supermarkets can offer merchandise at prices 40 percent lower than those at conventional supermarkets.[12]

Although conventional supermarkets still sell the majority of food merchandise, they are under substantial competitive pressure on multiple sides: from supercenters, warehouse clubs, extreme-value retailers, convenience stores, and even drug stores.[13] All these types of retailers have increased the amount of space they devote to consumables.

To compete successfully against intrusions by other food retailing formats, conventional supermarkets are differentiating their offerings by (1) emphasizing fresh perishables; (2) targeting green, ethnic, and Millennial consumers; (3) providing better value with private-label merchandise; (4) adding new value-added services such as online ordering and delivery options; and (5) providing a better shopping experience, such as by adding restaurant options or hosting social events.[14] One excellent example of some of these efforts comes in the form of a stellar grocer, Trader Joe's, as Adding Value 17.1 explains.

Supercenters

Supercenters are large stores (185,000 square feet) that combine a supermarket with a full-line discount store. Walmart operates almost 3,500 supercenters in the United States,[15] accounting for the vast majority of total supercenter sales—far outpacing its competitors Meijer, SuperTarget (Target), Fred Meyer (Kroger Co.), and Super Kmart Center (Sears Holding). By offering broad assortments of grocery and general merchandise products under one roof, supercenters provide a one-stop shopping convenience to customers.

Warehouse Clubs

Warehouse clubs are large retailers (100,000 to 150,000 square feet) that offer a limited and irregular assortment of food and general merchandise, little service, and low prices to the general public and small businesses. The largest warehouse club chains are Costco, Sam's Club (Walmart), and BJ's Wholesale Club (operating only on the U.S. East Coast). Customers are attracted to these stores because they can stock up on large packs of basics (e.g., paper towels), mega-sized packaged groceries (e.g., a quart of ketchup), best-selling books and CDs, fresh meat and produce, and an unpredictable assortment of upscale merchandise and services (e.g., jewelry, electronics, and home decor) at lower prices than are available at other retail stores. Typically, members pay an annual fee of around $50, which amounts to significant additional income for the chains.

Warehouse clubs also have had substantial influences on retailing and its structure. For example, the four biggest warehouse retailers accounted for approximately 8 percent of 2012 retail sales. That's nearly twice as much as e-commerce represented. E-commerce grew from $35 billion to $348 billion in sales between 1992 and 2013; in the same period, warehouse club sales increased from $40 billion to $420 billion. The growth of warehouse clubs appears largely dependent on

Warehouse clubs have expanded their assortment of products in the electronics category and are known for great prices.

© Bloomberg/Contributor/Getty Images

Adding Value 17.1   Meet the Captain and Visit the Island[ii]

The employees are wearing tropical shirts, the product labels feature puns and silly rhymes, and the manager goes by "Captain." But dismissing Trader Joe's as a joke is a bad idea, especially if you're another grocery store chain that wants to appeal to discerning shoppers. Just ask Whole Foods. The roots of its success are as diverse as the customers Trader Joe's attracts. For example, its product lines offer organic, gourmet, and multicultural options (and sometimes combinations of all three) rather than focusing on any one type of product appeal. Furthermore, those options rarely are available anywhere else, because 80 percent of Trader Joe's product assortment consists of its own private labels. The plentiful, unique options also tend to be relatively low priced—likely an artifact of Trader Joe's ownership by the same family that runs the low-priced ALDI chain.

With these product and price offerings, rather than being all things to everyone, Trader Joe's is a little something for anyone. Full, stock-up shopping trips still require another grocer, but for a little something special and tasty, Trader Joe's provides a compelling alternative. Accordingly, it attracts a diverse fan base, approximately equally split between households that earn more than $100,000 annually and those that average closer to $25,000. Still, many of the customers at Trader Joe's exhibit some appealing similarities for retailers, including high levels of education, a health emphasis, and a high level of comfort with technological innovations.

In these traits, Trader Joe's customers are remarkably similar to those who shop at Whole Foods, despite the vast differences in the price positions the two chains take. Whole Foods' CEO even has admitted that the company views Trader Joe's

If you don't think shopping for groceries is fun, try Trader Joe's.

© Zuma Press, Inc/Alamy

as its primary competitor and that its own "365" private label represents a direct response to the offerings on hand at Trader Joe's. Yet its unique positioning sets Trader Joe's apart from other grocers in consumers' minds; it also helps it stand alone when it comes to some pertinent measures of success— namely, in the grocery industry, the average rate of sales per square foot is $521. Whole Foods, with its high-end, pricey, trendy image, nearly doubles that rate, with sales per square foot of $973. And Trader Joe's, with its small, island-themed stores? It achieves an utterly astounding $1,723 per square foot on average.

demand in more heavily populated areas, as the store locations move from distant suburbs into more city centers.[16]

Although both Coach for Men and Eva's products could be sold in warehouse clubs, these retailers probably are not the best choices. Both product lines will have an upscale image, which is inconsistent with any warehouse club. If, however, either firm has overstock merchandise as a result of overestimating demand or underestimating returned merchandise from retailers, warehouse clubs are a potential outlet.

Convenience Stores **Convenience stores** provide a limited variety and assortment of merchandise at a convenient location in 3,000- to 5,000-square-foot stores with speedy checkout. 7-Eleven is the largest convenience store chain in North America, with more than 8,000 locations.[17] This type of retailer is the modern version of the neighborhood mom-and-pop grocery or general store. Convenience stores enable consumers to make purchases quickly without having to search through a large store and wait in a lengthy checkout line. Convenience store assortments are limited in terms of depth and breadth, and they charge higher prices than supermarkets

In addition to convenience, 7-Eleven is a trendy place for young consumers in Indonesia to hang out.

© Francis Dean/Corbis

do. Milk, eggs, and bread once represented the majority of their sales, but now most sales come from gasoline and cigarettes.

Convenience stores also face increased competition from other retail formats. In response to these competitive pressures, convenience stores are taking steps to decrease their dependency on gasoline sales by offering fresh food and healthy fast food, tailoring assortments to local markets, and making their stores even more convenient to shop. Finally, convenience stores are adding new services, such as financial service kiosks that give customers the opportunity to cash checks, pay bills, and buy prepaid telephone minutes, theater tickets, and gift cards.

Online Grocery Retailers Time-strapped customers are willing to pay more to access options for ordering groceries online and having them delivered (e.g., for a gallon of organic milk, Safeway charges $5.99, and the delivery service Instacart charges $7.39). As a result, online sales of groceries have grown by 14.1 percent annually for the past five years.[18] The set of retailers providing online capabilities continues to expand, with Amazon and Walmart joining the long-standing, online-only retailers such as Peapod and Fresh Direct.[19] Furthermore, these retailers are joined by companies seeking to add value to the grocery channel by providing delivery services. That is, companies such as Instacart, Shipt, Postmates, and Google's delivery arm promise to allow customers to place online orders for items from their preferred grocers.[20]

Still, approximately 30 percent of the online orders placed with grocery retailers involve non-food items such as paper products or cleaning items. In contrast, sales in stores generally feature only around 14 percent nonfood items. Consumers thus rely on online grocers for lower profit margin nonperishable items rather than higher margin fresh fruit or meats. As a result, slim margins continue to be a problem for retailers as well as delivery services. For example, Instacart earns a profit only if the order is for more than around $68. Finally, even as customers call for grocery delivery services—and the industry has grown from 1.9 percent to 2.9 percent of total grocery sales—online grocery remains much smaller than other online retailing. Part of the reason may be the limited availability of grocery delivery services, which thus far remain accessible mainly in large cities. Delivery costs are also a factor even as the task is outsourced to relatively low-cost individual private contractors. This factor also might reflect a barrier to the industry's growth: Delivering perishable groceries to many customers is a lot easier and more feasible in dense, urban settings than across vast, rural distances. The expansion of this type of food retailing has prompted various other innovations as well, as Marketing Analytics 17.1 describes.

Instacart enables customers to place online grocery orders to be delivered to their homes.

© Peter Dasilva/The New York Times/ Redux Pictures

Marketing Analytics 17.1 — How FreshDirect Figures Out How and When Customers Order[iii]

For consumers who do their grocery shopping through electronic channels, such as those maintained by FreshDirect, the device they use may make big differences in the items they order. Accordingly, FreshDirect acknowledges its need to understand where, when, and through which channels its customers are shopping during each interaction with the company.

As a simple example, the grocery delivery service has determined that when people place orders on Saturdays or Sundays, they are usually doing so on their mobile devices. During the work week though, they largely use computers, suggesting that they are ordering from their desks, during their lunch breaks or in the midst of their work day. This difference means that the mobile site could promote more products that appeal to lazy weekend activities. But the traditional website likely needs to be quick, so that consumers can place their orders before their supervisors notice that they are on a shopping site during work hours.

The company's chief consumer officer offers a range of scenarios in which multichannel and multi-device capabilities are critical for the retailer. In particular, she highlights questions about when and where consumers prefer to find recipes, as well as how they react to potential weather hazards, noting "Let's say snow is coming. We don't know exactly which day. We need to figure out when's the last time we can fulfill orders this week. Are we going to need to shut down? We know people are panicked and they want their food. So we have to figure out where they are at that moment. Do we need to give a snow message on their mobile devices? And then coordinate it with what's on the desktop?"

As people's time spent interacting with online and mobile content increases, trends suggest that, conversely, their interactions with each individual seller are getting shorter. Retailers have just a moment to appeal to these quick-moving shoppers, and a key element of that appeal is understanding how they use their various devices in specific ways.

FreshDirect uses sophisticated analytics to understand its customers' buying behavior so that it can serve them better.

Source: Fresh Direct

General Merchandise Retailers

The major types of general merchandise retailers are department stores, full-line discount stores, specialty stores, category specialists, home improvement centers, off-price retailers, and extreme-value retailers.

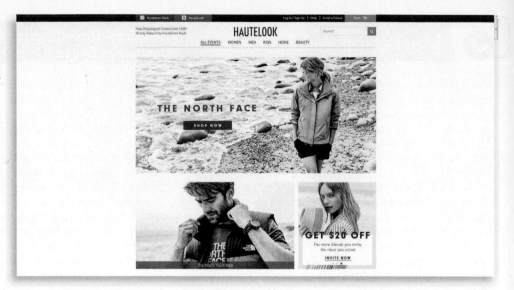

Department Stores

Department stores are retailers that carry a broad variety and deep assortment of merchandise, offer customer services, and organize their stores into distinct departments for displaying merchandise. The list of the largest department store chains in the United States includes Macy's, Kohl's, JCPenney, and Nordstrom.[21] Department stores would be an excellent retail channel for Coach for Men and Eva's new lines.

Even as some observers argue that the era of the department store has come to an end, several retailers have introduced innovative ideas to appeal better to their existing target markets, as well as attract young consumers who tend to show preferences for smaller specialty stores. For example, Nordstrom has transformed its image as a high-end destination for only the wealthiest of shoppers by integrating an online flash sale site, Haute Look. There, shoppers can find famous name brands for substantially discounted prices. To make the varied, discounted merchandise available for hands-on buyers too, Nordstrom maintains its Rack stores, as an off-price arm of its retail empire. The number of Nordstrom Rack stores continues to grow. Furthermore, Nordstrom has created strong links between these two "alternative" channels, such that consumers who order the wrong size on Haute Look can return the products to Nordstrom Rack without having to worry about shipping it back.[22]

Full-Line Discount Stores

Full-line discount stores are retailers that offer a broad variety of merchandise, limited service, and low prices. The largest full-line discount store chains are Walmart, Target, and Kmart (Sears Holding).

Although full-line discount stores typically might carry men's leather goods, accessories, and cosmetics, they are not good options for Coach for Men or Eva's new green cosmetics line. Customers do not expect higher-end products in full-line discount stores. Rather, they are looking for value prices and are willing to compromise on quality or cachet.

Walmart accounts for approximately two-thirds of full-line discount store retail sales in the United States.[23] Target has experienced considerable growth because its stores offer fashionable merchandise at low prices in a pleasant shopping environment. The retailer has developed an image of cheap chic by offering limited-edition exclusive apparel and cosmetic lines.

Specialty Stores

Specialty stores concentrate on a limited number of complementary merchandise categories targeted toward very specific market segments by offering deep but narrow assortments and sales associate expertise. Although such shops are familiar in brick-and-mortar forms, more retailers also are expanding their online specialty profile as well.

Estée Lauder's M-A-C line of cosmetics sells in the company's own retail specialty stores as well as in some department stores. Certain specialty stores would be excellent outlets for the new lines by Coach for Men and Eva. Customers likely expect to find Coach for Men leather goods and accessories in men's apparel or leather stores. Eva's line of green cosmetics would fit nicely in a cosmetics specialty store such as Sephora.

Drugstores Drugstores are specialty stores that concentrate on pharmaceuticals and health and personal grooming merchandise. Prescription pharmaceuticals represent almost 70 percent of drugstore sales. The largest drugstore chains in the United States are CVS and Walgreens Boots Alliance Inc.[24]

Drugstores face competition from pharmacies in discount stores and some food retailers and from pressure to reduce health care costs. In response, the major drugstore chains are offering a wider assortment of merchandise such as frequently purchased food items. They also offer services such as convenient drive-through windows and curbside pick-up for prescriptions, in-store medical clinics, and even makeovers and spa treatments.[25]

Although Estée Lauder's new line would not be consistent with the merchandise found in drugstores, Eva's green cosmetics may be a welcome addition. Some drugstores have recognized consumer demand for green products, although Eva's cosmetics may be priced higher than its competitors. Eva must decide whether her high-end products will suffer a tarnished image if she sells them in drugstores or whether drugstores could be a good channel for increasing her brand awareness.

Estée Lauder's M-A-C cosmetic lines sell in specialty stores such as Sephora.

© Rachel Murray/WireImage/Getty Images

Category Specialists Category specialists are big-box retailers or category killers that offer a narrow but deep assortment of merchandise. Most category specialists use a predominantly self-service approach, but they offer assistance to customers in some areas of the stores. For example, the office supply store Staples has a warehouse atmosphere with cartons of copy paper stacked on pallets, plus equipment in boxes on shelves. But in some departments, such as computers, electronics, and other high-tech products, salespeople staff the display area to answer questions and make suggestions. Other prominent category specialists are: Men's Warehouse, Best Buy, IKEA, Home Depot, and Bass Pro Shops.

By offering a complete assortment in a category at somewhat lower prices than their competition offers, category specialists can kill a category of merchandise for other retailers, which is why they are frequently called category killers. Using their category dominance, these retailers exploit their buying power to negotiate low prices.

Extreme-Value Retailers Extreme-value retailers are small, full-line discount stores that offer a limited merchandise assortment at very low prices. The largest extreme-value retailers are Dollar General and Dollar Tree (which purchased the Family Stores chain).[26]

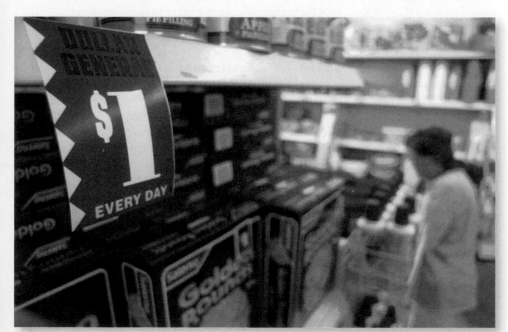

Dollar General is one of the United States' largest extreme-value retailers. It has small full-line discount stores that offer a limited assortment at very low prices.

© Mark Humphrey/AP Photo

Off-price retailers like Big Lots offer an inconsistent assort-ment of brand-name merchandise at a significant discount from the manufacturer's suggested retail price (MSRP).

© Chris Lee/MCT/Newscom

Like limited assortment food retailers, extreme-value re-tailers reduce costs and maintain low prices by buying oppor-tunistically from manufacturers with excess merchandise, offering a limited assortment, and operating in low-rent loca-tions. They offer a broad but shallow assortment of household goods, health and beauty aids, and groceries.

Many extreme-value retailers target low-income consum-ers, whose shopping behavior differs from that of typical dis-count store or warehouse club customers. Although these consumers might demand well-known national brands, they often cannot afford to buy large-sized packages. So vendors such as Procter & Gamble often create special, smaller pack-ages for extreme-value retailers, often using the reverse inno-vation approaches we discussed in Chapter 8. Also, higher-income consumers are increasingly patronizing these stores for the thrill of the hunt. Some shoppers regard the extreme-value retailers as an opportunity to find some hidden treasure among the household staples.

Extreme-value retailers would not be an obvious con-sumer choice for Coach for Men or Eva's new lines, because these stores are not consistent with the brands' image. But if these manufacturers find themselves in an overstock situation, they could use these retailers to reduce inventory. For the same reason, they might use off-price retailers.

Off-Price Retailers Off-price retailers offer an inconsistent assortment of brand-name merchandise at a significant discount from the manufacturer's suggested retail price (MSRP). In today's market, these off-price retailers may be brick-and-mortar stores, online outlets, or a combination of both. America's largest off-price retail chains are TJX Companies (which operates TJMaxx, Marshalls, Winners [Canada], HomeGoods, HomeSense [Canada]), Ross Stores, Burlington Coat Factory, Big Lots Inc., and Overstock.com.

To be able to sell at prices 20 to 60 percent lower than the MSRP,[27] most merchandise is bought opportunistically from manufacturers or other retailers with excess inventory at the end of the season. Therefore, customers cannot be confident that the same merchandise or even type of merchandise will be available each time they visit a store or website. The discounts off-price retailers receive from manufacturers reflect what they do not do as well: They do not ask suppliers to help them pay for advertising, make them take back unsold merchandise, charge them for markdowns, or ask them to delay payments.

Service Retailers

The retail firms discussed in the previous sections sell products to consumers.[28] However, service retailers, or firms that primarily sell services rather than merchandise, are a large and growing part of the retail industry. Consider a typical Saturday: After a bagel and cup of coffee at a nearby Peet's Coffee and Tea, you go to the Laundromat to wash and dry your clothes, drop off a suit at a dry cleaner, have a prescription filled at a CVS drugstore, and make your way to Jiffy Lube to have your car's oil changed. In a hurry, you drive through a Burger King so you can eat lunch quickly and be on time for your haircut at Supercuts. By midafternoon, you're ready for a workout at your health club. After stopping at home to change your clothes and meet the cleaning service that you hired through Amazon's online referral site to spiffy up your apartment, you're off to dinner, a movie, and dancing with a friend. Finally, you end your day with a café latte at Starbucks, having interacted with a dozen service retailers during the day.

There are a wide variety of service retailers, along with some national companies that provide these services. These companies are retailers because they sell goods and services to consumers. However, some are not just retailers. For example, airlines, banks, hotels, and insurance and express mail companies sell their services to businesses as well as consumers.

Service retailers, like this night-club, sell services rather than merchandise.

© Lane Oatey/Blue Jean Images/Getty Images RF

Several trends suggest considerable future growth in services retailing. For example, the aging population will increase demand for health care services. Younger people are also spending more time and money on health and fitness. Busy parents in two-income families are willing to pay to have their homes cleaned, lawns maintained, clothes washed and pressed, and meals prepared so they can spend more time with their families.

Now that we've explored the types of stores, we can examine how manufacturers and retailers coordinate their retail strategy using the four Ps.

PROGRESS CHECK

1. What strategies distinguish the different types of food retailers?
2. What strategies distinguish the different types of general merchandise retailers?
3. Are organizations that provide services to consumers retailers?

DEVELOPING A RETAIL STRATEGY USING THE FOUR Ps

 LO17-5 Describe the components of a retail strategy.

Like other marketers, retailers perform important functions that increase the value of the products and services they sell to consumers. We now examine these functions, classified into the four Ps: product, price, promotion, and place.

Product

A typical grocery store carries 30,000 to 40,000 items; a regional department store might carry as many as 100,000. Providing the right mix of merchandise and services that satisfies the needs of the target market is one of retailers' most fundamental activities. Offering assortments gives customers a choice. To reduce transportation costs and handling, manufacturers

Adding Value 17.2   Home Depot—Providing Customers Better Access to Products[iv]

By paying attention to what shoppers actually are buying in their stores, many big-box retailers that previously sought to stock a focused product assortment are shifting their inventories to feature more seemingly mismatched items. Shoppers at Home Depot wanted charcoal to go along with the new grills they had just bought, and laundry detergent to use with their new washer–dryer combos, so the home improvement store has expanded its offerings of such consumer goods. Other examples may seem even less convergent though. Staples now stocks coffee pods, because office employees and home-based workers rely on their single-serving machines for a caffeine boost. But it also provides personal deodorant and shaving cream. By stocking such items, Staples hopes that people popping in for toner will also appreciate the convenience of purchasing some basic necessities in the same store rather than visiting another retailer to gather such items.

Additionally, as customers continue to grow more comfortable with online buying, Home Depot is increasing its investment in its e-commerce operations. This provides customers access to more than 600,000 items, whereas the largest store can carry only 35,000 products. It also allows customers to enjoy in-home delivery of bulky products such as sinks or patio sets, rather than having to find a way to lug the heavy items home on their own. It also has set predictions for what it believes will be the fastest movers online: quick purchases such as lightbulbs and extension cords, combined with big, heavy items such as appliances.

With its online efforts, Home Depot also hopes to appeal to its business customers. Online ordering would enable a contractor to put together an e-commerce order for the project it has scheduled for the next day and then stop by the store to pick up the entire supply on the way to the project site.

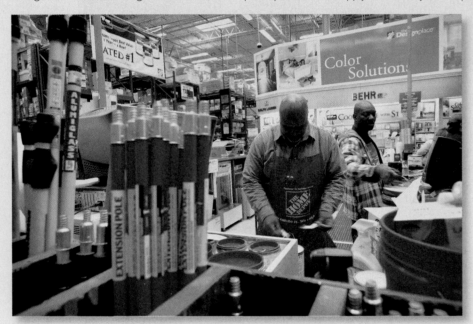

Why does Home Depot's Internet site carry more than 600,000 items, while its largest stores carry only 35,000?

© Scott Olson/Getty Images

typically ship cases of merchandise, such as cartons of mascara or boxes of leather jackets, to retailers. Because customers generally do not want or need to buy more than one of the same item, retailers break up the cases and sell customers the smaller quantities they desire. Adding Value 17.2 highlights how Home Depot is providing customers better access to more products both in the store and online.

Manufacturers don't like to store inventory because their factories and warehouses are typically not available or attractive shopping venues. Consumers don't want to purchase more than they need because storage consumes space. Neither group likes keeping inventory that isn't being used, because doing so ties up money that could be used for something else. Thus, in addition to other values to manufacturers and customers, retailers provide a storage function, though many retailers are beginning to push their suppliers to hold the inventory until they need it. (Recall our discussion of JIT inventory systems in Chapter 16.)

It is difficult for retailers to distinguish themselves from their competitors through the merchandise they carry, because competitors can purchase and sell many of the same popular brands. Thus, many retailers have developed **private-label brands** (also called **store brands**), which are products developed and marketed by a retailer and available only from that retailer. For example, if you want a Giani Bernini leather handbag, you have to go to Macy's.

Price

Price helps define the value of both the merchandise and the service, and the general price range of a particular store helps define its image. Although both Saks Fifth Avenue and JCPenney are department stores, their images could not be more different. Thus, when Coach considers which of these firms is most appropriate for its new line for men, it must keep in mind customers' perceived images of these retailers' price–quality relationship. The company does not, for instance, want to attempt to sell its new line at JCPenney if it is positioning the line with a relatively high price.

Price must always be aligned with the other elements of a retailer's strategy—that is, product, promotion, and place. A customer would not expect to pay $600 for a Coach for Men briefcase at a JCPenney store, but she might question the briefcase's quality if its price is significantly less than $600 at Neiman Marcus. As we discovered in Chapter 14, there is much more to pricing than simply adding a markup onto a product's cost. Manufacturers must consider at what price they will sell the product to retailers so that both the manufacturer and the retailer can make a reasonable profit. At the same time, both the manufacturer and the retailer are concerned about what the customer is willing and expecting to pay.

Given the price of a Coach bag, would you expect to find it in Saks Fifth Avenue or JCPenney?

© Peter Horree/Alamy

Promotion

Retailers and manufacturers know that good promotion, both within the retail environments and in the media, can mean the difference between flat sales and a growing consumer base. Advertising in traditional media such as newspapers, magazines, and television continues to be important to get customers into stores. Increasingly, electronic communications are being used for promotions as well. Some traditional approaches, such as direct mail, are being reevaluated by retailers, but many are still finding value in sending catalogs to customers and selected mailing lists. Companies also offer real-time promotions on their websites. For example, CVS.com contains in-store and online coupons that customers can use immediately on the website or print to use in the store. Coupons.com offers coupons that customers can use immediately for many grocery store items. Retailers are also investing heavily in **mobile commerce (M-commerce)**—product and service purchases through mobile devices.

A coordinated effort between the manufacturer and retailer helps guarantee that the customer receives a cohesive message and that both entities maintain their images. For example, Coach for Men might work with its most important retailers to develop advertising and point-of-sale signs. It may even help defray the costs of advertising by paying all or a portion of the advertising's production and media costs, an agreement called **cooperative (co-op) advertising**.

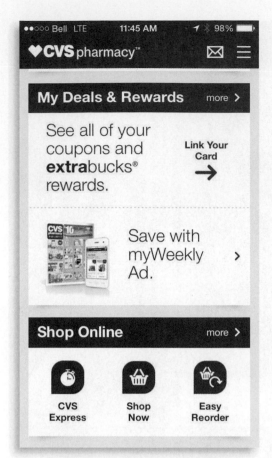

Customers receive promotions from CVS on their mobile devices that can be used immediately in the store.

Source: CVS

Store credit cards and gift cards are subtler forms of promotion that also facilitate shopping. Retailers might offer pricing promotions—such as coupons, rebates, and in-store or online discounts, or perhaps buy-one-get-one-free offers—to attract consumers and stimulate sales. These promotions play a very important role in driving traffic to retail locations, increasing average purchase size, and creating opportunities for repeat purchases. But retail promotions also are valuable to customers; they inform customers about what is new and available and how much it costs.

Another type of promotion occurs inside the store, where retailers use displays and signs placed at the point of purchase (POP) or in strategic areas such as the ends of aisles to inform customers and stimulate purchases of the featured products.

In addition to traditional forms of promotion, many retailers are devoting more resources to their overall retail environment as a means to promote and showcase what the store has to offer. These promotions may take the form of recognizable approaches, such as in-store and window displays, or they may be entirely new experiences designed to help retailers draw customers and add value to the shopping experience. Bass Pro Shops Outdoor World in Lawrenceville, Georgia, offers a 30,000-gallon aquarium stocked with fish for casting demonstrations, an indoor archery range, and a 43-foot climbing wall. These features enhance customers' visual experiences, provide them with educational information, and enhance the store's sales potential by enabling customers to try before they buy. In addition to adding fun to the shopping experience, these activities help offset the current drop in brick-and-mortar customers engendered by online shopping.

A variety of factors influence whether customers will actually buy once they are in the store. Some of these factors are quite subtle. Consumers' perceptions of value and their subsequent patronage are heavily influenced by their perceptions of the store's look and feel. Music, color, scent, aisle size, lighting, the availability of seating, and crowding can also significantly affect the overall shopping experience.[29] Therefore, the extent to which stores offer a more pleasant shopping experience fosters a better mood, resulting in greater spending.

Consider the funky C. Wonder emporium for example. This 7,000-square-foot store is divided into various nooks, each with its own

The customer experience is enhanced at C. Wonder by displaying merchandise in a variety of nooks with different personalities, having electronically enhanced fitting rooms, and using microchips embedded in the sales tags so customers can check out anywhere in the store.

Courtesy of C. Wonder

personality or feel, including English Town House, Vail Cabin, Palm Springs Modern, and Hollywood Regency. The separate sectors help customers navigate through the vast amount of merchandise available. To grant them control over their experience, C. Wonder's fitting rooms also come equipped with control panels that allow people trying on items to adjust the lighting as well as the type and volume of music played to suit their preferences.[30]

Personal selling and customer service representatives are also part of the overall promotional package. Retailers must provide services that make it easier to buy and use products, and retail associates—whether in the store, on the phone, or on the Internet—provide customers with information about product characteristics and availability. These individuals can also facilitate the sale of products or services that consumers perceive as complicated, risky, or expensive, such as an air conditioning unit, a computer, or a diamond ring. Manufacturers can play an important role in preparing retail sales and service associates to sell their products. Eva thus could conduct seminars or webinars about how to use and sell her new line of green cosmetics and supply printed educational materials to sales associates. Last but not least, sales reps handle the sales transactions.

Traditionally, retailers treated all their customers the same. Today, the most successful retailers concentrate on providing more value to their best customers. The knowledge retailers gain from their store personnel, the Internet browsing and buying activities of customers, and the data they collect on customer shopping habits can be used in customer relationship management (CRM). Using this information, retailers may modify product, price, and/or promotion to attempt to increase their share of wallet—the percentage of the customer's purchases made from that particular retailer. For instance, omnichannel retailers use consumer information collected from the customers' Internet browsing and buying behavior to send dedicated e-mails to customers promoting specific products or services. Retailers also may offer special discounts to good customers to help them become even more loyal.

Place

Retailers already have realized that convenience is a key ingredient to success, and an important aspect of this success is convenient locations.[31] As the old cliché claims, the three most important things in retailing are location, location, location. Many customers choose stores on the basis of where they are located, which makes great locations a competitive advantage that few rivals can duplicate. For instance, once Starbucks saturates a market by opening in the best locations, Peet's will have difficulty breaking into that same market—where would it put its stores?

In pursuit of better and better locations, retailers are experimenting with different options to reach their target markets. Walgreens has free-standing stores, unconnected to other retailers, so the stores can offer drive-up windows for customers to pick up their prescriptions. Walmart, Staples, and others are opening smaller stores in urban locations to serve those markets better.

To make their locations more convenient, Walgreens has some freestanding stores not connected to other retailers so the stores can offer a drive-up window for customers to pick up their prescriptions.

© McGraw-Hill Education/Andrew Resek, photographer

THE INTERNET AND OMNICHANNEL RETAILING

 LO17-6 Identify the benefits and challenges of omnichannel retailing.

The addition of the Internet channel to traditional store-based retailers has improved their ability to serve their customers and build a competitive advantage in several ways. According to Social and Mobile Marketing 17.1, IKEA effectively exemplifies these benefits.

Social & Mobile Marketing 17.1   In-Store and Online Analytics at IKEA[v]

IKEA's affordable, ready-to-assemble product line has made it the go-to place for furnishing a new home, apartment, or room. Much of its success stems from its unique store layouts, which force shoppers to walk past virtually every product offered, as displayed in sample rooms that have been modeled to inspire their design ideas. The layout also helps IKEA recognize which sorts of displays of what types of products invoke purchases—a sort of elemental analytics that benefits its strategy. Thus, when IKEA first decided to launch its website, it already recognized the importance of analytics as vital information that would enable it to serve its customers better.

Initially, IKEA's analytics-oriented focus was on website development. With its massive product range, the retailer had to find ways to discover pertinent patterns in consumers' product navigation and selection approaches. As it gathered such information, IKEA could begin to revise its site and successfully design a web page that encouraged customers to slow down during their online browsing, which would lead them to be inspired by new products, design ideas, and other services the company offers, but without ever sacrificing the convenience they demanded.

Having achieved that goal, IKEA turned its focus to increasing its online presence. For this feat, it needed to do more than analyze data that it had gathered from its own site. It needed data from social networking sites. These social media-derived

IKEA's analytics are used for website development and to improve its social media presence.
© Sergio Dionisio/Bloomberg/Getty Images

insights suggest channels and routes for improving consumers' perceptions of the brand. The influences of these analytics on many of IKEA's online actions are evident. For example, when "The Dress" became a vastly and inexplicably trending topic (is it white and gold or black and blue? and why could no one agree?), IKEA rapidly leveraged the social media sensation to plug its products by using the hashtag #TheDress.

First, the addition of an Internet channel has the potential to offer a greater selection of products. Second, an Internet channel enables retailers to provide customers with more personalized information about products and services. Third, it offers sellers the unique opportunity to collect information about consumer shopping behavior—information that they can use to improve the shopping experience across all channels. Fourth, the Internet channel allows sellers to enter new markets economically.

Deeper and Broader Selection

One benefit of adding the Internet channel is the vast number of alternatives retailers can make available to consumers without crowding their aisles or increasing their square footage. Stores and catalogs are limited by their size. By shopping on the Internet, consumers can easily visit and select merchandise from a broader array of retailers. Individual retailers' websites typically offer deeper assortments of merchandise (more colors, brands, and sizes) than are available in stores or catalogs. This expanded offering enables them to satisfy consumer demand for less popular styles, colors, or sizes. Many retailers also offer a broader assortment (more categories) on their websites. Staples.com, for instance, offers soft drinks and cleaning supplies, which are not available in stores, so that its business customers will view it as a one-stop shop.

Personalization

Another benefit of adding the Internet channel is the ability to personalize promotions and services economically, including heightened service or individualized offerings.

Personalized Customer Service Traditional Internet channel approaches for responding to customer questions—such as FAQ (frequently asked question) pages and offering an

800 number or e-mail address to ask questions—often do not provide the timely information customers are seeking. To improve customer service from an electronic channel, many firms offer live online chats, so that customers can click a button at any time and participate in an instant messaging conversation with a customer service representative. This technology also enables firms to send a proactive chat invitation at specific times to visitors to the site. Verizon Wireless programs its chat windows to appear at the moment a customer chooses a product, because its goal is to upsell these willing buyers to a more expensive plan.[32] Other online retailers use metrics such as the amount of time spent on the site or number of repeat visits to determine which customers will receive an invitation to chat.

Personalized Offering The interactive nature of the Internet also provides an opportunity for retailers to personalize their offerings for each of their customers, based on customers' behavior. Just as a well-trained salesperson would make recommendations to customers prior to checkout, an interactive web page can make suggestions to the shopper about items that he or she might like to see based on previous purchases, what other customers who purchased the same item purchased, or common web viewing behavior.

Some omnichannel retailers are able to personalize promotions and Internet home pages on the basis of several attributes tied to the shopper's current or previous web sessions, such as the time of day, time zone as determined by a computer's Internet address, and assumed gender.[33] However, some consumers worry about this ability to collect information about purchase histories, personal information, and search behavior on the Internet. How will this information be used in the future? Will it be sold to other firms? Will the consumer receive unwanted promotional materials online or in the mail?

Expanded Market Presence

The market for customers who shop in stores is typically limited to consumers living in close proximity to those stores. The market for catalogs is limited by the high cost of printing and mailing them and increasing consumer interest in environmentally friendly practices. By adding the Internet channel, retailers can expand their market without having to build new stores or incur the high cost of additional catalogs. Adding an Internet channel is particularly attractive to retailers that have strong brand names but limited locations and distribution. For example, retailers such as Nordstrom, REI, IKEA, and L.L.Bean are widely known for offering unique, high-quality merchandise. If these retailers had only a few stores, customers would have to travel vast distances to buy the merchandise they carry.

To ensure effective omnichannel retailing practices, modern retailers need to acknowledge modern consumers' preferences. That is, consumers desire a seamless experience when interacting with omnichannel retailers. They want to be recognized by a retailer, whether they interact with a sales associate, the retailer's website, or the retailer's call center by telephone. Customers want to buy a product through the retailer's Internet or catalog channels and pick it up or return it to a local store; find out if a product offered on the Internet channel is available at a local store; and, when unable to find a product in a store, determine if it is available for home delivery through the retailer's Internet channel.

However, providing this seamless experience for customers is not easy for retailers. Because each of the channels is somewhat different, a critical decision facing omnichannel retailers is the degree to which they should or are able to integrate the operations of the channels.[34] To determine how much integration is best, each retailer must address issues such as integrated CRM, brand image, pricing, and the supply chain.

Integrated CRM

Effective omnichannel operations require an integrated CRM (customer relationship management) system with a centralized customer data warehouse that houses a complete history of each customer's interaction with the retailer, regardless of whether the sale occurred in a store, on the Internet, or on the telephone.[35] This information storehouse allows retailers to efficiently handle complaints, expedite returns, target future promotions, and provide a seamless experience for customers when they interact with the retailer through multiple channels.

Multichannel retailers like Patagonia sell on the Internet, in catalogs, and in stores.

Source: Patagonia, Inc.

Brand Image

Retailers need to provide a consistent brand image across all channels. For example, Patagonia reinforces its image of selling high-quality, environmentally friendly sports equipment in its stores, catalogs, and website. Each of these channels emphasizes function, not fashion, in the descriptions of Patagonia's products. Patagonia's position about taking care of the environment is communicated by carefully lighting its stores and using recycled polyester and organic rather than pesticide-intensive cotton in many of its clothes.

Pricing

Pricing represents another difficult decision for omnichannel retailers. Customers expect pricing consistency for the same SKU across channels (excluding shipping charges and sales tax). However, in some cases, retailers need to adjust their pricing strategy because of the competition they face in different channels. For example, to compete effectively against Amazon.com, Barnes & Noble offers lower prices through its Internet channel (www.bn.com) than it offers in its stores.

Retailers with stores in multiple markets often set different prices for the same merchandise to compete better with local stores. Customers generally are not aware of these price differences because they are exposed to the prices only in their local markets. However, omnichannel retailers may have difficulties sustaining these regional price differences when customers can easily check prices on the Internet.

Supply Chain

Omnichannel retailers struggle to provide an integrated shopping experience across all their channels, because unique skills and resources are needed to manage each channel.[36] For example, store-based retail chains operate and manage many stores, each requiring the management of inventory and people. With Internet and catalog operations, inventory and telephone salespeople instead are typically centralized in one or two locations. Also, retail distribution centers (DCs) supporting a store channel are designed to ship many cartons of merchandise to stores. In contrast, the DCs supporting a catalog and Internet channel are designed to ship a few items at a time to many individual customers. The difference in shipping orientation for the two types of operations requires a completely different type of distribution center.

Due to these operational differences, many store-based retailers have a separate organization to manage their Internet and catalog operations. But as the omnichannel operation matures, retailers tend to integrate all operations under one organization. Both Walmart and JCPenney initially had separate organizations for their Internet channel but subsequently integrated them with stores and catalogs.

PROGRESS CHECK

1. What are the components of a retail strategy?
2. What are the advantages of traditional stores versus Internet-only stores?
3. What challenges do retailers face when marketing their products through multiple channels?

Reviewing Learning Objectives

 Discuss the four factors manufacturers should consider as they develop their strategy for working with retailers.

When they initiate the decision process for choosing retail partners, manufacturers determine how likely it is that certain retailers would carry their products and whether target customers expect to find their products for sale at those retail locations. Next, manufacturers need to identify types of retailers that would be appropriate locations for their products. After identifying likely and appropriate retailers, manufacturers work with their retailer partners to develop a strategy that comprises the four Ps. Finally, manufacturers, again with their retail partners, must determine which elements of an omnichannel strategy will be effective.

 Outline the considerations associated with choosing retail partners.

Manufacturers often start by noting the basic channel structure, which includes the level of vertical integration, the relative strength of the retailer and the manufacturer, and the strength of the brand. They also consider where their target customers expect to find products, which depends largely on the retailer's image. Channel member characteristics also are important inputs, as is the level of distribution intensity.

 List the three levels of distribution intensity.

Intensive distribution intensity means the product is available virtually everywhere, in as many places as

will agree to carry it. In an exclusive distribution intensity strategy, the manufacturer allows only one retailer (or retail chain) in each area to sell its products. Selective distribution is the middle ground option; several retailers carry the products, but not all of them.

 Describe the various types of retailers.

Retailers generally fall into one of three categories: food retailers, general merchandise retailers, or service retailers. Each of the categories consists of various formats, including supermarkets, supercenters, warehouse clubs, convenience stores, department stores, discount stores, specialty retailers, drugstores, category specialists, extreme-value retailers, and off-price stores. Although service retailers primarily sell services, if they sell to consumers, they are still retailers. Service retailers span the gambit from universities to automobile oil change shops.

 Describe the components of a retail strategy.

To develop a coordinated strategy—which represents a key goal for an effective channel partnership between retailers and manufacturers—retailers as well as manufacturers need to consider all of the four Ps in conjunction: product, place, promotion, and price.

Identify the benefits and challenges of omnichannel retailing.

The various types of retail channels—stores, catalogs, and the Internet—all offer their own benefits and limitations, including those related to availability, convenience, and safety, among others. If a retailer adopts an omnichannel strategy, it can exploit the benefits and mitigate the limitations of each channel and help expand its overall market presence. Furthermore, an omnichannel strategy offers the chance to gain a greater share of customers' wallets and more insight into their buying behaviors.

To function in multiple channels, retailers must organize their operations carefully to ensure an integrated customer experience. In particular, they have to have an integrated CRM system, determine how to maintain a consistent brand image across the various channels, whether to charge the same or different prices, and how best to deliver merchandise to multiple channels.

Key Terms

- big-box retailer, 531
- category killer, 531
- category specialist, 531
- convenience store, 527
- conventional supermarket, 526
- cooperative (co-op) advertising, 535
- department store, 530
- distribution intensity, 524
- drugstore, 531
- exclusive distribution, 524

- extreme-value food retailer, 526
- extreme-value retailer, 531
- full-line discount store, 530
- intensive distribution, 524
- limited-assortment supermarket, 526
- mobile commerce (M-commerce), 535
- off-price retailer, 532
- omnichannel or multichannel strategy, 521

- online chat, 539
- private-label brand, 535
- retailing, 520
- selective distribution, 524
- service retailer, 532
- share of wallet, 537
- store brand, 535
- specialty store, 530
- supercenter, 526
- warehouse club, 526

Marketing Digitally

1. How do JCrew.com and Gap.com provide value to their customers beyond the physical products they sell? Why would a customer purchase online instead of going to the store? Under what circumstances would the customer prefer a store-based experience?

2. Select a familiar omnichannel retailer. Evaluate its website in terms of how well it provides value to its customers. Do you believe that offering multiple selling channels to customers enhances their shopping experience? How does it help the retailer? Explain your answer.

Marketing Applications

1. Does Reebok pursue an intensive, an exclusive, or a selective distribution intensity strategy? Would you suggest any changes to this strategy?

2. Assume that AG, the designer jeans company, has decided to sell expensive wristwatches for men and women. What factors should it consider when developing its strategy for choosing retail partners?

3. Some argue that retailers can be eliminated from the distribution channel because they only add costs to the final product without creating any value-added services in the process. Do you agree with this perspective? Are consumers likely to make most purchases directly from manufacturers in the near future? Provide justification for your answers.

4. Assume you have been given some money but told that it must be invested in a retailer's stock. In which type of retailer would you choose to invest? Which specific retailer? Provide a rationale for your answers.

5. Provide examples of how manufacturers work with retailers to jointly plan and implement the four Ps.

6. Why have so many brick-and-mortar retailers adopted an omnichannel strategy?

7. You can purchase apparel at a discount store, specialty store, category specialist, off-price retailer, department store, or Internet-only store. From which of these types of stores do you shop? Explain why you prefer one type store over another.

8. Should Tana, a young entrepreneur who is launching a new line of environmentally friendly (green) cosmetics, sell through a physical store, catalog, or Internet? Explain two key benefits of each channel for her business.

9. Name a retailer from which you have received personalized service, product, or promotion offerings online. What form of personalization did you receive? Did the personalization influence your purchase decision? Explain why or why not.

Quiz Yourself

1. _____ reduce costs and maintain low prices by buying opportunistically from manufacturers with excess inventory, offering limited assortments of household goods and groceries, as well as health and beauty aids.

   a. Category killers

   b. Specialty stores

   c. Factory outlets

   d. Extreme-vlaue retailers

   e. Convenience stores

2. Jordan directs her salespeople to increase the company's share of wallet. Jordan is directing her salespeople to

   a. focus on increasing sales to their best customers.

   b. focus on male consumers and not female consumers.

   c. sell more store brands and fewer private-label products.

   d. become omnichannel salespeople.

   e. expand retailing elasticity.

(Answers to these two questions can be found in the Quiz Yourself Answer Key section.)

Chapter Case Study

MAKING MACY'S MEANINGFUL: MOVES BY THE RETAIL CHAIN TO MAINTAIN ITS COMPETITIVENESS

Faced with some surprising sales declines and threats to its status as the leading department store brand, Macy's has developed a multipronged strategy, seeking to leverage its existing advantages as well as some new retail options. Three key efforts reflect its expansion as an omnichannel retailer, its pursuit of relevant target customers, and its partnerships with other retail sources.

First, Macy's has a great online presence, and it simultaneously has adopted in-store technologies that help customers find the items they want, design fashionable outfits, make payments more easily, receive discounts, and even have their purchases delivered if they so choose. For example, with large Look Book displays, consumers interact with a sort of digital catalog in the store, finding fashionable ideas, ways to extend their existing wardrobes, and images from forward-thinking fashion icons. Touching the screen enables them to check the availability of various colors and sizes as well as receive more detailed information about items that are of interest. The POP (point-of-purchase) terminals in Macy's stores similarly are touchscreens that provide extensive inventory information, though they are more functional than fashionable. These smaller kiosks indicate which colors and styles are available and also identify which items have prompted the most Facebook likes or customer favorite rankings.

When it comes time to pay, Macy's is working to make the process easier and quicker by installing Apple Pay capabilities throughout its network of stores. As one of the earliest adopters of this new technology, Macy's is seeking to appeal to Apple fans who love to use their iPhones for nearly everything. With Macy's Wallet and the Shopkick app, customers have two methods to receive coupons and special offers. Once downloaded, the Shopkick app requires people to opt in, and then, as they enter a Macy's store, reminds them to open it so that they can receive personalized notifications. It tracks their movements through the store, so that a shopper in the outerwear department receives a discount offer on gloves rather than cosmetics, for example. The Macy's Wallet program is similar, except that it is unique to this retailer and links to consumers' loyalty cards. A shopper who has earned a percentage-off offer, on the basis of her or his prior purchases, thus no longer needs to worry about forgetting and leaving the paper coupon at home rather than bringing it on the current shopping trip.

Finally, using a crowdsourced delivery service called Deliv, Macy's offers customers the option of making their purchases in the store, then having them delivered to their homes, such that they no longer have to lug heavy packages through the mall.[37]

However, according to one analyst, the inventory in Macy's stores is often messy and seemingly overstocked, without sufficient on-duty personnel to keep the experience moving along nicely. Thus it might need to reorient its focus more on people and less on technology to maintain its high level of customer experience. As we discussed in the opening vignette to this chapter, to compete with Amazon, which continues to wow customers with its innovations, rapid delivery options, successful appeal to consumers, insurmountable product and service selection, and effective pricing, it needs to leverage its multiple channels and exploit its omnichannel potential to its full extent.[38]

Second, Macy's had determined that it needs to pursue those elusive young shoppers known as Millennials. Accordingly, it has implemented a $400 million renovation effort for its flagship New York City store, testing out various options that might attract more of the market of shoppers between the ages of 18 and 35 years. The basement level is newly designated "One Below," and it offers a notably different shopping experience. In addition to merchandise designed to appeal to Millennials, it provides services such as blow-drying stations, jean embroidering, and watch engraving. Shoppers can use a 3D printer to create their own custom jewelry, and a touchscreen wall allows them to take high-quality selfies.[39] These tests, if successful, are likely to spread to other locations as well. In the meantime, Macy's is opening more off-price stores, seemingly following the successful lead of Nordstrom with its Nordstrom Rack stores.

These moves reflect the conventional wisdom about what Millennials want. In particular, studies show that these young consumers tend to devote their spending more to personal or digital services than to apparel. They also suffer higher levels of debt, mostly due to student loans, and earn less on average than previous generations have. As a result, they generally seek lower-priced options for their fashion choices. This preference puts them in direct contrast with the previous big cohort of shoppers—namely, the Baby Boomers. The consumers in this age group, as they start to retire from the work force, exhibit strong spending patterns and have enviable levels of discretionary income and time. From this perspective, some observers suggest Macy's might be going after the wrong age demographic—unless Baby Boomers like selfie walls too.

At Macy's flagship New York City store, the newly designated "One Below" in the basement offers merchandise designed to appeal to Millennials, as well as services like this brow bar.

© Chris Goodney/Bloomberg/ Getty Images

Third, noting the success enjoyed by Best Buy when it opened dedicated stores within the stores, which reflect its strong relationships with vendors and ability to offer the kind of variety its customers demand, Macy's entered into a partnership with Best Buy but flipped their roles. That is, as the host location, Macy's opened several Best Buy operations within about a dozen of its department stores. The mini-Best Buys take up about 300 square feet of space and offer tablets, smartphones, smartwatches, audio devices, and accessories. As in traditional Best Buy stores, Samsung has a strong presence. Staffing the in-store stores will be Best Buy personnel, ready to answer shoppers' questions about high-tech devices. Best Buy's recent resurgence, as well as Macy's willingness to innovate, have contributed to the new initiative. In addition, Macy's notes that customers are seeking more variety in the items available to them, whether to purchase for themselves or as gifts. By adding the latest and coolest electronics gadgets—whether as tools to help people shop or as an expanded variety for consumers to purchase—Macy's seeks to ensure that it is a shopping destination for virtually anyone.[40]

Questions

1. In which channels is Macy's attempting to appeal to consumers?

2. What is Macy's plan to attract Millennials?

3. Do you shop at Macy's? Why or why not?

4. Using the factors for choosing retail partners outlined in the chapter, do you believe that Eva's line of green cosmetics should attempt to get placement in Macy's?

5. Develop a strategy for Macy's to promote Eva's line of green cosmetics.

Endnotes

1. Taylor Soper, "Amazon's Dominance of Online Shopping Starts with Product Searches, Study Shows," *Geek Wire*, October 6, 2015.

2. Dan Berthiaume, "Three Reasons Amazon Is Everyone's Competitor," *Chain Store Age*, November 9, 2015.

3. This chapter draws heavily from Michael Levy, Barton A. Weitz, and Dhruv Grewal, *Retailing Management*, 9th ed. (Burr Ridge, IL: McGraw-Hill/Irwin, 2015).

4. "Top 250 Global Retailers, 2016," *Store Magazine*, January 2016, https://nrf.com/2016/global250-table.

5. "Sales of Food at Home by Type of Outlet Table," USDA Economic Research Service, 2016, http://www.ers.usda.gov/datafiles/Food_Expenditures/Food_Expenditures/table14.xls.

6. "2016 Top 250 Global Powers of Retailing," *Stores*, January 2016, https://nrf.com/news/2016-top-250-global-powers-of-retailing#top10.

7. "Top 25 Global Food Retailers 2015," *Supermarket News*, 2015, http://supermarketnews.com/top-25-global-food-retailers-2015.

8. "2015 Top 75 U.S. & Canadian Food Retailers & Wholesalers," *Supermarket News*, 2015, http://supermarketnews.com/2015-top-75-us-canadian-food-retailers-wholesalers.

9. "Conventional Supermarket," TermWiki, http://en.termwiki.com/EN:conventional_supermarket (accessed April 27, 2016).

10. *Progressive Grocer*. "Share of Supermarket Sales in the United States in 2014, by Department," *Statista, The Statistics Portal*, July 2015, http://www.statista.com/statistics/240580/breakdown-of-us-supermarket-sales-by-department/.

11. Ashley Lutz, "Aldi's Secrets for Selling Cheaper Crockeries than Wal-Mart or Trader Joe's," *Business Insider*, April 8, 2015, http://www.businessinsider.com/why-aldi-is-so-cheap-2015-4.

12. Ibid.

13. George Anderson, "Supermarkets Continue to Give Ground to Other Channels," *Retail Wire*, February 19, 2014, http://www.retailwire.com/discussion/17340/supermarkets-continue-to-give-ground-to-other-channels.

14. Eliza Barclay, "Grocery Stores Are Losing You. Here's How They Plan to Win You Back," *NPR*, March 30, 2015, http://www.npr.org/sections/thesalt/2015/03/30/395774725/grocery-stores-are-losing-you-heres-how-they-plan-to-win-you-back.

15. http://corporate.walmart.com/our-story/locations/united-states#/united-states.

16. Sarah Halzack, "A Case for Costco and Other Warehouse Clubs Having Transformed Retail More than Amazon," *Washington Post*, September 2, 2015.

17. "2016 Top 101 Convenience Stores," *CPS*, http://www.cspdailynews.com/industry-news-analysis/top-convenience-stores.

18. Sarah Halzack, "The Staggering Challenges of the Online Grocery Business," *Washington Post*, January 20, 2015.

19. Tom Ryan, "Is Online Grocery Finally Ready for Launch?" *Retail Wire*, January 23, 2014.

20. Joseph Pisani, "What's Better for Grocery Delivery: Google, Instacart, or Postmates?" *Mercury News Business*, June 19, 2014.

21. "Fortune 500," *Fortune*, http://fortune.com/fortune500/.

22. Kelly Tackett, "An Evolutionary Tale from Nordstrom," *Retail Wire*, May 8, 2014.

23. *Forbes*, "Sales of the Leading Discount Store Companies Worldwide in 2014 (in Billion U.S. Dollars)," *Statista*, May 2015, http://www.statista.com/statistics/257983/sales-of-the-leading-discount-store-companies-worldwide/.

24. Corey Stern, "CVS and Walgreens Are Completely Dominating the US Drugstore Industry," *Business Insider*, July 29, 2015, http://www.businessinsider.com/cvs-and-walgreens-us-drug-store-market-share-2015-7.

25. Kate Taylor, "CVS Is Making an Unprecedented Move to Hook Millennial Moms," *Business Insider*, April 19, 2016, http://www.businessinsider.com/cvs-adds-curbside-pickup-service-2016-4; "12 New In-Store, Online, and Mobile Drugstore Services that Save You Time and Money," *Consumer Reports*, August 2014, http://www.consumerreports.org/cro/2014/08/new-pharmacy-services/index.htm.

26. Jenna Martin, "Top 10 Stories of 2015: Family Dollar Completes Merger with Dollar Tree," *Charlotte Business Journal*, December 15, 2015, http://www.bizjournals.com/charlotte/news/2015/12/15/top-10-stories-of-2015-family-dollar-completes.html.

27. http://www.wikinvest.com/industry/Off-price_Retail.

28. This section draws from Levy et al., *Retailing Management*, Chapter 2.

29. Nancy M. Pucinelli et al., "The Value of Knowing What Customers Really Want: Interpersonal Accuracy as an Environmental Cue," working paper (2012); Nancy Puccinelli et al., "Customer Experience Management in Retailing: Understanding the Buying Process," *Journal of Retailing* 85 (2009), pp. 15–30.

30. Patricia Marx, "C. Wonder," *The New Yorker*, November 21, 2011, p. 34.

31. Kathleen Seiders et al., "SERVCON: A Multidimensional Scale for Measuring Perceptions of Service Convenience," *Journal of the Academy of Marketing Science* 35, no. 1 (2007), pp. 144–56; Leonard Berry, Kathleen Seiders, and Dhruv Grewal, "Understanding Service Convenience," *Journal of Marketing* 66, no. 3 (July 2002).

32. http://www.verizonwireless.com/smartphones/.

33. "Sponsored Supplement: Expanding the Reach of Personalization," *Internet Retailer*, March 2010.

34. Christian Homburg, Josef Vollmayr, and Alexander Hahn, "Firm Value Creation through Major Channel Expansions: Evidence from an Event Study in the United States, Germany, and China," *Journal of Marketing*, 2014, http://dx.doi.org/10.1509/jm.12.0179.

35. Hongshuang (Alice) Li and P. K. Kannan, "Attributing Conversions in a Multichannel Online Marketing Environment: An Empirical Model and a Field Experiment," *Journal of Marketing Research* 51 (February 2014), pp. 40–56.

36. Jie Zhang et al., "Crafting Integrated Multichannel Retailing Strategies," *Journal of Interactive Marketing*, 2010.

37. Alexander Coolidge, "Hate Checkout Lines? Macy's Can Help," *Cincinnati Inquirer*, October 3, 2014.

38. Ken Lonyai, "Rivals Need to Up Customer Experiences to Compete with Amazon," *Retail Wire*, January 12, 2016.

39. Marina Nazario, "Macy's Has a Master Plan to Capture the Most Difficult Customers," *Business Insider*, October 3, 2015.

40. George Anderson, "Best Buy to Open Shops Inside Macy's Stores," *Retail Wire*, September 9, 2015.

 i. Tom Ryan, "Burberry Shocks the Industry, Going Direct from Runway to Consumer," *Retail Wire*, February 10, 2016.

 ii. Elaine Watson, "Quirky, Cult-Like, Aspirational, but Affordable: The Rise and Rise of Trader Joe's," *The Packaged Facts*, April 15, 2014.

 iii. David Orgel, "FreshDirect Targets Multi-Device Strategies," *Supermarket News*, January 20, 2016.

 iv. Shelly Banjo and Serena Ng, "Home Depot: The Place to Go for Toilet Paper?" *The Wall Street Journal*, June 6, 2014; Shelly Banjo, "Home Depot Lumbers into E-Commerce," *The Wall Street Journal*, April 16, 2014.

 v. Huge Inc., "Master Plan: IKEA," Huge Inc., 2012, http://hbs.hugeinc.com/casestudies/ikea; Case Studies, "IKEA and Brandwatch: Embedding Social across the Enterprise," PerformanceIN, March 9, 2015, http://performancein.com/news/2015/03/09/ikea-and-brandwatch-embedding-social-across-enterprise/; "IKEA: A Data Matching Love Story," Cream Global, 2012, https://www.creamglobal.com/case-studies/latest/17798/33834/ikea-a-data-matching-love-story/; Matt Kwong, "Building Your Career in Hashtags," *Toronto Star*, March 16, 2015,http://www.thestar.com/; James Ainsworth, "IKEA Speaks the Language of Emoticons," SmartData Collective, February 12, 2015,http://smartdatacollective.com/mike-longfellow/298876/ikea-speaks-language-emoticons-flat-packswords-mobile.

VALUE COMMUNICATION

In Section Seven we explore value communication. Today, value communication methods are more complex because of new technologies that have added e-mail, blogs, Internet, and podcasts to the advertising mix that once utilized only radio, television, newspapers, and magazines to relay messages to consumers. Chapter 18 introduces the breadth of integrated marketing communications. Chapter 19 discusses advertising, public relations, and sales promotions. The text concludes with a discussion of personal selling in Chapter 20.

CHAPTER 18

INTEGRATED MARKETING COMMUNICATIONS

LEARNING OBJECTIVES

After reading this chapter, you should be able to:

LO18-1 Identify the components of the communication process.

LO18-2 Explain the four steps in the AIDA model.

LO18-3 Describe the various integrative communication channels.

LO18-4 Explain the methods used to allocate the integrated marketing communications (IMC) budget.

LO18-5 Identify marketing metrics used to measure IMC success.

The incredible expansion of the Internet and on-line tools has radically changed the manner in which marketers communicate with customers. More and more, companies spread their messages over all sorts of media—television, print, radio, e-mail, Internet, and so on. To really stand out, then, a company may need to go further than ever.

To achieve success in a market, companies invariably must communicate the value of their offerings in diverse, well-rounded ways. When companies promote their brands through multiple channels, they stand a better chance of reaching their customers. Coordination across these platforms is the key to effective omnichannel (or multichannel) marketing communications. But it is difficult to ensure brand consistency when radio, television, online, and print ads each require different types of elements, unique voices, and varying styles. In addition, firms need to integrate their marketing communications even further by incorporating new opportunities to reach customers through social media sites such as Facebook and Twitter.

Even well-known brands need to consider these issues. As sales in the North American soft drink market have stagnated in recent years,[1] it has become ever more important for companies to create effective campaigns, seamlessly integrated across a wide variety of platforms. Therefore, Pepsi declared a "World Emoji Day," combined with a "Say It With Pepsi" campaign that ran in Canada. In one of the most successful integrated marketing campaigns of the year, Pepsi released cans and bottles of its Pepsi-branded soft drinks with emojis printed directly on them. The company also created its own emoji keyboard, with 35 new characters, and a PepsiMoji hashtag for customers to use on social media.

To integrate this campaign with its television advertising, Pepsi simultaneously released a television spot that featured a man proposing to his future spouse, using placards imprinted only with emojis.[2] The campaign was so successful in Canada that Pepsi rapidly geared it up globally.[3] Pepsi has supported this campaign with digital and traditional advertising as well as the communications created by its packaging.

Furthermore, Pepsi has tailored the campaign to each specific market. For example, in European markets, the "Say It With Pepsi" campaign includes soccer-inspired emojis and television ads featuring well-known players such as James Rodriguez and Davis de Gea.[4] The soccer-themed emojis are specific to this campaign, but they also reflect Pepsi's long tradition of featuring prominent celebrities and athletes in its advertising. Furthermore, Pepsi has created emojis for specific markets, such as one featuring a character dressed in a traditional Thai outfit.

In turn, the global campaign has extended emojis beyond bottles and cans, relying on collaborations with designers to create emoji-inspired fashion.[5] To remain consistent with Pepsi's overall marketing strategies, all of the emojis and fashion innovations use design elements from the traditional look of Pepsi, such as the shape of a globe and predominant colors of blue, red, and white.[6]

Pepsi's emoji-centered integrated marketing campaign thus is unique in several ways. Although widely popular, emojis have been restricted to the digital space. Yet studies show that more than 2 billion people send approximately 6 billion emojis every single day. By adding these popular visual communication tools to its products' labels,

Pepsi connects its retail efforts with digital marketing. Furthermore, emojis can act as a universal language. In Canada, a country with more than one official language, the campaign has showed just how effectively emojis have been able to break through language barriers.[7] In particular, emojis allow Pepsi to portray its message across nations and across promotion channels with far greater consistency.

Each element of an integrated marketing communications (IMC) strategy must have a well-defined purpose and support and extend the message delivered by all the other elements.

Throughout this book, we have focused our attention on how firms create value by developing products and services. However, consumers are not likely to come flocking to new products and services unless they are aware of them. Therefore, marketers must consider how to communicate the value of a product and/or service—or more specifically, the value proposition—to the target market. A firm must develop a communication strategy to demonstrate the value of its product. We begin our discussion by examining what IMC is, how it has developed, and how it contributes to value creation.

Integrated marketing communications (IMC) represents the promotion dimension of the four Ps. It encompasses a variety of communication disciplines—advertising, personal selling, sales promotion, public relations, direct marketing, and online marketing including social media—in combination to provide clarity, consistency, and maximum communicative impact.[8] Instead of consisting of separated marketing communications channels with no unified control, IMC programs regard each of the firm's marketing communications channels as part of a whole, each of which offers a different means to connect with the target audience. This integration of channels provides the firm with the best means to reach the target audience with the desired message, and it enhances the value story by offering a clear and consistent message.

There are three elements in any IMC strategy: the consumer, the channels through which the message is communicated, and the evaluation of the results of the communication. This chapter is organized around these three elements. In the first section, the focus is on consumers, so we examine how consumers receive communications, whether via media or other methods, as well as how the delivery of that communication affects a message's form and contents. The second section examines the various communication channels that make up the IMC arsenal and how each is used in an overall IMC strategy. The third section considers how the level of complexity in IMC strategies leads marketers to design new ways to measure the results of IMC campaigns.

LO18-1 Identify the components of the communication process.

COMMUNICATING WITH CONSUMERS

As the number of communication media have increased, the task of understanding how best to reach target consumers has become far more complex. In this section, we examine a model that describes how communications go from the firm to the consumer and the factors that affect the way the consumer perceives the message. Then we look at how marketing communications influence consumers—from making them aware that a product or service exists to moving them to buy.

The Communication Process

Exhibit 18.1 illustrates the communication process. Let's first define each component and then discuss how they interact.

The Sender The message originates from the sender, who must be clearly identified to the intended audience. As our opening vignette revealed, Pepsi seeks to communicate in

EXHIBIT 18.1   The Communication Process

new ways with customers, mainly through its packaging and promotional programs. With its emoji campaign and specialized emoji keyboard, for example, Pepsi establishes itself as a source of fun and different emojis that people can use in their daily activities. The Pepsi identity remains clear even with these innovative communications, because they consistently highlight its familiar blue, red, and white color scheme and logo images—and also portray happy consumers. Thus people who see and use the newly available emojis know precisely which company made them available. Similarly, when Pepsi introduces new versions—such as the stevia-sweetened True line or the 1893 brand with real sugar—it uses the same color- and shape-based visual reminders that they are Pepsi products, so the sender of the message remains clear and obvious at all times.

The Transmitter   The sender works with a creative department, whether in-house or from a marketing (or advertising) agency, to develop marketing communications to highlight the new beverage. With the assistance of its marketing department, Pepsi has developed new mobile and social media tools, together with websites, mobile apps, flyers, in-store displays, and televised commercials, to tout its brands and what they

Pepsi emojis encode the message that the iconic drink is associated with fun times and activities when people might likely drink carbonated beverages.

Source: PepsiMoji/Pepsico/YouTube

Pepsi has placed its products in mainstream, popular movies such as San Andreas *starring Paul Giamatti.*

Source: *San Andreas/Warner Bros. Entertainment Inc*

offer. The marketing department or external agency receives the information and transforms it for use in its role as the **transmitter**.

Encoding **Encoding** means converting the sender's ideas into a message, which could be verbal, visual, or both. Thus the Pepsi emojis signal fun times and activities during which people might be likely to drink carbonated beverages; the grinning face wearing sunglasses and headphones, as if it is ready to head to the beach, is one such emoji.[9] Although a picture can be worth a thousand words, the most important facet of encoding is not what is sent but rather what is received. Consumers must receive information that makes them want to try the new emojis, use Pepsi-linked symbols to communicate with their friends, and continue to purchase new versions of the beverages.

The Communication Channel The **communication channel** is the medium—print, broadcast, the Internet, and so forth—that carries the message. Pepsi could transmit through television, radio, and various print advertisements, but for its emoji campaign, it also made vast and clearly understandable use of social media. The media chosen must be appropriate to connect the sender with the desired recipients. Because the company believes its target market is broad, Pepsi has placed its products in mainstream, popular movies such as *Tomorrowland*, *San Andreas*, *Jurassic World*, and *The Perfect Guy*, as well as in the midst of a showdown of terminators in *Terminator: Genesis*. Social and Mobile Marketing 18.1 depicts how Snapchat offers another recently adopted communication channel.

The Receiver The **receiver** is the person who reads, hears, or sees and processes the information contained in the message and/or advertisement. The sender, of course, hopes that the person receiving it will be the one for whom it was originally intended. Pepsi wants its message received and decoded properly by a broad population that includes teens, young adults, and families. **Decoding** refers to the process by which the receiver interprets the sender's message.

Noise **Noise** is any interference that stems from competing messages, a lack of clarity in the message, or a flaw in the medium. It poses a problem for all communication channels. Pepsi may choose to advertise in newspapers that its target market doesn't read, which means the rate at which the message is received by those to whom it has relevance has been slowed considerably. As we have already defined, encoding is what the sender intends to say, and decoding is what the receiver hears. If there is a difference between them, it is probably due to noise.

Feedback Loop The **feedback loop** allows the receiver to communicate with the sender and thereby informs the sender whether the message was received and decoded properly. Feedback can take many forms: a customer's purchase of the item, the use of a Pepsi emoji, a complaint or compliment, the redemption of a coupon or rebate, a tweet about the product on Twitter, and so forth.

How Consumers Perceive Communication

The actual communication process is not as simple as the model in Exhibit 18.1 implies. Each receiver may interpret the sender's message differently, and senders often adjust their message according to the medium used and the receivers' level of knowledge about the product or service.

Receivers Decode Messages Differently Each receiver decodes a message in his or her own way, which is not necessarily the way the sender intended. Different people shown the same message will often take radically different meanings from it. For example, what does the image on page 554 to you?

Social & Mobile Marketing 18.1

Analyzing the Unmeasured: A Snapchat Experiment by Domino's to Test the Channel's Effectiveness[i]

Most marketing communications and advertising campaigns start with an idea, and then the appropriate channel to share it is chosen. In a recent Snapchat campaign by the UK arm of Domino's Pizza though, the pattern was reversed: Domino's wanted to experiment with using Snapchat, so it chose the channel first and then developed an idea that would enable it to test the success of the campaign.

The unique approach was necessary because Snapchat—as a primarily creative, rather than informative, messaging channel—lacks the analytical tools available in most other sources. Unlike other social media sites for example, it does not provide users with measures of reach or consumer responses. Yet it is an organic and popular social media application with great promise for reaching and appealing to young and savvy consumers.

Therefore, Domino's decided to undertake an experimental test, in which it posted a series of videos. The storyline featured a delivery driver beset by an alien invasion over multiple video uploads. Each entry in the series gave viewers a portion of a code; once they had the entire code, they could use it to receive a purchase voucher. Thus, the number of vouchers redeemed offered a good estimate of reach, because it signaled how many people were willing to watch the entire video series. After the 24-hour experiment, Domino's was pleasantly surprised by how many additional orders it received. As another measure of the campaign's success, Domino's also determined how far the video spread among various consumers.

Noting the gaps in its analytical capabilities, Snapchat is rumored to be working on developing better measurement and assessment tools. Some reports also suggest it might begin offering e-commerce capabilities and group messaging. Yet part of the appeal of Snapchat is the creativity it invokes. Other competitors already offer group messaging services, so expanding the services it offers could move Snapchat into more direct competition with new rivals and also disrupt its reputation as a fun site, not a commercial one.

The Domino's test thus remains just that; the pizza chain has not determined exactly how it will continue to use Snapchat in its marketing communications. But the promising results give it a good reason to continue experimenting. As Domino's head of digital marketing suggested, using Snapchat alongside other social media and traditional communications channels seemed like the way to go: "Our anticipation is that Snapchat will become a tool we add to our toolkit, rather than being the one that we use for everything."

Domino's is experimenting in the UK with Snapchat to test the effectiveness of its campaign "From Dough to Door."

Source: Domino's/Snapchat

If you are a user of this brand, it may convey satisfaction. If you recently went on a diet and gave up your soda, it may convey dismay or a sense of loss. If you have chosen to be a nonuser, it may convey some disgust. If you are a recently terminated employee, it may convey anger. The sender has little, if any, control over what meaning any individual receiver will take from the message.

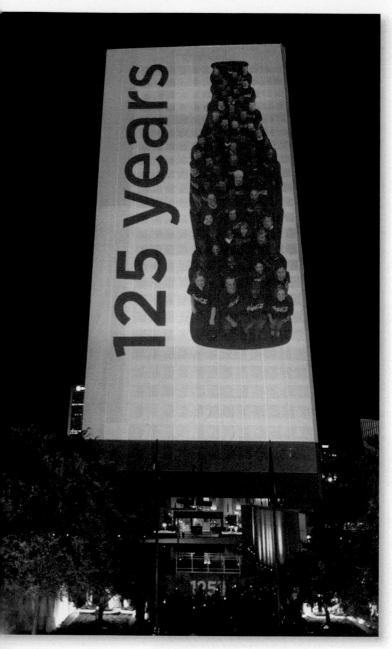

Consumers will perceive this giant billboard differently depending on their level of knowledge and attitude toward the brand.

© imago stock&people/Newscom

LO18-2 Explain the four steps in the AIDA model.

Senders Adjust Messages According to the Medium and Receivers' Traits
Different media communicate in varied ways, so marketers make adjustments to their messages and media depending on whether they want to communicate with suppliers, shareholders, customers, the general public, or even specific segments of those groups.[10]

For example, the high-technology firm Analtech sells thin layer chromatography plates to companies that need equipment to determine the ingredients of samples of virtually anything. It is not an easy product to explain and sell to laypeople, particularly when some purchasers might not have a science degree. Therefore, in addition to traditional marketing through trade shows and scientific conferences, Analtech developed a Monty Python–inspired YouTube video (https://www.youtube.com/watch?v=06gRhDMnPp8) that features a witch who overcomes threats to drown her by proving that the ink in the king's decree is actually from the sheriff's pen. It also highlights points in *CSI* episodes when the television detectives rely on its products. With these more broadly popular appeals, Analtech ensures its messages reach and can be received accurately by a wider audience, with less noise than might occur through more scientific appeals.

Pepsi has often solicited the talents of celebrities who are likely to appeal to various customer segments, such as those featured in the hit show *Empire*. Adding Value 18.1 describes this creative adjustment approach by Pepsi.

The AIDA Model
Clearly, IMC is not a straightforward process. After being exposed to marketing communications, consumers go through several steps before actually buying or taking some other action. There is not always a direct link between a particular form of marketing communications and a consumer's purchase.

To create effective IMC programs, marketers must understand how marketing communications work. Generally, marketing communications move consumers stepwise through a series of mental stages, for which there are several models. The most common is the **AIDA model** (Exhibit 18.2),[11] which suggests that **A**wareness leads to **I**nterest, which leads to **D**esire, which leads to **A**ction. At each stage, the consumer makes judgments about whether to take the next step in the process. Customers actually have three types of responses, so the AIDA model is also known as the think, feel, do model. In making a purchase decision, consumers go through each of the AIDA steps to some degree, but the steps may not always follow the AIDA order. For instance, during an impulse purchase, a consumer may feel and do before he or she thinks.

Awareness Even the best marketing communications can be wasted if the sender doesn't gain the attention of the consumer first. **Brand awareness** refers to a potential customer's ability to recognize or recall that the brand name is a particular type of retailer or product/service. Thus, brand awareness is the strength of the link between the brand name and the type of merchandise or service in the minds of customers.

There are several awareness metrics, including aided recall and top-of-mind awareness. **Aided recall** is when consumers indicate they know the brand when the name is presented to them. **Top-of-mind awareness**, the highest level of awareness, occurs when consumers mention a specific brand name first when they are asked about a product or service. For example, Harley-Davidson has top-of-mind awareness if a consumer responds

Adding Value **18.1**   Landing an Endorsement Contract on *Empire*: Fiction, Reality, and Pepsi[ii]

Product placements in popular films and television shows are a well-proven and relatively effective marketing tactic. But when it comes to *Empire*, everything is a little larger than life, leading Pepsi to recognize it needed to go big with its latest marketing innovation. That is, it would not be enough just to have Cookie drinking a Pepsi. The brand wanted to become part of the story, thus ensuring that fans of the Lyon family would be exposed to its products throughout the show, whenever they get around to watching it.

This potential market is huge: *Empire* attracts an estimated 13.5 million viewers when each new episode airs, and then another 9.2 million viewers who watch at their leisure through different on-demand services (e.g., DVRs, Hulu). These latter viewers constitute an ongoing challenge for marketers though, because in many cases, they do not see the same commercials, and with some services, they even can fast-forward or avoid the advertising altogether.

What they cannot miss though is a three-episode storyline in which Jamal, the young *Empire* character played by Jussie Smollett, earns himself an endorsement contract with Pepsi, shoots the commercial, and then presents it to other musicians during an industry event. Throughout these three episodes, Pepsi is a constant and aspirational presence; the fictional endorsement is a signal of success for Jamal's emerging music career. Furthermore, the pitch that the fictional Pepsi executives make to Jamal, to convince him that the endorsement is in his best interest, includes the assertion that Pepsi has a long and storied history of working with cutting-edge musicians and artists. The line serves to "sell" Jamal on the idea of the endorsement, even as it sells viewers on the image of Pepsi as cool and iconic.

Moving beyond these fictional elements, the commercial that Jamal shoots in the show then appears during the actual commercial breaks of the show. The advertisement itself was directed by the show's creator, Lee Daniels, which helped ensure consistency in the tone and image between the show and the marketing communication. Calling it gritty and raw, Daniels promises that the ad, appearing both in the show and during its commercial breaks, would not be "an experience that's been experienced by the regular Pepsi commercial viewer before." This thematic consistency is part of what Pepsi is counting on, to make sure that consumers do not regard the endorsement storyline and associated marketing as a sell-out by their beloved show or its creators.

The deal actually required several agreements. First, Pepsi paid Fox, the network that airs *Empire*, a reported $20 million for the right to enter the show and advertise in and through it. Second, Pepsi entered into separate contracts with Smollett, the actor who plays Jamal and is thus endorsing the company indirectly, and with Daniels, the director creating the vision for the marketing plan by directing both the show and the advertisement.

The experiment thus has required substantial resources from Pepsi. But the company considers the innovative marketing a risk worth taking, especially in response to information from Nielsen about advertising retention. Recent Nielsen data reveal that when a product appears both in the show's content and during a commercial broadcast during the show, viewers remember that product 18 percent more than they would if it is solely advertised in a traditional way.

Moreover, *Empire*'s primary audience is exactly the consumers that Pepsi hopes to attract. Young and hip, these viewers also seem fine with watching a family whose moral compass is a bit off center at times. Still, Pepsi chose Jamal, among the least controversial or violent of the members of the Lyon family, as its linked character, likely to avoid any brand damage that might result if Lucious were seen holding a Pepsi bottle while threatening to murder his uncle.

Pepsi's product placement on Empire *has been a huge success. Over three episodes, Jamal, played by Jussie Smollett, earns himself an endorsement contract with Pepsi, shoots the commercial, and then presents it to other musicians during an industry event.*

EXHIBIT 18.2 The AIDA Model

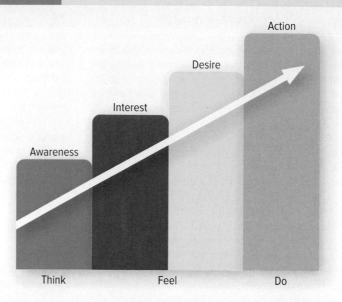

"Harley" when asked about American-made motorcycles. High top-of-mind awareness means that the brand probably enters the evoked set of brands (see Chapter 6) when customers decide to shop for that particular product or service. Manufacturers, retailers, and service providers build top-of-mind awareness by having memorable names; repeatedly exposing their name to customers through advertising, locations, and sponsorships; and using memorable symbols.

As an excellent example of the last method, imagine two smaller circles, sitting on opposite sides atop a larger circle. Did you see Mickey Mouse ears? Did you think of Disney? In addition, the company has moved on to images brighter than circles to ensure that its name comes easily to the front of young consumers' minds. Whether individual acts—such as Austin Mahone, Selena Gomez, and Demi Lovato—or groups—such as R5, Lemonade Mouth, and Allstar Weekend—Disney starts off its stars with Disney Channel shows, records them on the Disney-owned Hollywood Record label, plays the songs in heavy rotation on Radio Disney and Disney movie soundtracks, organizes concert tours with Disney-owned Buena Vista Concerts, and sells tie-in merchandise throughout Disney stores. Each of these marketing elements reminds the various segments of the target market about both the brand (e.g., One Direction) and its owner, Disney. With this omnichannel approach, Disney gets the same product into more markets than would be possible with a more conservative approach, which further builds top-of-mind awareness for both Disney and its stars.[12]

Interest Once the consumer is aware that the company or product exists, communication must work to increase the consumer's interest level. It isn't enough to let people know that the product exists; consumers must be persuaded that it is a product worth investigating. Because Stouffer's was suffering from a reputation of offering poor-quality meal options, it reoriented its marketing campaigns to focus on its "real food" ingredients that lead to meals good enough to make even a teenager put down her phone to join her family at dinnertime.[13] Thus, the ads' messages include attributes that are of interest to the target audience—in this case, parents who want to sit down to a nice dinner with their children. Disney increases interest in an upcoming tour or record by including a mention, whether casual or not, in the stars' television shows. Because the primary target market for the tour is also probably watching the show, the message is received by the correct recipient. As Ethical and Societal Dilemma 18.1 proposes, interest also can be sparked by a little controversy.

Ethical & Societal Dilemma 18.1   The Need to Take Risks in IMC[iii]

According to recommendations from a panel of marketing experts, if companies want their communications to resonate and stick with modern customers, they need to run the risk of angering or alienating them too. When marketing campaigns are just regular, "up the middle," or boring, they have little chance of prompting the sorts of behaviors advertisers seek, whether that means getting people to talk or actual sales.

Instead, the goal needs to be to spark interest in the campaign, which then will spark interest in the product or service. Interest might result from an unusual or unexpected presentation—or even a seemingly conventional approach with just a little difference. A key example comes from Honey Maid crackers, which ran a traditional advertising campaign that featured families to communicate a message of wholesomeness. What made the campaign different was the type of families being featured, which included gay parents, single parents, and a multiracial family. For many viewers, the difference

was appealing; for those who objected, Honey Maid transformed their often hateful comments into an art piece it could use to further its brand image as wholesome and welcoming.

Rather than challenging biases, other examples are just a little weird, such as a General Electric campaign to introduce an innovation it developed with the social network Quirty, in which an executive gives a foot massage to the inventor of their newly introduced Aros air conditioners. Then there are the fake infomercials directed by the comedy duo behind *Tim & Eric's Bedtime Stories*, which feature the famously distinctive actor Jeff Goldblum, hawking GE's new Link LED light bulbs.

Weird does not work for everybody, but according to these marketing experts, everybody needs to try it. If a marketing communication is not interesting enough to get consumers talking about it, warns one expert, then it is not interesting enough to run.

Honey Maid crackers ran an advertising campaign that featured multiracial and other nontraditional families to communicate a message of wholesomeness.

Source: Little Brother/Honey Maid/YouTube

Desire After the firm has piqued the interest of its target market, the goal of subsequent IMC messages should move the consumer from "I like it" to "I want it." If Lucy Hale (star of *Pretty Little Liars*) appears on *Good Morning America* (on ABC, which is owned by Disney) and talks about her upcoming album and how great it is going to be, the viewing audience is all the more likely to demand access—in this case, probably parents who hope to score points with their adolescent children by buying the latest single or reserving seats to an upcoming tour. Stouffer's aims to enhance consumers' desire through its food truck initiatives, which offer free samples of various frozen entrees, dressed up with extra ingredients, to show families how delicious a frozen dinner can be with just a few extra steps.[14]

If consumers watch Fox's Empire or visit Fox's website to see what Cookie wore on the show, they might in turn actually purchase the Empire original soundtrack on iTunes

© Fox Network/Photofest

Action The ultimate goal of any form of marketing communications is to drive the receiver to action. Thus Stouffer's likely hands out coupons for its products from its food trucks, to help push customers to make the purchase during their next trip to the grocery store. As long as the message has caught consumers' attention and made them interested enough to consider the product as a means to satisfy a specific desire of theirs, they likely will act on that interest by either searching for the product or making a purchase. If consumers watch Fox's *Empire* or visit Fox's website to see what Cookie wore on the show, they might in turn actually purchase the *Empire* original soundtrack on iTunes.

The Lagged Effect Sometimes consumers don't act immediately after receiving a form of marketing communications because of the lagged effect—a delayed response to a marketing communications campaign. It generally takes several exposures to a campaign before a consumer fully processes its message.[15] In turn, measuring the effect of a current campaign becomes more difficult because of the possible lagged response to a previous one. The recurrent presence of De Beers' advertising campaign for diamond jewelry resonates with consumers over time. So when the occasion arises to buy jewelry for oneself or for a loved one, the consumer will think of diamonds. But De Beers doesn't know if any particular marketing communication will lead consumers to check out or purchase a new diamond.

Now that we've examined various aspects of the communication process, let's look at how specific media are used in an IMC program.

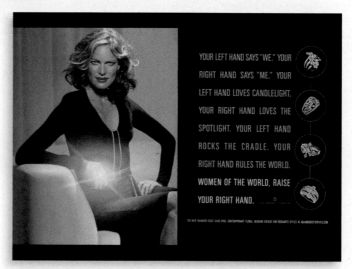

The recurrent presence of De Beers' advertising campaign for diamond jewelry resonates with consumers over time. So, when the occasion arises to buy jewelry for oneself or for a loved one, the consumer will think of diamonds.

Source: De Beers

PROGRESS CHECK

1. What are the different steps in the communication process?
2. What is the AIDA model?

CHANNELS USED IN AN INTEGRATED MARKETING COMMUNICATIONS STRATEGY

For any communications campaign to succeed, the firm must deliver the right message to the right audience through the right media, with the ultimate goal of profiting from long-term customer relationships rather than just short-term transactions. Reaching the right audience is becoming more difficult, however, as the media environment grows more complicated.

No single channel is necessarily better than another channel; the goal of IMC is to use the channels in conjunction so that the sum exceeds the total of the individual channels. However, advances in technology have led to a variety of new and traditional media channel options for consumers, all of which vie for consumers' attention. Print media have also grown and become more specialized. This proliferation of media has led many firms to shift their promotional dollars from advertising to direct marketing, website development, product placements, and other forms of promotion, all in search of the best way to deliver messages to their target audiences.

We now examine the individual channels of IMC and the way each contributes to a successful IMC campaign (see Exhibit 18.3). The channels can be viewed on two axes: passive and interactive (from the consumer's perspective) and offline and online. Some channels (e.g., advertising, sales promotion, public relations, personal selling, direct and online marketing) are discussed in far more detail in subsequent chapters, so we discuss them here only briefly.

LO18-3 Describe the various integrative communication channels.

Note that as the marketer's repertoire of IMC channels has expanded, so too have the ways in which marketers can communicate with their customers. So, for instance, direct marketing appears in all four boxes. Firms have expanded their use of these traditional media (e.g., advertising, public relations, and sales promotions) from pure offline approaches to a combination of offline and online.

Advertising

Perhaps the most visible of the IMC channels, advertising entails the placement of announcements and persuasive messages in time or space purchased in any of the mass media by business firms, nonprofit organizations, government agencies, and individuals who seek to inform and/or persuade members of a particular target market or audience about their products, services, organizations, or ideas.[16] In Chapter 19, we discuss the purpose of advertising and its various types but, for now, note that advertising is extremely effective for

EXHIBIT 18.3 Channels of an IMC Strategy

Interactive

- Personal selling
- Sales promotions
  (e.g., contests)
- Direct marketing
  (e.g., telemarketing)

- Direct marketing
  (e.g., mobile marketing)
- Online marketing
  (e.g., blogs, social media)

Offline / Online

- Advertising
- Sales promotions
  (e.g., coupons)
- Public relations
- Direct marketing
  (e.g., catalogs)

- Direct marketing
  (e.g., e-mail marketing)

Passive

creating awareness of a product or service and generating interest. Mass advertising can entice consumers into a conversation with marketers, though it does not necessarily require much action by consumers, which places it on the passive end of the spectrum. Traditionally, advertising has been passive and offline (e.g., television, magazines, newspapers; see Exhibit 18.3), though recently there has been a growth in online advertising and interactive features. Advertising thus must break through the clutter of other messages to reach its intended audience.

Public Relations

Public relations (PR) is the organizational function that manages the firm's communications to achieve a variety of objectives, including building and maintaining a positive image, handling or heading off unfavorable stories or events, and maintaining positive relationships with the media. Like advertising, this tactic is relatively passive in that customers do not have to take any action to receive it. Public relations activities support the other promotional efforts by the firm by generating free media attention, as we discuss further in Chapter 19.

Sales Promotions

Sales promotions are special incentives or excitement-building programs, such as coupons, rebates, contests, free samples, and point-of-purchase (POP) displays, that encourage the purchase of a product or service. Marketers typically design these incentives for use in conjunction with other advertising or personal selling programs. Many sales promotions, such as free samples or POP displays, are designed to build short-term sales. Others, such as contests and sweepstakes, have become integral tactics of some firms' CRM programs as a means to build customer loyalty. We discuss such sales promotions in more detail in Chapter 19.

Personal Selling

Personal selling is the two-way flow of communication between a buyer and a seller that is designed to influence the buyer's purchase decision. Personal selling can take place in various settings: face-to-face, video teleconferencing, on the telephone, or over the Internet. Although consumers don't often interact with professional salespeople, personal selling represents an important channel in many IMC programs, especially in business-to-business (B2B) settings.

The cost of communicating directly with a potential customer is quite high compared with other forms of promotion, but it is simply the best and most efficient way to sell certain products and services. Customers can buy many products and services without the help of a salesperson, but salespeople simplify the buying process by providing information and services that save customers time and effort. In many cases, sales representatives add significant value, which makes the added expense of employing them worthwhile. We devote Chapter 20 to personal selling and sales management.

Direct Marketing

The IMC channel that has received the greatest increase in aggregate spending recently is direct marketing, or marketing that communicates directly with target customers to generate a response or transaction.[17] Direct marketing contains a variety of traditional and new forms of marketing communications initiatives. Traditional direct marketing includes mail and catalogs sent through the mail; direct marketing also includes e-mail and mobile marketing.

Internet-based technologies have had a profound effect on direct marketing initiatives. E-mail, for instance, can be directed to a specific consumer. Firms use e-mail to inform customers of new merchandise and special promotions, confirm the receipt of an order, and indicate when an order has been shipped. Currently available technologies also mean mobile devices can function as a payment medium: Just tap your cell phone, and the transaction occurs in much the same way it occurs with a credit card.[18]

EXHIBIT 18.4	Illustrative Mobile Marketing Campaigns
Company	**Campaign**
Calvin Klein "Raw texts, real stories"	When Calvin Klein launched its new line of jeans in 2015, it became the first company to advertise on the dating app Tinder. The ads were designed to keep in line with the feel of the app's culture by including suggestive images and text-messaging conversations.
Hard Rock "World Burger Tour"	To promote its World Burger Tour, the Hard Rock Café used geo-targeted rich mobile ads directed at customers within a specific radius of the restaurant. The Hard Rock was also able to access customer information that helped identify vacationers, who would be more likely to be eating out. The campaign was a huge success, leading to a 220 percent increase in traffic.
Maytag ESPN	In November 2015, the appliance brand took over ESPN's mobile site for a day. On that day, visitors of the site viewed an ad that showed the Maytag repairman and famous spokesmen working on an assembly line. Maytag also went beyond the typical mobile ad by creating an experience that enabled customers to feel the physical movements felt by the Maytag repairman in the factory.
T-Mobile Social mobile ads	The Super Bowl is generally the biggest opportunity for television ads, so why didn't T-Mobile run its Super Bowl ad on TV? Instead, T-Mobile opted to run its ad on NBC's mobile and tablet apps, as well as on its website. T-Mobile made this decision after reviewing data that showed that Millennials prefer to stream television programs on other devices.

Source: Adapted from Brielle Jaekel, "Top 10 Mobile Advertising Campaigns of 2015," Mobile Marketer, January 5, 2016, http://www.mobilemarketer.com.

The increased use of customer databases has enabled marketers to identify and track consumers over time and across purchase situations, which has contributed to the rapid growth of direct marketing. Marketers have been able to build these databases, thanks to consumers' increased use of credit and debit cards, store-specific credit and loyalty cards, and online shopping, all of which require the buyer to give the seller personal information that becomes part of its database. Because firms understand customers' purchases better when they possess such information, they can more easily focus their direct marketing efforts appropriately.

Direct marketing retailers try to target their customers carefully so they will be more receptive to their messages. Omaha Steaks, for example, sends e-mail coupons for items that customers have purchased previously, mails slick pictures of gourmet steaks and meal packages to addresses that have received orders in the past, and calls customers personally during likely gift-giving occasions, such as the holidays, to offer to repeat a previous gift order. These different forms of direct marketing demonstrate how this IMC format can vary on both the interactivity and online–offline dimensions of the matrix.

Mobile marketing is marketing through wireless handheld devices such as cellular telephones.[19] Smartphones have become far more than tools to place calls; they offer a kind of mobile computer with the ability to obtain sports scores, weather, music, videos, and text messages as well as purchase merchandise. Marketing success rests on integrating marketing communications with fun, useful apps that are consistent with these consumer attitudes toward mobile devices. In response, firms are steadily improving customers' potential experience with their mobile interface. Exhibit 18.4 highlights five successful mobile marketing campaigns.

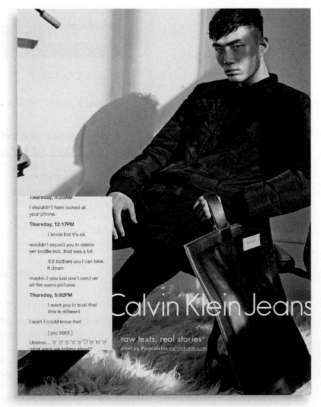

Calvin Klein's "Raw texts, real stories" mobile campaign was designed to keep in line with the feel of the app's culture by including suggestive images and text messaging conversations.
Source: Calvin Klein Jeans

Online Marketing

We now examine several electronic media vehicles: websites, blogs, and social media.

Websites Firms have increased their emphasis on communicating with customers through their websites. They use their websites to build their brand image and educate customers about their products or services as well as where they can be purchased. Retailers and some manufacturers sell merchandise directly to consumers over the Internet. For example, in addition to selling merchandise, Office Depot's website hosts a Business Resource Center for its business customers that provides advice, product knowledge, and connections to networking contacts in other businesses. It also provides forms that businesses can use to comply with Occupational Safety and Health Act (OSHA) requirements, check job applicant records, estimate cash flow, and develop a sexual harassment policy; posts workshops for running a business; and summarizes local and national business news. By providing this information, Office Depot reinforces its image as an essential source of products, services, and information for small businesses.

Many firms operate websites devoted to community building. These sites offer an opportunity for customers with similar interests to learn about products and services that support their hobbies and share information with others. Visitors can also post questions seeking information and/or comments about issues, products, and services. Many firms, especially retailers (e.g., Amazon), encourage customers to post reviews of products they have bought or used and even have visitors to their websites rate the quality of the reviews. Research has shown that these online product reviews increase customer loyalty and provide a competitive advantage for sites that offer them.[20]

Blogs A **blog (weblog)** contains periodic posts on a common web page. A well-received blog can communicate trends, announce special events, create positive word of mouth,

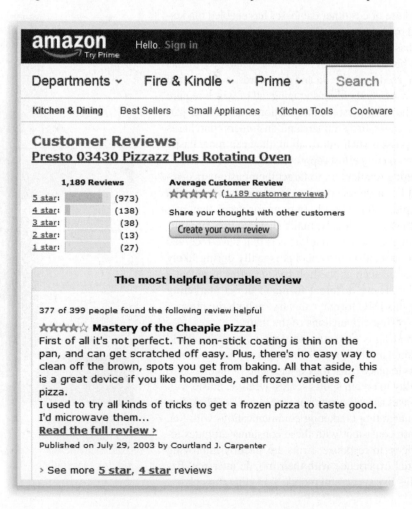

To increase customer loyalty and provide a competitive advantage, firms like Amazon encourage customers to post reviews of products or services they have bought or used.

Source: Amazon.com, Inc.

connect customers by forming a community, allow the company to respond directly to customers' comments, and develop a long-term relationship with the company. By its very nature, a blog is supposed to be transparent and contain authors' honest observations, which can help customers determine their trust and loyalty levels. Nowadays, blogs are becoming more interactive as the communication between bloggers and customers has increased. In addition, blogs can be linked to other social media such as the microblog Twitter. See Chapter 3 for further discussion.

Social Media The term social media refers to online and mobile technologies that distribute content to facilitate interpersonal interactions (see Chapter 3). The three most popular facilitators of social media are YouTube, Facebook, and Twitter. In these online sites, consumers review, communicate about, and aggregate information about products, prices, and promotions. These social media also allow users to interact among themselves (e.g., form a community) as well as provide other like-minded consumers (i.e., members of their community) and marketers their thoughts and evaluations about a firm's products or services. Thus, social media help facilitate the consumer decision process (Chapter 6) by encouraging need recognition, information search, alternative evaluation, purchase, and postpurchase reviews.

PROGRESS CHECK

1. What are the different elements of an IMC program?

PLANNING FOR AND MEASURING IMC SUCCESS

We begin this section by examining how marketers set strategic goals before they implement any IMC campaign. After they have established those goals, marketers can set the budget for the campaign and choose the marketing metrics they will use to evaluate whether it has achieved its strategic objectives.

Goals

As with any strategic undertaking, firms need to understand the outcome they hope to achieve before they begin. These goals can be short term, such as generating inquiries, increasing awareness, and prompting trial. Or they can be long term in nature, such as increasing sales, market share, and customer loyalty. Some other goals are outlined in Exhibit 18.5.

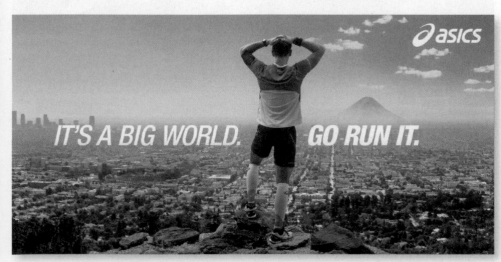

Running-shoe manufacturer ASICS devised the "It's a big world. Go run it" campaign to branch out beyond serious runners and to target casual runners.

Source: ASICS

EXHIBIT 18.5   Illustrative Marketing Goals and Related Campaigns

Company and Campaign	Goal	Target Market	Media Used	Outcome
ASICS "It's a big world. Go run it."	Branch out beyond serious runner market segment and target casual runners.	Even split males and females, aged 30–49	Television and print ads, online advertising	17% increase in sales
Columbia Sportswear Company "Tested Tough"	Showcase Columbia's technical innovation ability.	60% males, aged 20–59	Print ads, mobile media, social media, videos, online advertising	11% increase in sales
Southwest Airlines "Nonstop Love"	To show that Southwest is "an airline with a heart."	Even split males and females, all ages	Television, radio, print, billboard, and in-airport ads	4% increase in revenue
BMW "#DrivingLuxury"	To highlight the new technology of the redesigned 7 series sedan.	Mostly men, ages 35 and up	Social media, blog posts, videos	Posts reached up to 13,500 likes on Instagram

Source: "ASICS Launches New Global Advertising Campaign, Inspiring People Everywhere to Run with 'It's a big world. Go run it,'" PR Newswire, February 19, 2015; ASICS, 2015 Annual Report, ASICS, February 12, 2016; Karl Greenberg, "Columbia's New Global Campaign Is 'Tested Tough,'" Marketing Daily, October 7, 2015; Columbia Sportswear, 2015 Annual Report, Columbia SportSwear, 2016; David Gianatasio, "Southwest Airlines Is Completely, Hopelessly, Head over Heels in Love in New Ads," Ad Week, July 8, 2014; Southwest Airlines, 2014 Annual Report, March 15, 2015; "BMW's Instagram Influencer Marketing Campaign," Media Kix, http://mediakix.com/2015/12/instagram-influencer-marketing-bmw-campaign/.

Such goals, both short and long term, should be explicitly defined and measured. Regardless of their measure or changes, though, goals constitute part of the overall promotional plan, which is usually a subsection of the firm's marketing plan. Another part of the promotional plan is the budget.

Columbia Sportswear Company's "Tested Tough" campaign's goal is to showcase Columbia's technical innovation ability, here featuring its 93-year-old chairwoman Gert Boyle.

Source: Columbia

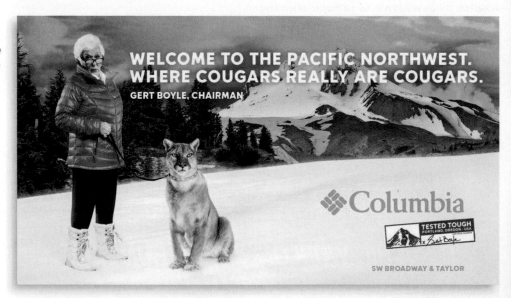

Setting and Allocating the IMC Budget

LO18-4 Explain the methods used to allocate the integrated marketing communications (IMC) budget.

Firms use a variety of methods to plan their marketing communications budgets. Because all the methods of setting a promotional budget have advantages as well as disadvantages, no one method should be used in isolation.[21]

EXHIBIT 18.6	Rule-of-Thumb Methods	
Method	**Definition**	**Limitations**
Competitive parity	The communication budget is set so that the firm's share of communication expenses equals its share of the market.	Does not allow firms to exploit the unique opportunities or problems they confront in a market. If all competitors use this method to set communication budgets, their market shares will stay approximately the same over time.
Percentage-of-sales	The communication budget is a fixed percentage of forecasted sales.	Assumes the same percentage used in the past, or by competitors, is still appropriate for the firm. Does not take into account new plans (e.g., to introduce a new line of products in the current year).
Available budget	Marketers forecast their sales and expenses, excluding communication, during the budgeting period. The difference between the forecast sales and expenses plus desired profit is reserved for the communication budget. That is, the communication budget is the money available after operating costs and profits have been budgeted.	Assumes communication expenses do not stimulate sales and profit.

The **objective-and-task method** determines the budget required to undertake specific tasks to accomplish communication objectives. To use this method, marketers first establish a set of communication objectives, then determine which media best reach the target market and how much it will cost to run the number and types of communications necessary to achieve the objectives. This process—set objectives, choose media, and determine costs—must be repeated for each product or service. The sum of all the individual communication plan budgets becomes the firm's total marketing communications budget. In addition to the objective-and-task method, various **rule-of-thumb methods** can be used to set budgets (see Exhibit 18.6).

These rule-of-thumb methods use prior sales and communication activities to determine the present communication budget. Although they are easy to implement, they have various limitations, as noted in Exhibit 18.6. Clearly, budgeting—not a simple process—may take several rounds of negotiations among the various managers, who are each competing for resources for their own areas of responsibility, to devise a final IMC budget.

Measuring Success Using Marketing Metrics

Once a firm has decided how to set its budget for marketing communications and its campaigns have been developed and implemented, it reaches the point that it must measure the success of the campaigns, using various marketing metrics.[22] Each step in the IMC process can be measured to determine how effective it has been in motivating consumers to move to the next step in the buying process. Such measures become particularly challenging when marketing efforts include creative and new forms of communication, as Adding Value 18.2 describes. Furthermore, recall that the lagged effect influences and complicates marketers' evaluations of a promotion's effectiveness as well as the best way to allocate marketing communications budgets. Because of the cumulative effect of marketing communications, it may take several exposures before consumers are moved to buy, so firms cannot expect too much too soon. They must invest in the marketing communications campaign with the idea that it may not reach its full potential for some time. In the same way, if firms cut marketing communications expenditures, it may take time before they experience a decrease in sales.

LO18-5 Identify marketing metrics used to measure IMC success.

Adding Value 18.2   America's Dream Team, Brought to You by Kia[iv]

In North America, spectator sports represent a nearly $64 billion market. Some of that revenue comes from ticket sales to fans who cannot get close enough to the action. But the right to broadcast those sports accounts for an ever-increasing portion of the market's revenue, and as those interests grow, some key priorities are changing too. In particular, the National Basketball Association (NBA) is breaking away from some of its traditional peers by taking a page from soccer and racing leagues: They are considering new sponsorship agreements that place company logos right on the players' uniforms.

Thus far, the new agreement applies only to the uniforms for the 2016 and 2017 All-Star Games, for which the NBA players' uniforms will feature a small, 3.25" × 1.6" patch with the name and logo of the automotive brand Kia. Individual teams do not have the league's permission to alter their jerseys similarly, and as of now there are no plans to add advertising patches to regular-season uniforms.

But even in this limited form, the move is still a dramatic change, considering that the NBA—along with its peers, the National Football League, Major League Baseball, and the National Hockey League—has never used them in the past. The uniforms in all these leagues feature logos for the manufacturer of the uniforms, and they often sport commemorative patches to honor important people and personalities who have recently died.

But advertising for other brands has not existed, for several reasons. The uniform manufacturers have resisted it in particular, worried that other ads on the jerseys would compete for consumers' attention. There is also the difficulty of finding an external sponsor that is acceptable to all the teams in the league. In addition, leagues have struggled to define a profit-sharing plan that would be fair. That is, how much of the revenue created by such advertising would go to the league, to the team, or to the players themselves?

For the NBA, Kia's All-Star jersey sponsorship actually was the result of negotiations between the league and Turner

In an unusual partnership between KIA and the NBA, a small KIA logo will appear on players' uniforms.
Source: Kia K900 LeBron James Commercial/Kia Motors America/YouTube

Sports, which is the network that owns the broadcast rights for games. When the two parties entered into their most recent contract, Turner asked for the right to negotiate with sponsors and sell advertising space on the players' uniforms. In turn, it entered into the two-year marketing agreement with Kia.

Although the NBA and other major sports leagues have little experience with this form of marketing communication, others are far more familiar with it. Drivers as well as their cars are festooned with sponsorship logos in most car-racing leagues. European soccer players also often display logos on their jerseys. One professional—and entrepreneurial—marathon runner sells space on his race kits and bibs to advertisers when he enters big races like the New York Marathon.

Moreover, it isn't as if sponsorships are anything new in sports—on virtually all levels. Another car company, Nissan, recently announced that it had entered into "the widest-reaching sponsorship in the history of collegiate sports." This agreement gives Nissan the rights to place its name and logos in the stadiums of 100 different universities throughout the United States, as well as to use those schools' names in its own advertising.

Traditional Media When measuring IMC success, the firm should examine when and how often consumers have been exposed to various marketing communications. Specifically, the firm uses measures of frequency and reach to gauge consumers' exposure to marketing communications. For most products and situations, a single exposure to a communication is hardly enough to generate the desired response. Therefore, marketers measure the **frequency** of exposure—how often the audience is exposed to a communication within a specified period of time. The other measure used to measure consumers' exposure to marketing communications is **reach**, which describes the percentage of the target population exposed to a specific marketing communication, such as an advertisement, at least once.[23] Marketing communications managers usually state their media objectives in terms of **gross rating points (GRP)**, which represent reach multiplied by frequency (GRP = Reach × Frequency).

This GRP measure can refer to print, radio, or television, but any comparisons require a single medium. Suppose that Kenneth Cole places seven advertisements in *Vogue* magazine, which reaches 50 percent of the fashion-forward target segment. The total GRP generated

When calculating the gross rating points (GRP) of The Voice, the advertiser would multiply the reach times the frequency.

© NBC/Photofest

by these seven magazine advertisements is 50 reach × 7 advertisements = 350 GRP. Now suppose Kenneth Cole includes 15 television ads as part of the same campaign, run during the program *America's Next Top Model,* which has a rating (reach) of 9.2. The total GRP generated by these 15 advertisements is 138 (9.2 × 15 = 138). However, advertisements typically appear in more than one television program. So, if Kenneth Cole also advertises 12 times during *The Voice,* which earns a rating of 1.8, its GRP would be 1.8 × 12 = 21.6, and the total GRP for both programs would be 138 + 21.6 = 159.6.

Web-Based Media Taken together, firms are spending close to $160 billion annually on online advertising, which includes paid search, display ads, e-mail, and sponsorships.[24] As shown in Exhibit 18.7, while the percentage increase of digital ad spending to total spending

| **EXHIBIT 18.7** | Digital Ad Spending Worldwide, 2010–2016 *(billions, % change and % of total media ad spending)* |

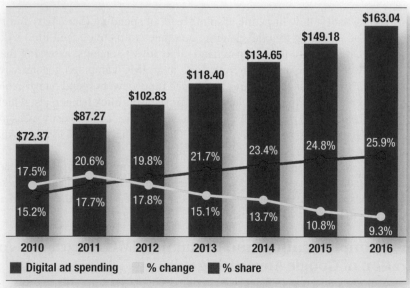

Note: Includes advertising that appears on desktop and laptop computers as well as mobile phones and tablets, and includes all the various formats of advertising on those platforms; excludes SMS, MMS, and P2P messaging-based advertising.

Source: eMarketer.com, December 2012

Marketing Analytics 18.1 | Puma's Use of Google Analytics[v]

The international sports brand Puma offers clothing and accessories alongside its iconic shoes. It enjoys continued success mainly because it has turned to analytics to define its integrated marketing strategies and develop its advertising. When Puma first partnered with Google Analytics, its primary goals were to showcase the breadth of its products online and centralize its online presence. But to compete in the modern age among customers who are accustomed to shopping anywhere at any time, it needed to do more than update its website. Thus, Puma integrated its advertising with its online marketing strategy to devise an overall branded content online strategy.

The insights gained from Google Analytics drive these new advertising and online strategies. For example, Puma launched a new photo-driven site with multiple profiles of famous athletes such as Olympian Usain Bolt and soccer star Mario Balotelli. Instead of traditional web formats, the site weaves the featured apparel together with buy buttons that appear interspersed throughout the content. The new site also was integrated with the brand's "Forever Faster" campaign—a campaign that also featured the same athletes in television commercials and social media campaigns. Although Puma.com is still a relatively small player in the online world, it saw a significant increase in engagement and the number of site visits as a result of these efforts.

Google Analytics also helped Puma develop another aspect of its marketing strategy: By analyzing each product line individually, Puma came to recognize exactly which products and lines were most popular. This analysis in turn revealed the

The insights gained from Google Analytics were used to launch a photo-driven site with profiles of famous athletes such as Olympian Usain Bolt and introduce the brand's "Forever Faster" campaign used in television commercials and social media campaigns.

© Jamie McCarthy/Getty Images

need to improve the visibility of its women's lines. To address this need, Puma decided to add inspirational women to its list of celebrity endorsements, alongside the mostly male athletes it had been featuring. In the hope of reaching more young female customers for example, Puma named Rihanna as a brand ambassador and creative director of its women's line.

---

is slowing somewhat (yellow line), the absolute level of spending (bar chart) and relative share of digital ad spending to total spending continues to increase (red line). Although GRP is an adequate measure for television and radio advertisements, assessing the effectiveness of any web-based communication efforts in an IMC campaign generally requires **web-tracking software**, which measures how much time viewers spend on particular web pages, the number of pages they view, how many times users click banner ads, which website they came from, and so on. All these performance metrics can be easily measured and assessed using a variety of software, including Google Analytics. Marketing Analytics 18.1 describes how Puma makes use of Google Analytics.

Facebook also helps companies see who has been visiting their fan pages, what those people are doing on the fan pages, and who is clicking their advertisements.[25] By keeping track of who is visiting their fan pages, marketers can better customize the material on their pages by getting to know the people visiting.

Planning, Implementing, and Evaluating IMC Programs—An Illustration of Google Advertising

Imagine a hypothetical upscale sneaker store in New York City, called Transit, that is modeled after vintage New York City subway trains. Transit's target market is young, well-educated, hip men and women aged 17 to 34 years. The owner's experience indicates the importance of personal selling for this market because these consumers (1) make large

Advertisers pay Google to be listed in the Sponsored Links section in the right-hand column of this screen grab, based on the keywords customers use in their searches.

Source: Google, Inc.

purchases and (2) seek considerable information before making a decision. Thus, Jay Oliver, the owner, spends part of his communication budget on training his sales associates. Oliver has realized his communication budget is considerably less than that of other sneaker stores in the area. He has therefore decided to concentrate his limited budget on a specific segment and use electronic media exclusively in his IMC program.

The IMC program Oliver has developed emphasizes his store's distinctive image and uses his website, social shopping, and some interesting community-building techniques. **Social shopping** is the use of the Internet to communicate about product preferences with other shoppers. For instance, he has an extensive customer database as part of his CRM system, from which he draws information for matching new merchandise with his customers' past purchase behaviors. He also has little personal nuggets of information that he or other sales associates have collected on the customers. He then e-mails specific customers information about new products that he believes will be of interest to them. He also encourages customers to use blogs hosted on his website. Customers chat about the hot new sneakers, club events, and races. He does everything with a strong sense of style.

To reach new customers, he is using **search engine marketing (SEM)**. In particular, he is using Google AdWords, a search engine marketing tool offered by Google that allows advertisers to show up in the Sponsored Links section of the search results page based on the keywords potential customers use (see the sponsored link section in the right-hand column of the Google screen grab above).

Oliver must determine the best keywords to use for his sponsored link advertising program. Some potential customers might search using the keywords "sneakers," "sneakers in New York City," "athletic shoes," or other such versions. Using Google AdWords, Oliver can assess the effectiveness of his advertising expenditures by measuring the reach, relevance, and return on investment for each of the keywords that potential customers used during their Internet searches.

To estimate reach, Oliver uses the number of **impressions** (the number of times the ad appears in front of the user) and the **click-through rate (CTR)**. To calculate CTR, he divides the number of times a user clicks an ad by the number of impressions.[26] For example, if a sponsored link was delivered 100 times and 10 people clicked on it, then the number of impressions is 100, the number of clicks is 10, and the CTR would be 10 percent.

The **relevance** of the ad describes how useful an ad message is to the consumer doing the search. Google provides a measure of relevance through its AdWords system

EXHIBIT 18.8	ROMI Assessment

(1) Keyword	(2) Clicks	(3) Marketing Expenditure	(4) Sales	(5) Gross Margin = Sales × Gross Margin% = Sales × 50%	(6) Gross Margin ($) (Col. 5) − Marketing Expenditure (Col. 3)	(7) ROMI = (Col. 6/Col. 3) × 100
Sneaker store	110	$10/day	$70/day	$35/day	$25	250%
New York City sneakers	40	$25/day	$80/day	$40/day	$15	60%

Note: The cost of the sneakers is 50 percent of the sale price.

using a quality score. The quality score looks at a variety of factors to measure how relevant a keyword is to an ad's text and to a user's search query. In general, a high-quality score means that a keyword will trigger ads in a higher position and at a lower cost-per-click.[27] In a search for "sneaker store," the Transit ad showed up fourth, suggesting high relevance.

Using the following formula, Oliver also can determine an ad's **return on marketing investment (ROMI)**:

$$\text{ROMI} = \frac{\text{Gross Margin} - \text{Marketing Expenditure}}{\text{Marketing Expenditure}} \times 100$$

For the two keyword searches in Exhibit 18.8, Oliver finds how much the advertising cost him (Column 3), the sales produced as a result (Column 4), the gross margin in dollars (Column 5), and the ROMI (Column 7). For "sneaker store," the Transit website had a lot more clicks (110) than the clicks received from "New York City sneakers" (40) (see Column 2, Exhibit 18.8). Even though the sales were lower for the keywords "sneaker store" at $35/day, versus $40/day for the keywords "New York City sneakers," the ROMI was much greater for the "sneaker store" keyword combination. In the future, Oliver should continue this keyword combination, in addition to producing others that are similar to it, in the hope that he will attain an even greater return on investment.

To evaluate his IMC program, Oliver compares the results of the program with his objectives (Exhibit 18.9). To measure his program's effectiveness, he conducted an inexpensive online survey using the questions in Exhibit 18.9, which shows the survey results for one year.

The results show a steady increase in awareness, knowledge of the store, and choice of the store as a primary source of sneakers. This research provides evidence that the IMC program was conveying the intended message to the target audience.

EXHIBIT 18.9	Program Effectiveness Results

Communication Objective	Question	Before Campaign	Six Months After	One Year After
Awareness (% mentioning store)	What stores sell sneakers?	38%	46%	52%
Knowledge (% giving outstanding rating for sales assistance)	Which stores would you rate outstanding on the following characteristics?	9	17	24
Attitude (% first choice)	On your next shopping trip for sneakers, which store would you visit first?	13	15	19
Visit (% visited store)	Which of the following stores have you been to?	8	15	19

PROGRESS CHECK

1. Why is the objective-and-task method of setting an IMC budget better than the rule-of-thumb methods?
2. How do firms use GRP to evaluate the effectiveness of traditional media?
3. How would a firm evaluate the effectiveness of its Google advertising?

Reviewing Learning Objectives

 Identify the components of the communication process.

The communication process begins with a sender, which provides the message to a transmitter, which develops or encodes the message for transmission through a communication channel. When a recipient receives the message, it may have been altered by noise in the environment. To find out, the sender needs to receive some form of feedback from the recipient.

 Explain the four steps in the AIDA model.

Awareness is the first "thinking" step, during which the consumer simply recognizes a brand or product. During the **I**nterest step, the consumer starts to "feel" and become intrigued enough to explore the product or brand. This interest then leads to another feeling, namely, **D**esire for the marketed item. Finally, to be successful, marketing communication must prompt an **A**ction: a purchase, a commitment, a recommendation, or whatever else the company is trying to get consumers to do.

 Describe the various integrative communication channels.

Advertising has long been the primary channel for marketing communication and is still a constant presence, but other media channels have become more and more prominent. For example, direct marketing media options, particularly online options, have increased in recent years. Outbound direct marketing telephone calls have declined, but Internet-based technologies like e-mail and m-commerce have increased. Public relations also has become increasingly important as other media forms become more expensive and as consumers grow more skeptical of commercial messages. With regard to new and electronic media, the wealth of recent options includes websites, corporate blogs, and social media such as YouTube, Facebook, and Twitter.

 Explain the methods used to allocate the integrated marketing communications (IMC) budget.

Various rule-of-thumb methods rely on prior sales and communication activities to determine the best allocation. For example, the competitive parity method sets the budget so that the share of communication expenses equals the firm's share of the market. The percentage-of-sales method, just as it sounds, uses a fixed percentage of sales as the amount of the budget. In contrast, the objective-and-task method establishes specific communication objectives, identifies which media can best attain those objectives, and then determines the related costs to expend.

 Identify marketing metrics used to measure IMC success.

Marketers rely on a mix of traditional and nontraditional measures to determine IMC success. Because potential customers generally need to be exposed to IMC messages several times before they will buy, firms estimate the degree to which customers are exposed to a message by multiplying frequency (the number of times an audience is exposed to a message) by reach (the percentage of the target population exposed to a specific marketing communication). Measuring Internet IMC effectiveness requires different measures, such as click-through tracking that measures how many times users click on banner advertising on websites.

Key Terms

■LEARNSMART

- advertising, 559
- AIDA model, 554
- aided recall, 554
- blog (weblog), 562
- brand awareness, 554
- click-through rate (CTR), 569

Marketing Digitally

1. Visit http://phelpsagency.com/ and click on the "Work" tab at the top. Compare the IMC for the different companies. What were the goals of the integrated marketing campaign? Which IMC channels were used in that particular campaign? How do those channels contribute to the success of the IMC campaign in achieving its stated goals?

Marketing Applications

1. Assume that the contemporary apparel company rag & bone has embarked on a new IMC strategy. It has chosen to advertise on TV during *NBC Nightly News* and in print in *Time* magazine. The message is designed to announce new styles for the season and uses a 17-year-old woman as the model. Evaluate this strategy and, if appropriate, propose an alternative.

2. Using the steps in the AIDA model, explain why a potential consumer in question 1 who views rag & bone's advertising may not be ready to go out and purchase a new pair of jeans.

3. Suppose a snack company introduces a new product called SumSeeds—sunflower seeds with energy boosters like caffeine, taurine, lysine, and ginseng. How would you expect this product's IMC program to differ from that for regular sunflower seeds sold as snacks?

4. Procter & Gamble sends new parents home from the hospital with a sample of Pampers diapers, and it has started sending Fusion ProGlide razors to each young man in America on his 18th birthday. What are the likely goals of such marketing tactics? How could Procter & Gamble measure how well it has achieved these goals with its free giveaways?

5. Suppose you saw your instructor for this course being interviewed on TV about the impact of a big storm on an upcoming holiday's sales. Is this interview part of your college's IMC program? If so, do you believe it benefits the college? How?

6. A hotel runs several advertisements in the student newspaper of a local university, promoting its Sunday brunch menu. The ads increase the number of people visiting its restaurant, but only slightly. Is the campaign necessarily a failure? What other goals might the hotel have for this advertising campaign?

7. As an intern for Pepsi, you have been asked to help with developing an IMC budget. The objective of the IMC strategy is to raise Diet Pepsi's market share by 2 percent in the United States in the next 18 months. Your manager explains, "It's real simple; just increase the budget 2 percent over last year's." Evaluate your manager's strategy.

8. You were sitting in the school cafeteria yesterday, and a young man from your marketing class, whom you don't know well, asked if he could sit down. He then started telling you about this very cool new Google app, "WordLens," that allows you to translate signs into different languages in real time using the camera on your smartphone. Although you recognize the merit in the product, you later find out that he works for Google. Do you believe his action constitutes an ethical IMC strategy? How will it affect your attitude toward Google and the potential that you will purchase the product?

Quiz Yourself

1. Home Depot hired an advertising agency to develop television ads for its grand opening in southern Maine. The advertising agency represents which of the following components of the communication process?
   a. sender
   b. transmitter
   c. communication channel
   d. receiver
   e. feedback

2. Which of the following formulas is accurate for calculating gross rating points (GRP)?
   a. Impressions multiplied by frequency
   b. Reach multiplied by impressions
   c. Reach multiplied by frequency
   d. Reach divided by impressions
   e. Reach divided by frequency

(Answers to these two questions can be found in the Quiz Yourself Answer Key section.)

Chapter Case Study

TAKING IMC TO THE MAX: PEPSI MAX AND MODERN COMMUNICATIONS

As we explained in the opener to this chapter, Pepsi has embraced the communication capabilities of emojis in a big way—you might even say, in a maximal way. Actually, PepsiCo would love it if you used that description, because for its Pepsi Max line of beverages, it actively seeks to establish a consistently cool, cutting-edge perception among consumers, mainly by using integrated marketing campaigns that revolve around the notion of living life "to the max." Let's consider a few of the ways it presents consistent messages across a range of channels.

The very name of the product line provides the foundation for the consistent message. By referring to the carbonated beverage as Pepsi Max, PepsiCo signals that this brand will offer more, greater, and bigger things to consumers. Thus every communication needs to be "to the max" as well—grander, louder, more exciting, more thrilling. In this effort, PepsiCo uses the tagline "Maximum Taste, No Sugar" in combination with hashtags such as #LiveforNow and #Unbelievable on social media.

On its dedicated YouTube channel, Pepsi Max posts videos of people living up to the philosophies embedded in the hashtags, including the "Human Loop the Loop" Damien Walters—a man who seemingly defies gravity (and offers an excellent lesson in centripetal force) in his unbelievable physical feat of running all the way around a vertical loop-the-loop.[28] Other videos on the channel highlight "Amazing Trampoline Tricks" and cool JumpCam shots of remarkable feats. The efforts have vastly increased the number of followers and views earned by adrenaline junkies, as well as those who simply find enjoyment in watching seemingly normal people be unbelievable.[29]

Rather than amazing feats by regular people, Pepsi Max's #Maxfootball campaign relies on some of the biggest names in men's soccer, including Sergio Agüero from Man City, James Rodríguez of Real Madrid, Arsenal's Alexis Sánchez, and the goalkeeper David de Gea for Manchester United. In televised advertisements, the players are flashed blue cards (rather than the yellow and red cards that stop play in the game), prompting adventures and fun for the regular people holding them up. One television spot, for example, tells the story of two regular delivery drivers who raise their blue cards and thereby gain magical access to a shooting session with the all-star players, who show off their acrobatic moves and enviable ball-handling skills.[30]

With a linked app, Pepsi Max allows users to enter contests to win similar "Blue Card Experiences," including tickets to the championship game. To increase the coordination across campaigns, the app also features a function that lets users scan the Pepsi emojis on Pepsi Max cans to win other prizes and contest entries.

As if those innovations were not "max" enough, PepsiCo is entering some of the newest channels in unusual ways. Whereas outdoor advertising traditionally has been static and relatively straightforward, Pepsi Max is changing the relationship between this marketing channel and social media. On digital billboards, Pepsi Max posts videos submitted by users to the entertainment network Vine that detail how they #LiveForNow (remember that hashtag?).[31] Drivers passing the billboards thus get to see a quick and exciting video, which they can access again when they get home and log in to their Vine accounts.

With another example of marrying traditional communication forms with modern technology, Pepsi Max also transformed bus stops into adventure zones. Using augmented reality techniques, it has created a system to allow remarkably realistic videos to play in the windows surrounding bus stops. Thus when a rider sits down to wait for the next bus and glances to the right, it appears as though a tiger were literally walking down the street, headed right toward the bus stop. Other videos show a massive meteor ready to obliterate the city street or an alien-looking tentacle grabbing pedestrians nearby.[32] The videos are very short, to avoid truly scaring people, but in those brief moments, more than a few people have experienced some thrilling terror. Of course, Pepsi Max also tapes their reactions and posts those videos to its YouTube channel.

Questions

1. Which channels is Pepsi Max using to communicate its marketing messages? Rank order your impression of how effective they are and justify your answer.

2. How are those various channels integrated?

3. Which IMC channels do these campaigns by Pepsi Max make use of?

Endnotes

1. Mike Esterl, "Coke Sticks to Its Strategy While Soda Sales Slide," *The Wall Street Journal,* April 9, 2014, http://online.wsj.com.

2. Alan Cassinelli, "The 15 Best Social Media Campaigns of 2015," *Business to Community,* December 31, 2015, http://www.business2community.com/social-media/15-best-social-media-campaigns-2015-01415014#klBUQ1dYj8W3mQkG.97.

3. Tim Nudd, "Pepsi Is About to Unleash Emojis on Its Bottles and Cans Globally This Summer," *Ad Week,* February 19, 2016, http://www.adweek.com/news/advertising-branding/pepsi-about-unleash-emojis-its-bottles-and-cans-globally-summer-169782.

4. E.J. Schultz and Jessica Wohl, "Pepsi Preps Global Emojiu Can and Bottle Campaign," *Advertising Age,* February 19, 2016, http://adage.com/article/cmo-strategy/pepsi-preps-global-emoji-bottle-campaign/302748/.

5. Ibid.

6. Cassinelli, "The 15 Best Social Media Campaigns of 2015."

7. Schultz and Wohl, "Pepsi Preps Global Emojiu Can and Bottle Campaign."

8. Terence Shimp and J. Craig Andrews, *Advertising Promotion and Other Aspects of Integrated Marketing Communications* (Boston: Cengage Learning, 2013).

9. PepsiCo, "Universal Language," http://design.pepsico.com/pepsimoji.php?v=20#section5.

10. Shimp and Andrews, *Advertising Promotion and Other Aspects of Integrated Marketing Communications.*

11. E. K. Strong, *The Psychology of Selling* (New York: McGraw-Hill, 1925).

12. Disney, "Music," http://music.disney.com; Phil Gallo, "Disney Music Tops Interscope in Album Market Share, Enters the EDM Fray," *Billboard,* May 10, 2014, http://www.billboard.com.

13. Andrew Adam Newman, "Trying to Bolster the Image of Frozen Meals as Sales Lag," *The New York Times,* April 23, 2014, http://www.nytimes.com.

14. Ibid.

15. John Philip Jones, "What Makes Advertising Work?" *The Economic Times,* July 24, 2002.

16. American Marketing Association, "Advertising," *Dictionary of Marketing Terms,* https://www.ama.org/resources/Pages/Dictionary.aspx.

17. Teri Evans, "Firms Hold Fast to Snail Mail Marketing," *The Wall Street Journal,* January 12, 2010, http://online.wsj.com; George E. Belch and Michael A. Belch, *Advertising and Promotion: An Integrated Marketing Communications Perspective* (New York: McGraw-Hill, 2007).

18. Rebecca Lieb, "Q&A: Cindy Krum Cuts through the Mobile Marketing Alphabet Soup of NFC and RFID," http://econsultancy.com, March 16, 2010.

19. Akihisa Fujita, "Mobile Marketing in Japan: The Acceleration of Integrated Marketing Communications," *Journal of Integrated Marketing Communications* (2008), pp. 41–46; Mobile update, http://www.businessinsider.com; http://www.informationweek.com; http://www.nearbynow.com (accessed May 26, 2010).

20. Yubo Chen, Scott Fay, and Qi Wang, "The Role of Marketing in Social Media: How Online Consumer Reviews Evolve," *Journal of Interactive Marketing* 25, no. 2 (May 2011), pp. 85–94.

21. This section draws from Michael Levy, Barton A. Weitz, and Dhruv Grewal, *Retailing Management,* 9th ed. (Burr Ridge, IL: McGraw-Hill /Irwin, 2015).

22. Megan Halscheid, Micheline Sabatté, and Sejal Sura, "Beyond the Last Click: Measuring ROI and Consumer Engagement with Clickstream Analysis," *Journal of Integrated Marketing Communications,* 2009, pp. 43–50; Vikram Mahidhar and Christine Cutten, "Navigating the Marketing Measurement Maze," *Journal of Integrated Marketing Communications,* 2007, pp. 41–46.

23. http://www.riger.com.

24. Sydney Ember, "Digital Ad Spending Expected to Soon Surpass TV," *The New York Times,* December 7, 2015.

25. "Facebook Pages: Insights for Your Facebook Page," http://www.facebook.com.

26. "Marketing and Advertising Using Google," Google 2007.

27. http://publishing2.com.

28. https://www.youtube.com/watch?v=OTcdutlcEJ4.

29. "How Pepsi Max's 'Unbelievable' YouTube Channel Helped Increase Market Share," *Think with Google,* November 2014, https://www.thinkwithgoogle.com/intl/en-gb/case-studies/how-pepsi-maxs-unbelievable-youtube-channel-helped-increase-market-share.html.

30. Tony Connelly, "Pepsi Max Launches Star-Studded Football Ad Campaign to Coincide with Its Emoji Marketing," *The Drum,* February 23, 2016, http://www.thedrum.com/news/2016/02/23/pepsi-max-launches-star-studded-football-ad-campaign-coincide-its-emoji-marketing.

31. Emma Hall, "Pepsi Max Puts Vine Videos on U.K. Billboards," *Advertising Age,* February 20, 2014.

32. Jessica Gioglio, "Pepsi Max Shocks and Delights Londoners with Augmented Reality Stunt," *Convince and Convert,* n.d., http://www.convinceandconvert.com/social-media-case-studies/pepsi-max-shocks-and-delights-londoners-with-augmented-reality-stunt/.

i. Seb Joseph, "Domino's Says Its Snapchat Test Led to a 'Surprising' Surge in Pizza Orders," *Business Insider,* February 18, 2016.

ii. Joe Flint, "Pepsi Gets Taste of 'Empire' Drama," *The Wall Street Journal,* November 19, 2015, http://adage.com/article/media/pepsi-s-meta-integration-fox-s-empire/301420/.

iii. Stuart Elliot, "Marketers Are Urged to Become Fearless," *The New York Times,* September 30, 2014, http://www.nytimes.com.

iv. Sarah Germano, "NBA to Put Kia Logo on Front of All-Star Jerseys," *The Wall Street Journal,* October 28, 2015; E.J. Schultz, "Nissan Goes Big with College Sports in New Sponsorship Deal," *Advertising Age,* November 6, 2015.

v. Google Analytics, "Case Study: Puma Kicks Up Order Rate 7% with Insights from Google Analytics and Viget," Google, 2013, https://static.googleusercontent.com/media/www.google.com/en/us/analytics/customers/pdfs/puma.pdf; Caitlin Carter, "Rihanna Signs on as Puma's New Creative Director," *Music Times,* December 16, 2014, http://www.musictimes.com/articles/20450/20141216/rihanna-pumas-new-creative-director-new-album-global-ambassador-fashion-icon.htm; Puma, "Rihanna: Gamechanger," Puma.com,http://us.puma.com/en_US/sports/ambassadors/rihanna; Lucia Moses, "Inside Puma's Branded Content Strategy," *Digiday,* December 15, 2014, http://digiday.com/brands/nielsenes-puma-branded-content/; Aaron Ricadela, "Puma's Marketing Strategy Is a Whole New Ball Game," *Business World,* September 19, 2014, http://www.independent.ie/business/world/pumas-marketing-strategy-is-a-whole-new-ball-game-30598229.html; Larissa Faw, "Puma Adds New Channels to Its 'Forever Faster' Campaign," *Media Post,* August 26, 2014, http://www.mediapost.com/publications/article/232889/puma-adds-new-channels-to-its-forever-faster-cam.html.

ADVERTISING, PUBLIC RELATIONS, AND SALES PROMOTIONS

LEARNING OBJECTIVES

After reading this chapter, you should be able to:

LO19-1   Describe the steps in designing and executing an advertising campaign.

LO19-2   Identify three objectives of advertising.

LO19-3   Describe the different ways that advertisers appeal to consumers.

LO19-4   Identify the various types of media.

LO19-5   Identify agencies that regulate advertising.

LO19-6   Describe the elements of a public relations toolkit.

LO19-7   Identify the various types of sales promotions.

"When McDonald say "we use 100% beef" is the 100% a percentage or is it a the name of a beef manufacturer that is named 100% ?"

LITTLE_RICEMAN
from Canada

"Do you use palm oil and if so is it derived ethically?"

KUNNENFLEUR
from Lower Sackville

that a McDonalds
es not rot?"

JRA B.
n Toronto, ON

"where does mcdonalds buy the beef it uses in its canadian mcdonalds hamburgers?"

JOSH W.
from Kitchener

"Is 100% Canadian Real Beef, a store or the content of your burgers?"

HONORVERITAS
from Thornhill

our burgers not rot"

NIEL J.
m Prairieville

"Will you be switching to beef from South America at any point in the future as all these rumours suggest?"

VLAD M.
from Kanata

the nutritional values
dium iced coffee sugar
lla and 2% milk instead
?"

"When you say 100% pure beef, is that 'pure beef' only beef or

Source: *YourQuestions.McDonalds.ca*

Lots of companies say that they listen to their customers. To prove its claim, McDonald's has initiated a marketing campaign in which it created channels for consumers to ask questions, then made the answers readily available. The risk in the strategy was that they would lack control over what kinds of questions people asked, but as the company's senior director of U.S. marketing explained recently, the campaign is about more than advertising; it is "fundamentally about an ongoing two-way communication with our customers."

The "Our Food. Your Questions" campaign places kiosks in major cities, where passersby can ask challenging questions, such as "What's really in your hamburgers?" or "Do you use dye in your shakes?" McDonald's then issues immediate responses to the individual questioners, and also posts the questions and answers online. At the same time, it broadcasts recordings of these interactions as television commercials and on YouTube, seeking to expand the reach of its truth-telling campaigns. In just a few months, McDonald's has posted responses to more than 25,000 questions through various social media, and it announced that 19 million people watched question videos through YouTube.

Furthermore, it relies on the insights it gains from this two-way conversation to refocus its ongoing communications on clearing up some misconceptions. For example, following up on a frequently asked question, McDonald's began running television ads depicting eggs being freshly cracked for Egg McMuffins. The recipe for the breakfast favorite had always required McDonald's kitchen staff to break fresh eggs, but when consumers asked, "What is in an Egg McMuffin?" McDonald's knew that it had not communicated that benefit sufficiently in its previous advertising.

Along with advertising what it already does, McDonald's is presenting itself as responsive to customers by announcing that it is revising the recipe for Chicken McNuggets. The question-and-answer session that focused on "What is really in Chicken McNuggets?" was the second most widely watched answer session on its U.S. YouTube site.[1] In addition, related questions signaled that consumers were worried about antibiotics and the healthfulness of the Happy Meal favorites. Therefore, the revised McNuggets will contain fewer ingredients, exclude artificial preservatives, and come from sources that do not add antibiotics to their poultry meal. In advertisements introducing the new McNuggets, McDonald's makes the "cleaner label" a key element.[2] The advertising thus has a lot of work to do, and McDonald's seeks to ensure that it covers all the bases.

Building on the notion of the "Your Questions" campaign, McDonald's announced that it has a new brand vision. Rather than highlighting the billions of customers it has served—long a standard on the brightly lit signs for the restaurant—it wants to focus on the billions of customers it heard. The new brand vision is designed to fit with its existing advertising tagline, "I'm lovin' it," to ensure consistency and flow across all its brand communications.[3]

Advertising is a paid form of communication delivered through media from an identifiable source about an organization, product, service, or idea designed to persuade the receiver to take some action now or in the future.[4] This definition provides some important distinctions between advertising and other forms of promotion, which we discussed in the previous chapter. First, advertising is not free; someone has paid, with money, trade, or other means, to get the message shown. Second, advertising must be carried by some medium—television, radio, print, the web, T-shirts, sidewalks, and so on. Third, legally, the source of the message must be known or knowable. Fourth, advertising represents a persuasive form of communication, designed to get the consumer to take some action. That desired action can range from "ask us questions" to "perceive us as responsive" to "buy more McNuggets for your kids."

Advertising encompasses an enormous industry and clearly is the most visible form of marketing communications—so much so that many people think of marketing and advertising as synonymous. Global advertising expenditures are approximately $570 billion, and almost half that amount is spent in North America. Although expenditures dropped somewhat during the global downturn, advertising remains virtually everywhere, and predictions are that it will continue to grow.[5]

This billboard will get your attention. Produced by the nonprofit organization Women's Aid, this interactive billboard for battered women changes as people walk by and notice. The bruises heal.

Source: WomensAid.org

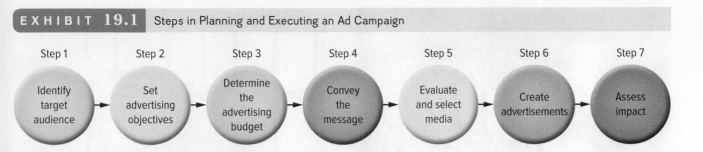

| EXHIBIT 19.1 | Steps in Planning and Executing an Ad Campaign |

Step 1 Identify target audience → **Step 2** Set advertising objectives → **Step 3** Determine the advertising budget → **Step 4** Convey the message → **Step 5** Evaluate and select media → **Step 6** Create advertisements → **Step 7** Assess impact

Yet how many of the advertisements you were exposed to yesterday do you remember today? Probably not more than three or four. As you learned in Chapter 6, perception is a highly selective process. Consumers simply screen out messages that are not relevant to them, and young consumers appear particularly good at doing so. For example, an astounding 92 percent of Millennial consumers indicated that while they watch television, they simultaneously and constantly check their mobile devices.[6] Thus, televised ads are unlikely to capture their attention for long, if at all. Then, if you do notice an advertisement, you may not react to it. Even if you react to it, you may not remember it later. Even if you remember the ad, you may not remember the brand or sponsor—or worse yet from the advertiser's point of view, you may remember it as an advertisement for another brand.[7]

To get you to remember their ad and the brand, advertisers must first get your attention. As we discussed in Chapter 18, the increasing number of communication channels and changes in consumers' media usage have made the job of advertisers far more difficult.[8] Advertisers continually endeavor to use creativity and various media to reach their target markets. In a public service campaign against domestic violence, the nonprofit organization Women's Aid raised interactive billboards, picturing a battered woman's face and the words "Look At Me." When people walking by stopped to look, facial recognition software embedded in the billboard recognized their actions, and the picture changed, such that the bruises healed. The creative approach not only attracted people's attention but also resonated with the underlying message—namely, that attention to a societal problem can be meaningful for solving the problem.[9]

As a consumer, you are exposed only to the end product—the finished advertisement, but many actions must take place before you actually get to see an ad. In this chapter, we examine the ingredients of a successful advertising campaign from identifying a target audience to creating the actual ad to assessing performance. Although our discussion is generally confined to advertising, much of the process for developing an advertising campaign is applicable to the IMC media vehicles discussed in Chapter 18. We conclude with some regulatory and ethical issues for advertising, then move on to public relations and sales promotions and their use.

Designing and carrying out a successful advertising program requires much planning and effort. Exhibit 19.1 shows the key steps in the process, each of which helps ensure that the intended message reaches the right audience and has the desired effect. We examine these steps in the sections that follow.

STEP 1: IDENTIFY TARGET AUDIENCE

The success of an advertising program depends on how well the advertiser can identify its target audience. Firms conduct research to identify their target audience, then use the information they gain to set the tone for the advertising program and help them select the media they will use to deliver the message to that audience.

 Describe the steps in designing and executing an advertising campaign.

During this research, firms must keep in mind that their target audience may or may not be the same as current users of the product. For example, adidas knows that FIFA fans likely are at least familiar with its offerings, even if they do not currently purchase sports gear from adidas. Thus some advertisements feature the international football (or soccer) stars Jozy Altidore and Lionel Messi to encourage them to buy more of the brand's products.[10] But teen-aged pop music fans might be less likely to pay attention to sporting goods. So adidas also brought in Selena Gomez to put her name on its Neo line and appear in related advertising.[11]

adidas uses different ads to appeal to different target markets. Jozy Altidore (left) appeals to soccer fans, while Selena Gomez (right) attracts teenaged pop music fans.

Source: adidas

LO19-2 Identify three objectives of advertising.

STEP 2: SET ADVERTISING OBJECTIVES

The objectives of an advertising campaign are derived from the overall objectives of the marketing program and clarify the specific goals that the ads are designed to accomplish. Generally, these objectives appear in the advertising plan, a subsection of the firm's overall marketing plan that explicitly analyzes the marketing and advertising situation, identifies the objectives of the advertising campaign, clarifies a specific strategy for accomplishing those objectives, and indicates how the firm can determine whether the campaign was successful.[12] An advertising plan is crucial because it will later serve as the yardstick against which advertising success or failure is measured.

Generally, in advertising to consumers, the objective is a pull strategy, in which the goal is to get consumers to pull the product into the marketing channel by demanding it. Push strategies also exist and are designed to increase demand by focusing on wholesalers, retailers, or salespeople. These campaigns attempt to motivate the seller to highlight the product, rather than the products of competitors, and thereby push the product to consumers. In this chapter, we focus on pull strategies. Push strategies are examined in Chapters 15, 16, and 20.

All advertising campaigns aim to achieve certain objectives: to inform, persuade, and remind customers. Another way of looking at advertising objectives is to examine an ad's focus. Is the ad designed to stimulate demand for a particular product or service or more broadly for the institution in general? Also, ads can be used to stimulate demand for a product category or an entire industry or for a specific brand, firm, or item. We first look at the broad overall objectives: to inform, persuade, and remind. Then we examine advertising objectives based on the focus of the ad: product versus institutional.

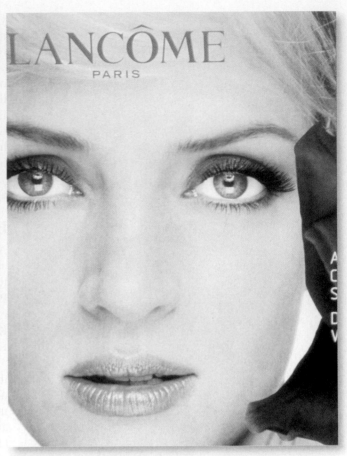

Is this product-focused advertisement designed to inform, persuade, or remind consumers about Pepsi Max?

Source: Pepsi-Cola Company

Lancôme's persuasive ads attempt to motivate consumers to take action: Try the product, switch brands, or continue to buy the product.

© Bill Aron/PhotoEdit

Informative Advertising

Informative advertising is a communication used to create and build brand awareness, with the ultimate goal of moving the consumer through the buying cycle to a purchase. Such advertising helps determine some important early stages of a product's life cycle (see Chapter 12), particularly when consumers have little information about the specific product or type of product. Retailers often use informative advertising to tell their customers about an upcoming sales event or the arrival of new merchandise.

Persuasive Advertising

When a product has gained a certain level of brand awareness, firms use persuasive advertising to motivate consumers to take action. Persuasive advertising generally occurs in the growth and early maturity stages of the product life cycle, when competition is most intense, and attempts to accelerate the market's acceptance of the product. In later stages of the product life cycle, persuasive advertising may be used to reposition an established brand by persuading consumers to change their existing perceptions of the advertised product. Consumer goods firms such as Lancôme often use persuasive advertising to convince consumers to take action—switch brands,[13] try a new product, or even continue to buy the advertised product.

Reminder Advertising

Finally, reminder advertising is a communication used to remind or prompt repurchases, especially for products that have gained market acceptance and are in the maturity stage of their life cycles. Such advertising certainly appears in traditional media, such as television or print commercials, but it also encompasses other forms of advertising. For example, if

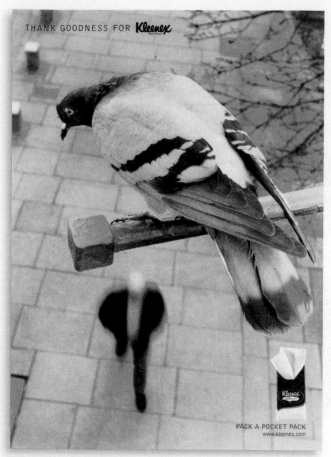

THANK GOODNESS FOR *Kleenex*

PACK A POCKET PACK
www.kleenex.com

This ad is designed to remind consumers that when you need tissues, don't think too hard. Just pick up a box of Kleenex.

Image Courtesy of The Advertising Archives

you decide to buy facial tissue, do you carefully consider all the options, comparing their sizes, prices, and performance, or do you just grab the first thing you see on the shelf? When your grocery store places a display of Kleenex facial tissues on the end of the paper products aisle, it relies on your top-of-the-mind awareness of the Kleenex brand, which the manufacturer has achieved through advertising. That is, Kleenex tissue maintains a prominent place in people's memories and triggers their response without them having to put any thought into it. The advertising and the end cap display thus prompt you and many other consumers to respond by buying a package, just the response Kleenex hoped to attain.

Focus of Advertisements

An ad campaign's objectives determine each specific ad's focus. The ad can be product focused, might have an institutional focus, or could have a public service focus. **Product-focused advertisements** inform, persuade, or remind consumers about a specific product or service. The Kleenex ad shown here is designed to generate sales for Kleenex.

An **institutional advertisement** is a type of advertising that promotes a company, corporation, business, institution, or organization. Unlike product-focused advertisements, it is not intended to sell a particular product or service. An ongoing and well-known institutional advertising campaign promotes GE's Ecomagination.[14] In the past, GE was thought to be one of the world's least "green" companies. Since 2005 GE, through its Ecomagination program, has devoted millions of dollars toward cleaner technologies including water purification technology and lower emission aircraft engines, and the development of cleaner energy like wind and solar power. The program has been so successful that *Fortune* named it as one of the world's top global green brands.[15]

A specific category of institutional advertising is **public service advertising (PSA)**. PSAs focus on public welfare; generally they are sponsored by nonprofit institutions, civic groups, religious organizations, trade associations, or political groups.[16] Like product and institutionally focused advertising, PSAs also inform, persuade, or remind consumers, but the focus is for the betterment of society. As such, PSAs represent a form of **social marketing**,

The GE Ecomagination program is institutional advertising in that it promotes the company and its "green" programs, not specific products.

Source: GE.com/about-us/ecomagination.com

Ecomagination 10 Year Anniversary: Driving Big Impacts for our Customers and Community

Power
~40 GW
Clean Energy Installed

Water
1B Gallons/Day
Wastewater Treated

Transportation
3T Ton
Rail Miles Traveled

defined as the application of marketing principles to a social issue to bring about attitudinal and behavioral change among the general public or a specific population segment.

Entertainer Reba McEntire is the spokesperson for a PSA for Outnumber Hunger, which was designed to raise awareness of the hunger problem in America. Sponsored by General Mills, Big Machine Label Group, and Feeding America, McEntire has appeared in special concert events and has been featured on more than 60 million General Mills packages, including Cheerios. For each General Mills product code entered by its customers at OutnumberHunger.com, five meals are acquired for local Feeding America food banks.[17]

Because PSAs are a special class of advertising that falls under Federal Communications Commission (FCC) rules, broadcasters must devote a specific amount of free airtime to them. Also, since they often are designed by top advertising agencies for nonprofit clients, PSAs usually are quite creative and stylistically appealing.

Regardless of whether the advertising campaign's objective is to inform, persuade, or remind, with a focus on a particular product or the institution in general, each campaign's objectives must be specific and measurable. For a brand awareness campaign, for example, the objective might be to increase brand awareness among the target market by 50 percent within six months. Another campaign's goal may be to persuade 10 percent of a competitor's customers to switch to the advertised brand. Once the advertising campaign's objectives are set, the firm sets the advertising budget.

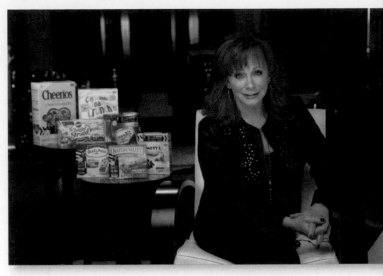

Entertainer Reba McEntire is the spokesperson for a PSA called Outnumber Hunger, designed to raise awareness of the hunger problem in America.

© Rick Diamond/WireImage/Getty Images

STEP 3: DETERMINE THE ADVERTISING BUDGET

The various budgeting methods for marketing communications (Chapter 18) also apply to budgeting for advertising. First, firms must consider the role that advertising plays in their attempt to meet their overall promotional objectives. Second, advertising expenditures vary over the course of the product life cycle. Third, the nature of the market and the product influence the size of advertising budgets. The nature of the market also determines the amount of money spent on advertising. For instance, less money is spent on advertising in B2B (business-to-business) marketing contexts than in B2C (business-to-consumer) markets. Personal selling, as we discuss in Chapter 20, likely is more important in B2B markets.

STEP 4: CONVEY THE MESSAGE

In this step, marketers determine what they want to convey about the product or service. First, the firm determines the key message it wants to communicate to the target audience. Second, the firm decides what appeal would most effectively convey the message. We present these decisions sequentially, but in reality they must be considered simultaneously.

The Message

The message provides the target audience with reasons to respond in the desired way. A logical starting point for deciding on the advertising message is to tout the key benefits of the product or service. The message should communicate its problem-solving ability clearly and in a compelling fashion. In this context, advertisers must remember that products and services solve problems, whether real or perceived. That is, people are not looking for 1/4-inch drill bits; they are looking for 1/4-inch holes to hang a picture on the wall.[18] Because there are many ways to make a 1/4-inch hole, a firm like Black & Decker must convey to consumers that its drill bit is the best way to get that hole.

Unique selling propositions like these by YouTube and Wrangler send powerful messages about the benefits of their offerings.

(Left): © Realimage/Alamy; (Right): © Tom Donoghue/Polaris/Newscom

Another common strategy differentiates a product by establishing its unique benefits. This distinction forms the basis for the **unique selling proposition (USP)** or the value proposition (as discussed in Chapter 9), which is often the common theme or slogan in an advertising campaign. A good USP communicates the unique attributes of the product and thereby becomes a snapshot of the entire campaign. Some of the most famous USPs include the following:

> Red Bull . . . Gives You Wings
>
> Ford . . . Built Tough
>
> Oreo . . . Milk's Favorite Cookie
>
> TNT . . . We Know Drama
>
> Kellogg's Corn Flakes Is The Original and Best Cereal
>
> *The New York Times* . . . All The News That's Fit to Print
>
> Trek . . . We Believe in Bikes
>
> Vail . . . Like Nothing On Earth
>
> YouTube . . . Broadcast Yourself
>
> Wrangler . . . Long Live Cowboys

The selling proposition communicated by the advertising must be not only unique to the brand but also meaningful to the consumer. It furthermore must be sustainable over time, even with repetition.

LO19-3 Describe the different ways that advertisers appeal to consumers.

The Appeal

Advertisers use different appeals to portray their products or services and persuade consumers to purchase them, though advertising tends to combine the types of appeals into two categories: informational and emotional.

Informational Appeals   **Informational appeals** help consumers make purchase decisions by offering factual information that encourages consumers to evaluate the brand favorably on the basis of the key benefits it provides.[19] Thus, ads for the Sexy Green Car Show in Cornwall, UK, espouse multiple ways in which consumers can educate themselves and act in a more environmentally conscious manner when it comes to their automobiles. This appeal is well suited to this type of product: By informing consumers about a potential source of its competitive advantage, including tangible features and images of science, the advertising copy directly delivers an informational, persuasive message.

Emotional Appeals   An **emotional appeal** aims to satisfy consumers' emotional desires rather than their utilitarian needs. These appeals therefore focus on feelings about the self.[20] The key to a successful emotional appeal is the use of emotion to create a bond

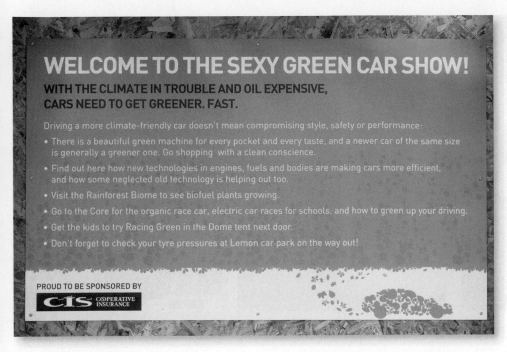

Ads for the Sexy Green Car Show in Cornwall, UK, espouse multiple ways in which consumers can educate themselves and act in a more environmentally conscious manner when it comes to their automobiles.

© Global Warming Images/Alamy

between the consumer and the brand. In its advertising, the UK insurance agency John Lewis highlights what really makes homeowner's insurance important, like the daughter in a family who simply must dance to "Tiny Dancer" but whose embellished twirls and leaps put everything in the home at risk of being broken. With both humor and tenderness (see https://www.youtube.com/watch?v=YqgoUWPx4eE), the advertising gives an emotional appeal to a service that many consumers regard as boring and unappealing.[21] Exhibit 19.2 shows firms and examples of the most common types of emotional appeals: fear/safety, humor, happiness, love (or sex),[22] comfort, and nostalgia.[23]

The UK insurance agency John Lewis uses a tender emotional appeal in an ad featuring a little girl dancing to "Tiny Dancer" while almost breaking everything in the room.

Source: Tiny Dancer/John Lewis Home Insurance/YouTube

EXHIBIT 19.2   Emotional Appeals in Advertising

Emotional Appeal	Company	Example
Fear/safety	Wandsworth	"Partied too hard? Do you know who you're leaving with?
Humor	Ocean Spray	"10 hours of cleansing and purifying . . . in one glass."
Happiness	Tropicana	"Awake to Alive"
Love/sex	Axe Body Spray	"Unleash the Chaos"
Comfort	Kleenex	"Softness Worth Sharing"
Nostalgia	Chevrolet	"Find New Roads"

Which emotional appeals are these ads using?

(Left): Source Axe Body Spray by Unilever; (Middle, right): Image Courtesy of The Advertising Archives

STEP 5: EVALUATE AND SELECT MEDIA

The content of an advertisement is tied closely to the characteristics of the media that firms select to carry the message, and vice versa. Media planning refers to the process of evaluating and selecting the media mix—the combination of the media used and the frequency of advertising in each medium—that will deliver a clear, consistent, compelling message to the intended audience.[24] For example, Macy's may determine that a heavy dose of television, radio, print, and billboards is appropriate for the holiday selling season between Thanksgiving and the end of the year.

Because the media buy, the actual purchase of airtime or print pages, is generally the largest expense in the advertising budget, marketers must make their decisions carefully. Television advertising is by far the most expensive. To characterize these various types of media, we use a dichotomy: mass and niche media.

Mass and Niche Media

Mass media channels include outdoor/billboards, newspapers, magazines, radio, and television and are ideal for reaching large numbers of anonymous audience members. Niche media channels are more focused and generally used to reach narrower segments, often with unique demographic characteristics or interests. Specialty television channels (e.g., Home and Garden TV) and specialty magazines (e.g., *Skateboarder* or *Cosmo Girl*) all provide examples of niche media. The Internet provides an opportunity to appeal to the masses through ads on the home page of Internet sites such as www.comcast.net or www.yahoo.com or more niched opportunities such as an American Express business card on the *Wall Street Journal* site (wsjonline.com).

Choosing the Right Medium

For each class of media, each alternative has specific characteristics that make it suitable for meeting specific objectives (see Exhibit 19.3).[25] For example, consumers use different media for different purposes, to which advertisers should match their messages. Television is used primarily for escapism and entertainment, so most television advertising relies on a mix of visual and auditory techniques.

LO19-4 Identify the various types of media.

EXHIBIT 19.3	Types of Media Available for Advertising	
Medium	Advantages	Disadvantages
Television	Wide reach; incorporates sound and video.	High cost; several channel and program options; may increase awareness of competitors' products.
Radio	Relatively inexpensive; can be selectively targeted; wide reach.	No video, which limits presentation; consumers give less focused attention than TV; exposure periods are short.
Magazines	Very targeted; subscribers pass along to others.	Relatively inflexible; takes some time for the magazine to be available.
Newspapers	Flexible; timely; able to localize.	Can be expensive in some markets; advertisements have short life span.
Internet/mobile	Can be linked to detailed content; highly flexible and interactive; allows for specific targeting.	Becoming cluttered; the ad may be blocked by software on the computer.
Outdoor/billboard	Relatively inexpensive; offers opportunities for repeat exposure.	Is not easily targeted; has placement problems in some markets; exposure time is very short.
Direct marketing	Highly targeted; allows for personalization.	Cost can vary depending on type of direct marketing used; traditional media, like mail, will be more expensive than newer media.

Communication media also vary in their ability to reach the desired audience. For instance, radio is a good medium for products such as grocery purchases or fast food because many consumers decide what to purchase either on the way to the store or while in the store. Because many people listen to the radio in their cars, it becomes a highly effective means to reach consumers at a crucial point in their decision process. Mobile advertising also is becoming more important, as Social and Mobile Marketing 19.1 explains. As we discussed in Chapter 18, each medium also varies in its reach and frequency. Advertisers can determine how effective their media mix has been in reaching their target audience by calculating the total GRP (Reach × Frequency) of the advertising schedule, which we discuss next.

Determining the Advertising Schedule

Another important decision for the media planner is the advertising schedule, which specifies the timing and duration of advertising. There are three types of schedules:

- A continuous schedule runs steadily throughout the year and therefore is suited to products and services that are consumed continually at relatively steady rates and that require a steady level of persuasive and/or reminder advertising. For example, Procter & Gamble advertises its Tide brand of laundry detergent continuously.

- Flighting refers to an advertising schedule implemented in spurts, with periods of heavy advertising followed by periods of no advertising. This pattern generally functions for products whose demand fluctuates, such as suntan lotion, which manufacturers may advertise heavily in the months leading up to and during the summer.

- Pulsing combines the continuous and flighting schedules by maintaining a base level of advertising but increasing advertising intensity during certain periods. For example, airlines, hotels, and car rental companies might continuously advertise to ensure brand awareness but might increase the advertising in spikes during certain low-demand periods.

Social & Mobile Marketing 19.1

What Comes Around: Just as Digital Has Pushed Out Traditional, Mobile Is Pushing Out Digital Advertising[i]

The signs of the growth of mobile advertising, at the expense of digital forms, have long been evident. But the speed with which this shift is occurring seemingly is taking many marketers by surprise, because it is virtually unprecedented.

Consider some of the numbers: In 2015, spending on mobile advertising increased by more than half of its 2014 rate. At the same time, spending on digital advertising dropped approximately 5 percent. Within just a couple of years, mobile advertising will be a bigger market than digital advertising.

Both forms are similar, in the sense that they are clearly distinct from traditional advertising and seek to reach technologically savvy shoppers. But they require unique approaches and marketing plans, because a campaign that works well on a user's desktop computer might not function effectively on a tablet or smartphone. Furthermore, mobile advertising offers functionalities and advertising tactics that digital ads cannot

provide. Mobile advertising also allows brands and marketers to send timely, location-based communications to consumers at the moment they enter a store or begin a search for a nearby restaurant on their phones.

Another trend occurring apace with this shift is the rise of ad-blocking technology. Apple now allows users to install software to block banner ads in digital channels. Although consumers indicate that they would like the ability to block advertising in mobile settings as well, marketing messages contained within apps continue to be prevalent. In this sense, advertisers might seek to expand their mobile marketing so as to avoid the barriers that consumers can implement on their desktops.

In the longer term though, the shift to more mobile advertising likely implies the need for new forms of marketing communication, including game-oriented, social content, and informational advertising that does not really look like advertising at all.

STEP 6: CREATE ADVERTISEMENTS

After the advertiser has decided on the message, type of ad, and appeal, its attention shifts to the actual creation of the advertisement. During this step, the message and appeal are translated creatively into words, pictures, colors, and/or music. (Adding Value 19.1 highlights the pro and cons of using popular music in television advertising campaigns.) Often,

Image Courtesy of The Advertising Archives

the execution style for the ad will dictate the type of medium used to deliver the message. To demonstrate an image, advertisers can use television and magazines. To promote price, they can use newspapers and radio. To appeal to specific target markets, they can use some of the electronic media vehicles described in Chapter 18. When using multiple media to deliver the same message, however, they must maintain consistency across styles—that is, integrated marketing—so that the different executions deliver a consistent and compelling message to the target audience.

How do advertisers go about creating advertisements? They simultaneously consider the objectives of the ad, the targeted customer segment(s), the product or service's value proposition or the unique selling proposition, and how the ad will be coordinated with other IMC elements.

They then go about creating an ad or the ad campaign. Using the print ad for the Ila DUSK Personal Alarm shown here as an example, the first component that the reader generally notices is the visual, and as such it should be eye-catching. The picture of the personal alarm on a chain is attractive and feminine. Although it is not always possible to meet all possible objectives with the visual, other important purposes are to identify the subject of the ad, show the product being used and its unique features, create a favorable impression of the product or advertiser, and arouse the readers' interest in the headline, which is generally noticed second.[26]

Adding Value 19.1   Selling Out or Selling Well? The Use and Choice of Popular Music in Advertising Campaigns[ii]

What's your reaction when one of your favorite songs by one of your favorite brands pops up in a commercial for a brand you might or might not love? Do you groan, annoyed that some hard-rocking rebel or cutting-edge artist has sold the rights to the song for advertising purposes? Or do you smile, pleased to hear your preferred song, and thus feel more affection for the brand being advertised? Obviously, marketers hope that your reaction is the latter one, but in many cases, consumers express attitudes more in line with the former.

The hits keep coming though. During the most recent Super Bowl, Acura relied on Van Halen's "Runnin' with the Devil" to introduce the latest model of its NSX sports car. Other advertisers use cover versions of popular songs or seek out relatively unknown artists with a cool sound to add an appropriate vibe to their marketing communications. The various options come with different costs: Licensing a popular song by a well-known musician can cost hundreds of thousands of dollars for a single use with a massive audience, like a Super Bowl commercial. If the brand chooses to use the song in an extended campaign, the licensing costs can easily reach millions. Cover versions of popular songs generally are more affordable, though the song writer still earns licensing fees. Most affordable of all is new music by

unfamiliar artists, because many of these musicians are happy mainly for the exposure that the advertising campaign offers them. As it becomes increasingly challenging to succeed in the music industry , such benefits, together with the promise of long-term residual income, make the licensing of music a popular and compelling option for struggling (or not-so-struggling) artists.

But choosing the right song for a marketing campaign involves more than considering the price. If the tone of the song does not match the marketing context, it can create cognitive dissonance. Thus for example, using "Cat's in the Cradle," the melancholy Jim Croce song about fathers and sons that makes virtually every listener cry, might not have been the best choice for a Nissan advertisement. Furthermore, reactions to songs are intensely personal, which makes it difficult for marketers to predict consumers' reactions. Many people obviously love Van Halen, but there are those for whom the sound of David Lee Roth's voice is deeply annoying. A song might remind an individual listener of a particularly good or particularly bad time in his or her life, with parallel effects on the consumer's perception of the product being advertised with that song. So will the effect be wonderful, or will it be terrible, and how are marketers to predict the answer in advance?

Was Van Halen's "Runnin' with the Devil" a good song to accompany a Super Bowl ad to introduce a new model of its NSX sports car?

Source: Acura NSX-What He Said/Acura/YouTube

The **headline** is the large type in an ad that is designed to draw attention. In the Ila DUSK Personal Alarm ad, the headline "ILA PERSONAL ALARM" simply identifies the product. But the **subhead**, a smaller headline, provides more information about the alarm it is selling; specifically, "it screams for your safety." Headlines and subheads should be short and use simple words and include the primary product or service benefits, the name of the brand, and an interest-provoking idea. They should ideally contain an action verb and give enough information for learning even if only the headline is read.

The **body copy** represents the main text portion of the ad. It is used to build on the interest generated by the visual and headlines, explains in more depth what the headline and subheads introduced, arouses desire for the product, and provides enough information to move the target consumer to action. In this case, the body copy, "Protect yourself this party season with the Ila DUSK personal alarm. As well as looking pretty, it emits a high decibel human scream for help. The only fashion accessory you need to be seen out with this Christmas," tells the story of this product and its use. This particular body copy is necessarily longer than for other products because it requires some explanation—the other ad elements are insufficient to explain and sell the product.

Finally, the ad typically has a number of **brand elements** that identify the sponsor of the ad, typically through a logo (M&S, which is the logo for Marks & Spencer department store in the United Kingdom) and a unique selling proposition (not found in this ad). Thus the advertiser must convey its message using compelling visuals, headlines, body copy, and identifying brand elements.

Although creativity plays a major role in the execution stage, advertisers must remain careful not to let their creativity overshadow the message. Whatever the execution style, the advertisement must be able to attract the audience's attention, provide a reason for the audience to spend its time viewing the advertisement, and accomplish what it set out to do. In the end, the execution style must match the medium and objectives.

Automobile manufacturers and dealers are among the most active advertisers and use very different messages in their advertising campaigns. Consider, for instance, two well-known car companies that have popular four-door sedan models, each with very different advertising campaigns.

- **Chevrolet Malibu.** Another entry into the hybrid market, the Malibu employs a battery pack and offers good gas mileage. It is also positioned as a family sedan, though the most recent revamping reduced the size of the backseat. Likely advertising outlets include family-oriented magazines and television spots.

- **Ford Fusion.** With a focus on fuel economy, ads for the Fusion promise its availability with both a hybrid and a conventional engine. Furthermore, it emphasizes Ford's SYNC technology, which uses voice recognition to make phone calls, find and play music, and get directions. With these appeals, Ford is focusing largely on social media to get young consumers, who tend to care about technology and environmental concerns, attached to the new model.[27]

At times, though, even when advertisers think they have done their best to appeal to consumers, their actions can backfire, as Ethical and Societal Dilemma 19.1 describes.

Although the Chevy Malibu offers a fuel-efficient hybrid model, it is positioned as a family sedan.

Source: General Motors

Ads for the new Ford Fusion emphasize fuel economy as well as interesting technology that it hopes will appeal to young consumers.

© Ford Motor Company

Ethical & Societal Dilemma 19.1   When Makeup Companies Really Do Make Up Models' Faces[iii]

Is Julia Roberts really that good looking? Of course, she's beautiful, but the portrayal of her face in advertising has, more likely than not, been given a Photoshop fix. Airbrushing may be as old as advertising, but improved technology makes the changes nearly imperceptible—it is difficult to tell the difference between the normal thickness of an eyelash and the version that Taylor Swift sported in a CoverGirl NatureLuxe Mousse Mascara ad. Ultimately, the National Advertising Division of the Council of Better Business Bureaus ruled the ad was misleading, prompting the brand to pull the ad.

But in other cases, cosmetics and fashion companies claim that fixing elements of appearance is both ubiquitous and expected by consumers. They assert they are not misleading anyone but rather creating a perfect image for their brand. For example, advertising for toothpaste features models with bright, white teeth. That's just a given. But if the advertising reveals unnaturally white teeth, beyond what could possibly be achieved by a toothpaste, is that false advertising? Is it wrong for cosmetic companies to retouch ads, brushing away wrinkles and skin imperfections digitally?

The UK Advertising Standards Agency considers touching up photos in ads to be wrong. That oversight agency banned two ads by L'Oréal, charging that they were misleading. One ad featured Julia Roberts promoting Teint Miracle, a new Lancôme skin product that, according to the company, provides "luminosity to the skin." The other featured the model Christy Turlington promoting a cosmetic concealer called Eraser that promises to hide wrinkles and skin discoloration. Although the company protested that the ads did not exaggerate their product effectiveness, the UK Advertising Standards Agency was not convinced.

In China, whose expanding consumer market has become an increasingly appealing target for advertisers, the central government is working to crack down on what it considers misleading advertising that overpromises what the featured products can do. Thus it fined Crest, the toothpaste brand owned by Procter & Gamble, close to one million dollars for using digital tools to retouch photos and make the models' teeth look whiter than they actually were.

When selling cosmetics, is it ethical to touch up photos of models and celebrities like Julia Roberts to make them even more beautiful?

© Gregg DeGuire/FilmMagic/Getty Images

Crest is not the only company to come under fire in China, which also has critiqued Nikon, Apple, and Volkswagen for failing to meet its standards. Thus for global brands, the question of international standardization has shifted a little. In addition to adjusting their products to appeal to the consumers of each nation, do they also need to adjust their marketing and advertising strategies to align with each country's distinct rules and standards for truth in advertising?

Do consumers want realistic images and measured promises, or do they accept and even prefer exaggerated claims and unrealistic images of beauty?

And ultimately, when selling cosmetics, is it ethical to touch up photos of models and celebrities like Julia Roberts to make them even more beautiful?

STEP 7: ASSESS IMPACT USING MARKETING METRICS

The effectiveness of an advertising campaign must be assessed before, during, and after the campaign has run. **Pretesting** refers to assessments performed before an ad campaign is implemented to ensure that the various elements are working in an integrated fashion and doing what they are intended to do.[28] **Tracking** includes monitoring key indicators such as daily or weekly sales volume while the advertisement is running to shed light on any problems with the message or the medium. **Posttesting** is the evaluation of the campaign's impact after it has been implemented. At this last stage, advertisers assess the sales and/or communication impact of the advertisement or campaign.

EXHIBIT 19.4   Hypothetical Sales History for Red Bull in a Grocery Store Chain

Sales volume is a good indicator of advertising effectiveness for frequently purchased consumer goods in the maturity stage of the product life cycle, such as Red Bull energy drink.

© McGraw-Hill Education/Jill Braaten, photographer

Measuring sales impact can be especially challenging because of the many influences other than advertising on consumers' choices, purchase behavior, and attitudes. These influences include the level of competitors' advertising, economic conditions in the target market, sociocultural changes, in-store merchandise availability, and even the weather—all of which can influence consumer purchasing behavior. For instance, the sales resulting from even the best ads can be foiled by a lack of merchandise in the stores or a blizzard. Advertisers must try to identify these influences and isolate those of the particular advertising campaign.

For frequently purchased consumer goods in the maturity stage of the product life cycle, such as soda, sales volume offers a good indicator of advertising effectiveness. Because their sales are relatively stable, and if we assume that the other elements of the marketing mix and the environment have not changed, we can attribute changes in sales volume to changes in advertising. Exhibit 19.4 illustrates a hypothetical sales history for Red Bull in a grocery store chain. Using a statistical technique called time-series analysis, sales data from the past is used to forecast the future. The data in Exhibit 19.4 can be decomposed into its basic trend (red), the seasonal influences (orange), and the **lift** or additional sales caused by the advertising (yellow). In this case, the lift caused by the advertising campaign is substantial.

For other types of goods in other stages of the product life cycle, sales data offer only one of the many indicators that marketers need to examine to determine advertising effectiveness. For instance, in high-growth markets, sales growth alone can be misleading because the market as a whole is growing. In such a situation, marketers measure sales relative to those of competitors to determine their relative market share. Firms find creative ways to identify advertising effectiveness. For example, digital cable allows firms to present a specific advertisement to certain neighborhoods and then track sales by local or regional retailers.

PROGRESS CHECK

1. What are the steps involved in planning an ad campaign?
2. What is the difference between informational, persuasive, and reminder advertising?
3. What are the pros and cons of the different media types?
4. How can the effectiveness of advertising be evaluated?

REGULATORY AND ETHICAL ISSUES IN ADVERTISING

In the United States, the regulation of advertising involves a complex mix of formal laws and informal restrictions designed to protect consumers from deceptive practices.[29] Many federal and state laws, as well as a wide range of self-regulatory agencies and agreements, affect advertising (Exhibit 19.5). The primary federal agencies that regulate advertising activities are the Federal Trade Commission (FTC), the Federal Communications Commission (FCC), and the Food and Drug Administration (FDA). In addition to these agencies, others such as the Bureau of Alcohol, Tobacco, Firearms, and Explosives and the U.S. Postal Service regulate advertising to some degree.

The FTC is the primary enforcement agency for most mass media advertising, although occasionally it cooperates with other agencies to investigate and enforce regulations on particular advertising practices. In one recent case, the FTC charged Pure Green Coffee, a Florida company, with false advertising and misrepresentation in its efforts to sell green coffee beans as a weight-loss aid. The company not only promised more benefits of the coffee beans than have been proven but also created fake websites designed to look like news outlets. They also used logos from *The Dr. Oz Show* to imply that the popular television personality endorsed the product.[30]

Many product categories fall under self-regulatory restrictions or guidelines. For example, advertising to children is regulated primarily through self-regulatory mechanisms designed by the National Association of Broadcasters and the Better Business Bureau's Children's Advertising Review Unit. The only formal regulation of children's advertising appears in the Children's Television Act of 1990, which limits the amount of advertising broadcast during children's viewing hours.[31]

Recently, to make matters even more complicated for advertisers, state attorney general offices have begun to inquire into various advertising practices and assert their authority to regulate advertising in their states. The European Union also has increased its regulation of advertising for member nations. Many of these state and European regulations are more restrictive than existing U.S. federal requirements.

The line between what is legal and illegal is more difficult to discern when it comes to **puffery**, which is the legal exaggeration of praise, stopping just short of deception, lavished on a product. When Match.com claims that it leads to "better first dates," it's puffery because *better* is a subjective measure. But if it claims it produces "more second dates," it

EXHIBIT 19.5	Federal Agencies That Regulate Advertising	
Federal Agency	**General Purpose**	**Specific Jurisdiction**
Federal Trade Commission (FTC) (1914)	Enforces federal consumer protection laws.	Enforces truth in advertising laws; defines deceptive and unfair advertising practices.
Federal Communications Commission (FCC) (1934)	Regulates interstate and international communications by radio, television, wire, satellite, and cable.	Enforces restrictions on broadcasting material that promotes lotteries (with some exceptions); cigarettes, little cigars, or smokeless tobacco products; or that perpetuates a fraud. Also enforces laws that prohibit or limit obscene, indecent, or profane language.
Food and Drug Administration (1930)	Regulates food, dietary supplements, drugs, cosmetics, medical devices (including radiation-emitting devices such as cell phones), biologics (biological issues), and blood products.	Regulates package labeling and inserts, definition of terms such as *light* and *organic*, and required disclosure statements (warning labels, dosage requirements, etc.).

Helps prevent clothes ageing.

The new Samsung washing machine range with gentle Aqua Shower, anti-bobble Diamond Drum and revitalising Air Refresh. Smart thinking. Simple living. samsungwashing.co.uk

SAMSUNG

Is this ad an example of puffery or deception?
Image Courtesy of The Advertising Archives

Prada garnered positive public relations when Lupita Nyong'o wore its gown to the Academy Awards.
© Jason LaVeris/Getty Images

must be able to back up its numerical, quantitative assertion. Even cartoon bears must follow the rules: Charmin's animated spokescharacters need to be drawn with a few pieces of toilet paper on their rears, instead of none, to ensure that Charmin's claims extend only to leaving less toilet paper behind than other brands (puffery), not eliminating the problem altogether (deception).[32]

How do the courts determine what makes an ad deceptive rather than simply puffery? The FTC's position is that it "will not pursue cases involving obviously exaggerated or puffing representations, i.e., those that ordinary consumers do not take seriously."[33] In general, the less specific the claim, the less likely it is considered to be deceptive. In the end, puffery is acceptable as long as consumers know that the firm is stretching the truth through exaggeration.[34]

PUBLIC RELATIONS

As you may recall from Chapter 18, **public relations (PR)** involves managing communications and relationships to achieve various objectives such as building and maintaining a positive image of the firm, handling or heading off unfavorable stories or events, and maintaining positive relationships with the media. In many cases, public relations activities support other promotional efforts by generating free media attention and general goodwill.

Designers, for example, vie to have celebrities, especially those nominated for awards, wear their fashions on the red carpet. Their brands offer intangible benefits, not just functional benefits. Events such as the Oscars, with its 35 million annual viewers, provide an unparalleled opportunity to showcase the emotional benefits of the brand and make others want to be a part of it. Thus, the celebrities whom designers pursue and offer their items to are those who will sell the most or provide the best iconic images. Lupita Nyong'o's great popularity meant that she could wear Ralph Lauren to the Golden Globes, then switch to Prada for the Academy Awards, and garner press for both design firms.[35] The placement of designer apparel at media events benefits both the designer and the celebrity. And neither happens by accident. Public relations people on both sides help orchestrate the events to get the maximum benefit for both parties.

Good PR has always been an important success factor. Yet in recent years, the importance of PR has grown as the costs of other forms of marketing communications have increased. At the same time, the influence of PR has become more powerful as consumers have become increasingly skeptical of marketing claims made in other media.[36] In many instances, consumers view media coverage generated through PR as more credible and objective than any other aspects of an IMC program because the firm does not buy the space in print media or time on radio or television.

Eight-year-old Neftali and singer Yunel Cruz (right) hold up colored-in peppers as they support Chili's "Create-A-Pepper to Fight Childhood Cancer" for St Jude Children's Research Hospital.

© Taylor Hill/Getty Images

Certainly the Chili's restaurant chain conducts plenty of media buys in traditional advertising spaces. But it also has partnered with St. Jude's Children's Research Hospital in one of the most successful examples of **cause-related marketing** (i.e., commercial activity in which businesses and charities form a partnership to market an image, product, or service for their mutual benefit)[37] in history. For several years, the restaurant has offered customers the opportunity to purchase a paper icon—in the shape of a chili pepper, natch—that they may color and hang on restaurant walls. The cause marketing campaign runs in September, which is also National Childhood Cancer Awareness Month. On the last Monday of the month, the restaurant puts its money where its mouth is and donates all its profits on sales during the day to St. Jude. Starting in 2016, Chili's took part in a Super Bowl Give Back event and the St. Jude Thanks and Giving® campaign. Chili's has raised more than $54 million for St. Jude.[38]

Another very popular PR tool is event sponsorship. **Event sponsorship** occurs when corporations support various activities (financially or otherwise), usually in the cultural or sports and entertainment sectors. Red Bull is a frequent sponsor of various kinds of sports events, such as Red Bull Air Race and numerous extreme sports events (e.g., cliff diving). Some of them are big-name events; the titles of most college football playoff games now include the name of their sponsors (e.g., the Allstate Sugar Bowl). Others are slightly less famous; for example, Rollerblade USA, the maker of Rollerblade in-line skates, sponsors Skate-In-School, a program it developed with the National Association for Sport and Physical Education (NASPE) to promote the inclusion of rollerblading in physical education curricula.

Firms often distribute PR toolkits to communicate with various audiences. Some toolkit elements are designed to inform specific groups directly, whereas others are created to generate media attention and disseminate information. We describe the various elements of a PR toolkit in Exhibit 19.6.

LO19-6 Describe the elements of a public relations toolkit.

Part of Red Bull's PR toolkit is its event sponsorship of a cliff-diving event.

© James Davies/Alamy

EXHIBIT 19.6   Elements of a Public Relations Toolkit

PR Element	Function
Publications: brochures, special-purpose single-issue publications such as books	Inform various constituencies about the activities of the organization and highlight specific areas of expertise.
Video and audio: programs, public service announcements	Highlight the organization or support cause-related marketing efforts.
Annual reports	Give required financial performance data and inform investors and others about the unique activities of the organization.
Media relations: press kits, news releases, speeches, event sponsorships	Generate news coverage of the organization's activities or products/services.
Electronic media: websites, e-mail campaigns	Websites can contain all the previously mentioned toolbox elements; e-mail directs PR efforts to specific target groups.

PROGRESS CHECK

1. Why do companies use public relations as part of their IMC strategy?
2. What are the elements of a public relations toolkit?

LO19-7 Identify the various types of sales promotions.

SALES PROMOTION

Advertising rarely provides the only means to communicate with target customers. As we discussed in Chapter 18, a natural link appears between advertising and sales promotion. **Sales promotions** are special incentives or excitement-building programs that encourage consumers to purchase a particular product or service, typically used in conjunction with other advertising or personal selling programs. Many sales promotions, like free samples or point-of-purchase (POP) displays, attempt to build short-term sales; others, such as loyalty programs, contests, and sweepstakes, have become integral components of firms' long-term customer relationship management (CRM) programs, which they use to build customer loyalty.

We present these sales promotion tools next. The tools of any sales promotion can be focused on any channel member—wholesalers, retailers, or end-user consumers. Just as we delineated for advertising, when sales promotions are targeted at channel members, the marketer is employing a push strategy; when it targets consumers themselves, it is using a pull strategy. Some sales promotion tools can be used with either a push or pull strategy. We now consider each of the tools and how they are used.

Types of Sales Promotion

Coupons Coupons offer a discount on the price of specific items when the items are purchased. Coupons are used to stimulate demand and are issued by manufacturers and retailers in newspapers, on products, on the shelf, at in-store kiosks, at the cash register, over the Internet, through the mail, and on mobile devices even when customers are in the store. Some retailers have linked their coupons directly to their loyalty programs. As Marketing Analytics 19.1 describes, the drugstore chain CVS tracks customers' purchases when they use their ExtraCare loyalty card and gives them coupons that are tailored just for them and their unique needs.[39] If a customer typically spends a small amount during each shopping trip, he or she might receive coupons to encourage larger purchases, such as buy one, get one free.

Marketing Analytics 19.1   How CVS Uses Loyalty Data to Define Coupons[iv]

In general, loyalty programs offer an effective means to provide more value to customers. In particular, the CVS ExtraCare program represents a flagship loyalty program—it is one of the oldest and largest in the United States. The program has been running for nearly 20 years; one in every three people in the United States has an ExtraCare card. Thus, more than 90 million households use it in a typical year.

The primary focus of the ExtraCare program has been to provide personalized offers that are relevant to and appreciated by customers while also encouraging their consistent shopping behavior. In recent developments, the program has spread across multiple channels, allowing customers to connect with offers in print, online, or through a mobile app. For example, customers can access the newly launched, omnichannel MyWeeklyAd program online or from a mobile device, or they can visit coupon kiosks in stores to scan their loyalty program cards and print coupons on the spot.

To support a unique, relevant, and well-appreciated shopping experience that encourages these customers to interact with the program and undertake additional sales, CVS relies heavily on customer data analytics. It collects vast amounts of data on the purchases that each ExtraCare member makes, and then it analyzes those data to uncover interesting or unexpected relationships among the items purchased. For example, customers who buy skin and hair products also purchase cosmetics, though not always at CVS. Furthermore, CVS discovered notable and helpful purchase timing patterns, such as its recognition that people typically buy toothpaste every five weeks.

By using the established relationships among the items that appear together in market baskets, CVS can obtain valuable insights, which in turn inform the personalized offers it sends to customers in an effort to adjust their behaviors. Thus, if an ExtraCare member buys face wash or conditioner, she might receive a coupon for lipstick. If another customer hasn't bought toothpaste in four and a half weeks, he will receive a coupon that provides him with a special incentive to purchase a high-end brand of toothpaste. CVS also uses these analytics to encourage customers to buy more each trip, such that a customer who typically spends $20 may receive a special offer if she

Marketing analytics are used to analyze data on the purchases of each ExtraCare customer, uncover interesting or unexpected relationships among items purchased, and use the information to provide personalized offers that are relevant to and appreciated by customers.

© McGraw-Hill Education/Mark Dierker, photographer

spends $30 the next time she shops. Finally, the data analytics give CVS important insights into which types of loyalty program offers are most successful—as well as which ones are not. For example, it determined that brand-specific coupons (e.g., for Pantene shampoo) were less effective than promotions geared toward the whole category (i.e., shampoos of various brands).

Internet sites also provide customers with instant coupons of their choosing. Imagine a customer who visits her local Walmart and finds a Hot Wheels video game for $29.99. By scanning the bar code using her cell phone, she connects to ShopSavvy.com and finds that the same item at a Target store a mile away is only $19.99. Another scan and a connection to MyCoupons.com provides her with a $10 coupon—which means she's saved $20 in a matter of minutes and just a few clicks.

Some coupons, whether printed from the Internet or sent to mobile phones, also contain information about the customer who uses it.[40] The bar code may identify the customer, his or her Internet address, Facebook page information, and even the search terms the customer used to find the coupon in the first place. These new breeds of coupons may look standard, but they offer up a startling amount of data, which promises benefits for advertisers who want to target their marketing more closely. Traditionally, coupons had low redemption rates and were therefore a relatively inexpensive sales promotion tool, but using customer data to create more targeted promotions has resulted in higher redemption rates, increasing their expense.

Deals A **deal** refers generally to a type of short-term price reduction that can take several forms, such as a featured price, a price lower than the regular price; a certain percentage more free offer contained in larger packaging; or a buy one, get one half off offer as shown in the nearby Payless ad. Another form of a deal involves a special financing arrangement such as reduced percentage interest rates or extended repayment terms. Deals encourage customers to try a product because they lower the risk for consumers by reducing the cost of the good.

But deals can also alter perceptions of value—a short-term price reduction may signal a different price–quality relationship than would be ideal from the manufacturer's perspective. In addition, as Old Spice learned, offering too many deals can offset likely gains. Its popular Old Spice Guy campaign attracted consumer attention through funny television commercials and interactive online campaigns, and sales of Old Spice jumped. But the company offered so many buy one, get one free deals at the same time that the potential profit impact of the great ads was essentially eliminated by the costs of the deals.[41]

Premiums A **premium** offers an item for free or at a bargain price to reward some type of behavior, such as buying, sampling, or testing. These rewards build goodwill among consumers, who often perceive high value in them. Premiums can be distributed in a variety of ways: They can be included in the product packaging, such as the toys inside cereal boxes; placed visibly on the package, such as a coupon for free milk on a box of Cheerios; handed out in the store; or delivered in the mail, such as the free perfume offers Victoria's Secret mails to customers. Furthermore, premiums can be very effective if they are consistent with the brand's message and image and highly desirable to the target market. However, finding a premium that meets these criteria at a reasonable cost can be a serious challenge.

Contests A **contest** refers to a brand-sponsored competition that requires some form of skill or effort. McGraw-Hill Education, the publisher of this textbook, held a "Get Connected and Win" contest and a "LearnSmart and Win" contest. Students were asked to

Source: CreateWP.Customer.
MHEducation.com

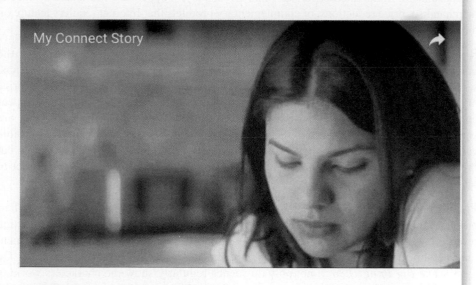

My Connect Story

We asked students across the country to create a video about McGraw-Hill Connect and how it has helped them. So many excellent videos came in that it was hard for our panel of judges to decide, but the winners have been posted! Check them out at GetConnectedandWin.com.

share their Connect and LearnSmart learning experiences via videos. The winners received scholarships, iPads, and other prizes.

Sweepstakes A form of sales promotion that offers prizes based on a chance drawing of entrants' names, **sweepstakes** do not require the entrant to complete a task other than buying a ticket or filling out a form. Often the key benefit of sweepstakes is that they encourage current consumers to consume more if the sweepstakes form appears inside the packaging or with the product. Many states, however, specify that no purchase can be required to enter sweepstakes.

Samples **Sampling** offers potential customers the opportunity to try a product or service before they make a buying decision. Distributing samples is one of the most costly sales promotion tools but also one of the most effective. Quick-service restaurants and grocery stores frequently use sampling. For instance, Starbucks provides samples of new products to customers. Costco uses so many samples that customers can have an entire meal. Sometimes trial-sized samples come in the mail or are distributed in stores.

Loyalty Programs As part of a sales promotion program, **loyalty programs** are specifically designed to retain customers by offering premiums or other incentives to customers who make multiple purchases over time. Well-designed loyalty programs encourage consumers to increase their engagement and purchases from a given firm. Such sales promotions are growing increasingly popular and are tied to long-term CRM systems. (Loyalty programs are examined in Chapters 2 and 3.) These programs need to be carefully managed because they can be quite costly.

Point-of-Purchase Displays

Point-of-purchase (POP) displays are merchandise displays located at the point of purchase, such as at the checkout counter in a supermarket. Retailers have long recognized that the most valuable real estate in the store is at the POP since they increase product visibility and encourage trial. Customers see products such as a magazine or a candy bar while they are waiting to pay for their purchases and impulsively purchase them. In the Internet version of a POP display, shoppers are stimulated by special merchandise, price reductions, or complementary products that Internet retailers feature on the checkout screen.

Rebates

Rebates are a particular type of price reduction in which a portion of the purchase price is returned by the seller to the buyer in the form of cash. Many products, such as consumer electronics, offer significant mail-in rebates that may lower the price of the item significantly. Some companies enjoy the added exposure when they appear on consumer websites like PriceGrabber.com and Nextag.com, where products are sorted by the price, with links to the retailer's website. The firms garner considerable value from rebates because they attract consumers and therefore stimulate sales, but they may not have to pay off all the rebates offered because consumers don't bother to redeem them.

Product Placement

When marketers use **product placement**, they pay to have their product included in nontraditional situations, such as in a scene in a movie or television program.[42] By doing so, they increase the visibility of their products. Product placement may be subtle, such as when *American Idol* judges are seen drinking Coca-Cola. On CBS's *The Big Bang Theory,* not only do scenes regularly show the characters working and eating there, but Sheldon also asserts his need to get "access to the Cheesecake Factory walk-in freezer." Although many firms would embrace product placement in hit shows and movies and are willing to pay for it, for Apple, the challenge is a little less stringent. U.S. film and television directors seem to love its sleek white laptops, earbudded iPods, and ubiquitous iPhones. Thus more than one-third of all top-grossing films at the U.S. box office—129 of 374 movies—have included Apple-branded products in the past decade. Recent appearances include popular offerings as well as critically acclaimed broadcasts, from Phil's desperate efforts to score an iPad on *Modern Family* to more nefarious uses depicted in *House of Cards*.[43] Apple is also unique in that it claims it does not pay for product placement, nor does it comment on film appearances. An analytics firm that estimates the dollar value of product placements has reported that Apple's five-minute screen time in *Mission Impossible* alone was worth more than $23 million.[44] Apple seemingly can earn those returns without paying for the placements, but not all companies are so lucky.

It is not an accident that this Apple iPad is the center of attention on this episode of Modern Family. *It is product placement. Even better, Apple does not pay for the placement!*

Source: Modern Family/ABC Television Network

Using Sales Promotion Tools

Marketers must be careful in their use of sales promotions, especially those that focus on lowering prices. Depending on the item, consumers may stock up when items are offered at a lower price, which simply shifts sales from the future to now and thereby leads to short-run benefits at the expense of long-term sales stability. For instance, using sales promotions such as coupons to stimulate sales of household cleaning supplies may cause consumers to stockpile the products and decrease demand for those products in the future. But a similar promotion used with a perishable product such as Dannon yogurt should increase its demand at the expense of competitors like Yoplait.

Many firms are also realizing the value of cross-promoting, when two or more firms join to reach a specific target market. To achieve a successful cross-promotion, the two products must appeal to the same target market and together create value for consumers. J.Crew has teamed up with several famous brands, including Lacoste, Barbour, Timex, New Balance, Ray-Ban, and Saint James, to offer well-known brands in the J.Crew stores and website.[45]

The goal of any sales promotion is to create value for both the consumers and the firm. By understanding the needs of its customers, as well as how best to entice them to purchase or consume a particular product or service, a firm can develop promotional messages and events that are of interest to and achieve the desired response from those customers. Traditionally, the role of sales promotion has been to generate short-term results, whereas the goal of advertising was to generate long-term results. As this chapter demonstrates, though, sales promotion as well as advertising can generate both long- and short-term effects. The effective combination of both types of activities leads to impressive results for the firm and the consumers.

PROGRESS CHECK

1. What are various forms of sales promotions?
2. What factors should a firm consider when evaluating a sales promotion?

Reviewing Learning Objectives

LO19-1 Describe the steps in designing and executing an advertising campaign.

Firms (1) identify their target market, (2) set advertising objectives, (3) set the advertising budget, (4) depict their product or service, (5) evaluate and select the media, (6) create the ad, and (7) assess the impact of the ad.

LO19-2 Identify three objectives of advertising.

All advertising campaigns are designed to inform, persuade, or remind customers. Informative advertising is communication used to create and build brand awareness. Persuasive advertising is communication used to motivate consumers to take action. Finally, reminder advertising is communication used to remind or prompt repurchases.

LO19-3 Describe the different ways that advertisers appeal to consumers.

Advertising appeals are either informational or emotional. Informational appeals influence pur-

chase decisions with factual information and strong arguments built around relevant key benefits that encourage consumers to evaluate the brand favorably. Emotional appeals indicate how the product satisfies emotional desires rather than utilitarian needs.

LO19-4 Identify the various types of media.

Firms can use mass media channels like newspapers or television to reach large numbers of anonymous audience members. Niche media, such as cable television and specialty magazines, are generally used to reach narrower segments that have unique demographic characteristics or interests. When choosing media, firms must match their objectives to that channel. Also, certain media are better at reaching a particular target audience than are others.

LO19-5 Identify agencies that regulate advertising.

Advertising is regulated by a plethora of federal and state agencies. The most important federal agencies are the FTC, which protects consumers against general deceptive advertising; the FCC, which has jurisdiction over radio, television, wire, satellite, and cable and covers issues regarding the use of tobacco products and objectionable language; and the FDA, which regulates food, dietary supplements, drugs, cosmetics, and medical devices.

 Describe the elements of a public relations toolkit.

A variety of elements compose a firm's public relations toolkit. They include publications, video and audio programs, public service announcements, annual reports, media kits (e.g., press kits), news releases, and electronic media (e.g., websites).

 Identify the various types of sales promotions.

Sales promotions are special incentives or excitement-building programs that encourage purchase and include coupons, deals, premiums, contests, sweepstakes, samples, POP displays, rebates, and product placement. They either push sales through the channel, as is the case with contests directed toward retail salespeople, or pull sales through the channel, as coupons and rebates do.

Key Terms   ■ SMARTBOOK

- advertising, 578
- advertising plan, 580
- advertising schedule, 587
- body copy, 590
- brand elements, 590
- cause-related marketing, 595
- contest, 598
- continuous schedule, 587
- coupon, 596
- cross-promoting, 601
- deal, 598
- emotional appeal, 584
- event sponsorship, 595
- flighting, 587
- headline, 589
- informational appeal, 584
- informative advertising, 581

- institutional advertisement, 582
- lift, 592
- loyalty program, 599
- mass media, 586
- media buy, 586
- media mix, 586
- media planning, 586
- niche media, 586
- persuasive advertising, 581
- point-of-purchase (POP) display, 600
- posttesting, 591
- premium, 598
- pretesting, 591
- product placement, 600
- product-focused advertisement, 582
- public relations (PR), 594

- public service advertising (PSA), 582
- puffery, 593
- pull strategy, 580
- pulsing, 587
- push strategy, 580
- rebate, 600
- reminder advertising, 581
- sales promotion, 596
- sampling, 599
- social marketing, 582
- subhead, 589
- sweepstakes, 599
- tracking, 591
- unique selling proposition (USP), 584

Marketing Digitally

1. Go to the website for the Children's Advertising Review Unit (CARU), one of the major self-regulatory bodies for children's advertising, at http://www.asrcreviews.org. Click on "CARU" and then "About Us—CARU" and examine the activities of CARU. How does this form of regulation complement the more formal regulation of federal and state agencies? Now look under the "Press Releases" link. Choose one of the press releases and discuss what action CARU took against the identified company or group. What was the main issue in the case?

2. *PR Newswire* attempts to provide information for "professional communicators." Visit its website at http://www.prnewswire.com and click on the "PR Newswire Services" link to explore the services it has to offer. What would you consider this organization's primary purpose to be? To whom does *PR Newswire* address the advertising appeals on its website?

Marketing Applications

1. What are the objectives of the McDonald's ad in the chapter opener? Does the ad have more than one objective? Explain your answer.

2. Using the same ad, explain what kind of appeal it uses.

3. Verizon spends millions of dollars each year on advertising for many different purposes. Provide an example

of how it might design an informative ad, a persuasive ad, and a reminder ad.

4. Name a current advertising slogan you believe is particularly effective for developing a unique selling proposition.

5. Bernard's, a local furniture company, target markets to college students with apartments and households of young people purchasing their first furniture items. If you worked for Bernard's, what type of media would you use for your advertising campaign? Justify your answer.

6. Should Bernard's use continuous, pulsing, or flighting for its advertising schedule? Why?

7. Suppose Porsche is introducing a new line of light trucks and has already created the advertising campaign. How would you assess the effectiveness of the campaign?

8. Suppose now that Porsche is planning a sales promotion campaign to augment its advertising campaign for the new line of light trucks. Which push and pull sales promotion tools do you believe would be most effective? Why?

9. Consider all the diet products that are currently advertised on television today, including weight-loss supplements, weight-loss programs, and fitness equipment. Do you believe that some of these ads overstate what the product or service can actually do? Do you think any of these ads are actually deceptive or puffery?

10. You are invited to your 6-year-old niece's birthday party and bring her the new superhero doll being advertised on television. She's thrilled when she unwraps the gift but is in tears a short time later because her new doll is broken. She explains that on TV, the doll flies and does karate kicks, but when she tried to play with the doll this way, it broke. You decide to call the manufacturer, and a representative tells you he is sorry your niece is so upset but that the ad clearly states the doll does not fly. The next time you see the televised ad, you notice very small print at the bottom stating that the doll does not fly. You decide to write a letter to the FTC about this practice. What information should you include in your letter?

Quiz Yourself

1. Firms often use _____ advertising to convince consumers to take action such as switching brands, trying a new product, or even continuing to buy the advertised product.
   a. pull
   b. push
   c. reminder
   d. persuasive
   e. informative

2. _____ is a tool used to communicate the distinct attributes of a product; it can be used as a slogan or a theme and often becomes a snapshot of the entire advertising campaign.
   a. The media mix
   b. A unique selling proposition
   c. An informational appeal
   d. Puffery
   e. A headline

(Answers to these two questions can be found in the Quiz Yourself Answer Key section.)

Chapter Case Study

MAKING MASTERCARD PRICELESS

How do you pay for books, clothing, groceries, or travel? For many consumers, the answer is MasterCard, which has more than 200 million cards in circulation.[46] Yet despite the credit card's popularity, it lags behind its major competitor, Visa, by nearly 100 million cards. It is also outstripped by American Express for both monthly and annual purchases and spending volume. Because MasterCard's primary function is to process transactions between each customer's bank and each merchant's bank, the company must appeal to two customer bases to build market share: the merchants who accept MasterCard for payment and the purchasers who use the card. These audiences are closely related, which implies that a single campaign can target both, likely even for an extended period. However, even the most successful campaigns can grow stale.

In 1997, MasterCard International and the advertising agency McCann Erickson Worldwide launched the emotion-based "Priceless" campaign, which celebrated life's most precious moments with the tagline, "There are some things money can't buy. For everything else, there's MasterCard."[47] The campaign was hugely successful, saving MasterCard from disaster, even in direct competition with the more widely accepted Visa card.[48] However, as consumer values and needs changed and the marketplace evolved, MasterCard faced a new challenge: how to retain customer loyalty and brand identification while reinvigorating its advertising.

Expanding Services to Meet Market Demand In 1966, a group of California banks created a member-owned association called the Interbank Card Association. This association grew its services, changing its name to MasterCard in 1979 to reflect a commitment to international growth.[49] As it reached new markets across the globe, MasterCard also focused on technology innovation to help make economic transactions faster, more convenient, and more secure. The company acquired interest in the international credit card EuroCard (known today as Europay International), as well as Cirrus, a worldwide interbank network that links MasterCard, Maestro, and Diner's Club credit, debit, and prepaid cards to an international network of ATMs. The company also added fraud/risk management providers to its network of services.

Today MasterCard's technology platform can handle more than 160 million transactions every hour with a 99.9 percent reliability rate,[50] and the company has issued a contactless, or smart, card that communicates with terminals via radio waves. This payment method does not require a signature and can be a card or key fob that is tapped rather than swiped; it also appears as a smartphone app. To provide even more value to customers, the company has added sophisticated consulting and information services that help merchants gain insight into consumer spending, according to their transaction data and in-depth analyses.[51] These efforts have dovetailed with changes in consumer behavior as shoppers have begun relying more on electronic payment options and less on paper-based currency. In 2006, the company transitioned to a new corporate governance and ownership structure and began trading on the New York Stock Exchange.

"Priceless" Revisited MasterCard began its "Priceless" campaign by identifying its target audience, which in this case focused on consumers. Hoping to persuade shoppers to keep their MasterCard at the top of their wallets, the campaign stressed the relationship between the card and experiences, as opposed to possessions. In early television ads, the narration linked the price of beauty parlor visits and new outfits to the "priceless" expression on an ex-boyfriend's face at a reunion, to create positive self-assessment feelings.[52] In another, the cost of tickets, refreshments, and souvenirs at a game was tied to the "priceless" opportunity for meaningful conversation between father and son, to invoke both happiness and love.[53] The "Priceless" campaign included various promotions and competitions in addition to these television spots.

In 2004, "Priceless" print ads took a new tack, weaving well-known retailers into the ads, together with MasterCard's theme. These retailers—which represented another of MasterCard's target audiences—received value from the prominent placement of their names and product images in the ads. Messaging moved from the general to the specific; an ad showing a teenaged rock band playing in a garage that might once have said, "extra-long extension cord, $11; moving them out of the living room: priceless," was modified to indicate that the extension cord was from Radio Shack. The result was a form of symbiotic marketing in which well-known brand names helped attract consumer attention to MasterCard ads, and each brand appeared to be endorsing the other.[54]

Magic Moments In July 2011, MasterCard launched an expanded campaign, called "Priceless Cities." This campaign, kicked off initially in New York, offers cardholders special experiences in major cities that can be shared with family and friends.[55] Designed to provide busy consumers with memorable opportunities in the realms of sports, music, entertainment, shopping, travel, arts, culture, and dining out, the campaign touted early opening times at the toy store FAO Schwartz, a safari sleepover at the Bronx Zoo, prime tickets to a Yankees game with an ex-Yankee, and VIP dining experiences designed by a famed chef.[56] The idea, says MasterCard's chief marketing officer, is to transform consumers' perceptions of the card from simply part of a priceless moment to being the force that enables such experiences. In competitive markets, when most competitors focus on deals and discounts, the MasterCard campaign attracts attention by appealing to emotions rather than to wallets and stressing unforgettable experiences rather than cost savings. The campaign forges an additional bond with card users, because it places MasterCard at the center of these memorable social activities.

The ads ran in more than 100 countries and aired in more than 50 languages, and the overall campaign uses print, radio, transit, outdoor advertising, and television. It also includes digital platforms to drive home its message, including a new section of the MasterCard website created specifically for the campaign, as well as social media channels such as Facebook and Twitter. Cardholders register at the site to access special offers; World Elite MasterCard holders get special offers as well as preferred access to the events.

With its continued efforts to keep the campaign fresh and interesting, MasterCard followed up on the Cities function with "Priceless Surprises," an initiative in which famous company endorsers surprise their fans. The resulting advertising, especially a spot in which Justin Timberlake knocked on the door of a woman who claimed to be his biggest fan, led others to believe that using MasterCard could someday lead to a similar surprise.[57]

Marketers must continuously evaluate their advertising campaigns and update them to ensure they are effectively communicating with their customers. New channels like social marketing can change shopping behaviors, creating opportunities that must be considered as part of any marketing strategy. In announcing plans for the future, MasterCard notes the potential of virtual reality platforms and interactions as a way to keep its promises "Priceless."[58] Thus, as MasterCard continues to demonstrate, even the best ideas need new infusions and innovations to keep appealing to their targets.

An endless entrée: £5
A slow spaghetti: £8.50
A leisurely latte: £2.95

A quick bite with a friend: Priceless

There are some things money can't buy, for everything else there's MasterCard

MasterCard

Accepted wherever friends meet and time flies.

The MasterCard "Priceless" IMC campaign has been going strong for more than 20 years, continuously adjusting to appeal to different target markets through multiple media channels.

Source: Mastercard

Questions

1. What is the primary objective of the "Priceless" campaign?

2. Does the "Priceless" campaign use an informational or an emotional appeal?

3. Given its various target markets, which media are most appropriate for each market?

4. How can MasterCard integrate the "Priceless" campaign into a public relations program?

5. Which sales promotion tactics could MasterCard employ?

Endnotes

1. Greg Jarboe, "McDonald's 'Our Food Your Questions' Video Campaign Is Changing Hearts, Minds, and Actions," *ReelSEO*, March 16, 2015, http://www.reelseo.com/mcdonalds-our-food-your-questions-video-campaign/.

2. Peter Frost, "McDonald's Plans to Launch 'Cleaner' Chicken McNuggets," *Crain's Chicago Business*, April 27, 2016, http://www.chicagobusiness.com/article/20160427/NEWS07/160429854/mcdonalds-plans-to-launch-cleaner-chicken-mcnuggets.

3. Christine Birkner, "McDonald's Moves from 'Billions Served' to 'Billions Heard'," *Marketing News Weekly,* January 20, 2015, https://www.ama.org/publications/eNewsletters/Marketing-News-Weekly.

4. George E. Belch and Michael A. Belch, *Advertising and Promotion: An Integrated Marketing Communications Perspective* (New York: McGraw-Hill, 2007); Jef I. Richards and Catherine M. Curran, "Oracles on 'Advertising': Searching for a Definition," *Journal of Advertising* 31, no. 2 (Summer 2002), pp. 63–77.

5. "Total Media Ad Spending Growth Slows Worldwide," *eMarketer,* September 15, 2015, http://www.emarketer.com/Article/Total-Media-Ad-Spending-Growth-Slows-Worldwide/1012981.

6. Christine Birkner, "Millennials' Attention Divided Across Devices More than Any Other Age Group, Study Finds," *Marketing News Weekly,* March 17, 2015, http://www.ama.org.

7. Dan Zigmond et al., "Measuring Advertising Quality on Television: Deriving Meaningful Metrics from Audience Retention Data," *Journal of Advertising Research* 49, no. 4 (December 2009), pp. 419–28; Robert G. Heath, Agnes C. Nairn, and Paul A. Bottomley, "How Effective Is Creativity? Emotive Content in TV Advertising Does Not Increase Attention," *Journal of Advertising Research* 49, no. 4 (December 2009), pp. 450–63; Raymond R. Burke and Thomas K. Srull, "Competitive Interference and Consumer Memory for Advertising," *Journal of Consumer Research* 15 (June 1988), pp. 55–68; Kevin Lane Keller, "Memory Factors in Advertising: The Effect of Advertising Retrieval Cues on Brand Evaluation," *Journal of Consumer Research* 14 (December 1987), pp. 316–33.

8. Markus Pfeiffer and Markus Zinnbauer, "Can Old Media Enhance New Media? How Traditional Advertising Pays Off for an Online Social Network," *Journal of Advertising Research* 50, no. 1 (2010), pp. 42–49; Terry Daugherty, Matthew Eastin, and Laura Bright, "Exploring Consumer Motivations for Creating User-Generated Content," *Journal of Interactive Advertising* 8, no. 2 (2008); Anthony Bianco, "The Vanishing Mass Market," *BusinessWeek,* July 12, 2004, pp. 61–68.

9. Leonie Roderick, "The Marketing Year: The Top Campaigns of 2015," *Marketing Week,* December 4, 2015, https://www.marketingweek.com/2015/12/04/the-marketing-year-the-top-campaigns-of-2015/; Adam Davidi, "The Best Ads of 2015: The Professionals Pick Their Favourites," *The Guardian,* December 4, 2015, http://www.theguardian.com/media-network/2015/dec/04/best-ads-advertising-2015-favourite.

10. Brendan Greeley, "World Cup Shootout: Can Nike Beat adidas at Soccer?" *Bloomberg Businessweek,* May 15, 2014, http://www.businessweek.com.

11. adidas, "Neo," http://www.adidas.com/us/content/selenagomez.

12. William F. Arens, Michael F. Weigold, and Christian Arens, *Contemporary Advertising,* 12th ed. (New York: McGraw-Hill, 2008).

13. Tulin Erdem, Michael Keane, and Baohong Sun, "The Impact of Advertising on Consumer Price Sensitivity in Experience Goods Markets," *Quantitative Marketing and Economics* 6 (June 2008), pp. 139–76; Xiaojing Yang and Robert E. Smith, "Beyond Attention Effects: Modeling the Persuasive and Emotional Effects of Advertising Creativity," *Marketing Science* 28 (September/October 2009), pp. 935–49; Matthew Shum, "Does Advertising Overcome Brand Loyalty? Evidence from the Breakfast Cereal Market," *Journal of Economics and Management Strategy* 13, no. 2 (2004), pp. 77–85.

14. Alexander Haldermann, "GE's Ecomagination Turns 10: How a Brand Can Be a Driver for Change," *Huffpost Business,* September 16, 2015.

15. Brian Dumaine, "Is Apple 'Greener' Than Starbucks?" *Fortune,* June 24, 2014.

16. http://www.marketingpower.com/_layouts/Dictionary.aspx?dLetter=P.

17. https://www.outnumberhunger.com/

18. Theodore Levitt, *The Marketing Imagination* (New York: Free Press, 1986).

19. Belch and Belch, *Advertising and Promotion.*

20. Katherine White and John Peloza, "Self-Benefit versus Other-Benefit Marketing Appeals: Their Effectiveness in Generating Charitable Support," *Journal of Marketing* 73 (July 2009), pp. 109–24.

21. Davidi, "The Best Ads of 2015."

22. Darren W. Dahl, Jaideep Sengupta, and Kathleen D. Vohs, "Sex in Advertising: Gender Differences and the Role of Relationship Commitment," *Journal of Consumer Research* 36, no. 2 (2009), pp. 215–31; Jaideep Sengupta and Darren W. Dahl, "Gender-Related Reactions to Gratuitous Sex Appeals in Advertising," *Journal of Consumer Psychology* 18, no. 1 (2008), pp. 62–78.

23. Jack Loftus, "ADT Ad Campaign Scares Homeowners into Buying ADT Security," *Gizmodo,* http://gizmodo.com; Jack Neff, "What the Stylish Garbage Can Is Wearing," *Advertising Age,* November 3, 2011, http://adage.com; Natalie Zmuda, "Best Buy Ups Holiday Spending, Introduces 'Game On, Santa' Campaign," *Advertising Age,* November 17, 2011, http://adage.com; Andrew Adam Newman, "Axe Adds Fragrance for Women to Its Lineup," *The New York Times,* January 8, 2012, http://www.nytimes.com.

24. *AMA Dictionary,* http://www.marketingpower.com/_layouts/Dictionary.aspx?dLetter=M.

25. Some illustrative articles look at the effectiveness of given media: H. Risselada, P. C. Verhoef, and T. H. Bijmolt, "Dynamic Effects of Social Influence and Direct Marketing on the Adoption of High-Technology Products," *Journal of Marketing* 78, no. 4 (2014); Robert Heath, "Emotional Engagement: How Television Builds Big Brands at Low Attention," *Journal of Advertising Research* 49, no. 1 (March 2009), pp. 62–73; Lex van Meurs and Mandy Aristoff, "Split-Second Recognition: What Makes Outdoor Advertising Work?" *Journal of Advertising Research* 49, no. 1 (March 2009), pp. 82–92.

26. William F. Arens, David H. Schaefer, and Michael F. Weigold, *Advertising, M-Series* (Burr Ridge: Irwin/McGraw-Hill, 2012).

27. Stephen Williams, "New Sedans Aim to Break Out of the Pack," *Advertising Age,* February 20, 2012, http://adage.com.

28. Dean M. Krugman et al., *Advertising: Its Role in Modern Marketing* (New York: Dryden Press, 1994), pp. 221–26.

29. Herbert Jack Rotfeld and Charles R. Taylor, "The Need for Interdisciplinary Research of Advertising Regulation: A Roadmap for Avoiding Confusion and Errors," *Journal of Advertising,* Winter 2009.

30. "FTC Charges Green Coffee Bean Sellers with Deceiving Consumers through Fake News Sites and Bogus Weight Loss Claims," May 19, 2014, http://www.ftc.gov/news-events/press-releases.

31. Debra Harker, Michael Harker, and Robert Burns, "Tackling Obesity: Developing a Research Agenda for Advertising Researchers," *Journal of Current Issues & Research in Advertising* 29, no. 2 (2007), pp. 39–51; N. Kapoor and D. P. S. Verma, "Children's Understanding of TV Advertisements: Influence of Age, Sex and Parents," *Vision* 9, no. 1 (2005), pp. 21–36; Catharine M. Curran and Jef I. Richards, "The Regulation of Children's Advertising in the U.S.," *International Journal of Advertising and Marketing to Children* 2, no. 2 (2002).

32. Irina Slutsky, "Nine Things You Can't Do in Advertising If You Want to Stay on the Right Side of the Law," *Advertising Age*, March 7, 2011, http://adage.com.

33. Bob Hunt, "Truth in Your Advertising: Avoid Puffery?" *Realty Times*, June 20, 2007.

34. Ibid.

35. Blue Carreon, "The 2014 Oscars Best Dressed List," *Forbes*, March 2, 2014, http://www.forbes.com.

36. Diego Rinallo and Suman Basuroy, "Does Advertising Spending Influence Media Coverage of the Advertiser?" *Journal of Marketing* 73 (November 2009), pp. 33–46; Carl Obermiller and Eric R. Spangenberg, "On the Origin and Distinctness of Skepticism toward Advertising," *Marketing Letters* 11, no. 4 (2000), p. 311.

37. Jackie Huba, "A Just Cause Creating Emotional Connections with Customers," http://www.inc.com.

38. https://www.stjude.org/get-involved/other-ways/partner-with-st-jude/corporate-partners/chili-s-grill-bar.html.

39. Personal communication with Rob Price, VP of Retail Marketing, CVS, June 16, 2009; Carol Angrisani, "CVS Moves to Personalization," *SN: Supermarket News* 56, no. 2 (March 24, 2008), p. 29.

40. Stephanie Clifford, "Web Coupons Know Lots about You, and They Tell," *The New York Times*, April 16, 2010.

41. Jack Neff, "Old Spice Is Killing It on YouTube Again, but Sales Are Down Double-Digits," *Advertising Age*, August 4, 2011, http://adage.com.

42. Eva A. van Reijmersdal, Peter C. Neijens, and Edith G. Smit, "A New Branch of Advertising: Reviewing Factors That Influence Reactions to Product Placement," *Journal of Advertising Research* 49, no. 4 (December 2009), pp. 429–49; Pamela Mills Homer, "Product Placement: The Impact of Placement Type and Repetition on Attitude," *Journal of Advertising*, Fall 2009.

43. Abe Sauer, "Beats and Apple: A Match Made in Product Placement Heaven," *Brandchannel.com*, May 28, 2014, http://www.brandchannel.com; Abe Sauer, "The Envelope, Please: The 2014 Brandcameo Product Placement Awards," *Brandchannel.com*, February 27, 2014, http://www.brandchannel.com; Abe Sauer, "Announcing the 2012 Brandcameo Product Placement Award Winners," *Brandchannel.com*, February 13, 2012, http://www.brandchannel.com.

44. Sauer, "The Envelope, Please."

45. http://www.jcrew.com.

46. http://www.cardhub.com/edu/market-share-by-credit-card-network/.

47. http://www.youtube.com/watch?v=3dcxQ2dvqmc.

48. http://marketingpractice.blogspot.com/2006/11/mastercard-priceless.html.

49. http://www.mastercard.com/us/company/en/docs/CorporateOverview_FINAL.pdf.

50. Ibid.

51. http://www.mastercardadvisors.com/.

52. http://www.youtube.com/watch?v=3dcxQ2dvqmc.

53. http://www.youtube.com/watch?v=Q_6stXKGuHo.

54. Stuart Elliott, "MasterCard Revamps Print Ads," *The New York Times*, August 11, 2004.

55. Stuart Elliott, "MasterCard Brings 'Priceless' to a Pricey Place," *The New York Times*, July 7, 2011; http://www.creditcardeducation.com/news/mastercard-offers-priceless-city-experiences.html.

56. http://newsroom.mastercard.com/press-releases/priceless-new-york-gives-mastercard-cardholders-privileged-access-to-the-citys-preeminent-experiences/.

57. Beth Snyder Bulik, "MasterCard CMO: How We Keep 'Priceless' Fresh After 17 Years," *Advertising Age*, February 4, 2014.

58. Dale Buss, "'Priceless' Evolution: 5 Questions with MasterCard CMO Raja Rajamannar," *Brand Channel*, January 4, 2016, http://www.brandchannel.com/2016/01/04/5-questions-mastercard-010416/.

i. Miriam Gottfried, "Publishers Face Moving Target in Mobile," *The Wall Street Journal*, July 7, 2015.

ii. Michael McCarthy, "Acura Taps Van Halen for a Hard-Driving Super Bowl Commercial," *The New York Times*, January 28, 2016.

iii. "Crest Is Fined Nearly $1 Million in China," *The New York Times*, March 10, 2015, http://www.nytimes.com; David Kiefaber, "Taylor Swift's CoverGirl Ad Is Pulled over Bogus Eyelashes," *Adweek*, December 23, 2011, http://www.adweek.com; David Gianastasio, "Turlington Ads: So Photoshopped They're Misleading?" *Adweek*, July 28, 2011, http://www.adweek.com; Tanzina Vega, "British Authority Bans Two Ads by L'Oréal," *The New York Times*, July 27, 2011, http://mediadecoder.blogs.nytimes.com.

iv. Elyse Dupré, "CVS/Pharmacy Devotes Extracare to Its Loyalty Program," *DM News* 36, no. 8 (2014), pp. 19–22; Stephanie Clifford, "Using Data to Stage-Manage Paths to the Prescription Counter," *The New York Times*, June 19, 2013, http://bits.blogs.nytimes.com.

CHAPTER 20

PERSONAL SELLING AND SALES MANAGEMENT

Everyone sells something, sometime. But selling well, efficiently, effectively, and with the ability to add value requires thoughtful considerations combined with insights based on experience and perhaps a natural sales ability that gives sellers a good feel for buyers. Personal selling is always and inevitably personal.

But it also can be greatly improved by advanced analytical technologies. In this sense, IBM's Watson offers one of the best sales tools available today to sellers in virtually any setting.

Watson can do much more than beat all comers at *Jeopardy.*[1] In IBM's Watson unit, more than 2,000 employees collaborate on providing software, hardware, and services related to the advanced technology service. With a budget of approximately $100 million, the unit also can fund venture projects to develop apps based on Watson's technology platform.[2]

With this dedicated support system, Watson gives clients of IBM access to some of the most powerful computing capabilities in the world, all available in the cloud. For example, the Singaporean bank DBS Group Holdings uses Watson to provide up-to-date insights and lessons to its financial planners and salespeople, who share that information with high net worth clients. As Watson analyzes massive amounts of financial data available in nearly real time, DBS provides more customized advising services to wealthy clients, who then may agree to do more of their investing with the bank. To gain this access, DBS pays around $12 million over three years. It also shares its own data with IBM, contributing and updating Watson's knowledge stores constantly.[3]

Supported by these updates and cloud accessibility, Watson lessens the challenges associated with selling by providing more in-depth and actionable information that salespeople and their managers can use. As an example of the benefits and value that Watson provides, IBM offers its own use of the tool as a prime example.[4]

When IBM analyzes sales of its software offerings across industries, customers, or regions, it relies on Watson to inform salespeople about whether customers in the banking or retail sector are more likely to buy a particular software solution, for example. With a few clicks, salespeople in the field also can learn how much of a particular customer's overall budget is devoted to IT software and how much IBM accounts for in that total. With the cloud capabilities, all members of a sales team can access immediately updated information at any time.

Then the analytical capabilities that are inherent to Watson help IBM develop and design new sales initiatives, promotions, and sales plans. For example, by combining historical sales data, budget details, and industry trends, Watson can reveal patterns to sales teams that signal which customers are most likely to respond to which sales campaigns. With this "pattern selling" approach, "The sales patterns can be easily customized for each sales team or for each individual sales rep to help them focus on the customers with the best potential for their specific product lines, for new engagements or for cross-selling and up-selling to existing accounts."⁵

Watson's output is strongly graphical as well, making it easy for salespeople to gain a sense of patterns and trends quickly and easily, without having to perform intricate calculations or analyses on their own. The Watson unit is dedicated to expanding its abilities even further by, for example, providing sales opportunities with new customers and prescriptions for how to sell to new and existing customers in dynamic markets.

Just like advertising, which we discussed in Chapter 19, personal selling is so important to integrated marketing communications that it deserves its own chapter. Almost everyone is engaged in some form of selling. On a personal level, you sell your ideas or opinions to your friends, family, employers, and professors. Even if you have no interest in personal selling as a career, a strong grounding in the topic will help you in numerous career choices. Consider, for instance, Harry Turk, a very successful labor attorney. He worked his way through college selling sweaters to fraternities across the country. Although he loved his part-time job, Harry decided to become an attorney. When asked whether he misses selling, he said, "I use my selling skills every day. I have to sell new clients on the idea that I'm the best attorney for the job. I have to sell my partners on my legal point of view. I even use selling skills when I'm talking to a judge or jury."

LO20-1 Describe the value added of personal selling.

THE SCOPE AND NATURE OF PERSONAL SELLING

Personal selling is the two-way flow of communication between a buyer or buyers and a seller, designed to influence the buyer's purchase decision. Personal selling can take place in various situations: face-to-face, via video teleconferencing, on the telephone, or over the Internet, for example. More than 11 million people are employed in sales positions in the United States,⁶ including those involved in business-to-business (B2B) transactions, such as manufacturer's representatives selling to retailers or other businesses, and those completing business-to-consumer (B2C) transactions, such as retail salespeople, real estate agents, and insurance agents. Salespeople are referred to in many ways: sales representatives or reps, account executives, agents. And as Harry Turk found, most professions rely on personal selling to some degree.

Salespeople don't always get the best coverage in popular media. In Arthur Miller's famous play *Death of a Salesman,* the main character, Willie Loman, leads a pathetic existence and suffers from the loneliness inherent in being a traveling salesman.⁷ The characters in David Mamet's play *Glengarry Glen Ross* portray salespeople as crude, ruthless, and of questionable character. Unfortunately, these powerful Pulitzer Prize–winning pieces of literature weigh heavily on our collective consciousness and often overshadow the millions of hardworking professional salespeople who have fulfilling and rewarding careers and who add value to their firm and provide value for their customers.

Personal Selling as a Career

Personal or professional selling can be a satisfying career for several reasons. First, many people love the lifestyle. Salespeople are typically out on their own. Although they occasionally work with their managers and other colleagues, salespeople tend to be responsible for planning their own days. This flexibility translates into an easier balance between work and family than many office-bound jobs can offer. Many salespeople now can rely on virtual offices, which enable them to communicate from anywhere and at any time with their colleagues and customers. Because salespeople are evaluated primarily on the results they produce, as long as they meet and exceed their goals, they experience little day-to-day supervision. You might find a salesperson at the gym in the middle of the day, when few other people are there, because no one keeps track of the length of his or her lunch break.

Second, the variety in the job often attracts people to sales. Every day is different, bringing different clients and customers, often in a variety of places. Their issues and problems and the solutions to those problems all differ and require creativity.[8] Third, professional selling and sales management can be a very lucrative career. Sales is among the highest-paying careers for college graduates, and compensation often includes perks such as the use of a company car or bonuses for high performance. A top performer can have a total compensation package of over $150,000; even starting salespeople can make well over $50,000. Although the monetary compensation can be significant, the satisfaction of being involved in interesting, challenging, and creative work is rewarding in and of itself.

Fourth, because salespeople are the frontline emissaries for their firms, they are very visible to management. Furthermore, their performance is fairly straightforward to measure, which means that high-performing salespeople who aspire to management positions are in a good position to be promoted.

Many salespeople now can rely on virtual offices, which enable them to communicate via the Internet with colleagues and customers.

© perfectlab/Shutterstock RF

The Value Added by Personal Selling

The benefits for salespeople mean that they are expensive for firms. Experts estimate that the average cost of a single B2B sales call is about $600.[9] So why include them in the marketing channel at all? In response to this question, some firms have turned to the Internet and technology to lower the costs of personal selling. Other firms, especially retailers, have made the decision not to use a sales force and thus require customers to perform the sales function on their own. But firms that continue to use personal selling as part of their integrated marketing communications program recognize the value it adds to their product or service mix. That is, personal selling is worth more than it costs. Personal selling adds value by educating customers and providing advice, saving the customer time, making things easier for customers, and building long-term strategic relationships with customers.[10]

Salespeople Provide Information and Advice Imagine how difficult it would be to buy a custom suit, a house, or a car without the help of a salesperson. UPS wouldn't dream of investing in a new fleet of airplanes without the benefit of Boeing's selling team. Boeing's sales team can provide UPS with the technical aspects of the aircraft as well as the economic justification for the purchase. If you need formalwear for your friend's upcoming wedding or a school dance, you might find it helpful to solicit the input of a retail sales associate who can tell you what colors are hot this season, how to tie a bowtie, how each garment tends to fit, what the latest fashions are in formalwear, and how long your dress should be for a function that starts at 6:00 p.m. Certainly you could figure out most of this information on your

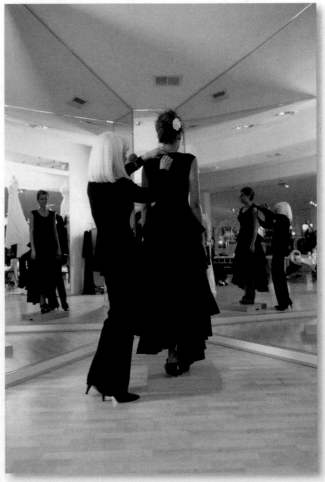

Salespeople provide information and advice.

© Mark Edward Atkinson/Getty Images RF

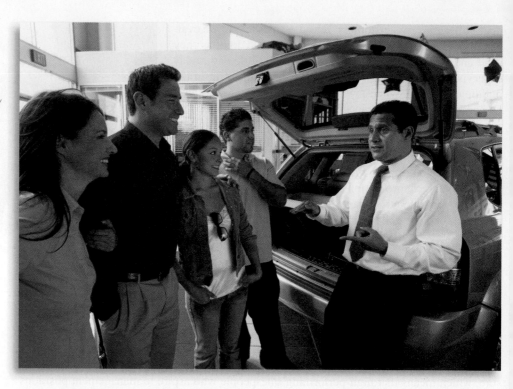

own, but many customers find value in and are willing to pay for the education and advice that salespeople provide.

Salespeople Save Time and Simplify Buying

Time is money! Customers perceive value in time and labor savings. In many grocery and drugstore chains, salespeople employed by the vendor that supplies the merchandise straighten stock, set up displays, assess inventory levels, and write orders. In some cases, such as bakeries or soft drink sales, salespeople and truck drivers even bring in the merchandise and stock the shelves. These are all tasks that retail employees would otherwise have to do. To appeal to end customers, manufacturers might send salespeople into stores to provide cooking demonstrations or free samples in the case of grocery stores, or trunk or made-to-measure shows in the case of apparel or shoe retailers. In this case, the vendor increases convenience for both its immediate customer (the retailer) and the end consumer.

Salespeople Build Relationships

As we discussed in Chapter 16, building strong marketing channel relationships is a critical success factor. Who in the organization is better equipped to manage this relationship than the salesperson, the frontline emissary for the firm? The most successful salespeople are those who build strong relationships with their customers—a rule that holds across all sorts of sales. That is, whether you are selling yourself as a job candidate, a product produced by your company, or a concept to a client, your sale is not successful if it leads to just a one-time transaction. Instead, good salespeople of all stripes consistently take a long-term perspective. This long-term perspective in turn demands effective customer relationship management, a goal that is being transformed with mobile approaches to what has long been a dreaded responsibility of salespeople, as described in Social and Mobile Marketing 20.1.

Building on the relationship concept introduced in Chapter 16, relationship selling refers to a sales philosophy and process that emphasizes a commitment to maintaining the relationship over the long term and investing in opportunities that are mutually beneficial to all parties.[11] Relationship-oriented salespeople work with their customers to find mutually beneficial solutions to their wants and needs. As we described in Chapter 7, colleges often negotiate long-term agreements with apparel companies to supply their sports teams. Similarly, a Lenovo sales team might be working with your university to provide you with the computer support and security you need during the years you spend working on the school's network.

Social & Mobile Marketing 20.1   Managing Relationships While Mobile: Sales Reports from the Field[i]

Effective sales demand in-depth, extensive knowledge about customers, which suggests the need for customer relationship marketing (CRM), a topic we have covered throughout this book. In turn, CRM demands data, because these systems cannot work without information being put in to them, for salespeople to take out later, as they need it. But convincing salespeople to take time out of their schedules to file CRM reports (rather than engaging in more lucrative sales efforts) has long been a challenge for managers and companies.

The challenge has been particularly acute for sales reps in the field. Because these sales reps rarely come into the office, the firms cannot support them as well in their efforts to make informed pitches to customers, and sales managers have little insight into what the sales reps are doing, when, how, and with whom. Not only does this leave the firm unable to monitor its employees, but it also makes the calculation of incentives or bonuses more difficult and less accurate, which ultimately could diminish sales performance overall.

In an effort to address these persistent issues, sales companies increasingly are relying on mobile technologies to make the reporting task and updates to the CRM system easy and nearly automatic. Rather than waiting until the end of the day—when they might have forgotten some of the details of an interaction with a client, or might forget to file their report altogether—mobile access to the firm's CRM system means that sales reps can input information immediately, possibly even before they leave the client site.

Some of the best mobile CRM offerings even gather data automatically. For example, mobile apps can gather immediate data about phone calls and e-mails between the sales rep and each client. These data then get catalogued and entered into the CRM system, without the salesperson needing to do anything further. Voice recognition technology also enables them to dictate a summary of their meetings and interactions, without having to fill in forms or write a formal report. All of these technologies in turn help sales managers keep tabs on what sales reps are doing, provide immediate feedback on their successful and unsuccessful efforts, and offer suggestions or training as needed.

With geolocaters, the mobile CRM systems also can make recommendations to salespeople in the field, such as when they happen to be in proximity to a customer whose purchase history suggests that this customer might be ready to buy again. Accordingly, the sales reps likely achieve better sales, which benefits them in the form of increased commissions or bonuses. Then they may be more likely to rely on and contribute to the CRM system in other ways. And finally, the increase in sales benefits the firm, which gains not only more sales in the short term but also greatly enhanced data to improve its sales performance in the long term.

THE PERSONAL SELLING PROCESS

LO20-2 Define the steps in the personal selling process.

Although selling may appear to be a rather straightforward process, successful salespeople must follow several steps. Depending on the sales situation and the buyer's readiness to purchase, the salesperson might not use every step, and the time required for each step varies with the situation. For example, if a customer goes into The Gap already prepared to purchase some chinos, the selling process will be fairly quick. But if Lenovo is attempting to sell personal computers for the first time to your university, the process may take several months. With this in mind, let's examine each step of the selling process (Exhibit 20.1).

Step 1: Generate and Qualify Leads

The first step in the selling process is to generate a list of potential customers (**leads**) and assess their potential (**qualify**). Salespeople who already have an established relationship with a customer will skip this step, and it is not used extensively in retail settings. In B2B situations, however, it is important to work continually to find new and potentially profitable customers.

Salespeople can generate and qualify leads in a variety of ways.[12] They might discover potential leads by talking to current customers, doing research on the Internet, or networking at events such as trade shows, industry conferences, or chamber of commerce meetings. Salespeople can also generate leads through cold calls and social media.

The Internet, and sites like LinkedIn and Twitter in particular, have been a boon for generating and qualifying leads.

Trade shows like the Consumer Electronics Show in Las Vegas are an excellent way to generate and qualify leads.

© Paul Sakuma/AP Photo

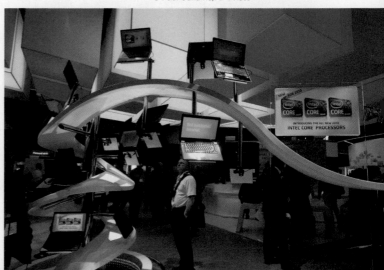

EXHIBIT 20.1 The Personal Selling Process

- Generate and qualify leads
- Preapproach
- Sales presentation and overcoming reservations
- Closing the sale
- Follow-up

Prior to the explosion of Internet use, it was cumbersome to perform research on products, customers, or competitors. Salespeople would rely on a research staff for this information, and it could take weeks for the research to be completed and sent through the mail. Today, salespeople connect with potential customers through Twitter and LinkedIn. Salespeople curate blogs to draw in customers and generate leads, a process known as **inbound marketing**. While these are all important tools, they are unlikely to replace cold calling anytime soon, as many customers still cannot be reached via social media.[13]

Trade shows also offer an excellent forum for finding leads. These major events are attended by buyers who choose to be exposed to products and services offered by potential suppliers in an industry. Consumer electronics buyers always make sure that they attend the annual Consumer Electronics Show (CES) in Las Vegas, the world's largest trade show for consumer technology (http://www.cesweb.org). The most recent show was attended by 165,000 people (representing more than 150 countries) such as vendors; developers; and suppliers of consumer-technology hardware, content, technology delivery systems, and related products and services.[14] Nearly 3,700 vendor exhibits took up close to 2 million net square feet of exhibit space, spread over three separate Las Vegas locations, showcasing the very latest products and services. Vendors often use CES to introduce new products, including the first camcorder (1981), high-definition television (HDTV, 1998), Internet protocol television (IP TV, 2005), and 3D printers (2014).[15] In addition to providing an opportunity for retail buyers to see the latest products, the CES conference program features prominent speakers from the technology sector.

Cold calls are a method of prospecting in which salespeople telephone or go to see potential customers without appointments.[16] **Telemarketing** is similar to a cold call, but it always occurs over the telephone. Sometimes professional telemarketing firms rather than the firm's salespeople make such calls. Adding Value 20.1 examines how colleges use it to boost attendance at sports events.

However, cold calls and telemarketing have become less popular over time, primarily because their success rate is fairly low. During cold calls, the salesperson is not able to establish the potential customer's specific needs because the receiver of the call is not expecting it and therefore may not be willing to participate in it. Accordingly, these methods can be very expensive. Second, federal as well as state governments are regulating the activities of telemarketers. Federal rules prohibit telemarketing to consumers whose names appear on the national Do-Not-Call list, which is maintained by the Federal Trade Commission. Even for those consumers whose names are not on the list, the rules prohibit calling before 8:00 a.m. or after 9:00 p.m. (in the consumer's time zone) or after the consumer has told the telemarketer not to call. Federal rules also prohibit unsolicited fax messages, calls, or messages to cell phones.

After salespeople generate leads, they must qualify those leads by determining whether it is worthwhile to pursue them and attempt to turn them into customers. In B2B settings, the costs of preparing and making a presentation are so substantial that the seller must assess a lead's potential. Salespeople consider, for example, whether the potential customer's needs

Telemarketing is a type of cold call in which salespeople generate or qualify leads on the telephone.

© Guillermo Legaria/Getty Images

Adding Value 20.1   College Athletics Turn to the Pros for Sales Help[ii]

Not that long ago, a few billboards and word of mouth were enough to sell out tickets for a college game. Demand for tickets to college basketball and football games was so high that many schools added seats as fast as they could and still had to turn fans away. But a dip in the economy, increased demands on leisure time, rising gas prices, and better television technology have combined to diminish ticket sales, leaving colleges with empty seats and a diminishing revenue stream, even as they face other budget constraints. In response, some athletic programs are outsourcing ticket sales to commission-driven experts in the hopes of bringing fans back to the bleachers.

Ticket marketing companies catering to colleges use the model adopted by professional sports organizations: Sales staff work for commissions and make as many as 100 calls a day to students, alumni, faculty, and anyone else connected to the university. As these callers chat about the team, the school, or college athletics, they listen for clues to customers' personalities and needs, then adjust their sales strategy accordingly. The commission structure ensures the strong motivation of the sales force, which benefits the schools, because every ticket sold promises additional potential income in the form of concessions. Furthermore, filled stadiums significantly improve the public perception of the team, team spirit, and the likelihood of national publicity.

Some ticketing companies also provide related services to help generate revenue. Callers versed in the specifics of the college's athletics program might request donations for athletic scholarships or sport-related programming. Sport marketers with contacts in the world of professional athletics can help schools pull together appropriate fundraising events. They provide research and insights, coordinate print production for programs and signage, assist with challenging media situations, help build sales of apparel and merchandise, and even rent seat cushions for homecoming games. Sophisticated software programs link ticketing, fundraising, and marketing functions to help track interactions, increase ticket sales, and improve the college's brand.

Other athletic departments prefer to hire and manage their own ticket sales staff. This approach gives the school greater control over its brand. It also avoids privacy concerns about sharing university databases with an external seller, which may be too aggressive for the school's educational environment, or running afoul of complex NCAA rules. However, internal sales might not be as effective, considering the competing priorities that confront the athletic department, the limited experience of the sales staff, the prohibitions on commission-based incentives for university employees, and ineffective channels of communication.

To fill football stadiums like this one at the University of Iowa, some universities have hired professional sales companies to call prospective ticket buyers.

Source: Phil Roeder/University of Iowa/Flickr/CC BY 2.0

pertain to a product or a service. They should assess whether the lead has the financial resources to pay for the product or service.[17] Clients looking to sell multimillion-dollar properties want real estate agents to qualify potential buyers first. Therefore, the sales agents might create a password-protected website that features floor plans and inside views for the shopping convenience of interested buyers. But to obtain the password, the customer must be prequalified as someone who could actually afford to buy the property. Such qualifications save both the agent and the seller the trouble of showing properties to curious people who could never actually afford to buy.

In a retail setting, though, qualifying potential customers is both dangerous and potentially illegal. Retail salespeople should never judge a book by its cover and assume that a person in the store doesn't fit the store's image or cannot afford to purchase there. Such actions can quickly rise to the level of unethical and illegal discrimination, as recently alleged by several African American shoppers against such well-known retail names as Macy's and Barneys.[18] Although not illegal, imagine the frustration you might feel if you visit an upscale jewelry store to purchase an engagement ring, only to be snubbed because you are dressed in your everyday, casual school clothes.

Step 2: Preapproach and the Use of CRM Systems

The **preapproach** occurs prior to meeting the customer for the first time and extends the qualification of leads procedure described in Step 1. Although the salesperson has learned about the customer during the qualification stage, in this step he or she must conduct additional research and develop plans for meeting with the customer. Suppose, for example, a management consulting firm wants to sell a bank a new system for finding checking account errors. The consulting firm's salesperson should first find out everything possible about the bank: How many checks does it process? What system is the bank using now? What are the benefits of the consultant's proposed system compared with the competition? The answers to these questions provide the basis for establishing value for the customer.

When Vonage decided to increase its sales of its voice over Internet protocol (VoIP) services to business customers rather than focusing only on consumers, it recognized that it needed information about how these buyers differed from its existing clients. Therefore, it purchased three firms that already function in business markets: Simple Signal, which provides unified communications-as-a-service solutions to small businesses; Telesphere Networks, which offers similar solutions to larger companies; and Vocalocity, which offers cloud-based communication services. Not only do those acquisitions provide it with customer data it can use in its preapproach planning, but they also provide introductions to potential business customers, leading Vonage to predict that it would be able to increase its B2B revenue by 40 percent.[19]

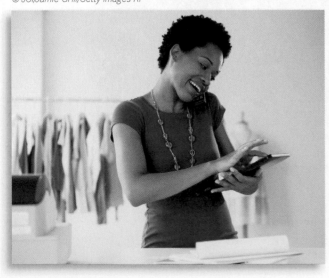

Salespeople input customer information into their tablets to develop a customer database for CRM systems.

© JGI/Jamie Grill/Getty Images RF

In the past, this customer information, if it was available at all, was typically included in a manual system that each individual salesperson kept, using a notebook or a series of cards. Today, salespeople often can access all this information immediately and conveniently from their firm's customer relationship management (CRM) system.

In most cases, these CRM systems have several components. There is a customer database or data warehouse. Whether the salesperson is working for a retail store or manages a selling team for an aerospace contractor, he or she can record transaction information, customer contact information, customer preferences, and market segment information about the customer. Once the data have been analyzed and CRM programs developed, salespeople can help implement the programs. Adding Value 20.2 describes the success of the most popular CRM system today, Salesforce.com.

Adding Value 20.2 | Selling in the Cloud: The Growth and Success of Salesforce.com[iii]

At one time, CRM systems were the exclusive domain of wealthy companies. With costs running into hundreds of thousands of dollars, CRM systems represented a massive investment in both money and the time required to establish them. Each system needed its own servers and support from vendors to ensure its maintenance and consistent functioning.

This scenario clearly represented an opportunity for a company that could offer easier, less expensive, leaner services. Enter Salesforce.com. Instead of complete, onsite CRM solutions, it promised to host all computing and data storage on its own servers, in the cloud. Clients did not need to find massive funds to purchase the system, because Salesforce.com initiated the first CRM-related software-as-a-service (SaaS) model. That is, client firms did not buy any software but instead paid Salesforce.com a subscription fee that varied according to the number of licenses they needed. Each user license cost approximately $75 a month, representing a substantial cost savings compared with full CRM systems. Moreover, because the software was in the cloud, salespeople could access their customer data anywhere, through their smartphones or

tablets, rather than having to return to the office to link into an in-house system.

And Salesforce.com didn't stop there. To build the most comprehensive service possible, the company created an entire section on its website that enabled clients to build and trade apps that would integrate with and extend the functionality of its system. To add value to its platform, it also has acquired dozens of firms that have developed innovative CRM technology. In recognition of its innovative, aggressive efforts, *Forbes* named Salesforce.com as one of the most innovative companies in practice today.

The move to an SaaS cloud-based CRM model in turn opened doors for vast segments of companies that never would have been able to purchase a full system. For several years, Salesforce.com thus has enjoyed a leading position in the CRM service market in terms of total revenue, revenue growth, and market share growth, and these growth rates continue to range in the 30 percent range across the board. As Salesforce.com's president and vice chair Keith Block asserts, "Salesforce.com's CRM market share leadership is a reflection of the consistent innovation we deliver to our customers."

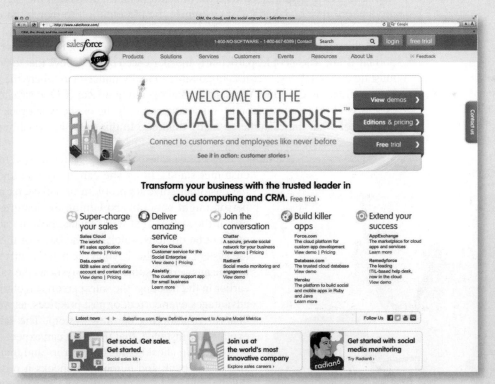

Salesforce.com offers its clients CRM solutions at a price most businesses can afford.

© Studio 101/Alamy

Having done the additional research, the salesperson establishes goals for meeting with the customer. It is important that the salesperson knows ahead of time exactly what should be accomplished. For instance, the consulting firm's salesperson cannot expect to get a purchase commitment from the bank after just the first visit. But a demonstration of the system and a short presentation about how the system would benefit the customer would be appropriate. It is often a good idea to practice the presentation prior to the meeting, using a technique known as **role playing**, in which the salesperson acts out a simulated buying situation while a colleague or manager acts as the buyer. Afterward, the practice sales presentation can be critiqued and adjustments can be made.

Step 3: Sales Presentation and Overcoming Reservations

The Presentation   Once all the background information has been obtained and the objectives for the meeting are set, the salesperson is ready for a person-to-person meeting. Let's continue with our bank example. During the first part of the meeting, the salesperson needs to get to know the customer, get the customer's attention, and create interest in the presentation to follow. The beginning of the presentation may be the most important part of the entire selling process, because it is when the salesperson establishes exactly where the customer is in the buying process (Exhibit 20.2). (For a refresher on the B2B buying process, see Chapter 7.)

Suppose, for instance, that the bank is in the first stage of the buying process: need recognition. It would not be prudent for the salesperson to discuss the pros and cons of different potential suppliers, because doing so would assume that the customer already had reached Step 4 (of the B2B buying process), proposal analysis and customer selection. By asking a series of questions though, the salesperson can assess the bank's need for the product or service and adapt or customize the presentation to match the customer's need and stage in the decision process.[20]

Asking questions is only half the battle; carefully listening to the answers is equally important. Some salespeople, particularly inexperienced ones, believe that to be in control, they must do all the talking. Yet it is impossible to really understand where the customer stands without listening carefully. What if the chief operating officer (COO) says, "It seems kind of expensive"? If the salesperson isn't listening carefully, he or she won't pick up on the subtle nuances of what the customer is really thinking. In this case, it probably means the COO doesn't see the value in the offering.

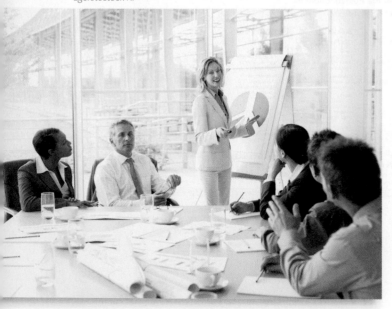

It is important to ask questions at the beginning of a sales presentation to establish where the customer is in the buying process.

© Chris Ryan/OJO Images/ agefotostock RF

When the salesperson has gotten a good feel for where the customer stands, he or she can apply that knowledge to help the customer solve its problem or satisfy its need. The salesperson might begin by explaining the features or characteristics of the system that will reduce checking account errors. It may not be obvious, solely on the basis of these features, that the system adds value beyond the bank's current practices. Using the answers to some of the questions the salesperson posed earlier in the meeting, the salesperson can clarify the product's advantages over current or past practices, as well as the overall benefits of adopting the new system. The salesperson might explain, for instance, that the bank can expect a 20 percent improvement in checking account errors and that, because of the size of the bank and number of checks it processes per year, this improvement would represent $2 million in annual savings. Because the system costs $150,000 per year and will take only three weeks to integrate into the current system, it will add significant and almost immediate value.

As this hypothetical example hints, personal selling often relies on an old-fashioned skill: storytelling. Even if they use advanced technologies and Internet-based communication

EXHIBIT 20.2 Aligning the Personal Selling Process with the B2B Buying Process

Personal selling process

- Generate and qualify leads
- Preapproach
- Sales presentation and overcoming reservations
- Closing the sale
- Follow-up

B2B buying process

- Need recognition
- Product specification
- RFP process
- Proposal analysis and supplier selection
- Order specification
- Performance assessment

media, salespeople must communicate their messages and sales pitches in ways that resonate with their audience of potential customers. As research in neuroscience continues to affirm, virtually everyone uses at least some level of emotional reaction in determining their choices. To appeal to customers, salespeople thus need to tell a story that engages people's imaginations.[21]

Handling Reservations An integral part of the sales presentation is handling reservations or objections that the buyer might have about the product or service. Although reservations can arise during each stage of the selling process, they are very likely to occur during the sales presentation. Customers may raise reservations pertaining to a variety of issues, but they usually relate in some way to value, such as that the price is too high for the level of quality or service.

Good salespeople know the types of reservations buyers are likely to raise. They may know, for instance, that their service is slower than competitors' or that their selection is limited. Although not all reservations can be forestalled, effective salespeople can anticipate and handle some. For example, when the bank COO said the check service seemed expensive, the salesperson was ready with information about how quickly the investment would be recouped.

As in other aspects of the selling process, the best way to handle reservations is to relax and listen, then ask questions to clarify any reservations.[22] For example, the salesperson could respond to the COO's reservation by asking, "How much do you think the bank is losing through checking account errors?" Her answer might open up a conversation about the positive trends in a cost–benefit analysis. Such questions are usually more effective than trying to prove the customer's reservation is not valid, because the latter approach implies the salesperson isn't really listening and could lead to an argument—the last thing a customer usually wants.

Step 4: Closing the Sale

Closing the sale means obtaining a commitment from the customer to make a purchase. Without a successful close, the salesperson goes away empty-handed, so many salespeople find this part of the sales process very stressful. Although losing a sale is never pleasant, salespeople who are involved in a relationship with their customers must view any specific sales presentation as part of the progression toward ultimately making the sale or building the relationship. An unsuccessful close on one day may just be a means of laying the groundwork for a successful close during the next meeting.

Although we have presented the selling process as a series of steps, closing the sale rarely follows so neatly. However, good salespeople listen carefully to what potential customers say and pay attention to their body language. By reading these signals, they can achieve an earlier close. Suppose that our hypothetical bank, instead of being in the first step of the buying process, were in the final step of negotiation and selection. An astute salesperson would pick up on these signals and ask for the sale.

Step 5: Follow-Up

> "It ain't over till it's over."
> —Yogi Berra[23]

With relationship selling, it is never really over, even after the sale is closed. The attitudes customers develop after the sale become the basis for how they purchase in the future. The follow-up therefore offers a prime opportunity for a salesperson to solidify the customer relationship through great service quality. Let's apply the five service quality dimensions we discussed in Chapter 13 to understand the follow-up:[24]

- **Reliability.** The salesperson and the supporting organization must deliver the right product or service on time.

- **Responsiveness.** The salesperson and support group must be ready to deal quickly with any issue, question, or problem that may arise.

- **Assurance.** Customers must be assured through adequate guarantees that their purchase will perform as expected.

- **Empathy.** The salesperson and support group must have a good understanding of the problems and issues faced by their customers. Otherwise, they cannot give them what they want.

- **Tangibles.** Because tangibles reflect the physical characteristics of the seller's business, such as its website, marketing communications, and delivery materials, their influence is subtler than that of the other four service quality dimensions. That doesn't mean it is any less important. Retail customers are generally more pleased with a purchase if it is carefully wrapped in nice paper instead of being haphazardly thrown into a crumpled plastic bag. The tangibles offer a signal that the product is of high quality, even though the packaging has nothing to do with the product's actual performance.

When customers' expectations are not met, they often complain—about deliveries, the billing amount or process, the product's performance, or after-sale services such as installation or training (recall the Gaps Model from Chapter 13). Effectively handling complaints

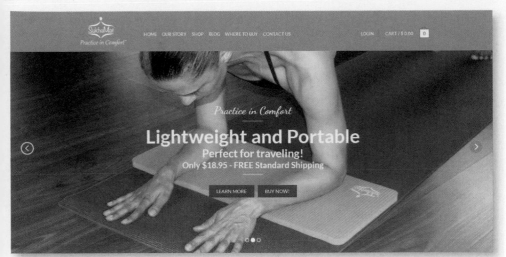

SukhaMat's owner, Barbara Merrill, sends handwritten thank-you notes to each of her customers.

Source: SukhaMat.com

is critical to the future of the relationship. As we noted in Chapter 13, the best way to handle complaints is to listen to the customer, provide a fair solution to the problem, and resolve the problem quickly.

The best way to nip a postsale problem in the bud is to check with the customer right after he or she takes possession of the product or immediately after the service has been completed. This speed demonstrates responsiveness and empathy. It also shows the customer that the salesperson and the firm care about customer satisfaction. Finally, a postsale follow-up call, e-mail, or letter takes the salesperson back to the first step in the sales process for initiating a new order and sustaining the relationship.

Such efforts are critical, no matter the size of the selling firm. From the moment Barbara Merrill first started her company SukhaMat, to sell the innovative knee pads she had invented along with other yoga products, she recognized the need for personal attention and follow-up efforts. Therefore, she hand wrote appreciative notes to each buyer from her home office, assuring them that she would be happy to hear from them with any questions or issues. As her company grew, with an expanding web presence and sales through Amazon, writing the full notes for each purchase became oppressively time consuming. Yet she was unwilling to give up the personal link to her customers, so she moved to a printed card, featuring the company's web address (www.sukhamat.com), as well as a personalized address line and signature. Such effort does not go unnoticed by customers; one Amazon review even explains a five-star rating by noting not just that "The SukhaMat is absolutely wonderful. It's just the right thickness and has just the right softness," but also that "P.S. The handwritten thank-you note from the seller was unexpected and very much appreciated touch."[25]

PROGRESS CHECK

1. Why is personal selling important to an IMC strategy?
2. What are the steps in the personal selling process?

MANAGING THE SALES FORCE

 LO20-3 Describe the key functions involved in managing a sales force.

Like any business activity involving people, the sales force requires management. **Sales management** involves the planning, direction, and control of personal selling activities, including recruiting, selecting, training, motivating, compensating, and evaluating, as they apply to the sales force.

Managing a sales force is a rewarding yet complicated undertaking. In this section, we examine how sales forces can be structured, some of the most important issues in recruiting and selecting salespeople, sales training issues, ways to compensate salespeople, and finally how to supervise and evaluate salespeople.

Sales Force Structure

Imagine the daunting task of putting together a sales force from scratch. Will you hire your own salespeople, or should they be manufacturer's representatives? What will each salesperson's primary duties be: order takers, order getters, sales support? Finally, will they work together in teams? In this section, we examine each of these issues.

Company Sales Force or Manufacturer's Representative

A **company sales force** comprises people who are employees of the selling company. **Independent agents**, also known as **manufacturer's representatives, or reps**, are salespeople who sell a manufacturer's products on an extended contract basis but are not employees of the manufacturer. They are compensated by commissions and do not take ownership or physical possession of the merchandise.

Manufacturer's representatives are useful for smaller firms or firms expanding into new markets, because such companies can achieve instant and extensive sales coverage without having to pay full-time personnel. Good sales representatives have many established contacts and can sell multiple products from noncompeting manufacturers during the same sales call. Also, the use of manufacturer's reps facilitates flexibility; it is much easier to replace a rep than an employee and much easier to expand or contract coverage in a market with a sales rep than with a company sales force.

Company sales forces are more typically used for established product lines. Because the salespeople are company employees, the manufacturer has more control over what they do. If, for example, the manufacturer's strategy is to provide extensive customer service, the sales manager can specify exactly what actions a company sales force must take. In contrast, because manufacturer's reps are paid on a commission basis, it is difficult to persuade them to take any action that doesn't directly lead to sales.

Salesperson Duties

Although the life of a professional salesperson is highly varied, salespeople generally play three important roles: order getting, order taking, and sales support.

Order Getting An **order getter** is a salesperson whose primary responsibilities are identifying potential customers and engaging those customers in discussions to attempt to make a sale. An order getter is also responsible for following up to ensure that the customer is satisfied and to build the relationship. In B2B settings, order getters are primarily involved in new buy and modified new buy situations (see Chapter 7). As a result, they require extensive sales and product knowledge training. The Pepsi salesperson who goes to Safeway's headquarters to sell a special promotion of Pepsi emojis is an order getter.

Order takers process routine orders, reorders, or rebuys for products.

© Mark Tuschman Photography

Order Taking An **order taker** is a salesperson whose primary responsibility is to process routine orders, reorders, or rebuys for products. Colgate employs order takers around the globe who go into stores and distribution centers that already carry Colgate products to check inventory, set up displays, write new orders, and make sure everything is going smoothly.

Sales Support **Sales support personnel** enhance and help with the overall selling effort. For example, if a Best Buy customer begins to experience computer problems, the company has a Geek Squad door-to-door service as well as support in the store. Those employees who respond to the customer's technical questions and repair the computer serve to support the overall sales process.

Combination Duties Although some salespeople's primary function may be order getting, order taking, or sales support, others fill a combination of roles. For instance, a computer salesperson at Staples may spend an hour with a

Customers like centenarian Ivy Bean can rely on sales support from Best Buy's Geek Squad.
© Bob Collier/PA Wire/AP Photo

customer educating him or her about the pros and cons of various systems and then make the sale. The next customer might simply need a specific printer cartridge. A third customer might bring in a computer and seek advice about an operating system problem. The salesperson was first an order getter, next an order taker, and finally a sales support person.

Some firms use **selling teams** that combine sales specialists whose primary duties are order getting, order taking, or sales support but who work together to service important accounts. As companies become larger and products more complicated, it is nearly impossible for one person to perform all the necessary sales functions.

Recruiting and Selecting Salespeople

When the firm has determined how the sales force will be structured, it must find and hire salespeople. Although superficially this task may sound as easy as posting the job opening on the Internet or running an ad in a newspaper, it must be performed carefully, because firms don't want to hire the wrong person. Salespeople are very expensive to train. Among other creative hiring tactics, Zappos' famously considers finding the right people so important that it will pay them to leave after a few weeks if they are not a good fit.[26]

In their critical efforts to find the right person for the job though, companies must take care to avoid biased practices such as hiring on the basis of stereotypes instead of qualifications. For most people, the picture of someone selling Avon products likely involves a middle-aged woman—namely, the "Avon Lady." But sales revenues for these products continue to provide salespeople a successful living, prompting plenty of women and men to try their hand at selling Avon.[27] Hiring based on misplaced assumptions about gender or other categories can be damaging to the company, as well as discriminatory.

The most important activity in the recruiting process is to determine exactly what the salesperson will be doing and what personal traits and abilities a person should have to do the job well. For instance, the Pepsi order getter who goes to Safeway to pitch a new product will typically need significant sales experience, coupled with great communication and analytical skills. Pepsi's order takers need to be reliable and able to get along with lots of different types of people in the stores, from managers to customers.

Many firms give candidates personality tests, but they stress different personality attributes, depending on the requisite traits for the position and the personality characteristics of their most successful salespeople.[28] For instance, impatience is often a positive characteristic for sales because it creates a sense of urgency to close the sale. But for very large, complicated sales targeting large institutions, like the bank in our previous example, an impatient salesperson may irritate the decision makers and kill the deal.

When recruiting salespeople, it helps to possess certain personal traits. What are those personal traits? Managers and sales experts generally agree on the following:[29]

- **Personality.** Good salespeople are friendly, sociable, and, in general, like being around people. Customers won't buy from someone they don't like.

- **Optimism.** Good salespeople tend to look at the bright side of things. Optimism also may help them be resilient—the third trait.

- **Resilience.** Good salespeople don't easily take no for an answer. They keep coming back until they get a yes.

- **Self-motivation.** As we have already mentioned, salespeople have lots of freedom to spend their days the way they believe will be most productive. But if the salespeople are not self-motivated to get the job done, it probably won't get done.

- **Empathy.** Empathy is one of the five dimensions of service quality discussed previously in this chapter and in Chapter 13. Good salespeople must care about their customers, their issues, and their problems.

Sales Training

Even people who possess all these personal traits need training. All salespeople benefit from training about selling and negotiation techniques, product and service knowledge, technologies used in the selling process, time and territory management, and company policies and procedures.

Firms use varied delivery methods to train their salespeople, depending on the topic of the training, what type of salesperson is being trained, and the cost versus the value of the training. For instance, an on-the-job training program is excellent for communicating selling and negotiation skills, because managers can observe the sales trainees in real selling situations and provide instant feedback. They can also engage in role-playing exercises in which the salesperson acts out a simulated buying situation and the manager critiques the salesperson's performance.

A much less expensive, but for some purposes equally valuable, training method is the Internet. Online training programs have revolutionized the way training happens in many firms. Firms can provide new product and service knowledge, spread the word about changes in company policies and procedures, and share selling tips in a user-friendly environment that salespeople can access anytime and anywhere. Distance learning sales training programs through teleconferencing enable a group of salespeople to participate with their instructor or manager in a virtual classroom. And testing can occur online as well. Online sales training may never replace the one-on-one interaction of on-the-job training for advanced selling skills, but it is quite effective and efficient for many other aspects of the sales training task.[30]

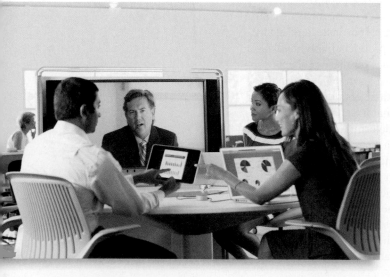

Technology has changed the lives of salespeople and the delivery methods of sales training. Companies can conduct distance learning and training through videoconferencing.

© Blend Images/Ariel Skelley/Getty Images RF

Motivating and Compensating Salespeople

An important goal for any effective sales manager is to get to know his or her salespeople and determine what motivates them to be effective. Some salespeople prize their freedom and like to be left alone; others want attention and are more productive when they receive accolades for a job well done. Still others are motivated primarily by monetary compensation. As Adding Value 20.3 reveals, these motives vary according to the selling context. Great sales managers determine how best to motivate each of their salespeople according to what is most important to each individual. Although sales managers can

Adding Value 20.3 — When Tupperware Does More Than Store Food: Sales as Empowerment among Indonesian Women[iv]

Tupperware may have started as an American company, but its primary sales markets have been overseas for years. Germany took top place for a while; today though, the biggest market for the plastic food container systems is Indonesia, where the company earned approximately $200 million in sales last year.

The reasons for its growth in Asia include some familiar notions but also some relatively notable distinctions. For example, a growing middle class leads consumers of virtually every country to look for ways to use their disposable income. Tupperware offers a target that is both fun and practical. In addition, as economies grow and consumers gain access to modern conveniences such as refrigerators, food storage products become a newly discovered need.

But Indonesia is unique in that it has strongly mandated and legally established roles for women that requires them to serve as caretakers in their families, while their husbands take the position of head of the household. Required to remain at home to care for their families, many middle-class women seek approved social interactions such as those created by Tupperware parties. Friends can come together to shop and chat, allowing the women a break from their daily routines.

This combination also makes Tupperware an ideal means for women to enter the workforce. Despite conservative social attitudes against women working, the at-home operations enable many of them to make a career out of selling Tupperware and convincing others to do the same. Thus the sales force in Indonesia currently includes about 250,000 women.

The social networks that enable the sales of Tupperware also resonate well in Indonesia, which has a long tradition of *arisans*, or gatherings in which women pool their money, then award the pot to a different member at each meeting. When the arisans include a Tupperware component, the pot of money usually helps the winner purchase a full set of products, which she would not have been able to afford otherwise.

Finally, the career prospects offered by Tupperware represent a viable means for women to escape poverty. One woman reports earning approximately US$2400 per month, six times what she and her husband combined earned previously. Thus, whereas "Initially, my husband refused to let me sell Tupperware even part-time. . . . Now he works for me."

Why is Indonesia Tupperwear's biggest market?

Source: Tupperware

emphasize different motivating factors, except in the smallest companies, the methods used to compensate salespeople must be fairly standardized and can be divided into two categories: financial and nonfinancial.

Financial Rewards   Salespeople's compensation usually has several components. Most salespeople receive at least part of their compensation as a **salary**, a fixed sum of money paid at regular intervals. Another common financial incentive is a **commission**, which is money paid as a percentage of the sales volume or profitability. A **bonus** is a payment made at management's discretion when the salesperson attains certain goals. Bonuses usually are given only periodically, such as at the end of the year. A **sales contest** is a short-term incentive designed to elicit a specific response from the sales force. Prizes might be cash or other types of financial incentives. For instance, Volkswagen may give a free trip to Germany for the salesperson who sells the most Touaregs.

The bulk of any compensation package is made up of salary, commission, or a combination of the two. The advantage of a salary plan is that salespeople know exactly what they will be paid, and sales managers have more control. Salaried salespeople can be directed to spend a certain percentage of their time handling customer service issues. Under a commission system, however, salespeople have only one objective—make the sale! Thus, a commission system provides the most incentive for the sales force to sell.

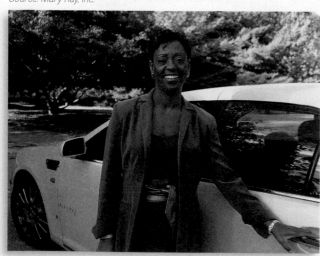

Nonfinancial Rewards   As we have noted, good salespeople are self-motivated. They want to do a good job and make the sale because it makes them feel good. But this good feeling also can be accentuated by recognition from peers and management. For instance, the internal monthly magazine and blog at the cosmetics firm Mary Kay provides an outlet for not only selling advice but also companywide recognition of individual salespeople's accomplishments.[31]

Nonfinancial rewards should have high symbolic value, as plaques, pens, or rings do. Free trips or days off are also effective rewards. More important than what the reward is, however, is the way it is operationalized. For instance, an award should be given at a sales meeting and publicized in the company newsletter. It should also be done in good taste, because if the award is perceived as tacky, no one will take it seriously.[32] Mary Kay recognizes salespeople's success with unusually large rewards that have both high symbolic and high material value. More than 130,000 independent beauty consultants and sales directors have earned the use of one of the famous pink Cadillacs, but it is also possible to gain rewards and recognition such as a set of faux pearl earrings within the first week of becoming a consultant.[33]

Evaluating Salespeople by Using Marketing Metrics

Salespeople's evaluation process must be tied to their reward structure. If salespeople do well, they should receive their rewards the way you do if you do well on your exams and assignments in a class: you earn good grades. However, salespeople should be evaluated and rewarded for only those activities and outcomes that fall under their control. If Nordstrom makes a unilateral decision to put Diesel jeans in all its stores after a negotiation with Diesel's corporate headquarters in Italy, the Diesel sales representatives responsible for individual Nordstrom stores should not receive credit for making the sale, nor should they get all the windfall commission that would ensue from the added sales.

Considering this guiding principle—evaluate and reward salespeople for what they do and not for what they don't do—how should sales managers evaluate salespeople? The answer is never easy because measures must be tied to performance, and there are many ways to measure performance in a complex job such as selling. For example, evaluating performance on the basis of monthly sales alone fails to consider how profitable the sales were, whether any progress was made to build new business that will be realized sometime in the future, or the level of customer service the salesperson provided. Because the sales job is multifaceted with many contributing success factors, sales managers should use multiple measures.[34]

In business practice, salesperson evaluation measures can be objective or subjective. Sales, profits, and the number of orders represent examples of objective measures. Although each is somewhat useful to managers, such measures do not provide an adequate perspective for a thorough evaluation, because there is no means of comparison with other salespeople. For instance, suppose salesperson A generated $1 million last year, but salesperson B generated $1.5 million. Should salesperson B automatically receive a significantly higher evaluation? Now consider that salesperson B's territory has twice as much potential as salesperson A's. Knowing this, we might suppose that salesperson A has actually done a better job. For this reason, firms use ratios such as profit per customer, orders per call, sales per hour, or expenses compared to sales as their objective measures.

Whereas objective measures are quantitative, subjective measures seek to assess salespeople's behavior: what they do and how well they do it. By their very nature, subjective measures reflect one person's opinion about another's performance. Thus, subjective evaluations can be biased and should be used cautiously and only in conjunction with multiple objective measures.

PROGRESS CHECK

1. What do sales managers need to do to manage their sales force successfully?
2. What is the difference between monetary and nonmonetary incentives?

ETHICAL AND LEGAL ISSUES IN PERSONAL SELLING

LO20-4 Describe the ethical and legal issues in personal selling.

Although ethical and legal issues permeate all aspects of marketing, they are particularly important for personal selling. Unlike advertising and other communications with customers, which are planned and executed on a corporate level, personal selling involves a one-to-one, and often face-to-face, encounter with the customer. Therefore, sellers' actions are not only highly visible to customers but also to other stakeholders, such as the communities in which they work.

Ethical and legal issues arise in three main areas. First, there is the relationship between the sales manager and the sales force. Second, in some situations, an inconsistency

Salespeople must live within their own ethical comfort zone. Should insurance salespeople disclose inadequate hurricane coverage and risk not making the sale?

© Charlie Riedel/AP Photo

might exist between corporate policy and the salesperson's ethical comfort zone. Third, ethical as well as legal issues can arise when the salesperson interacts with the customer, especially if that salesperson or the selling firm collects significant information about the customer. To maintain trustworthy customer relationships, companies must take care that they respect customer privacy and respect the information comfort zone—that is, the amount of information a customer feels comfortable providing.[35]

The Sales Manager and the Sales Force

Like any manager, a sales manager must treat people fairly and equally in everything he or she does. With regard to the sales force, this fairness must apply to hiring, promotion, supervision, training, assigning duties and quotas, compensation and incentives, and firing.[36] Federal laws cover many of these issues. For instance, equal employment opportunity laws make it unlawful to discriminate against a person in hiring, promotion, or firing because of race, religion, nationality, sex, or age.

The Sales Force and Corporate Policy

Sometimes salespeople face a conflict between what they believe represents ethical selling and what their company asks them to do to make a sale. Suppose an insurance agent whose compensation is based on commission sells a homeowner's policy to a family that has just moved to New Orleans, an area prone to flooding as a result of hurricanes. Even though the policy covers hurricane damage, it does not cover water damage from hurricanes. If the salesperson discloses the inadequate coverage, the sale might be lost because additional flood insurance is very expensive. What should the salesperson do? Salespeople must live within their own ethical comfort zone. If this or any other situation is morally repugnant to the salesperson, he or she must question the choice to be associated with such a company.[37]

Salespeople also can be held accountable for illegal actions sanctioned by the employer. If the homeowner asks if the home is above the floodplain or whether water damage from flooding is covered by the policy, and it is company policy to intentionally mislead potential customers, both the salesperson and the insurance dealership could be susceptible to legal action.

The Salesperson and the Customer

As the frontline emissaries for a firm, salespeople have a duty to be ethically and legally correct in all their dealings with their customers. Not only is it the right thing to do, it simply means good business. Long-term relationships can deteriorate quickly if customers believe that they have not been treated in an ethically proper manner. Unfortunately, salespeople sometimes get mixed signals from their managers or simply do not know when their behaviors might be considered unethical or illegal. Formal guidelines can help, but it is also important to integrate these guidelines into training programs in which salespeople can discuss various issues that arise in the field with their peers and managers.[38] Most important, however, is for sales managers to lead by example. If managers are known to cut ethical corners in their dealings with customers, it shouldn't surprise them when their salespeople do the same. Ethical and Societal Dilemma 20.1 considers the ethical issues that realtors face.

PROGRESS CHECK

1. What are three areas of personal selling in which ethical and legal issues are more likely to arise?

Ethical & Societal Dilemma 20.1 When Realtors Become Reality Stars[v]

Reality television has spread to nearly every facet of life, and real estate is no exception. On shows such as *Million Dollar Listing, House Hunters, Designed to Sell,* and *Property Brothers,* viewers can watch as homeowners try to sell their properties and potential buyers search for their perfect home. Helping them every step of the way are real estate professionals, some of whom have gained notoriety as reality television stars themselves.

The *Million Dollar Listing* series, with versions in New York and Los Angeles, has made household names out of agents such as Ryan Serhant and Josh Altman. The handsome young realtors not only broker massive real estate deals but also share stories about their personal lives and even allow cameras to catch them in the shower, in at least one memorable episode. As Altman recognized, "Nobody wants to see the guy who just sells houses every week. They want to see that drama between the realtors." As a result, some of the featured realtors have developed such an extensive fan base that they have hired publicists, managers, and drivers, as well as assistants whose sole job is to respond to contacts from fans.

The depictions of real estate transactions clearly make for great television. Consumers enjoy the voyeuristic glimpse into other people's financial affairs and living conditions, especially when those conditions include multimillion-dollar homes. The *Million Dollar Listing* episodes each average around 1.25 million viewers, leading networks such as Bravo and HGTV to keep adding new versions and twists to their lineups of real estate reality television shows.

But according to some observers, the shows create a destructive and potentially dangerous impression of what real estate transactions involve and what the responsibilities of professional realtors are. The agents often are presented in a less-than-flattering light, which could be damaging for their reputation. For example, one cast member on *The Real Housewives of Orange County* who was a real estate agent left the show mainly because she believed that participating in bickering and being subjected to wine thrown on her ultimately would be too professionally embarrassing to be healthy for her business.

Agencies that prohibit their brokers from appearing on such shows also note that discretion and clients' privacy are central goals for realtors—aspects that rarely are prioritized on reality television. Furthermore, if the agent becomes the star, the broker might come to overshadow the agency's brand as well as the sale itself.

The shows also present a condensed, highly edited version of the real estate process, naturally. Sales of big properties—and even smaller ones—can take months to complete, and much of the activity involves paperwork, e-mailing, and research. None of these elements are particularly compelling in video, so the shows tend to exclude them and focus more on loud negotiations, flashy open houses, or snarky interactions.

Yet for many of the star realtors, these potentially negative effects fade away in the face of the massive marketing bump they receive from their notoriety. Bravo asserts that every broker who has appeared on one of its shows has enjoyed increased business through the association. The well-known agents agree: One indicated that his business had jumped by 20 percent, and another noted that he moved from selling midrange condos to dealing in luxury estates, which earned him $200 million in commissions in a single recent year.

Do reality shows like Property Brothers, *starring Jonathan Silver Scott (left) and Drew Scott (right), portray the real estate industry and its salespeople in an ethically responsible manner?*
© HGTV/Photofest

Reviewing Learning Objectives

 Describe the value added of personal selling.

Although the cost of an average B2B sales call is expensive, many firms believe they couldn't do business without their sales forces. Customers can buy many products and services without the help of a salesperson, but in many other cases, it is worth the extra cost built into the price of a product to be educated about the product or get valuable advice. Salespeople can also simplify the buying process and therefore save the customer time and hassle.

 Define the steps in the personal selling process.

Although we discuss selling in terms of steps, it truly represents a process, and the time spent in each step varies according to the situation. In the first step, the salesperson generates a list of viable customers. During the second step, the preapproach, the salesperson gathers information about the customer and prepares for the presentation. The third step, the sales presentation, consists of a personal meeting between the salesperson and the customer. Through discussion and by asking questions, the salesperson learns where the customer is in the buying process and tailors the discussion around what the firm's product or service can do to meet that customer's needs. During the fourth step, the close, the salesperson asks for the order. Finally, during the follow-up, the salesperson and support staff solidify the long-term relationship by making sure the customer is satisfied with the purchase and addressing any complaints. The follow-up therefore sets the stage for the next purchase.

 Describe the key functions involved in managing a sales force.

The first task of a sales manager, assuming a firm is starting a sales force from scratch, is to determine whether to use a company sales force or manufacturer's representatives. Then sales managers must determine what the primary selling responsibilities will be—order getter, order taker, or sales support. The sales manager recruits and selects salespeople, but because there are all sorts of sales jobs, the sales manager must determine what it takes to be successful and then go after people with those attributes. In the next step, training, firms can choose between on-the-job and online training. Sales managers are also responsible for motivating and compensating salespeople. Most salespeople appreciate a balance of financial and nonfinancial rewards for doing a good job. Finally, sales managers are responsible for evaluating their salespeople. Normally, salespeople should be evaluated on a combination of objective measures, such as sales per hour, and subjective measures, such as how friendly they appear to customers.

 Describe the ethical and legal issues in personal selling.

Ethical and legal issues arise in three areas in personal selling. First, ethical and legal issues could arise based on how the sales manager interacts with the sales force. Second, there might be inconsistencies between corporate policy and the salesperson's ethical comfort zone. Finally, ethical and legal issues can arise as the salesperson interacts with customers.

Key Terms

LEARNSMART

- bonus, 626
- closing the sale, 620
- cold calls, 614
- commission, 626
- company sales force, 622
- inbound marketing, 614
- independent agents, 622
- leads, 613

- manufacturer's representatives (reps), 622
- order getter, 622
- order taker, 622
- personal selling, 610
- preapproach, 616
- qualify, 613
- relationship selling, 612

- role playing, 618
- salary, 626
- sales contest, 626
- sales management, 621
- sales support personnel, 622
- selling teams, 623
- telemarketing, 614
- trade shows, 614

Marketing Digitally

1. Go to Salesforce.com's YouTube channel at http://www .youtube.com/user/salesforce. Watch a few of the short videos and discuss how the tools described would help you as a salesperson.

2. To learn more about careers in sales, go to http://www.bls
.gov/oco/, the website for the Bureau of Labor Statistics.
This site contains a wealth of information about careers in
all fields. Click on "Sales." Choose any of the sales fields
listed, and explore that career field. What experience is
necessary to be hired for that job? What is the median salary? What do earners in the highest 10 percent of performance earn? Is job growth anticipated in that field?

Marketing Applications

1. How has your perception of what it would be like to have
a career in sales changed since you read this chapter?

2. "Salespeople just make products cost more." Do you
agree or disagree with this statement? Discuss why
you've taken that position.

3. Choose an industry or a specific company that you
would like to work for as a salesperson. How would
you generate and qualify leads?

4. Why is it important for salespeople to be good listeners? To be good at asking questions?

5. Suppose you are a salesperson at a high-end jewelry
store. What can you do to ensure that your customers are
satisfied? Now imagine you are the store manager of the
same store; what can you do in your position to guarantee
customers remain happy with the service they receive?

6. Imagine that a time machine has transported you back
to 1961. How was a day in the life of a salesperson selling appliances such as washing machines different in
1961 than it is now?

7. What are some of the potentially ethically troubling
and illegal situations facing professional salespeople,
and how should they deal with them?

8. Why would Gillette use a company sales force, while a
small independent manufacturer of organic shaving
cream uses manufacturer's representatives?

9. Similar to the way a sales manager evaluates a salesperson, your instructors evaluate your performance to assign you a grade. Choose one of your classes and analyze
the advantages and disadvantages of the objective and
subjective bases used to evaluate your performance.

10. A customer has the following reservations. How do
you respond?
    a. "I really like all the things this copier does, but I
    don't think it's going to be very reliable. With all
    those features, something's got to go wrong."
    b. "Your price for this printer is higher than the price
    I saw advertised on the Internet."

11. Imagine that you have just been hired by the school
newspaper to sell ad space. You are asked what you
think would be a "fair" compensation package for you.
Using the information from the chapter, make a list of
all the elements that should be included in your compensation package. How would this compensation
package change over time and with continued strong
performance?

12. You have taken a summer job in the windows and
doors department of a large home improvement store.
During sales training, you learn about the products,
how to best address customers' needs, and how to sell
the customer the best product to fit their needs regardless of price point. One day your manager informs you
that you are to recommend Smith Windows to every
window customer. Smith Windows are more expensive
and don't really provide superior benefit except in limited circumstances. The manager is insistent that you
recommend Smith. Not knowing what else to do, you
recommend Smith Windows to customers who would
have been better served by lower-cost windows. The
manager rewards you with a sales award. Later the
manager tells you that he received an all-expenses-
paid cruise for his family from Smith Windows. What,
if anything, should you do with this information?

Quiz Yourself

1. One of the advantages of personal selling over other
types of marketing communication is that
    a. salespeople can build strong relationships with
    customers.
    b. personal selling almost always costs less than other
    marketing communication alternatives.
    c. personal selling has greater reach than advertising.
    d. cold calling is easier than direct mail advertising.
    e. personal selling requires less training than other
    types of selling.

2. All of the following are service quality dimensions related to follow-up *except*
    a. ethics
    b. reliability
    c. tangibles
    d. responsiveness
    e. empathy

(Answers to these two questions can be found in the Quiz
Yourself Answer Key section.)

Chapter Case Study

ALTA DATA SOLUTIONS: MAKING THE SALE[39]

When Vicki Nguyen reached her office, she had a message from Mike Smith, the regional sales manager, to meet him in his office regarding the Burtell Inc. order. Vicki Nguyen is a senior sales associate for Alta Data Solutions Inc., a firm that markets software and hardware designed for data storage. The Burtell order represents a multimillion-dollar contract for Alta Data Solutions and would help Burtell boost its productivity levels and revenue for the region. To prepare for the meeting, Nguyen reviews her sales call report notes on the Burtell account.

Alta Data Solutions Alta Data Solutions provides software and hardware solutions to large firms and has an established track record for delivering an exceptional standard of quality and high levels of customer service. This excellent reputation allows Alta Data Solutions to charge a substantial premium, ranging from 10 to 20 percent above the market leader.

The data storage software services market has been dominated for two decades by this market leader. Alta Data Solutions holds the second position in the marketplace, with a considerably lower but growing market share. Only one other competitor, an aggressive, small, low-price player, holds a significant market share; this provider has made inroads into the market in the past several years through its aggressive sales tactics.

Alta Data Solutions has just built a new facility and hired 50 new software programmers. Therefore, the company must generate new business to meet its higher financial goals; even more important in the short run, it must keep the new programmers working on interesting projects to retain them.

Burtell Inc. Burtell Inc. is a division of a major U.S.-based consumer products firm. Its purchasing department negotiates contracts for software services and coordinates the interface among a variety of members from different departments. The business environment for consumer products has become highly competitive in recent years, leading to tight budgets and higher levels of scrutiny of the value added by vendors. Competition is fierce, as large numbers of end-user customers are considering vendors that provide the most data analysis with their products.

Burtell Inc. has been consistently buying software development services from the market leader since 1991 and is generally satisfied with its service. A recent change in corporate leadership, however, has increased concerns about its overreliance on one vendor for a particular service. Also, because of the difficult economic climate, the company is concerned about the cost of software services and whether it is necessary to provide such a high service level.

Vicki Nguyen's Call Report A call report is like a diary of sales calls made to a particular client. The notes in Vicki Nguyen's Burtell file pertaining to the current negotiations began on June 4 read as follows:

> June 4: I contacted Bethany O'Meara, chief purchasing officer at Burtell, to introduce myself to her and get a sense of what their future software needs might be. She told me that the slowed business climate had caused Burtell to institute a program for increased efficiency in operations and that they would be looking to negotiate a new contract for software solutions. She gave me some insights into the technological aspects of their needs.

> June 18: Met with Jon Aaronson, head of R&D, to explain our productivity-enhancing solutions. Went into considerable depth explaining how Alta could service their needs and learned what they were looking for in a provider. I went over some specific product specification issues, but Jon did not seem impressed. But he did ask for a price and told me that the final decision rested with Brad Alexander, the chief financial officer.

July 2: Presented to Bethany O'Meara and Jon Aaronson. They first asked about the price. I gave them a quote of $10 million. They suggested that other services were much cheaper. I explained that our price reflected the latest technology and that the price differential was an investment that could pay for itself several times over through faster communication speeds. I also emphasized our reputation for high-quality customer service. While the presentation appeared to meet their software needs, they did not seem impressed with the overall value. I also sent a copy of the presentation in report form to Brad Alexander and attempted to get an appointment to see him.

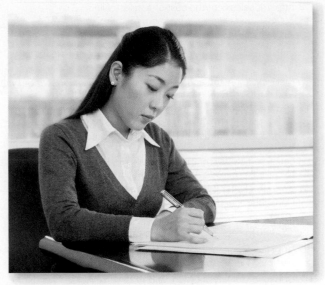

What are the key points Vicki Nguyen should make in her presentation?

© Lane Oatey/blue jean images/ Getty Images RF

July 9: Contacted Jon Aaronson by phone. He told me that we were in contention with three other firms and the debate was heated. He stated that the other firms were also touting their state-of-the-art technology. Discussed a lower price of $7 million. Also encouraged him to visit Alta Data Solutions headquarters to meet with the product manager who oversaw the product development efforts and would manage the implementation of the product. He wasn't interested in making the two-day trip even though it would spotlight our core competencies.

July 15: Received a conference call from Brad Alexander and Jon Aaronson to discuss the price. Brad said the price was still too high and that he could not depreciate that amount over the life of the software and meet target levels of efficiency. He wanted a final quote by August 6.

The Final Pitch Vicki Nguyen prepared for her meeting with Mike Smith, Alta's regional sales manager, by going over her notes and market data about the competitors. Smith's voicemail had said they'd be meeting to put together their best possible proposal.

Questions

Help Vicki Nguyen prepare her sales presentation.

1. Who should be at the presentation?
2. How should she start the meeting?
3. What are the key points she should make in her presentation?
4. What reservations should she expect? How should she handle them?

Endnotes

1. Alex Barinka, "IBM's Watson to Help Rich DBS Clients with 'Jeopardy' Smarts," *Bloomberg Technology*, January 8, 2014, http://www.bloomberg.com/.

2. Quentin Harvey, "IBM Plans Big Spending for the Cloud," *The New York Times*, January 17, 2014.

3. Barinka, "IBM's Watson to Help Rich DBS Clients with 'Jeopardy' Smarts."

4. Debra Pesek, "How IBM Uses Watson Analytics for Pattern Selling," Watson Analytics blog, November 17, 2015, https:// community.watsonanalytics.com/watson-analytics-blog/ how-ibm-uses-watson-analytics-for-pattern-selling/.

5. Ibid.

6. Bureau of Labor Statistics, http://www.bls.gov.

7. This section draws from Mark W. Johnston and Greg W. Marshall, *Relationship Selling*, 3rd ed. (Burr Ridge, IL: Irwin/ McGraw-Hill, 2009); Mark W. Johnston and Greg W. Marshall, *Relationship Selling and Sales Management*, 2nd ed. (Burr Ridge, IL: Irwin/McGraw-Hill, 2007).

8. Geoffrey James, "Selling Gets Complex," *Strategy+Business*, August 27, 2009; Dale Carnegie, *How to Win Friends and Influence People* (New York: Pocket, 1990); Neil Rackham, *SPIN Selling* (New York: McGraw-Hill, 1988).

9. http://4dsales.com/the-cost-of-a-sales-call/.

10. Bill Stinnett, *Think Like Your Customer* (Burr Ridge, IL: McGraw-Hill, 2004).

11. Pam Baker, "Best Sales Practices: Build Lasting Relationships," *CRM Buyer,* January 27, 2009.

12. Mark W. Johnston and Greg W. Marshall, *Relationship Selling,* 2nd ed. (Burr Ridge, IL: Irwin/McGraw-Hill, 2008).

13. S. Anthony Iannarino, "The Last Word on Cold Calling versus Social Media," *The Sales Blog,* April 21, 2014, http://www.thesalesblog.com; Justin Fishaw, "Has LinkedIn Replaced Cold Calling?" *SocialMediaToday,* August 21, 2013, http://www.socialmediatoday.com; Ken Krogue, "Cold Calling Is Dead, Thanks to LinkedIn," *Forbes,* August 9, 2013, http://www.forbes.com.

14. Andrew Mach, "10 Cutting Edge Gadgets from the 2016 Consumer Electronics Show," *PBS NewsHour,* January 9, 2016.

15. "CES 2016 Fact Sheet," CESweb.org.

16. Christine Comaford, "Sales Stuck? Try Sticking to a Script," *BusinessWeek,* April 4, 2008.

17. Christine Comaford-Lynch, "A Bad Lead Is Worse Than No Lead at All," *BusinessWeek,* March 26, 2008.

18. J. David Goodman, "Profiling Complaints by Black Shoppers Followed Changes to Stores' Security Policies," *The New York Times,* October 29, 2013, http://www.nytimes.com.

19. Kate Maddox, "New CMO at Vonage Will Make 'Aggressive' B-to-B Push," *Advertising Age,* April 28, 2015, http://www.adage.com.

20. Barton A. Weitz, Harish Sujan, and Mita Sujan, "Knowledge, Motivation, and Adaptive Behavior: A Framework for Improving Selling Effectiveness," *Journal of Marketing,* October 1986, pp. 174–91.

21. Dennis Nishi, "To Persuade People, Tell Them a Story," *The Wall Street Journal,* November 9, 2013, http://online.wsj.com.

22. Robert Keller, "Handling Objections in Today's Tough Environment," *SMM,* March 30, 2009.

23. http://www.quotedb.com/quotes/1303.

24. Mark W. Johnston and Greg W. Marshall, *Churchill/Ford/Walker's Sales Force Management,* 9th ed. (Burr Ridge, IL: McGraw-Hill/Irwin, 2009).

25. "Oh, What a Relief," review, May 28, 2015, http://www.amazon.com/SukhaMat-practice-Cushions-Complements-full-size/dp/B000055GRI?ie=UTF8&keywords=sukhamat&qid=1463250532&ref_=sr_1_1&sr=8-1.

26. Benjamin Snyder, "14% of Zappos Staff Left After Being Offered Exit Pay," *Fortune,* May 8, 2015.

27. Lynn Huber, "Can Men Sell Avon?" *Online Beauty Biz,* May 25, 2014, http://www.onlinebeautybiz.com; Sadie Whitelocks, "I'm an Avon Laddie! Salesman, 21, Is Part of the New Breed of Men Muscling in on Door-to-Door Trade," *DailyMail,* December 14, 2011, http://www.dailymail.co.uk.

28. Susan Greco, "Personality Testing for Sales Recruits," *INC.,* March 1, 2009.

29. Ned Smith, "10 Traits of Successful Salespeople," *Business News Daily,* March 20, 2013, http://www.businessnewsdaily.com; Steven W. Martin, "Seven Personality Traits of Top Salespeople," *Harvard Business Review,* June 27, 2011, http://blogs.hbr.org; Julie Chang, "Born to Sell?" *Sales and Marketing Management,* July 2003, p. 36.

30. Felicia G. Lassk et al., "The Future of Sales Training: Challenges and Related Research Questions," *Journal of Personal Selling and Sales Management* 32, no. 1 (2012), pp. 141–54.

31. http://blog.marykay.com/; https://www.shanisoffice.com/uploads/5/0/9/8/5098161/march_applause_en.pdf.

32. Johnston and Marshall, *Relationship Selling and Sales Management,* 2nd ed.

33. http://www.marykay.com/en-US/beabeautyconsultant/Pages/money-rewards.aspx.

34. For a discussion of common measures used to evaluate salespeople, see Mark W. Johnston and Greg W. Marshall, *Churchill/Ford/Walker's Sales Force Management,* 9th ed. (Burr Ridge, IL: McGraw-Hill/Irwin, 2009).

35. David H. Holtzman, "Big Business Knows Us Too Well," *BusinessWeek,* June 22, 2007.

36. Johnston and Marshall, *Churchill/Ford/Walker's Sales Force Management,* 9th ed.

37. Nicolas McClaren, "The Personal Selling and Sales Management Ethics Research: Managerial Implications and Research Directions from a Comprehensive Review of the Empirical Literature," *Journal of Business Ethics* 112, no. 1 (January 2013), pp. 101–25; Sean R. Valentine and Connie R. Bateman, "The Impact of Ethical Ideologies, Moral Intensity, and Social Context on Sales-Based Ethical Reasoning," *Journal of Business Ethics* 102, no. 1 (August 2011), pp. 155–68.

38. Casey Donoho and Timothy Heinze, "The Personal Selling Ethics Scale: Revisions and Expansions for Teaching Sales Ethics," *Journal of Marketing Education* 33, no. 1 (April 2011), pp. 107–22.

39. This case was written by Jeanne Munger in conjunction with the textbook authors Dhruv Grewal and Michael Levy as the basis of class discussion rather than to illustrate either effective or ineffective marketing practice. For a discussion of common measures used to evaluate salespeople, see Johnston and Marshall, *Churchill/Ford/Walker's Sales Force Management,* 9th ed.

i. Oscar Macia, "How Mobile Is Driving the Future of Field Sales," *Sales and Marketing,* March 11, 2016, https://salesandmarketing.com/content/how-mobile-driving-future-field-sales.

ii. Steve Berkowitz, "Marketers Reshape How College Teams Sell Tickets," *USA Today,* August 5, 2011, http://www.usatoday.com; "Accelerating the Trend toward Outsourcing Athletic Event Ticket Sales, Two More Universities Partner with IMG College," press release, May 31, 2011, http://www.imgworld.com; IMG College, http://www.imgcollege.com.

iii. "Salesforce Announces Fiscal 2015 Fourth Quarter and Full Year Results," Salesforce.com, February 25, 2016, http://investor.salesforce.com/about-us/investor/investor-news/investor-news-details/2015/Salesforce-Announces-Fiscal-2015-Fourth-Quarter-and-Full-Year-Results/default.aspx; Trefis Team, "Here Is the Reason Behind Salesforce.com's Unabated Growth," *Forbes,* November 25, 2015; "Salesforce.com Named #1 CRM Software Provider in Gartner's Worldwide CRM Market Share Report for Second Consecutive Year," *The Wall Street Journal,* April 29, 2014, http://online.wsj.com; Victoria Barret, "Why Salesforce.com Ranks #1 on Forbes' Most Innovative List," *Forbes,* September 5, 2012, http://www.forbes.com; Mi Ji et al., "Salesforce.com: Creating a Blue Ocean in the B2B Space," *INSEAD Case# INS255,* 2013.

iv. Joe Cochrane, "Tupperware's Sweet Spot Shifts to Indonesia," *The New York Times,* February 28, 2015, http://www.nytimes.com.

v. Candace Jackson, "A Real Estate Star Is Born," *The Wall Street Journal,* August 1, 2013.

actual product The physical attributes of a product including the brand name, features/design, quality level, and packaging.

ad-supported app Apps that are free to download, but place ads on the screen when using the program to generate revenue.

administered vertical marketing system A *supply chain* system in which there is no common ownership and no contractual relationships, but the dominant channel member controls the channel relationship.

advanced shipping notice (ASN) An electronic document that the supplier sends the retailer in advance of a shipment to tell the retailer exactly what to expect in the shipment.

advertising A paid form of communication from an identifiable source, delivered through a communication channel, and designed to persuade the receiver to take some action now or in the future.

advertising allowance Tactic of offering a price reduction to channel members if they agree to feature the manufacturer's product in their advertising and promotional efforts.

advertising plan A section of the firm's overall marketing plan that explicitly outlines the objectives of the advertising campaign, how the campaign might accomplish those objectives, and how the firm can determine whether the campaign was successful.

advertising schedule The specification of the timing and duration of advertising.

affective component A component of *attitude* that reflects what a person feels about the issue at hand—his or her like or dislike of something.

AIDA model A common model of the series of mental stages through which consumers move as a result of marketing communications: *Awareness* leads to *Interests*, which lead to *Desire*, which leads to *Action*.

aided recall An awareness metric that occurs when consumers recognize a name (e.g., of a brand) that has been presented to them.

alpha testing An attempt by the firm to determine whether a product will perform according to its design and whether it satisfies the need for which it was intended; occurs in the firm's research and development (R&D) department.

associated services (also called augmented product) The nonphysical attributes of the product including product warranties, financing, product support, and after-sale service. Also called *augmented product*.

attitude A person's enduring evaluation of his or her feelings about and behavioral tendencies toward an object or idea; consists of three components: *cognitive, affective,* and *behavioral*.

augmented product See *associated services*.

autocratic buying center A buying center in which one person makes the decision alone, though there may be multiple participants.

Baby Boomers Generational cohort of people born after World War II, between 1946 and 1964.

bait and switch A deceptive practice of luring customers into the store with a very low advertised price on an item (the bait), only to aggressively pressure them into purchasing a higher-priced model (the switch) by disparaging the lower-priced item, comparing it unfavorably with the higher-priced model, or professing an inadequate supply of the lower-priced item.

behavioral component A component of *attitude* that comprises the actions a person takes with regard to the issue at hand.

behavioral segmentation A segmentation method that divides customers into groups based on how they use the product or service. Some common behavioral measures include occasion and loyalty.

benefit segmentation The grouping of consumers on the basis of the benefits they derive from products or services.

beta testing Having potential consumers examine a product prototype in a real-use setting to determine its functionality, performance, potential problems, and other issues specific to its use.

big box retailer Discount stores that offer a narrow but deep assortment of merchandise; see also *category killer*.

big data Data sets that are too large and complex to analyze with conventional data management and data mining software.

blog (weblog) An online diary with periodic posts; corporate blogs are a new form of marketing communications.

body copy The main text portion of an ad.

bonus A payment made at management's discretion when the salesperson attains certain goals; usually given only periodically, such as at the end of the year.

bottom of the pyramid A term used for economic settings in which consumers earn very low wages.

bounce rate The percentage of times a visitor leaves the website almost immediately, such as after viewing only one page.

boycott A group's refusal to deal commercially with some organization to protest against its policies.

brainstorming A group activity used to generate ideas.

brand association The mental links that consumers make between a brand and its key product attributes; can involve a logo, slogan, or famous personality.

brand awareness Measures how many consumers in a market are familiar with the brand and what it stands for; created through repeated exposures of the various brand elements (brand name, logo, symbol, character, packaging, or slogan) in the firm's communications to consumers.

brand dilution Occurs when a brand extension adversely affects consumer perceptions about the attributes the core brand is believed to hold.

brand elements Characteristics that identify the sponsor of a specific ad.

brand equity The set of assets and liabilities linked to a brand that add to or subtract from the value provided by the product or service.

brand extension The use of the same brand name for new products being introduced to the same or new markets.

brand licensing A contractual arrangement between firms, whereby one firm allows another to use its brand name, logo, symbols, or characters in exchange for a negotiated fee.

brand loyalty Occurs when a consumer buys the same brand's product or service repeatedly over time rather than buying from multiple suppliers within the same category.

brand repositioning (rebranding) A strategy in which marketers change a brand's focus to target new markets or realign the brand's core emphasis with changing market preferences.

breadth Number of product lines offered by a firm; also known as variety.

break-even analysis Technique used to examine the relationships among cost, price, revenue, and profit over different levels of production and sales to determine the *break-even point*.

break-even point The point at which the number of units sold generates just enough revenue to equal the total costs; at this point, profits are zero.

breakthroughs See *pioneers*.

business ethics Refers to a branch of ethical study that examines ethical rules and principles within a commercial context, the various moral or ethical problems that might arise in a business setting, and any special duties or obligations that apply to persons engaged in commerce.

business-to-business (B2B) marketing The process of buying and selling goods or services to be used in the production of other goods and services, for consumption by the buying organization, or for resale by wholesalers and retailers.

business-to-consumer (B2C) marketing The process in which businesses sell to consumers.

buyer The buying center participant who handles the paperwork of the actual purchase.

buying center The group of people typically responsible for the buying decisions in large organizations.

cannibalize From a marketing perspective, it is the negative impact on a firm's sales, profits, or market share when one product competes closely with a similar product offered by the same company.

cash discount Tactic of offering a reduction in the invoice cost if the buyer pays the invoice prior to the end of the discount period.

category killer A specialist that offers an extensive assortment in a particular category so overwhelming the category that other retailers have difficulty competing.

category specialist A retailer that offers a narrow variety but a deep assortment of merchandise.

cause-related marketing Commercial activity in which businesses and charities form a partnership to market an image, a product, or a service for their mutual benefit; a type of promotional campaign.

checking The process of going through the goods upon receipt to ensure they arrived undamaged and that the merchandise ordered was the merchandise received.

churn The number of consumers who stop using a product or service, divided by the average number of consumers of that product or service.

click path Shows how users proceed through the information on a website—not unlike how grocery stores try to track the way shoppers move through their aisles.

click-through rate (CTR) The number of times a user clicks on an online ad divided by the number of impressions.

closing the sale Obtaining a commitment from the customer to make a purchase.

co-branding The practice of marketing two or more brands together, on the same package or promotion.

coercive power A type of marketing channel power that occurs when a member uses threats or punishment of the other channel member for not undertaking certain tasks. Delaying payment for late delivery would be an example.

cognitive component A component of *attitude* that reflects what a person believes to be true.

cold calls A method of prospecting in which salespeople telephone or go to see potential customers without appointments.

commission Compensation or financial incentive for salespeople based on a fixed percentage of their sales.

communication channel The medium—print, broadcast, the Internet—that carries the message.

communication gap A type of *service gap*; refers to the difference between the actual service provided to customers and the service that the firm's promotion program promises.

company sales force The people who are employees of the selling company and are engaged in the selling process.

compensatory decision rule At work when the consumer is evaluating alternatives and trades off one characteristic against another such that good characteristics compensate for bad ones.

competition-based pricing method An approach that attempts to reflect how the firm wants consumers to interpret its products relative to the competitors' offerings; for example, setting a price close to a competitor's price signals to consumers that the product is similar, whereas setting the price much higher signals greater features, better quality, or some other valued benefit.

competitive parity A firm's strategy of setting prices that are similar to those of major competitors.

competitor orientation A company objective based on the premise that the firm should measure itself primarily against its competition.

complementary products Products whose demand curves are positively related, such that they rise or fall together; a percentage increase in demand for one results in a percentage increase in demand for the other.

concentrated targeting strategy A marketing strategy of selecting a single, primary target market and focusing all energies on providing a product to fit that market's needs.

concept Brief written description of a product or service; its technology, working principles, and forms; and what customer needs it would satisfy.

concept testing The process in which a concept statement that describes a product or a service is presented to potential buyers or users to obtain their reactions.

connected effect With regard to the Wheel of Social Media Engagement, the connected effect is an outcome of social media that satisfies humans' innate need to connect with other people.

conscious marketing An approach to marketing that acknowledges four key principles: a higher purpose, stakeholders, conscious leadership, and a conscious culture

consensus buying center A buying center in which all members of the team must reach a collective agreement that they can support a particular purchase.

consultative buying center A buying center in which one person makes the decision but he or she solicits input from others before doing so.

consumer decision rules The set of criteria that consumers use consciously or subconsciously to quickly and efficiently select from among several alternatives.

consumer product Products and services used by people for their personal use.

consumer-to-consumer (C2C) marketing The process in which consumers sell to other consumers.

contest A brand-sponsored competition that requires some form of skill or effort.

continuous advertising schedule An advertising schedule that runs steadily throughout the year and therefore is suited to products and services that are consumed continually at relatively steady rates and that require a steady level of persuasive or reminder advertising.

contractual vertical marketing system A system in which independent firms at different levels of the supply chain join together through contracts to obtain economies of scale and coordination and to reduce conflict.

contribution per unit The price less the variable cost per unit. Variable used to determine the break-even point in units.

control phase The part of the strategic marketing planning process when managers evaluate the performance of the marketing strategy and take any necessary corrective actions.

convenience products/services Those for which the consumer is not willing to spend any effort to evaluate prior to purchase.

convenience store Type of retailer that provides a limited number of items at a convenient location in a small store with speedy checkout.

conventional supermarket Type of retailer that offers groceries, meat, and produce with limited sales of nonfood items, such as health and beauty aids and general merchandise, in a self-service format.

conversion rate Percentage of consumers who buy a product after viewing it.

cooperative (co-op) advertising An agreement between a manufacturer and retailer in which the manufacturer agrees to defray some advertising costs.

core customer value The basic problem-solving benefits that consumers are seeking.

corporate blog A website created by a company and often used to educate customers.

corporate social responsibility (CSR) Refers to the voluntary actions taken by a company to address the ethical, social, and environmental impacts of its business operations and the concerns of its stakeholders.

corporate vertical marketing system A system in which the parent company has complete control and can dictate the priorities and objectives of the supply chain; it may own facilities such as manufacturing plants, warehouse facilities, retail outlets, and design studios.

cost-based pricing method An approach that determines the final price to charge by starting with the cost, without recognizing the role that consumers or competitors' prices play in the marketplace.

cost-of-ownership method A value-based method for setting prices that determines the total cost of owning the product over its useful life.

country culture Similar to culture in general, but at a country level. Entails easy-to-spot visible nuances that are particular to a country, such as dress, symbols, ceremonies, language, colors, and food preferences, and subtler aspects, which are trickier to identify.

coupon Provides a stated discount to consumers on the final selling price of a specific item; the retailer handles the discount.

cross-docking distribution center A distribution center to which vendors ship merchandise prepackaged and ready for sale. The merchandise goes to a staging area rather than into storage. When all the merchandise going to a particular store has arrived in the staging area, it is loaded onto a truck, and away it goes. Thus, merchandise goes from the receiving dock to the shipping dock—cross dock.

cross-price elasticity The percentage change in demand for product A that occurs in response to a percentage change in price of product B; see also *complementary products*.

cross-promoting Efforts of two or more firms joining together to reach a specific target market.

culture The shared meanings, beliefs, morals, values, and customs of a group of people. It is transmitted by words, literature, and institutions and is passed down from generation to generation and learned over time.

cumulative quantity discount Pricing tactic that offers a discount based on the amount purchased over a specified period and usually involves several transactions; encourages resellers to maintain their current supplier because the cost to switch must include the loss of the discount.

customer excellence Involves a focus on retaining loyal customers and excellent customer service.

customer lifetime value The expected financial contribution from a particular customer to the firm's profits over the course of their entire relationship.

customer orientation A company objective based on the premise that the firm should measure itself primarily according to whether it meets its customers' needs.

customer relationship management (CRM) A business philosophy and set of strategies, programs, and systems that focus on identifying and building loyalty among the firm's most valued customers.

customer service Specifically refers to human or mechanical activities firms undertake to help satisfy their customers' needs and wants.

data Raw numbers or facts.

data mining The use of a variety of statistical analysis tools to uncover previously unknown patterns in the data stored in databases or relationships among variables.

data warehouses Large computer files that store millions and even billions of pieces of individual data.

deal A type of short-term price reduction that can take several forms, such as a "featured price," a price lower than the regular price; a "buy one, get one free" offer; or a certain percentage "more free" offer contained in larger packaging; can involve a special financing arrangement, such as reduced percentage interest rates or extended repayment terms.

decider The buying center participant who ultimately determines any part of or the entire buying decision—whether to buy, what to buy, how to buy, or where to buy.

decline stage Stage of the product life cycle when sales decline and the product eventually exits the market.

decoding The process by which the receiver interprets the sender's message.

delivery gap A type of *service gap;* the difference between the firm's service standards and the actual service it provides to customers.

demand curve Shows how many units of a product or service consumers will demand during a specific period at different prices.

democratic buying center A buying center in which the majority rules in making decisions.

demographic segmentation The grouping of consumers according to easily measured, objective characteristics such as age, gender, income, and education.

demographics Information about the characteristics of human populations and segments, especially those used to identify consumer markets such as by age, gender, income, and education.

department store A retailer that carries many different types of merchandise (broad variety) and lots of items within each type (deep assortment); offers some customer services; and is organized into separate departments to display its merchandise.

depth The number of categories within a product line.

derived demand The linkage between consumers' demand for a company's output and its purchase of necessary inputs to manufacture or assemble that particular output.

determinant attributes Product or service features that are important to the buyer and on which competing brands or stores are perceived to differ.

differentiated targeting strategy A strategy through which a firm targets several market segments with a different offering for each.

diffusion of innovation The process by which the use of an innovation, whether a product or a service, spreads throughout a market group over time and over various categories of adopters.

Digital Natives See *Generation Z.*

direct investment When a firm maintains 100 percent ownership of its plants, operation facilities, and offices in a foreign country, often through the formation of wholly owned subsidiaries.

direct marketing Sales and promotional techniques that communicate directly with target customers to generate a response or transaction

direct marketing channel A marketing channel in which there are no intermediaries; the manufacturer sells directly to the buyer.

dispatcher The person who coordinates deliveries to distribution centers.

distribution center A facility for the receipt, storage, and redistribution of goods to company stores or customers; may be operated by retailers, manufacturers, or distribution specialists.

distribution intensity The number of supply chain members to use at each level of the supply chain.

distributive fairness Pertains to a customer's perception of the benefits he or she received compared with the costs (inconvenience or loss) that resulted from a service failure.

distributor A type of reseller or marketing intermediary that resells manufactured products without significantly altering their form. Distributors often buy from manufacturers and sell to other businesses like retailers in a B2B transaction.

diversification strategy A growth strategy whereby a firm introduces a new product or service to a market segment that it does not currently serve.

drugstore A specialty store that concentrates on health and personal grooming merchandise, though pharmaceuticals may represent almost 70 percent of its sales.

duty See *tariff.*

dynamic effect With regard to the Wheel of Social Media Engagement, the *dynamic effect* describes the way in which information is exchanged to network participants through back-and-forth communications in an active and effective manner. It also expands the impact of the network effect by examining how people flow in and out of networked communities as their interests change (see *network effect.*)

dynamic pricing Refers to the process of charging different prices for goods or services based on the type of customer, time of the day, week, or even season, and level of demand. Also called *individualized pricing.*

early adopters The second group of consumers in the diffusion of innovation model, after *innovators,* to use a product or service innovation represent about 13.5 percent of the population. They generally don't like to take as much risk as innovators but instead wait and purchase the product after careful review.

early majority A group of consumers in the diffusion of innovation model that represents approximately 34 percent of the population; members don't like to take much risk and therefore tend to wait until bugs are worked out of a particular product or service; few new products and services can be profitable until this large group buys them.

economic situation Macroeconomic factor that affects the way consumers buy merchandise and spend money, both in a marketer's home country and abroad; see also *inflation, foreign currency fluctuations,* and *interest rates.*

elastic Refers to a market for a product or service that is price sensitive; that is, relatively small changes in price will generate fairly large changes in the quantity demanded.

electronic data interchange (EDI) The computer-to-computer exchange of business documents from a retailer to a vendor and back.

emotional appeal An appeal that aims to satisfy consumers' emotional desires rather than their utilitarian needs.

emotional support Concern for others' well-being and support of their decisions in a job setting.

empowerment In context of service delivery, means allowing employees to make decisions about how service is provided to customers.

encoding The process of converting the sender's ideas into a message, which could be verbal, visual, or both.

entrepreneur A person who organizes, operates, and assumes the risk of a new business venture.

esteem needs Part of Maslow's hierarchy, these are needs that enable people to fulfill inner desires.

evaluative criteria Consist of a set of salient, or important, attributes about a particular product.

event sponsorship Popular PR tool that occurs when corporations support various activities (financially or otherwise), usually in the cultural or sports and entertainment sectors.

everyday low pricing (EDLP) A strategy companies use to emphasize the continuity of their retail prices at a level somewhere between the regular, nonsale price and the deep-discount sale prices their competitors may offer.

evoked set Comprises the alternative brands or stores that the consumer states he or she would consider when making a purchase decision.

exchange The trade of things of value between the buyer and the seller so that each is better off as a result.

exchange control The regulation of a country's currency *exchange rate*.

exchange rate The measure of how much one currency is worth in relation to another.

exclusive distribution Strategy in which only selected retailers can sell a manufacturer's brand.

experience curve effect The drop in unit cost as the accumulated volume sold increases; as sales continue to grow, the costs continue to drop, allowing even further reductions in the price.

experiment See *experimental research*.

experimental research (experiment) A type of conclusive and quantitative research that systematically manipulates one or more variables to determine which variables have a causal effect on another variable.

expertise power A type of marketing channel power that occurs when a channel member uses its expertise as leverage to influence the actions of another channel member.

exporting Producing goods in one country and selling them in another.

extended problem solving A purchase decision process during which the consumer devotes considerable time and effort to analyzing alternatives; often occurs when the consumer perceives that the purchase decision entails a lot of risk.

external locus of control Refers to when consumers believe that fate or other external factors control all outcomes.

external search for information Occurs when the buyer seeks information outside his or her personal knowledge base to help make the buying decision.

extreme-value food retailer See *limited-assortment supermarkets*.

extreme-value retailer A general merchandise discount store found in lower-income urban or rural areas.

facial recognition software Software that can automatically identify or verify individuals from video or digital images.

family brand A firm's own corporate name used to brand its product lines and products.

feedback loop Allows the receiver to communicate with the sender and thereby informs the sender whether the message was received and decoded properly.

financial risk Risk associated with a monetary outlay; includes the initial cost of the purchase as well as the costs of using the item or service.

first movers Product pioneers that are the first to create a market or product category, making them readily recognizable to consumers and thus establishing a commanding and early market share lead.

fixed costs Those costs that remain essentially at the same level, regardless of any changes in the volume of production.

flighting (advertising schedule) An advertising schedule implemented in spurts, with periods of heavy advertising followed by periods of no advertising.

floor-ready merchandise Merchandise that is ready to be placed on the selling floor immediately.

focus group interview A research technique in which a small group of persons (usually 8 to 12) comes together for an intensive discussion about a particular topic, with the conversation guided by a trained moderator using an unstructured method of inquiry.

foreign currency fluctuations Changes in the value of a country's currency relative to the currency of another country; can influence consumer spending.

franchisee See *franchising*.

franchising A contractual agreement between a *franchisor* and a *franchisee* that allows the franchisee to operate a business using a name and format developed and supported by the franchisor.

franchisor See *franchising*.

freemium app Apps that are free to download, but include in-app purchases (see also *in-app purchase*).

frequency Measure of how often the audience is exposed to a communication within a specified period of time.

fulfillment center Warehouse facilities used to ship merchandise directly to customers.

full-line discount stores Retailers that offer low prices, limited service, and a broad variety of merchandise.

functional needs Pertain to the performance of a product or service.

gatekeeper The buying center participant who controls information or access to decision makers and influencers.

Generation X (Gen X) Generational cohort of people born between 1965 and 1976.

Generation Y (Gen Y) Generational cohort of people born between 1977 and 2000; biggest cohort since the original postwar baby boom. Also called *Millennials*.

Generation Z (Gen Z) Generational cohort of people born between 2001 and 2014. Also known as *Digital Natives* because people in this group were born into a world that already was full of electronic gadgets and digital technologies, such as the Internet and social networks.

generational cohort A group of people of the same generation—typically have similar purchase behaviors because they have shared experiences and are in the same stage of life.

geodemographic segmentation The grouping of consumers on the basis of a combination of geographic, demographic, and lifestyle characteristics.

geographic segmentation The grouping of consumers on the basis of where they live.

globalization The processes by which goods, services, capital, people, information, and ideas flow across national borders.

glocalization The process of firms standardizing their products globally, but using different promotional campaigns to sell them.

goods Items that can be physically touched.

gray market Employs irregular but not necessarily illegal methods; generally, it legally circumvents authorized channels of distribution to sell goods at prices lower than those intended by the manufacturer.

green marketing A strategic effort by firms to supply customers with environmentally friendly merchandise.

greenwashing Exploiting consumers by disingenuously marketing products or services as environmentally friendly, with the goal of gaining public approval and sales.

gross domestic product (GDP) Defined as the market value of the goods and services produced by a country in a year; the most widely used standardized measure of output.

gross national income (GNI) Consists of GDP plus the net income earned from investments abroad (minus any payments made to nonresidents who contribute to the domestic economy).

gross rating points (GRP) Measure used for various media advertising—print, radio, or television; GRP = Reach × Frequency.

growth stage Stage of the product life cycle when the product gains acceptance, demand and sales increase, and competitors emerge in the product category.

habitual decision making A purchase decision process in which consumers engage with little conscious effort.

headline In an advertisement, large type designed to draw attention.

heterogeneity As it refers to the differences between the marketing of products and services, the delivery of services is more variable.

high/low pricing A *pricing strategy* that relies on the promotion of sales, during which prices are temporarily reduced to encourage purchases.

hit A request for a file made by web browsers and search engines. Hits are commonly misinterpreted as a metric for website success; however, the number of hits typically is much larger than the number of people visiting a website.

horizontal channel conflict A type of channel conflict in which members at the same level of a marketing channel, for example, two competing retailers or two competing manufacturers, are in disagreement or discord, such as when they are in a price war.

horizontal price fixing Occurs when competitors that produce and sell competing products collude, or work together, to control prices, effectively taking price out of the decision process for consumers.

ideal point The position at which a particular market segment's ideal product would lie on a *perceptual map*.

ideas Intellectual concepts—thoughts, opinions, and philosophies.

implementation phase The part of the strategic marketing planning process when marketing managers (1) identify and evaluate different opportunities by engaging in segmentation, targeting, and positioning (see also *segmentation, targeting, and positioning*) and (2) implement the marketing mix using the four Ps.

impressions The number of times an advertisement appears in front of the user.

improvement value Represents an estimate of how much more (or less) consumers are willing to pay for a product relative to other comparable products.

impulse buying A buying decision made by customers on the spot when they see the merchandise.

in-app purchase A purchase made on a freemium app that enables the user to enhance the app or game.

in-depth interview An exploratory research technique in which trained researchers ask questions, listen to and record the answers, and then pose additional questions to clarify or expand on a particular issue.

inbound marketing Marketing activities that draw the attention of customers through blogs, Twitter, LinkedIn, and other online sources, rather than using more traditional activities that require having to go out to get customers' attention, such as making a sales call.

income effect The change in the quantity of a product demanded by consumers due to a change in their income.

independent agents Salespeople who sell a manufacturer's products on an extended contract basis but are not employees of the manufacturer; also known as *manufacturer's representatives* or *reps*.

independent (conventional) marketing channel A marketing channel in which several independent members—a manufacturer, a wholesaler, and a retailer—each attempts to satisfy its own objectives and maximize its profits, often at the expense of the other members.

indirect marketing channel When one or more intermediaries work with manufacturers to provide goods and services to customers.

individual brands The use of individual brand names for each of a firm's products.

individualized pricing See *dynamic pricing*.

inelastic Refers to a market for a product or service that is price insensitive; that is, relatively small changes in price will not generate large changes in the quantity demanded.

inflation Refers to the persistent increase in the prices of goods and services.

influencer The buying center participant whose views influence other members of the buying center in making the final decision.

information Organized, analyzed, interpreted data that offer value to marketers.

information effect With regard to the Wheel of Social Media Engagement, the *information effect* is the outcome of social media in which relevant information is spread by firms or individuals to other members of its social network.

information power A type of marketing channel power within an administered vertical marketing system in which one party (e.g., the manufacturer) provides or withholds important information to influence the actions of another party (e.g., the retailer).

informational appeal Used in a promotion to help consumers make purchase decisions by offering factual information and strong arguments built around relevant issues that encourage them to evaluate the brand favorably on the basis of the key benefits it provides.

informative advertising Communication used to create and build brand awareness, with the ultimate goal of moving the consumer through the buying cycle to a purchase.

infrastructure The basic facilities, services, and installations needed for a community or society to function, such as transportation and communications systems, water and power lines, and public institutions like schools, post offices, and prisons.

initiator The buying center participant who first suggests buying the particular product or service.

innovation The process by which ideas are transformed into new products and services that will help firms grow.

innovators Those buyers, representing approximately 2.5 percent of the population, who want to be the first to have the new product or service.

inseparable A characteristic of a service: it is produced and consumed at the same time; that is, service and consumption are inseparable.

institutional advertisement A type of advertising that promotes a company, corporation, business, institution, or organization. Unlike product-focused advertisements, it is not intended to sell a particular product or service

instrumental support Providing the equipment or systems needed to perform a task in a job setting.

intangible A characteristic of a service; it cannot be touched, tasted, or seen like a pure product can.

integrated marketing communications (IMC) Represents the promotion dimension of the four Ps; encompasses a variety of communication disciplines—general advertising, personal selling, sales promotion, public relations, direct marketing, and electronic media—in combination to provide clarity, consistency, and maximum communicative impact.

intensive distribution A strategy designed to get products into as many outlets as possible.

interest rates The cost of borrowing money; the cost to the customer or the fee the bank charges those customers for borrowing the money.

internal locus of control Refers to when consumers believe they have some control over the outcomes of their actions, in which case they generally engage in more search activities.

internal search for information Occurs when the buyer examines his or her own memory and knowledge about the product or service, gathered through past experiences.

introduction stage Stage of the product life cycle when innovators start buying the product.

involvement Consumer's interest in a product or service.

joint venture Formed when a firm entering a new market pools its resources with those of a local firm to form a new company in which ownership, control, and profits are shared.

just-in-time (JIT) inventory system Inventory management system designed to deliver less merchandise on a more frequent basis than traditional inventory systems; the firm gets the merchandise "just in time" for it to be used in the manufacture of another product, in the case of parts or components, or for sale when the customer wants it, in the case of consumer goods; also known as *quick response (QR) inventory system* in retailing.

keyword analysis An evaluation of what keywords people use to search on the Internet for their products and services.

knowledge gap A type of *service gap;* reflects the difference between customers' *expectations* and the firm's perception of those expectations.

laggards Consumers, representing approximately 16 percent of the population, who like to avoid change and rely on traditional products until they are no longer available. Sometimes laggards never adopt a product or service.

lagged effect A delayed response to a marketing communication campaign.

late majority The last group of buyers to enter a new product market, representing approximately 34% of the population; when they do, the product has achieved its full market potential.

lead time The amount of time between the recognition that an order needs to be placed and the arrival of the needed merchandise at the seller's store, ready for sale.

lead users Innovative product users who modify existing products according to their own ideas to suit their specific needs.

leader pricing Consumer pricing tactic that attempts to build store traffic by aggressively pricing and advertising a regularly purchased item, often priced at or just above the store's cost.

leads A list of potential customers.

learning A person's thought process or behavior that arises from experience and takes place throughout the consumer decision process.

lease A written agreement under which the owner of an item or property allows its use for a specified period of time in exchange for a fee.

legitimate power A type of marketing channel power that occurs if the channel member exerting the power has a contractual agreement with the other channel member that requires the other channel member to behave in a certain way. This type of power occurs in an administered vertical marketing system.

licensing A method used in developing new products in which a firm buys the rights to use a technology or idea from another firm.

lifestyles The way a person lives his or her life to achieve goals.

lift Additional sales caused by advertising.

limited problem solving Occurs during a purchase decision that calls for, at most, a moderate amount of effort and time.

limited-assortment supermarkets Retailers that offer only one or two brands or sizes of most products (usually including a store brand) and attempt to achieve great efficiency to lower costs and prices. See also *extreme-value food retailer.*

line extension The use of the same brand name within the same product line and represents an increase in a product line's depth.

locational excellence A method of achieving excellence by having a strong physical location and/or Internet presence.

loss-leader pricing Loss leader pricing takes the tactic of *leader pricing* one step further by lowering the price below the store's cost.

love needs Part of Maslow's hierarchy, needs are expressed through interactions with others.

loyalty program Specifically designed to retain customers by offering premiums or other incentives to customers who make multiple purchases over time.

loyalty segmentation Strategy of investing in loyalty initiatives to retain the firm's most profitable customers.

macroenvironmental factors Aspects of the external environment that affect a company's business, such as the culture, demographics, social trends, technological advances, economic situation, and political/regulatory environment (CDSTEP).

manufacturer brands (national brands) Brands owned and managed by the manufacturer.

manufacturer's representatives (reps) See *independent agents.*

manufacturer's suggested retail price (MSRP) The price that manufacturers suggest retailers use to sell their merchandise.

markdowns Reductions retailers take on the initial selling price of the product or service.

market development strategy A growth strategy that employs the existing marketing offering to reach new market segments, whether domestic or international.

market growth rate The annual rate of growth of the specific market in which the product competes.

market positioning The process of defining the marketing mix variables so that target customers have a clear, distinctive, desirable understanding of what the product does or represents in comparison with competing products.

market segment A group of consumers who respond similarly to a firm's marketing efforts.

market segmentation The process of dividing the market into groups of customers with different needs, wants, or characteristics—who therefore might appreciate products or services geared especially for them.

market share Percentage of a market accounted for by a specific entity.

marketing An organizational function and a set of processes for creating, *capturing*, communicating, and delivering value to customers and for managing customer relationships in ways that benefit the organization and its stakeholders.

marketing channel The set of institutions that transfer the ownership of and move goods from the point of production to the point of consumption; consists of all the institutions and marketing activities in the marketing process.

marketing channel management Also called *supply chain management*, refers to a set of approaches and techniques firms employ to efficiently and effectively integrate their suppliers.

marketing ethics Refers to those ethical problems that are specific to the domain of marketing.

marketing mix (four Ps) Product, price, place, and promotion—the controllable set of activities that a firm uses to respond to the wants of its target markets.

marketing plan A written document composed of an analysis of the current marketing situation, opportunities and threats for the firm, marketing objectives and strategy specified in terms of the four Ps, action programs, and projected or pro forma income (and other financial) statements.

marketing research A set of techniques and principles for systematically collecting, recording, analyzing, and interpreting data that can aid decision makers involved in marketing goods, services, or ideas.

marketing strategy A firm's target market, marketing mix, and method of obtaining a sustainable competitive advantage.

Maslow's hierarchy of needs A paradigm for classifying people's motives. It argues that when lower-level, more basic needs (physiological and safety) are fulfilled, people turn to satisfying their higher-level human needs (social and personal); see also *physiological, safety, love,* and *personal needs*.

mass media Channels that are ideal for reaching large numbers of anonymous audience members; include national newspapers, magazines, radio, and television.

maturity stage Stage of the product life cycle when industry sales reach their peak, so firms try to rejuvenate their products by adding new features or repositioning them.

maximizing profits A profit strategy that relies primarily on economic theory. If a firm can accurately specify a mathematical model that captures all the factors required to explain and predict sales and profits, it should be able to identify the price at which its profits are maximized.

media buy The actual purchase of airtime or print pages.

media mix The combination of the media used and the frequency of advertising in each medium.

media planning The process of evaluating and selecting the *media mix* that will deliver a clear, consistent, compelling message to the intended audience.

metric A measuring system that quantifies a trend, dynamic, or characteristic.

microblog Differs from a traditional blog in size. Consists of short sentences, short videos, or individual images. Twitter is an example of a microblog.

micromarketing An extreme form of segmentation that tailors a product or service to suit an individual customer's wants or needs; also called *one-to-one marketing*.

Millennials See *Generation Y*.

mission statement A broad description of a firm's objectives and the scope of activities it plans to undertake; attempts to answer two main questions: What type of business is it? What does it need to do to accomplish its goals and objectives?

mobile commerce (M-commerce) Communicating with or selling to consumers through wireless handheld devices such as cellular phones.

mobile marketing Marketing through wireless handheld devices.

mobile task management Mobile task management technology is a wireless network and a mobile device that receives demand notification and enables a speedy response.

modified rebuy In a B2B setting, refers to when the buyer has purchased a similar product in the past but has decided to change some specifications, such as the desired price, quality level, customer service level, options, and so forth.

monopolistic competition Competition that occurs when there are many firms that sell closely related but not homogeneous products; these products may be viewed as substitutes but are not perfect substitutes.

monopoly One firm provides the product or service in a particular industry.

motive A need or want that is strong enough to cause the person to seek satisfaction.

multi-attribute model A compensatory model of customer decision making based on the notion that customers see a product as a collection of attributes or characteristics. The model uses a weighted average score based on the importance of various attributes and performance on those issues.

need recognition The beginning of the consumer decision process; occurs when consumers recognize they have an unsatisfied need and want to go from their actual, needy state to a different, desired state.

negative word of mouth Occurs when consumers spread negative information about a product, service, or store to others.

network effect With regard to the Wheel of Social Media Engagement, the *network effect* is the outcome of social media engagement in which every time a firm or person posts information, it is transferred to the poster's vast connections across social media, causing the information to spread instantaneously.

neuromarketing the process of examining consumers' brain patterns to determine their responses to marketing communications, products, or services for the purpose of developing marketing tactics or strategies

new buy In a B2B setting, a purchase of a good or service for the first time; the buying decision is likely to be quite involved because the buyer or the buying organization does not have any experience with the item.

niche media Channels that are focused and generally used to reach narrow segments, often with unique demographic characteristics or interests.

noise Any interference that stems from competing messages, a lack of clarity in the message, or a flaw in the medium; a problem for all communication channels.

noncompensatory decision rule At work when consumers choose a product or service on the basis of a subset of its characteristics, regardless of the values of its other attributes.

noncumulative quantity discount Pricing tactic that offers a discount based on only the amount purchased in a single order; provides the buyer with an incentive to purchase more merchandise immediately.

objective-and-task method An IMC budgeting method that determines the cost required to undertake specific tasks to accomplish communication objectives; process entails setting objectives, choosing media, and determining costs.

observation An exploratory research method that entails examining purchase and consumption behaviors through personal or video camera scrutiny.

occasion segmentation A type of behavioral segmentation based on when a product or service is purchased or consumed.

off-price retailer A type of retailer that offers an inconsistent assortment of merchandise at relatively low prices.

oligopolistic competition Competition that occurs when only a few firms dominate a market.

omnichannel (multichannel) strategy Selling in more than one channel (e.g., stores, Internet, catalog).

one-to-one marketing See *micromarketing*.

online chat Instant messaging or voice conversation with an online sales representative.

operational excellence Involves a firm's focus on efficient operations, excellent supply chain management, and strong relationships with its suppliers.

order getter A salesperson whose primary responsibilities are identifying potential customers and engaging those customers in discussions to attempt to make a sale.

order taker A salesperson whose primary responsibility is to process routine orders or reorders or rebuys for products.

organizational culture Reflects the set of values, traditions, and customs that guide a firm's employees' behavior.

outsourcing A practice in which the client firm hires an outside firm to facilitate some aspect of their business. In the context of new product development, the outsourced firm helps their client develop new products or services.

page view The number of times an Internet page gets viewed by any visitor.

paid app Apps that charge the customer an upfront price to download the app ($0.99 is the most common), but offer full functionality once downloaded.

paid apps with in-app purchase Apps that require the consumer to pay initially to download the app and then offer the ability to buy additional functionality.

panel data Information collected from a group of consumers.

partnering (strategic) relationship A supply chain relationship that the members are committed to maintaining long term, investing in opportunities that are mutually beneficial; requires mutual trust, open communication, common goals, and credible commitments. See *strategic relationships*.

penetration pricing strategy A new product or service pricing strategy in which the initial price is set relatively low with the objective of building sales, market share, and profits quickly and to deter competition from entering the market.

perceived value The relationship between a product's or service's benefits and its cost.

perception The process by which people select, organize, and interpret information to form a meaningful picture of the world.

perceptual map Displays, in two or more dimensions, the position of products or brands in the consumer's mind.

performance risk The perceived danger inherent in a poorly performing product or service.

perishability A characteristic of a service: it cannot be stored for use in the future.

personal blog Website written by a person who receives no products or remuneration for his or her efforts.

personal selling The two-way flow of communication between a buyer and a seller that is designed to influence the buyer's purchase decision.

persuasive advertising Communication used to motivate consumers to take action.

physiological needs Those relating to the basic biological necessities of life: food, drink, rest, and shelter. This is part of Maslow's hierarchy.

physiological risk The fear of an actual harm should a product not perform properly.

pick ticket A document or display on a screen in a forklift truck indicating how much of each item to get from specific storage areas.

pioneers New product introductions that establish a completely new market or radically change both the rules of competition and consumer preferences in a market; also called *breakthroughs*.

planner In a retailing context, an employee who is responsible for the financial planning and analysis of merchandise, and its allocation to stores.

planning phase The part of the strategic marketing planning process when marketing executives, in conjunction with other top managers (1) define the mission or vision of the business and (2) evaluate the situation by assessing how various players, both in and outside the organization, affect the firm's potential for success.

point-of-purchase (POP) display A merchandise display located at the point of purchase, such as at the checkout counter in a grocery store.

political/regulatory environment Comprises political parties, government organizations, and legislation and laws.

postpurchase cognitive dissonance The psychologically uncomfortable state produced by an inconsistency between beliefs and behaviors that in turn evokes a motivation to reduce the dissonance; buyers' remorse.

posttesting The evaluation of an IMC campaign's impact after it has been implemented.

power A situation that occurs in a marketing channel in which one member has the means or ability to have control over the actions of another member in a channel at a different level of distribution, such as if a retailer has power or control over a supplier.

preapproach In the personal selling process, occurs prior to meeting the customer for the first time and extends the qualification of leads procedure; in this step, the salesperson conducts additional research and develops plans for meeting with the customer.

predatory pricing A firm's practice of setting a very low price for one or more of its products with the intent to drive its competition out of business; illegal under both the Sherman Antitrust Act and the Federal Trade Commission Act.

predictive analytics The use of statistics on data to determine patterns and predict future outcomes and trends.

premarket test Conducted before a product or service is brought to market to determine how many customers will try and then continue to use it.

premium An item offered for free or at a bargain price to reward some type of behavior, such as buying, sampling, or testing.

premium pricing A competitor-based pricing method by which the firm deliberately prices a product above the prices set for competing products to capture those consumers who always shop for the best or for whom price does not matter.

prestige products or services Products and services that consumers purchase for status rather than functionality.

pretesting Assessments performed before an ad campaign is implemented to ensure that the various elements are working in an integrated fashion and doing what they are intended to do.

price The overall sacrifice a consumer is willing to make—money, time, energy—to acquire a specific product or service.

price bundling Consumer pricing tactic of selling more than one product for a single, lower price than what the items would cost sold separately; can be used to sell slow-moving items, to encourage customers to stock up so they won't purchase competing brands, to encourage trial of a new product, or to provide an incentive to purchase a less desirable product or service to obtain a more desirable one in the same bundle.

price discrimination The practice of selling the same product to different resellers (wholesalers, distributors, or retailers) or to the ultimate consumer at different prices; some, but not all, forms of price discrimination are illegal.

price elasticity of demand Measures how changes in a price affect the quantity of the product demanded; specifically, the ratio of the percentage change in quantity demanded to the percentage change in price.

price fixing The practice of colluding with other firms to control prices.

price lining Consumer market pricing tactic of establishing a price floor and a price ceiling for an entire line of similar products and then setting a few other price points in between to represent distinct differences in quality.

price skimming A strategy of selling a new product or service at a high price that *innovators* and *early adopters* are willing to pay in order to obtain it; after the high-price market segment becomes saturated and sales begin to slow down, the firm generally lowers the price to capture (or skim) the next most price-sensitive segment.

price war A situation [or competition] that occurs when two or more firms compete primarily by lowering their prices.

pricing strategy A long-term approach to setting prices for the firms' products.

pricing tactics Short-term methods, in contrast to long-term *pricing strategies*, used to focus on company objectives, costs, customers, competition, or channel members; can be responses to competitive threats (e.g., lowering price temporarily to meet a competitor's price reduction) or broadly accepted methods of calculating a final price for the customer that is short term in nature.

primary data Data collected to address specific research needs.

primary package The packaging the consumer uses, such as the toothpaste tube, from which he or she typically seeks convenience in terms of storage, use, and consumption.

private-label brands Brands developed and marketed by a retailer and available only from that retailer; also called *store brands*.

procedural fairness Refers to the customer's perception of the fairness of the process used to resolve complaints about service.

product Anything that is of value to a consumer and can be offered through a voluntary marketing exchange.

product design See *product development*.

product development Also called *product design;* entails a process of balancing various engineering, manufacturing, marketing, and economic considerations to develop a product's form and features or a service's features.

product development strategy A growth strategy that offers a new product or service to a firm's current target market.

product excellence Involves a focus on achieving high-quality products; effective branding and positioning is key.

product life cycle Defines the stages that new products move through as they enter, get established in, and ultimately leave the marketplace and thereby offers marketers a starting point for their strategy planning.

product lines Groups of associated items, such as those that consumers use together or think of as part of a group of similar products.

product mix The complete set of all products offered by a firm.

product placement Inclusion of a product in nontraditional situations, such as in a scene in a movie or television program.

product-focused advertisements Advertisements used to inform, persuade, or remind consumers about a specific product or service.

professional blog Website written by a person who reviews and gives recommendations on products and services.

profit orientation A company objective that can be implemented by focusing on *target profit pricing, maximizing profits,* or *target return pricing.*

prototype The first physical form or service description of a new product, still in rough or tentative form, that has the same properties as a new product but is produced through different manufacturing processes, sometimes even crafted individually.

psychographic segmentation A method of segmenting customers based on how they spend their time and money, what activities they pursue, and their attitudes and opinions about the world in which they live.

psychographics Used in segmentation; delves into how consumers describe themselves; allows people to describe themselves using those characteristics that help them choose how they occupy their time (behavior) and what underlying psychological reasons determine those choices.

psychological needs Pertain to the personal gratification consumers associate with a product or service.

psychological risk Associated with the way people will feel if the product or service does not convey the right image.

public relations (PR) The organizational function that manages the firm's communications to achieve a variety of objectives, including building and maintaining a positive image, handling or heading off unfavorable stories or events, and maintaining positive relationships with the media.

public service advertising (PSA) Advertising that focuses on public welfare and generally is sponsored by nonprofit institutions, civic groups, religious organizations, trade associations, or political groups; a form of *social marketing*.

puffery The legal exaggeration of praise, stopping just short of deception, lavished on a product.

pull strategy A strategy in which the goal is to get consumers to pull the product through the marketing channel by demanding it.

pulsing (advertising schedule) An advertising schedule that combines the continuous and flighting schedules by maintaining a base level of advertising but increasing advertising intensity during certain periods.

purchasing power parity (PPP) A theory that states that if the exchange rates of two countries are in equilibrium, a product purchased in one will cost the same in the other, expressed in the same currency.

pure competition Competition that occurs when different companies sell commodity products that consumers perceive as substitutable; price usually is set according to the laws of supply and demand.

push strategy A strategy designed to increase demand by motivating sellers—wholesalers, distributors, or salespeople—to highlight the product, rather than the products of competitors, and thereby push the product onto consumers.

qualify The process of assessing the potential of sales leads.

qualitative research Informal research methods, including observation, following social media sites, in-depth interviews, focus groups, and projective techniques.

quantitative research Structured responses that can be statistically tested to confirm insights and hypotheses generated via qualitative research or secondary data.

quantity discount Pricing tactic of offering a reduced price according to the amount purchased; the more the buyer purchases, the higher the discount and, of course, the greater the value.

questionnaire A form that features a set of questions designed to gather information from respondents and thereby accomplish the researchers' objectives; questions can be either unstructured or structured.

quick response (QR) inventory system An inventory management system used in retailing; merchandise is received just in time for sale when the customer wants it; see also *just-in-time (JIT) inventory system*.

quota Designates the maximum quantity of a product that may be brought into a country during a specified time period.

R&D consortia A group of firms and institutions, possibly including government and educational institutions, that explore new ideas or obtain solutions for developing new products.

radio frequency identification (RFID) tag Tiny computer chip that automatically transmits to a special scanner all the information about a container's contents or individual products.

reach Measure of consumers' exposure to marketing communications; the percentage of the target population exposed to a specific marketing communication, such as an advertisement, at least once.

rebate A consumer discount in which a portion of the purchase price is returned to the buyer in cash; the manufacturer, not the retailer, issues the refund.

receiver The person who reads, hears, or sees and processes the information contained in the message or advertisement.

receiving The process of recording the receipt of merchandise as it arrives at a distribution center or store.

reference group One or more persons whom an individual uses as a basis for comparison regarding beliefs, feelings, and behaviors.

reference price The price against which buyers compare the actual selling price of the product and that facilitates their evaluation process.

referent power A type of marketing channel power that occurs if one channel member wants to be associated with another channel member. The channel member with whom the others wish to be associated has the power and can get them to do what they want.

regional culture Similar to culture in general, but at a regional level. The influence of the area within a country in which people live.

related diversification A growth strategy whereby the current target market and/or marketing mix shares something in common with the new opportunity.

relational orientation A method of building a relationship with customers based on the philosophy that buyers and sellers should develop a long-term relationship.

relationship selling A sales philosophy and process that emphasizes a commitment to maintaining the relationship over the long term and investing in opportunities that are mutually beneficial to all parties.

relative market share A measure of the product's strength in a particular market, defined as the sales of the focal product divided by the sales achieved by the largest firm in the industry.

relevance In the context of search engine marketing (SEM), it is a metric used to determine how useful an advertisement is to the consumer.

reminder advertising Communication used to remind consumers of a product or to prompt repurchases, especially for products that have gained market acceptance and are in the maturity stage of their life cycle.

request for proposals (RFP) A process through which buying organizations invite alternative suppliers to bid on supplying their required components.

reseller Marketing intermediary that resells manufactured products without significantly altering their form.

retailer/store brands Products developed by retailers. Also called *private-label brands*.

retailers' cooperative A marketing channel intermediary that buys collectively for a group of retailers to achieve price and promotion economies of scale. It is similar to a wholesaler, except that the retailer members have some control over, and sometimes ownership of, the cooperative's operations.

retailing The set of business activities that add value to products and services sold to consumers for their personal or family use; includes products bought at stores, through catalogs, and over the Internet, as well as services like fast-food restaurants, airlines, and hotels.

retrieval set Those brands or stores that the consumer can readily bring forth from memory.

return on marketing investment (ROMI) The amount of profit divided by the value of the investment. In the case of an advertisement, the ROI is (Sales revenue generated by ad − Ad's cost) ÷ Ad's cost.

reverse engineering Taking apart a competitor's product, analyzing it, and creating an improved product that does not infringe on the competitor's patents, if any exist.

reverse innovation When companies initially develop products for niche or underdeveloped markets, and then expand them into their original or home markets.

reward power A type of marketing channel power that occurs when the channel member exerting the power offers rewards to gain power, often a monetary incentive, for getting another channel member to do what it wants it to do.

role playing A good technique for practicing the sales presentation prior to meeting with a customer; the salesperson acts out a simulated buying situation while a colleague or manager acts as the buyer.

rule-of-thumb methods Budgeting methods that base the IMC budget on either the firm's share of the market in relation to competition, a fixed percentage of forecasted sales, or what is left after other operating costs and forecasted sales have been budgeted.

safety needs One of the needs in Maslow's hierarchy of needs; pertain to protection and physical well-being.

safety risk See *physiological risk*.

salary Compensation in the form of a fixed sum of money paid at regular intervals.

sales contest A short-term incentive designed to elicit a specific response from the sales force.

sales management The planning, direction, and control of personal selling activities, including recruiting, selecting, training, motivating, compensating, and evaluating, as they apply to the sales force.

sales orientation A company objective based on the belief that increasing sales will help the firm more than will increasing profits.

sales promotions Special incentives or excitement-building programs that encourage the purchase of a product or service, such as coupons, rebates, contests, free samples, and point-of-purchase displays.

sales support personnel Employees who enhance and help with a firm's overall selling effort, such as by responding to the customer's technical questions or facilitating repairs.

sample A group of customers who represent the customers of interest in a research study.

sampling Offers potential customers the opportunity to try a product or service before they make a buying decision.

scanner data A type of syndicated external secondary data used in quantitative research that is obtained from scanner readings of UPC codes at check-out counters.

search engine marketing (SEM) A type of web advertising whereby companies pay for keywords that are used to catch consumers' attention while browsing a search engine.

seasonal discount Seasonal discounts that are offered to consumers are price reductions offered on products and services to stimulate demand during off-peak seasons; whereas a seasonal discount in B2B settings is a pricing tactic that offers an additional reduction as an incentive to retailers to order merchandise in advance of the normal buying season.

secondary data Pieces of information that have already been collected from other sources and usually are readily available.

secondary package The wrapper or exterior carton that contains the primary package and provides the UPC label used by retail scanners; can contain additional product information that may not be available on the primary package.

segmentation, targeting, and positioning (STP) Firms use these processes to identify and evaluate opportunities for increasing sales and profits.

selective distribution Lies between the intensive and exclusive distribution strategies; uses a few selected customers in a territory.

self-actualization When a person is completely satisfied with his or her life.

self-concept The image a person has of himself or herself; a component of *psychographics*.

self-values Goals for life, not just the goals one wants to accomplish in a day; a component of *psychographics* that refers to overriding desires that drive how a person lives his or her life.

selling teams Combinations of sales specialists whose primary duties are order getting, order taking, or sales support but who work together to service important accounts.

sender The firm from which an IMC message originates; the sender must be clearly identified to the intended audience.

sentiment analysis A technique that allows marketers to analyze data from social media sites to collect consumer comments about companies and their products.

sentiment mining Data gathered by evaluating customer comments posted through social media sites such as Facebook and Twitter.

service Any intangible offering that involves a deed, performance, or effort that cannot be physically possessed; intangible customer benefits that are produced by people or machines and cannot be separated from the producer.

service gap Results when a service fails to meet the expectations that customers have about how it should be delivered.

Service Gaps Model A managerial tool designed to encourage the systematic examination of all aspects of the service delivery process and prescribes the steps needed to develop an optimal service strategy.

service quality Customers' perceptions of how well a service meets or exceeds their expectations.

service retailer A firm that primarily sells services rather than merchandise.

share of wallet The percentage of the customer's purchases made from a particular retailer.

shopping products/services Those for which consumers will spend time comparing alternatives, such as apparel, fragrances, and appliances.

showrooming Customers visit a store to touch, feel, and even discuss a product's features with a sales associate, and then purchase it online from another retailer at a lower price.

situation analysis Second step in a marketing plan; uses a SWOT analysis that assesses both the internal environment with regard to its **S**trengths and **W**eaknesses and the external environment in terms of its **O**pportunities and **T**hreats.

situational factors Factors affecting the consumer decision process; those that are specific to the situation that may override, or at least influence, psychological and social issues.

size discount The most common implementation of a quantity discount at the consumer level; the larger the quantity bought, the less the cost per unit (e.g., per ounce).

slotting allowances Fees firms pay to retailers simply to get new products into stores or to gain more or better shelf space for their products.

social marketing The content distributed through online and mobile technologies to facilitate interpersonal interactions.

social media The online and mobile technologies that distribute content to facilitate interpersonal interactions.

social risk The fears that consumers suffer when they worry others might not regard their purchases positively.

social shopping Using the Internet to communicate about product preferences with other shoppers.

specialty products/services Products or services toward which the customer shows a strong preference and for which he or she will expend considerable effort to search for the best suppliers.

specialty store A type of retailer that concentrates on a limited number of complementary merchandise categories in a relatively small store.

stakeholders The broad set of people who might be affected by a firm's actions, including not just corporate shareholders and customers but also employees (past, current, and prospective) and their families, supply chain partners, government agencies, the physical environment, and members of the communities in which the firm operates (defined either locally or on a global scale).

standards gap A type of *service gap;* pertains to the difference between the firm's perceptions of customers' expectations and the service standards it sets.

status quo pricing A competitor-oriented strategy in which a firm changes prices only to meet those of competition.

store brand Brands developed and marketed by a retailer and available only from that retailer; also called *private-label brands*.

straight rebuy In a B2B setting, refers to when the buyer or buying organization simply buys additional units of products that have previously been purchased.

strategic alliance A collaborative relationship between independent firms, though the partnering firms do not create an equity partnership; that is, they do not invest in one another.

strategic business unit (SBU) A division of the firm itself that can be managed and operated somewhat independently from other divisions and may have a different mission or objectives.

strategic (partnering) relationship A supply chain relationship that the members are committed to maintaining long term, investing in opportunities that are mutually beneficial; requires mutual trust, open communication, common goals, and credible commitments. Also called *partnering relationship*.

structured questions Closed-ended questions for which a discrete set of response alternatives, or specific answers, is provided for respondents to evaluate.

subhead An additional smaller headline in an ad that provides a great deal of information through the use of short and simple words.

substitute products Products for which changes in demand are negatively related; that is, a percentage increase in the quantity demanded for product A results in a percentage decrease in the quantity demanded for product B.

substitution effect Consumers' ability to substitute other products for the focal brand, thus increasing the price elasticity of demand for the focal brand.

supercenter Large stores combining full-line discount stores with supermarkets in one place.

supply chain The group of firms that make and deliver a given set of goods and services.

supply chain management A set of approaches and techniques firms employ to efficiently and effectively integrate their suppliers, manufacturers, warehouses, stores, and transportation intermediaries into a seamless value chain in which merchandise is produced and distributed in the right quantities, to the right locations, and at the right time, as well as to minimize system-wide costs while satisfying the service levels their customers require. Also called *marketing channel management*.

survey A systematic means of collecting information from people that generally uses a *questionnaire*.

sustainable competitive advantage Something the firm can persistently do better than its competitors.

sustainable packaging Product packaging that has less of a negative impact on the environment.

sweepstakes A form of sales promotion that offers prizes based on a chance drawing of entrants' names.

SWOT analysis A method of conducting a situation analysis within a marketing plan in which both the internal environment with regard to its **S**trengths and **W**eaknesses and the external environment in terms of its **O**pportunities and **T**hreats are examined.

syndicated data Data available for a fee from commercial research firms such as Information Resources Inc. (IRI), National Purchase Diary Panel, and Nielsen.

target marketing or targeting The process of evaluating the attractiveness of various segments and then deciding which to pursue as a market.

target profit pricing A pricing strategy implemented by firms when they have a particular profit goal as their overriding concern; uses price to stimulate a certain level of sales at a certain profit per unit.

target return pricing A pricing strategy implemented by firms less concerned with the absolute level of profits and more interested in the rate at which their profits are generated relative to their investments; designed to produce a specific return on investment, usually expressed as a percentage of sales.

tariff A tax levied on a good imported into a country; also called a *duty*.

technological advances Macroenvironmental factor that has greatly contributed to the improvement of the value of both products and services in the past few decades.

telemarketing A method of prospecting in which salespeople telephone potential customers.

test marketing A method of determining the success potential of a new product; it introduces the offering to a limited geographical area prior to a national launch.

ticketing and marking Creating price and identification labels and placing them on the merchandise.

timeliness effect With regard to the Wheel of Social Media Engagement, the *timeliness effect* of social media engagement is concerned with the firm being able to engage with the customer at the right place/time—their ability to do so 24/7 from any location.

top-of-mind awareness A prominent place in people's memories that triggers a response without them having to put any thought into it.

total cost The sum of the *variable* and *fixed costs*.

tracking Assessments that monitor key indicators, such as daily or weekly sales volume, while the advertisement is running to shed light on any problems with the message or the medium.

trade agreement Intergovernmental agreement designed to manage and promote trade activities for specific regions.

trade deficit Results when a country imports more goods than it exports.

trade shows Major events attended by buyers who choose to be exposed to products and services offered by potential suppliers in an industry.

trade surplus Occurs when a country has a higher level of exports than imports.

trading bloc Consists of those countries that have signed a particular trade agreement.

transmitter An agent or intermediary with which the sender works to develop the marketing communications; for example, a firm's creative department or an advertising agency.

triple bottom line A means to measure performance according to economic, environmental, and societal criteria.

undifferentiated targeting strategy (mass marketing) A marketing strategy a firm can use if the product or service is perceived to provide the same benefits to everyone, with no need to develop separate strategies for different groups.

uniform delivered pricing The shipper charges one rate, no matter where the buyer is located.

unique selling proposition (USP) A strategy of differentiating a product by communicating its unique attributes; often becomes the common theme or slogan in the entire advertising campaign.

Universal Product Code (UPC) The black-and-white bar code found on most merchandise. It contains a 13-digit code that indicates the manufacturer of the item, a description of the item, information about special packaging, and special promotions.

universal set All possible choices for a product category.

unrelated diversification A growth strategy whereby a new business lacks any common elements with the present business.

unsought products/services Products or services consumers either do not normally think of buying or do not know about.

unstructured questions Open-ended questions that allow respondents to answer in their own words.

user The person who consumes or uses the product or service purchased by the buying center.

value Reflects the relationship of benefits to costs, or what the consumer *gets* for what he or she *gives*.

Value and Lifestyle Survey (VALS) A psychographic tool developed by SRI Consulting Business Intelligence; classifies consumers into eight segments: innovators, thinkers, believers, achievers, strivers, experiencers, makers, or survivors.

value cocreation Customers act as collaborators with a manufacturer or retailer to create the product or service.

value proposition The unique value that a product or service provides to its customers and how it is better than and different from those of competitors.

value-based pricing method An approach that focuses on the overall value of the product offering as perceived by consumers, who determine value by comparing the benefits they expect the product to deliver with the sacrifice they will need to make to acquire the product.

variable costs Those costs, primarily labor and materials, that vary with production volume.

vendor-managed inventory (VMI) An approach for improving supply chain efficiency in which the manufacturer is responsible for maintaining the retailer's inventory levels in each of its stores.

vertical channel conflict A type of channel conflict in which members of the same marketing channel, for example, manufacturers, wholesalers, and retailers, are in disagreement or discord.

vertical marketing system A supply chain in which the members act as a unified system; there are three types: *administered, contractual,* and *corporate.*

vertical price fixing Occurs when parties at different levels of the same marketing channel (e.g., manufacturers and retailers) collude to control the prices passed on to consumers.

viral marketing program A promotional strategy that encourages people to pass along a marketing message to other potential consumers.

virtual community Online networks of people who communicate about specific topics.

voice-of-customer (VOC) program An ongoing marketing research system that collects customer inputs and integrates them into managerial decisions.

warehouse clubs Large retailers with an irregular assortment, low service levels, and low prices that often require membership for shoppers.

web portal An Internet site whose purpose is to be a major starting point for users when they connect to the web.

web-tracking software Software used to assess how much time viewers spend on particular web pages and the number of pages they view.

white papers In a B2B context, white papers are a promotional technique used by B2B sellers to provide information about a product or service in an educational context, thereby not appearing like a promotion or propaganda.

wholesaler Firm engaged in buying, taking title to, often storing, and physically handling goods in large quantities, then reselling the goods (usually in smaller quantities) to retailers or industrial or business users.

zone of tolerance The area between customers' expectations regarding their desired service and the minimum level of acceptable service—that is, the difference between what the customer really wants and what he or she will accept before going elsewhere.

zone pricing The shipper sets different prices depending on a geographic division of the delivery areas.

Chapter 1

1. Which of the following illustrates marketing's direct impact on consumers?

   Answer: (d) Marketing helps consumers learn about new products and services.

2. The _____ consists of the product, price, place, and promotion of an offering.

   Answer: (b) marketing mix

Chapter 2

1. After a firm has conducted a SWOT analysis, it would typically progress to the next step of marketing planning, which is _____ and involves using STP (segmentation, targeting, and positioning).

   Answer: (c) identifying and evaluating opportunities

2. Which of the following is a marketing metric that might be used to evaluate the performance of a company's implementation of its marketing plan?

   Answer: (d) GM (gross margin)

Chapter 3

1. Through its Facebook page, a major restaurant chain is offering its customers a Groupon coupon for 50 percent off the purchase of a meal. In doing so, the restaurant is focusing on which aspect of the 4E framework?

   Answer: (e) exciting

2. To get customers excited about a social media–related offer, the offer must be:

   Answer: (c) relevant and aimed at a target audience.

Chapter 4

1. As noted in your text, which of the following ranks as the top unethical behavior by employees as reported by chief marketing officers?

   Answer: (c) Participating in misleading or deceptive sales tactics.

2. A firm makes generous donations to charities, but its employees are always being scrutinized for engaging in questionable sales practices. This firm would be considered:

   Answer: (c) unethical but socially responsible.

Chapter 5

1. ABC Company knew that its customers were interested in environmentally friendly business practices, so it began marking all of its products as environmentally friendly because they were made with all-natural ingredients, even though ABC's plant was one of the worst polluters in town. The new term for this practice is

   Answer: (b) greenwashing.

2. One of the goals of value-based marketing is

   Answer: (c) to offer greater value than competitors offer.

Chapter 6

1. The salient or important attributes about a particular product that consumers use to make product evaluations are called

   Answer: (c) evaluative criteria

2. Because not all purchase intentions result in an actual purchase, marketers calculate the _____ to measure how

effectively a decision to purchase a specific product results in a completed purchase.

Answer: (e) conversion rate

Chapter 7

1. Which of the following statements regarding the B2B buying process is true?

   Answer: (e) In the B2B buying process, the search for information and evaluation of alternatives is more formal and structured.

2. In a _____ situation, the buying center is likely to proceed through all six steps in the buying process and involve many people in the buying decision.

   Answer: (d) new buy

Chapter 8

1. The shift of population from rural to urban areas in countries such as India helps global marketers by:

   Answer: (b) simplifying the supply chain needed to make goods and services available.

2. Why should marketers be aware of the BRIC countries?

   Answer: (c) They are likely to be the source of most market growth.

Chapter 9

1. For the _____ criteria to be met when evaluating segment attractiveness, the consumer must know the product or service exists, understand what it can do for him or her, and recognize how to buy it.

   Answer: (c) reachable

2. Which step in the STP process develops descriptions of the different segments, which helps firms better understand the customer profiles in each segment?

   Answer: (b) Select segmentation method

Chapter 10

1. Which of the following is not a disadvantage of using secondary research data?

   Answer: (b) The process is costly and time-consuming.

2. The key difference between scanner and panel research is that scanner research typically focuses on a particular _____, while panel research typically focuses on a particular _____.

   Answer: (a) product; person or household

Chapter 11

1. As the size of retail firms has increased through growth and consolidation, more retailers have developed _____ merchandise, which they use to establish a distinctive identity.

   Answer: (c) private-label

2. Brand equity is determined by four aspects of a brand. Which of the following is not one of the four aspects?

   Answer: (d) brand quality

Chapter 12

1. In the United States, most consumer packaged goods found in grocery and discount stores are already in the _____ stage, which is characterized by the adoption of the product by the late majority and intense competition for market share among firms.

   Answer: (c) maturity

2. Although they enjoy novelty and are considered to be opinion leaders, _____ are not the first to purchase new product innovations.

Answer: (c) early adopters

Chapter 13

1. Which of the following represents the most fundamental difference between a product and a service?

Answer: (b) tangibility

2. The Gaps Model is designed as a diagnostic tool to highlight specific areas where

Answer: (c) marketers are falling short in their service delivery.

Chapter 14

1. A _____ orientation explicitly invokes the concept of value such as when a firm uses a "no-haggle" pricing structure to make the purchase process simpler and easier.

Answer: (d) customer

2. The most common form of competition is _____, where many firms compete for customers in a given market but with differentiated products.

Answer: (e) monopolistic competition

Chapter 15

1. A(n) _____ strategy is attractive because it attracts two distinct market segments: customers who are not price-sensitive customers and customers who are price sensitive.

Answer: (b) high/low pricing

2. When using a market penetration strategy, as sales continue to grow, the costs continue to drop, allowing even further reductions in the price. This is due to

Answer: (e) experience curve effects.

Chapter 16

1. All of the following are examples of the value provided by a supply chain in the production of kitchen stoves except

Answer: (c) the product design team develops initial drawings for a new product offering.

2. When supply chain members that buy and sell to one another are not in agreement about their goals, _____ channel conflict can occur.

Answer: (a) vertical

Chapter 17

1. _____ reduce costs and maintain low prices by buying opportunistically from manufacturers with excess inventory, offering limited assortments of household goods and groceries, as well as health and beauty aids.

Answer: (d) Extreme value retailers

2. Jordan directs her salespeople to increase the company's share of wallet. Jordan is directing her salespeople to

Answer: (a) focus on increasing sales to their best customers.

Chapter 18

1. Home Depot hired an advertising agency to develop television ads for its grand opening in southern Maine. The advertising agency represents which of the following components of the communication process?

Answer: (b) transmitter

2. Which of the following formulas is accurate for calculating gross rating points (GRP)?

Answer: (c) Reach multiplied by frequency

Chapter 19

1. Firms often use _____ advertising to convince consumers to take action such as switching brands, trying a new product, or even continuing to buy the advertised product.

Answer: (d) persuasive

2. _____ is a tool used to communicate the distinct attributes of a product; it can be used as a slogan or a theme and often becomes a snapshot of the entire advertising campaign.

Answer: (b) A unique selling proposition

Chapter 20

1. One of the advantages of personal selling over other types of marketing communication is that

Answer: (a) salespeople can build strong relationships with customers.

2. All of the following are service quality dimensions related to follow-up *except*

Answer: (a) ethics

name index

Fleck, Nathalie, 367n43
Fleishman, Hannah, 263n65
Flint, Joe, 575nii
Florida, Rana, 140n24
Fok, Dennis, 401n20
Ford, Henry, 12
Fowler, Floyd J., 330n30
Fowler, Geoffrey, 403nii
French, Alan, 403ni
Friday, Mim, 44n
Friedman, Andrew, 394
Friedman, Milton, 140n15
Fritz, Ben, 403ni
Frohlich, Thomas C., 140n19
Frost, Lerinda L., 403niii
Frost, Peter, 403nv, 605n2
Fu, Guoqun, 367n36
Fuhrmans, Vanessa, 299n29
Fujita, Akihisa, 575n19
Fukada, Shiho, 257n
Fuller, Bonnie, 171ni
Fulton, Scott M. III, 171niv
Fung, Brian, 171n42

G

Gagliardi, Nancy, 170n1
Galbraith, Dan, 171n33
Galinsky, Adam D., 206n14
Gallay, Charley, 3n
Gallo, Carmine, 57n12, 206n43
Gallo, Phil, 575n12
Gallup, Sean, 34n
Gandhi, Mahatma, 135
Ganesh, Jaishankar, 299n17
Gannam, Tom, 384n
Garrett, Daniel M., 483n18, 483n21
Garrett, Jason, 517n22
Gasparro, Annie, 263n60, 367nv
Gates, Bill, 386
Gauri, Dinesh K., 482n3
Geller, Martinne, 263n48
George, M., 334n52
Germain, Richard, 517n23
Germano, Sarah, 112n1, 112n2, 575niv
Gessinger, Gernot H., 402n47
Giamatti, Paul, 552n
Gianastasio, David, 564n, 606niii
Gibs, Samuel, 232n10
Gilbert, David, 401n3
Gilly, Mary C., 262n19, 263n46
Gilson, Dave, 170n20
Gingerich, Mike, 113n34
Gioglio, Jessica, 575n32
Giriprakash, K., 263niii
Goel, Vindu, 483niii

Gold, Jon, 403n59
Goldblum, Jeff, 557
Goldenberg, Jacob, 402n26
Golder, Peter, 403n65
Golicic, Susan, 517n23
Gomez, Selena, 556, 579, 580
Goode, Lauren, 233ni
Goodman, J. David, 634n18
Goodney, Chris, 544n
Goodstein, Ronald, 299n22
Gosling, Samuel D., 299n15
Gottfried, Miriam, 27niv, 606ni
Goukens, Caroline, 206n19
Goulding, Matt, 263n67
Graham, John L., 170n8, 262n19, 263n46
Graham, Luke, 27n39
Greco, Susan, 634n28
Greeley, Brendan, 171n41, 605n10
Greenberg, Jeff, 317n, 465n, 472n
Greenberg, Karl, 564n
Greene, M. V., 429n24
Greenfield, Jerry, 21
Greenfield, Richard, 457n20
Greengard, Samuel, 115nv
Greenley, Gordon E., 263n52
Greenough, John, 171nv
Greenspan, Nick, 206n44
Grégoire, Yany, 429n27
Gregory, Paul, 262n36
Greifeneder, Rainer, 206n15
Gremler, Dwayne D., 57n10, 428n2, 429n6, 429n13
Gress, John, 19n
Gretler, Corinne, 27n45
Grewal, Dhruv, 26n21, 65n1, 113n20, 113n22, 206n31, 207n52, 330n29, 429n10, 429n26, 429n28, 456n5, 456n7, 457n19, 457n22, 482n3, 483n4, 483n9, 517n6, 517n7, 517n22, 545n3, 546n31, 575n21, 634n39
Griffin, Mitch, 205n5
Griffith, David A., 517n18
Grönroos, Christian, 429n26
Gross, Rachel, 207niii
Grossman, John, 367n44
Guarini, Drew, 457n20
Gundlach, Gregory T., 26n10, 57n13
Gupta, S., 335n52, 335n54
Guthrie, Amy, 517nv

H

Hacker, Lee, 506n
Hackett, Robert, 232n31
Hackmann, Britt, 65n1

Hagerty, James M., 299n11
Hahn, Alexander, 546n34
Haldermann, Alexander, 605n14
Hale, Lucy, 267, 557
Hale, Todd, 206n33
Hall, Emma, 575n31
Halscheid, Megan, 575n22
Halzack, Sarah, 299nii, 545n16, 545n18
Hamilton, R., 482n3
Hamilton, Rebecca W., 483n11
Hamilton, Ryan, 206n44
Hanssens, D., 335n52
Hao, Cui, 459n
Hardie, B., 335n52
Harding, Ian, 267
Hardt, Oliver, 212n
Hardy, J., 243n
Hardy, Quentin, 330n19
Hargrave, Marshall, 232n5
Harker, Debra, 605n31
Harker, Michael, 605n31
Harmon, Amy, 140n23
Harper, Bryce, 346, 347
Harrington, Blaine III, 437n
Harris, Derrick, 171niv
Harris, Elizabeth A., 140n35, 206n36, 483nii
Harris, Melissa, 331n47, 331n48, 403nv
Hartley, Steven W., 58n39, 65n3
Harvey, Quentin, 232ni, 633n2
Harvey, Steve, 159
Hastings, Reed, 21, 235
Hauser, John R., 402n35
Hawkins, Del I., 170n8
Haws, Kelly L., 330n10
Hay, Timothy, 401n12
Heath, Alex, 26n30
Heath, Robert G., 605n7, 605n25
Heerde, Harald J. van, 402n21
Heinze, Timothy, 634n38
Heisler, Toss, 470n
Heitjans, Torsten, 366n28
Henderson, Kirk, 207n47
Henderson, Mike, 146
Hendrix, Jimi, 441
Hennig-Thurau, Thorsen, 366n28
Henry, Thierry, 112
Herrmann, Andreas, 403n65
Herzog, Walter, 429n19
Hider, Ben, 609n
Highsmith, Jim, 402n38
Hill, Jonah, 434
Hill, Ronald Paul, 206n26
Hippel, Eric von, 402n38

Hoeffler, Steven, 402n42
Hofstede, Geert, 244, 245n, 262n23
Hofstede, Geert Jan, 245n
Hogan, John E., 482n2
Hogg, Erin, 232n23
Hogsholt, David, 476n
Hollister, Sean, 403n73
Holtzman, David H., 634n35
Homburg, Christian, 546n34
Homer, Pamela Mills, 606n42
Hong, Jae C., 122n
Horree, Peter, 535n
Hoshino, Kimihiro, 379n
Hotten, Russell, 59niv
Houson, Mark B., 366n28
Howell, Vandy, 483n18, 483n21
Hruby, Michael J., 184e, 184n, 289n, 305n, 317n, 355n, 373n, 437n, 469n
Hsu, Tiffany, 367niii
Huang, Rong, 366n18
Huba, Jackie, 606n37
Huber, Lynn, 634n27
Hughes, Robert, 464n
Humphrey, Mark, 531n
Hunt, Bob, 606n33, 606n34
Hussain, Sajjad, 252n
Hwang, Bang-Ning, 456n7

I

Iannarino, S. Anthony, 634n13
Iezzi, Teressa, 59n54, 59n58
Inman, J. Jeffrey, 207n51
Ip, Melissa, 262n10
Irwin, Julie R., 206n18
Isakson, Erik, 17n, 449n
Isidore, Chris, 483n32, 483n33, 483n38, 483n40
Iyer, Karthik, 517n23
Izquierdo, Ignacio, 91n

J

Jackson, Candace, 634nv
Jacobsohn, Jed, 293n
Jacobson, Robert, 366n18
Jaekel, Brielle, 561n
Jae-Won, Lee, 15n
Jaffe, Joseph, 299n16
James, Geoffrey, 633n8
James, Ken, 408n
James, LeBron, 82, 566n
Janiszewski, Chris, 207n49
Janofsky, Adam, 517n17
Jansen, Myra, 134–135, 136
Jarboe, Greg, 605n1
Jargon, Julie, 171n28, 263n48, 263n62, 483n37
Jayson, Sharon, 170n17

company index

subject index

TV viewership, 311
Twitter music marketing, 108
2-in-1 iPotty, 139

U

Uncertainty avoidance, 244
Underwear advertising, 300–302
Undifferentiated targeting strategies, 283
Unethical behavior. *See* Ethics; Marketing ethics
Unethical decision making, 130–131
Uniform delivered pricing, 470e, 471
Uniforms, 566
Unique selling propositions, 584
Universal product codes, 310, 501, 508
Universal sets, 181
Universities, student surveys, 307
University logo apparel, 225–228
University of Alabama, 225, 226
University of Michigan, 226
University of Southern California, 225
Unrelated diversification, 52
Unsought products/services, 342
Unstructured questions, 318
UPC codes, 310, 501, 508
URLs, 348e. *See also* Websites
U.S. Census data, 309
U.S. Food Waste Challenge, 162
U.S. Postal Service, 593
Users, in buying centers, 219, 220
USPs, 584

V

Vacuum cleaners, 381
VALS tool, 274–276
Value. *See also* Pricing
of brands, 347–352, 349e
buying decisions based on, 176
defined, 13
importance of innovation to, 375–376
perceived, 351
of personal selling for firms, 611–612
positioning based on, 286–290, 436–437
prices versus, 42, 434, 461–462, 463
Value cocreation, 13
Value creation
as basic marketing function, 6–8, 12–13
by channel members, 490–491
importance of innovation to, 375–376
by retailers, 521–522
Value proposition
defined, 43, 286
positioning based on, 286–290
unique, 584
Value-based marketing concepts, 13, 14–17, 150
Value-based marketing era, 13
Value-based pricing, 461–462, 463
Values, individual, 273
Vanilla farmers, 162
Variability of services, 410
Variable costs, 447, 448
vCath training tool, 180
Vendor Flex program (Amazon), 494, 501

Vendor-managed inventories, 503
Vendors. *See* Suppliers
Venezuela, currency valuation, 238
Verbal communications, 245
Versant 2100 printer, 214
Vertical channel conflict, 494, 495
Vertical marketing systems, 495–499, 523
Vertical price fixing, 474
Video sites, 105–107
Videoconferencing, 624
Vinyl LPs, 396
VIP service (Universal), 446
Viral marketing, 489
Virtual communities, 316–317
Virtual offices, 610–611
The Voice (TV show), 567
Voice, in marketing plans, 64
Voice recognition technology, 613
Voice-of-customer programs, 415
VoIP services, 616
VoluntEAR program, 125

W

Wait times, 415
Walking sticks, 372
Walkman players, 393
Wants, needs versus, 177
Warehouse clubs, 526–527
Water Is Life microblog, 97–98
Watson computer, 213, 608–610
Weaknesses of firms, 38
Wealth, target markets based on, 157, 237
Wear-now option (Burberry), 522
Weather, 174–175, 213
Web browsers, 393

Web portals, 217
Web surveys, 320
Webcams, 389
Webinars, 223
Websites. *See also* Internet
of brands, 348e
marketing communications through, 561–562
print versus, 156
restaurant, 420
use of predictive analytics with, 345
Web-tracking software, 568
Weight loss industry, 151–152, 203–205, 316–317
Weird communications, 557
Weixin app, 99
Wellness concerns, 148–150, 159–160
Wheel of Social Media Engagement, 88–92
White papers, 224–225
Wholesalers, 213, 488, 490, 520
Wholly owned subsidiaries, 252
WiFi access, 8
Wireless devices. *See* Mobile devices
Wireless payment systems, 164
Women, marketing to, 158, 271, 297
Word of mouth, 187
Workplace climates, 131
World cars, 254
World Emoji Day, 549–550

Y

Yoga, 160
YouTube videos, 84, 95–96, 111

Z

Zone pricing, 470e, 471–472
Zones of tolerance, 415–416